get with the programming

Through the power of practice and immediate personalized feedback, MyProgrammingLab improves your performance.

PEARSON
myprogramminglab™

Learn more at **www.myprogramminglab.com**

STARTING OUT WITH

C++

From Control Structures through Objects

SEVENTH EDITION

Tony Gaddis

Haywood Community College

Addison-Wesley

Boston   Columbus   Indianapolis   New York   San Francisco   Upper Saddle River
Amsterdam   Cape Town   Dubai   London   Madrid   Milan   Munich   Paris   Montreal   Toronto
Delhi   Mexico City   Sao Paulo   Sydney   Hong Kong   Seoul   Singapore   Taipei   Tokyo

Editorial Director: Marcia Horton
Editor-in-Chief: Michael Hirsch
Editorial Assistant: Stephanie Sellinger
Vice President, Marketing: Patrice Jones
Marketing Manager: Yezan Alayan
Marketing Coordinator: Kathryn Ferranti
Vice President, Production: Vince O'Brien
Managing Editor: Jeff Holcomb
Senior Production Project Manager: Marilyn Lloyd
Senior Operations Supervisor: Alan Fischer

Manufacturing Buyer: Lisa McDowell
Art Director: Linda Knowles
Cover Designer: Joyce Cosentino Wells
Cover Image: © Fotosearch/Rubberball Photos
Media Editor: Daniel Sandin
Media Project Manager: Wanda Rockwell
Full-Service Vendor: Aptara®, Inc.
Project Management: Dennis Free/Aptara®, Inc.
Printer/Binder: Edwards Brothers
Cover Printer: Lehigh-Phoenix Color

Contents at a Glance

v

Contents

Preface

Welcome to *Starting Out with C++: From Control Structures through Objects, 7th edition*. This book is intended for use in a two-semester C++ programming sequence, or an accelerated one-semester course. Students new to programming, as well as those with prior course work in other languages, will find this text beneficial. The fundamentals of programming are covered for the novice, while the details, pitfalls, and nuances of the C++ language are explored in-depth for both the beginner and more experienced student. The book is written with clear, easy-to-understand language and it covers all the necessary topics for an introductory programming course. This text is rich in example programs that are concise, practical, and real-world oriented, ensuring that the student not only learns how to implement the features and constructs of C++, but why and when to use them.

Changes in the Seventh Edition

This book's pedagogy, organization, and clear writing style remain the same as in the previous edition. Many improvements have been made, which are summarized here:

- This edition uses `string` objects, instead of `char` arrays, as the preferred way to store strings. This change has been made throughout the entire book. A thorough discussion of C-strings and the technique of storing them in `char` arrays is provided as a topic in Chapter 10.

- All of the introductory file I/O material has been consolidated and moved to Chapter 5. In previous editions, this material was gradually introduced in Chapters 3 through 5. Many reviewers requested that all the material be given in one place, after loops have been covered.

- Named constants are now introduced in Chapter 2, after variables.

- In Chapter 2 an additional *In the Spotlight* section demonstrating the modulus operator has been added.

- Chapter 4 has been reorganized so that all the fundamental decision structure topics appear early in the chapter.

- A discussion of passing arrays using `const` references has been added to Chapter 7.

- An *In the Spotlight* section giving an additional example of inheritance has been added to Chapter 15.

- Template examples for stacks, queues, and binary search trees have been added to Chapters 18 and 20.

- The Serendipity Booksellers project has been moved to the book's online resource page at www.pearsonhighered.com/gaddis.

Organization of the Text

This text teaches C++ in a step-by-step fashion. Each chapter covers a major set of topics and builds knowledge as the student progresses through the book. Although the chapters can be easily taught in their existing sequence, some flexibility is provided. The diagram shown in Figure P-1 suggests possible sequences of instruction.

Chapter 1 covers fundamental hardware, software, and programming concepts. You may choose to skip this chapter if the class has already mastered those topics. Chapters 2 through 7 cover basic C++ syntax, data types, expressions, selection structures, repetition structures, functions, and arrays. Each of these chapters builds on the previous chapter and should be covered in the order presented.

After Chapter 7 has been covered, you may proceed to Chapter 8, or jump to either Chapter 9 or Chapter 12. (If you jump to Chapter 12 at this point, you will need to postpone sections 12.7, 12.8, and 12.10 until Chapters 9 and 11 have been covered.)

After Chapter 9 has been covered, either of Chapters 10 or 11 may be covered. After Chapter 11, you may cover Chapters 13 through 17 in sequence. Next you can proceed to either Chapter 18 or Chapter 19. Finally, Chapter 20 may be covered.

This text's approach starts with a firm foundation in structured, procedural programming before delving fully into object-oriented programming and advanced data structures.

Brief Overview of Each Chapter

Chapter 1: Introduction to Computers and Programming

This chapter provides an introduction to the field of computer science and covers the fundamentals of programming, problem solving, and software design. The components of programs, such as key words, variables, operators, and punctuation are covered. The tools of the trade, such as pseudocode, flow charts, and hierarchy charts are also presented.

Chapter 2: Introduction to C++

This chapter gets the student started in C++ by introducing data types, identifiers, variable declarations, constants, comments, program output, simple arithmetic operations, and C-strings. Programming style conventions are introduced and good programming style is modeled here, as it is throughout the text. An optional section explains the difference between ANSI standard and pre-standard C++ programs.

Figure P-1

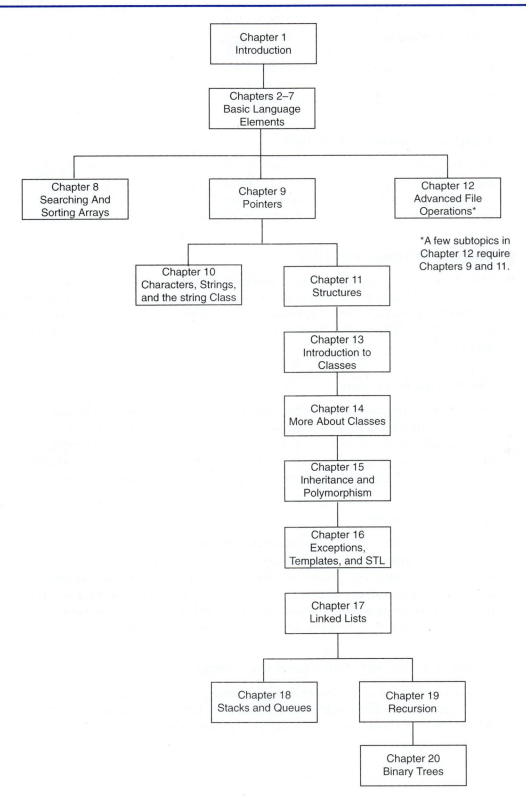

Chapter 3: Expressions and Interactivity

In this chapter the student learns to write programs that input and handle numeric, character, and string data. The use of arithmetic operators and the creation of mathematical expressions are covered in greater detail, with emphasis on operator precedence. Debugging is introduced, with a section on hand tracing a program. Sections are also included on simple output formatting, on data type conversion and type casting, and on using library functions that work with numbers.

Chapter 4: Making Decisions

Here the student learns about relational operators, relational expressions and how to control the flow of a program with the `if`, `if/else`, and `if/else if` statements. The conditional operator and the `switch` statement are also covered. Crucial applications of these constructs are covered, such as menu-driven programs and the validation of input.

Chapter 5: Loops and Files

This chapter covers repetition control structures. The `while` loop, `do-while` loop, and `for` loop are taught, along with common uses for these devices. Counters, accumulators, running totals, sentinels, and other application-related topics are discussed. Sequential file I/O is also introduced. The student learns to read and write text files, and use loops to process the data in a file.

Chapter 6: Functions

In this chapter the student learns how and why to modularize programs, using both `void` and value returning functions. Argument passing is covered, with emphasis on when arguments should be passed by value versus when they need to be passed by reference. Scope of variables is covered and sections are provided on local versus global variables and on static local variables. Overloaded functions are also introduced and demonstrated.

Chapter 7: Arrays

In this chapter the student learns to create and work with single and multidimensional arrays. Many examples of array processing are provided including examples illustrating how to find the sum, average, highest and lowest values in an array and how to sum the rows, columns, and all elements of a two-dimensional array. Programming techniques using parallel arrays are also demonstrated and the student is shown how to use a data file as an input source to populate an array. STL vectors are introduced and compared to arrays.

Chapter 8: Sorting and Searching Arrays

Here the student learns the basics of sorting arrays and searching for data stored in them. The chapter covers the Bubble Sort, Selection Sort, Linear Search, and Binary Search algorithms. There is also a section on sorting and searching STL `vector` objects.

Chapter 9: Pointers

This chapter explains how to use pointers. Pointers are compared to and contrasted with reference variables. Other topics include pointer arithmetic, initialization of pointers, relational comparison of pointers, pointers and arrays, pointers and functions, dynamic memory allocation, and more.

Chapter 10: Characters, C-strings, and More About the `string` Class

This chapter discusses various ways to process text at a detailed level. Library functions for testing and manipulating characters are introduced. C-strings are discussed, and the technique of storing C-strings in `char` arrays is covered. An extensive discussion of the `string` class methods is also given.

Chapter 11: Structured Data

The student is introduced to abstract data types and taught how to create them using structures, unions, and enumerated data types. Discussions and examples include using pointers to structures, passing structures to functions, and returning structures from functions.

Chapter 12: Advanced File Operations

This chapter covers sequential access, random access, text, and binary files. The various modes for opening files are discussed, as well as the many methods for reading and writing file contents. Advanced output formatting is also covered.

Chapter 13: Introduction to Classes

The student now shifts focus to the object-oriented paradigm. This chapter covers the fundamental concepts of classes. Member variables and functions are discussed. The student learns about private and public access specifications, and reasons to use each. The topics of constructors, overloaded constructors, and destructors are also presented. The chapter presents a section modeling classes with UML, and how to find the classes in a particular problem.

Chapter 14: More About Classes

This chapter continues the study of classes. Static members, friends, memberwise assignment, and copy constructors are discussed. The chapter also includes in-depth sections on operator overloading, object conversion, and object aggregation. There is also a section on class collaborations and the use of CRC cards.

Chapter 15: Inheritance and Polymorphism

The study of classes continues in this chapter with the subjects of inheritance, polymorphism, and virtual member functions. The topics covered include base and derived class constructors and destructors, virtual member functions, base class pointers, static and dynamic binding, multiple inheritance, and class hierarchies.

Chapter 16: Exceptions, Templates, and the Standard Template Library (STL)

The student learns to develop enhanced error trapping techniques using exceptions. Discussion then turns to function and class templates as a method for reusing code. Finally, the student is introduced to the containers, iterators, and algorithms offered by the Standard Template Library (STL).

Chapter 17: Linked Lists

This chapter introduces concepts and techniques needed to work with lists. A linked list ADT is developed and the student is taught to code operations such as creating a linked list, appending a node, traversing the list, searching for a node, inserting a node, deleting a node, and destroying a list. A linked list class template is also demonstrated.

Chapter 18: Stacks and Queues

In this chapter the student learns to create and use static and dynamic stacks and queues. The operations of stacks and queues are defined, and templates for each ADT are demonstrated.

Chapter 19: Recursion

This chapter discusses recursion and its use in problem solving. A visual trace of recursive calls is provided and recursive applications are discussed. Many recursive algorithms are presented, including recursive functions for finding factorials, finding a greatest common denominator (GCD), performing a binary search, and sorting (QuickSort). The classic Towers of Hanoi example is also presented. For students who need more challenge, there is a section on exhaustive algorithms.

Chapter 20: Binary Trees

This chapter covers the binary tree ADT, and demonstrates many binary tree operations. The student learns to traverse a tree, insert an element, delete an element, replace an element, test for an element, and destroy a tree.

Appendix A: Getting Started with Alice

This appendix gives a quick introduction to Alice. Alice is free software that can be used to teach fundamental programming concepts using 3D graphics.

Appendix B: ASCII Character Set

A list of the ASCII and Extended ASCII characters and their codes.

Appendix C: Operator Precedence and Associativity

A chart showing the C++ operators and their precedence.

The following appendices are available online at www.pearsonhighered.com/gaddis.

Appendix D: Introduction to Flowcharting

A brief introduction to flowcharting. This tutorial discusses sequence, selection, case, repetition, and module structures.

Appendix E: Using UML in Class Design

This appendix shows the student how to use the Unified Modeling Language to design classes. Notation for showing access specification, data types, parameters, return values, overloaded functions, composition, and inheritance are included.

Appendix F: Namespaces

This appendix explains namespaces and their purpose. Examples showing how to define a namespace and access its members are given.

Appendix G: Writing Managed C++ Code for the .NET Framework

This appendix introduces the student to the concepts surrounding managed C++ in Microsoft's .NET environment.

Appendix H: Passing Command Line Arguments

Teaches the student how to write a C++ program that accepts arguments from the command line. This appendix will be useful to students working in a command line environment, such as Unix, Linux, or the Windows command prompt.

Appendix I: Header File and Library Function Reference

This appendix provides a reference for the C++ library functions and header files discussed in the book.

Appendix J: Binary Numbers and Bitwise Operations

A guide to the C++ bitwise operators, as well as a tutorial on the internal storage of integers.

Appendix K: Multi-Source File Programs

Provides a tutorial on creating programs that consist of multiple source files. Function header files, class specification files, and class implementation files are discussed.

Appendix L: Stream Member Functions for Formatting

Covers stream member functions for formatting such as `setf`.

Appendix M: Introduction to Microsoft Visual C++ 2010 Express Edition

A tutorial on how to start a project in Microsoft Visual C++ 2010 Express Edition, compile a program, save source files, and more.

Appendix N: Answers to Checkpoints

Students may test their own progress by comparing their answers to the checkpoint exercises against this appendix. The answers to all Checkpoints are included.

Appendix O: Solutions to Odd-Numbered Review Questions

Another tool that students can use to gauge their progress.

Features of the Text

Concept Statements	Each major section of the text starts with a concept statement. This statement summarizes the ideas of the section.
Example Programs	The text has hundreds of complete example programs, each designed to highlight the topic currently being studied. In most cases, these are practical, real-world examples. Source code for these programs is provided so that students can run the programs themselves.
Program Output	After each example program there is a sample of its screen output. This immediately shows the student how the program should function.
In the Spotlight	Each of these sections provides a programming problem and a detailed, step by step analysis showing the student how to solve it.
VideoNotes	A series of online videos, developed specifically for this book, is available for viewing at www.pearsonhighered.com/gaddis. Icons appear throughout the text alerting the student to videos about specific topics.
Checkpoints	Checkpoints are questions placed throughout each chapter as a self-test study aid. Answers for all Checkpoint questions can be downloaded from the book's Companion Website at www.pearsonhighered.com/gaddis. This allows students to check how well they have learned a new topic.
Notes	Notes appear at appropriate places throughout the text. They are short explanations of interesting or often misunderstood points relevant to the topic at hand.
Warnings	Warnings are notes that caution the student about certain C++ features, programming techniques, or practices that can lead to malfunctioning programs or lost data.

Case Studies

Case studies that simulate real-world applications appear in many chapters throughout the text. These case studies are designed to highlight the major topics of the chapter in which they appear.

Review Questions and Exercises

Each chapter presents a thorough and diverse set of review questions, such as fill-in-the-blank and short answer, that check the student's mastery of the basic material presented in the chapter. These are followed by exercises requiring problem solving and analysis, such as the *Algorithm Workbench*, *Predict the Output*, and *Find the Errors* sections. Answers to the odd numbered review questions and review exercises can be downloaded from the book's Companion Website at www.pearsonhighered.com/gaddis.

Programming Challenges

Each chapter offers a pool of programming exercises designed to solidify the student's knowledge of the topics currently being studied. In most cases the assignments present real-world problems to be solved. When applicable, these exercises include input validation rules.

Group Projects

There are several group programming projects throughout the text, intended to be constructed by a team of students. One student might build the program's user interface, while another student writes the mathematical code, and another designs and implements a class the program uses. This process is similar to the way many professional programs are written and encourages team work within the classroom.

Software Development Project: Serendipity Booksellers

Available for download from the book's Companion Website at www.pearsonhighered.com/gaddis. This is an on-going project that instructors can optionally assign to teams of students. It systematically develops a "real-world" software package: a point-of-sale program for the fictitious Serendipity Booksellers organization. The Serendipity assignment for each chapter adds more functionality to the software, using constructs and techniques covered in that chapter. When complete, the program will act as a cash register, manage an inventory database, and produce a variety of reports.

C++ Quick Reference Guide

For easy access, a quick reference guide to the C++ language is printed on the last two pages of Appendix C in the book.

Supplements

Student Online Resources

Many student resources are available for this book from the publisher. The following items are available on the Gaddis Series Companion Website at www.pearsonhighered.com/gaddis:

- The source code for each example program in the book
- Access to the book's companion VideoNotes
- A full set of appendices, including answers to the Checkpoint questions, and answers to the odd-numbered review questions
- A collection of valuable Case Studies
- The complete Serendipity Booksellers Project

Integrated Development Environment (IDE) Resource Kits

Professors who adopt this text can order it for students with a kit containing five popular C++ IDEs (Microsoft® Visual Studio 2010 Express Edition, Dev C++, NetBeans, Eclipse, and CodeLite) and access to a Web site containing written and video tutorials for getting started in each IDE.   For ordering information, please contact your campus Pearson Education representative or visit www.pearsonhighered.com/cs.

Online Practice and Assessment with MyProgrammingLab

MyProgrammingLab helps students fully grasp the logic, semantics, and syntax of programming. Through practice exercises and immediate, personalized feedback, MyProgrammingLab improves the programming competence of beginning students who often struggle with the basic concepts and paradigms of popular high-level programming languages.

A self-study and homework tool, a MyProgrammingLab course consists of hundreds of small practice problems organized around the structure of this textbook. For students, the system automatically detects errors in the logic and syntax of their code submissions and offers targeted hints that enable students to figure out what went wrong—and why. For instructors, a comprehensive gradebook tracks correct and incorrect answers and stores the code inputted by students for review.

MyProgrammingLab is offered to users of this book in partnership with Turing's Craft, the makers of the CodeLab interactive programming exercise system. For a full demonstration, to see feedback from instructors and students, or to get started using MyProgrammingLab in your course, visit www.myprogramminglab.com.

Instructor Resources

The following supplements are available to qualified instructors only:

- Answers to all Review Questions in the text
- Solutions for all Programming Challenges in the text
- PowerPoint presentation slides for every chapter

- Computerized test bank
- Answers to all Student Lab Manual questions
- Solutions for all Student Lab Manual programs

Visit the Pearson Instructor Resource Center (www.pearsonhighered.com/irc) or send an email to computing@pearson.com for information on how to access them.

Textbook Web site

Student and instructor resources, including links to download Microsoft® Visual C++ 2010 Express and other popular IDEs, for all the books in the Gaddis *Starting Out With* series can be accessed at the following URL:

http://www.pearsonhighered.com/gaddis

Get this book the way you want it!

This book is part of Pearson Education's custom database for Computer Science textbooks. Use our online PubSelect system to select just the chapters you need from this, and other, Pearson Education CS textbooks. You can edit the sequence to exactly match your course organization and teaching approach. Visit www.pearsoncustom.com/cs for details.

Which Gaddis C++ book is right for you?

The Starting Out with C++ Series includes three books, one of which is sure to fit your course:

- *Starting Out with C++: From Control Structures through Objects*
- *Starting Out with C++: Early Objects*
- *Starting Out with C++: Brief Version.*

The following chart will help you determine which book is right for your course.

■ FROM CONTROL STRUCTURES THROUGH OBJECTS ■ BRIEF VERSION	■ EARLY OBJECTS
LATE INTRODUCTION OF OBJECTS Classes are introduced in Chapter 13 of the standard text and Chapter 11 of the brief text, after control structures, functions, arrays, and pointers. Advanced OOP topics, such as inheritance and polymorphism, are covered in the following two chapters.	**EARLIER INTRODUCTION OF OBJECTS** Classes are introduced in Chapter 7, after control structures and functions, but before arrays and pointers. Their use is then integrated into the remainder of the text. Advanced OOP topics, such as inheritance and polymorphism, are covered in Chapters 11 and 15.
INTRODUCTION OF DATA STRUCTURES AND RECURSION Linked lists, stacks and queues, and binary trees are introduced in the final chapters of the standard text. Recursion is covered after stacks and queues, but before binary trees. These topics are not covered in the brief text, though it does have appendices dealing with linked lists and recursion.	**INTRODUCTION OF DATA STRUCTURES AND RECURSION** Linked lists, stacks and queues, and binary trees are introduced in the final chapters of the text, after the chapter on recursion.

Acknowledgments

There have been many helping hands in the development and publication of this text. We would like to thank the following faculty reviewers for their helpful suggestions and expertise.

Ahmad Abuhejleh
University of Wisconsin, River Falls

David Akins
El Camino College

Steve Allan
Utah State University

Vicki Allan
Utah State University

Karen M. Arlien
Bismark State College

Mary Astone
Troy University

Ijaz A. Awan
Savannah State University

Robert Baird
Salt Lake Community College

Don Biggerstaff
Fayetteville Technical Community College

Michael Bolton
Northeastern Oklahoma State University

Bill Brown
Pikes Peak Community College

Charles Cadenhead
Richland Community College

Randall Campbell
Morningside College

Wayne Caruolo
Red Rocks Community College

Cathi Chambley-Miller
Aiken Technical College

C.C. Chao
Jacksonville State University

Joseph Chao
Bowling Green State University

Royce Curtis
Western Wisconsin Technical College

Joseph DeLibero
Arizona State University

Jeanne Douglas
University of Vermont

Michael Dowell
Augusta State U

William E. Duncan
Louisiana State University

Judy Etchison
Southern Methodist University

Dennis Fairclough
Utah Valley State College

Mark Fienup
University of Northern Iowa

Richard Flint
North Central College

Ann Ford Tyson
Florida State University

Jeanette Gibbons
South Dakota State University

James Gifford
University of Wisconsin, Stevens Point

Leon Gleiberman
Touro College

Barbara Guillott
Louisiana State University

Ranette Halverson, Ph.D.
Midwestern State University

Carol Hannahs
University of Kentucky

Dennis Heckman
Portland Community College

Ric Heishman
George Mason University

Michael Hennessy
University of Oregon

Ilga Higbee
Black Hawk College

Patricia Hines
Brookdale Community College

Mike Holland
Northern Virginia Community College

Mary Hovik
Lehigh Carbon Community College

Richard Hull
Lenoir-Rhyne College

Chris Kardaras
North Central College

Willard Keeling
Blue Ridge Community College

A.J. Krygeris
Houston Community College

Sheila Lancaster
Gadsden State Community College

Ray Larson
Inver Hills Community College

Jennifer Li
Ohlone College

Norman H. Liebling
San Jacinto College

Zhu-qu Lu
University of Maine, Presque Isle

Heidar Malki
University of Houston

Debbie Mathews
J. Sargeant Reynolds

Rick Matzen
Northeastern State University

Robert McDonald
East Stroudsburg University

James McGuffee
Austin Community College

Dean Mellas
Cerritos College

Lisa Milkowski
Milwaukee School of Engineering

Marguerite Nedreberg
Youngstown State University

Lynne O'Hanlon
Los Angeles Pierce College

Frank Paiano
Southwestern Community College

Theresa Park
Texas State Technical College

Mark Parker
Shoreline Community College

Tino Posillico
SUNY Farmingdale

Frederick Pratter
Eastern Oregon University

Susan L. Quick
Penn State University

Alberto Ramon
Diablo Valley College

Bazlur Rasheed
Sault College of Applied Arts and Technology

Farshad Ravanshad
Bergen Community College

Dolly Samson
Weber State University

Ruth Sapir
SUNY Farmingdale

Jason Schatz
City College of San Francisco

Dr. Sung Shin
South Dakota State University

Bari Siddique
University of Texas at Brownsville

William Slater
Collin County Community College

Shep Smithline
University of Minnesota

Caroline St. Claire
North Central College

Kirk Stephens
Southwestern Community College

Cherie Stevens
South Florida Community College

Dale Suggs
Campbell University

Mark Swanson
Red Wing Technical College

Ann Sudell Thorn
Del Mar College

Martha Tillman
College of San Mateo

Ralph Tomlinson
Iowa State University

David Topham
Ohlone College

Robert Tureman
Paul D. Camp Community College

Arisa K. Ude
Richland College

Peter van der Goes
Rose State College

Stewart Venit
California State University, Los Angeles

Judy Walters
North Central College

John H. Whipple
Northampton Community College

Aurelia Williams
Norfolk State University

Vida Winans
Illinois Institute of Technology

I would like to thank my family for their love and support in all of my many projects. I would also like to thank Christopher Rich for his assistance in this revision. I am extremely fortunate to have Michael Hirsch as my editor, and Stephanie Sellinger as editorial assistant. Michael's support and encouragement makes it a pleasure to write chapters and meet deadlines. I am also fortunate to have Yez Alayan as marketing manager, and Kathryn Ferranti as marketing coordinator. They do a great job getting my books out to the academic community. I had a great production team led by Jeff Holcomb, Managing Editor, and Marilyn Lloyd, Senior Production Project Manager. Thanks to you all!

About the Author

Tony Gaddis is the principal author of the *Starting Out with* series of textbooks. He has nearly two decades of experience teaching computer science courses, primarily at Haywood Community College. Tony is a highly acclaimed instructor who was previously selected as the North Carolina Community College Teacher of the Year, and has received the Teaching Excellence award from the National Institute for Staff and Organizational Development. The *Starting Out With* series includes introductory textbooks covering Programming Logic and Design, Alice, C++, Java^{TM}, Microsoft® Visual Basic®, Microsoft® Visual C#, and Python, all published by Pearson Addison-Wesley.

1

Introduction to Computers and Programming

1.1   Why Program?

CONCEPT: Computers can do many different jobs because they are programmable.

Think about some of the different ways that people use computers. In school, students use computers for tasks such as writing papers, searching for articles, sending e-mail, and participating in online classes. At work, people use computers to analyze data, make presentations, conduct business transactions, communicate with customers and coworkers, control machines in manufacturing facilities, and do many other things. At home, people use computers for tasks such as paying bills, shopping online, social networking, and playing computer games. And don't forget that smart phones, iPods®, car navigation systems, and many other devices are computers as well. The uses of computers are almost limitless in our everyday lives.

Computers can do such a wide variety of things because they can be programmed. This means that computers are not designed to do just one job, but any job that their programs tell them to do. A *program* is a set of instructions that a computer follows to perform a task. For example, Figure 1-1 shows screens using Microsoft Word and PowerPoint, two commonly used programs.

Figure 1-1   A word processing program and a presentation program

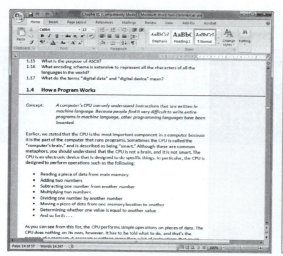
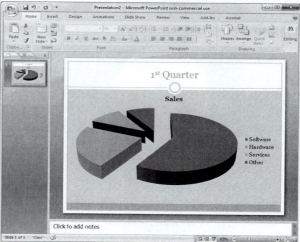

Programs are commonly referred to as *software*. Software is essential to a computer because without software, a computer can do nothing. All of the software that we use to make our computers useful is created by individuals known as programmers or software developers. A *programmer*, or *software developer*, is a person with the training and skills necessary to design, create, and test computer programs. Computer programming is an exciting and rewarding career. Today, you will find programmers working in business, medicine, government, law enforcement, agriculture, academics, entertainment, and almost every other field.

Computer programming is both an art and a science. It is an art because every aspect of a program should be carefully designed. Listed below are a few of the things that must be designed for any real-world computer program:

- The logical flow of the instructions
- The mathematical procedures
- The appearance of the screens
- The way information is presented to the user
- The program's "user-friendliness"
- Manuals and other forms of written documentation

There is also a scientific, or engineering, side to programming. Because programs rarely work right the first time they are written, a lot of testing, correction, and redesigning is required. This demands patience and persistence from the programmer. Writing software demands discipline as well. Programmers must learn special languages like C++ because computers do not understand English or other human languages. Languages such as C++ have strict rules that must be carefully followed.

Both the artistic and scientific nature of programming make writing computer software like designing a car: Both cars and programs should be functional, efficient, powerful, easy to use, and pleasing to look at.

1.2 Computer Systems: Hardware and Software

CONCEPT: All computer systems consist of similar hardware devices and software components. This section provides an overview of standard computer hardware and software organization.

Hardware

Hardware refers to the physical components that a computer is made of. A computer, as we generally think of it, is not an individual device, but a system of devices. Like the instruments in a symphony orchestra, each device plays its own part. A typical computer system consists of the following major components:

1. The central processing unit (CPU)
2. Main memory
3. Secondary storage devices
4. Input devices
5. Output devices

The organization of a computer system is depicted in Figure 1-2.

Figure 1-2

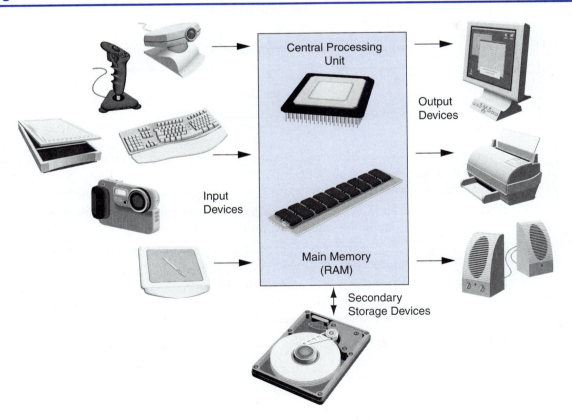

The CPU

When a computer is performing the tasks that a program tells it to do, we say that the computer is *running* or *executing* the program. The *central processing unit*, or *CPU*, is the part of a computer that actually runs programs. The CPU is the most important component in a computer because without it, the computer could not run software.

In the earliest computers, CPUs were huge devices that weighed tons. They were made of electrical and mechanical components such as vacuum tubes and switches. Today, CPUs are small chips, known as *microprocessors*, that can be held in the palm of your hand. In addition to being much smaller than the old electromechanical CPUs in early computers, today's microprocessors are also much more powerful.

The CPU's job is to fetch instructions, follow the instructions, and produce some result. Internally, the central processing unit consists of two parts: the *control unit* and the *arithmetic and logic unit (ALU)*. The control unit coordinates all of the computer's operations. It is responsible for determining where to get the next instruction and regulating the other major components of the computer with control signals. The arithmetic and logic unit, as its name suggests, is designed to perform mathematical operations. The organization of the CPU is shown in Figure 1-3.

Figure 1-3

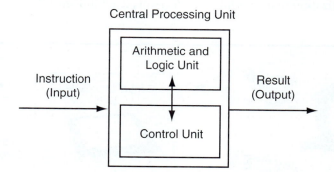

A program is a sequence of instructions stored in the computer's memory. When a computer is running a program, the CPU is engaged in a process known formally as the *fetch/decode/execute cycle*. The steps in the fetch/decode/execute cycle are as follows:

Fetch   The CPU's control unit fetches, from main memory, the next instruction in the sequence of program instructions.

Decode   The instruction is encoded in the form of a number. The control unit decodes the instruction and generates an electronic signal.

Execute   The signal is routed to the appropriate component of the computer (such as the ALU, a disk drive, or some other device). The signal causes the component to perform an operation.

These steps are repeated as long as there are instructions to perform.

Main Memory

You can think of main memory as the computer's work area. This is where the computer stores a program while the program is running, as well as the data that the program is working with. For example, suppose you are using a word processing program to write an essay for one of your classes. While you do this, both the word processing program and the essay are stored in main memory.

Main memory is commonly known as *random-access memory* or *RAM*. It is called this because the CPU is able to quickly access data stored at any random location in RAM. RAM is usually a *volatile* type of memory that is used only for temporary storage while a program is running. When the computer is turned off, the contents of RAM are erased. Inside your computer, RAM is stored in small chips.

A computer's memory is divided into tiny storage locations known as bytes. One *byte* is enough memory to store only a letter of the alphabet or a small number. In order to do anything meaningful, a computer must have lots of bytes. Most computers today have millions, or even billions, of bytes of memory.

Each byte is divided into eight smaller storage locations known as bits. The term *bit* stands for *binary digit*. Computer scientists usually think of bits as tiny switches that can be either on or off. Bits aren't actual "switches," however, at least not in the conventional sense. In most computer systems, bits are tiny electrical components that can hold either a positive or a negative charge. Computer scientists think of a positive charge as a switch in the *on* position and a negative charge as a switch in the *off* position.

Each byte is assigned a unique number known as an *address*. The addresses are ordered from lowest to highest. A byte is identified by its address in much the same way a post office box is identified by an address. Figure 1-4 shows a group of memory cells with their addresses. In the illustration, sample data is stored in memory. The number 149 is stored in the cell with the address 16, and the number 72 is stored at address 23.

Figure 1-4

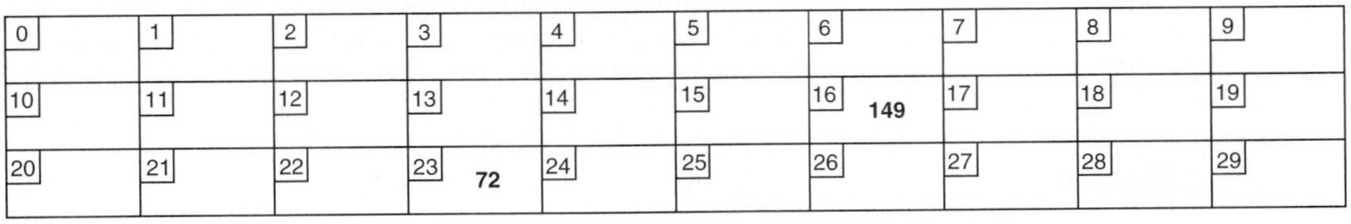

0	1	2	3	4	5	6	7	8	9
10	11	12	13	14	15	16 149	17	18	19
20	21	22	23 72	24	25	26	27	28	29

Secondary Storage

Secondary storage is a type of memory that can hold data for long periods of time—even when there is no power to the computer. Frequently used programs are stored in secondary memory and loaded into main memory as needed. Important information, such as word processing documents, payroll data, and inventory figures, is saved to secondary storage as well.

The most common type of secondary storage device is the disk drive. A *disk drive* stores data by magnetically encoding it onto a circular disk. Most computers have a disk drive mounted inside their case. External disk drives, which connect to one of the computer's communication ports, are also available. External disk drives can be used to create backup copies of important data or to move data to another computer.

In addition to external disk drives, many types of devices have been created for copying data, and for moving it to other computers. For many years floppy disk drives were popular. A *floppy disk drive* records data onto a small floppy disk, which can be removed from the drive. The use of floppy disk drives has declined dramatically in recent years, in favor of superior devices such as USB drives. *USB drives* are small devices that plug into the computer's USB (universal serial bus) port, and appear to the system as a disk drive. USB drives, which use *flash memory* to store data, are inexpensive, reliable, and small enough to be carried in your pocket.

Optical devices such as the *CD* (compact disc) and the *DVD* (digital versatile disc) are also popular for data storage. Data is not recorded magnetically on an optical disc, but is encoded as a series of pits on the disc surface. CD and DVD drives use a laser to detect the pits and thus read the encoded data. Optical discs hold large amounts of data, and because recordable CD and DVD drives are now commonplace, they are good mediums for creating backup copies of data.

Input Devices

Input is any information the computer collects from the outside world. The device that collects the information and sends it to the computer is called an *input device*. Common input devices are the keyboard, mouse, scanner, digital camera, and microphone. Disk drives, CD/DVD drives, and USB drives can also be considered input devices because programs and information are retrieved from them and loaded into the computer's memory.

Output Devices

Output is any information the computer sends to the outside world. It might be a sales report, a list of names, or a graphic image. The information is sent to an *output device*, which formats and presents it. Common output devices are monitors, printers, and speakers. Output sent to a monitor is sometimes called "softcopy," while output sent to a printer is called "hardcopy." Disk drives, USB drives, and CD/DVD recorders can also be considered output devices because the CPU sends them information to be saved.

Software

If a computer is to function, software is not optional. Everything that a computer does, from the time you turn the power switch on until you shut the system down, is under the control of software. There are two general categories of software: system software and application software. Most computer programs clearly fit into one of these two categories. Let's take a closer look at each.

System Software

The programs that control and manage the basic operations of a computer are generally referred to as *system software*. System software typically includes the following types of programs:

- *Operating Systems*
  An operating system is the most fundamental set of programs on a computer. The operating system controls the internal operations of the computer's hardware, manages all the devices connected to the computer, allows data to be saved to and retrieved from storage devices, and allows other programs to run on the computer.

- *Utility Programs*
  A *utility program* performs a specialized task that enhances the computer's operation or safeguards data. Examples of utility programs are virus scanners, file-compression programs, and data-backup programs.

- *Software Development Tools*
  The software tools that programmers use to create, modify, and test software are referred to as *software development tools*. Compilers and integrated development environments, which we discuss later in this chapter, are examples of programs that fall into this category.

Application Software

Programs that make a computer useful for everyday tasks are known as *application software*. These are the programs that people normally spend most of their time running on their computers. Figure 1-1, at the beginning of this chapter, shows screens from two commonly used applications—Microsoft Word, a word processing program, and Microsoft PowerPoint, a presentation program. Some other examples of application software are spreadsheet programs, e-mail programs, Web browsers, and game programs.

 ## Checkpoint

myprogramminglab *www.myprogramminglab.com*

1.1   Why is the computer used by so many different people, in so many different professions?

1.2   List the five major hardware components of a computer system.

1.3   Internally, the CPU consists of what two units?

1.4   Describe the steps in the fetch/decode/execute cycle.

1.5   What is a memory address? What is its purpose?

1.6   Explain why computers have both main memory and secondary storage.

1.7   What are the two general categories of software?

1.8   What fundamental set of programs control the internal operations of the computer's hardware?

1.9   What do you call a program that performs a specialized task, such as a virus scanner, a file-compression program, or a data-backup program?

1.10   Word processing programs, spreadsheet programs, e-mail programs, Web browsers, and game programs belong to what category of software?

1.3 Programs and Programming Languages

CONCEPT: A program is a set of instructions a computer follows in order to perform a task. A programming language is a special language used to write computer programs.

What Is a Program?

Computers are designed to follow instructions. A computer program is a set of instructions that tells the computer how to solve a problem or perform a task. For example, suppose we want the computer to calculate someone's gross pay. Here is a list of things the computer should do:

1. Display a message on the screen asking "How many hours did you work?"

2. Wait for the user to enter the number of hours worked. Once the user enters a number, store it in memory.

3. Display a message on the screen asking "How much do you get paid per hour?"

4. Wait for the user to enter an hourly pay rate. Once the user enters a number, store it in memory.

5. Multiply the number of hours by the amount paid per hour, and store the result in memory.

6. Display a message on the screen that tells the amount of money earned. The message must include the result of the calculation performed in Step 5.

Collectively, these instructions are called an *algorithm*. An algorithm is a set of well-defined steps for performing a task or solving a problem. Notice these steps are sequentially ordered. Step 1 should be performed before Step 2, and so forth. It is important that these instructions be performed in their proper sequence.

Although you and I might easily understand the instructions in the pay-calculating algorithm, it is not ready to be executed on a computer. A computer's CPU can only process instructions that are written in *machine language*. If you were to look at a machine language program, you would see a stream of *binary numbers* (numbers consisting of only 1s and 0s). The binary numbers form machine language instructions, which the CPU interprets as commands. Here is an example of what a machine language instruction might look like:

```
1011010000000101
```

As you can imagine, the process of encoding an algorithm in machine language is very tedious and difficult. In addition, each different type of CPU has its own machine language. If you wrote a machine language program for computer *A* and then wanted to run it on computer *B*, which has a different type of CPU, you would have to rewrite the program in computer B's machine language.

Programming languages, which use words instead of numbers, were invented to ease the task of programming. A program can be written in a programming language, such as C++, which is much easier to understand than machine language. Programmers save their programs in text files, and then use special software to convert their programs to machine language.

Program 1-1 shows how the pay-calculating algorithm might be written in C++.

The "Program Output with Example Input" shows what the program will display on the screen when it is running. In the example, the user enters 10 for the number of hours worked and 15 for the hourly pay rate. The program displays the earnings, which are $150.

 NOTE: The line numbers that are shown in Program 1-1 are *not* part of the program. This book shows line numbers in all program listings to help point out specific parts of the program.

Program 1-1

```
1   // This program calculates the user's pay.
2   #include <iostream>
3   using namespace std;
4
5   int main()
6   {
7      double hours, rate, pay;
8
9      // Get the number of hours worked.
10     cout << "How many hours did you work? ";
11     cin >> hours;
12
13     // Get the hourly pay rate.
14     cout << "How much do you get paid per hour? ";
15     cin >> rate;
16
17     // Calculate the pay.
18     pay = hours * rate;
19
20     // Display the pay.
21     cout << "You have earned $" << pay << endl;
22     return 0;
23  }
```

Program Output with Example Input Shown in Bold
How many hours did you work? **10 [Enter]**
How much do you get paid per hour? **15 [Enter]**
You have earned $150

Programming Languages

In a broad sense, there are two categories of programming languages: low-level and high-level. A low-level language is close to the level of the computer, which means it resembles the numeric machine language of the computer more than the natural language of humans. The easiest languages for people to learn are *high-level languages*. They are called "high-level" because they are closer to the level of human-readability than computer-readability. Figure 1-5 illustrates the concept of language levels.

Many high-level languages have been created. Table 1-1 lists a few of the well-known ones.

In addition to the high-level features necessary for writing applications such as payroll systems and inventory programs, C++ also has many low-level features. C++ is based on

Figure 1-5

High level (Easily read by humans)

Low level (machine language)
10100010 11101011

Table 1-1

Language	Description
BASIC	Beginners All-purpose Symbolic Instruction Code. A general programming language originally designed to be simple enough for beginners to learn.
FORTRAN	Formula Translator. A language designed for programming complex mathematical algorithms.
COBOL	Common Business-Oriented Language. A language designed for business applications.
Pascal	A structured, general-purpose language designed primarily for teaching programming.
C	A structured, general-purpose language developed at Bell Laboratories. C offers both high-level and low-level features.
C++	Based on the C language, C++ offers object-oriented features not found in C. Also invented at Bell Laboratories.
C#	Pronounced "C sharp." A language invented by Microsoft for developing applications based on the Microsoft .NET platform.
Java	An object-oriented language invented at Sun Microsystems. Java may be used to develop programs that run over the Internet, in a Web browser.
JavaScript	JavaScript can be used to write small programs that run in Web pages. Despite its name, JavaScript is not related to Java.
Python	Python is a general purpose language created in the early 1990s. It has become popular in both business and academic applications.
Ruby	Ruby is a general purpose language that was created in the 1990s. It is increasingly becoming a popular language for programs that run on Web servers.
Visual Basic	A Microsoft programming language and software development environment that allows programmers to quickly create Windows-based applications.

the C language, which was invented for purposes such as writing operating systems and compilers. Since C++ evolved from C, it carries all of C's low-level capabilities with it.

C++ is popular not only because of its mixture of low- and high-level features, but also because of its *portability*. This means that a C++ program can be written on one type of computer and then run on many other types of systems. This usually requires the program to be recompiled on each type of system, but the program itself may need little or no change.

> **NOTE:** Programs written for specific graphical environments often require significant changes when moved to a different type of system. Examples of such graphical environments are Windows, the X-Window System, and the Mac OS operating system.

Source Code, Object Code, and Executable Code

When a C++ program is written, it must be typed into the computer and saved to a file. A *text editor*, which is similar to a word processing program, is used for this task. The statements written by the programmer are called *source code*, and the file they are saved in is called the *source file*.

After the source code is saved to a file, the process of translating it to machine language can begin. During the first phase of this process, a program called the *preprocessor* reads the source code. The preprocessor searches for special lines that begin with the # symbol. These lines contain commands that cause the preprocessor to modify the source code in some way. During the next phase the *compiler* steps through the preprocessed source code, translating each source code instruction into the appropriate machine language instruction. This process will uncover any *syntax errors* that may be in the program. Syntax errors are illegal uses of key words, operators, punctuation, and other language elements. If the program is free of syntax errors, the compiler stores the translated machine language instructions, which are called *object code*, in an *object file*.

Although an object file contains machine language instructions, it is not a complete program. Here is why: C++ is conveniently equipped with a library of prewritten code for performing common operations or sometimes-difficult tasks. For example, the library contains hardware-specific code for displaying messages on the screen and reading input from the keyboard. It also provides routines for mathematical functions, such as calculating the square root of a number. This collection of code, called the *run-time library*, is extensive. Programs almost always use some part of it. When the compiler generates an object file, however, it does not include machine code for any run-time library routines the programmer might have used. During the last phase of the translation process, another program called the *linker* combines the object file with the necessary library routines. Once the linker has finished with this step, an *executable file* is created. The executable file contains machine language instructions, or *executable code*, and is ready to run on the computer.

Figure 1-6 illustrates the process of translating a C++ source file into an executable file.

The entire process of invoking the preprocessor, compiler, and linker can be initiated with a single action. For example, on a Linux system, the following command causes the C++ program named `hello.cpp` to be preprocessed, compiled, and linked. The executable code is stored in a file named `hello`.

```
g++ -o hello hello.cpp
```

Figure 1-6

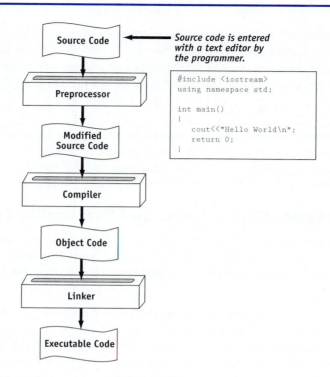

Appendix G explains how compiling works in .Net. You can download Appendix G from the book's companion Web site at www.pearsonhighered.com/gaddis.

Many development systems, particularly those on personal computers, have *integrated development environments (IDEs)*. These environments consist of a text editor, compiler, debugger, and other utilities integrated into a package with a single set of menus. Preprocessing, compiling, linking, and even executing a program is done with a single click of a button, or by selecting a single item from a menu. Figure 1-7 shows a screen from the Microsoft Visual Studio IDE.

✔ Checkpoint

myprogramminglab   *www.myprogramminglab.com*

1.11   What is an algorithm?

1.12   Why were computer programming languages invented?

1.13   What is the difference between a high-level language and a low-level language?

1.14   What does *portability* mean?

1.15   Explain the operations carried out by the preprocessor, compiler, and linker.

1.16   Explain what is stored in a source file, an object file, and an executable file.

1.17   What is an integrated development environment?

Figure 1-7

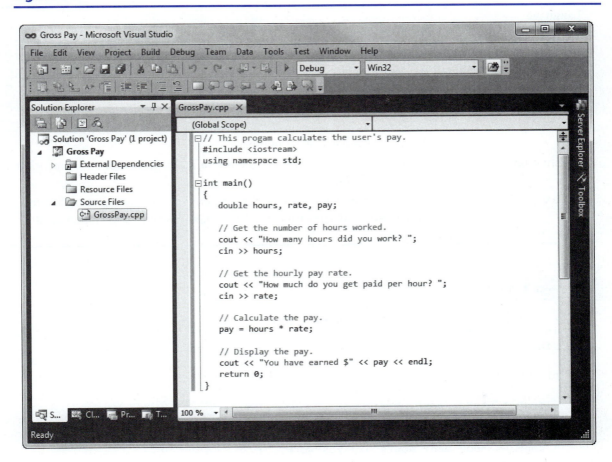

What Is a Program Made of?

CONCEPT: There are certain elements that are common to all programming languages.

Language Elements

All programming languages have a few things in common. Table 1-2 lists the common elements you will find in almost every language.

Let's look at some specific parts of Program 1-1 (the pay-calculating program) to see examples of each element listed in the table above. For your convenience, Program 1-1 is listed again.

Table 1-2

Language Element	Description
Key Words	Words that have a special meaning. Key words may only be used for their intended purpose. Key words are also known as reserved words.
Programmer-Defined Identifiers	Words or names defined by the programmer. They are symbolic names that refer to variables or programming routines.
Operators	Operators perform operations on one or more operands. An operand is usually a piece of data, like a number.
Punctuation	Punctuation characters that mark the beginning or ending of a statement, or separate items in a list.
Syntax	Rules that must be followed when constructing a program. Syntax dictates how key words and operators may be used, and where punctuation symbols must appear.

Program 1-1

```
1    // This program calculates the user's pay.
2    #include <iostream>
3    using namespace std;
4
5    int main()
6    {
7        double hours, rate, pay;
8
9        // Get the number of hours worked.
10       cout << "How many hours did you work? ";
11       cin >> hours;
12
13       // Get the hourly pay rate.
14       cout << "How much do you get paid per hour? ";
15       cin >> rate;
16
17       // Calculate the pay.
18       pay = hours * rate;
19
20       // Display the pay.
21       cout << "You have earned $" << pay << endl;
22       return 0;
23   }
```

Key Words (Reserved Words)

Three of C++'s key words appear on lines 3 and 5: using, namespace, and int. The word double, which appears on line 7, is also a C++ key word. These words, which are always written in lowercase, each have a special meaning in C++ and can only be used for their intended purposes. As you will see, the programmer is allowed to make up his or her own names for certain things in a program. Key words, however, are reserved and cannot be used for anything other than their designated purposes. Part of learning a programming language is learning what the key words are, what they mean, and how to use them.

NOTE: The `#include <iostream>` statement in line 2 is a preprocessor directive.

NOTE: In C++, key words are written in all lowercase.

Programmer-Defined Identifiers

The words `hours`, `rate`, and `pay` that appear in the program on lines 7, 11, 15, 18, and 21 are programmer-defined identifiers. They are not part of the C++ language but rather are names made up by the programmer. In this particular program, these are the names of variables. As you will learn later in this chapter, variables are the names of memory locations that may hold data.

Operators

On line 18 the following code appears:

```
pay = hours * rate;
```

The = and * symbols are both operators. They perform operations on pieces of data known as operands. The * operator multiplies its two operands, which in this example are the variables `hours` and `rate`. The = symbol is called the assignment operator. It takes the value of the expression on the right and stores it in the variable whose name appears on the left. In this example, the = operator stores in the `pay` variable the result of the `hours` variable multiplied by the `rate` variable. In other words, the statement says, "Make the `pay` variable equal to `hours` times `rate`, or "`pay` is assigned the value of `hours` times `rate`."

Punctuation

Notice that lines 3, 7, 10, 11, 14, 15, 18, 21, and 22 all end with a semicolon. A semicolon in C++ is similar to a period in English: It marks the end of a complete sentence (or statement, as it is called in programming jargon). Semicolons do not appear at the end of every line in a C++ program, however. There are rules that govern where semicolons are required and where they are not. Part of learning C++ is learning where to place semicolons and other punctuation symbols.

Lines and Statements

Often, the contents of a program are thought of in terms of lines and statements. A "line" is just that—a single line as it appears in the body of a program. Program 1-1 is shown with each of its lines numbered. Most of the lines contain something meaningful; however, some of the lines are empty. The blank lines are only there to make the program more readable.

A statement is a complete instruction that causes the computer to perform some action. Here is the statement that appears in line 10 of Program 1-1:

```
cout << "How many hours did you work? ";
```

This statement causes the computer to display the message "How many hours did you work?" on the screen. Statements can be a combination of key words, operators, and programmer-defined symbols. Statements often occupy only one line in a program, but sometimes they are spread out over more than one line.

Variables

A variable is a named storage location in the computer's memory for holding a piece of information. The information stored in variables may change while the program is running (hence the name "variable"). Notice that in Program 1-1 the words hours, rate, and pay appear in several places. All three of these are the names of variables. The hours variable is used to store the number of hours the user has worked. The rate variable stores the user's hourly pay rate. The pay variable holds the result of hours multiplied by rate, which is the user's gross pay.

NOTE: Notice the variables in Program 1-1 have names that reflect their purpose. In fact, it would be easy to guess what the variables were used for just by reading their names. This is discussed further in Chapter 2.

Variables are symbolic names that represent locations in the computer's random-access memory (RAM). When information is stored in a variable, it is actually stored in RAM. Assume a program has a variable named length. Figure 1-8 illustrates the way the variable name represents a memory location.

Figure 1-8

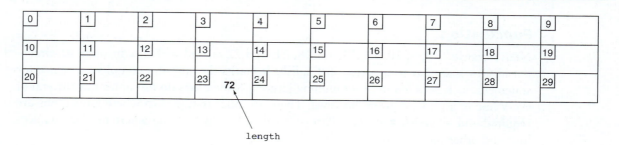

In Figure 1-8, the variable length is holding the value 72. The number 72 is actually stored in RAM at address 23, but the name length symbolically represents this storage location. If it helps, you can think of a variable as a box that holds information. In Figure 1-8, the number 72 is stored in the box named length. Only one item may be stored in the box at any given time. If the program stores another value in the box, it will take the place of the number 72.

Variable Definitions

In programming, there are two general types of data: numbers and characters. Numbers are used to perform mathematical operations and characters are used to print data on the screen or on paper.

Numeric data can be categorized even further. For instance, the following are all whole numbers, or integers:

```
5
7
-129
32154
```

The following are real, or floating-point numbers:

```
3.14159
6.7
1.0002
```

When creating a variable in a C++ program, you must know what type of data the program will be storing in it. Look at line 7 of Program 1-1:

```
double hours, rate, pay;
```

The word `double` in this statement indicates that the variables `hours`, `rate`, and `pay` will be used to hold double precision floating-point numbers. This statement is called a *variable definition*. It is used to *define* one or more variables that will be used in the program, and to indicate the type of data they will hold. The variable definition causes the variables to be created in memory, so all variables must be defined before they can be used. If you review the listing of Program 1-1, you will see that the variable definitions come before any other statements using those variables.

NOTE: Programmers often use the term "variable declaration" to mean the same thing as "variable definition." Strictly speaking, there is a difference between the two terms. A definition statement always causes a variable to be created in memory. Some types of declaration statements, however, do not cause a variable to be created in memory. You will learn more about declarations later in this book.

1.5 Input, Processing, and Output

CONCEPT: The three primary activities of a program are input, processing, and output.

Computer programs typically perform a three-step process of gathering input, performing some process on the information gathered, and then producing output. Input is information a program collects from the outside world. It can be sent to the program from the user, who is entering data at the keyboard or using the mouse. It can also be read from disk files or hardware devices connected to the computer. Program 1-1 allows the user to enter two pieces of information: the number of hours worked and the hourly pay rate. Lines 11 and 15 use the `cin` (pronounced "see in") object to perform these input operations:

```
cin >> hours;
cin >> rate;
```

Once information is gathered from the outside world, a program usually processes it in some manner. In Program 1-1, the hours worked and hourly pay rate are multiplied in line 18 and the result is assigned to the `pay` variable:

```
pay = hours * rate;
```

Output is information that a program sends to the outside world. It can be words or graphics displayed on a screen, a report sent to the printer, data stored in a file, or information sent to any device connected to the computer. Lines 10, 14, and 21 in Program 1-1 all perform output:

```
cout << "How many hours did you work? ";
cout << "How much do you get paid per hour? ";
cout << "You have earned $" << pay << endl;
```

These lines use the `cout` (pronounced "see out") object to display messages on the computer's screen. You will learn more details about the `cin` and `cout` objects in Chapter 2.

 ## Checkpoint

myprogramminglab *www.myprogramminglab.com*

1.18   Describe the difference between a key word and a programmer-defined identifier.

1.19   Describe the difference between operators and punctuation symbols.

1.20   Describe the difference between a program line and a statement.

1.21   Why are variables called "variable"?

1.22   What happens to a variable's current contents when a new value is stored there?

1.23   What must take place in a program before a variable is used?

1.24   What are the three primary activities of a program?

 ## 1.6 The Programming Process

CONCEPT: The programming process consists of several steps, which include design, creation, testing, and debugging activities.

Designing and Creating a Program

Now that you have been introduced to what a program is, it's time to consider the process of creating a program. Quite often, when inexperienced students are given programming assignments, they have trouble getting started because they don't know what to do first. If you find yourself in this dilemma, the steps listed in Figure 1-9 may help. These are the steps recommended for the process of writing a program.

Figure 1-9

---

1. Clearly define what the program is to do.
2. Visualize the program running on the computer.
3. Use design tools such as a hierarchy chart, flowcharts, or pseudocode to create a model of the program.
4. Check the model for logical errors.
5. Type the code, save it, and compile it.
6. Correct any errors found during compilation. Repeat Steps 5 and 6 as many times as necessary.
7. Run the program with test data for input.
8. Correct any errors found while running the program. Repeat Steps 5 through 8 as many times as necessary.
9. Validate the results of the program.

The steps listed in Figure 1-9 emphasize the importance of planning. Just as there are good ways and bad ways to paint a house, there are good ways and bad ways to create a program. A good program always begins with planning.

With the pay-calculating program as our example, let's look at each of the steps in more detail.

1. Clearly define what the program is to do.

This step requires that you identify the purpose of the program, the information that is to be input, the processing that is to take place, and the desired output. Let's examine each of these requirements for the example program:

Purpose	To calculate the user's gross pay.
Input	Number of hours worked, hourly pay rate.
Process	Multiply number of hours worked by hourly pay rate. The result is the user's gross pay.
Output	Display a message indicating the user's gross pay.

2. Visualize the program running on the computer.

Before you create a program on the computer, you should first create it in your mind. Step 2 is the visualization of the program. Try to imagine what the computer screen looks like while the program is running. If it helps, draw pictures of the screen, with sample input and output, at various points in the program. For instance, here is the screen produced by the pay-calculating program:

```
How many hours did you work? 10
How much do you get paid per hour? 15
You have earned $150
```

In this step, you must put yourself in the shoes of the user. What messages should the program display? What questions should it ask? By addressing these concerns, you will have already determined most of the program's output.

3. **Use design tools such as a hierarchy chart, flowcharts, or pseudocode to create a model of the program.**

While planning a program, the programmer uses one or more design tools to create a model of the program. Three common design tools are hierarchy charts, flowcharts, and pseudocode. A *hierarchy chart* is a diagram that graphically depicts the structure of a program. It has boxes that represent each step in the program. The boxes are connected in a way that illustrates their relationship to one another. Figure 1-10 shows a hierarchy chart for the pay-calculating program.

Figure 1-10

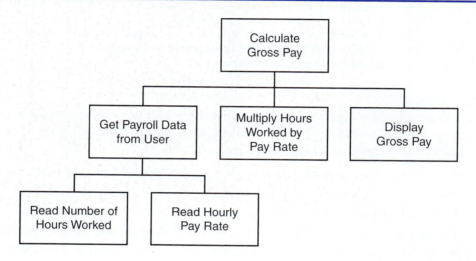

A hierarchy chart begins with the overall task, and then refines it into smaller subtasks. Each of the subtasks is then refined into even smaller sets of subtasks, until each is small enough to be easily performed. For instance, in Figure 1-10, the overall task "Calculate Gross Pay" is listed in the top-level box. That task is broken into three subtasks. The first subtask, "Get Payroll Data from User," is broken further into two subtasks. This process of "divide and conquer" is known as *top-down design.*

VideoNote

Introduction to Flowcharting

A *flowchart* is a diagram that shows the logical flow of a program. It is a useful tool for planning each operation a program performs, and the order in which the operations are to occur. For more information see Appendix D, Introduction to Flowcharting.

Pseudocode is a cross between human language and a programming language. Although the computer can't understand pseudocode, programmers often find it helpful to write an algorithm in a language that's "almost" a programming language, but still very similar to natural language. For example, here is pseudocode that describes the pay-calculating program:

VideoNote

Designing a Program with Pseudocode

Get payroll data.
Calculate gross pay.
Display gross pay.

Although the pseudocode above gives a broad view of the program, it doesn't reveal all the program's details. A more detailed version of the pseudocode follows.

Display "How many hours did you work?".
Input hours.
Display "How much do you get paid per hour?".
Input rate.
Store the value of hours times rate in the pay variable.
Display the value in the pay variable.

Notice the pseudocode contains statements that look more like commands than the English statements that describe the algorithm in Section 1.4 (What Is a Program Made of?). The pseudocode even names variables and describes mathematical operations.

4. **Check the model for logical errors.**

Logical errors are mistakes that cause the program to produce erroneous results. Once a hierarchy chart, flowchart, or pseudocode model of the program is assembled, it should be checked for these errors. The programmer should trace through the charts or pseudocode, checking the logic of each step. If an error is found, the model can be corrected before the next step is attempted.

5. **Type the code, save it, and compile it.**

Once a model of the program (hierarchy chart, flowchart, or pseudocode) has been created, checked, and corrected, the programmer is ready to write source code on the computer. The programmer saves the source code to a file, and begins the process of translating it to machine language. During this step the compiler will find any syntax errors that may exist in the program.

6. **Correct any errors found during compilation. Repeat Steps 5 and 6 as many times as necessary.**

If the compiler reports any errors, they must be corrected. Steps 5 and 6 must be repeated until the program is free of compile-time errors.

7. **Run the program with test data for input.**

Once an executable file is generated, the program is ready to be tested for run-time errors. A run-time error is an error that occurs while the program is running. These are usually logical errors, such as mathematical mistakes.

Testing for run-time errors requires that the program be executed with sample data or sample input. The sample data should be such that the correct output can be predicted. If the program does not produce the correct output, a logical error is present in the program.

8. **Correct any run-time errors found while running the program. Repeat Steps 5 through 8 as many times as necessary.**

When run-time errors are found in a program, they must be corrected. You must identify the step where the error occurred and determine the cause. Desk-checking is a process that can help locate run-time errors. The term *desk-checking* means the programmer starts reading the program, or a portion of the program, and steps through each statement. A sheet of paper is often used in this process to jot down the current contents of all variables and sketch what the screen looks like after each output operation. When a variable's contents change, or information is displayed on the screen, this is noted. By stepping through each statement, many errors can be located and corrected. If an error is a result of incorrect logic (such as an improperly stated math formula), you must correct the statement or statements involved in the logic. If an error is due to an incomplete understanding of the program requirements, then you must restate the program purpose and modify the hierarchy and/or flowcharts, pseudocode, and source code. The program must then be saved, recompiled and retested. This means Steps 5 though 8 must be repeated until the program reliably produces satisfactory results.

9. **Validate the results of the program.**

When you believe you have corrected all the run-time errors, enter test data and determine whether the program solves the original problem.

What Is Software Engineering?

The field of software engineering encompasses the whole process of crafting computer software. It includes designing, writing, testing, debugging, documenting, modifying, and maintaining complex software development projects. Like traditional engineers, software engineers use a number of tools in their craft. Here are a few examples:

- Program specifications
- Charts and diagrams of screen output
- Hierarchy charts and flowcharts
- Pseudocode
- Examples of expected input and desired output
- Special software designed for testing programs

Most commercial software applications are very large. In many instances one or more teams of programmers, not a single individual, develop them. It is important that the program requirements be thoroughly analyzed and divided into subtasks that are handled by individual teams, or individuals within a team.

In Step 3 of the programming process, you were introduced to the hierarchy chart as a tool for top-down design. The subtasks that are identified in a top-down design can easily become modules, or separate components of a program. If the program is very large or complex, a team of software engineers can be assigned to work on the individual modules. As the project develops, the modules are coordinated to finally become a single software application.

1.7 Procedural and Object-Oriented Programming

CONCEPT: Procedural programming and object-oriented programming are two ways of thinking about software development and program design.

C++ is a language that can be used for two methods of writing computer programs: *procedural programming* and *object-oriented programming*. This book is designed to teach you some of both.

In procedural programming, the programmer constructs procedures (or functions, as they are called in C++). The procedures are collections of programming statements that perform a specific task. The procedures each contain their own variables and commonly share variables with other procedures. This is illustrated by Figure 1-11.

Figure 1-11

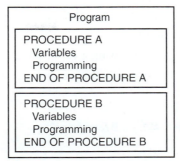

Procedural programming is centered on the procedure, or function. Object-oriented programming (OOP), on the other hand, is centered on the object. An object is a programming element that contains data and the procedures that operate on the data. It is a self-contained unit. This is illustrated in Figure 1-12.

Figure 1-12

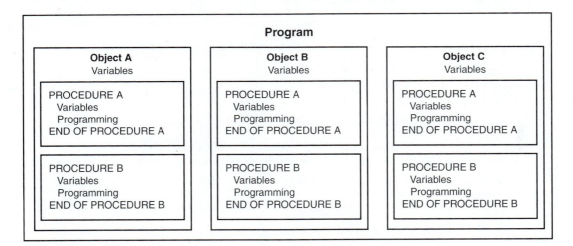

The objects contain, within themselves, both information and the ability to manipulate the information. Operations are carried out on the information in an object by sending the object a *message*. When an object receives a message instructing it to perform some operation, it carries out the instruction. As you study this text, you will encounter many other aspects of object-oriented programming.

 Checkpoint

myprogramminglab *www.myprogramminglab.com*

1.25   What four items should you identify when defining what a program is to do?

1.26   What does it mean to "visualize a program running"? What is the value of such an activity?

1.27   What is a hierarchy chart?

1.28   Describe the process of desk-checking.

1.29   Describe what a compiler does with a program's source code.

1.30   What is a run-time error?

1.31   Is a syntax error (such as misspelling a key word) found by the compiler or when the program is running?

1.32   What is the purpose of testing a program with sample data or input?

1.33   Briefly describe the difference between procedural and object-oriented programming.

Review Questions and Exercises

Short Answer

1. Both main memory and secondary storage are types of memory. Describe the difference between the two.

2. What is the difference between system software and application software?

3. What type of software controls the internal operations of the computer's hardware?

4. Why must programs written in a high-level language be translated into machine language before they can be run?

5. Why is it easier to write a program in a high-level language than in machine language?

6. Explain the difference between an object file and an executable file.

7. What is the difference between a syntax error and a logical error?

Fill-in-the-Blank

8. Computers can do many different jobs because they can be _____.

9. The job of the _____ is to fetch instructions, carry out the operations commanded by the instructions, and produce some outcome or resultant information.

10. Internally, the CPU consists of the _____ and the _____.

11. A(n) _____ is an example of a secondary storage device.

12. The two general categories of software are _____ and _____.

13. A program is a set of _____.

14. Since computers can't be programmed in natural human language, algorithms must be written in a(n) _____ language.

15. _____ is the only language computers really process.

16. _____ languages are close to the level of humans in terms of readability.

17. _____ languages are close to the level of the computer.

18. A program's ability to run on several different types of computer systems is called _____.

19. Words that have special meaning in a programming language are called _____.

20. Words or names defined by the programmer are called _____.

21. _____ are characters or symbols that perform operations on one or more operands.

22. _____ characters or symbols mark the beginning or ending of programming statements, or separate items in a list.

23. The rules that must be followed when constructing a program are called _____.

24. A(n) _____ is a named storage location.

25. A variable must be _____ before it can be used in a program.

26. The three primary activities of a program are _____, _____, and _____.

27. _____ is information a program gathers from the outside world.

28. _____ is information a program sends to the outside world.

29. A(n) _____ is a diagram that graphically illustrates the structure of a program.

Algorithm Workbench

Draw hierarchy charts or flowcharts that depict the programs described below. (See Appendix D for instructions on creating flowcharts.)

30. Available Credit

    The following steps should be followed in a program that calculates a customer's available credit:

    1. Display the message "Enter the customer's maximum credit."
    2. Wait for the user to enter the customer's maximum credit.
    3. Display the message "Enter the amount of credit used by the customer."
    4. Wait for the user to enter the customer's credit used.
    5. Subtract the used credit from the maximum credit to get the customer's available credit.
    6. Display a message that shows the customer's available credit.

31. Sales Tax

    Design a hierarchy chart or flowchart for a program that calculates the total of a retail sale. The program should ask the user for:
    – The retail price of the item being purchased
    – The sales tax rate

    Once these items have been entered, the program should calculate and display:
    – The sales tax for the purchase
    – The total of the sale

32. Account Balance

    Design a hierarchy chart or flowchart for a program that calculates the current balance in a savings account. The program must ask the user for:
    – The starting balance
    – The total dollar amount of deposits made
    – The total dollar amount of withdrawals made
    – The monthly interest rate

    Once the program calculates the current balance, it should be displayed on the screen.

VideoNote
Designing the Account Balance Program

Predict the Result

Questions 33–35 are programs expressed as English statements. What would each display on the screen if they were actual programs?

VideoNote
Predicting the Result of Problem 33

33. The variable x starts with the value 0.
    The variable y starts with the value 5.
    Add 1 to x.
    Add 1 to y.
    Add x and y, and store the result in y.
    Display the value in y on the screen.

34. The variable j starts with the value 10.
    The variable k starts with the value 2.
    The variable l starts with the value 4.
    Store the value of j times k in j.
    Store the value of k times l in l.
    Add j and l, and store the result in k.
    Display the value in k on the screen.

35. The variable a starts with the value 1.
    The variable b starts with the value 10.
    The variable c starts with the value 100.
    The variable x starts with the value 0.
    Store the value of c times 3 in x.
    Add the value of b times 6 to the value already in x.
    Add the value of a times 5 to the value already in x.
    Display the value in x on the screen.

Find the Error

36. The following *pseudocode algorithm* has an error. The program is supposed to ask the user for the length and width of a rectangular room, and then display the room's area. The program must multiply the width by the length in order to determine the area. Find the error.

    area = width × length.
    Display "What is the room's width?".
    Input width.
    Display "What is the room's length?".
    Input length.
    Display area.

2 Introduction to C++

2.1   The Parts of a C++ Program

CONCEPT: C++ programs have parts and components that serve specific purposes.

Every C++ program has an anatomy. Unlike human anatomy, the parts of C++ programs are not always in the same place. Nevertheless, the parts are there and your first step in learning C++ is to learn what they are. We will begin by looking at Program 2-1.

Let's examine the program line by line. Here's the first line:

```
// A simple C++ program
```

The // marks the beginning of a *comment*. The compiler ignores everything from the double slash to the end of the line. That means you can type anything you want on that line and the compiler will never complain! Although comments are not required, they are

27

very important to programmers. Most programs are much more complicated than the example in Program 2-1, and comments help explain what's going on.

Program 2-1

```
1   // A simple C++ program
2   #include <iostream>
3   using namespace std;
4
5   int main()
6   {
7      cout << "Programming is great fun!";
8      return 0;
9   }
```

The output of the program is shown below. This is what appears on the screen when the program runs.

Program Output
Programming is great fun!

Line 2 looks like this:

```
#include <iostream>
```

Because this line starts with a #, it is called a *preprocessor directive*. The preprocessor reads your program before it is compiled and only executes those lines beginning with a # symbol. Think of the preprocessor as a program that "sets up" your source code for the compiler.

The #include directive causes the preprocessor to include the contents of another file in the program. The word inside the brackets, iostream, is the name of the file that is to be included. The iostream file contains code that allows a C++ program to display output on the screen and read input from the keyboard. Because this program uses cout to display screen output, the iostream file must be included. The contents of the iostream file are included in the program at the point the #include statement appears. The iostream file is called a *header file,* so it should be included at the head, or top, of the program.

Line 3 reads:

```
using namespace std;
```

Programs usually contain several items with unique names. In this chapter you will learn to create variables. In Chapter 6 you will learn to create functions. In Chapter 13 you will learn to create objects. Variables, functions, and objects are examples of program entities that must have names. C++ uses *namespaces* to organize the names of program entities. The statement using namespace std; declares that the program will be accessing entities whose names are part of the namespace called std. (Yes, even namespaces have names.) The reason the program needs access to the std namespace is because every name created by the iostream file is part of that namespace. In order for a program to use the entities in iostream, it must have access to the std namespace.

Line 5 reads:

```
int main()
```

This marks the beginning of a function. A *function* can be thought of as a group of one or more programming statements that collectively has a name. The name of this function is *main*, and the set of parentheses that follows the name indicate that it is a function. The word `int` stands for "integer." It indicates that the function sends an integer value back to the operating system when it is finished executing.

Although most C++ programs have more than one function, every C++ program must have a function called `main`. It is the starting point of the program. If you are ever reading someone else's C++ program and want to find where it starts, just look for the function named `main`.

NOTE: C++ is a case-sensitive language. That means it regards uppercase letters as being entirely different characters than their lowercase counterparts. In C++, the name of the function `main` must be written in all lowercase letters. C++ doesn't see "Main" the same as "main," or "INT" the same as "int." This is true for all the C++ key words.

Line 6 contains a single, solitary character:

```
{
```

This is called a left-brace, or an opening brace, and it is associated with the beginning of the function `main`. All the statements that make up a function are enclosed in a set of braces. If you look at the third line down from the opening brace you'll see the closing brace. Everything between the two braces is the contents of the function `main`.

WARNING! Make sure you have a closing brace for every opening brace in your program!

After the opening brace you see the following statement in line 7:

```
cout << "Programming is great fun!";
```

To put it simply, this line displays a message on the screen. You will read more about `cout` and the `<<` operator later in this chapter. The message "Programming is great fun!" is printed without the quotation marks. In programming terms, the group of characters inside the quotation marks is called a *string literal* or *string constant*.

NOTE: This is the only line in the program that causes anything to be printed on the screen. The other lines, like `#include <iostream>` and `int main()`, are necessary for the framework of your program, but they do not cause any screen output. Remember, a program is a set of instructions for the computer. If something is to be displayed on the screen, you must use a programming statement for that purpose.

At the end of the line is a semicolon. Just as a period marks the end of a sentence, a semicolon marks the end of a complete statement in C++. Comments are ignored by the compiler, so the semicolon isn't required at the end of a comment. Preprocessor directives, like `#include` statements, simply end at the end of the line and never require semicolons. The beginning of a function, like `int main()`, is not a complete statement, so you don't place a semicolon there either.

It might seem that the rules for where to put a semicolon are not clear at all. Rather than worry about it now, just concentrate on learning the parts of a program. You'll soon get a feel for where you should and should not use semicolons.

Line 8 reads:

```
return 0;
```

This sends the integer value 0 back to the operating system upon the program's completion. The value 0 usually indicates that a program executed successfully.

Line 9 contains the closing brace:

```
}
```

This brace marks the end of the main function. Since main is the only function in this program, it also marks the end of the program.

In the sample program you encountered several sets of special characters. Table 2-1 provides a short summary of how they were used.

Table 2-1   Special Characters

Character	Name	Description
//	Double slash	Marks the beginning of a comment.
#	Pound sign	Marks the beginning of a preprocessor directive.
< >	Opening and closing brackets	Encloses a filename when used with the #include directive.
( )	Opening and closing parentheses	Used in naming a function, as in int main()
{ }	Opening and closing braces	Encloses a group of statements, such as the contents of a function.
" "	Opening and closing quotation marks	Encloses a string of characters, such as a message that is to be printed on the screen.
;	Semicolon	Marks the end of a complete programming statement.

 ## Checkpoint

myprogramminglab   *www.myprogramminglab.com*

2.1   The following C++ program will not compile because the lines have been mixed up.

```
int main()
}
// A crazy mixed up program
return 0;
#include <iostream>
cout << "In 1492 Columbus sailed the ocean blue.";
{
using namespace std;
```

When the lines are properly arranged the program should display the following on the screen:

```
In 1492 Columbus sailed the ocean blue.
```

Rearrange the lines in the correct order. Test the program by entering it on the computer, compiling it, and running it.

2.2   The cout Object

CONCEPT: Use the **cout** object to display information on the computer's screen.

In this section you will learn to write programs that produce output on the screen. The simplest type of screen output that a program can display is *console output*, which is merely plain text. The word *console* is an old computer term. It comes from the days when a computer operator interacted with the system by typing on a terminal. The terminal, which consisted of a simple screen and keyboard, was known as the *console*.

On modern computers, running graphical operating systems such as Windows or Mac OS X, console output is usually displayed in a window such as the one shown in Figure 2-1. In C++ you use the **cout** object to produce console output. (You can think of the word **cout** as meaning console **out**put.)

Figure 2-1   A Console Window

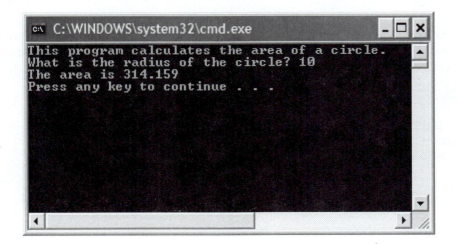

cout is classified as a *stream object*, which means it works with streams of data. To print a message on the screen, you send a stream of characters to **cout**. Let's look at line 7 from Program 2-1:

```
cout << "Programming is great fun!";
```

VideoNote
Using cout

Notice that the **<<** operator is used to send the string "Programming is great fun!" to **cout**. When the **<<** symbol is used this way, it is called the *stream insertion operator*. The item immediately to the right of the operator is sent to **cout** and then displayed on the screen.

The stream insertion operator is always written as two less-than signs with no space between them. Because you are using it to send a stream of data to the cout object, you can think of the stream insertion operator as an arrow that must point toward cout. This is illustrated in Figure 2-2.

Program 2-2 is another way to write the same program.

Figure 2-2

```
cout << "Programming is great fun!";
```
Think of the stream insertion operator as an
arrow that points toward cout.
```
cout ◄─── "Programming is great fun!";
```

Program 2-2

```
1   // A simple C++ program
2   #include <iostream>
3   using namespace std;
4
5   int main()
6   {
7      cout << "Programming is " << "great fun!";
8      return 0;
9   }
```

Program Output
```
Programming is great fun!
```

As you can see, the stream-insertion operator can be used to send more than one item to cout. The output of this program is identical to that of Program 2-1. Program 2-3 shows yet another way to accomplish the same thing.

Program 2-3

```
1   // A simple C++ program
2   #include <iostream>
3   using namespace std;
4
5   int main()
6   {
7      cout << "Programming is ";
8      cout << "great fun!";
9      return 0;
10  }
```

Program Output
```
Programming is great fun!
```

An important concept to understand about Program 2-3 is that, although the output is broken up into two programming statements, this program will still display the message on a single line. Unless you specify otherwise, the information you send to cout is displayed in a continuous stream. Sometimes this can produce less-than-desirable results. Program 2-4 is an example.

The layout of the actual output looks nothing like the arrangement of the strings in the source code. First, notice there is no space displayed between the words "sellers" and "during," or between "June:" and "Computer." cout displays messages exactly as they are sent. If spaces are to be displayed, they must appear in the strings.

Program 2-4

```
1   // An unruly printing program
2   #include <iostream>
3   using namespace std;
4
5   int main()
6   {
7      cout << "The following items were top sellers";
8      cout << "during the month of June:";
9      cout << "Computer games";
10     cout << "Coffee";
11     cout << "Aspirin";
12     return 0;
13  }
```

Program Output

```
The following items were top sellersduring the month of June:Computer gamesCoff
eeAspirin
```

Second, even though the output is broken into five lines in the source code, it comes out as one long line of output. Because the output is too long to fit on one line on the screen, it wraps around to a second line when displayed. The reason the output comes out as one long line is because cout does not start a new line unless told to do so. There are two ways to instruct cout to start a new line. The first is to send cout a *stream manipulator* called endl (which is pronounced "end-line" or "end-L"). Program 2-5 is an example.

Program 2-5

```
1   // A well-adjusted printing program
2   #include <iostream>
3   using namespace std;
4
5   int main()
6   {
7      cout << "The following items were top sellers" << endl;
8      cout << "during the month of June:" << endl;
9      cout << "Computer games" << endl;
10     cout << "Coffee" << endl;
11     cout << "Aspirin" << endl;
12     return 0;
13  }
```

(program output continues)

Program 2-5 *(continued)*

Program Output

```
The following items were top sellers
during the month of June:
Computer games
Coffee
Aspirin
```

 NOTE: The last character in endl is the lowercase letter L, *not* the number one.

Every time cout encounters an endl stream manipulator it advances the output to the beginning of the next line for subsequent printing. The manipulator can be inserted anywhere in the stream of characters sent to cout, outside the double quotes. The following statements show an example.

```
cout << "My pets are" << endl << "dog";
cout << endl << "cat" << endl << "bird" << endl;
```

Another way to cause cout to go to a new line is to insert an *escape sequence* in the string itself. An escape sequence starts with the backslash character (\), and is followed by one or more control characters. It allows you to control the way output is displayed by embedding commands within the string itself. Program 2-6 is an example.

Program 2-6

```
 1   // Yet another well-adjusted printing program
 2   #include <iostream>
 3   using namespace std;
 4
 5   int main()
 6   {
 7      cout << "The following items were top sellers\n";
 8      cout << "during the month of June:\n";
 9      cout << "Computer games\nCoffee";
10      cout << "\nAspirin\n";
11      return 0;
12   }
```

Program Output

```
The following items were top sellers
during the month of June:
Computer games
Coffee
Aspirin
```

The *newline escape sequence* is \n. When cout encounters \n in a string, it doesn't print it on the screen, but interprets it as a special command to advance the output cursor to the next line. You have probably noticed inserting the escape sequence requires less typing than inserting endl. That's why many programmers prefer it.

A common mistake made by beginning C++ students is to use a forward slash (/) instead of a backslash (\) when trying to write an escape sequence. This will not work. For example, look at the following code.

```
// Error!
cout << "Four Score/nAnd seven/nYears ago./n";
```

In this code, the programmer accidentally wrote /n when he or she meant to write \n. The cout object will simply display the /n characters on the screen. This code will display the following output:

```
Four Score/nAnd seven/nYears ago./n
```

Another common mistake is to forget to put the \n inside quotation marks. For example, the following code will not compile.

```
// Error! This code will not compile.
cout << "Good" << \n;
cout << "Morning" << \n;
```

This code will result in an error because the \n sequences are not inside quotation marks. We can correct the code by placing the \n sequences inside the string literals, as shown here:

```
// This will work.
cout << "Good\n";
cout << "Morning\n";
```

There are many escape sequences in C++. They give you the ability to exercise greater control over the way information is output by your program. Table 2-2 lists a few of them.

Table 2-2   Common Escape Sequences

Escape Sequence	Name	Description
\n	Newline	Causes the cursor to go to the next line for subsequent printing.
\t	Horizontal tab	Causes the cursor to skip over to the next tab stop.
\a	Alarm	Causes the computer to beep.
\b	Backspace	Causes the cursor to back up, or move left one position.
\r	Return	Causes the cursor to go to the beginning of the current line, not the next line.
\\	Backslash	Causes a backslash to be printed.
\'	Single quote	Causes a single quotation mark to be printed.
\"	Double quote	Causes a double quotation mark to be printed.

 WARNING! When using escape sequences, do not put a space between the backslash and the control character.

When you type an escape sequence in a string, you type two characters (a backslash followed by another character). However, an escape sequence is stored in memory as a single character. For example, consider the following string literal:

```
"One\nTwo\nThree\n"
```

The diagram in Figure 2-3 breaks this string into its individual characters. Notice how each of the \n escape sequences are considered one character.

Figure 2-3

| O | n | e | \n | T | w | o | \n | T | h | r | e | e | \n |

 2.3   # The #include Directive

> **CONCEPT:** The #include directive causes the contents of another file to be inserted into the program.

Now is a good time to expand our discussion of the #include directive. The following line has appeared near the top of every example program.

```
#include <iostream>
```

The header file iostream must be included in any program that uses the cout object. This is because cout is not part of the "core" of the C++ language. Specifically, it is part of the *input–output stream library*. The header file, iostream, contains information describing iostream objects. Without it, the compiler will not know how to properly compile a program that uses cout.

Preprocessor directives are not C++ statements. They are commands to the preprocessor, which runs prior to the compiler (hence the name "preprocessor"). The preprocessor's job is to set programs up in a way that makes life easier for the programmer.

For example, any program that uses the cout object must contain the extensive setup information found in iostream. The programmer could type all this information into the program, but it would be too time consuming. An alternative would be to use an editor to "cut and paste" the information into the program, but that would quickly become tiring as well. The solution is to let the preprocessor insert the contents of iostream automatically.

 WARNING! Do not put semicolons at the end of processor directives. Because preprocessor directives are not C++ statements, they do not require semicolons. In many cases an error will result from a preprocessor directive terminated with a semicolon.

An #include directive must always contain the name of a file. The preprocessor inserts the entire contents of the file into the program at the point it encounters the #include directive. The compiler doesn't actually see the #include directive. Instead it sees the code that was inserted by the preprocessor, just as if the programmer had typed it there.

The code contained in header files is C++ code. Typically it describes complex objects like cout. Later you will learn to create your own header files.

 ## Checkpoint

myprogramminglab   *www.myprogramminglab.com*

2.2   The following C++ program will not compile because the lines have been mixed up.

```
cout << "Success\n";
cout << " Success\n\n";
int main()
cout << "Success";
}
```

```
using namespace std;
// It's a mad, mad program
#include <iostream>
cout << "Success\n";
{
return 0;
```

When the lines are properly arranged the program should display the following on the screen:

Program Output
```
Success
Success Success

Success
```

Rearrange the lines in the correct order. Test the program by entering it on the computer, compiling it, and running it.

2.3   Study the following program and show what it will print on the screen.

```
// The Works of Wolfgang
#include <iostream>
using namespace std;

int main()
{
    cout << "The works of Wolfgang\ninclude the following";
    cout << "\nThe Turkish March" << endl;
    cout << "and Symphony No. 40 ";
    cout << "in G minor." << endl;
    return 0;
}
```

2.4   On paper, write a program that will display your name on the first line, your street address on the second line, your city, state, and ZIP code on the third line, and your telephone number on the fourth line. Place a comment with today's date at the top of the program. Test your program by entering, compiling, and running it.

2.4 Variables and Literals

> **CONCEPT:** Variables represent storage locations in the computer's memory. Literals are constant values that are assigned to variables.

As you discovered in Chapter 1, variables allow you to store and work with data in the computer's memory. They provide an "interface" to RAM. Part of the job of programming is to determine how many variables a program will need and what types of information they will hold. Program 2-7 is an example of a C++ program with a variable. Take a look at line 7:

```
    int number;
```

This is called a *variable definition*. It tells the compiler the variable's name and the type of data it will hold. This line indicates the variable's name is number. The word int stands for integer, so number will only be used to hold integer numbers. Later in this chapter you will learn all the types of data that C++ allows.

Program 2-7

```
 1   // This program has a variable.
 2   #include <iostream>
 3   using namespace std;
 4
 5   int main()
 6   {
 7      int number;
 8
 9      number = 5;
10      cout << "The value in number is " << number << endl;
11      return 0;
12   }
```

Program Output

```
The value in number is 5
```

 NOTE: You must have a definition for every variable you intend to use in a program. In C++, variable definitions can appear at any point in the program. Later in this chapter, and throughout the book, you will learn the best places to define variables.

Notice that variable definitions end with a semicolon. Now look at line 9:

```
number = 5;
```

This is called an *assignment*. The equal sign is an operator that copies the value on its right (5) into the variable named on its left (number). After this line executes, number will be set to 5.

 NOTE: This line does not print anything on the computer's screen. It runs silently behind the scenes, storing a value in RAM.

Look at line 10.

```
cout << "The value in number is " << number << endl;
```

The second item sent to cout is the variable name number. When you send a variable name to cout it prints the variable's contents. Notice there are no quotation marks around number. Look at what happens in Program 2-8.

Program 2-8

```
 1   // This program has a variable.
 2   #include <iostream>
 3   using namespace std;
 4
 5   int main()
 6   {
 7      int number;
 8
```

```
 9      number = 5;
10      cout << "The value in number is " << "number" << endl;
11      return 0;
12   }
```

Program Output

The value in number is number

When double quotation marks are placed around the word number it becomes a string literal, and is no longer a variable name. When string literals are sent to cout they are printed exactly as they appear inside the quotation marks. You've probably noticed by now that the endl stream manipulator has no quotation marks around it, for the same reason.

Sometimes a Number Isn't a Number

As shown in Program 2-8, just placing quotation marks around a variable name changes the program's results. In fact, placing double quotation marks around anything that is not intended to be a string literal will create an error of some type. For example, in Program 2-8 the number 5 was assigned to the variable number. It would have been incorrect to perform the assignment this way:

```
number = "5";
```

In this line, 5 is no longer an integer, but a string literal. Because number was defined as an integer variable, you can only store integers in it. The integer 5 and the string literal "5" are not the same thing.

The fact that numbers can be represented as strings frequently confuses students who are new to programming. Just remember that strings are intended for humans to read. They are to be printed on computer screens or paper. Numbers, however, are intended primarily for mathematical operations. You cannot perform math on strings. Before numbers can be displayed on the screen, they must first be converted to strings. (Fortunately, cout handles the conversion automatically when you send a number to it.)

Literals

A variable is called a "variable" because its value may be changed. A literal, on the other hand, is a value that does not change during the program's execution. Program 2-9 contains both literals and a variable.

Program 2-9

```
1   // This program has literals and a variable.
2   #include <iostream>
3   using namespace std;
4
5   int main()
6   {
```

(program continues)

Program 2-9 *(continued)*

```
7     int apples;
8
9     apples = 20;
10    cout << "Today we sold " << apples << " bushels of apples.\n";
11    return 0;
12  }
```

Program Output
Today we sold 20 bushels of apples.

Of course, the variable is apples. It is defined as an integer. Table 2-3 lists the literals found in the program.

Table 2-3

Literal	Type of Literal
20	Integer literal
"Today we sold "	String literal
"bushels of apples.\n"	String literal
0	Integer literal

What are literals used for? As you can see from this program, they are commonly used to store known values in variables and display messages on the screen or a printout.

NOTE: Literals are also called constants.

Checkpoint

myprogramminglab *www.myprogramminglab.com*

2.5   Examine the following program.

```
// This program uses variables and literals.
#include <iostream>
using namespace std;

int main()
{
    int little;
    int big;

    little = 2;
    big = 2000;
    cout << "The little number is " << little << endl;
    cout << "The big number is " << big << endl;
    return 0;
}
```

List all the variables and literals that appear in the program.

2.6   What will the following program display on the screen?

```
#include <iostream>
using namespace std;
```

```
int main()
{
    int number;

    number = 712;
    cout << "The value is " << "number" << endl;
    return 0;
}
```

2.5 Identifiers

CONCEPT: Choose variable names that indicate what the variables are used for.

An *identifier* is a programmer-defined name that represents some element of a program. Variable names are examples of identifiers. You may choose your own variable names in C++, as long as you do not use any of the C++ *key words*. The key words make up the "core" of the language and have specific purposes. Table 2-4 shows a complete list of the C++ key words. Note that they are all lowercase.

Table 2-4   The C++ Key Words

and	continue	goto	public	try
and_eq	default	if	register	typedef
asm	delete	inline	reinterpret_cast	typeid
auto	do	int	return	typename
bitand	double	long	short	union
bitor	dynamic_cast	mutable	signed	unsigned
bool	else	namespace	sizeof	using
break	enum	new	static	virtual
case	explicit	not	static_cast	void
catch	export	not_eq	struct	volatile
char	extern	operator	switch	wchar_t
class	false	or	template	while
compl	float	or_eq	this	xor
const	for	private	throw	xor_eq
const_cast	friend	protected	true	

You should always choose names for your variables that give an indication of what the variables are used for. You may be tempted to define variables with names like this:

```
int x;
```

The rather nondescript name, x, gives no clue as to the variable's purpose. Here is a better example.

```
int itemsOrdered;
```

The name `itemsOrdered` gives anyone reading the program an idea of the variable's use. This way of coding helps produce self-documenting programs, which means you get an understanding of what the program is doing just by reading its code. Because real-world programs usually have thousands of lines, it is important that they be as self-documenting as possible.

You probably have noticed the mixture of uppercase and lowercase letters in the name `itemsOrdered`. Although all of C++'s key words must be written in lowercase, you may use uppercase letters in variable names.

The reason the O in `itemsOrdered` is capitalized is to improve readability. Normally "items ordered" is two words. Unfortunately you cannot have spaces in a variable name, so the two words must be combined into one. When "items" and "ordered" are stuck together you get a variable definition like this:

```
int itemsordered;
```

Capitalization of the first letter of the second word and succeeding words makes `itemsOrdered` easier to read. It should be mentioned that this style of coding is not required. You are free to use all lowercase letters, all uppercase letters, or any combination of both. In fact, some programmers use the underscore character to separate words in a variable name, as in the following.

```
int items_ordered;
```

Legal Identifiers

Regardless of which style you adopt, be consistent and make your variable names as sensible as possible. Here are some specific rules that must be followed with all identifiers.

- The first character must be one of the letters a through z, A through Z, or an underscore character (_).
- After the first character you may use the letters a through z or A through Z, the digits 0 through 9, or underscores.
- Uppercase and lowercase characters are distinct. This means `ItemsOrdered` is not the same as `itemsordered`.

Table 2-5 lists variable names and tells whether each is legal or illegal in C++.

Table 2-5   Some Variable Names

Variable Name	Legal or Illegal?
dayOfWeek	Legal.
3dGraph	Illegal. Variable names cannot begin with a digit.
_employee_num	Legal.
June1997	Legal.
Mixture#3	Illegal. Variable names may only use letters, digits, or underscores.

2.6   Integer Data Types

CONCEPT: There are many different types of data. Variables are classified according to their data type, which determines the kind of information that may be stored in them. Integer variables can only hold whole numbers.

Computer programs collect pieces of data from the real world and manipulate them in various ways. There are many different types of data. In the realm of numeric information, for example, there are whole numbers and fractional numbers. There are negative numbers and positive numbers. And there are numbers so large, and others so small, that they don't even have a name. Then there is textual information. Names and addresses, for instance, are stored as groups of characters. When you write a program you must determine what types of information it will be likely to encounter.

If you are writing a program to calculate the number of miles to a distant star, you'll need variables that can hold very large numbers. If you are designing software to record microscopic dimensions, you'll need to store very small and precise numbers. Additionally, if you are writing a program that must perform thousands of intensive calculations, you'll want variables that can be processed quickly. The data type of a variable determines all of these factors.

Although C++ offers many data types, in the very broadest sense there are only two: numeric and character. Numeric data types are broken into two additional categories: integer and floating point. Integers are whole numbers like 12, 157, –34, and 2. Floating point numbers have a decimal point, like 23.7, 189.0231, and 0.987. Additionally, the integer and floating point data types are broken into even more classifications. Before we discuss the character data type, let's carefully examine the variations of numeric data.

Your primary considerations for selecting a numeric data type are:

- The largest and smallest numbers that may be stored in the variable
- How much memory the variable uses
- Whether the variable stores signed or unsigned numbers
- The number of decimal places of precision the variable has

The size of a variable is the number of bytes of memory it uses. Typically, the larger a variable is, the greater the range it can hold.

Table 2-6 shows the C++ integer data types with their typical sizes and ranges.

 NOTE: The data type sizes and ranges shown in Table 2-6 are typical on many systems. Depending on your operating system, the sizes and ranges may be different.

Table 2-6   Integer Data Types, Sizes, and Ranges

Data Type	Size	Range
short	2 bytes	–32,768 to +32,767
unsigned short	2 bytes	0 to +65,535
int	4 bytes	–2,147,483,648 to +2,147,483,647
unsigned int	4 bytes	0 to 4,294,967,295
long	4 bytes	–2,147,483,648 to +2,147,483,647
unsigned long	4 bytes	0 to 4,294,967,295

Here are some examples of variable definitions:

```
int days;
unsigned speed;
short month;
unsigned short amount;
long deficit;
unsigned long insects;
```

Unsigned data types can only store nonnegative values. They can be used when you know your program will not encounter negative values. For example, variables that hold ages or weights would rarely hold numbers less than 0.

> **NOTE:** An unsigned int variable can also be defined using only the word unsigned. For example, the following variable definitions are equivalent.
>
>   unsigned int days;
>   unsigned days;

Notice in Table 2-6 that the int and long data types have the same sizes and ranges, and that the unsigned int data type has the same size and range as the unsigned long data type. This is not always true because the size of integers is dependent on the type of system you are using. Here are the only guarantees:

- Integers are at least as big as short integers.
- Long integers are at least as big as integers.
- Unsigned short integers are the same size as short integers.
- Unsigned integers are the same size as integers.
- Unsigned long integers are the same size as long integers.

Later in this chapter you will learn to use the sizeof operator to determine how large all the data types are on your computer.

As mentioned before, variables are defined by stating the data type key word followed by the name of the variable. In Program 2-10 an integer, an unsigned integer, and a long integer have been defined.

Program 2-10

```
1   // This program has variables of several of the integer types.
2   #include <iostream>
3   using namespace std;
4
5   int main()
6   {
7       int checking;
8       unsigned int miles;
9       long days;
10
11      checking = -20;
12      miles = 4276;
13      days = 189000;
14      cout << "We have made a long journey of " << miles;
15      cout << " miles.\n";
16      cout << "Our checking account balance is " << checking;
17      cout << "\nAbout " << days << " days ago Columbus ";
18      cout << "stood on this spot.\n";
19      return 0;
20  }
```

Program Output
```
We have made a long journey of 4276 miles.
Our checking account balance is -20
About 189000 days ago Columbus stood on this spot.
```

In most programs you will need more than one variable of any given data type. If a program uses two integers, length and width, they could be defined separately, like this:

```
int length;
int width;
```

It is easier, however, to combine both variable definitions on one line:

```
int length, width;
```

You can define several variables of the same type like this, simply separating their names with commas. Program 2-11 illustrates this.

Program 2-11
```
 1   // This program shows three variables defined on the same line.
 2   #include <iostream>
 3   using namespace std;
 4
 5   int main()
 6   {
 7       int floors, rooms, suites;
 8
 9       floors = 15;
10       rooms = 300;
11       suites = 30;
12       cout << "The Grande Hotel has " << floors << " floors\n";
13       cout << "with " << rooms << " rooms and " << suites;
14       cout << " suites.\n";
15       return 0;
16   }
```

Program Output
```
The Grande Hotel has 15 floors
with 300 rooms and 30 suites.
```

Integer and Long Integer Literals

Look at lines 9, 10, and 11 in Program 2-11:

```
floors = 15;
rooms = 300;
suites = 30;
```

Each of these lines contains an integer literal. In C++, integer literals are normally stored in memory just as an int. On a system that uses 2 byte integers and 4 byte longs, the literal 50000 is too large to be stored as an int, so it is stored as a long.

One of the pleasing characteristics of the C++ language is that it allows you to control almost every aspect of your program. If you need to change the way something is stored in memory, the tools are provided to do that. For example, what if you are in a situation where you have an integer literal, but you need it to be stored in memory as a long integer? (Rest assured, this is a situation that does arise.) C++ allows you to force an integer literal to be stored as a long integer by placing the letter L at the end of the number. Here is an example:

```
32L
```

On a computer that uses 2-byte integers and 4-byte long integers, this literal will use 4 bytes. This is called a long integer literal.

NOTE: You can use either an uppercase or lowercase L. The lowercase l looks too much like the number 1, so you should always use the uppercase L.

If You Plan to Continue in Computer Science: Hexadecimal and Octal Literals

Programmers commonly express values in numbering systems other than decimal (or base 10). Hexadecimal (base 16) and octal (base 8) are popular because they make certain programming tasks more convenient than decimal numbers do.

By default, C++ assumes that all integer literals are expressed in decimal. You express hexadecimal numbers by placing 0x in front of them. (This is zero-x, not oh-x.) Here is how the hexadecimal number F4 would be expressed in C++:

```
0xF4
```

Octal numbers must be preceded by a 0 (zero, not oh). For example, the octal 31 would be written

```
031
```

NOTE: You will not be writing programs for some time that require this type of manipulation. It is important, however, that you understand this material. Good programmers should develop the skills for reading other people's source code. You may find yourself reading programs that use items like long integer, hexadecimal, or octal literals.

Checkpoint

myprogramminglab   *www.myprogramminglab.com*

2.7   Which of the following are illegal variable names, and why?

```
x
99bottles
july97
theSalesFigureForFiscalYear98
r&d
grade_report
```

2.8   Is the variable name Sales the same as sales? Why or why not?

2.9   Refer to the data types listed in Table 2-6 for these questions.

A) If a variable needs to hold numbers in the range 32 to 6,000, what data type would be best?

B) If a variable needs to hold numbers in the range –40,000 to +40,000, what data type would be best?

C) Which of the following literals uses more memory? 20 or 20L

2.10   On any computer, which data type uses more memory, an integer or an unsigned integer?

2.7 The char Data Type

You might be wondering why there isn't a 1-byte integer data type. Actually there is. It is called the char data type, which gets its name from the word "character." As its name suggests, it is primarily for storing characters, but strictly speaking, it is an integer data type.

NOTE: On some systems the char data type is larger than 1 byte.

The reason an integer data type is used to store characters is because characters are internally represented by numbers. Each printable character, as well as many nonprintable characters, is assigned a unique number. The most commonly used method for encoding characters is ASCII, which stands for the American Standard Code for Information Interchange. (There are other codes, such as EBCDIC, which is used by many IBM mainframes.)

When a character is stored in memory, it is actually the numeric code that is stored. When the computer is instructed to print the value on the screen, it displays the character that corresponds with the numeric code.

You may want to refer to Appendix B, which shows the ASCII character set. Notice that the number 65 is the code for A, 66 is the code for B, and so on. Program 2-12 demonstrates that when you work with characters, you are actually working with numbers.

Program 2-12

```
1   // This program demonstrates the close relationship between
2   // characters and integers.
3   #include <iostream>
4   using namespace std;
5
6   int main()
7   {
8      char letter;
9
10     letter = 65;
11     cout << letter << endl;
12     letter = 66;
13     cout << letter << endl;
14     return 0;
15  }
```

(program output continues)

Program 2-12 *(continued)*

Program Output
```
A
B
```

Figure 2-4 illustrates that when characters, such as A, B, and C, are stored in memory, it is really the numbers 65, 66, and 67 that are stored.

Figure 2-4

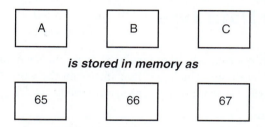

Character and String Literals

Although Program 2-12 nicely illustrates the way characters are represented by numbers, you do not have to work with the ASCII codes themselves. Program 2-13 is another version that works that same way.

Program 2-13 assigns character literals to the variable `letter`. Any time a program works with a character, it internally works with the code that represents that character, so this program is still assigning the values 65 and 66 to `letter`.

Program 2-13

```cpp
 1   // This program uses character literals.
 2   #include <iostream>
 3   using namespace std;
 4
 5   int main()
 6   {
 7      char letter;
 8
 9      letter = 'A';
10      cout << letter << endl;
11      letter = 'B';
12      cout << letter << endl;
13      return 0;
14   }
```

Program Output
```
A
B
```

Notice in lines 9 and 11 that the character literals are enclosed in single quotation marks. It is important that you do not confuse character literals with string literals, which are enclosed in double quotation marks. String literals cannot be assigned to char variables, because of the way string literals are stored internally.

Strings, which are a series of characters stored in consecutive memory locations, can be virtually any length. This means that there must be some way for the program to know how long a string is. In C++ an extra byte is appended to the end of string literals when they are stored in memory. In this last byte, the number 0 is stored. It is called the *null terminator* or *null character*, and it marks the end of the string.

Don't confuse the null terminator with the character '0'. If you look at Appendix B, you will see that ASCII code 48 corresponds to the character '0', whereas the null terminator is the same as the ASCII code 0. If you want to print the character 0 on the screen, you use ASCII code 48. If you want to mark the end of a string, however, you use ASCII code 0.

Let's look at an example of how a string literal is stored in memory. Figure 2-5 depicts the way the string literal "Sebastian" would be stored.

Figure 2-5

First, notice the quotation marks are not stored with the string. They are simply a way of marking the beginning and end of the string in your source code. Second, notice the very last byte of the string. It contains the null terminator, which is represented by the \0 character. The addition of this last byte means that although the string "Sebastian" is 9 characters long, it occupies 10 bytes of memory.

The null terminator is another example of something that sits quietly in the background. It doesn't print on the screen when you display a string, but nevertheless, it is there silently doing its job.

NOTE: C++ automatically places the null terminator at the end of string literals.

Now let's compare the way a string and a char are stored. Suppose you have the literals 'A' and "A" in a program. Figure 2-6 depicts their internal storage.

Figure 2-6

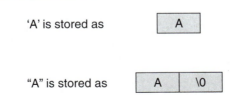

As you can see, 'A' is a 1-byte element and "A" is a 2-byte element. Since characters are really stored as ASCII codes, Figure 2-7 shows what is actually being stored in memory.

Figure 2-7

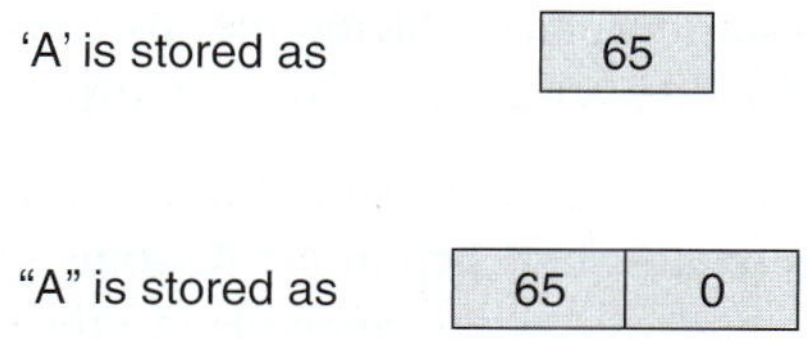

'A' is stored as | 65 |

"A" is stored as | 65 | 0 |

Because char variables are only large enough to hold one character, you cannot assign string literals to them. For example, the following code defines a char variable named letter. The character literal 'A' can be assigned to the variable, but the string literal "A" cannot.

```
char letter;
letter = 'A';  // This will work.
letter = "A";  // This will not work!
```

One final topic about characters should be discussed. You have learned that some strings look like a single character but really aren't. It is also possible to have a character that looks like a string. A good example is the newline character, \n. Although it is represented by two characters, a slash and an n, it is internally represented as one character. In fact, all escape sequences, internally, are just 1 byte.

Program 2-14 shows the use of \n as a character literal, enclosed in single quotation marks. If you refer to the ASCII chart in Appendix B, you will see that ASCII code 10 is the linefeed character. This is the code C++ uses for the newline character.

Program 2-14

```
 1   // This program uses character literals.
 2   #include <iostream>
 3   using namespace std;
 4
 5   int main()
 6   {
 7      char letter;
 8
 9      letter = 'A';
10      cout << letter << '\n';
11      letter = 'B';
12      cout << letter << '\n';
13      return 0;
14   }
```

Program Output

```
A
B
```

Let's review some important points regarding characters and strings:

- Printable characters are internally represented by numeric codes. Most computers use ASCII codes for this purpose.
- Characters normally occupy a single byte of memory.

- Strings are consecutive sequences of characters that occupy consecutive bytes of memory.
- String literals are always stored in memory with a null terminator at the end. This marks the end of the string.
- Character literals are enclosed in single quotation marks.
- String literals are enclosed in double quotation marks.
- Escape sequences such as `'\n'` are stored internally as a single character.

2.8 The C++ string Class

CONCEPT: Standard C++ provides a special data type for storing and working with strings.

Because a `char` variable can store only one character in its memory location, another data type is needed for a variable able to hold an entire string. Although C++ does not have a built-in data type able to do this, standard C++ provides something called the `string` class that allows the programmer to create a `string` type variable.

Using the string Class

The first step in using the `string` class is to `#include` the `string` header file. This is accomplished with the following preprocessor directive:

```
#include <string>
```

The next step is to define a `string` type variable, called a `string` object. Defining a `string` object is similar to defining a variable of a primitive type. For example, the following statement defines a `string` object named `movieTitle`.

```
string movieTitle;
```

You can assign a string literal to `movieTitle` with the assignment operator:

```
movieTitle = "Wheels of Fury";
```

You can use `cout` to display the value of the `movieTitle` object, as shown in the next statement:

```
cout << "My favorite movie is " << movieTitle << endl;
```

Program 2-15 is a complete program that demonstrates the preceding statements.

Program 2-15

```
1   // This program demonstrates the string class.
2   #include <iostream>
3   #include <string> // Required for the string class.
4   using namespace std;
```

(program continues)

Program 2-15   *(continued)*

```
 5
 6  int main()
 7  {
 8      string movieTitle;
 9
10      movieTitle = "Wheels of Fury";
11      cout << "My favorite movie is " << movieTitle << endl;
12      return 0;
13  }
```

Program Output

```
My favorite movie is Wheels of Fury
```

As you can see, working with string objects is similar to working with variables of other types. Throughout this text we will continue to discuss string class features and capabilities.

 ## Checkpoint

myprogramminglab *www.myprogramminglab.com*

2.11   What are the ASCII codes for the following characters? (Refer to Appendix B)

```
C
F
W
```

2.12   Which of the following is a character literal?

```
'B'
"B"
```

2.13   Assuming the char data type uses 1 byte of memory, how many bytes do the following literals use?

```
'Q'
"Q"
"Sales"
'\n'
```

2.14   Write a program that has the following character variables: first, middle, and last. Store your initials in these variables and then display them on the screen.

2.15   What is wrong with the following program statement?

```
char letter = "Z";
```

2.16   What header file must you include in order to use string objects?

2.17   Write a program that stores your name, address, and phone number in three separate string objects. Display the contents of the string objects on the screen.

2.9 Floating-Point Data Types

CONCEPT: Floating-point data types are used to define variables that can hold real numbers.

Whole numbers are not adequate for many jobs. If you are writing a program that works with dollar amounts or precise measurements, you need a data type that allows fractional values. In programming terms, these are called *floating-point* numbers.

Internally, floating-point numbers are stored in a manner similar to *scientific notation*. Take the number 47,281.97. In scientific notation this number is 4.728197×10^4. (10^4 is equal to 10,000, and $4.728197 \times 10,000$ is 47,281.97.) The first part of the number, 4.728197, is called the *mantissa*. The mantissa is multiplied by a power of ten.

Computers typically use *E notation* to represent floating-point values. In E notation, the number 47,281.97 would be 4.728197E4. The part of the number before the E is the mantissa, and the part after the E is the power of 10. When a floating point number is stored in memory, it is stored as the mantissa and the power of 10.

Table 2-7 shows other numbers represented in scientific and E notation.

Table 2-7   Floating Point Representations

Decimal Notation	Scientific Notation	E Notation
247.91	2.4791×10^2	`2.4791E2`
0.00072	7.2×10^{-4}	`7.2E-4`
2,900,000	2.9×10^6	`2.9E6`

In C++ there are three data types that can represent floating-point numbers. They are

```
float
double
long double
```

The `float` data type is considered *single precision*. The `double` data type is usually twice as big as `float`, so it is considered *double precision*. As you've probably guessed, the `long double` is intended to be larger than the `double`. Of course, the exact sizes of these data types are dependent on the computer you are using. The only guarantees are:

- A `double` is at least as big as a `float`.
- A `long double` is at least as big as a `double`.

Table 2-8 shows the sizes and ranges of floating-point data types usually found on PCs.

Table 2-8   Floating Point Data Types on PCs

Data Type	Key Word	Description
Single precision	`float`	4 bytes. Numbers between ±3.4E-38 and ±3.4E38
Double precision	`double`	8 bytes. Numbers between ±1.7E-308 and ±1.7E308
Long double precision	`long double*`	8 bytes. Numbers between ±1.7E-308 and ±1.7E308

*Some compilers use 10 bytes for long doubles. This allows a range of ±3.4E-4932 to ±1.1E4832

You will notice there are no unsigned floating point data types. On all machines, variables of the `float`, `double`, and `long double` data types can store positive or negative numbers.

Floating Point Literals

Floating point literals may be expressed in a variety of ways. As shown in Program 2-16, E notation is one method. When you are writing numbers that are extremely large or extremely small, this will probably be the easiest way. E notation numbers may be expressed with an uppercase E or a lowercase e. Notice that in the source code the literals were written as 1.495979E11 and 1.989E30, but the program printed them as 1.49598e+011 and 1.989e+30. The two sets of numbers are equivalent. (The plus sign in front of the exponent is also optional.) In Chapter 3 you will learn to control the way `cout` displays E notation numbers.

Program 2-16

```
 1   // This program uses floating point data types.
 2   #include <iostream>
 3   using namespace std;
 4
 5   int main()
 6   {
 7      float distance;
 8      double mass;
 9
10      distance = 1.495979E11;
11      mass = 1.989E30;
12      cout << "The Sun is " << distance << " meters away.\n";
13      cout << "The Sun\'s mass is " << mass << " kilograms.\n";
14      return 0;
15   }
```

Program Output
```
The Sun is 1.49598e+011 meters away.
The Sun's mass is 1.989e+030 kilograms.
```

You can also express floating-point literals in decimal notation. The literal 1.495979E11 could have been written as

```
149597900000.00
```

Obviously the E notation is more convenient for lengthy numbers, but for numbers like 47.39, decimal notation is preferable to 4.739E1.

All of the following floating-point literals are equivalent:

```
1.4959E11
1.4959e11
1.4959E+11
1.4959e+11
149590000000.00
```

Floating-point literals are normally stored in memory as `doubles`. But remember, C++ provides tools for handling just about any situation. Just in case you need to force a literal to be stored as a `float`, you can append the letter F or f to the end of it. For example, the following literals would be stored as `floats`:

```
1.2F
45.907f
```

> **NOTE:** Because floating-point literals are normally stored in memory as `doubles`, many compilers issue a warning message when you assign a floating-point literal to a `float` variable. For example, assuming num is a `float`, the following statement might cause the compiler to generate a warning message:
>
> ```
> num = 14.725;
> ```
>
> You can suppress the warning message by appending the f suffix to the floating-point literal, as shown below:
>
> ```
> num = 14.725f;
> ```

If you want to force a value to be stored as a `long double`, append an L or l to it, as in the following examples:

```
1034.56L
89.21
```

The compiler won't confuse these with long integers because they have decimal points. (Remember, the lowercase L looks so much like the number 1 that you should always use the uppercase L when suffixing literals.)

Assigning Floating-Point Values to Integer Variables

When a floating-point value is assigned to an integer variable, the fractional part of the value (the part after the decimal point) is discarded. For example, look at the following code.

```
int number;
number = 7.5;    // Assigns 7 to number
```

This code attempts to assign the floating-point value 7.5 to the integer variable `number`. As a result, the value 7 will be assigned to `number`, with the fractional part discarded. When part of a value is discarded, it is said to be *truncated*.

Assigning a floating-point variable to an integer variable has the same effect. For example, look at the following code.

```
int i;
float f;
f = 7.5;
i = f;            // Assigns 7 to i.
```

When the `float` variable `f` is assigned to the `int` variable `i`, the value being assigned (7.5) is truncated. After this code executes `i` will hold the value 7 and `f` will hold the value 7.5.

NOTE: When a floating-point value is truncated, it is not rounded. Assigning the value 7.9 to an `int` variable will result in the value 7 being stored in the variable.

WARNING! Floating-point variables can hold a much larger range of values than integer variables can. If a floating-point value is being stored in an integer variable, and the whole part of the value (the part before the decimal point) is too large for the integer variable, an invalid value will be stored in the integer variable.

2.10   The `bool` Data Type

CONCEPT: Boolean variables are set to either `true` or `false`.

Expressions that have a `true` or `false` value are called *Boolean* expressions, named in honor of English mathematician George Boole (1815–1864).

The `bool` data type allows you to create small integer variables that are suitable for holding `true` or `false` values. Program 2-17 demonstrates the definition and assignment of a `bool` variable.

Program 2-17

```
 1   // This program demonstrates boolean variables.
 2   #include <iostream>
 3   using namespace std;
 4
 5   int main()
 6   {
 7      bool boolValue;
 8
 9      boolValue = true;
10      cout << boolValue << endl;
11      boolValue = false;
12      cout << boolValue << endl;
13      return 0;
14   }
```

Program Output
```
1
0
```

As you can see from the program output, the value `true` is represented in memory by the number 1, and `false` is represented by 0. You will not be using `bool` variables until Chapter 4, however, so just remember they are useful for evaluating conditions that are either true or false.

2.11   Determining the Size of a Data Type

CONCEPT: The `sizeof` operator may be used to determine the size of a data type on any system.

Chapter 1 discussed the portability of the C++ language. As you have seen in this chapter, one of the problems of portability is the lack of common sizes of data types on all machines. If you are not sure what the sizes of data types are on your computer, C++ provides a way to find out.

A special operator called `sizeof` will report the number of bytes of memory used by any data type or variable. Program 2-18 illustrates its use. The first line that uses the operator is line 10:

```
cout << "The size of an integer is " << sizeof(int);
```

The name of the data type or variable is placed inside the parentheses that follow the operator. The operator "returns" the number of bytes used by that item. This operator can be invoked anywhere you can use an unsigned integer, including in mathematical operations.

Program 2-18

```
 1   // This program determines the size of integers, long
 2   // integers, and long doubles.
 3   #include <iostream>
 4   using namespace std;
 5
 6   int main()
 7   {
 8      long double apple;
 9
10      cout << "The size of an integer is " << sizeof(int);
11      cout << " bytes.\n";
12      cout << "The size of a long integer is " << sizeof(long);
13      cout << " bytes.\n";
14      cout << "An apple can be eaten in " << sizeof(apple);
15      cout << " bytes!\n";
16      return 0;
17   }
```

Program Output
```
The size of an integer is 4 bytes.
The size of a long integer is 4 bytes.
An apple can be eaten in 8 bytes!
```

Checkpoint

myprogramminglab   *www.myprogramminglab.com*

2.18   Yes or No: Is there an unsigned floating point data type? If so, what is it?

2.19   How would the following number in scientific notation be represented in E notation?

$$6.31 \times 10^{17}$$

2.20   Write a program that defines an integer variable named `age` and a `float` variable named `weight`. Store your age and weight, as literals, in the variables. The program should display these values on the screen in a manner similar to the following:

Program Output
My age is 26 and my weight is 180 pounds.

(Feel free to lie to the computer about your age and your weight—it'll never know!)

2.12   Variable Assignments and Initialization

CONCEPT: An assignment operation assigns, or copies, a value into a variable. When a value is assigned to a variable as part of the variable's definition, it is called an initialization.

As you have already seen in several examples, a value is stored in a variable with an *assignment statement*. For example, the following statement copies the value 12 into the variable `unitsSold`.

```
unitsSold = 12;
```

The = symbol is called the *assignment operator*. Operators perform operations on data. The data that operators work with are called *operands*. The assignment operator has two operands. In the previous statement, the operands are `unitsSold` and 12.

In an assignment statement, C++ requires the name of the variable receiving the assignment to appear on the left side of the operator. The following statement is incorrect.

```
12 = unitsSold;     // Incorrect!
```

In C++ terminology, the operand on the left side of the = symbol must be an *lvalue*. It is called an lvalue because it is a value that may appear on the left side of an assignment operator. An lvalue is something that identifies a place in memory whose contents may be changed. Most of the time this will be a variable name. The operand on the right side of the = symbol must be an *rvalue*. An rvalue is any expression that has a value. The assignment statement takes the value of the rvalue and puts it in the memory location of the object identified by the lvalue.

You may also assign values to variables as part of the definition. This is called *initialization*. Program 2-19 shows how it is done.

Program 2-19

```
1   // This program shows variable initialization.
2   #include <iostream>
3   using namespace std;
4
5   int main()
6   {
7       int month = 2, days = 28;
8
9       cout << "Month " << month << " has " << days << " days.\n";
10      return 0;
11  }
```

Program Output
Month 2 has 28 days.

As you can see, this simplifies the program and reduces the number of statements that must be typed by the programmer. Here are examples of other definition statements that perform initialization.

```
double interestRate = 12.9;
char stockode = 'D';
long customerNum = 459L;
```

Of course, there are always variations on a theme. C++ allows you to define several variables and only initialize some of them. Here is an example of such a definition:

```
int flightNum = 89, travelTime, departure = 10, distance;
```

The variable `flightNum` is initialized to 89 and `departure` is initialized to 10. The variables `travelTime` and `distance` remain uninitialized.

2.13 Scope

CONCEPT: A variable's scope is the part of the program that has access to the variable.

Every variable has a *scope*. The scope of a variable is the part of the program where the variable may be used. The rules that define a variable's scope are complex, and you will only be introduced to the concept here. In other sections of the book we will revisit this topic and expand on it.

The first rule of scope you should learn is that a variable cannot be used in any part of the program before the definition. Program 2-20 illustrates this.

Program 2-20

```
 1  // This program can't find its variable.
 2  #include <iostream>
 3  using namespace std;
 4
 5  int main()
 6  {
 7     cout << value; // ERROR! value not defined yet!
 8
 9     int value = 100;
10     return 0;
11  }
```

The program will not work because line 7 attempts to send the contents of the variable value to cout before the variable is defined. The compiler reads your program from top to bottom. If it encounters a statement that uses a variable before the variable is defined, an error will result. To correct the program, the variable definition must be put before any statement that uses it.

2.14   Arithmetic Operators

CONCEPT: There are many operators for manipulating numeric values and performing arithmetic operations.

C++ offers a multitude of operators for manipulating data. Generally, there are three types of operators: *unary*, *binary*, and *ternary*. These terms reflect the number of operands an operator requires.

VideoNote
Assignment Statements and Simple Math Expressions

Unary operators only require a single operand. For example, consider the following expression:

−5

Of course, we understand this represents the value negative five. The literal 5 is preceded by the minus sign. The minus sign, when used this way, is called the *negation operator*. Since it only requires one operand, it is a unary operator.

Binary operators work with two operands. The assignment operator is in this category. Ternary operators, as you may have guessed, require three operands. C++ only has one ternary operator, which will be discussed in Chapter 4.

Arithmetic operations are very common in programming. Table 2-9 shows the common arithmetic operators in C++.

Table 2-9 Fundamental Arithmetic Operators

Operator	Meaning	Type	Example
+	Addition	Binary	`total = cost + tax;`
−	Subtraction	Binary	`cost = total - tax;`
*	Multiplication	Binary	`tax = cost * rate;`
/	Division	Binary	`salePrice = original / 2;`
%	Modulus	Binary	`remainder = value % 3;`

Each of these operators works as you probably expect. The addition operator returns the sum of its two operands. In the following assignment statement, the variable `amount` will be assigned the value 12:

```
amount = 4 + 8;
```

The subtraction operator returns the value of its right operand subtracted from its left operand. This statement will assign the value 98 to `temperature`:

```
temperature = 112 - 14;
```

The multiplication operator returns the product of its two operands. In the following statement, `markUp` is assigned the value 3:

```
markUp = 12 * 0.25;
```

The division operator returns the quotient of its left operand divided by its right operand. In the next statement, `points` is assigned the value 5:

```
points = 100 / 20;
```

It is important to note that when both of the division operator's operands are integers, the result of the division will also be an integer. If the result has a fractional part, it will be thrown away. We will discuss this behavior, which is known as *integer division*, in greater detail later in this section.

The modulus operator, which only works with integer operands, returns the remainder of an integer division. The following statement assigns 2 to `leftOver`:

```
leftOver = 17 % 3;
```

In Chapter 3 you will learn how to use these operators in more complex mathematical formulas. For now we will concentrate on their basic usage. For example, suppose we need to write a program that calculates and displays an employee's total wages for the week. The regular hours for the work week are 40, and any hours worked over 40 are considered overtime. The employee earns $18.25 per hour for regular hours, and $27.78 per hour for overtime hours. The employee has worked 50 hours this week. The following pseudocode algorithm shows the program's logic.

Regular wages = base pay rate × regular hours
Overtime wages = overtime pay rate × overtime hours
Total wages = regular wages + overtime wages
Display the total wages

Program 2-21 shows the C++ code for the program.

Program 2-21

```
 1   // This program calculates hourly wages, including overtime.
 2   #include <iostream>
 3   using namespace std;
 4
 5   int main()
 6   {
 7      double regularWages,              // To hold regular wages
 8             basePayRate = 18.25,       // Base pay rate
 9             regularHours = 40.0,       // Hours worked less overtime
10             overtimeWages,             // To hold overtime wages
11             overtimePayRate = 27.78,   // Overtime pay rate
12             overtimeHours = 10,        // Overtime hours worked
13             totalWages;                // To hold total wages
14
15      // Calculate the regular wages.
16      regularWages = basePayRate * regularHours;
17
18      // Calculate the overtime wages.
19      overtimeWages = overtimePayRate * overtimeHours;
20
21      // Calculate the total wages.
22      totalWages = regularWages + overtimeWages;
23
24      // Display the total wages.
25      cout << "Wages for this week are $" << totalWages << endl;
26      return 0;
27   }
```

Program Output
```
Wages for this week are $1007.8
```

Let's take a closer look at the program. As mentioned in the comments, there are variables for regular wages, base pay rate, regular hours worked, overtime wages, overtime pay rate, overtime hours worked, and total wages.

Here is line 16, which multiplies `basePayRate` times `regularHours` and stores the result in `regularWages`:

```
regularWages = basePayRate * regularHours;
```

Here is line 19, which multiplies `overtimePayRate` times `overtimeHours` and stores the result in `overtimeWages`:

```
overtimeWages = overtimePayRate * overtimeHours;
```

Line 22 adds the regular wages and the overtime wages and stores the result in `totalWages`:

```
totalWages = regularWages + overtimeWages;
```

Line 25 displays the message on the screen reporting the week's wages.

Integer Division

When both operands of a division statement are integers, the statement will result in *integer division*. This means the result of the division will be an integer as well. If there is a remainder, it will be discarded. For example, look at the following code:

```
double number;
number = 5 / 2;
```

This code divides 5 by 2 and assigns the result to the number variable. What will be stored in number? You would probably assume that 2.5 would be stored in number because that is the result your calculator shows when you divide 5 by 2. However, that is not what happens when the previous C++ code is executed. Because the numbers 5 and 2 are both integers, the fractional part of the result will be thrown away, or truncated. As a result, the value 2 will be assigned to the number variable.

In the previous code, it doesn't matter that the number variable is declared as a double because the fractional part of the result is discarded before the assignment takes place. In order for a division operation to return a floating-point value, one of the operands must be of a floating-point data type. For example, the previous code could be written as follows:

```
double number;
number = 5.0 / 2;
```

In this code, 5.0 is treated as a floating-point number, so the division operation will return a floating-point number. The result of the division is 2.5.

In the Spotlight:
Calculating Percentages and Discounts

Determining percentages is a common calculation in computer programming. Although the % symbol is used in general mathematics to indicate a percentage, most programming languages (including C++) do not use the % symbol for this purpose. In a program, you have to convert a percentage to a floating-point number, just as you would if you were using a calculator. For example, 50 percent would be written as 0.5 and 2 percent would be written as 0.02.

Let's look at an example. Suppose you earn $6,000 per month and you are allowed to contribute a portion of your gross monthly pay to a retirement plan. You want to determine the amount of your pay that will go into the plan if you contribute 5 percent, 7 percent, or 10 percent of your gross wages. To make this determination you write the program shown in Program 2-22.

Program 2-22

```
1   // This program calculates the amount of pay that
2   // will be contributed to a retirement plan if 5%,
3   // 7%, or 10% of monthly pay is withheld.
4   #include <iostream>
5   using namespace std;
6
```

(program continues)

Program 2-22   *(continued)*

```
 7   int main()
 8   {
 9       // Variables to hold the monthly pay and the
10       // amount of contribution.
11       double monthlyPay = 6000.0, contribution;
12
13       // Calculate and display a 5% contribution.
14       contribution = monthlyPay * 0.05;
15       cout << "5 percent is $" << contribution
16           << " per month.\n";
17
18       // Calculate and display a 7% contribution.
19       contribution = monthlyPay * 0.07;
20       cout << "7 percent is $" << contribution
21           << " per month.\n";
22
23       // Calculate and display a 10% contribution.
24       contribution = monthlyPay * 0.1;
25       cout << "10 percent is $" << contribution
26           << " per month.\n";
27
28       return 0;
29   }
```

Program Output
```
5 percent is $300 per month.
7 percent is $420 per month.
10 percent is $600 per month.
```

Line 11 defines two variables: `monthlyPay` and `contribution`. The `monthlyPay` variable, which is initialized with the value 6000.0, holds the amount of your monthly pay. The `contribution` variable will hold the amount of a contribution to the retirement plan.

The statements in lines 14 through 16 calculate and display 5 percent of the monthly pay. The calculation is done in line 14, where the `monthlyPay` variable is multiplied by 0.05. The result is assigned to the `contribution` variable, which is then displayed in line 15.

Similar steps are taken in Lines 18 through 21, which calculate and display 7 percent of the monthly pay, and lines 24 through 26, which calculate and display 10 percent of the monthly pay.

Calculating a Percentage Discount

Another common calculation is determining a percentage discount. For example, suppose a retail business sells an item that is regularly priced at $59.95, and is planning to have a sale where the item's price will be reduced by 20 percent. You have been asked to write a program to calculate the sale price of the item.

To determine the sale price you perform two calculations:

- First, you get the amount of the discount, which is 20 percent of the item's regular price.
- Second, you subtract the discount amount from the item's regular price. This gives you the sale price.

Program 2-23 shows how this is done in C++.

Program 2-23

```
 1  // This program calculates the sale price of an item
 2  // that is regularly priced at $59.95, with a 20 percent
 3  // discount subtracted.
 4  #include <iostream>
 5  using namespace std;
 6
 7  int main()
 8  {
 9      // Variables to hold the regular price, the
10      // amount of a discount, and the sale price.
11      double regularPrice = 59.95, discount, salePrice;
12
13      // Calculate the amount of a 20% discount.
14      discount = regularPrice * 0.2;
15
16      // Calculate the sale price by subtracting the
17      // discount from the regular price.
18      salePrice = regularPrice - discount;
19
20      // Display the results.
21      cout << "Regular price: $" << regularPrice << endl;
22      cout << "Discount amount: $" << discount << endl;
23      cout << "Sale price: $" << salePrice << endl;
24      return 0;
25  }
```

Program Output
```
Regular price: $59.95
Discount amount: $11.99
Sale price: $47.96
```

Line 11 defines three variables. The `regularPrice` variable holds the item's regular price, and is initialized with the value 59.95. The `discount` variable will hold the amount of the discount once it is calculated. The `salePrice` variable will hold the item's sale price.

Line 14 calculates the amount of the 20 percent discount by multiplying `regularPrice` by 0.2. The result is stored in the `discount` variable. Line 18 calculates the sale price by subtracting `discount` from `regularPrice`. The result is stored in the `salePrice` variable. The cout statements in lines 21 through 23 display the item's regular price, the amount of the discount, and the sale price.

In the Spotlight:
Using the Modulus Operator and Integer Division

The modulus operator (%) is surprisingly useful. For example, suppose you need to extract the rightmost digit of a number. If you divide the number by 10, the remainder will be the rightmost digit. For instance, 123 ÷ 10 = 12 with a remainder of 3. In a computer program you would use the modulus operator to perform this operation. Recall that the modulus operator divides an integer by another integer, and gives the remainder. This is demonstrated in Program 2-24. The program extracts the rightmost digit of the number 12345.

Program 2-24

```
1  // This program extracts the rightmost digit of a number.
2  #include <iostream>
3  using namespace std;
4
5  int main()
6  {
7      int number = 12345;
8      int rightMost = number % 10;
9
10     cout << "The rightmost digit in "
11          << number << " is "
12          << rightMost << endl;
13
14     return 0;
15 }
```

Program Output

```
The rightmost digit in 12345 is 5
```

Interestingly, the expression number % 100 will give you the rightmost two digits in number, the expression number % 1000 will give you the rightmost three digits in number, etc.

The modulus operator (%) is useful in many other situations. For example, Program 2-25 converts 125 seconds to an equivalent number of minutes, and seconds.

Program 2-25

```
1  // This program converts seconds to minutes and seconds.
2  #include <iostream>
3  using namespace std;
4
5  int main()
6  {
7      // The total seconds is 125.
8      int totalSeconds = 125;
9
```

```
10      // Variables for the minutes and seconds
11      int minutes, seconds;
12
13      // Get the number of minutes.
14      minutes = totalSeconds / 60;
15
16      // Get the remaining seconds.
17      seconds = totalSeconds % 60;
18
19      // Display the results.
20      cout << totalSeconds << " seconds is equivalent to:\n";
21      cout << "Minutes: " << minutes << endl;
22      cout << "Seconds: " << seconds << endl;
23      return 0;
24 }
```

Program Output

```
125 seconds is equivalent to:
Minutes: 2
Seconds: 5
```

Let's take a closer look at the code:

- Line 8 defines an int variable named totalSeconds, initialized with the value 125.
- Line 11 declares the int variables minutes and seconds.
- Line 14 calculates the number of minutes in the specified number of seconds. There are 60 seconds in a minute, so this statement divides totalSeconds by 60. Notice that we are performing integer division in this statement. Both totalSeconds and the numeric literal 60 are integers, so the division operator will return an integer result. This is intentional because we want the number of minutes with no fractional part.
- Line 17 calculates the number of remaining seconds. There are 60 seconds in a minute, so this statement uses the % operator to divide the totalSeconds by 60, and get the remainder of the division. The result is the number of remaining seconds.
- Lines 20 through 22 display the number of minutes and seconds.

Checkpoint

myprogramminglab *www.myprogramminglab.com*

2.21   Is the following assignment statement valid or invalid? If it is invalid, why?

```
72 = amount;
```

2.22   How would you consolidate the following definitions into one statement?

```
int x = 7;
int y = 16;
int z = 28;
```

2.23   What is wrong with the following program? How would you correct it?

```cpp
#include <iostream>
using namespace std;

int main()
{
    number = 62.7;
    double number;
    cout << number << endl;
    return 0;
}
```

2.24   Is the following an example of integer division or floating-point division? What value will be stored in `portion`?

```cpp
portion = 70 / 3;
```

2.15   Comments

CONCEPT: Comments are notes of explanation that document lines or sections of a program. Comments are part of the program, but the compiler ignores them. They are intended for people who may be reading the source code.

It may surprise you that one of the most important parts of a program has absolutely no impact on the way it runs. In fact, the compiler ignores this part of a program. Of course, I'm speaking of the comments.

As a beginning programmer, you might be resistant to the idea of liberally writing comments in your programs. After all, it can seem more productive to write code that actually does something! It is crucial, however, that you develop the habit of thoroughly annotating your code with descriptive comments. It might take extra time now, but it will almost certainly save time in the future.

Imagine writing a program of medium complexity with about 8,000 to 10,000 lines of C++ code. Once you have written the code and satisfactorily debugged it, you happily put it away and move on to the next project. Ten months later you are asked to make a modification to the program (or worse, track down and fix an elusive bug). You open the file that contains your source code and stare at thousands of statements that now make no sense at all. If only you had left some notes to yourself explaining the program's code. Of course it's too late now. All that's left to do is decide what will take less time: figuring out the old program or completely rewriting it!

This scenario might sound extreme, but it's one you don't want to happen to you. Real world programs are big and complex. Thoroughly documented code will make your life easier, not to mention the other programmers who may have to read your code in the future.

Single-Line Comments

You have already seen one way to place comments in a C++ program. You simply place two forward slashes (//) where you want the comment to begin. The compiler ignores everything from that point to the end of the line. Program 2-26 shows that comments may be placed liberally throughout a program.

Program 2-26

```
1   // PROGRAM: PAYROLL.CPP
2   // Written by Herbert Dorfmann
3   // This program calculates company payroll
4   // Last modification: 8/20/2008
5   #include <iostream>
6   using namespace std;
7
8   int main()
9   {
10     double payRate;   // Holds the hourly pay rate
11     double hours;     // Holds the hours worked
12     int employNumber; // Holds the employee number
```

(The remainder of this program is left out.)

In addition to telling who wrote the program and describing the purpose of variables, comments can also be used to explain complex procedures in your code.

Multi-Line Comments

The second type of comment in C++ is the multi-line comment. *Multi-line comments* start with /* (a forward slash followed by an asterisk) and end with */ (an asterisk followed by a forward slash). Everything between these markers is ignored. Program 2-27 illustrates how multi-line comments may be used. Notice that a multi-line comment starts in line 1 with the /* symbol, and it ends in line 6 with the */ symbol.

Program 2-27

```
1   /*
2       PROGRAM: PAYROLL.CPP
3       Written by Herbert Dorfmann
4       This program calculates company payroll
5       Last modification: 8/20/2008
6   */
7
8   #include <iostream>
9   using namespace std;
10
11  int main()
12  {
13     double payRate;   // Holds the hourly pay rate
14     double hours;     // Holds the hours worked
15     int employNumber; // Holds the employee number
```

(The remainder of this program is left out.)

Unlike a comment started with `//`, a multi-line comment can span several lines. This makes it more convenient to write large blocks of comments because you do not have to mark every line. Consequently, the multi-line comment is inconvenient for writing single-line comments because you must type both a beginning and ending comment symbol.

NOTE: Many programmers use a combination of single-line comments and multi-line comments in their programs. Convenience usually dictates which style to use.

Remember the following advice when using multi-line comments:

- Be careful not to reverse the beginning symbol with the ending symbol.
- Be sure not to forget the ending symbol.

Both of these mistakes can be difficult to track down, and will prevent the program from compiling correctly.

2.16 Named Constants

CONCEPT: Literals may be given names that symbolically represent them in a program.

Assume the following statement appears in a banking program that calculates data pertaining to loans:

```
amount = balance * 0.069;
```

In such a program, two potential problems arise. First, it is not clear to anyone other than the original programmer what 0.069 is. It appears to be an interest rate, but in some situations there are fees associated with loan payments. How can the purpose of this statement be determined without painstakingly checking the rest of the program?

The second problem occurs if this number is used in other calculations throughout the program and must be changed periodically. Assuming the number is an interest rate, what if the rate changes from 6.9 percent to 7.2 percent? The programmer will have to search through the source code for every occurrence of the number.

Both of these problems can be addressed by using named constants. A *named constant* is like a variable, but its content is read-only, and cannot be changed while the program is running. Here is a definition of a named constant:

```
const double INTEREST_RATE = 0.069;
```

It looks just like a regular variable definition except that the word `const` appears before the data type name, and the name of the variable is written in all uppercase characters. The key word `const` is a qualifier that tells the compiler to make the variable read-only. Its value will remain constant throughout the program's execution. It is not required that the variable name be written in all uppercase characters, but many programmers prefer to write them this way so they are easily distinguishable from regular variable names.

An initialization value must be given when defining a constant with the const qualifier, or an error will result when the program is compiled. A compiler error will also result if there are any statements in the program that attempt to change the value of a named constant.

An advantage of using named constants is that they make programs more self-documenting. The following statement

```
amount = balance * 0.069;
```

can be changed to read

```
amount = balance * INTEREST_RATE;
```

A new programmer can read the second statement and know what is happening. It is evident that balance is being multiplied by the interest rate. Another advantage to this approach is that widespread changes can easily be made to the program. Let's say the interest rate appears in a dozen different statements throughout the program. When the rate changes, the initialization value in the definition of the named constant is the only value that needs to be modified. If the rate increases to 7.2%, the definition is changed to the following:

```
const double INTEREST_RATE = 0.072;
```

The program is then ready to be recompiled. Every statement that uses INTEREST_RATE will then use the new value.

Named constants can also help prevent typographical errors in a program's code. For example, suppose you use the number 3.14159 as the value of *pi* in a program that performs various geometric calculations. Each time you type the number 3.14159 in the program's code, there is a chance that you will make a mistake with one or more of the digits. As a result, the program will not produce the correct results. To help prevent a mistake such as this, you can define a named constant for *pi*, initialized with the correct value, and then use that constant in all of the formulas that require its value. Program 2-28 shows an example. It calculates the circumference of a circle that has a diameter of 10.

Program 2-28

```
 1 // This program calculates the circumference of a circle.
 2 #include <iostream>
 3 using namespace std;
 4
 5 int main()
 6 {
 7     // Constants
 8     const double PI = 3.14159;
 9     const double DIAMETER = 10.0;
10
11     // Variable to hold the circumference
12     double circumference;
13
14     // Calculate the circumference.
15     circumference = PI * DIAMETER;
16
```

(program continues)

Program 2-28   *(continued)*

```
17    // Display the circumference.
18    cout << "The circumference is: " << circumference << endl;
19    return 0;
20 }
```

Program Output
The circumference is: 31.4159

Let's take a closer look at the program. Line 8 defines a constant `double` named `PI`, initialized with the value 3.14159. This constant will be used for the value of *pi* in the program's calculation. Line 9 defines a constant `double` named `DIAMETER`, initialized with the value 10. This will be used for the circle's diameter. Line 12 defines a `double` variable named `circumference`, which will be used to hold the circle's circumference. Line 15 calculates the circle's circumference by multiplying `PI` by `DIAMETER`. The result of the calculation is assigned to the `circumference` variable. Line 18 displays the circle's circumference.

 Checkpoint

myprogramminglab   *www.myprogramminglab.com*

2.25   Write statements using the `const` qualifier to create named constants for the following literal values:

Literal Value	Description
2.71828	Euler's number (known in mathematics as *e*)
5.256E5	Number of minutes in a year
32.2	The gravitational acceleration constant (in feet per second^2)
9.8	The gravitational acceleration constant (in meters per second^2)
1609	Number of meters in a mile

2.17

Programming Style

CONCEPT: Programming style refers to the way a programmer uses identifiers, spaces, tabs, blank lines, and punctuation characters to visually arrange a program's source code. These are some, but not all, of the elements of programming style.

In Chapter 1 you learned that syntax rules govern the way a language may be used. The syntax rules of C++ dictate how and where to place key words, semicolons, commas, braces, and other components of the language. The compiler's job is to check for syntax errors and, if there are none, generate object code.

When the compiler reads a program it processes it as one long stream of characters. The compiler doesn't care that each statement is on a separate line, or that spaces separate operators from operands. Humans, on the other hand, find it difficult to read programs that aren't written in a visually pleasing manner. Consider Program 2-29 for example.

Program 2-29

```
1   #include <iostream>
2   using namespace std;int main(){double shares=220.0;
3   double avgPrice=14.67;cout<<"There were "<<shares
4   <<" shares sold at $"<<avgPrice<<" per share.\n";
5   return 0;}
```

Program Output

There were 220 shares sold at $14.67 per share.

Although the program is syntactically correct (it doesn't violate any rules of C++), it is very difficult to read. The same program is shown in Program 2-30, written in a more reasonable style.

Program 2-30

```
1    // This example is much more readable than Program 2-29.
2    #include <iostream>
3    using namespace std;
4
5    int main()
6    {
7       double shares = 220.0;
8       double avgPrice = 14.67;
9
10      cout << "There were " << shares << " shares sold at $";
11      cout << avgPrice << " per share.\n";
12      return 0;
13   }
```

Program Output

There were 220 shares sold at $14.67 per share.

Programming style refers to the way source code is visually arranged. Ideally, it is a consistent method of putting spaces and indentions in a program so visual cues are created. These cues quickly tell a programmer important information about a program.

For example, notice in Program 2-30 that inside the function main's braces each line is indented. It is a common C++ style to indent all the lines inside a set of braces. You will also notice the blank line between the variable definitions and the cout statements. This is intended to visually separate the definitions from the executable statements.

 NOTE: Although you are free to develop your own style, you should adhere to common programming practices. By doing so, you will write programs that visually make sense to other programmers.

Another aspect of programming style is how to handle statements that are too long to fit on one line. Because C++ is a free-flowing language, it is usually possible to spread a statement over several lines. For example, here is a cout statement that uses five lines:

```
cout << "The Fahrenheit temperature is "
     << fahrenheit
     << " and the Celsius temperature is "
     << celsius
     << endl;
```

This statement will work just as if it were typed on one line. Here is an example of variable definitions treated similarly:

```
int fahrenheit,
    celsius,
    kelvin;
```

There are many other issues related to programming style. They will be presented throughout the book.

2.18 If You Plan to Continue in Computer Science: Standard and Prestandard C++

CONCEPT: C++ programs written before the language became standardized may appear slightly different from programs written today.

C++ is a standardized programming language, but it hasn't always been. The language has evolved over the years and, as a result, there is a "newer style" and an "older style" of writing C++ code. The newer style is the way programs are written with standard C++, while the older style is the way programs were typically written using prestandard C++. Although the differences between the older and newer styles are subtle, it is important that you recognize them. When you go to work as a computer science professional, it is likely that you will see programs written in the older style. It is also possible that your workplace's programming tools only support the older conventions, and you may need to write programs using the older style.

Older Style Header Files

In older style C++, all header files end with the ".h" extension. For example, in a prestandard C++ program the statement that includes the `iostream.h` header file is written as:

```
#include <iostream.h>
```

Absence of `using namespace std;`

Another difference between the newer and older styles is that older style programs typically do not use the `using namespace std;` statement. In fact, some older compilers do not support namespaces at all, and will produce an error message if a program has that statement.

Using `#define` Directives Instead of `const` Definitions

The older C-style method of creating named constants is with the `#define` preprocessor directive. Although it is preferable to use the `const` modifier, there are programs with the `#define` directive still in use. In addition, Chapter 13 teaches other uses of the `#define` directive, so it is important to understand.

Let's look at an example. Program 2-31 is a modified version of Program 2-27. Instead of using `const` definitions, this program uses `#define` directives to create the PI and DIAMETER named constants.

Program 2-31

```
 1 // This program calculates the circumference of a circle.
 2 #include <iostream>
 3 using namespace std;
 4
 5 #define PI 3.14159
 6 #define DIAMETER 10.0
 7
 8 int main()
 9 {
10    // Variable to hold the circumference
11    double circumference;
12
13    // Calculate the circumference.
14    circumference = PI * DIAMETER;
15
16    // Display the circumference.
17    cout << "The circumference is: " << circumference << endl;
18    return 0;
19 }
```

Program Output
```
The circumference is: 31.4159
```

Remember, the preprocessor scans your program before it is compiled. It looks for directives, which are lines that begin with the # symbol. Preprocessor directives cause your source code to be modified prior to being compiled. The `#define` directives in lines 5 and 6 read:

```
#define PI 3.14159

#define DIAMETER 10.0
```

These two directives create the named constants PI and DIAMETER, and specify their values. Anytime PI is used in the program, it will be replaced by the value 3.14159. Likewise, any time DIAMETER is used in the program, it will be replaced by the value 10.0. So, Line 14, which reads

```
circumference = PI * DIAMETER;
```

will be modified by the preprocessor to read

```
circumference = 3.14159 * 10.0;
```

It is important to realize the difference between const definitions and constants created with the #define directive. Constants that are created with the const key word exist in memory just like variables. They have a data type and a specific storage location in memory. They are like regular variables in every way except that you cannot change their value while the program is running. Constants created with the #define directive, however, are not variables at all, but text substitutions. Each occurrence of the named constant in your source code is removed and the value of the constant is written in its place.

Be careful not to put a semicolon at the end of a #define directive. The semicolon will actually become part of the constant's value. For example, if the #define directives in lines 5 and 6 of Program 2-31 had been written like this:

```
#define PI 3.14159;          // ERROR!
#define DIAMETER 10.0;       // ERROR!
```

the mathematical statement in line 14

```
circumference = PI * DIAMETER;
```

would have been modified to read:

```
circumference = 3.14159; * 10.0;;
```

Because of the semicolons that were written at the end of the #define directives, the preprocessor would have created a syntax error in line 14 and the compiler would have given an error message when trying to process this statement.

> **NOTE:** #define directives are intended for the preprocessor; C++ statements are intended for the compiler. The preprocessor does not look for semicolons to terminate directives.

Review Questions and Exercises

Short Answer

1. How many operands does each of the following types of operators require?

   _____ Unary

   _____ Binary

   _____ Ternary

2. How may the float variables temp, weight, and age be defined in one statement?

3. How may the int variables months, days, and years be defined in one statement, with months initialized to 2 and years initialized to 3?

4. Write assignment statements that perform the following operations with the variables a, b, and c.

   A) Adds 2 to a and stores the result in b.

   B) Multiplies b times 4 and stores the result in a.

   C) Divides a by 3.14 and stores the result in b.

   D) Subtracts 8 from b and stores the result in a.

   E) Stores the value 27 in a.

   F) Stores the character 'K' in c.

   G) Stores the ASCII code for 'B' in c.

5. Is the following comment written using single-line or multi-line comment symbols?

   ```
   /* This program was written by M. A. Codewriter*/
   ```

6. Is the following comment written using single-line or multi-line comment symbols?

   ```
   // This program was written by M. A. Codewriter
   ```

7. Modify the following program so it prints two blank lines between each line of text.

   ```cpp
   #include <iostream>
   using namespace std;

   int main()
   {
      cout << "Two mandolins like creatures in the";
      cout << "dark";
      cout << "Creating the agony of ecstasy.";
      cout << "                    - George Barker";
      return 0;
   }
   ```

8. What will the following programs print on the screen?

   A)
   ```cpp
   #include <iostream>
   using namespace std;

   int main()
   {
      int freeze = 32, boil = 212;
      freeze = 0;
      boil = 100;
      cout << freeze << endl << boil << endl;
      return 0;
   }
   ```

   B)
   ```cpp
   #include <iostream>
   using namespace std;

   int main()
   {
      int x = 0, y = 2;
      x = y * 4;
      cout << x << endl << y << endl;
      return 0;
   }
   ```

   C)
   ```cpp
   #include <iostream>
   using namespace std;

   int main()
   {
      cout << "I am the incredible";
      cout << "computing\nmachine";
      cout << "\nand I will\namaze\n";
      cout << "you.";
      return 0;
   }
   ```

D)
```
#include <iostream>
using namespace std;

int main()
{
    cout << "Be careful\n";
    cout << "This might/n be a trick ";
    cout << "question\n";
    return 0;
}
```

E)
```
#include <iostream>
using namespace std;

int main()
{
    int a, x = 23;

    a = x % 2;
    cout << x << endl << a << endl;
    return 0;
}
```

Multiple Choice

9. Every complete statement ends with a
   A) period
   B) # symbol
   C) semicolon
   D) ending brace

10. Which of the following statements is correct?
   A) `#include (iostream)`
   B) `#include {iostream}`
   C) `#include <iostream>`
   D) `#include [iostream]`
   E) All of the above

11. Every C++ program must have a
   A) `cout` statement.
   B) function `main`.
   C) `#include` statement.
   D) All of the above

12. Preprocessor directives begin with a
   A) #
   B) !
   C) <
   D) *
   E) None of the above

13. The following data
    ```
    72
    'A'
    "Hello World"
    2.8712
    ```
    are all examples of

    A) Variables

    B) Literals or constants

    C) Strings

    D) None of the above

14. A group of statements, such as the contents of a function, is enclosed in

    A) Braces `{}`

    B) Parentheses `()`

    C) Brackets `<>`

    D) All of the above will do

15. Which of the following are *not* valid assignment statements? (Circle all that apply.)

    A) `total = 9;`

    B) `72 = amount;`

    C) `profit = 129`

    D) `letter = 'W';`

16. Which of the following are *not* valid `cout` statements? (Circle all that apply.)

    A) `cout << "Hello World";`

    B) `cout << "Have a nice day"\n;`

    C) `cout < value;`

    D) `cout << Programming is great fun;`

17. Assume w = 5, x = 4, y = 8, and z = 2. What value will be stored in `result` in each of the following statements?

    A) `result = x + y;`

    B) `result = z * 2;`

    C) `result = y / x;`

    D) `result = y - z;`

    E) `result = w % 2;`

18. How would each of the following numbers be represented in E notation?

    A) 3.287×10^{6}

    B) -978.65×10^{12}

    C) 7.65491×10^{-3}

    D) -58710.23×10^{-4}

19. The negation operator is

    A) Unary

    B) Binary

C) Ternary

D) None of the above

20. A(n) _____ is like a variable, but its value is read-only and cannot be changed during the program's execution.

A) secure variable

B) uninitialized variable

C) named constant

D) locked variable

21. When do preprocessor directives execute?

A) Before the compiler compiles your program

B) After the compiler compiles your program

C) At the same time as the compiler compiles your program

D) None of the above

True or False

22. T F A variable must be defined before it can be used.

23. T F Variable names may begin with a number.

24. T F Variable names may be up to 31 characters long.

25. T F A left brace in a C++ program should always be followed by a right brace later in the program.

26. T F You cannot initialize a named constant that is declared with the `const` modifier.

Algorithm Workbench

27. Convert the following pseudocode to C++ code. Be sure to define the appropriate variables.

> Store 20 in the *speed* variable.
> Store 10 in the *time* variable.
> Multiply *speed* by time and store the result in the *distance* variable.
> Display the contents of the *distance* variable.

28. Convert the following pseudocode to C++ code. Be sure to define the appropriate variables.

> Store 172.5 in the *force* variable.
> Store 27.5 in the *area* variable.
> Divide area by *force* and store the result in the *pressure* variable.
> Display the contents of the *pressure* variable.

Find the Error

29. There are a number of syntax errors in the following program. Locate as many as you can.

```
*/ What's wrong with this program? /*
#include iostream
using namespace std;
```

```
int main();
}
    int a, b, c\\ Three integers
    a = 3
    b = 4
    c = a + b
    Cout < "The value of c is %d" < C;
    return 0;
{
```

Programming Challenges

Visit www.myprogramminglab.com to complete many of these Programming Challenges online and get instant feedback.

1. Sum of Two Numbers

Write a program that stores the integers 62 and 99 in variables, and stores the sum of these two in a variable named `total`.

2. Sales Prediction

The East Coast sales division of a company generates 62 percent of total sales. Based on that percentage, write a program that will predict how much the East Coast division will generate if the company has $4.6 million in sales this year.

3. Sales Tax

Write a program that will compute the total sales tax on a $52 purchase. Assume the state sales tax is 4 percent and the county sales tax is 2 percent.

VideoNote
Solving the Restaurant Bill Problem

4. Restaurant Bill

Write a program that computes the tax and tip on a restaurant bill for a patron with a $44.50 meal charge. The tax should be 6.75 percent of the meal cost. The tip should be 15 percent of the total after adding the tax. Display the meal cost, tax amount, tip amount, and total bill on the screen.

5. Average of Values

To get the average of a series of values, you add the values up and then divide the sum by the number of values. Write a program that stores the following values in five different variables: 28, 32, 37, 24, and 33. The program should first calculate the sum of these five variables and store the result in a separate variable named `sum`. Then, the program should divide the `sum` variable by 5 to get the average. Display the average on the screen.

TIP: Use the `double` data type for all variables in this program.

6. Annual Pay

Suppose an employee gets paid every two weeks and earns $1700.00 each pay period. In a year the employee gets paid 26 times. Write a program that defines the following variables:

`payAmount`   This variable will hold the amount of pay the employee earns each pay period. Initialize the variable with 1700.0.

`payPeriods`   This variable will hold the number of pay periods in a year. Initialize the variable with 26.

`annualPay`   This variable will hold the employee's total annual pay, which will be calculated.

The program should calculate the employee's total annual pay by multiplying the employee's pay amount by the number of pay periods in a year, and store the result in the `annualPay` variable. Display the total annual pay on the screen.

7. **Ocean Levels**

Assuming the ocean's level is currently rising at about 1.5 millimeters per year, write a program that displays:

- The number of millimeters higher than the current level that the ocean's level will be in 5 years
- The number of millimeters higher than the current level that the ocean's level will be in 7 years
- The number of millimeters higher than the current level that the ocean's level will be in 10 years

8. **Total Purchase**

A customer in a store is purchasing five items. The prices of the five items are:

Price of item 1 = $12.95
Price of item 2 = $24.95
Price of item 3 = $6.95
Price of item 4 = $14.95
Price of item 5 = $3.95

Write a program that holds the prices of the five items in five variables. Display each item's price, the subtotal of the sale, the amount of sales tax, and the total. Assume the sales tax is 6%.

9. **Cyborg Data Type Sizes**

You have been given a job as a programmer on a Cyborg supercomputer. In order to accomplish some calculations, you need to know how many bytes the following data types use: `char`, `int`, `float`, and `double`. You do not have any manuals, so you can't look this information up. Write a C++ program that will determine the amount of memory used by these types and display the information on the screen.

10. **Miles per Gallon**

A car holds 12 gallons of gasoline and can travel 350 miles before refueling. Write a program that calculates the number of miles per gallon the car gets. Display the result on the screen.

Hint: Use the following formula to calculate miles per gallon (MPG):

MPG = Miles Driven / Gallons of Gas Used

11. **Distance per Tank of Gas**

    A car with a 20-gallon gas tank averages 21.5 miles per gallon when driven in town and 26.8 miles per gallon when driven on the highway. Write a program that calculates and displays the distance the car can travel on one tank of gas when driven in town and when driven on the highway.

    Hint: The following formula can be used to calculate the distance:

    Distance = Number of Gallons × Average Miles per Gallon

12. **Land Calculation**

    One acre of land is equivalent to 43,560 square feet. Write a program that calculates the number of acres in a tract of land with 389,767 square feet.

13. **Circuit Board Price**

    An electronics company sells circuit boards at a 40 percent profit. Write a program that will calculate the selling price of a circuit board that costs $12.67. Display the result on the screen.

14. **Personal Information**

    Write a program that displays the following pieces of information, each on a separate line:

    Your name
    Your address, with city, state, and ZIP code
    Your telephone number
    Your college major

    Use only a single cout statement to display all of this information.

15. **Triangle Pattern**

    Write a program that displays the following pattern on the screen:

    ```
         *
        ***
       *****
      *******
    ```

16. **Diamond Pattern**

    Write a program that displays the following pattern:

    ```
       *
      ***
     *****
    *******
     *****
      ***
       *
    ```

17. Stock Commission

Kathryn bought 600 shares of stock at a price of $21.77 per share. She must pay her stock broker a 2 percent commission for the transaction. Write a program that calculates and displays the following:

- The amount paid for the stock alone (without the commission)
- The amount of the commission
- The total amount paid (for the stock plus the commission)

18. Energy Drink Consumption

A soft drink company recently surveyed 12,467 of its customers and found that approximately 14 percent of those surveyed purchase one or more energy drinks per week. Of those customers who purchase energy drinks, approximately 64 percent of them prefer citrus flavored energy drinks. Write a program that displays the following:

- The approximate number of customers in the survey who purchase one or more energy drinks per week
- The approximate number of customers in the survey who prefer citrus flavored energy drinks

Expressions and Interactivity

TOPICS

3.1   The cin Object

CONCEPT: The cin object can be used to read data typed at the keyboard.

VideoNote

Reading Input with cin

So far you have written programs with built-in data. Without giving the user an opportunity to enter his or her own data, you have initialized the variables with the necessary starting values. These types of programs are limited to performing their task with only a single set of starting data. If you decide to change the initial value of any variable, the program must be modified and recompiled.

In reality, most programs ask for values that will be assigned to variables. This means the program does not have to be modified if the user wants to run it several times with different sets of data. For example, a program that calculates payroll for a small business might ask the user to enter the name of the employee, the hours worked, and the hourly pay rate. When the paycheck for that employee has been printed, the program could start over again and ask for the name, hours worked, and hourly pay rate of the next employee.

Just as `cout` is C++'s standard output object, `cin` is the standard input object. It reads input from the console (or keyboard) as shown in Program 3-1.

Program 3-1

```
 1   // This program asks the user to enter the length and width of
 2   // a rectangle. It calculates the rectangle's area and displays
 3   // the value on the screen.
 4   #include <iostream>
 5   using namespace std;
 6
 7   int main()
 8   {
 9       int length, width, area;
10
11       cout << "This program calculates the area of a ";
12       cout << "rectangle.\n";
13       cout << "What is the length of the rectangle? ";
14       cin >> length;
15       cout << "What is the width of the rectangle? ";
16       cin >> width;
17       area = length * width;
18       cout << "The area of the rectangle is " << area << ".\n";
19       return 0;
20   }
```

Program Output with Example Input Shown in Bold
```
This program calculates the area of a rectangle.
What is the length of the rectangle? 10 [Enter]
What is the width of the rectangle? 20 [Enter]
The area of the rectangle is 200.
```

Instead of calculating the area of one rectangle, this program can be used to get the area of any rectangle. The values that are stored in the `length` and `width` variables are entered by the user when the program is running. Look at lines 13 and 14:

```
cout << "What is the length of the rectangle? ";
cin >> length;
```

In line 13, the `cout` object is used to display the question "What is the length of the rectangle?" This question is known as a *prompt*, and it tells the user what data he or she should enter. Your program should always display a prompt before it uses `cin` to read input. This way, the user will know that he or she must type a value at the keyboard.

Line 14 uses the `cin` object to read a value from the keyboard. The >> symbol is the *stream extraction operator*. It gets characters from the stream object on its left and stores them in the variable whose name appears on its right. In this line, characters are taken from the `cin` object (which gets them from the keyboard) and are stored in the `length` variable.

Gathering input from the user is normally a two-step process:

1. Use the `cout` object to display a prompt on the screen.

2. Use the `cin` object to read a value from the keyboard.

The prompt should ask the user a question, or tell the user to enter a specific value. For example, the code we just examined from Program 3-1 displays the following prompt:

```
What is the length of the rectangle?
```

When the user sees this prompt, he or she knows to enter the rectangle's length. After the prompt is displayed, the program uses the cin object to read a value from the keyboard and store the value in the length variable.

Notice that the << and >> operators appear to point in the direction that data is flowing. In a statement that uses the cout object, the << operator always points toward cout. This indicates that data is flowing from a variable or a literal to the cout object. In a statement that uses the cin object, the >> operator always points toward the variable that is receiving the value. This indicates that data is flowing from cin to a variable. This is illustrated in Figure 3-1.

Figure 3-1

```
cout << "What is the length of the rectangle? ";
cin >> length;
```

Think of the << and >> operators as arrows that point in
the direction that data is flowing.

```
cout ← "What is the length of the rectangle? ";
cin → length;
```

The cin object causes a program to wait until data is typed at the keyboard and the **[Enter]** key is pressed. No other lines in the program will be executed until cin gets its input.

cin automatically converts the data read from the keyboard to the data type of the variable used to store it. If the user types 10, it is read as the characters '1' and '0'. cin is smart enough to know this will have to be converted to an int value before it is stored in the length variable. cin is also smart enough to know a value like 10.7 cannot be stored in an integer variable. If the user enters a floating-point value for an integer variable, cin will not read the part of the number after the decimal point.

NOTE: You must include the iostream file in any program that uses cin.

Entering Multiple Values

The cin object may be used to gather multiple values at once. Look at Program 3-2, which is a modified version of Program 3-1.

Line 15 waits for the user to enter two values. The first is assigned to length and the second to width.

```
cin >> length >> width;
```

Program 3-2

```
 1   // This program asks the user to enter the length and width of
 2   // a rectangle. It calculates the rectangle's area and displays
 3   // the value on the screen.
 4   #include <iostream>
 5   using namespace std;
 6
 7   int main()
 8   {
 9      int length, width, area;
10
11      cout << "This program calculates the area of a ";
12      cout << "rectangle.\n";
13      cout << "Enter the length and width of the rectangle ";
14      cout << "separated by a space.\n";
15      cin >> length >> width;
16      area = length * width;
17      cout << "The area of the rectangle is " << area << endl;
18      return 0;
19   }
```

Program Output with Example Input Shown in Bold
```
This program calculates the area of a rectangle.
Enter the length and width of the rectangle separated by a space.
10 20 [Enter]
The area of the rectangle is 200
```

In the example output, the user entered 10 and 20, so 10 is stored in `length` and 20 is stored in `width`.

Notice the user separates the numbers by spaces as they are entered. This is how `cin` knows where each number begins and ends. It doesn't matter how many spaces are entered between the individual numbers. For example, the user could have entered

    10   20

 NOTE: The **[Enter]** key is pressed after the last number is entered.

`cin` will also read multiple values of different data types. This is shown in Program 3-3.

Program 3-3

```
 1   // This program demonstrates how cin can read multiple values
 2   // of different data types.
 3   #include <iostream>
 4   using namespace std;
 5
```

```
 6   int main()
 7   {
 8       int whole;
 9       double fractional;
10       char letter;
11
12       cout << "Enter an integer, a double, and a character: ";
13       cin >> whole >> fractional >> letter;
14       cout << "Whole: " << whole << endl;
15       cout << "Fractional: " << fractional << endl;
16       cout << "Letter: " << letter << endl;
17       return 0;
18   }
```

Program Output with Example Input Shown in Bold
Enter an integer, a double, and a character: **4 5.7 b [Enter]**
Whole: 4
Fractional: 5.7
Letter: b

As you can see in the example output, the values are stored in their respective variables. But what if the user had responded in the following way?

Enter an integer, a double, and a character: **5.7 4 b [Enter]**

When the user types values at the keyboard, those values are first stored in an area of memory known as the *keyboard buffer*. So, when the user enters the values 5.7, 4, and b, they are stored in the keyboard buffer as shown in Figure 3-2.

Figure 3-2

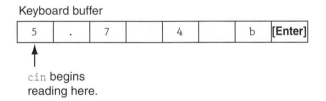

When the user presses the Enter key, cin reads the value 5 into the variable whole. It does not read the decimal point because whole is an integer variable. Next it reads .7 and stores that value in the double variable fractional. The space is skipped and 4 is the next value read. It is stored as a character in the variable letter. Because this cin statement reads only three values, the b is left in the keyboard buffer. So, in this situation the program would have stored 5 in whole, 0.7 in fractional, and the character '4' in letter. It is important that the user enters values in the correct order.

Checkpoint

myprogramminglab *www.myprogramminglab.com*

3.1   What header file must be included in programs using cin?

3.2   TRUE or FALSE: cin requires the user to press the **[Enter]** key when finished entering data.

3.3 Assume `value` is an integer variable. If the user enters 3.14 in response to the following programming statement, what will be stored in `value`?

```
cin >> value;
```

A) 3.14

B) 3

C) 0

D) Nothing. An error message is displayed.

3.4 A program has the following variable definitions.

```
long miles;
int feet;
float inches;
```

Write one `cin` statement that reads a value into each of these variables.

3.5 The following program will run, but the user will have difficulty understanding what to do. How would you improve the program?

```
// This program multiplies two numbers and displays the result.
#include <iostream>
using namespace std;

int main()
{
   double first, second, product;

   cin >> first >> second;
   product = first * second;
   cout << product;
   return 0;
}
```

3.6 Complete the following program skeleton so it asks for the user's weight (in pounds) and displays the equivalent weight in kilograms.

```
#include <iostream>
using namespace std;

int main()
{
   double pounds, kilograms;

   // Write code here that prompts the user
   // to enter his or her weight and reads
   // the input into the pounds variable.

   // The following line does the conversion.
   kilograms = pounds / 2.2;

   // Write code here that displays the user's weight
   // in kilograms.
   return 0;
}
```

3.2 Mathematical Expressions

CONCEPT: C++ allows you to construct complex mathematical expressions using multiple operators and grouping symbols.

In Chapter 2 you were introduced to the basic mathematical operators, which are used to build mathematical expressions. An *expression* is a programming statement that has a value. Usually, an expression consists of an operator and its operands. Look at the following statement:

```
sum = 21 + 3;
```

Since 21 + 3 has a value, it is an expression. Its value, 24, is stored in the variable sum. Expressions do not have to be in the form of mathematical operations. In the following statement, 3 is an expression.

```
number = 3;
```

Here are some programming statements where the variable result is being assigned the value of an expression:

```
result = x;
result = 4;
result = 15 / 3;
result = 22 * number;
result = sizeof(int);
result = a + b + c;
```

In each of these statements, a number, variable name, or mathematical expression appears on the right side of the = symbol. A value is obtained from each of these and stored in the variable result. These are all examples of a variable being assigned the value of an expression.

Program 3-4 shows how mathematical expressions can be used with the cout object.

Program 3-4

```
 1   // This program asks the user to enter the numerator
 2   // and denominator of a fraction and it displays the
 3   // decimal value.
 4
 5   #include <iostream>
 6   using namespace std;
 7
 8   int main()
 9   {
10       double numerator, denominator;
11
```

(program continues)

Program 3-4 *(continued)*

```
12      cout << "This program shows the decimal value of ";
13      cout << "a fraction.\n";
14      cout << "Enter the numerator: ";
15      cin >> numerator;
16      cout << "Enter the denominator: ";
17      cin >> denominator;
18      cout << "The decimal value is ";
19      cout << (numerator / denominator) << endl;
20      return 0;
21  }
```

Program Output with Example Input Shown in Bold
```
This program shows the decimal value of a fraction.
Enter the numerator: 3 [Enter]
Enter the denominator: 16 [Enter]
The decimal value is 0.1875
```

The cout object will display the value of any legal expression in C++. In Program 3-4, the value of the expression numerator / denominator is displayed.

NOTE: The example input for Program 3-4 shows the user entering 3 and 16. Since these values are assigned to double variables, they are stored as the double values 3.0 and 16.0.

NOTE: When sending an expression that consists of an operator to cout, it is always a good idea to put parentheses around the expression. Some advanced operators will yield unexpected results otherwise.

Operator Precedence

It is possible to build mathematical expressions with several operators. The following statement assigns the sum of 17, x, 21, and y to the variable answer.

```
answer = 17 + x + 21 + y;
```

Some expressions are not that straightforward, however. Consider the following statement:

```
outcome = 12 + 6 / 3;
```

What value will be stored in outcome? 6 is used as an operand for both the addition and division operators. outcome could be assigned either 6 or 14, depending on whether the addition operation or the division operation takes place first. The answer is 14 because the division operator has higher *precedence* than the addition operator.

Mathematical expressions are evaluated from left to right. When two operators share an operand, the operator with the highest precedence works first. Multiplication and division have higher precedence than addition and subtraction, so the statement above works like this:

A) 6 is divided by 3, yielding a result of 2

B) 12 is added to 2, yielding a result of 14

It could be diagrammed in the following way:

```
outcome = 12 + 6 / 3
                \ /
outcome = 12 +   2

outcome = 14
```

Table 3-1 shows the precedence of the arithmetic operators. The operators at the top of the table have higher precedence than the ones below them.

Table 3-1   Precedence of Arithmetic Operators (Highest to Lowest)

(unary negation) –
* / %
+   –

The multiplication, division, and modulus operators have the same precedence. This is also true of the addition and subtraction operators. Table 3-2 shows some expressions with their values.

Table 3-2   Some Simple Expressions and Their Values

Expression	Value
5 + 2 * 4	13
10 / 2 – 3	2
8 + 12 * 2 – 4	28
4 + 17 % 2 – 1	4
6 – 3 * 2 + 7 – 1	6

Associativity

An operator's *associativity* is either left to right, or right to left. If two operators sharing an operand have the same precedence, they work according to their associativity. Table 3-3 lists the associativity of the arithmetic operators. As an example, look at the following expression:

```
5 – 3 + 2
```

Both the – and + operators in this expression have the same precedence, and they have left to right associativity. So, the operators will work from left to right. This expression is the same as:

```
((5 – 3) + 2)
```

Here is another example:

```
12 / 6 * 4
```

Because the / and * operators have the same precedence, and they have left to right associativity, they will work from left to right. This expression is the same as:

```
((12 / 6) * 4)
```

Table 3-3   Associativity of Arithmetic Operators

Operator	Associativity
(unary negation) –	Right to left
* / %	Left to right
+ –	Left to right

Grouping with Parentheses

Parts of a mathematical expression may be grouped with parentheses to force some operations to be performed before others. In the following statement, the sum of a + b is divided by 4.

```
result = (a + b) / 4;
```

Without the parentheses, however, b would be divided by 4 and the result added to a. Table 3-4 shows more expressions and their values.

Table 3-4   More Simple Expressions and Their Values

Expression	Value
(5 + 2) * 4	28
10 / (5 – 3)	5
8 + 12 * (6 – 2)	56
(4 + 17) % 2 – 1	0
(6 – 3) * (2 + 7) / 3	9

Converting Algebraic Expressions to Programming Statements

In algebra it is not always necessary to use an operator for multiplication. C++, however, requires an operator for any mathematical operation. Table 3-5 shows some algebraic expressions that perform multiplication and the equivalent C++ expressions.

Table 3-5   Algebraic and C++ Multiplication Expressions

Algebraic Expression	Operation	C++ Equivalent
$6B$	6 times B	6 * B
$(3)(12)$	3 times 12	3 * 12
$4xy$	4 times x times y	4 * x * y

When converting some algebraic expressions to C++, you may have to insert parentheses that do not appear in the algebraic expression. For example, look at the following expression:

$$x = \frac{a + b}{c}$$

To convert this to a C++ statement, $a + b$ will have to be enclosed in parentheses:

```
x = (a + b) / c;
```

Table 3-6 shows more algebraic expressions and their C++ equivalents.

Table 3-6 Algebraic and C++ Expressions

Algebraic Expression	C++ Expression
$y = 3\dfrac{x}{2}$	`y = x / 2 * 3;`
$z = 3bc + 4$	`z = 3 * b * c + 4;`
$a = \dfrac{3x + 2}{4a - 1}$	`a = (3 * x + 2) / (4 * a - 1)`

No Exponents Please!

Unlike many programming languages, C++ does not have an exponent operator. Raising a number to a power requires the use of a *library function*. The C++ library isn't a place where you check out books, but a collection of specialized functions. Think of a library function as a "routine" that performs a specific operation. One of the library functions is called `pow`, and its purpose is to raise a number to a power. Here is an example of how it's used:

```
area = pow(4.0, 2.0);
```

This statement contains a *call* to the pow function. The numbers inside the parentheses are *arguments*. Arguments are data being sent to the function. The pow function always raises the first argument to the power of the second argument. In this example, 4 is raised to the power of 2. The result is *returned* from the function and used in the statement where the function call appears. In this case, the value 16 is returned from pow and assigned to the variable `area`. This is illustrated in Figure 3-3.

Figure 3-3

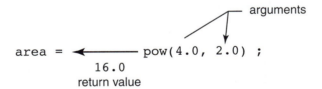

The statement `area = pow(4.0, 2.0)` is equivalent to the following algebraic statement:

$$\text{area} = 4^2$$

Here is another example of a statement using the pow function. It assigns 3 times 6^3 to `x`:

```
x = 3 * pow(6.0, 3.0);
```

And the following statement displays the value of 5 raised to the power of 4:

```
cout << pow(5.0, 4.0);
```

It might be helpful to think of pow as a "black box" that you plug two numbers into, and that then sends a third number out. The number that comes out has the value of the first number raised to the power of the second number, as illustrated in Figure 3-4:

Figure 3-4

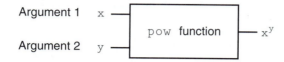

There are some guidelines that should be followed when the pow function is used. First, the program must include the cmath header file. Second, the arguments that you pass to the pow function should be doubles. Third, the variable used to store pow's return value should be defined as a double. For example, in the following statement the variable area should be a double:

```
area = pow(4.0, 2.0);
```

Program 3-5 solves a simple algebraic problem. It asks the user to enter the radius of a circle and then calculates the area of the circle. The formula is

$$Area = \pi r^2$$

which is expressed in the program as

```
area = PI * pow(radius, 2.0);
```

Program 3-5

```
 1   // This program calculates the area of a circle.
 2   // The formula for the area of a circle is Pi times
 3   // the radius squared. Pi is 3.14159.
 4   #include <iostream>
 5   #include <cmath>    // needed for pow function
 6   using namespace std;
 7
 8   int main()
 9   {
10      const double PI = 3.14159;
11      double area, radius;
12
13      cout << "This program calculates the area of a circle.\n";
14      cout << "What is the radius of the circle? ";
15      cin >> radius;
16      area = PI * pow(radius, 2.0);
17      cout << "The area is " << area << endl;
18      return 0;
19   }
```

Program Output with Example Input Shown in Bold

```
This program calculates the area of a circle.
What is the radius of the circle? 10 [Enter]
The area is 314.159
```

NOTE: Program 3-5 is presented as a demonstration of the pow function. In reality, there is no reason to use the pow function in such a simple operation. The math statement could just as easily be written as

```
area = PI * radius * radius;
```

The pow function is useful, however, in operations that involve larger exponents.

In the Spotlight:
Calculating an Average

Determining the average of a group of values is a simple calculation: You add all of the values and then divide the sum by the number of values. Although this is a straightforward calculation, it is easy to make a mistake when writing a program that calculates an average. For example, let's assume that a, b, and c are double variables. Each of the variables holds a value and we want to calculate the average of those values. If we are careless, we might write a statement such as the following to perform the calculation:

```
average = a + b + c / 3.0;
```

Can you see the error in this statement? When it executes, the division will take place first. The value in c will be divided by 3.0, and then the result will be added to the sum of a + b. That is not the correct way to calculate an average. To correct this error we need to put parentheses around a + b + c, as shown here:

```
average = (a + b + c) / 3.0;
```

Let's step through the process of writing a program that calculates an average. Suppose you have taken three tests in your computer science class, and you want to write a program that will display the average of the test scores. Here is the algorithm in pseudocode:

Get the first test score.
Get the second test score.
Get the third test score.
Calculate the average by adding the three test scores and dividing the sum by 3.
Display the average.

In the first three steps we prompt the user to enter three test scores. Let's say we store those test scores in the double variables test1, test2, and test3. Then in the fourth step we calculate the average of the three test scores. We will use the following statement to perform the calculation and store the result in the average variable, which is a double:

```
average = (test1 + test2 + test3) / 3.0;
```

The last step is to display the average. Program 3-6 shows the program.

Program 3-6

```
 1  // This program calculates the average
 2  // of three test scores.
 3  #include <iostream>
 4  #include <cmath>
 5  using namespace std;
 6
 7  int main()
 8  {
 9      double test1, test2, test3;   // To hold the scores
10      double average;               // To hold the average
11
12      // Get the three test scores.
13      cout << "Enter the first test score: ";
14      cin >> test1;
15      cout << "Enter the second test score: ";
16      cin >> test2;
17      cout << "Enter the third test score: ";
18      cin >> test3;
19
20      // Calculate the average of the scores.
21      average = (test1 + test2 + test3) / 3.0;
22
23      // Display the average.
24      cout << "The average score is: " << average << endl;
25      return 0;
26  }
```

Program Output with Example Input Shown in Bold
```
Enter the first test score: 90 [Enter]
Enter the second test score: 80 [Enter]
Enter the third test score: 100 [Enter]
The average score is 90
```

 Checkpoint

myprogramminglab   *www.myprogramminglab.com*

3.7   Complete the table below by writing the value of each expression in the "Value" column.

Expression	Value
6 + 3 * 5	
12 / 2 - 4	
9 + 14 * 2 - 6	
5 + 19 % 3 - 1	
(6 + 2) * 3	
14 / (11 - 4)	
9 + 12 * (8 - 3)	
(6 + 17) % 2 - 1	
(9 - 3) * (6 + 9) / 3	

3.8 Write C++ expressions for the following algebraic expressions:

$$y = 6x$$
$$a = 2b + 4c$$
$$y = x^2$$
$$g = \frac{x + 2}{z^2}$$
$$y = \frac{x^2}{z^2}$$

3.9 Study the following program and complete the table.

```cpp
#include <iostream>
#include <cmath>
using namespace std;

int main()
{
    double value1, value2, value3;

    cout << "Enter a number: ";
    cin >> value1;
    value2 = 2 * pow(value1, 2.0);
    value3 = 3 + value2 / 2 - 1;
    cout << value3 << endl;
    return 0;
}
```

If the User Enters...	The Program Will Display What Number (Stored in `value3`)?
2	
5	
4.3	
6	

3.10 Complete the following program skeleton so it displays the volume of a cylindrical fuel tank. The formula for the volume of a cylinder is

Volume = $\pi r^2 h$

where
π is 3.14159
r is the radius of the tank
h is the height of the tank

```cpp
#include <iostream>
#include <cmath>
using namespace std;
```

```
int main()
{
    double volume, radius, height;

    cout << "This program will tell you the volume of\n";
    cout << "a cylinder-shaped fuel tank.\n";
    cout << "How tall is the tank? ";
    cin >> height;
    cout << "What is the radius of the tank? ";
    cin >> radius;

    // You must complete the program.
}
```

3.3 When You Mix Apples and Oranges: Type Conversion

CONCEPT: When an operator's operands are of different data types, C++ will automatically convert them to the same data type. This can affect the results of mathematical expressions.

If an `int` is multiplied by a `float`, what data type will the result be? What if a `double` is divided by an `unsigned int`? Is there any way of predicting what will happen in these instances? The answer is yes. C++ follows a set of rules when performing mathematical operations on variables of different data types. It's helpful to understand these rules to prevent subtle errors from creeping into your programs.

Just like officers in the military, data types are ranked. One data type outranks another if it can hold a larger number. For example, a `float` outranks an `int`. Table 3-7 lists the data types in order of their rank, from highest to lowest.

Table 3-7 Data Type Ranking

`long double`
`double`
`float`
`unsigned long`
`long`
`unsigned int`
`int`

One exception to the ranking in Table 3-7 is when an `int` and a `long` are the same size. In that case, an `unsigned int` outranks `long` because it can hold a higher value.

When C++ is working with an operator, it strives to convert the operands to the same type. This automatic conversion is known as *type coercion*. When a value is converted to a higher data type, it is said to be *promoted*. To *demote* a value means to convert it to a lower data type. Let's look at the specific rules that govern the evaluation of mathematical expressions.

Rule 1: `char`s, `short`s, and `unsigned short`s are automatically promoted to `int`.

You will notice that `char`, `short`, and `unsigned short` do not appear in Table 3-7. That's because anytime they are used in a mathematical expression, they are automatically promoted to an `int`. The only exception to this rule is when an `unsigned short` holds a value larger than can be held by an `int`. This can happen on systems where `shorts` are the same size as `ints`. In this case, the `unsigned short` is promoted to `unsigned int`.

Rule 2: When an operator works with two values of different data types, the lower-ranking value is promoted to the type of the higher-ranking value.

In the following expression, assume that `years` is an `int` and `interestRate` is a `float`:

```
years * interestRate
```

Before the multiplication takes place, `years` will be promoted to a `float`.

Rule 3: When the final value of an expression is assigned to a variable, it will be converted to the data type of that variable.

In the following statement, assume that `area` is a `long int`, while `length` and `width` are both `ints`:

```
area = length * width;
```

Since `length` and `width` are both `ints`, they will not be converted to any other data type. The result of the multiplication, however, will be converted to `long` so it can be stored in `area`.

Watch out for situations where an expression results in a fractional value being assigned to an integer variable. Here is an example:

```
int x, y = 4;
float z = 2.7;
x = y * z;
```

In the expression `y * z`, `y` will be promoted to `float` and 10.8 will result from the multiplication. Since `x` is an integer, however, 10.8 will be truncated and 10 will be stored in `x`.

Integer Division

When you divide an integer by another integer in C++, the result is always an integer. If there is a remainder, it will be discarded. For example, in the following code, `parts` is assigned the value 2.0:

```
double parts;
parts = 15 / 6;
```

Even though 15 divided by 6 is really 2.5, the .5 part of the result is discarded because we are dividing an integer by an integer. It doesn't matter that `parts` is declared as a `double` because the fractional part of the result is discarded *before* the assignment takes place. In order for a division operation to return a floating-point value, at least one of the operands must be of a floating-point data type. For example, the previous code could be written as:

```
double parts;
parts = 15.0 / 6;
```

In this code the literal value 15.0 is interpreted as a floating-point number, so the division operation will return a floating-point number. The value 2.5 will be assigned to `parts`.

3.4   Overflow and Underflow

CONCEPT: When a variable is assigned a value that is too large or too small in range for that variable's data type, the variable overflows or underflows.

Trouble can arise when a variable is being assigned a value that is too large for its type. Here is a statement where a, b, and c are all short integers:

```
a = b * c;
```

If b and c are set to values large enough, the multiplication will produce a number too big to be stored in a. To prepare for this, a should have been defined as an int, or a long int.

When a variable is assigned a number that is too large for its data type, it *overflows*. Likewise, assigning a value that is too small for a variable causes it to *underflow*. Program 3-7 shows what happens when an integer overflows or underflows. (The output shown is from a system with two-byte short integers.)

Program 3-7

```cpp
 1    // This program demonstrates integer overflow and underflow.
 2    #include <iostream>
 3    using namespace std;
 4
 5    int main()
 6    {
 7        // testVar is initialized with the maximum value for a short.
 8        short testVar = 32767;
 9
10        // Display testVar.
11        cout << testVar << endl;
12
13        // Add 1 to testVar to make it overflow.
14        testVar = testVar + 1;
15        cout << testVar << endl;
16
17        // Subtract 1 from testVar to make it underflow.
18        testVar = testVar - 1;
19        cout << testVar << endl;
20        return 0;
21    }
```

Program Output
```
32767
-32768
32767
```

Typically, when an integer overflows, its contents wrap around to that data type's lowest possible value. In Program 3-7, testVar wrapped around from 32,767 to –32,768 when 1 was added to it. When 1 was subtracted from testVar, it underflowed, which caused its contents to wrap back around to 32,767. No warning or error message is given, so be careful when working with numbers close to the maximum or minimum range of an integer. If an overflow or underflow occurs, the program will use the incorrect number, and therefore produce incorrect results.

When floating-point variables overflow or underflow, the results depend upon how the compiler is configured. Your system may produce programs that do any of the following:

- Produces an incorrect result and continues running.
- Prints an error message and immediately stops when either floating point overflow or underflow occurs.
- Prints an error message and immediately stops when floating point overflow occurs, but stores a 0 in the variable when it underflows.
- Gives you a choice of behaviors when overflow or underflow occurs.

You can find out how your system reacts by compiling and running Program 3-8.

Program 3-8

```
1   // This program can be used to see how your system handles
2   // floating point overflow and underflow.
3   #include <iostream>
4   using namespace std;
5
6   int main()
7   {
8       float test;
9
10      test = 2.0e38 * 1000;    // Should overflow test.
11      cout << test << endl;
12      test = 2.0e-38 / 2.0e38; // Should underflow test.
13      cout << test << endl;
14      return 0;
15  }
```

3.5 Type Casting

CONCEPT: Type casting allows you to perform manual data type conversion.

A *type cast expression* lets you manually promote or demote a value. The general format of a type cast expression is

```
static_cast<DataType>(Value)
```

where *Value* is a variable or literal value that you wish to convert and *DataType* is the data type you wish to convert *Value* to. Here is an example of code that uses a type cast expression:

```
double number = 3.7;
int val;
val = static_cast<int>(number);
```

This code defines two variables: number, a double, and val, an int. The type cast expression in the third statement returns a copy of the value in number, converted to an int. When a double is converted to an int, the fractional part is truncated so this statement stores 3 in val. The original value in number is not changed, however.

Type cast expressions are useful in situations where C++ will not perform the desired conversion automatically. Program 3-9 shows an example where a type cast expression is used to prevent integer division from taking place. The statement that uses the type cast expression is

```
perMonth = static_cast<double>(books) / months;
```

Program 3-9

```
 1   // This program uses a type cast to avoid integer division.
 2   #include <iostream>
 3   using namespace std;
 4
 5   int main()
 6   {
 7      int books;        // Number of books to read
 8      int months;       // Number of months spent reading
 9      double perMonth;  // Average number of books per month
10
11      cout << "How many books do you plan to read? ";
12      cin >> books;
13      cout << "How many months will it take you to read them? ";
14      cin >> months;
15      perMonth = static_cast<double>(books) / months;
16      cout << "That is " << perMonth << " books per month.\n";
17      return 0;
18   }
```

Program Output with Example Input Shown in Bold
```
How many books do you plan to read? 30 [Enter]
How many months will it take you to read them? 7 [Enter]
That is 4.28571 books per month.
```

The variable books is an integer, but its value is converted to a double before the division takes place. Without the type cast expression in line 15, integer division would have been performed resulting in an incorrect answer.

 WARNING! In Program 3-9, the following statement would still have resulted in integer division:

```
perMonth = static_cast<double>(books / months);
```

The result of the expression books / months is 4. When 4 is converted to a double, it is 4.0. To prevent the integer division from taking place, one of the operands should be converted to a double prior to the division operation. This forces C++ to automatically convert the value of the other operand to a double.

Program 3-10 further demonstrates the type cast expression.

Program 3-10

```cpp
 1  // This program uses a type cast expression to print a character
 2  // from a number.
 3  #include <iostream>
 4  using namespace std;
 5
 6  int main()
 7  {
 8     int number = 65;
 9
10     // Display the value of the number variable.
11     cout << number << endl;
12
13     // Display the value of number converted to
14     // the char data type.
15     cout << static_cast<char>(number) << endl;
16     return 0;
17  }
```

Program Output

```
65
A
```

Let's take a closer look at this program. In line 8 the `int` variable `number` is initialized with the value 65. In line 11, `number` is sent to `cout`, causing 65 to be displayed. In line 15, a type cast expression is used to convert the value in `number` to the `char` data type. Recall from Chapter 2 that characters are stored in memory as integer ASCII codes. The number 65 is the ASCII code for the letter 'A', so this statement causes the letter 'A' to be displayed.

 NOTE: C++ provides several different type cast expressions. `static_cast` is the most commonly used type cast expression, so we will primarily use it in this book.

If You Plan to Continue in Computer Science: C-Style and Prestandard Type Cast Expressions

C++ also supports two older methods of creating type cast expressions: the C-style form and the prestandard C++ form. The C-style cast is the name of a data type enclosed in parentheses, preceding the value that is to be converted. For example, the following statement converts the value in `number` to an `int`.

```cpp
val = (int)number;
```

The following statement shows another example.

```cpp
perMonth = (double)books / months;
```

In this statement the value in the `books` variable is converted to a `double` before the division takes place.

The prestandard C++ form of the type cast expression appears as a data type name followed by a value inside a set of parentheses. Here is an example:

```
val = int(number);
```

The type cast in this statement returns a copy of the value in `number`, converted to an `int`. Here is another example:

```
perMonth = double(books) / months;
```

Although the `static_cast` expression is preferable to either the C-style or the prestandard C++ form of the type cast expression, you will probably see code in the workplace that uses these older styles.

 Checkpoint

myprogramminglab *www.myprogramminglab.com*

3.11   Assume the following variable definitions:

```
int a = 5, b = 12;
double x = 3.4, z = 9.1;
```

What are the values of the following expressions?

A) `b / a`

B) `x * a`

C) `static_cast<double>(b / a)`

D) `static_cast<double>(b) / a`

E) `b / static_cast<double>(a)`

F) `static_cast<double>(b) / static_cast<double>(a)`

G) `b / static_cast<int>(x)`

H) `static_cast<int>(x) * static_cast<int>(z)`

I) `static_cast<int>(x * z)`

J) `static_cast<double>(static_cast<int>(x) *`
                             `static_cast<int>(z))`

3.12   Complete the following program skeleton so it asks the user to enter a character. Store the character in the variable letter. Use a type cast expression with the variable in a cout statement to display the character's ASCII code on the screen.

```
#include <iostream>
using namespace std;
int main()
{
    char letter;

    //  Finish this program
    //  as specified above.
    return 0;
}
```

3.13   What will the following program display?

```cpp
#include <iostream>
using namespace std;

int main()
{
    int integer1, integer2;
    double result;

    integer1 = 19;
    integer2 = 2;
    result = integer1 / integer2;
    cout << result << endl;
    result = static_cast<double>(integer1) / integer2;
    cout << result << endl;
    result = static_cast<double>(integer1 / integer2);
    cout << result << endl;
    return 0;
}
```

3.6 Multiple Assignment and Combined Assignment

CONCEPT: Multiple assignment means to assign the same value to several variables with one statement.

C++ allows you to assign a value to multiple variables at once. If a program has several variables, such as a, b, c, and d, and each variable needs to be assigned a value, such as 12, the following statement may be constructed:

```cpp
a = b = c = d = 12;
```

The value 12 will be assigned to each variable listed in the statement.*

Combined Assignment Operators

Quite often, programs have assignment statements of the following form:

```cpp
number = number + 1;
```

The expression on the right side of the assignment operator gives the value of number plus 1. The result is then assigned to number, replacing the value that was previously stored there. Effectively, this statement adds 1 to number. In a similar fashion, the following statement subtracts 5 from number.

```cpp
number = number - 5;
```

---

* The assignment operator works from right to left. 12 is first assigned to d, then to c, then to b, then to a.

If you have never seen this type of statement before, it might cause some initial confusion because the same variable name appears on both sides of the assignment operator. Table 3-8 shows other examples of statements written this way.

Table 3-8 (Assume x = 6)

Statement	What It Does	Value of x After the Statement
x = x + 4;	Adds 4 to x	10
x = x - 3;	Subtracts 3 from x	3
x = x * 10;	Multiplies x by 10	60
x = x / 2;	Divides x by 2	3
x = x % 4	Makes x the remainder of x / 4	2

These types of operations are very common in programming. For convenience, C++ offers a special set of operators designed specifically for these jobs. Table 3-9 shows the *combined assignment operators*, also known as *compound operators*, and *arithmetic assignment operators*.

Table 3-9

Operator	Example Usage	Equivalent to
+=	x += 5;	x = x + 5;
-=	y -= 2;	y = y - 2;
*=	z *= 10;	z = z * 10;
/=	a /= b;	a = a / b;
%=	c %= 3;	c = c % 3;

As you can see, the combined assignment operators do not require the programmer to type the variable name twice. Also, they give a clear indication of what is happening in the statement. Program 3-11 uses combined assignment operators.

Program 3-11

```
 1  // This program tracks the inventory of three widget stores
 2  // that opened at the same time. Each store started with the
 3  // same number of widgets in inventory. By subtracting the
 4  // number of widgets each store has sold from its inventory,
 5  // the current inventory can be calculated.
 6  #include <iostream>
 7  using namespace std;
 8
 9  int main()
10  {
11      int begInv,     // Beginning inventory for all stores
12          sold,       // Number of widgets sold
13          store1,     // Store 1's inventory
14          store2,     // Store 2's inventory
15          store3;     // Store 3's inventory
16
17      // Get the beginning inventory for all the stores.
18      cout << "One week ago, 3 new widget stores opened\n";
```

```
19       cout << "at the same time with the same beginning\n";
20       cout << "inventory. What was the beginning inventory? ";
21       cin >> begInv;
22
23       // Set each store's inventory.
24       store1 = store2 = store3 = begInv;
25
26       // Get the number of widgets sold at store 1.
27       cout << "How many widgets has store 1 sold? ";
28       cin >> sold;
29       store1 -= sold; // Adjust store 1's inventory.
30
31       // Get the number of widgets sold at store 2.
32       cout << "How many widgets has store 2 sold? ";
33       cin >> sold;
34       store2 -= sold; // Adjust store 2's inventory.
35
36       // Get the number of widgets sold at store 3.
37       cout << "How many widgets has store 3 sold? ";
38       cin >> sold;
39       store3 -= sold; // Adjust store 3's inventory.
40
41       // Display each store's current inventory.
42       cout << "\nThe current inventory of each store:\n";
43       cout << "Store 1: " << store1 << endl;
44       cout << "Store 2: " << store2 << endl;
45       cout << "Store 3: " << store3 << endl;
46       return 0;
47   }
```

Program Output with Example Input Shown in Bold

```
One week ago, 3 new widget stores opened
at the same time with the same beginning
inventory. What was the beginning inventory? 100 [Enter]
How many widgets has store 1 sold? 25 [Enter]
How many widgets has store 2 sold? 15 [Enter]
How many widgets has store 3 sold? 45 [Enter]


The current inventory of each store:
Store 1: 75
Store 2: 85
Store 3: 55
```

More elaborate statements may be expressed with the combined assignment operators. Here is an example:

```
result *= a + 5;
```

In this statement, result is multiplied by the sum of a + 5. When constructing such statements, you must realize the precedence of the combined assignment operators is lower than that of the regular math operators. The statement above is equivalent to

```
result = result * (a + 5);
```

which is different from

```
result = result * a + 5;
```

Table 3-10 shows other examples of such statements and their assignment statement equivalencies.

Table 3-10

Example Usage	Equivalent to
`x += b + 5;`	`x = x + (b + 5);`
`y -= a * 2;`	`y = y - (a * 2);`
`z *= 10 - c;`	`z = z * (10 - c);`
`a /= b + c;`	`a = a / (b + c);`
`c %= d - 3;`	`c = c % (d - 3);`

 Checkpoint

myprogramminglab *www.myprogramminglab.com*

3.14   Write a multiple assignment statement that assigns 0 to the variables `total`, `subtotal`, `tax`, and `shipping`.

3.15   Write statements using combined assignment operators to perform the following:

A)   Add 6 to `x`.

B)   Subtract 4 from `amount`.

C)   Multiply `y` by 4.

D)   Divide `total` by 27.

E)   Store in `x` the remainder of `x` divided by 7.

F)   Add `y * 5` to `x`.

G)   Subtract `discount` times 4 from `total`.

H)   Multiply `increase` by `salesRep` times 5.

I)   Divide `profit` by `shares` minus 1000.

3.16   What will the following program display?

```cpp
#include <iostream>
using namespace std;

int main()
{
    int unus, duo, tres;

    unus = duo = tres = 5;
    unus += 4;
    duo *= 2;
    tres -= 4;
    unus /= 3;
    duo += tres;
    cout << unus << endl;
    cout << duo << endl;
    cout << tres << endl;
    return 0;
}
```

3.7 Formatting Output

CONCEPT: The cout object provides ways to format data as it is being displayed. This affects the way data appears on the screen.

The same data can be printed or displayed in several different ways. For example, all of the following numbers have the same value, although they look different:

```
720
720.0
720.00000000
7.2e+2
+720.0
```

The way a value is printed is called its *formatting*. The cout object has a standard way of formatting variables of each data type. Sometimes, however, you need more control over the way data is displayed. Consider Program 3-12, for example, which displays three rows of numbers with spaces between each one.

Program 3-12

```
 1  // This program displays three rows of numbers.
 2  #include <iostream>
 3  using namespace std;
 4
 5  int main()
 6  {
 7     int num1 = 2897, num2 = 5,    num3 = 837,
 8         num4 = 34,   num5 = 7,    num6 = 1623,
 9         num7 = 390,  num8 = 3456, num9 = 12;
10
11     // Display the first row of numbers
12     cout << num1 << "   " << num2 << "   " << num3 << endl;
13
14     // Display the second row of numbers
15     cout << num4 << "   " << num5 << "   " << num6 << endl;
16
17     // Display the third row of numbers
18     cout << num7 << "   " << num8 << "   " << num9 << endl;
19     return 0;
20  }
```

Program Output
```
2897   5   837
34   7   1623
390   3456   12
```

Unfortunately, the numbers do not line up in columns. This is because some of the numbers, such as 5 and 7, occupy one position on the screen, while others occupy two or three positions. cout uses just the number of spaces needed to print each number.

To remedy this, cout offers a way of specifying the minimum number of spaces to use for each number. A stream manipulator, setw, can be used to establish print fields of a specified width. Here is an example of how it is used:

```
value = 23;
cout << setw(5) << value;
```

The number inside the parentheses after the word setw specifies the *field width* for the value immediately following it. The field width is the minimum number of character positions, or spaces, on the screen to print the value in. In the example above, the number 23 will be displayed in a field of 5 spaces. Since 23 only occupies 2 positions on the screen, 3 blank spaces will be printed before it. To further clarify how this works, look at the following statements:

```
value = 23;
cout << "(" << setw(5) << value << ")";
```

This will cause the following output:

```
(   23)
```

Notice that the number occupies the last two positions in the field. Since the number did not use the entire field, cout filled the extra 3 positions with blank spaces. Because the number appears on the right side of the field with blank spaces "padding" it in front, it is said to be *right-justified*.

Program 3-13 shows how the numbers in Program 3-12 can be printed in columns that line up perfectly by using setw.

Program 3-13

```
 1   // This program displays three rows of numbers.
 2   #include <iostream>
 3   #include <iomanip>        // Required for setw
 4   using namespace std;
 5
 6   int main()
 7   {
 8      int num1 = 2897, num2 = 5,    num3 = 837,
 9          num4 = 34,    num5 = 7,    num6 = 1623,
10          num7 = 390,   num8 = 3456, num9 = 12;
11
12      // Display the first row of numbers
13      cout << setw(6) << num1 << setw(6)
14           << num2 << setw(6) << num3 << endl;
15
16      // Display the second row of numbers
17      cout << setw(6) << num4 << setw(6)
18           << num5 << setw(6) << num6 << endl;
19
20      // Display the third row of numbers
21      cout << setw(6) << num7 << setw(6)
22           << num8 << setw(6) << num9 << endl;
23      return 0;
24   }
```

Program Output
```
2897     5    837
  34     7   1623
 390  3456     12
```

By printing each number in a field of 6 positions, they are displayed in perfect columns.

 NOTE: A new header file, `iomanip`, is included in Program 3-13. It must be used in any program that uses `setw`.

Notice how a `setw` manipulator is used with each value because `setw` only establishes a field width for the value immediately following it. After that value is printed, `cout` goes back to its default method of printing.

You might wonder what will happen if the number is too large to fit in the field, as in the following statement:

```
value = 18397;
cout << setw(2) << value;
```

In cases like this, `cout` will print the entire number. `setw` only specifies the minimum number of positions in the print field. Any number larger than the minimum will cause `cout` to override the `setw` value.

You may specify the field width of any type of data. Program 3-14 shows `setw` being used with an integer, a floating-point number, and a `string` object.

Program 3-14

```
 1   // This program demonstrates the setw manipulator being
 2   // used with values of various data types.
 3   #include <iostream>
 4   #include <iomanip>
 5   #include <string>
 6   using namespace std;
 7
 8   int main()
 9   {
10       int intValue = 3928;
11       double doubleValue = 91.5;
12       string stringValue = "John J. Smith";
13
14       cout << "(" << setw(5) << intValue << ")" << endl;
15       cout << "(" << setw(8) << doubleValue << ")" << endl;
16       cout << "(" << setw(16) << stringValue << ")" << endl;
17       return 0;
18   }
```

(program output continues)

Program 3-14 *(continued)*

Program Output
```
( 3928)
(   91.5)
(    John J. Smith)
```

Program 3-14 can be used to illustrate the following points:
- The field width of a floating-point number includes a position for the decimal point.
- The field width of a `string` object includes all characters in the string, including spaces.
- The values printed in the field are right-justified by default. This means they are aligned with the right side of the print field, and any blanks that must be used to pad it are inserted in front of the value.

VideoNote

Formatting Numbers with setprecision

The `setprecision` Manipulator

Floating-point values may be rounded to a number of *significant digits*, or *precision*, which is the total number of digits that appear before and after the decimal point. You can control the number of significant digits with which floating-point values are displayed by using the `setprecision` manipulator. Program 3-15 shows the results of a division operation displayed with different numbers of significant digits.

Program 3-15

```cpp
 1   // This program demonstrates how setprecision rounds a
 2   // floating point value.
 3   #include <iostream>
 4   #include <iomanip>
 5   using namespace std;
 6
 7   int main()
 8   {
 9       double quotient, number1 = 132.364, number2 = 26.91;
10
11       quotient = number1 / number2;
12       cout << quotient << endl;
13       cout << setprecision(5) << quotient << endl;
14       cout << setprecision(4) << quotient << endl;
15       cout << setprecision(3) << quotient << endl;
16       cout << setprecision(2) << quotient << endl;
17       cout << setprecision(1) << quotient << endl;
18       return 0;
19   }
```

Program Output
```
4.91877
4.9188
4.919
4.92
4.9
5
```

The first value is displayed in line 12 without the `setprecision` manipulator. (By default, the system in the illustration displays floating-point values with 6 significant digits.) The subsequent `cout` statements print the same value, but rounded to 5, 4, 3, 2, and 1 significant digits.

If the value of a number is expressed in fewer digits of precision than specified by `setprecision`, the manipulator will have no effect. In the following statements, the value of `dollars` only has four digits of precision, so the number printed by both `cout` statements is 24.51.

```
double dollars = 24.51;
cout << dollars << endl;                    // Displays 24.51
cout << setprecision(5) << dollars << endl; // Displays 24.51
```

Table 3-11 shows how `setprecision` affects the way various values are displayed.

Table 3-11

Number	Manipulator	Value Displayed
28.92786	setprecision(3)	28.9
21	setprecision(5)	21
109.5	setprecision(4)	109.5
34.28596	setprecision(2)	34

Unlike field width, the precision setting remains in effect until it is changed to some other value. As with all formatting manipulators, you must include the header file `iomanip` to use `setprecision`.

Program 3-16 shows how the `setw` and `setprecision` manipulators may be combined to fully control the way floating point numbers are displayed.

Program 3-16

```
 1  // This program asks for sales figures for 3 days. The total
 2  // sales are calculated and displayed in a table.
 3  #include <iostream>
 4  #include <iomanip>
 5  using namespace std;
 6
 7  int main()
 8  {
 9      double day1, day2, day3, total;
10
11      // Get the sales for each day.
12      cout << "Enter the sales for day 1: ";
13      cin >> day1;
14      cout << "Enter the sales for day 2: ";
15      cin >> day2;
16      cout << "Enter the sales for day 3: ";
17      cin >> day3;
18
19      // Calculate the total sales.
20      total = day1 + day2 + day3;
```

(program continues)

Program 3-16 *(continued)*

```
21
22      // Display the sales figures.
23      cout << "\nSales Figures\n";
24      cout << "-------------\n";
25      cout << setprecision(5);
26      cout << "Day 1: " << setw(8) << day1 << endl;
27      cout << "Day 2: " << setw(8) << day2 << endl;
28      cout << "Day 3: " << setw(8) << day3 << endl;
29      cout << "Total: " << setw(8) << total << endl;
30      return 0;
31   }
```

Program Output with Example Input Shown in Bold
```
Enter the sales for day 1: 321.57 [Enter]
Enter the sales for day 2: 269.62 [Enter]
Enter the sales for day 3: 307.77 [Enter]

Sales Figures
-------------
Day 1:   321.57
Day 2:   269.62
Day 3:   307.77
Total:   898.96
```

The `fixed` Manipulator

The `setprecision` manipulator can sometimes surprise you in an undesirable way. When the precision of a number is set to a lower value, numbers tend to be printed in scientific notation. For example, here is the output of Program 3-16 with larger numbers being input:

Program 3-16

Program Output with Example Input Shown in Bold
```
Enter the sales for day 1: 145678.99 [Enter]
Enter the sales for day 2: 205614.85 [Enter]
Enter the sales for day 3: 198645.22 [Enter]

Sales Figures
-------------
Day 1: 1.4568e+005
Day 2: 2.0561e+005
Day 3: 1.9865e+005
Total: 5.4994e+005
```

Another stream manipulator, `fixed`, forces `cout` to print the digits in *fixed-point notation*, or decimal. Program 3-17 shows how the `fixed` manipulator is used.

Program 3-17

```cpp
 1   // This program asks for sales figures for 3 days. The total
 2   // sales are calculated and displayed in a table.
 3   #include <iostream>
 4   #include <iomanip>
 5   using namespace std;
 6
 7   int main()
 8   {
 9      double day1, day2, day3, total;
10
11      // Get the sales for each day.
12      cout << "Enter the sales for day 1: ";
13      cin >> day1;
14      cout << "Enter the sales for day 2: ";
15      cin >> day2;
16      cout << "Enter the sales for day 3: ";
17      cin >> day3;
18
19      // Calculate the total sales.
20      total = day1 + day2 + day3;
21
22      // Display the sales figures.
23      cout << "\nSales Figures\n";
24      cout << "-------------\n";
25      cout << setprecision(2) << fixed;
26      cout << "Day 1: " << setw(8) << day1 << endl;
27      cout << "Day 2: " << setw(8) << day2 << endl;
28      cout << "Day 3: " << setw(8) << day3 << endl;
29      cout << "Total: " << setw(8) << total << endl;
30      return 0;
31   }
```

Program Output with Example Input Shown in Bold
```
Enter the sales for day 1:  1321.87 [Enter]
Enter the sales for day 2:  1869.26 [Enter]
Enter the sales for day 3:  1403.77 [Enter]

Sales Figures
-------------
Day 1:   1321.87
Day 2:   1869.26
Day 3:   1403.77
Total:   4594.90
```

The statement in line 25 uses the `fixed` manipulator:

```cpp
cout << setprecision(2) << fixed;
```

When the `fixed` manipulator is used, all floating point numbers that are subsequently printed will be displayed in fixed point notation, with the number of digits to the right of the decimal point specified by the `setprecision` manipulator.

When the `fixed` and `setprecision` manipulators are used together, the value specified by the `setprecision` manipulator will be the number of digits to appear after the decimal point, not the number of significant digits. For example, look at the following code.

```
double x = 123.4567;
cout << setprecision(2) << fixed << x << endl;
```

Because the `fixed` manipulator is used, the `setprecision` manipulator will cause the number to be displayed with two digits after the decimal point. The value will be displayed as 123.46.

The `showpoint` Manipulator

By default, floating-point numbers are not displayed with trailing zeroes, and floating-point numbers that do not have a fractional part are not displayed with a decimal point. For example, look at the following code.

```
double x = 123.4, y = 456.0;
cout << setprecision(6) << x << endl;
cout << y << endl;
```

The `cout` statements will produce the following output.

```
123.4
456
```

Although six significant digits are specified for both numbers, neither number is displayed with trailing zeroes. If we want the numbers padded with trailing zeroes, we must use the `showpoint` manipulator as shown in the following code.

```
double x = 123.4, y = 456.0;
cout << setprecision(6) << showpoint << x << endl;
cout << y << endl;
```

These `cout` statements will produce the following output.

```
123.400
456.000
```

 NOTE: With most compilers, trailing zeroes are displayed when the `setprecision` and `fixed` manipulators are used together.

The `left` and `right` Manipulators

Normally output is right justified. For example, look at the following code.

```
double x = 146.789, y = 24.2, z = 1.783;
cout << setw(10) << x << endl;
cout << setw(10) << y << endl;
cout << setw(10) << z << endl;
```

Each of the variables, x, y, and z, is displayed in a print field of 10 spaces. The output of the cout statements is

```
146.789
   24.2
  1.783
```

Notice that each value is right-justified, or aligned to the right of its print field. You can cause the values to be left-justified by using the left manipulator, as shown in the following code.

```
double x = 146.789, y = 24.2, z = 1.783;
cout << left << setw(10) << x << endl;
cout << setw(10) << y << endl;
cout << setw(10) << z << endl;
```

The output of these cout statements is

```
146.789
24.2
1.783
```

In this case, the numbers are aligned to the left of their print fields. The left manipulator remains in effect until you use the right manipulator, which causes all subsequent output to be right-justified.

Table 3-12 summarizes the manipulators we have discussed.

Table 3-12

Stream Manipulator	Description
setw(n)	Establishes a print field of n spaces.
fixed	Displays floating-point numbers in fixed point notation.
showpoint	Causes a decimal point and trailing zeroes to be displayed, even if there is no fractional part.
setprecision(n)	Sets the precision of floating-point numbers.
left	Causes subsequent output to be left justified.
right	Causes subsequent output to be right justified.

 Checkpoint

myprogramminglab *www.myprogramminglab.com*

3.17 Write cout statements with stream manipulators that perform the following:
   A) Display the number 34.789 in a field of nine spaces with two decimal places of precision.
   B) Display the number 7.0 in a field of five spaces with three decimal places of precision.
      The decimal point and any trailing zeroes should be displayed.
   C) Display the number 5.789e+12 in fixed point notation.
   D) Display the number 67 left justified in a field of seven spaces.

3.18   The following program will not compile because the lines have been mixed up.

```
#include <iomanip>
}
cout << person << endl;
string person = "Wolfgang Smith";
int main()
cout << person << endl;
{
#include <iostream>
return 0;
cout << left;
using namespace std;
cout << setw(20);
cout << right;
```

When the lines are properly arranged the program should display the following:

```
        Wolfgang Smith
Wolfgang Smith
```

Rearrange the lines in the correct order. Test the program by entering it on the computer, compiling it, and running it.

3.19   The following program skeleton asks for an angle in degrees and converts it to radians. The formatting of the final output is left to you.

```
#include <iostream>
#include <iomanip>
using namespace std;

int main()
{
    const double PI = 3.14159;
    double degrees, radians;

    cout << "Enter an angle in degrees and I will convert it\n";
    cout << "to radians for you: ";
    cin >> degrees;
    radians = degrees * PI / 180;
    // Display the value in radians left justified, in fixed
    // point notation, with 4 places of precision, in a field
    // 5 spaces wide, making sure the decimal point is always
    // displayed.
    return 0;
}
```

3.8   Working with Characters and `string` Objects

CONCEPT: Special functions exist for working with characters and **string** objects.

Although it is possible to use cin with the >> operator to input strings, it can cause problems that you need to be aware of. When cin reads input, it passes over and ignores any leading *whitespace* characters (spaces, tabs, or line breaks). Once it comes to the first nonblank character and starts reading, it stops reading when it gets to the next whitespace character. Program 3-18 illustrates this problem.

Program 3-18

```cpp
1   // This program illustrates a problem that can occur if
2   // cin is used to read character data into a string object.
3   #include <iostream>
4   #include <string>
5   using namespace std;
6
7   int main()
8   {
9       string name;
10      string city;
11
12      cout << "Please enter your name: ";
13      cin >> name;
14      cout << "Enter the city you live in: ";
15      cin >> city;
16
17      cout << "Hello, " << name << endl;
18      cout << "You live in " << city << endl;
19      return 0;
20  }
```

Program Output with Example Input Shown in Bold
```
Please enter your name: Kate Smith [Enter]
Enter the city you live in: Hello, Kate
You live in Smith
```

Notice that the user was never given the opportunity to enter the city. In the first input statement, when cin came to the space between Kate and Smith, it stopped reading, storing just Kate as the value of name. In the second input statement, cin used the leftover characters it found in the keyboard buffer and stored Smith as the value of city.

To work around this problem, you can use a C++ function named getline. The getline function reads an entire line, including leading and embedded spaces, and stores it in a string object. The getline function looks like the following, where cin is the input stream we are reading from and inputLine is the name of the string object receiving the input.

```cpp
getline(cin, inputLine);
```

Program 3-19 illustrates using the getline function.

Program 3-19

```cpp
1   // This program demonstrates using the getline function
2   // to read character data into a string object.
3   #include <iostream>
4   #include <string>
5   using namespace std;
6
```

(program continues)

Program 3-19   *(continued)*

```
 7  int main()
 8  {
 9     string name;
10     string city;
11
12     cout << "Please enter your name: ";
13     getline(cin, name);
14     cout << "Enter the city you live in: ";
15     getline(cin, city);
16
17     cout << "Hello, " << name << endl;
18     cout << "You live in " << city << endl;
19     return 0;
20  }
```

Program Output with Example Input Shown in Bold
```
Please enter your name: Kate Smith [Enter]
Enter the city you live in: Raleigh [Enter]
Hello, Kate Smith
You live in Raleigh
```

Inputting a Character

Sometimes you want to read only a single character of input. For example, some programs display a menu of items for the user to choose from. Often the selections are denoted by the letters A, B, C, and so forth. The user chooses an item from the menu by typing a character. The simplest way to read a single character is with cin and the >> operator, as illustrated in Program 3-20.

Program 3-20

```
 1  // This program reads a single character into a char variable.
 2  #include <iostream>
 3  using namespace std;
 4
 5  int main()
 6  {
 7     char ch;
 8
 9     cout << "Type a character and press Enter: ";
10     cin >> ch;
11     cout << "You entered " << ch << endl;
12     return 0;
13  }
```

Program Output with Example Input Shown in Bold
```
Type a character and press Enter: A [Enter]
You entered A
```

Using `cin.get`

As with string input, however, there are times when using `cin >>` to read a character does not do what you want. For example, because it passes over all leading whitespace, it is impossible to input just a blank or [**Enter**] with `cin >>`. The program will not continue past the `cin` statement until some character other than the spacebar, tab key, or [**Enter**] key has been pressed. (Once such a character is entered, the [**Enter**] key must still be pressed before the program can continue to the next statement.) Thus, programs that ask the user to "`Press the Enter key to continue.`" cannot use the `>>` operator to read only the pressing of the [**Enter**] key.

In those situations, the `cin` object has a built-in function named `get` that is helpful. Because the `get` function is built into the `cin` object, we say that it is a *member function* of `cin`. The `get` member function reads a single character, including any whitespace character. If the program needs to store the character being read, the `get` member function can be called in either of the following ways. In both examples, assume that `ch` is the name of a char variable that the character is being read into.

```
cin.get(ch);
ch = cin.get();
```

If the program is using the `cin.get` function simply to pause the screen until the [**Enter**] key is pressed and does not need to store the character, the function can also be called like this:

```
cin.get();
```

Program 3-21 illustrates all three ways to use the `cin.get` function.

Program 3-21

```
 1   // This program demonstrates three ways
 2   // to use cin.get() to pause a program.
 3   #include <iostream>
 4   using namespace std;
 5
 6   int main()
 7   {
 8      char ch;
 9
10      cout << "This program has paused. Press Enter to continue.";
11      cin.get(ch);
12      cout << "It has paused a second time. Please press Enter again.";
13      ch = cin.get();
14      cout << "It has paused a third time. Please press Enter again.";
15      cin.get();
16      cout << "Thank you!";
17      return 0;
18   }
```

Program Output with Example Input Shown in Bold

```
This program has paused. Press Enter to continue. [Enter]
It has paused a second time. Please press Enter again. [Enter]
It has paused a third time. Please press Enter again. [Enter]
Thank you!
```

Mixing `cin >>` and `cin.get`

Mixing `cin >>` with `cin.get` can cause an annoying and hard-to-find problem. For example, look at Program 3-22.

Program 3-22

```
 1   // This program demonstrates a problem that occurs
 2   // when you mix cin >> with cin.get().
 3   #include <iostream>
 4   using namespace std;
 5
 6   int main()
 7   {
 8       char ch;                        // Define a character variable
 9       int number;                     // Define an integer variable
10
11       cout << "Enter a number: ";
12       cin >> number;                  // Read an integer
13       cout << "Enter a character: ";
14       ch = cin.get();                 // Read a character
15       cout << "Thank You!\n";
16       return 0;
17   }
```

Program Output with Example Input Shown in Bold
```
Enter a number: 100 [Enter]
Enter a character: Thank You!
```

When this program runs, line 12 lets the user enter a number, but it appears as though the statement in line 14 is skipped. This happens because `cin >>` and `cin.get` use slightly different techniques for reading data.

In the example run of the program, when line 12 executed, the user entered 100 and pressed the [**Enter**] key. Pressing the [**Enter**] key causes a newline character (`'\n'`) to be stored in the keyboard buffer, as shown in Figure 3-5. The `cin >>` statement in line 12 begins reading the data that the user entered, and stops reading when it comes to the newline character. This is shown in Figure 3-6. The newline character is not read, but remains in the keyboard buffer.

Figure 3-5

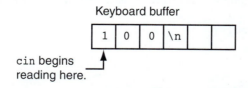

Figure 3-6

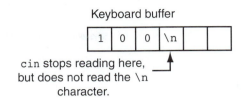

Keyboard buffer

| 1 | 0 | 0 | \n | | |

cin stops reading here,
but does not read the \n
character.

When the `cin.get` function in line 14 executes, it begins reading the keyboard buffer where the previous input operation stopped. That means that `cin.get` reads the newline character, without giving the user a chance to enter any more input. You can remedy this situation by using the `cin.ignore` function, described in the following section.

Using `cin.ignore`

To solve the problem previously described, you can use another of the `cin` object's member functions named `ignore`. The `cin.ignore` function tells the `cin` object to skip one or more characters in the keyboard buffer. Here is its general form:

```
cin.ignore(n, c);
```

The arguments shown in the parentheses are optional. If used, *n* is an integer and *c* is a character. They tell `cin` to skip *n* number of characters, or until the character *c* is encountered. For example, the following statement causes `cin` to skip the next 20 characters or until a newline is encountered, whichever comes first:

```
cin.ignore(20,'\n');
```

If no arguments are used, `cin` will skip only the very next character. Here's an example:

```
cin.ignore();
```

Program 3-23, which is a modified version of Program 3-22, demonstrates the function. Notice that a call to `cin.ignore` has been inserted in line 13, right after the `cin >>` statement.

Program 3-23

```
 1   // This program successfully uses both
 2   // cin >> and cin.get() for keyboard input.
 3   #include <iostream>
 4   using namespace std;
 5
 6   int main()
 7   {
 8      char ch;
 9      int number;
10
```

(program continues)

Program 3-23   *(continued)*

```
11      cout << "Enter a number: ";
12      cin >> number;
13      cin.ignore();                       // Skip the newline character
14      cout << "Enter a character: ";
15      ch = cin.get();
16      cout << "Thank You!\n";
17      return 0;
18   }
```

Program Output with Example Input Shown in Bold
```
Enter a number: 100 [Enter]
Enter a character: Z [Enter]
Thank You!
```

`string` Member Functions and Operators

C++ `string` objects also have a number of member functions. For example, if you want to know the length of the string that is stored in a `string` object, you can call the object's `length` member function. Here is an example of how to use it.

```
string state = "Texas";
int size = state.length();
```

The first statement creates a `string` object named `state`, and initializes it with the string `"Texas"`. The second statement defines an `int` variable named `size`, and initializes it with the length of the string in the `state` object. After this code executes, the size variable will hold the value 5.

Certain operators also work with `string` objects. One of them is the + operator. You have already encountered the + operator to add two numeric quantities. Because strings cannot be added, when this operator is used with string operands it *concatenates* them, or joins them together. Assume we have the following definitions and initializations in a program.

```
string greeting1 = "Hello ";
string greeting2;
string name1 = "World";
string name2 = "People";
```

The following statements illustrate how string concatenation works.

```
greeting2 = greeting1 + name1; // greeting2 now holds "Hello World"
greeting1 = greeting1 + name2; // greeting1 now holds "Hello People"
```

Notice that the string stored in `greeting1` has a blank as its last character. If the blank were not there, `greeting2` would have been assigned the string `"HelloWorld"`.

The last statement in the previous example could also have been written using the += combined assignment operator, to achieve the same result:

```
greeting1 += name2;
```

You will learn about other useful `string` member functions and operators in Chapter 10.

3.9 More Mathematical Library Functions

CONCEPT: The C++ runtime library provides several functions for performing complex mathematical operations.

Earlier in this chapter you learned to use the pow function to raise a number to a power. The C++ library has numerous other functions that perform specialized mathematical operations. These functions are useful in scientific and special-purpose programs. Table 3-13 shows several of these, each of which requires the cmath header file.

Table 3-13

Function	Example	Description
abs	y = abs(x);	Returns the absolute value of the argument. The argument and the return value are integers.
cos	y = cos(x);	Returns the cosine of the argument. The argument should be an angle expressed in radians. The return type and the argument are doubles.
exp	y = exp(x);	Computes the exponential function of the argument, which is x. The return type and the argument are doubles.
fmod	y = fmod(x, z);	Returns, as a double, the remainder of the first argument divided by the second argument. Works like the modulus operator, but the arguments are doubles. (The modulus operator only works with integers.) Take care not to pass zero as the second argument. Doing so would cause division by zero.
log	y = log(x);	Returns the natural logarithm of the argument. The return type and the argument are doubles.
log10	y = log10(x);	Returns the base-10 logarithm of the argument. The return type and the argument are doubles.
sin	y = sin(x);	Returns the sine of the argument. The argument should be an angle expressed in radians. The return type and the argument are doubles.
sqrt	y = sqrt(x);	Returns the square root of the argument. The return type and argument are doubles.
tan	y = tan(x);	Returns the tangent of the argument. The argument should be an angle expressed in radians. The return type and the argument are doubles.

Each of these functions is as simple to use as the pow function. The following program segment demonstrates the sqrt function, which returns the square root of a number:

```cpp
cout << "Enter a number: ";
cin >> num;
s = sqrt(num);
cout << "The square root of " << num << " is " << s << endl;
```

Here is the output of the program segment, with 25 as the number entered by the user:

```
Enter a number: 25
The square root of 25 is 5
```

Program 3-24 shows the sqrt function being used to find the hypotenuse of a right triangle. The program uses the following formula, taken from the Pythagorean theorem:

$$c = \sqrt{a^2 + b^2}$$

In the formula, c is the length of the hypotenuse, and a and b are the lengths of the other sides of the triangle.

Program 3-24

```cpp
 1   // This program asks for the lengths of the two sides of a
 2   // right triangle. The length of the hypotenuse is then
 3   // calculated and displayed.
 4   #include <iostream>
 5   #include <iomanip>    // For setprecision
 6   #include <cmath>      // For the sqrt and pow functions
 7   using namespace std;
 8
 9   int main()
10   {
11      double a, b, c;
12
13      cout << "Enter the length of side a: ";
14      cin >> a;
15      cout << "Enter the length of side b: ";
16      cin >> b;
17      c = sqrt(pow(a, 2.0) + pow(b, 2.0));
18      cout << "The length of the hypotenuse is ";
19      cout << setprecision(2) << c << endl;
20      return 0;
21   }
```

Program Output with Example Input Shown in Bold
```
Enter the length of side a: 5.0 [Enter]
Enter the length of side b: 12.0 [Enter]
The length of the hypotenuse is 13
```

The following statement, taken from Program 3-24, calculates the square root of the sum of the squares of the triangle's two sides:

```cpp
c = sqrt(pow(a, 2.0) + pow(b, 2.0));
```

Notice that the following mathematical expression is used as the sqrt function's argument:

```cpp
pow(a, 2.0) + pow(b, 2.0)
```

This expression calls the pow function twice: once to calculate the square of a and again to calculate the square of b. These two squares are then added together, and the sum is sent to the sqrt function.

Random Numbers

Some programming techniques require the use of randomly generated numbers. The C++ library has a function, rand(), for this purpose. (rand() requires the header file cstdlib). The number returned by the function is an int. Here is an example of its usage:

```
y = rand();
```

After this statement executes, the variable y will contain a random number. In actuality, the numbers produced by rand()are pseudorandom. The function uses an algorithm that produces the same sequence of numbers each time the program is repeated on the same system. For example, suppose the following statements are executed.

```
cout << rand() << endl;
cout << rand() << endl;
cout << rand() << endl;
```

The three numbers displayed will appear to be random, but each time the program runs, the same three values will be generated. In order to randomize the results of rand(), the srand() function must be used. srand() accepts an unsigned int argument, which acts as a seed value for the algorithm. By specifying different seed values, rand() will generate different sequences of random numbers.

A common practice for getting unique seed values is to call the time function, which is part of the standard library. The time function returns the number of seconds that have elapsed since midnight, January 1, 1970. The time function requires the ctime header file, and you pass 0 as an argument to the function. Program 3-25 demonstrates. The program should generate three different random numbers each time it is executed.

Program 3-25

```
 1   // This program demonstrates random numbers.
 2   #include <iostream>
 3   #include <cstdlib>   // For rand and srand
 4   #include <ctime>     // For the time function
 5   using namespace std;
 6
 7   int main()
 8   {
 9      // Get the system time.
10      unsigned seed = time(0);
11
12      // Seed the random number generator.
13      srand(seed);
14
15      // Display three random numbers.
16      cout << rand() << endl;
17      cout << rand() << endl;
18      cout << rand() << endl;
19      return 0;
20   }
```

Program Output
```
23861
20884
21941
```

NOTE: If you wish to limit the range of the random number, use the following formula.

```
y = 1 + rand() % maxRange;
```

The `maxRange` value is the upper limit of the range. For example, if you wish to generate a random number in the range of 1 through 100, use the following statement.

```
y = 1 + rand() % 100;
```

This is how the statement works: Look at the following expression.

```
rand() % 100
```

Assuming `rand()` returns 37894, the value of the expression above is 94. That is because 37894 divided by 100 is 378 with a remainder of 94. (The modulus operator returns the remainder.) But, what if `rand()` returns a number that is evenly divisible by 100, such as 500? The expression above will return a 0. If we want a number in the range 1 – 100, we must add 1 to the result. That is why we use the expression `1 + rand() % 100`.

 Checkpoint

myprogramminglab *www.myprogramminglab.com*

3.20   Write a short description of each of the following functions:

cos	log	sin
exp	log10	sqrt
fmod	pow	tan

3.21   Assume the variables `angle1` and `angle2` hold angles stored in radians. Write a statement that adds the sine of `angle1` to the cosine of `angle2`, and stores the result in the variable `x`.

3.22   To find the cube root (the third root) of a number, raise it to the power of $\frac{1}{3}$. To find the fourth root of a number, raise it to the power of $\frac{1}{4}$. Write a statement that will find the fifth root of the variable `x` and store the result in the variable `y`.

3.23   The cosecant of the angle *a* is

$$\frac{1}{\sin a}$$

Write a statement that calculates the cosecant of the angle stored in the variable `a`, and stores it in the variable `y`.

3.10   Focus on Debugging: Hand Tracing a Program

Hand tracing is a debugging process where you pretend that you are the computer executing a program. You step through each of the program's statements one by one. As you look at a statement, you record the contents that each variable will have after the statement executes. This process is often helpful in finding mathematical mistakes and other logic errors.

To hand trace a program you construct a chart with a column for each variable. The rows in the chart correspond to the lines in the program. For example, Program 3-26 is shown with a hand trace chart. The program uses the following four variables: num1, num2, num3, and avg. Notice that the hand trace chart has a column for each variable and a row for each line of code in function main.

Program 3-26

```
 1 // This program asks for three numbers, then
 2 // displays the average of the numbers.
 3 #include <iostream>
 4 using namespace std;

 5 int main()

 6 {

 7     double num1, num2, num3, avg;

 8     cout << "Enter the first number: ";

 9     cin >> num1;

10     cout << "Enter the second number: ";

11     cin >> num2;

12     cout << "Enter the third number: ";

13     cin >> num3;

14     avg = num1 + num2 + num3 / 3;

15     cout << "The average is " << avg << endl;

16     return 0;

17 }
```

num1	num2	num3	avg

This program, which asks the user to enter three numbers and then displays the average of the numbers, has a bug. It does not display the correct average. The output of a sample session with the program follows.

Program Output with Example Input Shown in Bold
```
Enter the first number: 10 [Enter]
Enter the second number: 20 [Enter]
Enter the third number: 30 [Enter]
The average is 40
```

The correct average of 10, 20, and 30 is 20, not 40. To find the error we will hand trace the program. To hand trace this program, you step through each statement, observing the operation that is taking place, and then record the contents of the variables after the statement executes. After the hand trace is complete, the chart will appear as follows. We have written question marks in the chart where we do not know the contents of a variable.

Program 3-26   **(with hand trace chart filled)**

```
 1 // This program asks for three numbers, then
 2 // displays the average of the numbers.
 3 #include <iostream>
 4 using namespace std;

 5 int main()

 6 {

 7     double num1, num2, num3, avg;

 8     cout << "Enter the first number: ";

 9     cin >> num1;

10     cout << "Enter the second number: ";

11     cin >> num2;

12     cout << "Enter the third number: ";

13     cin >> num3;

14     avg = num1 + num2 + num3 / 3;

15     cout << "The average is " << avg << endl;

16     return 0;

17 }
```

num1	num2	num3	avg
?	?	?	?
?	?	?	?
10	?	?	?
10	?	?	?
10	20	?	?
10	20	?	?
10	20	30	?
10	20	30	40
10	20	30	40

Do you see the error? By examining the statement that performs the math operation in line 14, we find a mistake. The division operation takes place before the addition operations, so we must rewrite that statement as

```
avg = (num1 + num2 + num3) / 3;
```

Hand tracing is a simple process that focuses your attention on each statement in a program. Often this helps you locate errors that are not obvious.

3.11

Focus on Problem Solving: A Case Study

General Crates, Inc. builds custom-designed wooden crates. With materials and labor, it costs GCI $0.23 per cubic foot to build a crate. In turn, they charge their customers $0.50 per cubic foot for the crate. You have been asked to write a program that calculates the volume (in cubic feet), cost, customer price, and profit of any crate GCI builds.

Variables

Table 3-14 shows the named constants and variables needed.

Table 3-14

Constant or Variable	Description
COST_PER_CUBIC_FOOT	A named constant, declared as a double and initialized with the value 0.23. This represents the cost to build a crate, per cubic foot.
CHARGE_PER_CUBIC_FOOT	A named constant, declared as a double and initialized with the value 0.5. This represents the amount charged for a crate, per cubic foot.
length	A double variable to hold the length of the crate, which is input by the user.
width	A double variable to hold the width of the crate, which is input by the user.
height	A double variable to hold the height of the crate, which is input by the user.
volume	A double variable to hold the volume of the crate. The value stored in this variable is calculated.
cost	A double variable to hold the cost of building the crate. The value stored in this variable is calculated.
charge	A double variable to hold the amount charged to the customer for the crate. The value stored in this variable is calculated.
profit	A double variable to hold the profit GCI makes from the crate. The value stored in this variable is calculated.

Program Design

The program must perform the following general steps:

1. Ask the user to enter the dimensions of the crate (the crate's length, width, and height).

2. Calculate the crate's volume, the cost of building the crate, the customer's charge, and the profit made.

3. Display the data calculated in Step 2.

A general hierarchy chart for this program is shown in Figure 3-7.

Figure 3-7

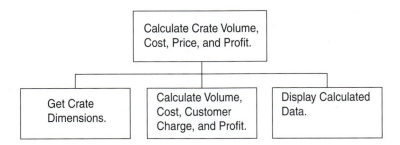

The "Get Crate Dimensions" step is shown in greater detail in Figure 3-8.

Figure 3-8

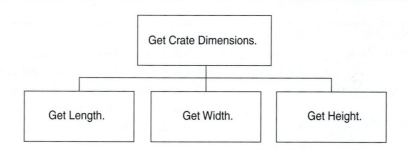

The "Calculate Volume, Cost, Customer Charge, and Profit" step is shown in greater detail in Figure 3-9.

Figure 3-9

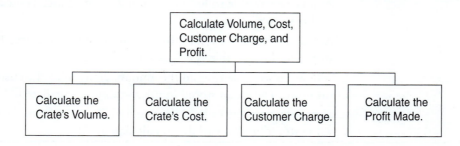

The "Display Calculated Data" step is shown in greater detail in Figure 3-10.

Figure 3-10

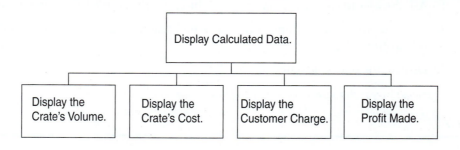

Pseudocode for the program is as follows:

```
Ask the user to input the crate's length.
Ask the user to input the crate's width.
Ask the user to input the crate's height.
Calculate the crate's volume.
Calculate the cost of building the crate.
Calculate the customer's charge for the crate.
Calculate the profit made from the crate.
Display the crate's volume.
```

Display the cost of building the crate.
Display the customer's charge for the crate.
Display the profit made from the crate.

Calculations

The following formulas will be used to calculate the crate's volume, cost, charge, and profit:

volume = length × width × height
cost = volume × 0.23
charge = volume × 0.5
profit = charge − cost

The Program

The last step is to expand the pseudocode into the final program, which is shown in Program 3-27.

Program 3-27

```
1   // This program is used by General Crates, Inc. to calculate
2   // the volume, cost, customer charge, and profit of a crate
3   // of any size. It calculates this data from user input, which
4   // consists of the dimensions of the crate.
5   #include <iostream>
6   #include <iomanip>
7   using namespace std;
8
9   int main()
10  {
11      // Constants for cost and amount charged
12      const double COST_PER_CUBIC_FOOT = 0.23;
13      const double CHARGE_PER_CUBIC_FOOT = 0.5;
14
15      // Variables
16      double length,   // The crate's length
17             width,    // The crate's width
18             height,   // The crate's height
19             volume,   // The volume of the crate
20             cost,     // The cost to build the crate
21             charge,   // The customer charge for the crate
22             profit;   // The profit made on the crate
23
24      // Set the desired output formatting for numbers.
25      cout << setprecision(2) << fixed << showpoint;
26
```

(program continues)

Program 3-27 *(continued)*

```
27      // Prompt the user for the crate's length, width, and height
28      cout << "Enter the dimensions of the crate (in feet):\n";
29      cout << "Length: ";
30      cin >> length;
31      cout << "Width: ";
32      cin >> width;
33      cout << "Height: ";
34      cin >> height;
35
36      // Calculate the crate's volume, the cost to produce it,
37      // the charge to the customer, and the profit.
38      volume = length * width * height;
39      cost = volume * COST_PER_CUBIC_FOOT;
40      charge = volume * CHARGE_PER_CUBIC_FOOT;
41      profit = charge - cost;
42
43      // Display the calculated data.
44      cout << "The volume of the crate is ";
45      cout << volume << " cubic feet.\n";
46      cout << "Cost to build: $" << cost << endl;
47      cout << "Charge to customer: $" << charge << endl;
48      cout << "Profit: $" << profit << endl;
49      return 0;
50   }
```

Program Output with Example Input Shown in Bold
```
Enter the dimensions of the crate (in feet):
Length: 10 [Enter]
Width: 8 [Enter]
Height: 4 [Enter]
The volume of the crate is 320.00 cubic feet.
Cost to build: $73.60
Charge to customer: $160.00
Profit: $86.40
```

Program Output with Different Example Input Shown in Bold
```
Enter the dimensions of the crate (in feet):
Length: 12.5 [Enter]
Width: 10.5 [Enter]
Height: 8 [Enter]
The volume of the crate is 1050.00 cubic feet.
Cost to build: $241.50
Charge to customer: $525.00
Profit: $283.50
```

Review Questions and Exercises

Short Answer

1. Assume that the following variables are defined:

```
int age;
double pay;
char section;
```

   Write a single `cin` statement that will read input into each of these variables.

2. Assume a `string` object has been defined as follows:

```
string description;
```

   A) Write a `cin` statement that reads in a one-word string.

   B) Write a statement that reads in a string that can contain multiple words separated by blanks.

3. What header files must be included in the following program?

```
int main()
{
    double amount = 89.7;
    cout << showpoint << fixed;
    cout << setw(8) << amount << endl;
    return 0;
}
```

4. Complete the following table by writing the value of each expression in the Value column.

Expression	Value
`28 / 4 - 2`	
`6 + 12 * 2 - 8`	
`4 + 8 * 2`	
`6 + 17 % 3 - 2`	
`2 + 22 * (9 - 7)`	
`(8 + 7) * 2`	
`(16 + 7) % 2 - 1`	
`12 / (10 - 6)`	
`(19 - 3) * (2 + 2) / 4`	

5. Write C++ expressions for the following algebraic expressions:

$$a = 12x$$

$$z = 5x + 14y + 6k$$

$$y = x^4$$

$$g = \frac{h + 12}{4k}$$

$$c = \frac{a^3}{b^2 k^4}$$

6. Assume a program has the following variable definitions:

```
int units;
float mass;
double weight;
```

and the following statement:

```
weight = mass * units;
```

Which automatic data type conversion will take place?

A) `mass` is demoted to an `int`, `units` remains an `int`, and the result of `mass * units` is an `int`.

B) `units` is promoted to a `float`, `mass` remains a `float`, and the result of `mass * units` is a `float`.

C) `units` is promoted to a `float`, `mass` remains a `float`, and the result of `mass * units` is a `double`.

7. Assume a program has the following variable definitions:

```
int a, b = 2;
float c = 4.2;
```

and the following statement:

```
a = b * c;
```

What value will be stored in `a`?

A) 8.4

B) 8

C) 0

D) None of the above

8. Assume that `qty` and `salesReps` are both integers. Use a type cast expression to rewrite the following statement so it will no longer perform integer division.

```
unitsEach = qty / salesReps;
```

9. Rewrite the following variable definition so the variable is a named constant.

```
int rate;
```

10. Complete the following table by writing statements with combined assignment operators in the right-hand column. The statements should be equivalent to the statements in the left-hand column.

Statements with Assignment Operator	Statements with Combined Assignment Operator

`x = x + 5;`
`total = total + subtotal;`
`dist = dist / rep;`
`ppl = ppl * period;`
`inv = inv - shrinkage;`
`num = num % 2;`	

11. Write a multiple assignment statement that can be used instead of the following group of assignment statements:

```
east = 1;
west = 1;
north = 1;
south = 1;
```

12. Write a `cout` statement so the variable `divSales` is displayed in a field of 8 spaces, in fixed point notation, with a precision of 2 decimal places. The decimal point should always be displayed.

13. Write a `cout` statement so the variable `totalAge` is displayed in a field of 12 spaces, in fixed point notation, with a precision of 4 decimal places.

14. Write a `cout` statement so the variable `population` is displayed in a field of 12 spaces, left-justified, with a precision of 8 decimal places. The decimal point should always be displayed.

Fill-in-the-Blank

15. The _____ library function returns the cosine of an angle.

16. The _____ library function returns the sine of an angle.

17. The _____ library function returns the tangent of an angle.

18. The _____ library function returns the exponential function of a number.

19. The _____ library function returns the remainder of a floating point division.

20. The _____ library function returns the natural logarithm of a number.

21. The _____ library function returns the base-10 logarithm of a number.

22. The _____ library function returns the value of a number raised to a power.

23. The _____ library function returns the square root of a number.

24. The _____ file must be included in a program that uses the mathematical functions.

Algorithm Workbench

25. A retail store grants its customers a maximum amount of credit. Each customer's available credit is his or her maximum amount of credit minus the amount of credit used. Write a pseudocode algorithm for a program that asks for a customer's maximum amount of credit and amount of credit used. The program should then display the customer's available credit.

    After you write the pseudocode algorithm, convert it to a complete C++ program.

26. Write a pseudocode algorithm for a program that calculates the total of a retail sale. The program should ask for the amount of the sale and the sales tax rate. The sales tax rate should be entered as a floating-point number. For example, if the sales tax rate is 6 percent, the user should enter 0.06. The program should display the amount of sales tax and the total of the sale.

    After you write the pseudocode algorithm, convert it to a complete C++ program.

27. Write a pseudocode algorithm for a program that asks the user to enter a golfer's score for three games of golf, and then displays the average of the three scores.

    After you write the pseudocode algorithm, convert it to a complete C++ program.

Find the Errors

Each of the following programs has some errors. Locate as many as you can.

28.
```cpp
using namespace std;
int main ()
{
    double number1, number2, sum;

    Cout << "Enter a number: ";
    Cin << number1;
    Cout << "Enter another number: ";
    Cin << number2;
    number1 + number2 = sum;
    Cout "The sum of the two numbers is " << sum
    return 0;
}
```

29.
```cpp
#include <iostream>
using namespace std;

int main()
{
    int number1, number2;
    float quotient;
    cout << "Enter two numbers and I will divide\n";
    cout << "the first by the second for you.\n";
    cin >> number1, number2;
    quotient = float<static_cast>(number1) / number2;
    cout << quotient
    return 0;
}
```

30.
```cpp
#include <iostream>;
using namespace std;

int main()
{
    const int number1, number2, product;

    cout << "Enter two numbers and I will multiply\n";
    cout << "them for you.\n";
    cin >> number1 >> number2;
    product = number1 * number2;
    cout << product
    return 0;
}
```

31.
```cpp
#include <iostream>;
using namespace std;

main
{
    int number1, number2;

    cout << "Enter two numbers and I will multiply\n"
    cout << "them by 50 for you.\n"
    cin >> number1 >> number2;
    number1 =* 50;
    number2 =* 50;
    cout << number1 << " " << number2;
    return 0;
}
```

32.
```cpp
#include <iostream>;
using namespace std;

main
{
    double number, half;

    cout << "Enter a number and I will divide it\n"
    cout << "in half for you.\n"
    cin >> number1;
    half =/ 2;
    cout << fixedpoint << showpoint << half << endl;
    return 0;
}
```

33.
```cpp
#include <iostream>;
using namespace std;

int main()
{
    char name, go;

    cout << "Enter your name: ";
    getline >> name;
    cout << "Hi " << name << endl;
    return 0;
}
```

Predict the Output

What will each of the following programs display? (Some should be hand traced, and require a calculator.)

34. (*Assume the user enters 38700. Use a calculator.*)
```cpp
#include <iostream>
using namespace std;
```

```cpp
int main()
{
    double salary, monthly;
    cout << "What is your annual salary? ";
    cin >> salary;
    monthly = static_cast<int>(salary) / 12;
    cout << "Your monthly wages are " << monthly << endl;
    return 0;
}
```

35.
```cpp
#include <iostream>
using namespace std;
int main()
{
    long x, y, z;

    x = y = z = 4;
    x += 2;
    y -= 1;
    z *= 3;
    cout << x << " " << y << " " << z << endl;
    return 0;
}
```

36. (*Assume the user enters George Washington.*)
```cpp
#include <iostream>
#include <iomanip>
#include <string>
using namespace std;

int main()
{
    string userInput;
    cout << "What is your name? ";
    getline(cin, userInput);
    cout << "Hello " << userInput << endl;
    return 0;
}
```

37. (*Assume the user enters 36720152. Use a calculator.*)
```cpp
#include <iostream>
#include <iomanip>
using namespace std;

int main()
{
    long seconds;
    double minutes, hours, days, months, years;

    cout << "Enter the number of seconds that have\n";
    cout << "elapsed since some time in the past and\n";
    cout << "I will tell you how many minutes, hours,\n";
    cout << "days, months, and years have passed: ";
    cin >> seconds;
```

```
    minutes = seconds / 60;
    hours = minutes / 60;
    days = hours / 24;
    years = days / 365;
    months = years * 12;

    cout << setprecision(4) << fixed << showpoint << right;
    cout << "Minutes: " << setw(6) << minutes << endl;
    cout << "Hours: " << setw(6) << hours << endl;
    cout << "Days: " << setw(6) << days << endl;
    cout << "Months: " << setw(6) << months << endl;
    cout << "Years: " << setw(6) << years << endl;
    return 0;
}
```

Programming Challenges

Visit www.myprogramminglab.com to complete many of these Programming Challenges online and get instant feedback.

1. **Miles per Gallon**

   Write a program that calculates a car's gas mileage. The program should ask the user to enter the number of gallons of gas the car can hold, and the number of miles it can be driven on a full tank. It should then display the number of miles that may be driven per gallon of gas.

2. **Stadium Seating**

   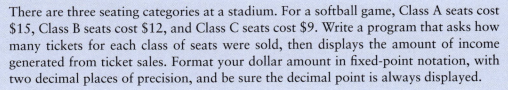

   There are three seating categories at a stadium. For a softball game, Class A seats cost $15, Class B seats cost $12, and Class C seats cost $9. Write a program that asks how many tickets for each class of seats were sold, then displays the amount of income generated from ticket sales. Format your dollar amount in fixed-point notation, with two decimal places of precision, and be sure the decimal point is always displayed.

   VideoNote
   Solving the Stadium Seating Problem

3. **Test Average**

   Write a program that asks for five test scores. The program should calculate the average test score and display it. The number displayed should be formatted in fixed-point notation, with one decimal point of precision.

4. **Average Rainfall**

   Write a program that calculates the average rainfall for three months. The program should ask the user to enter the name of each month, such as June or July, and the amount of rain (in inches) that fell each month. The program should display a message similar to the following:

   The average rainfall for June, July, and August is 6.72 inches.

5. **Box Office**

   A movie theater only keeps a percentage of the revenue earned from ticket sales. The remainder goes to the movie distributor. Write a program that calculates a theater's gross and net box office profit for a night. The program should ask for the name of the movie, and how many adult and child tickets were sold. (The price of an adult ticket is $6.00 and a child's ticket is $3.00.) It should display a report similar to

Movie Name:	"Wheels of Fury"
Adult Tickets Sold:	382
Child Tickets Sold:	127
Gross Box Office Profit:	$ 2673.00
Net Box Office Profit:	$ 534.60
Amount Paid to Distributor:	$ 2138.40

NOTE: Assume the theater keeps 20 percent of the gross box office profit.

6. **How Many Widgets?**

The Yukon Widget Company manufactures widgets that weigh 9.2 pounds each. Write a program that calculates how many widgets are stacked on a pallet, based on the total weight of the pallet. The program should ask the user how much the pallet weighs by itself and with the widgets stacked on it. It should then calculate and display the number of widgets stacked on the pallet.

7. **How Many Calories?**

A bag of cookies holds 40 cookies. The calorie information on the bag claims that there are 10 "servings" in the bag and that a serving equals 300 calories. Write a program that asks the user to input how many cookies he or she actually ate and then reports how many total calories were consumed.

8. **How Much Insurance?**

Many financial experts advise that property owners should insure their homes or buildings for at least 80 percent of the amount it would cost to replace the structure. Write a program that asks the user to enter the replacement cost of a building and then displays the minimum amount of insurance he or she should buy for the property.

9. **Automobile Costs**

Write a program that asks the user to enter the monthly costs for the following expenses incurred from operating his or her automobile: loan payment, insurance, gas, oil, tires, and maintenance. The program should then display the total monthly cost of these expenses, and the total annual cost of these expenses.

10. **Celsius to Fahrenheit**

Write a program that converts Celsius temperatures to Fahrenheit temperatures. The formula is

$$F = \frac{9}{5}C + 32$$

F is the Fahrenheit temperature and C is the Celsius temperature.

11. **Currency**

Write a program that will convert U.S. dollar amounts to Japanese yen and to euros, storing the conversion factors in the constants YEN_PER_DOLLAR and EUROS_PER_DOLLAR. To get the most up-to-date exchange rates, search the Internet using the term "currency exchange rate". If you cannot find the most recent exchange rates, use the following:

> 1 Dollar = 83.14 Yen
> 1 Dollar = 0.7337 Euros

Format your currency amounts in fixed-point notation, with two decimal places of precision, and be sure the decimal point is always displayed.

12. **Monthly Sales Tax**

A retail company must file a monthly sales tax report listing the sales for the month and the amount of sales tax collected. Write a program that asks for the month, the year, and the total amount collected at the cash register (that is, sales plus sales tax). Assume the state sales tax is 4 percent and the county sales tax is 2 percent.

If the total amount collected is known and the total sales tax is 6 percent, the amount of product sales may be calculated as:

$$S = \frac{T}{1.06}$$

S is the product sales and T is the total income (product sales plus sales tax).

The program should display a report similar to

```
Month: October
--------------------
Total Collected:     $ 26572.89
Sales:               $ 25068.76
County Sales Tax:    $   501.38
State Sales Tax:     $  1002.75
Total Sales Tax:     $  1504.13
```

13. **Property Tax**

A county collects property taxes on the assessment value of property, which is 60 percent of the property's actual value. If an acre of land is valued at $10,000, its assessment value is $6,000. The property tax is then 64¢ for each $100 of the assessment value. The tax for the acre assessed at $6,000 will be $38.40. Write a program that asks for the actual value of a piece of property and displays the assessment value and property tax.

14. **Senior Citizen Property Tax**

Madison County provides a $5,000 homeowner exemption for its senior citizens. For example, if a senior's house is valued at $158,000 its assessed value would be $94,800, as explained above. However, he would only pay tax on $89,800. At last year's tax rate of $2.64 for each $100 of assessed value, the property tax would be $2,370.72. In addition to the tax break, senior citizens are allowed to pay their property tax in four equal payments. The quarterly payment due on this property would be $592.68. Write a program that asks the user to input the actual value of a piece of property and the current tax rate for each $100 of assessed value. The program should then calculate and report how much annual property tax a senior homeowner will be charged for this property and what the quarterly tax bill will be.

15. **Math Tutor**

Write a program that can be used as a math tutor for a young student. The program should display two random numbers to be added, such as

```
  247
+ 129
```

The program should then pause while the student works on the problem. When the student is ready to check the answer, he or she can press a key and the program will display the correct solution:

```
  247
+ 129
  376
```

16. **Interest Earned**

Assuming there are no deposits other than the original investment, the balance in a savings account after one year may be calculated as

$$\texttt{Amount} = \texttt{Principal} * \left(1 + \frac{\texttt{Rate}}{\texttt{T}}\right)^{\texttt{T}}$$

`Principal` is the balance in the savings account, `Rate` is the interest rate, and `T` is the number of times the interest is compounded during a year (`T` is 4 if the interest is compounded quarterly).

Write a program that asks for the principal, the interest rate, and the number of times the interest is compounded. It should display a report similar to

```
Interest Rate:            4.25%
Times Compounded:           12
Principal:         $ 1000.00
Interest:          $   43.34
Amount in Savings: $ 1043.34
```

17. **Monthly Payments**

The monthly payment on a loan may be calculated by the following formula:

$$\texttt{Payment} = \frac{\texttt{Rate} * (1 + \texttt{Rate})^{\texttt{N}}}{((1 + \texttt{Rate})^{\texttt{N}} - 1)} * \texttt{L}$$

`Rate` is the monthly interest rate, which is the annual interest rate divided by 12. (12% annual interest would be 1 percent monthly interest.) `N` is the number of payments and `L` is the amount of the loan. Write a program that asks for these values and displays a report similar to

```
Loan Amount:            $ 10000.00
Monthly Interest Rate:          1%
Number of Payments:             36
Monthly Payment:        $   332.14
Amount Paid Back:       $ 11957.15
Interest Paid:          $  1957.15
```

18. Pizza Pi

Joe's Pizza Palace needs a program to calculate the number of slices a pizza of any size can be divided into. The program should perform the following steps:

A) Ask the user for the diameter of the pizza in inches.

B) Calculate the number of slices that may be taken from a pizza of that size.

C) Display a message telling the number of slices.

To calculate the number of slices that may be taken from the pizza, you must know the following facts:

- Each slice should have an area of 14.125 inches.
- To calculate the number of slices, simply divide the area of the pizza by 14.125.
- The area of the pizza is calculated with this formula:

Area = πr^2

> **NOTE:** π is the Greek letter pi. 3.14159 can be used as its value. The variable r is the radius of the pizza. Divide the diameter by 2 to get the radius.

Make sure the output of the program displays the number of slices in fixed point notation, rounded to one decimal place of precision. Use a named constant for pi.

19. How Many Pizzas?

Modify the program you wrote in Programming Challenge 18 (Pizza Pi) so that it reports the number of pizzas you need to buy for a party if each person attending is expected to eat an average of four slices. The program should ask the user for the number of people who will be at the party and for the diameter of the pizzas to be ordered. It should then calculate and display the number of pizzas to purchase.

20. Angle Calculator

Write a program that asks the user for an angle, entered in radians. The program should then display the sine, cosine, and tangent of the angle. (Use the `sin`, `cos`, and `tan` library functions to determine these values.) The output should be displayed in fixed-point notation, rounded to four decimal places of precision.

21. Stock Transaction Program

Last month Joe purchased some stock in Acme Software, Inc. Here are the details of the purchase:

- The number of shares that Joe purchased was 1,000.
- When Joe purchased the stock, he paid $32.87 per share.
- Joe paid his stock broker a commission that amounted to 2% of the amount he paid for the stock.

Two weeks later Joe sold the stock. Here are the details of the sale:

- The number of shares that Joe sold was 1,000.
- He sold the stock for $33.92 per share.
- He paid his stock broker another commission that amounted to 2% of the amount he received for the stock.

Write a program that displays the following information:

- The amount of money Joe paid for the stock.
- The amount of commission Joe paid his broker when he bought the stock.
- The amount that Joe sold the stock for.
- The amount of commission Joe paid his broker when he sold the stock.
- Display the amount of profit that Joe made after selling his stock and paying the two commissions to his broker. (If the amount of profit that your program displays is a negative number, then Joe lost money on the transaction.)

22. **Word Game**

Write a program that plays a word game with the user. The program should ask the user to enter the following:

- His or her name
- His or her age
- The name of a city
- The name of a college
- A profession
- A type of animal
- A pet's name

After the user has entered these items, the program should display the following story, inserting the user's input into the appropriate locations:

```
There once was a person named NAME who lived in CITY. At the age of
AGE, NAME went to college at COLLEGE. NAME graduated and went to work
as a PROFESSION. Then, NAME adopted a(n) ANIMAL named PETNAME. They
both lived happily ever after!
```

4 Making Decisions

TOPICS

4.1 Relational Operators

CONCEPT: Relational operators allow you to compare numeric and **char** values and determine whether one is greater than, less than, equal to, or not equal to another.

So far, the programs you have written follow this simple scheme:

- Gather input from the user.
- Perform one or more calculations.
- Display the results on the screen.

Computers are good at performing calculations, but they are also quite adept at comparing values to determine if one is greater than, less than, or equal to the other. These types of operations are valuable for tasks such as examining sales figures, determining profit and loss, checking a number to ensure it is within an acceptable range, and validating the input given by a user.

Numeric data is compared in C++ by using relational operators. Each relational operator determines whether a specific relationship exists between two values. For example, the greater-than operator (>) determines if a value is greater than another. The equality operator (==) determines if two values are equal. Table 4-1 lists all of C++'s relational operators.

Table 4-1

Relational Operators	Meaning
>	Greater than
<	Less than
>=	Greater than or equal to
<=	Less than or equal to
==	Equal to
!=	Not equal to

All of the relational operators are binary, which means they use two operands. Here is an example of an expression using the greater-than operator:

    x > y

This expression is called a *relational expression*. It is used to determine whether x is greater than y. The following expression determines whether x is less than y:

    x < y

Table 4-2 shows examples of several relational expressions that compare the variables x and y.

Table 4-2

Expression	What the Expression Means
x > y	Is x greater than y?
x < y	Is x less than y?
x >= y	Is x greater than or equal to y?
x <= y	Is x less than or equal to y?
x == y	Is x equal to y?
x != y	Is x not equal to y?

 NOTE: All the relational operators have left-to-right associativity. Recall that associativity is the order in which an operator works with its operands.

The Value of a Relationship

So, how are relational expressions used in a program? Remember, all expressions have a value. Relational expressions are also known as *Boolean expressions*, which means their value can only be *true* or *false*. If x is greater than y, the expression x > y will be true, while the expression y == x will be false.

The == operator determines whether the operand on its left is equal to the operand on its right. If both operands have the same value, the expression is true. Assuming that a is 4, the following expression is true:

```
a == 4
```

But the following is false:

```
a == 2
```

> **WARNING!** Notice the equality operator is two = symbols together. Don't confuse this operator with the assignment operator, which is one = symbol. The == operator determines whether a variable is equal to another value, but the = operator assigns the value on the operator's right to the variable on its left. There will be more about this later in the chapter.

A couple of the relational operators actually test for two relationships. The >= operator determines whether the operand on its left is greater than *or* equal to the operand on the right. Assuming that a is 4, b is 6, and c is 4, both of the following expressions are true:

```
b >= a
a >= c
```

But the following is false:

```
a >= 5
```

The <= operator determines whether the operand on its left is less than *or* equal to the operand on its right. Once again, assuming that a is 4, b is 6, and c is 4, both of the following expressions are true:

```
a <= c
b <= 10
```

But the following is false:

```
b <= a
```

The last relational operator is !=, which is the not-equal operator. It determines whether the operand on its left is not equal to the operand on its right, which is the opposite of the == operator. As before, assuming a is 4, b is 6, and c is 4, both of the following expressions are true:

```
a != b
b != c
```

These expressions are true because a is *not* equal to b and b is *not* equal to c. But the following expression is false because a *is* equal to c:

```
a != c
```

Table 4-3 shows other relational expressions and their true or false values.

Table 4-3 **(Assume x is 10 and y is 7.)**

Expression	Value
x < y	False, because x is not less than y.
x > y	True, because x is greater than y.
x >= y	True, because x is greater than or equal to y.
x <= y	False, because x is not less than or equal to y.
y != x	True, because y is not equal to x.

What Is Truth?

The question "what is truth?" is one you would expect to find in a philosophy book, not a C++ programming text. It's a good question for us to consider, though. If a relational expression can be either true or false, how are those values represented internally in a program? How does a computer store *true* in memory? How does it store *false*?

As you saw in Program 2-17, those two abstract states are converted to numbers. In C++, relational expressions represent true states with the number 1 and false states with the number 0.

 NOTE: As you will see later in this chapter, 1 is not the only value regarded as true.

To illustrate this more fully, look at Program 4-1.

Program 4-1

```cpp
 1   // This program displays the values of true and false states.
 2   #include <iostream>
 3   using namespace std;
 4
 5   int main()
 6   {
 7      bool trueValue, falseValue;
 8      int x = 5, y = 10;
 9
10      trueValue = x < y;
11      falseValue = y == x;
12
13      cout << "True is  " << trueValue << endl;
14      cout << "False is  " << falseValue << endl;
15      return 0;
16   }
```

Program Output
```
True is 1
False is 0
```

Let's examine the statements containing the relational expressions, in lines 10 and 11, a little closer:

```
trueValue = x < y;
falseValue = y == x;
```

These statements may seem odd because they are assigning the value of a comparison to a variable. In line 10 the variable `trueValue` is being assigned the result of x < y. Since x is less than y, the expression is true, and the variable `trueValue` is assigned the value 1. In line 11 the expression y == x is false, so the variable `falseValue` is set to 0. Table 4-4 shows examples of other statements using relational expressions and their outcomes.

NOTE: Relational expressions have a higher precedence than the assignment operator. In the statement

```
z = x < y;
```

the expression x < y is evaluated first, and then its value is assigned to z.

Table 4-4   (Assume x is 10, y is 7, and z, a, and b are `ints` or `bools`)

Statement	Outcome
`z = x < y`	z is assigned 0 because x is not less than y.
`cout << (x > y);`	Displays 1 because x is greater than y.
`a = x >= y;`	a is assigned 1 because x is greater than or equal to y.
`cout << (x <= y);`	Displays 0 because x is not less than or equal to y.
`b = y != x;`	b is assigned 1 because y is not equal to x.

When writing statements such as these, it sometimes helps to enclose the relational expression in parentheses, such as:

```
trueValue = (x < y);
falseValue = (y == x);
```

As interesting as relational expressions are, we've only scratched the surface of how to use them. In this chapter's remaining sections you will see how to get the most from relational expressions by using them in statements that take action based on the results of the comparison.

 Checkpoint

myprogramminglab *www.myprogramminglab.com*

4.1   Assuming x is 5, y is 6, and z is 8, indicate by circling the T or F whether each of the following relational expressions is true or false:

A) x == 5   T   F

B) 7 <= (x + 2)   T   F

C) z < 4   T   F

D) (2 + x) != y   T   F

E) z != 4   T   F

F) x >= 9   T   F

G) x <= (y * 2)   T   F

4.2   Indicate whether the following statements about relational expressions are correct or incorrect.

A)   `x <= y` is the same as `y > x`.

B)   `x != y` is the same as `y >= x`.

C)   `x >= y` is the same as `y <= x`.

4.3   Answer the following questions with a yes or no.

A)   If it is true that `x > y` and it is also true that `x < z`, does that mean `y < z` is true?

B)   If it is true that `x >= y` and it is also true that `z == x`, does that mean that `z == y` is true?

C)   If it is true that `x != y` and it is also true that `x != z`, does that mean that `z != y` is true?

4.4   What will the following program display?

```cpp
#include <iostream>
using namespace std;

int main ()
{
    int a = 0, b = 2, x = 4, y = 0;

    cout << (a == b) << endl;
    cout << (a != y) << endl;
    cout << (b <= x) << endl;
    cout << (y > a) << endl;
    return 0;
}
```

4.2   The `if` Statement

CONCEPT: The `if` statement can cause other statements to execute only under certain conditions.

VideoNote

The `if` Statement

You might think of the statements in a procedural program as individual steps taken as you are walking down a road. To reach the destination, you must start at the beginning and take each step, one after the other, until you reach the destination. The programs you have written so far are like a "path" of execution for the program to follow.

The type of code in Figure 4-1 is called a *sequence structure*, because the statements are executed in sequence, without branching off in another direction. Programs often need more than one path of execution, however. Many algorithms require a program to execute some statements only under certain circumstances. This can be accomplished with a *decision structure*.

In a decision structure's simplest form, a specific action is taken only when a specific condition exists. If the condition does not exist, the action is not performed. The flowchart in Figure 4-2 shows the logic of a decision structure. The diamond symbol represents a yes/no

Figure 4-1

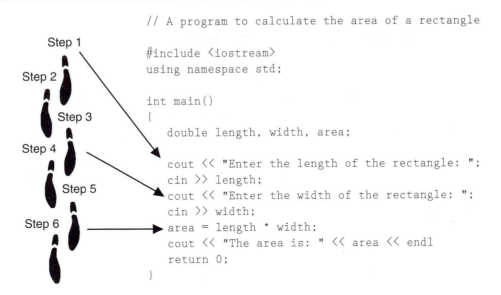

```
// A program to calculate the area of a rectangle

#include <iostream>
using namespace std;

int main()
{
    double length, width, area;

    cout << "Enter the length of the rectangle: ";
    cin >> length;
    cout << "Enter the width of the rectangle: ";
    cin >> width;
    area = length * width;
    cout << "The area is: " << area << endl
    return 0;
}
```

question or a true/false condition. If the answer to the question is yes (or if the condition is true), the program flow follows one path, which leads to an action being performed. If the answer to the question is no (or the condition is false), the program flow follows another path, which skips the action.

Figure 4-2

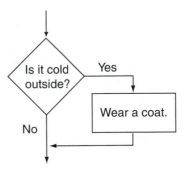

In the flowchart, the action "Wear a coat" is performed only when it is cold outside. If it is not cold outside, the action is skipped. The action is *conditionally executed* because it is performed only when a certain condition (cold outside) exists. Figure 4-3 shows a more elaborate flowchart, where three actions are taken only when it is cold outside.

We perform mental tests like these every day. Here are some other examples:

If the car is low on gas, stop at a service station and get gas.
If it's raining outside, go inside.
If you're hungry, get something to eat.

Figure 4-3

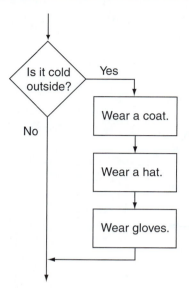

One way to code a decision structure in C++ is with the `if` statement. Here is the general format of the `if` statement:

```
if (expression)
    statement;
```

The `if` statement is simple in the way it works: If the value of the expression inside the parentheses is true, the very next *statement* is executed. Otherwise, it is skipped. The *statement* is *conditionally executed* because it only executes under the condition that the expression in the parentheses is true. Program 4-2 shows an example of an `if` statement. The user enters three test scores and the program calculates their average. If the average is greater than 95, the program congratulates the user on obtaining a high score.

Program 4-2

```
 1  // This program averages three test scores
 2  #include <iostream>
 3  #include <iomanip>
 4  using namespace std;
 5
 6  int main()
 7  {
 8     const int HIGH_SCORE = 95;    // A high score is 95 or greater
 9     int score1, score2, score3;   // To hold three test scores
10     double average;               // TO hold the average score
11
```

```
12      // Get the three test scores.
13      cout << "Enter 3 test scores and I will average them: ";
14      cin >> score1 >> score2 >> score3;
15
16      // Calculate and display the average score.
17      average = (score1 + score2 + score3) / 3.0;
18      cout << fixed << showpoint << setprecision(1);
19      cout << "Your average is " << average << endl;
20
21      // If the average is a high score, congratulate the user.
22      if (average > HIGH_SCORE)
23          cout << "Congratulations! That's a high score!\n";
24      return 0;
25  }
```

Program Output with Example Input Shown in Bold
Enter 3 test scores and I will average them: **80 90 70 [Enter]**
Your average is 80.0

Program Output with Different Example Input Shown in Bold
Enter 3 test scores and I will average them: **100 100 100 [Enter]**
Your average is 100.0
Congratulations! That's a high score!

Lines 22 and 23 cause the congratulatory message to be printed:

```
if (average > HIGH_SCORE)
    cout << "Congratulations! That's a high score!\n";
```

The cout statement in line 23 is executed only if the average is greater than 95, the value of the HIGH_SCORE constant. If the average is not greater than 95, the cout statement is skipped. Figure 4-4 shows the logic of this if statement.

Figure 4-4

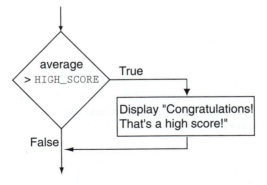

Table 4-5 shows other examples of if statements and their outcomes.

Table 4-5

Statement	Outcome
`if (hours > 40)` `    overTime = true;`	Assigns `true` to the `bool` variable `overTime` only if `hours` is greater than 40
`if (value > 32)` `    cout << "Invalid number\n";`	Displays the message "Invalid number" only if `value` is greater than 32
`if (overTime == true)` `    payRate *= 2;`	Multiplies `payRate` by 2 only if `overTime` is equal to `true`

Be Careful with Semicolons

Semicolons do not mark the end of a line, but the end of a complete C++ statement. The `if` statement isn't complete without the conditionally executed statement that comes after it. So, you must not put a semicolon after the `if (expression)` portion of an `if` statement.

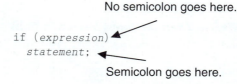

No semicolon goes here.

`if (expression)`
`    statement;`

Semicolon goes here.

If you inadvertently put a semicolon after the `if` part, the compiler will assume you are placing a null statement there. The *null statement* is an empty statement that does nothing. This will prematurely terminate the `if` statement, which disconnects it from the statement that follows it. The statement following the `if` will always execute, as shown in Program 4-3.

Program 4-3

```
 1  // This program demonstrates how a misplaced semicolon
 2  // prematurely terminates an if statement.
 3  #include <iostream>
 4  using namespace std;
 5
 6  int main()
 7  {
 8      int x = 0, y = 10;
 9
10      cout << "x is " << x << " and y is " << y << endl;
11      if (x > y);     // Error! Misplaced semicolon
12          cout << "x is greater than y\n"; //This is always executed.
13      return 0;
14  }
```

Program Output

```
x is 0 and y is 10
x is greater than y
```

Programming Style and the `if` Statement

Even though `if` statements usually span more than one line, they are technically one long statement. For instance, the following `if` statements are identical except in style:

```
if (a >= 100)
    cout << "The number is out of range.\n";
if (a >= 100) cout << "The number is out of range.\n";
```

In both the examples above, the compiler considers the `if` part and the `cout` statement as one unit, with a semicolon properly placed at the end. Indention and spacing are for the human readers of a program, not the compiler. Here are two important style rules you should adopt for writing `if` statements:

- The conditionally executed statement should appear on the line after the `if` statement.
- The conditionally executed statement should be indented one "level" from the `if` statement.

> **NOTE:** In most editors, each time you press the tab key, you are indenting one level.

By indenting the conditionally executed statement you are causing it to stand out visually. This is so you can tell at a glance what part of the program the `if` statement executes. This is a standard way of writing `if` statements and is the method you should use.

> **NOTE:** Indentation and spacing are for the human readers of a program, not the compiler. Even though the `cout` statement following the `if` statement in Program 4-3 is indented, the semicolon still terminates the `if` statement.

Comparing Floating-Point Numbers

Because of the way that floating-point numbers are stored in memory, rounding errors sometimes occur. This is because some fractional numbers cannot be exactly represented using binary. So, you should be careful when using the equality operator (`==`) to compare floating point numbers. For example, Program 4-4 uses two `double` variables, a and b. Both variables are initialized to the value 1.5. Then, the value 0.0000000000000001 is added to a. This should make a's contents different than b's contents. Because of a round-off error, however, the two variables are still the same.

Program 4-4

```
 1   // This program demonstrates how floating-point
 2   // round-off errors can make equality operations unreliable.
 3   #include <iostream>
 4   using namespace std;
 5
```

(program continues)

Program 4-4   *(continued)*

```
 6  int main()
 7  {
 8     double a = 1.5;          // a is 1.5.
 9     double b = 1.5;          // b is 1.5.
10
11     a += 0.0000000000000001;    // Add a little to a.
12     if (a == b)
13        cout << "Both a and b are the same.\n";
14     else
15        cout << "a and b are not the same.\n";
16
17     return 0;
18  }
```

Program Output

```
Both a and b are the same.
```

To prevent round-off errors from causing this type of problem, you should stick with greater-than and less-than comparisons with floating-point numbers.

And Now Back to Truth

Now that you've gotten your feet wet with relational expressions and `if` statements, let's look at the subject of truth again. You have seen that a relational expression has the value 1 when it is true and 0 when false. In the world of the `if` statement, however, the concept of truth is expanded. 0 is still false, but all values other than 0 are considered true. This means that any value, even a negative number, represents true as long as it is not 0.

Just as in real life, truth is a complicated thing. Here is a summary of the rules you have seen so far:

- When a relational expression is true it has the value 1.
- When a relational expression is false it has the value 0.
- Any expression that has the value 0 is considered false by the `if` statement. This includes the `bool` value `false`, which is equivalent to 0.
- Any expression that has any value other than 0 is considered true by the `if` statement. This includes the `bool` value `true`, which is equivalent to 1.

The fact that the `if` statement considers any nonzero value as true opens many possibilities. Relational expressions are not the only conditions that may be tested. For example, the following is a legal `if` statement in C++:

```
if (value)
    cout << "It is True!";
```

The `if` statement above does not test a relational expression, but rather the contents of a variable. If the variable, `value`, contains any number other than 0, the message "`It is True!`" will be displayed. If `value` is set to 0, however, the `cout` statement will be skipped. Here is another example:

```
if (x + y)
    cout << "It is True!";
```

In this statement the sum of x and y is tested like any other value in an if statement: 0 is false and all other values are true. You may also use the return value of function calls as conditional expressions. Here is an example that uses the pow function:

```
if (pow(a, b))
    cout << "It is True!";
```

This if statement uses the pow function to raise a to the power of b. If the result is anything other than 0, the cout statement is executed. This is a powerful programming technique that you will learn more about in Chapter 6.

Don't Confuse == With =

Earlier you saw a warning not to confuse the equality operator (==) with the assignment operator (=), as in the following statement:

```
if (x = 2)  //Caution here!
    cout << "It is True!";
```

The statement above does not determine whether x is equal to 2, it assigns x the value 2! Furthermore, the cout statement will *always* be executed because the expression x = 2 is always true.

This occurs because the value of an assignment expression is the value being assigned to the variable on the left side of the = operator. That means the value of the expression x = 2 is 2. Since 2 is a nonzero value, it is interpreted as a true condition by the if statement. Program 4-5 is a version of Program 4-2 that attempts to test for a perfect average of 100. The = operator, however, was mistakenly used in the if statement.

Program 4-5

```
 1   // This program averages 3 test scores. The if statement
 2   // uses the = operator, but the == operator was intended.
 3   #include <iostream>
 4   #include <iomanip>
 5   using namespace std;
 6
 7   int main()
 8   {
 9       int score1, score2, score3;  // To hold three test scores
10       double average;              // TO hold the average score
11
12       // Get the three test scores.
13       cout << "Enter 3 test scores and I will average them: ";
14       cin >> score1 >> score2 >> score3;
15
16       // Calculate and display the average score.
17       average = (score1 + score2 + score3) / 3.0;
18       cout << fixed << showpoint << setprecision(1);
19       cout << "Your average is " << average << endl;
20
```

(program continues)

Program 4-5   *(continued)*

```
21      // Our intention is to congratulate the user
22      // for having a perfect score. But, this doesn't work.
23      if (average = 100)  // WRONG! This is an assignment!
24         cout << "Congratulations! That's a perfect score!\n";
25      return 0;
26   }
```

Program Output with Example Input Shown in Bold
```
Enter three test scores and I will average them: 80 90 70 [Enter]
Your average is 80.0
Congratulations! That's a perfect score!
```

Regardless of the average score, this program will print the message congratulating the user on a perfect score.

 ## Checkpoint

myprogramminglab *www.myprogramminglab.com*

4.5   Write an `if` statement that performs the following logic: if the variable x is equal to 20, then assign 0 to the variable y.

4.6   Write an `if` statement that performs the following logic: if the variable `price` is greater than 500, then assign 0.2 to the variable `discountRate`.

4.7   Write an `if` statement that multiplies `payRate` by 1.5 if hours is greater than 40.

4.8   TRUE or FALSE: Both of the following `if` statements perform the same operation.

```
if (sales > 10000)
    commissionRate = 0.15;

if (sales > 10000) commissionRate = 0.15;
```

4.9   TRUE or FALSE: Both of the following `if` statements perform the same operation.

```
if (calls == 20)
    rate *= 0.5;

if (calls = 20)
    rate *= 0.5;
```

 4.3

Expanding the `if` Statement

CONCEPT: The `if` statement can conditionally execute a block of statements enclosed in braces.

What if you want an `if` statement to conditionally execute a group of statements, not just one line? For instance, what if the test averaging program needed to use several cout statements when a high score was reached? The answer is to enclose all of the conditionally executed statements inside a set of braces. Here is the format:

```
if (expression)
{
   statement;
   statement;
   // Place as many statements here as necessary.
}
```

Program 4-6, another modification of the test-averaging program, demonstrates this type of if statement.

Program 4-6

```
 1 // This program averages 3 test scores.
 2 // It demonstrates an if statement executing
 3 // a block of statements.
 4 #include <iostream>
 5 #include <iomanip>
 6 using namespace std;
 7
 8 int main()
 9 {
10    const int HIGH_SCORE = 95;    // A high score is 95 or greater
11    int score1, score2, score3;   // To hold three test scores
12    double average;               // TO hold the average score
13
14    // Get the three test scores.
15    cout << "Enter 3 test scores and I will average them: ";
16    cin >> score1 >> score2 >> score3;
17
18    // Calculate and display the average score.
19    average = (score1 + score2 + score3) / 3.0;
20    cout << fixed << showpoint << setprecision(1);
21    cout << "Your average is " << average << endl;
22
23    // If the average is high, congratulate the user.
24    if (average > HIGH_SCORE)
25    {
26       cout << "Congratulations!\n";
27       cout << "That's a high score.\n";
28       cout << "You deserve a pat on the back!\n";
29    }
30    return 0;
31 }
```

Program Output with Example Input Shown in Bold
Enter 3 test scores and I will average them: **100 100 100 [Enter]**
Your average is 100.0
Congratulations!
That's a high score.
You deserve a pat on the back!

(program output continues)

Program 4-6 *(continued)*

Program Output with Different Example Input Shown in Bold
Enter 3 test scores and I will average them: **80 90 70 [Enter]**
Your average is 80.0

Program 4-6 prints a more elaborate message when the average score is greater than 95. The if statement was expanded to execute three cout statements when highScore is set to true. Enclosing a group of statements inside a set of braces creates a *block* of code. The if statement will execute all the statements in the block, in the order they appear, only when average is greater than 95. Otherwise, the block will be skipped.

Notice all the statements inside the braces are indented. As before, this visually separates the statements from lines that are not indented, making it more obvious they are part of the if statement.

 NOTE: Anytime your program has a block of code, all the statements inside the braces should be indented.

Don't Forget the Braces!

If you intend to conditionally execute a block of statements with an if statement, don't forget the braces. Remember, without a set of braces, the if statement only executes the very next statement. Program 4-7 shows the test-averaging program with the braces inadvertently left out of the if statement's block.

Program 4-7

```
1  // This program averages 3 test scores. The braces
2  // were inadvertently left out of the if statement.
3  #include <iostream>
4  #include <iomanip>
5  using namespace std;
6
7  int main()
8  {
9     const int HIGH_SCORE = 95;    // A high score is 95 or greater
10    int score1, score2, score3;   // To hold three test scores
11    double average;               // To hold the average score
12
13    // Get the three test scores.
14    cout << "Enter 3 test scores and I will average them: ";
15    cin >> score1 >> score2 >> score3;
16
17    // Calculate and display the average score.
18    average = (score1 + score2 + score3) / 3.0;
19    cout << fixed << showpoint << setprecision(1);
20    cout << "Your average is " << average << endl;
21
```

```
22      // ERROR! This if statement is missing its braces!
23      if (average > HIGH_SCORE)
24          cout << "Congratulations!\n";
25          cout << "That's a high score.\n";
26          cout << "You deserve a pat on the back!\n";
27      return 0;
28  }
```

Program Output with Example Input Shown in Bold

```
Enter 3 test scores and I will average them: 80 90 70 [Enter]
Your average is 80
That's a high score.
You deserve a pat on the back!
```

The cout statements in lines 25 and 26 are always executed, even when average is not greater than 95. Because the braces have been removed, the if statement only controls execution of line 24. This is illustrated in Figure 4-5.

Figure 4-5

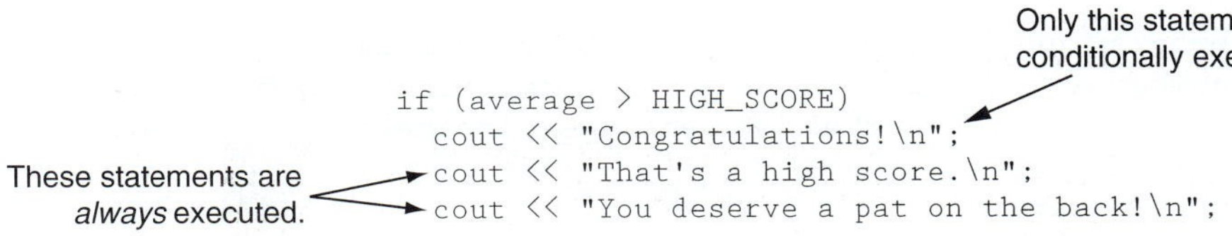

```
                              Only this statement is
                              conditionally executed.

             if (average > HIGH_SCORE)
                 cout << "Congratulations!\n";
These statements are    cout << "That's a high score.\n";
always executed.        cout << "You deserve a pat on the back!\n";
```

Checkpoint

myprogramminglab   *www.myprogramminglab.com*

4.10   Write an if statement that performs the following logic: if the variable sales is greater than 50,000, then assign 0.25 to the commissionRate variable, and assign 250 to the bonus variable.

4.11   The following code segment is syntactically correct, but it appears to contain a logic error. Can you find the error?

```
if (interestRate > .07)
    cout << "This account earns a $10 bonus.\n";
    balance += 10.0;
```

4.4   The `if/else` Statement

CONCEPT: The `if/else` statement will execute one group of statements if the expression is true, or another group of statements if the expression is false.

VideoNote

The `if/else`
Statement

The `if/else` statement is an expansion of the `if` statement. Here is its format:

```
if (expression)
    statement or block
else
    statement or block
```

As with the `if` statement, an expression is evaluated. If the expression is true, a statement or block of statements is executed. If the expression is false, however, a separate group of statements is executed. Program 4-8 uses the `if/else` statement along with the modulus operator to determine if a number is odd or even.

Program 4-8

```
 1   // This program uses the modulus operator to determine
 2   // if a number is odd or even. If the number is evenly divisible
 3   // by 2, it is an even number. A remainder indicates it is odd.
 4   #include <iostream>
 5   using namespace std;
 6
 7   int main()
 8   {
 9      int number;
10
11      cout << "Enter an integer and I will tell you if it\n";
12      cout << "is odd or even. ";
13      cin >> number;
14      if (number % 2 == 0)
15         cout << number << " is even.\n";
16      else
17         cout << number << " is odd.\n";
18      return 0;
19   }
```

Program Output with Example Input Shown in Bold
```
Enter an integer and I will tell you if it
is odd or even. 17 [Enter]
17 is odd.
```

The `else` part at the end of the `if` statement specifies a statement that is to be executed when the expression is false. When `number % 2` does not equal 0, a message is printed indicating the number is odd. Note that the program will only take one of the two paths in the `if/else` statement. If you think of the statements in a computer program as steps taken down a road, consider the `if/else` statement as a fork in the road. Instead of being a momentary detour, like an `if` statement, the `if/else` statement causes program execution to follow one of two exclusive paths. The flowchart in Figure 4-6 shows the logic of this `if/else` statement.

Figure 4-6

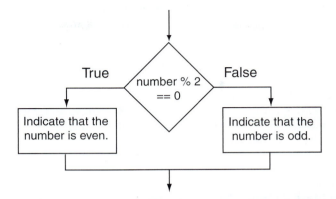

Notice the programming style used to construct the if/else statement. The word else is at the same level of indention as if. The statement whose execution is controlled by else is indented one level. This visually depicts the two paths of execution that may be followed.

Like the if part, the else part controls a single statement. If you wish to control more than one statement with the else part, create a block by writing the lines inside a set of braces. Program 4-9 shows this as a way of handling a classic programming problem: *division by zero*.

Division by zero is mathematically impossible to perform and it normally causes a program to crash. This means the program will prematurely stop running, sometimes with an error message. Program 4-9 shows a way to test the value of a divisor before the division takes place.

Program 4-9

```
 1   // This program asks the user for two numbers, num1 and num2.
 2   // num1 is divided by num2 and the result is displayed.
 3   // Before the division operation, however, num2 is tested
 4   // for the value 0. If it contains 0, the division does not
 5   // take place.
 6   #include <iostream>
 7   using namespace std;
 8
 9   int main()
10   {
11       double num1, num2, quotient;
12
13       // Get the first number.
14       cout << "Enter a number: ";
15       cin >> num1;
16
17       // Get the second number.
18       cout << "Enter another number: ";
19       cin >> num2;
20
21       // If num2 is not zero, perform the division.
22       if (num2 == 0)
23       {
```

(program continues)

Program 4-9   *(continued)*

```
24          cout << "Division by zero is not possible.\n";
25          cout << "Please run the program again and enter\n";
26          cout << "a number other than zero.\n";
27       }
28       else
29       {
30          quotient = num1 / num2;
31          cout << "The quotient of " << num1 << " divided by ";
32          cout << num2 << " is " << quotient << ".\n";
33       }
34       return 0;
35    }
```

Program Output with Example Input Shown in Bold
```
Enter a number: 10 [Enter]
Enter another number: 0 [Enter]
Division by zero is not possible.
Please run the program again and enter
a number other than zero.
```

The value of num2 is tested in line 22 before the division is performed. If the user enters 0, the lines controlled by the if part execute, displaying a message which indicates that the program cannot perform a division by zero. Otherwise, the else part takes control, which divides num1 by num2 and displays the result.

 Checkpoint

myprogramminglab   *www.myprogramminglab.com*

4.12   TRUE or FALSE: The following if/else statements cause the same output to display.

```
A)  if (x > y)
        cout << "x is the greater.\n";
    else
        cout << "x is not the greater.\n";
B)  if (y <= x)
        cout << "x is not the greater.\n";
    else
        cout << "x is the greater.\n";
```

4.13   Write an if/else statement that assigns 1 to x if y is equal to 100. Otherwise it should assign 0 to x.

4.14   Write an if/else statement that assigns 0.10 to commissionRate unless sales is greater than or equal to 50000.00, in which case it assigns 0.20 to commissionRate.

4.5   Nested `if` Statements

CONCEPT: To test more than one condition, an `if` statement can be nested inside another `if` statement.

Sometimes an `if` statement must be nested inside another `if` statement. For example, consider a banking program that determines whether a bank customer qualifies for a special, low interest rate on a loan. To qualify, two conditions must exist: (1) the customer must be currently employed, and (2) the customer must have recently graduated from college (in the past two years). Figure 4-7 shows a flowchart for an algorithm that could be used in such a program.

Figure 4-7

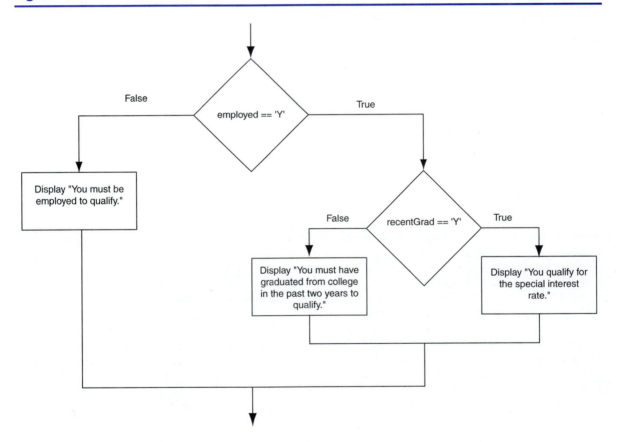

If we follow the flow of execution in the flowchart, we see that the expression `employed == 'Y'` is tested. If this expression is false, there is no need to perform further tests; we know that the customer does not qualify for the special interest rate. If the expression is true, however, we need to test the second condition. This is done with a nested decision structure that tests the expression `recentGrad == 'Y'`. If this expression is true, then the customer qualifies for the special interest rate. If this expression is false, then the customer does not qualify. Program 4-10 shows the code for the complete program.

Program 4-10

```
 1   // This program demonstrates the nested if statement.
 2   #include <iostream>
 3   using namespace std;
 4
 5   int main()
 6   {
 7      char employed,    // Currently employed, Y or N
 8           recentGrad; // Recent graduate, Y or N
 9
10      // Is the user employed and a recent graduate?
11      cout << "Answer the following questions\n";
12      cout << "with either Y for Yes or ";
13      cout << "N for No.\n";
14      cout << "Are you employed? ";
15      cin >> employed;
16      cout << "Have you graduated from college ";
17      cout << "in the past two years? ";
18      cin >> recentGrad;
19
20      // Determine the user's loan qualifications.
21      if (employed == 'Y')
22      {
23         if (recentGrad == 'Y') //Nested if
24         {
25            cout << "You qualify for the special ";
26            cout << "interest rate.\n";
27         }
28      }
29      return 0;
30   }
```

Program Output with Example Input Shown in Bold
```
Answer the following questions
with either Y for Yes or N for No.
Are you employed? Y [Enter]
Have you graduated from college in the past two years? Y [Enter]
You qualify for the special interest rate.
```

Program Output with Different Example Input Shown in Bold
```
Answer the following questions
with either Y for Yes or N for No.
Are you employed? Y [Enter]
Have you graduated from college in the past two years? N [Enter]
```

Look at the if statement that begins in line 21. It tests the expression employed == 'Y'. If this expression is true, the if statement that begins in line 23 is executed. Otherwise the program jumps to the return statement in line 29 and the program ends.

Notice in the second sample execution of Program 4-10 that the program output does not inform the user whether he or she qualifies for the special interest rate. If the user enters an 'N' (or any character other than 'Y') for employed or recentGrad, the program does not print a message letting the user know that he or she does not qualify. An else statement should be able to remedy this, as illustrated by Program 4-11.

Program 4-11

```cpp
1    // This program demonstrates the nested if statement.
2    #include <iostream>
3    using namespace std;
4
5    int main()
6    {
7       char employed,    // Currently employed, Y or N
8            recentGrad; // Recent graduate, Y or N
9
10      // Is the user employed and a recent graduate?
11      cout << "Answer the following questions\n";
12      cout << "with either Y for Yes or ";
13      cout << "N for No.\n";
14      cout << "Are you employed? ";
15      cin >> employed;
16      cout << "Have you graduated from college ";
17      cout << "in the past two years? ";
18      cin >> recentGrad;
19
20      // Determine the user's loan qualifications.
21      if (employed == 'Y')
22      {
23         if (recentGrad == 'Y') // Nested if
24         {
25            cout << "You qualify for the special ";
26            cout << "interest rate.\n";
27         }
28         else // Not a recent grad, but employed
29         {
30            cout << "You must have graduated from ";
31            cout << "college in the past two\n";
32            cout << "years to qualify.\n";
33         }
34      }
35      else // Not employed
36      {
37         cout << "You must be employed to qualify.\n";
38      }
39      return 0;
40   }
```

Program Output with Example Input Shown in Bold

```
Answer the following questions
with either Y for Yes or N for No.
Are you employed? N [Enter]
Have you graduated from college in the past two years? Y [Enter]
You must be employed to qualify.
```

(program output continues)

Program 4-11 *(continued)*

Program Output with Different Example Input Shown in Bold
```
Answer the following questions
with either Y for Yes or N for No.
Are you employed? Y [Enter]
Have you graduated from college in the past two years? N [Enter]
You must have graduated from college in the past two years to qualify.
```

Program Output with Different Example Input Shown in Bold
```
Answer the following questions
with either Y for Yes or N for No.
Are you employed? Y [Enter]
Have you graduated from college in the past two years? Y [Enter]
You qualify for the special interest rate.
```

In this version of the program, both `if` statements have `else` clauses that inform the user why he or she does not qualify for the special interest rate.

Programming Style and Nested Decision Structures

For readability and easier debugging, it's important to use proper alignment and indentation in a set of nested `if` statements. This makes it easier to see which actions are performed by each part of the decision structure. For example, the following code is functionally equivalent to lines 21 through 38 in Program 4-11. Although this code is logically correct, it is very difficult to read, and would be very difficult to debug because it is not properly indented.

```cpp
if (employed == 'Y')
{
if (recentGrad == 'Y') // Nested if
{
cout << "You qualify for the special ";
cout << "interest rate.\n";
}
else // Not a recent grad, but employed
{
cout << "You must have graduated from ";
cout << "college in the past two\n";
cout << "years to qualify.\n";
}
}
else // Not employed
{
cout << "You must be employed to qualify.\n";
}
```

> *Don't write code
> like this!*

Proper indentation and alignment also makes it easier to see which `if` and `else` clauses belong together, as shown in Figure 4-8.

Figure 4-8

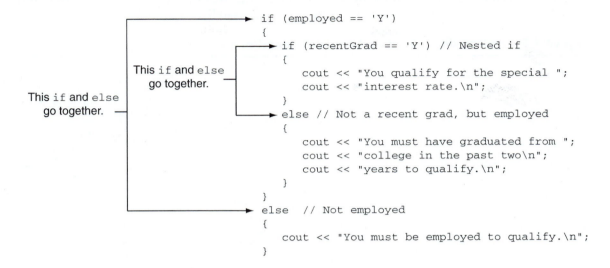

```
                                      if (employed == 'Y')
                                      {
                                          if (recentGrad == 'Y') // Nested if
              This if and else             {
              go together.                     cout << "You qualify for the special ";
                                                cout << "interest rate.\n";
                                            }
   This if and else                       else // Not a recent grad, but employed
   go together.                           {
                                              cout << "You must have graduated from ";
                                              cout << "college in the past two\n";
                                              cout << "years to qualify.\n";
                                          }
                                      }
                                      else  // Not employed
                                      {
                                          cout << "You must be employed to qualify.\n";
                                      }
```

Testing a Series of Conditions

In the previous example you saw how a program can use nested decision structures to test more than one condition. It is not uncommon for a program to have a series of conditions to test, and then perform an action depending on which condition is true. One way to accomplish this is to have a decision structure with numerous other decision structures nested inside it. For example, consider the program presented in the following *In the Spotlight* section.

In the Spotlight:
Multiple Nested Decision Structures

Dr. Suarez teaches a literature class and uses the following 10 point grading scale for all of his exams:

Test Score	Grade
90 and above	A
80–89	B
70–79	C
60–69	D
Below 60	F

He has asked you to write a program that will allow a student to enter a test score and then display the grade for that score. Here is the algorithm that you will use:

Ask the user to enter a test score.
Determine the grade in the following manner:
If the score is greater than or equal to 90, then the grade is A.
  Otherwise, if the score is greater than or equal to 80, then the grade is B.
    Otherwise, if the score is greater than or equal to 70, then the grade is C.
      Otherwise, if the score is greater than or equal to 60, then the grade is D.
      Otherwise, the grade is F.

You decide that the process of determining the grade will require several nested decisions structures, as shown in Figure 4-9. Program 4-12 shows the code for the complete program. The code for the nested decision structures is in lines 17 through 45.

Figure 4-9   Nested decision structure to determine a grade

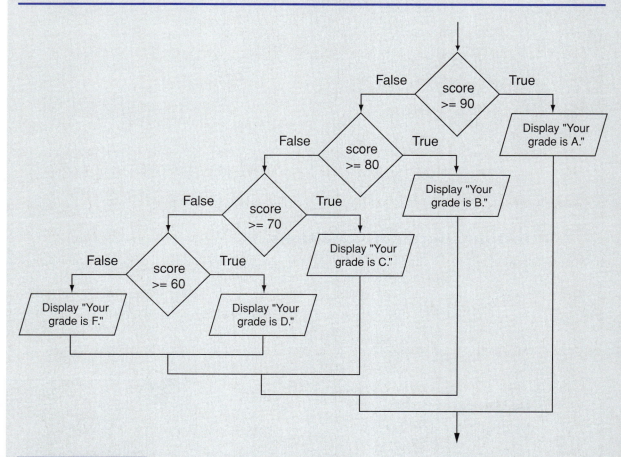

Program 4-12

```cpp
 1 // This program uses nested if/else statements to assign a
 2 // letter grade (A, B, C, D, or F) to a numeric test score.
 3 #include <iostream>
 4 using namespace std;
 5
 6 int main()
 7 {
 8    // Constants for grade thresholds
 9    const int A_SCORE = 90,
10               B_SCORE = 80,
11               C_SCORE = 70,
12               D_SCORE = 60;
13
14    int testScore;  // To hold a numeric test score
15
16    // Get the numeric test score.
17    cout << "Enter your numeric test score and I will\n";
```

```
18      cout << "tell you the letter grade you earned: ";
19      cin >> testScore;
20
21      // Determine the letter grade.
22      if (testScore >= A_SCORE)
23      {
24         cout << "Your grade is A.\n";
25      }
26      else
27      {
28          if (testScore >= B_SCORE)
29          {
30              cout << "Your grade is B.\n";
31          }
32          else
33          {
34              if (testScore >= C_SCORE)
35              {
36                  cout << "Your grade is C.\n";
37              }
38              else
39              {
40                  if (testScore >= D_SCORE)
41                  {
42                      cout << "Your grade is D.\n";
43                  }
44                  else
45                  {
46                      cout << "Your grade is F.\n";
47                  }
48              }
49          }
50      }
51
52      return 0;
53 }
```

Program Output with Example Input Shown in Bold
```
Enter your numeric test score and I will
tell you the letter grade you earned: 78 [Enter]
Your grade is C.
```

Program Output with Different Example Input Shown in Bold
```
Enter your numeric test score and I will
tell you the letter grade you earned: 84 [Enter]
Your grade is B.
```

 Checkpoint

myprogramminglab *www.myprogramminglab.com*

4.15   If you executed the following code, what would it display if the user enters 5?
        What if the user enters 15? What if the user enters 30? What if the user enters -1?

```
      int number;
      cout << "Enter a number: ";
      cin >> number;

      if (number > 0)
      {
          cout << "Zero\n";

          if (number > 10)
          {
              cout << "Ten\n";

              if (number > 20)
              {
                  cout << "Twenty\n";
              }
          }
      }
```

4.6   The `if/else if` Statement

> **CONCEPT:** The **if/else if** statement tests a series of conditions. It is often simpler to test a series of conditions with the **if/else if** statement than with a set of nested **if/else** statements.

VideoNote

The `if/else if` Statement

Even though Program 4-12 is a simple example, the logic of the nested decision structure is fairly complex. In C++, and many other languages, you can alternatively test a series of conditions using the `if/else if` statement. The `if/else if` statement makes certain types of nested decision logic simpler to write. Here is the general format of the `if/else if` statement:

```
if (expression_1)
{
    statement
    statement
    etc.
}
```
⎫ If `expression_1` is *true these state-ments are executed, and the rest of the structure is ignored.*

```
else if (expression_2)
{
    statement
    statement
    etc.
}
```
⎬ *Otherwise, if* `expression_2` *is true these statements are executed, and the rest of the structure is ignored.*

Insert as many `else if` *clauses as necessary*

```
else
{
    statement
    statement
    etc.
}
```
⎬ *These statements are executed if none of the expressions above are true.*

When the statement executes, *expression_1* is tested. If *expression_1* is true, the block of statements that immediately follows is executed, and the rest of the structure is ignored. If *expression_1* is false, however, the program jumps to the very next else if clause and tests *expression_2*. If it is true, the block of statements that immediately follows is executed, and then the rest of the structure is ignored. This process continues, from the top of the structure to the bottom, until one of the expressions is found to be true. If none of the expressions are true, the last else clause takes over and the block of statements immediately following it is executed.

The last else clause, which does not have an if statement following it, is referred to as the *trailing else*. The trailing else is optional, but in most cases you will use it.

NOTE: The general format shows braces surrounding each block of conditionally executed statements. As with other forms of the if statement, the braces are required only when more than one statement is conditionally executed.

Program 4-13 shows an example of the if/else if statement. This program is a modification of Program 4-12, which appears in the previous *In the Spotlight* section.

Program 4-13

```cpp
 1  // This program uses an if/else if statement to assign a
 2  // letter grade (A, B, C, D, or F) to a numeric test score.
 3  #include <iostream>
 4  using namespace std;
 5
 6  int main()
 7  {
 8     // Constants for grade thresholds
 9     const int A_SCORE = 90,
10               B_SCORE = 80,
11               C_SCORE = 70,
12               D_SCORE = 60;
13
14     int testScore;  // To hold a numeric test score
15
16     // Get the numeric test score.
17     cout << "Enter your numeric test score and I will\n"
18          << "tell you the letter grade you earned: ";
19     cin >> testScore;
20
21     // Determine the letter grade.
22     if (testScore >= A_SCORE)
23        cout << "Your grade is A.\n";
24     else if (testScore >= B_SCORE)
25        cout << "Your grade is B.\n";
26     else if (testScore >= C_SCORE)
27        cout << "Your grade is C.\n";
28     else if (testScore >= D_SCORE)
29        cout << "Your grade is D.\n";
30     else
31        cout << "Your grade is F.\n";
32
33     return 0;
34  }
```

(program output continues)

Program 4-13 *(continued)*

Program Output with Example Input Shown in Bold
```
Enter your numeric test score and I will
tell you the letter grade you earned: 78 [Enter]
Your grade is C.
```

Program Output with Different Example Input Shown in Bold
```
Enter your numeric test score and I will
tell you the letter grade you earned: 84 [Enter]
Your grade is B.
```

Let's analyze how the `if/else if` statement in lines 22 through 31 works. First, the expression `testScore >= A_SCORE` is tested in line 22:

```
→   if (testScore >= A_SCORE)
        cout << "Your grade is A.\n";
    else if (testScore >= B_SCORE)
        cout << "Your grade is B.\n";
    else if (testScore >= C_SCORE)
        cout << "Your grade is C.\n";
    else if (testScore >= D_SCORE)
        cout << "Your grade is D.\n";
    else
        cout << "Your grade is F.\n";
```

If `testScore` is greater than or equal to 90, the message `"Your grade is A.\n"` is displayed and the rest of the `if/else if` statement is skipped. If `testScore` is not greater than or equal to 90, the `else` clause in line 24 takes over and causes the next `if` statement to be executed:

```
    if (testScore >= A_SCORE)
        cout << "Your grade is A.\n";
→   else if (testScore >= B_SCORE)
        cout << "Your grade is B.\n";
    else if (testScore >= C_SCORE)
        cout << "Your grade is C.\n";
    else if (testScore >= D_SCORE)
        cout << "Your grade is D.\n";
    else
        cout << "Your grade is F.\n";
```

The first `if` statement handles all of the grades greater than or equal to 90, so when this `if` statement executes, `testScore` will have a value of 89 or less. If `testScore` is greater than or equal to 80, the message `"Your grade is B.\n"` is displayed and the rest of the `if/else if` statement is skipped. This chain of events continues until one of the expressions is found to be true, or the last `else` clause at the end of the statement is encountered.

Notice the alignment and indentation that is used with the `if/else if` statement: The starting `if` clause, the `else if` clauses, and the trailing `else` clause are all aligned, and the conditionally executed statements are indented.

Using the Trailing `else` To Catch Errors

The trailing `else` clause, which appears at the end of the `if/else if` statement, is optional, but in many situations you will use it to catch errors. For example, Program 4-13 will assign a grade to any number that is entered as the test score, including negative numbers. If a negative test score is entered, however, the user has probably made a mistake. We can modify the code as shown in Program 4-14 so the trailing else clause catches any test score that is less then 0 and displays an error message.

Program 4-14

```cpp
1 // This program uses an if/else if statement to assign a
2 // letter grade (A, B, C, D, or F) to a numeric test score.
3 #include <iostream>
4 using namespace std;
5
6 int main()
7 {
8    // Constants for grade thresholds
9    const int A_SCORE = 90,
10             B_SCORE = 80,
11             C_SCORE = 70,
12             D_SCORE = 60;
13
14    int testScore;  // To hold a numeric test score
15
16    // Get the numeric test score.
17    cout << "Enter your numeric test score and I will\n"
18         << "tell you the letter grade you earned: ";
19    cin >> testScore;
20
21    // Determine the letter grade.
22    if (testScore >= A_SCORE)
23       cout << "Your grade is A.\n";
24    else if (testScore >= B_SCORE)
25       cout << "Your grade is B.\n";
26    else if (testScore >= C_SCORE)
27       cout << "Your grade is C.\n";
28    else if (testScore >= D_SCORE)
29       cout << "Your grade is D.\n";
30    else if (testScore >= 0)
31       cout << "Your grade is F.\n";
32    else
33       cout << "Invalid test score.\n";
34
35    return 0;
36 }
```

Program Output with Example Input Shown in Bold

```
Enter your numeric test score and I will
tell you the letter grade you earned: -1 [Enter]
Invalid test score.
```

The if/else if Statement Compared to a Nested Decision Structure

You never have to use the if/else if statement because its logic can be coded with nested if/else statements. However, a long series of nested if/else statements has two particular disadvantages when you are debugging code:

- The code can grow complex and become difficult to understand.
- Because indenting is important in nested statements, a long series of nested if/ else statements can become too long to be displayed on the computer screen without horizontal scrolling. Also, long statements tend to "wrap around" when printed on paper, making the code even more difficult to read.

The logic of an if/else if statement is usually easier to follow than that of a long series of nested if/else statements. And, because all of the clauses are aligned in an if/else if statement, the lengths of the lines in the statement tend to be shorter.

Checkpoint

myprogramminglab *www.myprogramminglab.com*

4.16 What will the following code display?

```cpp
int funny = 7, serious = 15;
funny = serious % 2;

if (funny != 1)
{
    funny = 0;
    serious = 0;
}
else if (funny == 2)
{
    funny = 10;
    serious = 10;
}
else
{
    funny = 1;
    serious = 1;
}
cout << funny << "" << serious << endl;
```

4.17 The following code is used in a bookstore program to determine how many discount coupons a customer gets. Complete the table that appears after the program.

```cpp
int numBooks, numCoupons;
cout << "How many books are being purchased? ";
cin >> numBooks;

if (numBooks < 1)
    numCoupons = 0;
else if (numBooks < 3)
    numCoupons = 1;
else if (numBooks < 5)
    numCoupons = 2;
else
    numCoupons = 3;

cout << "The number of coupons to give is "
        << numCoupons << endl;
```

If the customer purchases this many books	This many coupons are given.
1	
3	
4	
5	
10	

4.7 Flags

CONCEPT: A flag is a Boolean or integer variable that signals when a condition exists.

A *flag* is typically a `bool` variable that signals when some condition exists in the program. When the flag variable is set to `false`, it indicates that the condition does not exist. When the flag variable is set to `true`, it means the condition does exist.

For example, suppose a program that calculates sales commissions has a `bool` variable, defined and initialized as shown here:

```
bool salesQuotaMet = false;
```

In the program, the `salesQuotaMet` variable is used as a flag to indicate whether a salesperson has met the sales quota. When we define the variable, we initialize it with `false` because we do not yet know if the salesperson has met the sales quota. Assuming a variable named `sales` holds the amount of sales, code similar to the following might be used to set the value of the `salesQuotaMet` variable:

```
if (sales >= QUOTA_AMOUNT)
    salesQuotaMet = true;
else
    salesQuotaMet = false;
```

As a result of this code, the `salesQuotaMet` variable can be used as a flag to indicate whether the sales quota has been met. Later in the program we might test the flag in the following way:

```
if (salesQuotaMet)
    cout << "You have met your sales quota!\n";
```

This code displays *You have met your sales quota!* if the `bool` variable `salesQuotaMet` is true. Notice that we did not have to use the `==` operator to explicitly compare the `salesQuotaMet` variable with the value `true`. This code is equivalent to the following:

```
if (salesQuotaMet == true)
    cout << "You have met your sales quota!\n";
```

Integer Flags

Integer variables may also be used as flags. This is because in C++ the value 0 is considered false, and any nonzero value is considered true. In the sales commission program previously described, we could define the `salesQuotaMet` variable with the following statement:

```
int salesQuotaMet = 0;          // 0 means false.
```

As before, we initialize the variable with 0 because we do not yet know if the sales quota has been met. After the sales have been calculated, we can use code similar to the following to set the value of the `salesQuotaMet` variable:

```
if (sales >= QUOTA_AMOUNT)
    salesQuotaMet = 1;
else
    salesQuotaMet = 0;
```

Later in the program we might test the flag in the following way:

```
if (salesQuotaMet)
    cout << "You have met your sales quota!\n";
```

4.8 Logical Operators

CONCEPT: Logical operators connect two or more relational expressions into one or reverse the logic of an expression.

In the previous section you saw how a program tests two conditions with two `if` statements. In this section you will see how to use logical operators to combine two or more relational expressions into one. Table 4-6 lists C++'s logical operators.

Table 4-6

Operator	Meaning	Effect
`&&`	AND	Connects two expressions into one. Both expressions must be true for the overall expression to be true.
`||`	OR	Connects two expressions into one. One or both expressions must be true for the overall expression to be true. It is only necessary for one to be true, and it does not matter which.
`!`	NOT	The ! operator reverses the "truth" of an expression. It makes a true expression false, and a false expression true.

The `&&` Operator

The `&&` operator is known as the logical AND operator. It takes two expressions as operands and creates an expression that is true only when both sub-expressions are true. Here is an example of an `if` statement that uses the `&&` operator:

```
if (temperature < 20 && minutes > 12)
    cout << "The temperature is in the danger zone.";
```

In the statement above the two relational expressions are combined into a single expression. The `cout` statement will only be executed if `temperature` is less than 20 AND `minutes` is greater than 12. If either relational test is false, the entire expression is false and the `cout` statement is not executed.

TIP: You must provide complete expressions on both sides of the && operator. For example, the following is not correct because the condition on the right side of the && operator is not a complete expression.

```
temperature > 0 && < 100
```

The expression must be rewritten as

```
temperature > 0 && temperature < 100
```

Table 4-7 shows a truth table for the && operator. The truth table lists all the possible combinations of values that two expressions may have, and the resulting value returned by the && operator connecting the two expressions.

Table 4-7

Expression	Value of Expression
true && false	false (0)
false && true	false (0)
false && false	false (0)
true && true	true (1)

As the table shows, both sub-expressions must be true for the && operator to return a true value.

NOTE: If the sub-expression on the left side of an && operator is false, the expression on the right side will not be checked. Since the entire expression is false if only one of the sub-expressions is false, it would waste CPU time to check the remaining expression. This is called *short circuit evaluation*.

The && operator can be used to simplify programs that otherwise would use nested if statements. Program 4-15 performs a similar operation as Program 4-11, which qualifies a bank customer for a special interest rate. This program uses a logical operator.

Program 4-15

```
 1  // This program demonstrates the && logical operator.
 2  #include <iostream>
 3  using namespace std;
 4
 5  int main()
 6  {
 7     char employed,     // Currently employed, Y or N
 8          recentGrad;   // Recent graduate, Y or N
 9
10     // Is the user employed and a recent graduate?
11     cout << "Answer the following questions\n";
12     cout << "with either Y for Yes or N for No.\n";
13
```

(program continues)

Program 4-15 *(continued)*

```
14    cout << "Are you employed? ";
15    cin >> employed;
16
17    cout << "Have you graduated from college "
18         << "in the past two years? ";
19    cin >> recentGrad;
20
21    // Determine the user's loan qualifications.
22    if (employed == 'Y' && recentGrad == 'Y')
23    {
24        cout << "You qualify for the special "
25             << "interest rate.\n";
26    }
27    else
28    {
29        cout << "You must be employed and have\n"
30             << "graduated from college in the\n"
31             << "past two years to qualify.\n";
32    }
33    return 0;
34 }
```

Program Output with Example Input Shown in Bold
```
Answer the following questions
with either Y for Yes or N for No.
Are you employed? Y [Enter]
Have you graduated from college in the past two years? N [Enter]
You must be employed and have
graduated from college in the
past two years to qualify.
```

Program Output with Example Input Shown in Bold
```
Answer the following questions
with either Y for Yes or N for No.
Are you employed? N [Enter]
Have you graduated from college in the past two years? Y [Enter]
You must be employed and have
graduated from college in the
past two years to qualify.
```

Program Output with Example Input Shown in Bold
```
Answer the following questions
with either Y for Yes or N for No.
Are you employed? Y [Enter]
Have you graduated from college in the past two years? Y [Enter]
You qualify for the special interest rate.
```

The message "You qualify for the special interest rate" is displayed only when both the expressions employed == 'Y' and recentGrad == 'Y' are true. If either of these is false, the message "You must be employed and have graduated from college in the past two years to qualify." is printed.

NOTE: Although it is similar, Program 4-15 is not the logical equivalent of Program 4-11. For example, Program 4-15 doesn't display the message "You must be employed to qualify."

The || Operator

The || operator is known as the logical OR operator. It takes two expressions as operands and creates an expression that is true when either of the sub-expressions are true. Here is an example of an `if` statement that uses the || operator:

```
if (temperature < 20 || temperature > 100)
    cout << "The temperature is in the danger zone.";
```

The `cout` statement will be executed if `temperature` is less than 20 OR `temperature` is greater than 100. If either relational test is true, the entire expression is true and the `cout` statement is executed.

TIP: You must provide complete expressions on both sides of the || operator. For example, the following is not correct because the condition on the right side of the || operator is not a complete expression.

```
temperature < 0 || > 100
```

The expression must be rewritten as

```
temperature < 0 || temperature > 100
```

Table 4-8 shows a truth table for the || operator.

Table 4-8

Expression	Value of the Expression
`true || false`	`true  (1)`
`false || true`	`true  (1)`
`false || false`	`false (0)`
`true || true`	`true  (1)`

All it takes for an OR expression to be true is for one of the sub-expressions to be true. It doesn't matter if the other sub-expression is false or true.

NOTE: The || operator also performs short circuit evaluation. If the sub-expression on the left side of an || operator is true, the expression on the right side will not be checked. Since it's only necessary for one of the sub-expressions to be true, it would waste CPU time to check the remaining expression.

Program 4-16 performs different tests to qualify a person for a loan. This one determines if the customer earns at least $35,000 per year, or has been employed for more than five years.

Program 4-16

```cpp
 1  // This program demonstrates the logical || operator.
 2  #include <iostream>
 3  using namespace std;
 4
 5  int main()
 6  {
 7     // Constants for minimum income and years
 8     const double MIN_INCOME = 35000.0;
 9     const int MIN_YEARS = 5;
10
11     double income;  // Annual income
12     int years;      // Years at the current job
13
14     // Get the annual income
15     cout << "What is your annual income? ";
16     cin >> income;
17
18     // Get the number of years at the current job.
19     cout << "How many years have you worked at "
20          << "your current job? ";
21     cin >> years;
22
23     // Determine the user's loan qualifications.
24     if (income >= MIN_INCOME || years > MIN_YEARS)
25        cout << "You qualify.\n";
26     else
27     {
28        cout << "You must earn at least $"
29             << MIN_INCOME << " or have been "
30             << "employed more than " << MIN_YEARS
31             << " years.\n";
32     }
33     return 0;
34  }
```

Program Output with Example Input Shown in Bold

What is your annual income? **40000 [Enter]**
How many years have you worked at your current job? **2 [Enter]**
You qualify.

Program Output with Example Input Shown in Bold

What is your annual income? **20000 [Enter]**
How many years have you worked at your current job? **7 [Enter]**
You qualify.

Program Output with Example Input Shown in Bold

What is your annual income? **30000 [Enter]**
How many years have you worked at your current job? **3 [Enter]**
You must earn at least $35000 or have been employed more than 5 years.

The message "You qualify\n." is displayed when either or both the expressions income >= 35000 or years > 5 are true. If both of these are false, the disqualifying message is printed.

The ! Operator

The ! operator performs a logical NOT operation. It takes an operand and reverses its truth or falsehood. In other words, if the expression is true, the ! operator returns false, and if the expression is false, it returns true. Here is an if statement using the ! operator:

```
if (!(temperature > 100))
    cout << "You are below the maximum temperature.\n";
```

First, the expression (temperature > 100) is tested to be true or false. Then the ! operator is applied to that value. If the expression (temperature > 100) is true, the ! operator returns false. If it is false, the ! operator returns true. In the example, it is equivalent to asking "is the temperature not greater than 100?"

Table 4-9 shows a truth table for the ! operator.

Table 4-9

Expression	Value of the Expression
!true	false (0)
!false	true (1)

Program 4-17 performs the same task as Program 4-16. The if statement, however, uses the ! operator to determine if the user does *not* make at least $35,000 or has *not* been on the job more than five years.

Program 4-17

```
 1  // This program demonstrates the logical ! operator.
 2  #include <iostream>
 3  using namespace std;
 4
 5  int main()
 6  {
 7      // Constants for minimum income and years
 8      const double MIN_INCOME = 35000.0;
 9      const int MIN_YEARS = 5;
10
11      double income;  // Annual income
12      int years;      // Years at the current job
13
14      // Get the annual income
15      cout << "What is your annual income? ";
16      cin >> income;
17
18      // Get the number of years at the current job.
19      cout << "How many years have you worked at "
20           << "your current job? ";
21      cin >> years;
22
```

(program continues)

Program 4-17   *(continued)*

```
23      // Determine the user's loan qualifications.
24      if (!(income >= MIN_INCOME || years > MIN_YEARS))
25      {
26         cout << "You must earn at least $"
27              << MIN_INCOME << " or have been "
28              << "employed more than " << MIN_YEARS
29              << " years.\n";
30      }
31      else
32         cout << "You qualify.\n";
33      return 0;
34 }
```

The output of Program 4-17 is the same as Program 4-16.

Precedence and Associativity of Logical Operators

Table 4-10 shows the precedence of C++'s logical operators, from highest to lowest.

Table 4-10

Logical Operators in Order of Precedence
!
&&
||

The ! operator has a higher precedence than many of the C++ operators. To avoid an error, you should always enclose its operand in parentheses unless you intend to apply it to a variable or a simple expression with no other operators. For example, consider the following expressions:

```
!(x > 2)
!x > 2
```

The first expression applies the ! operator to the expression x > 2. It is asking "is x not greater than 2?" The second expression, however, applies the ! operator to x only. It is asking "is the logical negation of x greater than 2?" Suppose x is set to 5. Since 5 is non-zero, it would be considered true, so the ! operator would reverse it to false, which is 0. The > operator would then determine if 0 is greater than 2. To avoid a catastrophe like this, always use parentheses!

The && and || operators rank lower in precedence than the relational operators, so precedence problems are less likely to occur. If you feel unsure, however, it doesn't hurt to use parentheses anyway.

```
(a > b) && (x < y)      is the same as    a > b && x < y
(x == y) || (b > a)     is the same as    x == y || b > a
```

The logical operators have left-to-right associativity. In the following expression, a < b is evaluated before y == z.

```
a < b || y == z
```

In the following expression, `y == z` is evaluated first, however, because the `&&` operator has higher precedence than `||`.

```
a < b || y == z && m > j
```

The expression is equivalent to

```
(a < b) || ((y == z) && (m > j))
```

4.9 Checking Numeric Ranges with Logical Operators

CONCEPT: Logical operators are effective for determining whether a number is in or out of a range.

When determining whether a number is inside a numeric range, it's best to use the `&&` operator. For example, the following `if` statement checks the value in `x` to determine whether it is in the range of 20 through 40:

```
if (x >= 20 && x <= 40)
    cout << x << " is in the acceptable range.\n";
```

The expression in the `if` statement will be true only when `x` is both greater than or equal to 20 AND less than or equal to 40. `x` must be within the range of 20 through 40 for this expression to be true.

When determining whether a number is outside a range, the `||` operator is best to use. The following statement determines whether `x` is outside the range of 20 to 40:

```
if (x < 20 || x > 40)
    cout << x << " is outside the acceptable range.\n";
```

It's important not to get the logic of these logical operators confused. For example, the following `if` statement would never test true:

```
if (x < 20 && x > 40)
    cout << x << " is outside the acceptable range.\n";
```

Obviously, `x` cannot be less than 20 and at the same time greater than 40.

NOTE: C++ does not allow you to check numeric ranges with expressions such as `5 < x < 20`. Instead, you must use a logical operator to connect two relational expressions, as previously discussed.

Checkpoint

myprogramminglab *www.myprogramminglab.com*

4.18   The following truth table shows various combinations of the values `true` and `false` connected by a logical operator. Complete the table by indicating if the result of such a combination is TRUE or FALSE.

Logical Expression	Result (true or false)
`true && false`	
`true && true`	
`false && true`	
`false && false`	
`true || false`	
`true || true`	
`false || true`	
`false || false`	
`!true`	
`!false`	

4.19 Assume the variables a = 2, b = 4, and c = 6. Indicate by circling the T or F if each of the following conditions is true or false:

```
a == 4 || b > 2          T    F
6 <= c && a > 3          T    F
1 != b && c != 3         T    F
a >= -1 || a <= b        T    F
!(a > 2)                 T    F
```

4.20 Write an `if` statement that prints the message "The number is valid" if the variable `speed` is within the range 0 through 200.

4.21 Write an `if` statement that prints the message "The number is not valid" if the variable `speed` is outside the range 0 through 200.

4.10 Menus

CONCEPT: You can use nested `if/else` statements or the `if/else if` statement to create menu-driven programs. A *menu-driven* program allows the user to determine the course of action by selecting it from a list of actions.

A menu is a screen displaying a set of choices the user selects from. For example, a program that manages a mailing list might give you the following menu:

1. Add a name to the list.

2. Remove a name from the list.

3. Change a name in the list.

4. Print the list.

5. Quit the program.

The user selects one of the operations by entering its number. Entering 4, for example, causes the mailing list to be printed, and entering 5 causes the program to end. Nested `if/else` statements or an `if/else if` structure can be used to set up such a menu. After the user enters a number, the program compares the number with the available selections and executes the statements that perform that operation.

Program 4-18 calculates the charges for membership in a health club. The club has three membership packages to choose from: standard adult membership, child membership, and senior citizen membership. The program presents a menu that allows the user to choose the desired package and then calculates the cost of the membership.

Program 4-18

```cpp
1  // This program displays a menu and asks the user to make a
2  // selection. An if/else if statement determines which item
3  // the user has chosen.
4  #include <iostream>
5  #include <iomanip>
6  using namespace std;
7
8  int main()
9  {
10     int choice;        // To hold a menu choice
11     int months;        // To hold the number of months
12     double charges;    // To hold the monthly charges
13
14     // Constants for membership rates
15     const double ADULT = 40.0,
16                  SENIOR = 30.0,
17                  CHILD = 20.0;
18
19     // Constants for menu choices
20     const int ADULT_CHOICE = 1,
21               CHILD_CHOICE = 2,
22               SENIOR_CHOICE = 3,
23               QUIT_CHOICE = 4;
24
25     // Display the menu and get a choice.
26     cout << "\t\tHealth Club Membership Menu\n\n"
27          << "1. Standard Adult Membership\n"
28          << "2. Child Membership\n"
29          << "3. Senior Citizen Membership\n"
30          << "4. Quit the Program\n\n"
31          << "Enter your choice: ";
32     cin >> choice;
33
34     // Set the numeric output formatting.
35     cout << fixed << showpoint << setprecision(2);
36
37     // Respond to the user's menu selection.
38     if (choice == ADULT_CHOICE)
39     {
40        cout << "For how many months? ";
41        cin >> months;
42        charges = months * ADULT;
43        cout << "The total charges are $" << charges << endl;
44     }
```

(program continues)

Program 4-18 *(continued)*

```
45      else if (choice == CHILD_CHOICE)
46      {
47         cout << "For how many months? ";
48         cin >> months;
49         charges = months * CHILD;
50         cout << "The total charges are $" << charges << endl;
51      }
52      else if (choice == SENIOR_CHOICE)
53      {
54         cout << "For how many months? ";
55         cin >> months;
56         charges = months * SENIOR;
57         cout << "The total charges are $" << charges << endl;
58      }
59      else if (choice == QUIT_CHOICE)
60      {
61          cout << "Program ending.\n";
62      }
63      else
64      {
65         cout << "The valid choices are 1 through 4. Run the\n"
66              << "program again and select one of those.\n";
67      }
68      return 0;
69 }
```

Program Output with Example Input Shown in Bold
```
      Health Club Membership Menu

1. Standard Adult Membership
2. Child Membership
3. Senior Citizen Membership
4. Quit the Program

Enter your choice: 3 [Enter]
For how many months? 6 [Enter]
The total charges are $180.00
```

Let's take a closer look at the program:

- Lines 10–12 define the following variables:
  - The choice variable will hold the user's menu choice
  - The months variable will hold the number of months of health club membership
  - The charges variable will hold the total charges
- Lines 15–17 define named constants for the monthly membership rates for adult, senior citizen, and child memberships.
- Lines 20–23 define named constants for the menu choices.
- Lines 26–32 display the menu and get the user's choice.
- Line 35 sets the numeric output formatting for floating point numbers.

- Lines 38–67 is an `if/else if` statement that determines the user's menu choice in the following manner:
  - If the user selected 1 from the menu (adult membership), the statements in lines 40–43 are executed.
  - Otherwise, if the user selected 2 from the menu (child membership), the statements in lines 47–50 are executed.
  - Otherwise, if the user selected 3 from the menu (senior citizen membership), the statements in lines 54–57 are executed.
  - Otherwise, if the user selected 4 from the menu (quit the program), the statement in line 61 is executed.
  - If the user entered any choice other than 1, 2, 3, or 4, the `else` clause in lines 63–67 executes, displaying an error message.

4.11 Focus on Software Engineering: Validating User Input

CONCEPT: As long as the user of a program enters bad input, the program will produce bad output. Programs should be written to filter out bad input.

Perhaps the most famous saying of the computer world is "garbage in, garbage out." The integrity of a program's output is only as good as its input, so you should try to make sure garbage does not go into your programs. *Input validation* is the process of inspecting data given to a program by the user and determining if it is valid. A good program should give clear instructions about the kind of input that is acceptable, and not assume the user has followed those instructions. Here are just a few examples of input validations performed by programs:

- Numbers are checked to ensure they are within a range of possible values. For example, there are 168 hours in a week. It is not possible for a person to be at work longer than 168 hours in one week.
- Values are checked for their "reasonableness." Although it might be possible for a person to be at work for 168 hours per week, it is not probable.
- Items selected from a menu or other sets of choices are checked to ensure they are available options.
- Variables are checked for values that might cause problems, such as division by zero.

Program 4-19 is a test scoring program that rejects any test score less than 0 or greater than 100.

Program 4-19

```
1 // This test scoring program does not accept test scores
2 // that are less than 0 or greater than 100.
3 #include <iostream>
4 using namespace std;
5
6 int main()
7 {
8     // Constants for grade thresholds
```

(program continues)

Program 4-19 *(continued)*

```cpp
 9     const int A_SCORE = 90,
10               B_SCORE = 80,
11               C_SCORE = 70,
12               D_SCORE = 60,
13               MIN_SCORE = 0,    // Minimum valid score
14               MAX_SCORE = 100;  // Maximum valid score
15
16     int testScore;  // To hold a numeric test score
17
18     // Get the numeric test score.
19     cout << "Enter your numeric test score and I will\n"
20          << "tell you the letter grade you earned: ";
21     cin >> testScore;
22
23     // Validate the input and determine the grade.
24     if (testScore >= MIN_SCORE && testScore <= MAX_SCORE)
25     {
26        // Determine the letter grade.
27        if (testScore >= A_SCORE)
28          cout << "Your grade is A.\n";
29        else if (testScore >= B_SCORE)
30          cout << "Your grade is B.\n";
31        else if (testScore >= C_SCORE)
32          cout << "Your grade is C.\n";
33        else if (testScore >= D_SCORE)
34          cout << "Your grade is D.\n";
35        else
36          cout << "Your grade is F.\n";
37     }
38     else
39     {
40        // An invalid score was entered.
41        cout << "That is an invalid score. Run the program\n"
42             << "again and enter a value in the range of\n"
43             << MIN_SCORE << " through " << MAX_SCORE << ".\n";
44     }
45
46     return 0;
47 }
```

Program Output with Example Input Shown in Bold
```
Enter your numeric test score and I will
tell you the letter grade you earned: –1 [Enter]
That is an invalid score. Run the program
again and enter a value in the range of
0 through 100.
```

Program Output with Example Input Shown in Bold
```
Enter your numeric test score and I will
tell you the letter grade you earned: 81 [Enter]
Your grade is B.
```

4.12 Comparing Characters and Strings

> **CONCEPT:** Relational operators can also be used to compare characters and `string` objects.

Earlier in this chapter you learned to use relational operators to compare numeric values. They can also be used to compare characters and `string` objects.

Comparing Characters

As you learned in Chapter 3, characters are actually stored in memory as integers. On most systems, this integer is the ASCII value of the character. For example, the letter 'A' is represented by the number 65, the letter 'B' is represented by the number 66, and so on. Table 4-11 shows the ASCII numbers that correspond to some of the commonly used characters.

Table 4-11 ASCII Values of Commonly Used Characters

Character	ASCII Value
'0' – '9'	48 – 57
'A' – 'Z'	65 – 90
'a' – 'z'	97 – 122
blank	32
period	46

Notice that every character, even the blank, has an ASCII code associated with it. Notice also that the ASCII code of a character representing a digit, such as `'1'` or `'2'`, is not the same as the value of the digit itself. A complete table showing the ASCII values for all characters can be found in Appendix B.

When two characters are compared, it is actually their ASCII values that are being compared. `'A' < 'B'` because the ASCII value of `'A'` (65) is less than the ASCII value of `'B'` (66). Likewise `'1' < '2'` because the ASCII value of `'1'` (49) is less than the ASCII value of `'2'` (50). However, as shown in Table 4-11, lowercase letters have higher ASCII codes than uppercase letters, so `'a' > 'Z'`. Program 4-20 shows how characters can be compared with relational operators.

Program 4-20

```
1  // This program demonstrates how characters can be
2  // compared with the relational operators.
3  #include <iostream>
4  using namespace std;
5
6  int main()
7  {
8     char ch;
```

(program continues)

Program 4-20   *(continued)*

```
 9
10     // Get a character from the user.
11     cout << "Enter a digit or a letter: ";
12     ch = cin.get();
13
14     // Determine what the user entered.
15     if (ch >= '0' && ch <= '9')
16        cout << "You entered a digit.\n";
17     else if (ch >= 'A' && ch <= 'Z')
18        cout << "You entered an uppercase letter.\n";
19     else if (ch >= 'a' && ch <= 'z')
20        cout << "You entered a lowercase letter.\n";
21     else
22        cout << "That is not a digit or a letter.\n";
23
24     return 0;
25 }
```

Program Output with Example Input Shown in Bold
```
Enter a digit or a letter: t [Enter]
You entered a lowercase letter.
```

Program Output with Example Input Shown in Bold
```
Enter a digit or a letter: v [Enter]
You entered an uppercase letter.
```

Program Output with Example Input Shown in Bold
```
Enter a digit or a letter: 5 [Enter]
You entered a digit.
```

Program Output with Example Input Shown in Bold
```
Enter a digit or a letter: & [Enter]
That is not a digit or a letter.
```

Comparing `string` Objects

`string` objects can also be compared with relational operators. As with individual characters, when two `string` objects are compared, it is actually the ASCII value of the characters making up the strings that are being compared. For example, assume the following definitions exist in a program:

```
string str1 = "ABC";
string str2 = "XYZ";
```

The `string` object `str1` is considered less than the `string` object `str2` because the characters "ABC" alphabetically precede (have lower ASCII values than) the characters "XYZ". So, the following `if` statement will cause the message "str1 is less than str2." to be displayed on the screen.

```
if (str1 < str2)
    cout << "str1 is less than str2.";
```

One by one, each character in the first operand is compared with the character in the corresponding position in the second operand. If all the characters in both `string` objects match, the two strings are equal. Other relationships can be determined if two characters in corresponding positions do not match. The first operand is less than the second operand if the first mismatched character in the first operand is less than its counterpart in the second operand. Likewise, the first operand is greater than the second operand if the first mismatched character in the first operand is greater than its counterpart in the second operand.

For example, assume a program has the following definitions:

```
string name1 = "Mary";
string name2 = "Mark";
```

The value in `name1`, "Mary", is greater than the value in `name2`, "Mark". This is because the first three characters in `name1` have the same ASCII values as the first three characters in `name2`, but the `'y'` in the fourth position of `"Mary"` has a greater ASCII value than the `'k'` in the corresponding position of `"Mark"`.

Any of the relational operators can be used to compare two `string` objects. Here are some of the valid comparisons of `name1` and `name2`.

```
name1 > name2     // true
name1 <= name2    // false
name1 != name2    // true
```

`string` objects can also, of course, be compared to string literals:

```
name1 < "Mary Jane" // true
```

Program 4-21 further demonstrates how relational operators can be used with `string` objects.

Program 4-21

```
 1   // This program uses relational operators to compare a string
 2   // entered by the user with valid stereo part numbers.
 3   #include <iostream>
 4   #include <iomanip>
 5   #include <string>
 6   using namespace std;
 7
 8   int main()
 9   {
10      const double PRICE_A = 249.0,
11                   PRICE_B = 299.0;
12
13      string partNum; // Holds a stereo part number
14
15      // Display available parts and get the user's selection
16      cout << "The stereo part numbers are:\n"
17           << "Boom Box: part number S-29A \n"
18           << "Shelf Model: part number S-29B \n"
19           << "Enter the part number of the stereo you\n"
20           << "wish to purchase: ";
21      cin >> partNum;
```

(program continues)

Program 4-21   *(continued)*

```
22
23      // Set the numeric output formatting
24      cout << fixed << showpoint << setprecision(2);
25
26      // Determine and display the correct price
27      if (partNum == "S-29A")
28         cout << "The price is $" << PRICE_A << endl;
29      else if (partNum == "S-29B")
30         cout << "The price is $" << PRICE_B << endl;
31      else
32         cout << partNum << " is not a valid part number.\n";
33      return 0;
34 }
```

Program Output with Example Input Shown in Bold
```
The stereo part numbers are:
Boom Box: part number S-29A
Shelf Model: part number S-29B
Enter the part number of the stereo you
wish to purchase: S-29A [Enter]
The price is $249.00
```

 Checkpoint

[myprogramminglab] *www.myprogramminglab.com*

4.22   Indicate whether each of the following relational expressions is true or false. Refer to the ASCII table in Appendix A if necessary.

A)   'a' < 'z'

B)   'a' == 'A'

C)   '5' < '7'

D)   'a' < 'A'

E)   '1' == 1

F)   '1' == 49

4.23   Indicate whether each of the following relational expressions is true or false. Refer to the ASCII table in Appendix B if necessary.

A)   "Bill" == "BILL"

B)   "Bill" < "BILL"

C)   "Bill" < "Bob"

D)   "189" > "23"

E)   "189" > "Bill"

F)   "Mary" < "MaryEllen"

G)   "MaryEllen" < "Mary Ellen"

4.13   The Conditional Operator

CONCEPT: You can use the conditional operator to create short expressions that work like `if/else` statements.

The conditional operator is powerful and unique. It provides a shorthand method of expressing a simple `if/else` statement. The operator consists of the question-mark (?) and the colon (:). Its format is:

```
expression ? expression : expression;
```

Here is an example of a statement using the conditional operator:

```
x < 0 ? y = 10 : z = 20;
```

The statement above is called a *conditional expression* and consists of three sub-expressions separated by the ? and : symbols. The expressions are `x < 0`, `y = 10`, and `z = 20`, as illustrated here:

| x < 0 | ? | y = 10 | : | z = 20; |

NOTE: Since it takes three operands, the conditional operator is considered a *ternary* operator.

The conditional expression above performs the same operation as the following `if/else` statement:

```
if (x < 0)
    y = 10;
else
    z = 20;
```

The part of the conditional expression that comes before the question mark is the expression to be tested. It's like the expression in the parentheses of an `if` statement. If the expression is true, the part of the statement between the ? and the : is executed. Otherwise, the part after the : is executed. Figure 4-10 illustrates the roles played by the three sub-expressions.

Figure 4-10

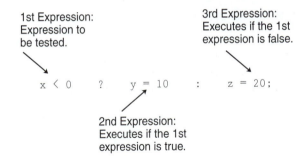

If it helps, you can put parentheses around the sub-expressions, as in the following:

```
(x < 0) ? (y = 10) : (z = 20);
```

Using the Value of a Conditional Expression

Remember, in C++ all expressions have a value, and this includes the conditional expression. If the first sub-expression is true, the value of the conditional expression is the value of the second sub-expression. Otherwise it is the value of the third sub-expression. Here is an example of an assignment statement using the value of a conditional expression:

```
a = x > 100 ? 0 : 1;
```

The value assigned to a will be either 0 or 1, depending upon whether x is greater than 100. This statement could be expressed as the following `if/else` statement:

```
if (x > 100)
    a = 0;
else
    a = 1;
```

Program 4-22 can be used to help a consultant calculate her charges. Her rate is $50.00 per hour, but her minimum charge is for five hours. The conditional operator is used in a statement that ensures the number of hours does not go below five.

Program 4-22

```cpp
 1 // This program calculates a consultant's charges at $50
 2 // per hour, for a minimum of 5 hours. The ?: operator
 3 // adjusts hours to 5 if less than 5 hours were worked.
 4 #include <iostream>
 5 #include <iomanip>
 6 using namespace std;
 7
 8 int main()
 9 {
10    const double PAY_RATE = 50.0;   // Hourly pay rate
11    const int MIN_HOURS = 5;        // Minimum billable hours
12    double hours,                   // Hours worked
13           charges;                 // Total charges
14
15    // Get the hours worked.
16    cout << "How many hours were worked? ";
17    cin >> hours;
18
19    // Determine the hours to charge for.
20    hours = hours < MIN_HOURS ? MIN_HOURS : hours;
21
22    // Calculate and display the charges.
23    charges = PAY_RATE * hours;
24    cout << fixed << showpoint << setprecision(2)
25         << "The charges are $" << charges << endl;
26    return 0;
27 }
```

Notice that in line 11 a constant named `MIN_HOURS` is defined to represent the minimum number of hours, which is 5. Here is the statement in line 20, with the conditional expression:

```
hours = hours < MIN_HOURS ? MIN_HOURS : hours;
```

If the value in hours is less than 5, then 5 is stored in hours. Otherwise hours is assigned the value it already has. The hours variable will not have a value less than 5 when it is used in the next statement, which calculates the consultant's charges.

As you can see, the conditional operator gives you the ability to pack decision-making power into a concise line of code. With a little imagination it can be applied to many other programming problems. For instance, consider the following statement:

```
cout << "Your grade is: " << (score < 60 ? "Fail." : "Pass.");
```

If you were to use an `if/else` statement, the statement above would be written as follows:

```
if (score < 60)
    cout << "Your grade is: Fail.";
else
    cout << "Your grade is: Pass.";
```

> **NOTE:** The parentheses are placed around the conditional expression because the `<<` operator has higher precedence than the `?:` operator. Without the parentheses, just the value of the expression `score < 60` would be sent to cout.

Checkpoint

 myprogramminglab *www.myprogramminglab.com*

4.24   Rewrite the following `if/else` statements as conditional expressions:

A)
```
if (x > y)
    z = 1;
else
    z = 20;
```
B)
```
if (temp > 45)
    population = base * 10;
else
    population = base * 2;
```
C)
```
if (hours > 40)
    wages *= 1.5;
else
    wages *= 1;
```
D)
```
if (result >= 0)
    cout << "The result is positive\n";
else
    cout << "The result is negative.\n";
```

4.25   The following statements use conditional expressions. Rewrite each with an `if/else` statement.

A) `j = k > 90 ? 57 : 12;`

B) `factor = x >= 10 ? y * 22 : y * 35;`

C) `total += count == 1 ? sales : count * sales;`

D) `cout << (((num % 2) == 0) ? "Even\n" : "Odd\n");`

4.26   What will the following program display?

```cpp
#include <iostream>
using namespace std;

int main()
{
    const int UPPER = 8, LOWER = 2;
    int num1, num2, num3 = 12, num4 = 3;

    num1 = num3 < num4 ? UPPER : LOWER;
    num2 = num4 > UPPER ? num3 : LOWER;
    cout << num1 << " " <<  num2 << endl;
    return 0;
}
```

4.14   The `switch` Statement

CONCEPT: The `switch` statement lets the value of a variable or expression determine where the program will branch.

A branch occurs when one part of a program causes another part to execute. The `if/else if` statement allows your program to branch into one of several possible paths. It performs a series of tests (usually relational) and branches when one of these tests is true. The `switch` statement is a similar mechanism. It, however, tests the value of an integer expression and then uses that value to determine which set of statements to branch to. Here is the format of the `switch` statement:

```cpp
switch (IntegerExpression)
{
   case ConstantExpression:
        // place one or more
        // statements here

   case ConstantExpression:
        // place one or more
        // statements here

   // case statements may be repeated as many
   // times as necessary

   default:
        // place one or more
        // statements here
}
```

The first line of the statement starts with the word `switch`, followed by an integer expression inside parentheses. This can be either of the following:

- a variable of any of the integer data types (including `char`)
- an expression whose value is of any of the integer data types

On the next line is the beginning of a block containing several `case` statements. Each `case` statement is formatted in the following manner:

```
case ConstantExpression:
      // place one or more
      // statements here
```

After the word `case` is a constant expression (which must be of an integer type), followed by a colon. The constant expression may be an integer literal or an integer named constant. The `case` statement marks the beginning of a section of statements. The program branches to these statements if the value of the `switch` expression matches that of the case expression.

WARNING! The expression of each `case` statement in the block must be unique.

NOTE: The expression following the word `case` must be an integer literal or constant. It cannot be a variable, and it cannot be an expression such as x < 22 or n == 50.

An optional `default` section comes after all the `case` statements. The program branches to this section if none of the `case` expressions match the `switch` expression. So, it functions like a trailing `else` in an `if/else if` statement.

Program 4-23 shows how a simple `switch` statement works.

Program 4-23

```
 1   // The switch statement in this program tells the user something
 2   // he or she already knows: the data just entered!
 3   #include <iostream>
 4   using namespace std;
 5
 6   int main()
 7   {
 8      char choice;
 9
10      cout << "Enter A, B, or C: ";
11      cin >> choice;
12      switch (choice)
13      {
14        case 'A': cout << "You entered A.\n";
15                  break;
16        case 'B': cout << "You entered B.\n";
17                  break;
18        case 'C': cout << "You entered C.\n";
19                  break;
20        default:  cout << "You did not enter A, B, or C!\n";
21      }
22      return 0;
23   }
```

(program continues)

Program 4-23   *(continued)*

Program Output with Example Input Shown in Bold
```
Enter A, B, or C: B [Enter]
You entered B.
```

Program Output with Example Input Shown in Bold
```
Enter A, B, or C: F [Enter]
You did not enter A, B, or C!
```

The first case statement is case 'A':, the second is case 'B':, and the third is case 'C':. These statements mark where the program is to branch to if the variable choice contains the values 'A', 'B', or 'C'. (Remember, character variables and literals are considered integers.) The default section is branched to if the user enters anything other than A, B, or C.

Notice the break statements that are in the case 'A', case 'B', and case 'C' sections.

```
switch (choice)
{
    case 'A':cout << "You entered A.\n";
            break; ←————
    case 'B':cout << "You entered B.\n";
            break; ←————
    case 'C':cout << "You entered C.\n";
            break; ←————
    default: cout << "You did not enter A, B, or C!\n";
}
```

The case statements show the program where to start executing in the block and the break statements show the program where to stop. Without the break statements, the program would execute all of the lines from the matching case statement to the end of the block.

 NOTE: The default section (or the last case section, if there is no default) does not need a break statement. Some programmers prefer to put one there anyway, for consistency.

Program 4-24 is a modification of Program 4-23, without the break statements.

Program 4-24

```
1   // The switch statement in this program tells the user something
2   // he or she already knows: the data just entered!
3   #include <iostream>
4   using namespace std;
5
6   int main()
7   {
8      char choice;
9
```

```
10       cout << "Enter A, B, or C: ";
11       cin >> choice;
12       // The following switch is
13       // missing its break statements!
14       switch (choice)
15       {
16          case 'A': cout << "You entered A.\n";
17          case 'B': cout << "You entered B.\n";
18          case 'C': cout << "You entered C.\n";
19          default:  cout << "You did not enter A, B, or C!\n";
20       }
21       return 0;
22    }
```

Program Output with Example Input Shown in Bold

Enter A, B, or C: **A [Enter]**
You entered A.
You entered B.
You entered C.
You did not enter A, B, or C!

Program Output with Example Input Shown in Bold

Enter A, B, or C: **C [Enter]**
You entered C.
You did not enter A, B, or C!

Without the break statement, the program "falls through" all of the statements below the one with the matching case expression. Sometimes this is what you want. Program 4-25 lists the features of three TV models a customer may choose from. The Model 100 has remote control. The Model 200 has remote control and stereo sound. The Model 300 has remote control, stereo sound, and picture-in-a-picture capability. The program uses a switch statement with carefully omitted breaks to print the features of the selected model.

Program 4-25

```
1    // This program is carefully constructed to use the "fall through"
2    // feature of the switch statement.
3    #include <iostream>
4    using namespace std;
5
6    int main()
7    {
8       int modelNum;   // Model number
9
10      // Get a model number from the user.
11      cout << "Our TVs come in three models:\n";
12      cout << "The 100, 200, and 300. Which do you want? ";
13      cin >> modelNum;
14
```

(program continues)

Program 4-25   *(continued)*

```
15       // Display the model's features.
16       cout << "That model has the following features:\n";
17       switch (modelNum)
18       {
19          case 300: cout << "\tPicture-in-a-picture.\n";
20          case 200: cout << "\tStereo sound.\n";
21          case 100: cout << "\tRemote control.\n";
22                    break;
23          default:  cout << "You can only choose the 100,";
24                    cout << "200, or 300.\n";
25       }
26       return 0;
27  }
```

Program Output with Example Input Shown in Bold
```
Our TVs come in three models:
The 100, 200, and 300. Which do you want? 100 [Enter]
That model has the following features:
    Remote control.
```

Program Output with Example Input Shown in Bold
```
Our TVs come in three models:
The 100, 200, and 300. Which do you want? 200 [Enter]
That model has the following features:
    Stereo sound.
    Remote control.
```

Program Output with Example Input Shown in Bold
```
Our TVs come in three models:
The 100, 200, and 300. Which do you want? 300 [Enter]
That model has the following features:
    Picture-in-a-picture.
    Stereo sound.
    Remote control.
```

Program Output with Example Input Shown in Bold
```
Our TVs come in three models:
The 100, 200, and 300. Which do you want? 500 [Enter]
That model has the following features:
You can only choose the 100, 200, or 300.
```

Another example of how useful this "fall through" capability can be is when you want the program to branch to the same set of statements for multiple case expressions. For instance, Program 4-26 asks the user to select a grade of pet food. The available choices are A, B, and C. The switch statement will recognize either upper or lowercase letters.

Program 4-26

```
1  // The switch statement in this program uses the "fall through"
2  // feature to catch both uppercase and lowercase letters entered
3  // by the user.
4  #include <iostream>
5  using namespace std;
6
```

```
 7   int main()
 8   {
 9      char feedGrade;
10
11      // Get the desired grade of feed.
12      cout << "Our pet food is available in three grades:\n";
13      cout << "A, B, and C. Which do you want pricing for? ";
14      cin >> feedGrade;
15
16      // Display the price.
17      switch(feedGrade)
18      {
19         case 'a':
20         case 'A': cout << "30 cents per pound.\n";
21                   break;
22         case 'b':
23         case 'B': cout << "20 cents per pound.\n";
24                   break;
25         case 'c':
26         case 'C': cout << "15 cents per pound.\n";
27                   break;
28         default:  cout << "That is an invalid choice.\n";
29      }
30      return 0;
31   }
```

Program Output with Example Input Shown in Bold
```
Our pet food is available in three grades:
A, B, and C. Which do you want pricing for? b [Enter]
20 cents per pound.
```

Program Output with Example Input Shown in Bold
```
Our pet food is available in three grades:
A, B, and C. Which do you want pricing for? B [Enter]
20 cents per pound.
```

When the user enters 'a' the corresponding case has no statements associated with it, so the program falls through to the next case, which corresponds with 'A'.

```
     case 'a':
     case 'A':  cout << "30 cents per pound.\n";
                break;
```

The same technique is used for 'b' and 'c'.

Using switch in Menu Systems

The switch statement is a natural mechanism for building menu systems. Recall that Program 4-18 gives a menu to select which health club package the user wishes to purchase. The program uses if/else if statements to determine which package the user has selected and displays the calculated charges. Program 4-27 is a modification of that program, using a switch statement instead of if/else if.

Program 4-27

```
1  // This program uses a switch statement to determine
2  // the item selected from a menu.
3  #include <iostream>
4  #include <iomanip>
5  using namespace std;
6
7  int main()
8  {
9     int choice;        // To hold a menu choice
10    int months;        // To hold the number of months
11    double charges;    // To hold the monthly charges
12
13    // Constants for membership rates
14    const double ADULT = 40.0,
15                 CHILD = 20.0,
16                 SENIOR = 30.0;
17
18    // Constants for menu choices
19    const int ADULT_CHOICE = 1,
20              CHILD_CHOICE = 2,
21              SENIOR_CHOICE = 3,
22              QUIT_CHOICE = 4;
23
24    // Display the menu and get a choice.
25    cout << "\t\tHealth Club Membership Menu\n\n"
26         << "1. Standard Adult Membership\n"
27         << "2. Child Membership\n"
28         << "3. Senior Citizen Membership\n"
29         << "4. Quit the Program\n\n"
30         << "Enter your choice: ";
31    cin >> choice;
32
33    // Set the numeric output formatting.
34    cout << fixed << showpoint << setprecision(2);
35
36    // Respond to the user's menu selection.
37    switch (choice)
38    {
39       case ADULT_CHOICE:
40          cout << "For how many months? ";
41          cin >> months;
42          charges = months * ADULT;
43          cout << "The total charges are $" << charges << endl;
44          break;
45
46       case CHILD_CHOICE:
47          cout << "For how many months? ";
48          cin >> months;
49          charges = months * CHILD;
50          cout << "The total charges are $" << charges << endl;
51          break;
52
```

```
53        case SENIOR_CHOICE:
54           cout << "For how many months? ";
55           cin >> months;
56           charges = months * SENIOR;
57           cout << "The total charges are $" << charges << endl;
58           break;
59
60        case QUIT_CHOICE:
61           cout << "Program ending.\n";
62           break;
63
64        default:
65           cout << "The valid choices are 1 through 4. Run the\n"
66                << "program again and select one of those.\n";
67    }
68
69    return 0;
70 }
```

Program Output with Example Input Shown in Bold
```
       Health Club Membership Menu

1. Standard Adult Membership
2. Child Membership
3. Senior Citizen Membership
4. Quit the Program

Enter your choice: 2 [Enter]
For how many months? 6 [Enter]
The total charges are $120.00
```

 Checkpoint

myprogramminglab *www.myprogramminglab.com*

4.27   Explain why you cannot convert the following if/else if statement into a switch statement.

```
if (temp == 100)
    x = 0;
else if (population > 1000)
    x = 1;
else if  (rate < .1)
    x = -1;
```

4.28   What is wrong with the following switch statement?

```
switch (temp)
{
    case temp < 0 : cout << "Temp is negative.\n";
                    break;
    case temp == 0: cout << "Temp is zero.\n";
                    break;
    case temp > 0 : cout << "Temp is positive.\n";
                    break;
}
```

4.29   What will the following program display?

```cpp
#include <iostream>
using namespace std;

int main()
{
    int funny = 7, serious = 15;

    funny = serious * 2;
    switch (funny)
    {    case 0 : cout << "That is funny.\n";
                break;
         case 30: cout << "That is serious.\n";
                break;
         case 32: cout << "That is seriously funny.\n";
                break;
         default: cout << funny << endl;
    }
    return 0;
}
```

4.30   Complete the following program skeleton by writing a switch statement that displays "one" if the user has entered 1, "two" if the user has entered 2, and "three" if the user has entered 3. If a number other than 1, 2, or 3 is entered, the program should display an error message.

```cpp
#include <iostream>
using namespace std;

int main()
{
    int userNum;

    cout << "Enter one of the numbers 1, 2, or 3: ";
    cin >> userNum;
    //
    // Write the switch statement here.
    //
    return 0;
}
```

4.31   Rewrite the following program. Use a switch statement instead of the if/else if statement.

```cpp
#include <iostream>
using namespace std;

int main()
{
    int selection;

    cout << "Which formula do you want to see?\n\n";
    cout << "1. Area of a circle\n";
    cout << "2. Area of a rectangle\n";
    cout << "3. Area of a cylinder\n"
    cout << "4. None of them!\n";
    cin >> selection;
    if (selection == 1)
        cout << "Pi times radius squared\n";
```

```
            else if (selection == 2)
               cout << "Length times width\n";
            else if (selection == 3)
               cout << "Pi times radius squared times height\n";
            else if (selection == 4)
               cout << "Well okay then, good bye!\n";
            else
               cout << "Not good with numbers, eh?\n";
            return 0;
      }
```

4.15 More About Blocks and Scope

CONCEPT: The scope of a variable is limited to the block in which it is defined.

C++ allows you to create variables almost anywhere in a program. Program 4-28 is a modification of Program 4-17, which determines if the user qualifies for a loan. The definitions of the variables income and years have been moved to later points in the program.

Program 4-28

```
 1 // This program demonstrates late variable definition
 2 #include <iostream>
 3 using namespace std;
 4
 5 int main()
 6 {
 7    // Constants for minimum income and years
 8    const double MIN_INCOME = 35000.0;
 9    const int MIN_YEARS = 5;
10
11    // Get the annual income.
12    cout << "What is your annual income? ";
13    double income;    // Variable definition
14    cin >> income;
15
16    // Get the number of years at the current job.
17    cout << "How many years have you worked at "
18         << "your current job? ";
19    int years;         // Variable definition
20    cin >> years;
21
22    // Determine the user's loan qualifications.
23    if (income >= MIN_INCOME || years > MIN_YEARS)
24       cout << "You qualify.\n";
25    else
26    {
27       cout << "You must earn at least $"
28            << MIN_INCOME << " or have been "
29            << "employed more than " << MIN_YEARS
30            << " years.\n";
31    }
32    return 0;
33 }
```

It is a common practice to define all of a function's variables at the top of the function. Sometimes, especially in longer programs, it's a good idea to define variables near the part of the program where they are used. This makes the purpose of the variable more evident.

Recall from Chapter 2 that the scope of a variable is defined as the part of the program where the variable may be used.

In Program 4-28, the scope of the income variable is the part of the program in lines 13 through 32. The scope of the years variable is the part of the program in lines 19 through 32.

The variables income and years are defined inside function main's braces. Variables defined inside a set of braces have *local scope* or *block scope*. They may only be used in the part of the program between their definition and the block's closing brace.

You may define variables inside any block. For example, look at Program 4-29. This version of the loan program has the variable years defined inside the block of the if statement. The scope of years is the part of the program in lines 21 through 31.

Program 4-29

```
 1  // This program demonstrates a variable defined in an inner block.
 2  #include <iostream>
 3  using namespace std;
 4
 5  int main()
 6  {
 7     // Constants for minimum income and years
 8     const double MIN_INCOME = 35000.0;
 9     const int MIN_YEARS = 5;
10
11     // Get the annual income.
12     cout << "What is your annual income? ";
13     double income;      // Variable definition
14     cin >> income;
15
16     if (income >= MIN_INCOME)
17     {
18        // Get the number of years at the current job.
19        cout << "How many years have you worked at "
20             << "your current job? ";
21        int years;      // Variable definition
22        cin >> years;
23
24        if (years > MIN_YEARS)
25           cout << "You qualify.\n";
26        else
27        {
28           cout << "You must have been employed for\n"
29                << "more than " << MIN_YEARS
30                << " years to qualify.\n";
31        }
32     }
33     else
```

```
34    {
35       cout << "You must earn at least $" << MIN_INCOME
36            << " to qualify.\n";
37    }
38    return 0;
39 }
```

Notice the scope of years is only within the block where it is defined. The variable is not visible before its definition or after the closing brace of the block. This is true of any variable defined inside a set of braces.

 NOTE: When a program is running and it enters the section of code that constitutes a variable's scope, it is said that the variable *comes into scope*. This simply means the variable is now visible and the program may reference it. Likewise, when a variable *leaves scope*, it may no longer be used.

Variables with the Same Name

When a block is nested inside another block, a variable defined in the inner block may have the same name as a variable defined in the outer block. As long as the variable in the inner block is visible, however, the variable in the outer block will be hidden. This is illustrated by Program 4-30.

Program 4-30

```
1  // This program uses two variables with the name number.
2  #include <iostream>
3  using namespace std;
4
5  int main()
6  {
7     // Define a variable named number.
8     int number;
9
10    cout << "Enter a number greater than 0: ";
11    cin >> number;
12    if (number > 0)
13    {
14       int number;  // Another variable named number.
15       cout << "Now enter another number: ";
16       cin >> number;
17       cout << "The second number you entered was "
18            << number << endl;
19    }
20    cout << "Your first number was " << number << endl;
21    return 0;
22 }
```

Program Output with Example Input Shown in Bold
```
Enter a number greater than 0: 2 [Enter]
Now enter another number: 7 [Enter]
The second number you entered was 7
Your first number was 2
```

Program 4-30 has two separate variables named `number`. The `cin` and `cout` statements in the inner block (belonging to the `if` statement) can only work with the `number` variable defined in that block. As soon as the program leaves that block, the inner `number` goes out of scope, revealing the outer `number` variable.

 WARNING! Although it's perfectly acceptable to define variables inside nested blocks, you should avoid giving them the same names as variables in the outer blocks. It's too easy to confuse one variable with another.

Case Study: See the Sales Commission Case Study on this book's companion Web site at www.pearsonhighered.com/gaddis.

Review Questions and Exercises

Short Answer

1. Describe the difference between the `if/else if` statement and a series of `if` statements.

2. In an `if/else if` statement, what is the purpose of a trailing `else`?

3. What is a flag and how does it work?

4. Can an `if` statement test expressions other than relational expressions? Explain.

5. Briefly describe how the `&&` operator works.

6. Briefly describe how the `||` operator works.

7. Why are the relational operators called relational?

8. Why do most programmers indent the conditionally executed statements in a decision structure?

Fill-in-the-Blank

9. An expression using the greater-than, less-than, greater-than-or-equal to, less-than-or-equal-to, equal, or not-equal to operator is called a(n) _____ expression.

10. A relational expression is either _____ or _____.

11. The value of a relational expression is 0 if the expression is _____ or 1 if the expression is _____.

12. The `if` statement regards an expression with the value 0 as _____.

13. The `if` statement regards an expression with a nonzero value as _____.

14. For an `if` statement to conditionally execute a group of statements, the statements must be enclosed in a set of _____.

15. In an `if/else` statement, the `if` part executes its statement or block if the expression is _____, and the `else` part executes its statement or block if the expression is _____.

16. The trailing `else` in an `if/else if` statement has a similar purpose as the _____ section of a `switch` statement.

17. The `if/else if` statement is actually a form of the _____ `if` statement.

18. If the sub-expression on the left of the _____ logical operator is false, the right sub-expression is not checked.

19. If the sub-expression on the left of the _____ logical operator is true, the right sub-expression is not checked.

20. The _____ logical operator has higher precedence than the other logical operators.

21. The logical operators have _____ associativity.

22. The _____ logical operator works best when testing a number to determine if it is within a range.

23. The _____ logical operator works best when testing a number to determine if it is outside a range.

24. A variable with _____ scope is only visible when the program is executing in the block containing the variable's definition.

25. You use the _____ operator to determine whether one `string` object is greater then another `string` object.

26. An expression using the conditional operator is called a(n) _____ expression.

27. The expression that is tested by a `switch` statement must have a(n) _____ value.

28. The expression following a `case` statement must be a(n) _____ _____.

29. A program will "fall through" a `case` section if it is missing the _____ statement.

30. What value will be stored in the variable `t` after each of the following statements executes?

    A) `t = (12 > 1);`_____

    B) `t = (2 < 0);`_____

    C) `t = (5 == (3 * 2));`_____

    D) `t = (5 == 5);`_____

Algorithm Workbench

31. Write an `if` statement that assigns 100 to x when y is equal to 0.

32. Write an `if/else` statement that assigns 0 to x when y is equal to 10. Otherwise it should assign 1 to x.

33. Using the following chart, write an `if/else if` statement that assigns .10, .15, or .20 to `commission`, depending on the value in `sales`.

Sales	Commission Rate
Up to $10,000	10%
$10,000 to $15,000	15%
Over $15,000	20%

34. Write an `if` statement that sets the variable `hours` to 10 when the flag variable `minimum` is set.

35. Write nested `if` statements that perform the following tests: If `amount1` is greater than 10 and `amount2` is less than 100, display the greater of the two.

36. Write an `if` statement that prints the message "The number is valid" if the variable `grade` is within the range 0 through 100.

37. Write an `if` statement that prints the message "The number is valid" if the variable `temperature` is within the range −50 through 150.

38. Write an `if` statement that prints the message "The number is not valid" if the variable `hours` is outside the range 0 through 80.

39. Assume `str1` and `str2` are `string` objects that have been initialized with different values. Write an `if/else` statement that compares the two objects and displays the one that is alphabetically greatest.

40. Convert the following `if/else if` statement into a `switch` statement:

```
if (choice == 1)
{
   cout << fixed << showpoint << setprecision(2);
}
else if (choice == 2 || choice == 3)
{
   cout << fixed << showpoint << setprecision(4);
}
else if (choice == 4)
{
   cout << fixed << showpoint << setprecision(6);
}
else
{
   cout << fixed << showpoint << setprecision(8);
}
```

41. Match the conditional expression with the `if/else` statement that performs the same operation.

A) `q = x < y ? a + b : x * 2;`

B) `q = x < y ? x * 2 : a + b;`

C) `x < y ? q = 0 : q = 1;`

```
_____   if (x < y)
            q = 0;
        else
            q = 1;

_____   if (x < y)
            q = a + b;
        else
            q = x * 2;

_____   if (x < y)
            q = x * 2;
        else
            q = a + b;
```

True or False

42. T   F   The = operator and the == operator perform the same operation when used in a Boolean expression.

43. T F A variable defined in an inner block may not have the same name as a variable defined in the outer block.

44. T F A conditionally executed statement should be indented one level from the `if` statement.

45. T F All lines in a block should be indented one level.

46. T F It's safe to assume that all uninitialized variables automatically start with 0 as their value.

47. T F When an `if` statement is nested in the `if` part of another statement, the only time the inner `if` is executed is when the expression of the outer `if` is true.

48. T F When an `if` statement is nested in the `else` part of another statement, as in an `if/else if`, the only time the inner `if` is executed is when the expression of the outer `if` is true.

49. T F The scope of a variable is limited to the block in which it is defined.

50. T F You can use the relational operators to compare `string` objects.

51. T F `x != y` is the same as `(x > y || x < y)`

52. T F `y < x` is the same as `x >= y`

53. T F `x >= y` is the same as `(x > y && x = y)`

Assume the variables x = 5, y = 6, and z = 8. Indicate by circling the T or F whether each of the following conditions is true or false:

54. T F `x == 5 || y > 3`

55. T F `7 <= x && z > 4`

56. T F `2 != y && z != 4`

57. T F `x >= 0 || x <= y`

Find the Errors

Each of the following programs has errors. Find as many as you can.

58.
```cpp
// This program averages 3 test scores.
// It uses the variable perfectScore as a flag.
include <iostream>
using namespace std;

int main()
{
    cout << "Enter your 3 test scores and I will ";
        << "average them:";
    int score1, score2, score3,
    cin >> score1 >> score2 >> score3;
    double average;
    average = (score1 + score2 + score3) / 3.0;
    if (average = 100);
        perfectScore = true;  // Set the flag variable
    cout << "Your average is " << average << endl;
    bool perfectScore;
    if (perfectScore);
    {
        cout << "Congratulations!\n";
        cout << "That's a perfect score.\n";
        cout << "You deserve a pat on the back!\n";
        return 0;
    }
}
```

59.
```cpp
// This program divides a user-supplied number by another
// user-supplied number. It checks for division by zero.
#include <iostream>
using namespace std;

int main()
{
    double num1, num2, quotient;

    cout << "Enter a number: ";
    cin >> num1;
    cout << "Enter another number: ";
    cin >> num2;
    if (num2 == 0)
        cout << "Division by zero is not possible.\n";
        cout << "Please run the program again ";
        cout << "and enter a number besides zero.\n";
    else
        quotient = num1 / num2;
        cout << "The quotient of " << num1 <<
        cout << " divided by " << num2 << " is ";
        cout << quotient << endl;
    return 0;
}
```

60.
```cpp
// This program uses an if/else if statement to assign a
// letter grade (A, B, C, D, or F) to a numeric test score.
#include <iostream>
using namespace std;

int main()
{
    int testScore;

    cout << "Enter your test score and I will tell you\n";
    cout << "the letter grade you earned: ";
    cin >> testScore;
    if (testScore < 60)
        cout << "Your grade is F.\n";
    else if (testScore < 70)
        cout << "Your grade is D.\n";
    else if (testScore < 80)
        cout << "Your grade is C.\n";
    else if (testScore < 90)
        cout << "Your grade is B.\n";
    else
        cout << "That is not a valid score.\n";
    else if (testScore <= 100)
        cout << "Your grade is A.\n";
    return 0;
}
```

61.
```cpp
// This program uses a switch-case statement to assign a
// letter grade (A, B, C, D, or F) to a numeric test score.
#include <iostream>
using namespace std;

int main()
{
    double testScore;
    cout << "Enter your test score and I will tell you\n";
    cout << "the letter grade you earned: ";
    cin >> testScore;
    switch (testScore)
    {
        case (testScore < 60.0):
                cout << "Your grade is F.\n";
                break;
        case (testScore < 70.0):
                cout << "Your grade is D.\n";
                break;
        case (testScore < 80.0):
                cout << "Your grade is C.\n";
                break;
        case (testScore < 90.0):
                cout << "Your grade is B.\n";
                break;
        case (testScore <= 100.0):
                cout << "Your grade is A.\n";
                break;
        default:
                cout << "That score isn't valid\n";
        return 0;
}
```

62. The following statement should determine if x is not greater than 20. What is wrong with it?

```cpp
if (!x > 20)
```

63. The following statement should determine if count is within the range of 0 through 100. What is wrong with it?

```cpp
if (count >= 0 || count <= 100)
```

64. The following statement should determine if count is outside the range of 0 through 100. What is wrong with it?

```cpp
if (count < 0 && count > 100)
```

65. The following statement should assign 0 to z if a is less than 10, otherwise it should assign 7 to z. What is wrong with it?

```cpp
z = (a < 10) : 0 ? 7;
```

Programming Challenges

Visit www.myprogramminglab.com to complete many of these Programming Challenges online and get instant feedback.

1. **Minimum/Maximum**

   Write a program that asks the user to enter two numbers. The program should use the conditional operator to determine which number is the smaller and which is the larger.

2. **Roman Numeral Converter**

   Write a program that asks the user to enter a number within the range of 1 through 10. Use a `switch` statement to display the Roman numeral version of that number.

   Input Validation: Do not accept a number less than 1 or greater than 10.

3. **Magic Dates**

   The date June 10, 1960 is special because when we write it in the following format, the month times the day equals the year.

   6/10/60

   Write a program that asks the user to enter a month (in numeric form), a day, and a two-digit year. The program should then determine whether the month times the day is equal to the year. If so, it should display a message saying the date is magic. Otherwise it should display a message saying the date is not magic.

4. **Areas of Rectangles**

   The area of a rectangle is the rectangle's length times its width. Write a program that asks for the length and width of two rectangles. The program should tell the user which rectangle has the greater area, or if the areas are the same.

5. **Body Mass Index**

   Write a program that calculates and displays a person's body mass index (BMI). The BMI is often used to determine whether a person with a sedentary lifestyle is overweight or underweight for his or her height. A person's BMI is calculated with the following formula:

   $BMI = weight \times 703 \, / \, height^2$

   where *weight* is measured in pounds and *height* is measured in inches. The program should display a message indicating whether the person has optimal weight, is underweight, or is overweight. A sedentary person's weight is considered to be optimal if his or her BMI is between 18.5 and 25. If the BMI is less than 18.5, the person is considered to be underweight. If the BMI value is greater than 25, the person is considered to be overweight.

6. **Mass and Weight**

   Scientists measure an object's mass in kilograms and its weight in newtons. If you know the amount of mass that an object has, you can calculate its weight, in newtons, with the following formula:

   $Weight = mass \times 9.8$

Write a program that asks the user to enter an object's mass, and then calculates and displays its weight. If the object weighs more than 1,000 newtons, display a message indicating that it is too heavy. If the object weighs less than 10 newtons, display a message indicating that the object is too light.

7. **Time Calculator**

Write a program that asks the user to enter a number of seconds.

- There are 60 seconds in a minute. If the number of seconds entered by the user is greater than or equal to 60, the program should display the number of minutes in that many seconds.
- There are 3,600 seconds in an hour. If the number of seconds entered by the user is greater than or equal to 3,600, the program should display the number of hours in that many seconds.
- There are 86,400 seconds in a day. If the number of seconds entered by the user is greater than or equal to 86,400, the program should display the number of days in that many seconds.

8. **Change for a Dollar Game**

Create a change-counting game that gets the user to enter the number of coins required to make exactly one dollar. The program should ask the user to enter the number of pennies, nickels, dimes, and quarters. If the total value of the coins entered is equal to one dollar, the program should congratulate the user for winning the game. Otherwise, the program should display a message indicating whether the amount entered was more than or less than one dollar.

9. **Math Tutor**

This is a modification of Programming Challenge 15 from Chapter 3. Write a program that can be used as a math tutor for a young student. The program should display two random numbers that are to be added, such as:

    247
  + 129

The program should wait for the student to enter the answer. If the answer is correct, a message of congratulations should be printed. If the answer is incorrect, a message should be printed showing the correct answer.

10. **Software Sales**

A software company sells a package that retails for $99. Quantity discounts are given according to the following table.

Quantity	Discount
10–19	20%
20–49	30%
50–99	40%
100 or more	50%

Write a program that asks for the number of units sold and computes the total cost of the purchase.

Input Validation: Make sure the number of units is greater than 0.

11. **Book Club Points**

Serendipity Booksellers has a book club that awards points to its customers based on the number of books purchased each month. The points are awarded as follows:

- If a customer purchases 0 books, he or she earns 0 points.
- If a customer purchases 1 book, he or she earns 5 points.
- If a customer purchases 2 books, he or she earns 15 points.
- If a customer purchases 3 books, he or she earns 30 points.
- If a customer purchases 4 or more books, he or she earns 60 points.

Write a program that asks the user to enter the number of books that he or she has purchased this month and then displays the number of points awarded.

12. **Bank Charges**

A bank charges $10 per month plus the following check fees for a commercial checking account:

$.10 each for fewer than 20 checks
$.08 each for 20–39 checks
$.06 each for 40–59 checks
$.04 each for 60 or more checks

The bank also charges an extra $15 if the balance of the account falls below $400 (before any check fees are applied). Write a program that asks for the beginning balance and the number of checks written. Compute and display the bank's service fees for the month.

Input Validation: Do not accept a negative value for the number of checks written. If a negative value is given for the beginning balance, display an urgent message indicating the account is overdrawn.

13. **Shipping Charges**

The Fast Freight Shipping Company charges the following rates:

Weight of Package (in Kilograms)	Rate per 500 Miles Shipped
2 Kg or less	$1.10
Over 2 Kg but not more than 6 kg	$2.20
Over 6 Kg but not more than 10 kg	$3.70
Over 10 Kg but not more than 20 kg	$4.80

Write a program that asks for the weight of the package and the distance it is to be shipped, and then displays the charges.

Input Validation: Do not accept values of 0 or less for the weight of the package. Do not accept weights of more than 20 Kg (this is the maximum weight the company will ship). Do not accept distances of less than 10 miles or more than 3,000 miles. These are the company's minimum and maximum shipping distances.

14. **Running the Race**

Write a program that asks for the names of three runners and the time it took each of them to finish a race. The program should display who came in first, second, and third place.

Input Validation: Only accept positive numbers for the times.

15. **Personal Best**

Write a program that asks for the name of a pole vaulter and the dates and vault heights (in meters) of the athlete's three best vaults. It should then report, in order of height (best first), the date on which each vault was made and its height.

Input Validation: Only accept values between 2.0 and 5.0 for the heights.

16. **Fat Gram Calculator**

Write a program that asks for the number of calories and fat grams in a food. The program should display the percentage of calories that come from fat. If the calories from fat are less than 30% of the total calories of the food, it should also display a message indicating that the food is low in fat.

One gram of fat has 9 calories, so

Calories from fat = fat grams * 9

The percentage of calories from fat can be calculated as

Calories from fat ÷ total calories

Input Validation: Make sure the number of calories and fat grams are not less than 0. Also, the number of calories from fat cannot be greater than the total number of calories. If that happens, display an error message indicating that either the calories or fat grams were incorrectly entered.

17. **Spectral Analysis**

If a scientist knows the wavelength of an electromagnetic wave, he or she can determine what type of radiation it is. Write a program that asks for the wavelength of an electromagnetic wave in meters and then displays what that wave is according to the chart below. (For example, a wave with a wavelength of 1E-10 meters would be an X-ray.)

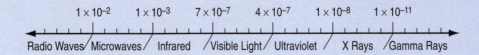

18. **The Speed of Sound**

The following table shows the approximate speed of sound in air, water, and steel.

Medium	Speed
Air	1,100 feet per second
Water	4,900 feet per second
Steel	16,400 feet per second

Write a program that displays a menu allowing the user to select air, water, or steel. After the user has made a selection, he or she should be asked to enter the distance a sound wave will travel in the selected medium. The program will then display the amount of time it will take. (Round the answer to four decimal places.)

Input Validation: Check that the user has selected one of the available choices from the menu. Do not accept distances less than 0.

19. **The Speed of Sound in Gases**

When sound travels through a gas, its speed depends primarily on the density of the medium. The less dense the medium, the faster the speed will be. The following table shows the approximate speed of sound at 0 degrees centigrade, measured in meters per second, when traveling through carbon dioxide, air, helium, and hydrogen.

Medium	Speed (Meters per Second)
Carbon Dioxide	258.0
Air	331.5
Helium	972.0
Hydrogen	1,270.0

Write a program that displays a menu allowing the user to select one of these four gases. After a selection has been made, the user should enter the number of seconds it took for the sound to travel in this medium from its source to the location at which it was detected. The program should then report how far away (in meters) the source of the sound was from the detection location.

Input Validation: Check that the user has selected one of the available menu choices. Do not accept times less than 0 seconds or more than 30 seconds.

20. **Freezing and Boiling Points**

The following table lists the freezing and boiling points of several substances. Write a program that asks the user to enter a temperature, and then shows all the substances that will freeze at that temperature and all that will boil at that temperature. For example, if the user enters –20 the program should report that water will freeze and oxygen will boil at that temperature.

Substance	Freezing Point (°F)	Boiling Point (°F)
Ethyl alcohol	–173	172
Mercury	–38	676
Oxygen	–362	–306
Water	32	212

21. Geometry Calculator

Write a program that displays the following menu:

```
Geometry Calculator

    1. Calculate the Area of a Circle
    2. Calculate the Area of a Rectangle
    3. Calculate the Area of a Triangle
    4. Quit

    Enter your choice (1-4):
```

If the user enters 1, the program should ask for the radius of the circle and then display its area. Use the following formula:

$$area = \pi r^2$$

Use 3.14159 for π and the radius of the circle for *r*. If the user enters 2, the program should ask for the length and width of the rectangle and then display the rectangle's area. Use the following formula:

```
area = length * width
```

If the user enters 3 the program should ask for the length of the triangle's base and its height, and then display its area. Use the following formula:

```
area = base * height * .5
```

If the user enters 4, the program should end.

Input Validation: Display an error message if the user enters a number outside the range of 1 through 4 when selecting an item from the menu. Do not accept negative values for the circle's radius, the rectangle's length or width, or the triangle's base or height.

22. Long-Distance Calls

A long-distance carrier charges the following rates for telephone calls:

Starting Time of Call	Rate per Minute
00:00–06:59	0.12
07:00–19:00	0.55
19:01–23:59	0.35

Write a program that asks for the starting time and the number of minutes of the call, and displays the charges. The program should ask for the time to be entered as a floating-point number in the form HH.MM. For example, 07:00 hours will be entered as 07.00, and 16:28 hours will be entered as 16.28.

Input Validation: The program should not accept times that are greater than 23:59. Also, no number whose last two digits are greater than 59 should be accepted. Hint: Assuming num is a floating-point variable, the following expression will give you its fractional part:

```
num − static_cast<int>(num)
```

23. **Internet Service Provider**

An Internet service provider has three different subscription packages for its customers:

Package A: For $9.95 per month 10 hours of access are provided. Additional hours are $2.00 per hour.

Package B: For $14.95 per month 20 hours of access are provided. Additional hours are $1.00 per hour.

Package C: For $19.95 per month unlimited access is provided.

Write a program that calculates a customer's monthly bill. It should ask which package the customer has purchased and how many hours were used. It should then display the total amount due.

Input Validation: Be sure the user only selects package A, B, or C. Also, the number of hours used in a month cannot exceed 744.

24. **Internet Service Provider, Part 2**

Modify the Program in Programming Challenge 23 so that it also displays how much money Package A customers would save if they purchased packages B or C, and how much money Package B customers would save if they purchased Package C. If there would be no savings, no message should be printed.

25. **Internet Service Provider, Part 3**

Months with 30 days have 720 hours, and months with 31 days have 744 hours. February, with 28 days, has 672 hours. Enhance the input validation of the Internet Service Provider program by asking the user for the month (by name), and validating that the number of hours entered is not more than the maximum for the entire month. Here is a table of the months, their days, and number of hours in each.

Month	Days	Hours
January	31	744
February	28	672
March	31	744
April	30	720
May	31	744
June	30	720
July	31	744
August	31	744
September	30	720
October	31	744
November	30	720
December	31	744

CHAPTER

5 Loops and Files

TOPICS

5.1 The Increment and Decrement Operators

CONCEPT: ++ and −− are operators that add and subtract 1 from their operands.

To *increment* a value means to increase it by one, and to *decrement* a value means to decrease it by one. Both of the following statements increment the variable num:

```
num = num + 1;
num += 1;
```

And num is decremented in both of the following statements:

```
num = num - 1;
num -= 1;
```

227

C++ provides a set of simple unary operators designed just for incrementing and decrementing variables. The increment operator is ++ and the decrement operator is --. The following statement uses the ++ operator to increment num:

```
num++;
```

And the following statement decrements num:

```
num--;
```

NOTE: The expression num++ is pronounced "num plus plus," and num-- is pronounced "num minus minus."

Our examples so far show the increment and decrement operators used in *postfix mode*, which means the operator is placed after the variable. The operators also work in *prefix mode*, where the operator is placed before the variable name:

```
++num;
--num;
```

In both postfix and prefix mode, these operators add 1 to or subtract 1 from their operand. Program 5-1 shows how they work.

Program 5-1

```
1   // This program demonstrates the ++ and -- operators.
2   #include <iostream>
3   using namespace std;
4
5   int main()
6   {
7       int num = 4;    // num starts out with 4.
8
9       // Display the value in num.
10      cout << "The variable num is " << num << endl;
11      cout << "I will now increment num.\n\n";
12
13      // Use postfix ++ to increment num.
14      num++;
15      cout << "Now the variable num is " << num << endl;
16      cout << "I will increment num again.\n\n";
17
18      // Use prefix ++ to increment num.
19      ++num;
20      cout << "Now the variable num is " << num << endl;
21      cout << "I will now decrement num.\n\n";
22
23      // Use postfix -- to decrement num.
24      num--;
25      cout << "Now the variable num is " << num << endl;
26      cout << "I will decrement num again.\n\n";
27
```

```
28      // Use prefix -- to increment num.
29      --num;
30      cout << "Now the variable num is " << num << endl;
31      return 0;
32  }
```

Program Output
```
The variable num is 4
I will now increment num.

Now the variable num is 5
I will increment num again.

Now the variable num is 6
I will now decrement num.

Now the variable num is 5
I will decrement num again.

Now the variable num is 4
```

The Difference Between Postfix and Prefix Modes

In the simple statements used in Program 5-1, it doesn't matter if the increment or decrement operator is used in postfix or prefix mode. The difference is important, however, when these operators are used in statements that do more than just incrementing or decrementing. For example, look at the following lines:

```
num = 4;
cout << num++;
```

This cout statement is doing two things: (1) displaying the value of num, and (2) incrementing num. But which happens first? cout will display a different value if num is incremented first than if num is incremented last. The answer depends on the mode of the increment operator.

Postfix mode causes the increment to happen after the value of the variable is used in the expression. In the example, cout will display 4, then num will be incremented to 5. Prefix mode, however, causes the increment to happen first. In the following statements, num will be incremented to 5, then cout will display 5:

```
num = 4;
cout << ++num;
```

Program 5-2 illustrates these dynamics further:

Program 5-2

```
1   // This program demonstrates the prefix and postfix
2   // modes of the increment and decrement operators.
3   #include <iostream>
4   using namespace std;
```

(program continues)

Program 5-2 *(continued)*

```
 5
 6   int main()
 7   {
 8      int num = 4;
 9
10      cout << num << endl;    // Displays 4
11      cout << num++ << endl;  // Displays 4, then adds 1 to num
12      cout << num << endl;    // Displays 5
13      cout << ++num << endl;  // Adds 1 to num, then displays 6
14      cout << endl;           // Displays a blank line
15
16      cout << num << endl;    // Displays 6
17      cout << num-- << endl;  // Displays 6, then subtracts 1 from num
18      cout << num << endl;    // Displays 5
19      cout << --num << endl;  // Subtracts 1 from num, then displays 4
20
21      return 0;
22   }
```

Program Output
```
4
4
5
6

6
6
5
4
```

Let's analyze the statements in this program. In line 8, num is initialized with the value 4, so the cout statement in line 10 displays 4. Then, line 11 sends the expression num++ to cout. Because the ++ operator is used in postfix mode, the value 4 is first sent to cout, and then 1 is added to num, making its value 5.

When line 12 executes, num will hold the value 5, so 5 is displayed. Then, line 13 sends the expression ++num to cout. Because the ++ operator is used in prefix mode, 1 is first added to num (making it 6), and then the value 6 is sent to cout. This same sequence of events happens in lines 16 through 19, except the -- operator is used.

For another example, look at the following code:

```
int x = 1;
int y
y = x++;      // Postfix increment
```

The first statement defines the variable x (initialized with the value 1) and the second statement defines the variable y. The third statement does two things:

- It assigns the value of x to the variable y.
- The variable x is incremented.

The value that will be stored in y depends on when the increment takes place. Because the ++ operator is used in postfix mode, it acts *after* the assignment takes place. So, this code will store 1 in y. After the code has executed, x will contain 2. Let's look at the same code, but with the ++ operator used in prefix mode:

```
int x = 1;
int y;
y = ++x;      // Prefix increment
```

In the third statement, the ++ operator is used in prefix mode, so it acts on the variable x before the assignment takes place. So, this code will store 2 in y. After the code has executed, x will also contain 2.

Using ++ and –– in Mathematical Expressions

The increment and decrement operators can also be used on variables in mathematical expressions. Consider the following program segment:

```
a = 2;
b = 5;
c = a * b++;
cout << a << " " << b << " " << c;
```

In the statement c = a * b++, c is assigned the value of a times b, which is 10. The variable b is then incremented. The cout statement will display

```
2 6 10
```

If the statement were changed to read

```
c = a * ++b;
```

The variable b would be incremented before it was multiplied by a. In this case c would be assigned the value of 2 times 6, so the cout statement would display

```
2 6 12
```

You can pack a lot of action into a single statement using the increment and decrement operators, but don't get too tricky with them. You might be tempted to try something like the following, thinking that c will be assigned 11:

```
a = 2;
b = 5;
c = ++(a * b);   // Error!
```

But this assignment statement simply will not work because the operand of the increment and decrement operators must be an lvalue. Recall from Chapter 2 that an lvalue identifies a place in memory whose contents may be changed. The increment and decrement operators usually have variables for their operands, but generally speaking, anything that can go on the left side of an = operator is legal.

Using ++ and –– in Relational Expressions

Sometimes you will see code where the ++ and –– operators are used in relational expressions. Just as in mathematical expressions, the difference between postfix and prefix mode is critical. Consider the following program segment:

```
x = 10;
if (x++ > 10)
    cout << "x is greater than 10.\n";
```

Two operations are happening in this `if` statement: (1) The value in `x` is tested to determine if it is greater than 10, and (2) `x` is incremented. Because the increment operator is used in postfix mode, the comparison happens first. Since 10 is not greater than 10, the `cout` statement won't execute. If the mode of the increment operator is changed, however, the `if` statement will compare 11 to 10 and the `cout` statement will execute:

```
x = 10;
if (++x > 10)
    cout << "x is greater than 10.\n";
```

 Checkpoint

myprogramminglab   *www.myprogramminglab.com*

5.1   What will the following program segments display?

A) ```
x = 2;
y = x++;
cout << x << y;
```

B) ```
x = 2;
y = ++x;
cout << x << y;
```

C) ```
x = 2;
y = 4;
cout << x++ << --y;
```

D) ```
x = 2;
y = 2 * x++;
cout << x << y;
```

E) ```
x = 99;
if (x++ < 100)
    cout "It is true!\n";
else
    cout << "It is false!\n";
```

F) ```
x = 0;
if (++x)
    cout << "It is true!\n";
else
    cout << "It is false!\n";
```

5.2   Introduction to Loops: The `while` Loop

CONCEPT: A loop is part of a program that repeats.

VideoNote
The `while` Loop

Chapter 4 introduced the concept of control structures, which direct the flow of a program. A *loop* is a control structure that causes a statement or group of statements to repeat. C++ has three looping control structures: the `while` loop, the `do-while` loop, and the `for` loop. The difference between these structures is how they control the repetition.

The while Loop

The while loop has two important parts: (1) an expression that is tested for a true or false value, and (2) a statement or block that is repeated as long as the expression is true. Figure 5-1 shows the logic of a while loop.

Figure 5-1

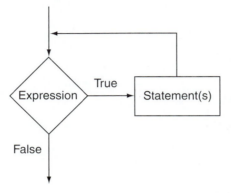

Here is the general format of the while loop:

```
while (expression)
   statement;
```

In the general format, *expression* is any expression that can be evaluated as true or false, and *statement* is any valid C++ statement. The first line shown in the format is sometimes called the *loop header*. It consists of the key word while followed by an *expression* enclosed in parentheses.

Here's how the loop works: the *expression* is tested, and if it is true, the *statement* is executed. Then, the *expression* is tested again. If it is true, the *statement* is executed. This cycle repeats until the *expression* is false.

The statement that is repeated is known as the *body* of the loop. It is also considered a conditionally executed statement, because it is executed only under the condition that the *expression* is true.

Notice there is no semicolon after the expression in parentheses. Like the if statement, the while loop is not complete without the statement that follows it.

If you wish the while loop to repeat a block of statements, its format is:

```
while (expression)
{
   statement;
   statement;
   // Place as many statements here
   // as necessary.
}
```

The while loop works like an if statement that executes over and over. As long as the expression inside the parentheses is true, the conditionally executed statement or block will repeat. Program 5-3 uses the while loop to print "Hello" five times.

Program 5-3

```
 1   // This program demonstrates a simple while loop.
 2   #include <iostream>
 3   using namespace std;
 4
 5   int main()
 6   {
 7      int number = 0;
 8
 9      while (number < 5)
10      {
11         cout << "Hello\n";
12         number++;
13      }
14      cout << "That's all!\n";
15      return 0;
16   }
```

Program Output
```
Hello
Hello
Hello
Hello
Hello
That's all!
```

Let's take a closer look at this program. In line 7 an integer variable, number, is defined and initialized with the value 0. In line 9 the while loop begins with this statement:

```
while (number < 5)
```

This statement tests the variable number to determine whether it is less than 5. If it is, then the statements in the body of the loop (lines 11 and 12) are executed:

```
cout << "Hello\n";
number++;
```

The statement in line 11 prints the word "Hello." The statement in line 12 uses the increment operator to add one to number. This is the last statement in the body of the loop, so after it executes, the loop starts over. It tests the expression number < 5 again, and if it is true, the statements in the body of the loop are executed again. This cycle repeats until the expression number < 5 is false. This is illustrated in Figure 5-2.

Each repetition of a loop is known as an *iteration*. This loop will perform five iterations because the variable number is initialized with the value 0, and it is incremented each time the body of the loop is executed. When the expression number < 5 is tested and found to be false, the loop will terminate and the program will resume execution at the statement that immediately follows the loop. Figure 5-3 shows the logic of this loop.

Figure 5-2

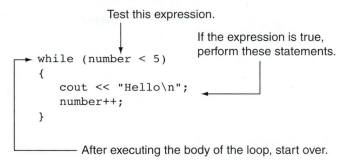

Figure 5-3

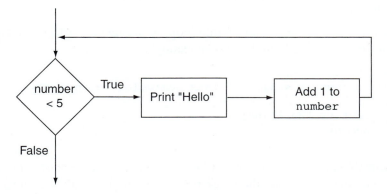

In this example, the number variable is referred to as the *loop control variable* because it controls the number of times that the loop iterates.

The while Loop Is a Pretest Loop

The while loop is known as a *pretest* loop, which means it tests its expression before each iteration. Notice the variable definition in line 7 of Program 5-3:

```
int number = 0;
```

The number variable is initialized with the value 0. If number had been initialized with the value 5 or greater, as shown in the following program segment, the loop would never execute:

```
int number = 6;
while (number < 5)
{
    cout << "Hello\n";
    number++;
}
```

An important characteristic of the while loop is that the loop will never iterate if the test expression is false to start with. If you want to be sure that a while loop executes the first time, you must initialize the relevant data in such a way that the test expression starts out as true.

Infinite Loops

In all but rare cases, loops must contain within themselves a way to terminate. This means that something inside the loop must eventually make the test expression false. The loop in Program 5-3 stops when the expression number < 5 is false.

If a loop does not have a way of stopping, it is called an infinite loop. An *infinite loop* continues to repeat until the program is interrupted. Here is an example of an infinite loop:

```
int number = 0;
while (number < 5)
{
    cout << "Hello\n";
}
```

This is an infinite loop because it does not contain a statement that changes the value of the number variable. Each time the expression number < 5 is tested, number will contain the value 0.

It's also possible to create an infinite loop by accidentally placing a semicolon after the first line of the while loop. Here is an example:

```
int number = 0;
while (number < 5);  // This semicolon is an ERROR!
{
    cout << "Hello\n";
    number++;
}
```

The semicolon at the end of the first line is assumed to be a null statement and disconnects the while statement from the block that comes after it. To the compiler, this loop looks like:

```
while (number < 5);
```

This while loop will forever execute the null statement, which does nothing. The program will appear to have "gone into space" because there is nothing to display screen output or show activity.

Don't Forget the Braces with a Block of Statements

If you write a loop that conditionally executes a block of statements, don't forget to enclose all of the statements in a set of braces. If the braces are accidentally left out, the while statement conditionally executes only the very next statement. For example, look at the following code.

```
int number = 0;
// This loop is missing its braces!
while (number < 5)
    cout << "Hello\n";
    number++;
```

In this code the number++ statement is not in the body of the loop. Because the braces are missing, the while statement only executes the statement that immediately follows it. This loop will execute infinitely because there is no code in its body that changes the number variable.

Another common pitfall with loops is accidentally using the = operator when you intend to use the == operator. The following is an infinite loop because the test expression assigns 1 to remainder each time it is evaluated instead of testing whether remainder is equal to 1.

```
while (remainder = 1) // Error: Notice the assignment
{
    cout << "Enter a number: ";
    cin >> num;
    remainder = num % 2;
}
```

Remember, any nonzero value is evaluated as true.

Programming Style and the while Loop

It's possible to create loops that look like this:

```
while (number < 5) { cout << "Hello\n"; number++; }
```

Avoid this style of programming. The programming style you should use with the while loop is similar to that of the if statement:

- If there is only one statement repeated by the loop, it should appear on the line after the while statement and be indented one additional level.
- If the loop repeats a block, each line inside the braces should be indented.

This programming style should visually set the body of the loop apart from the surrounding code. In general, you'll find a similar style being used with the other types of loops presented in this chapter.

In the Spotlight:

Designing a Program with a while Loop

A project currently underway at Chemical Labs, Inc. requires that a substance be continually heated in a vat. A technician must check the substance's temperature every 15 minutes. If the substance's temperature does not exceed 102.5 degrees Celsius, then the technician does nothing. However, if the temperature is greater than 102.5 degrees Celsius, the technician must turn down the vat's thermostat, wait 5 minutes, and check the temperature again. The technician repeats these steps until the temperature does not exceed 102.5 degrees Celsius. The director of engineering has asked you to write a program that guides the technician through this process.

Here is the algorithm:

1. *Prompt the user to enter the substance's temperature.*

2. *Repeat the following steps as long as the temperature is greater than 102.5 degrees Celsius:*

   a. *Tell the technician to turn down the thermostat, wait 5 minutes, and check the temperature again.*

   b. *Prompt the user to enter the substance's temperature.*

3. *After the loop finishes, tell the technician that the temperature is acceptable and to check it again in 15 minutes.*

After reviewing this algorithm, you realize that steps 2a and 2b should not be performed if the test condition (temperature is greater than 102.5) is false to begin with. The `while` loop will work well in this situation, because it will not execute even once if its condition is false. Program 5-4 shows the code for the program.

Program 5-4

```cpp
 1  // This program assists a technician in the process
 2  // of checking a substance's temperature.
 3  #include <iostream>
 4  using namespace std;
 5
 6  int main()
 7  {
 8     const double MAX_TEMP = 102.5;  // Maximum temperature
 9     double temperature;             // To hold the temperature
10
11     // Get the current temperature.
12     cout << "Enter the substance's Celsius temperature: ";
13     cin >> temperature;
14
15     // As long as necessary, instruct the technician
16     // to adjust the thermostat.
17     while (temperature > MAX_TEMP)
18     {
19        cout << "The temperature is too high. Turn the\n";
20        cout << "thermostat down and wait 5 minutes.\n";
21        cout << "Then take the Celsius temperature again\n";
22        cout << "and enter it here: ";
23        cin >> temperature;
24     }
25
26     // Remind the technician to check the temperature
27     // again in 15 minutes.
28     cout << "The temperature is acceptable.\n";
29     cout << "Check it again in 15 minutes.\n";
30
31     return 0;
32  }
```

Program Output with Example Input Shown in Bold
```
Enter the substance's Celsius temperature: 104.7 [Enter]
The temperature is too high. Turn the
thermostat down and wait 5 minutes.
Then take the Celsius temperature again
and enter it here: 103.2 [Enter]
The temperature is too high. Turn the
thermostat down and wait 5 minutes.
Then take the Celsius temperature again
and enter it here: 102.1 [Enter]
The temperature is acceptable.
Check it again in 15 minutes.
```

5.3

Using the `while` Loop for Input Validation

CONCEPT: The `while` loop can be used to create input routines that repeat until acceptable data is entered.

Perhaps the most famous saying of the computer industry is "garbage in, garbage out." The integrity of a program's output is only as good as its input, so you should try to make sure garbage does not go into your programs. *Input validation* is the process of inspecting data given to a program by the user and determining if it is valid. A good program should give clear instructions about the kind of input that is acceptable, and not assume the user has followed those instructions.

The `while` loop is especially useful for validating input. If an invalid value is entered, a loop can require that the user re-enter it as many times as necessary. For example, the following loop asks for a number in the range of 1 through 100:

```cpp
cout << "Enter a number in the range 1-100: ";
cin >> number;
while (number < 1 || number > 100)
{
    cout << "ERROR: Enter a value in the range 1-100: ";
    cin >> number;
}
```

This code first allows the user to enter a number. This takes place just before the loop. If the input is valid, the loop will not execute. If the input is invalid, however, the loop will display an error message and require the user to enter another number. The loop will continue to execute until the user enters a valid number. The general logic of performing input validation is shown in Figure 5-4.

Figure 5-4

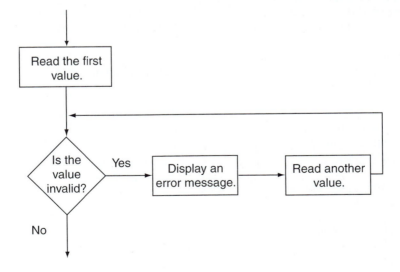

The read operation that takes place just before the loop is called a *priming read*. It provides the first value for the loop to test. Subsequent values are obtained by the loop.

Program 5-5 calculates the number of soccer teams a youth league may create, based on a given number of players and a maximum number of players per team. The program uses `while` loops (in lines 25 through 34 and lines 41 through 46) to validate the user's input.

Program 5-5

```
 1  // This program calculates the number of soccer teams
 2  // that a youth league may create from the number of
 3  // available players. Input validation is demonstrated
 4  // with while loops.
 5  #include <iostream>
 6  using namespace std;
 7
 8  int main()
 9  {
10     // Constants for minimum and maximum players
11     const int MIN_PLAYERS = 9,
12               MAX_PLAYERS = 15;
13
14     // Variables
15     int players,      // Number of available players
16         teamPlayers,  // Number of desired players per team
17         numTeams,     // Number of teams
18         leftOver;     // Number of players left over
19
20     // Get the number of players per team.
21     cout << "How many players do you wish per team? ";
22     cin >> teamPlayers;
23
24     // Validate the input.
25     while (teamPlayers < MIN_PLAYERS || teamPlayers > MAX_PLAYERS)
26     {
27        // Explain the error.
28        cout << "You should have at least " << MIN_PLAYERS
29             << " but no more than " << MAX_PLAYERS << " per team.\n";
30
31        // Get the input again.
32        cout << "How many players do you wish per team? ";
33        cin >> teamPlayers;
34     }
35
36     // Get the number of players available.
37     cout << "How many players are available? ";
38     cin >> players;
39
40     // Validate the input.
41     while (players <= 0)
42     {
43        // Get the input again.
44        cout << "Please enter 0 or greater: ";
45        cin >> players;
46     }
47
```

```
48      // Calculate the number of teams.
49      numTeams = players / teamPlayers;
50
51      // Calculate the number of leftover players.
52      leftOver = players % teamPlayers;
53
54      // Display the results.
55      cout << "There will be " << numTeams << " teams with "
56          << leftOver << " players left over.\n";
57      return 0;
58 }
```

Program Output with Example Input Shown in Bold
How many players do you wish per team? **4 [Enter]**
You should have at least 9 but no more than 15 per team.
How many players do you wish per team? **12 [Enter]**
How many players are available? **–142 [Enter]**
Please enter 0 or greater: **142 [Enter]**
There will be 11 teams with 10 players left over.

 Checkpoint

myprogramminglab *www.myprogramminglab.com*

5.2   Write an input validation loop that asks the user to enter a number in the range of 10 through 25.

5.3   Write an input validation loop that asks the user to enter 'Y', 'y', 'N', or 'n'.

5.4   Write an input validation loop that asks the user to enter "Yes" or "No".

5.4 Counters

CONCEPT: A counter is a variable that is regularly incremented or decremented each time a loop iterates.

Sometimes it's important for a program to control or keep track of the number of iterations a loop performs. For example, Program 5-6 displays a table consisting of the numbers 1 through 10 and their squares, so its loop must iterate 10 times.

Program 5-6

```
1 // This program displays a list of numbers and
2 // their squares.
3 #include <iostream>
4 using namespace std;
5
6 int main()
7 {
8     const int MIN_NUMBER = 1,   // Starting number to square
9               MAX_NUMBER = 10;  // Maximum number to square
10
```

(program continues)

Program 5-6 *(continued)*

```cpp
11     int num = MIN_NUMBER;          // Counter
12
13     cout << "Number Number Squared\n";
14     cout << "----------------------\n";
15     while (num <= MAX_NUMBER)
16     {
17         cout << num << "\t\t" << (num * num) << endl;
18         num++; //Increment the counter.
19     }
20     return 0;
21 }
```

Program Output

```
Number Number Squared
--------------------
1          1
2          4
3          9
4          16
5          25
6          36
7          49
8          64
9          81
10         100
```

In Program 5-6, the variable num, which starts at 1, is incremented each time through the loop. When num reaches 11 the loop stops. num is used as a *counter* variable, which means it is regularly incremented in each iteration of the loop. In essence, num keeps count of the number of iterations the loop has performed.

NOTE: It's important that num be properly initialized. Remember, variables defined inside a function have no guaranteed starting value.

5.5 **The do-while Loop**

CONCEPT: The do-while loop is a posttest loop, which means its expression is tested after each iteration.

The do-while loop looks something like an inverted while loop. Here is the do-while loop's format when the body of the loop contains only a single statement:

```cpp
do
    statement;
while (expression);
```

Here is the format of the do-while loop when the body of the loop contains multiple statements:

```
do
{
    statement;
    statement;
    // Place as many statements here
    // as necessary.
} while (expression);
```

NOTE: The do-while loop must be terminated with a semicolon.

The do-while loop is a *posttest* loop. This means it does not test its expression until it has completed an iteration. As a result, the do-while loop always performs at least one iteration, even if the expression is false to begin with. This differs from the behavior of a while loop, which you will recall is a pretest loop. For example, in the following while loop the cout statement will not execute at all:

```
int x = 1;
while (x < 0)
    cout << x << endl;
```

But the cout statement in the following do-while loop will execute once because the do-while loop does not evaluate the expression x < 0 until the end of the iteration.

```
int x = 1;
do
    cout << x << endl;
while (x < 0);
```

Figure 5-5 illustrates the logic of the do-while loop.

Figure 5-5

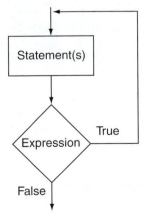

You should use the do-while loop when you want to make sure the loop executes at least once. For example, Program 5-7 averages a series of three test scores for a student. After the average is displayed, it asks the user if he or she wants to average another set of test scores. The program repeats as long as the user enters Y for yes.

Program 5-7

```cpp
 1   // This program averages 3 test scores. It repeats as
 2   // many times as the user wishes.
 3   #include <iostream>
 4   using namespace std;
 5
 6   int main()
 7   {
 8      int score1, score2, score3; // Three scores
 9      double average;             // Average score
10      char again;                 // To hold Y or N input
11
12      do
13      {
14         // Get three scores.
15         cout << "Enter 3 scores and I will average them: ";
16         cin >> score1 >> score2 >> score3;
17
18         // Calculate and display the average.
19         average = (score1 + score2 + score3) / 3.0;
20         cout << "The average is " << average << ".\n";
21
22         // Does the user want to average another set?
23         cout << "Do you want to average another set? (Y/N) ";
24         cin >> again;
25      } while (again == 'Y' || again == 'y');
26      return 0;
27   }
```

Program Output with Example Input Shown in Bold
```
Enter 3 scores and I will average them: 80 90 70 [Enter]
The average is 80.
Do you want to average another set? (Y/N) y [Enter]
Enter 3 scores and I will average them: 60 75 88 [Enter]
The average is 74.3333.
Do you want to average another set? (Y/N) n [Enter]
```

When this program was written, the programmer had no way of knowing the number of times the loop would iterate. This is because the loop asks the user if he or she wants to repeat the process. This type of loop is known as a *user-controlled loop*, because it allows the user to decide the number of iterations.

Using `do-while` with Menus

The `do-while` loop is a good choice for repeating a menu. Recall Program 4-27, which displayed a menu of health club packages. Program 5-8 is a modification of that program which uses a `do-while` loop to repeat the program until the user selects item 4 from the menu.

Program 5-8

```
1  // This program displays a menu and asks the user to make a
2  // selection. A do-while loop repeats the program until the
3  // user selects item 4 from the menu.
4  #include <iostream>
5  #include <iomanip>
6  using namespace std;
7
8  int main()
9  {
10     // Constants for menu choices
11     const int ADULT_CHOICE = 1,
12               CHILD_CHOICE = 2,
13               SENIOR_CHOICE = 3,
14               QUIT_CHOICE = 4;
15
16     // Constants for membership rates
17     const double ADULT = 40.0,
18                  CHILD = 20.0,
19                  SENIOR = 30.0;
20
21     // Variables
22     int choice;        // Menu choice
23     int months;        // Number of months
24     double charges;    // Monthly charges
25
26     // Set up numeric output formatting.
27     cout << fixed << showpoint << setprecision(2);
28
29     do
30     {
31        // Display the menu.
32        cout << "\n\t\tHealth Club Membership Menu\n\n"
33             << "1. Standard Adult Membership\n"
34             << "2. Child Membership\n"
35             << "3. Senior Citizen Membership\n"
36             << "4. Quit the Program\n\n"
37             << "Enter your choice: ";
38        cin >> choice;
39
40        // Validate the menu selection.
41        while (choice < ADULT_CHOICE || choice > QUIT_CHOICE)
42        {
43           cout << "Please enter a valid menu choice: ";
44           cin >> choice;
45        }
46
47        // Process the user's choice.
48        if (choice != QUIT_CHOICE)
49        {
50           // Get the number of months.
51           cout << "For how many months? ";
52           cin >> months;
53
```

(program continues)

Program 5-8 *(continued)*

```
54          // Respond to the user's menu selection.
55          switch (choice)
56          {
57             case ADULT_CHOICE:
58                charges = months * ADULT;
59                break;
60             case CHILD_CHOICE:
61                charges = months * CHILD;
62                break;
63             case SENIOR_CHOICE:
64                charges = months * SENIOR;
65          }
66
67          // Display the monthly charges.
68          cout << "The total charges are $"
69             << charges << endl;
70       }
71    } while (choice != QUIT_CHOICE);
72    return 0;
73 }
```

Program Output with Example Input Shown in Bold

```
           Health Club Membership Menu

1. Standard Adult Membership
2. Child Membership
3. Senior Citizen Membership
4. Quit the Program

Enter your choice: 1 [Enter]
For how many months? 12 [Enter]
The total charges are $480.00

           Health Club Membership Menu

1. Standard Adult Membership
2. Child Membership
3. Senior Citizen Membership
4. Quit the Program

Enter your choice: 4 [Enter]
Program ending.
```

 ## Checkpoint

myprogramminglab *www.myprogramminglab.com*

5.5 What will the following program segments display?

```
A) int count = 10;
   do
   {
       cout << "Hello World\n";
       count++;
   } while (count < 1);
```

```
B)  int v = 10;
    do
        cout << v << endl;
    while (v < 5);
C)  int count = 0, number = 0, limit = 4;
    do
    {
        number += 2;
        count++;
    } while (count < limit);
    cout << number << " " << count << endl;
```

5.6 The for Loop

CONCEPT: The for loop is ideal for performing a known number of iterations.

In general, there are two categories of loops: conditional loops and count-controlled loops. A *conditional loop* executes as long as a particular condition exists. For example, an input validation loop executes as long as the input value is invalid. When you write a conditional loop, you have no way of knowing the number of times it will iterate.

VideoNote
The for
Loop

Sometimes you know the exact number of iterations that a loop must perform. A loop that repeats a specific number of times is known as a *count-controlled loop*. For example, if a loop asks the user to enter the sales amounts for each month in the year, it will iterate twelve times. In essence, the loop counts to twelve and asks the user to enter a sales amount each time it makes a count. A count-controlled loop must possess three elements:

1. It must initialize a counter variable to a starting value.

2. It must test the counter variable by comparing it to a maximum value. When the counter variable reaches its maximum value, the loop terminates.

3. It must update the counter variable during each iteration. This is usually done by incrementing the variable.

Count-controlled loops are so common that C++ provides a type of loop specifically for them. It is known as the for loop. The for loop is specifically designed to initialize, test, and update a counter variable. Here is the format of the for loop when it is used to repeat a single statement:

```
for (initialization; test; update)
    statement;
```

The format of the for loop when it is used to repeat a block is

```
for (initialization; test; update)
{
    statement;
    statement;
    // Place as many statements here
    // as necessary.
}
```

The first line of the for loop is the *loop header.* After the key word for, there are three expressions inside the parentheses, separated by semicolons. (Notice there is not a semicolon after the third expression.) The first expression is the *initialization expression.* It is normally used to initialize a counter variable to its starting value. This is the first action performed by the loop, and it is only done once. The second expression is the *test expression.* This is an expression that controls the execution of the loop. As long as this expression is true, the body of the for loop will repeat. The for loop is a pretest loop, so it evaluates the test expression before each iteration. The third expression is the *update expression.* It executes at the end of each iteration. Typically, this is a statement that increments the loop's counter variable.

Here is an example of a simple for loop that prints "Hello" five times:

```
for (count = 0; count < 5; count++)
    cout << "Hello" << endl;
```

In this loop, the initialization expression is count = 0, the test expression is count < 5, and the update expression is count++. The body of the loop has one statement, which is the cout statement. Figure 5-6 illustrates the sequence of events that takes place during the loop's execution. Notice that Steps 2 through 4 are repeated as long as the test expression is true.

Figure 5-6

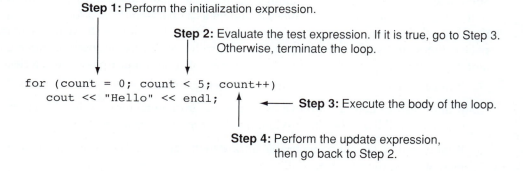

Step 1: Perform the initialization expression.

Step 2: Evaluate the test expression. If it is true, go to Step 3. Otherwise, terminate the loop.

```
for (count = 0; count < 5; count++)
    cout << "Hello" << endl;
```

Step 3: Execute the body of the loop.

Step 4: Perform the update expression, then go back to Step 2.

Figure 5-7 shows the loop's logic in the form of a flowchart.

Figure 5-7

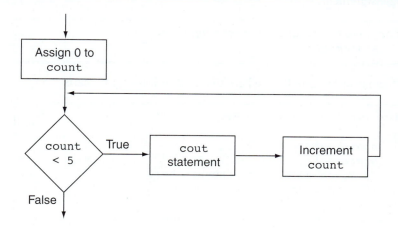

Notice how the counter variable, count, is used to control the number of times that the loop iterates. During the execution of the loop, this variable takes on the values 1 through 5, and when the test expression count < 5 is false, the loop terminates. Also notice that in this example the count variable is used only in the loop header, to control the number of loop iterations. It is not used for any other purpose. It is also possible to use the counter variable within the body of the loop. For example, look at the following code:

```
for (number = 1; number <= 10; number++)
    cout << number << " " << endl;
```

The counter variable in this loop is number. In addition to controlling the number of iterations, it is also used in the body of the loop. This loop will produce the following output:

```
1 2 3 4 5 6 7 8 9 10
```

As you can see, the loop displays the contents of the number variable during each iteration. Program 5-9 shows another example of a for loop that uses its counter variable within the body of the loop. This is yet another program that displays a table showing the numbers 1 through 10 and their squares.

Program 5-9

```cpp
 1  // This program displays the numbers 1 through 10 and
 2  // their squares.
 3  #include <iostream>
 4  using namespace std;
 5
 6  int main()
 7  {
 8      const int MIN_NUMBER = 1,    // Starting value
 9                MAX_NUMBER = 10;   // Ending value
10      int num;
11
12      cout << "Number Number Squared\n";
13      cout << "------------------------\n";
14
15      for (num = MIN_NUMBER; num <= MAX_NUMBER; num++)
16          cout << num << "\t\t" << (num * num) << endl;
17
18      return 0;
19  }
```

Program Output

```
Number Number Squared
--------------------
1            1
2            4
3            9
4            16
5            25
6            36
7            49
8            64
9            81
10           100
```

Figure 5-8 illustrates the sequence of events performed by this for loop, and Figure 5-9 shows the logic of the loop as a flowchart.

Figure 5-8

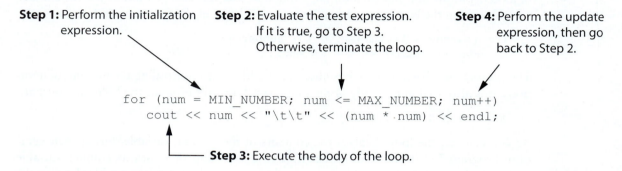

Step 1: Perform the initialization expression.

Step 2: Evaluate the test expression. If it is true, go to Step 3. Otherwise, terminate the loop.

Step 4: Perform the update expression, then go back to Step 2.

```
for (num = MIN_NUMBER; num <= MAX_NUMBER; num++)
    cout << num << "\t\t" << (num * num) << endl;
```

Step 3: Execute the body of the loop.

Figure 5-9

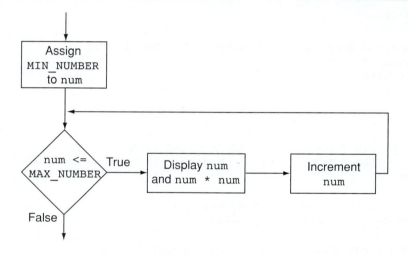

Using the `for` Loop Instead of `while` or `do-while`

You should use the `for` loop instead of the `while` or `do-while` loop in any situation that clearly requires an initialization, uses a false condition to stop the loop, and requires an update to occur at the end of each loop iteration. Program 5-9 is a perfect example. It requires that the num variable be initialized to 1, it stops the loop when num is greater than 10, and it increments num at the end of each loop iteration.

Recall that when we first introduced the idea of a counter variable we examined Program 5-6, which uses a `while` loop to display the table of numbers and their squares. Because the loop in that program requires an initialization, uses a false test expression to stop, and performs an increment at the end of each iteration, it can easily be converted to a `for` loop. Figure 5-10 shows how the `while` loop in Program 5-6 and the `for` loop in Program 5-9 each have initialization, test, and update expressions.

Figure 5-10

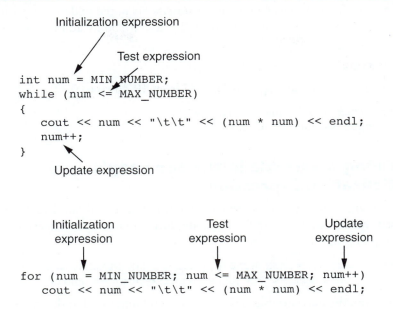

The `for` Loop Is a Pretest Loop

Because the `for` loop tests its test expression before it performs an iteration, it is a pretest loop. It is possible to write a `for` loop in such a way that it will never iterate. Here is an example:

```
for (count = 11; count <= 10; count++)
    cout << "Hello" << endl;
```

Because the variable `count` is initialized to a value that makes the test expression false from the beginning, this loop terminates as soon as it begins.

Avoid Modifying the Counter Variable in the Body of the `for` Loop

Be careful not to place a statement that modifies the counter variable in the body of the `for` loop. All modifications of the counter variable should take place in the update expression, which is automatically executed at the end of each iteration. If a statement in the body of the loop also modifies the counter variable, the loop will probably not terminate when you expect it to. The following loop, for example, increments x twice for each iteration:

```
for (x = 1; x <= 10; x++)
{
    cout << x << endl;
    x++;    // Wrong!
}
```

Other Forms of the Update Expression

You are not limited to using increment statements in the update expression. Here is a loop that displays all the even numbers from 2 through 100 by adding 2 to its counter:

```
for (num = 2; num <= 100; num += 2)
    cout << num << endl;
```

And here is a loop that counts backward from 10 down to 0:

```
for (num = 10; num >= 0; num--)
    cout << num << endl;
```

Defining a Variable in the *for* Loop's Initialization Expression

Not only may the counter variable be initialized in the initialization expression, it may be defined there as well. The following code shows an example. This is a modified version of the loop in Program 5-9.

```
for (int num = MIN_NUMBER; num <= MAX_NUMBER; num++)
    cout << num << "\t\t" << (num * num) << endl;
```

In this loop, the num variable is both defined and initialized in the initialization expression. If the counter variable is used only in the loop, it makes sense to define it in the loop header. This makes the variable's purpose more clear.

When a variable is defined in the initialization expression of a for loop, the scope of the variable is limited to the loop. This means you cannot access the variable in statements outside the loop. For example, the following program segment will not compile because the last cout statement cannot access the variable count.

```
for (int count = 1; count <= 10; count++)
    cout << count << endl;
cout << "count is now " << count << endl;    // ERROR!
```

Creating a User Controlled *for* Loop

Sometimes you want the user to determine the maximum value of the counter variable in a for loop, and therefore determine the number of times the loop iterates. For example, look at Program 5-10. This is another program that displays a list of numbers and their squares. Instead of displaying the numbers 1 through 10, this program allows the user to enter the minimum and maximum values to display.

Program 5-10

```
1  // This program demonstrates a user controlled for loop.
2  #include <iostream>
3  using namespace std;
4
5  int main()
6  {
7     int minNumber,    // Starting number to square
8         maxNumber;    // Maximum number to square
9
```

```
10       // Get the minimum and maximum values to display.
11       cout << "I will display a table of numbers and "
12            << "their squares.\n"
13            << "Enter the starting number: ";
14       cin >> minNumber;
15       cout << "Enter the ending number: ";
16       cin >> maxNumber;
17
18       // Display the table.
19       cout << "Number Number Squared\n"
20            << "------------------------\n";
21
22       for (int num = minNumber; num <= maxNumber; num++)
23          cout << num << "\t\t" << (num * num) << endl;
24
25       return 0;
26  }
```

Program Output with Example Input Shown in Bold
```
I will display a table of numbers and their squares.
Enter the starting number: 6 [Enter]
Enter the ending number: 12 [Enter]

Number Number Squared
--------------------
6            36
7            49
8            64
9            81
10           100
11           121
12           144
```

Before the loop, the code in lines 11 through 16 asks the user to enter the starting and ending numbers. These values are stored in the minNumber and maxNumber variables. These values are used in the for loop's initialization and test expressions:

```
for (int num = minNumber; num <= maxNumber; num++)
```

In this loop, the num variable takes on the values from maxNumber through maxValue, and then the loop terminates.

Using Multiple Statements in the Initialization and Update Expressions

It is possible to execute more than one statement in the initialization expression and the update expression. When using multiple statements in either of these expressions, simply separate the statements with commas. For example, look at the loop in the following code, which has two statements in the initialization expression.

```cpp
int x, y;
for (x = 1, y = 1; x <= 5; x++)
{
   cout << x << " plus " << y
        << " equals " << (x + y)
        << endl;
}
```

This loop's initialization expression is

```cpp
x = 1, y = 1
```

This initializes two variables, x and y. The output produced by this loop is

```
1 plus 1 equals 2
2 plus 1 equals 3
3 plus 1 equals 4
4 plus 1 equals 5
5 plus 1 equals 6
```

We can further modify the loop to execute two statements in the update expression. Here is an example:

```cpp
int x, y;
for (x = 1, y = 1; x <= 5; x++, y++)
{
    cout << x << " plus " << y
         << " equals " << (x + y)
         << endl;
}
```

The loop's update expression is

```cpp
x++, y++
```

This update expression increments both the x and y variables. The output produced by this loop is

```
1 plus 1 equals 2
2 plus 2 equals 4
3 plus 3 equals 6
4 plus 4 equals 8
5 plus 5 equals 10
```

Connecting multiple statements with commas works well in the initialization and update expressions, but do *not* try to connect multiple expressions this way in the test expression. If you wish to combine multiple expressions in the test expression, you must use the && or || operators.

Omitting the `for` Loop's Expressions

The initialization expression may be omitted from inside the for loop's parentheses if it has already been performed or no initialization is needed. Here is an example of the loop in Program 5-10 with the initialization being performed prior to the loop:

```cpp
int num = 1;
for ( ; num <= maxValue; num++)
   cout << num << "\t\t" << (num * num) << endl;
```

You may also omit the update expression if it is being performed elsewhere in the loop or if none is needed. Although this type of code is not recommended, the following for loop works just like a while loop:

```
int num = 1;
for ( ; num <= maxValue; )
{
    cout << num << "\t\t" << (num * num) << endl;
    num++;
}
```

You can even go so far as to omit all three expressions from the for loop's parentheses. Be warned, however, that if you leave out the test expression, the loop has no built-in way of terminating. Here is an example:

```
for ( ; ; )
    cout << "Hello World\n";
```

Because this loop has no way of stopping, it will display "Hello World\n" forever (or until something interrupts the program).

In the Spotlight:

Designing a Count-Controlled Loop with the for Statement

Your friend Amanda just inherited a European sports car from her uncle. Amanda lives in the United States, and she is afraid she will get a speeding ticket because the car's speedometer indicates kilometers per hour. She has asked you to write a program that displays a table of speeds in kilometers per hour with their values converted to miles per hour. The formula for converting kilometers per hour to miles per hour is:

$MPH = KPH * 0.6214$

In the formula, *MPH* is the speed in miles per hour and *KPH* is the speed in kilometers per hour.

The table that your program displays should show speeds from 60 kilometers per hour through 130 kilometers per hour, in increments of 10, along with their values converted to miles per hour. The table should look something like this:

KPH	MPH
60	37.3
70	43.5
80	49.7
etc. . . .	
130	80.8

After thinking about this table of values, you decide that you will write a for loop that uses a counter variable to hold the kilometer-per-hour speeds. The counter's starting value will be 60, its ending value will be 130, and you will add 10 to the counter variable after each iteration. Inside the loop you will use the counter variable to calculate a speed in miles-per-hour. Program 5-11 shows the code.

Program 5-11

```cpp
 1 // This program converts the speeds 60 kph through
 2 // 130 kph (in 10 kph increments) to mph.
 3 #include <iostream>
 4 #include <iomanip>
 5 using namespace std;
 6
 7 int main()
 8 {
 9    // Constants for the speeds
10    const int START_KPH = 60,   // Starting speed
11              END_KPH = 130,    // Ending speed
12              INCREMENT = 10;   // Speed increment
13
14    // Constant for the conversion factor
15    const double CONVERSION_FACTOR = 0.6214;
16
17    // Variables
18    int kph;        // To hold speeds in kph
19    double mph;     // To hold speeds in mph
20
21    // Set the numeric output formatting.
22    cout << fixed << showpoint << setprecision(1);
23
24    // Display the table headings.
25    cout << "KPH\tMPH\n";
26    cout << "--------------\n";
27
28    // Display the speeds.
29    for (kph = START_KPH; kph <= END_KPH; kph += INCREMENT)
30    {
31       // Calculate mph
32       mph = kph * CONVERSION_FACTOR;
33
34       // Display the speeds in kph and mph.
35       cout << kph << "\t" << mph << endl;
36
37    }
38    return 0;
39 }
```

Program Output

```
KPH       MPH
--------------
60        37.3
70        43.5
80        49.7
90        55.9
100       62.1
110       68.4
120       74.6
130       80.8
```

Checkpoint

myprogramminglab *www.myprogramminglab.com*

5.6   Name the three expressions that appear inside the parentheses in the `for` loop's header.

5.7   You want to write a `for` loop that displays "I love to program" 50 times. Assume that you will use a counter variable named `count`.

A) What initialization expression will you use?

B) What test expression will you use?

C) What update expression will you use?

D) Write the loop.

5.8   What will the following program segments display?

A) ```
for (int count = 0; count < 6; count++)
    cout << (count + count);
```

B)  ```
for (int value = -5; value < 5; value++)
    cout << value;
```

C) ```
int x;
for (x = 5; x <= 14; x += 3)
    cout << x << endl;
cout << x << endl;
```

5.9    Write a `for` loop that displays your name 10 times.

5.10   Write a `for` loop that displays all of the odd numbers, 1 through 49.

5.11   Write a `for` loop that displays every fifth number, zero through 100.

## 5.7  Keeping a Running Total

**CONCEPT:** A *running total* is a sum of numbers that accumulates with each iteration of a loop. The variable used to keep the running total is called an *accumulator*.

Many programming tasks require you to calculate the total of a series of numbers. For example, suppose you are writing a program that calculates a business's total sales for a week. The program would read the sales for each day as input and calculate the total of those numbers.

Programs that calculate the total of a series of numbers typically use two elements:

- A loop that reads each number in the series.
- A variable that accumulates the total of the numbers as they are read.

The variable that is used to accumulate the total of the numbers is called an *accumulator*. It is often said that the loop keeps a *running total* because it accumulates the total as it reads each number in the series. Figure 5-11 shows the general logic of a loop that calculates a running total.
```

Figure 5-11   Logic for calculating a running total

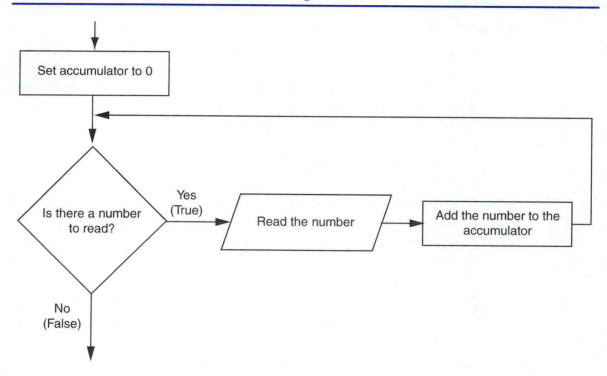

When the loop finishes, the accumulator will contain the total of the numbers that were read by the loop. Notice that the first step in the flowchart is to set the accumulator variable to 0. This is a critical step. Each time the loop reads a number, it adds it to the accumulator. If the accumulator starts with any value other than 0, it will not contain the correct total when the loop finishes.

Let's look at a program that calculates a running total. Program 5-12 calculates a company's total sales over a period of time by taking daily sales figures as input and calculating a running total of them as they are gathered.

Program 5-12

```
1   // This program takes daily sales figures over a period of time
2   // and calculates their total.
3   #include <iostream>
4   #include <iomanip>
5   using namespace std;
6
7   int main()
8   {
9       int days;              // Number of days
10      double total = 0.0;    // Accumulator, initialized with 0
11
12      // Get the number of days.
13      cout << "For how many days do you have sales figures? ";
```

```
14        cin >> days;
15
16        // Get the sales for each day and accumulate a total.
17        for (int count = 1; count <= days; count++)
18        {
19           double sales;
20           cout << "Enter the sales for day " << count << ": ";
21           cin >> sales;
22           total += sales;    // Accumulate the running total.
23        }
24
25        // Display the total sales.
26        cout << fixed << showpoint << setprecision(2);
27        cout << "The total sales are $" << total << endl;
28        return 0;
29  }
```

Program Output with Example Input Shown in Bold
For how many days do you have sales figures? **5 [Enter]**
Enter the sales for day 1: **489.32 [Enter]**
Enter the sales for day 2: **421.65 [Enter]**
Enter the sales for day 3: **497.89 [Enter]**
Enter the sales for day 4: **532.37 [Enter]**
Enter the sales for day 5: **506.92 [Enter]**
The total sales are $2448.15

Let's take a closer look at this program. Line 9 defines the days variable, which will hold the number of days that we have sales figures for. Line 10 defines the total variable, which will hold the total sales. Because total is an accumulator, it is initialized with 0.0.

In line 14 the user enters the number of days that he or she has sales figures for. The number is assigned to the days variable. Next, the for loop in lines 17 through 23 executes. In the loop's initialization expression, in line 17, the variable count is defined and initialized with 1. The test expression specifies the loop will repeat as long as count is less than or equal to days. The update expression increments count by one at the end of each loop iteration.

Line 19 defines a variable named sales. Because the variable is defined in the body of the loop, its scope is limited to the loop. During each loop iteration, the user enters the amount of sales for a specific day, which is assigned to the sales variable. This is done in line 21. Then, in line 22 the value of sales is added to the existing value in the total variable. (Note that line 22 does *not* assign sales to total, but *adds* sales to total. Put another way, this line increases total by the amount in sales.)

Because total was initially assigned 0.0, after the first iteration of the loop, total will be set to the same value as sales. After each subsequent iteration, total will be increased by the amount in sales. After the loop has finished, total will contain the total of all the daily sales figures entered. Now it should be clear why we assigned 0.0 to total before the loop executed. If total started at any other value, the total would be incorrect.

5.8 Sentinels

> **CONCEPT:** A *sentinel* is a special value that marks the end of a list of values.

Program 5-12, in the previous section, requires the user to know in advance the number of days he or she wishes to enter sales figures for. Sometimes the user has a list that is very long and doesn't know how many items there are. In other cases, the user might be entering several lists and it is impractical to require that every item in every list be counted.

A technique that can be used in these situations is to ask the user to enter a sentinel at the end of the list. A *sentinel* is a special value that cannot be mistaken as a member of the list and signals that there are no more values to be entered. When the user enters the sentinel, the loop terminates.

Program 5-13 calculates the total points earned by a soccer team over a series of games. It allows the user to enter the series of game points, then -1 to signal the end of the list.

Program 5-13

```
1   // This program calculates the total number of points a
2   // soccer team has earned over a series of games. The user
3   // enters a series of point values, then -1 when finished.
4   #include <iostream>
5   using namespace std;
6
7   int main()
8   {
9      int game = 1,    // Game counter
10         points,       // To hold a number of points
11         total = 0;    // Accumulator
12
13     cout << "Enter the number of points your team has earned\n";
14     cout << "so far in the season, then enter -1 when finished.\n\n";
15     cout << "Enter the points for game " << game << ": ";
16     cin >> points;
17
18     while (points != -1)
19     {
20        total += points;
21        game++;
22        cout << "Enter the points for game " << game << ": ";
23        cin >> points;
24     }
25     cout << "\nThe total points are " << total << endl;
26     return 0;
27  }
```

Program Output with Example Input Shown in Bold
```
Enter the number of points your team has earned
so far in the season, then enter -1 when finished.

Enter the points for game 1: 7 [Enter]
Enter the points for game 2: 9 [Enter]
Enter the points for game 3: 4 [Enter]
Enter the points for game 4: 6 [Enter]
Enter the points for game 5: 8 [Enter]
Enter the points for game 6: -1 [Enter]

The total points are 34
```

The value −1 was chosen for the sentinel in this program because it is not possible for a team to score negative points. Notice that this program performs a priming read in line 18 to get the first value. This makes it possible for the loop to immediately terminate if the user enters −1 as the first value. Also note that the sentinel value is not included in the running total.

 ### Checkpoint

myprogramminglab *www.myprogramminglab.com*

5.12   Write a for loop that repeats seven times, asking the user to enter a number. The loop should also calculate the sum of the numbers entered.

5.13   In the following program segment, which variable is the counter variable and which is the accumulator?

```
int a, x, y = 0;
for (x = 0; x < 10; x++)
{
    cout << "Enter a number: ";
    cin >> a;
    y += a;
}
cout << "The sum of those numbers is " << y << endl;
```

5.14   Why should you be careful when choosing a sentinel value?

5.15   How would you modify Program 5-13 so any negative value is a sentinel?

5.9

Focus on Software Engineering: Deciding Which Loop to Use

CONCEPT: Although most repetitive algorithms can be written with any of the three types of loops, each works best in different situations.

Each of the three C++ loops is ideal to use in different situations. Here's a short summary of when each loop should be used.

- **The while loop.** The while loop is a conditional loop, which means it repeats as long as a particular condition exists. It is also a pretest loop, so it is ideal in situations where you do not want the loop to iterate if the condition is false from the beginning. For example, validating input that has been read and reading lists of data terminated by a sentinel value are good applications of the while loop.
- **The do-while loop.** The do-while loop is also a conditional loop. Unlike the while loop, however, do-while is a posttest loop. It is ideal in situations where you always want the loop to iterate at least once. The do-while loop is a good choice for repeating a menu.
- **The for loop.** The for loop is a pretest loop that has built-in expressions for initializing, testing, and updating. These expressions make it very convenient to use a counter variable to control the number of iterations that the loop performs. The initialization expression can initialize the counter variable to a starting value, the test expression can test the counter variable to determine whether it holds the maximum value, and the update expression can increment the counter variable. The for loop is ideal in situations where the exact number of iterations is known.

5.10 Nested Loops

CONCEPT: A loop that is inside another loop is called a *nested loop*.

A nested loop is a loop that appears inside another loop. A clock is a good example of something that works like a nested loop. The second hand, minute hand, and hour hand all spin around the face of the clock. The hour hand, however, only makes one revolution for every 12 of the minute hand's revolutions. And it takes 60 revolutions of the second hand for the minute hand to make one revolution. This means that for every complete revolution of the hour hand, the second hand has revolved 720 times.

Here is a program segment with a for loop that partially simulates a digital clock. It displays the seconds from 0 to 59:

```
cout << fixed << right;
cout.fill('0');
for (int seconds = 0; seconds < 60; seconds++)
    cout << setw(2) << seconds << endl;
```

NOTE: The fill member function of cout changes the fill character, which is a space by default. In the program segment above, the fill function causes a zero to be printed in front of all single digit numbers.

We can add a minutes variable and nest the loop above inside another loop that cycles through 60 minutes:

```
cout << fixed << right;
cout.fill('0');
for (int minutes = 0; minutes < 60; minutes++)
{
    for (int seconds = 0; seconds < 60; seconds++)
    {
```

```
            cout << setw(2) << minutes << ":";
            cout << setw(2) << seconds << endl;
        }
    }
```

To make the simulated clock complete, another variable and loop can be added to count the hours:

```
cout << fixed << right;
cout.fill('0');
for (int hours = 0; hours < 24; hours++)
{
    for (int minutes = 0; minutes < 60; minutes++)
    {
        for (int seconds = 0; seconds < 60; seconds++)
        {
            cout << setw(2) << hours << ":";
            cout << setw(2) << minutes << ":";
            cout << setw(2) << seconds << endl;
        }
    }
}
```

The output of the previous program segment follows:

```
00:00:00
00:00:01
00:00:02
    .    (The program will count through each second of 24 hours.)
    .
    .
23:59:59
```

The innermost loop will iterate 60 times for each iteration of the middle loop. The middle loop will iterate 60 times for each iteration of the outermost loop. When the outermost loop has iterated 24 times, the middle loop will have iterated 1,440 times and the innermost loop will have iterated 86,400 times!

The simulated clock example brings up a few points about nested loops:

- An inner loop goes through all of its iterations for each iteration of an outer loop.
- Inner loops complete their iterations faster than outer loops.
- To get the total number of iterations of a nested loop, multiply the number of iterations of all the loops.

Program 5-14 is another test-averaging program. It asks the user for the number of students and the number of test scores per student. A nested inner loop, in lines 26 through 33, asks for all the test scores for one student, iterating once for each test score. The outer loop in lines 23 through 37 iterates once for each student.

Program 5-14

```
 1 // This program averages test scores. It asks the user for the
 2 // number of students and the number of test scores per student.
 3 #include <iostream>
 4 #include <iomanip>
 5 using namespace std;
```

(program continues)

Program 5-14 *(continued)*

```cpp
 6
 7  int main()
 8  {
 9     int numStudents,  // Number of students
10         numTests;     // Number of tests per student
11     double total,     // Accumulator for total scores
12            average;   // Average test score
13
14     // Set up numeric output formatting.
15     cout << fixed << showpoint << setprecision(1);
16
17     // Get the number of students.
18     cout << "This program averages test scores.\n";
19     cout << "For how many students do you have scores? ";
20     cin >> numStudents;
21
22     // Get the number of test scores per student.
23     cout << "How many test scores does each student have? ";
24     cin >> numTests;
25
26     // Determine each student's average score.
27     for (int student = 1; student <= numStudents; student++)
28     {
29        total = 0;       // Initialize the accumulator.
30        for (int test = 1; test <= numTests; test++)
31        {
32           double score;
33           cout << "Enter score " << test << " for ";
34           cout << "student " << student << ": ";
35           cin >> score;
36           total += score;
37        }
38        average = total / numTests;
39        cout << "The average score for student " << student;
40        cout << " is " << average << ".\n\n";
41     }
42     return 0;
43  }
```

Program Output with Example Input Shown in Bold

```
This program averages test scores.
For how many students do you have scores? 2 [Enter]
How many test scores does each student have? 3 [Enter]
Enter score 1 for student 1: 84 [Enter]
Enter score 2 for student 1: 79 [Enter]
Enter score 3 for student 1: 97 [Enter]
The average score for student 1 is 86.7.

Enter score 1 for student 2: 92 [Enter]
Enter score 2 for student 2: 88 [Enter]
Enter score 3 for student 2: 94 [Enter]
The average score for student 2 is 91.3.
```

5.11 Using Files for Data Storage

CONCEPT: When a program needs to save data for later use, it writes the data in a file. The data can then be read from the file at a later time.

The programs you have written so far require the user to reenter data each time the program runs, because data kept in variables and control properties is stored in RAM, and disappears once the program stops running. If a program is to retain data between the times it runs, it must have a way of saving it. Data is saved in a file, which is usually stored on a computer's disk. Once the data is saved in a file, it will remain there after the program stops running. Data that is stored in a file can be then retrieved and used at a later time.

Most of the commercial software that you use on a day-to-day basis store data in files. The following are a few examples.

- **Word processors:** Word processing programs are used to write letters, memos, reports, and other documents. The documents are then saved in files so they can be edited and printed.
- **Image editors:** Image editing programs are used to draw graphics and edit images such as the ones that you take with a digital camera. The images that you create or edit with an image editor are saved in files.
- **Spreadsheets:** Spreadsheet programs are used to work with numerical data. Numbers and mathematical formulas can be inserted into the rows and columns of the spreadsheet. The spreadsheet can then be saved in a file for use later.
- **Games:** Many computer games keep data stored in files. For example, some games keep a list of player names with their scores stored in a file. These games typically display the players' names in order of their scores, from highest to lowest. Some games also allow you to save your current game status in a file so you can quit the game and then resume playing it later without having to start from the beginning.
- **Web browsers:** Sometimes when you visit a Web page, the browser stores a small file known as a *cookie* on your computer. Cookies typically contain information about the browsing session, such as the contents of a shopping cart.

Programs that are used in daily business operations rely extensively on files. Payroll programs keep employee data in files, inventory programs keep data about a company's products in files, accounting systems keep data about a company's financial operations in files, and so on.

Programmers usually refer to the process of saving data in a file as *writing data* to the file. When a piece of data is written to a file, it is copied from a variable in RAM to the file. This is illustrated in Figure 5-12. An *output file* is a file that data is written to. It is called an output file because the program stores output in it.

Figure 5-12 Writing data to a file

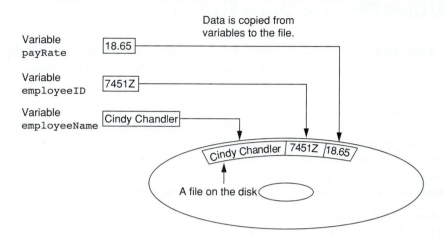

The process of retrieving data from a file is known as *reading data* from the file. When a piece of data is read from a file, it is copied from the file into a variable in RAM. Figure 5-13 illustrates this process. An *input file* is a file that data is read from. It is called an input file because the program gets input from the file.

Figure 5-13 Reading data from a file

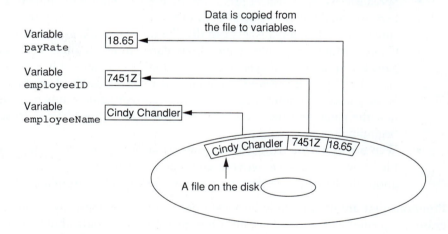

This section discusses ways to create programs that write data to files and read data from files. When a file is used by a program, three steps must be taken.

1. **Open the file**—Opening a file creates a connection between the file and the program. Opening an output file usually creates the file on the disk and allows the program to write data to it. Opening an input file allows the program to read data from the file.

2. **Process the file**—Data is either written to the file (if it is an output file) or read from the file (if it is an input file).

3. **Close the file**—After the program is finished using the file, the file must be closed. Closing a file disconnects the file from the program.

Types of Files

In general, there are two types of files: text and binary. A *text file* contains data that has been encoded as text, using a scheme such as ASCII or Unicode. Even if the file contains numbers, those numbers are stored in the file as a series of characters. As a result, the file may be opened and viewed in a text editor such as Notepad. A *binary file* contains data that has not been converted to text. Thus, you cannot view the contents of a binary file with a text editor. In this chapter we work only with text files. In Chapter 12 you will learn to work with binary files.

File Access Methods

There are two general ways to access data stored in a file: sequential access and direct access. When you work with a *sequential access file*, you access data from the beginning of the file to the end of the file. If you want to read a piece of data that is stored at the very end of the file, you have to read all of the data that comes before it—you cannot jump directly to the desired data. This is similar to the way cassette tape players work. If you want to listen to the last song on a cassette tape, you have to either fast-forward over all of the songs that come before it or listen to them. There is no way to jump directly to a specific song.

When you work with a *random access file* (also known as a *direct access file*), you can jump directly to any piece of data in the file without reading the data that comes before it. This is similar to the way a CD player or an MP3 player works. You can jump directly to any song that you want to listen to.

This chapter focuses on sequential access files. Sequential access files are easy to work with, and you can use them to gain an understanding of basic file operations. In Chapter 12 you will learn to work with random access files.

Filenames and File Stream Objects

Files on a disk are identified by a *filename*. For example, when you create a document with a word processor and then save the document in a file, you have to specify a filename. When you use a utility such as Windows Explorer to examine the contents of your disk, you see a list of filenames. Figure 5-14 shows how three files named cat.jpg, notes.txt, and resume.doc might be represented in Windows Explorer.

Figure 5-14   Three files

cat.jpg   notes.txt   resume.doc

Each operating system has its own rules for naming files. Many systems, including Windows, support the use of *filename extensions*, which are short sequences of characters that appear at the end of a filename preceded by a period (known as a "dot"). For example, the files depicted in Figure 5-14 have the extensions .jpg, .txt, and .doc. The extension usually indicates the type of data stored in the file. For example, the .jpg extension usually indicates that the file contains a graphic image that is compressed according to the JPEG image standard. The .txt extension usually indicates that the file contains text. The .doc extension usually indicates that the file contains a Microsoft Word document.

In order for a program to work with a file on the computer's disk, the program must create a file stream object in memory. A *file stream object* is an object that is associated with a specific file, and provides a way for the program to work with that file. It is called a "stream" object because a file can be thought of as a stream of data.

File stream objects work very much like the `cin` and `cout` objects. A stream of data may be sent to `cout`, which causes values to be displayed on the screen. A stream of data may be read from the keyboard by `cin`, and stored in variables. Likewise, streams of data may be sent to a file stream object, which writes the data to a file. When data is read from a file, the data flows from the file stream object that is associated with the file, into variables.

Setting Up a Program for File Input/Output

Just as `cin` and `cout` require the `iostream` file to be included in the program, C++ file access requires another header file. The file `fstream` contains all the declarations necessary for file operations. It is included with the following statement:

```
#include <fstream>
```

The `fstream` header file defines the data types `ofstream`, `ifstream`, and `fstream`. Before a C++ program can work with a file, it must define an object of one of these data types. The object will be "linked" with an actual file on the computer's disk, and the operations that may be performed on the file depend on which of these three data types you pick for the file stream object. Table 5-1 lists and describes the file stream data types.

Table 5-1

File Stream Data Type	Description
`ofstream`	Output file stream. You create an object of this data type when you want to create a file and write data to it.
`ifstream`	Input file stream. You create an object of this data type when you want to open an existing file and read data from it.
`fstream`	File stream. Objects of this data type can be used to open files for reading, writing, or both.

 NOTE: In this chapter we discuss only the `ofstream` and `ifstream` types. The `fstream` type is covered in Chapter 12.

Creating a File Object and Opening a File

Before data can be written to or read from a file, the following things must happen:

- A file stream object must be created
- The file must be opened and linked to the file stream object.

The following code shows an example of opening a file for input (reading).

```
ifstream inputFile;
inputFile.open("Customers.txt");
```

The first statement defines an `ifstream` object named `inputFile`. The second statement calls the object's `open` member function, passing the string `"Customers.txt"` as an argument. In this statement, the `open` member function opens the Customers.txt file and links it with the `inputFile` object. After this code executes, you will be able to use the `inputFile` object to read data from the Customers.txt file.

The following code shows an example of opening a file for output (writing).

```
ofstream outputFile;
outputFile.open("Employees.txt");
```

The first statement defines an `ofstream` object named `outputFile`. The second statement calls the object's `open` member function, passing the string `"Employees.txt"` as an argument. In this statement, the `open` member function creates the Employees.txt file and links it with the `outputFile` object. After this code executes, you will be able to use the `outputFile` object to write data to the Employees.txt file. It's important to remember that when you call an `ofstream` object's `open` member function, the specified file will be created. If the specified file already exists, it will be erased and a new file with the same name will be created.

Often, when opening a file, you will need to specify its path as well as its name. For example, on a Windows system the following statement opens the file `C:\data\inventory.txt`:

```
inputFile.open("C:\\data\\inventory.txt")
```

In this statement, the file `C:\data\inventory.txt` is opened and linked with `inputFile`.

 NOTE: Notice the use of two backslashes in the file's path. Two backslashes are needed to represent one backslash in a string literal.

It is possible to define a file stream object and open a file in one statement. Here is an example:

```
ifstream inputFile("Customers.txt");
```

This statement defines an `ifstream` object named `inputFile` and opens the Customer.txt file. Here is an example that defines an `ofstream` object named `outputFile` and opens the Employees.txt file:

```
ofstream outputFile("Employees.txt");
```

Closing a File

The opposite of opening a file is closing it. Although a program's files are automatically closed when the program shuts down, it is a good programming practice to write statements that close them. Here are two reasons a program should close files when it is finished using them:

- Most operating systems temporarily store data in a *file buffer* before it is written to a file. A file buffer is a small "holding section" of memory that file-bound data is first written to. When the buffer is filled, all the data stored there is written to the file. This technique improves the system's performance. Closing a file causes any unsaved data that may still be held in a buffer to be saved to its file. This means the data will be in the file if you need to read it later in the same program.

- Some operating systems limit the number of files that may be open at one time. When a program closes files that are no longer being used, it will not deplete more of the operating system's resources than necessary.

Calling the file stream object's `close` member function closes a file. Here is an example:

```
inputFile.close();
```

Writing Data to a File

You already know how to use the stream insertion operator (<<) with the cout object to write data to the screen. It can also be used with `ofstream` objects to write data to a file. Assuming `outputFile` is an `ofstream` object, the following statement demonstrates using the << operator to write a string literal to a file:

```
outputFile << "I love C++ programming\n";
```

This statement writes the string literal `"I love C++ programming\n"` to the file associated with `outputFile`. As you can see, the statement looks like a cout statement, except the name of the `ofstream` object name replaces cout. Here is a statement that writes both a string literal and the contents of a variable to a file:

```
outputFile << "Price: " << price << endl;
```

The statement above writes the stream of data to `outputFile` exactly as cout would write it to the screen: It writes the string `"Price: "`, followed by the value of the `price` variable, followed by a newline character.

Program 5-15 demonstrates opening a file, writing data to the file, and closing the file. After this code has executed, we can open the demofile.txt file using a text editor and look at its contents. Figure 5-15 shows how the file's contents will appear in Notepad.

Program 5-15

```cpp
 1   // This program writes data to a file.
 2   #include <iostream>
 3   #include <fstream>
 4   using namespace std;
 5
 6   int main()
 7   {
 8      ofstream outputFile;
 9      outputFile.open("demofile.txt");
10
11      cout << "Now writing data to the file.\n";
12
```

```
13      // Write four names to the file.
14      outputFile << "Bach\n";
15      outputFile << "Beethoven\n";
16      outputFile << "Mozart\n";
17      outputFile << "Schubert\n";
18
19      // Close the file
20      outputFile.close();
21      cout << "Done.\n";
22      return 0;
23   }
```

Program Screen Output

```
Now writing data to the file.
Done.
```

Figure 5-15

Notice that in lines 14 through 17 of Program 5-15, each string that was written to the file ends with a newline escape sequence (\n). The newline specifies the end of a line of text. Because a newline is written at the end of each string, the strings appear on separate lines when viewed in a text editor, as shown in Figure 5-15.

Program 5-16 shows what happens if we write the same four names without the \n escape sequence. Figure 5-16 shows the contents of the file that Program 5-16 creates. As you can see, all of the names appear on the same line in the file.

Program 5-16

```
1   // This program writes data to a single line in a file.
2   #include <iostream>
3   #include <fstream>
4   using namespace std;
5
6   int main()
7   {
8       ofstream outputFile;
9       outputFile.open("demofile.txt");
10
```

(program continues)

Program 5-16   *(continued)*

```
11      cout << "Now writing data to the file.\n";
12
13      // Write four names to the file.
14      outputFile << "Bach";
15      outputFile << "Beethoven";
16      outputFile << "Mozart";
17      outputFile << "Schubert";
18
19      // Close the file
20      outputFile.close();
21      cout << "Done.\n";
22      return 0;
23  }
```

Program Screen Output

```
Now writing data to the file.
Done.
```

Figure 5-16

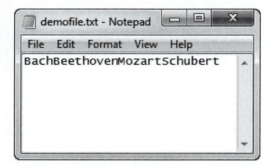

Program 5-17 shows another example. This program reads three numbers from the keyboard as input, and then saves those numbers in a file named Numbers.txt.

Program 5-17

```
1 // This program writes user input to a file.
2 #include <iostream>
3 #include <fstream>
4 using namespace std;
5
6 int main()
7 {
8    ofstream outputFile;
9    int number1, number2, number3;
10
11    // Open an output file.
12    outputFile.open("Numbers.txt");
13
```

```
14       // Get three numbers from the user.
15       cout << "Enter a number: ";
16       cin >> number1;
17       cout << "Enter another number: ";
18       cin >> number2;
19       cout << "One more time. Enter a number: ";
20       cin >> number3;
21
22       // Write the numbers to the file.
23       outputFile << number1 << endl;
24       outputFile << number2 << endl;
25       outputFile << number3 << endl;
26       cout << "The numbers were saved to a file.\n";
27
28       // Close the file
29       outputFile.close();
30       cout << "Done.\n";
31       return 0;
32 }
```

Program Screen Output with Example Input Shown in Bold

Enter a number: **100 [Enter]**
Enter another number: **200 [Enter]**
One more time. Enter a number: **300 [Enter]**
The numbers were saved to a file.
Done.

In Program 5-17, lines 23 through 25 write the contents of the number1, number2, and number3 variables to the file. Notice that the endl manipulator is sent to the outputFile object immediately after each item. Sending the endl manipulator causes a newline to be written to the file. Figure 5-17 shows the file's contents displayed in Notepad, using the example input values 100, 200, and 300. As you can see, each item appears on a separate line in the file because of the endl manipulators.

Figure 5-17

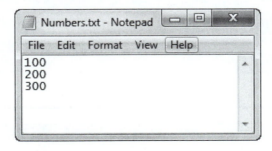

Program 5-18 shows an example that reads strings as input from the keyboard, and then writes those strings to a file. The program asks the user to enter the first names of three friends, and then it writes those names to a file named Friends.txt. Figure 5-18 shows an example of the Friends.txt file opened in Notepad.

Program 5-18

```cpp
1  // This program writes user input to a file.
2  #include <iostream>
3  #include <fstream>
4  #include <string>
5  using namespace std;
6
7  int main()
8  {
9     ofstream outputFile;
10    string name1, name2, name3;
11
12    // Open an output file.
13    outputFile.open("Friends.txt");
14
15    // Get the names of three friends.
16    cout << "Enter the names of three friends.\n";
17    cout << "Friend #1: ";
18    cin >> name1;
19    cout << "Friend #2: ";
20    cin >> name2;
21    cout << "Friend #3: ";
22    cin >> name3;
23
24    // Write the names to the file.
25    outputFile << name1 << endl;
26    outputFile << name2 << endl;
27    outputFile << name3 << endl;
28    cout << "The names were saved to a file.\n";
29
30    // Close the file
31    outputFile.close();
32    return 0;
33 }
```

Program Screen Output with Example Input Shown in Bold

```
Enter the names of three friends.
Friend #1: Joe [Enter]
Friend #2: Chris [Enter]
Friend #3: Geri [Enter]
The names were saved to a file.
```

Figure 5-18

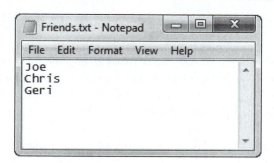

Reading Data from a File

VideoNote

Reading Data from a File

The >> operator not only reads user input from the cin object, but also data from a file. Assuming inputFile is an ifstream object, the following statement shows the >> operator reading data from the file into the variable name:

```
inputFile >> name;
```

Let's look at an example. Assume the file Friends.txt exists, and it contains the names shown in Figure 5-18. Program 5-19 opens the file, reads the names and displays them on the screen, and then closes the file.

Program 5-19

```
 1  // This program reads data from a file.
 2  #include <iostream>
 3  #include <fstream>
 4  #include <string>
 5  using namespace std;
 6
 7  int main()
 8  {
 9      ifstream inputFile;
10      string name;
11
12      inputFile.open("Friends.txt");
13      cout << "Reading data from the file.\n";
14
15      inputFile >> name;      // Read name 1 from the file
16      cout << name << endl;   // Display name 1
17
18      inputFile >> name;      // Read name 2 from the file
19      cout << name << endl;   // Display name 2
20
21      inputFile >> name;      // Read name 3 from the file
22      cout << name << endl;   // Display name 3
23
24      inputFile.close();      // Close the file
25      return 0;
26  }
```

Program Output

```
Reading data from the file.
Joe
Chris
Geri
```

The Read Position

When a file has been opened for input, the file stream object internally maintains a special value known as a *read position*. A file's read position marks the location of the next byte that will be read from the file. When an input file is opened, its read position is initially set to the first byte in the file. So, the first read operation extracts data starting at the first byte. As data is read from the file, the read position moves forward, toward the end of the file.

Let's see how this works with the example shown in Program 5-19. When the Friends.txt file is opened by the statement in line 12, the read position for the file will be positioned as shown in Figure 5-19.

Figure 5-19

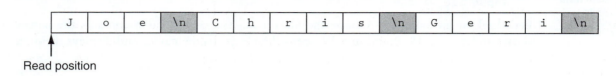

Keep in mind that when the >> operator extracts data from a file, it expects to read pieces of data that are separated by whitespace characters (spaces, tabs, or newlines). When the statement in line 15 executes, the >> operator reads data from the file's current read position, up to the \n character. The data that is read from the file is assigned to the name object. The \n character is also read from the file, but is not included as part of the data. So, the name object will hold the value "Joe" after this statement executes. The file's read position will then be at the location shown in Figure 5-20.

Figure 5-20

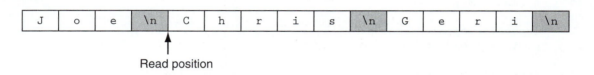

When the statement in line 18 executes, it reads the next item from the file, which is "Chris", and assigns that value to the name object. After this statement executes, the file's read position will be advanced to the next item, as shown in Figure 5-21.

Figure 5-21

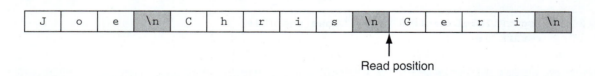

When the statement in line 21 executes, it reads the next item from the file, which is "Geri", and assigns that value to the name object. After this statement executes, the file's read position will be advanced to the end of the file, as shown in Figure 5-22.

Figure 5-22

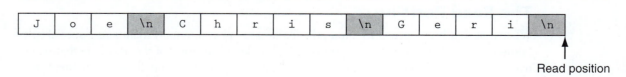

Reading Numeric Data From a Text File

Remember that when data is stored in a text file, it is encoded as text, using a scheme such as ASCII or Unicode. Even if the file contains numbers, those numbers are stored in the file as a series of characters. For example, suppose a text file contains numeric data, such as that shown in Figure 5-17. The numbers that you see displayed in the figure are stored in the file as the strings "10", "20", and "30". Fortunately, you can use the >> operator to read data such as this from a text file, into a numeric variable, and the >> operator will automatically convert the data to a numeric data type. Program 5-20 shows an example. It opens the file shown in Figure 5-23, reads the three numbers from the file into int variables, and calculates their sum.

Figure 5-23

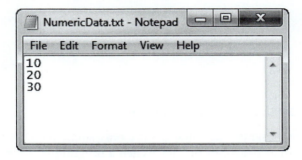

Program 5-20

```
 1 // This program reads numbers from a file.
 2 #include <iostream>
 3 #include <fstream>
 4 using namespace std;
 5
 6 int main()
 7 {
 8    ifstream inFile;
 9    int value1, value2, value3, sum;
10
11    // Open the file.
12    inFile.open("NumericData.txt");
13
14    // Read the three numbers from the file.
15    inFile >> value1;
16    inFile >> value2;
17    inFile >> value3;
18
19    // Close the file.
20    inFile.close();
21
```

(program continues)

Program 5-20 *(continued)*

```
22     // Calculate the sum of the numbers.
23     sum = value1 + value2 + value3;
24
25     // Display the three numbers.
26     cout << "Here are the numbers:\n"
27          << value1 << " " << value2
28          << " " << value3 << endl;
29
30     // Display the sum of the numbers.
31     cout << "Their sum is: " << sum << endl;
32     return 0;
33 }
```

Program Output

```
Here are the numbers:
10 20 30
Their sum is: 60
```

Using Loops to Process Files

Although some programs use files to store only small amounts of data, files are typically used to hold large collections of data. When a program uses a file to write or read a large amount of data, a loop is typically involved. For example, look at the code in Program 5-21. This program gets sales amounts for a series of days from the user and writes those amounts to a file named Sales.txt. The user specifies the number of days of sales data he or she needs to enter. In the sample run of the program, the user enters sales amounts for five days. Figure 5-24 shows the contents of the Sales.txt file containing the data entered by the user in the sample run.

Program 5-21

```
1 // This program reads data from a file.
2 #include <iostream>
3 #include <fstream>
4 using namespace std;
5
6 int main()
7 {
8    ofstream outputFile;   // File stream object
9    int numberOfDays;      // Number of days of sales
10   double sales;          // Sales amount for a day
11
12   // Get the number of days.
13   cout << "For how many days do you have sales? ";
14   cin >> numberOfDays;
15
```

```
16      // Open a file named Sales.txt.
17      outputFile.open("Sales.txt");
18
19      // Get the sales for each day and write it
20      // to the file.
21      for (int count = 1; count <= numberOfDays; count++)
22      {
23          // Get the sales for a day.
24          cout << "Enter the sales for day "
25              << count << ": ";
26          cin >> sales;
27
28          // Write the sales to the file.
29          outputFile << sales << endl;
30      }
31
32      // Close the file.
33      outputFile.close();
34      cout << "Data written to Sales.txt\n";
35      return 0;
36 }
```

Program Output (with Input Shown in Bold)

For how many days do you have sales? **5 [Enter]**
Enter the sales for day 1: **1000.00 [Enter]**
Enter the sales for day 2: **2000.00 [Enter]**
Enter the sales for day 3: **3000.00 [Enter]**
Enter the sales for day 4: **4000.00 [Enter]**
Enter the sales for day 5: **5000.00 [Enter]**
Data written to sales.txt.

Figure 5-24

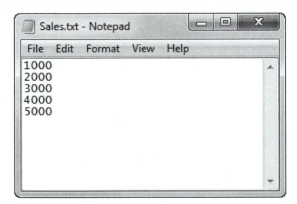

Detecting the End of the File

Quite often a program must read the contents of a file without knowing the number of items that are stored in the file. For example, suppose you need to write a program that displays all of the items in a file, but you do not know how many items the file contains.

You can open the file, and then use a loop to repeatedly read an item from the file and display it. However, an error will occur if the program attempts to read beyond the end of the file. The program needs some way of knowing when the end of the file has been reached so it will not try to read beyond it.

Fortunately, the >> operator not only reads data from a file, but also returns a true or false value indicating whether the data was successfully read or not. If the operator returns true, then a value was successfully read. If the operator returns false, it means that no value was read from the file.

Let's look at an example. A file named ListOfNumbers.txt, which is shown in Figure 5-25, contains a list of numbers. Without knowing how many numbers the file contains, Program 5-22 opens the file, reads all of the values it contains, and displays them.

Figure 5-25

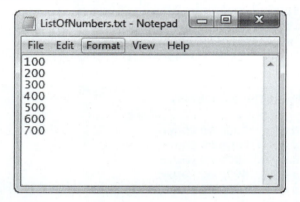

Program 5-22

```
 1 // This program reads data from a file.
 2 #include <iostream>
 3 #include <fstream>
 4 using namespace std;
 5
 6 int main()
 7 {
 8    ifstream inputFile;
 9    int number;
10
11    // Open the file.
12    inputFile.open("ListOfNumbers.txt");
13
14    // Read the numbers from the file and
15    // display them.
16    while (inputFile >> number)
17    {
18       cout << number << endl;
19    }
```

```
20
21    // Close the file.
22    inputFile.close();
23    return 0;
24 }
```

Program Output

```
100
200
300
400
500
600
700
```

Take a closer look at line 16:

```
while (inputFile >> number)
```

Notice that the statement that extracts data from the file is used as the Boolean expression in the `while` loop. It works like this:

- The expression `inputFile >> number` executes.
- If an item is successfully read from the file, the item is stored in the `number` variable, and the expression returns true to indicate that it succeeded. In that case, the statement in line 18 executes and the loop repeats.
- If there are no more items to read from the file, the expression `inputFile >> number` returns false, indicating that it did not read a value. In that case, the loop terminates.

Because the value returned from the `>>` operator controls the loop, it will read items from the file until the end of the file has been reached.

Testing for File Open Errors

Under certain circumstances, the open member function will not work. For example, the following code will fail if the file info.txt does not exist:

```
ifstream inputFile;
inputFile.open("info.txt");
```

There is a way to determine whether the open member function successfully opened the file. After you call the open member function, you can test the file stream object as if it were a Boolean expression. Program 5-23 shows an example.

Program 5-23

```
1 // This program tests for file open errors.
2 #include <iostream>
3 #include <fstream>
4 using namespace std;
5
```

(program continues)

Program 5-23   (continued)

```
 6 int main()
 7 {
 8    ifstream inputFile;
 9    int number;
10
11    // Open the file.
12    inputFile.open("BadListOfNumbers.txt");
13
14    // If the file successfully opened, process it.
15    if (inputFile)
16    {
17       // Read the numbers from the file and
18       // display them.
19       while (inputFile >> number)
20       {
21          cout << number << endl;
22       }
23
24       // Close the file.
25       inputFile.close();
26    }
27    else
28    {
29       // Display an error message.
30       cout << "Error opening the file.\n";
31    }
32    return 0;
33 }
```

Program Output (Assume BadListOfNumbers.txt does not exist)
```
Error opening the file.
```

Let's take a closer look at certain parts of the code. Line 12 calls the inputFile object's open member function to open the file ListOfNumbers.txt. Then the if statement in line 15 tests the value of the inputFile object as if it were a Boolean expression. When tested this way, the inputFile object will give a true value if the file was successfully opened. Otherwise it will give a false value. The example output shows this program will display an error message if it could not open the file.

Another way to detect a failed attempt to open a file is with the fail member function, as shown in the following code:

```
ifstream inputFile;
inputFile.open("customers.txt");
if (inputFile.fail())
{
   cout << "Error opening file.\n";
}
else
{
   // Process the file.
}
```

The `fail` member function returns true when an attempted file operation is unsuccessful. When using file I/O, you should always test the file stream object to make sure the file was opened successfully. If the file could not be opened, the user should be informed and appropriate action taken by the program.

Letting the User Specify a Filename

In each of the previous examples, the name of the file that is opened is hard-coded as a string literal into the program. In many cases, you will want the user to specify the name of a file for the program to open.

In standard C++, a file stream object's open member function will not accept a `string` object as an argument. The open member function requires that you pass the name of the file as a null-terminated string, which is also known as a *C-string*. String literals are stored in memory as null-terminated C-strings (which explains why you can pass them to the open function), but `string` objects are not.

Fortunately, `string` objects have a member function named `c_str` that returns the contents of the object formatted as a null-terminated C-string. Here is the general format of how you call the function:

```
stringObject.c_str()
```

In the general format, *stringObject* is the name of a `string` object. The `c_str` function returns the string that is stored in *stringObject* as a null-terminated C-string. Program 5-24 shows an example of how you can use the function. This is a modified version of Program 5-23. This version prompts the user to enter the name of the file. In line 15, the name that the user enters is stored in a `string` object named `filename`. In line 18, the value that is returned from `filename.c_str()` is passed as an argument to the open function.

Program 5-24

```cpp
 1  // This program lets the user enter a filename.
 2  #include <iostream>
 3  #include <string>
 4  #include <fstream>
 5  using namespace std;
 6
 7  int main()
 8  {
 9      ifstream inputFile;
10      string filename;
11      int number;
12
13      // Get the filename from the user.
14      cout << "Enter the filename: ";
15      cin >> filename;
16
17      // Open the file.
18      inputFile.open(filename.c_str());
19
20      // If the file successfully opened, process it.
21      if (inputFile)
```

(program continues)

Program 5-24   (continued)

```
22    {
23        // Read the numbers from the file and
24        // display them.
25        while (inputFile >> number)
26        {
27            cout << number << endl;
28        }
29
30        // Close the file.
31        inputFile.close();
32    }
33    else
34    {
35        // Display an error message.
36        cout << "Error opening the file.\n";
37    }
38    return 0;
39 }
```

Program Output with Example Input Shown in Bold
```
Enter the filename: ListOfNumbers.txt [Enter]
100
200
300
400
500
600
700
```

 Checkpoint

myprogramminglab *www.myprogramminglab.com*

5.16   What is an output file? What is an input file?

5.17   What three steps must be taken when a file is used by a program?

5.18   What is the difference between a text file and a binary file?

5.19   What is the difference between sequential access and random access?

5.20   What type of file stream object do you create if you want to write data to a file?

5.21   What type of file stream object do you create if you want to read data from a file?

5.22   Write a short program that uses a for loop to write the numbers 1 through 10 to a file.

5.23   Write a short program that opens the file created by the program you wrote for Checkpoint 5.22, reads all of the numbers from the file, and displays them.

5.24   The following code has an error. Can you correct it?

```
// Find the error and correct it.
ofstream outputFile;
string filename = "Test.txt";
outputFile.open(filename);
```

5.12 **Optional Topics: Breaking and Continuing a Loop**

CONCEPT: The `break` statement causes a loop to terminate early. The `continue` statement causes a loop to stop its current iteration and begin the next one.

WARNING! Use the `break` and `continue` statements with great caution. Because they bypass the normal condition that controls the loop's iterations, these statements make code difficult to understand and debug. For this reason, you should avoid using `break` and `continue` whenever possible. However, because they are part of the C++ language, we discuss them briefly in this section.

Sometimes it's necessary to stop a loop before it goes through all its iterations. The `break` statement, which was used with `switch` in Chapter 4, can also be placed inside a loop. When it is encountered, the loop stops and the program jumps to the statement immediately following the loop.

The `while` loop in the following program segment appears to execute 10 times, but the `break` statement causes it to stop after the fifth iteration.

```cpp
int count = 0;
while (count++ < 10)
{
    cout << count << endl;
    if (count == 5)
        break;
}
```

Program 5-25 uses the `break` statement to interrupt a `for` loop. The program asks the user for a number and then displays the value of that number raised to the powers of 0 through 10. The user can stop the loop at any time by entering Q.

Program 5-25

```cpp
 1   // This program raises the user's number to the powers
 2   // of 0 through 10.
 3   #include <iostream>
 4   #include <cmath>
 5   using namespace std;
 6
 7   int main()
 8   {
 9       double value;
10       char choice;
11
12       cout << "Enter a number: ";
13       cin >> value;
14       cout << "This program will raise " << value;
15       cout << " to the powers of 0 through 10.\n";
16       for (int count = 0; count <= 10; count++)
```

(program continues)

Program 5-25   *(continued)*

```
17    {
18        cout << value << " raised to the power of ";
19        cout << count << " is " << pow(value, count);
20        cout << "\nEnter Q to quit or any other key ";
21        cout << "to continue. ";
22        cin >> choice;
23        if (choice == 'Q' || choice == 'q')
24            break;
25    }
26    return 0;
27 }
```

Program Output with Example Input Shown in Bold
```
Enter a number: 2 [Enter]
This program will raise 2 to the powers of 0 through 10.
2 raised to the power of 0 is 1
Enter Q to quit or any other key to continue. C [Enter]
2 raised to the power of 1 is 2
Enter Q to quit or any other key to continue. C [Enter]
2 raised to the power of 2 is 4
Enter Q to quit or any other key to continue. Q [Enter]
```

Using break in a Nested Loop

In a nested loop, the break statement only interrupts the loop it is placed in. The following program segment displays five rows of asterisks on the screen. The outer loop controls the number of rows and the inner loop controls the number of asterisks in each row. The inner loop is designed to display 20 asterisks, but the break statement stops it during the eleventh iteration.

```
for (int row = 0; row < 5; row++)
{
    for (int star = 0; star < 20; star++)
    {
        cout << '*';
        if (star == 10)
            break;
    }
    cout << endl;
}
```

The output of the program segment above is:

```
***********
***********
***********
***********
***********
```

The continue Statement

The continue statement causes the current iteration of a loop to end immediately. When continue is encountered, all the statements in the body of the loop that appear after it are ignored, and the loop prepares for the next iteration.

In a `while` loop, this means the program jumps to the test expression at the top of the loop. As usual, if the expression is still true, the next iteration begins. In a `do-while` loop, the program jumps to the test expression at the bottom of the loop, which determines whether the next iteration will begin. In a `for` loop, `continue` causes the update expression to be executed, and then the test expression to be evaluated.

The following program segment demonstrates the use of `continue` in a `while` loop:

```
int testVal = 0;
while (testVal++ < 10)
{
   if (testVal == 4)
      continue;
   cout << testVal << " ";
}
```

This loop looks like it displays the integers 1 through 10. When `testVal` is equal to 4, however, the `continue` statement causes the loop to skip the `cout` statement and begin the next iteration. The output of the loop is

```
1 2 3 5 6 7 8 9 10
```

Program 5-26 demonstrates the `continue` statement. The program calculates the charges for DVD rentals, where current releases cost $3.50 and all others cost $2.50. If a customer rents several DVDs, every third one is free. The `continue` statement is used to skip the part of the loop that calculates the charges for every third DVD.

Program 5-26

```
 1 // This program calculates the charges for DVD rentals.
 2 // Every third DVD is free.
 3 #include <iostream>
 4 #include <iomanip>
 5 using namespace std;
 6
 7 int main()
 8 {
 9    int dvdCount = 1;    // DVD counter
10    int numDVDs;         // Number of DVDs rented
11    double total = 0.0;  // Accumulator
12    char current;        // Current release, Y or N
13
14    // Get the number of DVDs.
15    cout << "How many DVDs are being rented? ";
16    cin >> numDVDs;
17
18    // Determine the charges.
19    do
20    {
21       if ((dvdCount % 3) == 0)
22       {
23          cout << "DVD #" << dvdCount << " is free!\n";
24          continue;  // Immediately start the next iteration
25       }
```

(program continues)

Program 5-26 *(continued)*

```
26        cout << "Is DVD #" << dvdCount;
27        cout << " a current release? (Y/N) ";
28        cin >> current;
29        if (current == 'Y' || current == 'y')
30            total += 3.50;
31        else
32            total += 2.50;
33    } while (dvdCount++ < numDVDs);
34
35    // Display the total.
36    cout << fixed << showpoint << setprecision(2);
37    cout << "The total is $" << total << endl;
38    return 0;
39 }
```

Program Output with Example Input Shown in Bold
```
How many DVDs are being rented? 6 [Enter]
Is DVD #1 a current release? (Y/N) y [Enter]
Is DVD #2 a current release? (Y/N) n [Enter]
DVD #3 is free!
Is DVD #4 a current release? (Y/N) n [Enter]
Is DVD #5 a current release? (Y/N) y [Enter]
DVD #6 is free!
The total is $12.00
```

Case Study: See the Loan Amortization Case Study on this book's companion Web site at www.pearsonhighered.com/gaddis.

Review Questions and Exercises

Short Answer

1. Why should you indent the statements in the body of a loop?

2. Describe the difference between pretest loops and posttest loops.

3. Why are the statements in the body of a loop called conditionally executed statements?

4. What is the difference between the while loop and the do-while loop?

5. Which loop should you use in situations where you wish the loop to repeat until the test expression is false, and the loop should not execute if the test expression is false to begin with?

6. Which loop should you use in situations where you wish the loop to repeat until the test expression is false, but the loop should execute at least one time?

7. Which loop should you use when you know the number of required iterations?

8. Why is it critical that counter variables be properly initialized?

9. Why is it critical that accumulator variables be properly initialized?

10. Why should you be careful not to place a statement in the body of a `for` loop that changes the value of the loop's counter variable?

11. What header file do you need to include in a program that performs file operations?

12. What data type do you use when you want to create a file stream object that can write data to a file?

13. What data type do you use when you want to create a file stream object that can read data from a file?

14. Why should a program close a file when it's finished using it?

15. What is a file's read position? Where is the read position when a file is first opened for reading?

Fill-in-the-Blank

16. To _____ a value means to increase it by one, and to _____ a value means to decrease it by one.

17. When the increment or decrement operator is placed before the operand (or to the operand's left), the operator is being used in _____ mode.

18. When the increment or decrement operator is placed after the operand (or to the operand's right), the operator is being used in _____ mode.

19. The statement or block that is repeated is known as the _____ of the loop.

20. Each repetition of a loop is known as a(n) _____.

21. A loop that evaluates its test expression before each repetition is a(n) _____ loop.

22. A loop that evaluates its test expression after each repetition is a(n) _____ loop.

23. A loop that does not have a way of stopping is a(n) _____ loop.

24. A(n) _____ is a variable that "counts" the number of times a loop repeats.

25. A(n) _____ is a sum of numbers that accumulates with each iteration of a loop.

26. A(n) _____ is a variable that is initialized to some starting value, usually zero, and then has numbers added to it in each iteration of a loop.

27. A(n) _____ is a special value that marks the end of a series of values.

28. The _____ loop always iterates at least once.

29. The _____ and _____ loops will not iterate at all if their test expressions are false to start with.

30. The _____ loop is ideal for situations that require a counter.

31. Inside the `for` loop's parentheses, the first expression is the _____ , the second expression is the _____ , and the third expression is the _____.

32. A loop that is inside another is called a(n) _____ loop.

33. The _____ statement causes a loop to terminate immediately.

34. The _____ statement causes a loop to skip the remaining statements in the current iteration.

Algorithm Workbench

35. Write a `while` loop that lets the user enter a number. The number should be multiplied by 10, and the result stored in the variable `product`. The loop should iterate as long as `product` contains a value less than 100.

36. Write a `do-while` loop that asks the user to enter two numbers. The numbers should be added and the sum displayed. The user should be asked if he or she wishes to perform the operation again. If so, the loop should repeat; otherwise it should terminate.

37. Write a `for` loop that displays the following set of numbers:

    ```
    0, 10, 20, 30, 40, 50 . . . 1000
    ```

38. Write a loop that asks the user to enter a number. The loop should iterate 10 times and keep a running total of the numbers entered.

39. Write a nested loop that displays 10 rows of '#' characters. There should be 15 '#' characters in each row.

40. Convert the following `while` loop to a `do-while` loop:

    ```
    int x = 1;
    while (x > 0)
    {
        cout << "enter a number: ";
        cin >> x;
    }
    ```

41. Convert the following `do-while` loop to a `while` loop:

    ```
    char sure;
    do
    {
        cout << "Are you sure you want to quit? ";
        cin >> sure;
    } while (sure != 'Y' && sure != 'N');
    ```

42. Convert the following `while` loop to a `for` loop:

    ```
    int count = 0;
    while (count < 50)
    {
        cout << "count is " << count << endl;
        count++;
    }
    ```

43. Convert the following `for` loop to a `while` loop:

    ```
    for (int x = 50; x > 0; x--)
    {
        cout << x << " seconds to go.\n";
    }
    ```

44. Write code that does the following: Opens an output file with the filename Numbers.txt, uses a loop to write the numbers 1 through 100 to the file, and then closes the file.

45. Write code that does the following: Opens the Numbers.txt file that was created by the code you wrote in question 44, reads all of the numbers from the file and displays them, and then closes the file.

46. Modify the code that you wrote in question 45 so it adds all of the numbers read from the file and displays their total.

True or False

47. T   F   The operand of the increment and decrement operators can be any valid mathematical expression.

48. T   F   The `cout` statement in the following program segment will display 5:

```
int x = 5;
cout << x++;
```

49. T   F   The `cout` statement in the following program segment will display 5:

```
int x = 5;
cout << ++x;
```

50. T   F   The `while` loop is a pretest loop.

51. T   F   The `do-while` loop is a pretest loop.

52. T   F   The `for` loop is a posttest loop.

53. T   F   It is not necessary to initialize counter variables.

54. T   F   All three of the `for` loop's expressions may be omitted.

55. T   F   One limitation of the `for` loop is that only one variable may be initialized in the initialization expression.

56. T   F   Variables may be defined inside the body of a loop.

57. T   F   A variable may be defined in the initialization expression of the `for` loop.

58. T   F   In a nested loop, the outer loop executes faster than the inner loop.

59. T   F   In a nested loop, the inner loop goes through all of its iterations for every single iteration of the outer loop.

60. T   F   To calculate the total number of iterations of a nested loop, add the number of iterations of all the loops.

61. T   F   The `break` statement causes a loop to stop the current iteration and begin the next one.

62. T   F   The `continue` statement causes a terminated loop to resume.

63. T   F   In a nested loop, the `break` statement only interrupts the loop it is placed in.

64. T   F   When you call an `ofstream` object's `open` member function, the specified file will be erased if it already exists.

Find the Errors

Each of the following programs has errors. Find as many as you can.

65.
```
// Find the error in this program.
#include <iostream>
using namespace std;
```

```cpp
int main()
{
    int num1 = 0, num2 = 10, result;

    num1++;
    result = ++(num1 + num2);
    cout << num1 << " " << num2 << " " << result;
    return 0;
}
```

66.
```cpp
// This program adds two numbers entered by the user.
#include <iostream>
using namespace std;

int main()
{
    int num1, num2;
    char again;

    while (again == 'y' || again == 'Y')
        cout << "Enter a number: ";
        cin >> num1;
        cout << "Enter another number: ";
        cin >> num2;
        cout << "Their sum is << (num1 + num2) << endl;
        cout << "Do you want to do this again? ";
        cin >> again;
    return 0;
}
```

67.
```cpp
// This program uses a loop to raise a number to a power.
#include <iostream>
using namespace std;

int main()
{
    int num, bigNum, power, count;

    cout << "Enter an integer: ";
    cin >> num;
    cout << "What power do you want it raised to? ";
    cin >> power;
    bigNum = num;
    while (count++ < power);
        bigNum *= num;
    cout << "The result is << bigNum << endl;
    return 0;
}
```

68.
```cpp
// This program averages a set of numbers.
#include <iostream>
using namespace std;

int main()
{
    int numCount, total;
    double average;
```

```
      cout << "How many numbers do you want to average? ";
      cin >> numCount;
      for (int count = 0; count < numCount; count++)
      {
         int num;
         cout << "Enter a number: ";
         cin >> num;
         total += num;
         count++;
      }
      average = total / numCount;
      cout << "The average is << average << endl;
      return 0;
   }
```

69.
```
   // This program displays the sum of two numbers.
   #include <iostream>
   using namespace std;

   int main()
   {
      int choice, num1, num2;

      do
      {
         cout << "Enter a number: ";
         cin >> num1;
         cout << "Enter another number: ";
         cin >> num2;
         cout << "Their sum is " << (num1 + num2) << endl;
         cout << "Do you want to do this again?\n";
         cout << "1 = yes, 0 = no\n";
         cin >> choice;
      } while (choice = 1)
      return 0;
   }
```

70.
```
   // This program displays the sum of the numbers 1-100.
   #include <iostream>
   using namespace std;

   int main()
   {
      int count = 1, total;

      while (count <= 100)
         total += count;
      cout << "The sum of the numbers 1-100 is ";
      cout << total << endl;
      return 0;
   }
```

Programming Challenges

myprogramminglab *Visit www.myprogramminglab.com to complete many of these Programming Challenges online and get instant feedback.*

1. Sum of Numbers

Write a program that asks the user for a positive integer value. The program should use a loop to get the sum of all the integers from 1 up to the number entered. For example, if the user enters 50, the loop will find the sum of 1, 2, 3, 4, ... 50.

Input Validation: Do not accept a negative starting number.

2. Characters for the ASCII Codes

Write a program that uses a loop to display the characters for the ASCII codes 0 through 127. Display 16 characters on each line.

3. Ocean Levels

Assuming the ocean's level is currently rising at about 1.5 millimeters per year, write a program that displays a table showing the number of millimeters that the ocean will have risen each year for the next 25 years.

4. Calories Burned

**VideoNote
Solving the
Calories
Burned
Problem**

Running on a particular treadmill you burn 3.9 calories per minute. Write a program that uses a loop to display the number of calories burned after 10, 15, 20, 25, and 30 minutes.

5. Membership Fees Increase

A country club, which currently charges $2,500 per year for membership, has announced it will increase its membership fee by 4% each year for the next six years. Write a program that uses a loop to display the projected rates for the next six years.

6. Distance Traveled

The distance a vehicle travels can be calculated as follows:

```
distance = speed * time
```

For example, if a train travels 40 miles per hour for 3 hours, the distance traveled is 120 miles.

Write a program that asks the user for the speed of a vehicle (in miles per hour) and how many hours it has traveled. The program should then use a loop to display the distance the vehicle has traveled for each hour of that time period. Here is an example of the output:

```
What is the speed of the vehicle in mph? 40
How many hours has it traveled? 3
Hour    Distance Traveled
-------------------------------
  1             40
  2             80
  3             120
```

Input Validation: Do not accept a negative number for speed and do not accept any value less than 1 for time traveled.

7. **Pennies for Pay**

Write a program that calculates how much a person would earn over a period of time if his or her salary is one penny the first day and two pennies the second day, and continues to double each day. The program should ask the user for the number of days. Display a table showing how much the salary was for each day, and then show the total pay at the end of the period. The output should be displayed in a dollar amount, not the number of pennies.

Input Validation: Do not accept a number less than 1 for the number of days worked.

8. **Math Tutor**

This program started in Programming Challenge 15 of Chapter 3, and was modified in Programming Challenge 9 of Chapter 4. Modify the program again so it displays a menu allowing the user to select an addition, subtraction, multiplication, or division problem. The final selection on the menu should let the user quit the program. After the user has finished the math problem, the program should display the menu again. This process is repeated until the user chooses to quit the program.

Input Validation: If the user selects an item not on the menu, display an error message and display the menu again.

9. **Hotel Occupancy**

Write a program that calculates the occupancy rate for a hotel. The program should start by asking the user how many floors the hotel has. A loop should then iterate once for each floor. In each iteration, the loop should ask the user for the number of rooms on the floor and how many of them are occupied. After all the iterations, the program should display how many rooms the hotel has, how many of them are occupied, how many are unoccupied, and the percentage of rooms that are occupied. The percentage may be calculated by dividing the number of rooms occupied by the number of rooms.

NOTE: It is traditional that most hotels do not have a thirteenth floor. The loop in this program should skip the entire thirteenth iteration.

Input Validation: Do not accept a value less than 1 for the number of floors. Do not accept a number less than 10 for the number of rooms on a floor.

10. **Average Rainfall**

Write a program that uses nested loops to collect data and calculate the average rainfall over a period of years. The program should first ask for the number of years. The outer loop will iterate once for each year. The inner loop will iterate twelve times, once for each month. Each iteration of the inner loop will ask the user for the inches of rainfall for that month.

After all iterations, the program should display the number of months, the total inches of rainfall, and the average rainfall per month for the entire period.

Input Validation: Do not accept a number less than 1 for the number of years. Do not accept negative numbers for the monthly rainfall.

11. Population

Write a program that will predict the size of a population of organisms. The program should ask the user for the starting number of organisms, their average daily population increase (as a percentage), and the number of days they will multiply. A loop should display the size of the population for each day.

Input Validation: Do not accept a number less than 2 for the starting size of the population. Do not accept a negative number for average daily population increase. Do not accept a number less than 1 for the number of days they will multiply.

12. Celsius to Fahrenheit Table

In Programming Challenge 10 of Chapter 3 you were asked to write a program that converts a Celsius temperature to Fahrenheit. Modify that program so it uses a loop to display a table of the Celsius temperatures 0–20, and their Fahrenheit equivalents.

13. The Greatest and Least of These

Write a program with a loop that lets the user enter a series of integers. The user should enter −99 to signal the end of the series. After all the numbers have been entered, the program should display the largest and smallest numbers entered.

14. Student Line Up

A teacher has asked all her students to line up single file according to their first name. For example, in one class Amy will be at the front of the line and Yolanda will be at the end. Write a program that prompts the user to enter the number of students in the class, then loops to read in that many names. Once all the names have been read in it reports which student would be at the front of the line and which one would be at the end of the line. You may assume that no two students have the same name.

Input Validation: Do not accept a number less than 1 or greater than 25 for the number of students.

15. Payroll Report

Write a program that displays a weekly payroll report. A loop in the program should ask the user for the employee number, gross pay, state tax, federal tax, and FICA withholdings. The loop will terminate when 0 is entered for the employee number. After the data is entered, the program should display totals for gross pay, state tax, federal tax, FICA withholdings, and net pay.

Input Validation: Do not accept negative numbers for any of the items entered. Do not accept values for state, federal, or FICA withholdings that are greater than the gross pay. If the sum state tax + federal tax + FICA withholdings for any employee is greater than gross pay, print an error message and ask the user to re-enter the data for that employee.

16. Savings Account Balance

Write a program that calculates the balance of a savings account at the end of a period of time. It should ask the user for the annual interest rate, the starting balance, and the number of months that have passed since the account was established. A loop should then iterate once for every month, performing the following:

A) Ask the user for the amount deposited into the account during the month. (Do not accept negative numbers.) This amount should be added to the balance.

B) Ask the user for the amount withdrawn from the account during the month. (Do not accept negative numbers.) This amount should be subtracted from the balance.

C) Calculate the monthly interest. The monthly interest rate is the annual interest rate divided by twelve. Multiply the monthly interest rate by the balance, and add the result to the balance.

After the last iteration, the program should display the ending balance, the total amount of deposits, the total amount of withdrawals, and the total interest earned.

NOTE: If a negative balance is calculated at any point, a message should be displayed indicating the account has been closed and the loop should terminate.

17. Sales Bar Chart

Write a program that asks the user to enter today's sales for five stores. The program should then display a bar graph comparing each store's sales. Create each bar in the bar graph by displaying a row of asterisks. Each asterisk should represent $100 of sales.

Here is an example of the program's output.

```
Enter today's sales for store 1: 1000 [Enter]
Enter today's sales for store 2: 1200 [Enter]
Enter today's sales for store 3: 1800 [Enter]
Enter today's sales for store 4: 800 [Enter]
Enter today's sales for store 5: 1900 [Enter]

SALES BAR CHART
(Each * = $100)
Store 1: **********
Store 2: ************
Store 3: ******************
Store 4: ********
Store 5: *******************
```

18. Population Bar Chart

Write a program that produces a bar chart showing the population growth of Prairieville, a small town in the Midwest, at 20-year intervals during the past 100 years. The program should read in the population figures (rounded to the nearest 1,000 people) for 1900, 1920, 1940, 1960, 1980, and 2000 from a file. For each year it should display the date and a bar consisting of one asterisk for each 1,000 people. The data can be found in the `People.txt` file.

Here is an example of how the chart might begin:

```
PRAIRIEVILLE POPULATION GROWTH
(each * represents 1,000 people)
1900 **
1920 ****
1940 *****
```

19. Budget Analysis

Write a program that asks the user to enter the amount that he or she has budgeted for a month. A loop should then prompt the user to enter each of his or her expenses for the month, and keep a running total. When the loop finishes, the program should display the amount that the user is over or under budget.

20. Random Number Guessing Game

Write a program that generates a random number and asks the user to guess what the number is. If the user's guess is higher than the random number, the program should display "Too high, try again." If the user's guess is lower than the random number, the program should display "Too low, try again." The program should use a loop that repeats until the user correctly guesses the random number.

21. Random Number Guessing Game Enhancement

Enhance the program that you wrote for Programming Challenge 20 so it keeps a count of the number of guesses that the user makes. When the user correctly guesses the random number, the program should display the number of guesses.

22. Square Display

Write a program that asks the user for a positive integer no greater than 15. The program should then display a square on the screen using the character 'X'. The number entered by the user will be the length of each side of the square. For example, if the user enters 5, the program should display the following:

```
XXXXX
XXXXX
XXXXX
XXXXX
XXXXX
```

If the user enters 8, the program should display the following:

```
XXXXXXXX
XXXXXXXX
XXXXXXXX
XXXXXXXX
XXXXXXXX
XXXXXXXX
XXXXXXXX
XXXXXXXX
```

23. Pattern Displays

Write a program that uses a loop to display Pattern A below, followed by another loop that displays Pattern B.

Pattern A	Pattern B
+	++++++++++
++	+++++++++
+++	++++++++
++++	+++++++
+++++	++++++
++++++	+++++
+++++++	++++
++++++++	+++
+++++++++	++
++++++++++	+

24. **Using Files—Numeric Processing**

    If you have downloaded this book's source code from the companion Web site, you will find a file named Random.txt in the Chapter 05 folder. (The companion Web site is at www.pearsonhighered.com/gaddis.) This file contains a long list of random numbers. Copy the file to your hard drive and then write a program that opens the file, reads all the numbers from the file, and calculates the following:

    A) The number of numbers in the file

    B) The sum of all the numbers in the file (a running total)

    C) The average of all the numbers in the file

    The program should display the number of numbers found in the file, the sum of the numbers, and the average of the numbers.

25. **Using Files—Student Line Up**

    Modify the Student Line Up program described in Programming Challenge 14 so that it gets the names from a file. Names should be read in until there is no more data to read. If you have downloaded this book's source code from the companion Web site, you will find a file named LineUp.txt in the Chapter 05 folder. You can use this file to test the program. (The companion Web site is at www.pearsonhighered.com/gaddis.)

26. **Using Files—Savings Account Balance Modification**

    Modify the Savings Account Balance program described in Programming Challenge 16 so that it writes the final report to a file.

6 Functions

TOPICS

6.1 Focus on Software Engineering: Modular Programming

CONCEPT: A program may be broken up into manageable functions.

A function is a collection of statements that performs a specific task. So far you have experienced functions in two ways: (1) you have created a function named main in every program you've written, and (2) you have used library functions such as pow and strcmp. In this chapter you will learn how to create your own functions that can be used like library functions.

Functions are commonly used to break a problem down into small manageable pieces. Instead of writing one long function that contains all of the statements necessary to solve a problem, several small functions that each solve a specific part of the problem can be written. These small functions can then be executed in the desired order to solve the problem. This approach is sometimes called *divide and conquer* because a large problem is divided into several smaller problems that are easily solved. Figure 6-1 illustrates this idea by comparing two programs: one that uses a long complex function containing all of the statements necessary to solve a problem, and another that divides a problem into smaller problems, each of which are handled by a separate function.

Figure 6-1

This program has one long, complex function containing all of the statements necessary to solve a problem.

In this program the problem has been divided into smaller problems, each of which is handled by a separate function.

```
int main()
{
    statement;
    statement;
    statement;
    statement;
    statement;
    statement;
    statement;
    statement;
    statement;
    statement;
    statement;
    statement;
    statement;
    statement;
    statement;
    statement;
    statement;
    statement;
    statement;
    statement;
    statement;
    statement;
}
```

```
int main()
{
    statement;           main function
    statement;
    statement;
}
```

```
void function2()
{
    statement;
    statement;           function 2
    statement;
}
```

```
void function3()
{
    statement;
    statement;           function 3
    statement;
}
```

```
void function4()
{
    statement;
    statement;           function 4
    statement;
}
```

Another reason to write functions is that they simplify programs. If a specific task is performed in several places in a program, a function can be written once to perform that task, and then be executed anytime it is needed. This benefit of using functions is known as *code reuse* because you are writing the code to perform a task once and then reusing it each time you need to perform the task.

6.2   Defining and Calling Functions

CONCEPT: A function call is a statement that causes a function to execute. A function definition contains the statements that make up the function.

When creating a function, you must write its *definition*. All function definitions have the following parts:

Return type: A function can send a value to the part of the program that executed it. The return type is the data type of the value that is sent from the function.

Name: You should give each function a descriptive name. In general, the same rules that apply to variable names also apply to function names.

Parameter list: The program can send data into a function. The parameter list is a list of variables that hold the values being passed to the function.

Body: The body of a function is the set of statements that perform the function's operation. They are enclosed in a set of braces.

Figure 6-2 shows the definition of a simple function with the various parts labeled.

Figure 6-2

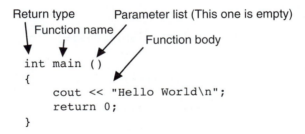

The line in the definition that reads `int main()` is called the *function header*.

void **Functions**

You already know that a function can return a value. The `main` function in all of the programs you have seen in this book is declared to return an `int` value to the operating system. The `return 0;` statement causes the value 0 to be returned when the `main` function finishes executing.

It isn't necessary for all functions to return a value, however. Some functions simply perform one or more statements which follows terminate. These are called *void functions*. The `displayMessage` function, which follows is an example.

```
void displayMessage()
{
    cout << "Hello from the function displayMessage.\n";
}
```

The function's name is `displayMessage`. This name gives an indication of what the function does: It displays a message. You should always give functions names that reflect their purpose. Notice that the function's return type is `void`. This means the function does not return a value to the part of the program that executed it. Also notice the function has no `return` statement. It simply displays a message on the screen and exits.

Calling a Function

A function is executed when it is *called*. Function `main` is called automatically when a program starts, but all other functions must be executed by *function call* statements. When a function is called, the program branches to that function and executes the statements in its body. Let's look at Program 6-1, which contains two functions: `main` and `displayMessage`.

Program 6-1

```
 1   // This program has two functions: main and displayMessage
 2   #include <iostream>
 3   using namespace std;
 4
 5   //*****************************************
 6   // Definition of function displayMessage  *
 7   // This function displays a greeting.     *
 8   //*****************************************
 9
10   void displayMessage()
11   {
12      cout << "Hello from the function displayMessage.\n";
13   }
14
15   //*****************************************
16   // Function main                         *
17   //*****************************************
18
19   int main()
20   {
21      cout << "Hello from main.\n";
22      displayMessage();
23      cout << "Back in function main again.\n";
24      return 0;
25   }
```

Program Output
```
Hello from main.
Hello from the function displayMessage.
Back in function main again.
```

The function `displayMessage` is called by the following statement in line 22:

```
displayMessage();
```

This statement is the function call. It is simply the name of the function followed by a set of parentheses and a semicolon. Let's compare this with the function header:

Function Header ⟶ `void displayMessage()`
Function Call ⟶ `displayMessage();`

The function header is part of the function definition. It declares the function's return type, name, and parameter list. It is not terminated with a semicolon because the definition of the function's body follows it.

The function call is a statement that executes the function, so it is terminated with a semicolon like all other C++ statements. The return type is not listed in the function call, and, if the program is not passing data into the function, the parentheses are left empty.

 NOTE: Later in this chapter you will see how data can be passed into a function by being listed inside the parentheses.

Even though the program starts executing at `main`, the function `displayMessage` is defined first. This is because the compiler must know the function's return type, the number of parameters, and the type of each parameter before the function is called. One way to ensure the compiler will know this information is to place the function definition before all calls to that function. (Later you will see an alternative, preferred method of accomplishing this.)

 NOTE: You should always document your functions by writing comments that describe what they do. These comments should appear just before the function definition.

Notice how Program 6-1 flows. It starts, of course, in function `main`. When the call to `displayMessage` is encountered, the program branches to that function and performs its statements. Once `displayMessage` has finished executing, the program branches back to function `main` and resumes with the line that follows the function call. This is illustrated in Figure 6-3.

Figure 6-3

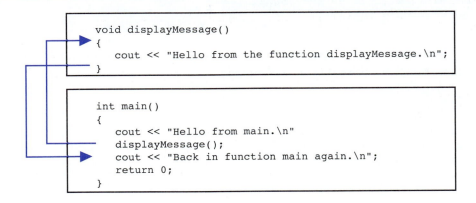

```
void displayMessage()
{
    cout << "Hello from the function displayMessage.\n";
}
```

```
int main()
{
    cout << "Hello from main.\n"
    displayMessage();
    cout << "Back in function main again.\n";
    return 0;
}
```

Function call statements may be used in control structures like loops, `if` statements, and `switch` statements. Program 6-2 places the `displayMessage` function call inside a loop.

Program 6-2

```
 1   // The function displayMessage is repeatedly called from a loop.
 2   #include <iostream>
 3   using namespace std;
 4
 5   //*****************************************
 6   // Definition of function displayMessage  *
 7   // This function displays a greeting.      *
 8   //*****************************************
 9
10   void displayMessage()
11   {
12      cout << "Hello from the function displayMessage.\n";
13   }
14
15   //*****************************************
16   // Function main                          *
17   //*****************************************
18
19   int main()
20   {
21      cout << "Hello from main.\n";
22      for (int count = 0; count < 5; count++)
23         displayMessage(); // Call displayMessage
24      cout << "Back in function main again.\n";
25      return 0;
26   }
```

Program Output

```
Hello from main.
Hello from the function displayMessage.
Hello from the function displayMessage.
Hello from the function displayMessage.
Hello from the function displayMessage.
Hello from the function displayMessage.
Back in function main again.
```

It is possible to have many functions and function calls in a program. Program 6-3 has three functions: `main`, `first`, and `second`.

Program 6-3

```
 1   // This program has three functions: main, first, and second.
 2   #include <iostream>
 3   using namespace std;
 4
```

```
 5   //*****************************************
 6   // Definition of function first          *
 7   // This function displays a message.      *
 8   //*****************************************
 9
10   void first()
11   {
12      cout << "I am now inside the function first.\n";
13   }
14
15   //*****************************************
16   // Definition of function second         *
17   // This function displays a message.      *
18   //*****************************************
19
20   void second()
21   {
22      cout << "I am now inside the function second.\n";
23   }
24
25   //*****************************************
26   // Function main                          *
27   //*****************************************
28
29   int main()
30   {
31      cout << "I am starting in function main.\n";
32      first();     // Call function first
33      second();    // Call function second
34      cout << "Back in function main again.\n";
35      return 0;
36   }
```

Program Output
```
I am starting in function main.
I am now inside the function first.
I am now inside the function second.
Back in function main again.
```

In lines 32 and 33 of Program 6-3, function main contains a call to first and a call to second:

```
first();
second();
```

Each call statement causes the program to branch to a function and then back to main when the function is finished. Figure 6-4 illustrates the paths taken by the program.

Figure 6-4

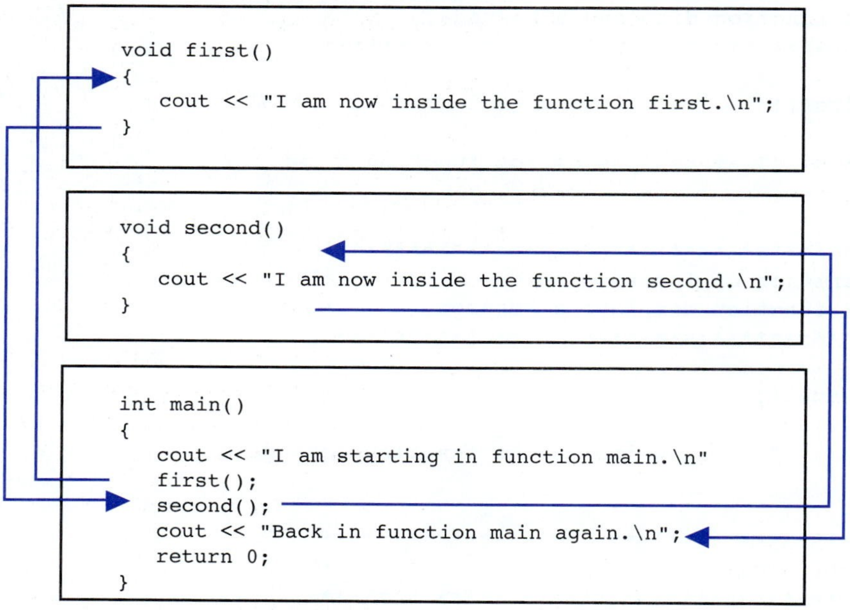

```cpp
void first()
{
    cout << "I am now inside the function first.\n";
}


void second()
{
    cout << "I am now inside the function second.\n";
}


int main()
{
    cout << "I am starting in function main.\n"
    first();
    second();
    cout << "Back in function main again.\n";
    return 0;
}
```

Functions may also be called in a hierarchical, or layered fashion. This is demonstrated by Program 6-4, which has three functions: main, deep, and deeper.

Program 6-4

```cpp
 1   // This program has three functions: main, deep, and deeper
 2   #include <iostream>
 3   using namespace std;
 4
 5   //*****************************************
 6   // Definition of function deeper          *
 7   // This function displays a message.      *
 8   //*****************************************
 9
10   void deeper()
11   {
12       cout << "I am now inside the function deeper.\n";
13   }
14
15   //*****************************************
16   // Definition of function deep            *
17   // This function displays a message.      *
18   //*****************************************
19
```

```
20   void deep()
21   {
22      cout << "I am now inside the function deep.\n";
23      deeper();   // Call function deeper
24      cout << "Now I am back in deep.\n";
25   }
26
27   //*****************************************
28   // Function main                         *
29   //*****************************************
30
31   int main()
32   {
33      cout << "I am starting in function main.\n";
34      deep();      // Call function deep
35      cout << "Back in function main again.\n";
36      return 0;
37   }
```

Program Output

```
I am starting in function main.
I am now inside the function deep.
I am now inside the function deeper.
Now I am back in deep.
Back in function main again.
```

In Program 6-4, function main only calls the function deep. In turn, deep calls deeper. The paths taken by the program are shown in Figure 6-5.

Figure 6-5

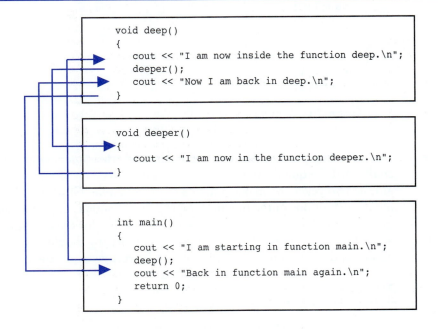

Checkpoint

myprogramminglab *www.myprogramminglab.com*

6.1 Is the following a function header or a function call?

```
calcTotal();
```

6.2 Is the following a function header or a function call?

```
void showResults()
```

6.3 What will the output of the following program be if the user enters 10?

```cpp
#include <iostream>
using namespace std;

void func1()
{
    cout << "Able was I\n";
}

void func2()
{
    cout << "I saw Elba\n";
}

int main()
{
    int input;
    cout << "Enter a number: ";
    cin >> input;
    if (input < 10)
    {
        func1();
        func2();
    }
    else
    {
        func2();
        func1();
    }
    return 0;
}
```

6.4 The following program skeleton determines whether a person qualifies for a credit card. To qualify, the person must have worked on his or her current job for at least two years and make at least $17,000 per year. Finish the program by writing the definitions of the functions qualify and noQualify. The function qualify should explain that the applicant qualifies for the card and that the annual interest rate is 12%. The function noQualify should explain that the applicant does not qualify for the card and give a general explanation why.

```cpp
#include <iostream>
using namespace std;

// You must write definitions for the two functions qualify
// and noQualify.
```

```
int main()
{
    double salary;
    int years;

    cout << "This program will determine if you qualify\n";
    cout << "for our credit card.\n";
    cout << "What is your annual salary? ";
    cin >> salary;
    cout << "How many years have you worked at your ";
    cout << "current job? ";
    cin >> years;
    if (salary >= 17000.0 && years >= 2)
        qualify();
    else
        noQualify();
    return 0;
}
```

6.3 Function Prototypes

CONCEPT: A function prototype eliminates the need to place a function definition before all calls to the function.

Before the compiler encounters a call to a particular function, it must already know the function's return type, the number of parameters it uses, and the type of each parameter. (You will learn how to use parameters in the next section.)

One way of ensuring that the compiler has this information is to place the function definition before all calls to that function. This was the approach taken in Programs 6-1, 6-2, 6-3, and 6-4. Another method is to declare the function with a *function prototype*. Here is a prototype for the `displayMessage` function in Program 6-1:

```
void displayMessage();
```

The prototype looks similar to the function header, except there is a semicolon at the end. The statement above tells the compiler that the function `displayMessage` has a `void` return type (it doesn't return a value) and uses no parameters.

NOTE: Function prototypes are also known as *function declarations*.

WARNING! You must place either the function definition or either/the function prototype ahead of all calls to the function. Otherwise the program will not compile.

Function prototypes are usually placed near the top of a program so the compiler will encounter them before any function calls. Program 6-5 is a modification of Program 6-3. The definitions of the functions `first` and `second` have been placed after `main`, and a function prototype has been placed after the `using namespace std` statement.

Program 6-5

```
1   // This program has three functions: main, first, and second.
2   #include <iostream>
3   using namespace std;
4
5   // Function Prototypes
6   void first();
7   void second();
8
9   int main()
10  {
11      cout << "I am starting in function main.\n";
12      first();    // Call function first
13      second();   // Call function second
14      cout << "Back in function main again.\n";
15      return 0;
16  }
17
18  //***********************************
19  // Definition of function first.    *
20  // This function displays a message. *
21  //***********************************
22
23  void first()
24  {
25      cout << "I am now inside the function first.\n";
26  }
27
28  //***********************************
29  // Definition of function second.   *
30  // This function displays a message. *
31  //***********************************
32
33  void second()
34  {
35      cout << "I am now inside the function second.\n";
36  }
```

Program Output

(The program's output is the same as the output of Program 6-3.)

When the compiler is reading Program 6-5, it encounters the calls to the functions first and second in lines 12 and 13 before it has read the definition of those functions. Because of the function prototypes, however, the compiler already knows the return type and parameter information of first and second.

NOTE: Although some programmers make main the last function in the program, many prefer it to be first because it is the program's starting point.

6.4 Sending Data into a Function

CONCEPT: When a function is called, the program may send values into the function.

VideoNote
Functions and Arguments

Values that are sent into a function are called *arguments*. You're already familiar with how to use arguments in a function call. In the following statement the function pow is being called and two arguments, 2.0 and 4.0, are passed to it:

```cpp
result = pow(2.0, 4.0);
```

By using *parameters*, you can design your own functions that accept data this way. A parameter is a special variable that holds a value being passed into a function. Here is the definition of a function that uses a parameter:

```cpp
void displayValue(int num)
{
    cout << "The value is " << num << endl;
}
```

Notice the integer variable definition inside the parentheses (int num). The variable num is a parameter. This enables the function displayValue to accept an integer value as an argument. Program 6-6 is a complete program using this function.

NOTE: In this text, the values that are passed into a function are called arguments, and the variables that receive those values are called parameters. There are several variations of these terms in use. Some call the arguments *actual parameters* and call the parameters *formal parameters*. Others use the terms *actual argument* and *formal argument*. Regardless of which set of terms you use, it is important to be consistent.

Program 6-6

```cpp
 1  // This program demonstrates a function with a parameter.
 2  #include <iostream>
 3  using namespace std;
 4
 5  // Function Prototype
 6  void displayValue(int);
 7
 8  int main()
 9  {
10      cout << "I am passing 5 to displayValue.\n";
11      displayValue(5);  // Call displayValue with argument 5
12      cout << "Now I am back in main.\n";
13      return 0;
14  }
15
```

(program continues)

Program 6-6   *(continued)*

```
16   //*********************************************************
17   // Definition of function displayValue.                  *
18   // It uses an integer parameter whose value is displayed. *
19   //*********************************************************
20
21   void displayValue(int num)
22   {
23      cout << "The value is " << num << endl;
24   }
```

Program Output
```
I am passing 5 to displayValue.
The value is 5
Now I am back in main.
```

First, notice the function prototype for `displayValue` in line 6:

```
void displayValue(int);
```

It is not necessary to list the name of the parameter variable inside the parentheses. Only its data type is required. The function prototype shown above could optionally have been written as:

```
void displayValue(int num);
```

However, the compiler ignores the name of the parameter variable in the function prototype.

In main, the `displayValue` function is called with the argument 5 inside the parentheses. The number 5 is passed into num, which is `displayValue`'s parameter. This is illustrated in Figure 6-6.

Figure 6-6

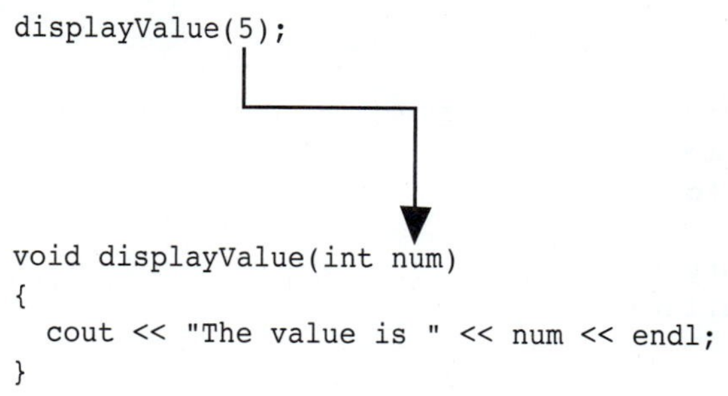

```
displayValue(5);



void displayValue(int num)
{
   cout << "The value is " << num << endl;
}
```

Any argument listed inside the parentheses of a function call is copied into the function's parameter variable. In essence, parameter variables are initialized to the value of their corresponding arguments. Program 6-7 shows the function `displayValue` being called several times with a different argument being passed each time.

Program 6-7

```
 1   // This program demonstrates a function with a parameter.
 2   #include <iostream>
 3   using namespace std;
 4
 5   // Function Prototype
 6   void displayValue(int);
 7
 8   int main()
 9   {
10      cout << "I am passing several values to displayValue.\n";
11      displayValue(5);  // Call displayValue with argument 5
12      displayValue(10); // Call displayValue with argument 10
13      displayValue(2);  // Call displayValue with argument 2
14      displayValue(16); // Call displayValue with argument 16
15      cout << "Now I am back in main.\n";
16      return 0;
17   }
18
19   //*********************************************************
20   // Definition of function displayValue.                 *
21   // It uses an integer parameter whose value is displayed. *
22   //*********************************************************
23
24   void displayValue(int num)
25   {
26      cout << "The value is " << num << endl;
27   }
```

Program Output
```
I am passing several values to displayValue.
The value is 5
The value is 10
The value is 2
The value is 16
Now I am back in main.
```

 WARNING! When passing a variable as an argument, simply write the variable name inside the parentheses of the function call. Do not write the data type of the argument variable in the function call. For example, the following function call will cause an error:

```
displayValue(int x); // Error!
```

The function call should appear as

```
displayValue(x);     // Correct
```

Each time the function is called in Program 6-7, num takes on a different value. Any expression whose value could normally be assigned to num may be used as an argument. For example, the following function call would pass the value 8 into num:

```
displayValue(3 + 5);
```

If you pass an argument whose type is not the same as the parameter's type, the argument will be promoted or demoted automatically. For instance, the argument in the following function call would be truncated, causing the value 4 to be passed to num:

```
displayValue(4.7);
```

Often, it's useful to pass several arguments into a function. Program 6-8 shows the definition of a function with three parameters.

Program 6-8

```
 1    // This program demonstrates a function with three parameters.
 2    #include <iostream>
 3    using namespace std;
 4
 5    // Function Prototype
 6    void showSum(int, int, int);
 7
 8    int main()
 9    {
10        int value1, value2, value3;
11
12        // Get three integers.
13        cout << "Enter three integers and I will display ";
14        cout << "their sum: ";
15        cin >> value1 >> value2 >> value3;
16
17        // Call showSum passing three arguments.
18        showSum(value1, value2, value3);
19        return 0;
20    }
21
22    //*************************************************************
23    // Definition of function showSum.                           *
24    // It uses three integer parameters. Their sum is displayed. *
25    //*************************************************************
26
27    void showSum(int num1, int num2, int num3)
28    {
29        cout << (num1 + num2 + num3) << endl;
30    }
```

Program Output with Example Input Shown in Bold
Enter three integers and I will display their sum: **4 8 7 [Enter]**
19

In the function header for showSum, the parameter list contains three variable definitions separated by commas:

```
void showSum(int num1, int num2, int num3)
```

WARNING! Each parameter variable in a parameter list must have a data type listed before its name. For example, a compiler error would occur if the parameter list for the showSum function were defined as shown in the following header:

```
void showSum(int num1, num2, num3) // Error!
```

A data type for all three of the parameter variables must be listed, as shown here:

```
void showSum(int num1, int num2, int num3) // Correct
```

In the function call in line 18, the variables value1, value2, and value3 are passed as arguments:

```
showSum(value1, value2, value3);
```

When a function with multiple parameters is called, the arguments are passed to the parameters in order. This is illustrated in Figure 6-7.

Figure 6-7

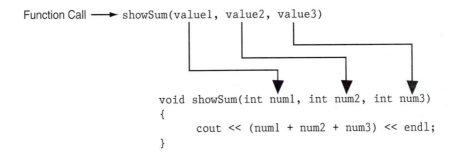

The following function call will cause 5 to be passed into the num1 parameter, 10 to be passed into num2, and 15 to be passed into num3:

```
showSum(5, 10, 15);
```

However, the following function call will cause 15 to be passed into the num1 parameter, 5 to be passed into num2, and 10 to be passed into num3:

```
showSum(15, 5, 10);
```

 NOTE: The function prototype must list the data type of each parameter.

 NOTE: Like all variables, parameters have a scope. The scope of a parameter is limited to the body of the function that uses it.

6.5   Passing Data by Value

CONCEPT: When an argument is passed into a parameter, only a copy of the argument's value is passed. Changes to the parameter do not affect the original argument.

As you've seen in this chapter, parameters are special-purpose variables that are defined inside the parentheses of a function definition. They are separate and distinct from the arguments that are listed inside the parentheses of a function call. The values that are stored in the parameter variables are copies of the arguments. Normally, when a parameter's value is changed inside a function it has no effect on the original argument. Program 6-9 demonstrates this concept.

Program 6-9

```
 1   // This program demonstrates that changes to a function parameter
 2   // have no effect on the original argument.
 3   #include <iostream>
 4   using namespace std;
 5
 6   // Function Prototype
 7   void changeMe(int);
 8
 9   int main()
10   {
11      int number = 12;
12
13      // Display the value in number.
14      cout << "number is " << number << endl;
15
16      // Call changeMe, passing the value in number
17      // as an argument.
18      changeMe(number);
19
20      // Display the value in number again.
21      cout << "Now back in main again, the value of ";
22      cout << "number is " << number << endl;
23      return 0;
24   }
25
26   //*************************************************************
27   // Definition of function changeMe.                         *
28   // This function changes the value of the parameter myValue. *
29   //*************************************************************
30
```

```
31   void changeMe(int myValue)
32   {
33       // Change the value of myValue to 0.
34       myValue = 0;
35
36       // Display the value in myValue.
37       cout << "Now the value is " << myValue << endl;
38   }
```

Program Output

```
number is 12
Now the value is 0
Now back in main again, the value of number is 12
```

Even though the parameter variable `myValue` is changed in the `changeMe` function, the argument `number` is not modified. The `myValue` variable contains only a copy of the `number` variable.

The `changeMe` function does not have access to the original argument. When only a copy of an argument is passed to a function, it is said to be *passed by value*. This is because the function receives a copy of the argument's value, and does not have access to the original argument.

Figure 6-8 illustrates that a parameter variable's storage location in memory is separate from that of the original argument.

Figure 6-8

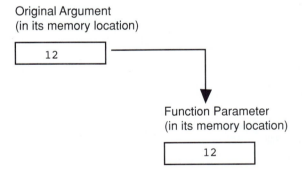

 NOTE: Later in this chapter you will learn ways to give a function access to its original arguments.

Focus on Software Engineering: Using Functions in a Menu-Driven Program

CONCEPT: Functions are ideal for use in menu-driven programs. When the user selects an item from a menu, the program can call the appropriate function.

In Chapters 4 and 5 you saw a menu-driven program that calculates the charges for a health club membership. Program 6-10 shows the program redesigned as a modular program. A *modular* program is broken up into functions that perform specific tasks.

Program 6-10

```
 1  // This is a menu-driven program that makes a function call
 2  // for each selection the user makes.
 3  #include <iostream>
 4  #include <iomanip>
 5  using namespace std;
 6
 7  // Function prototypes
 8  void showMenu();
 9  void showFees(double, int);
10
11  int main()
12  {
13     int choice;       // To hold a menu choice
14     int months;       // To hold a number of months
15
16     // Constants for the menu choices
17     const int ADULT_CHOICE = 1,
18               CHILD_CHOICE = 2,
19               SENIOR_CHOICE = 3,
20               QUIT_CHOICE = 4;
21
22     // Constants for membership rates
23     const double ADULT = 40.0,
24                  CHILD = 20.0;
25                  SENIOR = 30.0,
26
27     // Set up numeric output formatting.
28     cout << fixed << showpoint << setprecision(2);
29
30     do
31     {
32        // Display the menu and get the user's choice.
33        showMenu();
34        cin >> choice;
35
36        // Validate the menu selection.
37        while (choice < ADULT_CHOICE || choice > QUIT_CHOICE)
38        {
```

```
39                cout << "Please enter a valid menu choice: ";
40                cin >> choice;
41            }
42
43            // If the user does not want to quit, proceed.
44            if (choice != QUIT_CHOICE)
45            {
46                // Get the number of months.
47                cout << "For how many months? ";
48                cin >> months;
49
50                // Display the membership fees.
51                switch (choice)
52                {
53                    case ADULT_CHOICE:
54                        showFees(ADULT, months);
55                        break;
56                    case CHILD_CHOICE:
57                        showFees(CHILD, months);
58                        break;
59                    case SENIOR_CHOICE:
60                        showFees(SENIOR, months);
61                }
62            }
63        } while (choice != QUIT_CHOICE);
64        return 0;
65 }
66
67 //***************************************************************
68 // Definition of function showMenu which displays the menu.    *
69 //***************************************************************
70
71 void showMenu()
72 {
73    cout << "\n\t\tHealth Club Membership Menu\n\n"
74         << "1. Standard Adult Membership\n"
75         << "2. Child Membership\n"
76         << "3. Senior Citizen Membership\n"
77         << "4. Quit the Program\n\n"
78         << "Enter your choice: ";
79 }
80
81 //***************************************************************
82 // Definition of function showFees. The memberRate parameter holds *
83 // the monthly membership rate and the months parameter holds the  *
84 // number of months. The function displays the total charges.      *
85 //***************************************************************
86
87 void showFees(double memberRate, int months)
88 {
89     cout << "The total charges are $"
90          << (memberRate * months) << endl;
91 }
```

(program output continues)

Program 6-10 (continued)

Program Output with Example Input Shown in Bold

```
        Health Club Membership Menu

1. Standard Adult Membership
2. Child Membership
3. Senior Citizen Membership
4. Quit the Program

Enter your choice: 1 [Enter]
For how many months? 12 [Enter]
The total charges are $480.00

        Health Club Membership Menu

1. Standard Adult Membership
2. Child Membership
3. Senior Citizen Membership
4. Quit the Program

Enter your choice: 4 [Enter]
```

Let's take a closer look at this program. First notice the showMenu function in lines 71 through 79. This function displays the menu, and is called from the main function in line 33.

The showFees function appears in lines 87 through 91. Its purpose is to display the total fees for a membership lasting a specified number of months. The function accepts two arguments: the monthly membership fee (a double) and the number of months of membership (an int). The function uses these values to calculate and display the total charges. For example, if we wanted the function to display the fees for an adult membership lasting six months, we would pass the ADULT constant as the first argument and 6 as the second argument.

The showFees function is called from three different locations in the switch statement which is in the main function. The first location is line 54. This statement is executed when the user has selected item 1, standard adult membership, from the menu. The showFees function is called with the ADULT constant and the months variable passed as arguments. The second location is line 57. This statement is executed when the user has selected item 2, child membership, from the menu. The showFees function is called in this line with the CHILD constant and the months variable passed as arguments. The third location is line 60. This statement is executed when the user has selected item 3, senior citizen membership, from the menu. The showFees function is called with the SENIOR constant and the months variable passed as arguments. Each time the showFees function is called, it displays the total membership fees for the specified type of membership, for the specified number of months.

Checkpoint

myprogramminglab *www.myprogramminglab.com*

6.5 Indicate which of the following is the function prototype, the function header, and the function call:

```
void showNum(double num)

void showNum(double);

showNum(45.67);
```

6.6 Write a function named `timesTen`. The function should have an integer parameter named `number`. When `timesTen` is called, it should display the product of `number` times ten. (*Note*: just write the function. Do not write a complete program.)

6.7 Write a function prototype for the `timesTen` function you wrote in Question 6.6.

6.8 What is the output of the following program?

```cpp
#include <iostream>
using namespace std;

void showDouble(int); // Function prototype

int main()
{
    int num;

    for (num = 0; num < 10; num++)
        showDouble(num);
    return 0;
}

// Definition of function showDouble.
void showDouble(int value)
{
    cout << value << "\t" << (value * 2) << endl;
}
```

6.9 What is the output of the following program?

```cpp
#include <iostream>
using namespace std;

void func1(double, int); // Function prototype

int main()
{
    int x = 0;
    double y = 1.5;

    cout << x << " " << y << endl;
    func1(y, x);
    cout << x << " " << y << endl;
    return 0;
}
```

```
          void func1(double a, int b)
          {
             cout << a << " " << b << endl;
             a = 0.0;
             b = 10;
             cout << a << " " << b << endl;
          }
```

6.10   The following program skeleton asks for the number of hours you've worked and
        your hourly pay rate. It then calculates and displays your wages. The function
        showDollars, which you are to write, formats the output of the wages.

```
          #include <iostream>
          using namespace std;

          void showDollars(double); // Function prototype

          int main()
          {
             double payRate, hoursWorked, wages;

             cout << "How many hours have you worked? "
             cin >> hoursWorked;
             cout << "What is your hourly pay rate? ";
             cin >> payRate;
             wages = hoursWorked * payRate;
             showDollars(wages);
             return 0;
          }

          // You must write the definition of the function showDollars
          // here. It should take one parameter of the type double.
          // The function should display the message "Your wages are $"
          // followed by the value of the parameter. It should be displayed
          // with 2 places of precision after the decimal point, in fixed
          // notation, and the decimal point should always display.
```

6.7   The return Statement

CONCEPT: The return statement causes a function to end immediately.

When the last statement in a void function has finished executing, the function terminates
and the program returns to the statement following the function call. It's possible, however, to force a function to return before the last statement has been executed. When the
return statement is encountered, the function immediately terminates and control of the
program returns to the statement that called the function. This is demonstrated in Program 6-11. The function divide shows the quotient of arg1 divided by arg2. If arg2 is
set to zero, the function returns.

Program 6-11

```
 1   // This program uses a function to perform division. If division
 2   // by zero is detected, the function returns.
 3   #include <iostream>
 4   using namespace std;
 5
 6   // Function prototype.
 7   void divide(double, double);
 8
 9   int main()
10   {
11      double num1, num2;
12
13      cout << "Enter two numbers and I will divide the first\n";
14      cout << "number by the second number: ";
15      cin >> num1 >> num2;
16      divide(num1, num2);
17      return 0;
18   }
19
20   //************************************************************
21   // Definition of function divide.                          *
22   // Uses two parameters: arg1 and arg2. The function divides arg1*
23   // by arg2 and shows the result. If arg2 is zero, however, the  *
24   // function returns.                                        *
25   //************************************************************
26
27   void divide(double arg1, double arg2)
28   {
29      if (arg2 == 0.0)
30      {
31         cout << "Sorry, I cannot divide by zero.\n";
32         return;
33      }
34      cout << "The quotient is " << (arg1 / arg2) << endl;
35   }
```

Program Output with Example Input Shown in Bold
```
Enter two numbers and I will divide the first
number by the second number: 12 0 [Enter]
Sorry, I cannot divide by zero.
```

In the example running of the program, the user entered 12 and 0 as input. In line 16 the divide function was called, passing 12 into the arg1 parameter and 0 into the arg2 parameter. Inside the divide function, the if statement in line 29 executes. Because arg2 is equal to 0.0, the code in lines 31 and 32 execute. When the return statement in line 32 executes, the divide function immediately ends. This means the cout statement in line 34 does not execute. The program resumes at line 17 in the main function.

6.8 Returning a Value from a Function

> **CONCEPT:** A function may send a value back to the part of the program that called the function.

You've seen that data may be passed into a function by way of parameter variables. Data may also be returned from a function, back to the statement that called it. Functions that return a value are appropriately known as *value-returning functions*.

VideoNote
Value-Returning Functions

The pow function, which you have already seen, is an example of a value-returning function. Here is an example:

```
double x;
x = pow(4.0, 2.0);
```

The second line in this code calls the pow function, passing 4.0 and 2.0 as arguments. The function calculates the value of 4.0 raised to the power of 2.0 and returns that value. The value, which is 16.0, is assigned to the x variable by the = operator.

Although several arguments may be passed into a function, only one value may be returned from it. Think of a function as having multiple communication channels for receiving data (parameters), but only one channel for sending data (the return value). This is illustrated in Figure 6-9.

Figure 6-9

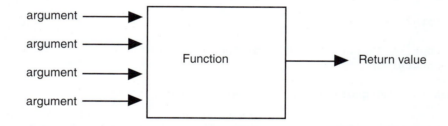

> **NOTE:** It is possible to return multiple values from a function, but they must be "packaged" in such a way that they are treated as a single value. This is a topic of Chapter 11.

Defining a Value-Returning Function

When you are writing a value-returning function, you must decide what type of value the function will return. This is because you must specify the data type of the return value in the function header, and in the function prototype. Recall that a void function, which does not return a value, uses the key word void as its return type in the function header. A value-returning function will use `int`, `double`, `bool`, or any other valid data type in its header. Here is an example of a function that returns an `int` value:

```
int sum(int num1, int num2)
{
   int result;

   result = num1 + num2;
   return result;
}
```

The name of this function is `sum`. Notice in the function header that the return type is `int`, as illustrated in Figure 6-10.

Figure 6-10

```
            Return Type
                 │
                 ▼
      int sum(int num1, int num2)
```

This code defines a function named `sum` that accepts two `int` arguments. The arguments are passed into the parameter variables `num1` and `num2`. Inside the function, a variable, `result`, is defined. Variables that are defined inside a function are called *local variables*. After the variable definition, the parameter variables `num1` and `num2` are added, and their sum is assigned to the `result` variable. The last statement in the function is

```
return result;
```

This statement causes the function to end, and it sends the value of the `result` variable back to the statement that called the function. A value-returning function must have a return statement written in the following general format:

```
return expression;
```

In the general format, *expression* is the value to be returned. It can be any expression that has a value, such as a variable, literal, or mathematical expression. The value of the expression is converted to the data type that the function returns, and is sent back to the statement that called the function. In this case, the `sum` function returns the value in the `result` variable.

However, we could have eliminated the `result` variable and returned the expression `num1 + num2`, as shown in the following code:

```
int sum(int num1, int num2)
{
   return num1 + num2;
}
```

When writing the prototype for a value-returning function, follow the same conventions that we have covered earlier. Here is the prototype for the `sum` function:

```
int sum(int, int);
```

Calling a Value-Returning Function

Program 6-12 shows an example of how to call the sum function.

Program 6-12

```
 1  // This program uses a function that returns a value.
 2  #include <iostream>
 3  using namespace std;
 4
 5  // Function prototype
 6  int sum(int, int);
 7
 8  int main()
 9  {
10     int value1 = 20,    // The first value
11         value2 = 40,    // The second value
12         total;          // To hold the total
13
14     // Call the sum function, passing the contents of
15     // value1 and value2 as arguments. Assign the return
16     // value to the total variable.
17     total = sum(value1, value2);
18
19     // Display the sum of the values.
20     cout << "The sum of " << value1 << " and "
21         << value2 << " is " << total << endl;
22     return 0;
23  }
24
25  //****************************************************
26  // Definition of function sum. This function returns  *
27  // the sum of its two parameters.                     *
28  //****************************************************
29
30  int sum(int num1, int num2)
31  {
32     return num1 + num2;
33  }
```

Program Output

```
The sum of 20 and 40 is 60
```

Here is the statement in line 17 that calls the sum function, passing value1 and value2 as arguments.

```
total = sum(value1, value2);
```

This statement assigns the value returned by the sum function to the total variable. In this case, the function will return 60. Figure 6-11 shows how the arguments are passed into the function and how a value is passed back from the function.

Figure 6-11

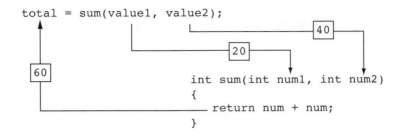

When you call a value-returning function, you usually want to do something meaningful with the value it returns. Program 6-12 shows a function's return value being assigned to a variable. This is commonly how return values are used, but you can do many other things with them. For example, the following code shows a mathematical expression that uses a call to the sum function:

```
int x = 10, y = 15;
double average;
average = sum(x, y) / 2.0;
```

In the last statement, the sum function is called with x and y as its arguments. The function's return value, which is 25, is divided by 2.0. The result, 12.5, is assigned to average. Here is another example:

```
int x = 10, y = 15;
cout << "The sum is " << sum(x, y) << endl;
```

This code sends the sum function's return value to cout so it can be displayed on the screen. The message "The sum is 25" will be displayed.

Remember, a value-returning function returns a value of a specific data type. You can use the function's return value anywhere that you can use a regular value of the same data type. This means that anywhere an int value can be used, a call to an int value-returning function can be used. Likewise, anywhere a double value can be used, a call to a double value-returning function can be used. The same is true for all other data types.

Let's look at another example. Program 6-13, which calculates the area of a circle, has two functions in addition to main. One of the functions is named square, and it returns the square of any number passed to it as an argument. The square function is called in a mathematical statement. The program also has a function named getRadius, which prompts the user to enter the circle's radius. The value entered by the user is returned from the function.

Program 6-13

```
1   // This program demonstrates two value-returning functions.
2   // The square function is called in a mathematical statement.
3   #include <iostream>
4   #include <iomanip>
5   using namespace std;
6
```

(program continues)

Program 6-13   *(continued)*

```
 7  //Function prototypes
 8  double getRadius();
 9  double square(double);
10
11  int main()
12  {
13     const double PI = 3.14159; // Constant for pi
14     double radius;             // To hold the circle's radius
15     double area;               // To hold the circle's area
16
17     // Set the numeric output formatting.
18     cout << fixed << showpoint << setprecision(2);
19
20     // Get the radius of the circle.
21     cout << "This program calculates the area of ";
22     cout << "a circle.\n";
23     radius = getRadius();
24
25     // Calculate the area of the circle.
26     area = PI * square(radius);
27
28     // Display the area.
29     cout << "The area is " << area << endl;
30     return 0;
31  }
32
33  //*****************************************************
34  // Definition of function getRadius.                 *
35  // This function asks the user to enter the radius of *
36  // the circle and then returns that number as a double.*
37  //*****************************************************
38
39  double getRadius()
40  {
41     double rad;
42
43     cout << "Enter the radius of the circle: ";
44     cin >> rad;
45     return rad;
46  }
47
48  //*****************************************************
49  // Definition of function square.                    *
50  // This function accepts a double argument and returns *
51  // the square of the argument as a double.           *
52  //*****************************************************
53
54  double square(double number)
55  {
56     return number * number;
57  }
```

Program Output with Example Input Shown in Bold
```
This program calculates the area of a circle.
Enter the radius of the circle: 10 [Enter]
The area is 314.16
```

First, look at the `getRadius` function defined in lines 39 through 46. The purpose of the function is to prompt the user to enter the radius of a circle. In line 41 the function defines a local variable, `rad`. Lines 43 and 44 prompt the user to enter the circle's radius, which is stored in the `rad` variable. In line 45 the value of the `rad` value is returned. The `getRadius` function is called in the `main` function, in line 23. The value that is returned from the function is assigned to the `radius` variable.

Next look at the `square` function, which is defined in lines 54 through 57. When the function is called, a `double` argument is passed to it. The function stores the argument in the `number` parameter. The `return` statement in line 56 returns the value of the expression `number * number`, which is the square of the `number` parameter. The `square` function is called in the `main` function, in line 26, with the value of `radius` passed as an argument. The function will return the square of the `radius` variable, and that value will be used in the mathematical expression.

Assuming the user has entered 10 as the radius, and this value is passed as an argument to the `square` function, the `square` function will return the value 100. Figure 6-12 illustrates how the value 100 is passed back to the mathematical expression in line 26. The value 100 will then be used in the mathematical expression.

Figure 6-12

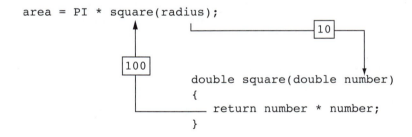

Functions can return values of any type. Both the `getRadius` and `square` functions in Program 6-13 return a `double`. The `sum` function you saw in Program 6-12 returned an `int`. When a statement calls a value-returning function, it should properly handle the return value. For example, if you assign the return value of the `square` function to a variable, the variable should be a `double`. If the return value of the function has a fractional portion and you assign it to an `int` variable, the value will be truncated.

In the Spotlight:

Using Functions

Your friend Michael runs a catering company. Some of the ingredients that his recipes require are measured in cups. When he goes to the grocery store to buy those ingredients, however, they are sold only by the fluid ounce. He has asked you to write a simple program that converts cups to fluid ounces.

You design the following algorithm:

1. *Display an introductory screen that explains what the program does.*

2. *Get the number of cups.*

3. *Convert the number of cups to fluid ounces and display the result.*

This algorithm lists the top level of tasks that the program needs to perform, and becomes the basis of the program's main function. The hierarchy chart shown in Figure 6-13 shows how the program will broken down into functions.

Figure 6-13   Hierarchy chart for the program

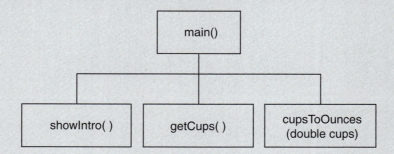

As shown in the hierarchy chart, the main function will call three other functions. Here are summaries of those functions:

- showIntro—This function will display a message on the screen that explains what the program does.
- getCups—This function will prompt the user to enter the number of cups and then will return that value as a double.
- cupsToOunces—This function will accept the number of cups as an argument and then return an equivalent number of fluid ounces as a double.

Program 6-14 shows the code for the program.

Program 6-14

```cpp
1   // This program converts cups to fluid ounces.
2   #include <iostream>
3   #include <iomanip>
4   using namespace std;
5
6   // Function prototypes
7   void showIntro();
8   double getCups();
9   double cupsToOunces(double);
10
11  int main()
12  {
13     // Variables for the cups and ounces.
14     double cups, ounces;
15
16     // Set up numeric output formatting.
17     cout << fixed << showpoint << setprecision(1);
18
19     // Display an intro screen.
20     showIntro();
21
22     // Get the number of cups.
23     cups = getCups();
24
25     // Convert cups to fluid ounces.
26     ounces = cupsToOunces(cups);
27
28     // Display the number of ounces.
29     cout << cups << " cups equals "
30          << ounces << " ounces.\n";
31
32     return 0;
33  }
34
35  //******************************************
36  // The showIntro function displays an       *
37  // introductory screen.                     *
38  //******************************************
39
40  void showIntro()
41  {
42     cout << "This program converts measurements\n"
43          << "in cups to fluid ounces. For your\n"
44          << "reference the formula is:\n"
45          << "    1 cup = 8 fluid ounces\n\n";
46  }
47
48  //******************************************
49  // The getCups function prompts the user    *
50  // to enter the number of cups and then     *
51  // returns that value as a double.          *
52  //******************************************
53
```

(program continues)

Program 6-14 *(continued)*

```
54 double getCups()
55 {
56     double numCups;
57
58     cout << "Enter the number of cups: ";
59     cin >> numCups;
60     return numCups;
61 }
62
63 //*****************************************
64 // The cupsToOunces function accepts a    *
65 // number of cups as an argument and      *
66 // returns the equivalent number of fluid *
67 // ounces as a double.                    *
68 //*****************************************
69
70 double cupsToOunces(double numCups)
71 {
72     return numCups * 8.0;
73 }
```

Program Output with Example Input Shown in Bold
```
This program converts measurements
in cups to fluid ounces. For your
reference the formula is:
    1 cup = 8 fluid ounces

Enter the number of cups: 2 [Enter]
2.0 cups equals 16.0 ounces.
```

6.9 Returning a Boolean Value

CONCEPT: Functions may return `true` or `false` values.

Frequently there is a need for a function that tests an argument and returns a `true` or `false` value indicating whether or not a condition exists. Such a function would return a `bool` value. For example, the following function accepts an `int` argument and returns `true` if the argument is within the range of 1 through 100, or `false` otherwise.

```
bool isValid(int number)
{
    bool status;

    if (number >= 1 && number <= 100)
        status = true;
    else
        status = false;
    return status;
}
```

The following code shows an if/else statement that uses a call to the function:

```
int value = 20;
if (isValid(value))
   cout << "The value is within range.\n";
else
   cout << "The value is out of range.\n";
```

When this code executes, the message "The value is within range." will be displayed.

Program 6-15 shows another example. This program has a function named isEven which returns true if its argument is an even number. Otherwise, the function returns false.

Program 6-15

```
 1  // This program uses a function that returns true or false.
 2  #include <iostream>
 3  using namespace std;
 4
 5  // Function prototype
 6  bool isEven(int);
 7
 8  int main()
 9  {
10     int val;
11
12     // Get a number from the user.
13     cout << "Enter an integer and I will tell you ";
14     cout << "if it is even or odd: ";
15     cin >> val;
16
17     // Indicate whether it is even or odd.
18     if (isEven(val))
19        cout << val << " is even.\n";
20     else
21        cout << val << " is odd.\n";
22     return 0;
23  }
24
25  //****************************************************************
26  // Definition of function isEven. This function accepts an      *
27  // integer argument and tests it to be even or odd. The function *
28  // returns true if the argument is even or false if the argument *
29  // is odd. The return value is a bool.                          *
30  //****************************************************************
31
32  bool isEven(int number)
33  {
34     bool status;
35
36     if (number % 2 == 0)
37        status = true;  // The number is even if there is no remainder.
38     else
39        status = false; // Otherwise, the number is odd.
40     return status;
41  }
```

(program output continues)

Program 6-15 (continued)

Program Output with Example Input Shown in Bold
```
Enter an integer and I will tell you if it is even or odd: 5 [Enter]
5 is odd.
```

The `isEven` function is called in line 18, in the following statement:

```
if (isEven(val))
```

When the `if` statement executes, `isEven` is called with `val` as its argument. If `val` is even, `isEven` returns `true` , otherwise it returns `false`.

 ## Checkpoint

myprogramminglab *www.myprogramminglab.com*

6.11 How many return values may a function have?

6.12 Write a header for a function named `distance`. The function should return a `double` and have two `double` parameters: `rate` and `time`.

6.13 Write a header for a function named `days`. The function should return an `int` and have three `int` parameters: `years`, `months`, and `weeks`.

6.14 Write a header for a function named `getKey`. The function should return a `char` and use no parameters.

6.15 Write a header for a function named `lightYears`. The function should return a `long` and have one `long` parameter: `miles`.

 ## 6.10 Local and Global Variables

CONCEPT: A local variable is defined inside a function and is not accessible outside the function. A global variable is defined outside all functions and is accessible to all functions in its scope.

Local Variables

Variables defined inside a function are *local* to that function. They are hidden from the statements in other functions, which normally cannot access them. Program 6-16 shows that because the variables defined in a function are hidden, other functions may have separate, distinct variables with the same name.

Program 6-16

```
 1   // This program shows that variables defined in a function
 2   // are hidden from other functions.
 3   #include <iostream>
 4   using namespace std;
 5
 6   void anotherFunction(); // Function prototype
```

```
 7
 8   int main()
 9   {
10      int num = 1;    // Local variable
11
12      cout << "In main, num is " << num << endl;
13      anotherFunction();
14      cout << "Back in main, num is " << num << endl;
15      return 0;
16   }
17
18   //****************************************************
19   // Definition of anotherFunction                    *
20   // It has a local variable, num, whose initial value *
21   // is displayed.                                     *
22   //****************************************************
23
24   void anotherFunction()
25   {
26      int num = 20;   // Local variable
27
28      cout << "In anotherFunction, num is " << num << endl;
29   }
```

Program Output
```
In main, num is 1
In anotherFunction, num is 20
Back in main, num is 1
```

Even though there are two variables named num, the program can only "see" one of them at a time because they are in different functions. When the program is executing in main, the num variable defined in main is visible. When anotherFunction is called, however, only variables defined inside it are visible, so the num variable in main is hidden. Figure 6-14 illustrates the closed nature of the two functions. The boxes represent the scope of the variables.

Figure 6-14

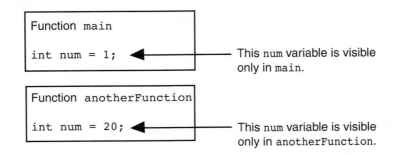

Local Variable Lifetime

A function's local variables exist only while the function is executing. This is known as the *lifetime* of a local variable. When the function begins, its local variables and its parameter variables are created in memory, and when the function ends, the local variables and parameter variables are destroyed. This means that any value stored in a local variable is lost between calls to the function in which the variable is declared.

Initializing Local Variables with Parameter Values

It is possible to use a parameter variable to initialize a local variable. Sometimes this simplifies the code in a function. For example, recall the first version of the sum function we discussed earlier:

```cpp
int sum(int num1, int num2)
{
   int result;

   result = num1 + num2;
   return result;
}
```

In the body of the function, the result variable is defined and then a separate assignment statement assigns num1 + num2 to result. We can combine these statements into one, as shown in the following modified version of the function.

```cpp
int sum(int num1, int num2)
{
   int result = num1 + num2;
   return result;
}
```

Because the scope of a parameter variable is the entire function in which it is declared, we can use parameter variables to initialize local variables.

Global Variables

A global variable is any variable defined outside all the functions in a program. The scope of a global variable is the portion of the program from the variable definition to the end. This means that a global variable can be accessed by all functions that are defined after the global variable is defined. Program 6-17 shows two functions, main and anotherFunction, that access the same global variable, num.

Program 6-17

```cpp
1   // This program shows that a global variable is visible
2   // to all the functions that appear in a program after
3   // the variable's declaration.
4   #include <iostream>
5   using namespace std;
6
7   void anotherFunction(); // Function prototype
8   int num = 2;            // Global variable
```

```
 9
10  int main()
11  {
12     cout << "In main, num is " << num << endl;
13     anotherFunction();
14     cout << "Back in main, num is " << num << endl;
15     return 0;
16  }
17
18  //*********************************************************
19  // Definition of anotherFunction                         *
20  // This function changes the value of the                *
21  // global variable num.                                  *
22  //*********************************************************
23
24  void anotherFunction()
25  {
26     cout << "In anotherFunction, num is " << num << endl;
27     num = 50;
28     cout << "But, it is now changed to " << num << endl;
29  }
```

Program Output

```
In main, num is 2
In anotherFunction, num is 2
But, it is now changed to 50
Back in main, num is 50
```

In Program 6-17, num is defined outside of all the functions. Because its definition appears before the definitions of main and anotherFunction, both functions have access to it.

Unless you explicitly initialize numeric global variables, they are automatically initialized to zero. Global character variables are initialized to NULL.* The variable globalNum in Program 6-18 is never set to any value by a statement, but because it is global, it is automatically set to zero.

Program 6-18

```
 1  // This program has an uninitialized global variable.
 2  #include <iostream>
 3  using namespace std;
 4
 5  int globalNum; // Global variable, automatically set to zero
 6
 7  int main()
 8  {
 9     cout << "globalNum is " << globalNum << endl;
10     return 0;
11  }
```

(program output continues)

---

* The NULL character is stored as ASCII code 0.

Program 6-18   *(continued)*

Program Output
globalNum is 0

Now that you've had a basic introduction to global variables, I must warn you to restrict your use of them. When beginning students first learn to write programs with multiple functions, they are sometimes tempted to make all their variables global. This is usually because global variables can be accessed by any function in the program without being passed as arguments. Although this approach might make a program easier to create, it usually causes problems later. The reasons are as follows:

- Global variables make debugging difficult. Any statement in a program can change the value of a global variable. If you find that the wrong value is being stored in a global variable, you have to track down every statement that accesses it to determine where the bad value is coming from. In a program with thousands of lines of code, this can be difficult.
- Functions that use global variables are usually dependent on those variables. If you want to use such a function in a different program, most likely you will have to redesign it so it does not rely on the global variable.
- Global variables make a program hard to understand. A global variable can be modified by any statement in the program. If you are to understand any part of the program that uses a global variable, you have to be aware of all the other parts of the program that access the global variable.

Because of this, you should not use global variables for the conventional purposes of storing, manipulating, and retrieving data. In most cases, you should declare variables locally and pass them as arguments to the functions that need to access them.

Global Constants

Although you should try to avoid the use of global variables, it is generally permissible to use global constants in a program. A *global constant* is a named constant that is available to every function in a program. Because a global constant's value cannot be changed during the program's execution, you do not have to worry about the potential hazards that are associated with the use of global variables.

Global constants are typically used to represent unchanging values that are needed throughout a program. For example, suppose a banking program uses a named constant to represent an interest rate. If the interest rate is used in several functions, it is easier to create a global constant, rather than a local named constant in each function. This also simplifies maintenance. If the interest rate changes, only the declaration of the global constant has to be changed, instead of several local declarations.

Program 6-19 shows an example of how global constants might be used. The program calculates an employee's gross pay, including overtime. In addition to main, this program has two functions: getBasePay and getOvertimePay. The getBasePay function accepts the number of hours worked and returns the amount of pay for the non-overtime hours. The getOvertimePay function accepts the number of hours worked and returns the amount of pay for the overtime hours, if any.

Program 6-19

```cpp
1    // This program calculates gross pay.
2    #include <iostream>
3    #include <iomanip>
4    using namespace std;
5
6    // Global constants
7    const double PAY_RATE = 22.55;      // Hourly pay rate
8    const double BASE_HOURS = 40.0;     // Max non-overtime hours
9    const double OT_MULTIPLIER = 1.5; // Overtime multiplier
10
11   // Function prototypes
12   double getBasePay(double);
13   double getOvertimePay(double);
14
15   int main()
16   {
17      double hours,           // Hours worked
18             basePay,         // Base pay
19             overtime = 0.0,  // Overtime pay
20             totalPay;        // Total pay
21
22      // Get the number of hours worked.
23      cout << "How many hours did you work? ";
24      cin >> hours;
25
26      // Get the amount of base pay.
27      basePay = getBasePay(hours);
28
29      // Get overtime pay, if any.
30      if (hours > BASE_HOURS)
31         overtime = getOvertimePay(hours);
32
33      // Calculate the total pay.
34      totalPay = basePay + overtime;
35
36      // Set up numeric output formatting.
37      cout << setprecision(2) << fixed << showpoint;
38
39      // Display the pay.
40      cout << "Base pay: $" << basePay << endl
41           << "Overtime pay $" << overtime << endl
42           << "Total pay $" << totalPay << endl;
43      return 0;
44   }
45
46   //**************************************************
47   // The getBasePay function accepts the number of *
48   // hours worked as an argument and returns the    *
49   // employee's pay for non-overtime hours.         *
50   //**************************************************
51
```

(program continues)

Program 6-19   *(continued)*

```
52   double getBasePay(double hoursWorked)
53   {
54      double basePay; // To hold base pay
55
56      // Determine base pay.
57      if (hoursWorked > BASE_HOURS)
58         basePay = BASE_HOURS * PAY_RATE;
59      else
60         basePay = hoursWorked * PAY_RATE;
61
62      return basePay;
63   }
64
65   //***************************************************
66   // The getOvertimePay function accepts the number  *
67   // of hours worked as an argument and returns the  *
68   // employee's overtime pay.                        *
69   //***************************************************
70
71   double getOvertimePay(double hoursWorked)
72   {
73      double overtimePay; // To hold overtime pay
74
75      // Determine overtime pay.
76      if (hoursWorked > BASE_HOURS)
77      {
78         overtimePay = (hoursWorked - BASE_HOURS) *
79                  PAY_RATE * OT_MULTIPLIER;
80      }
81      else
82         overtimePay = 0.0;
83
84      return overtimePay;
85   }
```

Program Output with Example Input Shown in Bold
```
How many hours did you work? 48 [Enter]
Base pay: $902.00
Overtime pay: $270.60
Total pay: $1172.60
```

Let's take a closer look at the program. Three global constants are defined in lines 7, 8, and 9. The PAY_RATE constant is set to the employee's hourly pay rate, which is 22.55. The BASE_HOURS constant is set to 40, which is the number of hours an employee can work in a week without getting paid overtime. The OT_MULTIPLIER constant is set to 1.5, which is the pay rate multiplier for overtime hours. This means that the employee's hourly pay rate is multiplied by 1.5 for all overtime hours.

Because these constants are global, and are defined before all of the functions in the program, all the functions may access them. For example, the getBasePay function accesses the BASE_HOURS constant in lines 57 and 58, and accesses the PAY_RATE constant in lines 58 and 60. The getOvertimePay function accesses the BASE_HOURS constant in lines 76 and 78, the PAY_RATE constant in line 79, and the OT_MULTIPLIER constant in line 79.

Local and Global Variables with the Same Name

You cannot have two local variables with the same name in the same function. This applies to parameter variables as well. A parameter variable is, in essence, a local variable. So, you cannot give a parameter variable and a local variable in the same function the same name.

However, you can have a local variable or a parameter variable with the same name as a global variable, or a global constant. When you do, the name of the local or parameter variable *shadows* the name of the global variable or global constant. This means that the global variable or constant's name is hidden by the name of the local or parameter variable. For example, look at Program 6-20. This program has a global constant named BIRDS, set to 500. The california function has a local constant named BIRDS, set to 10000.

Program 6-20

```
 1   // This program demonstrates how a local variable
 2   // can shadow the name of a global constant.
 3   #include <iostream>
 4   using namespace std;
 5
 6   // Global constant.
 7   const int BIRDS = 500;
 8
 9   // Function prototype
10   void california();
11
12   int main()
13   {
14      cout << "In main there are " << BIRDS
15           << " birds.\n";
16      california();
17      return 0;
18   }
19
20   //*******************************************
21   // california function                      *
22   //*******************************************
23
24   void california()
25   {
26      const int BIRDS = 10000;
27      cout << "In california there are " << BIRDS
28           << " birds.\n";
29   }
```

Program Output

```
In main there are 500 birds.
In california there are 10000 birds.
```

When the program is executing in the main function, the global constant BIRDS, which is set to 500, is visible. The cout statement in lines 14 and 15 displays "In main there are 500 birds." (My apologies to folks living in Maine for the difference in spelling.) When the program is executing in the california function, however, the local constant BIRDS shadows the global constant BIRDS. When the california function accesses BIRDS, it accesses the local constant. That is why the cout statement in lines 27 and 28 displays "In california there are 10000 birds."

6.11 Static Local Variables

If a function is called more than once in a program, the values stored in the function's local variables do not persist between function calls. This is because the local variables are destroyed when the function terminates and are then re-created when the function starts again. This is shown in Program 6-21.

Program 6-21

```
 1   // This program shows that local variables do not retain
 2   // their values between function calls.
 3   #include <iostream>
 4   using namespace std;
 5
 6   // Function prototype
 7   void showLocal();
 8
 9   int main()
10   {
11      showLocal();
12      showLocal();
13      return 0;
14   }
15
16   //***********************************************************
17   // Definition of function showLocal.                       *
18   // The initial value of localNum, which is 5, is displayed. *
19   // The value of localNum is then changed to 99 before the   *
20   // function returns.                                        *
21   //***********************************************************
22
23   void showLocal()
24   {
25      int localNum = 5; // Local variable
26
27      cout << "localNum is " << localNum << endl;
28      localNum = 99;
29   }
```

Program Output
```
localNum is 5
localNum is 5
```

Even though in line 28 the last statement in the showLocal function stores 99 in localNum, the variable is destroyed when the function returns. The next time the function is called, localNum is re-created and initialized to 5 again.

Sometimes it's desirable for a program to "remember" what value is stored in a local variable between function calls. This can be accomplished by making the variable static.

Static local variables are not destroyed when a function returns. They exist for the lifetime of the program, even though their scope is only the function in which they are defined. Program 6-22 demonstrates some characteristics of static local variables:

Program 6-22

```
 1   // This program uses a static local variable.
 2   #include <iostream>
 3   using namespace std;
 4
 5   void showStatic(); // Function prototype
 6
 7   int main()
 8   {
 9      // Call the showStatic function five times.
10      for (int count = 0; count < 5; count++)
11         showStatic();
12      return 0;
13   }
14
15   //*************************************************************
16   // Definition of function showStatic.                        *
17   // statNum is a static local variable. Its value is displayed *
18   // and then incremented just before the function returns.     *
19   //*************************************************************
20
21   void showStatic()
22   {
23      static int statNum;
24
25      cout << "statNum is " << statNum << endl;
26      statNum++;
27   }
```

Program Output
```
statNum is 0
statNum is 1
statNum is 2
statNum is 3
statNum is 4
```

In line 26 of Program 6-22, statNum is incremented in the showStatic function, and it retains its value between each function call. Notice that even though statNum is not explicitly initialized, it starts at zero. Like global variables, all static local variables are initialized to zero by default. (Of course, you can provide your own initialization value, if necessary.)

If you do provide an initialization value for a static local variable, the initialization only occurs once. This is because initialization normally happens when the variable is created, and static local variables are only created once during the running of a program. Program 6-23, which is a slight modification of Program 6-22, illustrates this point.

Program 6-23

```
 1   // This program shows that a static local variable is only
 2   // initialized once.
 3   #include <iostream>
 4   using namespace std;
 5
 6   void showStatic(); // Function prototype
 7
 8   int main()
 9   {
10      // Call the showStatic function five times.
11      for (int count = 0; count < 5; count++)
12         showStatic();
13      return 0;
14   }
15
16   //****************************************************************
17   // Definition of function showStatic.                          *
18   // statNum is a static local variable. Its value is displayed  *
19   // and then incremented just before the function returns.      *
20   //****************************************************************
21
22   void showStatic()
23   {
24      static int statNum = 5;
25
26      cout << "statNum is " << statNum << endl;
27      statNum++;
28   }
```

Program Output
```
statNum is 5
statNum is 6
statNum is 7
statNum is 8
statNum is 9
```

Even though the statement that defines statNum in line 24 initializes it to 5, the initialization does not happen each time the function is called. If it did, the variable would not be able to retain its value between function calls.

 Checkpoint

myprogramminglab   *www.myprogramminglab.com*

6.16   What is the difference between a static local variable and a global variable?

6.17   What is the output of the following program?

```
#include <iostream>
using namespace std;

void myFunc();  // Function prototype

int main()
{
```

```
    int var = 100;

    cout << var << endl;
    myFunc();
    cout << var << endl;
    return 0;
}

// Definition of function myFunc
void myFunc()
{
    int var = 50;

    cout << var << endl;
}
```

6.18   What is the output of the following program?

```
#include <iostream>
using namespace std;

void showVar(); // Function prototype

int main()
{
    for (int count = 0; count < 10; count++)
        showVar();
    return 0;
}

// Definition of function showVar
void showVar()
{
    static int var = 10;

    cout << var << endl;
    var++;
}
```

6.12 Default Arguments

CONCEPT: Default arguments are passed to parameters automatically if no argument
is provided in the function call.

It's possible to assign *default arguments* to function parameters. A default argument is
passed to the parameter when the actual argument is left out of the function call. The
default arguments are usually listed in the function prototype. Here is an example:

```
void showArea(double = 20.0, double = 10.0);
```

Default arguments are literal values or constants with an = operator in front of them,
appearing after the data types listed in a function prototype. Since parameter names are
optional in function prototypes, the example prototype could also be declared as

```
void showArea(double length = 20.0, double width = 10.0);
```

In both example prototypes, the function `showArea` has two `double` parameters. The first is assigned the default argument 20.0 and the second is assigned the default argument 10.0. Here is the definition of the function:

```cpp
void showArea(double length, double width)
{
   double area = length * width;
   cout << "The area is " << area << endl;
}
```

The default argument for `length` is 20.0 and the default argument for `width` is 10.0. Because both parameters have default arguments, they may optionally be omitted in the function call, as shown here:

```cpp
showArea();
```

In this function call, both default arguments will be passed to the parameters. The parameter `length` will take the value 20.0 and `width` will take the value 10.0. The output of the function will be

```
The area is 200
```

The default arguments are only used when the actual arguments are omitted from the function call. In the call below, the first argument is specified, but the second is omitted:

```cpp
showArea(12.0);
```

The value 12.0 will be passed to `length`, while the default value 10.0 will be passed to `width`. The output of the function will be

```
The area is 120
```

Of course, all the default arguments may be overridden. In the function call below, arguments are supplied for both parameters:

```cpp
showArea(12.0, 5.5);
```

The output of the function call above will be

```
The area is 66
```

NOTE: If a function does not have a prototype, default arguments may be specified in the function header. The `showArea` function could be defined as follows:

```cpp
void showArea(double length = 20.0, double width = 10.0)
{
   double area = length * width;
   cout << "The area is " << area << endl;
}
```

WARNING! A function's default arguments should be assigned in the earliest occurrence of the function name. This will usually be the function prototype.

Program 6-24 uses a function that displays asterisks on the screen. Arguments are passed to the function specifying how many columns and rows of asterisks to display. Default arguments are provided to display one row of 10 asterisks.

Program 6-24

```cpp
 1   // This program demonstrates default function arguments.
 2   #include <iostream>
 3   using namespace std;
 4
 5   // Function prototype with default arguments
 6   void displayStars(int = 10, int = 1);
 7
 8   int main()
 9   {
10      displayStars();        // Use default values for cols and rows.
11      cout << endl;
12      displayStars(5);       // Use default value for rows.
13      cout << endl;
14      displayStars(7, 3);    // Use 7 for cols and 3 for rows.
15      return 0;
16   }
17
18   //*********************************************************
19   // Definition of function displayStars.                  *
20   // The default argument for cols is 10 and for rows is 1.*
21   // This function displays a square made of asterisks.    *
22   //*********************************************************
23
24   void displayStars(int cols, int rows)
25   {
26      // Nested loop. The outer loop controls the rows
27      // and the inner loop controls the columns.
28      for (int down = 0; down < rows; down++)
29      {
30         for (int across = 0; across < cols; across++)
31            cout << "*";
32         cout << endl;
33      }
34   }
```

Program Output

```
**********

*****

*******
*******
*******
```

Although C++'s default arguments are very convenient, they are not totally flexible in their use. When an argument is left out of a function call, all arguments that come after it must be left out as well. In the `displayStars` function in Program 6-24, it is not possible to omit the argument for `cols` without also omitting the argument for `rows`. For example, the following function call would be illegal:

```cpp
displayStars(, 3); // Illegal function call.
```

It's possible for a function to have some parameters with default arguments and some without. For example, in the following function (which displays an employee's gross pay), only the last parameter has a default argument:

```
// Function prototype
void calcPay(int empNum, double payRate, double hours = 40.0);

// Definition of function calcPay
void calcPay(int empNum, double payRate, double hours)
{
   double wages;

   wages = payRate * hours;
   cout << fixed << showpoint << setprecision(2);
   cout << "Gross pay for employee number ";
   cout << empNum << " is " << wages << endl;
}
```

When calling this function, arguments must always be specified for the first two parameters (empNum and payRate) since they have no default arguments. Here are examples of valid calls:

```
calcPay(769, 15.75);       // Use default arg for 40 hours
calcPay(142, 12.00, 20);   // Specify number of hours
```

When a function uses a mixture of parameters with and without default arguments, the parameters with default arguments must be defined last. In the calcPay function, hours could not have been defined before either of the other parameters. The following prototypes are illegal:

```
// Illegal prototype
void calcPay(int empNum, double hours = 40.0, double payRate);

// Illegal prototype
void calcPay(double hours = 40.0, int empNum, double payRate);
```

Here is a summary of the important points about default arguments:

- The value of a default argument must be a literal value or a named constant.
- When an argument is left out of a function call (because it has a default value), all the arguments that come after it must be left out too.
- When a function has a mixture of parameters both with and without default arguments, the parameters with default arguments must be declared last.

6.13 Using Reference Variables as Parameters

CONCEPT: When used as parameters, reference variables allow a function to access the parameter's original argument. Changes to the parameter are also made to the argument.

Earlier you saw that arguments are normally passed to a function by value, and that the function cannot change the source of the argument. C++ provides a special type of variable called a *reference variable* that, when used as a function parameter, allows access to the original argument.

A reference variable is an alias for another variable. Any changes made to the reference variable are actually performed on the variable for which it is an alias. By using a reference variable as a parameter, a function may change a variable that is defined in another function.

Reference variables are defined like regular variables, except you place an ampersand (&) in front of the name. For example, the following function definition makes the parameter refVar a reference variable:

```
void doubleNum(int &refVar)
{
    refVar *= 2;
}
```

NOTE: The variable refVar is called "a reference to an int."

This function doubles refVar by multiplying it by 2. Since refVar is a reference variable, this action is actually performed on the variable that was passed to the function as an argument. When prototyping a function with a reference variable, be sure to include the ampersand after the data type. Here is the prototype for the doubleNum function:

```
void doubleNum(int &);
```

NOTE: Some programmers prefer not to put a space between the data type and the ampersand. The following prototype is equivalent to the one above:

```
void doubleNum(int&);
```

NOTE: The ampersand must appear in both the prototype and the header of any function that uses a reference variable as a parameter. It does not appear in the function call.

Program 6-25 demonstrates how the doubleNum function works.

Program 6-25

```
1   // This program uses a reference variable as a function
2   // parameter.
3   #include <iostream>
4   using namespace std;
5
6   // Function prototype. The parameter is a reference variable.
7   void doubleNum(int &);
8
9   int main()
```

(program continues)

Program 6-25 *(continued)*

```
10   {
11       int value = 4;
12
13       cout << "In main, value is " << value << endl;
14       cout << "Now calling doubleNum..." << endl;
15       doubleNum(value);
16       cout << "Now back in main. value is " << value << endl;
17       return 0;
18   }
19
20   //*********************************************************
21   // Definition of doubleNum.                               *
22   // The parameter refVar is a reference variable. The value *
23   // in refVar is doubled.                                   *
24   //*********************************************************
25
26   void doubleNum (int &refVar)
27   {
28       refVar *= 2;
29   }
```

Program Output

```
In main, value is 4
Now calling doubleNum...
Now back in main. value is 8
```

The parameter `refVar` in Program 6-25 "points" to the `value` variable in function `main`. When a program works with a reference variable, it is actually working with the variable it references, or points to. This is illustrated in Figure 6-15.

Figure 6-15

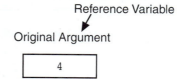

Recall that function arguments are normally passed by value, which means a copy of the argument's value is passed into the parameter variable. When a reference parameter is used, it is said that the argument is *passed by reference*.

Program 6-26 is a modification of Program 6-25. The function `getNum` has been added. The function asks the user to enter a number, which is stored in `userNum`. `userNum` is a reference to `main`'s variable `value`.

Program 6-26

```cpp
 1    // This program uses reference variables as function parameters.
 2    #include <iostream>
 3    using namespace std;
 4
 5    // Function prototypes. Both functions use reference variables
 6    // as parameters.
 7    void doubleNum(int &);
 8    void getNum(int &);
 9
10    int main()
11    {
12       int value;
13
14       // Get a number and store it in value.
15       getNum(value);
16
17       // Double the number stored in value.
18       doubleNum(value);
19
20       // Display the resulting number.
21       cout << "That value doubled is " << value << endl;
22       return 0;
23    }
24
25    //**************************************************************
26    // Definition of getNum.                                      *
27    // The parameter userNum is a reference variable. The user is *
28    // asked to enter a number, which is stored in userNum.       *
29    //**************************************************************
30
31    void getNum(int &userNum)
32    {
33       cout << "Enter a number: ";
34       cin >> userNum;
35    }
36
37    //**************************************************************
38    // Definition of doubleNum.                                   *
39    // The parameter refVar is a reference variable. The value    *
40    // in refVar is doubled.                                      *
41    //**************************************************************
42
43    void doubleNum (int &refVar)
44    {
45       refVar *= 2;
46    }
```

Program Output with Example Input Shown in Bold

```
Enter a number: 12 [Enter]
That value doubled is 24
```

NOTE: Only variables may be passed by reference. If you attempt to pass a nonvariable argument, such as a literal, a constant, or an expression, into a reference parameter, an error will result. Using the doubleNum function as an example, the following statements will generate an error.

```
doubleNum(5);            // Error
doubleNum(userNum + 10);  // Error
```

If a function uses more than one reference variable as a parameter, be sure to place the ampersand before each reference variable name. Here is the prototype and definition for a function that uses four reference variable parameters:

```
// Function prototype with four reference variables
// as parameters.
void addThree(int &, int &, int &, int &);

// Definition of addThree.
// All four parameters are reference variables.
void addThree(int &sum, int &num1, int &num2, int &num3)
{
    cout << "Enter three integer values: ";
    cin >> num1 >> num2 >> num3;
    sum = num1 + num2 + num3;
}
```

WARNING! Don't get carried away with using reference variables as function parameters. Any time you allow a function to alter a variable that's outside the function, you are creating potential debugging problems. Reference variables should only be used as parameters when the situation requires them.

Checkpoint

myprogramminglab *www.myprogramminglab.com*

6.19 What kinds of values may be specified as default arguments?

6.20 Write the prototype and header for a function called compute. The function should have three parameters: an int, a double, and a long (not necessarily in that order). The int parameter should have a default argument of 5, and the long parameter should have a default argument of 65536. The double parameter should not have a default argument.

6.21 Write the prototype and header for a function called calculate. The function should have three parameters: an int, a reference to a double, and a long (not necessarily in that order.) Only the int parameter should have a default argument, which is 47.

6.22 What is the output of the following program?

```
#include <iostream>
using namespace std;

void test(int = 2, int = 4, int = 6);
```

```
int main()
{
   test();
   test(6);
   test(3, 9);
   test(1, 5, 7);
   return 0;
}

void test (int first, int second, int third)
{
   first += 3;
   second += 6;
   third += 9;
   cout << first << " " << second << " " << third << endl;
}
```

6.23   The following program asks the user to enter two numbers. What is the output of the program if the user enters 12 and 14?

```
#include <iostream>
using namespace std;

void func1(int &, int &);
void func2(int &, int &, int &);
void func3(int, int, int);

int main()
{
   int x = 0, y = 0, z = 0;

   cout << x << " " << y << " " << z << endl;
   func1(x, y);
   cout << x << " " << y << " " << z << endl;
   func2(x, y, z);
   cout << x << " " << y << " " << z << endl;
   func3(x, y, z);
   cout << x << " " << y << " " << z << endl;
   return 0;
}

void func1(int &a, int &b)
{
   cout << "Enter two numbers: ";
   cin >> a >> b;
}
void func2(int &a, int &b, int &c)
{
   b++;
   c--;
   a = b + c;
}

void func3(int a, int b, int c)
{
   a = b - c;
}
```

6.14 Overloading Functions

CONCEPT: Two or more functions may have the same name, as long as their parameter lists are different.

Sometimes you will create two or more functions that perform the same operation, but use a different set of parameters or parameters of different data types. For instance, in Program 6-13 there is a `square` function that uses a `double` parameter. But, suppose you also wanted a `square` function that works exclusively with integers, accepting an `int` as its argument. Both functions would do the same thing: return the square of their argument. The only difference is the data type involved in the operation. If you were to use both these functions in the same program, you could assign a unique name to each function. For example, the function that squares an `int` might be named `squareInt`, and the one that squares a `double` might be named `squareDouble`. C++, however, allows you to *overload* function names. That means you may assign the same name to multiple functions, as long as their parameter lists are different. Program 6-27 uses two overloaded `square` functions.

Program 6-27

```
 1    // This program uses overloaded functions.
 2    #include <iostream>
 3    #include <iomanip>
 4    using namespace std;
 5
 6    // Function prototypes
 7    int square(int);
 8    double square(double);
 9
10    int main()
11    {
12       int userInt;
13       double userFloat;
14
15       // Get an int and a double.
16       cout << fixed << showpoint << setprecision(2);
17       cout << "Enter an integer and a floating-point value: ";
18       cin >> userInt >> userFloat;
19
20       // Display their squares.
21       cout << "Here are their squares: ";
22       cout << square(userInt) << " and " << square(userFloat);
23       return 0;
24    }
25
26    //************************************************************
27    // Definition of overloaded function square.                *
28    // This function uses an int parameter, number. It returns the *
29    // square of number as an int.                              *
30    //************************************************************
```

```
31
32   int square(int number)
33   {
34       return number * number;
35   }
36
37   //***************************************************************
38   // Definition of overloaded function square.                   *
39   // This function uses a double parameter, number. It returns   *
40   // the square of number as a double.                           *
41   //***************************************************************
42
43   double square(double number)
44   {
45       return number * number;
46   }
```

Program Output with Example Input Shown in Bold
Enter an integer and a floating-point value: **12 4.2 [Enter]**
Here are their squares: 144 and 17.64

Here are the headers for the square functions used in Program 6-27:

```
int square(int number)
```

```
double square(double number)
```

In C++, each function has a signature. The *function signature* is the name of the function and the data types of the function's parameters in the proper order. The square functions in Program 6-27 would have the following signatures:

```
square(int)
```

```
square(double)
```

When an overloaded function is called, C++ uses the function signature to distinguish it from other functions with the same name. In Program 6-27, when an int argument is passed to square, the version of the function that has an int parameter is called. Likewise, when a double argument is passed to square, the version with a double parameter is called.

Note that the function's return value is not part of the signature. The following functions could not be used in the same program because their parameter lists aren't different.

```
int square(int number)
{
    return number * number
}

double square(int number)  // Wrong! Parameter lists must differ
{
    return number * number
}
```

Overloading is also convenient when there are similar functions that use a different number of parameters. For example, consider a program with functions that return the sum of integers. One returns the sum of two integers, another returns the sum of three integers, and yet another returns the sum of four integers. Here are their function headers:

```cpp
int sum(int num1, int num2)

int sum(int num1, int num2, int num3)

int sum(int num1, int num2, int num3, int num4)
```

Because the number of parameters is different in each, they all may be used in the same program. Program 6-28 is an example that uses two functions, each named `calcWeeklyPay`, to determine an employee's gross weekly pay. One version of the function uses an `int` and a `double` parameter, while the other version only uses a `double` parameter.

Program 6-28

```cpp
 1  // This program demonstrates overloaded functions to calculate
 2  // the gross weekly pay of hourly paid or salaried employees.
 3  #include <iostream>
 4  #include <iomanip>
 5  using namespace std;
 6
 7  // Function prototypes
 8  void getChoice(char &);
 9  double calcWeeklyPay(int, double);
10  double calcWeeklyPay(double);
11
12  int main()
13  {
14      char selection;    // Menu selection
15      int worked;        // Hours worked
16      double rate;       // Hourly pay rate
17      double yearly;     // Yearly salary
18
19      // Set numeric output formatting.
20      cout << fixed << showpoint << setprecision(2);
21
22      // Display the menu and get a selection.
23      cout << "Do you want to calculate the weekly pay of\n";
24      cout << "(H) an hourly paid employee, or \n";
25      cout << "(S) a salaried employee?\n";
26      getChoice(selection);
27
28      // Process the menu selection.
29      switch (selection)
30      {
31          // Hourly paid employee
32          case 'H' :
33          case 'h' :  cout << "How many hours were worked? ";
```

```
34                       cin >> worked;
35                       cout << "What is the hourly pay rate? ";
36                       cin >> rate;
37                       cout << "The gross weekly pay is $";
38                       cout << calcWeeklyPay(worked, rate) << endl;
39                       break;
40
41          // Salaried employee
42          case 'S' :
43          case 's' :  cout << "What is the annual salary? ";
44                      cin >> yearly;
45                      cout << "The gross weekly pay is $";
46                      cout << calcWeeklyPay(yearly) << endl;
47                      break;
48       }
49       return 0;
50   }
51
52   //*********************************************************
53   // Definition of function getChoice.                     *
54   // The parameter letter is a reference to a char.        *
55   // This function asks the user for an H or an S and returns *
56   // the validated input.                                  *
57   //*********************************************************
58
59   void getChoice(char & letter)
60   {
61       // Get the user's selection.
62       cout << "Enter your choice (H or S): ";
63       cin >> letter;
64
65       // Validate the selection.
66       while (letter != 'H' && letter != 'h' &&
67              letter != 'S' && letter != 's')
68       {
69          cout << "Please enter H or S: ";
70          cin >> letter;
71       }
72   }
73
74   //*********************************************************
75   // Definition of overloaded function calcWeeklyPay.      *
76   // This function calculates the gross weekly pay of      *
77   // an hourly paid employee. The parameter hours holds the *
78   // number of hours worked. The parameter payRate holds the *
79   // hourly pay rate. The function returns the weekly salary. *
80   //*********************************************************
```

(program continues)

Program 6-28 *(continued)*

```
81
82   double calcWeeklyPay(int hours, double payRate)
83   {
84      return hours * payRate;
85   }
86
87   //**********************************************************
88   // Definition of overloaded function calcWeeklyPay.        *
89   // This function calculates the gross weekly pay of        *
90   // a salaried employee. The parameter holds the employee's *
91   // annual salary. The function returns the weekly salary.  *
92   //**********************************************************
93
94   double calcWeeklyPay(double annSalary)
95   {
96      return annSalary / 52;
97   }
```

Program Output with Example Input Shown in Bold
```
Do you want to calculate the weekly pay of
(H) an hourly paid employee, or
(S) a salaried employee?
Enter your choice (H or S): H [Enter]
How many hours were worked? 40 [Enter]
What is the hourly pay rate? 18.50 [Enter]
The gross weekly pay is $740.00
```

Program Output with Example Input Shown in Bold
```
Do you want to calculate the weekly pay of
(H) an hourly paid employee, or
(S) a salaried employee?
Enter your choice (H or S): S [Enter]
What is the annual salary? 68000.00 [Enter]
The gross weekly pay is $1307.69
```

6.15 The exit() Function

CONCEPT: The exit() function causes a program to terminate, regardless of which function or control mechanism is executing.

A C++ program stops executing when the return statement in function main is encountered. When other functions end, however, the program does not stop. Control of the program goes back to the place immediately following the function call. Sometimes, rare circumstances make it necessary to terminate a program in a function other than main. To accomplish this, the exit function is used.

When the exit function is called, it causes the program to stop, regardless of which function contains the call. Program 6-29 demonstrates its use.

Program 6-29

```cpp
 1   // This program shows how the exit function causes a program
 2   // to stop executing.
 3   #include <iostream>
 4   #include <cstdlib>   // Needed for the exit function
 5   using namespace std;
 6
 7   void function();     // Function prototype
 8
 9   int main()
10   {
11      function();
12      return 0;
13   }
14
15   //********************************************************
16   // This function simply demonstrates that exit can be used  *
17   // to terminate a program from a function other than main.   *
18   //********************************************************
19
20   void function()
21   {
22      cout << "This program terminates with the exit function.\n";
23      cout << "Bye!\n";
24      exit(0);
25      cout << "This message will never be displayed\n";
26      cout << "because the program has already terminated.\n";
27   }
```

Program Output

```
This program terminates with the exit function.
Bye!
```

To use the exit function, you must include the cstdlib header file. Notice the function takes an integer argument. This argument is the exit code you wish the program to pass back to the computer's operating system. This code is sometimes used outside of the program to indicate whether the program ended successfully or as the result of a failure. In Program 6-29, the exit code zero is passed, which commonly indicates a successful exit. If you are unsure which code to use with the exit function, there are two named constants, EXIT_FAILURE and EXIT_SUCCESS, defined in cstdlib for you to use. The constant EXIT_FAILURE is defined as the termination code that commonly represents an unsuccessful exit under the current operating system. Here is an example of its use:

```cpp
exit(EXIT_FAILURE);
```

The constant EXIT_SUCCESS is defined as the termination code that commonly represents a successful exit under the current operating system. Here is an example:

```cpp
exit(EXIT_SUCCESS);
```

NOTE: Generally, the exit code is important only if you know it will be tested outside the program. If it is not used, just pass zero, or EXIT_SUCCESS.

WARNING! The `exit()` function unconditionally shuts down your program. Because it bypasses a program's normal logical flow, you should use it with caution.

Checkpoint

myprogramminglab *www.myprogramminglab.com*

6.24 What is the output of the following program?

```cpp
#include <iostream>
#include <cstdlib>
using namespace std;

void showVals(double, double);

int main()
{
    double x = 1.2, y = 4.5;

    showVals(x, y);
    return 0;
}

void showVals(double p1, double p2)
{
    cout << p1 << endl;
    exit(0);
    cout << p2 << endl;
}
```

6.25 What is the output of the following program?

```cpp
#include <iostream>
using namespace std;

int manip(int);
int manip(int, int);
int manip(int, double);

int main()
{
    int x = 2, y= 4, z;
    double a = 3.1;

    z = manip(x) + manip(x, y) + manip(y, a);
    cout << z << endl;
    return 0;
}
int manip(int val)
{
    return val + val * 2;
}

int manip(int val1, int val2)
{
    return (val1 + val2) * 2;
}

int manip(int val1, double val2)
{
    return val1 * static_cast<int>(val2);
}
```

6.16 Stubs and Drivers

Stubs and *drivers* are very helpful tools for testing and debugging programs that use functions. They allow you to test the individual functions in a program, in isolation from the parts of the program that call the functions.

A *stub* is a dummy function that is called instead of the actual function it represents. It usually displays a test message acknowledging that it was called, and nothing more. For example, if a stub were used for the showFees function in Program 6-10 (the modular health club membership program), it might look like this:

```cpp
void showFees(double memberRate, int months)
{
    cout << "The showFees function was called with "
         << "the following arguments:\n"
         << "memberRate: " << memberRate << endl
         << "months: " << months << endl;
}
```

The following is an example output of the program if it were run with the stub instead of the actual showFees function. (A version of the health club program using this stub function is available from the book's companion Web site at www.pearsonhighered.com/gaddis. The program is named HealthClubWithStub.cpp.)

```
           Health Club Membership Menu

1. Standard Adult Membership
2. Child Membership
3. Senior Citizen Membership
4. Quit the Program

Enter your choice: 1 [Enter]
For how many months? 4 [Enter]
The showFees function was called with the following arguments:
memberRate: 40.00
months: 4

           Health Club Membership Menu

1. Standard Adult Membership
2. Child Membership
3. Senior Citizen Membership
4. Quit the Program

Enter your choice: 4 [Enter]
```

As you can see, by replacing an actual function with a stub, you can concentrate your testing efforts on the parts of the program that call the function. Primarily, the stub allows you to determine whether your program is calling a function when you expect it to, and to confirm that valid values are being passed to the function. If the stub represents a function that returns a value, then the stub should return a test value. This helps you confirm that the return value is being handled properly. When the parts of the program that call a function are debugged to your satisfaction, you can move on to testing and debugging the actual functions themselves. This is where *drivers* become useful.

A driver is a program that tests a function by simply calling it. If the function accepts arguments, the driver passes test data. If the function returns a value, the driver displays the return value on the screen. This allows you to see how the function performs in isolation from the rest of the program it will eventually be part of. Program 6-30 shows a driver for testing the showFees function in the health club membership program.

Program 6-30

```cpp
 1   // This program is a driver for testing the showFees function.
 2   #include <iostream>
 3   using namespace std;
 4
 5   // Prototype
 6   void showFees(double, int);
 7
 8   int main()
 9   {
10      // Constants for membership rates
11      const double ADULT = 40.0;
12      const double SENIOR = 30.0;
13      const double CHILD = 20.0;
14
15      // Perform a test for adult membership.
16      cout << "Testing an adult membership...\n"
17           << "Calling the showFees function with arguments "
18           << ADULT << " and 10.\n";
19      showFees(ADULT, 10);
20
21      // Perform a test for senior citizen membership.
22      cout << "\nTesting a senior citizen membership...\n"
23           << "Calling the showFees function with arguments "
24           << SENIOR << " and 10.\n";
25      showFees(SENIOR, 10);
26
27      // Perform a test for child membership.
28      cout << "\nTesting a child membership...\n"
29           << "\nCalling the showFees function with arguments "
30           << CHILD << " and 10.\n";
31      showFees(CHILD, 10);
32      return 0;
33   }
34
35   //*****************************************************************
36   // Definition of function showFees. The memberRate parameter holds*
37   // the monthly membership rate and the months parameter holds the *
38   // number of months. The function displays the total charges.    *
39   //*****************************************************************
40
41   void showFees(double memberRate, int months)
42   {
43       cout << "The total charges are $"
44            << (memberRate * months) << endl;
45   }
```

Program Output

```
Testing an adult membership...
Calling the showFees function with arguments 40 and 10.
The total charges are $400

Testing a senior citizen membership...
Calling the showFees function with arguments 30 and 10.
The total charges are $300

Testing a child membership...

Calling the showFees function with arguments 20 and 10.
The total charges are $200
```

As shown in Program 6-30, a driver can be used to thoroughly test a function. It can repeatedly call the function with different test values as arguments. When the function performs as desired, it can be placed into the actual program it will be part of.

Case Study: See High Adventure Travel Agency Part 1 Case Study on the book's companion Web site at www.pearsonhighered.com/gaddis.

Review Questions and Exercises

Short Answer

1. Why do local variables lose their values between calls to the function in which they are defined?

2. What is the difference between an argument and a parameter variable?

3. Where do you define parameter variables?

4. If you are writing a function that accepts an argument and you want to make sure the function cannot change the value of the argument, what do you do?

5. When a function accepts multiple arguments, does it matter in what order the arguments are passed in?

6. How do you return a value from a function?

7. What is the advantage of breaking your application's code into several small procedures?

8. How would a `static` local variable be useful?

9. Give an example where passing an argument by reference would be useful.

Fill-in-the-Blank

10. The _____ is the part of a function definition that shows the function name, return type, and parameter list.

11. If a function doesn't return a value, the word _____ will appear as its return type.

12. Either a function's _____ or its _____ must precede all calls to the function.

13. Values that are sent into a function are called _____.

14. Special variables that hold copies of function arguments are called _____.

15. When only a copy of an argument is passed to a function, it is said to be passed by _____.

16. A(n) _____ eliminates the need to place a function definition before all calls to the function.

17. A(n) _____ variable is defined inside a function and is not accessible outside the function.

18. _____ variables are defined outside all functions and are accessible to any function within their scope.

19. _____ variables provide an easy way to share large amounts of data among all the functions in a program.

20. Unless you explicitly initialize global variables, they are automatically initialized to _____.

21. If a function has a local variable with the same name as a global variable, only the _____ variable can be seen by the function.

22. _____ local variables retain their value between function calls.

23. The _____ statement causes a function to end immediately.

24. _____ arguments are passed to parameters automatically if no argument is provided in the function call.

25. When a function uses a mixture of parameters with and without default arguments, the parameters with default arguments must be defined _____.

26. The value of a default argument must be a(n) _____.

27. When used as parameters, _____ variables allow a function to access the parameter's original argument.

28. Reference variables are defined like regular variables, except there is a(n) _____ in front of the name.

29. Reference variables allow arguments to be passed by _____.

30. The _____ function causes a program to terminate.

31. Two or more functions may have the same name, as long as their _____ are different.

Algorithm Workbench

32. Examine the following function header, then write an example call to the function.

    ```
    void showValue(int quantity)
    ```

33. The following statement calls a function named `half`. The `half` function returns a value that is half that of the argument. Write the function.

    ```
    result = half(number);
    ```

34. A program contains the following function.

```
int cube(int num)
{
    return num * num * num;
}
```

Write a statement that passes the value 4 to this function and assigns its return value to the variable `result`.

35. Write a function named `timesTen` that accepts an argument. When the function is called, it should display the product of its argument multiplied times 10.

36. A program contains the following function.

```
void display(int arg1, double arg2, char arg3)
{
    cout << "Here are the values: "
         << arg1 << " " << arg2 << " "
         << arg3 << endl;
}
```

Write a statement that calls the procedure and passes the following variables to it:

```
int age;
double income;
char initial;
```

37. Write a function named `getNumber` that uses a reference parameter variable to accept an integer argument. The function should prompt the user to enter a number in the range of 1 through 100. The input should be validated and stored in the parameter variable.

True or False

38. T F   Functions should be given names that reflect their purpose.
39. T F   Function headers are terminated with a semicolon.
40. T F   Function prototypes are terminated with a semicolon.
41. T F   If other functions are defined before `main`, the program still starts executing at function `main`.
42. T F   When a function terminates, it always branches back to `main`, regardless of where it was called from.
43. T F   Arguments are passed to the function parameters in the order they appear in the function call.
44. T F   The scope of a parameter is limited to the function which uses it.
45. T F   Changes to a function parameter always affect the original argument as well.
46. T F   In a function prototype, the names of the parameter variables may be left out.
47. T F   Many functions may have local variables with the same name.
48. T F   Overuse of global variables can lead to problems.
49. T F   Static local variables are not destroyed when a function returns.
50. T F   All static local variables are initialized to –1 by default.

51. T   F   Initialization of static local variables only happens once, regardless of how many times the function in which they are defined is called.

52. T   F   When a function with default arguments is called and an argument is left out, all arguments that come after it must be left out as well.

53. T   F   It is not possible for a function to have some parameters with default arguments and some without.

54. T   F   The exit function can only be called from main.

55. T   F   A stub is a dummy function that is called instead of the actual function it represents.

Find the Errors

Each of the following functions has errors. Locate as many errors as you can.

56.
```cpp
void total(int value1, value2, value3)
{
    return value1 + value2 + value3;
}
```

57.
```cpp
double average(int value1, int value2, int value3)
{
    double average;

    average = value1 + value2 + value3 / 3;
}
```

58.
```cpp
void area(int length = 30, int width)
{
    return length * width;
}
```

59.
```cpp
void getValue(int value&)
{
    cout << "Enter a value: ";
    cin >> value&;
}
```

60. (*Overloaded functions*)
```cpp
int getValue()
{
    int inputValue;
    cout << "Enter an integer: ";
    cin >> inputValue;
    return inputValue;
}
double getValue()
{
    double inputValue;
    cout << "Enter a floating-point number: ";
    cin >> inputValue;
    return inputValue;
}
```

Programming Challenges

Visit www.myprogramminglab.com to complete many of these Programming Challenges online and get instant feedback.

1. **Markup**

   Write a program that asks the user to enter an item's wholesale cost and its markup percentage. It should then display the item's retail price. For example:

   - If an item's wholesale cost is 5.00 and its markup percentage is 100%, then the item's retail price is 10.00.
   - If an item's wholesale cost is 5.00 and its markup percentage is 50%, then the item's retail price is 7.50.

   The program should have a function named `calculateRetail` that receives the wholesale cost and the markup percentage as arguments, and returns the retail price of the item.

   Input Validation: Do not accept negative values for either the wholesale cost of the item or the markup percentage.

2. **Rectangle Area—Complete the Program**

   If you have downloaded this book's source code from the companion Web site, you will find a partially written program named `AreaRectangle.cpp` in the Chapter 06 folder. (The companion Web site is at www.pearsonhighered.com/gaddis.) Your job is to complete the program. When it is complete, the program will ask the user to enter the width and length of a rectangle, and then display the rectangle's area. The program calls the following functions, which have not been written:

   - `getLength` – This function should ask the user to enter the rectangle's length, and then return that value as a `double`.
   - `getWidth` – This function should ask the user to enter the rectangle's width, and then return that value as a `double`.
   - `getArea` – This function should accept the rectangle's length and width as arguments, and return the rectangle's area. The area is calculated by multiplying the length by the width.
   - `displayData` – This function should accept the rectangle's length, width, and area as arguments, and display them in an appropriate message on the screen.

3. **Winning Division**

   Write a program that determines which of a company's four divisions (Northeast, Southeast, Northwest, and Southwest) had the greatest sales for a quarter. It should include the following two functions, which are called by `main`.

   - `double getSales()` is passed the name of a division. It asks the user for a division's quarterly sales figure, validates the input, then returns it. It should be called once for each division.
   - `void findHighest()` is passed the four sales totals. It determines which is the largest and prints the name of the high grossing division, along with its sales figure.

   Input Validation: Do not accept dollar amounts less than $0.00.

4. **Safest Driving Area**

Write a program that determines which of five geographic regions within a major city (north, south, east, west, and central) had the fewest reported automobile accidents last year. It should have the following two functions, which are called by `main`.

- `int getNumAccidents()` is passed the name of a region. It asks the user for the number of automobile accidents reported in that region during the last year, validates the input, then returns it. It should be called once for each city region.
- `void findLowest()` is passed the five accident totals. It determines which is the smallest and prints the name of the region, along with its accident figure.

Input Validation: Do not accept an accident number that is less than 0.

5. **Falling Distance**

When an object is falling because of gravity, the following formula can be used to determine the distance the object falls in a specific time period:

$$d = \frac{1}{2} g t^2$$

The variables in the formula are as follows: d is the distance in meters, g is 9.8, and t is the amount of time, in seconds, that the object has been falling.

Write a function named `fallingDistance` that accepts an object's falling time (in seconds) as an argument. The function should return the distance, in meters, that the object has fallen during that time interval. Write a program that demonstrates the function by calling it in a loop that passes the values 1 through 10 as arguments, and displays the return value.

6. **Kinetic Energy**

In physics, an object that is in motion is said to have kinetic energy. The following formula can be used to determine a moving object's kinetic energy:

$$KE = \frac{1}{2} m v^2$$

The variables in the formula are as follows: KE is the kinetic energy, m is the object's mass in kilograms, and v is the object's velocity, in meters per second.

Write a function named `kineticEnergy` that accepts an object's mass (in kilograms) and velocity (in meters per second) as arguments. The function should return the amount of kinetic energy that the object has. Demonstrate the function by calling it in a program that asks the user to enter values for mass and velocity.

7. **Celsius Temperature Table**

The formula for converting a temperature from Fahrenheit to Celsius is

$$C = \frac{5}{9}(F - 32)$$

where F is the Fahrenheit temperature and C is the Celsius temperature. Write a function named `celsius` that accepts a Fahrenheit temperature as an argument. The function should return the temperature, converted to Celsius. Demonstrate the function by calling it in a loop that displays a table of the Fahrenheit temperatures 0 through 20 and their Celsius equivalents.

8. **Coin Toss**

   Write a function named `coinToss` that simulates the tossing of a coin. When you call the function, it should generate a random number in the range of 1 through 2. If the random number is 1, the function should display "heads." If the random number is 2, the function should display "tails." Demonstrate the function in a program that asks the user how many times the coin should be tossed, and then simulates the tossing of the coin that number of times.

9. **Present Value**

   Suppose you want to deposit a certain amount of money into a savings account, and then leave it alone to draw interest for the next 10 years. At the end of 10 years you would like to have $10,000 in the account. How much do you need to deposit today to make that happen? You can use the following formula, which is known as the present value formula, to find out:

   $$P = \frac{F}{(1 + r)^n}$$

   The terms in the formula are as follows:

   - *P* is the **present value**, or the amount that you need to deposit today.
   - *F* is the **future value** that you want in the account. (In this case, *F* is $10,000.)
   - *r* is the **annual interest rate**.
   - *n* is the **number of years** that you plan to let the money sit in the account.

   Write a program that has a function named `presentValue` that performs this calculation. The function should accept the future value, annual interest rate, and number of years as arguments. It should return the present value, which is the amount that you need to deposit today. Demonstrate the function in a program that lets the user experiment with different values for the formula's terms.

10. **Lowest Score Drop**

    Write a program that calculates the average of a group of test scores, where the lowest score in the group is dropped. It should use the following functions:

    - `void getScore()` should ask the user for a test score, store it in a reference parameter variable, and validate it. This function should be called by `main` once for each of the five scores to be entered.
    - `void calcAverage()` should calculate and display the average of the four highest scores. This function should be called just once by `main`, and should be passed the five scores.
    - `int findLowest()` should find and return the lowest of the five scores passed to it. It should be called by `calcAverage`, which uses the function to determine which of the five scores to drop.

    Input Validation: Do not accept test scores lower than 0 or higher than 100.

11. Star Search

A particular talent competition has five judges, each of whom awards a score between 0 and 10 to each performer. Fractional scores, such as 8.3, are allowed. A performer's final score is determined by dropping the highest and lowest score received, then averaging the three remaining scores. Write a program that uses this method to calculate a contestant's score. It should include the following functions:

- `void getJudgeData()` should ask the user for a judge's score, store it in a reference parameter variable, and validate it. This function should be called by `main` once for each of the five judges.
- `void calcScore()` should calculate and display the average of the three scores that remain after dropping the highest and lowest scores the performer received. This function should be called just once by `main`, and should be passed the five scores.

The last two functions, described below, should be called by `calcScore`, which uses the returned information to determine which of the scores to drop.

- `int findLowest()` should find and return the lowest of the five scores passed to it.
- `int findHighest()` should find and return the highest of the five scores passed to it.

Input Validation: Do not accept judge scores lower than 0 or higher than 10.

12. Days Out

Write a program that calculates the average number of days a company's employees are absent. The program should have the following functions:

- A function called by `main` that asks the user for the number of employees in the company. This value should be returned as an `int`. (The function accepts no arguments.)
- A function called by `main` that accepts one argument: the number of employees in the company. The function should ask the user to enter the number of days each employee missed during the past year. The total of these days should be returned as an `int`.
- A function called by `main` that takes two arguments: the number of employees in the company and the total number of days absent for all employees during the year. The function should return, as a `double`, the average number of days absent. (This function does not perform screen output and does not ask the user for input.)

Input Validation: Do not accept a number less than 1 for the number of employees. Do not accept a negative number for the days any employee missed.

13. Order Status

The Middletown Wholesale Copper Wire Company sells spools of copper wiring for $100 each. Write a program that displays the status of an order. The program should have a function that asks for the following data:

- The number of spools ordered.
- The number of spools in stock.
- Whether there are special shipping and handling charges.

(Shipping and handling is normally $10 per spool.) If there are special charges, the program should ask for the special charges per spool.

The gathered data should be passed as arguments to another function that displays

- The number of spools ready to ship from current stock.
- The number of spools on backorder (if the number ordered is greater than what is in stock).
- Subtotal of the portion ready to ship (the number of spools ready to ship times $100).
- Total shipping and handling charges on the portion ready to ship.
- Total of the order ready to ship.

The shipping and handling parameter in the second function should have the default argument 10.00.

Input Validation: Do not accept numbers less than 1 for spools ordered. Do not accept a number less than 0 for spools in stock or shipping and handling charges.

14. **Overloaded Hospital**

Write a program that computes and displays the charges for a patient's hospital stay. First, the program should ask if the patient was admitted as an in-patient or an out-patient. If the patient was an in-patient, the following data should be entered:

- The number of days spent in the hospital
- The daily rate
- Hospital medication charges
- Charges for hospital services (lab tests, etc.)

The program should ask for the following data if the patient was an out-patient:

- Charges for hospital services (lab tests, etc.)
- Hospital medication charges

The program should use two overloaded functions to calculate the total charges. One of the functions should accept arguments for the in-patient data, while the other function accepts arguments for out-patient information. Both functions should return the total charges.

Input Validation: Do not accept negative numbers for any data.

15. **Population**

In a population, the birth rate is the percentage increase of the population due to births and the death rate is the percentage decrease of the population due to deaths. Write a program that displays the size of a population for any number of years. The program should ask for the following data:

- The starting size of a population
- The annual birth rate
- The annual death rate
- The number of years to display

Write a function that calculates the size of the population for a year. The formula is

```
N = P + BP - DP
```

where N is the new population size, P is the previous population size, B is the birth rate, and D is the death rate.

Input Validation: Do not accept numbers less than 2 for the starting size. Do not accept negative numbers for birth rate or death rate. Do not accept numbers less than 1 for the number of years.

16. **Transient Population**

    Modify Programming Challenge 13 to also consider the effect on population caused by people moving into or out of a geographic area. Given as input a starting population size, the annual birth rate, the annual death rate, the number of individuals who typically move into the area each year, and the number of individuals who typically leave the area each year, the program should project what the population will be numYears from now. You can either prompt the user to input a value for numYears, or you can set it within the program.

    Input Validation: Do not accept numbers less than 2 for the starting size. Do not accept negative numbers for birth rate, death rate, arrivals, or departures.

17. **Paint Job Estimator**

    A painting company has determined that for every 115 square feet of wall space, one gallon of paint and eight hours of labor will be required. The company charges $18.00 per hour for labor. Write a modular program that allows the user to enter the number of rooms that are to be painted and the price of the paint per gallon. It should also ask for the square feet of wall space in each room. It should then display the following data:

    - The number of gallons of paint required
    - The hours of labor required
    - The cost of the paint
    - The labor charges
    - The total cost of the paint job

    Input validation: Do not accept a value less than 1 for the number of rooms. Do not accept a value less than $10.00 for the price of paint. Do not accept a negative value for square footage of wall space.

18. **Using Files—Hospital Report**

    Modify Programming Challenge 14, Overloaded Hospital, to write the report it creates to a file.

19. **Stock Profit**

    The profit from the sale of a stock can be calculated as follows:

    $$\text{Profit} = ((NS \times SP) - SC) - ((NS \times PP) + PC)$$

    where NS is the number of shares, SP is the sale price per share, SC is the sale commission paid, PP is the purchase price per share, and PC is the purchase commission paid. If the calculation yields a positive value, then the sale of the stock resulted in a profit. If the calculation yields a negative number, then the sale resulted in a loss.

    Write a function that accepts as arguments the number of shares, the purchase price per share, the purchase commission paid, the sale price per share, and the sale commission paid. The function should return the profit (or loss) from the sale of stock.

Demonstrate the function in a program that asks the user to enter the necessary data and displays the amount of the profit or loss.

20. **Multiple Stock Sales**

Use the function that you wrote for Programming Challenge 19 (Stock Profit) in a program that calculates the total profit or loss from the sale of multiple stocks. The program should ask the user for the number of stock sales, and the necessary data for each stock sale. It should accumulate the profit or loss for each stock sale and then display the total.

21. `isPrime` **Function**

A prime number is a number that is only evenly divisible by itself and 1. For example, the number 5 is prime because it can only be evenly divided by 1 and 5. The number 6, however, is not prime because it can be divided evenly by 1, 2, 3, and 6.

Write a function name `isPrime`, which takes an integer as an argument and returns true if the argument is a prime number, or false otherwise. Demonstrate the function in a complete program.

> **TIP:** Recall that the % operator divides one number by another, and returns the remainder of the division. In an expression such as num1 % num2, the % operator will return 0 if num1 is evenly divisible by num2.

22. **Prime Number List**

Use the `isPrime` function that you wrote in Programming Challenge 21 in a program that stores a list of all the prime numbers from 1 through 100 in a file.

23. **Rock, Paper, Scissors Game**

Write a program that lets the user play the game of Rock, Paper, Scissors against the computer. The program should work as follows.

1. When the program begins, a random number in the range of 1 through 3 is generated. If the number is 1, then the computer has chosen rock. If the number is 2, then the computer has chosen paper. If the number is 3, then the computer has chosen scissors. (Don't display the computer's choice yet.)

2. The user enters his or her choice of "rock", "paper", or "scissors" at the keyboard. (You can use a menu if you prefer.)

3. The computer's choice is displayed.

4. A winner is selected according to the following rules:

   - If one player chooses rock and the other player chooses scissors, then rock wins. (The rock smashes the scissors.)
   - If one player chooses scissors and the other player chooses paper, then scissors wins. (Scissors cuts paper.)
   - If one player chooses paper and the other player chooses rock, then paper wins. (Paper wraps rock.)
   - If both players make the same choice, the game must be played again to determine the winner.

Be sure to divide the program into functions that perform each major task.

Group Project

24. Travel Expenses

This program should be designed and written by a team of students. Here are some suggestions:

- One student should design function main, which will call the other functions in the program. The remainder of the functions will be designed by other members of the team.
- The requirements of the program should be analyzed so each student is given about the same work load.
- The parameters and return types of each function should be decided in advance.
- Stubs and drivers should be used to test and debug the program.
- The program can be implemented as a multifile program, or all the functions can be cut and pasted into the main file.

Here is the assignment: Write a program that calculates and displays the total travel expenses of a businessperson on a trip. The program should have functions that ask for and return the following:

- The total number of days spent on the trip
- The time of departure on the first day of the trip, and the time of arrival back home on the last day of the trip
- The amount of any round-trip airfare
- The amount of any car rentals
- Miles driven, if a private vehicle was used. Calculate the vehicle expense as $0.27 per mile driven
- Parking fees (The company allows up to $6 per day. Anything in excess of this must be paid by the employee.)
- Taxi fees, if a taxi was used anytime during the trip (The company allows up to $10 per day, for each day a taxi was used. Anything in excess of this must be paid by the employee.)
- Conference or seminar registration fees
- Hotel expenses (The company allows up to $90 per night for lodging. Anything in excess of this must be paid by the employee.)
- The amount of *each* meal eaten. On the first day of the trip, breakfast is allowed as an expense if the time of departure is before 7 a.m. Lunch is allowed if the time of departure is before 12 noon. Dinner is allowed on the first day if the time of departure is before 6 p.m. On the last day of the trip, breakfast is allowed if the time of arrival is after 8 a.m. Lunch is allowed if the time of arrival is after 1 p.m. Dinner is allowed on the last day if the time of arrival is after 7 p.m. The program should only ask for the amounts of allowable meals. (The company allows up to $9 for breakfast, $12 for lunch, and $16 for dinner. Anything in excess of this must be paid by the employee.)

The program should calculate and display the total expenses incurred by the businessperson, the total allowable expenses for the trip, the excess that must be reimbursed by the businessperson, if any, and the amount saved by the businessperson if the expenses were under the total allowed.

Input Validation: Do not accept negative numbers for any dollar amount or for miles driven in a private vehicle. Do not accept numbers less than 1 for the number of days. Only accept valid times for the time of departure and the time of arrival.

7 Arrays

TOPICS

7.1 Arrays Hold Multiple Values

CONCEPT: An array allows you to store and work with multiple values of the same data type.

The variables you have worked with so far are designed to hold only one value at a time. Each of the variable definitions in Figure 7-1 causes only enough memory to be reserved to hold one value of the specified data type.

An array works like a variable that can store a group of values, all of the same type. The values are stored together in consecutive memory locations. Here is a definition of an array of integers:

```
int days[6];
```

Figure 7-1

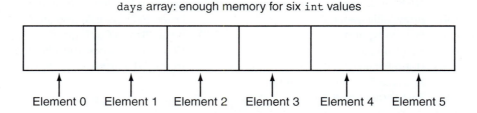

```
int count;      Enough memory for 1 int
                    12314

float price;    Enough memory for 1 float
                    56.981

char letter;    Enough memory for 1 char
                    A
```

The name of this array is days. The number inside the brackets is the array's *size declarator*. It indicates the number of *elements*, or values, the array can hold. The days array can store six elements, each one an integer. This is depicted in Figure 7-2.

Figure 7-2

days array: enough memory for six int values

Element 0   Element 1   Element 2   Element 3   Element 4   Element 5

An array's size declarator must be a constant integer expression with a value greater than zero. It can be either a literal, as in the previous example, or a named constant, as shown in the following:

```
const int NUM_DAYS = 6;
int days[NUM_DAYS];
```

Arrays of any data type can be defined. The following are all valid array definitions:

```
float temperatures[100];    // Array of 100 floats
string names[10];           // Array of 10 string objects
long units[50];             // Array of 50 long integers
double sizes[1200];         // Array of 1200 doubles
```

Memory Requirements of Arrays

The amount of memory used by an array depends on the array's data type and the number of elements. The hours array, defined here, is an array of six shorts.

```
short hours[6];
```

On a typical PC, a short uses two bytes of memory, so the hours array would occupy 12 bytes. This is shown in Figure 7-3.

Figure 7-3

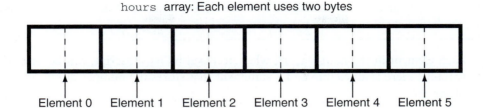

hours array: Each element uses two bytes

Element 0   Element 1   Element 2   Element 3   Element 4   Element 5

The size of an array can be calculated by multiplying the size of an individual element by the number of elements in the array. Table 7-1 shows the typical sizes of various arrays.

Table 7-1

Array Definition	Number of Elements	Size of Each Element	Size of the Array
char letters[25];	25	1 byte	25 bytes
short rings[100];	100	2 bytes	200 bytes
int miles[84];	84	4 bytes	336 bytes
float temp[12];	12	4 bytes	48 bytes
double distance[1000];	1000	8 bytes	8000 bytes

7.2 Accessing Array Elements

CONCEPT: The individual elements of an array are assigned unique subscripts. These subscripts are used to access the elements.

Even though an entire array has only one name, the elements may be accessed and used as individual variables. This is possible because each element is assigned a number known as a *subscript*. A subscript is used as an index to pinpoint a specific element within an array. The first element is assigned the subscript 0, the second element is assigned 1, and so forth. The six elements in the array hours would have the subscripts 0 through 5. This is shown in Figure 7-4.

Figure 7-4

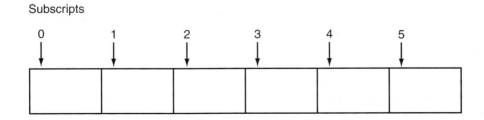

Subscripts

0   1   2   3   4   5

NOTE: Subscript numbering in C++ always starts at zero. The subscript of the last element in an array is one less than the total number of elements in the array. This means that in the array shown in Figure 7-4, the element `hours[6]` does not exist. `hours[5]` is the last element in the array.

Each element in the `hours` array, when accessed by its subscript, can be used as a `short` variable. Here is an example of a statement that stores the number 20 in the first element of the array:

```
hours[0] = 20;
```

NOTE: The expression `hours[0]` is pronounced "hours sub zero." You would read this assignment statement as "hours sub zero is assigned twenty."

Figure 7-5 shows the contents of the array `hours` after the statement assigns 20 to `hours[0]`.

Figure 7-5

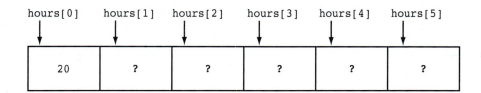

NOTE: Because values have not been assigned to the other elements of the array, question marks will be used to indicate that the contents of those elements are unknown. If an array is defined globally, all of its elements are initialized to zero by default. Local arrays, however, have no default initialization value.

The following statement stores the integer 30 in `hours[3]`.

```
hours[3] = 30;
```

Figure 7-6 shows the contents of the array after the previous statement executes:

Figure 7-6

hours[0]	hours[1]	hours[2]	hours[3]	hours[4]	hours[5]
20	?	?	30	?	?

NOTE: Understand the difference between the array size declarator and a subscript. The number inside the brackets of an array definition is the size declarator. The number inside the brackets of an assignment statement or any statement that works with the contents of an array is a subscript.

Inputting and Outputting Array Contents

Array elements may be used with the cin and cout objects like any other variable. Program 7-1 shows the array hours being used to store and display values entered by the user.

Program 7-1

```
 1 // This program asks for the number of hours worked
 2 // by six employees. It stores the values in an array.
 3 #include <iostream>
 4 using namespace std;
 5
 6 int main()
 7 {
 8    const int NUM_EMPLOYEES = 6;
 9    int hours[NUM_EMPLOYEES];
10
11    // Get the hours worked by each employee.
12    cout << "Enter the hours worked by "
13         << NUM_EMPLOYEES << " employees: ";
14    cin >> hours[0];
15    cin >> hours[1];
16    cin >> hours[2];
17    cin >> hours[3];
18    cin >> hours[4];
19    cin >> hours[5];
20
21    // Display the values in the array.
22    cout << "The hours you entered are:";
23    cout << " " << hours[0];
24    cout << " " << hours[1];
25    cout << " " << hours[2];
26    cout << " " << hours[3];
27    cout << " " << hours[4];
28    cout << " " << hours[5] << endl;
29    return 0;
30 }
```

Program Output with Example Input Shown in Bold
```
Enter the hours worked by 6 employees: 20 12 40 30 30 15 [Enter]
The hours you entered are: 20 12 40 30 30 15
```

Figure 7-7 shows the contents of the array hours with the values entered by the user in the example output above.

Figure 7-7

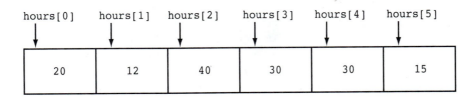

Even though the size declarator of an array definition must be a constant or a literal, subscript numbers can be stored in variables. This makes it possible to use a loop to "cycle through" an entire array, performing the same operation on each element. For example, look at the following code:

```cpp
const int ARRAY_SIZE = 5;
int numbers[ARRAY_SIZE];

for (int count = 0; count < ARRAY_SIZE; count++)
    numbers[count] = 99;
```

VideoNote
**Accessing
Array
Elements
with a Loop**

This code first defines a constant int named ARRAY_SIZE and initializes it with the value 5. Then it defines an int array named numbers, using ARRAY_SIZE as the size declarator. As a result, the numbers array will have five elements. The for loop uses a counter variable named count. This loop will iterate five times, and during the loop iterations the count variable will take on the values 0 through 4.

Notice that the statement inside the loop uses the count variable as a subscript. It assigns 99 to numbers[count]. During the first iteration, 99 is assigned to numbers[0]. During the next iteration, 99 is assigned to numbers[1]. This continues until 99 has been assigned to all of the array's elements. Figure 7-8 illustrates that the loop's initialization, test, and update expressions have been written so the loop starts and ends the counter variable with valid subscript values (0 through 4). This ensures that only valid subscripts are used in the body of the loop.

Figure 7-8

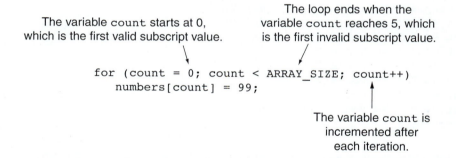

Program 7-1 could be simplified by using two for loops: one for inputting the values into the array and another for displaying the contents of the array. This is shown in Program 7-2.

Program 7-2

```cpp
1  // This program asks for the number of hours worked
2  // by six employees. It stores the values in an array.
3  #include <iostream>
4  using namespace std;
5
```

```
6  int main()
7  {
8     const int NUM_EMPLOYEES = 6; // Number of employees
9     int hours[NUM_EMPLOYEES];    // Each employee's hours
10    int count;                   // Loop counter
11
12    // Input the hours worked.
13    for (count = 0; count < NUM_EMPLOYEES; count++)
14    {
15       cout << "Enter the hours worked by employee "
16            << (count + 1) << ": ";
17       cin >> hours[count];
18    }
19
20    // Display the contents of the array.
21    cout << "The hours you entered are:";
22    for (count = 0; count < NUM_EMPLOYEES; count++)
23       cout << " " << hours[count];
24    cout << endl;
25    return 0;
26 }
```

Program Output with Example Input Shown in Bold
```
Enter the hours worked by employee 1: 20 [Enter]
Enter the hours worked by employee 2: 12 [Enter]
Enter the hours worked by employee 3: 40 [Enter]
Enter the hours worked by employee 4: 30 [Enter]
Enter the hours worked by employee 5: 30 [Enter]
Enter the hours worked by employee 6: 15 [Enter]
The hours you entered are: 20 12 40 30 30 15
```

The first for loop, in lines 13 through 18, prompts the user for each employee's hours. Take a closer look at lines 15 through 17:

```
cout << "Enter the hours worked by employee "
     << (count + 1) << ": ";
cin >> hours[count];
```

Notice that the cout statement uses the expression count + 1 to display the employee number, but the cin statement uses count as the array subscript. This is because the hours for employee number 1 are stored in hours[0], the hours for employee number 2 are stored in hours[1], and so forth.

The loop in lines 22 through 23 also uses the count variable to step through the array, displaying each element.

NOTE: You can use any integer expression as an array subscript. For example, the first loop in Program 7-2 could have been written like this:

```
for (count = 1; count <= NUM_EMPLOYEES; count++)
{
    cout << "Enter the hours worked by employee "
        << count << ": ";
    cin >> hours[count - 1];
}
```

In this code the `cin` statement uses the expression `count - 1` as a subscript.

Inputting data into an array must normally be done one element at a time. For example, the following `cin` statement will not input data into the `hours` array:

```
cin >> hours;   // Wrong! This will NOT work.
```

Instead, you must use multiple `cin` statements to read data into each array element, or use a loop to step through the array, reading data into its elements. Also, outputting an array's contents must normally be done one element at a time. For example, the following `cout` statement will not display the contents of the `hours` array:

```
cout << hours;   // Wrong! This will NOT work.
```

Instead, you must output each element of the array separately.

Reading Data from a File into an Array

Reading the contents of a file into an array is straightforward: Open the file and use a loop to read each item from the file, storing each item in an array element. The loop should iterate until either the array is filled or the end of the file is reached. Program 7-3 demonstrates by opening a file that has 10 numbers stored in it and then reading the file's contents into an array.

Program 7-3

```
 1  // This program reads data from a file into an array.
 2  #include <iostream>
 3  #include <fstream>
 4  using namespace std;
 5
 6  int main()
 7  {
 8      const int ARRAY_SIZE = 10;  // Array size
 9      int numbers[ARRAY_SIZE];    // Array with 10 elements
10      int count = 0;              // Loop counter variable
11      ifstream inputFile;         // Input file stream object
12
13      // Open the file.
14      inputFile.open("TenNumbers.txt");
15
```

```
16      // Read the numbers from the file into the array.
17      while (count < ARRAY_SIZE && inputFile >> numbers[count])
18          count++;
19
20      // Close the file.
21      inputFile.close();
22
23      // Display the numbers read:
24      cout << "The numbers are: ";
25      for (count = 0; count < ARRAY_SIZE; count++)
26          cout << numbers[count] << " ";
27      cout << endl;
28      return 0;
29 }
```

Program Output
The numbers are: 101 102 103 104 105 106 107 108 109 110

The while loop in lines 17 and 18 reads items from the file and assigns them to elements of the numbers array. Notice that the loop tests two Boolean expressions, connected by the && operator:

- The first expression is count < ARRAY_SIZE. The purpose of this expression is to prevent the loop from writing beyond the end of the array. If the expression is true, the second Boolean expression is tested. If this expression is false, however, the loop stops.
- The second expression is inputFile >> numbers[count]. This expression reads a value from the file and stores it in the numbers[count] array element. If a value is successfully read from the file, the expression is true and the loop continues. If no value can be read from the file, however, the expression is false and the loop stops.

Each time the loop iterates, it increments count in line 18.

Writing the Contents of an Array to a File

Writing the contents of an array to a file is also a straightforward matter. Use a loop to step through each element of the array, writing its contents to a file. Program 7-4 demonstrates.

Program 7-4

```
1  // This program writes the contents of an array to a file.
2  #include <iostream>
3  #include <fstream>
4  using namespace std;
5
6  int main()
7  {
8      const int ARRAY_SIZE = 10;  // Array size
9      int numbers[ARRAY_SIZE];    // Array with 10 elements
10     int count;                  // Loop counter variable
11     ofstream outputFile;        // Output file stream object
12
```

(program continues)

Program 7-4   *(continued)*

```
13      // Store values in the array.
14      for (count = 0; count < ARRAY_SIZE; count++)
15         numbers[count] = count;
16
17      // Open a file for output.
18      outputFile.open("SavedNumbers.txt");
19
20      // Write the array contents to the file.
21      for (count = 0; count < ARRAY_SIZE; count++)
22         outputFile << numbers[count] << endl;
23
24      // Close the file.
25      outputFile.close();
26
27      // That's it!
28      cout << "The numbers were saved to the file.\n ";
29      return 0;
30   }
```

Program Output

The numbers were saved to the file.

Contents of the File SavedNumbers.txt

```
0
1
2
3
4
5
6
7
8
9
```

7.3   No Bounds Checking in C++

CONCEPT: C++ does not prevent you from overwriting an array's bounds.

C++ is a popular language for software developers who have to write fast, efficient code. To increase runtime efficiency, C++ does not provide many of the common safeguards to prevent unsafe memory access found in other languages. For example, C++ does not perform array bounds checking. This means you can write programs with subscripts that go beyond the boundaries of a particular array. Program 7-5 demonstrates this capability.

WARNING! Think twice before you compile and run Program 7-5. The program will attempt to write to an area of memory outside the array. This is an invalid operation, and will most likely cause the program to crash.

Program 7-5

```cpp
 1  // This program unsafely accesses an area of memory by writing
 2  // values beyond an array's boundary.
 3  // WARNING: If you compile and run this program, it could crash.
 4  #include <iostream>
 5  using namespace std;
 6
 7  int main()
 8  {
 9     const int SIZE = 3;   // Constant for the array size
10     int values[SIZE];     // An array of 3 integers
11     int count;            // Loop counter variable
12
13     // Attempt to store five numbers in the three-element array.
14     cout << "I will store 5 numbers in a 3-element array!\n";
15     for (count = 0; count < 5; count++)
16        values[count] = 100;
17
18     // If the program is still running, display the numbers.
19     cout << "If you see this message, it means the program\n";
20     cout << "has not crashed! Here are the numbers:\n";
21     for (count = 0; count < 5; count++)
22        cout << values[count] << endl;
23     return 0;
24  }
```

The values array has three integer elements, with the subscripts 0, 1, and 2. The loop, however, stores the number 100 in elements 0, 1, 2, 3, and 4. The elements with subscripts 3 and 4 do not exist, but C++ allows the program to write beyond the boundary of the array, as if those elements were there. Figure 7-9 depicts the way the array is set up in memory when the program first starts to execute, and what happens when the loop writes data beyond the boundary of the array.

Figure 7-9

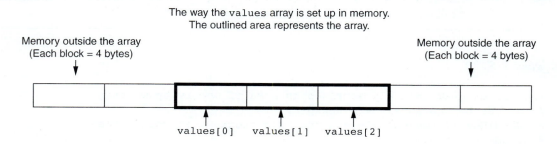

The way the `values` array is set up in memory.
The outlined area represents the array.

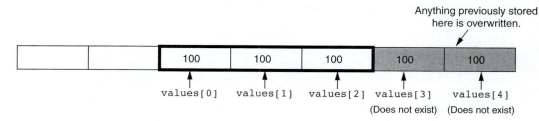

How the numbers assigned to the array overflow the array's boundaries.
The shaded area is the section of memory illegally written to.

Although C++ programs are fast and efficient, the absence of safeguards such as array bounds checking usually proves to be a bad thing. It's easy for C++ programmers to make careless mistakes that allow programs to access areas of memory that are supposed to be off-limits. You must always make sure that any time you assign values to array elements, the values are written within the array's boundaries.

Watch for Off-by-One Errors

In working with arrays, a common type of mistake is the *off-by-one error*. This is an easy mistake to make because array subscripts start at 0 rather than 1. For example, look at the following code:

```cpp
// This code has an off-by-one error.
const int SIZE = 100;
int numbers[SIZE];
for (int count = 1; count <= SIZE; count++)
    numbers[count] = 0;
```

The intent of this code is to create an array of integers with 100 elements, and store the value 0 in each element. However, this code has an off-by-one error. The loop uses its counter variable, `count`, as a subscript with the `numbers` array. During the loop's execution, the variable `count` takes on the values 1 through 100, when it should take on the values 0 through 99. As a result, the first element, which is at subscript 0, is skipped. In addition, the loop attempts to use 100 as a subscript during the last iteration. Because 100 is an invalid subscript, the program will write data beyond the array's boundaries.

Checkpoint

myprogramminglab *www.myprogramminglab.com*

7.1   Define the following arrays:

   A) `empNums`, a 100-element array of `int`s

   B) `payRates`, a 25-element array of `float`s

   C) `miles`, a 14-element array of `long`s

   D) `cityName`, a 26-element array of `string` objects

   E) `lightYears`, a 1,000-element array of `double`s

7.2   What's wrong with the following array definitions?

```
int readings[-1];
float measurements[4.5];
int size;
string names[size];
```

7.3   What would the valid subscript values be in a four-element array of `double`s?

7.4   What is the difference between an array's size declarator and a subscript?

7.5   What is "array bounds checking"? Does C++ perform it?

7.6   What is the output of the following code?

```
int values[5], count;
for (count = 0; count < 5; count++)
    values[count] = count + 1;
for (count = 0; count < 5; count++)
    cout << values[count] << endl;
```

7.7   The following program skeleton contains a 20-element array of `int`s called `fish`. When completed, the program should ask how many fish were caught by fishermen 1 through 20, and store this data in the array. Complete the program.

```
#include <iostream>
using namespace std;

int main()
{
    const int NUM_FISH = 20;
    int fish[NUM_FISH];
    // You must finish this program. It should ask how
    // many fish were caught by fishermen 1-20, and
    // store this data in the array fish.
    return 0;
}
```

7.4 Array Initialization

CONCEPT: Arrays may be initialized when they are defined.

Like regular variables, C++ allows you to initialize an array's elements when you create the array. Here is an example:

```
const int MONTHS = 12;
int days[MONTHS] = {31, 28, 31, 30, 31, 30, 31, 31, 30, 31, 30, 31};
```

The series of values inside the braces and separated with commas is called an *initialization list*. These values are stored in the array elements in the order they appear in the list. (The first value, 31, is stored in days[0], the second value, 28, is stored in days[1], and so forth.) Figure 7-10 shows the contents of the array after the initialization.

Figure 7-10

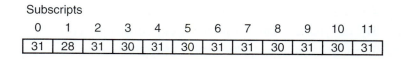

Subscripts

0	1	2	3	4	5	6	7	8	9	10	11
31	28	31	30	31	30	31	31	30	31	30	31

Program 7-6 demonstrates how an array may be initialized.

Program 7-6

```cpp
 1   // This program displays the number of days in each month.
 2   #include <iostream>
 3   using namespace std;
 4
 5   int main()
 6   {
 7      const int MONTHS = 12;
 8      int days[MONTHS] = { 31, 28, 31, 30,
 9                           31, 30, 31, 31,
10                           30, 31, 30, 31};
11
12      for (int count = 0; count < MONTHS; count++)
13      {
14         cout << "Month " << (count + 1) << " has ";
15         cout << days[count] << " days.\n";
16      }
17      return 0;
18   }
```

Program Output
```
Month 1 has 31 days.
Month 2 has 28 days.
Month 3 has 31 days.
Month 4 has 30 days.
Month 5 has 31 days.
Month 6 has 30 days.
Month 7 has 31 days.
Month 8 has 31 days.
Month 9 has 30 days.
Month 10 has 31 days.
Month 11 has 30 days.
Month 12 has 31 days.
```

> **NOTE:** Notice that C++ allows you to spread the initialization list across multiple lines. Both of the following array definitions are equivalent:
>
> ```
> double coins[5] = {0.05, 0.1, 0.25, 0.5, 1.0};
> double coins[5] = {0.05,
>                    0.1,
>                    0.25,
>                    0.5,
>                    1.0};
> ```

Program 7-7 shows an example with a `string` array that is initialized with strings.

Program 7-7

```
 1 // This program initializes a string array.
 2 #include <iostream>
 3 #include <string>
 4 using namespace std;
 5
 6 int main()
 7 {
 8     const int SIZE = 9;
 9     string planets[SIZE] = { "Mercury", "Venus", "Earth", "Mars",
10                              "Jupiter", "Saturn", "Uranus",
11                              "Neptune", "Pluto (a dwarf planet)" };
12
13     cout << "Here are the planets:\n";
14
15     for (int count = 0; count < SIZE; count++)
16        cout << planets[count] << endl;
17     return 0;
18 }
```

Program Output
```
Here are the planets:
Mercury
Venus
Earth
Mars
Jupiter
Saturn
Uranus
Neptune
Pluto (a dwarf planet)
```

Program 7-8 shows a character array being initialized with the first ten letters of the alphabet. The array is then used to display those characters' ASCII codes.

Program 7-8

```
1   // This program uses an array of ten characters to store the
2   // first ten letters of the alphabet. The ASCII codes of the
3   // characters are displayed.
4   #include <iostream>
5   using namespace std;
6
7   int main()
8   {
9       const int NUM_LETTERS = 10;
10      char letters[NUM_LETTERS] = {'A', 'B', 'C', 'D', 'E',
11                                   'F', 'G', 'H', 'I', 'J'};
12
13      cout << "Character" << "\t" << "ASCII Code\n";
14      cout << "---------" << "\t" << "----------\n";
15      for (int count = 0; count < NUM_LETTERS; count++)
16      {
17          cout << letters[count] << "\t\t";
18          cout << static_cast<int>(letters[count]) << endl;
19      }
20      return 0;
21  }
```

Program Output

Character	ASCII Code
A	65
B	66
C	67
D	68
E	69
F	70
G	71
H	72
I	73
J	74

NOTE: An array's initialization list cannot have more values than the array has elements.

Partial Array Initialization

When an array is being initialized, C++ does not require a value for every element. It's possible to only initialize part of an array, such as:

```
int numbers[7] = {1, 2, 4, 8};
```

This definition initializes only the first four elements of a seven-element array, as illustrated in Figure 7-11.

Figure 7-11

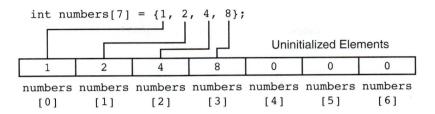

It's important to note that if an array is partially initialized, the uninitialized elements will be set to zero. The uninitialized elements of a string array will contain empty strings. This is true even if the array is defined locally. (If a local array is completely uninitialized, its elements will contain "garbage," like all other local variables.) Program 7-9 shows the contents of the array numbers after it is partially initialized.

Program 7-9

```
 1   // This program has a partially initialized array.
 2   #include <iostream>
 3   using namespace std;
 4
 5   int main()
 6   {
 7      const int SIZE = 7;
 8      int numbers[SIZE] = {1, 2, 4, 8}; // Initialize first 4 elements
 9
10      cout << "Here are the contents of the array:\n";
11      for (int index = 0; index < SIZE; index++)
12         cout << numbers[index] << " ";
13
14      cout << endl;
15      return 0;
16   }
```

Program Output
```
Here are the contents of the array:
1 2 4 8 0 0 0
```

If you leave an element uninitialized, you must leave all the elements that follow it uninitialized as well. C++ does not provide a way to skip elements in the initialization list. For example, the following is *not* legal:

```
int array[6] = {2, 4, , 8, , 12}; // NOT Legal!
```

Implicit Array Sizing

It's possible to define an array without specifying its size, as long as you provide an initialization list. C++ automatically makes the array large enough to hold all the initialization values. For example, the following definition creates an array with five elements:

```
double ratings[] = {1.0, 1.5, 2.0, 2.5, 3.0};
```

Because the size declarator is omitted, C++ counts the number of items in the initialization list and gives the array that many elements.

 NOTE: You *must* provide an initialization list if you leave out an array's size declarator. Otherwise, C++ doesn't know how large to make the array.

 7.5

Processing Array Contents

CONCEPT: Individual array elements are processed like any other type of variable.

Processing array elements is no different than processing other variables. For example, the following statement multiplies hours[3] by the variable rate:

```
pay = hours[3] * rate;
```

And the following are examples of pre-increment and post-increment operations on array elements:

```
int score[5] = {7, 8, 9, 10, 11};
++score[2];    // Pre-increment operation on the value in score[2]
score[4]++;    // Post-increment operation on the value in score[4]
```

 NOTE: When using increment and decrement operators, be careful not to confuse the subscript with the array element. For example, the following statement decrements the variable count, but does nothing to the value in amount[count]:

```
amount[count--];
```

To decrement the value stored in amount[count], use the following statement:

```
amount[count]--;
```

Program 7-10 demonstrates the use of array elements in a simple mathematical statement. A loop steps through each element of the array, using the elements to calculate the gross pay of five employees.

Program 7-10

```
1  // This program stores, in an array, the hours worked by
2  // employees who all make the same hourly wage.
3  #include <iostream>
4  #include <iomanip>
5  using namespace std;
6
```

```
 7   int main()
 8   {
 9      const int NUM_EMPLOYEES = 5;
10      int hours[NUM_EMPLOYEES];
11      double payrate;
12
13      // Input the hours worked.
14      cout << "Enter the hours worked by ";
15      cout << NUM_EMPLOYEES << " employees who all\n";
16      cout << "earn the same hourly rate.\n";
17      for (int index = 0; index < NUM_EMPLOYEES; index++)
18      {
19         cout << "Employee #" << (index + 1) << ": ";
20         cin >> hours[index];
21      }
22
23      // Input the hourly rate for all employees.
24      cout << "Enter the hourly pay rate for all the employees: ";
25      cin >> payrate;
26
27      // Display each employee's gross pay.
28      cout << "Here is the gross pay for each employee:\n";
29      cout << fixed << showpoint << setprecision(2);
30      for (int index = 0; index < NUM_EMPLOYEES; index++)
31      {
32         double grossPay = hours[index] * payrate;
33         cout << "Employee #" << (index + 1);
34         cout << ": $" << grossPay << endl;
35      }
36      return 0;
37   }
```

Program Output with Example Input Shown in Bold
```
Enter the hours worked by 5 employees who all
earn the same hourly rate.
Employee #1: 5 [Enter]
Employee #2: 10 [Enter]
Employee #3: 15 [Enter]
Employee #4: 20 [Enter]
Employee #5: 40 [Enter]
Enter the hourly pay rate for all the employees: 12.75 [Enter]
Here is the gross pay for each employee:
Employee #1: $63.75
Employee #2: $127.50
Employee #3: $191.25
Employee #4: $255.00
Employee #5: $510.00
```

The following statement in line 32 defines the variable grossPay and initializes it with the value of hours[index] times payRate:

```
double grossPay = hours[index] * payRate;
```

Array elements may also be used in relational expressions. For example, the following `if` statement tests `cost[20]` to determine whether it is less than `cost[0]`:

```
if (cost[20] < cost[0])
```

And the following statement sets up a `while` loop to iterate as long as `value[place]` does not equal 0:

```
while (value[place] != 0)
```

Thou Shall Not Assign

The following code defines two integer arrays: `newValues` and `oldValues`. `newValues` is uninitialized and `oldValues` is initialized with 10, 100, 200, and 300:

```
const int SIZE = 4;
int oldValues[SIZE] = {10, 100, 200, 300};
int newValues[SIZE];
```

At first glance, it might appear that the following statement assigns the contents of the array `oldValues` to `newValues`:

```
newValues = oldValues;          // Wrong!
```

Unfortunately, this statement will not work. The only way to assign one array to another is to assign the individual elements in the arrays. Usually, this is best done with a loop, such as:

```
for (int count = 0; count < SIZE; count++)
    newValues[count] = oldValues[count];
```

The reason the assignment operator will not work with an entire array at once is complex, but important to understand. Anytime the name of an array is used without brackets and a subscript, *it is seen as the array's beginning memory address*. To illustrate this, consider the definition of the arrays `newValues` and `oldValues` above. Figure 7-12 depicts the two arrays in memory.

Figure 7-12

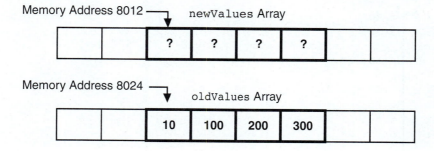

In the figure, `newValues` is shown starting at memory address 8012 and `oldValues` is shown starting at 8024. (Of course, these are just arbitrary addresses, picked for illustration purposes. In reality the addresses would probably be different.) Table 7-2 shows various expressions that use the names of these arrays, and their values.

Table 7-2

Expression	Value
oldValues[0]	10 (Contents of Element 0 of oldValues)
oldValues[1]	100 (Contents of Element 1 of oldValues)
oldValues[2]	200 (Contents of Element 2 of oldValues)
oldValues[3]	300 (Contents of Element 3 of oldValues)
newValues	8012 (Memory Address of newValues)
oldValues	8024 (Memory Address of oldValues)

Because the name of an array without the brackets and subscript stands for the array's starting memory address, the following statement

```
newValues = oldValues;
```

is interpreted by C++ as

```
8012 = 8024;
```

The statement will not work because you cannot change the starting memory address of an array.

Printing the Contents of an Array

Suppose we have the following array definition:

```
const int SIZE = 5;
int array[SIZE] = {10, 20, 30, 40, 50};
```

You now know that an array's name is seen as the array's beginning memory address. This explains why the following statement cannot be used to display the contents of array:

```
cout << array << endl;   //Wrong!
```

When this statement executes, cout will display the array's memory address, not the array's contents. You must use a loop to display the contents of each of the array's elements, as follows.

```
for (int count = 0; count < SIZE; count++)
    cout << array[count] << endl;
```

Summing the Values in a Numeric Array

To sum the values in an array, you must use a loop with an accumulator variable. The loop adds the value in each array element to the accumulator. For example, assume that the following statements appear in a program and that values have been stored in the units array.

```
const int NUM_UNITS = 24;
int units[NUM_UNITS];
```

The following loop adds the values of each element in the array to the `total` variable. When the code is finished, `total` will contain the sum of the `units` array's elements.

```
int total = 0;   // Initialize accumulator
for (int count = 0; count < NUM_UNITS; count++)
   total += units[count];
```

> **NOTE:** The first statement in the code segment sets `total` to 0. Recall from Chapter 5 that an accumulator variable must be set to 0 before it is used to keep a running total or the sum will not be correct.

Getting the Average of the Values in a Numeric Array

The first step in calculating the average of all the values in an array is to sum the values. The second step is to divide the sum by the number of elements in the array. Assume that the following statements appear in a program and that values have been stored in the `scores` array.

```
const int NUM_SCORES = 10;
double scores[NUM_SCORES];
```

The following code calculates the average of the values in the `scores` array. When the code completes, the average will be stored in the `average` variable.

```
double total = 0;   // Initialize accumulator
double average;      // Will hold the average
for (int count = 0; count < NUM_SCORES; count++)
   total += scores[count];
average = total / NUM_SCORES;
```

Notice that the last statement, which divides `total` by `numScores`, is not inside the loop. This statement should only execute once, after the loop has finished its iterations.

Finding the Highest and Lowest Values in a Numeric Array

The algorithms for finding the highest and lowest values in an array are very similar. First, let's look at code for finding the highest value in an array. Assume that the following code exists in a program, and that values have been stored in the array.

```
const int SIZE = 50;
int numbers[SIZE];
```

The code to find the highest value in the array is as follows.

```
int count;
int highest;

highest = numbers[0];
for (count = 1; count < SIZE; count++)
{
   if (numbers[count] > highest)
      highest = numbers[count];
}
```

First we copy the value in the first array element to the variable `highest`. Then the loop compares all of the remaining array elements, beginning at subscript 1, to the value in `highest`. Each time it finds a value in the array that is greater than `highest`, it copies that value to `highest`. When the loop has finished, `highest` will contain the highest value in the array.

The following code finds the lowest value in the array. As you can see, it is nearly identical to the code for finding the highest value.

```cpp
int count;
int lowest;

lowest = numbers[0];
for (count = 1; count < SIZE; count++)
{
    if (numbers[count] < lowest)
        lowest = numbers[count];
}
```

When the loop has finished, `lowest` will contain the lowest value in the array.

Partially Filled Arrays

Sometimes you need to store a series of items in an array, but you do not know the number of items that there are. As a result, you do not know the exact number of elements needed for the array. One solution is to make the array large enough to hold the largest possible number of items. This can lead to another problem, however. If the actual number of items stored in the array is less than the number of elements, the array will be only partially filled. When you process a partially filled array, you must only process the elements that contain valid data items.

A partially filled array is normally used with an accompanying integer variable that holds the number of items stored in the array. For example, suppose a program uses the following code to create an array with 100 elements, and an `int` variable named `count` that will hold the number of items stored in the array:

```cpp
const int SIZE = 100;
int array[SIZE];
int count = 0;
```

Each time we add an item to the array, we must increment `count`. The following code demonstrates.

```cpp
int number;
cout << "Enter a number or -1 to quit: ";
cin >> number;
while (number != -1 && count < SIZE)
{
    count++;
    array[count - 1] = number;
    cout << "Enter a number or -1 to quit: ";
    cin >> number;
}
```

Each iteration of this sentinel-controlled loop allows the user to enter a number to be stored in the array, or -1 to quit. The count variable is incremented, and then used to calculate the subscript of the next available element in the array. When the user enters -1, or count exceeds 99, the loop stops. The following code displays all of the valid items in the array.

```
for (int index = 0; index < count; index++)
{
    cout << array[index] << endl;
}
```

Notice that this code uses count to determine the maximum array subscript to use.

Program 7-11 shows how this technique can be used to read an unknown number of items from a file into an array. The program reads values from the file numbers.txt.

Program 7-11

```
 1  // This program reads data from a file into an array.
 2  #include <iostream>
 3  #include <fstream>
 4  using namespace std;
 5
 6  int main()
 7  {
 8      const int ARRAY_SIZE = 100; // Array size
 9      int numbers[ARRAY_SIZE];    // Array with 100 elements
10      int count = 0;              // Loop counter variable
11      ifstream inputFile;         // Input file stream object
12
13      inputFile.open("numbers.txt"); // Open the file.
14
15      // Read the numbers from the file into the array.
16      // After this loop executes, the count variable will hold
17      // the number of values that were stored in the array.
18      while (count < ARRAY_SIZE && inputFile >> numbers[count])
19          count++;
20
21      // Close the file.
22      inputFile.close();
23
24      // Display the numbers read.
25      cout << "The numbers are: ";
26      for (int index = 0; index < count; index++)
27          cout << numbers[index] << " ";
28      cout << endl;
29      return 0;
30  }
```

Program Output

The numbers are: 47 89 65 36 12 25 17 8 62 10 87 62

Look closer at the `while` loop that begins in line 18. It repeats as long as `count` is less than `ARRAY_SIZE` and the end of the file has not been encountered. The first part of the `while` loop's test expression, `count < ARRAY_SIZE`, prevents the loop from writing outside the array boundaries. Recall from Chapter 4 that the `&&` operator performs short-circuit evaluation, so the second part of the `while` loop's test expression, `inputFile >> values[count]`, will be executed only if `count` is less than `ARRAY_SIZE`.

Comparing Arrays

We have already noted that you cannot simply assign one array to another array. You must assign each element of the first array to an element of the second array. In addition, you cannot use the `==` operator with the names of two arrays to determine whether the arrays are equal. For example, the following code appears to compare two arrays, but in reality does not.

```cpp
int firstArray[] = { 5, 10, 15, 20, 25 };
int secondArray[] = { 5, 10, 15, 20, 25 };
if (firstArray == secondArray)         // This is a mistake.
   cout << "The arrays are the same.\n";
else
   cout << "The arrays are not the same.\n";
```

When you use the `==` operator with array names, the operator compares the beginning memory addresses of the arrays, not the contents of the arrays. The two array names in this code will obviously have different memory addresses. Therefore, the result of the expression `firstArray == secondArray` is false and the code reports that the arrays are not the same.

To compare the contents of two arrays, you must compare the elements of the two arrays. For example, look at the following code.

```cpp
const int SIZE = 5;
int firstArray[SIZE] = { 5, 10, 15, 20, 25 };
int secondArray[SIZE] = { 5, 10, 15, 20, 25 };
bool arraysEqual = true;  // Flag variable
int count = 0;            // Loop counter variable

// Determine whether the elements contain the same data.
while (arraysEqual && count < SIZE)
{
   if (firstArray[count] != secondArray[count])
      arraysEqual = false;
   count++;
}

if (arraysEqual)
   cout << "The arrays are equal.\n";
else
   cout << "The arrays are not equal.\n";
```

This code determines whether `firstArray` and `secondArray` contain the same values. A `bool` variable, `arraysEqual`, which is initialized to `true`, is used to signal whether the arrays are equal. Another variable, `count`, which is initialized to 0, is used as a loop counter variable.

Then a `while` loop begins. The loop executes as long as `arraysEqual` is `true` and the counter variable `count` is less than `SIZE`. During each iteration, it compares a different set of corresponding elements in the arrays. When it finds two corresponding elements that have different values, the `arraysEqual` variable is set to `false`. After the loop finishes, an `if` statement examines the `arraysEqual` variable. If the variable is `true`, then the arrays are equal and a message indicating so is displayed. Otherwise, they are not equal, so a different message is displayed.

7.6 Focus on Software Engineering: Using Parallel Arrays

CONCEPT: By using the same subscript, you can build relationships between data stored in two or more arrays.

Sometimes it's useful to store related data in two or more arrays. It's especially useful when the related data is of unlike types. For example, Program 7-12 is another variation of the payroll program. It uses two arrays: one to store the hours worked by each employee (as `int`s), and another to store each employee's hourly pay rate (as `double`s).

Program 7-12

```cpp
 1  // This program uses two parallel arrays: one for hours
 2  // worked and one for pay rate.
 3  #include <iostream>
 4  #include <iomanip>
 5  using namespace std;
 6
 7  int main()
 8  {
 9     const int NUM_EMPLOYEES = 5;   // Number of employees
10     int hours[NUM_EMPLOYEES];       // Holds hours worked
11     double payRate[NUM_EMPLOYEES]; // Holds pay rates
12
13     // Input the hours worked and the hourly pay rate.
14     cout << "Enter the hours worked by " << NUM_EMPLOYEES
15          << " employees and their\n"
16          << "hourly pay rates.\n";
17     for (int index = 0; index < NUM_EMPLOYEES; index++)
18     {
19        cout << "Hours worked by employee #" << (index+1) << ": ";
20        cin >> hours[index];
21        cout << "Hourly pay rate for employee #" << (index+1) << ": ";
22        cin >> payRate[index];
23     }
24
25     // Display each employee's gross pay.
```

```
26      cout << "Here is the gross pay for each employee:\n";
27      cout << fixed << showpoint << setprecision(2);
28      for (int index = 0; index < NUM_EMPLOYEES; index++)
29      {
30          double grossPay = hours[index] * payRate[index];
31          cout << "Employee #" << (index + 1);
32          cout << ": $" << grossPay << endl;
33      }
34      return 0;
35 }
```

Program Output with Example Input Shown in Bold
```
Enter the hours worked by 5 employees and their
hourly pay rates.
Hours worked by employee #1: 10 [Enter]
Hourly pay rate for employee #1: 9.75 [Enter]
Hours worked by employee #2: 15 [Enter]
Hourly pay rate for employee #2: 8.62 [Enter]
Hours worked by employee #3: 20 [Enter]
Hourly pay rate for employee #3: 10.50 [Enter]
Hours worked by employee #4: 40 [Enter]
Hourly pay rate for employee #4: 18.75 [Enter]
Hours worked by employee #5: 40 [Enter]
Hourly pay rate for employee #5: 15.65 [Enter]
Here is the gross pay for each employee:
Employee #1: $97.50
Employee #2: $129.30
Employee #3: $210.00
Employee #4: $750.00
Employee #5: $626.00
```

Notice in the loops that the same subscript is used to access both arrays. That's because the data for one employee is stored in the same relative position in each array. For example, the hours worked by employee #1 are stored in hours[0], and the same employee's pay rate is stored in payRate[0]. The subscript relates the data in both arrays.

This concept is illustrated in Figure 7-13.

Figure 7-13

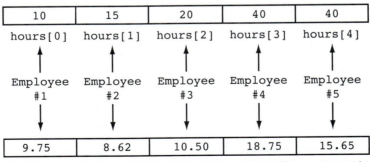

Checkpoint

myprogramminglab *www.myprogramminglab.com*

7.8 Define the following arrays:

A) `ages`, a 10-element array of `ints` initialized with the values 5, 7, 9, 14, 15, 17, 18, 19, 21, and 23.

B) `temps`, a 7-element array of `floats` initialized with the values 14.7, 16.3, 18.43, 21.09, 17.9, 18.76, and 26.7.

C) `alpha`, an 8-element array of `chars` initialized with the values 'J', 'B', 'L', 'A', '*', '$', 'H', and 'M'.

7.9 Is each of the following a valid or invalid array definition? (If a definition is invalid, explain why.)

```
int numbers[10] = {0, 0, 1, 0, 0, 1, 0, 0, 1, 1};
int matrix[5] = {1, 2, 3, 4, 5, 6, 7};
double radii[10] = {3.2, 4.7};
int table[7] = {2, , , 27, , 45, 39};
char codes[] = {'A', 'X', '1', '2', 's'};
int blanks[];
```

7.10 Given the following array definition:

```
int values[] = {2, 6, 10, 14};
```

What does each of the following display?

A) `cout << values[2];`

B) `cout << ++values[0];`

C) `cout << values[1]++;`

D) `x = 2;`
   `cout << values[++x];`

7.11 Given the following array definition:

```
int nums[5] = {1, 2, 3};
```

What will the following statement display?

```
cout << nums[3];
```

7.12 What is the output of the following code? (You may need to use a calculator.)

```
double balance[5] = {100.0, 250.0, 325.0, 500.0, 1100.0};
const double INTRATE = 0.1;

cout << fixed << showpoint << setprecision(2);
for (int count = 0; count < 5; count++)
    cout << (balance[count] * INTRATE) << endl;
```

7.13 What is the output of the following code? (You may need to use a calculator.)

```
const int SIZE = 5;
int time[SIZE] =   {1, 2, 3, 4, 5},
    speed[SIZE] = {18, 4, 27, 52, 100},
    dist[SIZE];
```

```
        for (int count = 0; count < SIZE; count++)
            dist[count] = time[count] * speed[count];
        for (int count = 0; count < SIZE; count++)
        {
            cout << time[count] << " ";
            cout << speed[count] << " ";
            cout << dist[count] << endl;
        }
```

7.7 Arrays as Function Arguments

CONCEPT: To pass an array as an argument to a function, pass the name of the array.

VideoNote

Passing an Array to a Function

Quite often you'll want to write functions that process the data in arrays. For example, functions could be written to put values in an array, display an array's contents on the screen, total all of an array's elements, or calculate their average. Usually, such functions accept an array as an argument.

When a single element of an array is passed to a function, it is handled like any other variable. For example, Program 7-13 shows a loop that passes one element of the array numbers to the function showValue each time the loop iterates.

Program 7-13

```
 1   // This program demonstrates that an array element is passed
 2   // to a function like any other variable.
 3   #include <iostream>
 4   using namespace std;
 5
 6   void showValue(int); // Function prototype
 7
 8   int main()
 9   {
10       const int SIZE = 8;
11       int numbers[SIZE] = {5, 10, 15, 20, 25, 30, 35, 40};
12
13       for (int index = 0; index < SIZE; index++)
14           showValue(numbers[index]);
15       return 0;
16   }
17
18   //*********************************************
19   // Definition of function showValue.          *
20   // This function accepts an integer argument.  *
21   // The value of the argument is displayed.     *
22   //*********************************************
23
24   void showValue(int num)
25   {
26       cout << num << " ";
27   }
```

Program Output

```
5 10 15 20 25 30 35 40
```

Each time showValue is called in line 14, a copy of an array element is passed into the parameter variable num. The showValue function simply displays the contents of num, and doesn't work directly with the array element itself. (In other words, the array element is passed by value.)

If the function were written to accept the entire array as an argument, however, the parameter would be set up differently. In the following function definition, the parameter nums is followed by an empty set of brackets. This indicates that the argument will be an array, not a single value.

```
void showValues(int nums[], int size)
{
   for (int index = 0; index < size; index++)
      cout << nums[index] << " ";
   cout << endl;
}
```

The reason there is no size declarator inside the brackets of nums is because nums is not actually an array. It's a special variable that can accept the address of an array. When an entire array is passed to a function, it is not passed by value, but passed by reference. Imagine the CPU time and memory that would be necessary if a copy of a 10,000-element array were created each time it was passed to a function! Instead, only the starting memory address of the array is passed. Program 7-14 shows the function showValues in use.

 NOTE: Notice that in the function prototype, empty brackets appear after the data type of the array parameter. This indicates that showValues accepts the address of an array of integers.

Program 7-14

```
 1   // This program demonstrates an array being passed to a function.
 2   #include <iostream>
 3   using namespace std;
 4
 5   void showValues(int [], int); // Function prototype
 6
 7   int main()
 8   {
 9      const int ARRAY_SIZE = 8;
10      int numbers[ARRAY_SIZE] = {5, 10, 15, 20, 25, 30, 35, 40};
11
12      showValues(numbers, ARRAY_SIZE);
13      return 0;
14   }
15
16   //*************************************************
17   // Definition of function showValue.              *
18   // This function accepts an array of integers and  *
19   // the array's size as its arguments. The contents *
20   // of the array are displayed.                     *
21   //*************************************************
22
```

```
23   void showValues(int nums[], int size)
24   {
25      for (int index = 0; index < size; index++)
26         cout << nums[index] << " ";
27      cout << endl;
28   }
```

Program Output

5 10 15 20 25 30 35 40

In Program 7-14, the function `showValues` is called in the following statement which appears in line 12:

```
showValues(numbers, ARRAY_SIZE);
```

The first argument is the name of the array. Remember, in C++ the name of an array without brackets and a subscript is actually the beginning address of the array. In this function call, the address of the `numbers` array is being passed as the first argument to the function. The second argument is the size of the array.

In the `showValues` function, the beginning address of the `numbers` array is copied into the `nums` parameter variable. The `nums` variable is then used to reference the `numbers` array. Figure 7-14 illustrates the relationship between the `numbers` array and the `nums` parameter variable. When the contents of `nums[0]` is displayed, it is actually the contents of `numbers[0]` that appears on the screen.

Figure 7-14

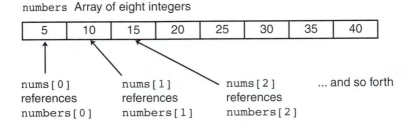

numbers Array of eight integers

| 5 | 10 | 15 | 20 | 25 | 30 | 35 | 40 |

nums[0] references numbers[0]

nums[1] references numbers[1]

nums[2] references numbers[2]

... and so forth

 NOTE: Although nums is not a reference variable, it works like one.

The `nums` parameter variable in the `showValues` function can accept the address of any integer array and can be used to reference that array. So, we can use the `showValues` function to display the contents of any integer array by passing the name of the array and its size as arguments. Program 7-15 uses the function to display the contents of two different arrays.

Program 7-15

```
1    // This program demonstrates the showValues function being
2    // used to display the contents of two arrays.
3    #include <iostream>
4    using namespace std;
5
```

(program continues)

Program 7-15   *(continued)*

```
 6   void showValues(int [], int); // Function prototype
 7
 8   int main()
 9   {
10      const int SIZE1 = 8; // Size of set1 array
11      const int SIZE2 = 5; // Size of set2 array
12      int set1[SIZE1] = {5, 10, 15, 20, 25, 30, 35, 40};
13      int set2[SIZE2] = {2, 4, 6, 8, 10};
14
15      // Pass set1 to showValues.
16      showValues(set1, SIZE1);
17
18      // Pass set2 to showValues.
19      showValues(set2, SIZE2);
20      return 0;
21   }
22
23   //*************************************************
24   // Definition of function showValues.            *
25   // This function accepts an array of integers and *
26   // the array's size as its arguments. The contents *
27   // of the array are displayed.                    *
28   //*************************************************
29
30   void showValues(int nums[], int size)
31   {
32      for (int index = 0; index < size; index++)
33         cout << nums[index] << " ";
34      cout << endl;
35   }
```

Program Output
```
5 10 15 20 25 30 35 40
2 4 6 8 10
```

Recall from Chapter 6 that when a reference variable is used as a parameter, it gives the function access to the original argument. Any changes made to the reference variable are actually performed on the argument referenced by the variable. Array parameters work very much like reference variables. They give the function direct access to the original array. Any changes made with the array parameter are actually made on the original array used as the argument. The function `doubleArray` in Program 7-16 uses this capability to double the contents of each element in the array.

Program 7-16

```
1   // This program uses a function to double the value of
2   // each element of an array.
3   #include <iostream>
4   using namespace std;
5
6   // Function prototypes
7   void doubleArray(int [], int);
```

```
 8   void showValues(int [], int);
 9
10   int main()
11   {
12      const int ARRAY_SIZE = 7;
13      int set[ARRAY_SIZE] = {1, 2, 3, 4, 5, 6, 7};
14
15      // Display the initial values.
16      cout << "The array's values are:\n";
17      showValues(set, ARRAY_SIZE);
18
19      // Double the values in the array.
20      doubleArray(set, ARRAY_SIZE);
21
22      // Display the resulting values.
23      cout << "After calling doubleArray the values are:\n";
24      showValues(set, ARRAY_SIZE);
25
26      return 0;
27   }
28
29   //*****************************************************
30   // Definition of function doubleArray                *
31   // This function doubles the value of each element   *
32   // in the array passed into nums. The value passed   *
33   // into size is the number of elements in the array. *
34   //*****************************************************
35
36   void doubleArray(int nums[], int size)
37   {
38      for (int index = 0; index < size; index++)
39         nums[index] *= 2;
40   }
41
42   //*****************************************************
43   // Definition of function showValues.                *
44   // This function accepts an array of integers and    *
45   // the array's size as its arguments. The contents   *
46   // of the array are displayed.                       *
47   //*****************************************************
48
49   void showValues(int nums[], int size)
50   {
51      for (int index = 0; index < size; index++)
52         cout << nums[index] << " ";
53      cout << endl;
54   }
```

Program Output

```
The array's values are:
1 2 3 4 5 6 7
After calling doubleArray the values are:
2 4 6 8 10 12 14
```

Using const **Array Parameters**

Sometimes you want a function to be able to modify the contents of an array that is passed to it as an argument, and sometimes you don't. You can prevent a function from making changes to an array argument by using the const key word in the parameter declaration. Here is an example of the showValues function, shown previously, rewritten with a const array parameter:

```cpp
void showValues(const int nums[], int size)
{
    for (int index = 0; index < size; index++)
        cout << nums[index] << " ";
    cout << endl;
}
```

When an array parameter is declared as const, the function is not allowed to make changes to the array's contents. If a statement in the function attempts to modify the array, an error will occur at compile time. As a precaution, you should always use const array parameters in any function that is not intended to modify its array argument. That way, the function will fail to compile if you inadvertently write code in it that modifies the array.

Some Useful Array Functions

Section 7.5 introduced you to algorithms such as summing an array and finding the highest and lowest values in an array. Now that you know how to pass an array as an argument to a function, you can write general purpose functions that perform those operations. The following In the Spotlight section shows an example.

In the Spotlight:
Processing an Array

Dr. LaClaire gives four exams during the semester in her chemistry class. At the end of the semester she drops each student's lowest test score before averaging the scores. She has asked you to write a program that will read a student's four test scores as input, and calculate the average with the lowest score dropped. Here is the pseudocode algorithm that you developed:

Read the student's four test scores.
Calculate the total of the scores.
Find the lowest score.
Subtract the lowest score from the total. This gives the adjusted total.
Divide the adjusted total by 3. This is the average.
Display the average.

Program 7-17 shows the program, which is modularized. Rather than presenting the entire program at once, let's first examine the main function, and then each additional function separately. Here is the first part of the program, including the main function:

Program 7-17   (`main` **function**)

```
 1  // This program gets a series of test scores and
 2  // calculates the average of the scores with the
 3  // lowest score dropped.
 4  #include <iostream>
 5  #include <iomanip>
 6  using namespace std;
 7
 8  // Function prototypes
 9  void getTestScores(double[], int);
10  double getTotal(const double[], int);
11  double getLowest(const double[], int);
12
13  int main()
14  {
15      const int SIZE = 4;         // Array size
16      double testScores[SIZE],    // Array of test scores
17             total,               // Total of the scores
18             lowestScore,         // Lowest test score
19             average;             // Average test score
20
21      // Set up numeric output formatting.
22      cout << fixed << showpoint << setprecision(1);
23
24      // Get the test scores from the user.
25      getTestScores(testScores, SIZE);
26
27      // Get the total of the test scores.
28      total = getTotal(testScores, SIZE);
29
30      // Get the lowest test score.
31      lowestScore = getLowest(testScores, SIZE);
32
33      // Subtract the lowest score from the total.
34      total -= lowestScore;
35
36      // Calculate the average. Divide by 3 because
37      // the lowest test score was dropped.
38      average = total / (SIZE - 1);
39
40      // Display the average.
41      cout << "The average with the lowest score "
42           << "dropped is " << average << ".\n";
43
44      return 0;
45  }
46
```

Lines 15 through 19 define the following items:

- `SIZE`, an `int` constant that is used as an array size declarator
- `testScores`, a `double` array to hold the test scores
- `total`, a `double` variable that will hold the test score totals
- `lowestScore`, a `double` variable that will hold the lowest test score
- `average`, a `double` variable that will hold the average of the test scores

Line 25 calls the `getTestScores` function, passing the `testScores` array and the value of the `SIZE` constant as arguments. The function gets the test scores from the user and stores them in the array.

Line 28 calls the `getTotal` function, passing the `testScores` array and the value of the `SIZE` constant as arguments. The function returns the total of the values in the array. This value is assigned to the `total` variable.

Line 31 calls the `getLowest` function, passing the `testScores` array and the value of the `SIZE` constant as arguments. The function returns the lowest value in the array. This value is assigned to the `lowestScore` variable.

Line 34 subtracts the lowest test score from the `total` variable. Then, line 38 calculates the average by dividing `total` by `SIZE` − 1. (The program divides by `SIZE` − 1 because the lowest test score was dropped.) Lines 41 and 42 display the average.

The `getTestScores` function appears next, as shown here:

Program 7-17   **(getTestScores function)**

```
47  //***********************************************************
48  // The getTestScores function accepts an array and its size *
49  // as arguments. It prompts the user to enter test scores,  *
50  // which are stored in the array.                           *
51  //***********************************************************
52
53  void getTestScores(double scores[], int size)
54  {
55     // Loop counter
56     int index;
57
58     // Get each test score.
59     for(index = 0; index <= size - 1; index++)
60     {
61        cout << "Enter test score number "
62             << (index + 1) << ": ";
63        cin >> scores[index];
64     }
65  }
66
```

The `getTestScores` function has two parameters:

- `scores[]`—A double array
- `size`—An int specifying the size of the array that is passed into the `scores[]` parameter

The purpose of this function is to get a student's test scores from the user and store them in the array that is passed as an argument into the `scores[]` parameter.

The getTotal function appears next, as shown here:

Program 7-17   (getTotal **function**)

```
67  //****************************************************
68  // The getTotal function accepts a double array     *
69  // and its size as arguments. The sum of the array's *
70  // elements is returned as a double.                 *
71  //****************************************************
72
73  double getTotal(const double array[], int size)
74  {
75     double total = 0; // Accumulator
76
77     // Add each element to total.
78     for (int count = 0; count < size; count++)
79        total += array[count];
80
81     // Return the total.
82     return total;
83  }
84
```

The getTotal function has two parameters:

- array[]—A const double array
- size—An int specifying the size of the array that is passed into the array[] parameter

This function returns the total of the values in the array that is passed as an argument into the array[] parameter.

The getLowest function appears next, as shown here:

Program 7-17   (getLowest **function**)

```
85   //****************************************************
86   // The getLowest function accepts a double array and *
87   // its size as arguments. The lowest value in the    *
88   // array is returned as a double.                    *
89   //****************************************************
90
91   double getLowest(const double array[], int size)
92   {
93      double lowest;  // To hold the lowest value
94
95      // Get the first array's first element.
96      lowest = array[0];
97
98      // Step through the rest of the array. When a
99      // value less than lowest is found, assign it
100     // to lowest.
```

(program continues)

Program 7-17   *(continued)*

```
101    for (int count = 1; count < size; count++)
102    {
103       if (array[count] < lowest)
104          lowest = array[count];
105    }
106
107    // Return the lowest value.
108    return lowest;
109 }
```

The `getLowest` function has two parameters:

- `array[]`—A `const double` array
- `size`—An `int` specifying the size of the array that is passed into the `array[]` parameter

This function returns the lowest value in the array that is passed as an argument into the `array[]` parameter. Here is an example of the program's output:

Program 7-17

Program Output with Example Input Shown in Bold
```
Enter test score number 1: 92 [Enter]
Enter test score number 2: 67 [Enter]
Enter test score number 3: 75 [Enter]
Enter test score number 4: 88 [Enter]
The average with the lowest score dropped is 85.0.
```

Checkpoint

myprogramminglab   *www.myprogramminglab.com*

7.14   Given the following array definitions

```
double array1[4] = {1.2, 3.2, 4.2, 5.2};
double array2[4];
```

will the following statement work? If not, why?

```
array2 = array1;
```

7.15   When an array name is passed to a function, what is actually being passed?

7.16   When used as function arguments, are arrays passed by value?

7.17   What is the output of the following program? (You may need to consult the ASCII table in Appendix B.)

```
#include <iostream>
using namespace std;

// Function prototypes
void fillArray(char [], int);
void showArray(const char [], int);
```

```cpp
int main ()
{
   const int SIZE = 8;
   char prodCode[SIZE] = {'0', '0', '0', '0', '0', '0', '0', '0'};

   fillArray(prodCode, SIZE);
   showArray(prodCode, SIZE);
   return 0;
}

// Definition of function fillArray.
// (Hint: 65 is the ASCII code for 'A')

void fillArray(char arr[], int size)
{
   char code = 65;

   for (int k = 0; k < size; code++, k++)
      arr[k] = code;
}

// Definition of function showArray.

void showArray(const char codes[], int size)
{
   for (int k = 0; k < size; k++)
      cout << codes[k];
   cout << endl;
}
```

7.18   The following program skeleton, when completed, will ask the user to enter 10 integers, which are stored in an array. The function avgArray, which you must write, is to calculate and return the average of the numbers entered.

```cpp
#include <iostream>
using namespace std;

// Write your function prototype here

int main()
{
   const int SIZE = 10;
   int userNums[SIZE];

   cout << "Enter 10 numbers: ";
   for (int count = 0; count < SIZE; count++)
   {
      cout << "#" << (count + 1) << " ";
      cin >> userNums[count];
   }
   cout << "The average of those numbers is ";
   cout << avgArray(userNums, SIZE) << endl;
   return 0;
}

//
// Write the function avgArray here.
//
```

7.8   Two-Dimensional Arrays

CONCEPT: A two-dimensional array is like several identical arrays put together. It is useful for storing multiple sets of data.

An array is useful for storing and working with a set of data. Sometimes, though, it's necessary to work with multiple sets of data. For example, in a grade-averaging program a teacher might record all of one student's test scores in an array of `doubles`. If the teacher has 30 students, that means she'll need 30 arrays of `doubles` to record the scores for the entire class. Instead of defining 30 individual arrays, however, it would be better to define a two-dimensional array.

The arrays that you have studied so far are one-dimensional arrays. They are called *one-dimensional* because they can only hold one set of data. Two-dimensional arrays, which are sometimes called *2D arrays*, can hold multiple sets of data. It's best to think of a two-dimensional array as having rows and columns of elements, as shown in Figure 7-15. This figure shows an array of test scores, having three rows and four columns.

Figure 7-15

	Column 0	Column 1	Column 2	Column 3
Row 0	scores[0] [0]	scores[0] [1]	scores[0] [2]	scores[0] [3]
Row 1	scores[1] [0]	scores[1] [1]	scores[1] [2]	scores[1] [3]
Row 2	scores[2] [0]	scores[2] [1]	scores[2] [2]	scores[2] [3]

The array depicted in Figure 7-15 has three rows (numbered 0 through 2), and four columns (numbered 0 through 3). There are a total of 12 elements in the array.

To define a two-dimensional array, two size declarators are required. The first one is for the number of rows and the second one is for the number of columns. Here is an example definition of a two-dimensional array with three rows and four columns:

```
double scores[3][4];
        └──┘  └──┘
       Rows  Columns
```

The first size declarator specifies the number of rows, and the second size declarator specifies the number of columns. Notice that each number is enclosed in its own set of brackets.

When processing the data in a two-dimensional array, each element has two subscripts: one for its row and another for its column. In the `scores` array defined above, the elements in row 0 are referenced as

```
scores[0][0]
scores[0][1]
scores[0][2]
scores[0][3]
```

The elements in row 1 are

```
scores[1][0]
scores[1][1]
scores[1][2]
scores[1][3]
```

And the elements in row 2 are

```
scores[2][0]
scores[2][1]
scores[2][2]
scores[2][3]
```

The subscripted references are used in a program just like the references to elements in a single-dimensional array, except now you use two subscripts. The first subscript represents the row position, and the second subscript represents the column position. For example, the following statement assigns the value 92.25 to the element at row 2, column 1 of the scores array:

```
scores[2][1] = 92.25;
```

And the following statement displays the element at row 0, column 2:

```
cout << scores[0][2];
```

Programs that cycle through each element of a two-dimensional array usually do so with nested loops. Program 7-18 is an example.

Program 7-18

```
 1  // This program demonstrates a two-dimensional array.
 2  #include <iostream>
 3  #include <iomanip>
 4  using namespace std;
 5
 6  int main()
 7  {
 8     const int NUM_DIVS = 3;              // Number of divisions
 9     const int NUM_QTRS = 4;              // Number of quarters
10     double sales[NUM_DIVS][NUM_QTRS];    // Array with 3 rows and 4 columns.
11     double totalSales = 0;               // To hold the total sales.
12     int div, qtr;                        // Loop counters.
13
14     cout << "This program will calculate the total sales of\n";
15     cout << "all the company's divisions.\n";
16     cout << "Enter the following sales information:\n\n";
17
18     // Nested loops to fill the array with quarterly
19     // sales figures for each division.
20     for (div = 0; div < NUM_DIVS; div++)
21     {
22        for (qtr = 0; qtr < NUM_QTRS; qtr++)
23        {
24           cout << "Division " << (div + 1);
25           cout << ", Quarter " << (qtr + 1) << ": $";
26           cin >> sales[div][qtr];
```

(program continues)

Program 7-18   *(continued)*

```
27          }
28        cout << endl; // Print blank line.
29      }
30
31      // Nested loops used to add all the elements.
32      for (div = 0; div < NUM_DIVS; div++)
33      {
34         for (qtr = 0; qtr < NUM_QTRS; qtr++)
35            totalSales += sales[div][qtr];
36      }
37
38      cout << fixed << showpoint << setprecision(2);
39      cout << "The total sales for the company are: $";
40      cout << totalSales << endl;
41      return 0;
42   }
```

Program Output with Example Input Shown in Bold

```
This program will calculate the total sales of
all the company's divisions.
Enter the following sales data:

Division 1, Quarter 1: $31569.45 [Enter]
Division 1, Quarter 2: $29654.23 [Enter]
Division 1, Quarter 3: $32982.54 [Enter]
Division 1, Quarter 4: $39651.21 [Enter]

Division 2, Quarter 1: $56321.02 [Enter]
Division 2, Quarter 2: $54128.63 [Enter]
Division 2, Quarter 3: $41235.85 [Enter]
Division 2, Quarter 4: $54652.33 [Enter]

Division 3, Quarter 1: $29654.35 [Enter]
Division 3, Quarter 2: $28963.32 [Enter]
Division 3, Quarter 3: $25353.55 [Enter]
Division 3, Quarter 4: $32615.88 [Enter]

The total sales for the company are: $456782.34
```

When initializing a two-dimensional array, it helps to enclose each row's initialization list in a set of braces. Here is an example:

```
int hours[3][2] = {{8, 5}, {7, 9}, {6, 3}};
```

The same definition could also be written as:

```
int hours[3][2] = {{8, 5},
                   {7, 9},
                   {6, 3}};
```

In either case, the values are assigned to hours in the following manner:

```
hours[0][0] is set to 8
hours[0][1] is set to 5
hours[1][0] is set to 7
```

```
hours[1][1] is set to 9
hours[2][0] is set to 6
hours[2][1] is set to 3
```

Figure 7-16 illustrates the initialization.

Figure 7-16

	Column 0	Column 1
Row 0	8	5
Row 1	7	9
Row 2	6	3

The extra braces that enclose each row's initialization list are optional. Both of the following statements perform the same initialization:

```
int hours[3][2] = {{8, 5}, {7, 9}, {6, 3}};
int hours[3][2] = {8, 5, 7, 9, 6, 3};
```

Because the extra braces visually separate each row, however, it's a good idea to use them. In addition, the braces give you the ability to leave out initializers within a row without omitting the initializers for the rows that follow it. For instance, look at the following array definition:

```
int table[3][2] = {{1}, {3, 4}, {5}};
```

table[0][0] is initialized to 1, table[1][0] is initialized to 3, table[1][1] is initialized to 4, and table[2][0] is initialized to 5. table[0][1] and table[2][1] are not initialized. Because some of the array elements are initialized, these two initialized elements are automatically set to zero.

Passing Two-Dimensional Arrays to Functions

Program 7-19 demonstrates passing a two-dimensional array to a function. When a two-dimensional array is passed to a function, the parameter type must contain a size declarator for the number of columns. Here is the header for the function showArray, from Program 7-19:

```
void showArray(const int array[][COLS], int rows)
```

COLS is a global named constant which is set to 4. The function can accept any two-dimensional integer array, as long as it consists of four columns. In the program, the contents of two separate arrays are displayed by the function.

Program 7-19

```
1   // This program demonstrates accepting a 2D array argument.
2   #include <iostream>
3   #include <iomanip>
4   using namespace std;
5
```

(program continues)

Program 7-19   *(continued)*

```
 6   // Global constants
 7   const int COLS = 4;       // Number of columns in each array
 8   const int TBL1_ROWS = 3; // Number of rows in table1
 9   const int TBL2_ROWS = 4; // Number of rows in table2
10
11   void showArray(const int [][COLS], int); // Function prototype
12
13   int main()
14   {
15      int table1[TBL1_ROWS][COLS] = {{1, 2, 3, 4},
16                                     {5, 6, 7, 8},
17                                     {9, 10, 11, 12}};
18      int table2[TBL2_ROWS][COLS] = {{10, 20, 30, 40},
19                                     {50, 60, 70, 80},
20                                     {90, 100, 110, 120},
21                                     {130, 140, 150, 160}};
22
23      cout << "The contents of table1 are:\n";
24      showArray(table1, TBL1_ROWS);
25      cout << "The contents of table2 are:\n";
26      showArray(table2, TBL2_ROWS);
27      return 0;
28   }
29
30   //**************************************************************
31   // Function Definition for showArray                          *
32   // The first argument is a two-dimensional int array with COLS  *
33   // columns. The second argument, rows, specifies the number of  *
34   // rows in the array. The function displays the array's contents. *
35   //**************************************************************
36
37   void showArray(const int array[][COLS], int rows)
38   {
39      for (int x = 0; x < rows; x++)
40      {
41         for (int y = 0; y < COLS; y++)
42         {
43            cout << setw(4) << array[x][y] << " ";
44         }
45         cout << endl;
46      }
47   }
```

Program Output

```
The contents of table1 are:
   1    2    3    4
   5    6    7    8
   9   10   11   12
The contents of table2 are:
  10   20   30   40
  50   60   70   80
  90  100  110  120
 130  140  150  160
```

C++ requires the columns to be specified in the function prototype and header because of the way two-dimensional arrays are stored in memory. One row follows another, as shown in Figure 7-17.

Figure 7-17

When the compiler generates code for accessing the elements of a two-dimensional array, it needs to know how many bytes separate the rows in memory. The number of columns is a critical factor in this calculation.

Summing All the Elements of a Two-Dimensional Array

To sum all the elements of a two-dimensional array, you can use a pair of nested loops to add the contents of each element to an accumulator. The following code is an example.

```cpp
const int NUM_ROWS = 5;        // Number of rows
const int NUM_COLS = 5;        // Number of columns
int total = 0;                 // Accumulator
int numbers[NUM_ROWS][NUM_COLS] = {{2, 7, 9, 6, 4},
                                   {6, 1, 8, 9, 4},
                                   {4, 3, 7, 2, 9},
                                   {9, 9, 0, 3, 1},
                                   {6, 2, 7, 4, 1}};

// Sum the array elements.
for (int row = 0; row < NUM_ROWS; row++)
{
   for (int col = 0; col < NUM_COLS; col++)
      total += numbers[row][col];
}

// Display the sum.
cout << "The total is " << total << endl;
```

Summing the Rows of a Two-Dimensional Array

Sometimes you may need to calculate the sum of each row in a two-dimensional array. For example, suppose a two-dimensional array is used to hold a set of test scores for a set of students. Each row in the array is a set of test scores for one student. To get the sum of a student's test scores (perhaps so an average may be calculated), you use a loop to add all the elements in one row. The following code shows an example.

```cpp
const int NUM_STUDENTS = 3;         // Number of students
const int NUM_SCORES = 5;           // Number of test scores
double total;                       // Accumulator is set in the loops
double average;                     // To hold each student's average
double scores[NUM_STUDENTS][NUM_SCORES] = {{88, 97, 79, 86, 94},
                                           {86, 91, 78, 79, 84},
                                           {82, 73, 77, 82, 89}};
```

```
// Get each student's average score.
for (int row = 0; row < NUM_STUDENTS; row++)
{
   // Set the accumulator.
   total = 0;

   // Sum a row.
   for (int col = 0; col < NUM_SCORES; col++)
      total += scores[row][col];

   // Get the average.
   average = total / NUM_SCORES;

   // Display the average.
   cout << "Score average for student "
        << (row + 1) << " is " << average <<endl;
}
```

Notice that the `total` variable, which is used as an accumulator, is set to zero just before the inner loop executes. This is because the inner loop sums the elements of a row and stores the sum in `total`. Therefore, the `total` variable must be set to zero before each iteration of the inner loop.

Summing the Columns of a Two-Dimensional Array

Sometimes you may need to calculate the sum of each column in a two-dimensional array. In the previous example a two-dimensional array is used to hold a set of test scores for a set of students. Suppose you wish to calculate the class average for each of the test scores. To do this, you calculate the average of each column in the array. This is accomplished with a set of nested loops. The outer loop controls the column subscript and the inner loop controls the row subscript. The inner loop calculates the sum of a column, which is stored in an accumulator. The following code demonstrates.

```
const int NUM_STUDENTS = 3;    // Number of students
const int NUM_SCORES = 5;      // Number of test scores
double total;                  // Accumulator is set in the loops
double average;                // To hold each score's class average
double scores[NUM_STUDENTS][NUM_SCORES] = {{88, 97, 79, 86, 94},
                                           {86, 91, 78, 79, 84},
                                           {82, 73, 77, 82, 89}};

// Get the class average for each score.
for (int col = 0; col < NUM_SCORES; col++)
{
   // Reset the accumulator.
   total = 0;

   // Sum a column.
   for (int row = 0; row < NUM_STUDENTS; row++)
      total += scores[row][col];

   // Get the average.
   average = total / NUM_STUDENTS;
```

```
            // Display the class average.
            cout << "Class average for test " << (col + 1)
                << " is " << average << endl;
        }
```

7.9 Arrays with Three or More Dimensions

CONCEPT: C++ does not limit the number of dimensions that an array may have. It is possible to create arrays with multiple dimensions, to model data that occur in multiple sets.

C++ allows you to create arrays with virtually any number of dimensions. Here is an example of a three-dimensional array definition:

```
double seats[3][5][8];
```

This array can be thought of as three sets of five rows, with each row containing eight elements. The array might be used to store the prices of seats in an auditorium, where there are eight seats in a row, five rows in a section, and a total of three sections.

Figure 7-18 illustrates the concept of a three-dimensional array as "pages" of two-dimensional arrays.

Figure 7-18

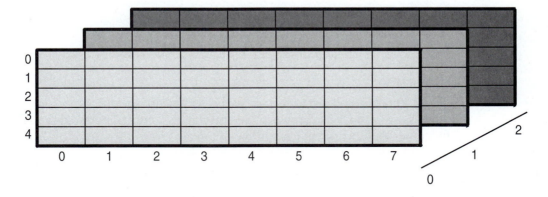

Arrays with more than three dimensions are difficult to visualize, but can be useful in some programming problems. For example, in a factory warehouse where cases of widgets are stacked on pallets, an array with four dimensions could be used to store a part number for each widget. The four subscripts of each element could represent the pallet number, case number, row number, and column number of each widget. Similarly, an array with five dimensions could be used if there were multiple warehouses.

 NOTE: When writing functions that accept multi-dimensional arrays as arguments, all but the first dimension must be explicitly stated in the parameter list.

Checkpoint

myprogramminglab *www.myprogramminglab.com*

7.19   Define a two-dimensional array of `ints` named `grades`. It should have 30 rows and 10 columns.

7.20   How many elements are in the following array?

```
double sales[6][4];
```

7.21   Write a statement that assigns the value 56893.12 to the first column of the first row of the array defined in Question 7.20.

7.22   Write a statement that displays the contents of the last column of the last row of the array defined in Question 7.20.

7.23   Define a two-dimensional array named `settings` large enough to hold the table of data below. Initialize the array with the values in the table.

12	24	32	21	42
14	67	87	65	90
19	1	24	12	8

7.24   Fill in the table below so it shows the contents of the following array:

```
int table[3][4] = {{2, 3}, {7, 9, 2}, {1}};
```


7.25   Write a function called `displayArray7`. The function should accept a two-dimensional array as an argument and display its contents on the screen. The function should work with any of the following arrays:

```
int hours[5][7];
int stamps[8][7];
int autos[12][7];
int cats[50][7];
```

7.26   A video rental store keeps DVDs on 50 racks with 10 shelves each. Each shelf holds 25 DVDs. Define a three-dimensional array large enough to represent the store's storage system.

 # 7.10   Focus on Problem Solving and Program Design: A Case Study

The National Commerce Bank has hired you as a contract programmer. Your first assignment is to write a function that will be used by the bank's automated teller machines (ATMs) to validate a customer's personal identification number (PIN).

Your function will be incorporated into a larger program that asks the customer to input his or her PIN on the ATM's numeric keypad. (PINs are seven-digit numbers. The program stores each digit in an element of an integer array.) The program also retrieves a copy of the customer's actual PIN from a database. (The PINs are also stored in the database as seven-element arrays.) If these two numbers match, then the customer's identity is validated. Your function is to compare the two arrays and determine whether they contain the same numbers.

Here are the specifications your function must meet:

Parameters   The function is to accept as arguments two integer arrays of seven elements each. The first argument will contain the number entered by the customer. The second argument will contain the number retrieved from the bank's database.

Return value   The function should return a Boolean `true` value if the two arrays are identical. Otherwise, it should return `false`.

Here is the pseudocode for the function:

```
For each element in the first array
    Compare the element with the element in the second array
    that is in the corresponding position.
    If the two elements contain different values
        Return false.
    End If.
End For.
Return true.
```

The C++ code is shown below.

```cpp
bool testPIN(const int custPIN[], const int databasePIN[], int size)
{
    for (int index = 0; index < size; index++)
    {
        if (custPIN[index] != databasePIN[index])
            return false;    // We've found two different values.
    }
    return true;    // If we make it this far, the values are the same.
}
```

Because you have only been asked to write a function that performs the comparison between the customer's input and the PIN that was retrieved from the database, you will also need to design a driver. Program 7-20 shows the complete program.

Program 7-20

```cpp
1  // This program is a driver that tests a function comparing the
2  // contents of two int arrays.
3  #include <iostream>
4  using namespace std;
5
6  // Function Prototype
7  bool testPIN(const int [], const int [], int);
8
```

(program continues)

Program 7-20   *(continued)*

```cpp
 9 int main ()
10 {
11    const int NUM_DIGITS = 7; // Number of digits in a PIN
12    int pin1[NUM_DIGITS] = {2, 4, 1, 8, 7, 9, 0}; // Base set of values.
13    int pin2[NUM_DIGITS] = {2, 4, 6, 8, 7, 9, 0}; // Only 1 element is
14                                              // different from pin1.
15    int pin3[NUM_DIGITS] = {1, 2, 3, 4, 5, 6, 7}; // All elements are
16                                              // different from pin1.
17    if (testPIN(pin1, pin2, NUM_DIGITS))
18       cout << "ERROR: pin1 and pin2 report to be the same.\n";
19    else
20       cout << "SUCCESS: pin1 and pin2 are different.\n";
21
22    if (testPIN(pin1, pin3, NUM_DIGITS))
23       cout << "ERROR: pin1 and pin3 report to be the same.\n";
24    else
25       cout << "SUCCESS: pin1 and pin3 are different.\n";
26
27    if (testPIN(pin1, pin1, NUM_DIGITS))
28       cout << "SUCCESS: pin1 and pin1 report to be the same.\n";
29    else
30       cout << "ERROR: pin1 and pin1 report to be different.\n";
31    return 0;
32 }
33
34 //******************************************************************
35 // The following function accepts two int arrays. The arrays are    *
36 // compared. If they contain the same values, true is returned.     *
37 // If they contain different values, false is returned.             *
38 //******************************************************************
39
40 bool testPIN(const int custPIN[], const int databasePIN[], int size)
41 {
42    for (int index = 0; index < size; index++)
43    {
44       if (custPIN[index] != databasePIN[index])
45          return false; // We've found two different values.
46    }
47    return true; // If we make it this far, the values are the same.
48 }
```

Program Output

```
SUCCESS: pin1 and pin2 are different.
SUCCESS: pin1 and pin3 are different.
SUCCESS: pin1 and pin1 report to be the same.
```

Case Study: See the Intersection of Sets Case Study on the book's companion Web site at www.pearsonhighered.com/gaddis.

7.11

If You Plan to Continue in Computer Science: Introduction to the STL vector

CONCEPT: The Standard Template Library offers a **vector** data type, which in many ways, is superior to standard arrays.

The *Standard Template Library* (STL) is a collection of data types and algorithms that you may use in your programs. These data types and algorithms are *programmer-defined*. They are not part of the C++ language, but were created in addition to the built-in data types. If you plan to continue your studies in the field of computer science, you should become familiar with the STL. This section introduces one of the STL data types. For more information on the STL, see Chapter 16.

> **NOTE:** Many older compilers do not support the STL.

The data types that are defined in the STL are commonly called *containers*. They are called containers because they store and organize data. There are two types of containers in the STL: sequence containers and associative containers. A *sequence container* organizes data in a sequential fashion, similar to an array. *Associative containers* organize data with keys, which allow rapid, random access to elements stored in the container.

In this section you will learn to use the vector data type, which is a sequence container. A vector is like an array in the following ways:

- A vector holds a sequence of values, or elements.
- A vector stores its elements in contiguous memory locations.
- You can use the array subscript operator [ ] to read the individual elements in the vector.

However, a vector offers several advantages over arrays. Here are just a few:

- You do not have to declare the number of elements that the vector will have.
- If you add a value to a vector that is already full, the vector will automatically increase its size to accommodate the new value.
- vectors can report the number of elements they contain.

Defining a vector

To use vectors in your program, you must include the vector header file with the following statement:

```
#include <vector>
```

> **NOTE:** To use the vector data type, you must have the using namespace std; statement in your program.

Now you are ready to define an actual `vector` object. The syntax for defining a `vector` is somewhat different from the syntax used in defining a regular variable or array. Here is an example:

```
vector<int> numbers;
```

This statement defines `numbers` as a `vector` of `int`s. Notice that the data type is enclosed in angled brackets, immediately after the word `vector`. Because the `vector` expands in size as you add values to it, there is no need to declare a size. You can define a starting size, if you prefer. Here is an example:

```
vector<int> numbers(10);
```

This statement defines `numbers` as a `vector` of 10 `int`s. This is only a starting size, however. Although the `vector` has 10 elements, its size will expand if you add more than 10 values to it.

 NOTE: If you specify a starting size for a `vector`, the size declarator is enclosed in parentheses, not square brackets.

When you specify a starting size for a `vector`, you may also specify an initialization value. The initialization value is copied to each element. Here is an example:

```
vector<int> numbers(10, 2);
```

In this statement, `numbers` is defined as a `vector` of 10 `int`s. Each element in `numbers` is initialized to the value 2.

You may also initialize a `vector` with the values in another `vector`. For example, look at the following statement. Assume that `set1` is a `vector` of `int`s that already has values stored in it.

```
vector<int> set2(set1);
```

After this statement executes, `set2` will be a copy of `set1`.

Table 7-3 summarizes the `vector` definition procedures we have discussed.

Table 7-3

Definition Format	Description
`vector<float> amounts;`	Defines `amounts` as an empty `vector` of `float`s.
`vector<string> names;`	Defines `names` as an empty `vector` of `string` objects.
`vector<int> scores(15);`	Defines `scores` as a `vector` of 15 `int`s.
`vector<char> letters(25, 'A');`	Defines `letters` as a `vector` of 25 characters. Each element is initialized with `'A'`.
`vector<double> values2(values1);`	Defines `values2` as a `vector` of `double`s. All the elements of `values1`, which is also a `vector` of `double`s, are copied to `value2`.

Storing and Retrieving Values in a `vector`

To store a value in an element that already exists in a `vector`, you may use the array subscript operator `[ ]`. For example, look at Program 7-21.

Program 7-21

```cpp
 1  // This program stores, in two vectors, the hours worked by 5
 2  // employees, and their hourly pay rates.
 3  #include <iostream>
 4  #include <iomanip>
 5  #include <vector>          // Needed to define vectors
 6  using namespace std;
 7
 8  int main()
 9  {
10      const int NUM_EMPLOYEES = 5;              // Number of employees
11      vector<int> hours(NUM_EMPLOYEES);         // A vector of integers
12      vector<double> payRate(NUM_EMPLOYEES);    // A vector of doubles
13      int index;                                // Loop counter
14
15      // Input the data.
16      cout << "Enter the hours worked by " << NUM_EMPLOYEES;
17      cout << " employees and their hourly rates.\n";
18      for (index = 0; index < NUM_EMPLOYEES; index++)
19      {
20          cout << "Hours worked by employee #" << (index + 1);
21          cout << ": ";
22          cin >> hours[index];
23          cout << "Hourly pay rate for employee #";
24          cout << (index + 1) << ": ";
25          cin >> payRate[index];
26      }
27
28      // Display each employee's gross pay.
29      cout << "\nHere is the gross pay for each employee:\n";
30      cout << fixed << showpoint << setprecision(2);
31      for (index = 0; index < NUM_EMPLOYEES; index++)
32      {
33          double grossPay = hours[index] * payRate[index];
34          cout << "Employee #" << (index + 1);
35          cout << ": $" << grossPay << endl;
36      }
37      return 0;
38  }
```

Program Output with Example Input Shown in Bold

Enter the hours worked by 5 employees and their hourly rates.
Hours worked by employee #1: **10 [Enter]**
Hourly pay rate for employee #1: **9.75 [Enter]**
Hours worked by employee #2: **15 [Enter]**
Hourly pay rate for employee #2: **8.62 [Enter]**
Hours worked by employee #3: **20 [Enter]**
Hourly pay rate for employee #3: **10.50 [Enter]**
Hours worked by employee #4: **40 [Enter]**
Hourly pay rate for employee #4: **18.75 [Enter]**
Hours worked by employee #5: **40 [Enter]**
Hourly pay rate for employee #5: **15.65 [Enter]**

(program output continues)

Program 7-21 *(continued)*

```
Here is the gross pay for each employee:
Employee #1: $97.50
Employee #2: $129.30
Employee #3: $210.00
Employee #4: $750.00
Employee #5: $626.00
```

Notice that Program 7-21 uses the following statements in lines 11 and 12 to define two vectors.

```
vector<int> hours(NUM_EMPLOYEES);       // A vector of integers
vector<double> payRate(NUM_EMPLOYEES); // A vector of doubles
```

Both of the vectors are defined with the starting size 5, which is the value of the named constant NUM_EMPLOYEES. The program uses the following loop in lines 18 through 26 to store a value in each element of both vectors:

```
for (index = 0; index < NUM_EMPLOYEES; index++)
{
    cout << "Hours worked by employee #" << (index + 1);
    cout << ": ";
    cin >> hours[index];
    cout << "Hourly pay rate for employee #";
    cout << (index + 1) << ": ";
    cin >> payRate[index];
}
```

Because the values entered by the user are being stored in vector elements that already exist, the program uses the array subscript operator [ ], as shown in the following statements, which appear in lines 22 and 25:

```
cin >> hours[index];
```

```
cin >> payRate[index];
```

Using the push_back Member Function

You cannot use the [ ] operator to access a vector element that does not exist. To store a value in a vector that does not have a starting size, or that is already full, use the push_back member function. The push_back member function accepts a value as an argument, and stores that value after the last element in the vector. (It pushes the value onto the back of the vector.) Here is an example:

```
numbers.push_back(25);
```

Assuming numbers is a vector of ints, this statement stores 25 as the last element. If numbers is full, the statement creates a new last element, and stores 25 in it. If there are no elements in numbers, this statement creates an element and stores 25 in it.

Program 7-22 is a modification of Program 7-21. This version, however, allows the user to specify the number of employees. The two vectors, hours and payRate, are defined without starting sizes. Because these vectors have no starting elements, the push_back member function is used to store values in the vectors.

Program 7-22

```cpp
1 // This program stores, in two arrays, the hours worked by 5
2 // employees, and their hourly pay rates.
3 #include <iostream>
4 #include <iomanip>
5 #include <vector>     // Needed to define vectors
6 using namespace std;
7
8 int main()
9 {
10    vector<int> hours;       // hours is an empty vector
11    vector<double> payRate; // payRate is an empty vector
12    int numEmployees;        // The number of employees
13    int index;               // Loop counter
14
15    // Get the number of employees.
16    cout << "How many employees do you have? ";
17    cin >> numEmployees;
18
19    // Input the payroll data.
20    cout << "Enter the hours worked by " << numEmployees;
21    cout << " employees and their hourly rates.\n";
22    for (index = 0; index < numEmployees; index++)
23    {
24       int tempHours;    // To hold the number of hours entered
25       double tempRate;  // To hold the pay rate entered
26
27       cout << "Hours worked by employee #" << (index + 1);
28       cout << ": ";
29       cin >> tempHours;
30       hours.push_back(tempHours);      // Add an element to hours
31       cout << "Hourly pay rate for employee #";
32       cout << (index + 1) << ": ";
33       cin >> tempRate;
34       payRate.push_back(tempRate);  // Add an element to payRate
35    }
36
37    // Display each employee's gross pay.
38    cout << "Here is the gross pay for each employee:\n";
39    cout << fixed << showpoint << setprecision(2);
40    for (index = 0; index < numEmployees; index++)
41    {
42       double grossPay = hours[index] * payRate[index];
43       cout << "Employee #" << (index + 1);
44       cout << ": $" << grossPay << endl;
45    }
46    return 0;
47 }
```

(program output continues)

Program 7-22 *(continued)*

Program Output with Example Input Shown in Bold
```
How many employees do you have? 3 [Enter]
Enter the hours worked by 3 employees and their hourly rates.
Hours worked by employee #1: 40 [Enter]
Hourly pay rate for employee #1: 12.63 [Enter]
Hours worked by employee #2: 25 [Enter]
Hourly pay rate for employee #2: 10.35 [Enter]
Hours worked by employee #3: 45 [Enter]
Hourly pay rate for employee #3: 22.65 [Enter]

Here is the gross pay for each employee:
Employee #1: $505.20
Employee #2: $258.75
Employee #3: $1019.2
```

Notice that in lines 40 through 45 the second loop, which calculates and displays each employee's gross pay, uses the `[]` operator to access the elements of the `hours` and `payRate` vectors:

```cpp
for (index = 0; index < numEmployees; index++)
{
    double grossPay = hours[index] * payRate[index];
    cout << "Employee #" << (index + 1);
    cout << ": $" << grossPay << endl;
}
```

This is possible because the first loop in lines 22 through 35 uses the `push_back` member function to create the elements in the two vectors.

Determining the Size of a `vector`

Unlike arrays, `vector`s can report the number of elements they contain. This is accomplished with the `size` member function. Here is an example of a statement that uses the `size` member function:

```cpp
numValues = set.size();
```

In this statement, assume that `numValues` is an `int` and `set` is a `vector`. After the statement executes, `numValues` will contain the number of elements in `set`.

The `size` member function is especially useful when you are writing functions that accept `vector`s as arguments. For example, look at the following code for the `showValues` function:

```cpp
void showValues(vector<int> vect)
{
    for (int count = 0; count < vect.size(); count++)
        cout << vect[count] << endl;
}
```

Because the `vector` can report its size, this function does not need to accept a second argument indicating the number of elements in the `vector`. Program 7-23 demonstrates this function.

Program 7-23

```cpp
 1  // This program demonstrates the vector size
 2  // member function.
 3  #include <iostream>
 4  #include <vector>
 5  using namespace std;
 6
 7  // Function prototype
 8  void showValues(vector<int>);
 9
10  int main()
11  {
12     vector<int> values;
13
14     // Put a series of numbers in the vector.
15     for (int count = 0; count < 7; count++)
16        values.push_back(count * 2);
17
18     // Display the numbers.
19     showValues(values);
20     return 0;
21  }
22
23  //*************************************************
24  // Definition of function showValues.           *
25  // This function accepts an int vector as its    *
26  // argument. The value of each of the vector's   *
27  // elements is displayed.                        *
28  //*************************************************
29
30  void showValues(vector<int> vect)
31  {
32     for (int count = 0; count < vect.size(); count++)
33        cout << vect[count] << endl;
34  }
```

Program Output

```
0
2
4
6
8
10
12
```

Removing Elements from a vector

Use the pop_back member function to remove the last element from a vector. In the following statement, assume that collection is the name of a vector.

```cpp
collection.pop_back();
```

This statement removes the last element from the collection vector. Program 7-24 demonstrates the function.

Program 7-24

```cpp
 1  // This program demonstrates the vector pop_back member function.
 2  #include <iostream>
 3  #include <vector>
 4  using namespace std;
 5
 6  int main()
 7  {
 8     vector<int> values;
 9
10     // Store values in the vector.
11     values.push_back(1);
12     values.push_back(2);
13     values.push_back(3);
14     cout << "The size of values is " << values.size() << endl;
15
16     // Remove a value from the vector.
17     cout << "Popping a value from the vector...\n";
18     values.pop_back();
19     cout << "The size of values is now " << values.size() << endl;
20
21     // Now remove another value from the vector.
22     cout << "Popping a value from the vector...\n";
23     values.pop_back();
24     cout << "The size of values is now " << values.size() << endl;
25
26     // Remove the last value from the vector.
27     cout << "Popping a value from the vector...\n";
28     values.pop_back();
29     cout << "The size of values is now " << values.size() << endl;
30     return 0;
31  }
```

Program Output

```
The size of values is 3
Popping a value from the vector...
The size of values is now 2
Popping a value from the vector...
The size of values is now 1
Popping a value from the vector...
The size of values is now 0
```

Clearing a vector

To completely clear the contents of a vector, use the clear member function, as shown in the following statement:

```cpp
    numbers.clear();
```

After this statement executes, numbers will be cleared of all its elements. Program 7-25 demonstrates the function.

Program 7-25

```
 1 // This program demonstrates the vector clear member function.
 2 #include <iostream>
 3 #include <vector>
 4 using namespace std;
 5
 6 int main()
 7 {
 8    vector<int> values(100);
 9
10    cout << "The values vector has "
11         << values.size() << " elements.\n";
12    cout << "I will call the clear member function...\n";
13    values.clear();
14    cout << "Now, the values vector has "
15         << values.size() << " elements.\n";
16    return 0;
17 }
```

Program Output

```
The values vector has 100 elements.
I will call the clear member function...
Now, the values vector has 0 elements.
```

Detecting an Empty vector

To determine if a vector is empty, use the empty member function. The function returns true if the vector is empty, and false if the vector has elements stored in it. Assuming set is a vector, here is an example of its use:

```
if (set.empty())
    cout << "No values in set.\n";
```

Program 7-26 uses a function named avgVector, which demonstrates the empty member function.

Program 7-26

```
 1 // This program demonstrates the vector's empty member function.
 2 #include <iostream>
 3 #include <vector>
 4 using namespace std;
 5
 6 // Function prototype
 7 double avgVector(vector<int>);
 8
 9 int main()
10 {
11    vector<int> values;    // A vector to hold values
12    int numValues;         // The number of values
13    double average;        // To hold the average
14
```

(program continues)

Program 7-26 *(continued)*

```
15      // Get the number of values to average.
16      cout << "How many values do you wish to average? ";
17      cin >> numValues;
18
19      // Get the values and store them in the vector.
20      for (int count = 0; count < numValues; count++)
21      {
22          int tempValue;
23          cout << "Enter a value: ";
24          cin >> tempValue;
25          values.push_back(tempValue);
26      }
27
28      // Get the average of the values and display it.
29      average = avgVector(values);
30      cout << "Average: " << average << endl;
31      return 0;
32  }
33
34  //***************************************************************
35  // Definition of function avgVector.                           *
36  // This function accepts an int vector as its argument. If     *
37  // the vector contains values, the function returns the        *
38  // average of those values. Otherwise, an error message is     *
39  // displayed and the function returns 0.0.                     *
40  //***************************************************************
41
42  double avgVector(vector<int> vect)
43  {
44      int total = 0;     // accumulator
45      double avg;        // average
46
47      if (vect.empty()) // Determine if the vector is empty
48      {
49          cout << "No values to average.\n";
50          avg = 0.0;
51      }
52      else
53      {
54          for (int count = 0; count < vect.size(); count++)
55              total += vect[count];
56          avg = total / vect.size();
57      }
58      return avg;
59  }
```

Program Output with Example Input Shown in Bold
```
How many values do you wish to average? 5 [Enter]
Enter a value: 12
Enter a value: 18
Enter a value: 3
Enter a value: 7
Enter a value: 9
Average: 9
```

Summary of vector Member Functions

Table 7-4 provides a summary of the vector member function we have discussed, as well as some additional ones.

Table 7-4

Member Function	Description
at(*element*)	Returns the value of the element located at *element* in the vector. *Example:* `x = vect.at(5);` This statement assigns the value of the fifth element of vect to x.
capacity()	Returns the maximum number of elements that may be stored in the vector without additional memory being allocated. (This is not the same value as returned by the size member function). *Example:* `x = vect.capacity();` This statement assigns the capacity of vect to x.
clear()	Clears a vector of all its elements. *Example:* `vect.clear();` This statement removes all the elements from vect.

empty()	Returns true if the vector is empty. Otherwise, it returns false.
	Example:
	
	`if (vect.empty())`
	`    cout << "The vector is empty.";`
	
	This statement displays the message if vect is empty.

pop_back()	Removes the last element from the vector. *Example:* `vect.pop_back();` This statement removes the last element of vect, thus reducing its size by 1.

(table continues)

Table 7-4 *(continued)*

Member Function	Description
push_back(*value*)	Stores a value in the last element of the vector. If the vector is full or empty, a new element is created. *Example:* vect.push_back(7); This statement stores 7 in the last element of vect.
reverse()	Reverses the order of the elements in the vector. (The last element becomes the first element, and the first element becomes the last element.) *Example:* vect.reverse(); This statement reverses the order of the element in vect.
resize(*elements, value*)	Resizes a vector by *elements* elements. Each of the new elements is initialized with the value in *value*. *Example:* vect.resize(5, 1); This statement increases the size of vect by five elements. The five new elements are initialized to the value 1.
swap(*vector2*)	Swaps the contents of the vector with the contents of *vector2*. *Example:* vect1.swap(vect2); This statement swaps the contents of vect1 and vect2

 ## Checkpoint

7.27   What header file must you #include in order to define vector objects?

7.28   Write a definition statement for a vector named frogs. frogs should be an empty vector of ints.

7.29   Write a definition statement for a vector named lizards. lizards should be a vector of 20 floats.

7.30   Write a definition statement for a vector named toads. toads should be a vector of 100 chars, with each element initialized to 'z'.

7.31   gators is an empty vector of ints. Write a statement that stores the value 27 in gators.

7.32   snakes is a vector of doubles, with 10 elements. Write a statement that stores the value 12.897 in element 4 of the snakes vector.

Review Questions and Exercises

Short Answer

1. What is the difference between a size declarator and a subscript?

2. Look at the following array definition.

   ```
   int values[10];
   ```

   How many elements does the array have?

   What is the subscript of the first element in the array?

   What is the subscript of the last element in the array?

   Assuming that an int uses four bytes of memory, how much memory does the array use?

3. Why should a function that accepts an array as an argument, and processes that array, also accept an argument specifying the array's size?

4. Consider the following array definition:

   ```
   int values[5] = { 4, 7, 6, 8, 2 };
   ```

   What does each of the following statements display?

   ```
   cout << values[4] << endl; _____
   ```

   ```
   cout << (values[2] + values[3]) << endl; _____
   ```

   ```
   cout << ++values[1] << endl; _____
   ```

5. How do you define an array without providing a size declarator?

6. Look at the following array definition.

   ```
   int numbers[5] = { 1, 2, 3 };
   ```

   What value is stored in numbers[2]?

   What value is stored in numbers[4]?

7. Assuming that array1 and array2 are both arrays, why is it not possible to assign the contents of array2 to array1 with the following statement?

   ```
   array1 = array2;
   ```

8. Assuming that numbers is an array of doubles, will the following statement display the contents of the array?

   ```
   cout << numbers << endl;
   ```

9. Is an array passed to a function by value or by reference?

10. When you pass an array name as an argument to a function, what is actually being passed?

11. How do you establish a parallel relationship between two or more arrays?

12. Look at the following array definition.

    ```
    double sales[8][10];
    ```

    How many rows does the array have?

    How many columns does the array have?

How many elements does the array have?

Write a statement that stores a number in the last column of the last row in the array.

13. When writing a function that accepts a two-dimensional array as an argument, which size declarator must you provide in the parameter for the array?

14. What advantages does a vector offer over an array?

Fill-in-the-Blank

15. The _____ indicates the number of elements, or values, an array can hold.

16. The size declarator must be a(n) _____ with a value greater than _____.

17. Each element of an array is accessed and indexed by a number known as a(n) _____.

18. Subscript numbering in C++ always starts at _____.

19. The number inside the brackets of an array definition is the _____, but the number inside an array's brackets in an assignment statement, or any other statement that works with the contents of the array, is the _____.

20. C++ has no array _____ checking, which means you can inadvertently store data past the end of an array.

21. Starting values for an array may be specified with a(n) _____ list.

22. If an array is partially initialized, the uninitialized elements will be set to _____.

23. If the size declarator of an array definition is omitted, C++ counts the number of items in the _____ to determine how large the array should be.

24. By using the same _____ for multiple arrays, you can build relationships between the data stored in the arrays.

25. You cannot use the _____ operator to copy data from one array to another in a single statement.

26. Any time the name of an array is used without brackets and a subscript, it is seen as _____.

27. To pass an array to a function, pass the _____ of the array.

28. A(n) _____ array is like several arrays of the same type put together.

29. It's best to think of a two-dimensional array as having _____ and _____.

30. To define a two-dimensional array, _____ size declarators are required.

31. When initializing a two-dimensional array, it helps to enclose each row's initialization list in _____.

32. When a two-dimensional array is passed to a function the _____ size must be specified.

33. The _____ is a collection of programmer-defined data types and algorithms that you may use in your programs

34. The two types of containers defined by the STL are _____ and _____.

35. The `vector` data type is a(n) _____ container.

36. To define a `vector` in your program, you must `#include` the _____ header file.

37. To store a value in a `vector` that does not have a starting size, or that is already full, use the _____ member function.

38. To determine the number of elements in a `vector`, use the _____ member function.

39. Use the _____ member function to remove the last element from a `vector`.

40. To completely clear the contents of a `vector`, use the _____ member function.

Algorithm Workbench

41. `names` is an integer array with 20 elements. Write a `for` loop that prints each element of the array.

42. The arrays `numberArray1` and `numberArray2` have 100 elements. Write code that copies the values in `numberArray1` to `numberArray2`.

43. In a program you need to store the identification numbers of 10 employees (as `int`s) and their weekly gross pay (as `double`s).

    A) Define two arrays that may be used in parallel to store the 10 employee identification numbers and gross pay amounts.

    B) Write a loop that uses these arrays to print each employee's identification number and weekly gross pay.

44. Define a two-dimensional array of integers named `grades`. It should have 30 rows and 10 columns.

45. In a program you need to store the populations of 12 countries.

    A) Define two arrays that may be used in parallel to store the names of the countries and their populations.

    B) Write a loop that uses these arrays to print each country's name and its population.

46. The following code totals the values in two arrays: `numberArray1` and `numberArray2`. Both arrays have 25 elements. Will the code print the correct sum of values for both arrays? Why or why not?

```
int total = 0;          // Accumulator
int count;              // Loop counter
// Calculate and display the total of the first array.
for (count = 0; count < 24; count++)
    total += numberArray1[count];
cout << "The total for numberArray1 is " << total << endl;
// Calculate and display the total of the second array.
for (count = 0; count < 24; count++)
    total += numberArray2[count];
cout << "The total for numberArray2 is " << total << endl;
```

47. Look at the following array definition.

```
int numberArray[9][11];
```

Write a statement that assigns 145 to the first column of the first row of this array.

Write a statement that assigns 18 to the last column of the last row of this array.

48. `values` is a two-dimensional array of `floats` with 10 rows and 20 columns. Write code that sums all the elements in the array and stores the sum in the variable `total`.

49. An application uses a two-dimensional array defined as follows.

```
int days[29][5];
```

Write code that sums each row in the array and displays the results.

Write code that sums each column in the array and displays the results.

True or False

50. T F An array's size declarator can be either a literal, a named constant, or a variable.

51. T F To calculate the amount of memory used by an array, multiply the number of elements by the number of bytes each element uses.

52. T F The individual elements of an array are accessed and indexed by unique numbers.

53. T F The first element in an array is accessed by the subscript 1.

54. T F The subscript of the last element in a single-dimensional array is one less than the total number of elements in the array.

55. T F The contents of an array element cannot be displayed with `cout`.

56. T F Subscript numbers may be stored in variables.

57. T F You can write programs that use invalid subscripts for an array.

58. T F Arrays cannot be initialized when they are defined. A loop or other means must be used.

59. T F The values in an initialization list are stored in the array in the order they appear in the list.

60. T F C++ allows you to partially initialize an array.

61. T F If an array is partially initialized, the uninitialized elements will contain "garbage."

62. T F If you leave an element uninitialized, you do not have to leave all the ones that follow it uninitialized.

63. T F If you leave out the size declarator of an array definition, you do not have to include an initialization list.

64. T F The uninitialized elements of a `string` array will automatically be set to the value `"0"`.

65. T F You cannot use the assignment operator to copy one array's contents to another in a single statement.

66. T F When an array name is used without brackets and a subscript, it is seen as the value of the first element in the array.

67. T F To pass an array to a function, pass the name of the array.

68. T F When defining a parameter variable to hold a single-dimensional array argument, you do not have to include the size declarator.

69. T F When an array is passed to a function, the function has access to the original array.

70. T F A two-dimensional array is like several identical arrays put together.

71. T   F   It's best to think of two-dimensional arrays as having rows and columns.

72. T   F   The first size declarator (in the declaration of a two-dimensional array) represents the number of columns. The second size definition represents the number of rows.

73. T   F   Two-dimensional arrays may be passed to functions, but the row size must be specified in the definition of the parameter variable.

74. T   F   C++ allows you to create arrays with three or more dimensions.

75. T   F   A vector is an associative container.

76. T   F   To use a vector, you must include the vector header file.

77. T   F   vectors can report the number of elements they contain.

78. T   F   You can use the [ ] operator to insert a value into a vector that has no elements.

79. T   F   If you add a value to a vector that is already full, the vector will automatically increase its size to accommodate the new value.

Find the Error

Each of the following definitions and program segments has errors. Locate as many as you can.

80.
```cpp
int size;
double values[size];
```

81.
```cpp
int collection[-20];
```

82.
```cpp
int table[10];
for (int x = 0; x < 20; x++)
{
    cout << "Enter the next value: ";
    cin >> table[x];
}
```

83.
```cpp
int hours[3] = 8, 12, 16;
```

84.
```cpp
int numbers[8] = {1, 2, , 4, , 5};
```

85.
```cpp
float ratings[];
```

86.
```cpp
char greeting[] = {'H', 'e', 'l', 'l', 'o'};
cout << greeting;
```

87.
```cpp
int array1[4], array2[4] = {3, 6, 9, 12};
array1 = array2;
```

88.
```cpp
void showValues(int nums)
{
    for (int count = 0; count < 8; count++)
        cout << nums[count];
}
```

89.
```cpp
void showValues(int nums[4][])
{
    for (rows = 0; rows < 4; rows++)
        for (cols = 0; cols < 5; cols++)
            cout << nums[rows][cols];
}
```

Programming Challenges

Visit www.myprogramminglab.com to complete many of these Programming Challenges online and get instant feedback.

1. Largest/Smallest Array Values

Write a program that lets the user enter 10 values into an array. The program should then display the largest and smallest values stored in the array.

2. Rainfall Statistics

Write a program that lets the user enter the total rainfall for each of 12 months into an array of `doubles`. The program should calculate and display the total rainfall for the year, the average monthly rainfall, and the months with the highest and lowest amounts.

Input Validation: Do not accept negative numbers for monthly rainfall figures.

3. Chips and Salsa

VideoNote
Solving the
Chips and
Salsa Problem

Write a program that lets a maker of chips and salsa keep track of sales for five different types of salsa: mild, medium, sweet, hot, and zesty. The program should use two parallel 5-element arrays: an array of strings that holds the five salsa names and an array of integers that holds the number of jars sold during the past month for each salsa type. The salsa names should be stored using an initialization list at the time the name array is created. The program should prompt the user to enter the number of jars sold for each type. Once this sales data has been entered, the program should produce a report that displays sales for each salsa type, total sales, and the names of the highest selling and lowest selling products.

Input Validation: Do not accept negative values for number of jars sold.

4. Monkey Business

A local zoo wants to keep track of how many pounds of food each of its three monkeys eats each day during a typical week. Write a program that stores this information in a two-dimensional 3×7 array, where each row represents a different monkey and each column represents a different day of the week. The program should first have the user input the data for each monkey. Then it should create a report that includes the following information:

- Average amount of food eaten per day by the whole family of monkeys.
- The least amount of food eaten during the week by any one monkey.
- The greatest amount of food eaten during the week by any one monkey.

Input Validation: Do not accept negative numbers for pounds of food eaten.

5. Rain or Shine

An amateur meteorologist wants to keep track of weather conditions during the past year's three-month summer season and has designated each day as either rainy ('R'), cloudy ('C'), or sunny ('S'). Write a program that stores this information in a 3×30 array of characters, where the row indicates the month (0 = June, 1 = July, 2 = August) and the column indicates the day of the month. Note that data are not being collected for the 31st of any month. The program should begin by reading the weather data in from a file. Then it should create a report that displays, for each month and for the whole three-month period, how many days were rainy, how many were cloudy, and how many were sunny. It should also report which of the three months had the largest number of rainy days. Data for the program can be found in the `RainOrShine.dat` file.

6. **Number Analysis Program**

Write a program that asks the user for a file name. Assume the file contains a series of numbers, each written on a separate line. The program should read the contents of the file into an array and then display the following data:

- The lowest number in the array
- The highest number in the array
- The total of the numbers in the array
- The average of the numbers in the array

If you have downloaded this book's source code from the companion Web site, you will find a file named numbers.txt in the Chapter 06 folder. You can use the file to test the program. (The companion Web site is at www.pearsonhighered.com/gaddis.)

7. **Quarterly Sales Statistics**

Write a program that lets the user enter four quarterly sales figures for six divisions of a company. The figures should be stored in a two-dimensional array. Once the figures are entered, the program should display the following data for each quarter:

- A list of the sales figures by division
- Each division's increase or decrease from the previous quarter (This will not be displayed for the first quarter.)
- The total sales for the quarter
- The company's increase or decrease from the previous quarter (This will not be displayed for the first quarter.)
- The average sales for all divisions that quarter
- The division with the highest sales for that quarter

The program should be modular, with functions that calculate the statistics above.

Input Validation: Do not accept negative numbers for sales figures.

8. **Payroll**

Write a program that uses the following arrays:

- `empId`: an array of seven long integers to hold employee identification numbers. The array should be initialized with the following numbers:

  ```
  5658845    4520125    7895122    8777541
  8451277    1302850    7580489
  ```

- `hours`: an array of seven integers to hold the number of hours worked by each employee
- `payRate`: an array of seven `doubles` to hold each employee's hourly pay rate
- `wages`: an array of seven `doubles` to hold each employee's gross wages

The program should relate the data in each array through the subscripts. For example, the number in element 0 of the `hours` array should be the number of hours worked by the employee whose identification number is stored in element 0 of the `empId` array. That same employee's pay rate should be stored in element 0 of the `payRate` array.

The program should display each employee number and ask the user to enter that employee's hours and pay rate. It should then calculate the gross wages for that employee (hours times pay rate) and store them in the `wages` array. After the data has been entered for all the employees, the program should display each employee's identification number and gross wages.

Input Validation: Do not accept negative values for hours or numbers less than 6.00 for pay rate.

9. **Driver's License Exam**

The local Driver's License Office has asked you to write a program that grades the written portion of the driver's license exam. The exam has 20 multiple choice questions. Here are the correct answers:

1. B	6. A	11. B	16. C
2. D	7. B	12. C	17. C
3. A	8. A	13. D	18. B
4. A	9. C	14. A	19. D
5. C	10. D	15. D	20. A

Your program should store the correct answers shown above in an array. It should ask the user to enter the student's answers for each of the 20 questions, and the answers should be stored in another array. After the student's answers have been entered, the program should display a message indicating whether the student passed or failed the exam. (A student must correctly answer 15 of the 20 questions to pass the exam.) It should then display the total number of correctly answered questions, the total number of incorrectly answered questions, and a list showing the question numbers of the incorrectly answered questions.

Input Validation: Only accept the letters A, B, C, or D as answers.

10. **Exam Grader**

One of your professors has asked you to write a program to grade her final exams, which consist of only 20 multiple-choice questions. Each question has one of four possible answers: A, B, C, or D. The file CorrectAnswers.txt contains the correct answers for all of the questions, with each answer written on a separate line. The first line contains the answer to the first question, the second line contains the answer to the second question, and so forth. (Download the book's source code from the companion Web site at www.pearsonhighered.com/gaddis. You will find the file in the Chapter 07 folder.)

Write a program that reads the contents of the CorrectAnswers.txt file into a `char` array, and then reads the contents of another file, containing a student's answers, into a second `char` array. (You can use the file StudentAnswers.txt for testing purposes. This file is also in the Chapter 07 source code folder, available on the book's companion Web site.) The program should determine the number of questions that the student missed, and then display the following:

- A list of the questions missed by the student, showing the correct answer and the incorrect answer provided by the student for each missed question
- The total number of questions missed
- The percentage of questions answered correctly. This can be calculated as

   Correctly Answered Questions ÷ Total Number of Questions

- If the percentage of correctly answered questions is 70% or greater, the program should indicate that the student passed the exam. Otherwise, it should indicate that the student failed the exam.

11. **Grade Book**

A teacher has five students who have taken four tests. The teacher uses the following grading scale to assign a letter grade to a student, based on the average of his or her four test scores.

Test Score	Letter Grade
90–100	A
80–89	B
70–79	C
60–69	D
0–59	F

Write a program that uses an array of `string` objects to hold the five student names, an array of five characters to hold the five students' letter grades, and five arrays of four `doubles` to hold each student's set of test scores.

The program should allow the user to enter each student's name and his or her four test scores. It should then calculate and display each student's average test score and a letter grade based on the average.

Input Validation: Do not accept test scores less than 0 or greater than 100.

12. **Grade Book Modification**

Modify the grade book application in Programming Challenge 13 so it drops each student's lowest score when determining the test score averages and letter grades.

13. **Lottery Application**

Write a program that simulates a lottery. The program should have an array of five integers named `lottery`, and should generate a random number in the range of 0 through 9 for each element in the array. The user should enter five digits which should be stored in an integer array named `user`. The program is to compare the corresponding elements in the two arrays and keep a count of the digits that match. For example, the following shows the `lottery` array and the `user` array with sample numbers stored in each. There are two matching digits (elements 2 and 4).

lottery array:

7	4	9	1	3

user array:

4	2	9	7	3

The program should display the random numbers stored in the `lottery` array and the number of matching digits. If all of the digits match, display a message proclaiming the user as a grand prize winner.

14. **vector Modification**

    Modify the National Commerce Bank case study presented in Program 7-21 so pin1, pin2, and pin3 are vectors instead of arrays. You must also modify the testPIN function to accept a vector instead of an array.

15. **Tic-Tac-Toe Game**

    Write a program that allows two players to play a game of tic-tac-toe. Use a two-dimensional char array with three rows and three columns as the game board. Each element of the array should be initialized with an asterisk (*). The program should run a loop that

    - Displays the contents of the board array
    - Allows player 1 to select a location on the board for an X. The program should ask the user to enter the row and column number.
    - Allows player 2 to select a location on the board for an O. The program should ask the user to enter the row and column number.
    - Determines whether a player has won, or a tie has occurred. If a player has won, the program should declare that player the winner and end. If a tie has occurred, the program should say so and end.

    Player 1 wins when there are three Xs in a row on the game board. The Xs can appear in a row, in a column, or diagonally across the board. A tie occurs when all of the locations on the board are full, but there is no winner.

16. **2D Array Operations**

    Write a program that creates a two-dimensional array initialized with test data. Use any data type you wish. The program should have the following functions:

    - **getTotal**. This function should accept a two-dimensional array as its argument and return the total of all the values in the array.
    - **getAverage**. This function should accept a two-dimensional array as its argument and return the average of all the values in the array.
    - **getRowTotal**. This function should accept a two-dimensional array as its first argument and an integer as its second argument. The second argument should be the subscript of a row in the array. The function should return the total of the values in the specified row.
    - **getColumnTotal**. This function should accept a two-dimensional array as its first argument and an integer as its second argument. The second argument should be the subscript of a column in the array. The function should return the total of the values in the specified column.
    - **getHighestInRow**. This function should accept a two-dimensional array as its first argument and an integer as its second argument. The second argument should be the subscript of a row in the array. The function should return the highest value in the specified row of the array.
    - **getLowestInRow**. This function should accept a two-dimensional array as its first argument and an integer as its second argument. The second argument should be the subscript of a row in the array. The function should return the lowest value in the specified row of the array.

    Demonstrate each of the functions in this program.

Group Project

17. Theater Seating

This program should be designed and written by a team of students. Here are some suggestions:

- One student should design function main, which will call the other functions in the program. The remainder of the functions will be designed by other members of the team.
- The requirements of the program should be analyzed so each student is given about the same work load.
- The parameters and return types of each function should be decided in advance.
- The program can be implemented as a multi-file program, or all the functions can be cut and pasted into the main file.

Here is the assignment: Write a program that can be used by a small theater to sell tickets for performances. The theater's auditorium has 15 rows of seats, with 30 seats in each row. The program should display a screen that shows which seats are available and which are taken. For example, the following screen shows a chart depicting each seat in the theater. Seats that are taken are represented by an * symbol, and seats that are available are represented by a # symbol:

```
                  Seats
          123456789012345678901234567890
Row  1    ***##***###*###############***####
Row  2    ####***************####********##
Row  3    **##**************###########***###
Row  4    **##############**********##******
Row  5    ***********###############*########
Row  6    ################****************####
Row  7    ########***************##########
Row  8    *************##*****###########
Row  9    ##########****##############****
Row 10    #####******************###########
Row 11    #**********##################**
Row 12    ###############********#########*
Row 13    ##***********#########**######
Row 14    ##############################
Row 15    ##############################
```

Here is a list of tasks this program must perform:

- When the program begins, it should ask the user to enter the seat prices for each row. The prices can be stored in a separate array. (Alternatively, the prices may be read from a file.)
- Once the prices are entered, the program should display a seating chart similar to the one shown above. The user may enter the row and seat numbers for tickets being sold. Every time a ticket or group of tickets is purchased, the program should display the total ticket prices and update the seating chart.
- The program should keep a total of all ticket sales. The user should be given an option of viewing this amount.

- The program should also give the user an option to see a list of how many seats have been sold, how many seats are available in each row, and how many seats are available in the entire auditorium.

Input Validation: When tickets are being sold, do not accept row or seat numbers that do not exist. When someone requests a particular seat, the program should make sure that seat is available before it is sold.

8 Searching and Sorting Arrays

8.1 Focus on Software Engineering: Introduction to Search Algorithms

CONCEPT: A search algorithm is a method of locating a specific item in a larger collection of data. This section discusses two algorithms for searching the contents of an array.

It's very common for programs not only to store and process data stored in arrays, but to search arrays for specific items. This section will show you two methods of searching an array: the linear search and the binary search. Each has its advantages and disadvantages.

The Linear Search

The *linear search* is a very simple algorithm. Sometimes called a *sequential search*, it uses a loop to sequentially step through an array, starting with the first element. It compares each element with the value being searched for, and stops when either the value is found or the end of the array is encountered. If the value being searched for is not in the array, the algorithm will unsuccessfully search to the end of the array.

Here is the pseudocode for a function that performs the linear search:

```
Set found to false.
Set position to -1.
Set index to 0.
While found is false and index < number of elements
    If list[index] is equal to search value
        found = true.
        position = index.
    End If
    Add 1 to index.
End While.
Return position.
```

The function searchList shown below is an example of C++ code used to perform a linear search on an integer array. The array list, which has a maximum of numElems elements, is searched for an occurrence of the number stored in value. If the number is found, its array subscript is returned. Otherwise, −1 is returned indicating the value did not appear in the array.

```
int searchList(const int list[], int numElems, int value)
{
    int index = 0;         // Used as a subscript to search array
    int position = -1;     // To record position of search value
    bool found = false;    // Flag to indicate if the value was found

    while (index < numElems && !found)
    {
        if (list[index] == value)    // If the value is found
        {
            found = true;            // Set the flag
            position = index;        // Record the value's subscript
        }
        index++;                     // Go to the next element
    }
    return position;                 // Return the position, or -1
}
```

 NOTE: The reason −1 is returned when the search value is not found in the array is because −1 is not a valid subscript.

Program 8-1 is a complete program that uses the searchList function. It searches the five-element array tests to find a score of 100.

Program 8-1

```
1 // This program demonstrates the searchList function, which
2 // performs a linear search on an integer array.
3 #include <iostream>
4 using namespace std;
5
```

```
 6  // Function prototype
 7  int searchList(const int [], int, int);
 8  const int SIZE = 5;
 9
10  int main()
11  {
12     int tests[SIZE] = {87, 75, 98, 100, 82};
13     int results;
14
15     // Search the array for 100.
16     results = searchList(tests, SIZE, 100);
17
18     // If searchList returned -1, then 100 was not found.
19     if (results == -1)
20        cout << "You did not earn 100 points on any test\n";
21     else
22     {
23        // Otherwise results contains the subscript of
24        // the first 100 found in the array.
25        cout << "You earned 100 points on test ";
26        cout << (results + 1) << endl;
27     }
28     return 0;
29  }
30
31  //***************************************************************
32  // The searchList function performs a linear search on an       *
33  // integer array. The array list, which has a maximum of numElems *
34  // elements, is searched for the number stored in value. If the *
35  // number is found, its array subscript is returned. Otherwise, *
36  // -1 is returned indicating the value was not in the array.    *
37  //***************************************************************
38
39  int searchList(const int list[], int numElems, int value)
40  {
41     int index = 0;       // Used as a subscript to search array
42     int position = -1;   // To record position of search value
43     bool found = false;  // Flag to indicate if the value was found
44
45     while (index < numElems && !found)
46     {
47        if (list[index] == value)  // If the value is found
48        {
49           found = true;           // Set the flag
50           position = index;       // Record the value's subscript
51        }
52        index++;                   // Go to the next element
53     }
54     return position;              // Return the position, or -1
55  }
```

Program Output

```
You earned 100 points on test 4
```

Inefficiency of the Linear Search

The advantage of the linear search is its simplicity. It is very easy to understand and implement. Furthermore, it doesn't require the data in the array to be stored in any particular order. Its disadvantage, however, is its inefficiency. If the array being searched contains 20,000 elements, the algorithm will have to look at all 20,000 elements in order to find a value stored in the last element (so the algorithm actually reads an element of the array 20,000 times).

In an average case, an item is just as likely to be found near the beginning of the array as near the end. Typically, for an array of N items, the linear search will locate an item in N/2 attempts. If an array has 50,000 elements, the linear search will make a comparison with 25,000 of them in a typical case. This is assuming, of course, that the search item is consistently found in the array. (N/2 is the average number of comparisons. The maximum number of comparisons is always N.)

When the linear search fails to locate an item, it must make a comparison with every element in the array. As the number of failed search attempts increases, so does the average number of comparisons. Obviously, the linear search should not be used on large arrays if the speed is important.

The Binary Search

VideoNote
The Binary Search

The *binary search* is a clever algorithm that is much more efficient than the linear search. Its only requirement is that the values in the array be sorted in order. Instead of testing the array's first element, this algorithm starts with the element in the middle. If that element happens to contain the desired value, then the search is over. Otherwise, the value in the middle element is either greater than or less than the value being searched for. If it is greater, then the desired value (if it is in the list) will be found somewhere in the first half of the array. If it is less, then the desired value (again, if it is in the list) will be found somewhere in the last half of the array. In either case, half of the array's elements have been eliminated from further searching.

If the desired value wasn't found in the middle element, the procedure is repeated for the half of the array that potentially contains the value. For instance, if the last half of the array is to be searched, the algorithm immediately tests *its* middle element. If the desired value isn't found there, the search is narrowed to the quarter of the array that resides before or after that element. This process continues until either the value being searched for is found or there are no more elements to test.

Here is the pseudocode for a function that performs a binary search on an array:

```
Set first index to 0.
Set last index to the last subscript in the array.
Set found to false.
Set position to -1.
While found is not true and first is less than or equal to last
    Set middle to the subscript halfway between array[first]
    and array[last].
    If array[middle] equals the desired value
```

```
        Set found to true.
        Set position to middle.
      Else If array[middle] is greater than the desired value
        Set last to middle - 1.
      Else
        Set first to middle + 1.
      End If.
    End While.
    Return position.
```

This algorithm uses three index variables: `first`, `last`, and `middle`. The `first` and `last` variables mark the boundaries of the portion of the array currently being searched. They are initialized with the subscripts of the array's first and last elements. The subscript of the element halfway between `first` and `last` is calculated and stored in the `middle` variable. If the element in the middle of the array does not contain the search value, the `first` or `last` variables are adjusted so that only the top or bottom half of the array is searched during the next iteration. This cuts the portion of the array being searched in half each time the loop fails to locate the search value.

The function `binarySearch` shown in the following example is used to perform a binary search on an integer array. The first parameter, `array`, which has a maximum of `numElems` elements, is searched for an occurrence of the number stored in `value`. If the number is found, its array subscript is returned. Otherwise, −1 is returned indicating the value did not appear in the array.

```cpp
int binarySearch(const int array[], int numElems, int value)
{
   int first = 0,                      // First array element
       last = numElems - 1,            // Last array element
       middle,                         // Midpoint of search
       position = -1;                  // Position of search value
   bool found = false;                 // Flag

   while (!found && first <= last)
   {
      middle = (first + last) / 2;     // Calculate midpoint
      if (array[middle] == value)      // If value is found at mid
      {
         found = true;
         position = middle;
      }
      else if (array[middle] > value)  // If value is in lower half
         last = middle - 1;
       else
         first = middle + 1;           // If value is in upper half
   }
   return position;
}
```

Program 8-2 is a complete program using the `binarySearch` function. It searches an array of employee ID numbers for a specific value.

Program 8-2

```cpp
 1 // This program demonstrates the binarySearch function, which
 2 // performs a binary search on an integer array.
 3 #include <iostream>
 4 using namespace std;
 5
 6 // Function prototype
 7 int binarySearch(const int [], int, int);
 8 const int SIZE = 20;
 9
10 int main()
11 {
12    // Array with employee IDs sorted in ascending order.
13    int idNums[SIZE] = {101, 142, 147, 189, 199, 207, 222,
14                        234, 289, 296, 310, 319, 388, 394,
15                        417, 429, 447, 521, 536, 600};
16    int results;   // To hold the search results
17    int empID;     // To hold an employee ID
18
19    // Get an employee ID to search for.
20    cout << "Enter the employee ID you wish to search for: ";
21    cin >> empID;
22
23    // Search for the ID.
24    results = binarySearch(idNums, SIZE, empID);
25
26    // If results contains -1 the ID was not found.
27    if (results == -1)
28       cout << "That number does not exist in the array.\n";
29    else
30    {
31       // Otherwise results contains the subscript of
32       // the specified employee ID in the array.
33       cout << "That ID is found at element " << results;
34       cout << " in the array.\n";
35    }
36    return 0;
37 }
38
39 //***************************************************************
40 // The binarySearch function performs a binary search on an     *
41 // integer array. array, which has a maximum of size elements,  *
42 // is searched for the number stored in value. If the number is *
43 // found, its array subscript is returned. Otherwise, -1 is     *
44 // returned indicating the value was not in the array.          *
45 //***************************************************************
46
```

```
47  int binarySearch(const int array[], int size, int value)
48  {
49     int first = 0,                // First array element
50         last = size - 1,          // Last array element
51         middle,                   // Midpoint of search
52         position = -1;            // Position of search value
53     bool found = false;           // Flag
54
55     while (!found && first <= last)
56     {
57        middle = (first + last) / 2;      // Calculate midpoint
58        if (array[middle] == value)       // If value is found at mid
59        {
60           found = true;
61           position = middle;
62        }
63        else if (array[middle] > value)   // If value is in lower half
64           last = middle - 1;
65        else
66           first = middle + 1;            // If value is in upper half
67     }
68     return position;
69  }
```

Program Output with Example Input Shown in Bold
Enter the employee ID you wish to search for: **199 [Enter]**
That ID is found at element 4 in the array.

 WARNING! Notice that the array in Program 8-2 is initialized with its values already sorted in ascending order. The binary search algorithm will not work properly unless the values in the array are sorted.

The Efficiency of the Binary Search

Obviously, the binary search is much more efficient than the linear search. Every time it makes a comparison and fails to find the desired item, it eliminates half of the remaining portion of the array that must be searched. For example, consider an array with 1,000 elements. If the binary search fails to find an item on the first attempt, the number of elements that remains to be searched is 500. If the item is not found on the second attempt, the number of elements that remains to be searched is 250. This process continues until the binary search has either located the desired item or determined that it is not in the array. With 1,000 elements, this takes no more than 10 comparisons. (Compare this to the linear search, which would make an average of 500 comparisons!)

Powers of 2 are used to calculate the maximum number of comparisons the binary search will make on an array of any size. (A power of 2 is 2 raised to the power of some number.) Simply find the smallest power of 2 that is greater than or equal to the number of elements in the array. For example, a maximum of 16 comparisons will be made on an array of 50,000 elements ($2^{16} = 65,536$), and a maximum of 20 comparisons will be made on an array of 1,000,000 elements ($2^{20} = 1,048,576$).

8.2 Focus on Problem Solving and Program Design: A Case Study

The Demetris Leadership Center (DLC, Inc.) publishes the books, DVDs, and audio CDs listed in Table 8-1.

Table 8-1

Product Title	Product Description	Product Number	Unit Price
Six Steps to Leadership	Book	914	$12.95
Six Steps to Leadership	Audio CD	915	$14.95
The Road to Excellence	DVD	916	$18.95
Seven Lessons of Quality	Book	917	$16.95
Seven Lessons of Quality	Audio CD	918	$21.95
Seven Lessons of Quality	DVD	919	$31.95
Teams Are Made, Not Born	Book	920	$14.95
Leadership for the Future	Book	921	$14.95
Leadership for the Future	Audio CD	922	$16.95

The manager of the Telemarketing Group has asked you to write a program that will help order-entry operators look up product prices. The program should prompt the user to enter a product number, and will then display the title, description, and price of the product.

Variables

Table 8-2 lists the variables needed:

Table 8-2

Variable	Description
NUM_PRODS	A constant integer initialized with the number of products the Demetris Leadership Center sells. This value will be used in the definition of the program's array.
MIN_PRODNUM	A constant integer initialized with the lowest product number.
MAX_PRODNUM	A constant integer initialized with the highest product number.
id	Array of integers. Holds each product's number.
title	Array of strings, initialized with the titles of products.
description	Array of strings, initialized with the descriptions of each product.
prices	Array of doubles. Holds each product's price.

Modules

The program will consist of the functions listed in Table 8-3.

Table 8-3

Function	Description
`main`	The program's `main` function. It calls the program's other functions.
`getProdNum`	Prompts the user to enter a product number. The function validates input and rejects any value outside the range of correct product numbers.
`binarySearch`	A standard binary search routine. Searches an array for a specified value. If the value is found, its subscript is returned. If the value is not found, −1 is returned.
`displayProd`	Uses a common subscript into the `title`, `description`, and `prices` arrays to display the title, description, and price of a product.

Function `main`

Function `main` contains the variable definitions and calls the other functions. Here is its pseudocode:

```
do
    Call getProdNum.
    Call binarySearch.
    If binarySearch returned -1
        Inform the user that the product number was not found.
    else
        Call displayProd.
    End If.
    Ask the user if the program should repeat.
While the user wants to repeat the program.
```

Here is its actual C++ code.

```cpp
do
{
    // Get the desired product number.
    prodNum = getProdNum();

    // Search for the product number.
    index = binarySearch(id, NUM_PRODS, prodNum);

    // Display the results of the search.
    if (index == -1)
        cout << "That product number was not found.\n";
    else
        displayProd(title, description, prices, index);

    // Does the user want to do this again?
    cout << "Would you like to look up another product? (y/n) ";
    cin >> again;
} while (again == 'y' || again == 'Y');
```

The named constant NUM_PRODS is defined globally and initialized with the value 9. The arrays id, title, description, and prices will already be initialized with data.

The getProdNum Function

The getProdNum function prompts the user to enter a product number. It tests the value to ensure it is in the range of 914–922 (which are the valid product numbers). If an invalid value is entered, it is rejected and the user is prompted again. When a valid product number is entered, the function returns it. The pseudocode is shown below.

```
Display a prompt to enter a product number.
Read prodNum.
While prodNum is invalid
    Display an error message.
    Read prodNum.
End While.
Return prodNum.
```

Here is the actual C++ code.

```cpp
int getProdNum()
{
    int prodNum;

    cout << "Enter the item's product number: ";
    cin >> prodNum;
    // Validate input.
    while (prodNum < MIN_PRODNUM || prodNum > MAX_PRODNUM)
    {
        cout << "Enter a number in the range of " << MIN_PRODNUM;
        cout <<" through " << MAX_PRODNUM << ".\n";
        cin >> prodNum;
    }
    return prodNum;
}
```

The binarySearch Function

The binarySearch function is identical to the function discussed earlier in this chapter.

The displayProd Function

The displayProd function has parameter variables named title, desc, price, and index. These accept as arguments (respectively) the title, description, and price arrays, and a subscript value. The function displays the data stored in each array at the subscript passed into index. Here is the C++ code.

```
void displayProd(const string title[], const string desc[],
                 const double price[], int index)
{
    cout << "Title: " << title[index] << endl;
    cout << "Description: " << desc[index] << endl;
    cout << "Price: $" << price[index] << endl;
}
```

The Entire Program

Program 8-3 shows the entire program's source code.

Program 8-3

```
 1   // Demetris Leadership Center (DLC) product lookup program
 2   // This program allows the user to enter a product number
 3   // and then displays the title, description, and price of
 4   // that product.
 5   #include <iostream>
 6   #include <string>
 7   using namespace std;
 8
 9   const int NUM_PRODS = 9;       // The number of products produced
10   const int MIN_PRODNUM = 914;   // The lowest product number
11   const int MAX_PRODNUM = 922;   // The highest product number
12
13   // Function prototypes
14   int getProdNum();
15   int binarySearch(const int [], int, int);
16   void displayProd(const string [], const string [], const double [], int);
17
18   int main()
19   {
20       // Array of product IDs
21       int id[NUM_PRODS] = {914, 915, 916, 917, 918, 919, 920,
22                            921, 922};
23
24       // Array of product titles
25       string title[NUM_PRODS] =
26           { "Six Steps to Leadership",
27             "Six Steps to Leadership",
28             "The Road to Excellence",
29             "Seven Lessons of Quality",
30             "Seven Lessons of Quality",
31             "Seven Lessons of Quality",
32             "Teams Are Made, Not Born",
33             "Leadership for the Future",
34             "Leadership for the Future"
35           };
36
```

(program continues)

Program 8-3   *(continued)*

```
37        // Array of product descriptions
38        string description[NUM_PRODS] =
39              { "Book", "Audio CD", "DVD",
40                "Book", "Audio CD", "DVD",
41                "Book", "Book", "Audio CD"
42              };
43
44        // Array of product prices
45        double prices[NUM_PRODS] = {12.95, 14.95, 18.95, 16.95, 21.95,
46                                    31.95, 14.95, 14.95, 16.95};
47
48        int prodNum;    // To hold a product number
49        int index;      // To hold search results
50        char again;     // To hold a Y or N answer
51
52        do
53        {
54           // Get the desired product number.
55           prodNum = getProdNum();
56
57           // Search for the product number.
58           index = binarySearch(id, NUM_PRODS, prodNum);
59
60           // Display the results of the search.
61           if (index == -1)
62              cout << "That product number was not found.\n";
63           else
64              displayProd(title, description, prices, index);
65
66           // Does the user want to do this again?
67           cout << "Would you like to look up another product? (y/n) ";
68           cin >> again;
69        } while (again == 'y' || again == 'Y');
70        return 0;
71  }
72
73  //****************************************************
74  // Definition of getProdNum function                *
75  // The getProdNum function asks the user to enter a  *
76  // product number. The input is validated, and when *
77  // a valid number is entered, it is returned.        *
78  //****************************************************
79
80  int getProdNum()
81  {
82     int prodNum; // Product number
83
84     cout << "Enter the item's product number: ";
85     cin >> prodNum;
86     // Validate input
87     while (prodNum < MIN_PRODNUM || prodNum > MAX_PRODNUM)
```

```
 88        {
 89           cout << "Enter a number in the range of " << MIN_PRODNUM;
 90           cout <<" through " << MAX_PRODNUM << ".\n";
 91           cin >> prodNum;
 92        }
 93        return prodNum;
 94    }
 95
 96    //***************************************************************
 97    // Definition of binarySearch function                        *
 98    // The binarySearch function performs a binary search on an    *
 99    // integer array. array, which has a maximum of numElems       *
100    // elements, is searched for the number stored in value. If the *
101    // number is found, its array subscript is returned. Otherwise, *
102    // -1 is returned indicating the value was not in the array.   *
103    //***************************************************************
104
105    int binarySearch(const int array[], int numElems, int value)
106    {
107        int first = 0,            // First array element
108            last = numElems - 1,  // Last array element
109            middle,               // Midpoint of search
110            position = -1;        // Position of search value
111        bool found = false;       // Flag
112
113        while (!found && first <= last)
114        {
115           middle = (first + last) / 2;  // Calculate midpoint
116           if (array[middle] == value)   // If value is found at mid
117           {
118               found = true;
119               position = middle;
120           }
121           else if (array[middle] > value) // If value is in lower half
122               last = middle - 1;
123           else
124               first = middle + 1;          // If value is in upper half
125        }
126        return position;
127    }
128
129    //***************************************************************
130    // The displayProd function accepts three arrays and an int. *
131    // The arrays parameters are expected to hold the title,      *
132    // description, and prices arrays defined in main. The index  *
133    // parameter holds a subscript. This function displays the    *
134    // information in each array contained at the subscript.      *
135    //***************************************************************
136
```

(program continues)

Program 8-3 (continued)

```
137   void displayProd(const string title[], const string desc[],
138                     const double price[], int index)
139   {
140      cout << "Title: " << title[index] << endl;
141      cout << "Description: " << desc[index] << endl;
142      cout << "Price: $" << price[index] << endl;
143   }
```

Program Output with Example Input Shown in Bold
```
Enter the item's product number: 916 [Enter]
Title: The Road to Excellence
Description: DVD
Price: $18.95
Would you like to look up another product? (y/n) y [Enter]
Enter the item's product number: 920 [Enter]
Title: Teams Are Made, Not Born
Description: Book
Price: $14.95
Would you like to look up another product? (y/n) n [Enter]
```

 Checkpoint

myprogramminglab *www.myprogramminglab.com*

8.1   Describe the difference between the linear search and the binary search.

8.2   On average, with an array of 20,000 elements, how many comparisons will the linear search perform? (Assume the items being searched for are consistently found in the array.)

8.3   With an array of 20,000 elements, what is the maximum number of comparisons the binary search will perform?

8.4   If a linear search is performed on an array, and it is known that some items are searched for more frequently than others, how can the contents of the array be reordered to improve the average performance of the search?

8.3

Focus on Software Engineering: Introduction to Sorting Algorithms

CONCEPT: Sorting algorithms are used to arrange data into some order.

Often the data in an array must be sorted in some order. Customer lists, for instance, are commonly sorted in alphabetical order. Student grades might be sorted from highest to lowest. Product codes could be sorted so all the products of the same color are stored together. To sort the data in an array, the programmer must use an appropriate *sorting algorithm*. A sorting algorithm is a technique for scanning through an array and rearranging its contents in some specific order. This section will introduce two simple sorting algorithms: the *bubble sort* and the *selection sort*.

The Bubble Sort

The bubble sort is an easy way to arrange data in *ascending* or *descending order*. If an array is sorted in ascending order, it means the values in the array are stored from lowest to highest. If the values are sorted in descending order, they are stored from highest to lowest. Let's see how the bubble sort is used in arranging the following array's elements in ascending order:

7	2	3	8	9	1
Element 0	Element 1	Element 2	Element 3	Element 4	Element 5

The bubble sort starts by comparing the first two elements in the array. If element 0 is greater than element 1, they are exchanged. After the exchange, the array shown above would appear as:

2	7	3	8	9	1
Element 0	Element 1	Element 2	Element 3	Element 4	Element 5

This method is repeated with elements 1 and 2. If element 1 is greater than element 2, they are exchanged. The array above would then appear as:

2	3	7	8	9	1
Element 0	Element 1	Element 2	Element 3	Element 4	Element 5

Next, elements 2 and 3 are compared. In this array, these two elements are already in the proper order (element 2 is less than element 3), so no exchange takes place.

As the cycle continues, elements 3 and 4 are compared. Once again, no exchange is necessary because they are already in the proper order.

When elements 4 and 5 are compared, however, an exchange must take place because element 4 is greater than element 5. The array now appears as:

2	3	7	8	1	9
Element 0	Element 1	Element 2	Element 3	Element 4	Element 5

At this point, the entire array has been scanned, but its contents aren't quite in the right order yet. So, the sort starts over again with elements 0 and 1. Because those two are in the proper order, no exchange takes place. Elements 1 and 2 are compared next, but once again, no exchange takes place. This continues until elements 3 and 4 are compared. Because element 3 is greater than element 4, they are exchanged. The array now appears as

2	3	7	1	8	9
Element 0	Element 1	Element 2	Element 3	Element 4	Element 5

By now you should see how the sort will eventually cause the elements to appear in the correct order. The sort repeatedly passes through the array until no exchanges are made. Ultimately, the array will appear as

1	2	3	7	8	9
Element 0	Element 1	Element 2	Element 3	Element 4	Element 5

Here is the bubble sort in pseudocode:

```
Do
    Set swap flag to false.
    For count is set to each subscript in array from 0 through the
            next-to-last subscript
        If array[count] is greater than array[count + 1]
            Swap the contents of array[count] and array[count + 1].
            Set swap flag to true.
        End If.
    End For.
While any elements have been swapped.
```

The C++ code below implements the bubble sort as a function. The parameter array is an integer array to be sorted. size contains the number of elements in array.

```cpp
void sortArray(int array[], int size)
{
    bool swap;
    int temp;

    do
    {
        swap = false;
        for (int count = 0; count < (size - 1); count++)
        {
            if (array[count] > array[count + 1])
            {
                temp = array[count];
                array[count] = array[count + 1];
                array[count + 1] = temp;
                swap = true;
            }
        }
    } while (swap);
}
```

Inside the function is a for loop nested inside a do-while loop. The for loop sequences through the entire array, comparing each element with its neighbor, and swapping them if necessary. Anytime two elements are exchanged, the flag variable swap is set to true.

The for loop must be executed repeatedly until it can sequence through the entire array without making any exchanges. This is why it is nested inside a do-while loop. The do-while loop sets swap to false, and then executes the for loop. If swap is set to true after the for loop has finished, the do-while loop repeats.

Here is the starting line of the `for` loop:

```
for (int count = 0; count < (size - 1); count++)
```

The variable `count` holds the array subscript values. It starts at zero and is incremented as long as it is less than `size` - 1. The value of `size` is the number of elements in the array, and `count` stops just short of reaching this value because the following line compares each element with the one after it:

```
if (array[count] > array[count + 1])
```

When `array[count]` is the next-to-last element, it will be compared to the last element. If the `for` loop were allowed to increment count past `size` - 1, the last element in the array would be compared to a value outside the array.

Let's look at the `if` statement in its entirety:

```
if (array[count] > array[count + 1])
{
    temp = array[count];
    array[count] = array[count + 1];
    array[count + 1] = temp;
    swap = true;
}
```

If `array[count]` is greater than `array[count + 1]`, the two elements must be exchanged. First, the contents of `array[count]` are copied into the variable `temp`. Then the contents of `array[count + 1]` is copied into `array[count]`. The exchange is made complete when the contents of `temp` (the previous contents of `array[count]`) are copied to `array[count + 1]`. Last, the `swap` flag variable is set to `true`. This indicates that an exchange has been made.

Program 8-4 demonstrates the bubble sort function in a complete program.

Program 8-4

```
 1 // This program uses the bubble sort algorithm to sort an
 2 // array in ascending order.
 3 #include <iostream>
 4 using namespace std;
 5
 6 // Function prototypes
 7 void sortArray(int [], int);
 8 void showArray(const int [], int);
 9
10 int main()
11 {
12    // Array of unsorted values
13    int values[6] = {7, 2, 3, 8, 9, 1};
14
15    // Display the values.
16    cout << "The unsorted values are:\n";
17    showArray(values, 6);
18
19    // Sort the values.
20    sortArray(values, 6);
```

(program continues)

Program 8-4   *(continued)*

```
21
22     // Display them again.
23     cout << "The sorted values are:\n";
24     showArray(values, 6);
25     return 0;
26 }
27
28 //*********************************************************
29 // Definition of function sortArray                      *
30 // This function performs an ascending order bubble sort on *
31 // array. size is the number of elements in the array.   *
32 //*********************************************************
33
34 void sortArray(int array[], int size)
35 {
36    bool swap;
37    int temp;
38
39    do
40    {
41       swap = false;
42       for (int count = 0; count < (size - 1); count++)
43       {
44          if (array[count] > array[count + 1])
45          {
46             temp = array[count];
47             array[count] = array[count + 1];
48             array[count + 1] = temp;
49             swap = true;
50          }
51       }
52    } while (swap);
53 }
54
55 //*********************************************************
56 // Definition of function showArray.                     *
57 // This function displays the contents of array. size is the *
58 // number of elements.                                   *
59 //*********************************************************
60
61 void showArray(const int array[], int size)
62 {
63    for (int count = 0; count < size; count++)
64       cout << array[count] << " ";
65    cout << endl;
66 }
```

Program Output

```
The unsorted values are:
7 2 3 8 9 1
The sorted values are:
1 2 3 7 8 9
```

The Selection Sort

The bubble sort is inefficient for large arrays because items only move by one element at a time. The selection sort, however, usually performs fewer exchanges because it moves items immediately to their final position in the array. It works like this: The smallest value in the array is located and moved to element 0. Then the next smallest value is located and moved to element 1. This process continues until all of the elements have been placed in their proper order.

VideoNote
The
Selection
Sort

Let's see how the selection sort works when arranging the elements of the following array:

5	7	2	8	9	1
Element 0	Element 1	Element 2	Element 3	Element 4	Element 5

The selection sort scans the array, starting at element 0, and locates the element with the smallest value. The contents of this element are then swapped with the contents of element 0. In this example, the 1 stored in element 5 is swapped with the 5 stored in element 0. After the exchange, the array would appear as

1	7	2	8	9	5
Element 0	Element 1	Element 2	Element 3	Element 4	Element 5

The algorithm then repeats the process, but because element 0 already contains the smallest value in the array, it can be left out of the procedure. This time, the algorithm begins the scan at element 1. In this example, the contents of element 2 are exchanged with those of element 1. The array would then appear as

1	2	7	8	9	5
Element 0	Element 1	Element 2	Element 3	Element 4	Element 5

Once again the process is repeated, but this time the scan begins at element 2. The algorithm will find that element 5 contains the next smallest value. This element's contents are exchanged with those of element 2, causing the array to appear as

1	2	5	8	9	7
Element 0	Element 1	Element 2	Element 3	Element 4	Element 5

Next, the scanning begins at element 3. Its contents are exchanged with those of element 5, causing the array to appear as

1	2	5	7	9	8
Element 0	Element 1	Element 2	Element 3	Element 4	Element 5

At this point there are only two elements left to sort. The algorithm finds that the value in element 5 is smaller than that of element 4, so the two are swapped. This puts the array in its final arrangement:

1	2	5	7	8	9
Element 0	Element 1	Element 2	Element 3	Element 4	Element 5

Here is the selection sort algorithm in pseudocode:

```
For startScan is set to each subscript in array from 0 through the
                next-to-last subscript
    Set index variable to startScan.
    Set minIndex variable to startScan.
    Set minValue variable to array[startScan].

    For index is set to each subscript in array from (startScan + 1)
                through the last subscript
        If array[index] is less than minValue
            Set minValue to array[index].
            Set minIndex to index.
        End If.
    End For.
    Set array[minIndex] to array[startScan].
    Set array[startScan] to minValue.
End For.
```

The following C++ code implements the selection sort in a function. It accepts two arguments: `array` and `size`. `array` is an integer array and `size` is the number of elements in the array. The function uses the selection sort to arrange the values in the array in ascending order.

```cpp
void selectionSort(int array[], int size)
{
    int startScan, minIndex, minValue;

    for (startScan = 0; startScan < (size - 1); startScan++)
    {
        minIndex = startScan;
        minValue = array[startScan];
        for(int index = startScan + 1; index < size; index++)
        {
            if (array[index] < minValue)
            {
                minValue = array[index];
                minIndex = index;
            }
        }
        array[minIndex] = array[startScan];
        array[startScan] = minValue;
    }
}
```

Inside the function are two `for` loops, one nested inside the other. The inner loop sequences through the array, starting at `array[startScan + 1]`, searching for the element with the smallest value. When the element is found, its subscript is stored in the variable `minIndex` and its value is stored in `minValue`. The outer loop then exchanges the contents of this element with `array[startScan]` and increments `startScan`. This procedure repeats until the contents of every element have been moved to their proper location.

Program 8-5 demonstrates the selection sort function in a complete program.

Program 8-5

```cpp
 1  // This program uses the selection sort algorithm to sort an
 2  // array in ascending order.
 3  #include <iostream>
 4  using namespace std;
 5
 6  // Function prototypes
 7  void selectionSort(int [], int);
 8  void showArray(const int [], int);
 9
10  int main()
11  {
12     // Define an array with unsorted values
13     const int SIZE = 6;
14     int values[SIZE] = {5, 7, 2, 8, 9, 1};
15
16     // Display the values.
17     cout << "The unsorted values are\n";
18     showArray(values, SIZE);
19
20     // Sort the values.
21     selectionSort(values, SIZE);
22
23     // Display the values again.
24     cout << "The sorted values are\n";
25     showArray(values, SIZE);
26     return 0;
27  }
28
29  //************************************************************
30  // Definition of function selectionSort.                    *
31  // This function performs an ascending order selection sort on *
32  // array. size is the number of elements in the array.       *
33  //************************************************************
34
35  void selectionSort(int array[], int size)
36  {
37     int startScan, minIndex, minValue;
38
39     for (startScan = 0; startScan < (size - 1); startScan++)
40     {
41        minIndex = startScan;
42        minValue = array[startScan];
43        for(int index = startScan + 1; index < size; index++)
44        {
45           if (array[index] < minValue)
46           {
47              minValue = array[index];
48              minIndex = index;
49           }
50        }
```

(program continues)

Program 8-5   *(continued)*

```
51          array[minIndex] = array[startScan];
52          array[startScan] = minValue;
53      }
54  }
55
56  //*************************************************************
57  // Definition of function showArray.                          *
58  // This function displays the contents of array. size is the  *
59  // number of elements.                                        *
60  //*************************************************************
61
62  void showArray(const int array[], int size)
63  {
64      for (int count = 0; count < size; count++)
65          cout << array[count] << " ";
66      cout << endl;
67  }
```

Program Output

```
The unsorted values are
5 7 2 8 9 1
The sorted values are
1 2 5 7 8 9
```

8.4 Focus on Problem Solving and Program Design: A Case Study

Like the previous case study, this is a program developed for the Demetris Leadership Center. Recall that DLC, Inc., publishes books, DVDs, and audio CDs. (See Table 8-1 for a complete list of products, with title, description, product number, and price.) Table 8-4 shows the number of units of each product sold during the past six months.

Table 8-4

Product Number	Units Sold
914	842
915	416
916	127
917	514
918	437
919	269
920	97
921	492
922	212

The vice president of sales has asked you to write a sales reporting program that displays the following information:

- A list of the products in the order of their sales dollars (NOT units sold), from highest to lowest
- The total number of all units sold
- The total sales for the six-month period

Variables

Table 8-5 lists the variables needed:

Table 8-5

Variable	Description
NUM_PRODS	A constant integer initialized with the number of products that DLC, Inc., sells. This value will be used in the definition of the program's array.
prodNum	Array of ints. Holds each product's number.
units	Array of ints. Holds each product's number of units sold.
prices	Array of doubles. Holds each product's price.
sales	Array of doubles. Holds the computed sales amounts (in dollars) of each product.

The elements of the four arrays, prodNum, units, prices, and sales will correspond with each other. For example, the product whose number is stored in prodNum[2] will have sold the number of units stored in units[2]. The sales amount for the product will be stored in sales[2].

Modules

The program will consist of the functions listed in Table 8-6.

Table 8-6

Function	Description
main	The program's main function. It calls the program's other functions.
calcSales	Calculates each product's sales.
dualSort	Sorts the sales array so the elements are ordered from highest to lowest. The prodNum array is ordered so the product numbers correspond with the correct sales figures in the sorted sales array.
showOrder	Displays a list of the product numbers and sales amounts from the sorted sales and prodNum arrays.
showTotals	Displays the total number of units sold and the total sales amount for the period.

Function `main`

Function `main` is very simple. It contains the variable definitions and calls the other functions. Here is the pseudocode for its executable statements:

```
Call calcSales.
Call dualSort.
Set display mode to fixed point output with two decimal places of
      precision.
Call showOrder.
Call showTotals.
```

Here is its actual C++ code:

```cpp
// Calculate each product's sales.
calcSales(units, prices, sales, NUM_PRODS);

// Sort the elements in the sales array in descending
// order and shuffle the ID numbers in the id array to
// keep them in parallel.
dualSort(id, sales, NUM_PRODS);

// Set the numeric output formatting.
cout << setprecision(2) << fixed << showpoint;

// Display the products and sales amounts.
showOrder(sales, id, NUM_PRODS);

// Display total units sold and total sales.
showTotals(sales, units, NUM_PRODS);
```

The named constant `NUM_PRODS` will be defined globally and initialized to the value 9.

The arrays `id`, `units`, and `prices` will already be initialized with data. (It will be left as an exercise for you to modify this program so the user may enter these values.)

The `calcSales` Function

The `calcSales` function multiplies each product's units sold by its price. The resulting amount is stored in the `sales` array. Here is the function's pseudocode:

```
For index is set to each subscript in the arrays from 0 through the
      last subscript.
   Set sales[index] to units[index] times prices[index].
End For.
```

And here is the function's actual C++ code:

```cpp
void calcSales(const int units[], const double prices[],
               double sales[], int num)
{
   for (int index = 0; index < num; index++)
      sales[index] = units[index] * prices[index];
}
```

The `dualSort` Function

The `dualSort` function is a modified version of the selection sort algorithm shown in Program 8-5. The `dualSort` function accepts two arrays as arguments: the `sales` array and the `id` array. The function actually performs the selection sort on the `sales` array. When the function moves an element in the `sales` array, however, it also moves the corresponding element in the `id` array. This is to ensure that the product numbers in the `id` array still have subscripts that match their sales figures in the `sales` array.

The `dualSort` function is also different in another way: It sorts the array in descending order.

Here is the pseudocode for the `dualSort` function:

```
For startScan variable is set to each subscript in array from 0 through
the next-to-last subscript
    Set index variable to startScan.
    Set maxIndex variable to startScan.
    Set tempId variable to id[startScan].
    Set maxValue variable to sales[startScan].
    For index variable is set to each subscript in array from
                  (startScan + 1) through the last subscript
        If sales[index] is greater than maxValue
            Set maxValue to sales[index].
            Set tempId to tempId[index].
            Set maxIndex to index.
        End If.
    End For.
    Set sales[maxIndex] to sales[startScan].
    Set id[maxIndex] = id[startScan].
    Set sales[startScan] to maxValue.
    Set id[startScan] = tempId.
End For.
```

Here is the actual C++ code for the `dualSort` function:

```cpp
void dualSort(int id[], double sales[], int size)
{
    int startScan, maxIndex, tempId;
    double maxValue;

    for (startScan = 0; startScan < (size - 1); startScan++)
    {
        maxIndex = startScan;
        maxValue = sales[startScan];
        tempId = id[startScan];
        for(int index = startScan + 1; index < size; index++)
        {
            if (sales[index] > maxValue)
            {
                maxValue = sales[index];
                tempId = id[index];
                maxIndex = index;
            }
        }
```

```
        sales[maxIndex] = sales[startScan];
        id[maxIndex] = id[startScan];
        sales[startScan] = maxValue;
        id[startScan] = tempId;
    }
}
```

 NOTE: Once the `dualSort` function is called, the `id` and `sales` arrays are no longer synchronized with the `units` and `prices` arrays. Because this program doesn't use `units` and `prices` together with `id` and `sales` after this point, it will not be noticed in the final output. However, it is never a good programming practice to sort parallel arrays in such a way that they are out of synchronization. It will be left as an exercise for you to modify the program so all the arrays are synchronized and used in the final output of the program.

The `showOrder` Function

The `showOrder` function displays a heading and the sorted list of product numbers and their sales amounts. It accepts the `id` and `sales` arrays as arguments. Here is its pseudocode:

```
Display heading.
For index variable is set to each subscript of the arrays from 0
through the last subscript
    Display id[index].
    Display sales[index].
End For.
```

Here is the function's actual C++ code:

```cpp
void showOrder(const double sales[], const int id[], int num)
{
    cout << "Product Number\tSales\n";

    cout << "---------------------------------\n";
    for (int index = 0; index < num; index++)
    {
        cout << id[index] << "\t\t$";
        cout << setw(8) << sales[index] << endl;
    }
    cout << endl;
}
```

The `showTotals` Function

The `showTotals` function displays the total number of units of all products sold and the total sales for the period. It accepts the `units` and `sales` arrays as arguments. Here is its pseudocode:

```
Set totalUnits variable to 0.
Set totalSales variable to 0.0.
For index variable is set to each subscript in the arrays from 0
through the last subscript
    Add units[index] to totalUnits[index].
    Add sales[index] to totalSales.
```

```
End For.
Display totalUnits with appropriate heading.
Display totalSales with appropriate heading.
```

Here is the function's actual C++ code:

```cpp
void showTotals(const double sales[], const int units[], int num)
{
   int totalUnits = 0;
   double totalSales = 0.0;
   for (int index = 0; index < num; index++)
   {
      totalUnits += units[index];
      totalSales += sales[index];
   }
   cout << "Total Units Sold:  " << totalUnits << endl;
   cout << "Total Sales:       $" << totalSales << endl;
}
```

The Entire Program

Program 8-6 shows the entire program's source code.

Program 8-6

```cpp
 1 // This program produces a sales report for DLC, Inc.
 2 #include <iostream>
 3 #include <iomanip>
 4 using namespace std;
 5
 6 // Function prototypes
 7 void calcSales(const int [], const double [], double [], int);
 8 void showOrder(const double [], const int [], int);
 9 void dualSort(int [], double [], int);
10 void showTotals(const double [], const int [], int);
11
12 // NUM_PRODS is the number of products produced.
13 const int NUM_PRODS = 9;
14
15 int main()
16 {
17    // Array with product ID numbers
18    int id[NUM_PRODS] = {914, 915, 916, 917, 918, 919, 920,
19                         921, 922};
20
21    // Array with number of units sold for each product
22    int units[NUM_PRODS] = {842, 416, 127, 514, 437, 269, 97,
23                            492, 212};
24
25    // Array with product prices
26    double prices[NUM_PRODS] = {12.95, 14.95, 18.95, 16.95, 21.95,
27                               31.95, 14.95, 14.95, 16.95};
28
```

(program continues)

Program 8-6 *(continued)*

```
29      // Array to hold the computed sales amounts
30      double sales[NUM_PRODS];
31
32      // Calculate each product's sales.
33      calcSales(units, prices, sales, NUM_PRODS);
34
35      // Sort the elements in the sales array in descending
36      // order and shuffle the ID numbers in the id array to
37      // keep them in parallel.
38      dualSort(id, sales, NUM_PRODS);
39
40      // Set the numeric output formatting.
41      cout << setprecision(2) << fixed << showpoint;
42
43      // Display the products and sales amounts.
44      showOrder(sales, id, NUM_PRODS);
45
46      // Display total units sold and total sales.
47      showTotals(sales, units, NUM_PRODS);
48      return 0;
49  }
50
51  //*****************************************************************
52  // Definition of calcSales. Accepts units, prices, and sales    *
53  // arrays as arguments. The size of these arrays is passed       *
54  // into the num parameter. This function calculates each         *
55  // product's sales by multiplying its units sold by each unit's  *
56  // price. The result is stored in the sales array.               *
57  //*****************************************************************
58
59  void calcSales(const int units[], const double prices[], double sales[], int num)
60  {
61      for (int index = 0; index < num; index++)
62          sales[index] = units[index] * prices[index];
63  }
64
65  //*****************************************************************
66  // Definition of function dualSort. Accepts id and sales arrays *
67  // as arguments. The size of these arrays is passed into size.   *
68  // This function performs a descending order selection sort on   *
69  // the sales array. The elements of the id array are exchanged   *
70  // identically as those of the sales array. size is the number   *
71  // of elements in each array.                                    *
72  //*****************************************************************
73
74  void dualSort(int id[], double sales[], int size)
75  {
76      int startScan, maxIndex, tempid;
77      double maxValue;
78
```

```
 79    for (startScan = 0; startScan < (size - 1); startScan++)
 80    {
 81       maxIndex = startScan;
 82       maxValue = sales[startScan];
 83       tempid = id[startScan];
 84       for(int index = startScan + 1; index < size; index++)
 85       {
 86          if (sales[index] > maxValue)
 87          {
 88             maxValue = sales[index];
 89             tempid = id[index];
 90             maxIndex = index;
 91          }
 92       }
 93       sales[maxIndex] = sales[startScan];
 94       id[maxIndex] = id[startScan];
 95       sales[startScan] = maxValue;
 96       id[startScan] = tempid;
 97    }
 98 }
 99
100 //*************************************************************
101 // Definition of showOrder function. Accepts sales and id arrays *
102 // as arguments. The size of these arrays is passed into num.    *
103 // The function first displays a heading, then the sorted list   *
104 // of product numbers and sales.                                 *
105 //*************************************************************
106
107 void showOrder(const double sales[], const int id[], int num)
108 {
109    cout << "Product Number\tSales\n";
110    cout << "--------------------------------\n";
111    for (int index = 0; index < num; index++)
112    {
113       cout << id[index] << "\t\t$";
114       cout << setw(8) << sales[index] << endl;
115    }
116    cout << endl;
117 }
118
119 //*************************************************************
120 // Definition of showTotals function. Accepts sales and id arrays *
121 // as arguments. The size of these arrays is passed into num.    *
122 // The function first calculates the total units (of all         *
123 // products) sold and the total sales. It then displays these    *
124 // amounts.                                                      *
125 //*************************************************************
126
```

(program continues)

Program 8-6 *(continued)*

```
127  void showTotals(const double sales[], const int units[], int num)
128  {
129      int totalUnits = 0;
130      double totalSales = 0.0;
131
132      for (int index = 0; index < num; index++)
133      {
134         totalUnits += units[index];
135         totalSales += sales[index];
136      }
137      cout << "Total Units Sold:  " << totalUnits << endl;
138      cout << "Total Sales:      $" << totalSales << endl;
139  }
```

Program Output

```
Product Number                Sales
-----------------------------------
914                       $10903.90
918                       $ 9592.15
917                       $ 8712.30
919                       $ 8594.55
921                       $ 7355.40
915                       $ 6219.20
922                       $ 3593.40
916                       $ 2406.65
920                       $ 1450.15
Total Units Sold:            3406
Total Sales:              $58827.70
```

8.5

If You Plan to Continue in Computer Science: Sorting and Searching vectors (Continued from Section 7.12)

CONCEPT: The sorting and searching algorithms you have studied in this chapter may be applied to STL **vectors** as well as arrays.

Once you have properly defined an STL vector and populated it with values, you may sort and search the vector with the algorithms presented in this chapter. Simply substitute the vector syntax for the array syntax when necessary. Program 8-7, which illustrates this, is a modification of the case study in Program 8-6.

Program 8-7

```
 1 // This program produces a sales report for DLC, Inc.
 2 // This version of the program uses STL vectors instead of arrays.
 3 #include <iostream>
 4 #include <iomanip>
 5 #include <vector>
 6 using namespace std;
 7
 8 // Function prototypes
 9 void initVectors(vector<int> &, vector<int> &, vector<double> &);
10 void calcSales(vector<int>, vector<double>, vector<double> &);
11 void showOrder(vector<double>, vector<int>);
12 void dualSort(vector<int> &, vector<double> &);
13 void showTotals(vector<double>, vector<int>);
14
15 int main()
16 {
17    vector<int> id;         // Product ID numbers
18    vector<int> units;      // Units sold
19    vector<double> prices;  // Product prices
20    vector<double> sales;   // To hold product sales
21
22    // Must provide an initialization routine.
23    initVectors(id, units, prices);
24
25    // Calculate each product's sales.
26    calcSales(units, prices, sales);
27
28    // Sort the elements in the sales array in descending
29    // order and shuffle the ID numbers in the id array to
30    // keep them in parallel.
31    dualSort(id, sales);
32
33    // Set the numeric output formatting.
34    cout << fixed << showpoint << setprecision(2);
35
36    // Display the products and sales amounts.
37    showOrder(sales, id);
38
39    // Display total units sold and total sales.
40    showTotals(sales, units);
41    return 0;
42 }
43
44 //*****************************************************************
45 // Definition of initVectors. Accepts id, units, and prices      *
46 // vectors as reference arguments. This function initializes each *
47 // vector to a set of starting values.                            *
48 //*****************************************************************
49
```

(program continues)

Program 8-7   *(continued)*

```
50  void initVectors(vector<int> &id, vector<int> &units,
51                  vector<double> &prices)
52  {
53     // Initialize the id vector with the ID numbers
54     // 914 through 922.
55     for (int value = 914; value <= 922; value++)
56        id.push_back(value);
57
58     // Initialize the units vector with data.
59     units.push_back(842);
60     units.push_back(416);
61     units.push_back(127);
62     units.push_back(514);
63     units.push_back(437);
64     units.push_back(269);
65     units.push_back(97);
66     units.push_back(492);
67     units.push_back(212);
68
69     // Initialize the prices vector.
70     prices.push_back(12.95);
71     prices.push_back(14.95);
72     prices.push_back(18.95);
73     prices.push_back(16.95);
74     prices.push_back(21.95);
75     prices.push_back(31.95);
76     prices.push_back(14.95);
77     prices.push_back(14.95);
78     prices.push_back(16.95);
79  }
80
81
82  //****************************************************************
83  // Definition of calcSales. Accepts units, prices, and sales    *
84  // vectors as arguments. The sales vector is passed into a       *
85  // reference parameter. This function calculates each product's  *
86  // sales by multiplying its units sold by each unit's price. The *
87  // result is stored in the sales vector.                         *
88  //****************************************************************
89
90  void calcSales(vector<int> units, vector<double> prices,
91                 vector<double> &sales)
92  {
93     for (int index = 0; index < units.size(); index++)
94        sales.push_back(units[index] * prices[index]);
95  }
96
```

```
 97   //***************************************************************
 98   // Definition of function dualSort. Accepts id and sales vectors *
 99   // as reference arguments. This function performs a descending   *
100   // order selection sort on the sales vector. The elements of the *
101   // id vector are exchanged identically as those of the sales     *
102   // vector.                                                        *
103   //***************************************************************
104
105   void dualSort(vector<int> &id, vector<double> &sales)
106   {
107      int startScan, maxIndex, tempid, size;
108      double maxValue;
109
110      size = id.size();
111      for (startScan = 0; startScan < (size - 1); startScan++)
112      {
113         maxIndex = startScan;
114         maxValue = sales[startScan];
115         tempid = id[startScan];
116         for(int index = startScan + 1; index < size; index++)
117         {
118            if (sales[index] > maxValue)
119            {
120               maxValue = sales[index];
121               tempid = id[index];
122               maxIndex = index;
123            }
124         }
125         sales[maxIndex] = sales[startScan];
126         id[maxIndex] = id[startScan];
127         sales[startScan] = maxValue;
128         id[startScan] = tempid;
129      }
130   }
131
132   //***************************************************************
133   // Definition of showOrder function. Accepts sales and id vectors *
134   // as arguments. The function first displays a heading, then the  *
135   // sorted list of product numbers and sales.                      *
136   //***************************************************************
137
138   void showOrder(vector<double> sales, vector<int> id)
139   {
140      cout << "Product Number\tSales\n";
141      cout << "----------------------------------\n";
142      for (int index = 0; index < id.size(); index++)
143      {
144         cout << id[index] << "\t\t$";
145         cout << setw(8) << sales[index] << endl;
146      }
147      cout << endl;
148   }
```

(program continues)

Program 8-7 *(continued)*

```
149
150  //**********************************************************************
151  // Definition of showTotals function. Accepts sales and id vectors   *
152  // as arguments. The function first calculates the total units (of   *
153  // all products) sold and the total sales. It then displays these    *
154  // amounts.                                                           *
155  //**********************************************************************
156
157  void showTotals(vector<double> sales, vector<int> units)
158  {
159     int totalUnits = 0;
160     double totalSales = 0.0;
161
162     for (int index = 0; index < units.size(); index++)
163     {
164        totalUnits += units[index];
165        totalSales += sales[index];
166     }
167     cout << "Total Units Sold:  " << totalUnits << endl;
168     cout << "Total Sales:      $" << totalSales << endl;
169  }
```

Program Output

```
Product Number                  Sales
----------------------------------------
914                        $10903.90
918                        $ 9592.15
917                        $ 8712.30
919                        $ 8594.55
921                        $ 7355.40
915                        $ 6219.20
922                        $ 3593.40
916                        $ 2406.65
920                        $ 1450.15
Total Units Sold:             3406
Total Sales:               $58827.70
```

There are some differences between this program and Program 8-6. First, the initVectors function was added. In Program 8-6, this was not necessary because the id, units, and prices arrays had initialization lists. vectors do not accept initialization lists, so this function stores the necessary initial values in the id, units, and prices vectors.

Now, look at the function header for initVectors:

```
void initVectors(vector<int> &id, vector<int> &units,
                 vector<double> &prices)
```

Notice that the vector parameters are references (as indicated by the & that precedes the parameter name). This brings up an important difference between vectors and arrays: By default, vectors are passed by value, whereas arrays are only passed by reference. If you want to change a value in a vector argument, it *must* be passed into a reference parameter. Reference vector parameters are also used in the calcSales and dualSort functions.

Also, notice that each time a value is added to a vector, the push_back member function is called. This is because the [] operator cannot be used to store a new element in a vector. It can only be used to store a value in an existing element or read a value from an existing element.

The code in this function appears cumbersome because it calls each vector's push_back member function once for each value that is to be stored in the vector. This code can be simplified by storing the vector initialization values in arrays, and then using loops to call the push_back member function, storing the values in the arrays in the vectors. The following code shows an alternative initVectors function that takes this approach.

```cpp
void initVectors(vector<int> &id, vector<int> &units,
                 vector<double> &prices)
{
   const int NUM_PRODS = 9;
   int count;
   int unitsSold[NUM_PRODS] = {842, 416, 127, 514, 437, 269, 97,
                               492, 212};
   double productPrices[NUM_PRODS] = {12.95, 14.95, 18.95, 16.95,
                                      21.95, 31.95, 14.95, 14.95,
                                      16.95};

   // Initialize the id vector
   for (int value = 914; value <= 922; value++)
      id.push_back(value);

   // Initialize the units vector
   for (count = 0; count < NUM_PRODS; count++)
     units.push_back(unitsSold[count]);

   // Initialize the prices vector
   for (count = 0; count < NUM_PRODS; count++)
      prices.push_back(productPrices[count]);
}
```

Next, notice that the calcSales, showOrder, dualSort, and showTotals functions do not accept an argument indicating the number of elements in the vectors. This is not necessary because vectors have the size member function, which returns the number of elements in the vector. The following code segment, which is taken from the calcSales function, shows the units.size() member function being used to control the number of loop iterations.

```cpp
for (int index = 0; index < units.size(); index++)
    sales.push_back(units[index] * prices[index]);
```

Review Questions and Exercises

Short Answer

1. Why is the linear search also called "sequential search"?

2. If a linear search function is searching for a value that is stored in the last element of a 10,000-element array, how many elements will the search code have to read to locate the value?

3. In an average case involving an array of N elements, how many times will a linear search function have to read the array to locate a specific value?

4. A binary search function is searching for a value that is stored in the middle element of an array. How many times will the function read an element in the array before finding the value?

5. What is the maximum number of comparisons that a binary search function will make when searching for a value in a 1,000-element array?

6. Why is the bubble sort inefficient for large arrays?

7. Why is the selection sort more efficient than the bubble sort on large arrays?

Fill-in-the-Blank

8. The _____ search algorithm steps sequentially through an array, comparing each item with the search value.

9. The _____ search algorithm repeatedly divides the portion of an array being searched in half.

10. The _____ search algorithm is adequate for small arrays but not large arrays.

11. The _____ search algorithm requires that the array's contents be sorted.

12. If an array is sorted in _____ order, the values are stored from lowest to highest.

13. If an array is sorted in _____ order, the values are stored from highest to lowest.

True or False

14. T   F   If data are sorted in ascending order, it means they are ordered from lowest value to highest value.

15. T   F   If data are sorted in descending order, it means they are ordered from lowest value to highest value.

16. T   F   The *average* number of comparisons performed by the linear search on an array of N elements is N/2 (assuming the search values are consistently found).

17. T   F   The *maximum* number of comparisons performed by the linear search on an array of N elements is N/2 (assuming the search values are consistently found).

18. Complete the following table calculating the average and maximum number of comparisons the linear search will perform, and the maximum number of comparisons the binary search will perform.

Array Size →	50 Elements	500 Elements	10,000 Elements	100,000 Elements	10,000,000 Elements
Linear Search (Average Comparisons)					
Linear Search (Maximum Comparisons)					
Binary Search (Maximum Comparisons)					

Programming Challenges

Visit www.myprogramminglab.com to complete many of these Programming Challenges online and get instant feedback.

1. **Charge Account Validation**

   Write a program that lets the user enter a charge account number. The program should determine if the number is valid by checking for it in the following list:

   ```
   5658845    4520125    7895122    8777541    8451277    1302850
   8080152    4562555    5552012    5050552    7825877    1250255
   1005231    6545231    3852085    7576651    7881200    4581002
   ```

   The list of numbers above should be initialized in a single-dimensional array. A simple linear search should be used to locate the number entered by the user. If the user enters a number that is in the array, the program should display a message saying that the number is valid. If the user enters a number that is not in the array, the program should display a message indicating that the number is invalid.

2. **Lottery Winners**

   A lottery ticket buyer purchases 10 tickets a week, always playing the same 10 5-digit "lucky" combinations. Write a program that initializes an array or a vector with these numbers and then lets the player enter this week's winning 5-digit number. The program should perform a linear search through the list of the player's numbers and report whether or not one of the tickets is a winner this week. Here are the numbers:

   ```
   13579    26791    26792    33445    55555
   62483    77777    79422    85647    93121
   ```

3. **Lottery Winners Modification**

   Modify the program you wrote for Programming Challenge 2 (Lottery Winners) so it performs a binary search instead of a linear search.

VideoNote
Solving the Charge Account Validation Modification Problem

4. **Charge Account Validation Modification**

   Modify the program you wrote for Problem 1 (Charge Account Validation) so it performs a binary search to locate valid account numbers. Use the selection sort algorithm to sort the array before the binary search is performed.

5. **Rainfall Statistics Modification**

   Modify the Rainfall Statistics program you wrote for Programming Challenge 2 of Chapter 7. The program should display a list of months, sorted in order of rainfall, from highest to lowest.

6. **String Selection Sort**

   Modify the selectionSort function presented in this chapter so it sorts an array of strings instead of an array of ints. Test the function with a driver program. Use Program 8-8 as a skeleton to complete.

Program 8-8

```cpp
#include <iostream>
#include <string>
using namespace std;

int main()
{
    const int NUM_NAMES = 20;
    string names[NUM_NAMES] = {"Collins, Bill", "Smith, Bart", "Allen, Jim",
                               "Griffin, Jim", "Stamey, Marty", "Rose, Geri",
                               "Taylor, Terri", "Johnson, Jill",
                               "Allison, Jeff", "Looney, Joe", "Wolfe, Bill",
                               "James, Jean", "Weaver, Jim", "Pore, Bob",
                               "Rutherford, Greg", "Javens, Renee",
                               "Harrison, Rose", "Setzer, Cathy",
                               "Pike, Gordon", "Holland, Beth" };

    // Insert your code to complete this program

    return 0;
}
```

7. **Binary String Search**

   Modify the binarySearch function presented in this chapter so it searches an array of strings instead of an array of ints. Test the function with a driver program. Use Program 8-8 as a skeleton to complete. (The array must be sorted before the binary search will work.)

8. **Search Benchmarks**

   Write a program that has an array of at least 20 integers. It should call a function that uses the linear search algorithm to locate one of the values. The function should keep a count of the number of comparisons it makes until it finds the value. The program then should call a function that uses the binary search algorithm to locate the same value. It should also keep count of the number of comparisons it makes. Display these values on the screen.

9. **Sorting Benchmarks**

   Write a program that uses two identical arrays of at least 20 integers. It should call a function that uses the bubble sort algorithm to sort one of the arrays in ascending order. The function should keep a count of the number of exchanges it makes. The program then should call a function that uses the selection sort algorithm to sort the other array. It should also keep count of the number of exchanges it makes. Display these values on the screen.

10. **Sorting Orders**

Write a program that uses two identical arrays of just eight integers. It should display the contents of the first array, then call a function to sort the array using an ascending order bubble sort modified to print out the array contents after each pass of the sort. Next, the program should display the contents of the second array, then call a function to sort the array using an ascending order selection sort modified to print out the array contents after each pass of the sort.

11. **Using Files—String Selection Sort Modification**

Modify the program you wrote for Programming Challenge 6 so it reads in 20 strings from a file. The data can be found in the `names.dat` file.

CHAPTER

9 Pointers

TOPICS

9.1 Getting the Address of a Variable

CONCEPT: The address operator (&) returns the memory address of a variable.

Every variable is allocated a section of memory large enough to hold a value of the variable's data type. On a PC, for instance, it's common for one byte to be allocated for chars, two bytes for shorts, four bytes for ints, longs, and floats, and eight bytes for doubles.

Each byte of memory has a unique *address*. A variable's address is the address of the first byte allocated to that variable. Suppose the following variables are defined in a program:

```
char letter;
short number;
float amount;
```

Figure 9-1 illustrates how they might be arranged in memory and shows their addresses.

Figure 9-1

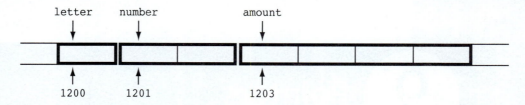

In Figure 9-1, the variable `letter` is shown at address 1200, `number` is at address 1201, and `amount` is at address 1203.

NOTE: The addresses of the variables shown in Figure 9-1 are arbitrary values used only for illustration purposes.

Getting the address of a variable is accomplished with an operator in C++. When the address operator (`&`) is placed in front of a variable name, it returns the address of that variable. Here is an expression that returns the address of the variable `amount`:

```
&amount
```

And here is a statement that displays the variable's address on the screen:

```
cout << &amount;
```

NOTE: Do not confuse the address operator with the `&` symbol used when defining a reference variable.

Program 9-1 demonstrates the use of the address operator to display the address, size, and contents of a variable.

Program 9-1

```
 1   // This program uses the & operator to determine a variable's
 2   // address and the sizeof operator to determine its size.
 3   #include <iostream>
 4   using namespace std;
 5
 6   int main()
 7   {
 8      int x = 25;
 9
10      cout << "The address of x is " << &x << endl;
11      cout << "The size of x is " << sizeof(x) << " bytes\n";
12      cout << "The value in x is " << x << endl;
13      return 0;
14   }
```

Program Output
```
The address of x is 0x8f05
The size of x is 4 bytes
The value in x is 25
```

NOTE: The address of the variable x is displayed in hexadecimal. This is the way addresses are normally shown in C++.

9.2 Pointer Variables

CONCEPT: *Pointer variables*, which are often just called *pointers*, are designed to hold memory addresses. With pointer variables you can indirectly manipulate data stored in other variables.

A *pointer variable*, which often is just called a *pointer*, is a special variable that holds a memory address. Just as int variables are designed to hold integers, and double variables are designed to hold floating-point numbers, pointer variables are designed to hold memory addresses.

Memory addresses identify specific locations in the computer's memory. Because a pointer variable holds a memory address, it can be used to hold the location of some other piece of data. This should give you a clue as to why it is called a pointer: It "points" to some piece of data that is stored in the computer's memory. Pointer variables also allow you to work with the data that they point to.

We've already used memory addresses in this book to work with data. Recall from Chapter 6 that when we pass an array as an argument to a function, we are actually passing the array's beginning address. For example, suppose we have an array named numbers and we call the showValues function as shown here.

```cpp
const int SIZE = 5;
int numbers[SIZE] = { 1, 2, 3, 4, 5 };
showValues(numbers, SIZE);
```

In this code we are passing the name of the array, numbers, and its size as arguments to the showValues function. Here is the definition for the showValues function:

```cpp
void showValues(int values[], int size)
{
    for (int count = 0; count < size; count++)
        cout << values[count] << endl;
}
```

In the function, the values parameter receives the address of the numbers array. It works like a pointer because it "points" to the numbers array, as shown in Figure 9-2.

Figure 9-2

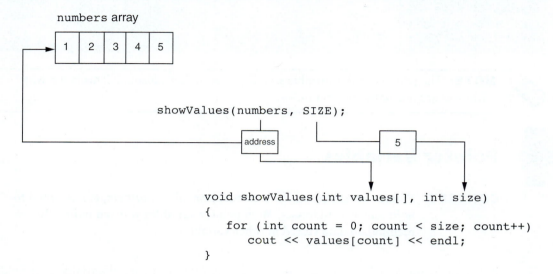

Inside the showValues function, anything that is done to the values parameter is actually done to the numbers array. We can say that the values parameter references the numbers array.

Also recall from Chapter 6 that we discussed reference variables. A reference variable acts as an alias for another variable. It is called a reference variable because it references another variable in the program. Anything that you do to the reference variable is actually done to the variable it references. For example, suppose we have the variable jellyDonuts and we pass the variable to the getOrder function, as shown here:

```
int jellyDonuts;
getOrder(jellyDonuts);
```

Here is the definition for the getOrder function:

```
void getOrder(int &donuts)
{
    cout << "How many doughnuts do you want? ";
    cin >> donuts;
}
```

In the function, the donuts parameter is a reference variable, and it receives the address of the jellyDonuts variable. It works like a pointer because it "points" to the jellyDonuts variable as shown in Figure 9-3.

Inside the getOrder function, the donuts parameter references the jellyDonuts variable. Anything that is done to the donuts parameter is actually done to the jellyDonuts variable. When the user enters a value, the cin statement uses the donuts reference variable to indirectly store the value in the jellyDonuts variable.

Notice that the connection between the donuts reference variable and the jellyDonuts argument is automatically established by C++ when the function is called. When you are writing this code, you don't have go to the trouble of finding the memory address of the

Figure 9-3

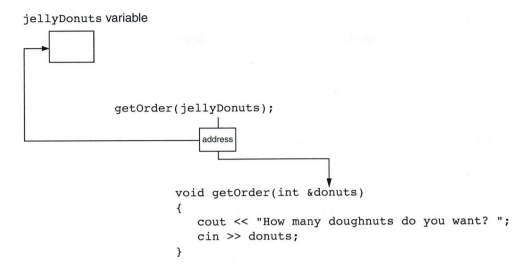

jellyDonuts variable and then properly storing that address in the donuts reference variable. When you are storing a value in the donuts variable, you don't have to specify that the value should actually be stored in the jellyDonuts variable. C++ handles all of that automatically.

In C++, pointer variables are yet another mechanism for using memory addresses to work with pieces of data. Pointer variables are similar to reference variables, but pointer variables operate at a lower level. By this, I mean that C++ does not automatically do as much work for you with pointer variables as it does with reference variables. In order to make a pointer variable reference another item in memory, you have to write code that fetches the memory address of that item and assigns the address to the pointer variable. Also, when you use a pointer variable to store a value in the memory location that the pointer references, your code has to specify that the value should be stored in the location referenced by the pointer variable, and not in the pointer variable itself.

Because reference variables are easier to work with, you might be wondering why you would ever use pointers at all. In C++, pointers are useful, and even necessary, for many operations. One such operation is dynamic memory allocation. When you are writing a program that will need to work with an unknown amount of data, dynamic memory allocation allows you to create variables, arrays, and more complex data structures in memory while the program is running. We will discuss dynamic memory allocation in greater detail in this chapter. Pointers are also very useful in algorithms that manipulate arrays and work with certain types of strings. In object-oriented programming, which you will learn about in Chapters 13, 14, and 15, pointers are very useful for creating and working with objects and for sharing access to those objects.

Creating and Using Pointer Variables

The definition of a pointer variable looks pretty much like any other definition. Here is an example:

```
int *ptr;
```

The asterisk in front of the variable name indicates that ptr is a pointer variable. The int data type indicates that ptr can be used to hold the address of an integer variable. The definition statement above would read "ptr is a pointer to an int."

NOTE: In this definition, the word int does not mean that ptr is an integer variable. It means that ptr can hold the address of an integer variable. Remember, pointers only hold one kind of value: an address.

Some programmers prefer to define pointers with the asterisk next to the type name, rather than the variable name. For example, the previous definition shown above could be written as:

```
int* ptr;
```

This style of definition might visually reinforce the fact that ptr's data type is not int, but pointer-to-int. Both definition styles are correct.

Program 9-2 demonstrates a very simple usage of a pointer: storing and printing the address of another variable.

Program 9-2

```
 1   // This program stores the address of a variable in a pointer.
 2   #include <iostream>
 3   using namespace std;
 4
 5   int main()
 6   {
 7      int x = 25;     // int variable
 8      int *ptr;       // Pointer variable, can point to an int
 9
10      ptr = &x;       // Store the address of x in ptr
11      cout << "The value in x is " << x << endl;
12      cout << "The address of x is " << ptr << endl;
13      return 0;
14   }
```

Program Output
```
The value in x is 25
The address of x is 0x7e00
```

In Program 9-2, two variables are defined: x and ptr. The variable x is an int and the variable ptr is a pointer to an int. The variable x is initialized with the value 25. The variable ptr is assigned the address of x with the following statement in line 10:

```
ptr = &x;
```

Figure 9-4 illustrates the relationship between ptr and x.

Figure 9-4

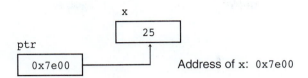

As shown in Figure 9-4, x, which is located at memory address 0x7e00, contains the number 25. ptr contains the address 0x7e00. In essence, it "points" to the variable x.

The real benefit of pointers is that they allow you to indirectly access and modify the variable being pointed to. In Program 9-2, for instance, ptr could be used to change the contents of the variable x. This is done with the *indirection operator*, which is an asterisk (*). When the indirection operator is placed in front of a pointer variable name, it *dereferences* the pointer. When you are working with a dereferenced pointer, you are actually working with the value the pointer is pointing to. This is demonstrated in Program 9-3.

Program 9-3

```
 1  // This program demonstrates the use of the indirection operator.
 2  #include <iostream>
 3  using namespace std;
 4
 5  int main()
 6  {
 7      int x = 25;     // int variable
 8      int *ptr;       // Pointer variable, can point to an int
 9
10      ptr = &x;       // Store the address of x in ptr
11
12      // Use both x and ptr to display the value in x.
13      cout << "Here is the value in x, printed twice:\n";
14      cout << x << endl;      // Displays the contents of x
15      cout << *ptr << endl;   // Displays the contents of x
16
17      // Assign 100 to the location pointed to by ptr. This
18      // will actually assign 100 to x.
19      *ptr = 100;
20
21      // Use both x and ptr to display the value in x.
22      cout << "Once again, here is the value in x:\n";
23      cout << x << endl;      // Displays the contents of x
24      cout << *ptr << endl;   // Displays the contents of x
25      return 0;
26  }
```

(program output continues)

Program 9-3 *(continued)*

Program Output
```
Here is the value in x, printed twice:
25
25
Once again, here is the value in x:
100
100
```

Take a closer look at the statement in line 10:

```
ptr = &x;
```

This statement assigns the address of the x variable to the ptr variable. Now look at line 15:

```
cout << *ptr << endl;  // Displays the contents of x
```

When you apply the indirection operator (*) to a pointer variable, you are working, not with the pointer variable itself, but with the item it points to. Because this statement sends the expression *ptr to the cout object, it does not display the value in ptr, but the value that ptr points to. Since ptr points to the x variable, this statement displays the contents of the x variable.

Suppose the statement did not use the indirection operator. Suppose that statement had been written as:

```
cout << ptr << endl;   // Displays an address
```

Because the indirection operator is not applied to ptr in this statement, it works directly with the ptr variable. This statement would display the address that is stored in ptr.

Now take a look at the following statement, which appears in line 19:

```
*ptr = 100;
```

Notice the indirection operator being used with ptr. That means the statement is not affecting ptr, but the item that ptr points to. This statement assigns 100 to the item ptr points to, which is the x variable. After this statement executes, 100 will be stored in the x variable.

Program 9-4 demonstrates that pointers can point to different variables.

Program 9-4

```
 1  // This program demonstrates a pointer variable referencing
 2  // different variables.
 3  #include <iostream>
 4  using namespace std;
 5
 6  int main()
 7  {
 8     int x = 25, y = 50, z = 75;  // Three int variables
 9     int *ptr;                    // Pointer variable
10
```

```
11      // Display the contents of x, y, and z.
12      cout << "Here are the values of x, y, and z:\n";
13      cout << x << " " << y << " " << z << endl;
14
15      // Use the pointer to manipulate x, y, and z.
16
17      ptr = &x;       // Store the address of x in ptr.
18      *ptr += 100;    // Add 100 to the value in x.
19
20      ptr = &y;       // Store the address of y in ptr.
21      *ptr += 100;    // Add 100 to the value in y.
22
23      ptr = &z;       // Store the address of z in ptr.
24      *ptr += 100;    // Add 100 to the value in z.
25
26      // Display the contents of x, y, and z.
27      cout << "Once again, here are the values of x, y, and z:\n";
28      cout << x << " " << y << " " << z << endl;
29      return 0;
30  }
```

Program Output
```
Here are the values of x, y, and z:
25 50 75
Once again, here are the values of x, y, and z:
125 150 175
```

Take a closer look at the statement in line 17:

```
ptr = &x;
```

This statement assigns the address of the x variable to the ptr variable. Now look at line 18:

```
*ptr += 100;
```

In this statement notice that the indirection operator (*) is used with the ptr variable. When we apply the indirection operator to ptr, we are working, not with ptr, but with the item that ptr points to. When this statement executes, ptr is pointing at x, so the statement in line 18 adds 100 to the contents of x. Then the following statement, in line 20, executes:

```
ptr = &y;
```

This statement assigns the address of the y variable to the ptr variable. After this statement executes, ptr is no longer pointing at x. Rather, it will be pointing at y. The statement in line 21, shown here, adds 100 to the y variable.

```
*ptr += 100;
```

These steps are repeated with the z variable in lines 23 and 24.

> **NOTE:** So far you've seen three different uses of the asterisk in C++:
>
> - As the multiplication operator, in statements such as
>   ```
>   distance = speed * time;
>   ```
> - In the definition of a pointer variable, such as
>   ```
>   int *ptr;
>   ```
> - As the indirection operator, in statements such as
>   ```
>   *ptr = 100;
>   ```

9.3 The Relationship Between Arrays and Pointers

CONCEPT: Array names can be used as constant pointers, and pointers can be used as array names.

You learned in Chapter 7 that an array name, without brackets and a subscript, actually represents the starting address of the array. This means that an array name is really a pointer. Program 9-5 illustrates this by showing an array name being used with the indirection operator.

Program 9-5

```
 1  // This program shows an array name being dereferenced with the *
 2  // operator.
 3  #include <iostream>
 4  using namespace std;
 5
 6  int main()
 7  {
 8      short numbers[] = {10, 20, 30, 40, 50};
 9
10      cout << "The first element of the array is ";
11      cout << *numbers << endl;
12      return 0;
13  }
```

Program Output
```
The first element of the array is 10
```

Because numbers works like a pointer to the starting address of the array, the first element is retrieved when numbers is dereferenced. So how could the entire contents of an array be retrieved using the indirection operator? Remember, array elements are stored together in memory, as illustrated in Figure 9-5.

It makes sense that if numbers is the address of numbers[0], values could be added to numbers to get the addresses of the other elements in the array. It's important to know, however, that pointers do not work like regular variables when used in mathematical statements. In C++, when you add a value to a pointer, you are actually adding that value *times the size of the data type being referenced by the pointer*. In other words, if you add

Figure 9-5

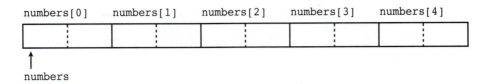

one to numbers, you are actually adding 1 * sizeof(short) to numbers. If you add two to numbers, the result is numbers + 2 * sizeof(short), and so forth. On a PC, this means the following are true, because short integers typically use two bytes:

```
*(numbers + 1) is actually *(numbers + 1 * 2)
*(numbers + 2) is actually *(numbers + 2 * 2)
*(numbers + 3) is actually *(numbers + 3 * 2)
```

and so forth.

This automatic conversion means that an element in an array can be retrieved by using its subscript or by adding its subscript to a pointer to the array. If the expression *numbers, which is the same as *(numbers + 0), retrieves the first element in the array, then *(numbers + 1) retrieves the second element. Likewise, *(numbers + 2) retrieves the third element, and so forth. Figure 9-6 shows the equivalence of subscript notation and pointer notation.

Figure 9-6

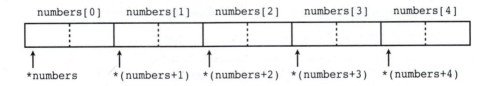

  NOTE: The parentheses are critical when adding values to pointers. The * operator has precedence over the + operator, so the expression *number + 1 is not equivalent to *(number + 1). *number + 1 adds one to the contents of the first element of the array, while *(number + 1) adds one to the address in number, then dereferences it.

Program 9-6 shows the entire contents of the array being accessed, using pointer notation.

Program 9-6

```
1   // This program processes an array using pointer notation.
2   #include <iostream>
3   using namespace std;
4
```

(program continues)

Program 9-6 *(continued)*

```
 5   int main()
 6   {
 7      const int SIZE = 5;   // Size of the array
 8      int numbers[SIZE];    // Array of integers
 9      int count;            // Counter variable
10
11      // Get values to store in the array.
12      // Use pointer notation instead of subscripts.
13      cout << "Enter " << SIZE << " numbers: ";
14      for (count = 0; count < SIZE; count++)
15         cin >> *(numbers + count);
16
17      // Display the values in the array.
18      // Use pointer notation instead of subscripts.
19      cout << "Here are the numbers you entered:\n";
20      for (count = 0; count < SIZE; count++)
21         cout << *(numbers + count)<< " ";
22      cout << endl;
23      return 0;
24   }
```

Program Output with Example Input Shown in Bold
```
Enter 5 numbers: 5 10 15 20 25 [Enter]
Here are the numbers you entered:
5 10 15 20 25
```

When working with arrays, remember the following rule:

array[index] is equivalent to *(*array* + index)

 WARNING! Remember that C++ performs no bounds checking with arrays. When stepping through an array with a pointer, it's possible to give the pointer an address outside of the array.

To demonstrate just how close the relationship is between array names and pointers, look at Program 9-7. It defines an array of doubles and a double pointer, which is assigned the starting address of the array. Not only is pointer notation then used with the array name, but subscript notation is used with the pointer!

Program 9-7

```
1   // This program uses subscript notation with a pointer variable and
2   // pointer notation with an array name.
3   #include <iostream>
4   #include <iomanip>
5   using namespace std;
6
```

```
 7   int main()
 8   {
 9      const int NUM_COINS = 5;
10      double coins[NUM_COINS] = {0.05, 0.1, 0.25, 0.5, 1.0};
11      double *doublePtr;    // Pointer to a double
12      int count;            // Array index
13
14      // Assign the address of the coins array to doublePtr.
15      doublePtr = coins;
16
17      // Display the contents of the coins array. Use subscripts
18      // with the pointer!
19      cout << "Here are the values in the coins array:\n";
20      for (count = 0; count < NUM_COINS; count++)
21         cout << doublePtr[count] << " ";
22
23      // Display the contents of the array again, but this time
24      // use pointer notation with the array name!
25      cout << "\nAnd here they are again:\n";
26      for (count = 0; count < NUM_COINS; count++)
27         cout << *(coins + count) << " ";
28      cout << endl;
29      return 0;
30   }
```

Program Output

```
Here are the values in the coins array:
0.05 0.1 0.25 0.5 1
And here they are again:
0.05 0.1 0.25 0.5 1
```

Notice that the address operator is not needed when an array's address is assigned to a pointer. Because the name of an array is already an address, use of the & operator would be incorrect. You can, however, use the address operator to get the address of an individual element in an array. For instance, &numbers[1] gets the address of numbers[1]. This technique is used in Program 9-8.

Program 9-8

```
 1   // This program uses the address of each element in the array.
 2   #include <iostream>
 3   #include <iomanip>
 4   using namespace std;
 5
 6   int main()
 7   {
 8      const int NUM_COINS = 5;
 9      double coins[NUM_COINS] = {0.05, 0.1, 0.25, 0.5, 1.0};
10      double *doublePtr; // Pointer to a double
11      int count;          // Array index
12
```

(program continues)

Program 9-8 *(continued)*

```
13      // Use the pointer to display the values in the array.
14      cout << "Here are the values in the coins array:\n";
15      for (count = 0; count < NUM_COINS; count++)
16      {
17         // Get the address of an array element.
18         doublePtr = &coins[count];
19
20         // Display the contents of the element.
21         cout << *doublePtr << " ";
22      }
23      cout << endl;
24      return 0;
25   }
```

Program Output
```
Here are the values in the coins array:
0.05 0.1 0.25 0.5 1
```

The only difference between array names and pointer variables is that you cannot change the address an array name points to. For example, consider the following definitions:

```
double readings[20], totals[20];
double *dptr;
```

These statements are legal:

```
dptr = readings; // Make dptr point to readings.
dptr = totals;   // Make dptr point to totals.
```

But these are illegal:

```
readings = totals;  // ILLEGAL! Cannot change readings.
totals = dptr;      // ILLEGAL! Cannot change totals.
```

Array names are *pointer constants*. You can't make them point to anything but the array they represent.

9.4 Pointer Arithmetic

CONCEPT: Some mathematical operations may be performed on pointers.

The contents of pointer variables may be changed with mathematical statements that perform addition or subtraction. This is demonstrated in Program 9-9. The first loop increments the pointer variable, stepping it through each element of the array. The second loop decrements the pointer, stepping it through the array backward.

Program 9-9

```cpp
 1   // This program uses a pointer to display the contents of an array.
 2   #include <iostream>
 3   using namespace std;
 4
 5   int main()
 6   {
 7      const int SIZE = 8;
 8      int set[SIZE] = {5, 10, 15, 20, 25, 30, 35, 40};
 9      int *numPtr;    // Pointer
10      int count;      // Counter variable for loops
11
12      // Make numPtr point to the set array.
13      numPtr = set;
14
15      // Use the pointer to display the array contents.
16      cout << "The numbers in set are:\n";
17      for (count = 0; count < SIZE; count++)
18      {
19         cout << *numPtr << " ";
20         numPtr++;
21      }
22
23      // Display the array contents in reverse order.
24      cout << "\nThe numbers in set backward are:\n";
25      for (count = 0; count < SIZE; count++)
26      {
27         numPtr--;
28         cout << *numPtr << " ";
29      }
30      return 0;
31   }
```

Program Output
```
The numbers in set are:
5 10 15 20 25 30 35 40
The numbers in set backward are:
40 35 30 25 20 15 10 5
```

 NOTE: Because numPtr is a pointer to an integer, the increment operator adds the size of one integer to numPtr, so it points to the next element in the array. Likewise, the decrement operator subtracts the size of one integer from the pointer.

Not all arithmetic operations may be performed on pointers. For example, you cannot multiply or divide a pointer. The following operations are allowable:

- The ++ and -- operators may be used to increment or decrement a pointer variable.
- An integer may be added to or subtracted from a pointer variable. This may be performed with the + and – operators, or the += and -= operators.
- A pointer may be subtracted from another pointer.

9.5   Initializing Pointers

CONCEPT: Pointers may be initialized with the address of an existing object.

Remember that a pointer is designed to point to an object of a specific data type. When a pointer is initialized with an address, it must be the address of an object the pointer can point to. For instance, the following definition of `pint` is legal because `myValue` is an integer:

```cpp
int myValue;
int *pint = &myValue;
```

The following is also legal because `ages` is an array of integers:

```cpp
int ages[20];
int *pint = ages;
```

But the following definition of `pint` is illegal because `myFloat` is not an `int`:

```cpp
float myFloat;
int *pint = &myFloat;   // Illegal!
```

Pointers may be defined in the same statement as other variables of the same type. The following statement defines an integer variable, `myValue`, and then defines a pointer, `pint`, which is initialized with the address of `myValue`:

```cpp
int myValue, *pint = &myValue;
```

And the following statement defines an array, `readings`, and a pointer, `marker`, which is initialized with the address of the first element in the array:

```cpp
double readings[50], *marker = readings;
```

Of course, a pointer can only be initialized with the address of an object that has already been defined. The following is illegal because `pint` is being initialized with the address of an object that does not exist yet:

```cpp
int *pint = &myValue;   // Illegal!
int myValue;
```

 Checkpoint

myprogramminglab   *www.myprogramminglab.com*

9.1   Write a statement that displays the address of the variable `count`.

9.2   Write the definition statement for a variable `fltPtr`. The variable should be a pointer to a `float`.

9.3   List three uses of the `*` symbol in C++.

9.4   What is the output of the following code?

```cpp
int x = 50, y = 60, z = 70;
int *ptr;

cout << x << "   " << y << "   " << z << endl;
ptr = &x;
```

```
*ptr *= 10;
ptr = &y;
*ptr *= 5;
ptr = &z;
*ptr *= 2;
cout << x << "   " << y << "   " << z << endl;
```

9.5   Rewrite the following loop so it uses pointer notation (with the indirection operator) instead of subscript notation.

```
for (int x = 0; x < 100; x++)
    cout << arr[x] << endl;
```

9.6   Assume `ptr` is a pointer to an `int`, and holds the address 12000. On a system with 4-byte integers, what address will be in `ptr` after the following statement?

```
ptr += 10;
```

9.7   Assume `pint` is a pointer variable. Is each of the following statements valid or invalid? If any is invalid, why?

A) `pint++;`

B) `--pint;`

C) `pint /= 2;`

D) `pint *= 4;`

E) `pint += x;   // Assume x is an int.`

9.8   Is each of the following definitions valid or invalid? If any is invalid, why?

A) `int ivar;`
    `int *iptr = &ivar;`

B) `int ivar, *iptr = &ivar;`

C) `float fvar;`
    `int *iptr = &fvar;`

D) `int nums[50], *iptr = nums;`

E) `int *iptr = &ivar;`
    `int ivar;`

9.6   Comparing Pointers

CONCEPT: If one address comes before another address in memory, the first address is considered "less than" the second. C++'s relational operators may be used to compare pointer values.

Pointers may be compared by using any of C++'s relational operators:

```
> < == != >= <=
```

In an array, all the elements are stored in consecutive memory locations, so the address of element 1 is greater than the address of element 0. This is illustrated in Figure 9-7.

Figure 9-7

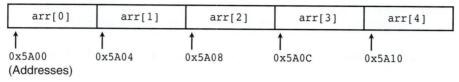

An array of five integers

| arr[0] | arr[1] | arr[2] | arr[3] | arr[4] |

0x5A00   0x5A04   0x5A08   0x5A0C   0x5A10
(Addresses)

Because the addresses grow larger for each subsequent element in the array, the following if statements are all true:

```
if (&arr[1] > &arr[0])
if (arr < &arr[4])
if (arr == &arr[0])
if (&arr[2] != &arr[3])
```

NOTE: Comparing two pointers is not the same as comparing the values the two pointers point to. For example, the following if statement compares the addresses stored in the pointer variables ptr1 and ptr2:

```
if (ptr1 < ptr2)
```

The following statement, however, compares the values that ptr1 and ptr2 point to:

```
if (*ptr1 < *ptr2)
```

The capability of comparing addresses gives you another way to be sure a pointer does not go beyond the boundaries of an array. Program 9-10 initializes the pointer nums with the starting address of the array set. The nums pointer is then stepped through the array set until the address it contains is equal to the address of the last element of the array. Then the pointer is stepped backward through the array until it points to the first element.

Program 9-10

```
 1  // This program uses a pointer to display the contents
 2  // of an integer array.
 3  #include <iostream>
 4  using namespace std;
 5
 6  int main()
 7  {
 8      int set[8] = {5, 10, 15, 20, 25, 30, 35, 40};
 9      int *nums = set;      // Make nums point to set
10
11      // Display the numbers in the array.
12      cout << "The numbers in set are:\n";
13      cout << *nums << " ";   // Display first element
```

```
14        while (nums < &set[7])
15        {
16            // Advance nums to point to the next element.
17            nums++;
18            // Display the value pointed to by nums.
19            cout << *nums << " ";
20        }
21
22        // Display the numbers in reverse order.
23        cout << "\nThe numbers in set backward are:\n";
24        cout << *nums << " ";    // Display first element
25        while (nums > set)
26        {
27            // Move backward to the previous element.
28            nums--;
29            // Display the value pointed to by nums.
30            cout << *nums << " ";
31        }
32        return 0;
33    }
```

Program Output
```
The numbers in set are:
5 10 15 20 25 30 35 40
The numbers in set backward are:
40 35 30 25 20 15 10 5
```

9.7 Pointers as Function Parameters

CONCEPT: A pointer can be used as a function parameter. It gives the function access to the original argument, much like a reference parameter does.

In Chapter 6 you were introduced to the concept of reference variables being used as function parameters. A reference variable acts as an alias to the original variable used as an argument. This gives the function access to the original argument variable, allowing it to change the variable's contents. When a variable is passed into a reference parameter, the argument is said to be passed by reference.

Another way to pass an argument by reference is to use a pointer variable as the parameter. Admittedly, reference variables are much easier to work with than pointers. Reference variables hide all the "mechanics" of dereferencing and indirection. You should still learn to use pointers as function arguments, however, because some tasks, especially when you are dealing with strings, are best done with pointers.* Also, the C++ library has many functions that use pointers as parameters.

---

* It is also important to learn this technique in case you ever need to write a C program. In C, the only way to pass a variable by reference is to use a pointer.

Here is the definition of a function that uses a pointer parameter:

```
void doubleValue(int *val)
{
    *val *= 2;
}
```

The purpose of this function is to double the variable pointed to by val with the following statement:

```
*val *= 2;
```

When val is dereferenced, the *= operator works on the variable pointed to by val. This statement multiplies the original variable, whose address is stored in val, by two. Of course, when the function is called, the address of the variable that is to be doubled must be used as the argument, not the variable itself. Here is an example of a call to the doubleValue function:

```
doubleValue(&number);
```

This statement uses the address operator (&) to pass the address of number into the val parameter. After the function executes, the contents of number will have been multiplied by two. The use of this function is illustrated in Program 9-11.

Program 9-11

```
 1   // This program uses two functions that accept addresses of
 2   // variables as arguments.
 3   #include <iostream>
 4   using namespace std;
 5
 6   // Function prototypes
 7   void getNumber(int *);
 8   void doubleValue(int *);
 9
10   int main()
11   {
12       int number;
13
14       // Call getNumber and pass the address of number.
15       getNumber(&number);
16
17       // Call doubleValue and pass the address of number.
18       doubleValue(&number);
19
20       // Display the value in number.
21       cout << "That value doubled is " << number << endl;
22       return 0;
23   }
24
```

```
25    //*************************************************************
26    // Definition of getNumber. The parameter, input, is a pointer. *
27    // This function asks the user for a number. The value entered   *
28    // is stored in the variable pointed to by input.                *
29    //*************************************************************
30
31    void getNumber(int *input)
32    {
33        cout << "Enter an integer number: ";
34        cin >> *input;
35    }
36
37    //*************************************************************
38    // Definition of doubleValue. The parameter, val, is a pointer. *
39    // This function multiplies the variable pointed to by val by    *
40    // two.                                                          *
41    //*************************************************************
42
43    void doubleValue(int *val)
44    {
45        *val *= 2;
46    }
```

Program Output with Example Input Shown in Bold
```
Enter an integer number: 10 [Enter]
That value doubled is 20
```

Program 9-11 has two functions that use pointers as parameters. Notice the function prototypes:

```
void getNumber(int *);
void doubleValue(int *);
```

Each one uses the notation int * to indicate the parameter is a pointer to an int. As with all other types of parameters, it isn't necessary to specify the name of the variable in the prototype. The * is required, though.

The getNumber function asks the user to enter an integer value. The following cin statement, in line 34, stores the value entered by the user in memory:

```
cin >> *input;
```

The indirection operator causes the value entered by the user to be stored, not in input, but in the variable pointed to by input.

WARNING! It's critical that the indirection operator be used in the statement above. Without it, cin would store the value entered by the user in input, as if the value were an address. If this happens, input will no longer point to the number variable in function main. Subsequent use of the pointer will result in erroneous, if not disastrous, results.

When the `getNumber` function is called in line 15, the address of the `number` variable in function `main` is passed as the argument. After the function executes, the value entered by the user is stored in `number`. Next, the `doubleValue` function is called in line 18, with the address of `number` passed as the argument. This causes `number` to be multiplied by two.

Pointer variables can also be used to accept array addresses as arguments. Either subscript or pointer notation may then be used to work with the contents of the array. This is demonstrated in Program 9-12.

Program 9-12

```
1    // This program demonstrates that a pointer may be used as a
2    // parameter to accept the address of an array.
3    #include <iostream>
4    #include <iomanip>
5    using namespace std;
6
7    // Function prototypes
8    void getSales(double *, int);
9    double totalSales(double *, int);
10
11   int main()
12   {
13      const int QTRS = 4;
14      double sales[QTRS];
15
16      // Get the sales data for all quarters.
17      getSales(sales, QTRS);
18
19      // Set the numeric output formatting.
20      cout << fixed << showpoint << setprecision(2);
21
22      // Display the total sales for the year.
23      cout << "The total sales for the year are $";
24      cout << totalSales(sales, QTRS) << endl;
25      return 0;
26   }
27
28   //****************************************************************
29   // Definition of getSales. This function uses a pointer to accept *
30   // the address of an array of doubles. The function asks the user *
31   // to enter sales figures and stores them in the array.          *
32   //****************************************************************
33   void getSales(double *arr, int size)
34   {
35      for (int count = 0; count < size; count++)
36      {
37         cout << "Enter the sales figure for quarter ";
38         cout << (count + 1) << ": ";
39         cin >> arr[count];
40      }
41   }
42
```

```
43  //************************************************************
44  // Definition of totalSales. This function uses a pointer to    *
45  // accept the address of an array. The function returns the total *
46  // of the elements in the array.                                 *
47  //************************************************************
48  double totalSales(double *arr, int size)
49  {
50      double sum = 0.0;
51
52      for (int count = 0; count < size; count++)
53      {
54         sum += *arr;
55         arr++;
56      }
57      return sum;
58  }
```

Program Output with Example Input Shown in Bold
```
Enter the sales figure for quarter 1: 10263.98 [Enter]
Enter the sales figure for quarter 2: 12369.69 [Enter]
Enter the sales figure for quarter 3: 11542.13 [Enter]
Enter the sales figure for quarter 4: 14792.06 [Enter]
The total sales for the year are $48967.86
```

Notice that in the `getSales` function in Program 9-12, even though the parameter `arr` is defined as a pointer, subscript notation is used in the `cin` statement in line 39:

```
cin >> arr[count];
```

In the `totalSales` function, `arr` is used with the indirection operator in line 54:

```
sum += *arr;
```

And in line 55, the address in `arr` is incremented to point to the next element:

```
arr++;
```

NOTE: The two previous statements could be combined into the following statement:

```
sum += *arr++;
```

The * operator will first dereference `arr`, then the ++ operator will increment the address in `arr`.

Pointers to Constants

You have seen how an item's address can be passed into a pointer parameter, and how the pointer can be used to modify the item that was passed as an argument. Sometimes it is necessary to pass the address of a `const` item into a pointer. When this is the case, the pointer must be defined as a pointer to a `const` item. For example, consider the following array definition:

```
const int SIZE = 6;
const double payRates[SIZE] = { 18.55, 17.45,
                                12.85, 14.97,
                                10.35, 18.89 };
```

In this code, payRates is an array of const doubles. This means that each element in the array is a const double, and the compiler will not allow us to write code that changes the array's contents. If we want to pass the payRates array into a pointer parameter, the parameter must be declared as a pointer to const double. The following function shows such an example:

```
void displayPayRates(const double *rates, int size)
{
    // Set numeric output formatting.
    cout << setprecision(2) << fixed << showpoint;

    // Display all the pay rates.
    for (int count = 0; count < size; count++)
    {
        cout << "Pay rate for employee " << (count + 1)
             << " is $" << *(rates + count) << endl;
    }
}
```

In the function header, notice that the rates parameter is defined as a pointer to const double. It should be noted that the word const is applied to the thing that rates points to, not rates itself. This is illustrated in Figure 9-8.

Figure 9-8

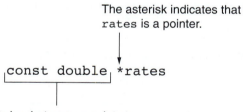

Because rates is a pointer to a const, the compiler will not allow us to write code that changes the thing that rates points to.

In passing the address of a constant into a pointer variable, the variable must be defined as a pointer to a constant. If the word const had been left out of the definition of the rates parameter, a compiler error would have resulted.

Passing a Nonconstant Argument into a Pointer to a Constant

Although a constant's address can be passed only to a pointer to const, a pointer to const can also receive the address of a nonconstant item. For example, look at Program 9-13.

Program 9-13

```cpp
 1   // This program demonstrates a pointer to const parameter
 2   #include <iostream>
 3   using namespace std;
 4
 5   void displayValues(const int *, int);
 6
 7   int main()
 8   {
 9      // Array sizes
10      const int SIZE = 6;
11
12      // Define an array of const ints.
13      const int array1[SIZE] = { 1, 2, 3, 4, 5, 6 };
14
15      // Define an array of nonconst ints.
16      int array2[SIZE] = { 2, 4, 6, 8, 10, 12 };
17
18      // Display the contents of the const array.
19      displayValues(array1, SIZE);
20
21      // Display the contents of the nonconst array.
22      displayValues(array2, SIZE);
23      return 0;
24   }
25
26   //****************************************************
27   // The displayValues function uses a pointer to     *
28   // parameter to display the contents of an array.   *
29   //****************************************************
30
31   void displayValues(const int *numbers, int size)
32   {
33      // Display all the values.
34      for (int count = 0; count < size; count++)
35      {
36         cout << *(numbers + count) << " ";
37      }
38      cout << endl;
39   }
```

Program Output
```
1 2 3 4 5 6
2 4 6 8 10 12
```

NOTE: When you are writing a function that uses a pointer parameter, and the function is not intended to change the data the parameter points to, it is always a good idea to make the parameter a pointer to const. Not only will this protect you from writing code in the function that accidentally changes the argument, but the function will be able to accept the addresses of both constant and nonconstant arguments.

Constant Pointers

In the previous section we discussed pointers to `const`. That is, pointers that point to `const` data. You can also use the `const` key word to define a constant pointer. Here is the difference between a pointer to `const` and a `const` pointer:

- A pointer to `const` points to a constant item. The data that the pointer points to cannot change, but the pointer itself can change.
- With a `const` pointer, it is the pointer itself that is constant. Once the pointer is initialized with an address, it cannot point to anything else.

The following code shows an example of a `const` pointer.

```
int value = 22;
int * const ptr = &value;
```

Notice in the definition of `ptr` the word `const` appears after the asterisk. This means that `ptr` is a `const` pointer. This is illustrated in Figure 9-9. In the code, `ptr` is initialized with the address of the `value` variable. Because `ptr` is a constant pointer, a compiler error will result if we write code that makes `ptr` point to anything else. An error will not result, however, if we use `ptr` to change the contents of `value`. This is because `value` is not constant, and `ptr` is not a pointer to `const`.

Figure 9-9

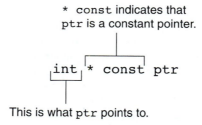

Constant pointers must be initialized with a starting value, as shown in the previous example code. If a constant pointer is used as a function parameter, the parameter will be initialized with the address that is passed as an argument into it, and cannot be changed to point to anything else while the function is executing. Here is an example that attempts to violate this rule:

```
void setToZero(int * const ptr)
{
    ptr = 0;  // ERROR!! Cannot change the contents of ptr.
}
```

This function's parameter, `ptr`, is a `const` pointer. It will not compile because we cannot have code in the function that changes the contents of `ptr`. However, `ptr` does not point to a `const`, so we can have code that changes the data that `ptr` points to. Here is an example of the function that will compile:

```
void setToZero(int * const ptr)
{
    *ptr = 0;
}
```

Although the parameter is const pointer, we can call the function multiple times with different arguments. The following code will successfully pass the addresses of x, y, and z to the setToZero function:

```
int x, y, z;
// Set x, y, and z to 0.
setToZero(&x);
setToZero(&y);
setToZero(&z);
```

Constant Pointers to Constants

So far, when using const with pointers we've seen pointers to constants and we've seen constant pointers. You can also have constant pointers to constants. For example, look at the following code:

```
int value = 22;
const int * const ptr = &value;
```

In this code ptr is a const pointer to a const int. Notice the word const appears before int, indicating that ptr points to a const int, and it appears after the asterisk, indicating that ptr is a constant pointer. This is illustrated in Figure 9-10.

Figure 9-10

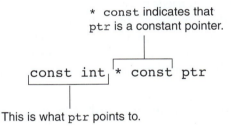

In the code, ptr is initialized with the address of value. Because ptr is a const pointer, we cannot write code that makes ptr point to anything else. Because ptr is a pointer to const, we cannot use it to change the contents of value. The following code shows one more example of a const pointer to a const. This is another version of the displayValues function in Program 9-13.

```
void displayValues(const int * const numbers, int size)
{
   // Display all the values.
   for (int count = 0; count < size; count++)
   {
      cout << *(numbers + count) << " ";
   }
   cout << endl;
}
```

In this code, the parameter numbers is a const pointer to a const int. Although we can call the function with different arguments, the function itself cannot change what numbers points to, and it cannot use numbers to change the contents of an argument.

Focus on Software Engineering: Dynamic Memory Allocation

CONCEPT: Variables may be created and destroyed while a program is running.

As long as you know how many variables you will need during the execution of a program, you can define those variables up front. For example, a program to calculate the area of a rectangle will need three variables: one for the rectangle's length, one for the rectangle's width, and one to hold the area. If you are writing a program to compute the payroll for 30 employees, you'll probably create an array of 30 elements to hold the amount of pay for each person.

But what about those times when you don't know how many variables you need? For instance, suppose you want to write a test-averaging program that will average any number of tests. Obviously the program would be very versatile, but how do you store the individual test scores in memory if you don't know how many variables to define? Quite simply, you allow the program to create its own variables "on the fly." This is called *dynamic memory allocation*, and is only possible through the use of pointers.

To dynamically allocate memory means that a program, while running, asks the computer to set aside a chunk of unused memory large enough to hold a variable of a specific data type. Let's say a program needs to create an integer variable. It will make a request to the computer that it allocate enough bytes to store an `int`. When the computer fills this request, it finds and sets aside a chunk of unused memory large enough for the variable. It then gives the program the starting address of the chunk of memory. The program can only access the newly allocated memory through its address, so a pointer is required to use those bytes.

The way a C++ program requests dynamically allocated memory is through the `new` operator. Assume a program has a pointer to an `int` defined as

```
int *iptr;
```

Here is an example of how this pointer may be used with the `new` operator:

```
iptr = new int;
```

This statement is requesting that the computer allocate enough memory for a new `int` variable. The operand of the `new` operator is the data type of the variable being created. Once the statement executes, `iptr` will contain the address of the newly allocated memory. This is illustrated in Figure 9-11. A value may be stored in this new variable by dereferencing the pointer:

```
*iptr = 25;
```

Any other operation may be performed on the new variable by simply using the dereferenced pointer. Here are some example statements:

```
cout << *iptr;      // Display the contents of the new variable.
cin >> *iptr;       // Let the user input a value.
total += *iptr;     // Use the new variable in a computation.
```

Figure 9-11

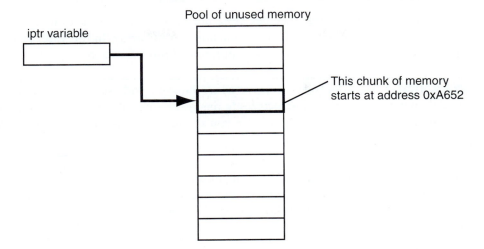

Pool of unused memory

iptr variable

This chunk of memory
starts at address 0xA652

Although the statements above illustrate the use of the new operator, there's little purpose in dynamically allocating a single variable. A more practical use of the new operator is to dynamically create an array. Here is an example of how a 100-element array of integers may be allocated:

```
iptr = new int[100];
```

VideoNote
**Dynamically
Allocating
an Array**

Once the array is created, the pointer may be used with subscript notation to access it. For instance, the following loop could be used to store the value 1 in each element:

```
for (int count = 0; count < 100; count++)
    iptr[count] = 1;
```

But what if there isn't enough free memory to accommodate the request? What if the program asks for a chunk large enough to hold a 100,000-element array of floats, and that much memory isn't available? When memory cannot be dynamically allocated, C++ throws an exception and terminates the program. *Throwing an exception* means the program signals that an error has occurred. You will learn more about exceptions in Chapter 16.

Programs created with older C++ compilers behave differently when memory cannot be dynamically allocated. Under older compilers, the new operator returns the address 0, or NULL when it fails to allocate the requested amount of memory. (NULL is a named constant, defined in the iostream file, that stands for address 0.) A program created with an older compiler should always check to see if the new operator returns NULL, as shown in the following code:

```
iptr = new int[100];
if (iptr == NULL)
{
    cout << "Error allocating memory!\n";
    return;
}
```

NOTE: A pointer that contains the address 0 is called a *null pointer*.

The `if` statement determines whether `iptr` points to address 0. If it does, then the `new` operator was unable to allocate enough memory for the array. In this case, an error message is displayed and the `return` statement terminates the function.

 WARNING! The address 0 is considered an unusable address. Most computers store special operating system data structures in the lower areas of memory. Anytime you use the `new` operator with an older compiler, you should always test the pointer for the `NULL` address before you use it.

When a program is finished using a dynamically allocated chunk of memory, it should release it for future use. The `delete` operator is used to free memory that was allocated with `new`. Here is an example of how `delete` is used to free a single variable, pointed to by `iptr`:

```
delete iptr;
```

If `iptr` points to a dynamically allocated array, the `[]` symbol must be placed between `delete` and `iptr`:

```
delete [] iptr;
```

 WARNING! Only use pointers with `delete` that were previously used with `new`. If you use a pointer with `delete` that does not reference dynamically allocated memory, unexpected problems could result!

Program 9-14 demonstrates the use of `new` and `delete`. It asks for sales figures for any number of days. The figures are stored in a dynamically allocated array, and then totaled and averaged.

 Appendix G discusses garbage collection in .NET. You can download Appendix G from the book's companion Web site at www.pearsonhighered.com/gaddis.

Program 9-14

```
 1  // This program totals and averages the sales figures for any
 2  // number of days. The figures are stored in a dynamically
 3  // allocated array.
 4  #include <iostream>
 5  #include <iomanip>
 6  using namespace std;
 7
 8  int main()
 9  {
10     double *sales,     // To dynamically allocate an array
11            total = 0.0, // Accumulator
12            average;     // To hold average sales
```

```
13      int numDays,         // To hold the number of days of sales
14          count;           // Counter variable
15
16      // Get the number of days of sales.
17      cout << "How many days of sales figures do you wish ";
18      cout << "to process? ";
19      cin >> numDays;
20
21      // Dynamically allocate an array large enough to hold
22      // that many days of sales amounts.
23      sales = new double[numDays];
24
25      // Get the sales figures for each day.
26      cout << "Enter the sales figures below.\n";
27      for (count = 0; count < numDays; count++)
28      {
29          cout << "Day " << (count + 1) << ": ";
30          cin >> sales[count];
31      }
32
33      // Calculate the total sales
34      for (count = 0; count < numDays; count++)
35      {
36          total += sales[count];
37      }
38
39      // Calculate the average sales per day
40      average = total / numDays;
41
42      // Display the results
43      cout << fixed << showpoint << setprecision(2);
44      cout << "\n\nTotal Sales: $" << total << endl;
45      cout << "Average Sales: $" << average << endl;
46
47      // Free dynamically allocated memory
48      delete [] sales;
49      sales = 0;           // Make sales point to null.
50
51      return 0;
52  }
```

Program Output with Example Input Shown in Bold

```
How many days of sales figures do you wish to process? 5 [Enter]
Enter the sales figures below.
Day 1: 898.63 [Enter]
Day 2: 652.32 [Enter]
Day 3: 741.85 [Enter]
Day 4: 852.96 [Enter]
Day 5: 921.37 [Enter]

Total Sales: $4067.13
Average Sales: $813.43
```

The statement in line 23 dynamically allocates memory for an array of `doubles`, using the value in `numDays` as the number of elements. The `new` operator returns the starting address of the chunk of memory, which is assigned to the `sales` pointer variable. The `sales` variable is then used throughout the program to store the sales amounts in the array and perform the necessary calculations. In line 48 the `delete` operator is used to free the allocated memory.

Notice that in line 49 the value 0 is assigned to the `sales` pointer. It is a good practice to store 0 in a pointer variable after using `delete` on it. First, it prevents code from inadvertently using the pointer to access the area of memory that was freed. Second, it prevents errors from occurring if `delete` is accidentally called on the pointer again. The `delete` operator is designed to have no effect when used on a null pointer.

9.9 Focus on Software Engineering: Returning Pointers from Functions

CONCEPT: Functions can return pointers, but you must be sure the item the pointer references still exists.

Like any other data type, functions may return pointers. For example, the following function locates the null terminator that appears at the end of a string (such as a string literal) and returns a pointer to it.

```
char *findNull(char *str)
{
    char *ptr = str;

    while (*ptr != '\0')
        ptr++;
    return ptr;
}
```

The `char *` return type in the function header indicates the function returns a pointer to a `char`:

```
char *findNull(char *str)
```

When writing functions that return pointers, you should take care not to create elusive bugs. For instance, see if you can determine what's wrong with the following function.

```
string *getFullName()
{
    string fullName[3];
    cout << "Enter your first name: ";
    getline(cin, fullName[0]);
    cout << "Enter your middle name: ";
    getline(cin, fullName[1]);
    cout << "Enter your last name: ";
    getline(cin, fullName[2]);
    return fullName;
}
```

The problem, of course, is that the function returns a pointer to an array that no longer exists. Because the `fullName` array is defined locally, it is destroyed when the function terminates. Attempting to use the pointer will result in erroneous and unpredictable results.

You should return a pointer from a function only if it is

- A pointer to an item that was passed into the function as an argument
- A pointer to a dynamically allocated chunk of memory

For instance, the following function is acceptable:

```
string *getFullName(string fullName[])
{
    cout << "Enter your first name: ";
    getline(cin, fullName[0]);
    cout << "Enter your middle name: ";
    getline(cin, fullName[1]);
    cout << "Enter your last name: ";
    getline(cin, fullName[2]);
    return fullName;
}
```

This function accepts a pointer to the memory location where the user's input is to be stored. Because the pointer references a memory location that was valid prior to the function being called, it is safe to return a pointer to the same location. Here is another acceptable function:

```
string *getFullName()
{
    string *fullName;
    fullName = new string[3];

    cout << "Enter your first name: ";
    getline(cin, fullName[0]);
    cout << "Enter your middle name: ";
    getline(cin, fullName[1]);
    cout << "Enter your last name: ";
    getline(cin, fullName[2]);
    return fullName;
}
```

This function uses the new operator to allocate a section of memory. This memory will remain allocated until the delete operator is used or the program ends, so it's safe to return a pointer to it.

Program 9-15 shows another example. This program uses a function, getRandomNumbers, to get a pointer to an array of random numbers. The function accepts an integer argument that is the number of random numbers in the array. The function dynamically allocates an array, uses the system clock to seed the random number generator, populates the array with random values, and then returns a pointer to the array.

Program 9-15

```
1  // This program demonstrates a function that returns
2  // a pointer.
3  #include <iostream>
4  #include <cstdlib>    // For rand and srand
5  #include <ctime>      // For the time function
6  using namespace std;
7
```

(program continues)

Program 9-15   *(continued)*

```cpp
 8   // Function prototype
 9   int *getRandomNumbers(int);
10
11   int main()
12   {
13      int *numbers;  // To point to the numbers
14
15      // Get an array of five random numbers.
16      numbers = getRandomNumbers(5);
17
18      // Display the numbers.
19      for (int count = 0; count < 5; count++)
20         cout << numbers[count] << endl;
21
22      // Free the memory.
23      delete [] numbers;
24      numbers = 0;
25      return 0;
26   }
27
28   //**************************************************
29   // The getRandomNumbers function returns a pointer *
30   // to an array of random integers. The parameter   *
31   // indicates the number of numbers requested.      *
32   //**************************************************
33
34   int *getRandomNumbers(int num)
35   {
36      int *arr;    // Array to hold the numbers
37
38      // Return null if num is zero or negative.
39      if (num <= 0)
40         return NULL;
41
42      // Dynamically allocate the array.
43      arr = new int[num];
44
45      // Seed the random number generator by passing
46      // the return value of time(0) to srand.
47      srand( time(0) );
48
49      // Populate the array with random numbers.
50      for (int count = 0; count < num; count++)
51         arr[count] = rand();
52
53      // Return a pointer to the array.
54      return arr;
55   }
```

Program Output

```
2712
9656
24493
12483
7633
```

In the Spotlight

Suppose you are developing a program that works with arrays of integers, and you find that you frequently need to duplicate the arrays. Rather than rewriting the array-duplicating code each time you need it, you decide to write a function that accepts an array and its size as arguments, creates a new array that is a copy of the argument array, and returns a pointer to the new array. The function will work as follows:

Accept an array and its size as arguments.
Dynamically allocate a new array that is the same size as the argument array.
Copy the elements of the argument array to the new array.
Return a pointer to the new array.

Program 9-16 demonstrates the function, which is named `duplicateArray`.

Program 9-16

```
 1   // This program uses a function to duplicate
 2   // an int array of any size.
 3   #include <iostream>
 4   using namespace std;
 5
 6   // Function prototype
 7   int *duplicateArray(const int *, int);
 8   void displayArray(const int[], int);
 9
10   int main()
11   {
12      // Define constants for the array sizes.
13      const int SIZE1 = 5, SIZE2 = 7, SIZE3 = 10;
14
15      // Define three arrays of different sizes.
16      int array1[SIZE1] = { 100, 200, 300, 400, 500 };
17      int array2[SIZE2] = { 10, 20, 30, 40, 50, 60, 70 };
18      int array3[SIZE3] = { 1, 2, 3, 4, 5, 6, 7, 8, 9, 10 };
19
20      // Define three pointers for the duplicate arrays.
21      int *dup1, *dup2, *dup3;
22
23      // Duplicate the arrays.
24      dup1 = duplicateArray(array1, SIZE1);
25      dup2 = duplicateArray(array2, SIZE2);
26      dup3 = duplicateArray(array3, SIZE3);
27
28      // Display the original arrays.
29      cout << "Here are the original array contents:\n";
30      displayArray(array1, SIZE1);
31      displayArray(array2, SIZE2);
32      displayArray(array3, SIZE3);
33
34      // Display the new arrays.
```

(program continues)

Program 9-16   *(continued)*

```
35      cout << "\nHere are the duplicate arrays:\n";
36      displayArray(dup1, SIZE1);
37      displayArray(dup2, SIZE2);
38      displayArray(dup3, SIZE3);
39
40      // Free the dynamically allocated memory and
41      // set the pointers to 0.
42      delete [] dup1;
43      delete [] dup2;
44      delete [] dup3;
45      dup1 = 0;
46      dup2 = 0;
47      dup3 = 0;
48      return 0;
49   }
50   //*********************************************************
51   // The duplicateArray function accepts an int array    *
52   // and an int that indicates the array's size. The     *
53   // function creates a new array that is a duplicate     *
54   // of the argument array and returns a pointer to the  *
55   // new array. If an invalid size is passed the          *
56   // function returns null.                               *
57   //*********************************************************
58
59   int *duplicateArray(const int *arr, int size)
60   {
61     int *newArray;
62
63     // Validate the size. If 0 or a negative
64     // number was passed, return null.
65     if (size <= 0)
66        return NULL;
67
68     // Allocate a new array.
69     newArray = new int[size];
70
71     // Copy the array's contents to the
72     // new array.
73     for (int index = 0; index < size; index++)
74        newArray[index] = arr[index];
75
76     // Return a pointer to the new array.
77     return newArray;
78   }
79
80   //*********************************************************
81   // The displayArray function accepts an int array   *
82   // and its size as arguments and displays the       *
83   // contents of the array.                           *
84   //*********************************************************
85
86   void displayArray(const int arr[], int size)
```

```
87  {
88    for (int index = 0; index < size; index++)
89       cout << arr[index] << " ";
90    cout << endl;
91  }
```

Program Output

```
Here are the original array contents:
100 200 300 400 500
10 20 30 40 50 60 70
1 2 3 4 5 6 7 8 9 10

Here are the duplicate arrays:
100 200 300 400 500
10 20 30 40 50 60 70
1 2 3 4 5 6 7 8 9 10
```

The `duplicateArray` function appears in lines 59 through 78. The `if` statement in lines 65 through 66 validates that `size` contains a valid array size. If `size` is 0 or less, the function immediately returns `NULL` to indicate that an invalid size was passed.

Line 69 allocates a new array and assigns its address to the `newArray` pointer. Then the loop in lines 73 through 74 copies the elements of the `arr` parameter to the new array. Then the `return` statement in line 77 returns a pointer to the new array.

 Checkpoint

myprogramminglab *www.myprogramminglab.com*

9.9   Assuming `arr` is an array of `int`s, will each of the following program segments display "True" or "False"?

A) `if (arr < &arr[1])`
      `cout << "True";`
   `else`
      `cout << "False";`

B) `if (&arr[4] < &arr[1])`
      `cout << "True";`
   `else`
      `cout << "False";`

C) `if (arr != &arr[2])`
      `cout << "True";`
   `else`
      `cout << "False";`

D) `if (arr != &arr[0])`
      `cout << "True";`
   `else`
      `cout << "False";`

9.10   Give an example of the proper way to call the following function:

```
void makeNegative(int *val)
{
    if (*val > 0)
```

```
                        *val = -(*val);
                }
```

9.11   Complete the following program skeleton. When finished, the program will ask
        the user for a length (in inches), convert that value to centimeters, and display the
        result. You are to write the function convert. (*Note:* 1 inch = 2.54 cm. Do not
        modify function main.)

```
#include <iostream>
#include <iomanip>
using namespace std;

// Write your function prototype here.

int main()
{
    double measurement;

    cout << "Enter a length in inches, and I will convert\n";
    cout << "it to centimeters: ";
    cin >> measurement;
    convert(&measurement);
    cout << fixed << setprecision(4);
    cout << "Value in centimeters: " << measurement << endl;
    return 0;
}
//
// Write the function convert here.
//
```

9.12   Look at the following array definition:

```
const int numbers[SIZE] = { 18, 17, 12, 14 };
```

Suppose we want to pass the array to the function processArray in the following manner:

```
processArray(numbers, SIZE);
```

Which of the following function headers is the correct one for the processArray
function?

A) void processArray(const int *arr, int size)

B) void processArray(int * const arr, int size)

9.13   Assume ip is a pointer to an int. Write a statement that will dynamically allocate
        an integer variable and store its address in ip. Write a statement that will free the
        memory allocated in the statement you wrote above.

9.14   Assume ip is a pointer to an int. Then, write a statement that will dynamically
        allocate an array of 500 integers and store its address in ip. Write a statement
        that will free the memory allocated in the statement you just wrote.

9.15   What is a null pointer?

9.16   Give an example of a function that correctly returns a pointer.

9.17   Give an example of a function that incorrectly returns a pointer.

Focus on Problem Solving and Program Design: A Case Study

9.10

CONCEPT: This case study demonstrates how an array of pointers can be used to display the contents of a second array in sorted order, without sorting the **second** array.

The United Cause, a charitable relief agency, solicits donations from businesses. The local United Cause office received the following donations from the employees of CK Graphics, Inc.:

$5, $100, $5, $25, $10, $5, $25, $5, $5, $100, $10, $15, $10, $5, $10

The donations were received in the order they appear. The United Cause manager has asked you to write a program that displays the donations in ascending order, as well as in their original order.

Variables

Table 9-1 shows the major variables needed.

Table 9-1

Variable	Description
NUM_DONATIONS	A constant integer initialized with the number of donations received from CK Graphics, Inc. This value will be used in the definition of the program's arrays.
donations	An array of integers containing the donation amounts.
arrPtr	An array of pointers to integers. This array has the same number of elements as the donations array. Each element of arrPtr will be initialized to point to an element of the donations array.

Programming Strategy

In this program the donations array will contain the donations in the order they were received. The elements of the arrPtr array are pointers to integers. They will point to the elements of the donations array, as illustrated in Figure 9-12.

Figure 9-12

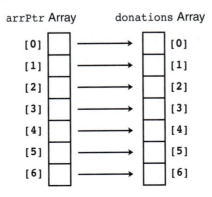

The `arrPtr` array will initially be set up to point to the elements of the `donations` array in their natural order. In other words, `arrPtr[0]` will point to `donations[0]`, `arrPtr[1]` will point to `donations[1]`, and so forth. In that arrangement, the following statement would cause the contents of `donations[5]` to be displayed:

```
cout << *(arrPtr[5]) << endl;
```

After the `arrPtr` array is sorted, however, `arrPtr[0]` will point to the smallest element of `donations`, `arrPtr[1]` will point to the next-to-smallest element of `donations`, and so forth. This is illustrated in Figure 9-13.

Figure 9-13

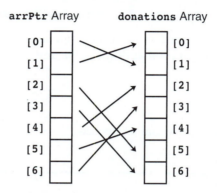

This technique gives us access to the elements of the `donations` array in a sorted order without actually disturbing the contents of the `donations` array itself.

Modules

The program will consist of the functions listed in Table 9-2.

Table 9-2

Function	Description
main	The program's main function. It calls the program's other functions.
arrSelectSort	Performs an ascending order selection sort on its parameter, `arr`, which is an array of pointers. Each element of `arr` points to an element of a second array. After the sort, `arr` will point to the elements of the second array in ascending order.
showArray	Displays the contents of its parameter, `arr`, which is an array of integers. This function is used to display the donations in their original order.
showArrPtr	Accepts an array of pointers to integers as an argument. Displays the contents of what each element of the array points to. This function is used to display the contents of the `donations` array in sorted order.

Function `main`

In addition to containing the variable definitions, function `main` sets up the `arrPtr` array to point to the elements of the `donations` array. Then the function `arrSelectSort` is called to sort the elements of `arrPtr`. Last, the functions `showArrPtr` and `showArray` are called to display the donations. Here is the pseudocode for `main`'s executable statements:

```
For count is set to the values 0 through the number of donations
    Set arrPtr[count] to the address of donations[count].
End For
Call arrSelectSort.
Call showArrPtr.
Call showArray.
```

The `arrSelectSort` Function

The `arrSelectSort` function is a modified version of the selection sort algorithm shown in Chapter 8. The only difference is that `arr` is now an array of pointers. Instead of sorting on the contents of `arr`'s elements, `arr` is sorted on the contents of what its elements point to. Here is the pseudocode:

```
For startScan is set to the values 0 up to (but not including) the
          next-to-last subscript in arr
    Set index variable to startScan.
    Set minIndex variable to startScan.
    Set minElem pointer to arr[startScan].
    For index variable is set to the values from (startScan + 1) through
                 the last subscript in arr
        If *(arr[index]) is less than *minElem
            Set minElem to arr[index].
            Set minIndex to index.
        End If.
    End For.
    Set arr[minIndex] to arr[startScan].
    Set arr[startScan] to minElem.
End For.
```

The `showArrPtr` Function

The `showArrPtr` function accepts an array of pointers as its argument. It displays the values pointed to by the elements of the array. Here is its pseudocode:

```
For every element in the arr
    Dereference the element and display what it points to.
End For.
```

The `showArray` Function

The `showArray` function simply displays the contents of `arr` sequentially. Here is its pseudocode:

```
For every element in arr
    Display the element's contents
End For.
```

The Entire Program

Program 9-17 shows the entire program's source code.

Program 9-17

```
 1  // This program shows the donations made to the United Cause
 2  // by the employees of CK Graphics, Inc. It displays
 3  // the donations in order from lowest to highest
 4  // and in the original order they were received.
 5  #include <iostream>
 6  using namespace std;
 7
 8  // Function prototypes
 9  void arrSelectSort(int *[], int);
10  void showArray(const int [], int);
11  void showArrPtr(int *[], int);
12
13  int main()
14  {
15     const int NUM_DONATIONS = 15;   // Number of donations
16
17     // An array containing the donation amounts.
18     int donations[NUM_DONATIONS] = {5,   100, 5,   25, 10,
19                                     5,   25,  5,   5,  100,
20                                     10,  15,  10,  5,  10 };
21
22     // An array of pointers to int.
23     int *arrPtr[NUM_DONATIONS];
24
25     // Each element of arrPtr is a pointer to int. Make each
26     // element point to an element in the donations array.
27     for (int count = 0; count < NUM_DONATIONS; count++)
28        arrPtr[count] = &donations[count];
29
30     // Sort the elements of the array of pointers.
31     arrSelectSort(arrPtr, NUM_DONATIONS);
32
33     // Display the donations using the array of pointers. This
34     // will display them in sorted order.
35     cout << "The donations, sorted in ascending order, are: \n";
36     showArrPtr(arrPtr, NUM_DONATIONS);
37
38     // Display the donations in their original order.
39     cout << "The donations, in their original order, are: \n";
40     showArray(donations, NUM_DONATIONS);
41     return 0;
42  }
43
```

```
44  //*****************************************************************
45  // Definition of function arrSelectSort.                         *
46  // This function performs an ascending order selection sort on   *
47  // arr, which is an array of pointers. Each element of arr       *
48  // points to an element of a second array. After the sort,       *
49  // arr will point to the elements of the second array in         *
50  // ascending order.                                              *
51  //*****************************************************************
52
53  void arrSelectSort(int *arr[], int size)
54  {
55     int startScan, minIndex;
56     int *minElem;
57
58     for (startScan = 0; startScan < (size - 1); startScan++)
59     {
60        minIndex = startScan;
61        minElem = arr[startScan];
62        for(int index = startScan + 1; index < size; index++)
63        {
64           if (*(arr[index]) < *minElem)
65           {
66              minElem = arr[index];
67              minIndex = index;
68           }
69        }
70        arr[minIndex] = arr[startScan];
71        arr[startScan] = minElem;
72     }
73  }
74
75  //*****************************************************************
76  // Definition of function showArray.                             *
77  // This function displays the contents of arr. size is the       *
78  // number of elements.                                           *
79  //*****************************************************************
80
81  void showArray(const int arr[], int size)
82  {
83     for (int count = 0; count < size; count++)
84        cout << arr[count] << " ";
85     cout << endl;
86  }
87
88  //*****************************************************************
89  // Definition of function showArrPtr.                            *
90  // This function displays the contents of the array pointed to   *
91  // by arr. size is the number of elements.                       *
92  //*****************************************************************
93
94  void showArrPtr(int *arr[], int size)
95  {
96     for (int count = 0; count < size; count++)
```

(program continues)

Program 9-17 *(continued)*

```
97          cout << *(arr[count]) << " ";
98      cout << endl;
99 }
```

Program Output
```
The donations, sorted in ascending order, are:
5 5 5 5 5 5 10 10 10 10 15 25 25 100 100
The donations, in their original order, are:
5 100 5 25 10 5 25 5 5 100 10 15 10 5 10
```

Review Questions and Exercises

Short Answer

1. What does the indirection operator do?

2. Look at the following code.

   ```
   int x = 7;
   int *iptr = &x;
   ```

   What will be displayed if you send the expression *iptr to cout? What happens if you send the expression ptr to cout?

3. So far you have learned three different uses for the * operator. What are they?

4. What math operations are allowed on pointers?

5. Assuming that ptr is a pointer to an int, what happens when you add 4 to ptr?

6. Look at the following array definition.

   ```
   int numbers[] = { 2, 4, 6, 8, 10 };
   ```

   What will the following statement display?

   ```
   cout << *(numbers + 3) << endl;
   ```

7. What is the purpose of the new operator?

8. What happens when a program uses the new operator to allocate a block of memory, but the amount of requested memory isn't available? How do programs written with older compilers handle this?

9. What is the purpose of the delete operator?

10. Under what circumstances can you successfully return a pointer from a function?

11. What is the difference between a pointer to a constant and a constant pointer?

12. What are two advantages of declaring a pointer parameter as a constant pointer?

Fill-in-the-Blank

13. Each byte in memory is assigned a unique _____.

14. The _____ operator can be used to determine a variable's address.

15. _____ variables are designed to hold addresses.

16. The _____ operator can be used to work with the variable a pointer points to.

17. Array names can be used as _____, and vice versa.

18. Creating variables while a program is running is called _____.

19. The _____ operator is used to dynamically allocate memory.

20. Under older compilers, if the new operator cannot allocate the amount of memory requested, it returns _____.

21. A pointer that contains the address 0 is called a(n) _____ pointer.

22. When a program is finished with a chunk of dynamically allocated memory, it should free it with the _____ operator.

23. You should only use pointers with delete that were previously used with _____.

Algorithm Workbench

24. Look at the following code.

```
double value = 29.7;
double *ptr = &value;
```

Write a cout statement that uses the ptr variable to display the contents of the value variable.

25. Look at the following array definition.

```
int set[10];
```

Write a statement using pointer notation that stores the value 99 in set[7];

26. Write code that dynamically allocates an array of 20 integers, then uses a loop to allow the user to enter values for each element of the array.

27. Assume that tempNumbers is a pointer that points to a dynamically allocated array. Write code that releases the memory used by the array.

28. Look at the following function definition.

```
void getNumber(int &n)
{
    cout << "Enter a number: ";
    cin >> n;
}
```

In this function, the parameter n is a reference variable. Rewrite the function so that n is a pointer.

29. Write the definition of ptr, a pointer to a constant int.

30. Write the definition of ptr, a constant pointer to an int.

True or False

31. T   F   Each byte of memory is assigned a unique address.

32. T   F   The * operator is used to get the address of a variable.

33. T   F   Pointer variables are designed to hold addresses.

34. T   F   The & symbol is called the indirection operator.

35. T   F   The & operator dereferences a pointer.

36. T   F   When the indirection operator is used with a pointer variable, you are actually working with the value the pointer is pointing to.

37. T   F   Array names cannot be dereferenced with the indirection operator.

38. T   F   When you add a value to a pointer, you are actually adding that number times the size of the data type referenced by the pointer.

39. T   F   The address operator is not needed to assign an array's address to a pointer.

40. T   F   You can change the address that an array name points to.

41. T   F   Any mathematical operation, including multiplication and division, may be performed on a pointer.

42. T   F   Pointers may be compared using the relational operators.

43. T   F   When used as function parameters, reference variables are much easier to work with than pointers.

44. T   F   The new operator dynamically allocates memory.

45. T   F   A pointer variable that has not been initialized is called a null pointer.

46. T   F   The address 0 is generally considered unusable.

47. T   F   In using a pointer with the delete operator, it is not necessary for the pointer to have been previously used with the new operator.

Find the Error

Each of the following definitions and program segments has errors. Locate as many as you can.

48. ```
int ptr*;
```

49. ```
int x, *ptr;
&x = ptr;
```

50. ```
int x, *ptr;
*ptr = &x;
```

51. ```
int x, *ptr;
ptr = &x;
ptr = 100; // Store 100 in x
cout << x << endl;
```

52. ```
int numbers[] = {10, 20, 30, 40, 50};
cout << "The third element in the array is ";
cout << *numbers + 3 << endl;
```

53. ```
int values[20], *iptr;
iptr = values;
iptr *= 2;
```

54. ```
float level;
int fptr = &level;
```

55. ```
int *iptr = &ivalue;
int ivalue;
```

56. ```
void doubleVal(int val)
{
    *val *= 2;
}
```
```

57. ```cpp
    int *pint;
    new pint;
    ```

58. ```cpp
    int *pint;
    pint = new int;
    if (pint == NULL)
       *pint = 100;
    else
       cout << "Memory allocation error\n";
    ```

59. ```cpp
    int *pint;
    pint = new int[100]; // Allocate memory
       .
       .
    ```
    Code that processes the array.
    ```cpp
       .
       .
    delete pint;    // Free memory
    ```

60. ```cpp
    int *getNum()
    {
        int wholeNum;

        cout << "Enter a number: ";
        cin >> wholeNum;
        return &wholeNum;
    }
    ```

61. ```cpp
    const int arr[] = { 1, 2, 3 };
    int *ptr = arr;
    ```

62. ```cpp
    void doSomething(int * const ptr)
    {
        int localArray[] = { 1, 2, 3 };
        ptr = localArray;
    }
    ```

Programming Challenges

Visit www.myprogramminglab.com to complete many of these Programming Challenges online and get instant feedback.

1. **Array Allocator**

    Write a function that dynamically allocates an array of integers. The function should accept an integer argument indicating the number of elements to allocate. The function should return a pointer to the array.

2. **Test Scores #1**

    Write a program that dynamically allocates an array large enough to hold a user-defined number of test scores. Once all the scores are entered, the array should be passed to a function that sorts them in ascending order. Another function should be called that calculates the average score. The program should display the sorted list of scores and averages with appropriate headings. Use pointer notation rather than array notation whenever possible.

    Input Validation: Do not accept negative numbers for test scores.

3. Drop Lowest Score

Modify Problem 2 above so the lowest test score is dropped. This score should not be included in the calculation of the average.

4. Test Scores #2

Modify the program of Programming Challenge 2 to allow the user to enter name-score pairs. For each student taking a test, the user types the student's name followed by the student's integer test score. Modify the sorting function so it takes an array holding the student names and an array holding the student test scores. When the sorted list of scores is displayed, each student's name should be displayed along with his or her score. In stepping through the arrays, use pointers rather than array subscripts.

5. Pointer Rewrite

VideoNote

Solving the Pointer Rewrite Problem

The following function uses reference variables as parameters. Rewrite the function so it uses pointers instead of reference variables, and then demonstrate the function in a complete program.

```
int doSomething(int &x, int &y)
{
    int temp = x;
    x = y * 10;
    y = temp * 10;
    return x + y;

}
```

6. Case Study Modification #1

Modify Program 9-17 (the United Cause case study program) so it can be used with any set of donations. The program should dynamically allocate the `donations` array and ask the user to input its values.

7. Case Study Modification #2

Modify Program 9-17 (the United Cause case study program) so the `arrptr` array is sorted in descending order instead of ascending order.

8. Mode Function

In statistics, the *mode* of a set of values is the value that occurs most often or with the greatest frequency. Write a function that accepts as arguments the following:

A) An array of integers

B) An integer that indicates the number of elements in the array

The function should determine the mode of the array. That is, it should determine which value in the array occurs most often. The mode is the value the function should return. If the array has no mode (none of the values occur more than once), the function should return -1. (Assume the array will always contain nonnegative values.)

Demonstrate your pointer prowess by using pointer notation instead of array notation in this function.

9. Median Function

In statistics, when a set of values is sorted in ascending or descending order, its *median* is the middle value. If the set contains an even number of values, the median is the mean, or average, of the two middle values. Write a function that accepts as arguments the following:

A) An array of integers

B) An integer that indicates the number of elements in the array

The function should determine the median of the array. This value should be returned as a `double`. (Assume the values in the array are already sorted.)

Demonstrate your pointer prowess by using pointer notation instead of array notation in this function.

10. **Reverse Array**

Write a function that accepts an `int` array and the array's size as arguments. The function should create a copy of the array, except that the element values should be reversed in the copy. The function should return a pointer to the new array. Demonstrate the function in a complete program.

11. **Array Expander**

Write a function that accepts an `int` array and the array's size as arguments. The function should create a new array that is twice the size of the argument array. The function should copy the contents of the argument array to the new array, and initialize the unused elements of the second array with 0. The function should return a pointer to the new array.

12. **Element Shifter**

Write a function that accepts an `int` array and the array's size as arguments. The function should create a new array that is one element larger than the argument array. The first element of the new array should be set to 0. Element 0 of the argument array should be copied to element 1 of the new array, element 1 of the argument array should be copied to element 2 of the new array, and so forth. The function should return a pointer to the new array.

13. **Movie Statistics**

Write a program that can be used to gather statistical data about the number of movies college students see in a month. The program should perform the following steps:

A) Ask the user how many students were surveyed. An array of integers with this many elements should then be dynamically allocated.

B) Allow the user to enter the number of movies each student saw into the array.

C) Calculate and display the average, median, and mode of the values entered. (Use the functions you wrote in Problems 8 and 9 to calculate the median and mode.)

Input Validation: Do not accept negative numbers for input.

10 Characters, C-Strings, and More About the **string** Class

TOPICS

10.1 Character Testing

> **CONCEPT:** The C++ library provides several functions for testing characters. To use these functions you must include the **cctype** header file.

The C++ library provides several functions that allow you to test the value of a character. These functions test a single char argument and return either true or false.* For example, the following program segment uses the isupper function to determine whether the character passed as an argument is an uppercase letter. If it is, the function returns true. Otherwise, it returns false.

```
char letter = 'a';
if (isupper(letter))
    cout << "Letter is uppercase.\n";
else
    cout << "Letter is lowercase.\n";
```

---

* These functions actually return an int value. The return value is nonzero to indicate true, or zero to indicate false.

541

Because the variable `letter`, in this example, contains a lowercase character, `isupper` returns `false`. The `if` statement will cause the message "Letter is lowercase" to be displayed.

Table 10-1 lists several character-testing functions. Each of these is prototyped in the `cctype` header file, so be sure to include that file when using the functions.

Table 10-1

Character Function	Description
`isalpha`	Returns true (a nonzero number) if the argument is a letter of the alphabet. Returns 0 if the argument is not a letter.
`isalnum`	Returns true (a nonzero number) if the argument is a letter of the alphabet or a digit. Otherwise it returns 0.
`isdigit`	Returns true (a nonzero number) if the argument is a digit from 0 through 9. Otherwise it returns 0.
`islower`	Returns true (a nonzero number) if the argument is a lowercase letter. Otherwise, it returns 0.
`isprint`	Returns true (a nonzero number) if the argument is a printable character (including a space). Returns 0 otherwise.
`ispunct`	Returns true (a nonzero number) if the argument is a printable character other than a digit, letter, or space. Returns 0 otherwise.
`isupper`	Returns true (a nonzero number) if the argument is an uppercase letter. Otherwise, it returns 0.
`isspace`	Returns true (a nonzero number) if the argument is a whitespace character. Whitespace characters are any of the following: space ' ' vertical tab '\v' newline '\n' tab '\t' Otherwise, it returns 0.

Program 10-1 uses several of the functions shown in Table 10-1. It asks the user to input a character and then displays various messages, depending upon the return value of each function.

Program 10-1

```
1   // This program demonstrates some character-testing functions.
2   #include <iostream>
3   #include <cctype>
4   using namespace std;
5
6   int main()
7   {
8       char input;
9
```

```
10      cout << "Enter any character: ";
11      cin.get(input);
12      cout << "The character you entered is: " << input << endl;
13      if (isalpha(input))
14         cout << "That's an alphabetic character.\n";
15      if (isdigit(input))
16         cout << "That's a numeric digit.\n";
17      if (islower(input))
18         cout << "The letter you entered is lowercase.\n";
19      if (isupper(input))
20         cout << "The letter you entered is uppercase.\n";
21      if (isspace(input))
22         cout << "That's a whitespace character.\n";
23      return 0;
24   }
```

Program Output with Example Input Shown in Bold
```
Enter any character: A [Enter]
The character you entered is: A
That's an alphabetic character.
The letter you entered is uppercase.
```

Program Output with Different Example Input Shown in Bold
```
Enter any character: 7 [Enter]
The character you entered is: 7
That's a numeric digit.
```

Program 10-2 shows a more practical application of the character testing functions. It tests a seven-character customer number to determine whether it is in the proper format.

Program 10-2

```
1   // This program tests a customer number to determine whether
2   // it is in the proper format.
3   #include <iostream>
4   #include <cctype>
5   using namespace std;
6
7   // Function prototype
8   bool testNum(char [], int);
9
10  int main()
11  {
12     const int SIZE = 8;   // Array size
13     char customer[SIZE];  // To hold a customer number
14
15     // Get the customer number.
16     cout << "Enter a customer number in the form ";
17     cout << "LLLNNNN\n";
18     cout << "(LLL = letters and NNNN = numbers): ";
19     cin.getline(customer, SIZE);
```

(program continues)

Program 10-2 *(continued)*

```
20
21      // Determine whether it is valid.
22      if (testNum(customer, SIZE))
23         cout << "That's a valid customer number.\n";
24      else
25      {
26         cout << "That is not the proper format of the ";
27         cout << "customer number.\nHere is an example:\n";
28         cout << "    ABC1234\n";
29      }
30      return 0;
31   }
32
33   //************************************************************
34   // Definition of function testNum.                          *
35   // This function determines whether the custNum parameter    *
36   // holds a valid customer number. The size parameter is      *
37   // the size of the custNum array.                            *
38   //************************************************************
39
40   bool testNum(char custNum[], int size)
41   {
42      int count;   // Loop counter
43
44      // Test the first three characters for alphabetic letters.
45      for (count = 0; count < 3; count++)
46      {
47         if (!isalpha(custNum[count]))
48            return false;
49      }
50
51      // Test the remaining characters for numeric digits.
52      for (count = 3; count < size - 1; count++)
53      {
54         if (!isdigit(custNum[count]))
55            return false;
56      }
57      return true;
58   }
```

Program Output with Example Input Shown in Bold
```
Enter a customer number in the form LLLNNNN
(LLL = letters and NNNN = numbers): RQS4567 [Enter]
That's a valid customer number.
```

Program Output with Different Example Input Shown in Bold
```
Enter a customer number in the form LLLNNNN
(LLL = letters and NNNN = numbers): AX467T9 [Enter]
That is not the proper format of the customer number.
Here is an example:
   ABC1234
```

In this program, the customer number is expected to consist of three alphabetic letters followed by four numeric digits. The testNum function accepts an array argument and tests the first three characters with the following loop in lines 45 through 49:

```
for (count = 0; count < 3; count++)
{
   if (!isalpha(custNum[count]))
      return false;
}
```

The isalpha function returns true if its argument is an alphabetic character. The ! operator is used in the if statement to determine whether the tested character is NOT alphabetic. If this is so for any of the first three characters, the function testNum returns false. Likewise, the next four characters are tested to determine whether they are numeric digits with the following loop in lines 52 through 56:

```
for (count = 3; count < size - 1; count++)
{
   if (!isdigit(custNum[count]))
      return false;
}
```

The isdigit function returns true if its argument is the character representation of any of the digits 0 through 9. Once again, the ! operator is used to determine whether the tested character is *not* a digit. If this is so for any of the last four characters, the function testNum returns false. If the customer number is in the proper format, the function will cycle through both the loops without returning false. In that case, the last line in the function is the return true statement, which indicates the customer number is valid.

10.2 Character Case Conversion

CONCEPT: The C++ library offers functions for converting a character to upper- or lowercase.

The C++ library provides two functions, toupper and tolower, for converting the case of a character. The functions are described in Table 10-2. (These functions are prototyped in the header file cctype, so be sure to include it.)

Table 10-2

Function	Description
toupper	Returns the uppercase equivalent of its argument.
tolower	Returns the lowercase equivalent of its argument.

Each of the functions in Table 10-2 accepts a single character argument. If the argument is a lowercase letter, the toupper function returns its uppercase equivalent. For example, the following statement will display the character A on the screen:

```
cout << toupper('a');
```

If the argument is already an uppercase letter, `toupper` returns it unchanged. The following statement causes the character `Z` to be displayed:

```
cout << toupper('Z');
```

Any nonletter argument passed to `toupper` is returned as it is. Each of the following statements display `toupper`'s argument without any change:

```
cout << toupper('*');    // Displays *
cout << toupper ('&');   // Displays &
cout << toupper('%');    // Displays %
```

`toupper` and `tolower` don't actually cause the character argument to change, they simply return the upper- or lowercase equivalent of the argument. For example, in the following program segment, the variable `letter` is set to the value 'A'. The `tolower` function returns the character 'a', but `letter` still contains 'A'.

```
char letter = 'A';
cout << tolower(letter) << endl;
cout << letter << endl;
```

These statements will cause the following to be displayed:

```
a
A
```

Program 10-3 demonstrates the `toupper` function in an input validation loop.

Program 10-3

```
 1  // This program calculates the area of a circle. It asks the user
 2  // if he or she wishes to continue. A loop that demonstrates the
 3  // toupper function repeats until the user enters 'y', 'Y',
 4  // 'n', or 'N'.
 5  #include <iostream>
 6  #include <cctype>
 7  #include <iomanip>
 8  using namespace std;
 9
10  int main()
11  {
12      const double PI = 3.14159;  // Constant for pi
13      double radius;              // The circle's radius
14      char goAgain;               // To hold Y or N
15
16      cout << "This program calculates the area of a circle.\n";
17      cout << fixed << setprecision(2);
18
19      do
20      {
21          // Get the radius and display the area.
22          cout << "Enter the circle's radius: ";
23          cin >> radius;
24          cout << "The area is " << (PI * radius * radius);
25          cout << endl;
```

```
26
27              // Does the user want to do this again?
28              cout << "Calculate another? (Y or N) ";
29              cin >> goAgain;
30
31              // Validate the input.
32              while (toupper(goAgain) != 'Y' && toupper(goAgain) != 'N')
33              {
34                  cout << "Please enter Y or N: ";
35                  cin >> goAgain;
36              }
37
38      } while (toupper(goAgain) == 'Y');
39      return 0;
40  }
```

Program Output with Example Input Shown in Bold
```
This program calculates the area of a circle.
Enter the circle's radius: 10 [Enter]
The area is 314.16
Calculate another? (Y or N) b Enter]
Please enter Y or N: y [Enter]
Enter the circle's radius: 1 [Enter]
The area is 3.14
Calculate another? (Y or N) n [Enter]
```

In lines 28 and 29 the user is prompted to enter either Y or N to indicate whether he or she wants to calculate another area. We don't want the program to be so picky that it accepts only uppercase Y or uppercase N. Lowercase y or lowercase n are also acceptable. The input validation loop must be written so to reject anything except 'Y', 'y', 'N', or 'n'. One way to do this would be to test the goAgain variable in four relational expressions, as shown here:

```
while (goAgain != 'Y' && goAgain != 'y' &&
       goAgain != 'N' && goAgain != 'N')
```

Although there is nothing wrong with this code, we could use the toupper function to get the uppercase equivalent of goAgain, and make only two comparisons. This is the approach taken in line 32:

```
while (toupper(goAgain) != 'Y' && toupper(goAgain) != 'N')
```

Another approach would have been to use the tolower function to get the lowercase equivalent of goAgain. Here is an example:

```
while (tolower(goAgain) != 'y' && tolower(goAgain) != 'n')
```

Either approach will yield the same results.

Checkpoint

myprogramminglab   *www.myprogramminglab.com*

10.1   Write a short description of each of the following functions:

```
isalpha
isalnum
isdigit
islower
isprint
ispunct
isupper
isspace
toupper
tolower
```

10.2   Write a statement that will convert the contents of the `char` variable `big` to lowercase. The converted value should be assigned to the variable `little`.

10.3   Write an `if` statement that will display the word "digit" if the variable `ch` contains a numeric digit. Otherwise, it should display "Not a digit."

10.4   What is the output of the following statement?

```
cout << toupper(tolower('A'));
```

10.5   Write a loop that asks the user `"Do you want to repeat the program or quit? (R/Q)"`. The loop should repeat until the user has entered an R or Q (either uppercase or lowercase).

10.3   C-Strings

CONCEPT: In C++, a C-string is a sequence of characters stored in consecutive memory locations, terminated by a null character.

String is a generic term that describes any consecutive sequence of characters. A word, a sentence, a person's name, and the title of a song are all strings. In the C++ language, there are two primary ways that strings are stored in memory: as `string` objects, or as C-strings. You have already been introduced to the `string` class, and by now, you have written several programs that use `string` objects. In this section, we will use C-strings, which are an alternative method for storing and working with strings.

A *C-string* is a string whose characters are stored in consecutive memory locations, and are followed by a null character, or null terminator. Recall from Chapter 2 that a null character or null terminator is a byte holding the ASCII code 0. Strings that are stored this way are called C-strings because this is the way strings are handled in the C programming language.

In C++, all string literals are stored in memory as C-strings. Recall that a string literal (or string constant) is the literal representation of a string in a program. In C++, string literals are enclosed in double quotation marks, such as:

```
"Bailey"
```

Figure 10-1 illustrates how the string literal `"Bailey"` is stored in memory, as a C-string.

Figure 10-1

| B | a | i | l | e | y | \0 |

NOTE: Remember that `\0` ("slash zero") is the escape sequence representing the null terminator. It stands for the ASCII code 0.

The purpose of the null terminator is to mark the end of the C-string. Without it, there would be no way for a program to know the length of a C-string.

More About String Literals

A string literal or string constant is enclosed in a set of double quotation marks (`" "`). For example, here are five string literals:

```
"Have a nice day."
"What is your name?"
"John Smith"
"Please enter your age:"
"Part Number 45Q1789"
```

All of a program's string literals are stored in memory as C-strings, with the null terminator automatically appended. For example, look at Program 10-4.

Program 10-4

```
 1   // This program contains string literals.
 2   #include <iostream>
 3   using namespace std;
 4
 5   int main()
 6   {
 7      char again;
 8
 9      do
10      {
11         cout << "C++ programming is great fun!" << endl;
12         cout << "Do you want to see the message again? ";
13         cin >> again;
14      } while (again == 'Y' || again == 'y');
15      return 0;
16   }
```

This program contains two string literals:

```
"C++ programming is great fun!"
"Do you want to see the message again? "
```

The first string occupies 30 bytes of memory (including the null terminator), and the second string occupies 39 bytes. They appear in memory in the following forms:

C	+	+		p	r	o	g	r	a	m	m	i	n	g		i	s		g	r	e	a	t		f	u	n	!	\0

D	o		y	o	u		w	a	n	t		t	o		s	e	e		t	h	e		m	e	s	s	a	g
e		a	g	a	i	n	?		\0																			

It's important to realize that a string literal has its own storage location, just like a variable or an array. When a string literal appears in a statement, it's actually its memory address that C++ uses. Look at the following example:

```
cout << "Do you want to see the message again? ";
```

In this statement, the memory address of the string literal "Do you want to see the message again? " is passed to the `cout` object. `cout` displays the consecutive characters found at this address. It stops displaying the characters when a null terminator is encountered.

C-Strings Stored in Arrays

The C programming language does not provide a `string` class like the one that C++ provides. In the C language, all strings are treated as C-strings. When a C programmer wants to store a string in memory, he or she has to create a `char` array that is large enough to hold the string, plus one extra element for the null character.

You might be wondering why this should matter to anyone learning C++. You need to know about C-strings for the following reasons:

- The `string` class has not always existed in the C++ language. Several years ago, C++ stored strings as C-strings. As a professional programmer, you might encounter older C++ code (known as *legacy code*) that uses C-strings.
- Some of the C++ library functions work only with C-strings. For example, when you use a file stream object to open a file, the `open` member function accepts a C-string argument for the filename.
- In the workplace, it is not unusual for C++ programmers to work with specialized libraries that are written in C. Any strings that C libraries work with will be C-strings.

As previously mentioned, if you want to store a C-string in memory, you have to define a `char` array that is large enough to hold the string, plus one extra element for the null character. Here is an example:

```
const int SIZE = 21;
char name[SIZE];
```

This code defines a `char` array that has 21 elements, so it is big enough to hold a C-string that is no more that 20 characters long.

You can initialize a `char` array with a string literal, as shown here:

```
const int SIZE = 21;
char name[SIZE] = "Jasmine";
```

After this code executes, the `name` array will be created with 21 elements. The first 8 elements will be initialized with the characters 'J', 'a', 's', 'm', 'i', 'n', 'e', and '\0'. The null character is automatically added as the last character. You can implicitly size a `char` array by initializing it with a string literal, as shown here:

```
char name[] = "Jasmine";
```

After this code executes, the `name` array will be created with 8 elements, initialized with the characters `'J'`, `'a'`, `'s'`, `'m'`, `'i'`, `'n'`, `'e'`, and `'\0'`.

C-string input can be performed by the `cin` object. For example, the following code allows the user to enter a string (with no whitespace characters) into the `name` array:

```
const int SIZE = 21;
char name[SIZE];
cin >> name;
```

Recall from Chapter 7 that an array name with no brackets and no subscript is converted into the beginning address of the array. In the previous statement, `name` indicates the address in memory where the string is to be stored. Of course, `cin` has no way of knowing that `name` has 21 elements. If the user enters a string of 30 characters, `cin` will write past the end of the array. This can be prevented by using `cin`'s `getline` member function. Assume the following array has been defined in a program:

```
const int SIZE = 80;
char line[SIZE];
```

The following statement uses `cin`'s `getline` member function to get a line of input (including whitespace characters) and store it in the `line` array:

```
cin.getline(line, SIZE);
```

The first argument tells `getline` where to store the string input. This statement indicates the starting address of the `line` array as the storage location for the string. The second argument indicates the maximum length of the string, including the null terminator. In this example, the `SIZE` constant is equal to 80, so `cin` will read 79 characters, or until the user presses the **[Enter]** key, whichever comes first. `cin` will automatically append the null terminator to the end of the string.

Once a string is stored in an array, it can be processed using standard subscript notation. For example, Program 10-5 displays a string stored in an array. It uses a loop to display each character in the array until the null terminator is encountered.

Program 10-5

```
 1   // This program displays a string stored in a char array.
 2   #include <iostream>
 3   using namespace std;
 4
 5   int main()
 6   {
 7      const int SIZE = 80;    // Array size
 8      char line[SIZE];        // To hold a line of input
 9      int count = 0;          // Loop counter variable
10
11      // Get a line of input.
12      cout << "Enter a sentence of no more than "
13           << (SIZE - 1) << " characters:\n";
14      cin.getline(line, SIZE);
15
```

(program continues)

Program 10-5   *(continued)*

```
16      // Display the input one character at a time.
17      cout << "The sentence you entered is:\n";
18      while (line[count] != '\0')
19      {
20         cout << line[count];
21         count++;
22      }
23      return 0;
24   }
```

Program Output with Example Input Shown in Bold

Enter a sentence of no more than 79 characters:
C++ is challenging but fun! [Enter]
The sentence you entered is:
C++ is challenging but fun!

10.4   Library Functions for Working with C-Strings

CONCEPT: The C++ library has numerous functions for handling C-strings. These functions perform various tests and manipulations, and require that the **cstring** header file be included.

The `strlen` Function

Because C-strings are stored in arrays, working with them is quite different than working with `string` objects. Fortunately, the C++ library provides many functions for manipulating and testing C-strings. These functions all require the `cstring` header file to be included, as shown here:

```
#include <cstring>
```

For instance, the following code segment uses the `strlen` function to determine the length of the string stored in the name array:

```
char name[] = "Thomas Edison";
int length;
length = strlen(name);
```

The `strlen` function accepts a pointer to a C-string as its argument. It returns the length of the string, which is the number of characters up to, but not including, the null terminator. As a result, the variable `length` will have the number 13 stored in it. The length of a string isn't to be confused with the size of the array holding it. Remember, the only information being passed to `strlen` is the beginning address of a C-string. It doesn't know where the array ends, so it looks for the null terminator to indicate the end of the string.

When using a C-string handling function, you must pass one or more C-strings as arguments. This means passing the address of the C-string, which may be accomplished by using any of the following as arguments:

- The name of the array holding the C-string
- A pointer variable that holds the address of the C-string
- A literal string

Anytime a literal string is used as an argument to a function, the address of the literal string is passed. Here is an example of the `strlen` function being used with such an argument:

```
length = strlen("Thomas Edison");
```

The `strcat` Function

The `strcat` function accepts two pointers to C-strings as its arguments. The function *concatenates*, or appends one string to another. The following code shows an example of its use:

```
const int SIZE = 13;
char string1[SIZE] = "Hello ";
char string2[] = "World!";

cout << string1 << endl;
cout << string2 << endl;
strcat(string1, string2);
cout << string1 << endl;
```

These statements will cause the following output:

```
Hello
World!
Hello World!
```

The `strcat` function copies the contents of `string2` to the end of `string1`. In this example, `string1` contains the string "Hello " before the call to `strcat`. After the call, it contains the string "Hello World!". Figure 10-2 shows the contents of both arrays before and after the function call.

Figure 10-2

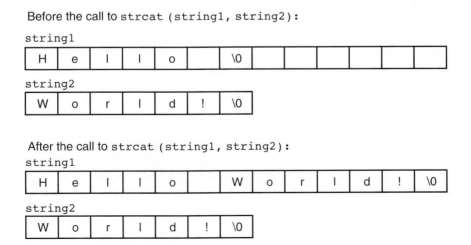

Notice the last character in string1 (before the null terminator) is a space. The strcat function doesn't insert a space, so it's the programmer's responsibility to make sure one is already there, if needed. It's also the programmer's responsibility to make sure the array holding string1 is large enough to hold string1 plus string2 plus a null terminator.

Here is a program segment that uses the sizeof operator to test an array's size before strcat is called:

```
if (sizeof(string1) >= (strlen(string1) + strlen(string2) + 1))
    strcat(string1, string2);
else
    cout << "String1 is not large enough for both strings.\n";
```

 WARNING! If the array holding the first string isn't large enough to hold both strings, strcat will overflow the boundaries of the array.

The strcpy Function

Recall from Chapter 7 that one array cannot be assigned to another with the = operator. Each individual element must be assigned, usually inside a loop. The strcpy function can be used to copy one string to another. Here is an example of its use:

```
const int SIZE = 13;
char name[SIZE];
strcpy(name, "Albert Einstein");
```

The strcpy function's two arguments are C-string addresses. The contents of the second argument are copied to the memory location specified by the first argument, including the null terminator. (The first argument usually references an array.) In this example, the strcpy function will copy the string "Albert Einstein" to the name array.

If anything is already stored in the location referenced by the first argument, it is overwritten, as shown in the following program segment:

```
const int SIZE = 10;
char string1[SIZE] = "Hello", string2[SIZE] = "World!";
cout << string1 << endl;
cout << string2 << endl;
strcpy(string1, string2);
cout << string1 << endl;
cout << string2 << endl;
```

Here is the output:

```
Hello
World!
World!
World!
```

 WARNING! Being true to C++'s nature, strcpy performs no bounds checking. The array specified by the first argument will be overflowed if it isn't large enough to hold the string specified by the second argument.

The `strncat` and `strncpy` Functions

Because the the `strcat` and `strcpy` functions can potentially overwrite the bounds of an array, they make it possible to write unsafe code. As an alternative, you should use `strncat` and `strncpy` whenever possible.

The `strncat` functions works like `strcat`, except it takes a third argument specifying the maximum number of characters from the second string to append to the first. Here is an example call to `strncat`:

```
strncat(string1, string2, 10);
```

When this statement executes, `strncat` will append no more than 10 characters from `string2` to `string1`. The following code shows an example of calculating the maximum number of characters that can be appended to an array.

```
 1   int maxChars;
 2   const int SIZE_1 = 17;
 3   const int SIZE_2 = 18;
 4
 5   char string1[SIZE_1] = "Welcome ";
 6   char string2[SIZE_2] = "to North Carolina";
 7
 8   cout << string1 << endl;
 9   cout << string2 << endl;
10   maxChars = sizeof(string1) - (strlen(string1) + 1);
11   strncat(string1, string2, maxChars);
12   cout << string1 << endl;
```

The statement in line 10 calculates the number of empty elements in `string1`. It does this by subtracting the length of the string stored in the array plus 1 for the null terminator. This code will cause the following output:

```
Welcome
to North Carolina
Welcome to North
```

The `strncpy` function allows you to copy a specified number of characters from a string to a destination. Calling `strncpy` is similar to calling `strcpy`, except you pass a third argument specifying the maximum number of characters from the second string to copy to the first. Here is an example call to `strncpy`:

```
strncpy(string1, string2, 5);
```

When this statement executes, `strncpy` will copy no more than five characters from `string2` to `string1`. However, if the specified number of characters is less than or equal to the length of `string2`, a null terminator is not appended to `string1`. If the specified number of characters is greater than the length of `string2`, then `string1` is padded with null terminators, up to the specified number of characters. The following code shows an example using the `strncpy` function.

```
 1   int maxChars;
 2   const int SIZE = 11;
 3
 4   char string1[SIZE];
 5   char string2[] = "I love C++ programming!";
 6
```

```
 7    maxChars = sizeof(string1) - 1;
 8    strncpy(string1, string2, maxChars);
 9    // Put the null terminator at the end.
10    string1[maxChars] = '\0';
11    cout << string1 << endl;
```

Notice that a statement was written in line 10 to put the null terminator at the end of
`string1`. This is because `maxChars` was less than the length of `string2`, and `strncpy` did
not automatically place a null terminator there.

The `strstr` Function

The `strstr` function searches for a string inside of a string. For instance, it could be used
to search for the string "seven" inside the larger string "Four score and seven years ago."
The function's first argument is the string to be searched, and the second argument is the
string to look for. If the function finds the second string inside the first, it returns the
address of the occurrence of the second string within the first string. Otherwise it returns
the address 0, or the NULL address. Here is an example:

```
char arr[] = "Four score and seven years ago";
char *strPtr;
cout << arr << endl;
strPtr = strstr(arr, "seven"); // search for "seven"
cout << strPtr << endl;
```

In this code, `strstr` will locate the string "seven" inside the string "Four score and seven
years ago." It will return the address of the first character in "seven" which will be stored
in the pointer variable `strPtr`. If run as part of a complete program, this segment will display the following:

```
Four score and seven years ago
seven years ago
```

The `strstr` function can be useful in any program that must locate data inside one or
more strings. Program 10-6, for example, stores a list of product numbers and descriptions in an array of C-strings. It allows the user to look up a product description by entering all or part of its product number.

Program 10-6

```
 1   // This program uses the strstr function to search an array.
 2   #include <iostream>
 3   #include <cstring>       // For strstr
 4   using namespace std;
 5
 6   int main()
 7   {
 8       // Constants for array lengths
 9       const int NUM_PRODS = 5;   // Number of products
10       const int LENGTH = 27;     // String length
11
```

```
12        // Array of products
13        char products[NUM_PRODS][LENGTH] =
14                       { "TV327 31-inch Television",
15                         "CD257 CD Player",
16                         "TA677 Answering Machine",
17                         "CS109 Car Stereo",
18                         "PC955 Personal Computer" };
19
20        char lookUp[LENGTH];   // To hold user's input
21        char *strPtr = NULL;   // To point to the found product
22        int index;             // Loop counter
23
24        // Prompt the user for a product number.
25        cout << "\tProduct Database\n\n";
26        cout << "Enter a product number to search for: ";
27        cin.getline(lookUp, LENGTH);
28
29        // Search the array for a matching substring
30        for (index = 0; index < NUM_PRODS; index++)
31        {
32           strPtr = strstr(products[index], lookUp);
33           if (strPtr != NULL)
34              break;
35        }
36
37        // If a matching substring was found, display the product info.
38        if (strPtr != NULL)
39           cout << products[index] << endl;
40        else
41           cout << "No matching product was found.\n";
42
43        return 0;
44   }
```

Program Output with Example Input Shown in Bold
```
     Product Database

Enter a product to search for: CS [Enter]
CS109  Car Stereo
```

Program Output with Different Example Input Shown in Bold
```
     Product Database

Enter a product to search for: AB [Enter]
No matching product was found.
```

Table 10-3 summarizes the string-handling functions discussed here, as well as the `strcmp` function that was discussed in Chapter 4. (All the functions listed require the `cstring` header file.)

In Program 10-6, the `for` loop in lines 30 through 35 cycles through each C-string in the array calling the following statement:

```
strPtr = strstr(prods[index], lookUp);
```

The `strstr` function searches the string referenced by `prods[index]` for the name entered by the user, which is stored in `lookUp`. If `lookUp` is found inside `prods[index]`, the function returns its address. In that case, the following `if` statement causes the `for` loop to terminate:

```
if (strPtr != NULL)
    break;
```

Outside the loop, the following `if else` statement in lines 38 through 41 determines whether the string entered by the user was found in the array. If not, it informs the user that no matching product was found. Otherwise, the product number and description are displayed:

```
if (strPtr == NULL)
    cout << "No matching product was found.\n";
else
    cout << prods[index] << endl;
```

The `strcmp` Function

Because C-strings are stored in `char` arrays, you cannot use the relational operators to compare two C-strings. To compare C-strings, you should use the library function `strcmp`. This function takes two C-strings as arguments and returns an integer that indicates how the two strings compare to each other. Here is the function's prototype:

```
int strcmp(char *string1, char *string2);
```

The function takes two C-strings as parameters (actually, pointers to C-strings) and returns an integer result. The value of the result is set accordingly:

- The result is *zero* if the two strings are *equal* on a character-by-character basis
- The result is *negative* if `string1` comes *before* `string2` in alphabetical order
- The result is *positive* if `string1` comes *after* `string2` in alphabetical order

Here is an example of the use of `strcmp` to determine if two strings are equal:

```
if (strcmp(string1, string2) == 0)
    cout << "The strings are equal.\n";
else
    cout << "The strings are not equal.\n";
```

Program 10-7 shows a complete example.

Program 10-7

```
 1 // This program tests two C-strings for equality
 2 // using the strcmp function.
 3 #include <iostream>
 4 #include <string>
 5 using namespace std;
 6
 7 int main()
 8 {
 9    // Two arrays for two strings.
10    const int LENGTH = 40;
11    char firstString[LENGTH], secondString[LENGTH];
12
```

```
13       // Read two strings.
14       cout << "Enter a string: ";
15       cin.getline(firstString, LENGTH);
16       cout << "Enter another string: ";
17       cin.getline(secondString, LENGTH);
18
19       // Compare the strings for equality with strcmp.
20       if (strcmp(firstString, secondString) == 0)
21          cout << "You entered the same string twice.\n";
22       else
23          cout << "The strings are not the same.\n";
24
25       return 0;
26  }
```

Program Output with Example Input Shown in Bold

Enter a string: **Alfonso [Enter]**
Enter another string: **Alfonso [Enter]**
You entered the same string twice.

The strcmp function is case sensitive when it compares strings. If the user enters "Dog" and "dog" in Program 10-7, it will report they are not the same. Most compilers provide nonstandard versions of strcmp that perform case-insensitive comparisons. For instance, some compilers provide a function named stricmp that works identically to strcmp except the case of the characters is ignored.

Program 10-8 is a more practical example of how strcmp can be used. It asks the user to enter the part number of the stereo they wish to purchase. The part number contains digits, letters, and a hyphen, so it must be stored as a string. Once the user enters the part number, the program displays the price of the stereo.

Program 10-8

```
1  // This program uses strcmp to compare the string entered
2  // by the user with the valid stereo part numbers.
3  #include <iostream>
4  #include <cstring>
5  #include <iomanip>
6  using namespace std;
7
8  int main()
9  {
10     // Price of parts.
11     const double A_PRICE = 249.0,
12                  B_PRICE = 299.0;
13
14     // Character array for part number.
15     const int PART_LENGTH = 8;
16     char partNum[PART_LENGTH];
17
```

(program continues)

Program 10-8 *(continued)*

```
18    // Instruct the user to enter a part number.
19    cout << "The stereo part numbers are:\n"
20         << "\tBoom Box, part number S147-29A\n"
21         << "\tShelf Model, part number S147-29B\n"
22         << "Enter the part number of the stereo you\n"
23         << "wish to purchase: ";
24
25    // Read a part number of at most 8 characters.
26    cin >> partNum;
27
28    // Determine what user entered using strcmp
29    // and print its price.
30    cout << showpoint << fixed << setprecision(2);
31    if (strcmp(partNum, "S147-29A") == 0)
32      cout << "The price is $" << A_PRICE << endl;
33    else if (strcmp(partNum, "S147-29B") == 0)
34      cout << "The price is $" << B_PRICE << endl;
35    else
36      cout << partNum << " is not a valid part number.\n";
37    return 0;
38 }
```

Program Output with Example Input Shown in Bold
```
The stereo part numbers are:
    Boom Box, part number S147-29A
    Shelf Model, part number S147-29B
Enter the part number of the stereo you
wish to purchase: S147-29B [Enter]
The price is $299.00
```

Using ! with `strcmp`

Some programmers prefer to use the logical NOT operator with `strcmp` when testing strings for equality. Because 0 is considered logically false, the `!` operator converts that value to true. The expression `!strcmp(string1, string2)` returns true when both strings are the same, and false when they are different. The two following statements perform the same operation:

```
if (strcmp(firstString, secondString) == 0)
if (!strcmp(firstString, secondString))
```

Sorting Strings

Programs are frequently written to print alphabetically sorted lists of items. For example, consider a department store computer system that keeps customers' names and addresses in a file. The names do not appear in the file alphabetically but in the order the operator entered them. If a list were to be printed in this order, it would be very difficult to locate any specific name. The list would have to be sorted before it was printed.

Because the value returned by `strcmp` is based on the relative alphabetic order of the two strings being compared, it can be used in programs that sort strings. Program 10-9 asks the user to enter two names, which are then printed in alphabetic order.

Program 10-9

```
 1  // This program uses the return value of strcmp to
 2  // alphabetically sort two strings entered by the user.
 3  #include <iostream>
 4  #include <string>
 5  using namespace std;
 6
 7  int main()
 8  {
 9     // Two arrays to hold two strings.
10     const int NAME_LENGTH = 30;
11     char name1[NAME_LENGTH], name2[NAME_LENGTH];
12
13     // Read two strings.
14     cout << "Enter a name (last name first): ";
15     cin.getline(name1, NAME_LENGTH);
16     cout << "Enter another name: ";
17     cin.getline(name2, NAME_LENGTH);
18
19     // Print the two strings in alphabetical order.
20     cout << "Here are the names sorted alphabetically:\n";
21     if (strcmp(name1, name2) < 0)
22        cout << name1 << endl << name2 << endl;
23     else if (strcmp(name1, name2) > 0)
24        cout << name2 << endl << name1 << endl;
25     else
26        cout << "You entered the same name twice!\n";
27
28     return 0;
29  }
```

Program Output with Example Input Shown in Bold
```
Enter a name (last name first): Smith, Richard [Enter]
Enter another name: Jones, John [Enter]
Here are the names sorted alphabetically:
Jones, John
Smith, Richard
```

Table 10-3 provides a summary of the C-string handling functions that we have discussed. All of the functions listed require the cstring header file.

Table 10-3

Function	Description
strlen	Accepts a C-string or a pointer to a C-string as an argument. Returns the length of the C-string (not including the null terminator.) *Example Usage:* len = strlen(name);
strcat	Accepts two C-strings or pointers to two C-strings as arguments. The function appends the contents of the second string to the first C-string. (The first string is altered, the second string is left unchanged.) *Example Usage:* strcat(string1, string2);

(table continues)

Table 10-3   *(continued)*

Function	Description
strcpy	Accepts two C-strings or pointers to two C-strings as arguments. The function copies the second C-string to the first C-string. The second C-string is left unchanged. *Example Usage:* `strcpy(string1, string2);`
strncat	Accepts two C-strings or pointers to two C-strings, and an integer argument. The third argument, an integer, indicates the maximum number of characters to copy from the second C-string to the first C-string. *Example Usage:* `strncat(string1, string2, n);`
strncpy	Accepts two C-strings or pointers to two C-strings, and an integer argument. The third argument, an integer, indicates the maximum number of characters to copy from the second C-string to the first C-string. If n is less than the length of `string2`, the null terminator is not automatically appended to `string1`. If n is greater than the length of `string2`, `string1` is padded with '\0' characters. *Example Usage:* `strncpy(string1, string2, n);`
strcmp	Accepts two C-strings or pointers to two C-strings arguments. If `string1` and `string2` are the same, this function returns 0. If `string2` is alphabetically greater than `string1`, it returns a negative number. If `string2` is alphabetically less than `string1`, it returns a positive number. *Example Usage:* `if (strcmp(string1, string2))`
strstr	Accepts two C-strings or pointers to two C-strings as arguments. Searches for the first occurrence of `string2` in `string1`. If an occurrence of `string2` is found, the function returns a pointer to it. Otherwise, it returns a NULL pointer (address 0). *Example Usage:* `cout << strstr(string1, string2);`

 Checkpoint

myprogramminglab *www.myprogramminglab.com*

10.6   Write a short description of each of the following functions:

```
strlen
strcat
strcpy
strncat
strncpy
strcmp
strstr
```

10.7   What will the following program segment display?

```
char dog[] = "Fido";
cout << strlen(dog) << endl;
```

10.8   What will the following program segment display?

```
char string1[16] = "Have a ";
char string2[9] = "nice day";
strcat(string1, string2);
cout << string1 << endl;
cout << string2 << endl;
```

10.9   Write a statement that will copy the string "Beethoven" to the array `composer`.

10.10   When complete, the following program skeleton will search for the string "Windy" in the array `place`. If `place` contains "Windy" the program will display the message "Windy found." Otherwise it will display "Windy not found."

```cpp
#include <iostream>
// include any other necessary header files
using namespace std;

int main()
{
    char place[] = "The Windy City";
    // Complete the program. It should search the array place
    // for the string "Windy" and display the message "Windy
    // found" if it finds the string. Otherwise, it should
    // display the message "Windy not found."
    return 0;
}
```

10.5 C-String/Numeric Conversion Functions

CONCEPT: The C++ library provides functions for converting a C-string representation of a number to a numeric data type and vice versa. These functions require the `cstdlib` header file to be included.

There is a great difference between a number that is stored as a string and one stored as a numeric value. The string "26792" isn't actually a number, but a series of ASCII codes representing the individual digits of the number. It uses six bytes of memory (including the null terminator). Because it isn't an actual number, it's not possible to perform mathematical operations with it, unless it is first converted to a numeric value.

Several functions exist in the C++ library for converting C-string representations of numbers into numeric values, and vice versa. Table 10-4 shows some of these. Note that all of these functions require the `cstdlib` header file.

Table 10-4

Function	Description
`atoi`	Accepts a C-string as an argument. The function converts the C-string to an integer and returns that value. *Example Usage:* `num = atoi("4569");`
`atol`	Accepts a C-string as an argument. The function converts the C-string to a `long` integer and returns that value. *Example Usage:* `lnum = atol("500000");`
`atof`	Accepts a C-string as an argument. The function converts the C-string to a `double` and returns that value. *Example Usage:* `fnum = atof("3.14159");`
`itoa`	Converts an integer to a C-string.* The first argument, `value`, is the integer. The result will be stored at the location pointed to by the second argument, `string`. The third argument, `base`, is an integer. It specifies the numbering system that the converted integer should be expressed in (8 = octal, 10 = decimal, 16 = hexadecimal, etc.). *Example Usage:* `itoa(value, string, base);`

*The `itoa` function is not supported by all compilers.

The `atoi` Function

The `atoi` function converts a string to an integer. It accepts a C-string argument and returns the converted integer value. Here is an example of how to use it:

```
int num;
num = atoi("1000");
```

In these statements, `atoi` converts the string "1000" into the integer 1000. Once the variable `num` is assigned this value, it can be used in mathematical operations or any task requiring a numeric value.

The `atol` Function

The `atol` function works just like `atoi`, except the return value is a `long` integer. Here is an example:

```
long bigNum;
bigNum = atol("500000");
```

The `atof` Function

The `atof` function accepts a C-string argument and converts it to a `double`. The numeric `double` value is returned, as shown here:

```
double num;
num = atof("12.67");
```

Although the `atof` function returns a `double`, you can still use it to convert a C-string to a `float`. For example, look at the following code.

```
float x;
x = atof("3.4");
```

The `atof` function converts the string "3.4" to the `double` value 3.4. Because 3.4 is within the range of a `float`, it can be stored in a `float` variable without the loss of data.

 NOTE: If a string that cannot be converted to a numeric value is passed to any of these functions, the function's behavior is undefined by C++. Many compilers, however, will perform the conversion process until an invalid character is encountered. For example, `atoi("123x5")` might return the integer 123. It is possible that these functions will return 0 if they cannot successfully convert their argument.

The `itoa` Function

The `itoa` function is similar to `atoi`, but it works in reverse. It converts a numeric integer into a string representation of the integer. The `itoa` function accepts three arguments: the integer value to be converted, a pointer to the location in memory where the string is to be stored, and a number that represents the base of the converted value. Here is an example:

```
const int SIZE = 10;
char numArray[SIZE];
itoa(1200, numArray, SIZE);
cout << numArray << endl;
```

This program segment converts the integer value 1200 to a string. The string is stored in the array numArray. The third argument, 10, means the number should be written in decimal, or base 10 notation. The output of the cout statement is

        1200

WARNING! As always, C++ performs no array bounds checking. Make sure the array whose address is passed to itoa is large enough to hold the converted number, including the null terminator.

Now let's look at Program 10-10, which uses a string-to-number conversion function, atoi. It allows the user to enter a series of values, or the letters Q or q to quit. The average of the numbers is then calculated and displayed.

Program 10-10

```cpp
1   // This program demonstrates the strcmp and atoi functions.
2   #include <iostream>
3   #include <cctype>         // For tolower
4   #include <cstring>        // For strcmp
5   #include <cstdlib>        // For atoi
6   using namespace std;
7
8   int main()
9   {
10      const int SIZE = 20;   // Array size
11      char input[SIZE];      // To hold user input
12      int total = 0;         // Accumulator
13      int count = 0;         // Loop counter
14      double average;        // To hold the average of numbers
15
16      // Get the first number.
17      cout << "This program will average a series of numbers.\n";
18      cout << "Enter the first number or Q to quit: ";
19      cin.getline(input, SIZE);
20
21      // Process the number and subsequent numbers.
22      while (tolower(input[0]) != 'q')
23      {
24         total += atoi(input);    // Keep a running total
25         count++;                 // Count the numbers entered
26         // Get the next number.
27         cout << "Enter the next number or Q to quit: ";
28         cin.getline(input, SIZE);
29      }
30
31      // If any numbers were entered, display their average.
32      if (count != 0)
33      {
34         average = static_cast<double>(total) / count;
35         cout << "Average: " << average << endl;
36      }
37      return 0;
38   }
```

(program output continues)

Program 10-10 *(continued)*

Program Output with Example Input Shown in Bold
```
This program will average a series of numbers.
Enter the first number or Q to quit: 74 [Enter]
Enter the next number or Q to quit: 98 [Enter]
Enter the next number or Q to quit: 23 [Enter]
Enter the next number or Q to quit: 54 [Enter]
Enter the next number or Q to quit: Q [Enter]
Average: 62.25
```

In line 22, the following `while` statement uses the `tolower` function to determine whether the first character entered by the user is "q" or "Q".

```
while (tolower(input[0]) != 'q')
```

If the user hasn't entered 'Q' or 'q' the loop performs an iteration. The following statement, in line 24, uses `atoi` to convert the string in input to an integer and adds its value to `total`:

```
total += atoi(input);  // Keep a running total
```

The counter is updated in line 25 and then the user is asked for the next number. When all the numbers are entered, the user terminates the loop by entering 'Q' or 'q'. If one or more numbers are entered, their average is displayed.

The string-to numeric conversion functions can also help with a common input problem. Recall from Chapter 3 that using `cin >>` and then calling `cin.get` causes problems because the `>>` operator leaves the newline character in the keyboard buffer. When the `cin.get` function executes, the first character it sees in the keyboard buffer is the newline character, so it reads no further.

The same problem exists when a program uses `cin >>` and then calls `cin.getline` to read a line of input. For example, look at the following code. (Assume `idNumber` is an `int` and name is a `char` array.)

```
1     // Get the user's ID number.
2     cout << "What is your ID number? ";
3     cin >> idNumber;
4
5     // Get the user's name.
6     cout << "What is your name? ";
7     cin.getline(name, NAME_SIZE);
```

Let's say the user enters 25 and presses Enter when the `cin >>` statement in line 3 executes. The value 25 will be stored in `idNumber`, and the newline character will be left in the keyboard buffer. When the `cin.getline` function is called in line 7, the first character it sees in the keyboard buffer is the newline character, so it reads no further. It will appear that the statement in line 7 was skipped.

One work-around that we have used in this book is to call `cin.ignore` to skip over the newline character just before calling `cin.getline`. Another approach is to use cin.getline to read all of a program's input, including numbers. When numeric input is needed, it is read into a char array as a string, and then converted to the appropriate numeric data type. Because you aren't mixing cin >> with cin.getline, the problem of the remaining newline character doesn't exist. Program 10-11 shows an example.

Program 10-11

```cpp
1   // This program demonstrates how the getline function can
2   // be used for all of a program's input.
3   #include <iostream>
4   #include <cstdlib>
5   #include <iomanip>
6   using namespace std;
7
8   int main()
9   {
10      const int INPUT_SIZE = 81;    // Size of input array
11      const int NAME_SIZE = 30;     // Size of name array
12      char input[INPUT_SIZE];       // To hold a line of input
13      char name[NAME_SIZE];         // To hold a name
14      int idNumber;                 // To hold an ID number
15      int age;                      // To hold an age
16      double income;                // To hold income
17
18      // Get the user's ID number.
19      cout << "What is your ID number? ";
20      cin.getline(input, INPUT_SIZE); // Read as a string
21      idNumber = atoi(input);         // Convert to int
22
23      // Get the user's name. No conversion necessary.
24      cout << "What is your name? ";
25      cin.getline(name, NAME_SIZE);
26
27      // Get the user's age.
28      cout << "How old are you? ";
29      cin.getline(input, INPUT_SIZE); // Read as a string
30      age = atoi(input);              // Convert to int
31
32      // Get the user's income.
33      cout << "What is your annual income? ";
34      cin.getline(input, INPUT_SIZE); // Read as a string
35      income = atof(input);           // Convert to double
36
37      // Show the resulting data.
38      cout << setprecision(2) << fixed << showpoint;
39      cout << "Your name is " << name
40          <<", you are " << age
41          << " years old,\nand you make $"
42          << income << " per year.\n";
43
44      return 0;
45  }
```

(program output continues)

Program 10-11   *(continued)*

Program Output with Example Input Shown in Bold
```
What is your ID number? 1234 [Enter]
What is your name? Janice Smith [Enter]
How old are you? 25 [Enter]
What is your annual income? 60000 [Enter]
Your name is Janice Smith, you are 25 years old,
and you make $60000.00 per year.
```

Checkpoint

myprogramminglab   *www.myprogramminglab.com*

10.11   Write a short description of each of the following functions:

```
atoi
atol
atof
itoa
```

10.12   Write a statement that will convert the string "10" to an integer and store the result in the variable num.

10.13   Write a statement that will convert the string "100000" to a long and store the result in the variable num.

10.14   Write a statement that will convert the string "7.2389" to a double and store the result in the variable num.

10.15   Write a statement that will convert the integer 127 to a string, stored in base-10 notation in the array value.

10.6

Focus on Software Engineering: Writing Your Own C-String-Handling Functions

CONCEPT: You can design your own specialized functions for manipulating strings.

VideoNote
Writing a C-String-Handling Function

By being able to pass arrays as arguments, you can write your own functions for processing C-strings. For example, Program 10-12 uses a function to copy a C-string from one array to another.

Program 10-12

```
 1   // This program uses a function to copy a C-string into an array.
 2   #include <iostream>
 3   using namespace std;
 4
 5   void stringCopy(char [], char []);  // Function prototype
 6
```

```
 7  int main()
 8  {
 9     const int LENGTH = 30;   // Size of the arrays
10     char first[LENGTH];      // To hold the user's input
11     char second[LENGTH];     // To hold the copy
12
13     // Get a string from the user and store in first.
14     cout << "Enter a string with no more than "
15          << (LENGTH - 1) << " characters:\n";
16     cin.getline(first, LENGTH);
17
18     // Copy the contents of first to second.
19     stringCopy(first, second);
20
21     // Display the copy.
22     cout << "The string you entered is:\n" << second << endl;
23     return 0;
24  }
25
26  //***********************************************************
27  // Definition of the stringCopy function.                  *
28  // This function copies the C-string in string1 to string2. *
29  //***********************************************************
30
31  void stringCopy(char string1[], char string2[])
32  {
33     int index = 0;   // Loop counter
34
35     // Step through string1, copying each element to
36     // string2. Stop when the null character is encountered.
37     while (string1[index] != '\0')
38     {
39        string2[index] = string1[index];
40        index++;
41     }
42
43     // Place a null character in string2.
44     string2[index] = '\0';
45  }
```

Program Output with Example Input Shown in Bold
```
Enter a string with no more than 29 characters:
```
Thank goodness it's Friday! [Enter]
```
The string you entered is:
Thank goodness it's Friday!
```

Notice the function stringCopy does not accept an argument indicating the size of the arrays. It simply copies the characters from string1 into string2 until it encounters a null terminator in string1. When the null terminator is found, the loop has reached the end of the C-string. The last statement in the function assigns a null terminator (the '\0' character) to the end of string2, so it is properly terminated.

WARNING! Because the stringCopy function doesn't know the size of the second array, it's the programmer's responsibility to make sure the second array is large enough to hold the string in the first array.

Program 10-13 uses another C-string-handling function: nameSlice. The program asks the user to enter his or her first and last names, separated by a space. The function searches the string for the space, and replaces it with a null terminator. In effect, this "cuts" the last name off of the string.

Program 10-13

```cpp
 1   // This program uses the function nameSlice to cut the last
 2   // name off of a string that contains the user's first and
 3   // last names.
 4   #include <iostream>
 5   using namespace std;
 6
 7   void nameSlice(char []); // Function prototype
 8
 9   int main()
10   {
11      const int SIZE = 41;  // Array size
12      char name[SIZE];      // To hold the user's name
13
14      cout << "Enter your first and last names, separated ";
15      cout << "by a space:\n";
16      cin.getline(name, SIZE);
17      nameSlice(name);
18      cout << "Your first name is: " << name << endl;
19      return 0;
20   }
21
22   //************************************************************
23   // Definition of function nameSlice. This function accepts a   *
24   // character array as its argument. It scans the array looking *
25   // for a space. When it finds one, it replaces it with a null  *
26   // terminator.                                                 *
27   //************************************************************
28
29   void nameSlice(char userName[])
30   {
31      int count = 0;  // Loop counter
32
33      // Locate the first space, or the null terminator if there
34      // are no spaces.
35      while (userName[count] != ' ' && userName[count] != '\0')
36         count++;
37
38      // If a space was found, replace it with a null terminator.
39      if (userName[count] == ' ')
40         userName[count] = '\0';
41   }
```

Program Output with Example Input Shown in Bold
```
Enter your first and last names, separated by a space:
```
Jimmy Jones [Enter]
```
Your first name is: Jimmy
```

The following loop in lines 35 and 36 starts at the first character in the array and scans the string searching for either a space or a null terminator:

```cpp
while (userName[count] != ' ' && userName[count] != '\0')
    count++;
```

If the character in userName[count] isn't a space or the null terminator, count is incremented, and the next character is examined. With the example input "Jimmy Jones," the loop finds the space separating "Jimmy" and "Jones" at userName[5]. When the loop stops, count is set to 5. This is illustrated in Figure 10-3.

Figure 10-3

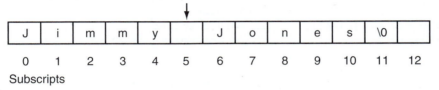

The loop stops when count reaches 5 because userName[5] contains a space

J	i	m	m	y		J	o	n	e	s	\0	
0	1	2	3	4	5	6	7	8	9	10	11	12

Subscripts

NOTE: The loop will also stop if it encounters a null terminator. This is so it will not go beyond the boundary of the array if the user didn't enter a space.

Once the loop has finished, userName[count] will either contain a space or a null terminator. If it contains a space, the following if statement, in lines 39 and 40, replaces it with a null terminator:

```cpp
if (userName[count] == ' ')
    userName[count] = '\0';
```

This is illustrated in Figure 10-4.

Figure 10-4

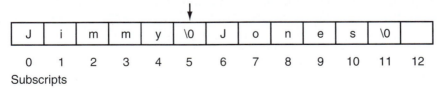

The space is replaced with a null terminator. This now becomes the end of the string.

J	i	m	m	y	\0	J	o	n	e	s	\0	
0	1	2	3	4	5	6	7	8	9	10	11	12

Subscripts

The new null terminator now becomes the end of the string.

Using Pointers to Pass C-String Arguments

Pointers are extremely useful for writing functions that process C-strings. If the starting address of a string is passed into a pointer parameter variable, it can be assumed that all the characters, from that address up to the byte that holds the null terminator, are part of the string. (It isn't necessary to know the length of the array that holds the string.)

Program 10-14 demonstrates a function, countChars, that uses a pointer to count the number of times a specific character appears in a C-string.

Program 10-14

```
 1   // This program demonstrates a function, countChars, that counts
 2   // the number of times a specific character appears in a string.
 3   #include <iostream>
 4   using namespace std;
 5
 6   int countChars(char *, char);   // Function prototype
 7
 8   int main()
 9   {
10      const int SIZE = 51;     // Array size
11      char userString[SIZE];   // To hold a string
12      char letter;             // The character to count
13
14      // Get a string from the user.
15      cout << "Enter a string (up to 50 characters): ";
16      cin.getline(userString, SIZE);
17
18      // Choose a character whose occurrences within the string will be counted.
19      cout << "Enter a character and I will tell you how many\n";
20      cout << "times it appears in the string: ";
21      cin >> letter;
22
23      // Display the number of times the character appears.
24      cout << letter << " appears ";
25      cout << countChars(userString, letter) << " times.\n";
26      return 0;
27   }
28
29   //****************************************************************
30   // Definition of countChars. The parameter strPtr is a pointer   *
31   // that points to a string. The parameter Ch is a character that *
32   // the function searches for in the string. The function returns *
33   // the number of times the character appears in the string.      *
34   //****************************************************************
35
36   int countChars(char *strPtr, char ch)
37   {
38      int times = 0;  // Number of times ch appears in the string
39
```

```
40        // Step through the string counting occurrences of ch.
41        while (*strPtr != '\0')
42        {
43           if (*strPtr == ch)   // If the current character equals ch...
44              times++;          // ... increment the counter
45           strPtr++;            // Go to the next char in the string.
46        }
47
48        return times;
49   }
```

Program Output with Example Input Shown in Bold

Enter a string (up to 50 characters): **Starting Out with C++ [Enter]**
Enter a character and I will tell you how many
times it appears in the string: **t [Enter]**
t appears 4 times.

In the function `countChars`, `strPtr` points to the C-string that is to be searched and `ch` contains the character to look for. The `while` loop in lines 41 through 46 repeats as long as the character that `strPtr` points to is not the null terminator:

```
while (*strPtr != '\0')
```

Inside the loop, the `if` statement in line 43 compares the character that `strPtr` points to with the character in `ch`:

```
if (*strPtr == ch)
```

If the two are equal, the variable `times` is incremented in line 44. (`times` keeps a running total of the number of times the character appears.) The last statement in the loop is

```
strPtr++;
```

This statement increments the address in `strPtr`. This causes `strPtr` to point to the next character in the string. Then, the loop starts over. When `strPtr` finally reaches the null terminator, the loop terminates and the function returns the value in `times`.

For another example, see the String Manipulation Case Study, available for download from the book's companion Web site at www.pearsonhighered.com/gaddis.

 ## Checkpoint

myprogramminglab *www.myprogramminglab.com*

10.16   What is the output of the following program?

```
#include <iostream>
using namespace std;

// Function Prototype
void mess(char []);

int main()
{
    char stuff[] = "Tom Talbert Tried Trains";
```

```
        cout << stuff << endl;
        mess(stuff);
        cout << stuff << endl;
        return 0;
    }

    // Definition of function mess
    void mess(char str[])
    {
        int step = 0;

        while (str[step] != '\0')
        {
            if (str[step] == 'T')
                str[step] = 'D';
            step++;
        }
    }
```

10.7 More About the C++ `string` Class

CONCEPT: Standard C++ provides a special data type for storing and working with strings.

**VideoNote
More About
the `string`
Class**

The `string` class is an abstract data type. This means it is not a built-in, primitive data type like `int` or `char`. Instead, it is a programmer-defined data type that accompanies the C++ language. It provides many capabilities that make storing and working with strings easy and intuitive.

Using the `string` Class

The first step in using the `string` class is to `#include` the `string` header file. This is accomplished with the following preprocessor directive:

```
#include <string>
```

Now you are ready to define a `string` object. Defining a `string` object is similar to defining a variable of a primitive type. For example, the following statement defines a `string` object named `movieTitle`.

```
string movieTitle;
```

You assign a string value to the `movieTitle` object with the assignment operator, as shown in the following statement.

```
movieTitle = "Wheels of Fury";
```

The contents of movieTitle is displayed on the screen with the cout object, as shown in the next statement:

```
cout << "My favorite movie is " << movieTitle << endl;
```

Program 10-15 is a complete program that demonstrates the statements shown above.

Program 10-15

```
 1   // This program demonstrates the string class.
 2   #include <iostream>
 3   #include <string>      // Required for the string class.
 4   using namespace std;
 5
 6   int main()
 7   {
 8      string movieTitle;
 9
10      movieTitle = "Wheels of Fury";
11      cout << "My favorite movie is " << movieTitle << endl;
12      return 0;
13   }
```

Program Output
```
My favorite movie is Wheels of Fury
```

As you can see, working with string objects is similar to working with variables of other types. For example, Program 10-16 demonstrates how you can use cin to read a value from the keyboard into a string object.

Program 10-16

```
 1   // This program demonstrates how cin can read a string into
 2   // a string class object.
 3   #include <iostream>
 4   #include <string>
 5   using namespace std;
 6
 7   int main()
 8   {
 9      string name;
10
11      cout << "What is your name? ";
12      cin >> name;
13      cout << "Good morning " << name << endl;
14      return 0;
15   }
```

Program Output with Example Input Shown in Bold
```
What is your name? Peggy [Enter]
Good morning Peggy
```

Reading a Line of Input into a `string` Object

If you want to read a line of input (with spaces) into a `string` object, use the `getline()` function. Here is an example:

```
string name;
cout << "What is your name? ";
getline(cin, name);
```

The `getline()` function's first argument is the name of a stream object you wish to read the input from. The function call above passes the `cin` object to `getline()`, so the function reads a line of input from the keyboard. The second argument is the name of a `string` object. This is where `getline()` stores the input that it reads.

Comparing and Sorting `string` Objects

There is no need to use a function such as `strcmp` to compare `string` objects. You may use the `<`, `>`, `<=`, `>=`, `==`, and `!=` relational operators. For example, assume the following definitions exist in a program:

```
string set1 = "ABC";
string set2 = "XYZ";
```

The object `set1` is considered less than the object `set2` because the characters "ABC" alphabetically precede the characters "XYZ." So, the following `if` statement will cause the message "set1 is less than set2" to be displayed on the screen.

```
if (set1 < set2)
    cout << "set1 is less than set2.\n";
```

Relational operators perform comparisons on `string` objects in a fashion similar to the way the `strcmp` function compares C-strings. One by one, each character in the first operand is compared with the character in the corresponding position in the second operand. If all the characters in both strings match, the two strings are equal. Other relationships can be determined if two characters in corresponding positions do not match. The first operand is less than the second operand if the mismatched character in the first operand is less than its counterpart in the second operand. Likewise, the first operand is greater than the second operand if the mismatched character in the first operand is greater than its counterpart in the second operand.

For example, assume a program has the following definitions:

```
string name1 = "Mary";
string name2 = "Mark";
```

The value in `name1`, "Mary," is greater than the value in `name2`, "Mark." This is because the "y" in "Mary" has a greater ASCII value than the "k" in "Mark."

`string` objects can also be compared to C-strings with relational operators. Assuming `str` is a `string` object, all of the following are valid relational expressions:

```
str > "Joseph"
"Kimberly" < str
str == "William"
```

Program 10-17 demonstrates string objects and relational operators.

Program 10-17

```cpp
 1  // This program uses the == operator to compare the string entered
 2  // by the user with the valid stereo part numbers.
 3  #include <iostream>
 4  #include <iomanip>
 5  #include <string>
 6  using namespace std;
 7
 8  int main()
 9  {
10      const double APRICE = 249.0;    // Price for part A
11      const double BPRICE = 299.0;    // Price for part B
12      string partNum;                 // Part number
13
14      cout << "The stereo part numbers are:\n";
15      cout << "\tBoom Box, part number S147-29A\n";
16      cout << "\tShelf Model, part number S147-29B\n";
17      cout << "Enter the part number of the stereo you\n";
18      cout << "wish to purchase: ";
19      cin >> partNum;
20      cout << fixed << showpoint << setprecision(2);
21
22      if (partNum == "S147-29A")
23         cout << "The price is $" << APRICE << endl;
24      else if (partNum == "S147-29B")
25         cout << "The price is $" << BPRICE << endl;
26      else
27         cout << partNum << " is not a valid part number.\n";
28      return 0;
29  }
```

Program Output with Example Input Shown in Bold
```
The stereo part numbers are:
        Boom Box, part number S147-29A
        Shelf Model, part number S147-29B
Enter the part number of the stereo you
wish to purchase: S147-29A [Enter]
The price is $249.00
```

You may also use relational operators to sort string objects. Program 10-18 demonstrates this.

Program 10-18

```
 1  // This program uses relational operators to alphabetically
 2  // sort two strings entered by the user.
 3  #include <iostream>
 4  #include <string>
 5  using namespace std;
 6
 7  int main ()
 8  {
 9     string name1, name2;
10
11     // Get a name.
12     cout << "Enter a name (last name first): ";
13     getline(cin, name1);
14
15     // Get another name.
16     cout << "Enter another name: ";
17     getline(cin, name2);
18
19     // Display them in alphabetical order.
20     cout << "Here are the names sorted alphabetically:\n";
21     if (name1 < name2)
22        cout << name1 << endl << name2 << endl;
23     else if (name1 > name2)
24        cout << name2 << endl << name1 << endl;
25     else
26        cout << "You entered the same name twice!\n";
27     return 0;
28  }
```

Program Output with Example Input Shown in Bold
```
Enter a name (last name first): Smith, Richard [Enter]
Enter another name: Jones, John [Enter]
Here are the names sorted alphabetically:
Jones, John
Smith, Richard
```

Other Ways to Define `string` Objects

There are a variety of ways to initialize a `string` object when you define it. Table 10-5 shows several example definitions, and describes each. Program 10-19 demonstrates a `string` object initialized with the string "William Smith."

Program 10-19

```
 1  // This program initializes a string object.
 2  #include <iostream>
 3  #include <string>
 4  using namespace std;
 5
```

```
 6    int main()
 7    {
 8       string greeting;
 9       string name("William Smith");
10
11       greeting = "Hello ";
12       cout << greeting << name << endl;
13       return 0;
14    }
```

Program Output

Hello William Smith

Table 10-5

Definition	Description
`string address;`	Defines an empty `string` object named `address`.
`string name("William Smith");`	Defines a `string` object named `name`, initialized with "William Smith."
`string person1(person2);`	Defines a `string` object named `person1`, which is a copy of `person2`. `person2` may be either a `string` object or character array.
`string set1(set2, 5);`	Defines a `string` object named `set1`, which is initialized to the first five characters in the character array `set2`.
`string lineFull('z', 10);`	Defines a `string` object named `lineFull` initialized with 10 `'z'` characters.
`string firstName(fullName, 0, 7);`	Defines a `string` object named `firstName`, initialized with a substring of the `string` `fullName`. The substring is seven characters long, beginning at position 0.

Notice in Program 10-16 the use of the = operator to assign a value to the `string` object. The `string` class supports several operators, which are described in Table 10-6.

Table 10-6

Supported Operator	Description
`>>`	Extracts characters from a stream and inserts them into the `string`. Characters are copied until a whitespace or the end of the string is encountered.
`<<`	Inserts the `string` into a stream.
`=`	Assigns the `string` on the right to the `string` object on the left.
`+=`	Appends a copy of the `string` on the right to the `string` object on the left.
`+`	Returns a `string` that is the concatenation of the two `string` operands.
`[]`	Implements array-subscript notation, as in `name[x]`. A reference to the character in the x position is returned.
Relational Operators	Each of the relational operators is implemented:
	`< > <= >= == !=`

Program 10-20 demonstrates some of the `string` operators.

Program 10-20

```
 1   // This program demonstrates the C++ string class.
 2   #include <iostream>
 3   #include <string>
 4   using namespace std;
 5
 6   int main ()
 7   {
 8      // Define three string objects.
 9      string str1, str2, str3;
10
11      // Assign values to all three.
12      str1 = "ABC";
13      str2 = "DEF";
14      str3 = str1 + str2;
15
16      // Display all three.
17      cout << str1 << endl;
18      cout << str2 << endl;
19      cout << str3 << endl;
20
21      // Concatenate a string onto str3 and display it.
22      str3 += "GHI";
23      cout << str3 << endl;
24      return 0;
25   }
```

Program Output

```
ABC
DEF
ABCDEF
ABCDEFGHI
```

Using `string` Class Member Functions

The `string` class also has member functions. For example, the `length` member function returns the length of the string stored in the object. The value is returned as an unsigned integer.

Assume the following `string` object definition exists in a program:

```
string town = "Charleston";
```

The following statement in the same program would assign the value 10 to the variable `x`.

```
x = town.length();
```

Program 10-21 further demonstrates the `length` member function.

Program 10-21

```cpp
1    // This program demonstrates a string
2    // object's length member function.
3    #include <iostream>
4    #include <string>
5    using namespace std;
6
7    int main ()
8    {
9       string town;
10
11       cout << "Where do you live? ";
12       cin >> town;
13       cout << "Your town's name has " << town.length() ;
14       cout << " characters\n";
15       return 0;
16   }
```

Program Output with Example Input Shown in Bold

```
Where do you live? Jacksonville [Enter]
Your town's name has 12 characters
```

The size function also returns the length of the string. It is demonstrated in the for loop in Program 10-22.

Program 10-22

```cpp
1    // This program demonstrates the C++ string class.
2    #include <iostream>
3    #include <string>
4    using namespace std;
5
6    int main()
7    {
8       // Define three string objects.
9       string str1, str2, str3;
10
11       // Assign values to all three.
12       str1 = "ABC";
13       str2 = "DEF";
14       str3 = str1 + str2;
15
16       // Use subscripts to display str3 one character
17       // at a time.
18       for (int x = 0; x < str3.size(); x++)
19          cout << str3[x];
20       cout << endl;
21
```

(program continues)

Program 10-22 *(continued)*

```
22      // Compare str1 with str2.
23      if (str1 < str2)
24          cout << "str1 is less than str2\n";
25      else
26          cout << "str1 is not less than str2\n";
27      return 0;
28  }
```

Program Output
```
ABCDEF
str1 is less than str2
```

Table 10-7 lists many of the `string` class member functions and their overloaded variations. In the examples, assume `theString` is the name of a `string` object.

Table 10-7

Member Function Example	Description
`theString.append(n, 'z');`	Appends n copies of 'z' to `theString`.
`theString.append(str);`	Appends `str` to `theString`. `str` can be a `string` object or character array.
`theString.append(str, n);`	The first n characters of the character array `str` are appended to `theString`.
`theString.append(str, x, n);`	n number of characters from `str`, starting at position x, are appended to `theString`. If `theString` is too small, the function will copy as many characters as possible.
`theString.assign(n, 'z');`	Assigns n copies of `'z'` to `theString`.
`theString.assign(str);`	Assigns `str` to `theString`. `str` can be a `string` object or character array.
`theString.assign(str, n);`	The first n characters of the character array `str` are assigned to `theString`.
`theString.assign(str, x, n);`	n number of characters from `str`, starting at position x, are assigned to `theString`. If `theString` is too small, the function will copy as many characters as possible.
`theString.at(x);`	Returns the character at position x in the `string`.
`theString.begin();`	Returns an iterator pointing to the first character in the string. (For more information on iterators, see Chapter 16.)
`theString.c_str();`	Converts the contents of `theString` to a C-string, and returns a pointer to the C-string.
`theString.capacity();`	Returns the size of the storage allocated for the `string`.
`theString.clear();`	Clears the `string` by deleting all the characters stored in it.

Table 10-7 *(continued)*

Member Function Example	Description
theString.compare(str);	Performs a comparison like the strcmp function (see Chapter 4), with the same return values. str can be a string object or a character array.
theString.compare(x, n, str);	Compares theString and str, starting at position x, and continuing for n characters. The return value is like strcmp. str can be a string object or character array.
theString.copy(str, x, n);	Copies the character array str to theString, beginning at position x, for n characters. If theString is too small, the function will copy as many characters as possible.
theString.empty();	Returns true if theString is empty.
theString.end();	Returns an iterator pointing to the last character of the string in theString. (For more information on iterators, see Chapter 15.)
theString.erase(x, n);	Erases n characters from theString, beginning at position x.
theString.find(str, x);	Returns the first position at or beyond position x where the string str is found in theString. str may be either a string object or a character array.
theString.find('z', x);	Returns the first position at or beyond position x where 'z' is found in theString.
theString.insert(x, n, 'z');	Inserts 'z' n times into theString at position x.
theString.insert(x, str);	Inserts a copy of str into theString, beginning at position x. str may be either a string object or a character array.
theString.length();	Returns the length of the string in theString.
theString.replace(x, n, str);	Replaces the n characters in theString beginning at position x with the characters in string object str.
theString.resize(n, 'z');	Changes the size of the allocation in theString to n. If n is less than the current size of the string, the string is truncated to n characters. If n is greater, the string is expanded and 'z' is appended at the end enough times to fill the new spaces.
theString.size();	Returns the length of the string in theString.
theString.substr(x, n);	Returns a copy of a substring. The substring is n characters long and begins at position x of theString.
theString.swap(str);	Swaps the contents of theString with str.

10.8   Focus on Problem Solving and Program Design: A Case Study

As a programmer for the Home Software Company, you are asked to develop a function named `dollarFormat` that inserts commas and a $ sign at the appropriate locations in a `string` object containing an unformatted dollar amount. As an argument, the function should accept a reference to a `string` object. You may assume the `string` object contains a value such as 1084567.89. The function should modify the `string` object so it contains a formatted dollar amount, such as $1,084,567.89.

The code for the `dollarFormat` function follows.

```
void dollarFormat(string &currency)
{
    int dp;

    dp = currency.find('.');   // Find decimal point
    if (dp > 3)                // Insert commas
    {
        for (int x = dp - 3; x > 0; x -= 3)
            currency.insert(x, ",");
    }
    currency.insert(0, "$");   // Insert dollar sign
}
```

The function defines an `int` variable named `dp`. This variable is used to hold the position of the unformatted number's decimal point. This is accomplished with the statement:

```
dp = currency.find('.');
```

The `string` class' `find` member function returns the position number in the string where the '.' character is found. An `if` statement determines if the number has more than three numbers preceding the decimal point:

```
if (dp > 3)
```

If the decimal point is at a position greater than 3, then the function inserts commas in the string with the following loop:

```
for (int x = dp - 3; x > 0; x -= 3)
    currency.insert(x, ",");
```

Finally, a $ symbol is inserted at position 0 (the first character in the `string`).

Program 10-23 demonstrates the function.

Program 10-23

```
 1   // This program lets the user enter a number. The
 2   // dollarFormat function formats the number as
 3   // a dollar amount.
 4   #include <iostream>
 5   #include <string>
 6   using namespace std;
 7
 8   // Function prototype
 9   void dollarFormat(string &);
10
11   int main ()
12   {
13      string input;
14
15      // Get the dollar amount from the user.
16      cout << "Enter a dollar amount in the form nnnnn.nn : ";
17      cin >> input;
18      dollarFormat(input);
19      cout << "Here is the amount formatted:\n";
20      cout << input << endl;
21      return 0;
22   }
23
24   //**********************************************************
25   // Definition of the dollarFormat function. This function   *
26   // accepts a string reference object, which is assumed      *
27   // to hold a number with a decimal point. The function      *
28   // formats the number as a dollar amount with commas and    *
29   // a $ symbol.                                              *
30   //**********************************************************
31
32   void dollarFormat(string &currency)
33   {
34      int dp;
35
36      dp = currency.find('.');   // Find decimal point
37      if (dp > 3)                // Insert commas
38      {
39         for (int x = dp - 3; x > 0; x -= 3)
40            currency.insert(x, ",");
41      }
42      currency.insert(0, "$");   // Insert dollar sign
43   }
```

Program Output with Example Input Shown in Bold

```
Enter a dollar amount in the form nnnnn.nn: 1084567.89 [Enter]
Here is the amount formatted:
$1,084,567.89
```

Review Questions and Exercises

Short Answer

1. What header file must you include in a program using character testing functions such as `isalpha` and `isdigit`?

2. What header file must you include in a program using the character conversion functions `toupper` and `tolower`?

3. Assume c is a `char` variable. What value does c hold after each of the following statements executes?

   Statement   Contents of c
   ```
   c = toupper('a');_____
   c = toupper('B');_____
   c = tolower('D');_____
   c = toupper('e');_____
   ```

4. Look at the following code. What value will be stored in s after the code executes?

   ```
   char name[10];
   int s;
   strcpy(name, "Jimmy");
   s = strlen(name);
   ```

5. What header file must you include in a program using string functions such as `strlen` and `strcpy`?

6. What header file must you include in a program using string/numeric conversion functions such as `atoi` and `atof`?

7. What header file must you include in a program using `string` class objects?

8. How do you compare `string` class objects?

Fill-in-the-Blank

9. The _____ function returns true if the character argument is uppercase.

10. The _____ function returns true if the character argument is a letter of the alphabet.

11. The _____ function returns true if the character argument is a digit.

12. The _____ function returns true if the character argument is a whitespace character.

13. The _____ function returns the uppercase equivalent of its character argument.

14. The _____ function returns the lowercase equivalent of its character argument.

15. The _____ file must be included in a program that uses character testing functions.

16. The _____ function returns the length of a string.

17. To _____ two strings means to append one string to the other.

18. The _____ function concatenates two strings.

19. The _____ function copies one string to another.

20. The _____ function searches for a string inside of another one.

21. The _____ function compares two strings.

22. The _____ function copies, at most, *n* number of characters from one string to another.

23. The _____ function returns the value of a string converted to an integer.

24. The _____ function returns the value of a string converted to a long integer.

25. The _____ function returns the value of a string converted to a float.

26. The _____ function converts an integer to a string.

Algorithm Workbench

27. The following `if` statement determines whether choice is equal to 'Y' or 'y'.

    ```
    if (choice == 'Y' || choice == 'y')
    ```

    Simplify this statement by using either the `toupper` or `tolower` function.

28. Assume `input` is a `char` array holding a C-string. Write code that counts the number of elements in the array that contain an alphabetic character.

29. Look at the following array definition.

    ```
    char str[10];
    ```

    Assume that `name` is also a `char` array, and it holds a C-string. Write code that copies the contents of `name` to `str` if the C-string in `name` is not too big to fit in `str`.

30. Look at the following statements.

    ```
    char str[] = "237.89";
    double value;
    ```

    Write a statement that converts the string in `str` to a double and stores the result in `value`.

31. Write a function that accepts a pointer to a C-string as its argument. The function should count the number of times the character 'w' occurs in the argument and return that number.

32. Assume that `str1` and `str2` are string class objects. Write code that displays "They are the same!" if the two objects contain the same string.

True or False

33. T F Character testing functions, such as `isupper`, accept strings as arguments and test each character in the string.

34. T F If `toupper`'s argument is already uppercase, it is returned as is, with no changes.

35. T F If `tolower`'s argument is already lowercase, it will be inadvertently converted to uppercase.

36. T F The `strlen` function returns the size of the array containing a string.

37. T F If the starting address of a string is passed into a pointer parameter, it can be assumed that all the characters, from that address up to the byte that holds the null terminator, are part of the string.

38. T F String-handling functions accept as arguments pointers to strings (array names or pointer variables), or literal strings.

39. T F   The `strcat` function checks to make sure the first string is large enough to hold both strings before performing the concatenation.

40. T F   The `strcpy` function will overwrite the contents of its first string argument.

41. T F   The `strcpy` function performs no bounds checking on the first argument.

42. T F   There is no difference between "847" and 847.

Find the Errors

Each of the following programs or program segments has errors. Find as many as you can.

43. ```
char str[] = "Stop";
if (isupper(str) == "STOP")
    exit(0);
```

44. ```
char numeric[5];
int x = 123;
numeric = atoi(x);
```

45. ```
char string1[] = "Billy";
char string2[] = " Bob Jones";
strcat(string1, string2);
```

46. ```
char x = 'a', y = 'a';
if (strcmp(x, y) == 0)
    exit(0);
```

Programming Challenges

Visit www.myprogramminglab.com to complete many of these Programming Challenges online and get instant feedback.

1. **String Length**

   Write a function that returns an integer and accepts a pointer to a C-string as an argument. The function should count the number of characters in the string and return that number. Demonstrate the function in a simple program that asks the user to input a string, passes it to the function, and then displays the function's return value.

2. **Backward String**

   Write a function that accepts a pointer to a C-string as an argument and displays its contents backward. For instance, if the string argument is "Gravity" the function should display "ytivarG". Demonstrate the function in a program that asks the user to input a string and then passes it to the function.

VideoNote
Solving the Backward String Problem

3. **Word Counter**

   Write a function that accepts a pointer to a C-string as an argument and returns the number of words contained in the string. For instance, if the string argument is "Four score and seven years ago" the function should return the number 6. Demonstrate the function in a program that asks the user to input a string and then passes it to the function. The number of words in the string should be displayed on the screen. *Optional Exercise:* Write an overloaded version of this function that accepts a string class object as its argument.

4. **Average Number of Letters**

   Modify the program you wrote for Problem 3 (Word Counter), so it also displays the average number of letters in each word.

5. **Sentence Capitalizer**

   Write a function that accepts a pointer to a C-string as an argument and capitalizes the first character of each sentence in the string. For instance, if the string argument is "hello. my name is Joe. what is your name?" the function should manipulate the string so it contains "Hello. My name is Joe. What is your name?" Demonstrate the function in a program that asks the user to input a string and then passes it to the function. The modified string should be displayed on the screen. *Optional Exercise:* Write an overloaded version of this function that accepts a string class object as its argument.

6. **Vowels and Consonants**

   Write a function that accepts a pointer to a C-string as its argument. The function should count the number of vowels appearing in the string and return that number.

   Write another function that accepts a pointer to a C-string as its argument. This function should count the number of consonants appearing in the string and return that number.

   Demonstrate these two functions in a program that performs the following steps:

   1. The user is asked to enter a string.

   2. The program displays the following menu:
      A) Count the number of vowels in the string
      B) Count the number of consonants in the string
      C) Count both the vowels and consonants in the string
      D) Enter another string
      E) Exit the program

   3. The program performs the operation selected by the user and repeats until the user selects E to exit the program.

7. **Name Arranger**

   Write a program that asks for the user's first, middle, and last names. The names should be stored in three different character arrays. The program should then store, in a fourth array, the name arranged in the following manner: the last name followed by a comma and a space, followed by the first name and a space, followed by the middle name. For example, if the user entered "Carol Lynn Smith", it should store "Smith, Carol Lynn" in the fourth array. Display the contents of the fourth array on the screen.

8. **Sum of Digits in a String**

   Write a program that asks the user to enter a series of single digit numbers with nothing separating them. Read the input as a C-string or a string object. The program should display the sum of all the single-digit numbers in the string. For example, if the user enters 2514, the program should display 12, which is the sum of 2, 5, 1, and 4. The program should also display the highest and lowest digits in the string.

9. **Most Frequent Character**

Write a function that accepts either a pointer to a C-string, or a string object, as its argument. The function should return the character that appears most frequently in the string. Demonstrate the function in a complete program.

10. **replaceSubstring Function**

Write a function named replaceSubstring. The function should accept three C-string or string object arguments. Let's call them *string1*, *string2*, and *string3*. It should search *string1* for all occurrences of *string2*. When it finds an occurrence of *string2*, it should replace it with *string3*. For example, suppose the three arguments have the following values:

string1:	"the dog jumped over the fence"
string2:	"the"
string3:	"that"

With these three arguments, the function would return a string object with the value "that dog jumped over that fence." Demonstrate the function in a complete program.

11. **Case Manipulator**

Write a program with three functions: upper, lower, and reverse. The upper function should accept a pointer to a C-string as an argument. It should step through each character in the string, converting it to uppercase. The lower function, too, should accept a pointer to a C-string as an argument. It should step through each character in the string, converting it to lowercase. Like upper and lower, reverse should also accept a pointer to a string. As it steps through the string, it should test each character to determine whether it is upper- or lowercase. If a character is uppercase, it should be converted to lowercase. Likewise, if a character is lowercase, it should be converted to uppercase.

Test the functions by asking for a string in function main, then passing it to them in the following order: reverse, lower, and upper.

12. **Password Verifier**

Imagine you are developing a software package that requires users to enter their own passwords. Your software requires that users' passwords meet the following criteria:

- The password should be at least six characters long.
- The password should contain at least one uppercase and at least one lowercase letter.
- The password should have at least one digit.

Write a program that asks for a password and then verifies that it meets the stated criteria. If it doesn't, the program should display a message telling the user why.

13. **Date Printer**

Write a program that reads a string from the user containing a date in the form mm/dd/yyyy. It should print the date in the form March 12, 2012.

14. **Word Separator**

    Write a program that accepts as input a sentence in which all of the words are run together, but the first character of each word is uppercase. Convert the sentence to a string in which the words are separated by spaces and only the first word starts with an uppercase letter. For example the string "StopAndSmellTheRoses." would be converted to "Stop and smell the roses."

15. **Character Analysis**

    If you have downloaded this book's source code from the companion Web site, you will find a file named `text.txt` in the Chapter 10 folder. (The companion Web site is at www.pearsonhighered.com/gaddis.) Write a program that reads the file's contents and determines the following:

    - The number of uppercase letters in the file
    - The number of lowercase letters in the file
    - The number of digits in the file

16. **Pig Latin**

    Write a program that reads a sentence as input and converts each word to "Pig Latin." In one version, to convert a word to Pig Latin you remove the first letter and place that letter at the end of the word. Then you append the string "ay" to the word. Here is an example:

    English: I SLEPT MOST OF THE NIGHT

    Pig Latin: IAY LEPTSAY OSTMAY FOAY HETAY IGHTNAY

17. **Morse Code Converter**

    Morse code is a code where each letter of the English alphabet, each digit, and various punctuation characters are represented by a series of dots and dashes. Table 10-8 shows part of the code.

    Write a program that asks the user to enter a string, and then converts that string to Morse code.

Table 10-8   Morse Code

Character	Code	Character	Code	Character	Code	Character	Code
space	*space*	6	−....	G	−−.	Q	−−.−
comma	−−..−−	7	−−...	H	....	R	.−.
period	.−.−.−	8	−−−..	I	..	S	...
question mark	..−−..	9	−−−−.	J	.−−−	T	−
0	−−−−−	A	.−	K	−.−	U	..−
1	.−−−−	B	−...	L	.−..	V	...−
2	..−−−	C	−.−.	M	−−	W	.−−
3	...−−	D	−..	N	−.	X	−..−
4	....−	E	.	O	−−−	Y	−.−−
5	.....	F	..−.	P	.−−.	Z	−−..

18. **Phone Number List**

Write a program that has an array of at least 10 `string` objects that hold people's names and phone numbers. You may make up your own strings, or use the following:

```
"Becky Warren, 555-1223"
"Joe Looney, 555-0097"
"Geri Palmer, 555-8787"
"Lynn Presnell, 555-1212"
"Holly Gaddis, 555-8878"
"Sam Wiggins, 555-0998"
"Bob Kain, 555-8712"
"Tim Haynes, 555-7676"
"Warren Gaddis, 555-9037"
"Jean James, 555-4939"
"Ron Palmer, 555-2783"
```

The program should ask the user to enter a name or partial name to search for in the array. Any entries in the array that match the string entered should be displayed. For example, if the user enters "Palmer" the program should display the following names from the list:

```
Geri Palmer, 555-8787
Ron Palmer, 555-2783
```

19. **Check Writer**

Write a program that displays a simulated paycheck. The program should ask the user to enter the date, the payee's name, and the amount of the check. It should then display a simulated check with the dollar amount spelled out, as shown here:

```
                                              Date: 11/24/2012


Pay to the Order of: John Phillips            $1920.85

One thousand nine hundred twenty and 85 cents
```

Be sure to format the numeric value of the check in fixed-point notation with two decimal places of precision. Be sure the decimal place always displays, even when the number is zero or has no fractional part. Use either C-strings or string class objects in this program.

Input Validation: Do not accept negative dollar amounts, or amounts over $10,000.

11 Structured Data

TOPICS

11.1 Abstract Data Types

CONCEPT: Abstract data types (ADTs) are data types created by the programmer. ADTs have their own range (or domain) of data and their own sets of operations that may be performed on them.

The term *abstract data type*, or ADT, is very important in computer science and is especially significant in object-oriented programming. This chapter introduces you to the structure, which is one of C++'s mechanisms for creating abstract data types.

Abstraction

An *abstraction* is a general model of something. It is a definition that includes only the general characteristics of an object. For example, the term "dog" is an abstraction. It defines a general type of animal. The term captures the essence of what all dogs are without specifying the detailed characteristics of any particular type of dog. According to *Webster's New Collegiate Dictionary*, a dog is a highly variable carnivorous domesticated mammal (*Canis familiaris*) probably descended from the common wolf.

In real life, however, there is no such thing as a mere "dog." There are specific types of dogs, each with its own set of characteristics. There are poodles, cocker spaniels, Great Danes, rottweilers, and many other breeds. There are small dogs and large dogs. There are gentle dogs and ferocious dogs. They come in all shapes, sizes, and dispositions. A real-life dog is not abstract. It is concrete.

Data Types

C++ has several *primitive data types*, or data types that are defined as a basic part of the language, as shown in Table 11-1.

Table 11-1

`bool`	`int`	`unsigned long int`
`char`	`long int`	`float`
`unsigned char`	`unsigned short int`	`double`
`short int`	`unsigned int`	`long double`

A data type defines what values a variable may hold. Each data type listed in Table 11-1 has its own range of values, such as –32,768 to +32,767 for `short`s, and so forth. Data types also define what values a variable may not hold. For example, integer variables may not be used to hold fractional numbers.

In addition to defining a range or domain of values that a variable may hold, data types also define the operations that may be performed on a value. All of the data types listed in Table 11-1 allow the following mathematical and relational operators to be used with them:

```
+  -  *  /  >  <  >=  <=  ==  !=
```

Only the integer data types, however, allow operations with the modulus operator (%). So, a data type defines what values an object may hold and the operations that may be performed on the object.

The primitive data types are abstract in the sense that a data type and an object of that data type are not the same thing. For example, consider the following variable definition:

```
int x = 1, y = 2, z = 3;
```

In the statement above the integer variables x, y, and z are defined. They are three separate instances of the data type `int`. Each variable has its own characteristics (x is set to 1, y is set to 2, and z is set to 3). In this example, the data type `int` is the abstraction and the variables x, y, and z are concrete occurrences.

Abstract Data Types

An abstract data type (ADT) is a data type created by the programmer and is composed of one or more primitive data types. The programmer decides what values are acceptable for the data type, as well as what operations may be performed on the data type. In many cases, the programmer designs his or her own specialized operations.

For example, suppose a program is created to simulate a 12-hour clock. The program could contain three ADTs: Hours, Minutes, and Seconds. The range of values for the Hours data type would be the integers 1 through 12. The range of values for the Minutes and Seconds data types would be 0 through 59. If an Hours object is set to 12 and then incremented, it will then take on the value 1. Likewise if a Minutes object or a Seconds object is set to 59 and then incremented, it will take on the value 0.

Abstract data types often combine several values. In the clock program, the Hours, Minutes, and Seconds objects could be combined to form a single Clock object. In this chapter you will learn how to combine variables of primitive data types to form your own data structures, or ADTs.

11.2 Focus on Software Engineering: Combining Data into Structures

> **CONCEPT:** C++ allows you to group several variables together into a single item known as a structure.

So far you've written programs that keep data in individual variables. If you need to group items together, C++ allows you to create arrays. The limitation of arrays, however, is that all the elements must be of the same data type. Sometimes a relationship exists between items of different types. For example, a payroll system might keep the variables shown in Table 11-2. These variables hold data for a single employee.

Table 11-2

Variable Definition	Data Held
int empNumber;	Employee number
string name;	Employee's name
double hours;	Hours worked
double payRate;	Hourly pay rate
double grossPay;	Gross pay

VideoNote
Creating a Structure

All of the variables listed in Table 11-2 are related because they can hold data about the same employee. Their definition statements, though, do not make it clear that they belong together. To create a relationship between variables, C++ gives you the ability to package them together into a *structure*.

Before a structure can be used, it must be declared. Here is the general format of a structure declaration:

```
struct tag
{
    variable declaration;
    // ... more declarations
    //    may follow...
};
```

The *tag* is the name of the structure. As you will see later, it's used like a data type name. The variable declarations that appear inside the braces declare *members* of the structure. Here is an example of a structure declaration that holds the payroll data listed in Table 11-2:

```cpp
struct PayRoll
{
    int empNumber;      // Employee number
    string name;        // Employee's name
    double hours;       // Hours worked
    double payRate;     // Hourly pay rate
    double grossPay;    // Gross pay
};
```

This declaration declares a structure named `PayRoll`. The structure has five members: `empNumber`, `name`, `hours`, `payRate`, and `grossPay`.

 WARNING! Notice that a semicolon is required after the closing brace of the structure declaration.

 NOTE: In this text we begin the names of structure tags with an uppercase letter. Later you will see the same convention used with unions. This visually differentiates these names from the names of variables.

 NOTE: The structure declaration shown contains three `double` members, each declared on a separate line. The three could also have been declared on the same line, as

```cpp
struct PayRoll
{
    int empNumber;
    string name;
    double hours, payRate, grossPay;
};
```

Many programmers prefer to place each member declaration on a separate line, however, for increased readability.

It's important to note that the structure declaration in our example does not define a variable. It simply tells the compiler what a `PayRoll` structure is made of. In essence, it creates a new data type named `PayRoll`. You can define variables of this type with simple definition statements, just as you would with any other data type. For example, the following statement defines a variable named `deptHead`:

```cpp
PayRoll deptHead;
```

The data type of `deptHead` is the `PayRoll` structure. The structure tag, `PayRoll`, is listed before the variable name just as the word `int` or `double` would be listed to define variables of those types.

Remember that structure variables are actually made up of other variables known as members. Because `deptHead` is a `PayRoll` structure it contains the following members:

```
empNumber, an int
name, a string object
hours, a double
payRate, a double
grossPay, a double
```

Figure 11-1 illustrates this.

Figure 11-1

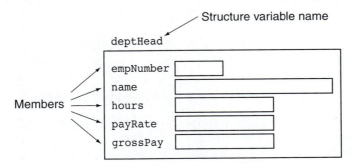

Just as it's possible to define multiple `int` or `double` variables, it's possible to define multiple structure variables in a program. The following statement defines three `PayRoll` variables: `deptHead`, `foreman`, and `associate`:

```
PayRoll deptHead, foreman, associate;
```

Figure 11-2 illustrates the existence of these three variables.

Figure 11-2

deptHead

empNumber	
name	
hours	
payRate	
grossPay	

foreman

empNumber	
name	
hours	
payRate	
grossPay	

associate

empNumber	
name	
hours	
payRate	
grossPay	

Each of the variables defined in this example is a separate *instance* of the `PayRoll` structure and contains its own members. An instance of a structure is a variable that exists in memory. It contains within it all the members described in the structure declaration.

Although the structure variables in the example are separate, each contains members with the same name. (In the next section you'll see how to access these members.) Here are some other examples of structure declarations and variable definitions:

```
struct Time                        struct Date
{                                  {
    int hour;                          int day;
    int minutes;                       int month;
    int seconds;                       int year;
};                                 };

// Definition of the              // Definition of the structure
// structure variable now.        // variable today.
Time now;                         Date today;
```

In review, there are typically two steps to implementing structures in a program:

- Create the structure declaration. This establishes the tag (or name) of the structure and a list of items that are members.
- Define variables (or instances) of the structure and use them in the program to hold data.

11.3 Accessing Structure Members

CONCEPT: The *dot operator* (.) allows you to access structure members in a program.

C++ provides the dot operator (a period) to access the individual members of a structure. Using our example of `deptHead` as a `PayRoll` structure variable, the following statement demonstrates how to access the `empNumber` member:

```
deptHead.empNumber = 475;
```

In this statement, the number 475 is assigned to the `empNumber` member of `deptHead`. The dot operator connects the name of the member variable with the name of the structure variable it belongs to. The following statements assign values to the `empNumber` members of the `deptHead`, `foreman`, and `associate` structure variables:

```
deptHead.empNumber = 475;
foreman.empNumber = 897;
associate.empNumber = 729;
```

With the dot operator you can use member variables just like regular variables. For example these statements display the contents of deptHead's members:

```
cout << deptHead.empNumber << endl;
cout << deptHead.name << endl;
cout << deptHead.hours << endl;
cout << deptHead.payRate << endl;
cout << deptHead.grossPay << endl;
```

Program 11-1 is a complete program that uses the PayRoll structure.

Program 11-1

```
 1  // This program demonstrates the use of structures.
 2  #include <iostream>
 3  #include <string>
 4  #include <iomanip>
 5  using namespace std;
 6
 7  struct PayRoll
 8  {
 9     int empNumber;     // Employee number
10     string name;       // Employee's name
11     double hours;      // Hours worked
12     double payRate;    // Hourly payRate
13     double grossPay;   // Gross pay
14  };
15
16  int main()
17  {
18     PayRoll employee; // employee is a PayRoll structure.
19
20     // Get the employee's number.
21     cout << "Enter the employee's number: ";
22     cin >> employee.empNumber;
23
24     // Get the employee's name.
25     cout << "Enter the employee's name: ";
26     cin.ignore();  // To skip the remaining '\n' character
27     getline(cin, employee.name);
28
29     // Get the hours worked by the employee.
30     cout << "How many hours did the employee work? ";
31     cin >> employee.hours;
32
33     // Get the employee's hourly pay rate.
34     cout << "What is the employee's hourly payRate? ";
35     cin >> employee.payRate;
36
37     // Calculate the employee's gross pay.
38     employee.grossPay = employee.hours * employee.payRate;
39
```

(program continues)

Program 11-1 *(continued)*

```
40      // Display the employee data.
41      cout << "Here is the employee's payroll data:\n";
42      cout << "Name: " << employee.name << endl;
43      cout << "Number: " << employee.empNumber << endl;
44      cout << "Hours worked: " << employee.hours << endl;
45      cout << "Hourly payRate: " << employee.payRate << endl;
46      cout << fixed << showpoint << setprecision(2);
47      cout << "Gross Pay: $" << employee.grossPay << endl;
48      return 0;
49  }
```

Program Output with Example Input Shown in Bold

```
Enter the employee's number: 489 [Enter]
Enter the employee's name: Jill Smith [Enter]
How many hours did the employee work? 40 [Enter]
What is the employee's hourly pay rate? 20 [Enter]
Here is the employee's payroll data:
Name: Jill Smith
Number: 489
Hours worked: 40
Hourly pay rate: 20
Gross pay: $800.00
```

NOTE: Program 11-1 has the following call, in line 26, to cin's ignore member function:

```
cin.ignore();
```

Recall that the ignore function causes cin to ignore the next character in the input buffer. This is necessary for the getline function to work properly in the program.

NOTE: The contents of a structure variable cannot be displayed by passing the entire variable to cout. For example, assuming employee is a PayRoll structure variable, the following statement will not work:

```
cout << employee << endl;  // Will not work!
```

Instead, each member must be separately passed to cout.

As you can see from Program 11-1, structure members that are of a primitive data type can be used with cin, cout, mathematical statements, and any operation that can be performed with regular variables. The only difference is that the structure variable name and the dot operator must precede the name of a member. Program 11-2 shows the member of a structure variable being passed to the pow function.

Program 11-2

```cpp
 1   // This program stores data about a circle in a structure.
 2   #include <iostream>
 3   #include <cmath>   // For the pow function
 4   #include <iomanip>
 5   using namespace std;
 6
 7   // Constant for pi.
 8   const double PI = 3.14159;
 9
10   // Structure declaration
11   struct Circle
12   {
13       double radius;       // A circle's radius
14       double diameter;     // A circle's diameter
15       double area;         // A circle's area
16   };
17
18   int main()
19   {
20       Circle c;     // Define a structure variable
21
22       // Get the circle's diameter.
23       cout << "Enter the diameter of a circle: ";
24       cin >> c.diameter;
25
26       // Calculate the circle's radius.
27       c.radius = c.diameter / 2;
28
29       // Calculate the circle's area.
30       c.area = PI * pow(c.radius, 2.0);
31
32       // Display the circle data.
33       cout << fixed << showpoint << setprecision(2);
34       cout << "The radius and area of the circle are:\n";
35       cout << "Radius: " << c.radius << endl;
36       cout << "Area: " << c.area << endl;
37       return 0;
38   }
```

Program Output with Example Input Shown in Bold

```
Enter the diameter of a circle: 10 [Enter]
The radius and area of the circle are:
Radius: 5
Area: 78.54
```

Comparing Structure Variables

You cannot perform comparison operations directly on structure variables. For example, assume that `circle1` and `circle2` are `Circle` structure variables. The following statement will cause an error.

```
if (circle1 == circle2)    // Error!
```

In order to compare two structures, you must compare the individual members, as shown in the following code.

```
if (circle1.radius == circle2.radius &&
    circle1.diameter == circle2.diameter &&
    circle1.area == circle2.area)
```

11.4 Initializing a Structure

CONCEPT: The members of a structure variable may be initialized with starting values when the structure variable is defined.

A structure variable may be initialized when it is defined, in a fashion similar to the initialization of an array. Assume the following structure declaration exists in a program:

```
struct CityInfo
{
    string cityName;
    string state;
    long population;
    int distance;
};
```

A variable may then be defined with an initialization list, as shown in the following:

```
CityInfo location = {"Asheville", "NC", 50000, 28};
```

This statement defines the variable `location`. The first value in the initialization list is assigned to the first declared member, the second value in the initialization list is assigned to the second member, and so on. The `location` variable is initialized in the following manner:

The string "Asheville" is assigned to `location.cityName`
The string "NC" is assigned to `location.state`
50000 is assigned to `location.population`
28 is assigned to `location.distance`

You do not have to provide initializers for all the members of a structure variable. For example, the following statement only initializes the `cityName` member of `location`:

```
CityInfo location = {"Tampa"};
```

The `state`, `population`, and `distance` members are left uninitialized. The following statement only initializes the `cityName` and `state` members, while leaving `population` and `distance` uninitialized:

```
CityInfo location = {"Atlanta", "GA"};
```

If you leave a structure member uninitialized, you must leave all the members that follow it uninitialized as well. C++ does not provide a way to skip members in a structure. For example, the following statement, which attempts to skip the initialization of the `population` member, is *not* legal:

```
CityInfo location = {"Knoxville", "TN", , 90};  // Illegal!
```

Program 11-3 demonstrates the use of partially initialized structure variables.

Program 11-3

```cpp
 1  // This program demonstrates partially initialized
 2  // structure variables.
 3  #include <iostream>
 4  #include <string>
 5  #include <iomanip>
 6  using namespace std;
 7
 8  struct EmployeePay
 9  {
10      string name;        // Employee name
11      int empNum;         // Employee number
12      double payRate;     // Hourly pay rate
13      double hours;       // Hours worked
14      double grossPay;    // Gross pay
15  };
16
17  int main()
18  {
19      EmployeePay employee1 = {"Betty Ross", 141, 18.75};
20      EmployeePay employee2 = {"Jill Sandburg", 142, 17.50};
21
22      cout << fixed << showpoint << setprecision(2);
23
24      // Calculate pay for employee1
25      cout << "Name: " << employee1.name << endl;
26      cout << "Employee Number: " << employee1.empNum << endl;
27      cout << "Enter the hours worked by this employee: ";
28      cin >> employee1.hours;
29      employee1.grossPay = employee1.hours * employee1.payRate;
30      cout << "Gross Pay: " << employee1.grossPay << endl << endl;
31
32      // Calculate pay for employee2
33      cout << "Name: " << employee2.name << endl;
34      cout << "Employee Number: " << employee2.empNum << endl;
35      cout << "Enter the hours worked by this employee: ";
```

(program continues)

Program 11-3 *(continued)*

```
36      cin >> employee2.hours;
37      employee2.grossPay = employee2.hours * employee2.payRate;
38      cout << "Gross Pay: " << employee2.grossPay << endl;
39      return 0;
40   }
```

Program Output with Example Input Shown in Bold
```
Name: Betty Ross
Employee Number: 141
Enter the hours worked by this employee: 40 [Enter]
Gross Pay: 750.00

Name: Jill Sandburg
Employee Number: 142
Enter the hours worked by this employee: 20 [Enter]
Gross Pay: 350.00
```

It's important to note that you cannot initialize a structure member in the declaration of the structure. For instance, the following declaration is illegal:

```
// Illegal structure declaration
struct CityInfo
{
    string cityName = "Asheville";    // Error!
    string state = "NC";              // Error!
    long population = 50000;          // Error!
    int distance = 28;                // Error!
};
```

Remember that a structure declaration doesn't actually create the member variables. It only declares what the structure "looks like." The member variables are created in memory when a structure variable is defined. Because no variables are created by the structure declaration, there's nothing that can be initialized there.

Checkpoint

myprogramminglab *www.myprogramminglab.com*

11.1 Write a structure declaration to hold the following data about a savings account:
Account Number (string object)
Account Balance (double)
Interest Rate (double)
Average Monthly Balance (double)

11.2 Write a definition statement for a variable of the structure you declared in Question 11.1. Initialize the members with the following data:
Account Number: ACZ42137-B12-7
Account Balance: $4512.59
Interest Rate: 4%
Average Monthly Balance: $4217.07

11.3　The following program skeleton, when complete, asks the user to enter these data about his or her favorite movie:

Name of movie
Name of the movie's director
Name of the movie's producer
The year the movie was released

Complete the program by declaring the structure that holds this data, defining a structure variable, and writing the individual statements necessary.

```
#include <iostream>
using namespace std;

// Write the structure declaration here to hold the movie data.

int main()
{
    // define the structure variable here.

    cout << "Enter the following data about your\n";
    cout << "favorite movie.\n";
    cout << "name: ";
    // Write a statement here that lets the user enter the
    // name of a favorite movie. Store the name in the
    // structure variable.
    cout << "Director: ";
    // Write a statement here that lets the user enter the
    // name of the movie's director. Store the name in the
    // structure variable.
    cout << "Producer: ";
    // Write a statement here that lets the user enter the
    // name of the movie's producer. Store the name in the
    // structure variable.
    cout << "Year of release: ";
    // Write a statement here that lets the user enter the
    // year the movie was released. Store the year in the
    // structure variable.
    cout << "Here is data on your favorite movie:\n";
    // Write statements here that display the data.
    // just entered into the structure variable.
    return 0;
}
```

11.5 Arrays of Structures

CONCEPT: Arrays of structures can simplify some programming tasks.

In Chapter 7 you saw that data can be stored in two or more arrays, with a relationship established between the arrays through their subscripts. Because structures can hold several items of varying data types, a single array of structures can be used in place of several arrays of regular variables.

An array of structures is defined like any other array. Assume the following structure declaration exists in a program:

```
struct BookInfo
{
    string title;
    string author;
    string publisher;
    double price;
};
```

The following statement defines an array, `bookList`, that has 20 elements. Each element is a `BookInfo` structure.

```
BookInfo bookList[20];
```

Each element of the array may be accessed through a subscript. For example, `bookList[0]` is the first structure in the array, `bookList[1]` is the second, and so forth. To access a member of any element, simply place the dot operator and member name after the subscript. For example, the following expression refers to the `title` member of `bookList[5]`:

```
bookList[5].title
```

The following loop steps through the array, displaying the data stored in each element:

```
for (int index = 0; index < 20; index++)
{
    cout << bookList[index].title << endl;
    cout << bookList[index].author << endl;
    cout << bookList[index].publisher << endl;
    cout << bookList[index].price << endl << endl;
}
```

Program 11-4 calculates and displays payroll data for three employees. It uses a single array of structures.

Program 11-4

```
 1   // This program uses an array of structures.
 2   #include <iostream>
 3   #include <iomanip>
 4   using namespace std;
 5
 6   struct PayInfo
 7   {
 8       int hours;          // Hours worked
 9       double payRate;     // Hourly pay rate
10   };
11
12   int main()
13   {
14       const int NUM_WORKERS = 3;      // Number of workers
15       PayInfo workers[NUM_WORKERS];   // Array of structures
16       int index;                      // Loop counter
17
```

```
18        // Get employee pay data.
19        cout << "Enter the hours worked by " << NUM_WORKERS
20             << " employees and their hourly rates.\n";
21
22        for (index = 0; index < NUM_WORKERS; index++)
23        {
24            // Get the hours worked by an employee.
25            cout << "Hours worked by employee #" << (index + 1);
26            cout << ": ";
27            cin >> workers[index].hours;
28
29            // Get the employee's hourly pay rate.
30            cout << "Hourly pay rate for employee #";
31            cout << (index + 1) << ": ";
32            cin >> workers[index].payRate;
33            cout << endl;
34        }
35
36        // Display each employee's gross pay.
37        cout << "Here is the gross pay for each employee:\n";
38        cout << fixed << showpoint << setprecision(2);
39        for (index = 0; index < NUM_WORKERS; index++)
40        {
41            double gross;
42            gross = workers[index].hours * workers[index].payRate;
43            cout << "Employee #" << (index + 1);
44            cout << ": $" << gross << endl;
45        }
46        return 0;
47    }
```

Program Output with Example Input Shown in Bold

```
Enter the hours worked by 3 employees and their hourly rates.
Hours worked by employee #1: 10 [Enter]
Hourly pay rate for employee #1: 9.75 [Enter]

Hours worked by employee #2: 20 [Enter]
Hourly pay rate for employee #2: 10.00 [Enter]

Hours worked by employee #3: 40 [Enter]
Hourly pay rate for employee #3: 20.00 [Enter]

Here is the gross pay for each employee:
Employee #1: $97.50
Employee #2: $200.00
Employee #3: $800.00
```

Initializing a Structure Array

To initialize a structure array, simply provide an initialization list for one or more of the elements. For example, the array in Program 11-4 could have been initialized as follows:

```
PayInfo workers[NUM_WORKERS] = {
                                {10, 9.75 },
                                {15, 8.62 },
                                {20, 10.50},
                                {40, 18.75},
                                {40, 15.65}
                               };
```

As in all single-dimensional arrays, you can initialize all or part of the elements in an array of structures, as long as you do not skip elements.

11.6 Focus on Software Engineering: Nested Structures

CONCEPT: It's possible for a structure variable to be a member of another structure variable.

Sometimes it's helpful to nest structures inside other structures. For example, consider the following structure declarations:

```
struct Costs
{
    double wholesale;
    double retail;
};

struct Item
{
    string partNum;
    string description;
    Costs pricing;
};
```

The `Costs` structure has two members: `wholesale` and `retail`, both `doubles`. Notice that the third member of the `Item` structure, `pricing`, is a `Costs` structure. Assume the variable `widget` is defined as follows:

```
Item widget;
```

The following statements show examples of accessing members of the `pricing` variable, which is inside `widget`:

```
widget.pricing.wholesale = 100.0;
widget.pricing.retail = 150.0;
```

Program 11-5 gives a more elaborate illustration of nested structures.

Program 11-5

```cpp
1   // This program uses nested structures.
2   #include <iostream>
3   #include <string>
4   using namespace std;
5
6   // The Date structure holds data about a date.
7   struct Date
8   {
9      int month;
10     int day;
11     int year;
12  };
13
14  // The Place structure holds a physical address.
15  struct Place
16  {
17     string address;
18     string city;
19     string state;
20     string zip;
21  };
22
23  // The EmployeeInfo structure holds an employee's data.
24  struct EmployeeInfo
25  {
26     string name;
27     int employeeNumber;
28     Date birthDate;          // Nested structure
29     Place residence;         // Nested structure
30  };
31
32  int main()
33  {
34     // Define a structure variable to hold info about the manager.
35     EmployeeInfo manager;
36
37     // Get the manager's name and employee number
38     cout << "Enter the manager's name: ";
39     getline(cin, manager.name);
40     cout << "Enter the manager's employee number: ";
41     cin >> manager.employeeNumber;
42
43     // Get the manager's birth date
44     cout << "Now enter the manager's date of birth.\n";
45     cout << "Month (up to 2 digits): ";
```

(program continues)

Program 11-5 *(continued)*

```
46        cin >> manager.birthDate.month;
47        cout << "Day (up to 2 digits): ";
48        cin >> manager.birthDate.day;
49        cout << "Year: ";
50        cin >> manager.birthDate.year;
51        cin.ignore();  // Skip the remaining newline character
52
53        // Get the manager's residence information
54        cout << "Enter the manager's street address: ";
55        getline(cin, manager.residence.address);
56        cout << "City: ";
57        getline(cin, manager.residence.city);
58        cout << "State: ";
59        getline(cin, manager.residence.state);
60        cout << "ZIP Code: ";
61        getline(cin, manager.residence.zip);
62
63        // Display the information just entered
64        cout << "\nHere is the manager's information:\n";
65        cout << manager.name << endl;
66        cout << "Employee number " << manager.employeeNumber << endl;
67        cout << "Date of birth: ";
68        cout << manager.birthDate.month << "-";
69        cout << manager.birthDate.day << "-";
70        cout << manager.birthDate.year << endl;
71        cout << "Place of residence:\n";
72        cout << manager.residence.address << endl;
73        cout << manager.residence.city << ", ";
74        cout << manager.residence.state << "   ";
75        cout << manager.residence.zip << endl;
76        return 0;
77 }
```

Program Output with Example Input Shown in Bold

```
Enter the manager's name: John Smith [Enter]
Enter the manager's employee number: 789 [Enter]
Now enter the manager's date of birth.
Month (up to 2 digits): 10 [Enter]
Day (up to 2 digits): 14 [Enter]
Year: 1970 [Enter]
Enter the manager's street address: 190 Disk Drive [Enter]
City: Redmond [Enter]
State: WA [Enter]
ZIP Code: 98052 [Enter]
```

```
Here is the manager's information:
John Smith
Employee number 789
Date of birth: 10-14-1970
Place of residence:
190 Disk Drive
Redmond, WA  98052
```

 Checkpoint

myprogramminglab *www.myprogramminglab.com*

For Questions 11.4–11.7 below, assume the `Product` structure is declared as follows:

```
struct Product
{
    string description;    // Product description
    int partNum;           // Part number
    double cost;           // Product cost
};
```

11.4   Write a definition for an array of 100 `Product` structures. Do not initialize the array.

11.5   Write a loop that will step through the entire array you defined in Question 11.4, setting all the product descriptions to an empty string, all part numbers to zero, and all costs to zero.

11.6   Write the statements that will store the following data in the first element of the array you defined in Question 11.4:

Description: Claw hammer
Part Number: 547
Part Cost: $8.29

11.7   Write a loop that will display the contents of the entire array you created in Question 11.4.

11.8   Write a structure declaration named `Measurement`, with the following members:

miles, an integer
meters, a long integer

11.9   Write a structure declaration named `Destination`, with the following members:

city, a string object
distance, a Measurement structure (declared in Question 11.8)

Also define a variable of this structure type.

11.10   Write statements that store the following data in the variable you defined in Question 11.9:

City: Tupelo
Miles: 375
Meters: 603,375

11.7 Structures as Function Arguments

CONCEPT: Structure variables may be passed as arguments to functions.

VideoNote

Passing a Structure to a Function

Like other variables, the individual members of a structure variable may be used as function arguments. For example, assume the following structure declaration exists in a program:

```
struct Rectangle
{
    double length;
    double width;
    double area;
};
```

Let's say the following function definition exists in the same program:

```
double multiply(double x, double y)
{
    return x * y;
}
```

Assuming that box is a variable of the Rectangle structure type, the following function call will pass box.length into x and box.width into y. The return value will be stored in box.area.

```
box.area = multiply(box.length, box.width);
```

Sometimes it's more convenient to pass an entire structure variable into a function instead of individual members. For example, the following function definition uses a Rectangle structure variable as its parameter:

```
void showRect(Rectangle r)
{
    cout << r.length << endl;
    cout << r.width << endl;
    cout << r.area << endl;
}
```

The following function call passes the box variable into r:

```
showRect(box);
```

Inside the function showRect, r's members contain a copy of box's members. This is illustrated in Figure 11-3.

Once the function is called, r.length contains a copy of box.length, r.width contains a copy of box.width, and r.area contains a copy of box.area.

Structures, like all variables, are normally passed by value into a function. If a function is to access the members of the original argument, a reference variable may be used as the parameter. Program 11-6 uses two functions that accept structures as arguments. Arguments are passed to the getItem function by reference, and to the showItem function by value.

Figure 11-3

```
                          showRect(box);


                    void showRect(Rectangle r)
                    {
                            cout << r.length << endl;
                            cout << r.width << endl;
                            cout << r.area << endl;
                    }
```

Program 11-6

```cpp
1   // This program has functions that accept structure variables
2   // as arguments.
3   #include <iostream>
4   #include <string>
5   #include <iomanip>
6   using namespace std;
7
8   struct InventoryItem
9   {
10      int partNum;                  // Part number
11      string description;           // Item description
12      int onHand;                   // Units on hand
13      double price;                 // Unit price
14  };
15
16  // Function Prototypes
17  void getItem(InventoryItem&);     // Argument passed by reference
18  void showItem(InventoryItem);     // Argument passed by value
19
20  int main()
21  {
22      InventoryItem part;
23
24      getItem(part);
25      showItem(part);
26      return 0;
27  }
28
29  //*********************************************************
30  // Definition of function getItem. This function uses     *
31  // a structure reference variable as its parameter. It asks *
32  // the user for information to store in the structure.     *
33  //*********************************************************
34
```

(program continues)

Program 11-6 *(continued)*

```
35  void getItem(InventoryItem &p)    // Uses a reference parameter
36  {
37     // Get the part number.
38     cout << "Enter the part number: ";
39     cin >> p.partNum;
40
41     // Get the part description.
42     cout << "Enter the part description: ";
43     cin.ignore();  // Ignore the remaining newline character
44     getline(cin, p.description);
45
46     // Get the quantity on hand.
47     cout << "Enter the quantity on hand: ";
48     cin >> p.onHand;
49
50     // Get the unit price.
51     cout << "Enter the unit price: ";
52     cin >> p.price;
53  }
54
55  //***********************************************************
56  // Definition of function showItem. This function accepts   *
57  // an argument of the InventoryItem structure type. The     *
58  // contents of the structure is displayed.                  *
59  //***********************************************************
60
61  void showItem(InventoryItem p)
62  {
63     cout << fixed << showpoint << setprecision(2);
64     cout << "Part Number: " << p.partNum << endl;
65     cout << "Description: " << p.description << endl;
66     cout << "Units On Hand: " << p.onHand << endl;
67     cout << "Price: $" << p.price << endl;
68  }
```

Program Output with Example Input Shown in Bold
```
Enter the part number: 800 [Enter]
Enter the part description: Screwdriver [Enter]
Enter the quantity on hand: 135 [Enter]
Enter the unit price: 1.25 [Enter]
Part Number: 800
Description: Screwdriver
Units on Hand: 135
Price: $1.25
```

Notice that the InventoryItem structure declaration in Program 11-6 appears before both the prototypes and the definitions of the getItem and showItem functions. This is because both functions use an InventoryItem structure variable as their parameter. The compiler must know what InventoryItem is before it encounters any definitions for variables of that type. Otherwise, an error will occur.

Constant Reference Parameters

Sometimes structures can be quite large. Passing large structures by value can decrease a program's performance because a copy of the structure has to be created. When a structure is passed by reference, however, it isn't copied. A reference that points to the original argument is passed instead. So, it's often preferable to pass large objects such as structures by reference.

Of course, the disadvantage of passing an object by reference is that the function has access to the original argument. It can potentially alter the argument's value. This can be prevented, however, by passing the argument as a constant reference. The showItem function from Program 11-6 is shown here, modified to use a constant reference parameter.

```
void showItem(const InventoryItem &p)
{
    cout << fixed << showpoint << setprecision(2);
    cout << "Part Number: " << p.partNum << endl;
    cout << "Description: " << p.description << endl;
    cout << "Units on Hand: " << p.onHand << endl;
    cout << "Price: $" << p.price << endl;
}
```

This version of the function is more efficient than the original version because the amount of time and memory consumed in the function call is reduced. Because the parameter is defined as a constant, the function cannot accidentally corrupt the value of the argument.

The prototype for this version of the function follows.

```
void showItem(const InventoryItem&);
```

11.8 Returning a Structure from a Function

CONCEPT: A function may return a structure.

Just as functions can be written to return an `int`, `long`, `double`, or other data type, they can also be designed to return a structure. Recall the following structure declaration from Program 11-2:

```
struct Circle
{
    double radius;
    double diameter;
    double area;
};
```

A function, such as the following, could be written to return a variable of the `Circle` data type:

```
Circle getCircleData()
{
    Circle temp;               // Temporary Circle structure

    temp.radius = 10.0;     // Store the radius
    temp.diameter = 20.0;   // Store the diameter
    temp.area = 314.159;    // Store the area
    return temp;            // Return the temporary structure
}
```

Notice that the getCircleData function has a return data type of Circle. That means the function returns an entire Circle structure when it terminates. The return value can be assigned to any variable that is a Circle structure. The following statement, for example, assigns the function's return value to the Circle structure variable named myCircle:

```
myCircle = getCircleData();
```

After this statement executes, myCircle.radius will be set to 10.0, myCircle.diameter will be set to 20.0, and myCircle.area will be set to 314.159.

When a function returns a structure, it is always necessary for the function to have a local structure variable to hold the member values that are to be returned. In the getCircleData function, the values for diameter, radius, and area are stored in the local variable temp. The temp variable is then returned from the function.

Program 11-7 is a modification of Program 11-2. The function getInfo gets the circle's diameter from the user and calculates the circle's radius. The diameter and radius are stored in a local structure variable, round, which is returned from the function.

Program 11-7

```
1   // This program uses a function to return a structure. This
2   // is a modification of Program 11-2.
3   #include <iostream>
4   #include <iomanip>
5   #include <cmath>   // For the pow function
6   using namespace std;
7
8   // Constant for pi.
9   const double PI = 3.14159;
10
11  // Structure declaration
12  struct Circle
13  {
14     double radius;       // A circle's radius
15     double diameter;     // A circle's diameter
16     double area;         // A circle's area
17  };
18
19  // Function prototype
20  Circle getInfo();
21
22  int main()
23  {
24     Circle c;       // Define a structure variable
```

```cpp
25
26      // Get data about the circle.
27      c = getInfo();
28
29      // Calculate the circle's area.
30      c.area = PI * pow(c.radius, 2.0);
31
32      // Display the circle data.
33      cout << "The radius and area of the circle are:\n";
34      cout << fixed << setprecision(2);
35      cout << "Radius: " << c.radius << endl;
36      cout << "Area: " << c.area << endl;
37      return 0;
38   }
39
40   //************************************************************
41   // Definition of function getInfo. This function uses a local   *
42   // variable, tempCircle, which is a circle structure. The user  *
43   // enters the diameter of the circle, which is stored in        *
44   // tempCircle.diameter. The function then calculates the radius *
45   // which is stored in tempCircle.radius. tempCircle is then     *
46   // returned from the function.                                  *
47   //************************************************************
48
49   Circle getInfo()
50   {
51      Circle tempCircle;  // Temporary structure variable
52
53      // Store circle data in the temporary variable.
54      cout << "Enter the diameter of a circle: ";
55      cin >> tempCircle.diameter;
56      tempCircle.radius = tempCircle.diameter / 2.0;
57
58      // Return the temporary variable.
59      return tempCircle;
60   }
```

Program Output with Example Input Shown in Bold
Enter the diameter of a circle: **10 [Enter]**
The radius and area of the circle are:
Radius: 5.00
Area: 78.54

NOTE: In Chapter 6 you learned that C++ only allows you to return a single value from a function. Structures, however, provide a way around this limitation. Even though a structure may have several members, it is technically a single value. By packaging multiple values inside a structure, you can return as many variables as you need from a function.

11.9 Pointers to Structures

CONCEPT: You may take the address of a structure variable and create variables that are pointers to structures.

Defining a variable that is a pointer to a structure is as simple as defining any other pointer variable: The data type is followed by an asterisk and the name of the pointer variable. Here is an example:

```
Circle *cirPtr;
```

This statement defines `cirPtr` as a pointer to a `Circle` structure. Look at the following code:

```
Circle myCircle = { 10.0, 20.0, 314.159 };
Circle *cirPtr;
cirPtr = &myCircle;
```

The first two lines define `myCircle`, a structure variable, and `cirPtr`, a pointer. The third line assigns the address of `myCircle` to `cirPtr`. After this line executes, `cirPtr` will point to the `myCircle` structure. This is illustrated in Figure 11-4.

Figure 11-4

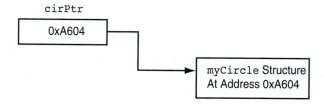

Indirectly accessing the members of a structure through a pointer can be clumsy, however, if the indirection operator is used. One might think the following statement would access the `radius` member of the structure pointed to by `cirPtr`, but it doesn't:

```
*cirPtr.radius = 10;
```

The dot operator has higher precedence than the indirection operator, so the indirection operator tries to dereference `cirPtr.radius`, not `cirPtr`. To dereference the `cirPtr` pointer, a set of parentheses must be used.

```
(*cirPtr).radius = 10;
```

Because of the awkwardness of this notation, C++ has a special operator for dereferencing structure pointers. It's called the *structure pointer operator*, and it consists of a hyphen (-) followed by the greater-than symbol (>). The previous statement, rewritten with the structure pointer operator, looks like this:

```
cirPtr->radius = 10;
```

The structure pointer operator takes the place of the dot operator in statements using pointers to structures. The operator automatically dereferences the structure pointer on its left. There is no need to enclose the pointer name in parentheses.

NOTE: The structure pointer operator is supposed to look like an arrow, thus visually indicating that a "pointer" is being used.

Program 11-8 shows that a pointer to a structure may be used as a function parameter, allowing the function to access the members of the original structure argument.

Program 11-8

```
1  // This program demonstrates a function that uses a
2  // pointer to a structure variable as a parameter.
3  #include <iostream>
4  #include <string>
5  #include <iomanip>
6  using namespace std;
7
8  struct Student
9  {
10     string name;          // Student's name
11     int idNum;            // Student ID number
12     int creditHours;      // Credit hours enrolled
13     double gpa;           // Current GPA
14  };
15
16  void getData(Student *);  // Function prototype
17
18  int main()
19  {
20     Student freshman;
21
22     // Get the student data.
23     cout << "Enter the following student data:\n";
24     getData(&freshman);     // Pass the address of freshman.
25     cout << "\nHere is the student data you entered:\n";
26
27     // Now display the data stored in freshman
28     cout << setprecision(3);
29     cout << "Name: " << freshman.name << endl;
30     cout << "ID Number: " << freshman.idNum << endl;
31     cout << "Credit Hours: " << freshman.creditHours << endl;
32     cout << "GPA: " << freshman.gpa << endl;
33     return 0;
34  }
35
```

(program continues)

Program 11-8 *(continued)*

```
36   //***********************************************************
37   // Definition of function getData. Uses a pointer to a    *
38   // Student structure variable. The user enters student    *
39   // information, which is stored in the variable.           *
40   //***********************************************************
41
42   void getData(Student *s)
43   {
44      // Get the student name.
45      cout << "Student name: ";
46      getline(cin, s->name);
47
48      // Get the student ID number.
49      cout << "Student ID Number: ";
50      cin >> s->idNum;
51
52      // Get the credit hours enrolled.
53      cout << "Credit Hours Enrolled: ";
54      cin >> s->creditHours;
55
56      // Get the GPA.
57      cout << "Current GPA: ";
58      cin >> s->gpa;
59   }
```

Program Output with Example Input Shown in Bold
```
Enter the following student data:
Student Name: Frank Smith [Enter]
Student ID Number: 4876 [Enter]
Credit Hours Enrolled: 12 [Enter]
Current GPA: 3.45 [Enter]

Here is the student data you entered:
Name: Frank Smith
ID Number: 4876
Credit Hours: 12
GPA: 3.45
```

Dynamically Allocating a Structure

You can also use a structure pointer and the new operator to dynamically allocate a structure. For example, the following code defines a Circle pointer named cirPtr and dynamically allocates a Circle structure. Values are then stored in the dynamically allocated structure's members.

```
Circle *cirPtr;            // Define a Circle pointer
cirPtr = new Circle;       // Dynamically allocate a Circle structure
cirPtr->radius = 10;       // Store a value in the radius member
cirPtr->diameter = 20;     // Store a value in the diameter member
cirPtr->area = 314.159;    // Store a value in the area member
```

You can also dynamically allocate an array of structures. The following code shows an array of five `Circle` structures being allocated.

```
Circle *circles;
circles = new Circle[5];
for (int count = 0; count < 5; count++)
{
    cout << "Enter the radius for circle "
         << (count + 1) << ": ";
    cin >> circles[count].radius;
}
```

11.10 Focus on Software Engineering: When to Use ., When to Use –>, and When to Use *

Sometimes structures contain pointers as members. For example, the following structure declaration has an `int` pointer member:

```
struct GradeInfo
{
    string name;            // Student names
    int *testScores;        // Dynamically allocated array
    float average;          // Test average
};
```

It is important to remember that the structure pointer operator (`->`) is used to dereference a pointer to a structure, not a pointer that is a member of a structure. If a program dereferences the `testScores` pointer in this structure, the indirection operator must be used. For example, assume that the following variable has been defined:

```
GradeInfo student1;
```

The following statement will display the value pointed to by the `testScores` member:

```
cout << *student1.testScores;
```

It is still possible to define a pointer to a structure that contains a pointer member. For instance, the following statement defines `stPtr` as a pointer to a `GradeInfo` structure:

```
GradeInfo *stPtr;
```

Assuming that `stPtr` points to a valid `GradeInfo` variable, the following statement will display the value pointed to by its `testScores` member:

```
cout << *stPtr->testScores;
```

In this statement, the `*` operator dereferences `stPtr->testScores`, while the `->` operator dereferences `stPtr`. It might help to remember that the following expression:

```
stPtr->testScores
```

is equivalent to

```
(*stPtr).testScores
```

So, the expression

```
*stPtr->testScores
```

is the same as

```
*(*stPtr).testScores
```

The awkwardness of this last expression shows the necessity of the `->` operator. Table 11-3 lists some expressions using the `*`, `->`, and `.` operators, and describes what each references.

Table 11-3

Expression	Description
`s->m`	s is a structure pointer and m is a member. This expression accesses the m member of the structure pointed to by s.
`*a.p`	a is a structure variable and p, a pointer, is a member. This expression dereferences the value pointed to by p.
`(*s).m`	s is a structure pointer and m is a member. The `*` operator dereferences s, causing the expression to access the m member of the structure pointed to by s. This expression is the same as `s->m`.
`*s->p`	s is a structure pointer and p, a pointer, is a member of the structure pointed to by s. This expression accesses the value pointed to by p. (The `->` operator dereferences s and the `*` operator dereferences p.)
`*(*s).p`	s is a structure pointer and p, a pointer, is a member of the structure pointed to by s. This expression accesses the value pointed to by p. `(*s)` dereferences s and the outermost `*` operator dereferences p. The expression `*s->p` is equivalent.

 Checkpoint

myprogramminglab   *www.myprogramminglab.com*

Assume the following structure declaration exists for Questions 11.11–11.15:

```
struct Rectangle
{
    int length;
    int width;
};
```

11.11   Write a function that accepts a `Rectangle` structure as its argument and displays the structure's contents on the screen.

11.12   Write a function that uses a `Rectangle` structure reference variable as its parameter and stores the user's input in the structure's members.

11.13   Write a function that returns a `Rectangle` structure. The function should store the user's input in the members of the structure before returning it.

11.14   Write the definition of a pointer to a `Rectangle` structure.

11.15   Assume `rptr` is a pointer to a `Rectangle` structure. Which of the expressions, A, B, or C, is equivalent to the following expression:

```
rptr->width
```

A)   `*rptr.width`

B)   `(*rptr).width`

C)   `rptr.(*width)`

11.11   Unions

CONCEPT: A *union* is like a structure, except all the members occupy the same memory area.

A union, in almost all regards, is just like a structure. The difference is that all the members of a union use the same memory area, so only one member can be used at a time. A union might be used in an application where the program needs to work with two or more values (of different data types), but only needs to use one of the values at a time. Unions conserve memory by storing all their members in the same memory location.

Unions are declared just like structures, except the key word union is used instead of struct. Here is an example:

```
union PaySource
{
    short hours;
    float sales;
};
```

A union variable of the data type shown above can then be defined as

```
PaySource employee1;
```

The `PaySource` union variable defined here has two members: `hours` (a `short`), and `sales` (a `float`). The entire variable will only take up as much memory as the largest member (in this case, a `float`). The way this variable is stored on a typical PC is illustrated in Figure 11-5.

Figure 11-5

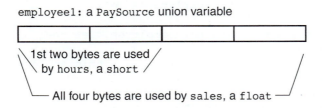

employee1: a PaySource union variable

1st two bytes are used by hours, a short

All four bytes are used by sales, a float

As shown in Figure 11-5, the union uses four bytes on a typical PC. It can store a `short` or a `float`, depending on which member is used. When a value is stored in the `sales` member, all four bytes are needed to hold the data. When a value is stored in the `hours` member, however, only the first two bytes are used. Obviously, both members can't hold values at the same time. This union is demonstrated in Program 11-9.

Program 11-9

```cpp
1   // This program demonstrates a union.
2   #include <iostream>
3   #include <iomanip>
4   using namespace std;
5
6   union PaySource
7   {
8      int hours;          // Hours worked
9      float sales;        // Amount of sales
10  };
11
12  int main()
13  {
14     PaySource employee1;     // Define a union variable
15     char payType;            // To hold the pay type
16     float payRate;           // Hourly pay rate
17     float grossPay;          // Gross pay
18
19     cout << fixed << showpoint << setprecision(2);
20     cout << "This program calculates either hourly wages or\n";
21     cout << "sales commission.\n";
22
23     // Get the pay type, hourly or commission.
24     cout << "Enter H for hourly wages or C for commission: ";
25     cin >> payType;
26
27     // Determine the gross pay, depending on the pay type.
28     if (payType == 'H' || payType == 'h')
29     {
30        // This is an hourly paid employee. Get the
31        // pay rate and hours worked.
32        cout << "What is the hourly pay rate? ";
33        cin >> payRate;
34        cout << "How many hours were worked? ";
35        cin >> employee1.hours;
36
37        // Calculate and display the gross pay.
38        grossPay = employee1.hours * payRate;
39        cout << "Gross pay: $" << grossPay << endl;
40     }
41     else if (payType == 'C' || payType == 'c')
42     {
43        // This is a commission-paid employee. Get the
44        // amount of sales.
45        cout << "What are the total sales for this employee? ";
46        cin >> employee1.sales;
47
48        // Calculate and display the gross pay.
49        grossPay = employee1.sales * 0.10;
50        cout << "Gross pay: $" << grossPay << endl;
51     }
```

```
52      else
53      {
54          // The user made an invalid selection.
55          cout << payType << " is not a valid selection.\n";
56      }
57      return 0;
58  }
```

Program Output with Example Input Shown in Bold
```
This program calculates either hourly wages or
sales commission.
Enter H for hourly wages or C for commission: C [Enter]
What are the total sales for this employee? 5000 [Enter]
Gross pay: $500.00
```

Program Output with Different Example Input Shown in Bold
```
This program calculates either hourly wages or
sales commission.
Enter H for hourly wages or C for commission: H [Enter]
What is the hourly pay rate? 20 [Enter]
How many hours were worked? 40 [Enter]
Gross pay: $800.00
```

Everything else you already know about structures applies to unions. For example, arrays of unions may be defined. A union may be passed as an argument to a function or returned from a function. Pointers to unions may be defined and the members of the union referenced by the pointer can be accessed with the -> operator.

Anonymous Unions

The members of an anonymous union have names, but the union itself has no name. Here is the general format of an anonymous union declaration:

```
union
{
    member declaration;
    ...
};
```

An anonymous union declaration actually creates the member variables in memory, so there is no need to separately define a union variable. Anonymous unions are simple to use because the members may be accessed without the dot operator. Program 11-10, which is a modification of Program 11-9, demonstrates the use of an anonymous union.

Program 11-10

```
1   // This program demonstrates an anonymous union.
2   #include <iostream>
3   #include <iomanip>
4   using namespace std;
```

(program continues)

Program 11-10   *(continued)*

```cpp
 5
 6  int main()
 7  {
 8     union                      // Anonymous union
 9     {
10        int hours;
11        float sales;
12     };
13
14     char payType;             // To hold the pay type
15     float payRate;            // Hourly pay rate
16     float grossPay;           // Gross pay
17
18     cout << fixed << showpoint << setprecision(2);
19     cout << "This program calculates either hourly wages or\n";
20     cout << "sales commission.\n";
21
22     // Get the pay type, hourly or commission.
23     cout << "Enter H for hourly wages or C for commission: ";
24     cin >> payType;
25
26     // Determine the gross pay, depending on the pay type.
27     if (payType == 'H' || payType == 'h')
28     {
29        // This is an hourly paid employee. Get the
30        // pay rate and hours worked.
31        cout << "What is the hourly pay rate? ";
32        cin >> payRate;
33        cout << "How many hours were worked? ";
34        cin >> hours; // Anonymous union member
35
36        // Calculate and display the gross pay.
37        grossPay = hours * payRate;
38        cout << "Gross pay: $" << grossPay << endl;
39     }
40     else if (payType == 'C' || payType == 'c')
41     {
42        // This is a commission-paid employee. Get the
43        // amount of sales.
44        cout << "What are the total sales for this employee? ";
45        cin >> sales; // Anonymous union member
46
47        // Calculate and display the gross pay.
48        grossPay = sales * 0.10;
49        cout << "Gross pay: $" << grossPay << endl;
50     }
51     else
52     {
53        // The user made an invalid selection.
54        cout << payType << " is not a valid selection.\n";
55     }
56     return 0;
57  }
```

Program Output with Example Input Shown in Bold
```
This program calculates either hourly wages or
sales commission.
Enter H for hourly wages or C for commission: C [Enter]
What are the total sales for this employee? 12000 [Enter]
Gross pay: $1200.00
```

NOTE: Notice the anonymous union in Program 11-10 is declared inside function `main`. If an anonymous union is declared globally (outside all functions), it must be declared static. This means the word `static` must appear before the word `union`.

 Checkpoint

myprogramminglab *www.myprogramminglab.com*

11.16 Declare a union named `ThreeTypes` with the following members:

    `letter:`   A character
    `whole:`   An integer
    `real:`   A double

11.17 Write the definition for an array of 50 of the `ThreeTypes` structures you declared in Question 11.16.

11.18 Write a loop that stores the floating point value 2.37 in all the elements of the array you defined in Question 11.17.

11.19 Write a loop that stores the character 'A' in all the elements of the array you defined in Question 11.17.

11.20 Write a loop that stores the integer 10 in all the elements of the array you defined in Question 11.17.

11.12 Enumerated Data Types

CONCEPT: An enumerated data type is a programmer-defined data type. It consists of values known as enumerators, which represent integer constants.

Using the enum key word you can create your own data type and specify the values that belong to that type. Such a type is known as an *enumerated data type*. Here is an example of an enumerated data type declaration:

```
enum Day { MONDAY, TUESDAY, WEDNESDAY, THURSDAY, FRIDAY };
```

An enumerated type declaration begins with the key word `enum`, followed by the name of the type, followed by a list of identifiers inside braces, and is terminated with a semicolon. The example declaration creates an enumerated data type named `Day`. The identifiers `MONDAY`, `TUESDAY`, `WEDNESDAY`, `THURSDAY`, and `FRIDAY`, which are listed inside the braces, are known as *enumerators*. They represent the values that belong to the Day data type. Here is the general format of an enumerated type declaration:

```
enum TypeName { One or more enumerators };
```

Note that the enumerators are not enclosed in quotation marks, therefore they are not strings. Enumerators must be legal C++ identifiers.

Once you have created an enumerated data type in your program, you can define variables of that type. For example, the following statement defines workDay as a variable of the Day type:

```
Day workDay;
```

Because workDay is a variable of the Day data type, we may assign any of the enumerators MONDAY, TUESDAY, WEDNESDAY, THURSDAY, or FRIDAY to it. For example, the following statement assigns the value WEDNESDAY to the workDay variable.

```
Day workDay = WEDNESDAY;
```

So just what are these enumerators MONDAY, TUESDAY, WEDNESDAY, THURSDAY, and FRIDAY? You can think of them as integer named constants. Internally, the compiler assigns integer values to the enumerators, beginning with 0. The enumerator MONDAY is stored in memory as the number 0, TUESDAY is stored in memory as the number 1, WEDNESDAY is stored in memory as the number 2, and so forth. To prove this, look at the following code.

```
cout << MONDAY << endl << TUESDAY << endl
     << WEDNESDAY << endl << THURSDAY << endl
     << FRIDAY << endl;
```

This statement will produce the following output:

```
0
1
2
3
4
```

 NOTE: When making up names for enumerators, it is not required that they be written in all uppercase letters. For example, we could have written the enumerators of the Days type as monday, tuesday, etc. Because they represent constant values, however, many programmers prefer to write them in all uppercase letters. This is strictly a preference of style.

Assigning an Integer to an enum Variable

Even though the enumerators of an enumerated data type are stored in memory as integers, you cannot directly assign an integer value to an enum variable. For example, assuming that workDay is a variable of the Day data type previously described, the following assignment statement is illegal.

```
workDay = 3;   // Error!
```

Compiling this statement will produce an error message such as "Cannot convert int to Day." When assigning a value to an enum variable, you should use a valid enumerator. However, if circumstances require that you store an integer value in an enum variable, you can do so by casting the integer. Here is an example:

```
workDay = static_cast<Day>(3);
```

This statement will produce the same results as:

```
workDay = THURSDAY;
```

Assigning an Enumerator to an int Variable

Although you cannot directly assign an integer value to an enum variable, you can directly assign an enumerator to an integer variable. For example, the following code will work just fine.

```
enum Day { MONDAY, TUESDAY, WEDNESDAY, THURSDAY, FRIDAY };
int x;
x = THURSDAY;
cout << x << endl;
```

When this code runs it will display 3. You can also assign a variable of an enumerated type to an integer variable, as shown here:

```
Day workDay = FRIDAY;
int x = workDay;
cout << x << endl;
```

When this code runs it will display 4.

Comparing Enumerator Values

Enumerator values can be compared using the relational operators. For example, using the Day data type we have been discussing, the following expression is true.

```
FRIDAY > MONDAY
```

The expression is true because the enumerator FRIDAY is stored in memory as 4 and the enumerator MONDAY is stored as 0. The following code will display the message "Friday is greater than Monday."

```
if (FRIDAY > MONDAY)
    cout << "Friday is greater than Monday.\n";
```

You can also compare enumerator values with integer values. For example, the following code will display the message "Monday is equal to zero."

```
if (MONDAY == 0)
    cout << "Monday is equal to zero.\n";
```

Let's look at a complete program that uses much of what we have learned so far. Program 11-11 uses the Day data type that we have been discussing.

Program 11-11

```cpp
 1   // This program demonstrates an enumerated data type.
 2   #include <iostream>
 3   #include <iomanip>
 4   using namespace std;
 5
 6   enum Day { MONDAY, TUESDAY, WEDNESDAY, THURSDAY, FRIDAY };
 7
 8   int main()
 9   {
10      const int NUM_DAYS = 5;     // The number of days
11      double sales[NUM_DAYS];     // To hold sales for each day
12      double total = 0.0;         // Accumulator
13      int index;                  // Loop counter
14
15      // Get the sales for each day.
16      for (index = MONDAY; index <= FRIDAY; index++)
17      {
18         cout << "Enter the sales for day "
19              << index << ": ";
20         cin >> sales[index];
21      }
22
23      // Calculate the total sales.
24      for (index = MONDAY; index <= FRIDAY; index++)
25         total += sales[index];
26
27      // Display the total.
28      cout << "The total sales are $" << setprecision(2)
29           << fixed << total << endl;
30
31      return 0;
32   }
```

Program Output with Example Input Shown in Bold
```
Enter the sales for day 0: 1525.00 [Enter]
Enter the sales for day 1: 1896.50 [Enter]
Enter the sales for day 2: 1975.63 [Enter]
Enter the sales for day 3: 1678.33 [Enter]
Enter the sales for day 4: 1498.52 [Enter]
The total sales are $8573.98
```

Anonymous Enumerated Types

Notice that Program 11-11 does not define a variable of the Day data type. Instead it uses the Day data type's enumerators in the for loops. The counter variable index is initialized to MONDAY (which is 0), and the loop iterates as long as index is less than or equal to FRIDAY (which is 4). When you do not need to define variables of an enumerated type, you can actually make the type anonymous. An *anonymous enumerated type* is simply one that does not have a name. For example, in Program 11-11 we could have declared the enumerated type as:

```cpp
enum { MONDAY, TUESDAY, WEDNESDAY, THURSDAY, FRIDAY };
```

This declaration still creates the enumerators. We just can't use the data type to define variables because the type does not have a name.

Using Math Operators to Change the Value of an enum Variable

Even though enumerators are really integers, and enum variables really hold integer values, you can run into problems when trying to perform math operations with them. For example, look at the following code.

```
Day day1, day2;    // Defines two Day variables.
day1 = TUESDAY;    // Assign TUESDAY to day1.
day2 = day1 + 1;   // ERROR! This will not work!
```

The third statement causes a problem because the expression day1 + 1 results in the integer value 2. The assignment operator then attempts to assign the integer value 2 to the enum variable day2. Because C++ cannot implicitly convert an int to a Day, an error occurs. You can fix this by using a cast to explicitly convert the result to Day, as shown here:

```
day2 = static_cast<Day>(day1 + 1);   // This works.
```

Using an enum Variable to Step Through an Array's Elements

Because enumerators are stored in memory as integers, you can use them as array subscripts. For example, look at the following code.

```
enum Day { MONDAY, TUESDAY, WEDNESDAY, THURSDAY, FRIDAY };
const int NUM_DAYS = 5;
double sales[NUM_DAYS];
sales[MONDAY] = 1525.0;      // Stores 1525.0 in sales[0].
sales[TUESDAY] = 1896.5;     // Stores 1896.5 in sales[1].
sales[WEDNESDAY] = 1975.63;  // Stores 1975.63 in sales[2].
sales[THURSDAY] = 1678.33;   // Stores 1678.33 in sales[3].
sales[FRIDAY] = 1498.52;     // Stores 1498.52 in sales[4].
```

This code stores values in all five elements of the sales array. Because enumerator values can be used as array subscripts, you can use an enum variable in a loop to step through the elements of an array. However, using an enum variable for this purpose is not as straightforward as using an int variable. This is because you cannot use the ++ or -- operators directly on an enum variable. To understand what I mean, first look at the following code taken from Program 11-11:

```
for (index = MONDAY; index <= FRIDAY; index++)
{
    cout << "Enter the sales for day "
         << index << ": ";
    cin >> sales[index];
}
```

In this code, index is an int variable used to step through each element of the array. It is reasonable to expect that we could use a Day variable instead, as shown in the following code.

```
Day workDay;  // Define a Day variable

// ERROR!!! This code will NOT work.
for (workDay = MONDAY; workDay <= FRIDAY; workDay++)
{
    cout << "Enter the sales for day "
        << workDay << ": ";
    cin >> sales[workDay];
}
```

Notice that the `for` loop's update expression uses the ++ operator to increment `workDay`. Although this works fine with an `int` variable, the ++ operator cannot be used with an enum variable. Instead, you must convert `workDay++` to an equivalent expression that will work. The expression `workDay++` attempts to do the same thing as:

```
workDay = workDay + 1;  // Good idea, but still won't work.
```

However, this still will not work. We have to use a cast to explicitly convert the expression `workDay + 1` to the `Day` data type, like this:

```
workDay = static_cast<Day>(workDay + 1);
```

This is the expression that we must use in the `for` loop instead of `workDay++`. The corrected `for` loop looks like this:

```
for (workDay = MONDAY; workDay <= FRIDAY;
            workDay = static_cast<Day>(workDay + 1))
{
    cout << "Enter the sales for day "
        << workDay << ": ";
    cin >> sales[workDay];
}
```

Program 11-12 is a version of Program 11-11 that is modified to use a `Day` variable to step through the elements of the `sales` array.

Program 11-12

```
 1   // This program demonstrates an enumerated data type.
 2   #include <iostream>
 3   #include <iomanip>
 4   using namespace std;
 5
 6   enum Day { MONDAY, TUESDAY, WEDNESDAY, THURSDAY, FRIDAY };
 7
 8   int main()
 9   {
10       const int NUM_DAYS = 5;      // The number of days
11       double sales[NUM_DAYS];      // To hold sales for each day
12       double total = 0.0;          // Accumulator
13       Day workDay;                 // Loop counter
14
```

```
15      // Get the sales for each day.
16      for (workDay = MONDAY; workDay <= FRIDAY;
17                           workDay = static_cast<Day>(workDay + 1))
18      {
19         cout << "Enter the sales for day "
20               << workDay << ": ";
21         cin >> sales[workDay];
22      }
23
24      // Calculate the total sales.
25      for (workDay = MONDAY; workDay <= FRIDAY;
26                           workDay = static_cast<Day>(workDay + 1))
27         total += sales[workDay];
28
29      // Display the total.
30      cout << "The total sales are $" << setprecision(2)
31            << fixed << total << endl;
32
33      return 0;
34  }
```

Program Output with Example Input Shown in Bold
```
Enter the sales for day 0: 1525.00 [Enter]
Enter the sales for day 1: 1896.50 [Enter]
Enter the sales for day 2: 1975.63 [Enter]
Enter the sales for day 3: 1678.33 [Enter]
Enter the sales for day 4: 1498.52 [Enter]
The total sales are $8573.98
```

Using Enumerators to Output Values

As you have already seen, sending an enumerator to cout causes the enumerator's integer value to be displayed. For example, assuming we are using the Day type previously described, the following statement displays 0.

```
cout << MONDAY << endl;
```

If you wish to use the enumerator to display a string such as "Monday," you'll have to write code that produces the desired string. For example, in the following code assume that workDay is a Day variable that has been initialized to some value. The switch statement displays the name of a day, based upon the value of the variable.

```
switch(workDay)
{
    case MONDAY    : cout << "Monday";
                     break;
    case TUESDAY   : cout << "Tuesday";
                     break;
    case WEDNESDAY : cout << "Wednesday";
                     break;
    case THURSDAY  : cout << "Thursday";
                     break;
    case FRIDAY    : cout << "Friday";
}
```

Program 11-13 shows this type of code used in a function. Instead of asking the user to enter the sales for day 0, day 1, and so forth, it displays the names of the days.

Program 11-13

```
 1   // This program demonstrates an enumerated data type.
 2   #include <iostream>
 3   #include <iomanip>
 4   using namespace std;
 5
 6   enum Day { MONDAY, TUESDAY, WEDNESDAY, THURSDAY, FRIDAY };
 7
 8   // Function prototype
 9   void displayDayName(Day);
10
11   int main()
12   {
13      const int NUM_DAYS = 5;    // The number of days
14      double sales[NUM_DAYS];    // To hold sales for each day
15      double total = 0.0;        // Accumulator
16      Day workDay;               // Loop counter
17
18      // Get the sales for each day.
19      for (workDay = MONDAY; workDay <= FRIDAY;
20                      workDay = static_cast<Day>(workDay + 1))
21      {
22         cout << "Enter the sales for day ";
23         displayDayName(workDay);
24         cout << ": ";
25         cin >> sales[workDay];
26      }
27
28      // Calculate the total sales.
29      for (workDay = MONDAY; workDay <= FRIDAY;
30                      workDay = static_cast<Day>(workDay + 1))
31         total += sales[workDay];
32
33      // Display the total.
34      cout << "The total sales are $" << setprecision(2)
35            << fixed << total << endl;
36
37      return 0;
38   }
39
40   //************************************************************
41   // Definition of the displayDayName function              *
42   // This function accepts an argument of the Day type and   *
43   // displays the corresponding name of the day.            *
44   //************************************************************
45
```

```
46   void displayDayName(Day d)
47   {
48      switch(d)
49      {
50         case MONDAY    : cout << "Monday";
51                          break;
52         case TUESDAY   : cout << "Tuesday";
53                          break;
54         case WEDNESDAY : cout << "Wednesday";
55                          break;
56         case THURSDAY  : cout << "Thursday";
57                          break;
58         case FRIDAY    : cout << "Friday";
59      }
60   }
```

Program Output with Example Input Shown in Bold
```
Enter the sales for Monday: 1525.00 [Enter]
Enter the sales for Tuesday: 1896.50 [Enter]
Enter the sales for Wednesday: 1975.63 [Enter]
Enter the sales for Thursday: 1678.33 [Enter]
Enter the sales for Friday: 1498.52 [Enter]
The total sales are $8573.98
```

Specifying Integer Values for Enumerators

By default, the enumerators in an enumerated data type are assigned the integer values 0, 1, 2, and so forth. If this is not appropriate, you can specify the values to be assigned, as in the following example.

```
enum Water { FREEZING = 32, BOILING = 212 };
```

In this example, the FREEZING enumerator is assigned the integer value 32 and the BOILING enumerator is assigned the integer value 212. Program 11-14 demonstrates how this enumerated type might be used.

Program 11-14

```
1   // This program demonstrates an enumerated data type.
2   #include <iostream>
3   #include <iomanip>
4   using namespace std;
5
6   int main()
7   {
8      enum Water { FREEZING = 32, BOILING = 212 };
9      int waterTemp; // To hold the water temperature
10
```

(program continues)

Program 11-14 *(continued)*

```
11      cout << "Enter the current water temperature: ";
12      cin >> waterTemp;
13      if (waterTemp <= FREEZING)
14         cout << "The water is frozen.\n";
15      else if (waterTemp >= BOILING)
16         cout << "The water is boiling.\n";
17      else
18         cout << "The water is not frozen or boiling.\n";
19
20      return 0;
21   }
```

Program Output with Example Input Shown in Bold
```
Enter the current water temperature: 10 [Enter]
The water is frozen.
```

Program Output with Example Input Shown in Bold
```
Enter the current water temperature: 300 [Enter]
The water is boiling.
```

Program Output with Example Input Shown in Bold
```
Enter the current water temperature: 92 [Enter]
The water is not frozen or boiling.
```

If you leave out the value assignment for one or more of the enumerators, it will be assigned a default value. Here is an example:

```
enum Colors { RED, ORANGE, YELLOW = 9, GREEN, BLUE };
```

In this example the enumerator RED will be assigned the value 0, ORANGE will be assigned the value 1, YELLOW will be assigned the value 9, GREEN will be assigned the value 10, and BLUE will be assigned the value 11.

Enumerators Must Be Unique Within the Same Scope

Enumerators are identifiers just like variable names, named constants, and function names. As with all identifiers, they must be unique within the same scope. For example, an error will result if both of the following enumerated types are declared within the same scope. The reason is that ROOSEVELT is declared twice.

```
enum Presidents { MCKINLEY, ROOSEVELT, TAFT };
enum VicePresidents { ROOSEVELT, FAIRBANKS, SHERMAN };  // Error!
```

The following declarations will also cause an error if they appear within the same scope.

```
enum Status { OFF, ON };
const int OFF = 0;          // Error!
```

Declaring the Type and Defining the Variables in One Statement

The following code uses two lines to declare an enumerated data type and define a variable of the type.

```
enum Car { PORSCHE, FERRARI, JAGUAR };
Car sportsCar;
```

C++ allows you to declare an enumerated data type and define one or more variables of the type in the same statement. The previous code could be combined into the following statement:

```
enum Car { PORSCHE, FERRARI, JAGUAR } sportsCar;
```

The following statement declares the `Car` data type and defines two variables: `myCar` and `yourCar`.

```
enum Car { PORSCHE, FERRARI, JAGUAR } myCar, yourCar;
```

For an additional example of this chapter's topics, see the High Adventure Travel Part 2 Case Study on this book's companion Web site at www.pearsonhighered.com/gaddis.

Checkpoint

myprogramminglab *www.myprogramminglab.com*

11.21 Look at the following declaration.
```
enum Flower { ROSE, DAISY, PETUNIA };
```
In memory, what value will be stored for the enumerator ROSE? For DAISY? For PETUNIA?

11.22 What will the following code display?
```
enum { HOBBIT, ELF = 7, DRAGON };
cout << HOBBIT << " " << ELF << " " << DRAGON << endl;
```

11.23 Does the enumerated data type declared in Checkpoint Question 11.22 have a name, or is it anonymous?

11.24 What will the following code display?
```
enum Letters { Z, Y, X };
if (Z > X)
    cout << "Z is greater than X.\n";
else
    cout << "Z is not greater than X.\n";
```

11.25 Will the following code cause an error, or will it compile without any errors? If it causes an error, rewrite it so it compiles.
```
enum Color { RED, GREEN, BLUE };
Color c;
c = 0;
```

11.26 Will the following code cause an error, or will it compile without any errors? If it causes an error, rewrite it so it compiles.
```
enum Color { RED, GREEN, BLUE };
Color c = RED;
c++;
```

Review Questions and Exercises

Short Answer

1. What is a primitive data type?

2. Does a structure declaration cause a structure variable to be created?

3. Both arrays and structures are capable of storing multiple values. What is the difference between an array and a structure?

4. Look at the following structure declaration.

```
struct Point
{
    int x;
    int y;
};
```

Write statements that

A) define a `Point` structure variable named `center`

B) assign 12 to the x member of `center`

C) assign 7 to the y member of `center`

D) display the contents of the x and y members of `center`

5. Look at the following structure declaration.

```
struct FullName
{
    string lastName;
    string middleName;
    string firstName;
};
```

Write statements that

A) Define a `FullName` structure variable named `info`

B) Assign your last, middle, and first name to the members of the `info` variable

C) Display the contents of the members of the `info` variable

6. Look at the following code.

```
struct PartData
{
    string partName;
    int idNumber;
};

PartData inventory[100];
```

Write a statement that displays the contents of the `partName` member of element 49 of the `inventory` array.

7. Look at the following code.

```
struct Town
{
    string townName;
    string countyName;
    double population;
    double elevation;
};
```

```
Town t = { "Canton", "Haywood", 9478 };
```

A) What value is stored in t.townName?

B) What value is stored in t.countyName?

C) What value is stored in t.population?

D) What value is stored in t.elevation?

8. Look at the following code.

```
structure Rectangle
{
    int length;
    int width;
};

Rectangle *r;
```

Write statements that

A) Dynamically allocate a Rectangle structure variable and use r to point to it.

B) Assign 10 to the structure's length member and 14 to the structure's width member.

9. What is the difference between a union and a structure?

10. Look at the following code.

```
union Values
{
    int ivalue;
    double dvalue;
};

Values v;
```

Assuming that an int uses four bytes and a double uses eight bytes, how much memory does the variable v use?

11. What will the following code display?

```
enum { POODLE, BOXER, TERRIER };
cout << POODLE << " " << BOXER << " " << TERRIER << endl;
```

12. Look at the following declaration.

```
enum Person { BILL, JOHN, CLAIRE, BOB };
Person p;
```

Indicate whether each of the following statements or expressions is valid or invalid.

A) p = BOB;

B) p++;

C) BILL > BOB

D) p = 0;

E) int x = BILL;

F) p = static_cast<Person>(3);

G) cout << CLAIRE << endl;

Fill-in-the-Blank

13. Before a structure variable can be created, the structure must be _____.

14. The _____ is the name of the structure type.

15. The variables declared inside a structure declaration are called _____.

16. A(n) _____ is required after the closing brace of a structure declaration.

17. In the definition of a structure variable, the _____ is placed before the variable name, just like the data type of a regular variable is placed before its name.

18. The _____ operator allows you to access structure members.

Algorithm Workbench

19. The structure Car is declared as follows:

```
struct Car
{
    string carMake;
    string carModel;
    int yearModel;
    double cost;
};
```

Write a definition statement that defines a Car structure variable initialized with the following data:

Make: Ford
Model: Mustang
Year Model: 1968
Cost: $20,000

20. Define an array of 25 of the Car structure variables (the structure is declared in Question 19).

21. Define an array of 35 of the Car structure variables. Initialize the first three elements with the following data:

Make	Model	Year	Cost
Ford	Taurus	1997	$21,000
Honda	Accord	1992	$11,000
Lamborghini	Countach	1997	$200,000

22. Write a loop that will step through the array you defined in Question 21, displaying the contents of each element.

23. Declare a structure named TempScale, with the following members:

fahrenheit: a double
centigrade: a double

Next, declare a structure named Reading, with the following members:

windSpeed: an int
humidity: a double
temperature: a TempScale structure variable

Next define a Reading structure variable.

24. Write statements that will store the following data in the variable you defined in Question 23.

    Wind Speed: 37 mph
    Humidity: 32%
    Fahrenheit temperature: 32 degrees
    Centigrade temperature: 0 degrees

25. Write a function called `showReading`. It should accept a `Reading` structure variable (see Question 23) as its argument. The function should display the contents of the variable on the screen.

26. Write a function called `findReading`. It should use a `Reading` structure reference variable (see Question 23) as its parameter. The function should ask the user to enter values for each member of the structure.

27. Write a function called `getReading`, which returns a `Reading` structure (see Question 23). The function should ask the user to enter values for each member of a `Reading` structure, then return the structure.

28. Write a function called `recordReading`. It should use a `Reading` structure pointer variable (see Question 23) as its parameter. The function should ask the user to enter values for each member of the structure pointed to by the parameter.

29. Rewrite the following statement using the structure pointer operator:

    ```
    (*rptr).windSpeed = 50;
    ```

30. Rewrite the following statement using the structure pointer operator:

    ```
    *(*strPtr).num = 10;
    ```

31. Write the declaration of a union called `Items` with the following members:

`alpha`	a character
`num`	an integer
`bigNum`	a `long` integer
`real`	a `float`

    Next, write the definition of an `Items` union variable.

32. Write the declaration of an anonymous union with the same members as the union you declared in Question 31.

33. Write a statement that stores the number 452 in the `num` member of the anonymous union you declared in Question 32.

34. Look at the following statement.

    ```
    enum Color { RED, ORANGE, GREEN, BLUE };
    ```

    A) What is the name of the data type declared by this statement?
    B) What are the enumerators for this type?
    C) Write a statement that defines a variable of this type and initializes it with a valid value.

35. A pet store sells dogs, cats, birds, and hamsters. Write a declaration for an anonymous enumerated data type that can represent the types of pets the store sells.

True or False

36. T F A semicolon is required after the closing brace of a structure or union declaration.

37. T F A structure declaration does not define a variable.

38. T F The contents of a structure variable can be displayed by passing the structure variable to the `cout` object.

39. T F Structure variables may not be initialized.

40. T F In a structure variable's initialization list, you do not have to provide initializers for all the members.

41. T F You may skip members in a structure's initialization list.

42. T F The following expression refers to the element 5 in the array `carInfo`:
`carInfo.model[5]`

43. T F An array of structures may be initialized.

44. T F A structure variable may not be a member of another structure.

45. T F A structure member variable may be passed to a function as an argument.

46. T F An entire structure may not be passed to a function as an argument.

47. T F A function may return a structure.

48. T F When a function returns a structure, it is always necessary for the function to have a local structure variable to hold the member values that are to be returned.

49. T F The indirection operator has higher precedence than the dot operator.

50. T F The structure pointer operator does not automatically dereference the structure pointer on its left.

51. T F In a union, all the members are stored in different memory locations.

52. T F All the members of a union may be used simultaneously.

53. T F You may define arrays of unions.

54. T F You may not define pointers to unions.

55. T F An anonymous union has no name.

56. T F If an anonymous union is defined globally (outside all functions), it must be declared `static`.

Find the Errors

Each of the following declarations, programs, and program segments has errors. Locate as many as you can.

57.
```
struct
{
    int x;
    float y;
};
```

58.
```
struct Values
{
    string name;
    int age;
}
```

59.
```cpp
struct TwoVals
{
    int a, b;
};
int main ()
{
    TwoVals.a = 10;
    TwoVals.b = 20;
    return 0;
}
```

60.
```cpp
#include <iostream>
using namespace std;

struct ThreeVals
{
    int a, b, c;
};
int main()
{
    ThreeVals vals = {1, 2, 3};
    cout << vals << endl;
    return 0;
}
```

61.
```cpp
#include <iostream>
#include <string>
using namespace std;

struct names
{
    string first;
    string last;
};
int main ()
{
    names customer = "Smith", "Orley";
    cout << names.first << endl;
    cout << names.last << endl;
    return 0;
}
```

62.
```cpp
struct FourVals
{
    int a, b, c, d;
};
int main ()
{
    FourVals nums = {1, 2, , 4};
    return 0;
}
```

63.
```cpp
#include <iostream>
using namespace std;
```

```
      struct TwoVals
      {
          int a = 5;
          int b = 10;
      };
      int main()
      {
          TwoVals v;

          cout << v.a << " " << v.b;
          return 0;
      }
```

64.
```
    struct TwoVals
    {
        int a = 5;
        int b = 10;
    };

    int main()
    {
        TwoVals varray[10];

        varray.a[0] = 1;
        return 0;
    }
```

65.
```
    struct TwoVals
    {
        int a;
        int b;
    };
    TwoVals getVals()
    {
        TwoVals.a = TwoVals.b = 0;
    }
```

66.
```
    struct ThreeVals
    {
        int a, b, c;
    };

    int main ()
    {
        TwoVals s, *sptr;
        sptr = &s;
        *sptr.a = 1;
        return 0;
    }
```

67.
```
    #include <iostream>
    using namespace std;

    union Compound
    {
        int x;
        float y;
    };
```

```
int main()
{
   Compound u;
   u.x = 1000;
   cout << u.y << endl;
   return 0;
}
```

Programming Challenges

Visit www.myprogramminglab.com to complete many of these Programming Challenges online and get instant feedback.

1. Movie Data

Write a program that uses a structure named `MovieData` to store the following information about a movie:

> Title
> Director
> Year Released
> Running Time (in minutes)

The program should create two `MovieData` variables, store values in their members, and pass each one, in turn, to a function that displays the information about the movie in a clearly formatted manner.

2. Movie Profit

Modify the Movie Data program written for Programming Challenge 1 to include two additional members that hold the movie's production costs and first-year revenues. Modify the function that displays the movie data to display the title, director, release year, running time, and first year's profit or loss.

3. Corporate Sales Data

Write a program that uses a structure to store the following data on a company division:

> Division Name (such as East, West, North, or South)
> First-Quarter Sales
> Second-Quarter Sales
> Third-Quarter Sales
> Fourth-Quarter Sales
> Total Annual Sales
> Average Quarterly Sales

The program should use four variables of this structure. Each variable should represent one of the following corporate divisions: East, West, North, and South. The user should be asked for the four quarters' sales figures for each division. Each division's total and average sales should be calculated and stored in the appropriate member of each structure variable. These figures should then be displayed on the screen.

Input Validation: Do not accept negative numbers for any sales figures.

VideoNote
**Solving the
Weather
Statistics
Problem**

4. **Weather Statistics**

Write a program that uses a structure to store the following weather data for a particular month:

Total Rainfall
High Temperature
Low Temperature
Average Temperature

The program should have an array of 12 structures to hold weather data for an entire year. When the program runs, it should ask the user to enter data for each month. (The average temperature should be calculated.) Once the data are entered for all the months, the program should calculate and display the average monthly rainfall, the total rainfall for the year, the highest and lowest temperatures for the year (and the months they occurred in), and the average of all the monthly average temperatures.

Input Validation: Only accept temperatures within the range between −100 and +140 degrees Fahrenheit.

5. **Weather Statistics Modification**

Modify the program that you wrote for Programming Challenge 4 so it defines an enumerated data type with enumerators for the months (JANUARY, FEBRUARY, etc.). The program should use the enumerated type to step through the elements of the array.

6. **Soccer Scores**

Write a program that stores the following data about a soccer player in a structure:

Player's Name
Player's Number
Points Scored by Player

The program should keep an array of 12 of these structures. Each element is for a different player on a team. When the program runs it should ask the user to enter the data for each player. It should then show a table that lists each player's number, name, and points scored. The program should also calculate and display the total points earned by the team. The number and name of the player who has earned the most points should also be displayed.

Input Validation: Do not accept negative values for players' numbers or points scored.

7. **Customer Accounts**

Write a program that uses a structure to store the following data about a customer account:

Name
Address
City, State, and ZIP
Telephone Number
Account Balance
Date of Last Payment

The program should use an array of at least 20 structures. It should let the user enter data into the array, change the contents of any element, and display all the data stored in the array. The program should have a menu-driven user interface.

Input Validation: When the data for a new account is entered, be sure the user enters data for all the fields. No negative account balances should be entered.

8. **Search Function for Customer Accounts Program**

   Add a function to Programming Challenge 7 that allows the user to search the structure array for a particular customer's account. It should accept part of the customer's name as an argument and then search for an account with a name that matches it. All accounts that match should be displayed. If no account matches, a message saying so should be displayed.

9. **Speakers' Bureau**

   Write a program that keeps track of a speakers' bureau. The program should use a structure to store the following data about a speaker:

   > Name
   > Telephone Number
   > Speaking Topic
   > Fee Required

   The program should use an array of at least 10 structures. It should let the user enter data into the array, change the contents of any element, and display all the data stored in the array. The program should have a menu-driven user interface.

   Input Validation: When the data for a new speaker is entered, be sure the user enters data for all the fields. No negative amounts should be entered for a speaker's fee.

10. **Search Function for the Speakers' Bureau Program**

    Add a function to Programming Challenge 9 that allows the user to search for a speaker on a particular topic. It should accept a key word as an argument and then search the array for a structure with that key word in the Speaking Topic field. All structures that match should be displayed. If no structure matches, a message saying so should be displayed.

11. **Monthly Budget**

    A student has established the following monthly budget:

Housing	500.00
Utilities	150.00
Household Expenses	65.00
Transportation	50.00
Food	250.00
Medical	30.00
Insurance	100.00
Entertainment	150.00
Clothing	75.00
Miscellaneous	50.00

Write a program that has a `MonthlyBudget` structure designed to hold each of these expense categories. The program should pass the structure to a function that asks the user to enter the amounts spent in each budget category during a month. The program should then pass the structure to a function that displays a report indicating the amount over or under in each category, as well as the amount over or under for the entire monthly budget.

12. **Course Grade**

Write a program that uses a structure to store the following data:

Member Name	Description
Name	Student name
Idnum	Student ID number
Tests	Pointer to an array of test scores
Average	Average test score
Grade	Course grade

The program should keep a list of test scores for a group of students. It should ask the user how many test scores there are to be and how many students there are. It should then dynamically allocate an array of structures. Each structure's `Tests` member should point to a dynamically allocated array that will hold the test scores.

After the arrays have been dynamically allocated, the program should ask for the ID number and all the test scores for each student. The average test score should be calculated and stored in the `average` member of each structure. The course grade should be computed on the basis of the following grading scale:

Average Test Grade	Course Grade
91–100	A
81–90	B
71–80	C
61–70	D
60 or below	F

The course grade should then be stored in the `Grade` member of each structure. Once all this data is calculated, a table should be displayed on the screen listing each student's name, ID number, average test score, and course grade.

Input Validation: Be sure all the data for each student is entered. Do not accept negative numbers for any test score.

13. **Drink Machine Simulator**

Write a program that simulates a soft drink machine. The program should use a structure that stores the following data:

Drink Name
Drink Cost
Number of Drinks in Machine

The program should create an array of five structures. The elements should be initialized with the following data:

Drink Name	Cost	Number in Machine
Cola	.75	20
Root Beer	.75	20
Lemon-Lime	.75	20
Grape Soda	.80	20
Cream Soda	.80	20

Each time the program runs, it should enter a loop that performs the following steps: A list of drinks is displayed on the screen. The user should be allowed to either quit the program or pick a drink. If the user selects a drink, he or she will next enter the amount of money that is to be inserted into the drink machine. The program should display the amount of change that would be returned and subtract one from the number of that drink left in the machine. If the user selects a drink that has sold out, a message should be displayed. The loop then repeats. When the user chooses to quit the program it should display the total amount of money the machine earned.

Input Validation: When the user enters an amount of money, do not accept negative values, or values greater than $1.00.

14. **Inventory Bins**

Write a program that simulates inventory bins in a warehouse. Each bin holds a number of the same type of parts. The program should use a structure that keeps the following data:

Description of the part kept in the bin
Number of parts in the bin

The program should have an array of 10 bins, initialized with the following data:

Part Description	Number of Parts in the Bin
Valve	10
Bearing	5
Bushing	15
Coupling	21
Flange	7
Gear	5
Gear Housing	5
Vacuum Gripper	25
Cable	18
Rod	12

The program should have the following functions:

AddParts: a function that increases a specific bin's part count by a specified number.

RemoveParts: a function that decreases a specific bin's part count by a specified number.

When the program runs, it should repeat a loop that performs the following steps: The user should see a list of what each bin holds and how many parts are in each bin. The user can choose to either quit the program or select a bin. When a bin is selected, the user can either add parts to it or remove parts from it. The loop then repeats, showing the updated bin data on the screen.

Input Validation: No bin can hold more than 30 parts, so don't let the user add more than a bin can hold. Also, don't accept negative values for the number of parts being added or removed.

15. **Multipurpose Payroll**

Write a program that calculates pay for either an hourly paid worker or a salaried worker. Hourly paid workers are paid their hourly pay rate times the number of hours worked. Salaried workers are paid their regular salary plus any bonus they may have earned. The program should declare two structures for the following data:

Hourly Paid:
HoursWorked
HourlyRate

Salaried:
Salary
Bonus

The program should also declare a union with two members. Each member should be a structure variable: one for the hourly paid worker and another for the salaried worker.

The program should ask the user whether he or she is calculating the pay for an hourly paid worker or a salaried worker. Regardless of which the user selects, the appropriate members of the union will be used to store the data that will be used to calculate the pay.

Input Validation: Do not accept negative numbers. Do not accept values greater than 80 for HoursWorked.

12 Advanced File Operations

TOPICS

12.1 File Operations

CONCEPT: A file is a collection of data that is usually stored on a computer's disk. Data can be saved to files and then later reused.

Almost all real-world programs use files to store and retrieve data. Here are a few examples of familiar software packages that use files extensively.

- **Word Processors:** Word processing programs are used to write letters, memos, reports, and other documents. The documents are then saved in files so they can be edited and reprinted.

- **Database Management Systems:** DBMSs are used to create and maintain databases. Databases are files that contain large collections of data, such as payroll records, inventories, sales statistics, and customer records.

- **Spreadsheets:** Spreadsheet programs are used to work with numerical data. Numbers and mathematical formulas can be inserted into the rows and columns of the spreadsheet. The spreadsheet can then be saved to a file for use later.

- **Compilers**: Compilers translate the source code of a program, which is saved in a file, into an executable file. Throughout the previous chapters of this book you have created many C++ source files and compiled them to executable files.

Chapter 5 provided enough information for you to write programs that perform simple file operations. This chapter covers more advanced file operations, and focuses primarily on the `fstream` data type. As a review, Table 12-1 compares the `ifstream`, `ofstream`, and `fstream` data types. All of these data types require the `fstream` header file.

Table 12-1   File Stream

Data Type	Description
`ifstream`	Input File Stream. This data type can be used only to read data from files into memory.
`ofstream`	Output File Stream. This data type can be used to create files and write data to them.
`fstream`	File Stream. This data type can be used to create files, write data to them, and read data from them.

Using the `fstream` Data Type

You define an `fstream` object just as you define objects of other data types. The following statement defines an `fstream` object named `dataFile`.

```
fstream dataFile;
```

As with `ifstream` and `ofstream` objects, you use an `fstream` object's open function to open a file. An `fstream` object's open function requires two arguments, however. The first argument is a string containing the name of the file. The second argument is a file access flag that indicates the mode in which you wish to open the file. Here is an example.

```
dataFile.open("info.txt", ios::out);
```

The first argument in this function call is the name of the file, `info.txt`. The second argument is the file access flag `ios::out`. This tells C++ to open the file in output mode. Output mode allows data to be written to a file. The following statement uses the `ios::in` access flag to open a file in input mode, which allows data to be read from the file.

```
dataFile.open("info.txt", ios::in);
```

There are many file access flags, as listed in Table 12-2.

Table 12-2

File Access Flag	Meaning
ios::app	Append mode. If the file already exists, its contents are preserved and all output is written to the end of the file. By default, this flag causes the file to be created if it does not exist.
ios::ate	If the file already exists, the program goes directly to the end of it. Output may be written anywhere in the file.
ios::binary	Binary mode. When a file is opened in binary mode, data are written to or read from it in pure binary format. (The default mode is text.)
ios::in	Input mode. Data will be read from the file. If the file does not exist, it will not be created and the open function will fail.
ios::out	Output mode. Data will be written to the file. By default, the file's contents will be deleted if it already exists.
ios::trunc	If the file already exists, its contents will be deleted (truncated). This is the default mode used by ios::out.

Several flags may be used together if they are connected with the | operator. For example, assume dataFile is an fstream object in the following statement:

```
dataFile.open("info.txt", ios::in | ios::out);
```

This statement opens the file info.txt in both input and output modes. This means data may be written to and read from the file.

NOTE: When used by itself, the ios::out flag causes the file's contents to be deleted if the file already exists. When used with the ios::in flag, however, the file's existing contents are preserved. If the file does not already exist, it will be created.

The following statement opens the file in such a way that data will only be written to its end:

```
dataFile.open("info.txt", ios::out | ios::app);
```

By using different combinations of access flags, you can open files in many possible modes.

Program 12-1 uses an fstream object to open a file for output, and then writes data to the file.

Program 12-1

```
1   // This program uses an fstream object to write data to a file.
2   #include <iostream>
3   #include <fstream>
4   using namespace std;
5
6   int main()
7   {
8       fstream dataFile;
9
```

(program continues)

Program 12-1   *(continued)*

```
10       cout << "Opening file...\n";
11       dataFile.open("demofile.txt", ios::out);    // Open for output
12       cout << "Now writing data to the file.\n";
13       dataFile << "Jones\n";                       // Write line 1
14       dataFile << "Smith\n";                       // Write line 2
15       dataFile << "Willis\n";                      // Write line 3
16       dataFile << "Davis\n";                       // Write line 4
17       dataFile.close();                            // Close the file
18       cout << "Done.\n";
19       return 0;
20   }
```

Program Output

```
Opening file...
Now writing data to the file.
Done.
```

Output to File `demofile.txt`

```
Jones
Smith
Willis
Davis
```

The file output is shown for Program 12-1 the way it would appear if the file contents were displayed on the screen. The \n characters cause each name to appear on a separate line. The actual file contents, however, appear as a stream of characters as shown in Figure 12-1.

Figure 12-1

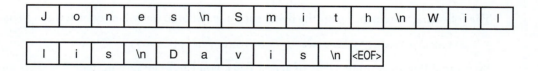

As you can see from the figure, \n characters are written to the file along with all the other characters. The characters are added to the file sequentially, in the order they are written by the program. The very last character is an *end-of-file marker*. It is a character that marks the end of the file and is automatically written when the file is closed. (The actual character used to mark the end of a file depends upon the operating system being used. It is always a nonprinting character. For example, some systems use control-Z.)

Program 12-2 is a modification of Program 12-1 that further illustrates the sequential nature of files. The file is opened, two names are written to it, and it is closed. The file is then reopened by the program in append mode (with the `ios::app` access flag). When a file is opened in append mode, its contents are preserved and all subsequent output is appended to the file's end. Two more names are added to the file before it is closed and the program terminates.

Program 12-2

```
1    // This program writes data to a file, closes the file,
2    // then reopens the file and appends more data.
3    #include <iostream>
4    #include <fstream>
5    using namespace std;
6
7    int main()
8    {
9       ofstream dataFile;
10
11      cout << "Opening file...\n";
12      // Open the file in output mode.
13      dataFile.open("demofile.txt", ios::out);
14      cout << "Now writing data to the file.\n";
15      dataFile << "Jones\n";                    // Write line 1
16      dataFile << "Smith\n";                    // Write line 2
17      cout << "Now closing the file.\n";
18      dataFile.close();                         // Close the file
19
20      cout << "Opening the file again...\n";
21      // Open the file in append mode.
22      dataFile.open("demofile.txt", ios::out | ios::app);
23      cout << "Writing more data to the file.\n";
24      dataFile << "Willis\n";                   // Write line 3
25      dataFile << "Davis\n";                    // Write line 4
26      cout << "Now closing the file.\n";
27      dataFile.close();                         // Close the file
28
29      cout << "Done.\n";
30      return 0;
31   }
```

Output to File demofile.txt
```
Jones
Smith
Willis
Davis
```

The first time the file is opened, the names are written as shown in Figure 12-2.

Figure 12-2

| J | o | n | e | s | \n | S | m | i | t | h | \n | <EOF> |

The file is closed and an end-of-file character is automatically written. When the file is reopened, the new output is appended to the end of the file, as shown in Figure 12-3.

Figure 12-3

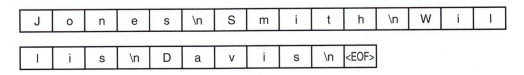

NOTE: If the `ios::out` flag had been alone, without `ios::app` the second time the file was opened, the file's contents would have been deleted. If this had been the case, the names Jones and Smith would have been erased and the file would only have contained the names Willis and Davis.

File Open Modes with `ifstream` and `ofstream` Objects

The `ifstream` and `ofstream` data types each have a default mode in which they open files. This mode determines the operations that may be performed on the file, and what happens if the file that is being opened already exists. Table 12-3 describes each data type's default open mode.

Table 12-3

File Type	Default Open Mode
ofstream	The file is opened for output only. Data may be written to the file, but not read from the file. If the file does not exist, it is created. If the file already exists, its contents are deleted (the file is truncated).
ifstream	The file is opened for input only. Data may be read from the file, but not written to it. The file's contents will be read from its beginning. If the file does not exist, the open function fails.

You cannot change the fact that `ifstream` files may only be read from, and `ofstream` files may only be written to. You can, however, vary the way operations are carried out on these files by providing a file access flag as an optional second argument to the open function. The following code shows an example using an `ofstream` object.

```
ofstream outputFile;
outputFile.open("values.txt", ios::out|ios::app);
```

The `ios::app` flag specifies that data written to the `values.txt` file should be appended to its existing contents.

Checking for a File's Existence Before Opening It

Sometimes you want to determine whether a file already exists before opening it for output. You can do this by first attempting to open the file for input. If the file does not exist, the open operation will fail. In that case, you can create the file by opening it for output. The following code gives an example.

```
fstream dataFile;
dataFile.open("values.txt", ios::in);
if (dataFile.fail())
{
        // The file does not exist, so create it.
        dataFile.open("values.txt", ios::out);
        //
        // Continue to process the file...
        //
}
```

```
else    // The file already exists.
{
        dataFile.close();
        cout << "The file values.txt already exists.\n";
}
```

Opening a File with the File Stream Object Definition Statement

An alternative to using the open member function is to use the file stream object definition statement to open the file. Here is an example:

```
fstream dataFile("names.txt", ios::in | ios::out);
```

This statement defines an fstream object named dataFile and uses it to open the file names.txt. The file is opened in both input and output modes. This technique eliminates the need to call the open function when your program knows the name and access mode of the file at the time the object is defined. You may also use this technique with ifstream and ofstream objects, as shown in the following examples.

```
ifstream inputFile("info.txt");
ofstream outputFile("addresses.txt");
ofstream dataFile("customers.txt", ios::out|ios::app);
```

You may also test for errors after you have opened a file with this technique. The following code shows an example.

```
ifstream inputFile("SalesData.txt");
if (!inputFile)
    cout << "Error opening SalesData.txt.\n";
```

 Checkpoint

myprogramminglab *www.myprogramminglab.com*

12.1 Which file access flag would you use if you want all output to be written to the end of an existing file?

12.2 How do you use more than one file access flag?

12.3 Assuming that diskInfo is an fstream object, write a statement that opens the file names.dat for output.

12.4 Assuming that diskInfo is an fstream object, write a statement that opens the file customers.txt for output, where all output will be written to the end of the file.

12.5 Assuming that diskInfo is an fstream object, write a statement that opens the file payable.txt for both input and output.

12.6 Write a statement that defines an fstream object named dataFile and opens a file named salesfigures.txt for input. (*Note:* The file should be opened with the definition statement, not an open function call.)

12.2 File Output Formatting

CONCEPT: File output may be formatted in the same way that screen output is formatted.

The same output formatting techniques that are used with cout, which are covered in Chapter 3, may also be used with file stream objects. For example, the setprecision and fixed manipulators may be called to establish the number of digits of precision that floating point values are rounded to. Program 12-3 demonstrates this.

Program 12-3

```
 1   // This program uses the setprecision and fixed
 2   // manipulators to format file output.
 3   #include <iostream>
 4   #include <iomanip>
 5   #include <fstream>
 6   using namespace std;
 7
 8   int main()
 9   {
10      fstream dataFile;
11      double num = 17.816392;
12
13      dataFile.open("numfile.txt", ios::out);   // Open in output mode
14
15      dataFile << fixed;              // Format for fixed-point notation
16      dataFile << num << endl;        // Write the number
17
18      dataFile << setprecision(4);    // Format for 4 decimal places
19      dataFile << num << endl;        // Write the number
20
21      dataFile << setprecision(3);    // Format for 3 decimal places
22      dataFile << num << endl;        // Write the number
23
24      dataFile << setprecision(2);    // Format for 2 decimal places
25      dataFile << num << endl;        // Write the number
26
27      dataFile << setprecision(1);    // Format for 1 decimal place
28      dataFile << num << endl;        // Write the number
29
30      cout << "Done.\n";
31      dataFile.close();               // Close the file
32      return 0;
33   }
```

Contents of File `numfile.txt`
```
17.816392
17.8164
17.816
17.82
17.8
```

Notice the file output is formatted just as cout would format screen output. Program 12-4 shows the setw stream manipulator being used to format file output into columns.

Program 12-4

```
 1   // This program writes three rows of numbers to a file.
 2   #include <iostream>
 3   #include <fstream>
 4   #include <iomanip>
 5   using namespace std;
 6
 7   int main()
 8   {
 9      const int ROWS = 3;    // Rows to write
10      const int COLS = 3;    // Columns to write
11      int nums[ROWS][COLS] = { 2897, 5, 837,
12                               34, 7, 1623,
13                               390, 3456, 12 };
14      fstream outFile("table.txt", ios::out);
15
16      // Write the three rows of numbers with each
17      // number in a field of 8 character spaces.
18      for (int row = 0; row < ROWS; row++)
19      {
20         for (int col = 0; col < COLS; col++)
21         {
22            outFile << setw(8) << nums[row][col];
23         }
24         outFile << endl;
25      }
26      outFile.close();
27      cout << "Done.\n";
28      return 0;
29   }
```

Contents of File `table.txt`

```
    2897       5      837
      34       7     1623
     390    3456       12
```

Figure 12-4 shows the way the characters appear in the file.

Figure 12-4

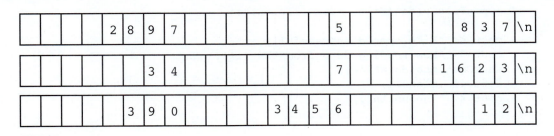

12.3 Passing File Stream Objects to Functions

CONCEPT: File stream objects may be passed by reference to functions.

When writing actual programs, you'll want to create modularized code for handling file operations. File stream objects may be passed to functions, but they should always be passed by reference. The openFile function shown below uses an fstream reference object parameter:

VideoNote

Passing File Stream Objects to Functions

```cpp
bool openFileIn(fstream &file, string name)
{
   bool status;

   file.open(name.c_str(), ios::in);
   if (file.fail())
      status = false;
   else
      status = true;
   return status;
}
```

The internal state of file stream objects changes with most every operation. They should always be passed to functions by reference to ensure internal consistency. Program 12-5 shows an example of how file stream objects may be passed as arguments to functions.

Program 12-5

```cpp
 1  // This program demonstrates how file stream objects may
 2  // be passed by reference to functions.
 3  #include <iostream>
 4  #include <fstream>
 5  #include <string>
 6  using namespace std;
 7
 8  // Function prototypes
 9  bool openFileIn(fstream &, string);
10  void showContents(fstream &);
11
12  int main()
13  {
14     fstream dataFile;
15
16     if (openFileIn(dataFile, "demofile.txt"))
17     {
18        cout << "File opened successfully.\n";
19        cout << "Now reading data from the file.\n\n";
20        showContents(dataFile);
21        dataFile.close();
22        cout << "\nDone.\n";
23     }
```

```
24       else
25           cout << "File open error!" << endl;
26
27       return 0;
28   }
29
30   //**************************************************************
31   // Definition of function openFileIn. Accepts a reference    *
32   // to an fstream object as an argument. The file is opened   *
33   // for input. The function returns true upon success, false  *
34   // upon failure.                                             *
35   //**************************************************************
36
37   bool openFileIn(fstream &file, string name)
38   {
39       file.open(name.c_str(), ios::in);
40       if (file.fail())
41           return false;
42       else
43           return true;
44   }
45
46   //**************************************************************
47   // Definition of function showContents. Accepts an fstream   *
48   // reference as its argument. Uses a loop to read each name  *
49   // from the file and displays it on the screen.              *
50   //**************************************************************
51
52   void showContents(fstream &file)
53   {
54       string line;
55
56       while (file >> line)
57       {
58           cout << line << endl;
59       }
60   }
```

Program Output

```
File opened successfully.
Now reading data from the file.

Jones
Smith
Willis
Davis

Done.
```

12.4 More Detailed Error Testing

CONCEPT: All stream objects have error state bits that indicate the condition of the stream.

All stream objects contain a set of bits that act as flags. These flags indicate the current state of the stream. Table 12-4 lists these bits.

Table 12-4

Bit	Description
ios::eofbit	Set when the end of an input stream is encountered.
ios::failbit	Set when an attempted operation has failed.
ios::hardfail	Set when an unrecoverable error has occurred.
ios::badbit	Set when an invalid operation has been attempted.
ios::goodbit	Set when all the flags above are not set. Indicates the stream is in good condition.

These bits can be tested by the member functions listed in Table 12-5. (You've already learned about the `fail()` function.) One of the functions listed in the table, `clear()`, can be used to set a status bit.

Table 12-5

Function	Description
eof()	Returns true (nonzero) if the `eofbit` flag is set, otherwise returns false.
fail()	Returns true (nonzero) if the `failbit` or `hardfail` flags are set, otherwise returns false.
bad()	Returns true (nonzero) if the `badbit` flag is set, otherwise returns false.
good()	Returns true (nonzero) if the `goodbit` flag is set, otherwise returns false.
clear()	When called with no arguments, clears all the flags listed above. Can also be called with a specific flag as an argument.

The function `showState`, shown here, accepts a file stream reference as its argument. It shows the state of the file by displaying the return values of the `eof()`, `fail()`, `bad()`, and `good()` member functions:

```
void showState(fstream &file)
{
    cout << "File Status:\n";
    cout << "   eof bit: " << file.eof() << endl;
    cout << "  fail bit: " << file.fail() << endl;
    cout << "   bad bit: " << file.bad() << endl;
    cout << "  good bit: " << file.good() << endl;
    file.clear();      // Clear any bad bits
}
```

Program 12-6 uses the `showState` function to display `testFile`'s status after various operations. First, the file is created and the integer value 10 is stored in it. The file is then closed and reopened for input. The integer is read from the file, and then a second read

operation is performed. Because there is only one item in the file, the second read operation will result in an error.

Program 12-6

```cpp
 1    // This program demonstrates the return value of the stream
 2    // object error testing member functions.
 3    #include <iostream>
 4    #include <fstream>
 5    using namespace std;
 6
 7    // Function prototype
 8    void showState(fstream &);
 9
10    int main()
11    {
12        int num = 10;
13
14        // Open the file for output.
15        fstream testFile("stuff.dat", ios::out);
16        if (testFile.fail())
17        {
18           cout << "ERROR: Cannot open the file.\n";
19           return 0;
20        }
21
22        // Write a value to the file.
23        cout << "Writing the value " << num << " to the file.\n";
24        testFile << num;
25
26        // Show the bit states.
27        showState(testFile);
28
29        // Close the file.
30        testFile.close();
31
32        // Reopen the file for input.
33        testFile.open("stuff.dat", ios::in);
34        if (testFile.fail())
35        {
36           cout << "ERROR: Cannot open the file.\n";
37           return 0;
38        }
39
40        // Read the only value from the file.
41        cout << "Reading from the file.\n";
42        testFile >> num;
43        cout << "The value " << num << " was read.\n";
44
45        // Show the bit states.
46        showState(testFile);
47
```

(program continues)

Program 12-6 *(continued)*

```
48       // No more data in the file, but force an invalid read operation.
49       cout << "Forcing a bad read operation.\n";
50       testFile >> num;
51
52       // Show the bit states.
53       showState(testFile);
54
55       // Close the file.
56       testFile.close();
57       return 0;
58   }
59
60   //*********************************************************************
61   // Definition of function showState. This function uses            *
62   // an fstream reference as its parameter. The return values of      *
63   // the eof(), fail(), bad(), and good() member functions are        *
64   // displayed. The clear() function is called before the function    *
65   // returns.                                                         *
66   //*********************************************************************
67
68   void showState(fstream &file)
69   {
70       cout << "File Status:\n";
71       cout << "  eof bit: " << file.eof() << endl;
72       cout << "  fail bit: " << file.fail() << endl;
73       cout << "  bad bit: " << file.bad() << endl;
74       cout << "  good bit: " << file.good() << endl;
75       file.clear();  // Clear any bad bits
76   }
```

Program Output

```
Writing the value 10 to the file.
File Status:
  eof bit: 0
  fail bit: 0
  bad bit: 0
  good bit: 1
Reading from the file.
The value 10 was read.
File Status:
  eof bit: 1
  fail bit: 0
  bad bit: 0
  good bit: 1
Forcing a bad read operation.
File Status:
  eof bit: 1
  fail bit: 1
  bad bit: 0
  good bit: 0
```

12.5 Member Functions for Reading and Writing Files

CONCEPT: File stream objects have member functions for more specialized file reading and writing.

If whitespace characters are part of the data in a file, a problem arises when the file is read by the >> operator. Because the operator considers whitespace characters as delimiters, it does not read them. For example, consider the file murphy.txt, which contains the following data:

Jayne Murphy
47 Jones Circle
Almond, NC 28702

Figure 12-5 shows the way the data is recorded in the file.

Figure 12-5

J	a	y	n	e		M	u	r	p	h	y	\n	4	7

	J	o	n	e	s		C	i	r	c	l	e	\n	A

l	m	o	n	d	,		N	C			2	8	7	0

2	\n	\<EOF\>

The problem that arises from the use of the >> operator is evident in the output of Program 12-7.

Program 12-7

```
 1  // This program demonstrates how the >> operator should not
 2  // be used to read data that contain whitespace characters
 3  // from a file.
 4  #include <iostream>
 5  #include <fstream>
 6  #include <string>
 7  using namespace std;
 8
 9  int main()
10  {
11      string input;     // To hold file input
12      fstream nameFile; // File stream object
13
14      // Open the file in input mode.
15      nameFile.open("murphy.txt", ios::in);
16
17      // If the file was successfully opened, continue.
18      if (nameFile)
```

(program continues)

Program 12-7   *(continued)*

```
19   {
20       // Read the file contents.
21       while (nameFile >> input)
22       {
23           cout << input;
24       }
25
26       // Close the file.
27       nameFile.close();
28    }
29    else
30    {
31       cout << "ERROR: Cannot open file.\n";
32    }
33    return 0;
34 }
```

Program Output

JayneMurphy47JonesCircleAlmond,NC28702

The `getline` Function

The problem with Program 12-7 can be solved by using the `getline` function. The function reads a "line" of data, including whitespace characters. Here is an example of the function call:

```
getline(dataFile, str,'\n');
```

The three arguments in this statement are explained as follows:

`dataFile`	This is the name of the file stream object. It specifies the stream object from which the data is to be read.
`str`	This is the name of a `string` object. The data read from the file will be stored here.
`'\n'`	This is a delimiter character of your choice. If this delimiter is encountered, it will cause the function to stop reading. (This argument is optional. If it's left out, `'\n'` is the default.)

The statement is an instruction to read a line of characters from the file. The function will read until it encounters a \n. The line of characters will be stored in the `str` object.

Program 12-8 is a modification of Program 12-7. It uses the `getline` function to read whole lines of data from the file.

Program 12-8

```
1 // This program uses the getline function to read a line of
2 // data from the file.
3 #include <iostream>
4 #include <fstream>
5 #include <string>
6 using namespace std;
7
8 int main()
```

```
 9 {
10    string input;      // To hold file input
11    fstream nameFile; // File stream object
12
13    // Open the file in input mode.
14    nameFile.open("murphy.txt", ios::in);
15
16    // If the file was successfully opened, continue.
17    if (nameFile)
18    {
19       // Read an item from the file.
20       getline(nameFile, input);
21
22       // While the last read operation
23       // was successful, continue.
24       while (nameFile)
25       {
26          // Display the last item read.
27          cout << input << endl;
28
29          // Read the next item.
30          getline(nameFile, input);
31       }
32
33       // Close the file.
34       nameFile.close();
35    }
36    else
37    {
38       cout << "ERROR: Cannot open file.\n";
39    }
40    return 0;
41 }
```

Program Output
```
Jayne Murphy
47 Jones Circle
Almond, NC 28702
```

Because the third argument of the getline function was left out in Program 12-8, its default value is \n. Sometimes you might want to specify another delimiter. For example, consider a file that contains multiple names and addresses, and that is internally formatted in the following manner:

Contents of names2.txt
```
Jayne Murphy$47 Jones Circle$Almond, NC 28702\n$Bobbie Smith$
217 Halifax Drive$Canton, NC 28716\n$Bill Hammet$PO Box 121$
Springfield, NC 28357\n$
```

Think of this file as consisting of three records. A record is a complete set of data about a single item. Also, the records in the file above are made of three fields. The first field is the person's name. The second field is the person's street address or PO box number. The third field contains the person's city, state, and ZIP code. Notice that each field ends with a $ character, and each record ends with a \n character. Program 12-9 demonstrates how a getline function can be used to detect the $ characters.

Program 12-9

```
 1  // This file demonstrates the getline function with
 2  // a specified delimiter.
 3  #include <iostream>
 4  #include <fstream>
 5  #include <string>
 6  using namespace std;
 7
 8  int main()
 9  {
10     string input;  // To hold file input
11
12     // Open the file for input.
13     fstream dataFile("names2.txt", ios::in);
14
15     // If the file was successfully opened, continue.
16     if (dataFile)
17     {
18        // Read an item using $ as a delimiter.
19        getline(dataFile, input, '$');
20
21        // While the last read operation
22        // was successful, continue.
23        while (dataFile)
24        {
25           // Display the last item read.
26           cout << input << endl;
27
28           // Read an item using $ as a delimiter.
29           getline(dataFile, input, '$');
30        }
31
32        // Close the file.
33        dataFile.close();
34     }
35     else
36     {
37        cout << "ERROR: Cannot open file.\n";
38     }
39     return 0;
40  }
```

Program Output

```
Jayne Murphy
47 Jones Circle
Almond, NC 28702

Bobbie Smith
217 Halifax Drive
Canton, NC 28716

Bill Hammet
PO Box 121
Springfield, NC 28357
```

Notice that the \n characters, which mark the end of each record, are also part of the output. They cause an extra blank line to be printed on the screen, separating the records.

 NOTE: When using a printable character, such as $, to delimit data in a file, be sure to select a character that will not actually appear in the data itself. Since it's doubtful that anyone's name or address contains a $ character, it's an acceptable delimiter. If the file contained dollar amounts, however, another delimiter would have been chosen.

The get **Member Function**

The file stream object's get member function is also useful. It reads a single character from the file. Here is an example of its usage:

```
inFile.get(ch);
```

In this example, ch is a char variable. A character will be read from the file and stored in ch. Program 12-10 shows the function used in a complete program. The user is asked for the name of a file. The file is opened and the get function is used in a loop to read the file's contents, one character at a time.

Program 12-10

```cpp
 1 // This program asks the user for a file name. The file is
 2 // opened and its contents are displayed on the screen.
 3 #include <iostream>
 4 #include <fstream>
 5 #include <string>
 6 using namespace std;
 7
 8 int main()
 9 {
10     string fileName;   // To hold the file name
11     char ch;           // To hold a character
12     fstream file;      // File stream object
13
14     // Get the file name
15     cout << "Enter a file name: ";
16     cin >> fileName;
17
18     // Open the file.
19     file.open(fileName.c_str(), ios::in);
20
21     // If the file was successfully opened, continue.
22     if (file)
23     {
24         // Get a character from the file.
25         file.get(ch);
26
27         // While the last read operation was
28         // successful, continue.
29         while (file)
30         {
```

(program continues)

Program 12-10 *(continued)*

```
31              // Display the last character read.
32              cout << ch;
33
34              // Read the next character
35              file.get(ch);
36          }
37
38          // Close the file.
39          file.close();
40      }
41      else
42          cout << fileName << " could not be opened.\n";
43      return 0;
44  }
```

Program 12-10 will display the contents of any file. The `get` function even reads whitespaces, so all the characters will be shown exactly as they appear in the file.

The `put` Member Function

The put member function writes a single character to the file. Here is an example of its usage:

```
outFile.put(ch);
```

In this statement, the variable `ch` is assumed to be a `char` variable. Its contents will be written to the file associated with the file stream object `outFile`. Program 12-11 demonstrates the put function.

Program 12-11

```
 1  // This program demonstrates the put member function.
 2  #include <iostream>
 3  #include <fstream>
 4  using namespace std;
 5
 6  int main()
 7  {
 8      char ch;  // To hold a character
 9
10      // Open the file for output.
11      fstream dataFile("sentence.txt", ios::out);
12
13      cout << "Type a sentence and be sure to end it with a ";
14      cout << "period.\n";
15
16      // Get a sentence from the user one character at a time
17      // and write each character to the file.
18      cin.get(ch);
19      while (ch != '.')
20      {
21          dataFile.put(ch);
22          cin.get(ch);
23      }
```

```
24          dataFile.put(ch); // Write the period.
25
26          // Close the file.
27          dataFile.close();
28          return 0;
29      }
```

Program Output with Example Input Shown in Bold

Type a sentence and be sure to end it with a period.
I am on my way to becoming a great programmer. [Enter]

Resulting Contents of the File sentence.txt:

I am on my way to becoming a great programmer.

 ## Checkpoint

myprogramminglab *www.myprogramminglab.com*

12.7   Assume the file input.txt contains the following characters:

R	u	n		S	p	o	t		r	u	n	\n	S	e

e		S	p	o	t		r	u	n	\n	<EOF>

What will the following program display on the screen?

```
#include <iostream>
#include <fstream>
#include <string>
using namespace std;

int main()
{
    fstream inFile("input.txt", ios::in);
    string item;

    inFile >> item;
    while (inFile)
    {
        cout << item << endl;
        inFile >> item;
    }
    inFile.close();
    return 0;
}
```

12.8   Describe the difference between reading a file with the >> operator and the getline function.

12.9   What will be stored in the file out.txt after the following program runs?

```
include <iostream>
#include <fstream>
#include <iomanip>
using namespace std;
```

```cpp
int main()
{
    const int SIZE = 5;
    ofstream outFile("out.txt");
    double nums[SIZE] = {100.279, 1.719, 8.602, 7.777, 5.099};

    outFile << fixed << setprecision(2);
    for (int count = 0; count < 5; count++)
    {
        outFile << setw(8) << nums[count];
    }
    outFile.close();
    return 0;
}
```

12.6 Focus on Software Engineering: Working with Multiple Files

CONCEPT: It's possible to have more than one file open at once in a program.

VideoNote
Working with Multiple Files

Quite often you will need to have multiple files open at once. In many real-world applications, data about a single item are categorized and written to several different files. For example, a payroll system might keep the following files:

emp.dat   A file that contains the following data about each employee: name, job title, address, telephone number, employee number, and the date hired.

pay.dat   A file that contains the following data about each employee: employee number, hourly pay rate, overtime rate, and number of hours worked in the current pay cycle.

withhold.dat   A file that contains the following data about each employee: employee number, dependents, and extra withholdings.

When the system is writing paychecks, you can see that it will need to open each of the files listed above and read data from them. (Notice that each file contains the employee number. This is how the program can locate a specific employee's data.)

In C++, you open multiple files by defining multiple file stream objects. For example, if you need to read from three files, you can define three file stream objects, such as:

```cpp
ifstream file1, file2, file3;
```

Sometimes you will need to open one file for input and another file for output. For example, Program 12-12 asks the user for a file name. The file is opened and read. Each character is converted to uppercase and written to a second file called out.txt. This type of program can be considered a *filter*. Filters read the input of one file, changing the data in some fashion, and write it out to a second file. The second file is a modified version of the first file.

Program 12-12

```cpp
1  // This program demonstrates reading from one file and writing
2  // to a second file.
3  #include <iostream>
4  #include <fstream>
5  #include <string>
6  #include <cctype> // Needed for the toupper function.
7  using namespace std;
8
9  int main()
10 {
11     string fileName;      // To hold the file name
12     char ch;              // To hold a character
13     ifstream inFile;      // Input file
14
15     // Open a file for output.
16     ofstream outFile("out.txt");
17
18     // Get the input file name.
19     cout << "Enter a file name: ";
20     cin >> fileName;
21
22     // Open the file for input.
23     inFile.open(fileName.c_str());
24
25     // If the input file opened successfully, continue.
26     if (inFile)
27     {
28         // Read a char from file 1.
29         inFile.get(ch);
30
31         // While the last read operation was
32         // successful, continue.
33         while (inFile)
34         {
35             // Write uppercase char to file 2.
36             outFile.put(toupper(ch));
37
38             // Read another char from file 1.
39             inFile.get(ch);
40         }
41
42         // Close the two files.
43         inFile.close();
44         outFile.close();
45         cout << "File conversion done.\n";
46     }
47     else
48         cout << "Cannot open " << fileName << endl;
49     return 0;
50 }
```

(program output continues)

Program 12-12 *(continued)*

Program Output with Example Input Shown in Bold
```
Enter a file name: hownow.txt [Enter]
File conversion done.
```

Contents of `hownow.txt`
```
how now brown cow.
How Now?
```

Resulting Contents of `out.txt`
```
HOW NOW BROWN COW.
HOW NOW?
```

12.7 Binary Files

CONCEPT: Binary files contain data that is not necessarily stored as ASCII text.

All the files you've been working with so far have been text files. That means the data stored in the files has been formatted as ASCII text. Even a number, when stored in a file with the << operator, is converted to text. For example, consider the following program segment:

```
ofstream file("num.dat");
short x = 1297;
file << x;
```

The last statement writes the contents of x to the file. When the number is written, however, it is stored as the characters '1', '2', '9', and '7'. This is illustrated in Figure 12-6.

Figure 12-6

| '1' | '2' | '9' | '7' | <EOF> |

1297 expressed in ASCII

| 49 | 50 | 57 | 55 | <EOF> |

The number 1297 isn't stored in memory (in the variable x) in the fashion depicted in the figure above, however. It is formatted as a binary number, occupying two bytes on a typical PC. Figure 12-7 shows how the number is represented in memory, using binary or hexadecimal.

Figure 12-7

1297 as a short integer, in binary

| 00000101 | 00010001 |

1297 as a short integer, in hexadecimal

| 05 | 11 |

The representation of the number shown in Figure 12-7 is the way the "raw" data is stored in memory. Data can be stored in a file in its pure, binary format. The first step is to open the file in binary mode. This is accomplished by using the `ios::binary` flag. Here is an example:

```
file.open("stuff.dat", ios::out | ios::binary);
```

Notice the `ios::out` and `ios::binary` flags are joined in the statement with the | operator. This causes the file to be opened in both output and binary modes.

> **NOTE:** By default, files are opened in text mode.

The `write` and `read` Member Functions

The file stream object's `write` member function is used to write binary data to a file. The general format of the `write` member function is

```
fileObject.write(address, size);
```

Let's look at the parts of this function call format.

- *fileObject* is the name of a file stream object.
- *address* is the starting address of the section of memory that is to be written to the file. This argument is expected to be the address of a `char` (or a pointer to a `char`).
- *size* is the number of bytes of memory to write. This argument must be an integer value.

For example, the following code uses a file stream object named `file` to write a character to a binary file.

```
char letter = 'A';
file.write(&letter, sizeof(letter));
```

The first argument passed to the `write` function is the address of the `letter` variable. This tells the `write` function where the data that is to be written to the file is located. The second argument is the size of the `letter` variable, which is returned from the `sizeof` operator. This tells the `write` function the number of bytes of data to write to the file. Because the sizes of data types can vary among systems, it is best to use the `sizeof` operator to determine the number of bytes to write. After this function call executes, the contents of the `letter` variable will be written to the binary file associated with the `file` object.

The following code shows another example. This code writes an entire `char` array to a binary file.

```
char data[] = {'A', 'B', 'C', 'D'};
file.write(data, sizeof(data));
```

In this code, the first argument is the name of the `data` array. By passing the name of the array we are passing a pointer to the beginning of the array. Because `data` is an array of `char` values, the name of the array is a pointer to a `char`. The second argument passes the name of the array to the `sizeof` operator. When the name of an array is passed to the `sizeof` operator, the operator returns the number of bytes allocated to the array. After this function call executes, the contents of the `data` array will be written to the binary file associated with the `file` object.

The `read` member function is used to read binary data from a file into memory. The general format of the `read` member function is

> *fileObject*.read(*address*, *size*);

Here are the parts of this function call format:

- *fileObject* is the name of a file stream object.
- *address* is the starting address of the section of memory where the data being read from the file is to be stored. This is expected to be the address of a `char` (or a pointer to a `char`).
- *size* is the number of bytes of memory to read from the file. This argument must be an integer value.

For example, suppose we want to read a single character from a binary file and store that character in the `letter` variable. The following code uses a file stream object named `file` to do just that.

```
char letter;
file.read(&letter, sizeof(letter));
```

The first argument passed to the `read` function is the address of the `letter` variable. This tells the `read` function where to store the value that is read from the file. The second argument is the size of the `letter` variable. This tells the `read` function the number of bytes to read from the file. After this function executes, the `letter` variable will contain a character that was read from the file.

The following code shows another example. This code reads enough data from a binary file to fill an entire `char` array.

```
char data[4];
file.read(data, sizeof(data));
```

In this code, the first argument is the address of the `data` array. The second argument is the number of bytes allocated to the array. On a system that uses 1-byte characters, this function will read four bytes from the file and store them in the `data` array.

Program 12-13 demonstrates writing a `char` array to a file and then reading the data from the file back into memory.

Program 12-13

```
 1   // This program uses the write and read functions.
 2   #include <iostream>
 3   #include <fstream>
 4   using namespace std;
 5
 6   int main()
 7   {
 8      const int SIZE = 4;
 9      char data[SIZE] = {'A', 'B', 'C', 'D'};
10      fstream file;
11
```

```
12      // Open the file for output in binary mode.
13      file.open("test.dat", ios::out | ios::binary);
14
15      // Write the contents of the array to the file.
16      cout << "Writing the characters to the file.\n";
17      file.write(data, sizeof(data));
18
19      // Close the file.
20      file.close();
21
22      // Open the file for input in binary mode.
23      file.open("test.dat", ios::in | ios::binary);
24
25      // Read the contents of the file into the array.
26      cout << "Now reading the data back into memory.\n";
27      file.read(data, sizeof(data));
28
29      // Display the contents of the array.
30      for (int count = 0; count < SIZE; count++)
31         cout << data[count] << " ";
32      cout << endl;
33
34      // Close the file.
35      file.close();
36      return 0;
37   }
```

Program Output
```
Writing the characters to the file.
Now reading the data back into memory.
A B C D
```

Writing Data Other Than `char` to Binary Files

Because the write and read member functions expect their first argument to be a pointer to a char, you must use a type cast when writing and reading items that are of other data types. To convert a pointer from one type to another you should use the reinterpret_cast type cast. The general format of the type cast is

```
reinterpret_cast<dataType>(value)
```

where *dataType* is the data type that you are converting to, and *value* is the value that you are converting. For example, the following code uses the type cast to store the address of an int in a char pointer variable.

```
int x = 65;
char *ptr;
ptr = reinterpret_cast<char *>(&x);
```

The following code shows how to use the type cast to pass the address of an integer as the first argument to the write member function.

```
int x = 27;
file.write(reinterpret_cast<char *>(&x), sizeof(x));
```

After the function executes, the contents of the variable x will be written to the binary file associated with the `file` object. The following code shows an `int` array being written to a binary file.

```
const int SIZE = 10;
int numbers[SIZE] = {1, 2, 3, 4, 5, 6, 7, 8, 9, 10};
file.write(reinterpret_cast<char *>(numbers), sizeof(numbers));
```

After this function call executes, the contents of the `numbers` array will be written to the binary file. The following code shows values being read from the file and stored into the numbers array.

```
const int SIZE = 10;
int numbers[SIZE];
file.read(reinterpret_cast<char *>(numbers), sizeof(numbers));
```

Program 12-14 demonstrates writing an `int` array to a file and then reading the data from the file back into memory.

Program 12-14

```
 1   // This program uses the write and read functions.
 2   #include <iostream>
 3   #include <fstream>
 4   using namespace std;
 5
 6   int main()
 7   {
 8      const int SIZE = 10;
 9      fstream file;
10      int numbers[SIZE] = {1, 2, 3, 4, 5, 6, 7, 8, 9, 10};
11
12      // Open the file for output in binary mode.
13      file.open("numbers.dat", ios::out | ios::binary);
14
15      // Write the contents of the array to the file.
16      cout << "Writing the data to the file.\n";
17      file.write(reinterpret_cast<char *>(numbers), sizeof(numbers));
18
19      // Close the file.
20      file.close();
21
22      // Open the file for input in binary mode.
23      file.open("numbers.dat", ios::in | ios::binary);
24
25      // Read the contents of the file into the array.
26      cout << "Now reading the data back into memory.\n";
27      file.read(reinterpret_cast<char *>(numbers), sizeof(numbers));
28
29      // Display the contents of the array.
30      for (int count = 0; count < SIZE; count++)
31         cout << numbers[count] << " ";
32      cout << endl;
33
34      // Close the file.
35      file.close();
36      return 0;
37   }
```

Program Output
```
Writing the data to the file.
Now reading the data back into memory.
1 2 3 4 5 6 7 8 9 10
```

12.8 Creating Records with Structures

CONCEPT: Structures may be used to store fixed-length records to a file.

Earlier in this chapter the concept of fields and records was introduced. A field is an individual piece of data pertaining to a single item. A record is made up of fields and is a complete set of data about a single item. For example, a set of fields might be a person's name, age, address, and phone number. Together, all those fields that pertain to one person make up a record.

In C++, structures provide a convenient way to organize data into fields and records. For example, the following code could be used to create a record containing data about a person.

```
const int NAME_SIZE = 51, ADDR_SIZE = 51, PHONE_SIZE = 14;

struct Info
{
    char name[NAME_SIZE];
    int  age;
    char address1[ADDR_SIZE];
    char address2[ADDR_SIZE];
    char phone[PHONE_SIZE];
};
```

Besides providing an organizational structure for data, structures also package data into a single unit. For example, assume the structure variable `person` is defined as

```
Info person;
```

Once the members (or fields) of `person` are filled with data, the entire variable may be written to a file using the `write` function:

```
file.write(reinterpret_cast<char *>(&person), sizeof(person));
```

The first argument is the address of the person variable. The `reinterpret_cast` operator is used to convert the address to a `char` pointer. The second argument is the `sizeof` operator with `person` as its `argument`. This returns the number of bytes used by the person structure. Program 12-15 demonstrates this technique.

 NOTE: Because structures can contain a mixture of data types, you should always use the `ios::binary` mode when opening a file to store them.

Program 12-15

```
1   // This program uses a structure variable to store a record to a file.
2   #include <iostream>
3   #include <fstream>
4   using namespace std;
5
6   // Array sizes
7   const int NAME_SIZE = 51, ADDR_SIZE = 51, PHONE_SIZE = 14;
8
9   // Declare a structure for the record.
10  struct Info
11  {
12     char name[NAME_SIZE];
13     int  age;
14     char address1[ADDR_SIZE];
15     char address2[ADDR_SIZE];
16     char phone[PHONE_SIZE];
17  };
18
19  int main()
20  {
21     Info person;    // To hold info about a person
22     char again;     // To hold Y or N
23
24     // Open a file for binary output.
25     fstream people("people.dat", ios::out | ios::binary);
26
27     do
28     {
29        // Get data about a person.
30        cout << "Enter the following data about a "
31             << "person:\n";
32        cout << "Name: ";
33        cin.getline(person.name, NAME_SIZE);
34        cout << "Age: ";
35        cin >> person.age;
36        cin.ignore(); // Skip over the remaining newline.
37        cout << "Address line 1: ";
38        cin.getline(person.address1, ADDR_SIZE);
39        cout << "Address line 2: ";
40        cin.getline(person.address2, ADDR_SIZE);
41        cout << "Phone: ";
42        cin.getline(person.phone, PHONE_SIZE);
43
44        // Write the contents of the person structure to the file.
45        people.write(reinterpret_cast<char *>(&person),
46                     sizeof(person));
47
48        // Determine whether the user wants to write another record.
49        cout << "Do you want to enter another record? ";
50        cin >> again;
51        cin.ignore();  // Skip over the remaining newline.
52     } while (again == 'Y' || again == 'y');
53
```

```
54        // Close the file.
55        people.close();
56        return 0;
57   }
```

Program Output with Example Input Shown in Bold
Enter the following data about a person:
Name: **Charlie Baxter [Enter]**
Age: **42 [Enter]**
Address line 1: **67 Kennedy Blvd. [Enter]**
Address line 2: **Perth, SC 38754 [Enter]**
Phone: **(803)555-1234 [Enter]**
Do you want to enter another record? **Y [Enter]**
Enter the following data about a person:
Name: **Merideth Murney [Enter]**
Age: **22 [Enter]**
Address line 1: **487 Lindsay Lane [Enter]**
Address line 2: **Hazelwood, NC 28737 [Enter]**
Phone: **(828)555-9999 [Enter]**
Do you want to enter another record? **N [Enter]**

Program 12-15 allows you to build a file by filling the members of the person variable, and then writing the variable to the file. Program 12-16 opens the file and reads each record into the person variable, then displays the data on the screen.

Program 12-16

```
1    // This program uses a structure variable to read a record from a file.
2    #include <iostream>
3    #include <fstream>
4    using namespace std;
5
6    const int NAME_SIZE = 51, ADDR_SIZE = 51, PHONE_SIZE = 14;
7
8    // Declare a structure for the record.
9    struct Info
10   {
11       char name[NAME_SIZE];
12       int age;
13       char address1[ADDR_SIZE];
14       char address2[ADDR_SIZE];
15       char phone[PHONE_SIZE];
16   };
17
18   int main()
19   {
20       Info person;     // To hold info about a person
21       char again;      // To hold Y or N
22       fstream people;  // File stream object
23
24       // Open the file for input in binary mode.
25       people.open("people.dat", ios::in | ios::binary);
26
```

(program continues)

Program 12-16 *(continued)*

```
27      // Test for errors.
28      if (!people)
29      {
30         cout << "Error opening file. Program aborting.\n";
31         return 0;
32      }
33
34
35      cout << "Here are the people in the file:\n\n";
36      // Read the first record from the file.
37      people.read(reinterpret_cast<char *>(&person),
38               sizeof(person));
39
40      // While not at the end of the file, display
41      // the records.
42      while (!people.eof())
43      {
44         // Display the record.
45         cout << "Name: ";
46         cout << person.name << endl;
47         cout << "Age: ";
48         cout << person.age << endl;
49         cout << "Address line 1: ";
50         cout << person.address1 << endl;
51         cout << "Address line 2: ";
52         cout << person.address2 << endl;
53         cout << "Phone: ";
54         cout << person.phone << endl;
55
56         // Wait for the user to press the Enter key.
57         cout << "\nPress the Enter key to see the next record.\n";
58         cin.get(again);
59
60         // Read the next record from the file.
61         people.read(reinterpret_cast<char *>(&person),
62                  sizeof(person));
63      }
64
65      cout << "That's all the data in the file!\n";
66      people.close();
67      return 0;
68   }
```

Program Output (Using the same file created by Program 12-15 as input)

```
Here are the people in the file:

Name: Charlie Baxter
Age: 42
Address line 1: 67 Kennedy Blvd.
Address line 2: Perth, SC  38754
Phone: (803)555-1234
```

```
Press the Enter key to see the next record.

Name: Merideth Murney
Age: 22
Address line 1: 487 Lindsay Lane
Address line 2: Hazelwood, NC  28737
Phone: (828)555-9999

Press the Enter key to see the next record.

That's all the data in the file!
```

NOTE: Structures containing pointers cannot be correctly stored to disk using the techniques of this section. This is because if the structure is read into memory on a subsequent run of the program, it cannot be guaranteed that all program variables will be at the same memory locations. Because `string` class objects contain implicit pointers, they cannot be a part of a structure that has to be stored.

12.9 Random-Access Files

CONCEPT: Random Access means nonsequentially accessing data in a file.

All of the programs created so far in this chapter have performed *sequential file access*. When a file is opened, the position where reading and/or writing will occur is at the file's beginning (unless the `ios::app` mode is used, which causes data to be written to the end of the file). If the file is opened for output, bytes are written to it one after the other. If the file is opened for input, data is read beginning at the first byte. As the reading or writing continues, the file stream object's read/write position advances sequentially through the file's contents.

The problem with sequential file access is that in order to read a specific byte from the file, all the bytes that precede it must be read first. For instance, if a program needs data stored at the hundredth byte of a file, it will have to read the first 99 bytes to reach it. If you've ever listened to a cassette tape player, you understand sequential access. To listen to a song at the end of the tape, you have to listen to all the songs that come before it, or fast-forward over them. There is no way to immediately jump to that particular song.

Although sequential file access is useful in many circumstances, it can slow a program down tremendously. If the file is very large, locating data buried deep inside it can take a long time. Alternatively, C++ allows a program to perform *random file access*. In random file access, a program may immediately jump to any byte in the file without first reading the preceding bytes. The difference between sequential and random file access is like the difference between a cassette tape and a compact disc. When listening to a CD, there is no need to listen to or fast forward over unwanted songs. You simply jump to the track that you want to listen to. This is illustrated in Figure 12-8.

The seekp and seekg Member Functions

File stream objects have two member functions that are used to move the read/write position to any byte in the file. They are `seekp` and `seekg`. The `seekp` function is used with

Figure 12-8

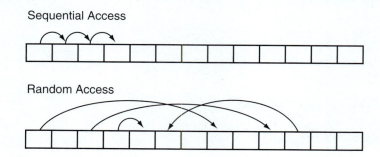

files opened for output and seekg is used with files opened for input. (It makes sense if you remember that "p" stands for "put" and "g" stands for "get." seekp is used with files that you put data into, and seekg is used with files you get data out of.)

Here is an example of seekp's usage:

```
file.seekp(20L, ios::beg);
```

The first argument is a long integer representing an offset into the file. This is the number of the byte you wish to move to. In this example, 20L is used. (Remember, the L suffix forces the compiler to treat the number as a long integer.) This statement moves the file's write position to byte number 20. (All numbering starts at 0, so byte number 20 is actually the twenty-first byte.)

The second argument is called the mode, and it designates where to calculate the offset *from*. The flag ios::beg means the offset is calculated from the beginning of the file. Alternatively, the offset can be calculated from the end of the file or the current position in the file. Table 12-6 lists the flags for all three of the random-access modes.

Table 12-6

Mode Flag	Description
ios::beg	The offset is calculated from the beginning of the file.
ios::end	The offset is calculated from the end of the file.
ios::cur	The offset is calculated from the current position.

Table 12-7 shows examples of seekp and seekg using the various mode flags.

Notice that some of the examples in Table 12-7 use a negative offset. Negative offsets result in the read or write position being moved backward in the file, while positive offsets result in a forward movement.

Assume the file letters.txt contains the following data:

```
abcdefghijklmnopqrstuvwxyz
```

Program 12-17 uses the seekg function to jump around to different locations in the file, retrieving a character after each stop.

Table 12-7

Statement	How It Affects the Read/Write Position
`file.seekp(32L, ios::beg);`	Sets the write position to the 33rd byte (byte 32) from the beginning of the file.
`file.seekp(-10L, ios::end);`	Sets the write position to the 10th byte from the end of the file.
`file.seekp(120L, ios::cur);`	Sets the write position to the 121st byte (byte 120) from the current position.
`file.seekg(2L, ios::beg);`	Sets the read position to the 3rd byte (byte 2) from the beginning of the file.
`file.seekg(-100L, ios::end);`	Sets the read position to the 100th byte from the end of the file.
`file.seekg(40L, ios::cur);`	Sets the read position to the 41st byte (byte 40) from the current position.
`file.seekg(0L, ios::end);`	Sets the read position to the end of the file.

Program 12-17

```
 1   // This program demonstrates the seekg function.
 2   #include <iostream>
 3   #include <fstream>
 4   using namespace std;
 5
 6   int main()
 7   {
 8      char ch;  // To hold a character
 9
10      // Open the file for input.
11      fstream file("letters.txt", ios::in);
12
13      // Move to byte 5 from the beginning of the file
14      // (the 6th byte) and read the character there.
15      file.seekg(5L, ios::beg);
16      file.get(ch);
17      cout << "Byte 5 from beginning: " << ch << endl;
18
19      // Move to the 10th byte from the end of the file
20      // and read the character there.
21      file.seekg(-10L, ios::end);
22      file.get(ch);
23      cout << "10th byte from end: " << ch << endl;
24
25      // Move to byte 3 from the current position
26      // (the 4th byte) and read the character there.
27      file.seekg(3L, ios::cur);
28      file.get(ch);
29      cout << "Byte 3 from current: " << ch << endl;
30
31      file.close();
32      return 0;
33   }
```

(program output continues)

Program 12-17   *(continued)*

Program Screen Output
```
Byte 5 from beginning: f
10th byte from end: q
Byte 3 from current: u
```

Program 12-18 shows a more robust example of the seekg function. It opens the people.dat file created by Program 12-15. The file contains two records. Program 12-18 displays record 1 (the second record) first, then displays record 0.

The program has two important functions other than main. The first, byteNum, takes a record number as its argument and returns that record's starting byte. It calculates the record's starting byte by multiplying the record number by the size of the Info structure. This returns the offset of that record from the beginning of the file. The second function, showRec, accepts an Info structure as its argument and displays its contents on the screen.

Program 12-18

```cpp
 1    // This program randomly reads a record of data from a file.
 2    #include <iostream>
 3    #include <fstream>
 4    using namespace std;
 5
 6    const int NAME_SIZE = 51, ADDR_SIZE = 51, PHONE_SIZE = 14;
 7
 8    // Declare a structure for the record.
 9    struct Info
10    {
11        char name[NAME_SIZE];
12        int age;
13        char address1[ADDR_SIZE];
14        char address2[ADDR_SIZE];
15        char phone[PHONE_SIZE];
16    };
17
18    // Function Prototypes
19    long byteNum(int);
20    void showRec(Info);
21
22    int main()
23    {
24        Info person;    // To hold info about a person
25        fstream people; // File stream object
26
27        // Open the file for input in binary mode.
28        people.open("people.dat", ios::in | ios::binary);
29
```

```
30      // Test for errors.
31      if (!people)
32      {
33         cout << "Error opening file. Program aborting.\n";
34         return 0;
35      }
36
37      // Read and display record 1 (the second record).
38      cout << "Here is record 1:\n";
39      people.seekg(byteNum(1), ios::beg);
40      people.read(reinterpret_cast<char *>(&person), sizeof(person));
41      showRec(person);
42
43      // Read and display record 0 (the first record).
44      cout << "\nHere is record 0:\n";
45      people.seekg(byteNum(0), ios::beg);
46      people.read(reinterpret_cast<char *>(&person), sizeof(person));
47      showRec(person);
48
49      // Close the file.
50      people.close();
51      return 0;
52   }
53
54   //*************************************************************
55   // Definition of function byteNum. Accepts an integer as    *
56   // its argument. Returns the byte number in the file of the *
57   // record whose number is passed as the argument.           *
58   //*************************************************************
59
60   long byteNum(int recNum)
61   {
62      return sizeof(Info) * recNum;
63   }
64
65   //*************************************************************
66   // Definition of function showRec. Accepts an Info structure *
67   // as its argument, and displays the structure's contents.   *
68   //*************************************************************
69
70   void showRec(Info record)
71   {
72      cout << "Name: ";
73      cout << record.name << endl;
74      cout << "Age: ";
75      cout << record.age << endl;
76      cout << "Address line 1: ";
77      cout << record.address1 << endl;
78      cout << "Address line 2: ";
79      cout << record.address2 << endl;
```

(program continues)

Program 12-18   *(continued)*

```
80      cout << "Phone: ";
81      cout << record.phone << endl;
82   }
```

Program Output (Using the same file created by Program 12–15 as input)
```
Here is record 1:
Name: Merideth Murney
Age: 22
Address line 1: 487 Lindsay Lane
Address line 2: Hazelwood, NC  28737
Phone: (828)555-9999

Here is record 0:
Name: Charlie Baxter
Age: 42
Address line 1: 67 Kennedy Blvd.
Address line 2: Perth, SC  38754
Phone: (803)555-1234
```

 WARNING! If a program has read to the end of a file, you must call the file stream object's `clear` member function before calling `seekg` or `seekp`. This clears the file stream object's `eof` flag. Otherwise, the `seekg` or `seekp` function will not work.

The `tellp` and `tellg` Member Functions

File stream objects have two more member functions that may be used for random file access: `tellp` and `tellg`. Their purpose is to return, as a long integer, the current byte number of a file's read and write position. As you can guess, `tellp` returns the write position and `tellg` returns the read position. Assuming `pos` is a long integer, here is an example of the functions' usage:

```
pos = outFile.tellp();
pos = inFile.tellg();
```

One application of these functions is to determine the number of bytes that a file contains. The following example demonstrates how to do this using the `tellg` function.

```
file.seekg(0L, ios::end);
numBytes = file.tellg();
cout << "The file has " << numBytes << " bytes.\n";
```

First the `seekg` member function is used to move the read position to the last byte in the file. Then the `tellg` function is used to get the current byte number of the read position.

Program 12-19 demonstrates the `tellg` function. It opens the `letters.txt` file, which was also used in Program 12-17. The file contains the following characters:

```
abcdefghijklmnopqrstuvwxyz
```

Program 12-19

```cpp
1   // This program demonstrates the tellg function.
2   #include <iostream>
3   #include <fstream>
4   using namespace std;
5
6   int main()
7   {
8      long offset;      // To hold an offset amount
9      long numBytes;    // To hold the file size
10     char ch;          // To hold a character
11     char again;       // To hold Y or N
12
13     // Open the file for input.
14     fstream file("letters.txt", ios::in);
15
16     // Determine the number of bytes in the file.
17     file.seekg(0L, ios::end);
18     numBytes = file.tellg();
19     cout << "The file has " << numBytes << " bytes.\n";
20
21     // Go back to the beginning of the file.
22     file.seekg(0L, ios::beg);
23
24     // Let the user move around within the file.
25     do
26     {
27        // Display the current read position.
28        cout << "Currently at position " << file.tellg() << endl;
29
30        // Get a byte number from the user.
31        cout << "Enter an offset from the beginning of the file: ";
32        cin >> offset;
33
34        // Move the read position to that byte, read the
35        // character there, and display it.
36        if (offset >= numBytes)     // Past the end of the file?
37           cout << "Cannot read past the end of the file.\n";
38        else
39        {
40           file.seekg(offset, ios::beg);
41           file.get(ch);
42           cout << "Character read: " << ch << endl;
43        }
44
45        // Does the user want to try this again?
46        cout << "Do it again? ";
47        cin >> again;
48     } while (again == 'Y' || again == 'y');
49
50     // Close the file.
51     file.close();
52     return 0;
53  }
```

(program output continues)

Program 12-19 *(continued)*

Program Output with Example Input Shown in Bold
```
The file has 26 bytes.
Currently at position 0
Enter an offset from the beginning of the file: 5 [Enter]
Character read: f
Do it again? y [Enter]
Currently at position 6
Enter an offset from the beginning of the file: 0 [Enter]
Character read: a
Do it again? y [Enter]
Currently at position 1
Enter an offset from the beginning of the file: 26 [Enter]
Cannot read past the end of the file.
Do it again? n [Enter]
```

Rewinding a Sequential-Access File with seekg

Sometimes when processing a sequential file, it is necessary for a program to read the contents of the file more than one time. For example, suppose a program searches a file for an item specified by the user. The program must open the file, read its contents, and determine if the specified item is in the file. If the user needs to search the file again for another item, the program must read the file's contents again.

One simple approach for reading a file's contents more than once is to close and reopen the file, as shown in the following code example.

```
dataFile.open("file.txt", ios::in);        // Open the file.

//
// Read and process the file's contents.
//

dataFile.close();                          // Close the file.
dataFile.open("file.txt", ios::in);        // Open the file again.

//
// Read and process the file's contents again.
//

dataFile.close();                          // Close the file.
```

Each time the file is reopened, its read position is located at the beginning of the file. The read position is the byte in the file that will be read with the next read operation.

Another approach is to "rewind" the file. This means moving the read position to the beginning of the file without closing and reopening it. This is accomplished with the file stream object's seekg member function to move the read position back to the beginning of the file. The following example code demonstrates.

```
dataFile.open("file.txt", ios::in);        // Open the file.

//
// Read and process the file's contents.
//
```

```
dataFile.clear();                    // Clear the eof flag.
dataFile.seekg(0L, ios::beg);        // Rewind the read position.

//
// Read and process the file's contents again.
//

dataFile.close();                    // Close the file.
```

Notice that prior to calling the `seekg` member function, the `clear` member function is called. As previously mentioned this clears the file object's `eof` flag and is necessary only if the program has read to the end of the file. This approach eliminates the need to close and reopen the file each time the file's contents are processed.

12.10 Opening a File for Both Input and Output

CONCEPT: You may perform input and output on an **fstream** file without closing it and reopening it.

Sometimes you'll need to perform both input and output on a file without closing and reopening it. For example, consider a program that allows you to search for a record in a file and then make changes to it. A read operation is necessary to copy the data from the file to memory. After the desired changes have been made to the data in memory, a write operation is necessary to replace the old data in the file with the new data in memory.

Such operations are possible with `fstream` objects. The `ios::in` and `ios::out` file access flags may be joined with the | operator, as shown in the following statement.

```
fstream file("data.dat", ios::in | ios::out)
```

The same operation may be accomplished with the `open` member function:

```
file.open("data.dat", ios::in | ios::out);
```

You may also specify the `ios::binary` flag if binary data is to be written to the file. Here is an example:

```
file.open("data.dat", ios::in | ios::out | ios::binary);
```

When an `fstream` file is opened with both the `ios::in` and `ios::out` flags, the file's current contents are preserved and the read/write position is initially placed at the beginning of the file. If the file does not exist, it is created.

Programs 12-20, 12-21, and 12-22 demonstrate many of the techniques we have discussed. Program 12-20 sets up a file with five blank inventory records. Each record is a structure with members for holding a part description, quantity on hand, and price. Program 12-21 displays the contents of the file on the screen. Program 12-22 opens the file in both input and output modes, and allows the user to change the contents of a specific record.

Program 12-20

```
1   // This program sets up a file of blank inventory records.
2   #include <iostream>
3   #include <fstream>
4   using namespace std;
5
6   // Constants
7   const int DESC_SIZE = 31;    // Description size
8   const int NUM_RECORDS = 5;   // Number of records
9
10  // Declaration of InventoryItem structure
11  struct InventoryItem
12  {
13     char desc[DESC_SIZE];
14     int qty;
15     double price;
16  };
17
18  int main()
19  {
20     // Create an empty InventoryItem structure.
21     InventoryItem record = { "", 0, 0.0 };
22
23     // Open the file for binary output.
24     fstream inventory("Inventory.dat", ios::out | ios::binary);
25
26     // Write the blank records
27     for (int count = 0; count < NUM_RECORDS; count++)
28     {
29        cout << "Now writing record " << count << endl;
30        inventory.write(reinterpret_cast<char *>(&record),
31                    sizeof(record));
32     }
33
34     // Close the file.
35     inventory.close();
36     return 0;
37  }
```

Program Output

```
Now writing record 0
Now writing record 1
Now writing record 2
Now writing record 3
Now writing record 4
```

Program 12-21 simply displays the contents of the inventory file on the screen. It can be used to verify that Program 12-20 successfully created the blank records, and that Program 12-22 correctly modified the designated record.

Program 12-21

```cpp
 1    // This program displays the contents of the inventory file.
 2    #include <iostream>
 3    #include <fstream>
 4    using namespace std;
 5
 6    const int DESC_SIZE = 31;   // Description size
 7
 8    // Declaration of InventoryItem structure
 9    struct InventoryItem
10    {
11       char desc[DESC_SIZE];
12       int qty;
13       double price;
14    };
15
16    int main()
17    {
18       InventoryItem record; // To hold an inventory record
19
20       // Open the file for binary input.
21       fstream inventory("Inventory.dat", ios::in | ios::binary);
22
23       // Now read and display the records
24       inventory.read(reinterpret_cast<char *>(&record),
25                   sizeof(record));
26       while (!inventory.eof())
27       {
28          cout << "Description: ";
29          cout << record.desc << endl;
30          cout << "Quantity: ";
31          cout << record.qty << endl;
32          cout << "Price: ";
33          cout << record.price << endl << endl;
34          inventory.read(reinterpret_cast<char *>(&record),
35                      sizeof(record));
36       }
37
38       // Close the file.
39       inventory.close();
40       return 0;
41    }
```

Here is the screen output of Program 12-21 if it is run immediately after Program 12-20 sets up the file of blank records.

Program 12-21

Program Output

```
Description:
Quantity: 0
Price: 0.0
```

(program output continues)

Program 12-21 *(continued)*

```
Description:
Quantity: 0
Price: 0.0

Description:
Quantity: 0
Price: 0.0

Description:
Quantity: 0
Price: 0.0

Description:
Quantity: 0
Price: 0.0
```

Program 12-22 allows the user to change the contents of an individual record in the inventory file.

Program 12-22

```cpp
 1   // This program allows the user to edit a specific record.
 2   #include <iostream>
 3   #include <fstream>
 4   using namespace std;
 5
 6   const int DESC_SIZE = 31;   // Description size
 7
 8   // Declaration of InventoryItem structure
 9   struct InventoryItem
10   {
11      char desc[DESC_SIZE];
12      int qty;
13      double price;
14   };
15
16   int main()
17   {
18      InventoryItem record;   // To hold an inventory record
19      long recNum;            // To hold a record number
20
21      // Open the file in binary mode for input and output
22      fstream inventory("Inventory.dat",
23                       ios::in | ios::out | ios::binary);
24
25      // Get the record number of the desired record.
26      cout << "Which record do you want to edit? ";
27      cin >> recNum;
28
29      // Move to the record and read it.
30      inventory.seekg(recNum * sizeof(record), ios::beg);
31      inventory.read(reinterpret_cast<char *>(&record),
32                    sizeof(record));
```

```
33
34        // Display the record contents.
35        cout << "Description: ";
36        cout << record.desc << endl;
37        cout << "Quantity: ";
38        cout << record.qty << endl;
39        cout << "Price: ";
40        cout << record.price << endl;
41
42        // Get the new record data.
43        cout << "Enter the new data:\n";
44        cout << "Description: ";
45        cin.ignore();
46        cin.getline(record.desc, DESC_SIZE);
47        cout << "Quantity: ";
48        cin >> record.qty;
49        cout << "Price: ";
50        cin >> record.price;
51
52        // Move back to the beginning of this record's position.
53        inventory.seekp(recNum * sizeof(record), ios::beg);
54
55        // Write the new record over the current record.
56        inventory.write(reinterpret_cast<char *>(&record),
57                    sizeof(record));
58
59        // Close the file.
60        inventory.close();
61        return 0;
62    }
```

Program Output with Example Input Shown in Bold
```
Which record do you want to edit? 2 [Enter]
Description:
Quantity: 0
Price: 0.0
Enter the new data:
Description: Wrench [Enter]
Quantity: 10 [Enter]
Price: 4.67 [Enter]
```

Checkpoint

myprogramminglab   *www.myprogramminglab.com*

12.10   Describe the difference between the seekg and the seekp functions.

12.11   Describe the difference between the tellg and the tellp functions.

12.12   Describe the meaning of the following file access flags:
        ios::beg
        ios::end
        ios::cur

12.13   What is the number of the first byte in a file?

12.14 Briefly describe what each of the following statements does:
```
file.seekp(100L, ios::beg);
file.seekp(-10L, ios::end);
file.seekg(-25L, ios::cur);
file.seekg(30L, ios::cur);
```

12.15 Describe the mode that each of the following statements causes a file to be opened in:
```
file.open("info.dat", ios::in | ios::out);
file.open("info.dat", ios::in | ios::app);
file.open("info.dat", ios::in | ios::out | ios::ate);
file.open("info.dat", ios::in | ios::out | ios::binary);
```

For another example of this chapter's topics, see the High Adventure Travel Part 3 Case Study, available on the book's companion Web site at www.pearsonhighered.com/gaddis.

Review Questions and Exercises

Short Answer

1. What capability does the fstream data type provide that the ifstream and ofstream data types do not?

2. Which file access flag do you use to open a file when you want all output written to the end of the file's existing contents?

3. Assume that the file data.txt already exists, and the following statement executes. What happens to the file?

   ```
   fstream file("data.txt", ios::out);
   ```

4. How do you combine multiple file access flags when opening a file?

5. Should file stream objects be passed to functions by value or by reference? Why?

6. Under what circumstances is a file stream object's ios::hardfail bit set? What member function reports the state of this bit?

7. Under what circumstances is a file stream object's ios::eofbit bit set? What member function reports the state of this bit?

8. Under what circumstances is a file stream object's ios::badbit bit set? What member function reports the state of this bit?

9. How do you read the contents of a text file that contains whitespace characters as part of its data?

10. What arguments do you pass to a file stream object's write member function?

11. What arguments do you pass to a file stream object's read member function?

12. What type cast do you use to convert a pointer from one type to another?

13. What is the difference between the seekg and seekp member functions?

14. How do you get the byte number of a file's current read position? How do you get the byte number of a file's current write position?

15. If a program has read to the end of a file, what must you do before using either the seekg or seekp member functions?

16. How do you determine the number of bytes that a file contains?

17. How do you rewind a sequential-access file?

Fill-in-the-Blank

18. The _____ file stream data type is for output files, input files, or files that perform both input and output.

19. If a file fails to open, the file stream object will be set to _____.

20. The same formatting techniques used with _____ may also be used when writing data to a file.

21. The _____ function reads a line of text from a file.

22. The _____ member function reads a single character from a file.

23. The _____ member function writes a single character to a file.

24. _____ files contain data that is unformatted and not necessarily stored as ASCII text.

25. _____ files contain data formatted as _____.

26. A(n) _____ is a complete set of data about a single item and is made up of _____.

27. In C++, _____ provide a convenient way to organize data into fields and records.

28. The _____ member function writes "raw" binary data to a file.

29. The _____ member function reads "raw" binary data from a file.

30. The _____ operator is necessary if you pass anything other than a pointer-to-char as the first argument of the two functions mentioned in questions 26 and 27.

31. In _____ file access, the contents of the file are read in the order they appear in the file, from the file's start to its end.

32. In _____ file access, the contents of a file may be read in any order.

33. The _____ member function moves a file's read position to a specified byte in the file.

34. The _____ member function moves a file's write position to a specified byte in the file.

35. The _____ member function returns a file's current read position.

36. The _____ member function returns a file's current write position.

37. The _____ mode flag causes an offset to be calculated from the beginning of a file.

38. The _____ mode flag causes an offset to be calculated from the end of a file.

39. The _____ mode flag causes an offset to be calculated from the current position in the file.

40. A negative offset causes the file's read or write position to be moved _____ in the file from the position specified by the mode.

Algorithm Workbench

41. Write a statement that defines a file stream object named `places`. The object will be used for both output and input.

42. Write two statements that use a file stream object named `people` to open a file named `people.dat`. (Show how to open the file with a member function and at the definition of the file stream object.) The file should be opened for output.

43. Write two statements that use a file stream object named `pets` to open a file named `pets.dat`. (Show how to open the file with a member function and at the definition of the file stream object.) The file should be opened for input.

44. Write two statements that use a file stream object named `places` to open a file named `places.dat`. (Show how to open the file with a member function and at the definition of the file stream object.) The file should be opened for both input and output.

45. Write a program segment that defines a file stream object named `employees`. The file should be opened for both input and output (in binary mode). If the file fails to open, the program segment should display an error message.

46. Write code that opens the file `data.txt` for both input and output, but first determines if the file exists. If the file does not exist, the code should create it, then open it for both input and output.

47. Write code that determines the number of bytes contained in the file associated with the file stream object `dataFile`.

48. The `infoFile` file stream object is used to sequentially access data. The program has already read to the end of the file. Write code that rewinds the file.

True or False

49. T F   Different operating systems have different rules for naming files.

50. T F   `fstream` objects are only capable of performing file output operations.

51. T F   `ofstream` objects, by default, delete the contents of a file if it already exists when opened.

52. T F   `ifstream` objects, by default, create a file if it doesn't exist when opened.

53. T F   Several file access flags may be joined by using the | operator.

54. T F   A file may be opened in the definition of the file stream object.

55. T F   If a file is opened in the definition of the file stream object, no mode flags may be specified.

56. T F   A file stream object's `fail` member function may be used to determine if the file was successfully opened.

57. T F   The same output formatting techniques used with `cout` may also be used with file stream objects.

58. T F   The >> operator expects data to be delimited by whitespace characters.

59. T F   The `getline` member function can be used to read text that contains whitespaces.

60. T F   It is not possible to have more than one file open at once in a program.

61. T F   Binary files contain unformatted data, not necessarily stored as text.

62. T F   Binary is the default mode in which files are opened.

63. T F   The `tellp` member function tells a file stream object which byte to move its write position to.

64. T F   It is possible to open a file for both input and output.

Find the Error

Each of the following programs or program segments has errors. Find as many as you can.

```
65. fstream file(ios::in | ios::out);
    file.open("info.dat");
    if (!file)
    {
        cout << "Could not open file.\n";
    }
```

```
66. ofstream file;
    file.open("info.dat", ios::in);
    if (file)
    {
        cout << "Could not open file.\n";
    }
```

```
67. fstream file("info.dat");
    if (!file)
    {
        cout << "Could not open file.\n";
    }
```

```
68. fstream dataFile("info.dat", ios:in | ios:binary);
    int x = 5;
    dataFile << x;
```

```
69. fstream dataFile("info.dat", ios:in);
    char stuff[81];
    dataFile.get(stuff);
```

```
70. fstream dataFile("info.dat", ios:in);
    char stuff[81] = "abcdefghijklmnopqrstuvwxyz";
    dataFile.put(stuff);
```

```
71. fstream dataFile("info.dat", ios:out);
    struct Date
    {
        int month;
        int day;
        int year;
    };
    Date dt = { 4, 2, 98 };
    dataFile.write(&dt, sizeof(int));
```

```
72. fstream inFile("info.dat", ios:in);
    int x;
    inFile.seekp(5);
    inFile >> x;
```

Programming Challenges

Visit www.myprogramminglab.com to complete many of these Programming Challenges online and get instant feedback.

1. File Head Program

Write a program that asks the user for the name of a file. The program should display the first 10 lines of the file on the screen (the "head" of the file). If the file has fewer than 10 lines, the entire file should be displayed, with a message indicating the entire file has been displayed.

> **NOTE:** Using an editor, you should create a simple text file that can be used to test this program.

2. File Display Program

Write a program that asks the user for the name of a file. The program should display the contents of the file on the screen. If the file's contents won't fit on a single screen, the program should display 24 lines of output at a time, and then pause. Each time the program pauses, it should wait for the user to strike a key before the next 24 lines are displayed.

> **NOTE:** Using an editor, you should create a simple text file that can be used to test this program.

3. Punch Line

Write a program that reads and prints a joke and its punch line from two different files. The first file contains a joke, but not its punch line. The second file has the punch line as its last line, preceded by "garbage." The `main` function of your program should open the two files and then call two functions, passing each one the file it needs. The first function should read and display each line in the file it is passed (the joke file). The second function should display only the last line of the file it is passed (the punch line file). It should find this line by seeking to the end of the file and then backing up to the beginning of the last line. Data to test your program can be found in the `joke.txt` and `punchline.txt` files.

4. Tail Program

Write a program that asks the user for the name of a file. The program should display the last 10 lines of the file on the screen (the "tail" of the file). If the file has fewer than 10 lines, the entire file should be displayed, with a message indicating the entire file has been displayed.

> **NOTE:** Using an editor, you should create a simple text file that can be used to test this program.

5. Line Numbers

(This assignment could be done as a modification of the program in Programming Challenge 2.) Write a program that asks the user for the name of a file. The program should display the contents of the file on the screen. Each line of screen output should be preceded with a line number, followed by a colon. The line numbering should start at 1. Here is an example:

```
1:George Rolland
2:127 Academy Street
3:Brasstown, NC  28706
```

If the file's contents won't fit on a single screen, the program should display 24 lines of output at a time, and then pause. Each time the program pauses, it should wait for the user to strike a key before the next 24 lines are displayed.

NOTE: Using an editor, you should create a simple text file that can be used to test this program.

6. String Search

Write a program that asks the user for a file name and a string to search for. The program should search the file for every occurrence of a specified string. When the string is found, the line that contains it should be displayed. After all the occurrences have been located, the program should report the number of times the string appeared in the file.

NOTE: Using an editor, you should create a simple text file that can be used to test this program.

7. Sentence Filter

Write a program that asks the user for two file names. The first file will be opened for input and the second file will be opened for output. (It will be assumed that the first file contains sentences that end with a period.) The program will read the contents of the first file and change all the letters to lowercase except the first letter of each sentence, which should be made uppercase. The revised contents should be stored in the second file.

NOTE: Using an editor, you should create a simple text file that can be used to test this program.

8. Array/File Functions

Write a function named `arrayToFile`. The function should accept three arguments: the name of a file, a pointer to an `int` array, and the size of the array. The function should open the specified file in binary mode, write the contents of the array to the file, and then close the file.

Write another function named `fileToArray`. This function should accept three arguments: the name of a file, a pointer to an `int` array, and the size of the array. The function should open the specified file in binary mode, read its contents into the array, and then close the file.

Write a complete program that demonstrates these functions by using the `arrayToFile` function to write an array to a file, and then using the `fileToArray` function to read the data from the same file. After the data are read from the file into the array, display the array's contents on the screen.

VideoNote
**Solving
the File
Encryption
Filter Problem**

9. **File Encryption Filter**

File encryption is the science of writing the contents of a file in a secret code. Your encryption program should work like a filter, reading the contents of one file, modifying the data into a code, and then writing the coded contents out to a second file. The second file will be a version of the first file, but written in a secret code.

Although there are complex encryption techniques, you should come up with a simple one of your own. For example, you could read the first file one character at a time, and add 10 to the ASCII code of each character before it is written to the second file.

10. **File Decryption Filter**

Write a program that decrypts the file produced by the program in Programming Challenge 9. The decryption program should read the contents of the coded file, restore the data to its original state, and write it to another file.

11. **Corporate Sales Data Output**

Write a program that uses a structure to store the following data on a company division:

> Division Name (such as East, West, North, or South)
> Quarter (1, 2, 3, or 4)
> Quarterly Sales

The user should be asked for the four quarters' sales figures for the East, West, North, and South divisions. The data for each quarter for each division should be written to a file.

Input Validation: Do not accept negative numbers for any sales figures.

12. **Corporate Sales Data Input**

Write a program that reads the data in the file created by the program in Programming Challenge 11. The program should calculate and display the following figures:

- Total corporate sales for each quarter
- Total yearly sales for each division
- Total yearly corporate sales
- Average quarterly sales for the divisions
- The highest and lowest quarters for the corporation

13. **Inventory Program**

Write a program that uses a structure to store the following inventory data in a file:

> Item Description
> Quantity on Hand
> Wholesale Cost
> Retail Cost
> Date Added to Inventory

The program should have a menu that allows the user to perform the following tasks:

- Add new records to the file.
- Display any record in the file.
- Change any record in the file.

Input Validation: The program should not accept quantities, or wholesale or retail costs, less than 0. The program should not accept dates that the programmer determines are unreasonable.

14. **Inventory Screen Report**

Write a program that reads the data in the file created by the program in Programming Challenge 13. The program should calculate and display the following data:

- The total wholesale value of the inventory
- The total retail value of the inventory
- The total quantity of all items in the inventory

15. **Average Number of Words**

If you have downloaded this book's source code from the companion Web site, you will find a file named `text.txt` in the Chapter 12 folder. (The companion Web site is at www.pearsonhighered.com/gaddis.) The text that is in the file is stored as one sentence per line. Write a program that reads the file's contents and calculates the average number of words per sentence.

Group Project

16. **Customer Accounts**

This program should be designed and written by a team of students. Here are some suggestions:

- One student should design function `main`, which will call other program functions. The remainder of the functions will be designed by other members of the team.
- The requirements of the program should be analyzed so each student is given about the same workload.

Write a program that uses a structure to store the following data about a customer account:

> Name
> Address
> City, State, and ZIP
> Telephone Number
> Account Balance
> Date of Last Payment

The structure should be used to store customer account records in a file. The program should have a menu that lets the user perform the following operations:

- Enter new records into the file.
- Search for a particular customer's record and display it.
- Search for a particular customer's record and delete it.
- Search for a particular customer's record and change it.
- Display the contents of the entire file.

Input Validation: When the data for a new account is entered, be sure the user enters data for all the fields. No negative account balances should be entered.

13 Introduction to Classes

TOPICS

13.1 Procedural and Object-Oriented Programming

CONCEPT: Procedural programming is a method of writing software. It is a programming practice centered on the procedures or actions that take place in a program. Object-oriented programming is centered around the object. Objects are created from abstract data types that encapsulate data and functions together.

There are two common programming methods in practice today: procedural programming and object-oriented programming (or OOP). Up to this chapter, you have learned to write procedural programs.

In a procedural program, you typically have data stored in a collection of variables and/or structures, coupled with a set of functions that perform operations on the data. The data and the functions are separate entities. For example, in a program that works with the geometry of a rectangle you might have the variables in Table 13-1:

Table 13-1

Variable Definition	Description
`double width;`	Holds the rectangle's width
`double length;`	Holds the rectangle's length

In addition to the variables listed in Table 13-1, you might also have the functions listed in Table 13-2:

Table 13-2

Function Name	Description
`setData()`	Stores values in `width` and `length`
`displayWidth()`	Displays the rectangle's width
`displayLength()`	Displays the rectangle's length
`displayArea()`	Displays the rectangle's area

Usually the variables and data structures in a procedural program are passed to the functions that perform the desired operations. As you might imagine, the focus of procedural programming is on creating the functions that operate on the program's data.

Procedural programming has worked well for software developers for many years. However, as programs become larger and more complex, the separation of a program's data and the code that operates on the data can lead to problems. For example, the data in a procedural program are stored in variables, as well as more complex structures that are created from variables. The procedures that operate on the data must be designed with those variables and data structures in mind. But, what happens if the format of the data is altered? Quite often, a program's specifications change, resulting in redesigned data structures. When the structure of the data changes, the code that operates on the data must also change to accept the new format. This results in additional work for programmers and a greater opportunity for bugs to appear in the code.

This problem has helped influence the shift from procedural programming to object-oriented programming (OOP). Whereas procedural programming is centered on creating procedures or functions, object-oriented programming is centered on creating objects. An *object* is a software entity that contains both data and procedures. The data that are contained in an object are known as the object's *attributes*. The procedures that an object performs are called *member functions*. The object is, conceptually, a self-contained unit consisting of attributes (data) and procedures (functions). This is illustrated in Figure 13-1.

OOP addresses the problems that can result from the separation of code and data through encapsulation and data hiding. *Encapsulation* refers to the combining of data and code into a single object. *Data hiding* refers to an object's ability to hide its data from code that

Figure 13-1

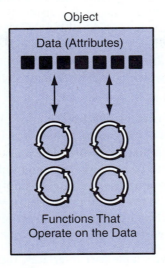

Object

Data (Attributes)

Functions That
Operate on the Data

 NOTE: In other programming languages, the procedures that an object performs are often called *methods*.

is outside the object. Only the object's member functions may directly access and make changes to the object's data. An object typically hides its data, but allows outside code to access its member functions. As shown in Figure 13-2, the object's member functions provide programming statements outside the object with indirect access to the object's data.

Figure 13-2

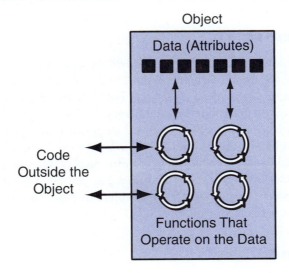

Object

Data (Attributes)

Code
Outside the
Object

Functions That
Operate on the Data

When an object's internal data are hidden from outside code, and access to that data is restricted to the object's member functions, the data are protected from accidental corruption. In addition, the programming code outside the object does not need to know about the format or internal structure of the object's data. The code only needs to interact with the object's functions. When a programmer changes the structure of an object's internal data, he or she also modifies the object's member functions so they may properly operate on the data. The way in which outside code interacts with the member functions, however, does not change.

An everyday example of object-oriented technology is the automobile. It has a rather simple interface that consists of an ignition switch, steering wheel, gas pedal, brake pedal, and a gear shift. Vehicles with manual transmissions also provide a clutch pedal. If you want to drive an automobile (to become its user), you only have to learn to operate these elements of its interface. To start the motor, you simply turn the key in the ignition switch. What happens internally is irrelevant to the user. If you want to steer the auto to the left, you rotate the steering wheel left. The movements of all the linkages connecting the steering wheel to the front tires occur transparently.

Because automobiles have simple user interfaces, they can be driven by people who have no mechanical knowledge. This is good for the makers of automobiles because it means more people are likely to become customers. It's good for the users of automobiles because they can learn just a few simple procedures and operate almost any vehicle.

These are also valid concerns in software development. A real-world program is rarely written by only one person. Even the programs you have created so far weren't written entirely by you. If you incorporated C++ library functions, or objects like cin and cout, you used code written by someone else. In the world of professional software development, programmers commonly work in teams, buy and sell their code, and collaborate on projects. With OOP, programmers can create objects with powerful engines tucked away "under the hood," protected by simple interfaces that safeguard the object's algorithms.

Object Reusability

In addition to solving the problems of code/data separation, the use of OOP has also been encouraged by the trend of *object reusability*. An object is not a stand-alone program, but is used by programs that need its service. For example, Sharon is a programmer who has developed an object for rendering 3D images. She is a math whiz and knows a lot about computer graphics, so her object is coded to perform all the necessary 3D mathematical operations and handle the computer's video hardware. Tom, who is writing a program for an architectural firm, needs his application to display 3D images of buildings. Because he is working under a tight deadline and does not possess a great deal of knowledge about computer graphics, he can use Sharon's object to perform the 3D rendering (for a small fee, of course!).

Classes and Objects

Now let's discuss how objects are created in software. Before an object can be created, it must be designed by a programmer. The programmer determines the attributes and functions that are necessary, and then creates a class. A *class* is code that specifies the attributes and member functions that a particular type of object may have. Think of a class as a "blueprint" that objects may be created from. It serves a similar purpose as the blueprint for a house. The blueprint itself is not a house, but is a detailed description of a house. When we use the blueprint to build an actual house, we could say we are building an instance of the house described by the blueprint. If we so desire, we can build several identical houses from the same blueprint. Each house is a separate instance of the house described by the blueprint. This idea is illustrated in Figure 13-3.

Figure 13-3

Blueprint that describes a house.

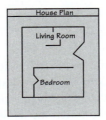

Instances of the house described by the blueprint.

So, a class is not an object, but it is a description of an object. When the program is running, it uses the class to create, in memory, as many objects of a specific type as needed. Each object that is created from a class is called an *instance* of the class.

For example, Jessica is an entomologist (someone who studies insects) and she also enjoys writing computer programs. She designs a program to catalog different types of insects. As part of the program, she creates a class named `Insect`, which specifies attributes and member functions for holding and manipulating data common to all types of insects. The `Insect` class is not an object, but a specification that objects may be created from. Next, she writes programming statements that create a `housefly` object, which is an instance of the `Insect` class. The `housefly` object is an entity that occupies computer memory and stores data about a housefly. It has the attributes and member functions specified by the `Insect` class. Then she writes programming statements that create a `mosquito` object. The `mosquito` object is also an instance of the `Insect` class. It has its own area in memory, and stores data about a mosquito. Although the `housefly` and `mosquito` objects are two separate entities in the computer's memory, they were both created from the `Insect` class. This means that each of the objects has the attributes and member functions described by the `Insect` class. This is illustrated in Figure 13-4.

Figure 13-4

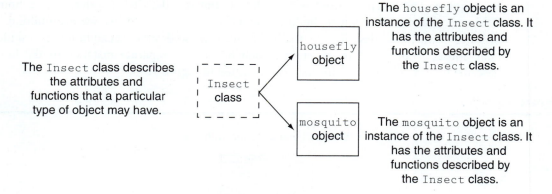

The Insect class describes the attributes and functions that a particular type of object may have.

Insect class

housefly object

The housefly object is an instance of the Insect class. It has the attributes and functions described by the Insect class.

mosquito object

The mosquito object is an instance of the Insect class. It has the attributes and functions described by the Insect class.

At the beginning of this section we discussed how a procedural program that works with rectangles might have variables to hold the rectangle's width and length, and separate functions to do things like store values in the variables and make calculations. The program would pass the variables to the functions as needed. In an object-oriented program, we would create a Rectangle class which would encapsulate the data (width and length) and the functions that work with the data. Figure 13-5 shows a representation of such a class.

Figure 13-5

```
Member Variables
     double width;
     double length;

Member Functions
     void setWidth(double w)
     { ... function code ...}

     void setLength(double len)
     { ... function code ...}

     double getWidth()
     { ... function code ...}

     double getLength()
     { ... function code ...}

     double getArea()
     { ... function code ...}
```

In the object-oriented approach, the variables and functions are all members of the Rectangle class. When we need to work with a rectangle in our program, we create a Rectangle object, which is an instance of the Rectangle class. When we need to perform an operation on the Rectangle object's data, we use that object to call the appropriate member function. For example, if we need to get the area of the rectangle, we use the object to call the getArea member function. The getArea member function would be designed to calculate the area of that object's rectangle, and return the value.

Using a Class You Already Know

Before we go any further, let's review the basics of a class that you have already learned something about: the `string` class. First, recall that you must have the following `#include` directive in any program that uses the `string` class:

```
#include <string>
```

This is necessary because the `string` class is declared in the `string` header file. Next, you can define a `string` object with a statement such as

```
string cityName;
```

This creates a `string` object named `cityName`. The `cityName` object is an instance of the `string` class.

Once a `string` object has been created, you can store data in it. Because the `string` class is designed to work with the assignment operator, you can assign a string literal to a `string` object. Here is an example:

```
cityName = "Charleston";
```

After this statement executes, the string `"Charleston"` will be stored in the `cityName` object. `"Charleston"` will become the object's data.

The `string` class specifies numerous member functions that perform operations on the data that a `string` object holds. For example, it has a member function named `length`, which returns the length of the string stored in a `string` object. The following code demonstrates:

```
string cityName;              // Create a string object named cityName
int strSize;                  // To hold the length of a string
cityName = "Charleston";      // Assign "Charleston" to cityName
strSize = cityName.length();  // Store the string length in strSize
```

The last statement calls the `length` member function, which returns the length of a string. The expression `cityName.length()` returns the length of the string stored in the `cityName` object. After this statement executes, the `strSize` variable will contain the value 10, which is the length of the string `"Charleston"`.

The `string` class also specifies a member function named `append`, which appends an additional string onto the string already stored in an object. The following code demonstrates.

```
string cityName;
cityName = "Charleston";
cityName.append(" South Carolina");
```

In the second line, the string `"Charleston"` is assigned to the `cityName` object. In the third line, the `append` member function is called and `" South Carolina"` is passed as an argument. The argument is appended to the string that is already stored in `cityName`. After this statement executes, the `cityName` object will contain the string `"Charleston South Carolina"`.

13.2 Introduction to Classes

> **CONCEPT:** In C++, the class is the construct primarily used to create objects.

A *class* is similar to a structure. It is a data type defined by the programmer, consisting of variables and functions. Here is the general format of a class declaration:

VideoNote
Writing a Class

```
class ClassName
{
    declaration;
    // ... more declarations
    // may follow...
};
```

The declaration statements inside a class declaration are for the variables and functions that are members of that class. For example, the following code declares a class named `Rectangle` with two member variables: `width` and `length`.

```
class Rectangle
{
    double width;
    double length;
};                      // Don't forget the semicolon.
```

There is a problem with this class, however. Unlike structures, the members of a class are *private* by default. Private class members cannot be accessed by programming statements outside the class. So, no statements outside this `Rectangle` class can access the `width` and `length` members.

Recall from our earlier discussion on object-oriented programming that an object can perform data hiding, which means that critical data stored inside the object are protected from code outside the object. In C++, a class's private members are hidden, and can be accessed only by functions that are members of the same class. A class's *public* members may be accessed by code outside the class.

Access Specifiers

C++ provides the key words `private` and `public` which you may use in class declarations. These key words are known as *access specifiers* because they specify how class members may be accessed. The following is the general format of a class declaration that uses the `private` and `public` access specifiers.

```
class ClassName
{
    private:
        // Declarations of private
        // members appear here.
    public:
        // Declarations of public
        // members appear here.
};
```

Notice that the access specifiers are followed by a colon (:), and then followed by one or more member declarations. In this general format, the private access specifier is used first. All of the declarations that follow it, up to the public access specifier, are for private members. Then, all of the declarations that follow the public access specifier are for public members.

Public Member Functions

To allow access to a class's private member variables, you create public member functions that work with the private member variables. For example, consider the Rectangle class. To allow access to a Rectangle object's width and length member variables, we will add the member functions listed in Table 13-3.

Table 13-3

Member Function	Description
setWidth	This function accepts an argument which is assigned to the width member variable.
setLength	This function accepts an argument which is assigned to the length member variable.
getWidth	This function returns the value stored in the width member variable.
getLength	This function returns the value stored in the length member variable.
getArea	This function returns the product of the width member variable multiplied by the length member variable. This value is the area of the rectangle.

For the moment we will not actually define the functions described in Table 13-3. We leave that for later. For now we will only include declarations, or prototypes, for the functions in the class declaration:

```
class Rectangle
{
    private:
        double width;
        double length;
    public:
        void setWidth(double);
        void setLength(double);
        double getWidth() const;
        double getLength() const;
        double getArea() const;
};
```

In this declaration, the member variables width and length are declared as private, which means they can be accessed only by the class's member functions. The member functions, however, are declared as public, which means they can be called from statements outside the class. If code outside the class needs to store a width or a length in a Rectangle object, it must do so by calling the object's setWidth or setLength member functions. Likewise, if code outside the class needs to retrieve a width or length stored in a Rectangle object, it must do so with the object's getWidth or getLength member functions. These public functions provide an interface for code outside the class to use Rectangle objects.

NOTE: Even though the default access of a class is private, it's still a good idea to use the `private` key word to explicitly declare private members. This clearly documents the access specification of all the members of the class.

Using `const` with Member Functions

Notice that the key word `const` appears in the declarations of the `getWidth`, `getLength`, and `getArea` member functions, as shown here:

```
double getWidth() const;
double getLength() const;
double getArea() const;
```

When the key word `const` appears after the parentheses in a member function declaration, it specifies that the function will not change any data stored in the calling object. If you inadvertently write code in the function that changes the calling object's data, the compiler will generate an error. As you will see momentarily, the `const` key word must also appear in the function header.

Placement of `public` and `private` Members

There is no rule requiring you to declare private members before public members. The `Rectangle` class could be declared as follows:

```
class Rectangle
{
    public:
        void setWidth(double);
        void setLength(double);
        double getWidth() const;
        double getLength() const;
        double getArea() const;
    private:
        double width;
        double length;
};
```

In addition, it is not required that all members of the same access specification be declared in the same place. Here is yet another declaration of the `Rectangle` class.

```
class Rectangle
{
    private:
        double width;
    public:
        void setWidth(double);
        void setLength(double);
        double getWidth() const;
        double getLength() const;
        double getArea() const;
    private:
        double length;
};
```

Although C++ gives you freedom in arranging class member declarations, you should adopt a consistent standard. Most programmers choose to group member declarations of the same access specification together.

 NOTE: Notice in our example that the first character of the class name is written in uppercase. This is not required, but serves as a visual reminder that the class name is not a variable name.

Defining Member Functions

The `Rectangle` class declaration contains declarations or prototypes for five member functions: `setWidth`, `setLength`, `getWidth`, `getLength`, and `getArea`. The definitions of these functions are written outside the class declaration:

```
//***********************************************************
// setWidth assigns its argument to the private member width. *
//***********************************************************

void Rectangle::setWidth(double w)
{
    width = w;
}



//*************************************************************
// setLength assigns its argument to the private member length. *
//*************************************************************

void Rectangle::setLength(double len)
{
    length = len;
}

//**********************************************************
// getWidth returns the value in the private member width.   *
//**********************************************************

double Rectangle::getWidth() const
{
    return width;
}

//*********************************************************
// getLength returns the value in the private member length. *
//*********************************************************

double Rectangle::getLength() const
{
    return length;
}
```

```
//*********************************************************
// getArea returns the product of width times length.   *
//*********************************************************

double Rectangle::getArea() const
{
    return width * length;
}
```

In each function definition, the following precedes the name of each function:

```
Rectangle::
```

The two colons are called the *scope resolution operator*. When `Rectangle::` appears before the name of a function in a function header, it identifies the function as a member of the `Rectangle` class.

Here is the general format of the function header of any member function defined outside the declaration of a class:

```
ReturnType ClassName::functionName(ParameterList)
```

In the general format, `ReturnType` is the function's return type. `ClassName` is the name of the class that the function is a member of. `functionName` is the name of the member function. `ParameterList` is an optional list of parameter variable declarations.

 WARNING! Remember, the class name and scope resolution operator extends the name of the function. They must appear after the return type and immediately before the function name in the function header. The following would be incorrect:

```
Rectangle::double getArea() //Incorrect!
```

In addition, if you leave the class name and scope resolution operator out of a member function's header, the function will not become a member of the class.

```
double getArea() // Not a member of the Rectangle class!
```

Accessors and Mutators

As mentioned earlier, it is a common practice to make all of a class's member variables private and to provide public member functions for accessing and changing them. This ensures that the object owning the member variables is in control of all changes being made to them. A member function that gets a value from a class's member variable but does not change it is known as an *accessor*. A member function that stores a value in member variable or changes the value of member variable in some other way is known as a *mutator*. In the `Rectangle` class, the member functions `getLength` and `getWidth` are accessors, and the member functions `setLength` and `setWidth` are mutators.

Some programmers refer to mutators as *setter functions* because they set the value of an attribute, and accessors as *getter functions* because they get the value of an attribute.

Using `const` with Accessors

Notice that the key word `const` appears in the headers of the `getWidth`, `getLength`, and `getArea` member functions, as shown here:

```
double Rectangle::getWidth() const
double Rectangle::getLength() const
double Rectangle::getArea() const
```

Recall that these functions were also declared in the class with the `const` key word. When you mark a member function as `const`, the `const` key word must appear in both the declaration and the function header.

In essence, when you mark a member function as `const`, you are telling the compiler that the calling object is a constant. The compiler will generate an error if you inadvertently write code in the function that changes the calling object's data. Because this decreases the chances of having bugs in your code, it is a good practice to mark all accessor functions as `const`.

The Importance of Data Hiding

As a beginning student, you might be wondering why you would want to hide the data that is inside the classes you create. As you learn to program, you will be the user of your own classes, so it might seem that you are putting forth a great effort to hide data from yourself. If you write software in industry, however, the classes that you create will be used as components in large software systems; programmers other than yourself will use your classes. By hiding a class's data, and allowing it to be accessed through only the class's member functions, you can better ensure that the class will operate as you intended it to.

13.3

Defining an Instance of a Class

CONCEPT: Class objects must be defined after the class is declared.

VideoNote

Defining an Instance of a Class

Like structure variables, class objects are not created in memory until they are defined. This is because a class declaration by itself does not create an object, but is merely the description of an object. We can use it to create one or more objects, which are instances of the class.

Class objects are created with simple definition statements, just like variables. Here is the general format of a simple object definition statement:

```
ClassName objectName;
```

In the general format, *ClassName* is the name of a class and *objectName* is the name we are giving the object.

For example, the following statement defines `box` as an object of the `Rectangle` class:

```
Rectangle box;
```

Defining a class object is called the *instantiation* of a class. In this statement, `box` is an *instance* of the `Rectangle` class.

Accessing an Object's Members

The box object that we previously defined is an instance of the Rectangle class. Suppose we want to change the value in the box object's width variable. To do so, we must use the box object to call the setWidth member function, as shown here:

```
box.setWidth(12.7);
```

Just as you use the dot operator to access a structure's members, you use the dot operator to call a class's member functions. This statement uses the box object to call the setWidth member function, passing 12.7 as an argument. As a result, the box object's width variable will be set to 12.7. Here are other examples of statements that use the box object to call member functions:

```
box.setLength(4.8);       // Set box's length to 4.8.
x = box.getWidth();       // Assign box's width to x.
cout << box.getLength();  // Display box's length.
cout << box.getArea();    // Display box's area.
```

NOTE: Notice that inside the Rectangle class's member functions, the dot operator is not used to access any of the class's member variables. When an object is used to call a member function, the member function has direct access to that object's member variables.

A Class Demonstration Program

Program 13-1 is a complete program that demonstrates the Rectangle class.

Program 13-1

```
 1   // This program demonstrates a simple class.
 2   #include <iostream>
 3   using namespace std;
 4
 5   // Rectangle class declaration.
 6   class Rectangle
 7   {
 8      private:
 9         double width;
10         double length;
11      public:
12         void setWidth(double);
13         void setLength(double);
14         double getWidth() const;
15         double getLength() const;
16         double getArea() const;
17   };
18
19   //*************************************************
20   // setWidth assigns a value to the width member.  *
21   //*************************************************
22
```

```
23   void Rectangle::setWidth(double w)
24   {
25      width = w;
26   }
27
28   //***************************************************
29   // setLength assigns a value to the length member. *
30   //***************************************************
31
32   void Rectangle::setLength(double len)
33   {
34      length = len;
35   }
36
37   //***************************************************
38   // getWidth returns the value in the width member. *
39   //***************************************************
40
41   double Rectangle::getWidth() const
42   {
43      return width;
44   }
45
46   //****************************************************
47   // getLength returns the value in the length member. *
48   //****************************************************
49
50   double Rectangle::getLength() const
51   {
52      return length;
53   }
54
55   //****************************************************
56   // getArea returns the product of width times length. *
57   //****************************************************
58
59   double Rectangle::getArea() const
60   {
61      return width * length;
62   }
63
64   //*****************************************************
65   // Function main                                      *
66   //*****************************************************
67
68   int main()
69   {
70      Rectangle box;      // Define an instance of the Rectangle class
71      double rectWidth;   // Local variable for width
72      double rectLength;  // Local variable for length
73
74      // Get the rectangle's width and length from the user.
75      cout << "This program will calculate the area of a\n";
76      cout << "rectangle. What is the width? ";
```

(program continues)

Program 13-1   *(continued)*

```
77       cin >> rectWidth;
78       cout << "What is the length? ";
79       cin >> rectLength;
80
81       // Store the width and length of the rectangle
82       // in the box object.
83       box.setWidth(rectWidth);
84       box.setLength(rectLength);
85
86       // Display the rectangle's data.
87       cout << "Here is the rectangle's data:\n";
88       cout << "Width: " << box.getWidth() << endl;
89       cout << "Length: " << box.getLength() << endl;
90       cout << "Area: " << box.getArea() << endl;
91       return 0;
92   }
```

Program Output with Example Input Shown in Bold
```
This program will calculate the area of a
rectangle. What is the width? 10 [Enter]
What is the length? 5 [Enter]
Here is the rectangle's data:
Width: 10
Length: 5
Area: 50
```

The `Rectangle` class declaration, along with the class's member functions, appears in lines 6 through 62. Inside the `main` function, in line 70, the following statement creates a `Rectangle` object named `box`.

```
Rectangle box;
```

The `box` object is illustrated in Figure 13-6. Notice that the `width` and `length` member variables do not yet hold meaningful values. An object's member variables are not automatically initialized to 0. When an object's member variable is first created, it holds whatever random value happens to exist at the variable's memory location. We commonly refer to such a random value as "garbage."

Figure 13-6

The box object when first created

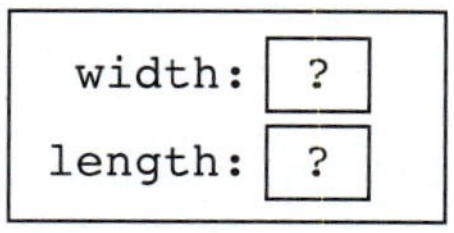

In lines 75 through 79 the program prompts the user to enter the width and length of a rectangle. The width that is entered is stored in the `rectWidth` variable, and the length that is entered is stored in the `rectLength` variable. In line 83 the following statement uses the box object to call the setWidth member function, passing the value of the rectWidth variable as an argument:

```
box.setWidth(rectWidth);
```

This sets box's width member variable to the value in rectWidth. Assuming rectWidth holds the value 10, Figure 13-7 shows the state of the box object after this statement executes.

Figure 13-7

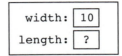

The box object with width set to 10

width: 10
length: ?

In line 84 the following statement uses the box object to call the setLength member function, passing the value of the rectLength variable as an argument.

```
box.setLength(rectLength);
```

This sets box's length member variable to the value in rectLength. Assuming rectLength holds the value 5, Figure 13-8 shows the state of the box object after this statement executes.

Figure 13-8

The box object with width set to 10
and length set to 5

width: 10
length: 5

Lines 88, 89, and 90 use the box object to call the getWidth, getLength, and getArea member functions, displaying their return values on the screen.

NOTE: Figures 13-6 through 13-8 show the state of the box object at various times during the execution of the program. An object's *state* is simply the data that is stored in the object's attributes at any given moment.

Program 13-1 creates only one Rectangle object. It is possible to create many instances of the same class, each with its own data. For example, Program 13-2 creates three Rectangle objects, named kitchen, bedroom, and den. Note that lines 6 through 62 have been left out of the listing because they contain the Rectangle class declaration and the definitions for the class's member functions. These lines are identical to those same lines in Program 13-1.

Program 13-2

```
 1  // This program creates three instances of the Rectangle class.
 2  #include <iostream>
 3  using namespace std;
 4
 5  // Rectangle class declaration.
```

Lines 6 through 62 have been left out.

```
63
64  //********************************************************
65  // Function main                                        *
66  //********************************************************
67
68  int main()
69  {
70     double number;        // To hold a number
71     double totalArea;     // The total area
72     Rectangle kitchen;    // To hold kitchen dimensions
73     Rectangle bedroom;    // To hold bedroom dimensions
74     Rectangle den;        // To hold den dimensions
75
76     // Get the kitchen dimensions.
77     cout << "What is the kitchen's length? ";
78     cin >> number;                              // Get the length
79     kitchen.setLength(number);                  // Store in kitchen object
80     cout << "What is the kitchen's width? ";
81     cin >> number;                              // Get the width
82     kitchen.setWidth(number);                   // Store in kitchen object
83
84     // Get the bedroom dimensions.
85     cout << "What is the bedroom's length? ";
86     cin >> number;                              // Get the length
87     bedroom.setLength(number);                  // Store in bedroom object
88     cout << "What is the bedroom's width? ";
89     cin >> number;                              // Get the width
90     bedroom.setWidth(number);                   // Store in bedroom object
91
92     // Get the den dimensions.
93     cout << "What is the den's length? ";
94     cin >> number;                              // Get the length
95     den.setLength(number);                      // Store in den object
96     cout << "What is the den's width? ";
97     cin >> number;                              // Get the width
98     den.setWidth(number);                       // Store in den object
99
100    // Calculate the total area of the three rooms.
101    totalArea = kitchen.getArea() + bedroom.getArea()
102            + den.getArea();
103
104    // Display the total area of the three rooms.
105    cout << "The total area of the three rooms is "
106         << totalArea << endl;
107
108    return 0;
109 }
```

Program Output with Example Input Shown in Bold
```
What is the kitchen's length? 10 [Enter]
What is the kitchen's width? 14 [Enter]
What is the bedroom's length? 15 [Enter]
What is the bedroom's width? 12 [Enter]
What is the den's length? 20 [Enter]
What is the den's width? 30 [Enter]
The total area of the three rooms is 920
```

In lines 72, 73, and 74, the following code defines three `Rectangle` variables. This creates three objects, each an instance of the `Rectangle` class:

```
Rectangle kitchen;    // To hold kitchen dimensions
Rectangle bedroom;    // To hold bedroom dimensions
Rectangle den;        // To hold den dimensions
```

In the example output, the user enters 10 and 14 as the length and width of the kitchen, 15 and 12 as the length and width of the bedroom, and 20 and 30 as the length and width of the den. Figure 13-9 shows the states of the objects after these values are stored in them.

Figure 13-9

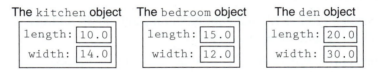

Notice from Figure 13-9 that each instance of the `Rectangle` class has its own `length` and `width` variables. Every instance of a class has its own set of member variables that can hold their own values. The class's member functions can perform operations on specific instances of the class. For example, look at the following statement in line 79 of Program 13-2:

```
kitchen.setLength(number);
```

This statement calls the `setLength` member function, which stores a value in the `kitchen` object's `length` variable. Now look at the following statement in line 87:

```
bedroom.setLength(number);
```

This statement also calls the `setLength` member function, but this time it stores a value in the `bedroom` object's `length` variable. Likewise, the following statement in line 95 calls the `setLength` member function to store a value in the `den` object's `length` variable:

```
den.setLength(number);
```

The `setLength` member function stores a value in a specific instance of the `Rectangle` class. All of the other `Rectangle` class member functions work in a similar way. They access one or more member variables of a specific `Rectangle` object.

Avoiding Stale Data

In the `Rectangle` class, the `getLength` and `getWidth` member functions return the values stored in member variables, but the `getArea` member function returns the result of a calculation. You might be wondering why the area of the rectangle is not stored in a member variable, like the length and the width. The area is not stored in a member variable because it could potentially become stale. When the value of an item is dependent on other data and that item is not updated when the other data are changed, it is said that the item has become *stale*. If the area of the rectangle were stored in a member variable, the value of the member variable would become incorrect as soon as either the `length` or `width` member variables changed.

When designing a class, you should take care not to store in a member variable calculated data that could potentially become stale. Instead, provide a member function that returns the result of the calculation.

Pointers to Objects

You can also define pointers to class objects. For example, the following statement defines a pointer variable named `rectPtr`:

```
Rectangle *rectPtr;
```

The `rectPtr` variable is not an object, but it can hold the address of a `Rectangle` object. The following code shows an example.

```
Rectangle myRectangle;   // A Rectangle object
Rectangle *rectPtr;      // A Rectangle pointer
rectPtr = &myRectangle;  // rectPtr now points to myRectangle
```

The first statement creates a `Rectangle` object named `myRectangle`. The second statement creates a `Rectangle` pointer named `rectPtr`. The third statement stores the address of the `myRectangle` object in the `rectPtr` pointer. This is illustrated in Figure 13-10.

Figure 13-10

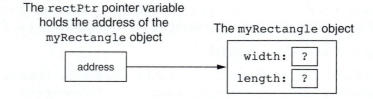

The `rectPtr` pointer variable holds the address of the `myRectangle` object

The `myRectangle` object

The `rectPtr` pointer can then be used to call member functions by using the `->` operator. The following statements show examples.

```
rectPtr->setWidth(12.5);
rectPtr->setLength(4.8);
```

The first statement calls the `setWidth` member function, passing 12.5 as an argument. Because `rectPtr` points to the `myRectangle` object, this will cause 12.5 to be stored in the `myRectangle` object's `width` variable. The second statement calls the `setLength` member function, passing 4.8 as an argument. This will cause 4.8 to be stored in the myRectangle object's `length` variable. Figure 13-11 shows the state of the `myRectangle` object after these statements have executed.

Figure 13-11

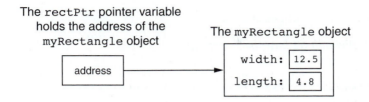

The `rectPtr` pointer variable holds the address of the `myRectangle` object

The `myRectangle` object

address

width: 12.5
length: 4.8

Class object pointers can be used to dynamically allocate objects. The following code shows an example.

```
1   // Define a Rectangle pointer.
2   Rectangle *rectPtr;
3
4   // Dynamically allocate a Rectangle object.
5   rectPtr = new Rectangle;
6
7   // Store values in the object's width and length.
8   rectPtr->setWidth(10.0);
9   rectPtr->setLength(15.0);
10
11  // Delete the object from memory.
12  delete rectPtr;
13  rectPtr = 0;
```

Line 2 defines `rectPtr` as a `Rectangle` pointer. Line 5 uses the `new` operator to dynamically allocate a `Rectangle` object and assign its address to `rectPtr`. Lines 8 and 9 store values in the dynamically allocated object's `width` and `length` variables. Figure 13-12 shows the state of the dynamically allocated object after these statements have executed.

Figure 13-12

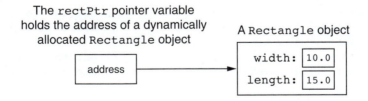

The `rectPtr` pointer variable holds the address of a dynamically allocated `Rectangle` object

A `Rectangle` object

address

width: 10.0
length: 15.0

Line 12 deletes the object from memory and line 13 stores the address 0 in `rectPtr`. Recall from Chapter 9 that this prevents code from inadvertently using the pointer to access the area of memory that has been freed. It also prevents errors from occurring if `delete` is accidentally called on the pointer again.

Program 13-3 is a modification of Program 13-2. In this program, `kitchen`, `bedroom`, and `den` are `Rectangle` pointers. They are used to dynamically allocate `Rectangle` objects. The output is the same as Program 13-2.

Program 13-3

```
 1 // This program creates three instances of the Rectangle class.
 2 #include <iostream>
 3 using namespace std;
 4
 5 // Rectangle class declaration.
```

Lines 6 through 62 have been left out.

```
 63
 64 //*****************************************************
 65 // Function main                                     *
 66 //*****************************************************
 67
 68 int main()
 69 {
 70     double number;         // To hold a number
 71     double totalArea;      // The total area
 72     Rectangle *kitchen;    // To point to kitchen dimensions
 73     Rectangle *bedroom;    // To point to bedroom dimensions
 74     Rectangle *den;        // To point to den dimensions
 75
 76     // Dynamically allocate the objects.
 77     kitchen = new Rectangle;
 78     bedroom = new Rectangle;
 79     den = new Rectangle;
 80
 81     // Get the kitchen dimensions.
 82     cout << "What is the kitchen's length? ";
 83     cin >> number;                            // Get the length
 84     kitchen->setLength(number);               // Store in kitchen object
 85     cout << "What is the kitchen's width? ";
 86     cin >> number;                            // Get the width
 87     kitchen->setWidth(number);                // Store in kitchen object
 88
 89     // Get the bedroom dimensions.
 90     cout << "What is the bedroom's length? ";
 91     cin >> number;                            // Get the length
 92     bedroom->setLength(number);               // Store in bedroom object
 93     cout << "What is the bedroom's width? ";
 94     cin >> number;                            // Get the width
 95     bedroom->setWidth(number);                // Store in bedroom object
 96
 97     // Get the den dimensions.
 98     cout << "What is the den's length? ";
 99     cin >> number;                            // Get the length
100     den->setLength(number);                   // Store in den object
101     cout << "What is the den's width? ";
102     cin >> number;                            // Get the width
103     den->setWidth(number);                    // Store in den object
104
105     // Calculate the total area of the three rooms.
106     totalArea = kitchen->getArea() + bedroom->getArea()
107             + den->getArea();
108
```

```
109    // Display the total area of the three rooms.
110    cout << "The total area of the three rooms is "
111        << totalArea << endl;
112
113    // Delete the objects from memory.
114    delete kitchen;
115    delete bedroom;
116    delete den;
117    kitchen = 0;    // Make kitchen point to null.
118    bedroom = 0;    // Make bedroom point to null.
119    den = 0;        // Make den point to null.
120
121    return 0;
122 }
```

 Checkpoint

myprogramminglab *www.myprogramminglab.com*

13.1   True or False: You must declare all private members of a class before the public members.

13.2   Assume that `RetailItem` is the name of a class, and the class has a `void` member function named `setPrice` which accepts a `double` argument. Which of the following shows the correct use of the scope resolution operator in the member function definition?

A) `RetailItem::void setPrice(double p)`

B) `void RetailItem::setPrice(double p)`

13.3   An object's private member variables are accessed from outside the object by

A) public member functions

B) any function

C) the dot operator

D) the scope resolution operator

13.4   Assume that `RetailItem` is the name of a class, and the class has a `void` member function named `setPrice` which accepts a `double` argument. If `soap` is an instance of the `RetailItem` class, which of the following statements properly uses the `soap` object to call the `setPrice` member function?

A) `RetailItem::setPrice(1.49);`

B) `soap::setPrice(1.49);`

C) `soap.setPrice(1.49);`

D) `soap:setPrice(1.49);`

13.5   Complete the following code skeleton to declare a class named `Date`. The class should contain variables and functions to store and retrieve a date in the form 4/2/2012.

```
class Date
{
    private:

    public:

}
```

13.4 Why Have Private Members?

CONCEPT: In object-oriented programming, an object should protect its important data by making it private and providing a public interface to access that data.

You might be questioning the rationale behind making the member variables in the Rectangle class private. You might also be questioning why member functions were defined for such simple tasks as setting variables and getting their contents. After all, if the member variables were declared as public, the member functions wouldn't be needed.

As mentioned earlier in this chapter, classes usually have variables and functions that are meant only to be used internally. They are not intended to be accessed by statements outside the class. This protects critical data from being accidentally modified or used in a way that might adversely affect the state of the object. When a member variable is declared as private, the only way for an application to store values in the variable is through a public member function. Likewise, the only way for an application to retrieve the contents of a private member variable is through a public member function. In essence, the public members become an interface to the object. They are the only members that may be accessed by any application that uses the object.

In the Rectangle class, the width and length member variables hold critical data. Therefore they are declared as private and an interface is constructed with public member functions. If a program creates a Rectangle object, the program must use the setWidth and getWidth member functions to access the object's width member. To access the object's length member, the program must use the setLength and getLength member functions. This idea is illustrated in Figure 13-13.

Figure 13-13

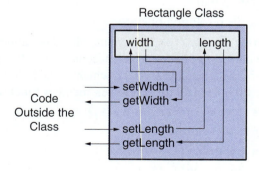

The public member functions can be written to filter out invalid data. For example, look at the following version of the setWidth member function.

```
void Rectangle::setWidth(double w)
{
    if (w >= 0)
        width = w;
```

```
   else
   {
      cout << "Invalid width\n";
      exit(EXIT_FAILURE);
   }

}
```

Notice that this version of the function doesn't just assign the parameter value to the width variable. It first tests the parameter to make sure it is 0 or greater. If a negative number was passed to the function, an error message is displayed and then the standard library function exit is called to abort the program. The setLength function could be written in a similar way:

```
void Rectangle::setLength(double len)
{
   if (len >= 0)
      length = len;
   else
   {
      cout << "Invalid length\n";
      exit(EXIT_FAILURE);
   }
}
```

The point being made here is that mutator functions can do much more than simply store values in attributes. They can also validate those values to ensure that only acceptable data is stored in the object's attributes. Keep in mind, however, that calling the exit function, as we have done in these examples, is not the best way to deal with invalid data. In reality, you would not design a class to abort the entire program just because invalid data were passed to a mutator function. In Chapter 15 we will discuss exceptions, which provide a much better way for classes to handle errors. Until we discuss exceptions, however, we will keep our code simple by using only rudimentary data validation techniques.

Focus on Software Engineering: Separating Class Specification from Implementation

CONCEPT: Usually class declarations are stored in their own header files. Member function definitions are stored in their own .cpp files.

In the programs we've looked at so far, the class declaration, member function definitions, and application program are all stored in one file. A more conventional way of designing C++ programs is to store class declarations and member function definitions in their own separate files. Typically, program components are stored in the following fashion:

- Class declarations are stored in their own header files. A header file that contains a class declaration is called a *class specification* file. The name of the class specification file is usually the same as the name of the class, with a .h extension. For example, the Rectangle class would be declared in the file Rectangle.h.

- The member function definitions for a class are stored in a separate .cpp file called the *class implementation* file. The file usually has the same name as the class, with the .cpp extension. For example, the Rectangle class's member functions would be defined in the file Rectangle.cpp.

- Any program that uses the class should #include the class's header file. The class's .cpp file (that which contains the member function definitions) should be compiled and linked with the main program. This process can be automated with a project or make utility. Integrated development environments such as Visual Studio also provide the means to create the multi-file projects.

Let's see how we could rewrite Program 13-1 using this design approach. First, the Rectangle class declaration would be stored in the following Rectangle.h file. (This file is stored in the Student Source Code Folder Chapter 13\Rectangle Version 1.)

Contents of Rectangle.h (Version 1)

```
 1  // Specification file for the Rectangle class.
 2  #ifndef RECTANGLE_H
 3  #define RECTANGLE_H
 4
 5  // Rectangle class declaration.
 6
 7  class Rectangle
 8  {
 9     private:
10        double width;
11        double length;
12     public:
13        void setWidth(double);
14        void setLength(double);
15        double getWidth() const;
16        double getLength() const;
17        double getArea() const;
18  };
19
20  #endif
```

This is the specification file for the Rectangle class. It contains only the declaration of the Rectangle class. It does not contain any member function definitions. When we write other programs that use the Rectangle class, we can have an #include directive that includes this file. That way, we won't have to write the class declaration in every program that uses the Rectangle class.

This file also introduces two new preprocessor directives: #ifndef and #endif. The #ifndef directive that appears in line 2 is called an *include guard*. It prevents the header file from accidentally being included more than once. When your main program file has an #include directive for a header file, there is always the possibility that the header file will have an #include directive for a second header file. If your main program file also has an #include directive for the second header file, then the preprocessor will include the second header file twice. Unless an include guard has been written into the second header file, an error will occur because the compiler will process the declarations in the second header file twice. Let's see how an include guard works.

The word `ifndef` stands for "if not defined." It is used to determine whether a specific constant has not been defined with a `#define` directive. When the `Rectangle.h` file is being compiled, the `#ifndef` directive checks for the existence of a constant named `RECTANGLE_H`. If the constant has not been defined, it is immediately defined in line 3 and the rest of the file is included. If the constant has been defined, it means that the file has already been included. In that case, everything between the `#ifndef` and `#endif` directives is skipped. This is illustrated in Figure 13-14.

Figure 13-14

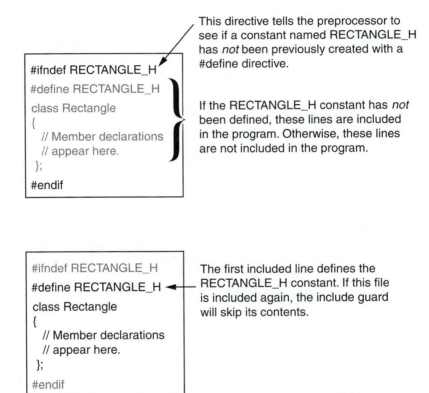

Next we need an implementation file that contains the class's member function definitions. The implementation file for the `Rectangle` class is `Rectangle.cpp`. (This file is stored in the Student Source Code Folder `Chapter 13\Rectangle Version 1`.)

Contents of `Rectangle.cpp` (Version 1)

```
1   // Implementation file for the Rectangle class.
2   #include "Rectangle.h"    // Needed for the Rectangle class
3   #include <iostream>       // Needed for cout
4   #include <cstdlib>        // Needed for the exit function
5   using namespace std;
6
7   //*********************************************************
8   // setWidth sets the value of the member variable width.   *
9   //*********************************************************
10
```

```
11   void Rectangle::setWidth(double w)
12   {
13      if (w >= 0)
14         width = w;
15      else
16      {
17         cout << "Invalid width\n";
18         exit(EXIT_FAILURE);
19      }
20   }
21
22   //************************************************************
23   // setLength sets the value of the member variable length.  *
24   //************************************************************
25
26   void Rectangle::setLength(double len)
27   {
28      if (len >= 0)
29         length = len;
30      else
31      {
32         cout << "Invalid length\n";
33         exit(EXIT_FAILURE);
34      }
35   }
36
37   //************************************************************
38   // getWidth returns the value in the member variable width. *
39   //************************************************************
40
41   double Rectangle::getWidth() const
42   {
43      return width;
44   }
45
46   //*************************************************************
47   // getLength returns the value in the member variable length. *
48   //*************************************************************
49
50   double Rectangle::getLength() const
51   {
52      return length;
53   }
54
55   //*************************************************************
56   // getArea returns the product of width times length.        *
57   //*************************************************************
58
59   double Rectangle::getArea() const
60   {
61      return width * length;
62   }
```

Look at line 2, which has the following #include directive:

```
#include "Rectangle.h"
```

This directive includes the Rectangle.h file, which contains the Rectangle class declaration. Notice that the name of the header file is enclosed in double-quote characters (" ") instead of angled brackets (< >). When you are including a C++ system header file, such as iostream, you enclose the name of the file in angled brackets. This indicates that the file is located in the compiler's *include file directory*. The include file directory is the directory or folder where all of the standard C++ header files are located. When you are including a header file that you have written, such as a class specification file, you enclose the name of the file in double-quote marks. This indicates that the file is located in the current project directory.

Any file that uses the Rectangle class must have an #include directive for the Rectangle.h file. We need to include Rectangle.h in the class specification file because the functions in this file belong to the Rectangle class. Before the compiler can process a function with Rectangle:: in its name, it must have already processed the Rectangle class declaration.

Now that we have the Rectangle class stored in its own specification and implementation files, we can see how to use them in a program. Program 13-4 shows a modified version of Program 13-1. This version of the program does not contain the Rectangle class declaration, or the definitions of any of the class's member functions. Instead, it is designed to be compiled and linked with the class specification and implementation files. (This file is stored in the Student Source Code Folder Chapter 13\Rectangle Version 1.)

Program 13-4

```
 1   // This program uses the Rectangle class, which is declared in
 2   // the Rectangle.h file. The member Rectangle class's member
 3   // functions are defined in the Rectangle.cpp file. This program
 4   // should be compiled with those files in a project.
 5   #include <iostream>
 6   #include "Rectangle.h"  // Needed for Rectangle class
 7   using namespace std;
 8
 9   int main()
10   {
11      Rectangle box;     // Define an instance of the Rectangle class
12      double rectWidth;  // Local variable for width
13      double rectLength; // Local variable for length
14
15      // Get the rectangle's width and length from the user.
16      cout << "This program will calculate the area of a\n";
17      cout << "rectangle. What is the width? ";
18      cin >> rectWidth;
19      cout << "What is the length? ";
20      cin >> rectLength;
21
```

(program continues)

Program 13-4 *(continued)*

```
22      // Store the width and length of the rectangle
23      // in the box object.
24      box.setWidth(rectWidth);
25      box.setLength(rectLength);
26
27      // Display the rectangle's data.
28      cout << "Here is the rectangle's data:\n";
29      cout << "Width: " << box.getWidth() << endl;
30      cout << "Length: " << box.getLength() << endl;
31      cout << "Area: " << box.getArea() << endl;
32      return 0;
33  }
```

Notice that Program 13-4 has an `#include` directive for the `Rectangle.h` file in line 6. This causes the declaration for the `Rectangle` class to be included in the file. To create an executable program from this file, the following steps must be taken:

- The implementation file, `Rectangle.cpp`, must be compiled. `Rectangle.cpp` is not a complete program, so you cannot create an executable file from it alone. Instead, you compile `Rectangle.cpp` to an object file which contains the compiled code for the `Rectangle` class. This file would typically be named `Rectangle.obj`.
- The main program file, `Pr13-4.cpp`, must be compiled. This file is not a complete program either, because it does not contain any of the implementation code for the `Rectangle` class. So, you compile this file to an object file such as `Pr13-4.obj`.
- The object files, `Pr13-4.obj` and `Rectangle.obj`, are linked together to create an executable file, which would be named something like `Pr13-4.exe`.

This process is illustrated in Figure 13-15.

The exact details on how these steps take place are different for each C++ development system. Fortunately, most systems perform all of these steps automatically for you. For example, in Microsoft Visual C++ you create a project, and then you simply add all of the files to the project. When you compile the project, the steps are taken care of for you and an executable file is generated.

NOTE: Appendix M gives step-by-step instructions for creating multi-file projects in Microsoft Visual C++ 2010 Express Edition. You can download Appendix M from the book's companion Web site at www.pearsonhighered.com/gaddis.

Separating a class into a specification file and an implementation file provides a great deal of flexibility. First, if you wish to give your class to another programmer, you don't have to share all of your source code with that programmer. You can give him or her the specification file and the compiled object file for the class's implementation. The other programmer simply inserts the necessary `#include` directive into his or her program, compiles it, and links it with your class's object file. This prevents the other programmer, who might not know all the details of your code, from making changes that will introduce bugs.

Figure 13-15

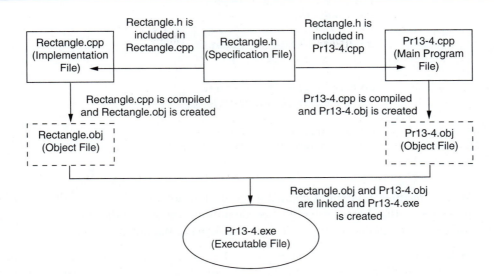

Separating a class into specification and implementation files also makes things easier when the class's member functions must be modified. It is only necessary to modify the implementation file and recompile it to a new object file. Programs that use the class don't have to be completely recompiled, just linked with the new object file.

13.6 Inline Member Functions

CONCEPT: When the body of a member function is written inside a class declaration, it is declared inline.

When the body of a member function is small, it is usually more convenient to place the function's definition, instead of its prototype, in the class declaration. For example, in the `Rectangle` class the member functions `getWidth`, `getLength`, and `getArea` each have only one statement. The `Rectangle` class could be revised as shown in the following listing. (This file is stored in the Student Source Code Folder `Chapter 13\Rectangle Version 2`.)

Contents of `Rectangle.h` (Version 2)

```
 1   // Specification file for the Rectangle class
 2   // This version uses some inline member functions.
 3   #ifndef RECTANGLE_H
 4   #define RECTANGLE_H
 5
 6   class Rectangle
 7   {
 8      private:
 9         double width;
10         double length;
```

```
11      public:
12          void setWidth(double);
13          void setLength(double);
14
15          double getWidth() const
16              { return width; }
17
18          double getLength() const
19              { return length; }
20
21          double getArea() const
22              { return width * length; }
23   };
24   #endif
```

When a member function is defined in the declaration of a class, it is called an *inline function*. Notice that because the function definitions are part of the class, there is no need to use the scope resolution operator and class name in the function header.

Notice that the getWidth, getLength, and getArea functions are declared inline, but the setWidth and setLength functions are not. They are still defined outside the class declaration. The following listing shows the implementation file for the revised Rectangle class. (This file is also stored in the Student Source Code Folder Chapter 13\ Rectangle Version 2.)

Contents of `Rectangle.cpp` (Version 2)

```
 1   // Implementation file for the Rectangle class.
 2   // In this version of the class, the getWidth, getLength,
 3   // and getArea functions are written inline in Rectangle.h.
 4   #include "Rectangle.h"   // Needed for the Rectangle class
 5   #include <iostream>      // Needed for cout
 6   #include <cstdlib>       // Needed for the exit function
 7   using namespace std;
 8
 9   //*********************************************************
10   // setWidth sets the value of the member variable width.   *
11   //*********************************************************
12
13   void Rectangle::setWidth(double w)
14   {
15      if (w >= 0)
16         width = w;
17      else
18      {
19         cout << "Invalid width\n";
20         exit(EXIT_FAILURE);
21      }
22   }
23
24   //*********************************************************
25   // setLength sets the value of the member variable length.   *
26   //*********************************************************
27
```

```
28   void Rectangle::setLength(double len)
29   {
30      if (len >= 0)
31         length = len;
32      else
33      {
34         cout << "Invalid length\n";
35         exit(EXIT_FAILURE);
36      }
37   }
```

Inline Functions and Performance

A lot goes on "behind the scenes" each time a function is called. A number of special items, such as the function's return address in the program and the values of arguments, are stored in a section of memory called the *stack*. In addition, local variables are created and a location is reserved for the function's return value. All this overhead, which sets the stage for a function call, takes precious CPU time. Although the time needed is minuscule, it can add up if a function is called many times, as in a loop.

Inline functions are compiled differently than other functions. In the executable code, inline functions aren't "called" in the conventional sense. In a process known as *inline expansion*, the compiler replaces the call to an inline function with the code of the function itself. This means that the overhead needed for a conventional function call isn't necessary for an inline function, and can result in improved performance.[*] Because the inline function's code can appear multiple times in the executable program, however, the size of the program can increase.[†]

Checkpoint

myprogramminglab *www.myprogramminglab.com*

13.6 Why would you declare a class's member variables `private`?

13.7 When a class's member variables are declared `private`, how does code outside the class store values in, or retrieve values from, the member variables?

13.8 What is a class specification file? What is a class implementation file?

13.9 What is the purpose of an include guard?

13.10 Assume the following class components exist in a program:

`BasePay` class declaration
`BasePay` member function definitions
`Overtime` class declaration
`Overtime` member function definitions

In what files would you store each of these components?

13.11 What is an inline member function?

---

[*] Because inline functions cause code to increase in size, they can decrease performance on systems that use paging.

[†] Writing a function inline is a request to the compiler. The compiler will ignore the request if inline expansion is not possible or practical.

13.7 Constructors

CONCEPT: A constructor is a member function that is automatically called when a class object is created.

A constructor is a member function that has the same name as the class. It is automatically called when the object is created in memory, or instantiated. It is helpful to think of constructors as initialization routines. They are very useful for initializing member variables or performing other setup operations.

To illustrate how constructors work, look at this Demo class declaration:

```cpp
class Demo
{
public:
    Demo(); // Constructor
};

Demo::Demo()
{
    cout << "Welcome to the constructor!\n";
}
```

The class Demo only has one member: a function also named Demo. This function is the constructor. When an instance of this class is defined, the function Demo is automatically called. This is illustrated in Program 13-5.

Program 13-5

```cpp
 1   // This program demonstrates a constructor.
 2   #include <iostream>
 3   using namespace std;
 4
 5   // Demo class declaration.
 6
 7   class Demo
 8   {
 9   public:
10      Demo();      // Constructor
11   };
12
13   Demo::Demo()
14   {
15      cout << "Welcome to the constructor!\n";
16   }
17
```

```
18    //*****************************************
19    // Function main.                         *
20    //*****************************************
21
22    int main()
23    {
24       Demo demoObject;   // Define a Demo object;
25
26       cout << "This program demonstrates an object\n";
27       cout << "with a constructor.\n";
28       return 0;
29    }
```

Program Output

```
Welcome to the constructor!
This program demonstrates an object
with a constructor.
```

Notice that the constructor's function header looks different than that of a regular member function. There is no return type—not even void. This is because constructors are not executed by explicit function calls and cannot return a value. The function header of a constructor's external definition takes the following form:

> *ClassName*::*ClassName*(*ParameterList*)

In the general format, *ClassName* is the name of the class and *ParameterList* is an optional list of parameter variable declarations.

In Program 13-5, demoObject's constructor executes automatically when the object is defined. Because the object is defined before the cout statements in function main, the constructor displays its message first. Suppose we had defined the Demo object between two cout statements, as shown here.

```
cout << "This is displayed before the object is created.\n";
Demo demoObject;// Define a Demo object.
cout << "\nThis is displayed after the object is created.\n";
```

This code would produce the following output:

```
This is displayed before the object is created.
Welcome to the constructor!
This is displayed after the object is created.
```

This simple Demo example illustrates when a constructor executes. More importantly, you should understand why a class should have a constructor. A constructor's purpose is to initialize an object's attributes. Because the constructor executes as soon as the object is created, it can initialize the object's data members to valid values before those members are used by other code. It is a good practice to always write a constructor for every class.

For example, the `Rectangle` class that we looked at earlier could benefit from having a constructor. A program could define a `Rectangle` object and then use that object to call the `getArea` function before any values were stored in `width` and `length`. Because the `width` and `length` member variables are not initialized, the function would return garbage. The following code shows a better version of the `Rectangle` class, equipped with a constructor. The constructor initializes both `width` and `length` to 0.0. (These files are stored in the Student Source Code Folder `Chapter 13\Rectangle Version 3`.)

Contents of `Rectangle.h` (Version 3)

```
 1   // Specification file for the Rectangle class
 2   // This version has a constructor.
 3   #ifndef RECTANGLE_H
 4   #define RECTANGLE_H
 5
 6   class Rectangle
 7   {
 8      private:
 9         double width;
10         double length;
11      public:
12         Rectangle();                // Constructor
13         void setWidth(double);
14         void setLength(double);
15
16         double getWidth() const
17            { return width; }
18
19         double getLength() const
20            { return length; }
21
22         double getArea() const
23            { return width * length; }
24   };
25   #endif
```

Contents of `Rectangle.cpp` (Version 3)

```
 1   // Implementation file for the Rectangle class.
 2   // This version has a constructor.
 3   #include "Rectangle.h"    // Needed for the Rectangle class
 4   #include <iostream>       // Needed for cout
 5   #include <cstdlib>        // Needed for the exit function
 6   using namespace std;
 7
 8   //*******************************************************
 9   // The constructor initializes width and length to 0.0.   *
10   //*******************************************************
11
12   Rectangle::Rectangle()
13   {
14      width = 0.0;
15      length = 0.0;
16   }
```

```
17
18   //*************************************************************
19   // setWidth sets the value of the member variable width.     *
20   //*************************************************************
21
22   void Rectangle::setWidth(double w)
23   {
24      if (w >= 0)
25         width = w;
26      else
27      {
28         cout << "Invalid width\n";
29         exit(EXIT_FAILURE);
30      }
31   }
32
33   //*************************************************************
34   // setLength sets the value of the member variable length.  *
35   //*************************************************************
36
37   void Rectangle::setLength(double len)
38   {
39      if (len >= 0)
40         length = len;
41      else
42      {
43         cout << "Invalid length\n";
44         exit(EXIT_FAILURE);
45      }
46   }
```

Program 13-6 demonstrates this new version of the class. It creates a `Rectangle` object and then displays the values returned by the `getWidth`, `getLength`, and `getArea` member functions. (This file is also stored in the Student Source Code Folder Chapter 13\Rectangle Version 3.)

Program 13-6

```
1    // This program uses the Rectangle class's constructor.
2    #include <iostream>
3    #include "Rectangle.h"  // Needed for Rectangle class
4    using namespace std;
5
6    int main()
7    {
8       Rectangle box;        // Define an instance of the Rectangle class
9
10      // Display the rectangle's data.
11      cout << "Here is the rectangle's data:\n";
12      cout << "Width: " << box.getWidth() << endl;
13      cout << "Length: " << box.getLength() << endl;
14      cout << "Area: " << box.getArea() << endl;
15      return 0;
16   }
```

(program output continues)

Program 13-6   *(continued)*

Program Output
```
Here is the rectangle's data:
Width: 0
Length: 0
Area: 0
```

The Default Constructor

All of the examples we have looked at in this section demonstrate default constructors. A *default constructor* is a constructor that takes no arguments. Like regular functions, constructors may accept arguments, have default arguments, be declared inline, and be overloaded. We will see examples of these as we progress through the chapter.

If you write a class with no constructor whatsoever, when the class is compiled C++ will automatically write a default constructor that does nothing. For example, the first version of the `Rectangle` class had no constructor; so, when the class was compiled C++ generated the following constructor:

```
Rectangle::Rectangle()
{ }
```

Default Constructors and Dynamically Allocated Objects

Earlier we discussed how class objects may be dynamically allocated in memory. For example, assume the following pointer is defined in a program:

```
Rectangle *rectPtr;
```

This statement defines `rectPtr` as a `Rectangle` pointer. It can hold the address of any `Rectangle` object. But because this statement does not actually create a `Rectangle` object, the constructor does not execute. Suppose we use the pointer in a statement that dynamically allocates a `Rectangle` object, as shown in the following code.

```
rectPtr = new Rectangle;
```

This statement creates a `Rectangle` object. When the `Rectangle` object is created by the new operator, its default constructor is automatically executed.

13.8 Passing Arguments to Constructors

CONCEPT: A constructor can have parameters, and can accept arguments when an object is created.

Constructors may accept arguments in the same way as other functions. When a class has a constructor that accepts arguments, you can pass initialization values to the constructor when you create an object. For example, the following code shows yet another version of the `Rectangle` class. This version has a constructor that accepts arguments for the rectangle's width and length. (These files are stored in the Student Source Code Folder `Chapter 13\Rectangle Version 4.`)

Contents of `Rectangle.h` (Version 4)

```
1   // Specification file for the Rectangle class
2   // This version has a constructor.
3   #ifndef RECTANGLE_H
4   #define RECTANGLE_H
5
6   class Rectangle
7   {
8      private:
9         double width;
10        double length;
11     public:
12        Rectangle(double, double);   // Constructor
13        void setWidth(double);
14        void setLength(double);
15
16        double getWidth() const
17           { return width; }
18
19        double getLength() const
20           { return length; }
21
22        double getArea() const
23           { return width * length; }
24   };
25   #endif
```

Contents of `Rectangle.cpp` (Version 4)

```
1   // Implementation file for the Rectangle class.
2   // This version has a constructor that accepts arguments.
3   #include "Rectangle.h"   // Needed for the Rectangle class
4   #include <iostream>      // Needed for cout
5   #include <cstdlib>       // Needed for the exit function
6   using namespace std;
7
8   //*********************************************************
9   // The constructor accepts arguments for width and length.  *
10  //*********************************************************
11
12  Rectangle::Rectangle(double w, double len)
13  {
14     width = w;
15     length = len;
16  }
17
18  //*********************************************************
19  // setWidth sets the value of the member variable width.   *
20  //*********************************************************
21
22  void Rectangle::setWidth(double w)
23  {
24     if (w >= 0)
25        width = w;
```

```
26       else
27       {
28           cout << "Invalid width\n";
29           exit(EXIT_FAILURE);
30       }
31   }
32
33   //**********************************************************
34   // setLength sets the value of the member variable length.  *
35   //**********************************************************
36
37   void Rectangle::setLength(double len)
38   {
39       if (len >= 0)
40           length = len;
41       else
42       {
43           cout << "Invalid length\n";
44           exit(EXIT_FAILURE);
45       }
46   }
```

The constructor, which appears in lines 12 through 16 of `Rectangle.cpp`, accepts two arguments, which are passed into the w and `len` parameters. The parameters are assigned to the `width` and `length` member variables. Because the constructor is automatically called when a `Rectangle` object is created, the arguments are passed to the constructor as part of the object definition. Here is an example:

```
Rectangle box(10.0, 12.0);
```

This statement defines `box` as an instance of the `Rectangle` class. The constructor is called with the value 10.0 passed into the w parameter and 12.0 passed into the `len` parameter. As a result, the object's `width` member variable will be assigned 10.0 and the `length` member variable will be assigned 12.0. This is illustrated in Figure 13-16.

Figure 13-16

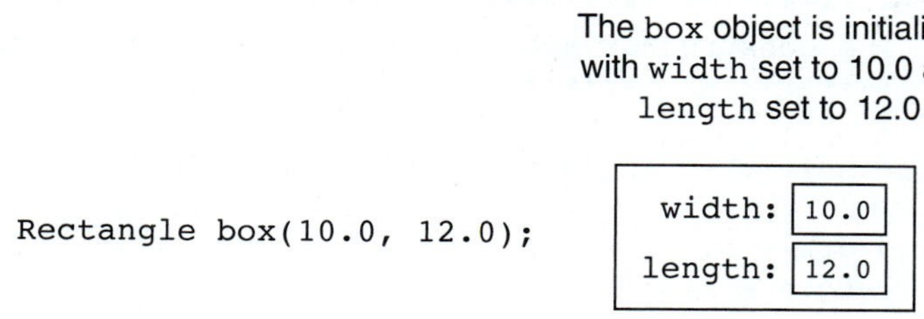

The box object is initialized
with width set to 10.0 and
length set to 12.0

```
Rectangle box(10.0, 12.0);
```

```
width:  10.0
length: 12.0
```

Program 13-7 demonstrates the class. (This file is also stored in the Student Source Code Folder `Chapter 13\Rectangle Version 4`.)

Program 13-7

```
 1   // This program calls the Rectangle class constructor.
 2   #include <iostream>
 3   #include <iomanip>
 4   #include "Rectangle.h"
 5   using namespace std;
 6
 7   int main()
 8   {
 9       double houseWidth,    // To hold the room width
10              houseLength;   // To hold the room length
11
12       // Get the width of the house.
13       cout << "In feet, how wide is your house? ";
14       cin >> houseWidth;
15
16       // Get the length of the house.
17       cout << "In feet, how long is your house? ";
18       cin >> houseLength;
19
20       // Create a Rectangle object.
21       Rectangle house(houseWidth, houseLength);
22
23       // Display the house's width, length, and area.
24       cout << setprecision(2) << fixed;
25       cout << "The house is " << house.getWidth()
26            << " feet wide.\n";
27       cout << "The house is " << house.getLength()
28            << " feet long.\n";
29       cout << "The house is " << house.getArea()
30            << " square feet in area.\n";
31       return 0;
32   }
```

Program Output with Example Input Shown in Bold
```
In feet, how wide is your house? 30 [Enter]
In feet, how long is your house? 60 [Enter]
The house is 30.00 feet wide.
The house is 60.00 feet long.
The house is 1800.00 square feet in area.
```

The statement in line 21 creates a Rectangle object, passing the values in houseWidth and houseLength as arguments.

The following code shows another example: the Sale class. This class might be used in a retail environment where sales transactions take place. An object of the Sale class represents the sale of an item. (This file is stored in the Student Source Code Folder Chapter 13\ Sale Version 1.)

Contents of `Sale.h` (Version 1)

```
1   // Specification file for the Sale class.
2   #ifndef SALE_H
3   #define SALE_H
4
5   class Sale
6   {
7   private:
8       double itemCost;      // Cost of the item
9       double taxRate;       // Sales tax rate
10  public:
11      Sale(double cost, double rate)
12          { itemCost = cost;
13            taxRate = rate; }
14
15      double getItemCost() const
16          { return itemCost; }
17
18      double getTaxRate() const
19          { return taxRate; }
20
21      double getTax() const
22          { return (itemCost * taxRate); }
23
24      double getTotal() const
25          { return (itemCost + getTax()); }
26  };
27  #endif
```

The `itemCost` member variable, declared in line 8, holds the selling price of the item. The `taxRate` member variable, declared in line 9, holds the sales tax rate. The constructor appears in lines 11 through 13. Notice that the constructor is written inline. It accepts two arguments, the item cost and the sales tax rate. These arguments are used to initialize the `itemCost` and `taxRate` member variables. The `getItemCost` member function, in lines 15 through 16, returns the value in `itemCost`, and the `getTaxRate` member function, in lines 18 through 19, returns the value in `taxRate`. The `getTax` member function, in lines 21 through 22, calculates and returns the amount of sales tax for the purchase. The `getTotal` member function, in lines 24 through 25, calculates and returns the total of the sale. The total is the item cost plus the sales tax. Program 13-8 demonstrates the class. (This file is stored in the Student Source Code Folder `Chapter 13\Sale Version 1`.)

Program 13-8

```
1   // This program demonstrates passing an argument to a constructor.
2   #include <iostream>
3   #include <iomanip>
4   #include "Sale.h"
5   using namespace std;
6
```

```
 7   int main()
 8   {
 9       const double TAX_RATE = 0.06;   // 6 percent sales tax rate
10       double cost;                    // To hold the item cost
11
12       // Get the cost of the item.
13       cout << "Enter the cost of the item: ";
14       cin >> cost;
15
16       // Create a Sale object for this transaction.
17       Sale itemSale(cost, TAX_RATE);
18
19       // Set numeric output formatting.
20       cout << fixed << showpoint << setprecision(2);
21
22       // Display the sales tax and total.
23       cout << "The amount of sales tax is $"
24            << itemSale.getTax() << endl;
25       cout << "The total of the sale is $";
26       cout << itemSale.getTotal() << endl;
27       return 0;
28   }
```

Program Output with Example Input Shown in Bold
Enter the cost of the item: **10.00 [Enter]**
The amount of sales tax is $0.60
The total of the sale is $10.60

In the example run of the program the user enters 10.00 as the cost of the item. This value is stored in the local variable cost. In line 17 the itemSale object is created. The values of the cost variable and the TAX_RATE constant are passed as arguments to the constructor. As a result, the object's cost member variable is initialized with the value 10.0 and the rate member variable is initialized with the value 0.06. This is illustrated in Figure 13-17.

Figure 13-17

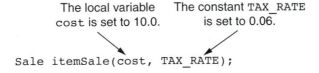

The local variable cost is set to 10.0.   The constant TAX_RATE is set to 0.06.

Sale itemSale(cost, TAX_RATE);

The itemSale object is initialized with the cost member set to 10.0 and the rate member set to 0.06

```
cost: 10.0
rate: 0.06
```

Using Default Arguments with Constructors

Like other functions, constructors may have default arguments. Recall from Chapter 6 that default arguments are passed to parameters automatically if no argument is provided in the function call. The default value is listed in the parameter list of the function's declaration or the function header. The following code shows a modified version of the Sale class. This version's constructor uses a default argument for the tax rate. (This file is stored in the Student Source Code Folder Chapter 13\Sale Version 2.)

Contents of Sale.h (Version 2)

```
1   // This version of the Sale class uses a default argument
2   // in the constructor.
3   #ifndef SALE_H
4   #define SALE_H
5
6   class Sale
7   {
8   private:
9      double itemCost;      // Cost of the item
10     double taxRate;       // Sales tax rate
11  public:
12     Sale(double cost, double rate = 0.05)
13        { itemCost = cost;
14          taxRate = rate; }
15
16     double getItemCost() const
17        { return itemCost; }
18
19     double getTaxRate() const
20        { return taxRate; }
21
22     double getTax() const
23        { return (itemCost * taxRate); }
24
25     double getTotal() const
26        { return (itemCost + getTax()); }
27  };
28  #endif
```

If an object of this Sale class is defined with only one argument (for the cost parameter) passed to the constructor, the default argument 0.05 will be provided for the rate parameter. This is demonstrated in Program 13-9. (This file is stored in the Student Source Code Folder Chapter 13\Sale Version 2.)

Program 13-9

```
1   // This program uses a constructor's default argument.
2   #include <iostream>
3   #include <iomanip>
4   #include "Sale.h"
5   using namespace std;
6
```

```
 7  int main()
 8  {
 9      double cost;    // To hold the item cost
10
11      // Get the cost of the item.
12      cout << "Enter the cost of the item: ";
13      cin >> cost;
14
15      // Create a Sale object for this transaction.
16      // Specify the item cost, but use the default
17      // tax rate of 5 percent.
18      Sale itemSale(cost);
19
20      // Set numeric output formatting.
21      cout << fixed << showpoint << setprecision(2);
22
23      // Display the sales tax and total.
24      cout << "The amount of sales tax is $"
25           << itemSale.getTax() << endl;
26      cout << "The total of the sale is $";
27      cout << itemSale.getTotal() << endl;
28      return 0;
29  }
```

Program Output with Example Input Shown in Bold
```
Enter the cost of the item: 10.00 [Enter]
The amount of sales tax is $0.50
The total of the sale is $10.50
```

More About the Default Constructor

It was mentioned earlier that when a constructor doesn't accept arguments, it is known as the default constructor. If a constructor has default arguments for all its parameters, it can be called with no explicit arguments. It then becomes the default constructor. For example, suppose the constructor for the Sale class had been written as the following:

```
Sale(double cost = 0.0, double rate = 0.05)
  { itemCost = cost;
    taxRate = rate; }
```

This constructor has default arguments for each of its parameters. As a result, the constructor can be called with no arguments, as shown here:

```
Sale itemSale;
```

This statement defines a Sale object. No arguments were passed to the constructor, so the default arguments for both parameters are used. Because this constructor can be called with no arguments, it is the default constructor.

Classes with No Default Constructor

When all of a class's constructors require arguments, then the class does not have a default constructor. In such a case you must pass the required arguments to the constructor when creating an object. Otherwise, a compiler error will result.

13.9 Destructors

CONCEPT: A destructor is a member function that is automatically called when an object is destroyed.

Destructors are member functions with the same name as the class, preceded by a tilde character (~). For example, the destructor for the `Rectangle` class would be named `~Rectangle`.

Destructors are automatically called when an object is destroyed. In the same way that constructors set things up when an object is created, destructors perform shutdown procedures when the object goes out of existence. For example, a common use of destructors is to free memory that was dynamically allocated by the class object.

Program 13-10 shows a simple class with a constructor and a destructor. It illustrates when, during the program's execution, each is called.

Program 13-10

```
 1   // This program demonstrates a destructor.
 2   #include <iostream>
 3   using namespace std;
 4
 5   class Demo
 6   {
 7   public:
 8       Demo();     // Constructor
 9       ~Demo();    // Destructor
10   };
11
12   Demo::Demo()
13   {
14       cout << "Welcome to the constructor!\n";
15   }
16
17   Demo::~Demo()
18   {
19       cout << "The destructor is now running.\n";
20   }
21
```

```
22  //*******************************************
23  // Function main.                           *
24  //*******************************************
25
26  int main()
27  {
28     Demo demoObject;  // Define a demo object;
29
30     cout << "This program demonstrates an object\n";
31     cout << "with a constructor and destructor.\n";
32     return 0;
33  }
```

Program Output

```
Welcome to the constructor!
This program demonstrates an object
with a constructor and destructor.
The destructor is now running.
```

The following code shows a more practical example of a class with a destructor. The
ContactInfo class holds the following data about a contact:

- The contact's name
- The contact's phone number

The constructor accepts arguments for both items. The name and phone number are
passed as a pointer to a C-string. Rather than storing the name and phone number in a
char array with a fixed size, the constructor gets the length of the C-string and
dynamically allocates just enough memory to hold it. The destructor frees the allocated
memory when the object is destroyed. (This file is stored in the Student Source Code Folder
Chapter 13\ContactInfo Version 1.)

Contents of ContactInfo.h (Version 1)

```
1  // Specification file for the Contact class.
2  #ifndef CONTACTINFO_H
3  #define CONTACTINFO_H
4  #include <cstring>   // Needed for strlen and strcpy
5
6  // ContactInfo class declaration.
7  class ContactInfo
8  {
9  private:
10     char *name;    // The name
11     char *phone;   // The phone number
12  public:
13     // Constructor
14     ContactInfo(char *n, char *p)
15     { // Allocate just enough memory for the name and phone number.
16       name = new char[strlen(n) + 1];
17       phone = new char[strlen(p) + 1];
18
```

```
19        // Copy the name and phone number to the allocated memory.
20        strcpy(name, n);
21        strcpy(phone, p); }
22
23     // Destructor
24     ~ContactInfo()
25     { delete [] name;
26       delete [] phone; }
27
28     const char *getName() const
29     { return name; }
30
31     const char *getPhoneNumber() const
32     { return phone; }
33  };
34  #endif
```

Notice that the return type of the getName and getPhoneNumber functions in lines 28 through 32 is const char *. This means that each function returns a pointer to a constant char. This is a security measure. It prevents any code that calls the functions from changing the string that the pointer points to.

Program 13-11 demonstrates the class. (This file is also stored in the Student Source Code Folder Chapter 13\ContactInfo Version 1.)

Program 13-11

```
1  // This program demonstrates a class with a destructor.
2  #include <iostream>
3  #include "ContactInfo.h"
4  using namespace std;
5
6  int main()
7  {
8     // Define a ContactInfo object with the following data:
9     // Name: Kristen Lee  Phone Number: 555-2021
10    ContactInfo entry("Kristen Lee", "555-2021");
11
12    // Display the object's data.
13    cout << "Name: " << entry.getName() << endl;
14    cout << "Phone Number: " << entry.getPhoneNumber() << endl;
15    return 0;
16  }
```

Program Output
```
Name: Kristen Lee
Phone Number: 555-2021
```

In addition to the fact that destructors are automatically called when an object is destroyed, the following points should be mentioned:

- Like constructors, destructors have no return type.
- Destructors cannot accept arguments, so they never have a parameter list.

Destructors and Dynamically Allocated Class Objects

If a class object has been dynamically allocated by the new operator, its memory should be released when the object is no longer needed. For example, in the following code objectPtr is a pointer to a dynamically allocated ContactInfo class object.

```
// Define a ContactInfo pointer.
ContactInfo *objectPtr;

// Dynamically create a ContactInfo object.
objectPtr = new ContactInfo("Kristen Lee", "555-2021");
```

The following statement shows the delete operator being used to destroy the dynamically created object.

```
delete objectPtr;
```

When the object pointed to by objectPtr is destroyed, its destructor is automatically called.

 Checkpoint

myprogramminglab   *www.myprogramminglab.com*

13.12   Briefly describe the purpose of a constructor.

13.13   Briefly describe the purpose of a destructor.

13.14   A member function that is never declared with a return data type, but that may have arguments is
   A) The constructor
   B) The destructor
   C) Both the constructor and the destructor
   D) Neither the constructor nor the destructor

13.15   A member function that is never declared with a return data type and can never have arguments is
   A) The constructor
   B) The destructor
   C) Both the constructor and the destructor
   D) Neither the constructor nor the destructor

13.16   Destructor function names always start with
   A) A number
   B) Tilde character (~)
   C) A data type name
   D) None of the above

13.17   A constructor that requires no arguments is called
   A) A default constructor
   B) An overloaded constructor
   C) A null constructor
   D) None of the above

13.18 TRUE or FALSE: Constructors are never declared with a return data type.

13.19 TRUE or FALSE: Destructors are never declared with a return type.

13.20 TRUE or FALSE: Destructors may take any number of arguments.

13.10 Overloading Constructors

CONCEPT: A class can have more than one constructor.

Recall from Chapter 6 that when two or more functions share the same name, the function is said to be overloaded. Multiple functions with the same name may exist in a C++ program, as long as their parameter lists are different.

A class's member functions may be overloaded, including the constructor. One constructor might take an integer argument, for example, while another constructor takes a `double`. There could even be a third constructor taking two integers. As long as each constructor takes a different list of parameters, the compiler can tell them apart. For example, the `string` class has several overloaded constructors. The following statement creates a `string` object with no arguments passed to the constructor:

```
string str;
```

This executes the `string` class's default constructor, which stores an empty string in the object. Another way to create a `string` object is to pass a string literal as an argument to the constructor, as shown here:

```
string str("Hello");
```

This executes an overloaded constructor, which stores the string "Hello" in the object.

Let's look at an example of how you can create overloaded constructors. The `InventoryItem` class holds the following data about an item that is stored in inventory:

- Item's description (a `string` object)
- Item's cost (a `double`)
- Number of units in inventory (an `int`)

The following code shows the class. To simplify the code, all the member functions are written inline. (This file is stored in the Student Source Code Folder `Chapter 13\InventoryItem`.)

Contents of `InventoryItem.h`

```
1   // This class has overloaded constructors.
2   #ifndef INVENTORYITEM_H
3   #define INVENTORYITEM_H
4   #include <string>
5   using namespace std;
6
7   class InventoryItem
```

```
 8   {
 9   private:
10       string description;  // The item description
11       double cost;         // The item cost
12       int units;           // Number of units on hand
13   public:
14       // Constructor #1
15       InventoryItem()
16          { // Initialize description, cost, and units.
17            description = "";
18            cost = 0.0;
19            units = 0; }
20
21       // Constructor #2
22       InventoryItem(string desc)
23          { // Assign the value to description.
24            description = desc;
25
26            // Initialize cost and units.
27            cost = 0.0;
28            units = 0; }
29
30       // Constructor #3
31       InventoryItem(string desc, double c, int u)
32         { // Assign values to description, cost, and units.
33           description = desc;
34           cost = c;
35           units = u; }
36
37       // Mutator functions
38       void setDescription(string d)
39          { description = d; }
40
41       void setCost(double c)
42          { cost = c; }
43
44       void setUnits(int u)
45          { units = u; }
46
47       // Accessor functions
48       string getDescription() const
49          { return description; }
50
51       double getCost() const
52          { return cost; }
53
54       int getUnits() const
55          { return units; }
56   };
57   #endif
```

The first constructor appears in lines 15 through 19. It takes no arguments, so it is the default constructor. It initializes the description variable to an empty string. The cost and units variables are initialized to 0.

The second constructor appears in lines 22 through 28. This constructor accepts only one argument, the item description. The `cost` and `units` variables are initialized to 0.

The third constructor appears in lines 31 through 35. This constructor accepts arguments for the description, cost, and units.

The mutator functions set values for `description`, `cost`, and `units`. Program 13-12 demonstrates the class. (This file is also stored in the Student Source Code Folder `Chapter 13\InventoryItem`.)

Program 13-12

```
 1  // This program demonstrates a class with overloaded constructors.
 2  #include <iostream>
 3  #include <iomanip>
 4  #include "InventoryItem.h"
 5
 6  int main()
 7  {
 8      // Create an InventoryItem object and call
 9      // the default constructor.
10      InventoryItem item1;
11      item1.setDescription("Hammer"); // Set the description
12      item1.setCost(6.95);            // Set the cost
13      item1.setUnits(12);             // Set the units
14
15      // Create an InventoryItem object and call
16      // constructor #2.
17      InventoryItem item2("Pliers");
18
19      // Create an InventoryItem object and call
20      // constructor #3.
21      InventoryItem item3("Wrench", 8.75, 20);
22
23      cout << "The following items are in inventory:\n";
24      cout << setprecision(2) << fixed << showpoint;
25
26      // Display the data for item 1.
27      cout << "Description: " << item1.getDescription() << endl;
28      cout << "Cost: $" << item1.getCost() << endl;
29      cout << "Units on Hand: " << item1.getUnits() << endl << endl;
30
31      // Display the data for item 2.
32      cout << "Description: " << item2.getDescription() << endl;
33      cout << "Cost: $" << item2.getCost() << endl;
34      cout << "Units on Hand: " << item2.getUnits() << endl << endl;
35
36      // Display the data for item 3.
37      cout << "Description: " << item3.getDescription() << endl;
38      cout << "Cost: $" << item3.getCost() << endl;
39      cout << "Units on Hand: " << item3.getUnits() << endl;
40      return 0;
41  }
```

Program Output
```
The following items are in inventory:
Description: Hammer
Cost: $6.95
Units on Hand: 12

Description: Pliers
Cost: $0.00
Units on Hand: 0

Description: Wrench
Cost: $8.75
Units on Hand: 20
```

Only One Default Constructor and One Destructor

When an object is defined without an argument list for its constructor, the compiler automatically calls the default constructor. For this reason, a class may have only one default constructor. If there were more than one constructor that could be called without an argument, the compiler would not know which one to call by default.

Remember, a constructor whose parameters all have a default argument is considered a default constructor. It would be an error to create a constructor that accepts no parameters along with another constructor that has default arguments for all its parameters. In such a case the compiler would not be able to resolve which constructor to execute.

Classes may also only have one destructor. Because destructors take no arguments, the compiler has no way to distinguish different destructors.

Other Overloaded Member Functions

Member functions other than constructors can also be overloaded. This can be useful because sometimes you need several different ways to perform the same operation. For example, in the `InventoryItem` class we could have overloaded the `setCost` function as shown here:

```cpp
void setCost(double c)
    { cost = c; }

void setCost(string c)
    { cost = atof(c.c_str()); }
```

The first version of the function accepts a `double` argument and assigns it to `cost`. The second version of the function accepts a `string` object. This could be used where you have the cost of the item stored in a `string` object. The function calls the `atof` function to convert the string to a `double`, and assigns its value to `cost`.

13.11 Private Member Functions

CONCEPT: A private member function may only be called from a function that is a member of the same class.

Sometimes a class will contain one or more member functions that are necessary for internal processing, but should not be called by code outside the class. For example, a class might have a member function that performs a calculation only when a value is stored in a particular member variable, and should not be performed at any other time. That function should not be directly accessible by code outside the class because it might get called at the wrong time. In this case, the member function should be declared `private`. When a member function is declared `private`, it may only be called internally.

For example, consider the following version of the `ContactInfo` class. (This file is stored in the Student Source Code Folder `Chapter 13\ContactInfo Version 2`.)

Contents of `ContactInfo.h` (Version 2)

```
 1  // Contact class specification file (version 2)
 2  #ifndef CONTACTINFO_H
 3  #define CONTACTINFO_H
 4  #include <cstring>    // Needed for strlen and strcpy
 5
 6  // ContactInfo class declaration.
 7  class ContactInfo
 8  {
 9  private:
10     char *name;    // The contact's name
11     char *phone;   // The contact's phone number
12
13     // Private member function: initName
14     // This function initializes the name attribute.
15     void initName(char *n)
16     {   name = new char[strlen(n) + 1];
17         strcpy(name, n); }
18
19     // Private member function: initPhone
20     // This function initializes the phone attribute.
21      void initPhone(char *p)
22     {   phone = new char[strlen(p) + 1];
23         strcpy(phone, p); }
24  public:
25     // Constructor
26     ContactInfo(char *n, char *p)
27     { // Initialize the name attribute.
28       initName(n);
29
30       // Initialize the phone attribute.
31       initPhone(n); }
32
```

```
33    // Destructor
34    ~ContactInfo()
35    { delete [] name;
36      delete [] phone; }
37
38    const char *getName() const
39    { return name; }
40
41    const char *getPhoneNumber() const
42    { return phone; }
43 };
44 #endif
```

In this version of the class, the logic in the constructor is modularized. It calls two private member functions, initName and initPhone. The initName function allocates memory for the name attribute and initializes it with the value pointed to by the n parameter. The initPhone function allocates memory for the phone attribute and initializes it with the value pointed to by the p parameter. These functions are private because they should be called only from the constructor. If they were ever called by code outside the class, they would change the values of the name and phone pointers without deallocating the memory that they currently point to.

13.12 Arrays of Objects

CONCEPT: You may define and work with arrays of class objects.

As with any other data type in C++, you can define arrays of class objects. An array of InventoryItem objects could be created to represent a business's inventory records. Here is an example of such a definition:

```
const int ARRAY_SIZE = 40;
InventoryItem inventory[ARRAY_SIZE];
```

This statement defines an array of 40 InventoryItem objects. The name of the array is inventory, and the default constructor is called for each object in the array.

If you wish to define an array of objects and call a constructor that requires arguments, you must specify the arguments for each object individually in an initializer list. Here is an example:

```
InventoryItem inventory[] = {"Hammer", "Wrench", "Pliers"};
```

The compiler treats each item in the initializer list as an argument for an array element's constructor. Recall that the second constructor in the InventoryItem class declaration takes the item description as an argument. So, this statement defines an array of three objects and calls that constructor for each object. The constructor for inventory[0] is called with "Hammer" as its argument, the constructor for inventory[1] is called with "Wrench" as its argument, and the constructor for inventory[2] is called with "Pliers" as its argument.

WARNING! If the class does not have a default constructor you must provide an initializer for each object in the array.

If a constructor requires more than one argument, the initializer must take the form of a function call. For example, look at the following definition statement.

```
InventoryItem inventory[] = { InventoryItem("Hammer", 6.95, 12),
                              InventoryItem("Wrench", 8.75, 20),
                              InventoryItem("Pliers", 3.75, 10) };
```

This statement calls the third constructor in the `InventoryItem` class declaration for each object in the `inventory` array.

It isn't necessary to call the same constructor for each object in an array. For example, look at the following statement.

```
InventoryItem inventory[] = { "Hammer",
                              InventoryItem("Wrench", 8.75, 20),
                              "Pliers" };
```

This statement calls the second constructor for `inventory[0]` and `inventory[2]`, and calls the third constructor for `inventory[1]`.

If you do not provide an initializer for all of the objects in an array, the default constructor will be called for each object that does not have an initializer. For example, the following statement defines an array of three objects, but only provides initializers for the first two. The default constructor is called for the third object.

```
const int SIZE = 3;
InventoryItem inventory [SIZE] = { "Hammer",
                                   InventoryItem("Wrench", 8.75, 20) };
```

In summary, if you use an initializer list for class object arrays, there are three things to remember:

- If there is no default constructor you must furnish an initializer for each object in the array.
- If there are fewer initializers in the list than objects in the array, the default constructor will be called for all the remaining objects.
- If a constructor requires more than one argument, the initializer takes the form of a constructor function call.

Accessing Members of Objects in an Array

Objects in an array are accessed with subscripts, just like any other data type in an array. For example, to call the `setUnits` member function of `inventory[2]`, the following statement could be used:

```
inventory[2].setUnits(30);
```

This statement sets the `units` variable of `inventory[2]` to the value 30. Program 13-13 shows an array of `InventoryItem` objects being used in a complete program. (This file is stored in the Student Source Code Folder `Chapter 13\InventoryItem`.)

Program 13-13

```
1   // This program demonstrates an array of class objects.
2   #include <iostream>
3   #include <iomanip>
4   #include "InventoryItem.h"
5   using namespace std;
6
7   int main()
8   {
9       const int NUM_ITEMS = 5;
10      InventoryItem inventory[NUM_ITEMS] = {
11                  InventoryItem("Hammer", 6.95, 12),
12                  InventoryItem("Wrench", 8.75, 20),
13                  InventoryItem("Pliers", 3.75, 10),
14                  InventoryItem("Ratchet", 7.95, 14),
15                  InventoryItem("Screwdriver", 2.50, 22) };
16
17      cout << setw(14) <<"Inventory Item"
18          << setw(8) << "Cost" << setw(8)
19          << setw(16) << "Units on Hand\n";
20      cout << "------------------------------------\n";
21
22      for (int i = 0; i < NUM_ITEMS; i++)
23      {
24          cout << setw(14) << inventory[i].getDescription();
25          cout << setw(8) << inventory[i].getCost();
26          cout << setw(7) << inventory[i].getUnits() << endl;
27      }
28
29      return 0;
30  }
```

Program Output

```
Inventory Item    Cost  Units on Hand
------------------------------------
        Hammer    6.95      12
        Wrench    8.75      20
        Pliers    3.75      10
       Ratchet    7.95      14
   Screwdriver    2.5       22
```

 Checkpoint

mygrogramminglab   *www.myprogramminglab.com*

13.21   What will the following program display on the screen?

```
#include <iostream>
using namespace std;

class Tank
```

```
{
private:
    int gallons;
public:
    Tank()
        { gallons = 50; }
    Tank(int gal)
        { gallons = gal; }
    int getGallons()
        { return gallons; }
};

int main()
{
    Tank storage[3] = { 10, 20 };

    for (int index = 0; index < 3; index++)
        cout << storage[index].getGallons() << endl;
    return 0;
}
```

13.22   What will the following program display on the screen?

```
#include <iostream>
using namespace std;

class Package
{
private:
    int value;
public:
    Package()
        { value = 7; cout << value << endl; }
    Package(int v)
        { value = v; cout << value << endl; }
    ~Package()
        { cout << value << endl; }
};

int main()
{
    Package obj1(4);
    Package obj2();
    Package obj3(2);
    return 0;
}
```

13.23   In your answer for Checkpoint 13.22 indicate for each line of output whether the line is displayed by constructor #1, constructor #2, or the destructor.

13.24   Why would a member function be declared private?

13.25   Define an array of three InventoryItem objects.

13.26   Complete the following program so it defines an array of Yard objects. The program should use a loop to ask the user for the length and width of each Yard.

```
#include <iostream>
using namespace std;
```

```
class Yard
{
private:
    int length, width;
public:
    Yard()
        { length = 0; width = 0; }
    setLength(int len)
        { length = len; }
    setWidth(int w)
        { width = w; }
};

int main()
{
    // Finish this program
}
```

13.13 Focus on Problem Solving and Program Design: An OOP Case Study

You are a programmer for the Home Software Company. You have been assigned to develop a class that models the basic workings of a bank account. The class should perform the following tasks:

- Save the account balance.
- Save the number of transactions performed on the account.
- Allow deposits to be made to the account.
- Allow withdrawals to be taken from the account.
- Calculate interest for the period.
- Report the current account balance at any time.
- Report the current number of transactions at any time.

Private Member Variables

Table 13-4 lists the private member variables needed by the class.

Table 13-4

Variable	Description
balance	A double that holds the current account balance.
interestRate	A double that holds the interest rate for the period.
interest	A double that holds the interest earned for the current period.
transactions	An integer that holds the current number of transactions.

Public Member Functions

Table 13-5 lists the public member functions needed by the class.

Table 13-5

Function	Description
Constructor	Takes arguments to be initially stored in the `balance` and `interestRate` members. The default value for the balance is zero and the default value for the interest rate is 0.045.
setInterestRate	Takes a `double` argument which is stored in the `interestRate` member.
makeDeposit	Takes a `double` argument, which is the amount of the deposit. This argument is added to `balance`.
withdraw	Takes a `double` argument which is the amount of the withdrawal. This value is subtracted from the balance, unless the withdrawal amount is greater than the balance. If this happens, the function reports an error.
calcInterest	Takes no arguments. This function calculates the amount of interest for the current period, stores this value in the `interest` member, and then adds it to the `balance` member.
getInterestRate	Returns the current interest rate (stored in the `interestRate` member).
getBalance	Returns the current balance (stored in the `balance` member).
getInterest	Returns the interest earned for the current period (stored in the `interest` member).
getTransactions	Returns the number of transactions for the current period (stored in the `transactions` member).

The Class Declaration

The following listing shows the class declaration.

Contents of `Account.h`

```
 1  // Specification file for the Account class.
 2  #ifndef ACCOUNT_H
 3  #define ACCOUNT_H
 4
 5  class Account
 6  {
 7  private:
 8     double balance;        // Account balance
 9     double interestRate;   // Interest rate for the period
10     double interest;       // Interest earned for the period
11     int transactions;      // Number of transactions
12  public:
13     Account(double iRate = 0.045, double bal = 0)
14        { balance = bal;
15          interestRate = iRate;
16          interest = 0;
17          transactions = 0; }
18
```

```
19      void setInterestRate(double iRate)
20          { interestRate = iRate; }
21
22      void makeDeposit(double amount)
23          { balance += amount; transactions++; }
24
25      void withdraw(double amount); // Defined in Account.cpp
26
27      void calcInterest()
28          { interest = balance * interestRate; balance += interest; }
29
30      double getInterestRate() const
31          { return interestRate; }
32
33      double getBalance() const
34          { return balance; }
35
36      double getInterest() const
37          { return interest; }
38
39      int getTransactions() const
40          { return transactions; }
41   };
42   #endif
```

The `withdraw` Member Function

The only member function not written `inline` in the class declaration is `withdraw`. The purpose of that function is to subtract the amount of a withdrawal from the `balance` member. If the amount to be withdrawn is greater than the current balance, however, no withdrawal is made. The function returns true if the withdrawal is made, or false if there is not enough in the account.

Contents of `Account.cpp`

```
1    // Implementation file for the Account class.
2    #include "Account.h"
3
4    bool Account::withdraw(double amount)
5    {
6       if (balance < amount)
7          return false; // Not enough in the account
8       else
9       {
10         balance -= amount;
11         transactions++;
12         return true;
13      }
14   }
```

The Class's Interface

The `balance`, `interestRate`, `interest`, and `transactions` member variables are private, so they are hidden from the world outside the class. The reason is that a programmer with direct access to these variables might unknowingly commit any of the following errors:

- A deposit or withdrawal might be made without the `transactions` member being incremented.
- A withdrawal might be made for more than is in the account. This will cause the `balance` member to have a negative value.
- The interest rate might be calculated and the `balance` member adjusted, but the amount of interest might not get recorded in the `interest` member.
- The wrong interest rate might be used.

Because of the potential for these errors, the class contains public member functions that ensure the proper steps are taken when the account is manipulated.

Implementing the Class

Program 13-14 shows an implementation of the `Account` class. It presents a menu for displaying a savings account's balance, number of transactions, and interest earned. It also allows the user to deposit an amount into the account, make a withdrawal from the account, and calculate the interest earned for the current period.

Program 13-14

```
 1 // This program demonstrates the Account class.
 2 #include <iostream>
 3 #include <cctype>
 4 #include <iomanip>
 5 #include "Account.h"
 6 using namespace std;
 7
 8 // Function prototypes
 9 void displayMenu();
10 void makeDeposit(Account &);
11 void withdraw(Account &);
12
13 int main()
14 {
15    Account savings;    // Savings account object
16    char choice;        // Menu selection
17
18    // Set numeric output formatting.
19     cout << fixed << showpoint << setprecision(2);
20
21    do
22    {
23       // Display the menu and get a valid selection.
24       displayMenu();
25       cin >> choice;
```

```
26          while (toupper(choice) < 'A' || toupper(choice) > 'G')
27          {
28             cout << "Please make a choice in the range "
29                  << "of A through G:";
30             cin >> choice;
31          }
32
33          // Process the user's menu selection.
34          switch(choice)
35          {
36          case 'a':
37          case 'A': cout << "The current balance is $";
38                    cout << savings.getBalance() << endl;
39                    break;
40          case 'b':
41          case 'B': cout << "There have been ";
42                    cout << savings.getTransactions()
43                         << " transactions.\n";
44                    break;
45          case 'c':
46          case 'C': cout << "Interest earned for this period: $";
47                    cout << savings.getInterest() << endl;
48                    break;
49          case 'd':
50          case 'D': makeDeposit(savings);
51                    break;
52          case 'e':
53          case 'E': withdraw(savings);
54                    break;
55          case 'f':
56          case 'F': savings.calcInterest();
57                    cout << "Interest added.\n";
58          }
59       } while (toupper(choice) != 'G');
60
61       return 0;
62 }
63
64 //**************************************************
65 // Definition of function displayMenu. This function *
66 // displays the user's menu on the screen.           *
67 //**************************************************
68
```

(program continues)

Program 13-14   *(continued)*

```
69  void displayMenu()
70  {
71     cout << "\n                     MENU\n";
72     cout << "----------------------------------------\n";
73     cout << "A) Display the account balance\n";
74     cout << "B) Display the number of transactions\n";
75     cout << "C) Display interest earned for this period\n";
76     cout << "D) Make a deposit\n";
77     cout << "E) Make a withdrawal\n";
78     cout << "F) Add interest for this period\n";
79     cout << "G) Exit the program\n\n";
80     cout << "Enter your choice: ";
81  }
82
83  //***************************************************************
84  // Definition of function makeDeposit. This function accepts  *
85  // a reference to an Account object. The user is prompted for *
86  // the dollar amount of the deposit, and the makeDeposit      *
87  // member of the Account object is then called.               *
88  //***************************************************************
89
90  void makeDeposit(Account &acnt)
91  {
92     double dollars;
93
94     cout << "Enter the amount of the deposit: ";
95     cin >> dollars;
96     cin.ignore();
97     acnt.makeDeposit(dollars);
98  }
99
100 //***************************************************************
101 // Definition of function withdraw. This function accepts     *
102 // a reference to an Account object. The user is prompted for *
103 // the dollar amount of the withdrawal, and the withdraw      *
104 // member of the Account object is then called.               *
105 //***************************************************************
106
107 void withdraw(Account &acnt)
108 {
109    double dollars;
110
111    cout << "Enter the amount of the withdrawal: ";
112    cin >> dollars;
113    cin.ignore();
114    if (!acnt.withdraw(dollars))
115       cout << "ERROR: Withdrawal amount too large.\n\n";
116 }
```

Program Output with Example Input Shown in Bold

```
                MENU
------------------------------------------
A) Display the account balance
B) Display the number of transactions
C) Display interest earned for this period
D) Make a deposit
E) Make a withdrawal
F) Add interest for this period
G) Exit the program

Enter your choice: d [Enter]
Enter the amount of the deposit: 500 [Enter]

                MENU
------------------------------------------
A) Display the account balance
B) Display the number of transactions
C) Display interest earned for this period
D) Make a deposit
E) Make a withdrawal
F) Add interest for this period
G) Exit the program

Enter your choice: a [Enter]
The current balance is $500.00

                MENU
------------------------------------------
A) Display the account balance
B) Display the number of transactions
C) Display interest earned for this period
D) Make a deposit
E) Make a withdrawal
F) Add interest for this period
G) Exit the program

Enter your choice: e [Enter]
Enter the amount of the withdrawal: 700 [Enter]
ERROR: Withdrawal amount too large.

                MENU
------------------------------------------
A) Display the account balance
B) Display the number of transactions
C) Display interest earned for this period
D) Make a deposit
E) Make a withdrawal
F) Add interest for this period
G) Exit the program

Enter your choice: e [Enter]
Enter the amount of the withdrawal: 200 [Enter]
```

(program output continues)

Program 13-14 *(continued)*

```
                    MENU
-----------------------------------------
A) Display the account balance
B) Display the number of transactions
C) Display interest earned for this period
D) Make a deposit
E) Make a withdrawal
F) Add interest for this period
G) Exit the program

Enter your choice: f [Enter]
Interest added.

                    MENU
-----------------------------------------
A) Display the account balance
B) Display the number of transactions
C) Display interest earned for this period
D) Make a deposit
E) Make a withdrawal
F) Add interest for this period
G) Exit the program

Enter your choice: a [Enter]
The current balance is $313.50

                    MENU
-----------------------------------------
A) Display the account balance
B) Display the number of transactions
C) Display interest earned for this period
D) Make a deposit
E) Make a withdrawal
F) Add interest for this period
G) Exit the program

Enter your choice: g [Enter]
```

13.14 Focus on Object-Oriented Programming: Creating an Abstract Array Data Type

CONCEPT: The absence of array bounds checking in C++ is a source of potential hazard. In this section we examine a simple integer list class that provides bounds checking.

One of the benefits of object-oriented programming is the ability to create abstract data types that are improvements on built-in data types. As you know, arrays provide no bounds checking in C++. You can, however, create a class that has array-like characteristics and performs bounds checking. For example, look at the following IntegerList class.

Contents of `IntegerList.h`

```
1   // Specification file for the IntegerList class.
2   #ifndef INTEGERLIST_H
3   #define INTEGERLIST_H
4
5   class IntegerList
6   {
7   private:
8      int *list;                // Pointer to the array.
9      int numElements;          // Number of elements.
10     bool isValid(int);        // Validates subscripts.
11  public:
12     IntegerList(int);          // Constructor
13     ~IntegerList();            // Destructor
14     void setElement(int, int);  // Sets an element to a value.
15     void getElement(int, int&); // Returns an element.
16  };
17  #endif
```

Contents of `IntegerList.cpp`

```
1  // Implementation file for the IntegerList class.
2  #include <iostream>
3  #include <cstdlib>
4  #include "IntegerList.h"
5  using namespace std;
6
7  //*********************************************************
8  // The constructor sets each element to zero.            *
9  //*********************************************************
10
11 IntegerList::IntegerList(int size)
12 {
13    list = new int[size];
14    numElements = size;
15    for (int ndx = 0; ndx < size; ndx++)
16       list[ndx] = 0;
17 }
18
19 //*********************************************************
20 // The destructor releases allocated memory.             *
21 //*********************************************************
22
23 IntegerList::~IntegerList()
24 {
25    delete [] list;
26 }
27
```

```
28  //***********************************************************
29  // isValid member function.                                *
30  // This private member function returns true if the argument *
31  // is a valid subscript, or false otherwise.               *
32  //***********************************************************
33
34  bool IntegerList::isValid(int element) const
35  {
36     bool status;
37
38     if (element < 0 || element >= numElements)
39        status = false;
40     else
41        status = true;
42     return status;
43  }
44
45  //***********************************************************
46  // setElement member function.                             *
47  // Stores a value in a specific element of the list. If an  *
48  // invalid subscript is passed, the program aborts.        *
49  //***********************************************************
50
51  void IntegerList::setElement(int element, int value)
52  {
53     if (isValid(element))
54        list[element] = value;
55     else
56     {
57        cout << "Error: Invalid subscript\n";
58        exit(EXIT_FAILURE);
59     }
60  }
61
62  //***********************************************************
63  // getElement member function.                             *
64  // Returns the value stored at the specified element.      *
65  // If an invalid subscript is passed, the program aborts.  *
66  //***********************************************************
67
68  int IntegerList::getElement(int element) const
69  {
70     if (isValid(element))
71        return list[element];
72     else
73     {
74        cout << "Error: Invalid subscript\n";
75        exit(EXIT_FAILURE);
76     }
77  }
```

The `IntegerList` class allows you to store and retrieve numbers in a dynamically allocated array of integers. Here is a synopsis of the members.

`list`	A pointer to an `int`. This member points to the dynamically allocated array of integers.
`numElements`	An integer that holds the number of elements in the dynamically allocated array.
`isValid`	This function validates a subscript into the array. It accepts a subscript value as an argument, and returns boolean `true` if the subscript is in the range 0 through `numElements` - 1. If the value is outside that range, boolean `false` is returned.
Constructor	The class constructor accepts an `int` argument that is the number of elements to allocate for the array. The array is allocated and each element is set to zero.
`setElement`	The `setElement` member function sets a specific element of the `list` array to a value. The first argument is the element subscript, and the second argument is the value to be stored in that element. The function uses `isValid` to validate the subscript. If an invalid subscript is passed to the function, the program aborts.
`getElement`	The `getElement` member function retrieves a value from a specific element in the `list` array. The argument is the subscript of the element whose value is to be retrieved. The function uses `isValid` to validate the subscript. If the subscript is valid, the value is returned. If the subscript is invalid, the program aborts.

Program 13-15 demonstrates the class. A loop uses the `setElement` member to fill the array with 9s and prints an asterisk on the screen each time a 9 is successfully stored. Then another loop uses the `getElement` member to retrieve the values from the array and prints them on the screen. Finally, a statement uses the `setElement` member to demonstrate the subscript validation by attempting to store a value in element 50.

Program 13-15

```
1   // This program demonstrates the IntegerList class.
2   #include <iostream>
3   #include "IntegerList.h"
4   using namespace std;
5
6   int main()
7   {
8      const int SIZE = 20;
9      IntegerList numbers(SIZE);
10     int val, x;
11
```

(program continues)

Program 13-15 *(continued)*

```
12     // Store 9s in the list and display an asterisk
13     // each time a 9 is successfully stored.
14     for (x = 0; x < SIZE; x++)
15     {
16        numbers.setElement(x, 9);
17        cout << "* ";
18     }
19     cout << endl;
20
21     // Display the 9s.
22     for (x = 0; x < SIZE; x++)
23     {
24        val = numbers.getElement(x);
25        cout << val << " ";
26     }
27     cout << endl;
28
29     // Attempt to store a value outside the list's bounds.
30     numbers.setElement(50, 9);
31
32     // Will this message display?
33     cout << "Element 50 successfully set.\n";
34     return 0;
35  }
```

Program Output

```
* * * * * * * * * * * * * * * * * * * *
9 9 9 9 9 9 9 9 9 9 9 9 9 9 9 9 9 9 9 9
Error: Invalid subscript
```

13.15 Focus on Object-Oriented Design: The Unified Modeling Language (UML)

CONCEPT: The Unified Modeling Language provides a standard method for graphically depicting an object-oriented system.

When designing a class it is often helpful to draw a UML diagram. *UML* stands for *Unified Modeling Language*. The UML provides a set of standard diagrams for graphically depicting object-oriented systems. Figure 13-18 shows the general layout of a UML diagram for a class. Notice that the diagram is a box that is divided into three sections. The top section is where you write the name of the class. The middle section holds a list of the class's member variables. The bottom section holds a list of the class's member functions.

Figure 13-18

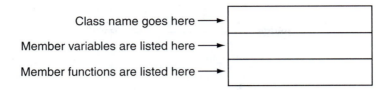

Class name goes here →
Member variables are listed here →
Member functions are listed here →

Earlier in this chapter you studied a `Rectangle` class that could be used in a program that works with rectangles. The first version of the `Rectangle` class that you studied had the following member variables:

- `width`
- `length`

The class also had the following member functions:

- `setWidth`
- `setLength`
- `getWidth`
- `getLength`
- `getArea`

From this information alone we can construct a simple UML diagram for the class, as shown in Figure 13-19.

Figure 13-19

Rectangle
width length
setWidth() setLength() getWidth() getLength() getArea()

The UML diagram in Figure 13-19 tells us the name of the class, the names of the member variables, and the names of the member functions. The UML diagram in Figure 13-19 does not convey many of the class details, however, such as access specification, member variable data types, parameter data types, and function return types. The UML provides optional notation for these types of details.

Showing Access Specification in UML Diagrams

The UML diagram in Figure 13-19 lists all of the members of the `Rectangle` class but does not indicate which members are private and which are public. In a UML diagram you may optionally place a − character before a member name to indicate that it is private, or a + character to indicate that it is public. Figure 13-20 shows the UML diagram modified to include this notation.

Figure 13-20

Rectangle
- width
- length
+ setWidth()
+ setLength()
+ getWidth()
+ getLength()
+ getArea()

Data Type and Parameter Notation in UML Diagrams

The Unified Modeling Language also provides notation that you may use to indicate the data types of member variables, member functions, and parameters. To indicate the data type of a member variable, place a colon followed by the name of the data type after the name of the variable. For example, the `width` variable in the `Rectangle` class is a `double`. It could be listed as follows in the UML diagram:

```
- width : double
```

NOTE: In UML notation the variable name is listed first, then the data type. This is the opposite of C++ syntax, which requires the data type to appear first.

The return type of a member function can be listed in the same manner: After the function's name, place a colon followed by the return type. The `Rectangle` class's `getLength` function returns a `double`, so it could be listed as follows in the UML diagram:

```
+ getLength() : double
```

Parameter variables and their data types may be listed inside a member function's parentheses. For example, the `Rectangle` class's `setLength` function has a `double` parameter named `len`, so it could be listed as follows in the UML diagram:

```
+ setLength(len : double) : void
```

Figure 13-21 shows a UML diagram for the `Rectangle` class with parameter and data type notation.

Figure 13-21

Rectangle
- width : double
- length : double
+ setWidth(w : double) : void
+ setLength(len : double) : void
+ getWidth() : double
+ getLength() : double
+ getArea() : double

Showing Constructors and Destructors in a UML Diagram

There is more than one accepted way of showing a class constructor in a UML diagram. In this book we will show a constructor just as any other function, except we will list no return type. For example, Figure 13-22 shows a UML diagram for the InventoryItem class that we looked at previously in this chapter.

Figure 13-22

InventoryItem
- description : string - cost : double - units : int
+ InventoryItem() : + InventoryItem(desc : string) : + InventoryItem(desc : string,   c : double, u : int) : + setDescription(d : string) : void + setCost(c : double) : void + setUnits(u : int) : void + getDescription() : string + getCost() : double + getUnits() : int

Focus on Object-Oriented Design: Finding the Classes and Their Responsibilities

CONCEPT: One of the first steps in creating an object-oriented application is determining the classes that are necessary, and their responsibilities within the application.

So far you have learned the basics of writing a class, creating an object from the class, and using the object to perform operations. This knowledge is necessary to create an object-oriented application, but it is not the first step in designing the application. The first step is to analyze the problem that you are trying to solve and determine the classes that you will need. In this section we will discuss a simple technique for finding the classes in a problem and determining their responsibilities.

Finding the Classes

When developing an object-oriented application, one of your first tasks is to identify the classes that you will need to create. Typically, your goal is to identify the different types of real-world objects that are present in the problem, and then create classes for those types of objects within your application.

Over the years, software professionals have developed numerous techniques for finding the classes in a given problem. One simple and popular technique involves the following steps.

1. Get a written description of the problem domain.

2. Identify all the nouns (including pronouns and noun phrases) in the description. Each of these is a potential class.

3. Refine the list to include only the classes that are relevant to the problem.

Let's take a closer look at each of these steps.

Write a Description of the Problem Domain

The *problem domain* is the set of real-world objects, parties, and major events related to the problem. If you adequately understand the nature of the problem you are trying to solve, you can write a description of the problem domain yourself. If you do not thoroughly understand the nature of the problem, you should have an expert write the description for you.

For example, suppose we are programming an application that the manager of Joe's Automotive Shop will use to print service quotes for customers. Here is a description that an expert, perhaps Joe himself, might have written:

Joe's Automotive Shop services foreign cars and specializes in servicing cars made by Mercedes, Porsche, and BMW. When a customer brings a car to the shop, the manager gets the customer's name, address, and telephone number. The manager then determines the make, model, and year of the car, and gives the customer a service quote. The service quote shows the estimated parts charges, estimated labor charges, sales tax, and total estimated charges.

The problem domain description should include any of the following:

- Physical objects such as vehicles, machines, or products
- Any role played by a person, such as manager, employee, customer, teacher, student, etc.
- The results of a business event, such as a customer order, or in this case a service quote
- Recordkeeping items, such as customer histories and payroll records

Identify All of the Nouns

The next step is to identify all of the nouns and noun phrases. (If the description contains pronouns, include them too.) Here's another look at the previous problem domain description. This time the nouns and noun phrases appear in bold.

Joe's Automotive Shop services **foreign cars**, and specializes in servicing **cars** made by **Mercedes**, **Porsche**, and **BMW**. When a **customer** brings a **car** to the **shop**, the **manager** gets the **customer's** **name**, **address**, and **telephone number**. The **manager** then determines the **make**, **model**, and **year** of the **car**, and gives the **customer** a **service quote**. The **service quote** shows the **estimated parts charges**, **estimated labor charges**, **sales tax**, and **total estimated charges**.

Notice that some of the nouns are repeated. The following list shows all of the nouns without duplicating any of them.

address
BMW
car
cars
customer
estimated labor charges
estimated parts charges
foreign cars
Joe's Automotive Shop
make
manager
Mercedes
model
name
Porsche
sales tax
service quote
shop
telephone number
total estimated charges
year

Refine the List of Nouns

The nouns that appear in the problem description are merely candidates to become classes. It might not be necessary to make classes for them all. The next step is to refine the list to include only the classes that are necessary to solve the particular problem at hand. We will look at the common reasons that a noun can be eliminated from the list of potential classes.

1. **Some of the nouns really mean the same thing.**

In this example, the following sets of nouns refer to the same thing:
- **cars** and **foreign cars**
  These both refer to the general concept of a car.
- **Joe's Automotive Shop** and **shop**
  Both of these refer to the company "Joe's Automotive Shop."

We can settle on a single class for each of these. In this example we will arbitrarily eliminate **foreign cars** from the list, and use the word **cars**. Likewise we will eliminate **Joe's Automotive Shop** from the list and use the word **shop**. The updated list of potential classes is:

address
BMW
car
cars
customer
estimated labor charges
estimated parts charges
~~foreign cars~~
~~Joe's Automotive Shop~~
make
manager
Mercedes
model
name
Porsche
sales tax
service quote
shop
telephone number
total estimated charges
year

Because **cars** and **foreign cars** mean the same thing in this problem, we have eliminated **foreign cars**. Also, because **Joe's Automotive Shop** and **shop** mean the same thing, we have eliminated **Joe's Automotive Shop**.

2. **Some nouns might represent items that we do not need to be concerned with in order to solve the problem.**

A quick review of the problem description reminds us of what our application should do: print a service quote. In this example we can eliminate two unnecessary classes from the list:

- We can cross **shop** off the list because our application only needs to be concerned with individual service quotes. It doesn't need to work with or determine any company-wide information. If the problem description asked us to keep a total of all the service quotes, then it would make sense to have a class for the shop.
- We will not need a class for the **manager** because the problem statement does not direct us to process any information about the manager. If there were multiple shop managers, and the problem description had asked us to record which manager generated each service quote, then it would make sense to have a class for the manager.

The updated list of potential classes at this point is:

address
BMW
car
cars
customer
estimated labor charges
estimated parts charges
~~foreign cars~~
~~Joe's Automotive Shop~~
make
~~manager~~
Mercedes
model
name
Porsche
sales tax
service quote
~~shop~~
telephone number
total estimated charges
year

Our problem description does not direct us to process any information about the **shop**, or any information about the **manager**, so we have eliminated those from the list.

3. Some of the nouns might represent objects, not classes.

We can eliminate **Mercedes, Porsche,** and **BMW** as classes because, in this example, they all represent specific cars, and can be considered instances of a **cars** class. Also, we can eliminate the word **car** from the list. In the description it refers to a specific car brought to the shop by a customer. Therefore, it would also represent an instance of a **cars** class. At this point the updated list of potential classes is:

address
~~BMW~~
~~car~~
cars
customer
estimated labor charges
estimated parts charges
~~foreign cars~~
~~Joe's Automotive Shop~~
~~manager~~
make
~~Mercedes~~
model
name
~~Porsche~~
sales tax
service quote
~~shop~~
telephone number
total estimated charges
year

We have eliminated **Mercedes, Porsche, BMW,** and **car** because they are all instances of a **cars** class. That means that these nouns identify objects, not classes.

NOTE: Some object-oriented designers take note of whether a noun is plural or singular. Sometimes a plural noun will indicate a class and a singular noun will indicate an object.

4.   **Some of the nouns might represent simple values that can be stored in a variable and do not require a class.**

Remember, a class contains attributes and member functions. Attributes are related items that are stored within an object of the class, and define the object's state. Member functions are actions or behaviors that may be performed by an object of the class. If a noun represents a type of item that would not have any identifiable attributes or member functions, then it can probably be eliminated from the list. To help determine whether a noun represents an item that would have attributes and member functions, ask the following questions about it:

- Would you use a group of related values to represent the item's state?
- Are there any obvious actions to be performed by the item?

If the answers to both of these questions are no, then the noun probably represents a value that can be stored in a simple variable. If we apply this test to each of the nouns that remain in our list, we can conclude that the following are probably not classes: **address, estimated labor charges, estimated parts charges, make, model, name, sales tax, telephone number, total estimated charges** and **year.** These are all simple string or numeric values that can be stored in variables. Here is the updated list of potential classes:

~~address~~
~~BMW~~
~~car~~
cars
customer
~~estimated labor charges~~
~~estimated parts charges~~
~~foreign cars~~
~~Joe's Automotive Shop~~
~~make~~
~~manager~~
~~Mercedes~~
~~model~~
~~name~~
~~Porsche~~
~~sales tax~~
service quote
~~shop~~
~~telephone number~~
~~total estimated charges~~
~~year~~

We have eliminated **address, estimated labor charges, estimated parts charges, make, model, name, sales tax, telephone number, total estimated charges,** and **year** as classes because they represent simple values that can be stored in variables.

As you can see from the list, we have eliminated everything except **cars, customer,** and **service quote.** This means that in our application, we will need classes to represent cars, customers, and service quotes. Ultimately, we will write a `Car` class, a `Customer` class, and a `ServiceQuote` class.

Identifying a Class's Responsibilities

Once the classes have been identified, the next task is to identify each class's responsibilities. A class's *responsibilities* are

- the things that the class is responsible for knowing
- the actions that the class is responsible for doing

When you have identified the things that a class is responsible for knowing, then you have identified the class's attributes. Likewise, when you have identified the actions that a class is responsible for doing, you have identified its member functions.

It is often helpful to ask the questions "In the context of this problem, what must the class know? What must the class do?" The first place to look for the answers is in the description of the problem domain. Many of the things that a class must know and do will be mentioned. Some class responsibilities, however, might not be directly mentioned in the problem domain, so brainstorming is often required. Let's apply this methodology to the classes we previously identified from our problem domain.

The `Customer` class

In the context of our problem domain, what must the `Customer` class know? The description directly mentions the following items, which are all attributes of a customer:

- the customer's name
- the customer's address
- the customer's telephone number

These are all values that can be represented as strings and stored in the class's member variables. The `Customer` class can potentially know many other things. One mistake that can be made at this point is to identify too many things that an object is responsible for knowing. In some applications, a `Customer` class might know the customer's email address. This particular problem domain does not mention that the customer's email address is used for any purpose, so we should not include it as a responsibility.

Now let's identify the class's member functions. In the context of our problem domain, what must the `Customer` class do? The only obvious actions are to

- create an object of the `Customer` class
- set and get the customer's name
- set and get the customer's address
- set and get the customer's telephone number

From this list we can see that the `Customer` class will have a constructor, as well as accessor and mutator functions for each of its attributes. Figure 13-23 shows a UML diagram for the `Customer` class.

Figure 13-23

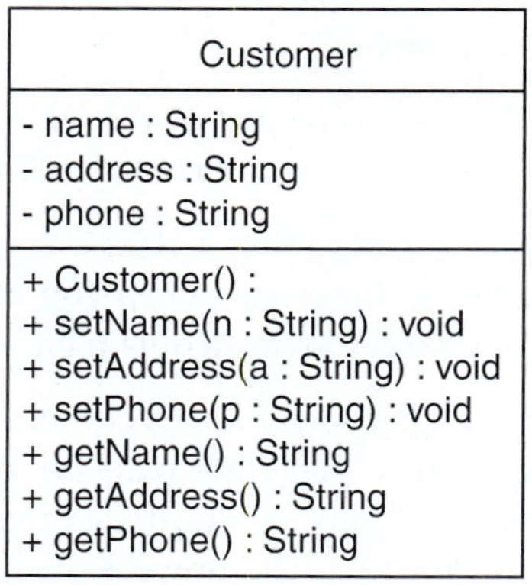

```
                    Customer
         ┌─────────────────────────────┐
         │         Customer            │
         ├─────────────────────────────┤
         │ - name : String             │
         │ - address : String          │
         │ - phone : String            │
         ├─────────────────────────────┤
         │ + Customer() :              │
         │ + setName(n : String) : void│
         │ + setAddress(a : String) : void│
         │ + setPhone(p : String) : void│
         │ + getName() : String        │
         │ + getAddress() : String     │
         │ + getPhone() : String       │
         └─────────────────────────────┘
```

The `Car` Class

In the context of our problem domain, what must an object of the `Car` class know? The following items are all attributes of a car, and are mentioned in the problem domain:

- the car's make
- the car's model
- the car's year

Now let's identify the class's member functions. In the context of our problem domain, what must the `Car` class do? Once again, the only obvious actions are the standard set of member functions that we will find in most classes (constructors, accessors, and mutators). Specifically, the actions are:

- create an object of the `Car` class
- set and get the car's make
- set and get the car's model
- set and get the car's year

Figure 13-24 shows a UML diagram for the `Car` class at this point.

Figure 13-24

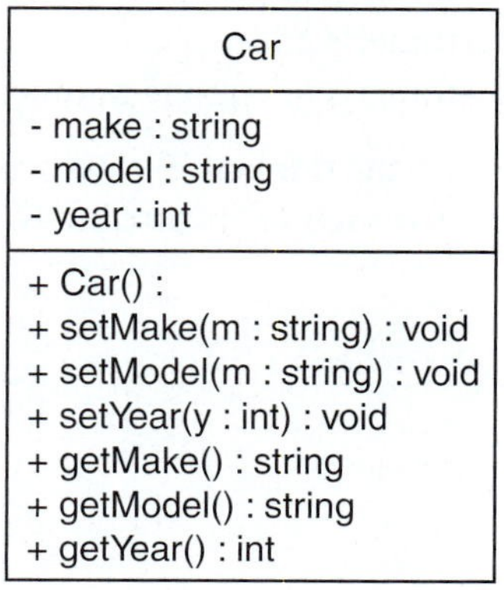

```
                    Car
         ┌─────────────────────────────┐
         │          Car                │
         ├─────────────────────────────┤
         │ - make : string             │
         │ - model : string            │
         │ - year : int                │
         ├─────────────────────────────┤
         │ + Car() :                   │
         │ + setMake(m : string) : void│
         │ + setModel(m : string) : void│
         │ + setYear(y : int) : void   │
         │ + getMake() : string        │
         │ + getModel() : string       │
         │ + getYear() : int           │
         └─────────────────────────────┘
```

The ServiceQuote Class

In the context of our problem domain, what must an object of the ServiceQuote class know? The problem domain mentions the following items:

- the estimated parts charges
- the estimated labor charges
- the sales tax
- the total estimated charges

Careful thought and a little brainstorming will reveal that two of these items are the results of calculations: sales tax and total estimated charges. These items are dependent on the values of the estimated parts and labor charges. In order to avoid the risk of holding stale data, we will not store these values in member variables. Rather, we will provide member functions that calculate these values and return them. The other member functions that we will need for this class are a constructor and the accessors and mutators for the estimated parts charges and estimated labor charges attributes. Figure 13-25 shows a UML diagram for the ServiceQuote class.

Figure 13-25

ServiceQuote
- partsCharges : double - laborCharges : double

+ ServiceQuote() :
+ setPartsCharges(c : double) :
    void
+ setLaborCharges(c : double) :
    void
+ getPartsCharges() : double
+ getLaborCharges() : double
+ getSalesTax() : double
+ getTotalCharges() : double

This Is Only the Beginning

You should look at the process that we have discussed in this section as merely a starting point. It's important to realize that designing an object-oriented application is an iterative process. It may take you several attempts to identify all of the classes that you will need, and determine all of their responsibilities. As the design process unfolds, you will gain a deeper understanding of the problem, and consequently you will see ways to improve the design.

 ## Checkpoint

myprogramminglab *www.myprogramminglab.com*

13.27   What is a problem domain?

13.28   When designing an object-oriented application, who should write a description of the problem domain?

13.29   How do you identify the potential classes in a problem domain description?

13.30 What are a class's responsibilities?

13.31 What two questions should you ask to determine a class's responsibilities?

13.32 Will all of a class's actions always be directly mentioned in the problem domain description?

13.33 Look at the following description of a problem domain:

A doctor sees patients in her practice. When a patient comes to the practice, the doctor performs one or more procedures on the patient. Each procedure that the doctor performs has a description and a standard fee. As the patient leaves the practice, he or she receives a statement from the office manager. The statement shows the patient's name and address, as well as the procedures that were performed, and the total charge for the procedures.

Assume that you are writing an application to generate a statement that can be printed and given to the patient.

A) Identify all of the potential classes in this problem domain.

B) Refine the list to include only the necessary class or classes for this problem.

C) Identify the responsibilities of the class or classes that you identified in step B.

Review Questions and Exercises

Short Answer

1. What is the difference between a class and an instance of the class?

2. What is the difference between the following `Person` structure and `Person` class?

```
struct Person
{
    string name;
    int age;
};

class Person
{
    string name;
    int age;
};
```

3. What is the default access specification of class members?

4. Look at the following function header for a member function.

```
void Circle::getRadius()
```

What is the name of the function?

What class is the function a member of?

5. A contractor uses a blueprint to build a set of identical houses. Are classes analogous to the blueprint or the houses?

6. What is a mutator function? What is an accessor function?

7. Is it a good idea to make member variables private? Why or why not?

8. Can you think of a good reason to avoid writing statements in a class member function that use `cout` or `cin`?

9. Under what circumstances should a member function be private?

10. What is a constructor? What is a destructor?

11. What is a default constructor? Is it possible to have more than one default constructor?

12. Is it possible to have more than one constructor? Is it possible to have more than one destructor?

13. If a class object is dynamically allocated in memory, does its constructor execute? If so, when?

14. When defining an array of class objects, how do you pass arguments to the constructor for each object in the array?

15. What are a class's responsibilities?

16. How do you identify the classes in a problem domain description?

Fill-in-the-Blank

17. The two common programming methods in practice today are _____ and _____.

18. _____ programming is centered around functions or procedures.

19. _____ programming is centered around objects.

20. _____ is an object's ability to contain and manipulate its own data.

21. In C++ the _____ is the construct primarily used to create objects.

22. A class is very similar to a(n) _____.

23. A(n) _____ is a key word inside a class declaration that establishes a member's accessibility.

24. The default access specification of class members is _____.

25. The default access specification of a struct in C++ is _____.

26. Defining a class object is often called the _____ of a class.

27. Members of a class object may be accessed through a pointer to the object by using the _____ operator.

28. If you were writing the declaration of a class named `Canine`, what would you name the file it was stored in? _____

29. If you were writing the external definitions of the `Canine` class's member functions, you would save them in a file named _____.

30. When a member function's body is written inside a class declaration, the function is _____.

31. A(n) _____ is automatically called when an object is created.

32. A(n) _____ is a member function with the same name as the class.

33. _____ are useful for performing initialization or setup routines in a class object.

34. Constructors cannot have a(n) _____ type.

35. A(n) _____ constructor is one that requires no arguments.

36. A(n) _____ is a member function that is automatically called when an object is destroyed.

37. A destructor has the same name as the class, but is preceded by a(n) _____ character.

38. Like constructors, destructors cannot have a(n) _____ type.

39. A constructor whose arguments all have default values is a(n) _____ constructor.

40. A class may have more than one constructor, as long as each has a different _____.

41. A class may only have one default _____ and one _____.

42. A(n) _____ may be used to pass arguments to the constructors of elements in an object array.

Algorithm Workbench

43. Write a class declaration named `Circle` with a private member variable named `radius`. Write set and get functions to access the `radius` variable, and a function named `getArea` that returns the area of the circle. The area is calculated as

    ```
    3.14159 * radius * radius
    ```

44. Add a default constructor to the `Circle` class in question 43. The constructor should initialize the `radius` member to 0.

45. Add an overloaded constructor to the `Circle` class in question 44. The constructor should accept an argument and assign its value to the `radius` member variable.

46. Write a statement that defines an array of five objects of the `Circle` class in question 45. Let the default constructor execute for each element of the array.

47. Write a statement that defines an array of five objects of the `Circle` class in question 45. Pass the following arguments to the elements' constructor: 12, 7, 9, 14, and 8.

48. Write a `for` loop that displays the radius and area of the circles represented by the array you defined in question 47.

49. If the items on the following list appeared in a problem domain description, which would be potential classes?

Animal	Medication	Nurse
Inoculate	Operate	Advertise
Doctor	Invoice	Measure
Patient	Client	Customer

50. Look at the following description of a problem domain:

    The bank offers the following types of accounts to its customers: savings accounts, checking accounts, and money market accounts. Customers are allowed to deposit money into an account (thereby increasing its balance), withdraw money from an account (thereby decreasing its balance), and earn interest on the account. Each account has an interest rate.

    Assume that you are writing an application that will calculate the amount of interest earned for a bank account.

    A) Identify the potential classes in this problem domain.

    B) Refine the list to include only the necessary class or classes for this problem.

    C) Identify the responsibilities of the class or classes.

True or False

51. T F Private members must be declared before public members.

52. T F Class members are private by default.

53. T F Members of a `struct` are private by default.

54. T F Classes and structures in C++ are very similar.

55. T F All private members of a class must be declared together.

56. T F All public members of a class must be declared together.

57. T F It is legal to define a pointer to a class object.

58. T F You can use the `new` operator to dynamically allocate an instance of a class.

59. T F A private member function may be called from a statement outside the class, as long as the statement is in the same program as the class declaration.

60. T F Constructors do not have to have the same name as the class.

61. T F Constructors may not have a return type.

62. T F Constructors cannot take arguments.

63. T F Destructors cannot take arguments.

64. T F Destructors may return a value.

65. T F Constructors may have default arguments.

66. T F Member functions may be overloaded.

67. T F Constructors may not be overloaded.

68. T F A class may not have a constructor with no parameter list, and a constructor whose arguments all have default values.

69. T F A class may only have one destructor.

70. T F When an array of objects is defined, the constructor is only called for the first element.

71. T F To find the classes needed for an object-oriented application, you identify all of the verbs in a description of the problem domain.

72. T F A class's responsibilities are the things the class is responsible for knowing, and actions the class must perform.

Find the Errors

Each of the following class declarations or programs contain errors. Find as many as possible.

73.
```cpp
class Circle:
   {
   private
      double centerX;
      double centerY;
      double radius;
   public
      setCenter(double, double);
      setRadius(double);
   }
```

74.
```cpp
#include <iostream>
using namespace std;

Class Moon;
{
Private;
    double earthWeight;
    double moonWeight;
Public;
    moonWeight(double ew);
        { earthWeight = ew; moonWeight = earthWeight / 6; }
    double getMoonWeight();
        { return moonWeight; }
}

int main()
{
    double earth;
    cout >> "What is your weight? ";
    cin << earth;
    Moon lunar(earth);
    cout << "On the moon you would weigh "
        <<lunar.getMoonWeight() << endl;
    return 0;
}
```

75.
```cpp
#include <iostream>
using namespace std;

class DumbBell;
{
    int weight;
public:
    void setWeight(int);
};
void setWeight(int w)
{
    weight = w;
}

int main()
{
    DumbBell bar;

    DumbBell(200);
    cout << "The weight is " << bar.weight << endl;
    return 0;
}
```

76.
```cpp
class Change
{
public:
    int pennies;
    int nickels;
    int dimes;
    int quarters;
    Change()
```

```
        { pennies = nickels = dimes = quarters = 0; }
    Change(int p = 100, int n = 50, d = 50, q = 25);
};

void Change::Change(int p, int n, d, q)
{
    pennies = p;
    nickels = n;
    dimes = d;
    quarters = q;
}
```

Programming Challenges

Visit www.myprogramminglab.com to complete many of these Programming Challenges online and get instant feedback.

1. **Date**

   Design a class called `Date`. The class should store a date in three integers: `month`, `day`, and `year`. There should be member functions to print the date in the following forms:

   12/25/2012
   December 25, 2012
   25 December 2012

   Demonstrate the class by writing a complete program implementing it.

   Input Validation: Do not accept values for the day greater than 31 or less than 1. Do not accept values for the month greater than 12 or less than 1.

2. **`Employee` Class**

   Write a class named `Employee` that has the following member variables:

VideoNote
Solving the Employee Class Problem

   - **`name`.** A string that holds the employee's name.
   - **`idNumber`.** An int variable that holds the employee's ID number.
   - **`department`.** A string that holds the name of the department where the employee works.
   - **`position`.** A string that holds the employee's job title.

   The class should have the following constructors:

   - A constructor that accepts the following values as arguments and assigns them to the appropriate member variables: employee's name, employee's ID number, department, and position.
   - A constructor that accepts the following values as arguments and assigns them to the appropriate member variables: employee's name and ID number. The `department` and `position` fields should be assigned an empty string (`""`).
   - A default constructor that assigns empty strings (`""`) to the `name`, `department`, and `position` member variables, and 0 to the `idNumber` member variable.

   Write appropriate mutator functions that store values in these member variables and accessor functions that return the values in these member variables. Once you have written the class, write a separate program that creates three `Employee` objects to hold the following data.

Name	ID Number	Department	Position
Susan Meyers	47899	Accounting	Vice President
Mark Jones	39119	IT	Programmer
Joy Rogers	81774	Manufacturing	Engineer

The program should store this data in the three objects and then display the data for each employee on the screen.

3. **Car Class**

Write a class named Car that has the following member variables:

- **yearModel.** An int that holds the car's year model.
- **make.** A string that holds the make of the car.
- **speed.** An int that holds the car's current speed.

In addition, the class should have the following constructor and other member functions.

- **Constructor.** The constructor should accept the car's year model and make as arguments. These values should be assigned to the object's yearModel and make member variables. The constructor should also assign 0 to the speed member variables.
- **Accessor.** Appropriate accessor functions to get the values stored in an object's yearModel, make, and speed member variables.
- **accelerate.** The accelerate function should add 5 to the speed member variable each time it is called.
- **brake.** The brake function should subtract 5 from the speed member variable each time it is called.

Demonstrate the class in a program that creates a Car object, and then calls the accelerate function five times. After each call to the accelerate function, get the current speed of the car and display it. Then, call the brake function five times. After each call to the brake function, get the current speed of the car and display it.

4. **Personal Information Class**

Design a class that holds the following personal data: name, address, age, and phone number. Write appropriate accessor and mutator functions. Demonstrate the class by writing a program that creates three instances of it. One instance should hold your information, and the other two should hold your friends' or family members' information.

5. **RetailItem Class**

Write a class named RetailItem that holds data about an item in a retail store. The class should have the following member variables:

- **description.** A string that holds a brief description of the item.
- **unitsOnHand.** An int that holds the number of units currently in inventory.
- **price.** A double that holds the item's retail price.

Write a constructor that accepts arguments for each member variable, appropriate mutator functions that store values in these member variables, and accessor functions that return the values in these member variables. Once you have written the class, write a separate program that creates three `RetailItem` objects and stores the following data in them.

	Description	Units On Hand	Price
Item #1	Jacket	12	59.95
Item #2	Designer Jeans	40	34.95
Item #3	Shirt	20	24.95

6. Inventory Class

Design an `Inventory` class that can hold information and calculate data for items in a retail store's inventory. The class should have the following *private* member variables:

Variable Name	Description
itemNumber	An int that holds the item's item number.
quantity	An int for holding the quantity of the items on hand.
cost	A double for holding the wholesale per-unit cost of the item
totalCost	A double for holding the total inventory cost of the item (calculated as quantity times cost).

The class should have the following *public* member functions:

Member Function	Description
Default Constructor	Sets all the member variables to 0.
Constructor #2	Accepts an item's number, cost, and quantity as arguments. The function should copy these values to the appropriate member variables and then call the setTotalCost function.
setItemNumber	Accepts an integer argument that is copied to the itemNumber member variable.
setQuantity	Accepts an integer argument that is copied to the quantity member variable.
setCost	Accepts a double argument that is copied to the cost member variable.
setTotalCost	Calculates the total inventory cost for the item (quantity times cost) and stores the result in totalCost.
getItemNumber	Returns the value in itemNumber.
getQuantity	Returns the value in quantity.
getCost	Returns the value in cost.
getTotalCost	Returns the value in totalCost.

Demonstrate the class in a driver program.

Input Validation: Do not accept negative values for item number, quantity, or cost.

7. **Widget Factory**

Design a class for a widget manufacturing plant. Assuming that 10 widgets may be produced each hour, the class object will calculate how many days it will take to produce any number of widgets. (The plant operates two shifts of eight hours each per day.) Write a program that asks the user for the number of widgets that have been ordered and then displays the number of days it will take to produce them.

Input Validation: Do not accept negative values for the number of widgets ordered.

8. **TestScores Class**

Design a `TestScores` class that has member variables to hold three test scores. The class should have a constructor, accessor, and mutator functions for the test score fields, and a member function that returns the average of the test scores. Demonstrate the class by writing a separate program that creates an instance of the class. The program should ask the user to enter three test scores, which are stored in the `TestScores` object. Then the program should display the average of the scores, as reported by the `TestScores` object.

9. **Circle Class**

Write a `Circle` class that has the following member variables:

- `radius`: a double
- `pi`: a double initialized with the value 3.14159

The class should have the following member functions:

- **Default Constructor.** A default constructor that sets `radius` to 0.0.
- **Constructor.** Accepts the radius of the circle as an argument.
- `setRadius`. A mutator function for the radius variable.
- `getRadius`. An accessor function for the radius variable.
- `getArea`. Returns the area of the circle, which is calculated as
  area = pi * radius * radius
- `getDiameter`. Returns the diameter of the circle, which is calculated as
  diameter = radius * 2
- `getCircumference`. Returns the circumference of the circle, which is calculated as
  circumference = 2 * pi * radius

Write a program that demonstrates the `Circle` class by asking the user for the circle's radius, creating a `Circle` object, and then reporting the circle's area, diameter, and circumference.

10. **Population**

In a population, the birth rate and death rate are calculated as follows:

Birth Rate = Number of Births ÷ Population
Death Rate = Number of Deaths ÷ Population

For example, in a population of 100,000 that has 8,000 births and 6,000 deaths per year, the birth rate and death rate are:

Birth Rate = 8,000 ÷ 100,000 = 0.08
Death Rate = 6,000 ÷ 100,000 = 0.06

Design a `Population` class that stores a population, number of births, and number of deaths for a period of time. Member functions should return the birth rate and death rate. Implement the class in a program.

Input Validation: Do not accept population figures less than 1, or birth or death numbers less than 0.

11. **Number Array Class**

Design a class that has an array of floating-point numbers. The constructor should accept an integer argument and dynamically allocate the array to hold that many numbers. The destructor should free the memory held by the array. In addition, there should be member functions to perform the following operations:

- Store a number in any element of the array
- Retrieve a number from any element of the array
- Return the highest value stored in the array
- Return the lowest value stored in the array
- Return the average of all the numbers stored in the array

Demonstrate the class in a program.

12. **Payroll**

Design a `PayRoll` class that has data members for an employee's hourly pay rate, number of hours worked, and total pay for the week. Write a program with an array of seven `PayRoll` objects. The program should ask the user for the number of hours each employee has worked and will then display the amount of gross pay each has earned.

Input Validation: Do not accept values greater than 60 for the number of hours worked.

13. **Mortgage Payment**

Design a class that will determine the monthly payment on a home mortgage. The monthly payment with interest compounded monthly can be calculated as follows:

$$\text{Payment} = \frac{\text{Loan} \times \dfrac{\text{Rate}}{12} \times \text{Term}}{\text{Term} - 1}$$

where

$$\text{Term} = \left(1 + \frac{\text{Rate}}{12}\right)^{12 \times \text{Years}}$$

Payment = the monthly payment
Loan = the dollar amount of the loan
Rate = the annual interest rate
Years = the number of years of the loan

The class should have member functions for setting the loan amount, interest rate, and number of years of the loan. It should also have member functions for returning the monthly payment amount and the total amount paid to the bank at the end of the loan period. Implement the class in a complete program.

Input Validation: Do not accept negative numbers for any of the loan values.

14. **Freezing and Boiling Points**

The following table lists the freezing and boiling points of several substances.

Substance	Freezing Point	Boiling Point
Ethyl Alcohol	–173	172
Oxygen	–362	–306
Water	32	212

Design a class that stores a temperature in a `temperature` member variable and has the appropriate accessor and mutator functions. In addition to appropriate constructors, the class should have the following member functions:

- **isEthylFreezing.** This function should return the `bool` value `true` if the temperature stored in the `temperature` field is at or below the freezing point of ethyl alcohol. Otherwise, the function should return `false`.
- **isEthylBoiling.** This function should return the `bool` value `true` if the temperature stored in the `temperature` field is at or above the boiling point of ethyl alcohol. Otherwise, the function should return `false`.
- **isOxygenFreezing.** This function should return the `bool` value `true` if the temperature stored in the `temperature` field is at or below the freezing point of oxygen. Otherwise, the function should return `false`.
- **isOxygenBoiling.** This function should return the `bool` value `true` if the temperature stored in the `temperature` field is at or above the boiling point of oxygen. Otherwise, the function should return `false`.
- **isWaterFreezing.** This function should return the `bool` value `true` if the temperature stored in the `temperature` field is at or below the freezing point of water. Otherwise, the function should return `false`.
- **isWaterBoiling.** This function should return the `bool` value `true` if the temperature stored in the `temperature` field is at or above the boiling point of water. Otherwise, the function should return `false`.

Write a program that demonstrates the class. The program should ask the user to enter a temperature, and then display a list of the substances that will freeze at that temperature and those that will boil at that temperature. For example, if the temperature is –20 the class should report that water will freeze and oxygen will boil at that temperature.

15. **Cash Register**

Design a `CashRegister` class that can be used with the `InventoryItem` class discussed in this chapter. The `CashRegister` class should perform the following:

1. Ask the user for the item and quantity being purchased.

2. Get the item's cost from the `InventoryItem` object.

3. Add a 30% profit to the cost to get the item's unit price.

4. Multiply the unit price times the quantity being purchased to get the purchase subtotal.

5. Compute a 6% sales tax on the subtotal to get the purchase total.

6. Display the purchase subtotal, tax, and total on the screen.

7. Subtract the quantity being purchased from the `onHand` variable of the `InventoryItem` class object.

Implement both classes in a complete program. Feel free to modify the `InventoryItem` class in any way necessary.

Input Validation: Do not accept a negative value for the quantity of items being purchased.

16. **Trivia Game**

In this programming challenge you will create a simple trivia game for two players. The program will work like this:

- Starting with player 1, each player gets a turn at answering five trivia questions. (There are a total of 10 questions.) When a question is displayed, four possible answers are also displayed. Only one of the answers is correct, and if the player selects the correct answer he or she earns a point.
- After answers have been selected for all of the questions, the program displays the number of points earned by each player and declares the player with the highest number of points the winner.

In this program you will design a `Question` class to hold the data for a trivia question. The `Question` class should have member variables for the following data:

- A trivia question
- Possible answer #1
- Possible answer #2
- Possible answer #3
- Possible answer #4
- The number of the correct answer (1, 2, 3, or 4)

The `Question` class should have appropriate constructor(s), accessor, and mutator functions.

The program should create an array of 10 `Question` objects, one for each trivia question. Make up your own trivia questions on the subject or subjects of your choice for the objects.

Group Project

17. **Patient Fees**

1. This program should be designed and written by a team of students. Here are some suggestions:

- One or more students may work on a single class.
- The requirements of the program should be analyzed so each student is given about the same workload.

– The parameters and return types of each function and class member function should be decided in advance.
– The program will be best implemented as a multi-file program.

2. You are to write a program that computes a patient's bill for a hospital stay. The different components of the program are

The `PatientAccount` class
The `Surgery` class
The `Pharmacy` class
The `main` program

– The `PatientAccount` class will keep a total of the patient's charges. It will also keep track of the number of days spent in the hospital. The group must decide on the hospital's daily rate.
– The `Surgery` class will have stored within it the charges for at least five types of surgery. It can update the charges variable of the `PatientAccount` class.
– The `Pharmacy` class will have stored within it the price of at least five types of medication. It can update the charges variable of the `PatientAccount` class.
– The student who designs the main program will design a menu that allows the user to enter a type of surgery and a type of medication, and check the patient out of the hospital. When the patient checks out, the total charges should be displayed.

14 More About Classes

TOPICS

14.1 Instance and Static Members

CONCEPT: Each instance of a class has its own copies of the class's instance variables. If a member variable is declared **static**, however, all instances of that class have access to that variable. If a member function is declared **static**, it may be called without any instances of the class being defined.

Instance Variables

Each class object (an instance of a class) has its own copy of the class's member variables. An object's member variables are separate and distinct from the member variables of other objects of the same class. For example, recall that the Rectangle class discussed in Chapter 13 has two member variables: width and length. Suppose that we define two objects of the Rectangle class and set their width and length member variables as shown in the following code.

```
Rectangle box1, box2;

// Set the width and length for box1.
box1.setWidth(5);
box1.setLength(10);
```

```
// Set the width and length for box2.
box2.setWidth(500);
box2.setLength(1000);
```

This code creates `box1` and `box2`, which are two distinct objects. Each has its own `width` and `length` member variables, as illustrated in Figure 14-1.

Figure 14-1

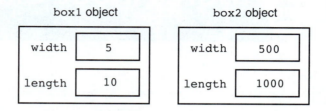

When the `getWidth` member function is called, it returns the value stored in the calling object's `width` member variable. For example, the following statement displays 5 500.

```
cout << box1.getWidth() << " " << box2.getWidth() << endl;
```

In object-oriented programming, member variables such as the `Rectangle` class's `width` and `length` members are known as *instance variables*. They are called instance variables because each instance of the class has its own copies of the variables.

Static Members

It is possible to create a member variable or member function that does not belong to any instance of a class. Such members are known as *static member variables* and *static member functions*. When a value is stored in a static member variable, it is not stored in an instance of the class. In fact, an instance of the class doesn't even have to exist in order for values to be stored in the class's static member variables. Likewise, static member functions do not operate on instance variables. Instead, they can operate only on static member variables. You can think of static member variables and static member functions as belonging to the class instead of to an instance of the class. In this section, we will take a closer look at static members. First we will examine static member variables.

Static Member Variables

When a member variable is declared with the key word `static`, there will be only one copy of the member variable in memory, regardless of the number of instances of the class that might exist. A single copy of a class's static member variable is shared by all instances of the class. For example, the following `Tree` class uses a static member variable to keep count of the number of instances of the class that are created.

Contents of `Tree.h`

```
1  // Tree class
2  class Tree
3  {
4  private:
5     static int objectCount;    // Static member variable.
```

```
 6    public:
 7       // Constructor
 8       Tree()
 9          { objectCount++; }
10
11       // Accessor function for objectCount
12       int getObjectCount() const
13          { return objectCount; }
14    };
15
16    // Definition of the static member variable, written
17    // outside the class.
18    int Tree::objectCount = 0;
```

First, notice in line 5 the declaration of the static member variable named `objectCount`: A static member variable is created by placing the key word `static` before the variable's data type. Also notice that in line 18 we have written a definition statement for the `objectCount` variable, and that the statement is outside the class declaration. This external definition statement causes the variable to be created in memory, and is required. In line 18 we have explicitly initialized the `objectCount` variable with the value 0. We could have left out the initialization because C++ automatically stores 0 in all uninitialized static member variables. It is a good practice to initialize the variable anyway, so it is clear to anyone reading the code that the variable starts out with the value 0.

Next, look at the constructor in lines 8 and 9. In line 9 the ++ operator is used to increment `objectCount`. Each time an instance of the `Tree` class is created, the constructor will be called and the `objectCount` member variable will be incremented. As a result, the `objectCount` member variable will contain the number of instances of the `Tree` class that have been created. The `getObjectCount` function, in lines 12 and 13, returns the value in `objectCount`. Program 14-1 demonstrates this class.

Program 14-1

```
 1    // This program demonstrates a static member variable.
 2    #include <iostream>
 3    #include "Tree.h"
 4    using namespace std;
 5
 6    int main()
 7    {
 8       // Define three Tree objects.
 9       Tree oak;
10       Tree elm;
11       Tree pine;
12
13       // Display the number of Tree objects we have.
14       cout << "We have " << pine.getObjectCount()
15            << " trees in our program!\n";
16       return 0;
17    }
```

Program Output
```
We have 3 trees in our program!
```

The program creates three instances of the `Tree` class, stored in the variables `oak`, `elm`, and `pine`. Although there are three instances of the class, there is only one copy of the static `objectCount` variable. This is illustrated in Figure 14-2.

Figure 14-2

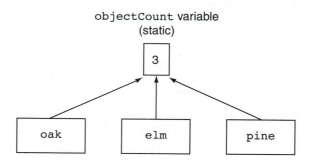

Instances of the `Tree` class

In line 14 the program calls the `getObjectCount` member function to retrieve the number of instances that have been created. Although the program uses the `pine` object to call the member function, the same value would be returned if any of the objects had been used. For example, all three of the following `cout` statements would display the same thing.

```
cout << "We have " << oak.getObjectCount() << " trees\n";
cout << "We have " << elm.getObjectCount() << " trees\n";
cout << "We have " << pine.getObjectCount() << " trees\n";
```

A more practical use of a static member variable is demonstrated in Program 14-2. The `Budget` class is used to gather the budget requests for all the divisions of a company. The class uses a static member, `corpBudget`, to hold the amount of the overall corporate budget. When the member function `addBudget` is called, its argument is added to the current contents of `corpBudget`. By the time the program is finished, `corpBudget` will contain the total of all the values placed there by all the `Budget` class objects. (These files are stored in the Student Source Code Folder `Chapter 14\Budget Version 1`.)

Contents of `Budget.h` (Version 1)

```
 1   #ifndef BUDGET_H
 2   #define BUDGET_H
 3
 4   // Budget class declaration
 5   class Budget
 6   {
 7   private:
 8       static double corpBudget;   // Static member
 9       double divisionBudget;      // Instance member
10   public:
11       Budget()
12           { divisionBudget = 0; }
13
```

```
14        void addBudget(double b)
15           { divisionBudget += b;
16             corpBudget += b; }
17
18        double getDivisionBudget() const
19           { return divisionBudget; }
20
21        double getCorpBudget() const
22           { return corpBudget; }
23   };
24
25   // Definition of static member variable corpBudget
26   double Budget::corpBudget = 0;
27
28   #endif
```

Program 14-2

```
 1   // This program demonstrates a static class member variable.
 2   #include <iostream>
 3   #include <iomanip>
 4   #include "Budget.h"
 5   using namespace std;
 6
 7   int main()
 8   {
 9      int count;                          // Loop counter
10      const int NUM_DIVISIONS = 4;        // Number of divisions
11      Budget divisions[NUM_DIVISIONS];    // Array of Budget objects
12
13      // Get the budget requests for each division.
14      for (count = 0; count < NUM_DIVISIONS; count++)
15      {
16         double budgetAmount;
17         cout << "Enter the budget request for division ";
18         cout << (count + 1) << ": ";
19         cin >> budgetAmount;
20         divisions[count].addBudget(budgetAmount);
21      }
22
23      // Display the budget requests and the corporate budget.
24      cout << fixed << showpoint << setprecision(2);
25      cout << "\nHere are the division budget requests:\n";
26      for (count = 0; count < NUM_DIVISIONS; count++)
27      {
28         cout << "\tDivision " << (count + 1) << "\t$ ";
29         cout << divisions[count].getDivisionBudget() << endl;
30      }
31      cout << "\tTotal Budget Requests:\t$ ";
32      cout << divisions[0].getCorpBudget() << endl;
33
34      return 0;
35   }
```

(program output continues)

Program 14-2 *(continued)*

Program Output with Example Input Shown in Bold
```
Enter the budget request for division 1: 100000 [Enter]
Enter the budget request for division 2: 200000 [Enter]
Enter the budget request for division 3: 300000 [Enter]
Enter the budget request for division 4: 400000 [Enter]

Here are the division budget requests:
     Division 1    $ 100000.00
     Division 2    $ 200000.00
     Division 3    $ 300000.00
     Division 4    $ 400000.00
     Total Budget Requests:  $ 1000000.00
```

Static Member Functions

You declare a static member function by placing the `static` keyword in the function's prototype. Here is the general form:

```
static ReturnType FunctionName (ParameterTypeList);
```

A function that is a static member of a class cannot access any nonstatic member data in its class. With this limitation in mind, you might wonder what purpose static member functions serve. The following two points are important for understanding their usefulness:

- Even though static member variables are declared in a class, they are actually defined outside the class declaration. The lifetime of a class's static member variable is the lifetime of the program. This means that a class's static member variables come into existence before any instances of the class are created.
- A class's static member functions can be called before any instances of the class are created. This means that a class's static member functions can access the class's static member variables *before* any instances of the class are defined in memory. This gives you the ability to create very specialized setup routines for class objects.

Program 14-3, a modification of Program 14-2, demonstrates this feature. It asks the user to enter the main office's budget request before any division requests are entered. The `Budget` class has been modified to include a static member function named `mainOffice`. This function adds its argument to the static `corpBudget` variable, and is called before any instances of the `Budget` class are defined. (These files are stored in the Student Source Code Folder `Chapter 14\Budget Version 2`.)

Contents of `Budget.h` (Version 2)

```
 1   #ifndef BUDGET_H
 2   #define BUDGET_H
 3
 4   // Budget class declaration
 5   class Budget
 6   {
 7   private:
 8       static double corpBudget;    // Static member variable
 9       double divisionBudget;       // Instance member variable
```

```
10   public:
11      Budget()
12         { divisionBudget = 0; }
13
14      void addBudget(double b)
15         { divisionBudget += b;
16           corpBudget += b; }
17
18      double getDivisionBudget() const
19         { return divisionBudget; }
20
21      double getCorpBudget() const
22         { return corpBudget; }
23
24      static void mainOffice(double);   // Static member function
25   };
26
27   #endif
```

Contents of `Budget.cpp`

```
1   #include "Budget.h"
2
3   // Definition of corpBudget static member variable
4   double Budget::corpBudget = 0;
5
6   //**********************************************************
7   // Definition of static member function mainOffice.        *
8   // This function adds the main office's budget request to  *
9   // the corpBudget variable.                                *
10  //**********************************************************
11
12  void Budget::mainOffice(double moffice)
13  {
14     corpBudget += moffice;
15  }
```

Program 14-3

```
1   // This program demonstrates a static member function.
2   #include <iostream>
3   #include <iomanip>
4   #include "Budget.h"
5   using namespace std;
6
7   int main()
8   {
9      int count;                      // Loop counter
10     double mainOfficeRequest;       // Main office budget request
11     const int NUM_DIVISIONS = 4;    // Number of divisions
12
```

(program continues)

Program 14-3   *(continued)*

```
13      // Get the main office's budget request.
14      // Note that no instances of the Budget class have been defined.
15      cout << "Enter the main office's budget request: ";
16      cin >> mainOfficeRequest;
17      Budget::mainOffice(mainOfficeRequest);
18
19      Budget divisions[NUM_DIVISIONS]; // An array of Budget objects.
20
21      // Get the budget requests for each division.
22      for (count = 0; count < NUM_DIVISIONS; count++)
23      {
24          double budgetAmount;
25          cout << "Enter the budget request for division ";
26          cout << (count + 1) << ": ";
27          cin >> budgetAmount;
28          divisions[count].addBudget(budgetAmount);
29      }
30
31      // Display the budget requests and the corporate budget.
32      cout << fixed << showpoint << setprecision(2);
33      cout << "\nHere are the division budget requests:\n";
34      for (count = 0; count < NUM_DIVISIONS; count++)
35      {
36          cout << "\tDivision " << (count + 1) << "\t$ ";
37          cout << divisions[count].getDivisionBudget() << endl;
38      }
39      cout << "\tTotal Budget Requests:\t$ ";
40      cout << divisions[0].getCorpBudget() << endl;
41
42      return 0;
43  }
```

Program Output with Example Input Shown in Bold
```
Enter the main office's budget request: 100000 [Enter]
Enter the budget request for division 1: 100000 [Enter]
Enter the budget request for division 2: 200000 [Enter]
Enter the budget request for division 3: 300000 [Enter]
Enter the budget request for division 4: 400000 [Enter]

Here are the division budget requests:
    Division 1     $ 100000.00
    Division 2     $ 200000.00
    Division 3     $ 300000.00
    Division 4     $ 400000.00
    Total Requests (including main office): $ 1100000.00
```

Notice in line 17 the statement that calls the static function mainOffice:

```
Budget::mainOffice(amount);
```

Calls to static member functions do not use the regular notation of connecting the function name to an object name with the dot operator. Instead, static member functions are called by connecting the function name to the class name with the scope resolution operator.

> **NOTE:** If an instance of a class with a static member function exists, the static member function can be called with the class object name and the dot operator, just like any other member function.

14.2 Friends of Classes

CONCEPT: A friend is a function or class that is not a member of a class, but has access to the private members of the class.

Private members are hidden from all parts of the program outside the class, and accessing them requires a call to a public member function. Sometimes you will want to create an exception to that rule. A *friend* function is a function that is not part of a class, but that has access to the class's private members. In other words, a friend function is treated as if it were a member of the class. A friend function can be a regular stand-alone function, or it can be a member of another class. (In fact, an entire class can be declared a friend of another class.)

In order for a function or class to become a friend of another class, it must be declared as such by the class granting it access. Classes keep a "list" of their friends, and only the external functions or classes whose names appear in the list are granted access. A function is declared a friend by placing the key word `friend` in front of a prototype of the function. Here is the general format:

```
friend ReturnType FunctionName (ParameterTypeList)
```

In the following declaration of the `Budget` class, the `addBudget` function of another class, `AuxiliaryOffice` has been declared a friend. (This file is stored in the Student Source Code Folder `Chapter 14\Budget Version 3`.)

Contents of `Budget.h` (Version 3)

```
 1   #ifndef BUDGET_H
 2   #define BUDGET_H
 3   #include "Auxil.h"
 4
 5   // Budget class declaration
 6   class Budget
 7   {
 8   private:
 9      static double corpBudget;    // Static member variable
10      double divisionBudget;       // Instance member variable
11   public:
12      Budget()
13         { divisionBudget = 0; }
14
15      void addBudget(double b)
16         { divisionBudget += b;
17           corpBudget += b; }
```

```
18
19      double getDivisionBudget() const
20         { return divisionBudget; }
21
22      double getCorpBudget() const
23         { return corpBudget; }
24
25      // Static member function
26      static void mainOffice(double);
27
28      // Friend function
29      friend void AuxiliaryOffice::addBudget(double, Budget &);
30   };
31
32   #endif
```

Let's assume another class, `AuxiliaryOffice`, represents a division's auxiliary office, perhaps in another country. The auxiliary office makes a separate budget request, which must be added to the overall corporate budget. The friend declaration of the `AuxiliaryOffice::addBudget` function tells the compiler that the function is to be granted access to `Budget`'s private members. Notice the function takes two arguments: a `double` and a reference object of the `Budget` class. The `Budget` class object that is to be modified by the function is passed to it, by reference, as an argument. The following code shows the declaration of the `AuxillaryOffice` class. (This file is stored in the Student Source Code Folder `Chapter 14\Budget Version 3`.)

Contents of `Auxil.h`

```
1    #ifndef AUXIL_H
2    #define AUXIL_H
3
4    class Budget;  // Forward declaration of Budget class
5
6    // Aux class declaration
7
8    class AuxiliaryOffice
9    {
10   private:
11      double auxBudget;
12   public:
13      AuxiliaryOffice()
14         { auxBudget = 0; }
15
16      double getDivisionBudget() const
17         { return auxBudget; }
18
19      void addBudget(double, Budget &);
20   };
21
22   #endif
```

Contents of `Auxil.cpp`

```
 1   #include "Auxil.h"
 2   #include "Budget.h"
 3
 4   //**********************************************************
 5   // Definition of member function mainOffice.             *
 6   // This function is declared a friend by the Budget class. *
 7   // It adds the value of argument b to the static corpBudget *
 8   // member variable of the Budget class.                  *
 9   //**********************************************************
10
11   void AuxiliaryOffice::addBudget(double b, Budget &div)
12   {
13      auxBudget += b;
14      div.corpBudget += b;
15   }
```

Notice the `Auxil.h` file contains the following statement in line 4:

```
class Budget; // Forward declaration of Budget class
```

This is a *forward declaration* of the `Budget` class. It simply tells the compiler that a class named `Budget` will be declared later in the program. This is necessary because the compiler will process the `Auxil.h` file before it processes the `Budget` class declaration. When it is processing the `Auxil.h` file it will see the following function declaration in line 19:

```
void addBudget(double, Budget &);
```

The `addBudget` function's second parameter is a `Budget` reference variable. At this point, the compiler has not processed the `Budget` class declaration, so, without the forward declaration, it wouldn't know what a `Budget` reference variable is.

The following code shows the definition of the `addBudget` function. (This file is also stored in the Student Source Code Folder `Chapter 14\Budget Version 3`.)

Contents of `Auxil.cpp`

```
 1   #include "Auxil.h"
 2   #include "Budget.h"
 3
 4   //**********************************************************
 5   // Definition of member function mainOffice.             *
 6   // This function is declared a friend by the Budget class. *
 7   // It adds the value of argument b to the static corpBudget *
 8   // member variable of the Budget class.                  *
 9   //**********************************************************
10
11   void AuxiliaryOffice::addBudget(double b, Budget &div)
12   {
13      auxBudget += b;
14      div.corpBudget += b;
15   }
```

The parameter `div`, a reference to a `Budget` class object, is used in line 14. This statement adds the parameter `b` to `div.corpBudget`. Program 14-4 demonstrates the classes.

Program 14-4

```
1    // This program demonstrates a static member function.
2    #include <iostream>
3    #include <iomanip>
4    #include "Budget.h"
5    using namespace std;
6
7    int main()
8    {
9       int count;                    // Loop counter
10      double mainOfficeRequest;     // Main office budget request
11      const int NUM_DIVISIONS = 4;  // Number of divisions
12
13      // Get the main office's budget request.
14      cout << "Enter the main office's budget request: ";
15      cin >> mainOfficeRequest;
16      Budget::mainOffice(mainOfficeRequest);
17
18      Budget divisions[NUM_DIVISIONS]; // Array of Budget objects
19      AuxiliaryOffice auxOffices[4];   // Array of AuxiliaryOffice
20
21      // Get the budget requests for each division
22      // and their auxiliary offices.
23      for (count = 0; count < NUM_DIVISIONS; count++)
24      {
25         double budgetAmount;  // To hold input
26
27         // Get the request for the division office.
28         cout << "Enter the budget request for division ";
29         cout << (count + 1) << ": ";
30         cin >> budgetAmount;
31         divisions[count].addBudget(budgetAmount);
32
33         // Get the request for the auxiliary office.
34         cout << "Enter the budget request for that division's\n";
35         cout << "auxiliary office: ";
36         cin >> budgetAmount;
37         auxOffices[count].addBudget(budgetAmount, divisions[count]);
38      }
39
40      // Display the budget requests and the corporate budget.
41      cout << fixed << showpoint << setprecision(2);
42      cout << "\nHere are the division budget requests:\n";
43      for (count = 0; count < NUM_DIVISIONS; count++)
44      {
45         cout << "\tDivision " << (count + 1) << "\t\t$";
46         cout << divisions[count].getDivisionBudget() << endl;
47         cout << "\tAuxiliary office:\t$";
48         cout << auxOffices[count].getDivisionBudget() << endl << endl;
49      }
50      cout << "Total Budget Requests:\t$ ";
51      cout << divisions[0].getCorpBudget() << endl;
52      return 0;
53   }
```

Program Output with Example Input Shown in Bold
```
Enter the main office's budget request: 100000 [Enter]
Enter the budget request for division 1: 100000 [Enter]
Enter the budget request for that division's
auxiliary office: 50000 [Enter]
Enter the budget request for division 2: 200000 [Enter]
Enter the budget request for that division's
auxiliary office: 40000 [Enter]
Enter the budget request for division 3: 300000 [Enter]
Enter the budget request for that division's
auxiliary office: 70000 [Enter]
Enter the budget request for division 4: 400000 [Enter]
Enter the budget request for that division's
auxiliary office: 65000 [Enter]

Here are the division budget requests:
        Division 1              $100000.00
        Auxiliary office:       $50000.00

        Division 2              $200000.00
        Auxiliary office:       $40000.00

        Division 3              $300000.00
        Auxiliary office:       $70000.00

        Division 4              $400000.00
        Auxiliary office:       $65000.00

Total Budget Requests:   $ 1325000.00
```

As mentioned before, it is possible to make an entire class a friend of another class. The Budget class could make the AuxiliaryOffice class its friend with the following declaration:

```
friend class AuxiliaryOffice;
```

This may not be a good idea, however. Every member function of AuxiliaryOffice (including ones that may be added later) would have access to the private members of Budget. The best practice is to declare as friends only those functions that must have access to the private members of the class.

 ## Checkpoint

myprogramminglab   *www.myprogramminglab.com*

14.1 What is the difference between an instance member variable and a static member variable?

14.2 Static member variables are declared inside the class declaration. Where are static member variables defined?

14.3 Does a static member variable come into existence in memory before, at the same time as, or after any instances of its class?

14.4 What limitation does a static member function have?

14.5   What action is possible with a static member function that isn't possible with an instance member function?

14.6   If class x declares function f as a friend, does function f become a member of class x?

14.7   Class Y is a friend of class X, which means the member functions of class Y have access to the private members of class X. Does the friend key word appear in class Y's declaration or in class X's declaration?

14.3   Memberwise Assignment

CONCEPT: The = operator may be used to assign one object's data to another object, or to initialize one object with another object's data. By default, each member of one object is copied to its counterpart in the other object.

Like other variables (except arrays), objects may be assigned to one another using the = operator. As an example, consider Program 14-5 which uses the Rectangle class (version 4) that we discussed in Chapter 13. Recall that the Rectangle class has two member variables: width and length. The constructor accepts two arguments, one for width and one for length.

Program 14-5

```
 1  // This program demonstrates memberwise assignment.
 2  #include <iostream>
 3  #include "Rectangle.h"
 4  using namespace std;
 5
 6  int main()
 7  {
 8     // Define two Rectangle objects.
 9     Rectangle box1(10.0, 10.0);   // width = 10.0, length = 10.0
10     Rectangle box2 (20.0, 20.0);  // width = 20.0, length = 20.0
11
12     // Display each object's width and length.
13     cout << "box1's width and length: " << box1.getWidth()
14          << " " << box1.getLength() << endl;
15     cout << "box2's width and length: " << box2.getWidth()
16          << " " << box2.getLength() << endl << endl;
17
18     // Assign the members of box1 to box2.
19     box2 = box1;
20
21     // Display each object's width and length again.
22     cout << "box1's width and length: " << box1.getWidth()
23          << " " << box1.getLength() << endl;
24     cout << "box2's width and length: " << box2.getWidth()
25          << " " << box2.getLength() << endl;
26
27     return 0;
28  }
```

The following statement, which appears in line 19, copies the width and length member variables of box1 directly into the width and length member variables of box2:

```
box2 = box1;
```

Memberwise assignment also occurs when one object is initialized with another object's values. Remember the difference between assignment and initialization: assignment occurs between two objects that already exist, and initialization happens to an object being created. Consider the following code:

```
// Define box1.
Rectangle box1(100.0, 50.0);

// Define box2, initialize with box1's values
Rectangle box2 = box1;
```

The last statement defines a Rectangle object, box2, and initializes it to the values stored in box1. Because memberwise assignment takes place, the box2 object will contain the exact same values as the box1 object.

14.4 Copy Constructors

CONCEPT: A copy constructor is a special constructor that is called whenever a new object is created and initialized with another object's data.

Most of the time, the default memberwise assignment behavior in C++ is perfectly acceptable. There are instances, however, where memberwise assignment cannot be used. For example, consider the following class. (This file is stored in the Student Source Code Folder Chapter 14\StudentTestScores Version 1.)

Contents of StudentTestScores.h (Version 1)

```
 1 #ifndef STUDENTTESTSCORES_H
 2 #define STUDENTTESTSCORES_H
 3 #include <string>
 4 using namespace std;
 5
 6 const double DEFAULT_SCORE = 0.0;
 7
 8 class StudentTestScores
 9 {
10 private:
11    string studentName;   // The student's name
12    double *testScores;   // Points to array of test scores
13    int numTestScores;    // Number of test scores
14
```

```
15        // Private member function to create an
16        // array of test scores.
17        void createTestScoresArray(int size)
18        { numTestScores = size;
19          testScores = new double[size];
20          for (int i = 0; i < size; i++)
21            testScores[i] = DEFAULT_SCORE; }
22
23 public:
24        // Constructor
25        StudentTestScores(string name, int numScores)
26        { studentName = name;
27          createTestScoresArray(numScores); }
28
29        // Destructor
30        ~StudentTestScores()
31        { delete [] testScores; }
32
33        // The setTestScore function sets a specific
34        // test score's value.
35        void setTestScore(double score, int index)
36        { testScores[index] = score; }
37
38        // Set the student's name.
39        void setStudentName(string name)
40        { studentName = name; }
41
42        // Get the student's name.
43        string getStudentName() const
44        { return studentName; }
45
46        // Get the number of test scores.
47        int getNumTestScores() const
48        { return numTestScores; }
49
50        // Get a specific test score.
51        double getTestScore(int index) const
52        { return testScores[index]; }
53 };
54 #endif
```

This class stores a student's name and a set of test scores. Let's take a closer look at the code:

- Lines 11 through 13 declare the class's attributes. The studentName attribute is a string object that holds a student's name. The testScores attribute is an int pointer. Its purpose is to point to a dynamically allocated int array that holds the student's test score. The numTestScore attribute is an int that holds the number of test scores.

- The createTestScoresArray private member function, in lines 17 through 21, creates an array to hold the student's test scores. It accepts an argument for the number of test scores, assigns this value to the numTestScores attribute (line 18), and then dynamically allocates an int array for the testScores attribute (line 19). The for loop in lines 20 through 21 initializes each element of the array to the default value 0.0.

- The constructor, in lines 25 through 27, accepts the student's name and the number of test scores as arguments. In line 26 the name is assigned to the `studentName` attribute, and in line 27 the number of test scores is passed to the `createTestScoresArray` member function.
- The destructor, in lines 30 through 31, deallocates the test score array.
- The `setTestScore` member function, in lines 35 through 36, sets a specific score in the `testScores` attribute. The function accepts arguments for the score and the index where the score should be stored in the `testScores` array.
- The `setStudentName` member function, in lines 39 through 40, accepts an argument that is assigned to the `studentName` attribute.
- The `getStudentName` member function, in lines 43 through 44, returns the value of the `studentName` attribute.
- The `getNumTestScores` member function, in lines 47 through 48, returns the number of test scores stored in the object.
- The `getTestScore` member function, in lines 51 through 52, returns a specific score (specified by the index parameter) from the `testScores` attribute.

A potential problem with this class lies in the fact that one of its members, `testScores`, is a pointer. The `createTestScoresArray` member function (called by the constructor) performs a critical operation with the pointer: it dynamically allocates a section of memory for the `testScores` array, and assigns default values to each of its element. For instance, the following statement creates a `StudentTestScores` object named `student1`, whose `testScores` member references dynamically allocated memory holding an array of 5 `double`'s:

```
StudentTestScores("Maria Jones Tucker", 5);
```

This is depicted in Figure 14-3.

Figure 14-3

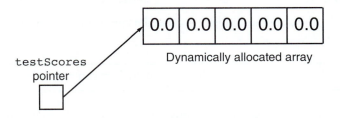

Consider what happens when another `StudentTestScores` object is created and initialized with the `student1` object, as in the following statement:

```
StudentTestScores student2 = student1;
```

In the statement above, `student2`'s constructor isn't called. Instead, memberwise assignment takes place, copying each of `student1`'s member variables into `student2`. This means that a separate section of memory is not allocated for `student2`'s `testScores` member. It simply gets a copy of the address stored in `student1`'s `testScores` member. Both pointers will point to the same address, as depicted in Figure 14-4.

In this situation, either object can manipulate the values stored in the array, causing the changes to show up in the other object. Likewise, one object can be destroyed, causing its destructor to be called, which frees the allocated memory. The remaining object's `testScores` pointer would still reference this section of memory, although it should no longer be used.

Figure 14-4

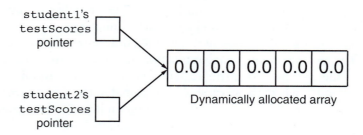

The solution to this problem is to create a *copy constructor* for the object. A copy constructor is a special constructor that's called when an object is initialized with another object's data. It has the same form as other constructors, except it has a reference parameter of the same class type as the object itself. For example, here is a copy constructor for the StudentTestScores class:

```
StudentTestScores(StudentTestScores &obj)
{ studentName = obj.studentName;
  numTestScores = obj.numTestScores;
  testScores = new double[numTestScores];
  for (int i = 0; i < length; i++)
      testScores[i] = obj.testScores[i]; }
```

When the = operator is used to initialize a StudentTestScores object with the contents of another StudentTestScores object, the copy constructor is called. The StudentTestScores object that appears on the right side of the = operator is passed as an argument to the copy constructor. For example, look at the following statement:

```
StudentTestScores student1 ("Molly McBride", 8);
StudentTestScores student2 = student1;
```

In this code, the student1 object is passed as an argument to the student2 object's copy constructor.

 NOTE: C++ requires that a copy constructor's parameter be a reference object.

As you can see from studying the copy constructor's code, student2's testScores member will properly reference its own dynamically allocated memory. There will be no danger of student1 inadvertently destroying or corrupting student2's data.

Using const Parameters in Copy Constructors

Because copy constructors are required to use reference parameters, they have access to their argument's data. Since the purpose of a copy constructor is to make a copy of the argument, there is no reason the constructor should modify the argument's data. With this in mind, it's a good idea to make copy constructors' parameters constant by specifying the const key word in the parameter list. Here is an example:

```
StudentTestScores(const StudentTestScores &obj)
{ studentName = obj.studentName;
  numTestScores = obj.numTestScores;
```

```
      testScores = new double[numTestScores];
      for (int i = 0; i < numTestScores; i++)
            testScores[i] = obj.testScores[i]; }
```

The const key word ensures that the function cannot change the contents of the parameter. This will prevent you from inadvertently writing code that corrupts data.

The complete listing for the revised StudentTestScores class is shown here. (This file is stored in the Student Source Code Folder Chapter 14\StudentTestScores Version 2.)

Contents of StudentTestScores.h (Version 2)

```
 1  #ifndef STUDENTTESTSCORES_H
 2  #define STUDENTTESTSCORES_H
 3  #include <string>
 4  using namespace std;
 5
 6  const double DEFAULT_SCORE = 0.0;
 7
 8  class StudentTestScores
 9  {
10  private:
11     string studentName;   // The student's name
12     double *testScores;   // Points to array of test scores
13     int numTestScores;    // Number of test scores
14
15      // Private member function to create an
16      // array of test scores.
17     void createTestScoresArray(int size)
18     { numTestScores = size;
19       testScores = new double[size];
20       for (int i = 0; i < size; i++)
21            testScores[i] = DEFAULT_SCORE; }
22
23  public:
24       // Constructor
25     StudentTestScores(string name, int numScores)
26     { studentName = name;
27       createTestScoresArray(numScores); }
28
29      // Copy constructor
30     StudentTestScores(const StudentTestScores &obj)
31     { studentName = obj.studentName;
32       numTestScores = obj.numTestScores;
33       testScores = new double[numTestScores];
34       for (int i = 0; i < numTestScores; i++)
35            testScores[i] = obj.testScores[i]; }
36
37       // Destructor
38     ~StudentTestScores()
39     { delete [] testScores; }
40
41      // The setTestScore function sets a specific
42      // test score's value.
43     void setTestScore(double score, int index)
```

```
44      { testScores[index] = score; }
45
46       // Set the student's name.
47      void setStudentName(string name)
48      { studentName = name; }
49
50       // Get the student's name.
51      string getStudentName() const
52      { return studentName; }
53
54       // Get the number of test scores.
55      int getNumTestScores() const
56      { return numTestScores; }
57
58       // Get a specific test score.
59      double getTestScore(int index) const
60      { return testScores[index]; }
61 };
62 #endif
```

Copy Constructors and Function Parameters

When a class object is passed by value as an argument to a function, it is passed to a parameter that is also a class object, and the copy constructor of the function's parameter is called. Remember that when a nonreference class object is used as a function parameter it is created when the function is called, and it is initialized with the argument's value.

This is why C++ requires the parameter of a copy constructor to be a reference object. If an object were passed to the copy constructor by value, the copy constructor would create a copy of the argument and store it in the parameter object. When the parameter object is created, its copy constructor will be called, thus causing another parameter object to be created. This process will continue indefinitely (or at least until the available memory fills up, causing the program to halt).

To prevent the copy constructor from calling itself an infinite number of times, C++ requires its parameter to be a reference object.

The Default Copy Constructor

Although you may not realize it, you have seen the action of a copy constructor before. If a class doesn't have a copy constructor, C++ creates a *default copy constructor* for it. The default copy constructor performs the memberwise assignment discussed in the previous section.

 ## Checkpoint

myprogramminglab *www.myprogramminglab.com*

14.8   Briefly describe what is meant by memberwise assignment.

14.9   Describe two instances when memberwise assignment occurs.

14.10   Describe a situation in which memberwise assignment should not be used.

14.11   When is a copy constructor called?

14.12   How does the compiler know that a member function is a copy constructor?

14.13   What action is performed by a class's default copy constructor?

14.5   Operator Overloading

CONCEPT: C++ allows you to redefine how standard operators work when used with class objects.

VideoNote

**Operator
Overloading**

C++ provides many operators to manipulate data of the primitive data types. However, what if you wish to use an operator to manipulate class objects? For example, assume that a class named `Date` exists, and objects of the `Date` class hold the month, day, and year in member variables. Suppose the `Date` class has a member function named `add`. The `add` member function adds a number of days to the date, and adjusts the member variables if the date goes to another month or year. For example, the following statement adds five days to the date stored in the `today` object:

```
today.add(5);
```

Although it might be obvious that the statement is adding five days to the date stored in `today`, the use of an operator might be more intuitive. For example, look at the following statement:

```
today += 5;
```

This statement uses the standard `+=` operator to add 5 to `today`. This behavior does not happen automatically, however. The `+=` operator must be *overloaded* for this action to occur. In this section, you will learn to overload many of C++'s operators to perform specialized operations on class objects.

> **NOTE:** You have already experienced the behavior of an overloaded operator. The `/` operator performs two types of division: floating point and integer. If one of the `/` operator's operands is a floating point type, the result will be a floating point value. If both of the `/` operator's operands are integers, however, a different behavior occurs: the result is an integer and any fractional part is thrown away.

Overloading the = Operator

Although copy constructors solve the initialization problems inherent with objects containing pointer members, they do not work with simple assignment statements. Copy constructors are just that—constructors. They are only invoked when an object is created. Statements like the following still perform memberwise assignment:

```
student2 = student1;
```

In order to change the way the assignment operator works, it must be overloaded. Operator overloading permits you to redefine an existing operator's behavior when used with a class object.

C++ allows a class to have special member functions called *operator functions*. If you wish to redefine the way a particular operator works with an object, you define a function for that operator. The Operator function is then executed any time the operator is used with an object of that class. For example, the following version of the `StudentTestScores` class overloads the `=` operator. (This file is stored in the Student Source Code Folder `Chapter 14\StudentTestScores Version 3`.)

Contents of StudentTestScores (Version 3)

```
 1 #ifndef STUDENTTESTSCORES_H
 2 #define STUDENTTESTSCORES_H
 3 #include <string>
 4 using namespace std;
 5
 6 const double DEFAULT_SCORE = 0.0;
 7
 8 class StudentTestScores
 9 {
10 private:
11    string studentName;   // The student's name
12    double *testScores;   // Points to array of test scores
13    int numTestScores;    // Number of test scores
14
15     // Private member function to create an
16     // array of test scores.
17    void createTestScoresArray(int size)
18    { numTestScores = size;
19      testScores = new double[size];
20      for (int i = 0; i < size; i++)
21         testScores[i] = DEFAULT_SCORE; }
22
23 public:
24     // Constructor
25    StudentTestScores(string name, int numScores)
26    { studentName = name;
27      createTestScoresArray(numScores); }
28
29     // Copy constructor
30    StudentTestScores(const StudentTestScores &obj)
31    { studentName = obj.studentName;
32      numTestScores = obj.numTestScores;
33      testScores = new double[numTestScores];
34      for (int i = 0; i < numTestScores; i++)
35         testScores[i] = obj.testScores[i]; }
36
37     // Destructor
38    ~StudentTestScores()
39    { delete [] testScores; }
40
41     // The setTestScore function sets a specific
42     // test score's value.
43    void setTestScore(double score, int index)
44    { testScores[index] = score; }
45
46     // Set the student's name.
47    void setStudentName(string name)
48    { studentName = name; }
49
50     // Get the student's name.
51    string getStudentName() const
52    { return studentName; }
53
```

```
54      // Get the number of test scores.
55      int getNumTestScores()
56      { return numTestScores; }
57
58      // Get a specific test score.
59      double getTestScore(int index) const
60      { return testScores[index]; }
61
62      // Overloaded = operator
63      void operator=(const StudentTestScores &right)
64      { delete [] testScores;
65        studentName = right.studentName;
66        numTestScores = right.numTestScores;
67        testScores = new double[numTestScores];
68        for (int i = 0; i < numTestScores; i++)
69            testScores[i] = right.testScores[i]; }
70 };
71 #endif
```

Let's examine the operator function to understand how it works. First look at the function header:

Return type   Function name   Parameter for object on the right side of operator

```
void operator=(const StudentTestScores &right)
```

The name of the function is `operator=`. This specifies that the function overloads the `=` operator. Because it is a member of the `StudentTestScores` class, this function will be called only when an assignment statement executes where the object on the left side of the `=` operator is a `StudentTestScores` object.

NOTE: You can, if you choose, put spaces around the operator symbol. For instance, the function header above could also read:

```
void operator = (const StudentTestScores &right)
```

The function has one parameter: a constant reference object named `right`. This parameter references the object on the right side of the operator. For example, when the following statement is executed, `right` will reference the `student1` object:

```
student2 = student1;
```

It is not required that the parameter of an operator function be a reference object. The `StudentTestScores` example declares `right` as a `const` reference for the following reasons:

- It was declared as a reference for efficiency purposes. This prevents the compiler from making a copy of the object being passed into the function.
- It was declared constant so the function will not accidentally change the contents of the argument.

NOTE: In the example, the parameter was named `right` simply to illustrate that it references the object on the right side of the operator. You can name the parameter anything you wish. It will always take the object on the operator's right as its argument.

In learning the mechanics of operator overloading, it is helpful to know that the following two statements do the same thing:

```
student2 = student1;        // Call operator= function
student2.operator=(student1);  // Call operator= function
```

In the last statement you can see exactly what is going on in the function call. The student1 object is being passed to the function's parameter, right. Inside the function, the values in right's members are used to initialize student2. Notice that the operator= function has access to the right parameter's private members. Because the operator= function is a member of the StudentTestScores class, it has access to the private members of any StudentTestScores object that is passed into it.

 NOTE: C++ allows operator functions to be called with regular function call notation, or by using the operator symbol.

Program 14-6 demonstrates the StudentTestScores class with its overloaded assignment operator. (This file is stored in the Student Source Code Folder Chapter 14\ StudentTestScores Version 3.)

Program 14-6

```
 1  // This program demonstrates the overloaded = operator
 2  #include <iostream>
 3  #include "StudentTestScores.h"
 4  using namespace std;
 5
 6  // Function prototype
 7  void displayStudent(StudentTestScores);
 8
 9  int main()
10  {
11      // Create a StudentTestScores object and
12      // assign test scores.
13      StudentTestScores student1("Kelly Thorton", 3);
14      student1.setTestScore(100.0, 0);
15      student1.setTestScore(95.0, 1);
16      student1.setTestScore(80, 2);
17
18      // Create another StudentTestScore object
19      // with default test scores.
20      StudentTestScores student2("Jimmy Griffin", 5);
21
22      // Assign the student1 object to student2
23      student2 = student1;
24
25      // Display both objects. They should
26      // contain the same data.
27      displayStudent(student1);
28      displayStudent(student2);
29      return 0;
30  }
31
```

```
32  // The displayStudent function accepts a
33  // StudentTestScores object's data.
34  void displayStudent(StudentTestScores s)
35  {
36      cout << "Name: " << s.getStudentName() << endl;
37      cout << "Test Scores: ";
38      for (int i = 0; i < s.getNumTestScores(); i++)
39          cout << s.getTestScore(i) << " ";
40      cout << endl;
41  }
```

Program Output
```
Name: Kelly Thorton
Test Scores: 100 95 80
Name: Kelly Thorton
Test Scores: 100 95 80
```

The = Operator's Return Value

There is only one problem with the overloaded = operator shown in Program 14-6: it has a void return type. C++'s built-in = operator allows multiple assignment statements such as:

```
a = b = c;
```

In this statement, the expression b = c causes c to be assigned to b and then returns the value of c. The return value is then stored in a. If a class object's overloaded = operator is to function this way, it too must have a valid return type.

For example, the StudentTestScores class's operator= function could be written as:

```
const StudentTestScores operator=(const StudentTestScores &right)
{ delete [] testScores;
  studentName = right.studentName;
  numTestScores = right.numTestScores;
  testScores = new double[numTestScores];
  for (int i = 0; i < numTestScores; i++)
      testScores[i] = right.testScores[i];
  return *this;  }
```

The data type of the operator function specifies that a const StudentTestScores object is returned. Look at the last statement in the function:

```
return *this;
```

This statement returns the value of a dereferenced pointer: this. But what is this? Read on.

The this Pointer

The this pointer is a special built-in pointer that is available to a class's member functions. It always points to the instance of the class making the function call. For example, if student1 and student2 are both StudentTestScores objects, the following statement causes the getStudentName function to operate on student1:

```
cout << student1.getStudentName() << endl;
```

Likewise, the following statement causes getStudentName to operate on student2:

```
cout << student2.getStudentName() << endl;
```

When getStudentName is operating on student1, the this pointer is pointing to student1. When getStudentName is operating on student2, this is pointing to student2. The this pointer always points to the object that is being used to call the member function.

 NOTE: The this pointer is passed as a hidden argument to all nonstatic member functions.

The overloaded = operator function is demonstrated in Program 14-7. The multiple assignment statement in line 21 causes the operator= function to execute. (This file and the revised version of the StudentTestScores class is stored in the Student Source Code Folder Chapter 14\StudentTestScores Version 4.)

Program 14-7

```
 1   // This program demonstrates the overloaded = operator
 2   // with a return value.
 3   #include <iostream>
 4   #include "StudentTestScores.h"
 5   using namespace std;
 6
 7   int main()
 8   {
 9      // Create and initialize the jim object
10      StudentTestScores jim("Jim Young", 1);
11      jim.setTestScore(95.5, 0);
12
13      // Create and initialize the bob object
14      StudentTestScores bob("Bob Faraday", 1);
15      bob.setTestScore(82.8, 0);
16
17      // Create the clone object and initialize with jim
18      StudentTestScores clone = jim;
19
20      // Assign jim to bob and clone
21      clone = bob = jim;
22
23      // Display the contents of the jim object
24      cout << "The jim object contains: ";
25      cout << jim.getName() << ", " ;
26      cout << jim.getTestScore(0) << endl;
27
28      // Display the contents of the bob object
29      cout << "The bob object contains: ";
30      cout << bob.getName() << ", " ;
31      cout << bob.getTestScore(0) << endl;
32
```

```
33        // Display the contents of the clone object
34        cout << "The clone object contains: ";
35        cout << clone.getName() << ", " ;
36        cout << clone.getTestScore(0) << endl;
37
38        return 0;
39   }
```

Program Output
```
Name: Kelly Thorton
Test Scores: 100 95 80
Name: Kelly Thorton
Test Scores: 100 95 80
Name: Kelly Thorton
Test Scores: 100 95 80
```

Some General Issues of Operator Overloading

Now that you have had a taste of operator overloading, let's look at some of the general issues involved in this programming technique.

Although it is not a good programming practice, you can change an operator's entire meaning if that's what you wish to do. There is nothing to prevent you from changing the = symbol from an assignment operator to a "display" operator. For instance, the following class does just that:

```
class Weird
{
private:
   int value;
public:
   Weird(int v)
      {value = v; }
   void operator=(const weird &right)
      { cout << right.value << endl; }
};
```

Although the operator= function in the Weird class overloads the assignment operator, the function doesn't perform an assignment. Instead, it displays the contents of right.value. Consider the following program segment:

```
Weird a(5), b(10);
a = b;
```

Although the statement a = b looks like an assignment statement, it actually causes the contents of b's value member to be displayed on the screen:

```
10
```

Another operator overloading issue is that you cannot change the number of operands taken by an operator. The = symbol must always be a binary operator. Likewise, ++ and -- must always be unary operators.

The last issue is that although you may overload most of the C++ operators, you cannot overload all of them. Table 14-1 shows all of the C++ operators that may be overloaded.

Table 14-1

+	–	*	/	%	^	&	|	~	!	=	<
>	+=	–=	*=	/=	%=	^=	&=	|=	<<	>>	>>=
<<=	==	!=	<=	>=	&&	||	++	––	->*	,	->
[]	()	new	delete								

> **NOTE:** Some of the operators in Table 14-1 are beyond the scope of this book and are not covered.

The only operators that cannot be overloaded are

```
?:    .    .*    ::    sizeof
```

Overloading Math Operators

Many classes would benefit not only from an overloaded assignment operator, but also from overloaded math operators. To illustrate this, consider the FeetInches class shown in the following two files. (These files are stored in the Student Source Code Folder Chapter 14\FeetInches Version 1.)

Contents of FeetInches.h (Version 1)

```
 1  #ifndef FEETINCHES_H
 2  #define FEETINCHES_H
 3
 4  // The FeetInches class holds distances or measurements
 5  // expressed in feet and inches.
 6
 7  class FeetInches
 8  {
 9  private:
10     int feet;      // To hold a number of feet
11     int inches;    // To hold a number of inches
12     void simplify(); // Defined in FeetInches.cpp
13  public:
14     // Constructor
15     FeetInches(int f = 0, int i = 0)
16        { feet = f;
17          inches = i;
18          simplify(); }
19
20     // Mutator functions
21     void setFeet(int f)
22        { feet = f; }
23
```

```
24       void setInches(int i)
25          { inches = i;
26            simplify(); }
27
28       // Accessor functions
29       int getFeet() const
30          { return feet; }
31
32       int getInches() const
33          { return inches; }
34
35       // Overloaded operator functions
36       FeetInches operator + (const FeetInches &); // Overloaded +
37       FeetInches operator - (const FeetInches &); // Overloaded -
38    };
39
40    #endif
```

Contents of `FeetInches.cpp` (Version 1)

```
1    // Implementation file for the FeetInches class
2    #include <cstdlib>        // Needed for abs()
3    #include "FeetInches.h"
4
5    //*************************************************************
6    // Definition of member function simplify. This function      *
7    // checks for values in the inches member greater than        *
8    // twelve or less than zero. If such a value is found,         *
9    // the numbers in feet and inches are adjusted to conform      *
10   // to a standard feet & inches expression. For example,        *
11   // 3 feet 14 inches would be adjusted to 4 feet 2 inches and *
12   // 5 feet -2 inches would be adjusted to 4 feet 10 inches.     *
13   //*************************************************************
14
15   void FeetInches::simplify()
16   {
17      if (inches >= 12)
18      {
19         feet += (inches / 12);
20         inches = inches % 12;
21      }
22      else if (inches < 0)
23      {
24         feet -= ((abs(inches) / 12) + 1);
25         inches = 12 - (abs(inches) % 12);
26      }
27   }
28
29   //*********************************************
30   // Overloaded binary + operator.              *
31   //*********************************************
32
```

```
33   FeetInches FeetInches::operator + (const FeetInches &right)
34   {
35      FeetInches temp;
36
37      temp.inches = inches + right.inches;
38      temp.feet = feet + right.feet;
39      temp.simplify();
40      return temp;
41   }
42
43   //*********************************************
44   // Overloaded binary - operator.              *
45   //*********************************************
46
47   FeetInches FeetInches::operator - (const FeetInches &right)
48   {
49      FeetInches temp;
50
51      temp.inches = inches - right.inches;
52      temp.feet = feet - right.feet;
53      temp.simplify();
54      return temp;
55   }
```

The `FeetInches` class is designed to hold distances or measurements expressed in feet and inches. It consists of eight member functions:

- A constructor that allows the `feet` and `inches` members to be set. The default values for these members is zero.
- A `setFeet` function for storing a value in the `feet` member.
- A `setInches` function for storing a value in the `inches` member.
- A `getFeet` function for returning the value in the `feet` member.
- A `getInches` function for returning the value in the `inches` member.
- A `simplify` function for normalizing the values held in `feet` and `inches`. This function adjusts any set of values where the `inches` member is greater than 12 or less than 0.
- An `operator +` function that overloads the standard + math operator.
- An `operator -` function that overloads the standard - math operator.

NOTE: The `simplify` function uses the standard library function `abs()` to get the absolute value of the `inches` member. The `abs()` function requires that `cstdlib` be included.

The overloaded + and - operators allow one `FeetInches` object to be added to or subtracted from another. For example, assume the `length1` and `length2` objects are defined and initialized as follows:

```
FeetInches length1(3, 5), length2(6, 3);
```

The `length1` object is holding the value 3 feet 5 inches, and the `length2` object is holding the value 6 feet 3 inches. Because the + operator is overloaded, we can add these two objects in a statement such as:

```
length3 = length1 + length2;
```

This statement will add the values of the `length1` and `length2` objects and store the result in the `length3` object. After the statement executes, the `length3` object will be set to 9 feet 8 inches.

The member function that overloads the + operator appears in lines 33 through 41 of the `FeetInches.cpp` file.

This function is called anytime the + operator is used with two `FeetInches` objects. Just like the overloaded = operator we defined in the previous section, this function has one parameter: a constant reference object named `right`. This parameter references the object on the right side of the operator. For example, when the following statement is executed, `right` will reference the `length2` object:

```
length3 = length1 + length2;
```

As before, it might be helpful to think of the statement above as the following function call:

```
length3 = length1.operator+(length2);
```

The `length2` object is being passed to the function's parameter, `right`. When the function finishes, it will return a `FeetInches` object to `length3`. Now let's see what is happening inside the function. First, notice that a `FeetInches` object named `temp` is defined locally in line 35:

```
FeetInches temp;
```

This object is a temporary location for holding the results of the addition. Next, line 37 adds `inches` to `right.inches` and stores the result in `temp.inches`:

```
temp.inches = inches + right.inches;
```

The `inches` variable is a member of `length1`, the object making the function call. It is the object on the left side of the operator. `right.inches` references the `inches` member of `length2`. The next statement, in line 38, is very similar. It adds `feet` to `right.feet` and stores the result in `temp.feet`:

```
temp.feet = feet + right.feet;
```

At this point in the function, `temp` contains the sum of the `feet` and `inches` members of both objects in the expression. The next step is to adjust the values so they conform to a normal value expressed in feet and inches. This is accomplished in line 39 by calling `temp.simplify()`:

```
temp.simplify();
```

The last step, in line 40, is to return the value stored in `temp`:

```
return temp;
```

In the statement length3 = length1 + length2, the return statement in the operator function causes the values stored in temp to be returned to the length3 object.

Program 14-8 demonstrates the overloaded operators. (This file is stored in the student source code folder Chapter 14\FeetInches Version 1.)

Program 14-8

```
 1   // This program demonstrates the FeetInches class's overloaded
 2   // + and - operators.
 3   #include <iostream>
 4   #include "FeetInches.h"
 5   using namespace std;
 6
 7   int main()
 8   {
 9      int feet, inches;  // To hold input for feet and inches
10
11      // Create three FeetInches objects. The default arguments
12      // for the constructor will be used.
13      FeetInches first, second, third;
14
15      // Get a distance from the user.
16      cout << "Enter a distance in feet and inches: ";
17      cin >> feet >> inches;
18
19      // Store the distance in the first object.
20      first.setFeet(feet);
21      first.setInches(inches);
22
23      // Get another distance from the user.
24      cout << "Enter another distance in feet and inches: ";
25      cin >> feet >> inches;
26
27      // Store the distance in second.
28      second.setFeet(feet);
29      second.setInches(inches);
30
31      // Assign first + second to third.
32      third = first + second;
33
34      // Display the result.
35      cout << "first + second = ";
36      cout << third.getFeet() << " feet, ";
37      cout << third.getInches() << " inches.\n";
38
```

```
39        // Assign first - second to third.
40        third = first - second;
41
42        // Display the result.
43        cout << "first - second = ";
44        cout << third.getFeet() << " feet, ";
45        cout << third.getInches() << " inches.\n";
46
47        return 0;
48   }
```

Program Output with Example Input Shown in Bold
Enter a distance in feet and inches: **6 5 [Enter]**
Enter another distance in feet and inches: **3 10 [Enter]**
first + second = 10 feet, 3 inches.
first - second = 2 feet, 7 inches.

Overloading the Prefix ++ Operator

Unary operators, such as ++ and −−, are overloaded in a fashion similar to the way binary operators are implemented. Because unary operators only affect the object making the operator function call, however, there is no need for a parameter. For example, let's say you wish to have a prefix increment operator for the FeetInches class. Assume the FeetInches object distance is set to the values 7 feet and 5 inches. A ++ operator function could be designed to increment the object's inches member. The following statement would cause distance to have the value 7 feet 6 inches:

```
++distance;
```

The following function overloads the prefix ++ operator to work in this fashion:

```
FeetInches FeetInches::operator++()
{
    ++inches;
    simplify();
    return *this;
}
```

This function first increments the object's inches member. The simplify() function is called and then the dereferenced this pointer is returned. This allows the operator to perform properly in statements like this:

```
distance2 = ++distance1;
```

Remember, the statement above is equivalent to

```
distance2 = distance1.operator++();
```

Overloading the Postfix ++ Operator

Overloading the postfix ++ operator is only slightly different than overloading the prefix version. Here is the function that overloads the postfix operator with the `FeetInches` class:

```
FeetInches FeetInches::operator++(int)
{
    FeetInches temp(feet, inches);
    inches++;
    simplify();
    return temp;
}
```

The first difference you will notice is the use of a *dummy parameter*. The word `int` in the function's parentheses establishes a nameless integer parameter. When C++ sees this parameter in an operator function, it knows the function is designed to be used in post-fix mode. The second difference is the use of a temporary local variable, the `temp` object. `temp` is initialized with the `feet` and `inches` values of the object making the function call. `temp`, therefore, is a copy of the object being incremented, but before the increment takes place. After `inches` is incremented and the `simplify` function is called, the con-tents of `temp` is returned. This causes the postfix operator to behave correctly in a state-ment like this:

```
distance2 = distance1++;
```

You will find a version of the `FeetInches` class with the overloaded prefix and postfix ++ operators stored in the Student Source Code Folder `Chapter 14\FeetInches Version 2`. In that folder you will also find Program 14-9, which demonstrates these overloaded operators.

Program 14-9

```
 1   // This program demonstrates the FeetInches class's overloaded
 2   // prefix and postfix ++ operators.
 3   #include <iostream>
 4   #include "FeetInches.h"
 5   using namespace std;
 6
 7   int main()
 8   {
 9       int count;   // Loop counter
10
11       // Define a FeetInches object with the default
12       // value of 0 feet, 0 inches.
13       FeetInches first;
14
15       // Define a FeetInches object with 1 foot 5 inches.
16       FeetInches second(1, 5);
17
```

```
18      // Use the prefix ++ operator.
19      cout << "Demonstrating prefix ++ operator.\n";
20      for (count = 0; count < 12; count++)
21      {
22          first = ++second;
23          cout << "first: " << first.getFeet() << " feet, ";
24          cout << first.getInches() << " inches. ";
25          cout << "second: " << second.getFeet() << " feet, ";
26          cout << second.getInches() << " inches.\n";
27      }
28
29      // Use the postfix ++ operator.
30      cout << "\nDemonstrating postfix ++ operator.\n";
31      for (count = 0; count < 12; count++)
32      {
33          first = second++;
34          cout << "first: " << first.getFeet() << " feet, ";
35          cout << first.getInches() << " inches. ";
36          cout << "second: " << second.getFeet() << " feet, ";
37          cout << second.getInches() << " inches.\n";
38      }
39
40      return 0;
41  }
```

Program Output

```
Demonstrating prefix ++ operator.
first: 1 feet 6 inches. second: 1 feet 6 inches.
first: 1 feet 7 inches. second: 1 feet 7 inches.
first: 1 feet 8 inches. second: 1 feet 8 inches.
first: 1 feet 9 inches. second: 1 feet 9 inches.
first: 1 feet 10 inches. second: 1 feet 10 inches.
first: 1 feet 11 inches. second: 1 feet 11 inches.
first: 2 feet 0 inches. second: 2 feet 0 inches.
first: 2 feet 1 inches. second: 2 feet 1 inches.
first: 2 feet 2 inches. second: 2 feet 2 inches.
first: 2 feet 3 inches. second: 2 feet 3 inches.
first: 2 feet 4 inches. second: 2 feet 4 inches.
first: 2 feet 5 inches. second: 2 feet 5 inches.

Demonstrating postfix ++ operator.
first: 2 feet 5 inches. second: 2 feet 6 inches.
first: 2 feet 6 inches. second: 2 feet 7 inches.
first: 2 feet 7 inches. second: 2 feet 8 inches.
first: 2 feet 8 inches. second: 2 feet 9 inches.
first: 2 feet 9 inches. second: 2 feet 10 inches.
first: 2 feet 10 inches. second: 2 feet 11 inches.
first: 2 feet 11 inches. second: 3 feet 0 inches.
first: 3 feet 0 inches. second: 3 feet 1 inches.
first: 3 feet 1 inches. second: 3 feet 2 inches.
first: 3 feet 2 inches. second: 3 feet 3 inches.
first: 3 feet 3 inches. second: 3 feet 4 inches.
first: 3 feet 4 inches. second: 3 feet 5 inches.
```

Checkpoint

myprogramminglab   *www.myprogramminglab.com*

14.14   Assume there is a class named `Pet`. Write the prototype for a member function of `Pet` that overloads the = operator.

14.15   Assume that `dog` and `cat` are instances of the `Pet` class, which has overloaded the = operator. Rewrite the following statement so it appears in function call notation instead of operator notation:

        `dog = cat;`

14.16   What is the disadvantage of an overloaded = operator returning `void`?

14.17   Describe the purpose of the `this` pointer.

14.18   The `this` pointer is automatically passed to what type of functions?

14.19   Assume there is a class named `Animal` that overloads the = and + operators. In the following statement, assume `cat`, `tiger`, and `wildcat` are all instances of the `Animal` class:

        `wildcat = cat + tiger;`

        Of the three objects, `wildcat`, `cat`, or `tiger`, which is calling the `operator+` function? Which object is passed as an argument into the function?

14.20   What does the use of a dummy parameter in a unary operator function indicate to the compiler?

Overloading Relational Operators

In addition to the assignment and math operators, relational operators may be overloaded. This capability allows classes to be compared in statements that use relational expressions such as:

```
if (distance1 < distance2)
{
    ... code ...
}
```

Overloaded relational operators are implemented like other binary operators. The only difference is that a relational operator function should always return a `true` or `false` value. The `FeetInches` class in the Student Source Code Folder `Chapter 14\FeetInches Version 3` contains functions to overload the >, <, and == relational operators. Here is the function for overloading the > operator:

```
bool FeetInches::operator > (const FeetInches &right)
{
    bool status;

    if (feet > right.feet)
        status = true;
    else if (feet == right.feet && inches > right.inches)
        status = true;
    else
        status = false;

    return status;
}
```

As you can see, the function compares the feet member (and if necessary, the inches member) with that of the parameter. If the calling object contains a value greater than that of the parameter, true is returned. Otherwise, false is returned.

Here is the code that overloads the < operator:

```
bool FeetInches::operator < (const FeetInches &right)
{
   bool status;

   if (feet < right.feet)
      status = true;
   else if (feet == right.feet && inches < right.inches)
      status = true;
   else
      status = false;

   return status;
}
```

Here is the code that overloads the == operator:

```
bool FeetInches::operator == (const FeetInches &right)
{
   bool status;

   if (feet == right.feet && inches == right.inches)
      status = true;
   else
      status = false;

   return status;
}
```

Program 14-10 demonstrates these overloaded operators. (This file is also stored in the Student Source Code Folder Chapter 14\FeetInches Version 3.)

Program 14-10

```
 1  // This program demonstrates the FeetInches class's overloaded
 2  // relational operators.
 3  #include <iostream>
 4  #include "FeetInches.h"
 5  using namespace std;
 6
 7  int main()
 8  {
 9     int feet, inches;  // To hold input for feet and inches
10
11     // Create two FeetInches objects. The default arguments
12     // for the constructor will be used.
13     FeetInches first, second;
14
15     // Get a distance from the user.
16     cout << "Enter a distance in feet and inches: ";
17     cin >> feet >> inches;
18
```

(program continues)

Program 14-10   *(continued)*

```
19        // Store the distance in first.
20        first.setFeet(feet);
21        first.setInches(inches);
22
23        // Get another distance.
24        cout << "Enter another distance in feet and inches: ";
25        cin >> feet >> inches;
26
27        // Store the distance in second.
28        second.setFeet(feet);
29        second.setInches(inches);
30
31        // Compare the two objects.
32        if (first == second)
33           cout << "first is equal to second.\n";
34        if (first > second)
35           cout << "first is greater than second.\n";
36        if (first < second)
37           cout << "first is less than second.\n";
38
39        return 0;
40   }
```

Program Output with Example Input Shown in Bold
Enter a distance in feet and inches: **6 5 [Enter]**
Enter another distance in feet and inches: **3 10 [Enter]**
first is greater than second.

Program Output with Different Example Input Shown in Bold
Enter a distance in feet and inches: **5 5 [Enter]**
Enter another distance in feet and inches: **5 5 [Enter]**
first is equal to second.

Program Output with Different Example Input Shown in Bold
Enter a distance in feet and inches: **3 4 [Enter]**
Enter another distance in feet and inches: **3 7 [Enter]**
first is less than second.

Overloading the << and >> Operators

Overloading the math and relational operators gives you the ability to write those types of expressions with class objects just as naturally as with integers, floats, and other built-in data types. If an object's primary data members are private, however, you still have to make explicit member function calls to send their values to cout. For example, assume distance is a FeetInches object. The following statements display its internal values:

```
cout << distance.getFeet() << " feet, ";
cout << distance.getInches() << "inches";
```

It is also necessary to explicitly call member functions to set a FeetInches object's data. For instance, the following statements set the distance object to user-specified values:

```
cout << "Enter a value in feet: ";
cin >> f;
distance.setFeet(f);
cout << "Enter a value in inches: ";
cin >> i;
distance.setInches(i);
```

By overloading the stream insertion operator (<<), you could send the `distance` object to `cout`, as shown in the following code, and have the screen output automatically formatted in the correct way.

```
cout << distance;
```

Likewise, by overloading the stream extraction operator (>>), the `distance` object could take values directly from `cin`, as shown here.

```
cin >> distance;
```

Overloading these operators is done in a slightly different way, however, than overloading other operators. These operators are actually part of the `ostream` and `istream` classes defined in the C++ runtime library. (The `cout` and `cin` objects are instances of `ostream` and `istream`.) You must write operator functions to overload the `ostream` version of `<<` and the `istream` version of `>>`, so they work directly with a class such as `FeetInches`. The `FeetInches` class in the Student Source Code Folder `Chapter 14\FeetInches Version 4` contains functions to overload the `<<` and `>>` operators. Here is the function that overloads the `<<` operator:

```
ostream &operator << (ostream &strm, const FeetInches &obj)
{
    strm << obj.feet << " feet, " << obj.inches << " inches";
    return strm;
}
```

Notice the function has two parameters: an `ostream` reference object and a `const FeetInches` reference object. The `ostream` parameter will be a reference to the actual `ostream` object on the left side of the `<<` operator. The second parameter is a reference to a `FeetInches` object. This parameter will reference the object on the right side of the `<<` operator. This function tells C++ how to handle any expression that has the following form:

```
ostreamObject << FeetInchesObject
```

So, when C++ encounters the following statement, it will call the overloaded `operator<<` function:

```
cout << distance;
```

Notice that the function's return type is `ostream &`. This means that the function returns a reference to an `ostream` object. When the `return strm;` statement executes, it doesn't return a copy of `strm`, but a reference to it. This allows you to chain together several expressions using the overloaded `<<` operator, such as:

```
cout << distance1 << " " << distance2 << endl;
```

Here is the function that overloads the stream extraction operator to work with the `FeetInches` class:

```
istream &operator >> (istream &strm, FeetInches &obj)
{
   // Prompt the user for the feet.
   cout << "Feet: ";
   strm >> obj.feet;

   // Prompt the user for the inches.
   cout << "Inches: ";
   strm >> obj.inches;

   // Normalize the values.
   obj.simplify();

   return strm;
}
```

The same principles hold true for this operator. It tells C++ how to handle any expression in the following form:

> *istreamObject* >> *FeetInchesObject*

Once again, the function returns a reference to an `istream` object so several of these expressions may be chained together.

You have probably realized that neither of these functions is quite ready to work, though. Both functions attempt to directly access the `FeetInches` object's private members. Because the functions aren't themselves members of the `FeetInches` class, they don't have this type of access. The next step is to make the operator functions friends of `FeetInches`. This is shown in the following listing of the `FeetInches` class declaration. (This file is stored in the Student Source Code Folder `Chapter 14\FeetInches Version 4`.)

> **NOTE:** Some compilers require you to prototype the `>>` and `<<` operator functions outside the class. For this reason, we have added the following statements to the `FeetInches.h` class specification file.
>
> ```
> class FeetInches;                        // Forward Declaration
>
> // Function Prototypes for Overloaded Stream Operators
> ostream &operator << (ostream &, const FeetInches &);
> istream &operator >> (istream &, FeetInches &);
> ```

Contents of `FeetInches.h` (Version 4)

```
 1   #ifndef FEETINCHES_H
 2   #define FEETINCHES_H
 3
 4   #include <iostream>
 5   using namespace std;
 6
 7   class FeetInches; // Forward Declaration
 8
 9   // Function Prototypes for Overloaded Stream Operators
10   ostream &operator << (ostream &, const FeetInches &);
11   istream &operator >> (istream &, FeetInches &);
```

```
12
13   // The FeetInches class holds distances or measurements
14   // expressed in feet and inches.
15
16   class FeetInches
17   {
18   private:
19      int feet;         // To hold a number of feet
20      int inches;       // To hold a number of inches
21      void simplify();  // Defined in FeetInches.cpp
22   public:
23      // Constructor
24      FeetInches(int f = 0, int i = 0)
25         { feet = f;
26           inches = i;
27           simplify(); }
28
29      // Mutator functions
30      void setFeet(int f)
31         { feet = f; }
32
33      void setInches(int i)
34         { inches = i;
35           simplify(); }
36
37      // Accessor functions
38      int getFeet() const
39         { return feet; }
40
41      int getInches() const
42         { return inches; }
43
44      // Overloaded operator functions
45      FeetInches operator + (const FeetInches &); // Overloaded +
46      FeetInches operator - (const FeetInches &); // Overloaded -
47      FeetInches operator ++ ();              // Prefix ++
48      FeetInches operator ++ (int);           // Postfix ++
49      bool operator > (const FeetInches &);    // Overloaded >
50      bool operator < (const FeetInches &);    // Overloaded <
51      bool operator == (const FeetInches &);   // Overloaded ==
52
53      // Friends
54      friend ostream &operator << (ostream &, const FeetInches &);
55      friend istream &operator >> (istream &, FeetInches &);
56   };
57
58   #endif
```

Lines 54 and 55 in the class declaration tell C++ to make the overloaded << and >> operator functions friends of the FeetInches class:

```
friend ostream &operator<<(ostream &, const FeetInches &);
friend istream &operator>>(istream &, FeetInches &);
```

These statements give the operator functions direct access to the FeetInches class's private members. Program 14-11 demonstrates how the overloaded operators work. (This file is also stored in the Student Source Code Folder Chapter 14\FeetInches Version 4.)

Program 14-11

```
 1  // This program demonstrates the << and >> operators,
 2  // overloaded to work with the FeetInches class.
 3  #include <iostream>
 4  #include "FeetInches.h"
 5  using namespace std;
 6
 7  int main()
 8  {
 9     FeetInches first, second;  // Define two objects.
10
11     // Get a distance for the first object.
12     cout << "Enter a distance in feet and inches.\n";
13     cin >> first;
14
15     // Get a distance for the second object.
16     cout << "Enter another distance in feet and inches.\n";
17     cin >> second;
18
19     // Display the values in the objects.
20     cout << "The values you entered are:\n";
21     cout << first << " and " << second << endl;
22     return 0;
23  }
```

Program Output with Example Input Shown in Bold
```
Enter a distance in feet and inches.
Feet: 6 [Enter]
Inches: 5 [Enter]
Enter another distance in feet and inches.
Feet: 3 [Enter]
Inches: 10 [Enter]
The values you entered are:
6 feet, 5 inches and 3 feet, 10 inches
```

Overloading the [] Operator

In addition to the traditional operators, C++ allows you to change the way the [] symbols work. This gives you the ability to write classes that have array-like behaviors. For example, the string class overloads the [] operator so you can access the individual characters stored in string class objects. Assume the following definition exists in a program:

```
string name = "William";
```

The first character in the string, 'W,' is stored at name[0], so the following statement will display W on the screen.

```
cout << name[0];
```

You can use the overloaded [ ] operator to create an array class, like the following one. The class behaves like a regular array, but performs the bounds-checking that C++ lacks.

Contents of `IntArray.h`

```
 1   // Specification file for the IntArray class
 2   #ifndef INTARRAY_H
 3   #define INTARRAY_H
 4
 5   class IntArray
 6   {
 7   private:
 8      int *aptr;                    // Pointer to the array
 9      int arraySize;                // Holds the array size
10      void subscriptError();        // Handles invalid subscripts
11   public:
12      IntArray(int);                // Constructor
13      IntArray(const IntArray &);   // Copy constructor
14      ~IntArray();                  // Destructor
15
16      int size() const              // Returns the array size
17         { return arraySize; }
18
19      int &operator[](const int &); // Overloaded [] operator
20   };
21   #endif
```

Contents of `IntArray.cpp`

```
 1   // Implementation file for the IntArray class
 2   #include <iostream>
 3   #include <cstdlib>   // For the exit function
 4   #include "IntArray.h"
 5   using namespace std;
 6
 7   //*******************************************************
 8   // Constructor for IntArray class. Sets the size of the *
 9   // array and allocates memory for it.                   *
10   //*******************************************************
11
12   IntArray::IntArray(int s)
13   {
14      arraySize = s;
15      aptr = new int [s];
16      for (int count = 0; count < arraySize; count++)
17         *(aptr + count) = 0;
18   }
19
20   //*******************************************************
21   // Copy Constructor for IntArray class.                 *
22   //*******************************************************
23
```

```
24    IntArray::IntArray(const IntArray &obj)
25    {
26       arraySize = obj.arraySize;
27       aptr = new int [arraySize];
28       for(int count = 0; count < arraySize; count++)
29          *(aptr + count) = *(obj.aptr + count);
30    }
31
32    //*****************************************************
33    // Destructor for IntArray class.                    *
34    //*****************************************************
35
36    IntArray::~IntArray()
37    {
38       if (arraySize > 0)
39          delete [] aptr;
40    }
41
42    //********************************************************
43    // subscriptError function. Displays an error message and   *
44    // terminates the program when a subscript is out of range. *
45    //********************************************************
46
47    void IntArray::subscriptError()
48    {
49       cout << "ERROR: Subscript out of range.\n";
50       exit(0);
51    }
52
53    //*****************************************************
54    // Overloaded [] operator. The argument is a subscript. *
55    // This function returns a reference to the element     *
56    // in the array indexed by the subscript.               *
57    //*****************************************************
58
59    int &IntArray::operator[](const int &sub)
60    {
61       if (sub < 0 || sub >= arraySize)
62          subscriptError();
63       return aptr[sub];
64    }
```

Before focusing on the overloaded operator, let's look at the constructors and the destructor. The code for the first constructor in lines 12 through 18 of the `IntArray.cpp` file follows:

```
IntArray::IntArray(int s)
{
   arraySize = s;
   aptr = new int [s];
   for (int count = 0; count < arraySize; count++)
      *(aptr + count) = 0;
}
```

When an instance of the class is defined, the number of elements the array is to have is passed into the constructor's parameter, s. This value is copied to the `arraySize` member, and then used to dynamically allocate enough memory for the array. The constructor's final step is to store zeros in all of the array's elements:

```
for (int count = 0; count < arraySize; count++)
    *(aptr + count) = 0;
```

The class also has a copy constructor in lines 24 through 30, which is used when a class object is initialized with another object's data:

```
IntArray::IntArray(const IntArray &obj)
{
    arraySize = obj.arraySize;
    aptr = new int [arraySize];
    for(int count = 0; count < arraySize; count++)
        *(aptr + count) = *(obj.aptr + count);
}
```

A reference to the initializing object is passed into the parameter obj. Once the memory is successfully allocated for the array, the constructor copies all the values in obj's array into the calling object's array.

The destructor, in lines 36 through 40, simply frees the memory allocated by the class's constructors. First, however, it checks the value in arraySize to be sure the array has at least one element:

```
IntArray::~IntArray()
{
    if (arraySize > 0)
        delete [] aptr;
}
```

The [] operator is overloaded similarly to other operators. The definition of the operator[] function appears in lines 59 through 64:

```
int &IntArray::operator[](const int &sub)
{
    if (sub < 0 || sub >= arraySize)
        subscriptError();
    return aptr[sub];
}
```

The operator[] function can have only a single parameter. The one shown uses a constant reference to an integer. This parameter holds the value placed inside the brackets in an expression. For example, if table is an IntArray object, the number 12 will be passed into the sub parameter in the following statement:

```
cout << table[12];
```

Inside the function, the value in the sub parameter is tested by the following if statement:

```
if (sub < 0 || sub >= arraySize)
    subscriptError();
```

This statement determines whether sub is within the range of the array's subscripts. If sub is less than 0 or greater than or equal to arraySize, it's not a valid subscript, so the subscriptError function is called. If sub is within range, the function uses it as an offset into the array, and returns a reference to the value stored at that location.

One critically important aspect of the function above is its return type. It's crucial that the function return not simply an integer, but a *reference* to an integer. The reason for this is that expressions such as the following must be possible:

```
table[5] = 27;
```

Remember, the built-in = operator requires the object on its left to be an lvalue. An lvalue must represent a modifiable memory location, such as a variable. The integer return value of a function is not an lvalue. If the operator[] function merely returns an integer, it cannot be used to create expressions placed on the left side of an assignment operator.

A reference to an integer, however, is an lvalue. If the operator[] function returns a reference, it can be used to create expressions like the following:

```
table[7] = 52;
```

In this statement, the operator[] function is called with 7 passed as its argument. Assuming 7 is within range, the function returns a reference to the integer stored at (aptr + 7). In essence, the statement above is equivalent to:

```
*(aptr + 7) = 52;
```

Because the operator[] function returns actual integers stored in the array, it is not necessary for math or relational operators to be overloaded. Even the stream operators << and >> will work just as they are with the IntArray class.

Program 14-12 demonstrates how the class works.

Program 14-12

```
 1   // This program demonstrates an overloaded [] operator.
 2   #include <iostream>
 3   #include "IntArray.h"
 4   using namespace std;
 5
 6   int main()
 7   {
 8      const int SIZE = 10;   // Array size
 9
10      // Define an IntArray with 10 elements.
11      IntArray table(SIZE);
12
13      // Store values in the array.
14      for (int x = 0; x < SIZE; x++)
15         table[x] = (x * 2);
16
17      // Display the values in the array.
18      for (int x = 0; x < SIZE; x++)
19         cout << table[x] << " ";
20      cout << endl;
21
22      // Use the standard + operator on array elements.
23      for (int x = 0; x < SIZE; x++)
24         table[x] = table[x] + 5;
25
```

```
26        // Display the values in the array.
27        for (int x = 0; x < SIZE; x++)
28           cout << table[x] << " ";
29        cout << endl;
30
31        // Use the standard ++ operator on array elements.
32        for (int x = 0; x < SIZE; x++)
33           table[x]++;
34
35        // Display the values in the array.
36        for (int x = 0; x < SIZE; x++)
37           cout << table[x] << " ";
38        cout << endl;
39
40        return 0;
41    }
```

Program Output
```
0 2 4 6 8 10 12 14 16 18
5 7 9 11 13 15 17 19 21 23
6 8 10 12 14 16 18 20 22 24
```

Program 14-13 demonstrates the IntArray class's bounds-checking capability.

Program 14-13

```
1  // This program demonstrates the IntArray class's bounds-checking ability.
2  #include <iostream>
3  #include "IntArray.h"
4  using namespace std;
5
6  int main()
7  {
8     const int SIZE = 10;   // Array size
9
10    // Define an IntArray with 10 elements.
11    IntArray table(SIZE);
12
13    // Store values in the array.
14    for (int x = 0; x < SIZE; x++)
15       table[x] = x;
16
17    // Display the values in the array.
18    for (int x = 0; x < SIZE; x++)
19       cout << table[x] << " ";
20    cout << endl;
21
22    // Attempt to use an invalid subscript.
23    cout << "Now attempting to use an invalid subscript.\n";
24    table[SIZE + 1] = 0;
25    return 0;
26 }
```

(program output continues)

Program 14-13   *(continued)*

Program Output
```
0 1 2 3 4 5 6 7 8 9
Now attempting to use an invalid subscript.
ERROR: Subscript out of range.
```

 Checkpoint

 myprogramminglab *www.myprogramminglab.com*

14.21   Describe the values that should be returned from functions that overload relational operators.

14.22   What is the advantage of overloading the << and >> operators?

14.23   What type of object should an overloaded << operator function return?

14.24   What type of object should an overloaded >> operator function return?

14.25   If an overloaded << or >> operator accesses a private member of a class, what must be done in that class's declaration?

14.26   Assume the class `NumList` has overloaded the `[ ]` operator. In the expression below, `list1` is an instance of the `NumList` class:

```
list1[25]
```

Rewrite the expression above to explicitly call the function that overloads the `[ ]` operator.

14.6 Object Conversion

CONCEPT: Special operator functions may be written to convert a class object to any other type.

As you've already seen, operator functions allow classes to work more like built-in data types. Another capability that operator functions can give classes is automatic type conversion.

Data type conversion happens "behind the scenes" with the built-in data types. For instance, suppose a program uses the following variables:

```
int i;
double d;
```

The statement below automatically converts the value in `i` to a floating-point number and stores it in `d`:

```
d = i;
```

Likewise, the following statement converts the value in `d` to an integer (truncating the fractional part) and stores it in `i`:

```
i = d;
```

The same functionality can also be given to class objects. For example, assuming `distance` is a `FeetInches` object and `d` is a `double`, the following statement would conveniently convert `distance`'s value into a floating-point number and store it in `d`, if `FeetInches` is properly written:

```
d = distance;
```

To be able to use a statement such as this, an operator function must be written to perform the conversion. The Student Source Code Folder `Chapter 14\FeetInches Version 5` contains a version of the `FeetInches` class with such an operator function. Here is the code for the operator function that converts a `FeetInches` object to a `double`:

```
FeetInches::operator double()
{
    double temp = feet;

    temp += (inches / 12.0);
    return temp;
}
```

This function contains an algorithm that will calculate the decimal equivalent of a feet and inches measurement. For example, the value 4 feet 6 inches will be converted to 4.5. This value is stored in the local variable `temp`. The `temp` variable is then returned.

 NOTE: No return type is specified in the function header. Because the function is a `FeetInches-to-double` conversion function, it will always return a `double`. Also, because the function takes no arguments, there are no parameters.

The revised `FeetInches` class also has an operator function that converts a `FeetInches` object to an `int`. The function, shown here, simply returns the `feet` member, thus truncating the `inches` value:

```
FeetInches:: operator int()
{
    return feet;
}
```

Program 14-14 demonstrates both of these conversion functions. (This file is also stored in the Student Source Code Folder `Chapter 14\FeetInches Version 5`.)

Program 14-14

```
 1  // This program demonstrates the FeetInches class's
 2  // conversion functions.
 3  #include <iostream>
 4  #include "FeetInches.h"
 5  using namespace std;
 6
 7  int main()
 8  {
 9      double d;  // To hold double input
10      int i;     // To hold int input
11
```

(program continues)

Program 14-14   (continued)

```
12      // Define a FeetInches object.
13      FeetInches distance;
14
15      // Get a distance from the user.
16      cout << "Enter a distance in feet and inches:\n";
17      cin >> distance;
18
19      // Convert the distance object to a double.
20      d = distance;
21
22      // Convert the distance object to an int.
23      i = distance;
24
25      // Display the values.
26      cout << "The value " << distance;
27      cout << " is equivalent to " << d << " feet\n";
28      cout << "or " << i << " feet, rounded down.\n";
29      return 0;
30  }
```

Program Output with Example Input Shown in Bold
```
Enter a distance in feet and inches:
Feet: 8 [Enter]
Inches: 6 [Enter]
The value 8 feet, 6 inches is equivalent to 8.5 feet
or 8 feet, rounded down.
```

See the Case Study on Creating a String Class for another example. You can download the case study from the book's companion Web site at www.pearsonhighered.com/gaddis.

Checkpoint

myprogramminglab *www.myprogramminglab.com*

14.27   When overloading a binary operator such as + or −, what object is passed into the operator function's parameter?

14.28   Explain why overloaded prefix and postfix ++ and -- operator functions should return a value.

14.29   How does C++ tell the difference between an overloaded prefix and postfix ++ or -- operator function?

14.30   Write member functions of the FeetInches class that overload the prefix and postfix -- operators. Demonstrate the functions in a simple program similar to Program 14-14.

14.7 Aggregation

14.7

CONCEPT: Aggregation occurs when a class contains an instance of another class.

VideoNote

Class Aggregation

In real life, objects are frequently made of other objects. A house, for example, is made of door objects, window objects, wall objects, and much more. It is the combination of all these objects that makes a house object.

When designing software, it sometimes makes sense to create an object from other objects. For example, suppose you need an object to represent a course that you are taking in college. You decide to create a Course class, which will hold the following information:

- The course name
- The instructor's last name, first name, and office number
- The textbook's title, author, and publisher

In addition to the course name, the class will hold items related to the instructor and the textbook. You could put attributes for each of these items in the Course class. However, a good design principle is to separate related items into their own classes. In this example, an Instructor class could be created to hold the instructor-related data and a TextBook class could be created to hold the textbook-related data. Instances of these classes could then be used as attributes in the Course class.

Let's take a closer look at how this might be done. To keep things simple, the Instructor class will have only the following functions:

- A default constructor that assigns empty strings to the instructor's last name, first name, and office number.
- A constructor that accepts arguments for the instructor's last name, first name, and office number
- A set function that can be used to set all of the class's attributes
- A print function that displays the object's attribute values

The code for the Instructor class is shown here:

Contents of `Instructor.h`

```
 1  #ifndef INSTRUCTOR
 2  #define INSTRUCTOR
 3  #include <iostream>
 4  #include <string>
 5  using namespace std;
 6
 7  // Instructor class
 8  class Instructor
 9  {
10  private:
11     string lastName;     // Last name
12     string firstName;    // First name
13     string officeNumber; // Office number
14  public:
15     // The default constructor stores empty strings
16     // in the string objects.
```

```
17       Instructor()
18          { set("", "", ""); }
19
20       // Constructor
21       Instructor(string lname, string fname, string office)
22          { set(lname, fname, office); }
23
24       // set function
25       void set(string lname, string fname, string office)
26          { lastName = lname;
27            firstName = fname;
28            officeNumber = office; }
29
30       // print function
31       void print() const
32          { cout << "Last name: " << lastName << endl;
33            cout << "First name: " << firstName << endl;
34            cout << "Office number: " << officeNumber << endl; }
35    };
36    #endif
```

The code for the `TextBook` class is shown next. As before, we want to keep the class simple. The only functions it has are a default constructor, a constructor that accepts arguments, a `set` function, and a `print` function.

Contents of `TextBook.h`

```
1    #ifndef TEXTBOOK
2    #define TEXTBOOK
3    #include <iostream>
4    #include <string>
5    using namespace std;
6
7    // TextBook class
8    class TextBook
9    {
10   private:
11       string title;      // Book title
12       string author;     // Author name
13       string publisher;  // Publisher name
14   public:
15       // The default constructor stores empty strings
16       // in the string objects.
17       TextBook()
18          { set("", "", ""); }
19
20       // Constructor
21       TextBook(string textTitle, string auth, string pub)
22          { set(textTitle, auth, pub); }
23
24       // set function
25       void set(string textTitle, string auth, string pub)
26          { title = textTitle;
27            author = auth;
28            publisher = pub; }
29
```

```
30      // print function
31      void print() const
32          {  cout << "Title: " << title << endl;
33             cout << "Author: " << author << endl;
34             cout << "Publisher: " << publisher << endl; }
35  };
36  #endif
```

The `Course` class is shown next. Notice that the `Course` class has an `Instructor` object and a `TextBook` object as member variables. Those objects are used as attributes of the `Course` object. Making an instance of one class an attribute of another class is called *object aggregation*. The word *aggregate* means "a whole that is made of constituent parts." In this example, the `Course` class is an aggregate class because an instance of it is made of constituent objects.

When an instance of one class is a member of another class, it is said that there is a "has a" relationship between the classes. For example, the relationships that exist among the `Course`, `Instructor`, and `TextBook` classes can be described as follows:

- The course *has an* instructor.
- The course *has a* textbook.

The "has a" relationship is sometimes called a *whole–part relationship* because one object is part of a greater whole.

Contents of `Course.h`

```
1   #ifndef COURSE
2   #define COURSE
3   #include <iostream>
4   #include <string>
5   #include "Instructor.h"
6   #include "TextBook.h"
7   using namespace std;
8
9   class Course
10  {
11  private:
12      string courseName;      // Course name
13      Instructor instructor;  // Instructor
14      TextBook textbook;      // Textbook
15  public:
16      // Constructor
17      Course(string course, string instrLastName,
18             string instrFirstName, string instrOffice,
19             string textTitle, string author,
20             string publisher)
21        {  // Assign the course name.
22          courseName = course;
23
24          // Assign the instructor.
25          instructor.set(instrLastName, instrFirstName, instrOffice);
26
27          // Assign the textbook.
28          textbook.set(textTitle, author, publisher); }
29
```

```
30        // print function
31        void print() const
32        { cout << "Course name: " << courseName << endl << endl;
33          cout << "Instructor Information:\n";
34          instructor.print();
35          cout << "\nTextbook Information:\n";
36          textbook.print();
37          cout << endl; }
38     };
39     #endif
```

Program 14-15 demonstrates the Course class.

Program 14-15

```
1   // This program demonstrates the Course class.
2   #include "Course.h"
3
4   int main()
5   {
6      // Create a Course object.
7      Course myCourse("Intro to Computer Science", // Course name
8         "Kramer", "Shawn", "RH3010",          // Instructor info
9         "Starting Out with C++", "Gaddis", // Textbook title and author
10        "Addison-Wesley");                   // Textbook publisher
11
12     // Display the course info.
13     myCourse.print();
14     return 0;
15  }
```

Program Output
```
Course name: Intro to Computer Science

Instructor Information:
Last name: Kramer
First name: Shawn
Office number: RH3010

Textbook Information:
Title: Starting Out with C++
Author: Gaddis
Publisher: Addison-Wesley
```

Aggregation in UML Diagrams

In Chapter 13 you were introduced to the Unified Modeling Language (UML) as a tool for designing classes. You show aggregation in a UML diagram by connecting two classes with a line that has an open diamond at one end. The diamond is closest to the class that is the aggregate. Figure 14-5 shows a UML diagram depicting the relationship between the Course, Instructor, and TextBook classes. The open diamond is closest to the Course class because it is the aggregate (the whole).

Figure 14-5

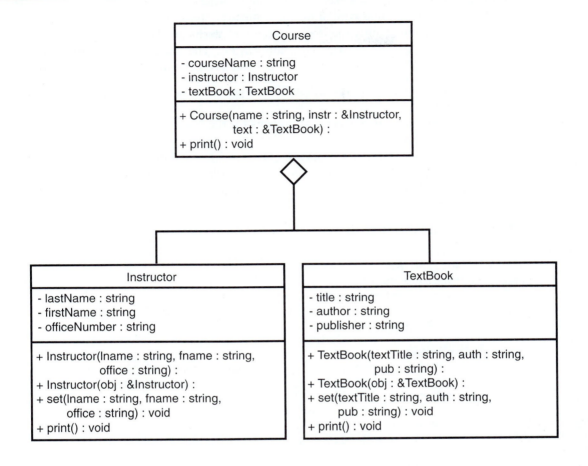

14.8 Focus on Object-Oriented Design: Class Collaborations

CONCEPT: It is common for classes to interact, or collaborate, with one another to perform their operations. Part of the object-oriented design process is identifying the collaborations between classes.

In an object-oriented application it is common for objects of different classes to collaborate. This simply means that objects interact with each other. Sometimes one object will need the services of another object in order to fulfill its responsibilities. For example, let's say an object needs to read a number from the keyboard and then format the number to appear as a dollar amount. The object might use the services of the cin object to read the number from the keyboard, and then use the services of another object that is designed to format the number.

If one object is to collaborate with another object, then it must know something about the other object's member functions and how to call them. Let's look at an example.

The following code shows a class named `Stock`. An object of this class holds data about a company's stock. This class has two attributes: `symbol` and `sharePrice`. The `symbol` attribute holds the trading symbol for the company's stock. This is a short series of characters that are used to identify the stock on the stock exchange. For example, the XYZ Company's stock might have the trading symbol XYZ. The `sharePrice` attribute holds the current price per share of the stock. The class also has the following member functions:

- A default constructor that initializes `symbol` to an empty string and `sharePrice` to 0.0.
- A constructor that accepts arguments for the symbol and share price.
- A copy constructor
- A `set` function that accepts arguments for the symbol and share price.
- A `getSymbol` function that returns the stock's trading symbol.
- A `getSharePrice` function that returns the current price of the stock.

Contents of `Stock.h`

```
 1   #ifndef STOCK
 2   #define STOCK
 3   #include <string>
 4   using namespace std;
 5
 6   class Stock
 7   {
 8   private:
 9       string symbol;       // Trading symbol of the stock
10       double sharePrice;   // Current price per share
11   public:
12       // Default constructor
13       Stock()
14           { set("", 0.0); }
15
16       // Constructor
17       Stock(const string sym, double price)
18           { set(sym, price); }
19
20       // Copy constructor
21       Stock(const Stock &obj)
22           { set(obj.symbol, obj.sharePrice); }
23
24       // Mutator function
25       void set(string sym, double price)
26           { symbol = sym;
27             sharePrice = price; }
28
29       // Accessor functions
30       string getSymbol() const
31           { return symbol; }
32
33       double getSharePrice() const
34           { return sharePrice; }
35   };
36   #endif
```

The following code shows another class named `StockPurchase` that uses an object of the `Stock` class to simulate the purchase of a stock. The `StockPurchase` class is responsible for calculating the cost of the stock purchase. To do that, the `StockPurchase` class must know how to call the `Stock` class's `getSharePrice` function to get the price per share of the stock.

Contents of `StockPurchase.h`

```
1   #ifndef STOCK_PURCHASE
2   #define STOCK_PURCHASE
3   #include "Stock.h"
4
5   class StockPurchase
6   {
7   private:
8      Stock stock;   // The stock that was purchased
9      int shares;    // The number of shares
10  public:
11     // The default constructor sets shares to 0. The stock
12     // object is initialized by its default constructor.
13     StockPurchase()
14        { shares = 0; }
15
16     // Constructor
17     StockPurchase(const Stock &stockObject, int numShares)
18        { stock = stockObject;
19          shares = numShares; }
20
21     // Accessor function
22     double getCost() const
23        { return shares * stock.getSharePrice(); }
24  };
25  #endif
```

The second constructor for the `StockPurchase` class accepts a `Stock` object representing the stock that is being purchased, and an `int` representing the number of shares to purchase. In line 18 we see the first collaboration: the `StockPurchase` constructor makes a copy of the `Stock` object by using the `Stock` class's copy constructor. The next collaboration takes place in the `getCost` function. This function calculates and returns the cost of the stock purchase. In line 23 it calls the `Stock` class's `getSharePrice` function to determine the stock's price per share. Program 14-16 demonstrates this class.

Program 14-16

```
1   // Stock trader program
2   #include <iostream>
3   #include <iomanip>
4   #include "Stock.h"
5   #include "StockPurchase.h"
6   using namespace std;
7
```

(program continues)

Program 14-16 *(continued)*

```cpp
 8   int main()
 9   {
10      int sharesToBuy;   // Number of shares to buy
11
12      // Create a Stock object for the company stock. The
13      // trading symbol is XYZ and the stock is currently
14      // priced at $9.62 per share.
15      Stock xyzCompany("XYZ", 9.62);
16
17      // Display the symbol and current share price.
18      cout << setprecision(2) << fixed << showpoint;
19      cout << "XYZ Company's trading symbol is "
20           << xyzCompany.getSymbol() << endl;
21      cout << "The stock is currently $"
22           << xyzCompany.getSharePrice()
23           << " per share.\n";
24
25      // Get the number of shares to purchase.
26      cout << "How many shares do you want to buy? ";
27      cin >> sharesToBuy;
28
29      // Create a StockPurchase object for the transaction.
30      StockPurchase buy(xyzCompany, sharesToBuy);
31
32      // Display the cost of the transaction.
33      cout << "The cost of the transaction is $"
34           << buy.getCost() << endl;
35      return 0;
36   }
```

Program Output with Example Input Shown in Bold
```
XYZ Company's trading symbol is XYZ
The stock is currently $9.62 per share.
How many shares do you want to buy? 100 [Enter]
The cost of the transaction is $962.00
```

Determining Class Collaborations with CRC Cards

During the object-oriented design process, you can determine many of the collaborations that will be necessary between classes by examining the responsibilities of the classes. In Chapter 13 we discussed the process of finding the classes and their responsibilities. Recall from that section that a class's responsibilities are

- the things that the class is responsible for knowing
- the actions that the class is responsible for doing

Often you will determine that the class must collaborate with another class in order to fulfill one or more of its responsibilities. One popular method of discovering a class's responsibilities and collaborations is by creating CRC cards. *CRC* stands for class, responsibilities, and collaborations.

You can use simple index cards for this procedure. Once you have gone through the process of finding the classes (which is discussed in Chapter 13), set aside one index card for each class. At the top of the index card, write the name of the class. Divide the rest of the card into two columns. In the left column, write each of the class's responsibilities. As you write each responsibility, think about whether the class needs to collaborate with another class to fulfill that responsibility. Ask yourself questions such as

- Will an object of this class need to get data from another object in order to fulfill this responsibility?
- Will an object of this class need to request another object to perform an operation in order to fulfill this responsibility?

If collaboration is required, write the name of the collaborating class in the right column, next to the responsibility that requires it. If no collaboration is required for a responsibility, simply write "None" in the right column, or leave it blank. Figure 14-6 shows an example CRC card for the `StockPurchase` class.

Figure 14-6

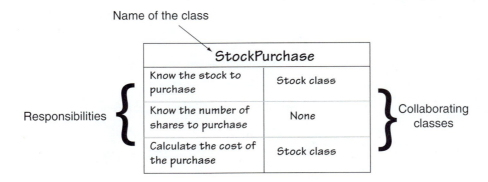

From the CRC card shown in the figure, we can see that the `StockPurchase` class has the following responsibilities and collaborations:

- Responsibility: To know the stock to purchase
  Collaboration: The `Stock` class
- Responsibility: To know the number of shares to purchase
  Collaboration: None
- Responsibility: To calculate the cost of the purchase
  Collaboration: The `Stock` class

When you have completed a CRC card for each class in the application, you will have a good idea of each class's responsibilities and how the classes must interact.

 Checkpoint

myprogramminglab *www.myprogramminglab.com*

14.31 What are the benefits of having operator functions that perform object conversion?

14.32 Why are no return types listed in the prototypes or headers of operator functions that perform data type conversion?

14.33 Assume there is a class named `BlackBox`. Write the header for a member function that converts a `BlackBox` object to an `int`.

14.34 Assume there are two classes, `Big` and `Small`. The `Big` class has, as a member, an instance of the `Small` class. Write a sentence that describes the relationship between the two classes.

Review Questions and Exercises

Short Answer

1. Describe the difference between an instance member variable and a static member variable.

2. Assume that a class named Numbers has the following static member function declaration:

   ```
   static void showTotal();
   ```

   Write a statement that calls the showTotal function.

3. A static member variable is declared in a class. Where is the static member variable defined?

4. What is a friend function?

5. Why is it not always a good idea to make an entire class a friend of another class?

6. What is memberwise assignment?

7. When is a copy constructor called?

8. How can the compiler determine if a constructor is a copy constructor?

9. Describe a situation where memberwise assignment is not desirable.

10. Why must the parameter of a copy constructor be a reference?

11. What is a default copy constructor?

12. Why would a programmer want to overload operators rather than use regular member functions to perform similar operations?

13. What is passed to the parameter of a class's operator= function?

14. Why shouldn't a class's overloaded = operator be implemented with a void operator function?

15. How does the compiler know whether an overloaded ++ operator should be used in prefix or postfix mode?

16. What is the this pointer?

17. What type of value should be returned from an overloaded relational operator function?

18. The class Stuff has both a copy constructor and an overloaded = operator. Assume that blob and clump are both instances of the Stuff class. For each statement below, indicate whether the copy constructor or the overloaded = operator will be called.

    ```
    Stuff blob = clump;
    clump = blob;
    blob.operator=(clump);
    showValues(blob);          // blob is passed by value.
    ```

19. Explain the programming steps necessary to make a class's member variable static.

20. Explain the programming steps necessary to make a class's member function static.

21. Consider the following class declaration:

    ```
    class Thing
    {
    private:
       int x;
    ```

```
        int y;
        static int z;
    public:
        Thing()
            { x = y = z; }
        static void putThing(int a)
            { z = a; }
};
```

Assume a program containing the class declaration defines three Thing objects with the following statement:

```
Thing one, two, three;
```

How many separate instances of the x member exist?

How many separate instances of the y member exist?

How many separate instances of the z member exist?

What value will be stored in the x and y members of each object?

Write a statement that will call the PutThing member function *before* the objects above are defined.

22. Describe the difference between making a class a member of another class (object aggregation), and making a class a friend of another class.

23. What is the purpose of a forward declaration of a class?

24. Explain why memberwise assignment can cause problems with a class that contains a pointer member.

25. Why is a class's copy constructor called when an object of that class is passed by value into a function?

Fill-in-the-Blank

26. If a member variable is declared _____, all objects of that class have access to the same variable.

27. Static member variables are defined _____ the class.

28. A(n) _____ member function cannot access any nonstatic member variables in its own class.

29. A static member function may be called _____ any instances of its class are defined.

30. A(n) _____ function is not a member of a class, but has access to the private members of the class.

31. A(n) _____ tells the compiler that a specific class will be declared later in the program.

32. _____ is the default behavior when an object is assigned the value of another object of the same class.

33. A(n) _____ is a special constructor, called whenever a new object is initialized with another object's data.

34. _____ is a special built-in pointer that is automatically passed as a hidden argument to all nonstatic member functions.

35. An operator may be _____ to work with a specific class.

36. When overloading the _____ operator, its function must have a dummy parameter.

37. Making an instance of one class a member of another class is called _____.

38. Object aggregation is useful for creating a(n) _____ relationship between two classes.

Algorithm Workbench

39. Assume a class named `Bird` exists. Write the header for a member function that overloads the = operator for that class.

40. Assume a class named `Dollars` exists. Write the headers for member functions that overload the prefix and postfix ++ operators for that class.

41. Assume a class named `Yen` exists. Write the header for a member function that overloads the < operator for that class.

42. Assume a class named `Length` exists. Write the header for a member function that overloads cout's << operator for that class.

43. Assume a class named `Collection` exists. Write the header for a member function that overloads the `[ ]` operator for that class.

True or False

44. T   F   Static member variables cannot be accessed by nonstatic member functions.

45. T   F   Static member variables are defined outside their class declaration.

46. T   F   A static member function may refer to nonstatic member variables of the same class, but only after an instance of the class has been defined.

47. T   F   When a function is declared a `friend` by a class, it becomes a member of that class.

48. T   F   A `friend` function has access to the private members of the class declaring it a `friend`.

49. T   F   An entire class may be declared a `friend` of another class.

50. T   F   In order for a function or class to become a friend of another class, it must be declared as such by the class granting it access.

51. T   F   If a class has a pointer as a member, it's a good idea to also have a copy constructor.

52. T   F   You cannot use the = operator to assign one object's values to another object, unless you overload the operator.

53. T   F   If a class doesn't have a copy constructor, the compiler generates a default copy constructor for it.

54. T   F   If a class has a copy constructor, and an object of that class is passed by value into a function, the function's parameter will *not* call its copy constructor.

55. T   F   The `this` pointer is passed to static member functions.

56. T   F   All functions that overload unary operators must have a dummy parameter.

57. T   F   For an object to perform automatic type conversion, an operator function must be written.

58. T   F   It is possible to have an instance of one class as a member of another class.

Find the Error

Each of the following class declarations has errors. Locate as many as you can.

59.
```
class Box
{
    private:
        double width;
        double length;
        double height;
    public:
        Box(double w, l, h)
            { width = w; length = l; height = h; }
        Box(Box b) // Copy constructor
            { width = b.width;
              length = b.length;
              height = b.height; }

        ... Other member functions follow ...
};
```

60.
```
class Circle
{
    private:
        double diameter;
        int centerX;
        int centerY;
    public:
        Circle(double d, int x, int y)
            { diameter = d; centerX = x; centerY = y; }
        // Overloaded = operator
        void Circle=(Circle &right)
            { diameter = right.diameter;
              centerX = right.centerX;
              centerY = right.centerY; }

            ... Other member functions follow ...
        };
```

61.
```
class Point
{
    private:
        int xCoord;
        int yCoord;
    public:
        Point (int x, int y)
            { xCoord = x; yCoord = y; }
        // Overloaded + operator
        void operator+(const &Point right)
            { xCoord += right.xCoord;
              yCoord += right.yCoord;
            }

        ... Other member functions follow ...
};
```

```
62. class Box
    {
        private:
           double width;
           double length;
           double height;
        public:
           Box(double w, l, h)
              { width = w; length = l; height = h; }
           // Overloaded prefix ++ operator
           void operator++()
              {    ++width; ++length; }
           // Overloaded postfix ++ operator
           void operator++()
              {    width++; length++; }

        ... Other member functions follow ...
    };
63. class Yard
    {
        private:
           float length;
        public:
           yard(float l)
              { length = l; }
           // float conversion function
           void operator float()
              { return length; }

        ... Other member functions follow ...
    };
```

Programming Challenges

Visit www.myprogramminglab.com to complete many of these Programming Challenges online and get instant feedback.

1. **Numbers** Class

   Design a class `Numbers` that can be used to translate whole dollar amounts in the range 0 through 9999 into an English description of the number. For example, the number 713 would be translated into the string *seven hundred thirteen*, and 8203 would be translated into *eight thousand two hundred three*. The class should have a single integer member variable:

   ```
   int number;
   ```

   and a static array of `string` objects that specify how to translate key dollar amounts into the desired format. For example, you might use static strings such as

   ```
   string lessThan20[20] = {"zero", "one", ..., "eighteen", "nineteen"};
   string hundred = "hundred";
   string thousand = "thousand";
   ```

   The class should have a constructor that accepts a nonnegative integer and uses it to initialize the `Numbers` object. It should have a member function `print()` that prints the English description of the `Numbers` object. Demonstrate the class by writing a main program that asks the user to enter a number in the proper range and then prints out its English description.

2. **Day of the Year**

Assuming that a year has 365 days, write a class named DayOfYear that takes an integer representing a day of the year and translates it to a string consisting of the month followed by day of the month. For example,

Day 2 would be *January 2.*
Day 32 would be *February 1.*
Day 365 would be *December 31.*

The constructor for the class should take as parameter an integer representing the day of the year, and the class should have a member function print() that prints the day in the month–day format. The class should have an integer member variable to represent the day, and should have static member variables holding string objects that can be used to assist in the translation from the integer format to the month-day format.

Test your class by inputting various integers representing days and printing out their representation in the month–day format.

3. **Day of the Year Modification**

Modify the DayOfYear class, written in Programming Challenge 2, to add a constructor that takes two parameters: a string object representing a month and an integer in the range 0 through 31 representing the day of the month. The constructor should then initialize the integer member of the class to represent the day specified by the month and day of month parameters. The constructor should terminate the program with an appropriate error message if the number entered for a day is outside the range of days for the month given.

Add the following overloaded operators:

++   **prefix and postfix increment operators.** These operators should modify the DayOfYear object so that it represents the next day. If the day is already the end of the year, the new value of the object will represent the first day of the year.

--   **prefix and postfix decrement operators.** These operators should modify the DayOfYear object so that it represents the previous day. If the day is already the first day of the year, the new value of the object will represent the last day of the year.

4. **NumDays Class**

VideoNote

Solving the NumDays Problem

Design a class called NumDays. The class's purpose is to store a value that represents a number of work hours and convert it to a number of days. For example, 8 hours would be converted to 1 day, 12 hours would be converted to 1.5 days, and 18 hours would be converted to 2.25 days. The class should have a constructor that accepts a number of hours, as well as member functions for storing and retrieving the hours and days. The class should also have the following overloaded operators:

+   *Addition operator.* When two NumDays objects are added together, the overloaded + operator should return the sum of the two objects' hours members.

- *Subtraction operator.* When one NumDays object is subtracted from another, the overloaded – operator should return the difference of the two objects' hours members.

++ *Prefix and postfix increment operators.* These operators should increment the number of hours stored in the object. When incremented, the number of days should be automatically recalculated.

-- *Prefix and postfix decrement operators.* These operators should decrement the number of hours stored in the object. When decremented, the number of days should be automatically recalculated.

5. **Time Off**

> **NOTE:** This assignment assumes you have already completed Programming Challenge 4.

Design a class named TimeOff. The purpose of the class is to track an employee's sick leave, vacation, and unpaid time off. It should have, as members, the following instances of the NumDays class described in Programming Challenge 4:

maxSickDays   A NumDays object that records the maximum number of days of sick leave the employee may take.

sickTaken   A NumDays object that records the number of days of sick leave the employee has already taken.

maxVacation   A NumDays object that records the maximum number of days of paid vacation the employee may take.

vacTaken   A NumDays object that records the number of days of paid vacation the employee has already taken.

maxUnpaid   A NumDays object that records the maximum number of days of unpaid vacation the employee may take.

unpaidTaken   A NumDays object that records the number of days of unpaid leave the employee has taken.

Additionally, the class should have members for holding the employee's name and identification number. It should have an appropriate constructor and member functions for storing and retrieving data in any of the member objects.

Input Validation: Company policy states that an employee may not accumulate more than 240 hours of paid vacation. The class should not allow the maxVacation object to store a value greater than this amount.

6. **Personnel Report**

> **NOTE:** This assignment assumes you have already completed Programming Challenges 4 and 5.

Write a program that uses an instance of the TimeOff class you designed in Programming Challenge 5. The program should ask the user to enter the number of months an employee has worked for the company. It should then use the TimeOff object to calculate and display the employee's maximum number of sick leave and vacation days. Employees earn 12 hours of vacation leave and 8 hours of sick leave per month.

7. **Month** Class

Design a class named `Month`. The class should have the following private members:

- `name` A `string` object that holds the name of a month, such as "January," "February," etc.
- `monthNumber` An integer variable that holds the number of the month. For example, January would be 1, February would be 2, etc. Valid values for this variable are 1 through 12.

In addition, provide the following member functions:

- A default constructor that sets `monthNumber` to 1 and `name` to "January."
- A constructor that accepts the name of the month as an argument. It should set `name` to the value passed as the argument and set `monthNumber` to the correct value.
- A constructor that accepts the number of the month as an argument. It should set `monthNumber` to the value passed as the argument and set `name` to the correct month name.
- Appropriate set and get functions for the `name` and `monthNumber` member variables.
- Prefix and postfix overloaded `++` operator functions that increment `monthNumber` and set `name` to the name of next month. If `monthNumber` is set to 12 when these functions execute, they should set `monthNumber` to 1 and `name` to "January."
- Prefix and postfix overloaded `--` operator functions that decrement `monthNumber` and set `name` to the name of previous month. If `monthNumber` is set to 1 when these functions execute, they should set `monthNumber` to 12 and `name` to "December."

Also, you should overload `cout`'s `<<` operator and `cin`'s `>>` operator to work with the `Month` class. Demonstrate the class in a program.

8. **Date** Class Modification

Modify the `Date` class in Programming Challenge 1 of Chapter 13. The new version should have the following overloaded operators:

`++`   *Prefix and postfix increment operators.* These operators should increment the object's `day` member.

`--`   *Prefix and postfix decrement operators.* These operators should decrement the object's `day` member.

`-`   *Subtraction operator.* If one `Date` object is subtracted from another, the operator should give the number of days between the two dates. For example, if April 10, 2012 is subtracted from April 18, 2012, the result will be 8.

`<<`   `cout`*'s stream insertion operator.* This operator should cause the date to be displayed in the form

```
April 18, 2012
```

`>>`   `cin`*'s stream extraction operator.* This operator should prompt the user for a date to be stored in a `Date` object.

The class should detect the following conditions and handle them accordingly:

- When a date is set to the last day of the month and incremented, it should become the first day of the following month.

- When a date is set to December 31 and incremented, it should become January 1 of the following year.
- When a day is set to the first day of the month and decremented, it should become the last day of the previous month.
- When a date is set to January 1 and decremented, it should become December 31 of the previous year.

Demonstrate the class's capabilities in a simple program.

Input Validation: The overloaded >> operator should not accept invalid dates. For example, the date 13/45/2012 should not be accepted.

9. **FeetInches** Modification

Modify the FeetInches class discussed in this chapter so it overloads the following operators:

```
<=
>=
!=
```

Demonstrate the class's capabilities in a simple program.

10. **Corporate Sales**

A corporation has six divisions, each responsible for sales to different geographic locations. Design a DivSales class that keeps sales data for a division, with the following members:

- An array with four elements for holding four quarters of sales figures for the division.
- A private static variable for holding the total corporate sales for all divisions for the entire year.
- A member function that takes four arguments, each assumed to be the sales for a quarter. The value of the arguments should be copied into the array that holds the sales data. The total of the four arguments should be added to the static variable that holds the total yearly corporate sales.
- A function that takes an integer argument within the range of 0–3. The argument is to be used as a subscript into the division quarterly sales array. The function should return the value of the array element with that subscript.

Write a program that creates an array of six DivSales objects. The program should ask the user to enter the sales for four quarters for each division. After the data are entered, the program should display a table showing the division sales for each quarter. The program should then display the total corporate sales for the year.

Input Validation: Only accept positive values for quarterly sales figures.

11. **FeetInches** Class Copy Constructor and **multiply** Function

Add a copy constructor to the FeetInches class. This constructor should accept a FeetInches object as an argument. The constructor should assign to the feet attribute the value in the argument's feet attribute, and assign to the inches attribute the value in the argument's `inches` attribute. As a result, the new object will be a copy of the argument object.

Next, add a `multiply` member function to the `FeetInches` class. The `multiply` function should accept a `FeetInches` object as an argument. The argument object's `feet` and `inches` attributes will be multiplied by the calling object's `feet` and `inches` attributes, and a `FeetInches` object containing the result will be returned.

12. **`LandTract` Class**

Make a `LandTract` class that is composed of two `FeetInches` objects, one for the tract's length and one for the width. The class should have a member function that returns the tract's area. Demonstrate the class in a program that asks the user to enter the dimensions for two tracts of land. The program should display the area of each tract of land and indicate whether the tracts are of equal size.

13. **Carpet Calculator**

The Westfield Carpet Company has asked you to write an application that calculates the price of carpeting for rectangular rooms. To calculate the price, you multiply the area of the floor (width times length) by the price per square foot of carpet. For example, the area of floor that is 12 feet long and 10 feet wide is 120 square feet. To cover that floor with carpet that costs $8 per square foot would cost $960. (12 × 10 × 8 = 960.)

First, you should create a class named `RoomDimension` that has two `FeetInches` objects as attributes: one for the length of the room and one for the width. (You should use the version of the `FeetInches` class that you created in Programming Challenge 11 with the addition of a `multiply` member function. You can use this function to calculate the area of the room.) The `RoomDimension` class should have a member function that returns the area of the room as a `FeetInches` object.

Next, you should create a `RoomCarpet` class that has a `RoomDimension` object as an attribute. It should also have an attribute for the cost of the carpet per square foot. The `RoomCarpet` class should have a member function that returns the total cost of the carpet.

Once you have written these classes, use them in an application that asks the user to enter the dimensions of a room and the price per square foot of the desired carpeting. The application should display the total cost of the carpet.

14. **Parking Ticket Simulator**

For this assignment you will design a set of classes that work together to simulate a police officer issuing a parking ticket. The classes you should design are:

• **The `ParkedCar` Class:** This class should simulate a parked car. The class's responsibilities are:
    – To know the car's make, model, color, license number, and the number of minutes that the car has been parked

- The **ParkingMeter** Class: This class should simulate a parking meter. The class's only responsibility is:
  - To know the number of minutes of parking time that has been purchased
- The **ParkingTicket** Class: This class should simulate a parking ticket. The class's responsibilities are:
  - To report the make, model, color, and license number of the illegally parked car
  - To report the amount of the fine, which is $25 for the first hour or part of an hour that the car is illegally parked, plus $10 for every additional hour or part of an hour that the car is illegally parked
  - To report the name and badge number of the police officer issuing the ticket
- The **PoliceOfficer** Class: This class should simulate a police officer inspecting parked cars. The class's responsibilities are:
  - To know the police officer's name and badge number
  - To examine a **ParkedCar** object and a **ParkingMeter** object, and determine whether the car's time has expired
  - To issue a parking ticket (generate a **ParkingTicket** object) if the car's time has expired

Write a program that demonstrates how these classes collaborate.

15. **Car Instrument Simulator**

For this assignment you will design a set of classes that work together to simulate a car's fuel gauge and odometer. The classes you will design are:

- The **FuelGauge** Class: This class will simulate a fuel gauge. Its responsibilities are
  - To know the car's current amount of fuel, in gallons.
  - To report the car's current amount of fuel, in gallons.
  - To be able to increment the amount of fuel by 1 gallon. This simulates putting fuel in the car. (The car can hold a maximum of 15 gallons.)
  - To be able to decrement the amount of fuel by 1 gallon, if the amount of fuel is greater than 0 gallons. This simulates burning fuel as the car runs.

- The **Odometer** Class: This class will simulate the car's odometer. Its responsibilities are:
  - To know the car's current mileage.
  - To report the car's current mileage.
  - To be able to increment the current mileage by 1 mile. The maximum mileage the odometer can store is 999,999 miles. When this amount is exceeded, the odometer resets the current mileage to 0.
  - To be able to work with a **FuelGauge** object. It should decrease the **FuelGauge** object's current amount of fuel by 1 gallon for every 24 miles traveled. (The car's fuel economy is 24 miles per gallon.)

Demonstrate the classes by creating instances of each. Simulate filling the car up with fuel, and then run a loop that increments the odometer until the car runs out of fuel. During each loop iteration, print the car's current mileage and amount of fuel.

CHAPTER

15 Inheritance, Polymorphism, and Virtual Functions

TOPICS

15.1 What Is Inheritance?

CONCEPT: Inheritance allows a new class to be based on an existing class. The new class inherits all the member variables and functions (except the constructors and destructor) of the class it is based on.

Generalization and Specialization

In the real world you can find many objects that are specialized versions of other more general objects. For example, the term "insect" describes a very general type of creature with numerous characteristics. Because grasshoppers and bumblebees are insects, they have all the general characteristics of an insect. In addition, they have special characteristics of their own. For example, the grasshopper has its jumping ability, and the bumblebee has its stinger. Grasshoppers and bumblebees are specialized versions of an insect. This is illustrated in Figure 15-1.

Figure 15-1

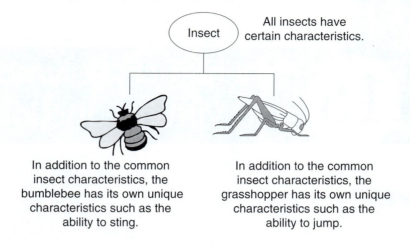

Insect — All insects have certain characteristics.

In addition to the common insect characteristics, the bumblebee has its own unique characteristics such as the ability to sting.

In addition to the common insect characteristics, the grasshopper has its own unique characteristics such as the ability to jump.

Inheritance and the "Is a" Relationship

When one object is a specialized version of another object, there is an *"is a" relationship* between them. For example, a grasshopper *is an* insect. Here are a few other examples of the "is a" relationship.

- A poodle *is a* dog.
- A car *is a* vehicle.
- A tree *is a* plant.
- A rectangle *is a* shape.
- A football player *is an* athlete.

When an "is a" relationship exists between classes, it means that the specialized class has all of the characteristics of the general class, plus additional characteristics that make it special. In object-oriented programming, *inheritance* is used to create an "is a" relationship between classes.

Inheritance involves a base class and a derived class. The *base class* is the general class and the *derived class* is the specialized class. The derived class is based on, or derived from, the base class. You can think of the base class as the parent and the derived class as the child. This is illustrated in Figure 15-2.

Figure 15-2

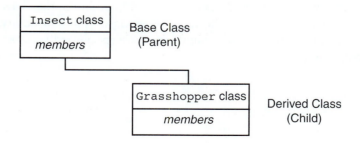

Insect class
members
Base Class (Parent)

Grasshopper class
members
Derived Class (Child)

The derived class inherits the member variables and member functions of the base class without any of them being rewritten. Furthermore, new member variables and functions may be added to the derived class to make it more specialized than the base class.

Let's look at an example of how inheritance can be used. Most teachers assign various graded activities for their students to complete. A graded activity can receive a numeric score such as 70, 85, 90, and so on, and a letter grade such as A, B, C, D, or F. The following `GradedActivity` class is designed to hold the numeric score and letter grade of a graded activity. When a numeric score is stored by the class, it automatically determines the letter grade. (These files are stored in the Student Source Code Folder `Chapter 15\GradedActivity Version 1`.)

Contents of `GradedActivity.h` (Version 1)

```
 1  #ifndef GRADEDACTIVITY_H
 2  #define GRADEDACTIVITY_H
 3
 4  // GradedActivity class declaration
 5
 6  class GradedActivity
 7  {
 8  private:
 9     double score;    // To hold the numeric score
10  public:
11     // Default constructor
12     GradedActivity()
13        { score = 0.0; }
14
15     // Constructor
16     GradedActivity(double s)
17        { score = s; }
18
19     // Mutator function
20     void setScore(double s)
21        { score = s; }
22
23     // Accessor functions
24     double getScore() const
25        { return score; }
26
27     char getLetterGrade() const;
28  };
29  #endif
```

Contents of `GradedActivity.cpp` (Version 1)

```
 1  #include "GradedActivity.h"
 2
 3  //*****************************************************
 4  // Member function GradedActivity::getLetterGrade      *
 5  //*****************************************************
 6
```

```
 7  char GradedActivity::getLetterGrade() const
 8  {
 9      char letterGrade; // To hold the letter grade
10
11      if (score > 89)
12          letterGrade = 'A';
13      else if (score > 79)
14          letterGrade = 'B';
15      else if (score > 69)
16          letterGrade = 'C';
17      else if (score > 59)
18          letterGrade = 'D';
19      else
20          letterGrade = 'F';
21
22      return letterGrade;
23  }
```

The GradedActivity class has a default constructor that initializes the score member variable to 0.0. A second constructor accepts an argument for score. The setScore member function also accepts an argument for the score variable, and the getLetterGrade member function returns the letter grade that corresponds to the value in score. Program 15-1 demonstrates the GradedActivity class. (This file is also stored in the Student Source Code Folder Chapter 15\GradedActivity Version 1.)

Program 15-1

```
 1  // This program demonstrates the GradedActivity class.
 2  #include <iostream>
 3  #include "GradedActivity.h"
 4  using namespace std;
 5
 6  int main()
 7  {
 8      double testScore;  // To hold a test score
 9
10      // Create a GradedActivity object for the test.
11      GradedActivity test;
12
13      // Get a numeric test score from the user.
14      cout << "Enter your numeric test score: ";
15      cin >> testScore;
16
17      // Store the numeric score in the test object.
18      test.setScore(testScore);
19
20      // Display the letter grade for the test.
21      cout << "The grade for that test is "
22          << test.getLetterGrade() << endl;
23
24      return 0;
25  }
```

Program Output with Example Input Shown in Bold
```
Enter your numeric test score: 89 [Enter]
The grade for that test is B
```

Program Output with Different Example Input Shown in Bold
```
Enter your numeric test score: 75 [Enter]
The grade for that test is C
```

The GradedActivity class represents the general characteristics of a student's graded activity. Many different types of graded activities exist, however, such as quizzes, midterm exams, final exams, lab reports, essays, and so on. Because the numeric scores might be determined differently for each of these graded activities, we can create derived classes to handle each one. For example, the following code shows the FinalExam class, which is derived from the GradedActivity class. It has member variables for the number of questions on the exam (numQuestions), the number of points each question is worth (pointsEach), and the number of questions missed by the student (numMissed). These files are also stored in the Student Source Code Folder Chapter 15\GradedActivity Version 1.

Contents of `FinalExam.h`

```
 1  #ifndef FINALEXAM_H
 2  #define FINALEXAM_H
 3  #include "GradedActivity.h"
 4
 5  class FinalExam : public GradedActivity
 6  {
 7  private:
 8     int numQuestions;    // Number of questions
 9     double pointsEach;   // Points for each question
10     int numMissed;       // Number of questions missed
11  public:
12     // Default constructor
13     FinalExam()
14        { numQuestions = 0;
15          pointsEach = 0.0;
16          numMissed = 0; }
17
18     // Constructor
19     FinalExam(int questions, int missed)
20        { set(questions, missed); }
21
22     // Mutator function
23     void set(int, int);  // Defined in FinalExam.cpp
24
25     // Accessor functions
26     double getNumQuestions() const
27        { return numQuestions; }
28
29     double getPointsEach() const
30        { return pointsEach; }
31
```

```
32       int getNumMissed() const
33          { return numMissed; }
34   };
35   #endif
```

Contents of `FinalExam.cpp`

```
1    #include "FinalExam.h"
2
3    //*********************************************************
4    // set function                                          *
5    // The parameters are the number of questions and the    *
6    // number of questions missed.                           *
7    //*********************************************************
8
9    void FinalExam::set(int questions, int missed)
10   {
11       double numericScore;  // To hold the numeric score
12
13       // Set the number of questions and number missed.
14       numQuestions = questions;
15       numMissed = missed;
16
17       // Calculate the points for each question.
18       pointsEach = 100.0 / numQuestions;
19
20       // Calculate the numeric score for this exam.
21       numericScore = 100.0 - (missed * pointsEach);
22
23       // Call the inherited setScore function to set
24       // the numeric score.
25       setScore(numericScore);
26   }
```

The only new notation in this code is in line 5 of the `FinalExam.h` file, which reads

```
class FinalExam : public GradedActivity
```

This line indicates the name of the class being declared and the name of the base class it is derived from. `FinalExam` is the name of the class being declared and `GradedActivity` is the name of the base class it inherits from.

If we want to express the relationship between the two classes, we can say that a `FinalExam` *is a* `GradedActivity`.

The word `public`, which precedes the name of the base class in line 5 of the `FinalExam.h` file, is the *base class access specification*. It affects how the members of the base class are inherited by the derived class. When you create an object of a derived class, you can think of it as being built on top of an object of the base class. The members of the base class object become members of the derived class object. How the base class members appear in the derived class is determined by the base class access specification.

Although we will discuss this topic in more detail in the next section, let's see how it works in this example. The `GradedActivity` class has both private members and public members. The `FinalExam` class is derived from the `GradedActivity` class, using `public` access specification. This means that the public members of the `GradedActivity` class will become public members of the `FinalExam` class. The private members of the `GradedActivity` class cannot be accessed directly by code in the `FinalExam` class. Although the private members of the `GradedActivity` class are inherited, it's as though they are invisible to the code in the `FinalExam` class. They can only be accessed by the member functions of the `GradedActivity` class. Here is a list of the members of the `FinalExam` class:

Private Members:

`int numQuestions`	Declared in the `FinalExam` class
`double pointsEach`	Declared in the `FinalExam` class
`int numMissed`	Declared in the `FinalExam` class

Public Members:

`FinalExam()`	Defined in the `FinalExam` class
`FinalExam(int, int)`	Defined in the `FinalExam` class
`set(int, int)`	Defined in the `FinalExam` class
`getNumQuestions()`	Defined in the `FinalExam` class
`getPointsEach()`	Defined in the `FinalExam` class
`getNumMissed()`	Defined in the `FinalExam` class
`setScore(double)`	Inherited from `GradedActivity`
`getScore()`	Inherited from `GradedActivity`
`getLetterGrade()`	Inherited from `GradedActivity`

The `GradedActivity` class has one private member, the variable `score`. Notice that it is not listed as a member of the `FinalExam` class. It is still inherited by the derived class, but because it is a private member of the base class, only member functions of the base class may access it. It is truly private to the base class. Because the functions `setScore`, `getScore`, and `getLetterGrade` are public members of the base class, they also become public members of the derived class.

You will also notice that the `GradedActivity` class constructors are not listed among the members of the `FinalExam` class. Although the base class constructors still exist, it makes sense that they are not members of the derived class because their purpose is to construct objects of the base class. In the next section we discuss in more detail how base class constructors operate.

Let's take a closer look at the `FinalExam` class constructors. The default constructor appears in lines 13 through 16 of the `FinalExam.h` file. It simply assigns 0 to each of the class's member variables. Another constructor appears in lines 19 through 20. This constructor accepts two arguments, one for the number of questions on the exam, and one for the number of questions missed. This constructor merely passes those values as arguments to the `set` function.

The set function is defined in `FinalExam.cpp`. It accepts two arguments: the number of questions on the exam, and the number of questions missed by the student. In lines 14 and 15 these values are assigned to the `numQuestions` and `numMissed` member variables. In line 18 the number of points for each question is calculated. In line 21 the numeric test score is calculated. In line 25, the last statement in the function reads:

```
setScore(numericScore);
```

This is a call to the `setScore` function. Although no `setScore` function appears in the `FinalExam` class, it is inherited from the `GradedActivity` class. Program 15-2 demonstrates the `FinalExam` class.

Program 15-2

```
 1   // This program demonstrates a base class and a derived class.
 2   #include <iostream>
 3   #include <iomanip>
 4   #include "FinalExam.h"
 5   using namespace std;
 6
 7   int main()
 8   {
 9      int questions;  // Number of questions on the exam
10      int missed;     // Number of questions missed by the student
11
12      // Get the number of questions on the final exam.
13      cout << "How many questions are on the final exam? ";
14      cin >> questions;
15
16      // Get the number of questions the student missed.
17      cout << "How many questions did the student miss? ";
18      cin >> missed;
19
20      // Define a FinalExam object and initialize it with
21      // the values entered.
22      FinalExam test(questions, missed);
23
24      // Display the test results.
25      cout << setprecision(2);
26      cout << "\nEach question counts " << test.getPointsEach()
27           << " points.\n";
28      cout << "The exam score is " << test.getScore() << endl;
29      cout << "The exam grade is " << test.getLetterGrade() << endl;
30
31      return 0;
32   }
```

Program Output with Example Input Shown in Bold
```
How many questions are on the final exam? 20 [Enter]
How many questions did the student miss? 3 [Enter]

Each question counts 5 points.
The exam score is 85
The exam grade is B
```

Notice in lines 28 and 29 that the public member functions of the `GradedActivity` class may be directly called by the `test` object:

```
cout << "The exam score is " << test.getScore() << endl;
cout << "The exam grade is " << test.getLetterGrade() << endl;
```

The `getScore` and `getLetterGrade` member functions are inherited as public members of the `FinalExam` class, so they may be accessed like any other public member.

Inheritance does not work in reverse. It is not possible for a base class to call a member function of a derived class. For example, the following classes will not compile in a program because the `BadBase` constructor attempts to call a function in its derived class:

```
class BadBase
{
   private:
       int x;
   public:
       BadBase() { x = getVal(); }    // Error!
};

class Derived : public BadBase
{
   private:
       int y;
   public:
       Derived(int z) { y = z; }
       int getVal() { return y; }
};
```

Checkpoint

myprogramminglab *www.myprogramminglab.com*

15.1 Here is the first line of a class declaration. Circle the name of the base class:
```
class Truck : public Vehicle
```

15.2 Circle the name of the derived class in the following declaration line:
```
class Truck : public Vehicle
```

15.3 Suppose a program has the following class declarations:

```
class Shape
{
private:
   double area;
public:
   void setArea(double a)
      { area = a; }

   double getArea()
      { return area; }
};

class Circle : public Shape
{
private:
   double radius;
```

```
   public:
      void setRadius(double r)
         { radius = r;
           setArea(3.14 * r * r); }

      double getRadius()
         { return radius; }
};
```

Answer the following questions concerning these classes:

A) When an object of the `Circle` class is created, what are its private members?

B) When an object of the `Circle` class is created, what are its public members?

C) What members of the `Shape` class are not accessible to member functions of the `Circle` class?

15.2 Protected Members and Class Access

CONCEPT: Protected members of a base class are like private members, but they may be accessed by derived classes. The base class access specification determines how private, public, and protected base class members are accessed when they are inherited by the derived classes.

Until now you have used two access specifications within a class: `private` and `public`. C++ provides a third access specification, `protected`. Protected members of a base class are like private members, except they may be accessed by functions in a derived class. To the rest of the program, however, protected members are inaccessible.

The following code shows a modified version of the `GradedActivity` class declaration. The private member of the class has been made protected. This file is stored in the Student Source Code Folder `Chapter 15\GradedActivity Version 2`. The implementation file, `GradedActivity.cpp` has not changed, so it is not shown again in this example.

Contents of `GradedActivity.h` (Version 2)

```
 1  #ifndef GRADEDACTIVITY_H
 2  #define GRADEDACTIVITY_H
 3
 4  // GradedActivity class declaration
 5
 6  class GradedActivity
 7  {
 8  protected:
 9     double score;    // To hold the numeric score
10  public:
11     // Default constructor
12     GradedActivity()
13        { score = 0.0; }
14
15     // Constructor
16     GradedActivity(double s)
17        { score = s; }
18
```

```
19       // Mutator function
20       void setScore(double s)
21          { score = s; }
22
23       // Accessor functions
24       double getScore() const
25          { return score; }
26
27       char getLetterGrade() const;
28    };
29    #endif
```

Now we will look at a modified version of the `FinalExam` class, which is derived from this version of the `GradedActivity` class. This version of the `FinalExam` class has a new member function named `adjustScore`. This function directly accesses the `GradedActivity` class's score member variable. If the content of the `score` variable has a fractional part of 0.5 or greater, the function rounds `score` up to the next whole number. The `set` function calls the `adjustScore` function after it calculates the numeric score. (These files are stored in the Student Source Code Folder `Chapter 15\GradedActivity Version 2`.)

Contents of `FinalExam.h` (Version 2)

```
1     #ifndef FINALEXAM_H
2     #define FINALEXAM_H
3     #include "GradedActivity.h"
4
5     class FinalExam : public GradedActivity
6     {
7     private:
8        int numQuestions;     // Number of questions
9        double pointsEach;    // Points for each question
10       int numMissed;        // Number of questions missed
11    public:
12       // Default constructor
13       FinalExam()
14          { numQuestions = 0;
15            pointsEach = 0.0;
16            numMissed = 0; }
17
18       // Constructor
19       FinalExam(int questions, int missed)
20          { set(questions, missed); }
21
22       // Mutator functions
23       void set(int, int);    // Defined in FinalExam.cpp
24       void adjustScore();    // Defined in FinalExam.cpp
25
26       // Accessor functions
27       double getNumQuestions() const
28          { return numQuestions; }
29
30       double getPointsEach() const
31          { return pointsEach; }
32
```

```
33      int getNumMissed() const
34         { return numMissed; }
35   };
36   #endif
```

Contents of `FinalExam.cpp` (Version 2)

```
 1   #include "FinalExam.h"
 2
 3   //**********************************************************
 4   // set function                                           *
 5   // The parameters are the number of questions and the     *
 6   // number of questions missed.                            *
 7   //**********************************************************
 8
 9   void FinalExam::set(int questions, int missed)
10   {
11      double numericScore;  // To hold the numeric score
12
13      // Set the number of questions and number missed.
14      numQuestions = questions;
15      numMissed = missed;
16
17      // Calculate the points for each question.
18      pointsEach = 100.0 / numQuestions;
19
20      // Calculate the numeric score for this exam.
21      numericScore = 100.0 - (missed * pointsEach);
22
23      // Call the inherited setScore function to set
24      // the numeric score.
25      setScore(numericScore);
26
27      // Call the adjustScore function to adjust
28      // the score.
29      adjustScore();
30   }
31
32   //**************************************************************
33   // Definition of Test::adjustScore. If score is within        *
34   // 0.5 points of the next whole point, it rounds the score up  *
35   // and recalculates the letter grade.                         *
36   //**************************************************************
37
38   void FinalExam::adjustScore()
39   {
40      double fraction = score - static_cast<int>(score);
41
42      if (fraction >= 0.5)
43      {
44         // Adjust the score variable in the GradedActivity class.
45         score += (1.0 - fraction);
46      }
47   }
```

Program 15-3 demonstrates these versions of the `GradedActivity` and `FinalExam` classes. (This file is also stored in the Student Source Code Folder `Chapter 15\ GradedActivity Version 2`.)

Program 15-3

```cpp
 1   // This program demonstrates a base class with a
 2   // protected member.
 3   #include <iostream>
 4   #include <iomanip>
 5   #include "FinalExam.h"
 6   using namespace std;
 7
 8   int main()
 9   {
10      int questions; // Number of questions on the exam
11      int missed;    // Number of questions missed by the student
12
13      // Get the number of questions on the final exam.
14      cout << "How many questions are on the final exam? ";
15      cin >> questions;
16
17      // Get the number of questions the student missed.
18      cout << "How many questions did the student miss? ";
19      cin >> missed;
20
21      // Define a FinalExam object and initialize it with
22      // the values entered.
23      FinalExam test(questions, missed);
24
25      // Display the adjusted test results.
26      cout << setprecision(2) << fixed;
27      cout << "\nEach question counts "
28           << test.getPointsEach() << " points.\n";
29      cout << "The adjusted exam score is "
30           << test.getScore() << endl;
31      cout << "The exam grade is "
32           << test.getLetterGrade() << endl;
33
34      return 0;
35   }
```

Program Output with Example Input Shown in Bold
```
How many questions are on the final exam? 16 [Enter]
How many questions did the student miss? 5 [Enter]

Each question counts 6.25 points.
The adjusted exam score is 69.00
The exam grade is D
```

The program works as planned. In the example run, the student missed five questions, which are worth 6.25 points each. The unadjusted score would be 68.75. The score was adjusted to 69.

More About Base Class Access Specification

The first line of the `FinalExam` class declaration reads:

```
class FinalExam : public GradedActivity
```

This declaration gives public access specification to the base class. Recall from our earlier discussion that base class access specification affects how inherited base class members are accessed. Be careful not to confuse base class access specification with member access specification. Member access specification determines how members that are *defined* within the class are accessed. Base class access specification determines how *inherited* members are accessed.

When you create an object of a derived class, it inherits the members of the base class. The derived class can have its own private, protected, and public members, but what is the access specification of the inherited members? This is determined by the base class access specification. Table 15-1 summarizes how base class access specification affects the way that base class members are inherited.

Table 15-1

Base Class Access Specification	How Members of the Base Class Appear in the Derived Class
private	Private members of the base class are inaccessible to the derived class.
	Protected members of the base class become private members of the derived class.
	Public members of the base class become private members of the derived class.
protected	Private members of the base class are inaccessible to the derived class.
	Protected members of the base class become protected members of the derived class.
	Public members of the base class become protected members of the derived class.
public	Private members of the base class are inaccessible to the derived class.
	Protected members of the base class become protected members of the derived class.
	Public members of the base class become public members of the derived class.

As you can see from Table 15-1, class access specification gives you a great deal of flexibility in determining how base class members will appear in the derived class. Think of a base class's access specification as a filter that base class members must pass through when becoming inherited members of a derived class. This is illustrated in Figure 15-3.

NOTE: If the base class access specification is left out of a declaration, the default access specification is `private`. For example, in the following declaration, `Grade` is declared as a `private` base class:

```
class Test : Grade
```

Figure 15-3

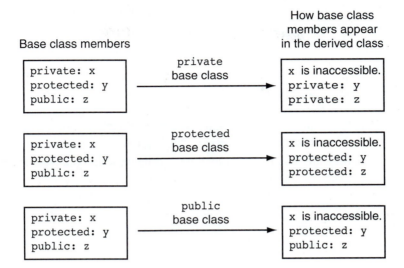

Checkpoint

myprogramminglab *www.myprogramminglab.com*

15.4   What is the difference between private members and protected members?

15.5   What is the difference between member access specification and class access specification?

15.6   Suppose a program has the following class declaration:

```
// Declaration of CheckPoint class.
class CheckPoint
{
   private:
      int a;
   protected:
      int b;
      int c;
      void setA(int x) { a = x;}
   public:
      void setB(int y) { b = y;}
      void setC(int z) { c = z;}
};
```

Answer the following questions regarding the class:

A) Suppose another class, Quiz, is derived from the CheckPoint class. Here is the first line of its declaration:

   class Quiz : private CheckPoint

Indicate whether each member of the CheckPoint class is private, protected, public, or inaccessible:

      a
      b
      c
      setA
      setB
      setC

B) Suppose the Quiz class, derived from the CheckPoint class, is declared as
    class Quiz : protected Checkpoint
Indicate whether each member of the CheckPoint class is private, protected, public, or inaccessible:

    a
    b
    c
    setA
    setB
    setC

C) Suppose the Quiz class, derived from the CheckPoint class, is declared as
    class Quiz : public Checkpoint
Indicate whether each member of the CheckPoint class is private, protected, public, or inaccessible:

    a
    b
    c
    setA
    setB
    setC

D) Suppose the Quiz class, derived from the CheckPoint class, is declared as
    class Quiz : Checkpoint
Is the CheckPoint class a private, public, or protected base class?

15.3   Constructors and Destructors in Base and Derived Classes

CONCEPT: The base class's constructor is called before the derived class's constructor. The destructors are called in reverse order, with the derived class's destructor being called first.

In inheritance, the base class constructor is called before the derived class constructor. Destructors are called in reverse order. Program 15-4 shows a simple set of demonstration classes, each with a default constructor and a destructor. The DerivedClass class is derived from the BaseClass class. Messages are displayed by the constructors and destructors to demonstrate when each is called.

Program 15-4

```
1   // This program demonstrates the order in which base and
2   // derived class constructors and destructors are called.
3   #include <iostream>
4   using namespace std;
5
6   //******************************
7   // BaseClass declaration        *
8   //******************************
9
```

```
10  class BaseClass
11  {
12  public:
13     BaseClass()  // Constructor
14        { cout << "This is the BaseClass constructor.\n"; }
15
16     ~BaseClass() // Destructor
17        { cout << "This is the BaseClass destructor.\n"; }
18  };
19
20  //*******************************
21  // DerivedClass declaration      *
22  //*******************************
23
24  class DerivedClass : public BaseClass
25  {
26  public:
27     DerivedClass()  // Constructor
28        { cout << "This is the DerivedClass constructor.\n"; }
29
30     ~DerivedClass()  // Destructor
31        { cout << "This is the DerivedClass destructor.\n"; }
32  };
33
34  //*******************************
35  // main function                *
36  //*******************************
37
38  int main()
39  {
40     cout << "We will now define a DerivedClass object.\n";
41
42     DerivedClass object;
43
44     cout << "The program is now going to end.\n";
45     return 0;
46  }
```

Program Output

```
We will now define a DerivedClass object.
This is the BaseClass constructor.
This is the DerivedClass constructor.
The program is now going to end.
This is the DerivedClass destructor.
This is the BaseClass destructor.
```

Passing Arguments to Base Class Constructors

In Program 15-4, both the base class and derived class have default constructors, that are called automatically. But what if the base class's constructor takes arguments? What if there is more than one constructor in the base class? The answer to these questions is to let the derived class constructor pass arguments to the base class constructor. For example, consider the following class:

Contents of `Rectangle.h`

```
 1   #ifndef RECTANGLE_H
 2   #define RECTANGLE_H
 3
 4   class Rectangle
 5   {
 6   private:
 7      double width;
 8      double length;
 9   public:
10      // Default constructor
11      Rectangle()
12         { width = 0.0;
13           length = 0.0; }
14
15      // Constructor #2
16      Rectangle(double w, double len)
17         { width = w;
18           length = len; }
19
20      double getWidth() const
21         { return width; }
22
23      double getLength() const
24         { return length; }
25
26      double getArea() const
27         { return width * length; }
28   };
29   #endif
```

This class is designed to hold data about a rectangle. It specifies two constructors. The default constructor, in lines 11 through 13, simply initializes the width and length member variables to 0.0. The second constructor, in lines 16 through 18, takes two arguments, which are assigned to the width and length member variables. Now let's look at a class that is derived from the Rectangle class:

Contents of `Cube.h`

```
 1   #ifndef CUBE_H
 2   #define CUBE_H
 3   #include "Rectangle.h"
 4
 5   class Cube : public Rectangle
 6   {
 7   protected:
 8      double height;
 9      double volume;
10   public:
11      // Default constructor
12      Cube() : Rectangle()
13         { height = 0.0; volume = 0.0; }
14
```

```
15        // Constructor #2
16        Cube(double w, double len, double h) : Rectangle(w, len)
17           { height = h;
18             volume = getArea() * h; }
19
20        double getHeight() const
21           { return height; }
22
23        double getVolume() const
24           { return volume; }
25     };
26     #endif
```

The Cube class is designed to hold data about cubes, which not only have a length and width, but a height and volume as well. Look at line 12, which is the first line of the Cube class's default constructor:

```
Cube() : Rectangle()
```

Notice the added notation in the header of the constructor. A colon is placed after the derived class constructor's parentheses, followed by a function call to a base class constructor. In this case, the base class's default constructor is being called. When this Cube class constructor executes, it will first call the Rectangle class's default constructor. This is illustrated here:

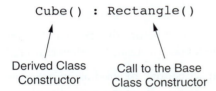

The general format of this type of constructor declaration is

ClassName::ClassName(ParameterList) : BaseClassName(ArgumentList)

You can also pass arguments to the base class constructor, as shown in the Cube class's second constructor. Look at line 16:

```
Cube(double w, double len, double h) : Rectangle(w, len)
```

This Cube class constructor has three parameters: w, len, and h. Notice that the Rectangle class's constructor is called, and the w and len parameters are passed as arguments. This causes the Rectangle class's second constructor to be called.

You only write this notation in the definition of a constructor, not in a prototype. In this example, the derived class constructor is written inline (inside the class declaration), so the notation that contains the call to the base class constructor appears there. If the constructor were defined outside the class, the notation would appear in the function header. For example, the Cube class could appear as follows.

```
class Cube : public Rectangle
{
protected:
   double height;
   double volume;
public:
   // Default constructor
   Cube() : Rectangle()
      { height = 0.0; volume = 0.0; }

   // Constructor #2
   Cube(double, double, double);

   double getHeight() const
      { return height; }

   double getVolume() const
      { return volume; }
};

// Cube class constructor #2
Cube::Cube(double w, double len, double h) : Rectangle(w, len)
{
   height = h;
   volume = getArea() * h;
}
```

The base class constructor is always executed before the derived class constructor. When the `Rectangle` constructor finishes, the `Cube` constructor is then executed.

Any literal value or variable that is in scope may be used as an argument to the derived class constructor. Usually, one or more of the arguments passed to the derived class constructor are, in turn, passed to the base class constructor. The values that may be used as base class constructor arguments are

- Derived class constructor parameters
- Literal values
- Global variables that are accessible to the file containing the derived class constructor definition
- Expressions involving any of these items

Program 15-5 shows the `Rectangle` and `Cube` classes in use.

Program 15-5

```
1  // This program demonstrates passing arguments to a base
2  // class constructor.
3  #include <iostream>
4  #include "Cube.h"
5  using namespace std;
6
```

```
 7  int main()
 8  {
 9     double cubeWidth;    // To hold the cube's width
10     double cubeLength;   // To hold the cube's length
11     double cubeHeight;   // To hold the cube's height
12
13     // Get the width, length, and height of
14     // the cube from the user.
15     cout << "Enter the dimensions of a cube:\n";
16     cout << "Width: ";
17     cin >> cubeWidth;
18     cout << "Length: ";
19     cin >> cubeLength;
20     cout << "Height: ";
21     cin >> cubeHeight;
22
23     // Define a Cube object and use the dimensions
24     // entered by the user.
25     Cube myCube(cubeWidth, cubeLength, cubeHeight);
26
27     // Display the Cube object's properties.
28     cout << "Here are the cube's properties:\n";
29     cout << "Width: " << myCube.getWidth() << endl;
30     cout << "Length: " << myCube.getLength() << endl;
31     cout << "Height: " << myCube.getHeight() << endl;
32     cout << "Base area: " << myCube.getArea() << endl;
33     cout << "Volume: " << myCube.getVolume() << endl;
34
35     return 0;
36  }
```

Program Output with Example Input Shown in Bold
```
Enter the dimensions of a cube:
Width: 10 [Enter]
Length: 15 [Enter]
Height: 12 [Enter]
Here are the cube's properties:
Width: 10
Length: 15
Height: 12
Base area: 150
Volume: 1800
```

 NOTE: If the base class has no default constructor, then the derived class must have a constructor that calls one of the base class constructors.

In the Spotlight:

The `Automobile`, `Car`, `Truck`, and `SUV` classes

Suppose we are developing a program that a car dealership can use to manage its inventory of used cars. The dealership's inventory includes three types of automobiles: cars, pickup trucks, and sport-utility vehicles (SUVs). Regardless of the type, the dealership keeps the following data about each automobile:

- Make
- Year model
- Mileage
- Price

Each type of vehicle that is kept in inventory has these general characteristics, plus its own specialized characteristics. For cars, the dealership keeps the following additional data:

- Number of doors (2 or 4)

For pickup trucks, the dealership keeps the following additional data:

- Drive type (two-wheel drive or four-wheel drive)

And, for SUVs, the dealership keeps the following additional data:

- Passenger capacity

In designing this program, one approach would be to write the following three classes:

- A `Car` class with attributes for the make, year model, mileage, price, and number of doors.
- A `Truck` class with attributes for the make, year model, mileage, price, and drive type.
- An `SUV` class with attributes for the make, year model, mileage, price, and passenger capacity.

This would be an inefficient approach, however, because all three classes have a large number of common data attributes. As a result, the classes would contain a lot of duplicated code. In addition, if we discover later that we need to add more common attributes, we would have to modify all three classes.

A better approach would be to write an `Automobile` base class to hold all the general data about an automobile, and then write derived classes for each specific type of automobile. The following code shows the `Automobile` class. (This file is stored in the Student Source Code Folder `Chapter 15\Automobile`.)

Contents of `Automobile.h`

```
1  #ifndef AUTOMOBILE_H
2  #define AUTOMOBILE_H
3  #include <string>
4  using namespace std;
5
6  // The Automobile class holds general data
7  // about an automobile in inventory.
8  class Automobile
```

```
 9 {
10 private:
11     string make;     // The auto's make
12     int model;       // The auto's year model
13     int mileage;     // The auto's mileage
14     double price;    // The auto's price
15
16 public:
17     // Default constructor
18     Automobile()
19     { make = "";
20       model = 0;
21       mileage = 0;
22       price = 0.0; }
23
24     // Constructor
25     Automobile(string autoMake, int autoModel,
26                int autoMileage, double autoPrice)
27     { make = autoMake;
28       model = autoModel;
29       mileage = autoMileage;
30       price = autoPrice; }
31
32     // Accessors
33     string getMake() const
34     { return make; }
35
36     int getModel() const
37     { return model; }
38
39     int getMileage() const
40     { return mileage; }
41
42     double getPrice() const
43     { return price; }
44 };
45 #endif
```

Notice that the class has a default constructor in lines 18 through 22, and a constructor that accepts arguments for all of the class's attributes in lines 25 through 30. The `Automobile` class is a complete class that we can create objects from. If we wish, we can write a program that creates instances of the `Automobile` class. However, the `Automobile` class holds only general data about an automobile. It does not hold any of the specific pieces of data that the dealership wants to keep about cars, pickup trucks, and SUVs. To hold data about those specific types of automobiles we will write derived classes that inherit from the `Automobile` class. The following shows the code for the `Car` class. (This file is also stored in the Student Source Code Folder `Chapter 15\Automobile`.)

Contents of `Car.h`

```
1 #ifndef CAR_H
2 #define CAR_H
3 #include "Automobile.h"
4 #include <string>
5 using namespace std;
```

```
 6
 7  // The Car class represents a car.
 8  class Car : public Automobile
 9  {
10  private:
11     int doors;
12
13  public:
14     // Default constructor
15     Car() : Automobile()
16     { doors = 0; }
17
18     // Constructor #2
19     Car(string carMake, int carModel, int carMileage,
20        double carPrice, int carDoors) :
21        Automobile(carMake, carModel, carMileage, carPrice)
22     { doors = carDoors; }
23
24     // Accessor for doors attribute
25     int getDoors()
26     { return doors; }
27  };
28  #endif
```

The Car class defines a doors attribute in line 11 to hold the car's number of doors. The class has a default constructor in lines 15 through 16 that sets the doors attribute to 0. Notice in line 15 that the default constructor calls the Automobile class's default constructor, which initializes all of the inherited attributes to their default values.

The Car class also has an overloaded constructor, in lines 19 through 22, that accepts arguments for the car's make, model, mileage, price, and number of doors. Line 21 calls the Automobile class's constructor, passing the make, model, mileage, and price as arguments. Line 22 sets the value of the doors attribute.

Now let's look at the Truck class, which also inherits from the Automobile class. (This file is also stored in the Student Source Code Folder Chapter 15\Automobile.)

Contents of Truck.h

```
 1  #ifndef TRUCK_H
 2  #define TRUCK_H
 3  #include "Automobile.h"
 4  #include <string>
 5  using namespace std;
 6
 7  // The Truck class represents a truck.
 8  class Truck : public Automobile
 9  {
10  private:
11     string driveType;
12
13  public:
14     // Default constructor
15     Truck() : Automobile()
16     { driveType = ""; }
17
```

```
18     // Constructor #2
19     Truck(string truckMake, int truckModel, int truckMileage,
20        double truckPrice, string truckDriveType) :
21        Automobile(truckMake, truckModel, truckMileage, truckPrice)
22     { driveType = truckDriveType; }
23
24     // Accessor for driveType attribute
25     string getDriveType()
26     { return driveType; }
27 };
28 #endif
```

The Truck class defines a driveType attribute in line 11 to hold a string describing the truck's drive type. The class has a default constructor in lines 15 through 16 that sets the driveType attribute to an empty string. Notice in line 15 that the default constructor calls the Automobile class's default constructor, which initializes all of the inherited attributes to their default values.

The Truck class also has an overloaded constructor, in lines 19 through 22, that accepts arguments for the truck's make, model, mileage, price, and drive type. Line 21 calls the Automobile class's constructor, passing the make, model, mileage, and price as arguments. Line 22 sets the value of the driveType attribute.

Now let's look at the SUV class, which also inherits from the Automobile class. (This file is also stored in the Student Source Code Folder Chapter 15\Automobile.)

Contents of SUV.h

```
 1 #ifndef SUV_H
 2 #define SUV_H
 3 #include "Automobile.h"
 4 #include <string>
 5 using namespace std;
 6
 7 // The SUV class represents a SUV.
 8 class SUV : public Automobile
 9 {
10 private:
11    int passengers;
12
13 public:
14    // Default constructor
15    SUV() : Automobile()
16    { passengers = 0; }
17
18    // Constructor #2
19    SUV(string SUVMake, int SUVModel, int SUVMileage,
20       double SUVPrice, int SUVPassengers) :
21       Automobile(SUVMake, SUVModel, SUVMileage, SUVPrice)
22    { passengers = SUVPassengers; }
23
24    // Accessor for passengers attribute
25    int getPassengers()
26    { return passengers; }
27 };
28 #endif
```

The SUV class defines a passengers attribute in line 11 to hold the number of passengers that the vehicle can accommodate. The class has a default constructor in lines 15 through 16 that sets the passengers attribute to 0. Notice in line 15 that the default constructor calls the Automobile class's default constructor, which initializes all of the inherited attributes to their default values.

The SUV class also has an overloaded constructor, in lines 19 through 22, that accepts arguments for the SUV's make, model, mileage, price, and number of passengers. Line 21 calls the Automobile class's constructor, passing the make, model, mileage, and price as arguments. Line 22 sets the value of the passengers attribute.

Program 15-6 demonstrates each of the derived classes. It creates a Car object, a Truck object, and an SUV object. (This file is also stored in the Student Source Code Folder Chapter 15\Automobile.)

Program 15-6

```cpp
 1  // This program demonstrates the Car, Truck, and SUV
 2  // classes that are derived from the Automobile class.
 3  #include <iostream>
 4  #include <iomanip>
 5  #include "Car.h"
 6  #include "Truck.h"
 7  #include "SUV.h"
 8  using namespace std;
 9
10  int main()
11  {
12      // Create a Car object for a used 2007 BMW with
13      // 50,000 miles, priced at $15,000, with 4 doors.
14      Car car("BMW", 2007, 50000, 15000.0, 4);
15
16      // Create a Truck object for a used 2006 Toyota
17      // pickup with 40,000 miles, priced at $12,000,
18      // with 4-wheel drive.
19      Truck truck("Toyota", 2006, 40000, 12000.0, "4WD");
20
21      // Create an SUV object for a used 2005 Volvo
22      // with 30,000 miles, priced at $18,000, with
23      // 5 passenger capacity.
24      SUV suv("Volvo", 2005, 30000, 18000.0, 5);
25
26      // Display the automobiles we have in inventory.
27      cout << fixed << showpoint << setprecision(2);
28      cout << "We have the following car in inventory:\n"
29           << car.getModel() << " " << car.getMake()
30           << " with " << car.getDoors() << " doors and "
31           << car.getMileage() << " miles.\nPrice: $"
32           << car.getPrice() << endl << endl;
33
```

```
34       cout << "We have the following truck in inventory:\n"
35            << truck.getModel() << " " << truck.getMake()
36            << " with " << truck.getDriveType()
37            << " drive type and " << truck.getMileage()
38            << " miles.\nPrice: $" << truck.getPrice()
39            << endl << endl;
40
41       cout << "We have the following SUV in inventory:\n"
42            << suv.getModel() << " " << suv.getMake()
43            << " with " << suv.getMileage() << " miles and "
44            << suv.getPassengers() << " passenger capacity.\n"
45            << "Price: $" << suv.getPrice() << endl;
46
47       return 0;
48 }
```

Program Output

```
We have the following car in inventory:
2007 BMW with 4 doors and 50000 miles.
Price: $15000.00

We have the following truck in inventory:
2006 Toyota with 4WD drive type and 40000 miles.
Price: $12000.00

We have the following SUV in inventory:
2005 Volvo with 30000 miles and 5 passenger capacity.
Price: $18000.00
```

 Checkpoint

myprogramminglab   *www.myprogramminglab.com*

15.7   What will the following program display?

```
#include <iostream>
using namespace std;

class Sky
{
public:
    Sky()
        { cout << "Entering the sky.\n"; }
    ~Sky()
        { cout << "Leaving the sky.\n"; }
};

class Ground : public Sky
{
public:
    Ground()
        { cout << "Entering the Ground.\n"; }
    ~Ground()
        { cout << "Leaving the Ground.\n"; }
};
```

```
int main()
{
   Ground object;
   return 0;
}
```

15.8   What will the following program display?

```
#include <iostream>
using namespace std;

class Sky
{
public:
   Sky()
      { cout << "Entering the sky.\n"; }
   Sky(string color)
      { cout << "The sky is " << color << endl; }
   ~Sky()
      { cout << "Leaving the sky.\n"; }
};

class Ground : public Sky
{
public:
   Ground()
      { cout << "Entering the Ground.\n"; }
   Ground(string c1, string c2) : Sky(c1)
      { cout << "The ground is " << c2 << endl; }
   ~Ground()
      { cout << "Leaving the Ground.\n"; }
};

int main()
{
   Ground object;
   return 0;
}
```

15.4   Redefining Base Class Functions

CONCEPT: A base class member function may be redefined in a derived class.

VideoNote
**Redefining
a Base Class
Function in a
Derived Class**

Inheritance is commonly used to extend a class or give it additional capabilities. Sometimes it may be helpful to overload a base class function with a function of the same name in the derived class. For example, recall the GradedActivity class that was presented earlier in this chapter:

```
class GradedActivity
{
protected:
   char letter;         // To hold the letter grade
   double score;        // To hold the numeric score
   void determineGrade(); // Determines the letter grade
```

```
public:
   // Default constructor
   GradedActivity()
      { letter = ' '; score = 0.0; }

   // Mutator function
   void setScore(double s)
      { score = s;
        determineGrade();}

   // Accessor functions
   double getScore() const
      { return score; }

   char getLetterGrade() const
      { return letter; }
};
```

This class holds a numeric score and determines a letter grade based on that score. The setScore member function stores a value in score, then calls the determineGrade member function to determine the letter grade.

Suppose a teacher wants to "curve" a numeric score before the letter grade is determined. For example, Dr. Harrison determines that in order to curve the grades in her class she must multiply each student's score by a certain percentage. This gives an adjusted score, which is used to determine the letter grade.

The following CurvedActivity class is derived from the GradedActivity class. It multiplies the numeric score by a percentage, and passes that value as an argument to the base class's setScore function. (This file is stored in the Student Source Code Folder Chapter 15\CurvedActivity.)

Contents of CurvedActivity.h

```
 1   #ifndef CURVEDACTIVITY_H
 2   #define CURVEDACTIVITY_H
 3   #include "GradedActivity.h"
 4
 5   class CurvedActivity : public GradedActivity
 6   {
 7   protected:
 8      double rawScore;       // Unadjusted score
 9      double percentage;     // Curve percentage
10   public:
11      // Default constructor
12      CurvedActivity() : GradedActivity()
13         { rawScore = 0.0; percentage = 0.0; }
14
15      // Mutator functions
16      void setScore(double s)
17         { rawScore = s;
18           GradedActivity::setScore(rawScore * percentage); }
19
```

```
20        void setPercentage(double c)
21           { percentage = c; }
22
23        // Accessor functions
24        double getPercentage() const
25           { return percentage; }
26
27        double getRawScore() const
28           { return rawScore; }
29    };
30    #endif
```

This `CurvedActivity` class has the following member variables:

- `rawScore`   This variable holds the student's unadjusted score.
- `percentage`   This variable holds the value that the unadjusted score must be multiplied by to get the curved score.

It also has the following member functions:

- A default constructor that calls the `GradedActivity` default constructor, then sets `rawScore` and `percentage` to 0.0.
- `setScore`   This function accepts an argument that is the student's unadjusted score. The function stores the argument in the `rawScore` variable, then passes `rawScore * percentage` as an argument to the base class's `setScore` function.
- `setPercentage`   This function stores a value in the `percentage` variable.
- `getPercentage`   This function returns the value in the `percentage` variable.
- `getRawScore`   This function returns the value in the `rawScore` variable.

 NOTE: Although we are not using the `CurvedActivity` class as a base class, it still has a protected member section. This is because we might want to use the `CurvedActivity` class itself as a base class, as you will see in the next section.

Notice that the `CurvedActivity` class has a `setScore` member function. This function has the same name as one of the base class member functions. When a derived class's member function has the same name as a base class member function, it is said that the derived class function *redefines* the base class function. When an object of the derived class calls the function, it calls the derived class's version of the function.

There is a distinction between redefining a function and overloading a function. An overloaded function is one with the same name as one or more other functions, but with a different parameter list. The compiler uses the arguments passed to the function to tell which version to call. Overloading can take place with regular functions that are not members of a class. Overloading can also take place inside a class when two or more member functions *of the same class* have the same name. These member functions must have different parameter lists for the compiler to tell them apart in function calls.

Redefining happens when a derived class has a function with the same name as a base class function. The parameter lists of the two functions can be the same because the derived class function is always called by objects of the derived class type.

Let's continue our look at the `CurvedActivity` class. Here is the `setScore` member function:

```
void setScore(double s)
   { rawScore = s;
     GradedActivity::setScore(rawScore * percentage); }
```

This function accepts an argument that should be the student's unadjusted numeric score, into the parameter s. This value is stored in the `rawScore` variable. Then the following statement is executed:

```
GradedActivity::setScore(rawScore * percentage);
```

This statement calls the base class's version of the `setScore` function with the expression `rawScore * percentage` passed as an argument. Notice that the name of the base class and the scope resolution operator precede the name of the function. This specifies that the base class's version of the `setScore` function is being called. A derived class function may call a base class function of the same name using this notation, which takes this form:

```
BaseClassName::functionName(ArgumentList);
```

Program 15-7 shows the `GradedActivity` and `CurvedActivity` classes used in a complete program. (This file is stored in the Student Source Code Folder `Chapter 15\ CurvedActivity`.)

Program 15-7

```
1   // This program demonstrates a class that redefines
2   // a base class function.
3   #include <iostream>
4   #include <iomanip>
5   #include "CurvedActivity.h"
6   using namespace std;
7
8   int main()
9   {
10      double numericScore;  // To hold the numeric score
11      double percentage;    // To hold curve percentage
12
13      // Define a CurvedActivity object.
14      CurvedActivity exam;
15
16      // Get the unadjusted score.
17      cout << "Enter the student's raw numeric score: ";
18      cin >> numericScore;
19
20      // Get the curve percentage.
21      cout << "Enter the curve percentage for this student: ";
22      cin >> percentage;
23
24      // Send the values to the exam object.
25      exam.setPercentage(percentage);
26      exam.setScore(numericScore);
27
```

(program continues)

Program 15-7 *(continued)*

```
28      // Display the grade data.
29      cout << fixed << setprecision(2);
30      cout << "The raw score is "
31           << exam.getRawScore() << endl;
32      cout << "The curved score is "
33           << exam.getScore() << endl;
34      cout << "The curved grade is "
35           << exam.getLetterGrade() << endl;
36
37      return 0;
38   }
```

Program Output with Example Input Shown in Bold
```
Enter the student's raw numeric score: 87 [Enter]
Enter the curve percentage for this student: 1.06 [Enter]
The raw score is 87.00
The curved score is 92.22
The curved grade is A
```

It is important to note that even though a derived class may redefine a function in the base class, objects that are defined of the base class type still call the base class version of the function. This is demonstrated in Program 15-8.

Program 15-8

```
1    // This program demonstrates that when a derived class function
2    // overrides a base class function, objects of the base class
3    // still call the base class version of the function.
4    #include <iostream>
5    using namespace std;
6
7    class BaseClass
8    {
9    public:
10      void showMessage()
11         { cout << "This is the Base class.\n"; }
12   };
13
14   class DerivedClass : public BaseClass
15   {
16   public:
17      void showMessage()
18         { cout << "This is the Derived class.\n"; }
19   };
20
21   int main()
22   {
23      BaseClass b;
24      DerivedClass d;
25
```

```
26      b.showMessage();
27      d.showMessage();
28
29      return 0;
30  }
```

Program Output
This is the Base class.
This is the Derived class.

In Program 15-8, a class named BaseClass is declared with a member function named showMessage. A class named DerivedClass is then declared, also with a showMessage member function. As their names imply, DerivedClass is derived from BaseClass. Two objects, b and d, are defined in function main. The object b is a BaseClass object and d is a DerivedClass object. When b is used to call the showMessage function, it is the BaseClass version that is executed. Likewise, when d is used to call showMessage, the DerivedClass version is used.

15.5 Class Hierarchies

CONCEPT: A base class can also be derived from another class.

Sometimes it is desirable to establish a hierarchy of classes in which one class inherits from a second class, which in turn inherits from a third class, as illustrated by Figure 15-4. In some cases, the inheritance of classes goes on for many layers.

Figure 15-4

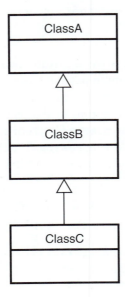

In Figure 15-4, `ClassC` inherits `ClassB`'s members, including the ones that `ClassB` inherited from `ClassA`. Let's look at an example of such a chain of inheritance. Consider the following `PassFailActivity` class, which inherits from the `GradedActivity` class. The class is intended to determine a letter grade of 'P' for passing, or 'F' for failing. (This file is stored in the Student Source Code Folder `Chapter 15\PassFailActivity`.)

Contents of `PassFailActivity.h`

```
 1  #ifndef PASSFAILACTIVITY_H
 2  #define PASSFAILACTIVITY_H
 3  #include "GradedActivity.h"
 4
 5  class PassFailActivity : public GradedActivity
 6  {
 7  protected:
 8     double minPassingScore;    // Minimum passing score.
 9  public:
10     // Default constructor
11     PassFailActivity() : GradedActivity()
12        { minPassingScore = 0.0; }
13
14     // Constructor
15     PassFailActivity(double mps) : GradedActivity()
16        { minPassingScore = mps; }
17
18     // Mutator
19     void setMinPassingScore(double mps)
20        { minPassingScore = mps; }
21
22     // Accessors
23     double getMinPassingScore() const
24        { return minPassingScore; }
25
26     char getLetterGrade() const;
27  };
28  #endif
```

The `PassFailActivity` class has a private member variable named `minPassingScore`. This variable holds the minimum passing score for an activity. The default constructor, in lines 11 through 12, sets `minPassingScore` to 0.0. An overloaded constructor in lines 15 through 16 accepts a `double` argument that is the minimum passing grade for the activity. This value is stored in the `minPassingScore` variable. The `getLetterGrade` member function is defined in the following `PassFailActivity.cpp` file. (This file is also stored in the Student Source Code Folder `Chapter 15\PassFailActivity`.)

Contents of `PassFailActivity.cpp`

```
 1  #include "PassFailActivity.h"
 2
 3  //*********************************************************
 4  // Member function PassFailActivity::getLetterGrade       *
 5  // This function returns 'P' if the score is passing,     *
 6  // otherwise it returns 'F'.                              *
 7  //*********************************************************
```

```
 8
 9   char PassFailActivity::getLetterGrade() const
10   {
11      char letterGrade;
12
13      if (score >= minPassingScore)
14         letterGrade = 'P';
15      else
16         letterGrade = 'F';
17
18      return letterGrade;
19   }
```

This `getLetterGrade` member function redefines the `getLetterGrade` member function of `GradedActivity` class. This version of the function returns a grade of `'P'` if the numeric score is greater than or equal to `minPassingScore`. Otherwise, the function returns a grade of `'F'`.

The `PassFailActivity` class represents the general characteristics of a student's pass-or-fail activity. There might be numerous types of pass-or-fail activities, however. Suppose we need a more specialized class, such as one that determines a student's grade for a pass-or-fail exam. The following `PassFailExam` class is an example. This class is derived from the `PassFailActivity` class. It inherits all of the members of `PassFailActivity`, including the ones that `PassFailActivity` inherits from `GradedActivity`. The `PassFailExam` class calculates the number of points that each question on the exam is worth, as well as the student's numeric score. (These files are stored in the Student Source Code Folder Chapter 15\PassFailActivity.)

Contents of `PassFailExam.h`

```
 1   #ifndef PASSFAILEXAM_H
 2   #define PASSFAILEXAM_H
 3   #include "PassFailActivity.h"
 4
 5   class PassFailExam : public PassFailActivity
 6   {
 7   private:
 8      int numQuestions;    // Number of questions
 9      double pointsEach;    // Points for each question
10      int numMissed;       // Number of questions missed
11   public:
12      // Default constructor
13      PassFailExam() : PassFailActivity()
14         { numQuestions = 0;
15           pointsEach = 0.0;
16           numMissed = 0; }
17
18      // Constructor
19      PassFailExam(int questions, int missed, double mps) :
20         PassFailActivity(mps)
21         { set(questions, missed); }
22
```

```
23        // Mutator function
24        void set(int, int);  // Defined in PassFailExam.cpp
25
26        // Accessor functions
27        double getNumQuestions() const
28           { return numQuestions; }
29
30        double getPointsEach() const
31           { return pointsEach; }
32
33        int getNumMissed() const
34           { return numMissed; }
35     };
36     #endif
```

Contents of `PassFailExam.cpp`

```
1     #include "PassFailExam.h"
2
3     //********************************************************
4     // set function                                         *
5     // The parameters are the number of questions and the   *
6     // number of questions missed.                          *
7     //********************************************************
8
9     void PassFailExam::set(int questions, int missed)
10    {
11       double numericScore;  // To hold the numeric score
12
13       // Set the number of questions and number missed.
14       numQuestions = questions;
15       numMissed = missed;
16
17       // Calculate the points for each question.
18       pointsEach = 100.0 / numQuestions;
19
20       // Calculate the numeric score for this exam.
21       numericScore = 100.0 - (missed * pointsEach);
22
23       // Call the inherited setScore function to set
24       // the numeric score.
25       setScore(numericScore);
26    }
```

The `PassFailExam` class inherits all of the `PassFailActivity` class's members, including the ones that `PassFailActivity` inherited from `GradedActivity`. Because the public base class access specification is used, all of the protected members of `PassFailActivity` become protected members of `PassFailExam`, and all of the public members of `PassFailActivity` become public members of `PassFailExam`. Table 15-2 lists all of the member variables of the `PassFailExam` class, and Table 15-3 lists all the member functions. These include the members that were inherited from the base classes.

Table 15-2

Member Variable of the PassFailExam Class	Access	Inherited?
numQuestions	protected	No
pointsEach	protected	No
numMissed	protected	No
minPassingScore	protected	Yes, from PassFailActivity
score	protected	Yes, from PassFailActivity, which inherited it from GradedActivity

Table 15-3

Member Function of the PassFailExam Class	Access	Inherited?
set	public	No
getNumQuestions	public	No
getPointsEach	public	No
getNumMissed	public	No
setMinPassingScore	public	Yes, from PassFailActivity
getMinPassingScore	public	Yes, from PassFailActivity
getLetterGrade	public	Yes, from PassFailActivity
setScore	public	Yes, from PassFailActivity, which inherited it from GradedActivity
getScore	public	Yes, from PassFailActivity, which inherited it from GradedActivity

Program 15-9 demonstrates the PassFailExam class. This file is also stored in the student source code folder Chapter 15\PassFailActivity.

Program 15-9

```
1   // This program demonstrates the PassFailExam class.
2   #include <iostream>
3   #include <iomanip>
4   #include "PassFailExam.h"
5   using namespace std;
6
7   int main()
8   {
9      int questions;      // Number of questions
10     int missed;         // Number of questions missed
11     double minPassing;  // The minimum passing score
12
13     // Get the number of questions on the exam.
14     cout << "How many questions are on the exam? ";
15     cin >> questions;
16
```

(program continues)

Program 15-9   (continued)

```
17        // Get the number of questions the student missed.
18        cout << "How many questions did the student miss? ";
19        cin >> missed;
20
21        // Get the minimum passing score.
22        cout << "Enter the minimum passing score for this test: ";
23        cin >> minPassing;
24
25        // Define a PassFailExam object.
26        PassFailExam exam(questions, missed, minPassing);
27
28        // Display the test results.
29        cout << fixed << setprecision(1);
30        cout << "\nEach question counts "
31             << exam.getPointsEach() << " points.\n";
32        cout << "The minimum passing score is "
33             << exam.getMinPassingScore() << endl;
34        cout << "The student's exam score is "
35             << exam.getScore() << endl;
36        cout << "The student's grade is "
37             << exam.getLetterGrade() << endl;
38        return 0;
39   }
```

Program Output with Example Input Shown in Bold
```
How many questions are on the exam? 100 [Enter]
How many questions did the student miss? 25 [Enter]
Enter the minimum passing score for this test: 60 [Enter]

Each question counts 1.0 points.
The minimum passing score is 60.0
The student's exam score is 75.0
The student's grade is P
```

This program uses the PassFailExam object to call the getLetterGrade member function in line 37. Recall that the PassFailActivity class redefines the getLetterGrade function to report only grades of 'P' or 'F'. Because the PassFailExam class is derived from the PassFailActivity class, it inherits the redefined getLetterGrade function.

Software designers often use class hierarchy diagrams. Like a family tree, a class hierarchy diagram shows the inheritance relationships between classes. Figure 15-5 shows a class hierarchy for the GradedActivity, FinalExam, PassFailActivity, and PassFailExam classes. The more general classes are toward the top of the tree and the more specialized classes are toward the bottom.

Figure 15-5

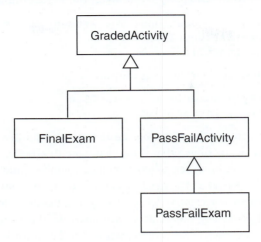

15.6 Polymorphism and Virtual Member Functions

CONCEPT: Polymorphism allows an object reference variable or an object pointer to reference objects of different types, and to call the correct member functions, depending upon the type of object being referenced.

VideoNote
Polymorphism

Look at the following code for a function named `displayGrade`:

```
void displayGrade(const GradedActivity &activity)
{
    cout << setprecision(1) << fixed;
    cout << "The activity's numeric score is "
        << activity.getScore() << endl;
    cout << "The activity's letter grade is "
        << activity.getLetterGrade() << endl;
}
```

This function uses a const `GradedActivity` reference variable as its parameter. When a `GradedActivity` object is passed as an argument to this function, the function calls the object's `getScore` and `getLetterGrade` member functions to display the numeric score and letter grade. The following code shows how we might call the function.

```
GradedActivity test(88.0);  // The score is 88
displayGrade(test);         // Pass test to displayGrade
```

This code will produce the following output:

```
The activity's numeric score is 88.0
The activity's letter grade is B
```

Recall that the `GradedActivity` class is also the base class for the `FinalExam` class. Because of the "is-a" relationship between a base class and a derived class, an object of the `FinalExam` class is not just a `FinalExam` object. It is also a `GradedActivity` object.

(A final exam *is a* graded activity.) Because of this relationship, we can also pass a `FinalExam` object to the `displayGrade` function. For example, look at the following code:

```
// There are 100 questions. The student missed 25.
FinalExam test2(100, 25);
displayGrade(test2);
```

This code will produce the following output:

```
The activity's numeric score is 75.0
The activity's letter grade is C
```

Because the parameter in the `displayGrade` function is a `GradedActivity` reference variable, it can reference any object that is derived from `GradedActivity`. A problem can occur with this type of code, however, when redefined member functions are involved. For example, recall that the `PassFailActivity` class is derived from the `GradedActivity` class. The `PassFailActivity` class redefines the `getLetterGrade` function. Although we can pass a `PassFailActivity` object as an argument to the `displayGrade` function, we will not get the results we wish. This is demonstrated in Program 15-10. (This file is stored in the Student Source Code Folder `Chapter 15\PassFailActivity`.)

Program 15-10

```
1   #include <iostream>
2   #include <iomanip>
3   #include "PassFailActivity.h"
4   using namespace std;
5
6   // Function prototype
7   void displayGrade(const GradedActivity &);
8
9   int main()
10  {
11      // Create a PassFailActivity object. Minimum passing
12      // score is 70.
13      PassFailActivity test(70);
14
15      // Set the score to 72.
16      test.setScore(72);
17
18      // Display the object's grade data. The letter grade
19      // should be 'P'. What will be displayed?
20      displayGrade(test);
21      return 0;
22  }
23
24  //*****************************************************************
25  // The displayGrade function displays a GradedActivity object's *
26  // numeric score and letter grade.                              *
27  //*****************************************************************
28
29  void displayGrade(const GradedActivity &activity)
```

```
30   {
31       cout << setprecision(1) << fixed;
32       cout << "The activity's numeric score is "
33            << activity.getScore() << endl;
34       cout << "The activity's letter grade is "
35            << activity.getLetterGrade() << endl;
36   }
```

Program Output
```
The activity's numeric score is 72.0
The activity's letter grade is C
```

As you can see from the example output, the getLetterGrade member function returned 'C' instead of 'P'. This is because the GradedActivity class's getLetterGrade function was executed instead of the PassFailActivity class's version of the function.

This behavior happens because of the way C++ matches function calls with the correct function. This process is known as *binding*. In Program 15-10, C++ decides at compile time which version of the getLetterGrade function to execute when it encounters the call to the function in line 35. Even though we passed a PassFailActivity object to the displayGrade function, the activity parameter in the displayGrade function is a GradedActivity reference variable. Because it is of the GradedActivity type, the compiler binds the function call in line 35 with the GradedActivity class's getLetterGrade function. When the program executes, it has already been determined by the compiler that the GradedActivity class's getLetterGrade function will be called. The process of matching a function call with a function at compile time is called *static binding*.

To remedy this, the getLetterGrade function can be made *virtual*. A *virtual function* is a member function that is dynamically bound to function calls. In *dynamic binding*, C++ determines which function to call at runtime, depending on the type of the object responsible for the call. If a GradedActivity object is responsible for the call, C++ will execute the GradedActivity::getLetterGrade function. If a PassFailActivity object is responsible for the call, C++ will execute the PassFailActivity::getLetterGrade function.

Virtual functions are declared by placing the key word virtual before the return type in the base class's function declaration, such as

```
virtual char getLetterGrade() const;
```

This declaration tells the compiler to expect getLetterGrade to be redefined in a derived class. The compiler does not bind calls to the function with the actual function. Instead, it allows the program to bind calls, at runtime, to the version of the function that belongs to the same class as the object responsible for the call.

 NOTE: You place the virtual key word only in the function's declaration or prototype. If the function is defined outside the class, you do not place the virtual key word in the function header.

The following code shows an updated version of the GradedActivity class, with the getLetterGrade function declared virtual. This file is stored in the Student Source Code Folder Chapter 15\GradedActivity Version 3. The GradedActivity.cpp file has not changed, so it is not shown again.

Contents of `GradedActivity.h` (Version 3)

```
 1   #ifndef GRADEDACTIVITY_H
 2   #define GRADEDACTIVITY_H
 3
 4   // GradedActivity class declaration
 5
 6   class GradedActivity
 7   {
 8   protected:
 9      double score;    // To hold the numeric score
10   public:
11      // Default constructor
12      GradedActivity()
13         { score = 0.0; }
14
15      // Constructor
16      GradedActivity(double s)
17         { score = s; }
18
19      // Mutator function
20      void setScore(double s)
21         { score = s; }
22
23      // Accessor functions
24      double getScore() const
25         { return score; }
26
27      virtual char getLetterGrade() const;
28   };
29   #endif
```

The only change we have made to this class is to declare `getLetterGrade` as `virtual` in line 27. This tells the compiler not to bind calls to `getLetterGrade` with the function at compile time. Instead, calls to the function will be bound dynamically to the function at runtime.

When a member function is declared `virtual` in a base class, any redefined versions of the function that appear in derived classes automatically become `virtual`. So, it is not necessary to declare the `getLetterGrade` function in the `PassFailActivity` class as `virtual`. It is still a good idea to declare the function `virtual` in the `PassFailActivity` class for documentation purposes. A new version of the `PassFailActivity` class is shown here. This file is stored in the Student Source Code Folder `Chapter 15\GradedActivity Version 3`. The `PassFailActivity.cpp` file has not changed, so it is not shown again.

Contents of `PassFailActivity.h`

```
 1   #ifndef PASSFAILACTIVITY_H
 2   #define PASSFAILACTIVITY_H
 3   #include "GradedActivity.h"
 4
 5   class PassFailActivity : public GradedActivity
```

```
 6  {
 7  protected:
 8     double minPassingScore;    // Minimum passing score
 9  public:
10     // Default constructor
11     PassFailActivity() : GradedActivity()
12        { minPassingScore = 0.0; }
13
14     // Constructor
15     PassFailActivity(double mps) : GradedActivity()
16        { minPassingScore = mps; }
17
18     // Mutator
19     void setMinPassingScore(double mps)
20        { minPassingScore = mps; }
21
22     // Accessors
23     double getMinPassingScore() const
24        { return minPassingScore; }
25
26     virtual char getLetterGrade() const;
27  };
28  #endif
```

The only change we have made to this class is to declare getLetterGrade as virtual in line 26. Program 15-11 is identical to Program 15-10, except it uses the corrected version of the GradedActivity and PassFailActivity classes. This file is also stored in the student source code folder Chapter 15\GradedActivity Version 3.

Program 15-11

```
 1  #include <iostream>
 2  #include <iomanip>
 3  #include "PassFailActivity.h"
 4  using namespace std;
 5
 6  // Function prototype
 7  void displayGrade(const GradedActivity &);
 8
 9  int main()
10  {
11     // Create a PassFailActivity object. Minimum passing
12     // score is 70.
13     PassFailActivity test(70);
14
15     // Set the score to 72.
16     test.setScore(72);
17
18     // Display the object's grade data. The letter grade
19     // should be 'P'. What will be displayed?
20     displayGrade(test);
21     return 0;
22  }
```

(program continues)

Program 15-11 *(continued)*

```
23
24   //*****************************************************************
25   // The displayGrade function displays a GradedActivity object's *
26   // numeric score and letter grade.                              *
27   //*****************************************************************
28
29   void displayGrade(const GradedActivity &activity)
30   {
31      cout << setprecision(1) << fixed;
32      cout << "The activity's numeric score is "
33           << activity.getScore() << endl;
34      cout << "The activity's letter grade is "
35           << activity.getLetterGrade() << endl;
36   }
```

Program Output

```
The activity's numeric score is 72.0
The activity's letter grade is P
```

Now that the getLetterGrade function is declared virtual, the program works properly. This type of behavior is known as polymorphism. The term *polymorphism* means the ability to take many forms. Program 15-12 demonstrates polymorphism by passing objects of the GradedActivity and PassFailExam classes to the displayGrade function. This file is stored in the Student Source Code Folder Chapter 15\GradedActivity Version 3.

Program 15-12

```
1    #include <iostream>
2    #include <iomanip>
3    #include "PassFailExam.h"
4    using namespace std;
5
6    // Function prototype
7    void displayGrade(const GradedActivity &);
8
9    int main()
10   {
11      // Create a GradedActivity object. The score is 88.
12      GradedActivity test1(88.0);
13
14      // Create a PassFailExam object. There are 100 questions,
15      // the student missed 25 of them, and the minimum passing
16      // score is 70.
17      PassFailExam test2(100, 25, 70.0);
18
19      // Display the grade data for both objects.
20      cout << "Test 1:\n";
21      displayGrade(test1);     // GradedActivity object
22      cout << "\nTest 2:\n";
```

```
23        displayGrade(test2);    // PassFailExam object
24        return 0;
25    }
26
27    //*******************************************************************
28    // The displayGrade function displays a GradedActivity object's *
29    // numeric score and letter grade.                              *
30    //*******************************************************************
31
32    void displayGrade(const GradedActivity &activity)
33    {
34        cout << setprecision(1) << fixed;
35        cout << "The activity's numeric score is "
36             << activity.getScore() << endl;
37        cout << "The activity's letter grade is "
38             << activity.getLetterGrade() << endl;
39    }
```

Program Output

```
Test 1:
The activity's numeric score is 88.0
The activity's letter grade is B

Test 2:
The activity's numeric score is 75.0
The activity's letter grade is P
```

Polymorphism Requires References or Pointers

The displayGrade function in Programs 15-11 and 15-12 uses a GradedActivity reference variable as its parameter. When we call the function, we pass an object by reference. Polymorphic behavior is not possible when an object is passed by value, however. For example, suppose the displayGrade function had been written as shown here:

```
// Polymorphic behavior is not possible with this function.
void displayGrade(const GradedActivity activity)
{
    cout << setprecision(1) << fixed;
    cout << "The activity's numeric score is "
         << activity.getScore() << endl;
    cout << "The activity's letter grade is "
         << activity.getLetterGrade() << endl;
}
```

In this version of the function the activity parameter is an object variable, not a reference variable. Suppose we call this version of the function with the following code:

```
// Create a GradedActivity object. The score is 88.
GradedActivity test1(88.0);

// Create a PassFailExam object. There are 100 questions,
// the student missed 25 of them, and the minimum passing
// score is 70.
PassFailExam test2(100, 25, 70.0);
```

```
                  // Display the grade data for both objects.
                  cout << "Test 1:\n";
                  displayGrade(test1);    // Pass the GradedActivity object
                  cout << "\nTest 2:\n";
                  displayGrade(&test2);   // Pass the PassFailExam object
```

This code will produce the following output:

```
    Test 1:
    The activity's numeric score is 88.0
    The activity's letter grade is B

    Test 2:
    The activity's numeric score is 75.0
    The activity's letter grade is C
```

Even though the `getLetterGrade` function is declared `virtual`, static binding still takes place because `activity` is not a reference variable or a pointer.

Alternatively we could have used a `GradedActivity` pointer in the `displayGrade` function, as shown in Program 15-13. This file is also stored in the Student Source Code Folder `Chapter 15\GradedActivity Version 3`.

Program 15-13

```
 1   #include <iostream>
 2   #include <iomanip>
 3   #include "PassFailExam.h"
 4   using namespace std;
 5
 6   // Function prototype
 7   void displayGrade(const GradedActivity *);
 8
 9   int main()
10   {
11      // Create a GradedActivity object. The score is 88.
12      GradedActivity test1(88.0);
13
14      // Create a PassFailExam object. There are 100 questions,
15      // the student missed 25 of them, and the minimum passing
16      // score is 70.
17      PassFailExam test2(100, 25, 70.0);
18
19      // Display the grade data for both objects.
20      cout << "Test 1:\n";
21      displayGrade(&test1);  // Address of the GradedActivity object
22      cout << "\nTest 2:\n";
23      displayGrade(&test2);  // Address of the PassFailExam object
24      return 0;
25   }
26
27   //****************************************************************
28   // The displayGrade function displays a GradedActivity object's *
29   // numeric score and letter grade. This version of the function *
30   // uses a GradedActivity pointer as its parameter.               *
31   //****************************************************************
```

```
32
33   void displayGrade(const GradedActivity *activity)
34   {
35      cout << setprecision(1) << fixed;
36      cout << "The activity's numeric score is "
37           << activity->getScore() << endl;
38      cout << "The activity's letter grade is "
39           << activity->getLetterGrade() << endl;
40   }
```

Program Output

```
Test 1:
The activity's numeric score is 88.0
The activity's letter grade is B

Test 2:
The activity's numeric score is 75.0
The activity's letter grade is P
```

Base Class Pointers

Pointers to a base class may be assigned the address of a derived class object. For example, look at the following code:

```
GradedActivity *exam = new PassFailExam(100, 25, 70.0);
```

This statement dynamically allocates a PassFailExam object and assigns its address to exam, which is a GradedActivity pointer. We can then use the exam pointer to call member functions, as shown here:

```
cout << exam->getScore() << endl;
cout << exam->getLetterGrade() << endl;
```

Program 15-14 is an example that uses base class pointers to reference derived class objects. This file is also stored in the Student Source Code Folder Chapter 15\ GradedActivity Version 3.

Program 15-14

```
1    #include <iostream>
2    #include <iomanip>
3    #include "PassFailExam.h"
4    using namespace std;
5
6    // Function prototype
7    void displayGrade(const GradedActivity *);
8
9    int main()
10   {
11      // Constant for the size of an array.
12      const int NUM_TESTS = 4;
13
```

(program continues)

Program 15-14 *(continued)*

```
14      // tests is an array of GradedActivity pointers.
15      // Each element of tests is initialized with the
16      // address of a dynamically allocated object.
17      GradedActivity *tests[NUM_TESTS] =
18         { new GradedActivity(88.0),
19           new PassFailExam(100, 25, 70.0),
20           new GradedActivity(67.0),
21           new PassFailExam(50, 12, 60.0)
22         };
23
24      // Display the grade data for each element in the array.
25      for (int count = 0; count < NUM_TESTS; count++)
26      {
27         cout << "Test #" << (count + 1) << ":\n";
28         displayGrade(tests[count]);
29         cout << endl;
30      }
31      return 0;
32   }
33
34   //*****************************************************************
35   // The displayGrade function displays a GradedActivity object's *
36   // numeric score and letter grade. This version of the function *
37   // uses a GradedActivity pointer as its parameter.              *
38   //*****************************************************************
39
40   void displayGrade(const GradedActivity *activity)
41   {
42      cout << setprecision(1) << fixed;
43      cout << "The activity's numeric score is "
44           << activity->getScore() << endl;
45      cout << "The activity's letter grade is "
46           << activity->getLetterGrade() << endl;
47   }
```

Program Output

```
Test #1:
The activity's numeric score is 88.0
The activity's letter grade is B

Test #2:
The activity's numeric score is 75.0
The activity's letter grade is P

Test #3:
The activity's numeric score is 67.0
The activity's letter grade is D

Test #4:
The activity's numeric score is 76.0
The activity's letter grade is P
```

Let's take a closer look at this program. An array named `tests` is defined in lines 17 through 22. This is an array of `GradedActivity` pointers. The array elements are initialized with the addresses of dynamically allocated objects. The `tests[0]` element is initialized with the address of the `GradedActivity` object returned from this expression:

```
new GradedActivity(88.0)
```

The `tests[1]` element is initialized with the address of the `GradedActivity` object returned from this expression:

```
new PassFailExam(100, 25, 70.0)
```

The `tests[2]` element is initialized with the address of the `GradedActivity` object returned from this expression:

```
new GradedActivity(67.0)
```

Finally, the `tests[3]` element is initialized with the address of the `GradedActivity` object returned from this expression:

```
new PassFailExam(50, 12, 60.0)
```

Although each element in the array is a `GradedActivity` pointer, some of the elements point to `GradedActivity` objects and some point to `PassFailExam` objects. The loop in lines 25 through 30 steps through the array, passing each pointer element to the `displayGrade` function.

Base Class Pointers and References Know Only About Base Class Members

Although a base class pointer can reference objects of any class that derives from the base class, there are limits to what the pointer can do with those objects. Recall that the `GradedActivity` class has, other than its constructors, only three member functions: `setScore`, `getScore`, and `getLetterGrade`. So, a `GradedActivity` pointer can be used to call only those functions, regardless of the type of object it points to. For example, look at the following code.

```
GradedActivity *exam = new PassFailExam(100, 25, 70.0);
cout << exam->getScore() << endl;       // This works.
cout << exam->getLetterGrade() << endl; // This works.
cout << exam->getPointsEach() << endl;  // ERROR! Won't work!
```

In this code, exam is a `GradedActivity` pointer, and is assigned the address of a `PassFailExam` object. The `GradedActivity` class has only the `setScore`, `getScore`, and `getLetterGrade` member functions, so those are the only member functions that the exam variable knows how to execute. The last statement in this code is a call to the `getPointsEach` member function, which is defined in the `PassFailExam` class. Because the exam variable only knows about member functions in the `GradedActivity` class, it cannot execute this function.

The "Is-a" Relationship Does Not Work in Reverse

It is important to note that the "is-a" relationship does not work in reverse. Although the statement "a final exam is a graded activity" is true, the statement "a graded activity is a final exam" is not true. This is because not all graded activities are final exams. Likewise, not all `GradedActivity` objects are `FinalExam` objects. So, the following code will not work.

```
// Create a GradedActivity object.
GradedActivity *gaPointer = new GradedActivity(88.0);

// Error! This will not work.
FinalExam *fePointer = gaPointer;
```

You cannot assign the address of a `GradedActivity` object to a `FinalExam` pointer. This makes sense because `FinalExam` objects have capabilities that go beyond those of a `GradedActivity` object. Interestingly, the C++ compiler will let you make such an assignment if you use a type cast, as shown here:

```
// Create a GradedActivity object.
GradedActivity *gaPointer = new GradedActivity(88.0);

// This will work, but with limitations.
FinalExam *fePointer = static_cast<FinalExam *>(gaPointer);
```

After this code executes, the derived class pointer `fePointer` will be pointing to a base class object. We can use the pointer to access members of the object, but only the members that exist. The following code demonstrates:

```
// This will work. The object has a getScore function.
cout << fePointer->getScore() << endl;

// This will work. The object has a getLetterGrade function.
cout << fePointer->getLetterGrade() << endl;

// This will compile, but an error will occur at runtime.
// The object does not have a getPointsEach function.
cout << fePointer->getPointsEach() << endl;
```

In this code `fePointer` is a `FinalExam` pointer, and it points to a `GradedActivity` object. The first two `cout` statements work because the `GradedActivity` object has `getScore` and a `getLetterGrade` member functions. The last `cout` statement will cause an error, however, because it calls the `getPointsEach` member function. The `GradedActivity` object does not have a `getPointsEach` member function.

Redefining vs. Overriding

Earlier in this chapter you learned how a derived class can redefine a base class member function. When a class redefines a virtual function, it is said that the class *overrides* the function. In C++, the difference between overriding and redefining base class functions is that overridden functions are dynamically bound, and redefined functions are statically bound. Only virtual functions can be overridden.

Virtual Destructors

When you write a class with a destructor, and that class could potentially become a base class, you should always declare the destructor `virtual`. This is because the compiler will perform static binding on the destructor if it is not declared `virtual`. This can lead to problems when a base class pointer or reference variable references a derived class object. If the derived class has its own destructor, it will not execute when the object is destroyed or goes out of scope. Only the base class destructor will execute. Program 15-15 demonstrates.

Program 15-15

```cpp
 1   #include <iostream>
 2   using namespace std;
 3
 4   // Animal is a base class.
 5   class Animal
 6   {
 7   public:
 8      // Constructor
 9      Animal()
10         { cout << "Animal constructor executing.\n"; }
11
12      // Destructor
13      ~Animal()
14         { cout << "Animal destructor executing.\n"; }
15   };
16
17   // The Dog class is derived from Animal
18   class Dog : public Animal
19   {
20   public:
21      // Constructor
22      Dog() : Animal()
23         { cout << "Dog constructor executing.\n"; }
24
25      // Destructor
26      ~Dog()
27         { cout << "Dog destructor executing.\n"; }
28   };
29
30   //***********************************************
31   // main function                                *
32   //***********************************************
33
34   int main()
35   {
36      // Create a Dog object, referenced by an
37      // Animal pointer.
38      Animal *myAnimal = new Dog;
39
40      // Delete the dog object.
41      delete myAnimal;
42      return 0;
43   }
```

Program Output

```
Animal constructor executing.
Dog constructor executing.
Animal destructor executing.
```

This program declares two classes: `Animal` and `Dog`. `Animal` is the base class and `Dog` is the derived class. Each class has its own constructor and destructor. In line 38, a `Dog` object is created and its address is stored in an `Animal` pointer. Both the `Animal` and the `Dog` constructors execute. In line 41 the object is deleted. When this statement executes, however, only the `Animal` destructor executes. The `Dog` destructor does not execute because the object is referenced by an `Animal` pointer. We can fix this problem by declaring the `Animal` class destructor `virtual`, as shown in Program 15-16.

Program 15-16

```
 1   #include <iostream>
 2   using namespace std;
 3
 4   // Animal is a base class.
 5   class Animal
 6   {
 7   public:
 8      // Constructor
 9      Animal()
10         { cout << "Animal constructor executing.\n"; }
11
12      // Destructor
13      virtual ~Animal()
14         { cout << "Animal destructor executing.\n"; }
15   };
16
17   // The Dog class is derived from Animal
18   class Dog : public Animal
19   {
20   public:
21      // Constructor
22      Dog() : Animal()
23         { cout << "Dog constructor executing.\n"; }
24
25      // Destructor
26      ~Dog()
27         { cout << "Dog destructor executing.\n"; }
28   };
29
30   //***********************************************
31   // main function                               *
32   //***********************************************
33
34   int main()
35   {
36      // Create a Dog object, referenced by an
37      // Animal pointer.
38      Animal *myAnimal = new Dog;
39
40      // Delete the dog object.
41      delete myAnimal;
42      return 0;
43   }
```

The only thing that has changed in this program is that the `Animal` class destructor is declared virtual in line 13. As a result, the destructor is dynamically bound at runtime. When the `Dog` object is destroyed, both the `Animal` and `Dog` destructors execute.

A good programming practice to follow is that any class that has a virtual member function should also have a virtual destructor. If the class doesn't require a destructor, it should have a virtual destructor that performs no statements. Remember, when a base class function is declared `virtual`, all overridden versions of the function in derived classes automatically become virtual. Including a virtual destructor in a base class, even one that does nothing, will ensure that any derived class destructors will also be virtual.

15.7 Abstract Base Classes and Pure Virtual Functions

CONCEPT: An abstract base class cannot be instantiated, but other classes are derived from it. A pure virtual function is a virtual member function of a base class that must be overridden. When a class contains a pure virtual function as a member, that class becomes an abstract base class.

Sometimes it is helpful to begin a class hierarchy with an *abstract base class*. An abstract base class is not instantiated itself, but serves as a base class for other classes. The abstract base class represents the generic, or abstract, form of all the classes that are derived from it.

For example, consider a factory that manufactures airplanes. The factory does not make a generic airplane, but makes three specific types of planes: two different models of prop-driven planes, and one commuter jet model. The computer software that catalogs the planes might use an abstract base class called `Airplane`. That class has members representing the common characteristics of all airplanes. In addition, it has classes for each of the three specific airplane models the factory manufactures. These classes have members representing the unique characteristics of each type of plane. The base class, `Airplane`, is never instantiated, but is used to derive the other classes.

A class becomes an abstract base class when one or more of its member functions is a *pure virtual function*. A pure virtual function is a virtual member function declared in a manner similar to the following:

```
virtual void showInfo() = 0;
```

The = 0 notation indicates that `showInfo` is a pure virtual function. Pure virtual functions have no body, or definition, in the base class. They must be overridden in derived classes. Additionally, the presence of a pure virtual function in a class prevents a program from instantiating the class. The compiler will generate an error if you attempt to define an object of an abstract base class.

For example, look at the following abstract base class `Student`. It holds data common to all students, but does not hold all the data needed for students of specific majors.

Contents of `Student.h`

```
1    // Specification file for the Student class
2    #ifndef STUDENT_H
3    #define STUDENT_H
4    #include <string>
5    using namespace std;
6
7    class Student
8    {
9    protected:
10       string name;          // Student name
11       string idNumber;      // Student ID
12       int yearAdmitted;     // Year student was admitted
13   public:
14       // Default constructor
15       Student()
16          { name = "";
17            idNumber = "";
18            yearAdmitted = 0; }
19
20       // Constructor
21       Student(string n, string id, int year)
22          { set(n, id, year); }
23
24       // The set function sets the attribute data.
25       void set(string n, string id, int year)
26          { name = n;                    // Assign the name
27            idNumber = id;               // Assign the ID number
28            yearAdmitted = year; }       // Assign the year admitted
29
30       // Accessor functions
31       const string getName() const
32          { return name; }
33
34       const string getIdNum() const
35          { return idNumber; }
36
37       int getYearAdmitted() const
38          { return yearAdmitted; }
39
40       // Pure virtual function
41       virtual int getRemainingHours() const = 0;
42   };
43   #endif
```

The `Student` class contains members for storing a student's name, ID number, and year admitted. It also has constructors and a mutator function for setting values in the `name`, `idNumber`, and `yearAdmitted` members. Accessor functions are provided that return the values in the `name`, `idNumber`, and `yearAdmitted` members. A pure virtual function named `getRemainingHours` is also declared.

The pure virtual function must be overridden in classes derived from the `Student` class. It was made a pure virtual function because this class is intended to be the base for classes that represent students of specific majors. For example, a `CsStudent` class might hold the data for a computer science student, and a `BiologyStudent` class might hold the data for a biology student. Computer science students must take courses in different disciplines than those taken by biology students. It stands to reason that the `CsStudent` class will calculate the number of hours taken in a different manner than the `BiologyStudent` class.

Let's look at an example of the `CsStudent` class.

Contents of `CsStudent.h`

```
1   // Specification file for the CsStudent class
2   #ifndef CSSTUDENT_H
3   #define CSSTUDENT_H
4   #include "Student.h"
5
6   // Constants for required hours
7   const int MATH_HOURS = 20;   // Math hours
8   const int CS_HOURS = 40;     // Computer science hours
9   const int GEN_ED_HOURS = 60; // General Ed hours
10
11  class CsStudent : public Student
12  {
13  private:
14      int mathHours;    // Hours of math taken
15      int csHours;      // Hours of Computer Science taken
16      int genEdHours;   // Hours of general education taken
17
18  public:
19      // Default constructor
20      CsStudent() : Student()
21          { mathHours = 0;
22            csHours = 0;
23            genEdHours = 0; }
24
25      // Constructor
26      CsStudent(string n, string id, int year) :
27        Student(n, id, year)
28          { mathHours = 0;
29            csHours = 0;
30            genEdHours = 0; }
31
32      // Mutator functions
33      void setMathHours(int mh)
34          { mathHours = mh; }
35
36      void setCsHours(int csh)
37          { csHours = csh; }
38
39      void setGenEdHours(int geh)
40          { genEdHours = geh; }
41
42      // Overridden getRemainingHours function,
43      // defined in CsStudent.cpp
44      virtual int getRemainingHours() const;
45  };
46  #endif
```

This file declares the following `const int` member variables in lines 7 through 9: `MATH_HOURS`, `CS_HOURS`, and `GEN_ED_HOURS`. These variables hold the required number of math, computer science, and general education hours for a computer science student. The `CsStudent` class, which derives from the `Student` class, declares the following member variables in lines 14 through 16: `mathHours`, `csHours`, and `genEdHours`. These variables hold the number of math, computer science, and general education hours taken by the student. Mutator functions are provided to store values in these variables. In addition, the class overrides the pure virtual `getRemainingHours` function in the `CsStudent.cpp` file.

Contents of `CsStudent.cpp`

```
 1   #include <iostream>
 2   #include "CsStudent.h"
 3   using namespace std;
 4
 5   //*******************************************************
 6   // The CsStudent::getRemainingHours function returns *
 7   // the number of hours remaining to be taken.         *
 8   //*******************************************************
 9
10   int CsStudent::getRemainingHours() const
11   {
12      int reqHours,      // Total required hours
13      remainingHours;    // Remaining hours
14
15      // Calculate the required hours.
16      reqHours = MATH_HOURS + CS_HOURS + GEN_ED_HOURS;
17
18      // Calculate the remaining hours.
19      remainingHours = reqHours - (mathHours + csHours +
20                       genEdHours);
21
22      // Return the remaining hours.
23      return remainingHours;
24   }
```

Program 15-17 provides a simple demonstration of the class.

Program 15-17

```
 1   // This program demonstrates the CsStudent class, which is
 2   // derived from the abstract base class, Student.
 3   #include <iostream>
 4   #include "CsStudent.h"
 5   using namespace std;
 6
 7   int main()
 8   {
 9      // Create a CsStudent object for a student.
10      CsStudent student("Jennifer Haynes", "167W98337", 2006);
11
12      // Store values for Math, Computer Science, and General
13      // Ed hours.
```

```
14      student.setMathHours(12);   // Student has taken 12 Math hours
15      student.setCsHours(20);     // Student has taken 20 CS hours
16      student.setGenEdHours(40); // Student has taken 40 Gen Ed hours
17
18      // Display the number of remaining hours.
19      cout << "The student " << student.getName()
20          << " needs to take " << student.getRemainingHours()
21          << " more hours to graduate.\n";
22
23      return 0;
24  }
```

Program Output

The student Jennifer Haynes needs to take 48 more hours to graduate.

Remember the following points about abstract base classes and pure virtual functions:

- When a class contains a pure virtual function, it is an abstract base class.
- Pure virtual functions are declared with the = 0 notation.
- Abstract base classes cannot be instantiated.
- Pure virtual functions have no body, or definition, in the base class.
- A pure virtual function *must* be overridden at some point in a derived class in order for it to become nonabstract.

 Checkpoint

myprogramminglab *www.myprogramminglab.com*

15.9   Explain the difference between overloading a function and redefining a function.

15.10   Explain the difference between static binding and dynamic binding.

15.11   Are virtual functions statically bound or dynamically bound?

15.12   What will the following program display?

```
#include <iostream.>
using namespace std;

class First
{
protected:
    int a;
public:
    First(int x = 1)
        { a = x; }

    int getVal()
        { return a; }
};

class Second : public First
{
private:
    int b;
```

```cpp
public:
    Second(int y = 5)
        { b = y; }
    int getVal()
        { return b; }
};

int main()
{
    First object1;
    Second object2;

    cout << object1.getVal() << endl;
    cout << object2.getVal() << endl;
    return 0;
}
```

15.13 What will the following program display?

```cpp
#include <iostream>
using namespace std;

class First
{
protected:
    int a;
public:
    First(int x = 1)
        { a = x; }

    void twist()
        { a *= 2; }
    int getVal()
        { twist(); return a; }
};

class Second : public First
{
private:
    int b;
public:
    Second(int y = 5)
        { b = y; }

    void twist()
        { b *= 10; }
};

int main()
{
    First object1;
    Second object2;

    cout << object1.getVal() << endl;
    cout << object2.getVal() << endl;
    return 0;
}
```

15.14   What will the following program display?

```cpp
#include <iostream>
using namespace std;

class First
{
protected:
    int a;
public:
    First(int x = 1)
        { a = x; }

    virtual void twist()
        { a *= 2; }

    int getVal()
        { twist(); return a; }
};

class Second : public First
{
private:
    int b;
public:
    Second(int y = 5)
        { b = y; }
    virtual void twist()
        { b *= 10; }
};

int main()
{
    First object1;
    Second object2;

    cout << object1.getVal() << endl;
    cout << object2.getVal() << endl;
    return 0;
}
```

15.15   What will the following program display?

```cpp
#include <iostream>
using namespace std;

class Base
{
protected:
    int baseVar;
public:
    Base(int val = 2)
        { baseVar = val; }

    int getVar()
        { return baseVar; }
};

class Derived : public Base
{
private:
    int derivedVar;
```

```
    public:
       Derived(int val = 100)
          { derivedVar = val; }
       int getVar()
          { return derivedVar; }
    };

    int main()
    {
       Base *optr;
       Derived object;

       optr = &object;
       cout << optr->getVar() << endl;
       return 0;
    }
```

15.8 Multiple Inheritance

CONCEPT: Multiple inheritance is when a derived class has two or more base classes.

Previously we discussed how a class may be derived from a second class that is itself derived from a third class. The series of classes establishes a chain of inheritance. In such a scheme, you might be tempted to think of the lowest class in the chain as having multiple base classes. A base class, however, should be thought of as the class that another class is directly derived from. Even though there may be several classes in a chain, each class (below the topmost class) only has one base class.

Another way of combining classes is through multiple inheritance. *Multiple inheritance* is when a class has two or more base classes. This is illustrated in Figure 15-6.

Figure 15-6

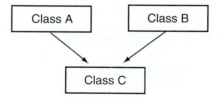

In Figure 15-6, class C is directly derived from classes A and B, and inherits the members of both. Neither class A nor B, however, inherits members from the other. Their members are only passed down to class C. Let's look at an example of multiple inheritance. Consider the two classes declared here:

Contents of `Date.h`

```
1    // Specification file for the Date class
2    #ifndef DATE_H
3    #define DATE_H
4
5    class Date
6    {
```

```
 7  protected:
 8      int day;
 9      int month;
10      int year;
11  public:
12      // Default constructor
13      Date(int d, int m, int y)
14          { day = 1; month = 1; year = 1900; }
15
16      // Constructor
17      Date(int d, int m, int y)
18          { day = d; month = m; year = y; }
19
20      // Accessors
21      int getDay() const
22          { return day; }
23
24      int getMonth() const
25          { return month; }
26
27      int getYear() const
28          { return year; }
29  };
30  #endif
```

Contents of `Time.h`

```
 1  // Specification file for the Time class
 2  #ifndef TIME_H
 3  #define TIME_H
 4
 5  class Time
 6  {
 7  protected:
 8      int hour;
 9      int min;
10      int sec;
11  public:
12      // Default constructor
13      Time()
14          { hour = 0; min = 0; sec = 0; }
15
16      // Constructor
17      Time(int h, int m, int s)
18          { hour = h; min = m; sec = s; }
19
20      // Accessor functions
21      int getHour() const
22          { return hour; }
23
```

```
24      int getMin() const
25          { return min; }
26
27      int getSec() const
28          { return sec; }
29  };
30  #endif
```

These classes are designed to hold integers that represent the date and time. They both can be used as base classes for a third class we will call `DateTime`:

Contents of `DateTime.h`

```
 1  // Specification file for the DateTime class
 2  #ifndef DATETIME_H
 3  #define DATETIME_H
 4  #include <string>
 5  #include "Date.h"
 6  #include "Time.h"
 7  using namespace std;
 8
 9  class DateTime : public Date, public Time
10  {
11  public:
12      // Default constructor
13      DateTime();
14
15      // Constructor
16      DateTime(int, int, int, int, int, int);
17
18      // The showDateTime function displays the
19      // date and the time.
20      void showDateTime() const;
21  };
22  #endif
```

In line 9, the first line in the `DateTime` declaration reads

```
class DateTime : public Date, public Time
```

Notice there are two base classes listed, separated by a *comma*. Each base class has its own access specification. The general format of the first line of a class declaration with multiple base classes is

```
class DerivedClassName : AccessSpecification BaseClassName,
                         AccessSpecification BaseClassName [, ...]
```

The notation in the square brackets indicates that the list of base classes with their access specifications may be repeated. (It is possible to have several base classes.)

Contents of `DateTime.cpp`

```
 1  // Implementation file for the DateTime class
 2  #include <iostream>
 3  #include <string>
 4  #include "DateTime.h"
 5  using namespace std;
 6
 7  //***************************************************
 8  // Default constructor                              *
 9  // Note that this constructor does nothing other    *
10  // than call default base class constructors.       *
11  //***************************************************
12  DateTime::DateTime() : Date(), Time()
13  { }
14
15  //***************************************************
16  // Constructor                                      *
17  // Note that this constructor does nothing other    *
18  // than call base class constructors.               *
19  //***************************************************
20  DateTime::DateTime(int dy, int mon, int yr, int hr, int mt, int sc) :
21       Date(dy, mon, yr), Time(hr, mt, sc)
22  { }
23
24  //***************************************************
25  // The showDateTime member function displays the    *
26  // date and the time.                               *
27  //***************************************************
28  void DateTime::showDateTime() const
29  {
30     // Display the date in the form MM/DD/YYYY.
31     cout << getMonth() << "/" << getDay() << "/" << getYear() << " ";
32
33     // Display the time in the form HH:MM:SS.
34     cout << getHour() << ":" << getMin() << ":" << getSec() << endl;
35  }
```

The class has two constructors: a default constructor and a constructor that accepts arguments for each component of a date and time. Let's look at the function header for the default constructor, in line 12:

```
DateTime::DateTime() : Date(), Time()
```

After the `DateTime` constructor's parentheses is a colon, followed by calls to the `Date` constructor and the `Time` constructor. The calls are separated by a comma. When using multiple inheritance, the general format of a derived class's constructor header is

```
DerivedClassName(ParameterList) : BaseClassName(ArgumentList),
                                  BaseClassName(ArgumentList)[, ...]
```

Look at the function header for the second constructor, which appears in lines 20 and 21:

```
DateTime::DateTime(int dy, int mon, int yr, int hr, int mt, int sc) :
    Date(dy, mon, yr), Time(hr, mt, sc)
```

This DateTime constructor accepts arguments for the day (dy), month (mon), year (yr), hour (hr), minute (mt), and second (sc). The dy, mon, and yr parameters are passed as arguments to the Date constructor. The hr, mt, and sc parameters are passed as arguments to the Time constructor.

The order that the base class constructor calls appear in the list does not matter. They are always called in the order of inheritance. That is, they are always called in the order they are listed in the first line of the class declaration. Here is line 9 from the DateTime.h file:

```
class DateTime : public Date, public Time
```

Because Date is listed before Time in the DateTime class declaration, the Date constructor will always be called first. If the classes use destructors, they are always called in reverse order of inheritance. Program 15-18 shows these classes in use.

Program 15-18

```
1  // This program demonstrates a class with multiple inheritance.
2  #include "DateTime.h"
3  using namespace std;
4
5  int main()
6  {
7     // Define a DateTime object and use the default
8     // constructor to initialize it.
9     DateTime emptyDay;
10
11    // Display the object's date and time.
12    emptyDay.showDateTime();
13
14    // Define a DateTime object and initialize it
15    // with the date 2/4/1960 and the time 5:32:27.
16    DateTime pastDay(2, 4, 1960, 5, 32, 27);
17
18    // Display the object's date and time.
19    pastDay.showDateTime();
20    return 0;
21 }
```

Program Output

```
1/1/1900 0:0:0
4/2/1960 5:32:27
```

 NOTE: It should be noted that multiple inheritance opens the opportunity for a derived class to have ambiguous members. That is, two base classes may have member variables or functions of the same name. In situations like these, the derived class should always redefine or override the member functions. Calls to the member functions of the appropriate base class can be performed within the derived class using the scope resolution operator (::). The derived class can also access the ambiguously named member variables of the correct base class using the scope resolution operator. If these steps aren't taken, the compiler will generate an error when it can't tell which member is being accessed.

Checkpoint

myprogramminglab *www.myprogramminglab.com*

15.16   Does the following diagram depict multiple inheritance or a chain of inheritance?

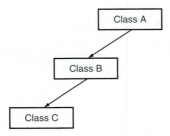

15.17   Does the following diagram depict multiple inheritance or a chain of inheritance?

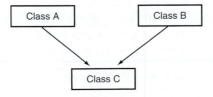

15.18   Examine the following classes. The table lists the variables that are members of the `Third` class (some are inherited). Complete the table by filling in the access specification each member will have in the `Third` class. Write "inaccessible" if a member is inaccessible to the `Third` class.

```
class First
{
    private:
        int a;
    protected:
        double b;
    public:
        long c;
};

class Second : protected First
{
    private:
        int d;
    protected:
        double e;
    public:
        long f;
};
```

```
class Third : public Second
{
    private:
        int g;
    protected:
        double h;
    public:
        long i;
};
```

Member Variable	Access Specification in Third Class
a	
b	
c	
d	
e	
f	
g	
h	
i	

15.19 Examine the following class declarations:

```
class Van
{
protected:
    int passengers;
public:
    Van(int p)
    { passengers = p; }
};

class FourByFour
{
protected:
    double cargoWeight;
public:
    FourByFour(float w)
        { cargoWeight = w; }
};
```

Write the declaration of a class named SportUtility. The class should be derived from both the Van and FourByFour classes above. (This should be a case of multiple inheritance, where both Van and FourByFour are base classes.)

Review Questions and Exercises

Short Answer

1. What is an "is a" relationship?

2. A program uses two classes: `Dog` and `Poodle`. Which class is the base class and which is the derived class?

3. How does base class access specification differ from class member access specification?

4. What is the difference between a protected class member and a private class member?

5. Can a derived class ever directly access the private members of its base class?

6. Which constructor is called first, that of the derived class or the base class?

7. What is the difference between redefining a base class function and overriding a base class function?

8. When does static binding take place? When does dynamic binding take place?

9. What is an abstract base class?

10. A program has a class `Potato`, which is derived from the class `Vegetable`, which is derived from the class `Food`. Is this an example of multiple inheritance? Why or why not?

11. What base class is named in the line below?

    ```
    class Pet : public Dog
    ```

12. What derived class is named in the line below?

    ```
    class Pet : public Dog
    ```

13. What is the class access specification of the base class named below?

    ```
    class Pet : public Dog
    ```

14. What is the class access specification of the base class named below?

    ```
    class Pet : Fish
    ```

15. Protected members of a base class are like _____ members, except they may be accessed by derived classes.

16. Complete the table below by filling in private, protected, public, or inaccessible in the right-hand column:

In a private base class, this base class MEMBER access specification…	…becomes this access specification in the derived class.
private	
protected	
public	

17. Complete the table on the next page by filling in private, protected, public, or inaccessible in the right-hand column:

In a protected base class, this base class MEMBE access specification...	...becomes this access specification in the derived class.
private	
protected	
public	

18. Complete the table below by filling in private, protected, public, or inaccessible in the right-hand column:

In a public base class, this base class MEMBER access specification...	...becomes this access specification in the derived class.
private	
protected	
public	

Fill-in-the-Blank

19. A derived class inherits the _____ of its base class.

20. When both a base class and a derived class have constructors, the base class's constructor is called _____ (first/last).

21. When both a base class and a derived class have destructors, the base class's constructor is called _____ (first/last).

22. An overridden base class function may be called by a function in a derived class by using the _____ operator.

23. When a derived class redefines a function in a base class, which version of the function do objects that are defined of the base class call? _____

24. A(n) _____ member function in a base class expects to be overridden in a derived class.

25. _____ binding is when the compiler binds member function calls at compile time.

26. _____ binding is when a function call is bound at runtime.

27. _____ is when member functions in a class hierarchy behave differently, depending upon which object performs the call.

28. When a pointer to a base class is made to point to a derived class, the pointer ignores any _____ the derived class performs, unless the function is _____.

29. A(n) _____ class cannot be instantiated.

30. A(n) _____ function has no body, or definition, in the class in which it is declared.

31. A(n) _____ of inheritance is where one class is derived from a second class, which in turn is derived from a third class.

32. _____ is where a derived class has two or more base classes.

33. In multiple inheritance, the derived class should always _____ a function that has the same name in more than one base class.

Algorithm Workbench

34. Write the first line of the declaration for a `Poodle` class. The class should be derived from the `Dog` class with public base class access.

35. Write the first line of the declaration for a `SoundSystem` class. Use multiple inheritance to base the class on the `CDplayer` class, the `Tuner` class, and the `CassettePlayer` class. Use public base class access in all cases.

36. Suppose a class named `Tiger` is derived from both the `Felis` class and the `Carnivore` class. Here is the first line of the `Tiger` class declaration:

    ```
    class Tiger : public Felis, public Carnivore
    ```

    Here is the function header for the Tiger constructor:

    ```
    Tiger(int x, int y) : Carnivore(x), Felis(y)
    ```

    Which base class constructor is called first, `Carnivore` or `Felis`?

37. Write the declaration for class `B`. The class's members should be

    - `m`, an integer. This variable should not be accessible to code outside the class or to member functions in any class derived from class `B`.
    - `n`, an integer. This variable should not be accessible to code outside the class, but should be accessible to member functions in any class derived from class `B`.
    - `setM`, `getM`, `setN`, and `getN`. These are the set and get functions for the member variables m and n. These functions should be accessible to code outside the class.
    - `calc`, a public virtual member function that returns the value of m times n.

    Next write the declaration for class `D`, which is derived from class `B`. The class's members should be
    - `q`, a float. This variable should not be accessible to code outside the class but should be accessible to member functions in any class derived from class `D`.
    - `r`, a float. This variable should not be accessible to code outside the class, but should be accessible to member functions in any class derived from class `D`.
    - `setQ`, `getQ`, `setR`, and `getR`. These are the set and get functions for the member variables q and r. These functions should be accessible to code outside the class.
    - `calc`, a public member function that overrides the base class `calc` function. This function should return the value of q times r.

True or False

38. T F   The base class's access specification affects the way base class member functions may access base class member variables.

39. T F   The base class's access specification affects the way the derived class inherits members of the base class.

40. T F   Private members of a private base class become inaccessible to the derived class.

41. T F   Public members of a private base class become private members of the derived class.

42. T F   Protected members of a private base class become public members of the derived class.

43. T F   Public members of a protected base class become private members of the derived class.

44. T   F   Private members of a protected base class become inaccessible to the derived class.

45. T   F   Protected members of a public base class become public members of the derived class.

46. T   F   The base class constructor is called after the derived class constructor.

47. T   F   The base class destructor is called after the derived class destructor.

48. T   F   It isn't possible for a base class to have more than one constructor.

49. T   F   Arguments are passed to the base class constructor by the derived class constructor.

50. T   F   A member function of a derived class may not have the same name as a member function of the base class.

51. T   F   Pointers to a base class may be assigned the address of a derived class object.

52. T   F   A base class may not be derived from another class.

Find the Errors

Each of the class declarations and/or member function definitions below has errors. Find as many as you can.

53.
```cpp
class Car, public Vehicle
{
    public:
        Car();
        ~Car();
    protected:
        int passengers;
}
```

54.
```cpp
class Truck, public : Vehicle, protected
{
    private:
        double cargoWeight;
    public:
        Truck();
        ~Truck();
};
```

55.
```cpp
class SnowMobile : Vehicle
{
    protected:
        int horsePower;
        double weight;
    public:
        SnowMobile(int h, double w), Vehicle(h)
            { horsePower = h; }
        ~SnowMobile();
};
```

56.
```cpp
class Table : public Furniture
{
    protected:
        int numSeats;
```

```
      public:
          Table(int n) : Furniture(numSeats)
              { numSeats = n; }
          ~Table();
      };
```

57.
```
class Tank : public Cylinder
    {
        private:
            int fuelType;
            double gallons;
        public:
            Tank();
            ~Tank();
            void setContents(double);
            void setContents(double);
    };
```

58.
```
class Three : public Two : public One
    {
        protected:
            int x;
        public:
            Three(int a, int b, int c), Two(b), Three(c)
                { x = a; }
            ~Three();
    };
```

Programming Challenges

Visit www.myprogramminglab.com to complete many of these Programming Challenges online and get instant feedback.

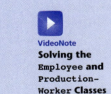

VideoNote
Solving the Employee and Production-Worker Classes Problem

1 `Employee` and `ProductionWorker` Classes

Design a class named `Employee`. The class should keep the following information in member variables:

- Employee name
- Employee number
- Hire date

Write one or more constructors and the appropriate accessor and mutator functions for the class.

Next, write a class named `ProductionWorker` that is derived from the `Employee` class. The `ProductionWorker` class should have member variables to hold the following information:

- Shift (an integer)
- Hourly pay rate (a `double`)

The workday is divided into two shifts: day and night. The shift variable will hold an integer value representing the shift that the employee works. The day shift is shift 1 and the night shift is shift 2. Write one or more constructors and the appropriate accessor and mutator functions for the class. Demonstrate the classes by writing a program that uses a `ProductionWorker` object.

2. `ShiftSupervisor` Class

In a particular factory a shift supervisor is a salaried employee who supervises a shift. In addition to a salary, the shift supervisor earns a yearly bonus when his or her shift meets production goals. Design a `ShiftSupervisor` class that is derived from the `Employee` class you created in Programming Challenge 1. The `ShiftSupervisor` class should have a member variable that holds the annual salary and a member variable that holds the annual production bonus that a shift supervisor has earned. Write one or more constructors and the appropriate accessor and mutator functions for the class. Demonstrate the class by writing a program that uses a `ShiftSupervisor` object.

3. `TeamLeader` Class

In a particular factory, a team leader is an hourly paid production worker who leads a small team. In addition to hourly pay, team leaders earn a fixed monthly bonus. Team leaders are required to attend a minimum number of hours of training per year. Design a `TeamLeader` class that extends the `ProductionWorker` class you designed in Programming Challenge 1. The `TeamLeader` class should have member variables for the monthly bonus amount, the required number of training hours, and the number of training hours that the team leader has attended. Write one or more constructors and the appropriate accessor and mutator functions for the class. Demonstrate the class by writing a program that uses a `TeamLeader` object.

4. Time Format

In Program 15-18, the file `Time.h` contains a `Time` class. Design a class called `MilTime` that is derived from the `Time` class. The `MilTime` class should convert time in military (24-hour) format to the standard time format used by the `Time` class. The class should have the following member variables:

`milHours:`	Contains the hour in 24-hour format. For example, 1:00 pm would be stored as 1300 hours, and 4:30 pm would be stored as 1630 hours.
`milSeconds:`	Contains the seconds in standard format.

The class should have the following member functions:

`Constructor:`	The constructor should accept arguments for the hour and seconds, in military format. The time should then be converted to standard time and stored in the `hours`, `min`, and `sec` variables of the `Time` class.
`setTime:`	Accepts arguments to be stored in the `milHours` and `milSeconds` variables. The time should then be converted to standard time and stored in the `hours`, `min`, and `sec` variables of the `Time` class.
`getHour:`	Returns the hour in military format.
`getStandHr:`	Returns the hour in standard format.

Demonstrate the class in a program that asks the user to enter the time in military format. The program should then display the time in both military and standard format.

Input Validation: The `MilTime` *class should not accept hours greater than 2359, or less than 0. It should not accept seconds greater than 59 or less than 0.*

5. Time Clock

Design a class named `TimeClock`. The class should be derived from the `MilTime` class you designed in Programming Challenge 4. The class should allow the programmer to pass two times to it: starting time and ending time. The class should have a member function that returns the amount of time elapsed between the two times. For example, if the starting time is 900 hours (9:00 am), and the ending time is 1300 hours (1:00 pm), the elapsed time is 4 hours.

Input Validation: The class should not accept hours greater than 2359 or less than 0.

6. Essay class

Design an `Essay` class that is derived from the `GradedActivity` class presented in this chapter. The `Essay` class should determine the grade a student receives on an essay. The student's essay score can be up to 100, and is determined in the following manner:

- Grammar: 30 points
- Spelling: 20 points
- Correct length: 20 points
- Content: 30 points

Demonstrate the class in a simple program.

7. PersonData and CustomerData classes

Design a class named `PersonData` with the following member variables:

- `lastName`
- `firstName`
- `address`
- `city`
- `state`
- `zip`
- `phone`

Write the appropriate accessor and mutator functions for these member variables.

Next, design a class named `CustomerData`, which is derived from the `PersonData` class. The `CustomerData` class should have the following member variables:

- `customerNumber`
- `mailingList`

The `customerNumber` variable will be used to hold a unique integer for each customer. The `mailingList` variable should be a `bool`. It will be set to `true` if the customer wishes to be on a mailing list, or `false` if the customer does not wish to be on a mailing list. Write appropriate accessor and mutator functions for these member variables. Demonstrate an object of the `CustomerData` class in a simple program.

8. PreferredCustomer Class

A retail store has a preferred customer plan where customers may earn discounts on all their purchases. The amount of a customer's discount is determined by the amount of the customer's cumulative purchases in the store.

- When a preferred customer spends $500, he or she gets a 5% discount on all future purchases.

- When a preferred customer spends $1,000, he or she gets a 6% discount on all future purchases.
- When a preferred customer spends $1,500, he or she gets a 7% discount on all future purchases.
- When a preferred customer spends $2,000 or more, he or she gets a 10% discount on all future purchases.

Design a class named `PreferredCustomer`, which is derived from the `CustomerData` class you created in Programming Challenge 7. The `PreferredCustomer` class should have the following member variables:

- `purchasesAmount` (a double)
- `discountLevel` (a double)

The `purchasesAmount` variable holds the total of a customer's purchases to date. The `discountLevel` variable should be set to the correct discount percentage, according to the store's preferred customer plan. Write appropriate member functions for this class and demonstrate it in a simple program.

Input Validation: Do not accept negative values for any sales figures.

9. **File Filter**

A file filter reads an input file, transforms it in some way, and writes the results to an output file. Write an abstract file filter class that defines a pure virtual function for transforming a character. Create one derived class of your file filter class that performs encryption, another that transforms a file to all uppercase, and another that creates an unchanged copy of the original file. The class should have the following member function:

```
void doFilter(ifstream &in, ofstream &out)
```

This function should be called to perform the actual filtering. The member function for transforming a single character should have the prototype:

```
char transform(char ch)
```

The encryption class should have a constructor that takes an integer as an argument and uses it as the encryption key.

10. **File Double-Spacer**

Create a derived class of the abstract filter class of Programming Challenge 9 that double-spaces a file: that is, it inserts a blank line between any two lines of the file.

11. **Course Grades**

In a course, a teacher gives the following tests and assignments:

- A **lab activity** that is observed by the teacher and assigned a numeric score.
- A **pass/fail exam** that has 10 questions. The minimum passing score is 70.
- An **essay** that is assigned a numeric score.
- A **final exam** that has 50 questions.

Write a class named `CourseGrades`. The class should have a member named `grades` that is an array of `GradedActivity` pointers. The `grades` array should have four elements, one for each of the assignments previously described. The class should have the following member functions:

setLab: This function should accept the address of a `GradedActivity` object as its argument. This object should already hold the student's score for the lab activity. Element 0 of the `grades` array should reference this object.

setPassFailExam: This function should accept the address of a `PassFailExam` object as its argument. This object should already hold the student's score for the pass/fail exam. Element 1 of the `grades` array should reference this object.

setEssay: This function should accept the address of an `Essay` object as its argument. (See Programming Challenge 6 for the `Essay` class. If you have not completed Programming Challenge 6, use a `GradedActivity` object instead.) This object should already hold the student's score for the essay. Element 2 of the `grades` array should reference this object.

setPassFailExam: This function should accept the address of a `FinalExam` object as its argument. This object should already hold the student's score for the final exam. Element 3 of the `grades` array should reference this object.

print: This function should display the numeric scores and grades for each element in the `grades` array.

Demonstrate the class in a program.

12. **`Ship`, `CruiseShip`, and `CargoShip` Classes**

Design a `Ship` class that has the following members:

- A member variable for the name of the ship (a string)
- A member variable for the year that the ship was built (a string)
- A constructor and appropriate accessors and mutators
- A virtual `print` function that displays the ship's name and the year it was built.

Design a `CruiseShip` class that is derived from the `Ship` class. The `CruiseShip` class should have the following members:

- A member variable for the maximum number of passengers (an int)
- A constructor and appropriate accessors and mutators
- A `print` function that overrides the `print` function in the base class. The `CruiseShip` class's print function should display only the ship's name and the maximum number of passengers.

Design a `CargoShip` class that is derived from the `Ship` class. The `CargoShip` class should have the following members:

- A member variable for the cargo capacity in tonnage (an int).
- A constructor and appropriate accessors and mutators.
- A `print` function that overrides the `print` function in the base class. The `CargoShip` class's print function should display only the ship's name and the ship's cargo capacity.

Demonstrate the classes in a program that has an array of `Ship` pointers. The array elements should be initialized with the addresses of dynamically allocated `Ship`,

CruiseShip, and CargoShip objects. (See Program 15-14, lines 17 through 22, for an example of how to do this.) The program should then step through the array, calling each object's print function.

13. **Pure Abstract Base Class Project**

Define a pure abstract base class called BasicShape. The BasicShape class should have the following members:

Private Member Variable:

  area, a double used to hold the shape's area.

Public Member Functions:

  getArea. This function should return the value in the member variable area.

  calcArea. This function should be a pure virtual function.

Next, define a class named Circle. It should be derived from the BasicShape class. It should have the following members:

Private Member Variables:

  centerX, a long integer used to hold the x coordinate of the circle's center.

  centerY, a long integer used to hold the y coordinate of the circle's center.

  radius, a double used to hold the circle's radius.

Public Member Functions:

  constructor—accepts values for centerX, centerY, and radius. Should call the overridden calcArea function described below.

  getCenterX—returns the value in centerX.

  getCenterY—returns the value in centerY.

  calcArea—calculates the area of the circle (area = 3.14159 * radius * radius) and stores the result in the inherited member area.

Next, define a class named Rectangle. It should be derived from the BasicShape class. It should have the following members:

Private Member Variables:

  width, a long integer used to hold the width of the rectangle.

  length, a long integer used to hold the length of the rectangle.

Public Member Functions:

  constructor—accepts values for width and length. Should call the overridden calcArea function described below.

`getWidth`—returns the value in width.

`getLength`—returns the value in length.

`calcArea`—calculates the area of the rectangle (area = length * width) and stores the result in the inherited member area.

After you have created these classes, create a driver program that defines a `Circle` object and a `Rectangle` object. Demonstrate that each object properly calculates and reports its area.

Group Project

14. **Bank Accounts**

This program should be designed and written by a team of students. Here are some suggestions:

- One or more students may work on a single class.
- The requirements of the program should be analyzed so each student is given about the same work load.
- The parameters and return types of each function and class member function should be decided in advance.
- The program will be best implemented as a multi-file program.

Design a generic class to hold the following information about a bank account:

Balance

Number of deposits this month

Number of withdrawals

Annual interest rate

Monthly service charges

The class should have the following member functions:

`Constructor:` Accepts arguments for the balance and annual interest rate.

`deposit:` A virtual function that accepts an argument for the amount of the deposit. The function should add the argument to the account balance. It should also increment the variable holding the number of deposits.

`withdraw:` A virtual function that accepts an argument for the amount of the withdrawal. The function should subtract the argument from the balance. It should also increment the variable holding the number of withdrawals.

`calcInt:` A virtual function that updates the balance by calculating the monthly interest earned by the account, and adding this interest to the balance. This is performed by the following formulas:

Monthly Interest Rate = (Annual Interest Rate / 12)
Monthly Interest = Balance * Monthly Interest Rate
Balance = Balance + Monthly Interest

monthlyProc: A virtual function that subtracts the monthly service charges from the balance, calls the `calcInt` function, and then sets the variables that hold the number of withdrawals, number of deposits, and monthly service charges to zero.

Next, design a savings account class, derived from the generic account class. The savings account class should have the following additional member:

    `status` (to represent an active or inactive account)

If the balance of a savings account falls below $25, it becomes inactive. (The `status` member could be a flag variable.) No more withdrawals may be made until the balance is raised above $25, at which time the account becomes active again. The savings account class should have the following member functions:

withdraw: A function that checks to see if the account is inactive before a withdrawal is made. (No withdrawal will be allowed if the account is not active.) A withdrawal is then made by calling the base class version of the function.

deposit: A function that checks to see if the account is inactive before a deposit is made. If the account is inactive and the deposit brings the balance above $25, the account becomes active again. The deposit is then made by calling the base class version of the function.

monthlyProc: Before the base class function is called, this function checks the number of withdrawals. If the number of withdrawals for the month is more than 4, a service charge of $1 for each withdrawal above 4 is added to the base class variable that holds the monthly service charges. (Don't forget to check the account balance after the service charge is taken. If the balance falls below $25, the account becomes inactive.)

Next, design a checking account class, also derived from the generic account class. It should have the following member functions:

withdraw: Before the base class function is called, this function will determine if a withdrawal (a check written) will cause the balance to go below $0. If the balance goes below $0, a service charge of $15 will be taken from the account. (The withdrawal will not be made.) If there isn't enough in the account to pay the service charge, the balance will become negative and the customer will owe the negative amount to the bank.

monthlyProc: Before the base class function is called, this function adds the monthly fee of $5 plus $0.10 per withdrawal (check written) to the base class variable that holds the monthly service charges.

Write a complete program that demonstrates these classes by asking the user to enter the amounts of deposits and withdrawals for a savings account and checking account. The program should display statistics for the month, including beginning balance, total amount of deposits, total amount of withdrawals, service charges, and ending balance.

 NOTE: You may need to add more member variables and functions to the classes than those listed above.

16 Exceptions, Templates, and the Standard Template Library (STL)

TOPICS

16.1 Exceptions

CONCEPT: Exceptions are used to signal errors or unexpected events that occur while a program is running.

Error testing is usually a straightforward process involving `if` statements or other control mechanisms. For example, the following code segment will trap a division-by-zero error before it occurs:

```
if (denominator == 0)
    cout << "ERROR: Cannot divide by zero.\n";
else
    quotient = numerator / denominator;
```

But what if similar code is part of a function that returns the quotient, as in the following example?

```
// An unreliable division function
double divide(int numerator, int denominator)
{
    if (denominator == 0)
    {
        cout << "ERROR: Cannot divide by zero.\n";
        return 0;
    }
        else
            return static_cast<double>(numerator) / denominator;
}
```

Functions commonly signal error conditions by returning a predetermined value. Apparently, the function in this example returns 0 when division by zero has been attempted. This is unreliable, however, because 0 is a valid result of a division operation. Even though the function displays an error message, the part of the program that calls the function will not know when an error has occurred. Problems like these require sophisticated error handling techniques.

Throwing an Exception

One way of handling complex error conditions is with *exceptions*. An exception is a value or an object that signals an error. When the error occurs, an exception is "thrown." For example, the following code shows the `divide` function, modified to throw an exception when division by zero has been attempted.

VideoNote
Throwing an Exception

```
double divide(int numerator, int denominator)
{
    if (denominator == 0)
        throw "ERROR: Cannot divide by zero.\n";
    else
        return static_cast<double>(numerator) / denominator;
}
```

The following statement causes the exception to be thrown.

```
throw "ERROR: Cannot divide by zero.\n";
```

The `throw` key word is followed by an argument, which can be any value. As you will see, the value of the argument is used to determine the nature of the error. The function above simply throws a string containing an error message.

The line containing a `throw` statement is known as the *throw point*. When a `throw` statement is executed, control is passed to another part of the program known as an *exception handler*. When an exception is thrown by a function, the function aborts.

Handling an Exception

To handle an exception, a program must have a *try/catch* construct. The general format of the try/catch construct is:

```
try
{
    // code here calls functions or object member
    // functions that might throw an exception.
}
catch(ExceptionParameter)
{
    // code here handles the exception
}
// Repeat as many catch blocks as needed.
```

The first part of the construct is the *try block*. This starts with the key word `try` and is followed by a block of code executing any statements that might directly or indirectly cause an exception to be thrown. The try block is immediately followed by one or more *catch blocks*, which are the exception handlers. A catch block starts with the key word `catch`, followed by a set of parentheses containing the definition of an exception parameter. For example, here is a try/catch construct that can be used with the `divide` function:

```
try
{
    quotient = divide(num1, num2);
    cout << "The quotient is " << quotient << endl;
}
catch (string exceptionString)
{
    cout << exceptionString;
}
```

Because the `divide` function throws an exception whose value is a string, there must be an exception handler that catches a string. The catch block shown catches the error message in the `exceptionString` parameter, and then displays it with `cout`. Now let's look at an entire program to see how `throw`, `try`, and `catch` work together. In the first sample run of Program 16-1, valid data are given. This shows how the program should run with no errors. In the second sample running, a denominator of 0 is given. This shows the result of the exception being thrown.

Program 16-1

```
1  // This program demonstrates an exception being thrown and caught.
2  #include <iostream>
3  #include <string>
4  using namespace std;
5
6  // Function prototype
7  double divide(int, int);
8
9  int main()
```

(program continues)

Program 16-1   *(continued)*

```
10   {
11       int num1, num2;  // To hold two numbers
12       double quotient; // To hold the quotient of the numbers
13
14       // Get two numbers.
15       cout << "Enter two numbers: ";
16       cin >> num1 >> num2;
17
18       // Divide num1 by num2 and catch any
19       // potential exceptions.
20       try
21       {
22          quotient = divide(num1, num2);
23          cout << "The quotient is " << quotient << endl;
24       }
25       catch (string exceptionString)
26       {
27          cout << exceptionString;
28       }
29
30       cout << "End of the program.\n";
31       return 0;
32   }
33
34   //*********************************************
35   // The divide function divides the numerator *
36   // by the denominator. If the denominator is *
37   // zero, the  function throws an exception.   *
38   //*********************************************
39
40   double divide(int numerator, int denominator)
41   {
42       if (denominator == 0)
43       {
44          string exceptionString = "ERROR: Cannot divide by zero.\n";
45          throw exceptionString;
46       }
47
48       return static_cast<double>(numerator) / denominator;
49   }
```

Program Output with Example Input Shown in Bold
```
Enter two numbers: 12 2 [Enter]
The quotient is 6
End of the program.
```

Program Output with Different Example Input Shown in Bold
```
Enter two numbers: 12 0 [Enter]
ERROR: Cannot divide by zero.
End of the program.
```

As you can see from the second output screen, the exception caused the program to jump out of the divide function and into the catch block. After the catch block has finished, the program resumes with the first statement after the try/catch construct. This is illustrated in Figure 16-1.

Figure 16-1

```
                            try
If this statement           {
throws an exception...           quotient = divide(num1, num2);
                                 cout << "The quotient is " << quotient << endl;
... then this statement     }
is skipped.                 catch (string exceptionString)
If the exception is a string,    {
the program jumps to             cout << exceptionString;
this catch clause.               }
After the catch block is    cout << "End of the program.\n";
finished, the program       return 0;
resumes here.
```

In the first output screen the user entered nonnegative values. No exception was thrown in the try block, so the program skipped the catch block and jumped to the statement immediately following the try/catch construct, which is in line 30. This is illustrated in Figure 16-2.

Figure 16-2

```
                            try
                            {
                                 quotient = divide(num1, num2);
                                 cout << "The quotient is " << quotient << endl;
                            }
If no exception is thrown in the    catch (string exceptionString)
try block, the program jumps        {
to the statement that immediately        cout << exceptionString;
follows the try/catch construct.    }
                            cout << "End of the program.\n";
                            return 0;
```

What if an Exception Is Not Caught?

There are two possible ways for a thrown exception to go uncaught. The first possibility is for the try/catch construct to contain no catch blocks with an exception parameter of the right data type. The second possibility is for the exception to be thrown from outside a try block. In either case, the exception will cause the entire program to abort execution.

Object-Oriented Exception Handling with Classes

Now that you have an idea of how the exception mechanism in C++ works, we will examine an object-oriented approach to exception handling. Recall the Rectangle class that was introduced in Chapter 13. That class had the mutator functions setWidth and setLength for setting the rectangle's width and length. If a negative value was passed to either of these functions, the class displayed an error message and aborted the program. The following code shows an improved version of the Rectangle class. This version throws an exception when a negative value is passed to setWidth or setLength. (These files are stored in the Student Source Code Folder Chapter 16\Rectangle Version 1.)

Contents of Rectangle.h (Version 1)

```
 1   // Specification file for the Rectangle class
 2   #ifndef RECTANGLE_H
 3   #define RECTANGLE_H
 4
 5   class Rectangle
 6   {
 7      private:
 8         double width;      // The rectangle's width
 9         double length;     // The rectangle's length
10      public:
11         // Exception class
12         class NegativeSize
13            { };                // Empty class declaration
14
15         // Default constructor
16         Rectangle()
17            { width = 0.0; length = 0.0; }
18
19         // Mutator functions, defined in Rectangle.cpp
20         void setWidth(double);
21         void setLength(double);
22
23         // Accessor functions
24         double getWidth() const
25            { return width; }
26
27         double getLength() const
28            { return length; }
29
30         double getArea() const
31            { return width * length; }
32   };
33   #endif
```

Notice the empty class declaration that appears in the public section, in lines 12 and 13. The NegativeSize class has no members. The only important part of the class is its name, which will be used in the exception-handling code. Now look at the Rectangle.cpp file, where the setWidth and setLength member functions are defined.

Contents of Rectangle.cpp (Version 1)

```
 1   // Implementation file for the Rectangle class.
 2   #include "Rectangle.h"
 3
 4   //***********************************************************
 5   // setWidth sets the value of the member variable width.   *
 6   //***********************************************************
 7
 8   void Rectangle::setWidth(double w)
```

```
 9  {
10      if (w >= 0)
11          width = w;
12      else
13          throw NegativeSize();
14  }
15
16  //*********************************************************
17  // setLength sets the value of the member variable length.  *
18  //*********************************************************
19
20  void Rectangle::setLength(double len)
21  {
22      if (len >= 0)
23          length = len;
24      else
25          throw NegativeSize();
26  }
```

In the setWidth function, the parameter w is tested by the if statement in line 10. If w is greater than or equal to 0, its value is assigned to the width member variable. If w holds a negative number, however, the statement in line 13 is executed:

```
throw NegativeSize();
```

The throw statement's argument, NegativeSize(), causes an instance of the NegativeSize class to be created and thrown as an exception.

The same series of events takes place in the setLength function. If the value in the len parameter is greater than or equal to 0, its value is assigned to the length member variable. If len holds a negative number, an instance of the NegativeSize class is thrown as an exception in line 25.

This way of reporting errors is much more graceful than simply aborting the program. Any code that uses the Rectangle class must simply have a catch block to handle the NegativeSize exceptions that the Rectangle class might throw. Program 16-2 shows an example. (This file is stored in the Student Source Code Folder Chapter 16\ Rectangle Version 1.)

Program 16-2

```
 1  // This program demonstrates Rectangle class exceptions.
 2  #include <iostream>
 3  #include "Rectangle.h"
 4  using namespace std;
 5
 6  int main()
 7  {
 8      double width;
 9      double length;
10
11      // Create a Rectangle object.
12      Rectangle myRectangle;
13
```

(program continues)

Program 16-2 *(continued)*

```
14      // Get the width and length.
15      cout << "Enter the rectangle's width: ";
16      cin >> width;
17      cout << "Enter the rectangle's length: ";
18      cin >> length;
19
20      // Store these values in the Rectangle object.
21      try
22      {
23         myRectangle.setWidth(width);
24         myRectangle.setLength(length);
25         cout << "The area of the rectangle is "
26              << myRectangle.getArea() << endl;
27      }
28      catch (Rectangle::NegativeSize)
29      {
30         cout << "Error: A negative value was entered.\n";
31      }
32      cout << "End of the program.\n";
33
34      return 0;
35  }
```

Program Output with Example Input Shown in Bold
```
Enter the rectangle's width: 10 [Enter]
Enter the rectangle's length: 20 [Enter]
The area of the rectangle is 200
End of the program.
```

Program Output with Different Example Input Shown in Bold
```
Enter the rectangle's width: 5 [Enter]
Enter the rectangle's length: –5 [Enter]
Error: A negative value was entered.
End of the program.
```

The catch statement in line 28 catches the NegativeSize exception when it is thrown by any of the statements in the try block. Inside the catch statement's parentheses is the name of the NegativeSize class. Because the NegativeSize class is declared inside the Rectangle class, we have to fully qualify the class name with the scope resolution operator.

Notice that we did not define a parameter of the NegativeSize class in the catch statement. In this case the catch statement only needs to specify the type of exception it handles.

Multiple Exceptions

The programs we have studied so far test only for a single type of error and throw only a single type of exception. In many cases a program will need to test for several different types of errors, and signal which one has occurred. C++ allows you to throw and catch multiple exceptions. The only requirement is that each different exception be of a different type. You then code a separate catch block for each type of exception that may be thrown in the try block.

For example, suppose we wish to expand the `Rectangle` class so it throws one type of exception when a negative value is specified for the `width`, and another type of exception when a negative value is specified for the `length`. First, we declare two different exception classes, such as:

```
// Exception class for a negative width
class NegativeWidth
    { };

// Exception class for a negative length
class NegativeLength
    { };
```

An instance of `NegativeWidth` will be thrown when a negative value is specified for the `width`, and an instance of `NegativeLength` will be thrown when a negative value is specified for the `length`. The code for the modified `Rectangle` class is shown here. (These files are stored in the Student Source Code Folder `Chapter 16\Rectangle Version 2`.)

Contents of `Rectangle.h` (Version 2)

```
 1   // Specification file for the Rectangle class
 2   #ifndef RECTANGLE_H
 3   #define RECTANGLE_H
 4
 5   class Rectangle
 6   {
 7      private:
 8         double width;      // The rectangle's width
 9         double length;     // The rectangle's length
10      public:
11         // Exception class for a negative width
12         class NegativeWidth
13            { };
14
15         // Exception class for a negative length
16         class NegativeLength
17            { };
18
19         // Default constructor
20         Rectangle()
21            { width = 0.0; length = 0.0; }
22
23         // Mutator functions, defined in Rectangle.cpp
24         void setWidth(double);
25         void setLength(double);
26
27         // Accessor functions
28         double getWidth() const
29            { return width; }
30
31         double getLength() const
32            { return length; }
33
```

```
34        double getArea() const
35            { return width * length; }
36   };
37   #endif
```

Contents of `Rectangle.cpp` (Version 2)

```
 1   // Implementation file for the Rectangle class.
 2   #include "Rectangle.h"
 3
 4   //*********************************************************
 5   // setWidth sets the value of the member variable width.   *
 6   //*********************************************************
 7
 8   void Rectangle::setWidth(double w)
 9   {
10       if (w >= 0)
11           width = w;
12       else
13           throw NegativeWidth();
14   }
15
16   //*********************************************************
17   // setLength sets the value of the member variable length.  *
18   //*********************************************************
19
20   void Rectangle::setLength(double len)
21   {
22       if (len >= 0)
23           length = len;
24       else
25           throw NegativeLength();
26   }
```

Notice that in the definition of the `setWidth` function (in `Rectangle.cpp`) that an instance of the `NegativeWidth` class is thrown in line 13. In the definition of the `setLength` function an instance of the `NegativeLength` class is thrown in line 25. Program 16-3 demonstrates this class. (This file is stored in the Student Source Code Folder `Chapter 16\Rectangle Version 2`.)

Program 16-3

```
 1   // This program demonstrates Rectangle class exceptions.
 2   #include <iostream>
 3   #include "Rectangle.h"
 4   using namespace std;
 5
 6   int main()
 7   {
 8       double width;
 9       double length;
10
```

```
11      // Create a Rectangle object.
12      Rectangle myRectangle;
13
14      // Get the width and length.
15      cout << "Enter the rectangle's width: ";
16      cin >> width;
17      cout << "Enter the rectangle's length: ";
18      cin >> length;
19
20      // Store these values in the Rectangle object.
21      try
22      {
23         myRectangle.setWidth(width);
24         myRectangle.setLength(length);
25         cout << "The area of the rectangle is "
26              << myRectangle.getArea() << endl;
27      }
28      catch (Rectangle::NegativeWidth)
29      {
30         cout << "Error: A negative value was given "
31              << "for the rectangle's width.\n";
32      }
33      catch (Rectangle::NegativeLength)
34      {
35         cout << "Error: A negative value was given "
36              << "for the rectangle's length.\n";
37      }
38
39      cout << "End of the program.\n";
40      return 0;
41  }
```

Program Output with Example Input Shown in Bold

Enter the rectangle's width: **10 [Enter]**
Enter the rectangle's length: **20 [Enter]**
The area of the rectangle is 200
End of the program.

Program Output with Different Example Input Shown in Bold

Enter the rectangle's width: **−5 [Enter]**
Enter the rectangle's length: **5 [Enter]**
Error: A negative value was given for the rectangle's width.
End of the program.

Program Output with Different Example Input Shown in Bold

Enter the rectangle's width: **5 [Enter]**
Enter the rectangle's length: **−5 [Enter]**
Error: A negative value was given for the rectangle's length.
End of the program.

The try block, in lines 21 through 27, contains code that can throw two different types of exceptions. The statement in line 23 can potentially throw a `NegativeWidth` exception, and the statement in line 24 can potentially throw a `NegativeLength` exception. To handle each of these types of exception, there are two `catch` statements. The statement in line 28 catches `NegativeWidth` exceptions, and the statement in line 33 catches `NegativeLength` exceptions.

When an exception is thrown by code in the try block, C++ searches the try/catch construct for a `catch` statement that can handle the exception. If the construct contains a `catch` statement that is compatible with the exception, control of the program is passed to the catch block.

Using Exception Handlers to Recover from Errors

Program 16-3 demonstrates how a try/catch construct can have several `catch` statements in order to handle different types of exceptions. However, the program does not use the exception handlers to recover from any of the errors. When the user enters a negative value for either the width or the length, this program still halts. Program 16-4 shows a better example of effective exception handling. It attempts to recover from the exceptions and get valid data from the user. (This file is stored in the Student Source Code Folder Chapter 16\Rectangle Version 2.)

Program 16-4

```
 1   // This program handles the Rectangle class exceptions.
 2   #include <iostream>
 3   #include "Rectangle.h"
 4   using namespace std;
 5
 6   int main()
 7   {
 8      double width;            // Rectangle's width
 9      double length;           // Rectangle's length
10      bool tryAgain = true;    // Flag to reread input
11
12      // Create a Rectangle object.
13      Rectangle myRectangle;
14
15      // Get the rectangle's width.
16      cout << "Enter the rectangle's width: ";
17      cin >> width;
18
19      // Store the width in the myRectangle object.
20      while (tryAgain)
21      {
22         try
23         {
24            myRectangle.setWidth(width);
25            // If no exception was thrown, then the
26            // next statement will execute.
27            tryAgain = false;
28         }
```

```
29          catch (Rectangle::NegativeWidth)
30          {
31              cout << "Please enter a nonnegative value: ";
32              cin >> width;
33          }
34      }
35
36      // Get the rectangle's length.
37      cout << "Enter the rectangle's length: ";
38      cin >> length;
39
40      // Store the length in the myRectangle object.
41      tryAgain = true;
42      while (tryAgain)
43      {
44          try
45          {
46              myRectangle.setLength(length);
47              // If no exception was thrown, then the
48              // next statement will execute.
49              tryAgain = false;
50          }
51          catch (Rectangle::NegativeLength)
52          {
53              cout << "Please enter a nonnegative value: ";
54              cin >> length;
55          }
56      }
57
58      // Display the area of the rectangle.
59      cout << "The rectangle's area is "
60          << myRectangle.getArea() << endl;
61      return 0;
62  }
```

Program Output with Example Input Shown in Bold
```
Enter the rectangle's width: –1 [Enter]
Please enter a nonnegative value: 10 [Enter]
Enter the rectangle's length: –5 [Enter]
Please enter a nonnegative value: 50 [Enter]
The rectangle's area is 500
```

Let's look at how this program recovers from a NegativeWidth exception. In line 10 a bool flag variable, tryAgain, is defined and initialized with the value true. This variable will indicate whether we need to get a value from the user again. Lines 16 and 17 prompt the user to enter the rectangle's width. Then the program enters the while loop in lines 20 through 34. The loop repeats as long as tryAgain is true. Inside the loop, the Rectangle class's setWidth member function is called in line 24. This statement is in a try block. If a NegativeWidth exception is thrown, the program will jump to the catch statement in line 29. In the catch block that follows, the user is asked to enter a nonnegative number.

The program then jumps out of the try/catch construct. Because `tryAgain` is still `true`, the loop will repeat.

If a nonnegative number is passed to the `setWidth` member function in line 24, no exception will be thrown. In that case, the statement in line 27 will execute, which sets `tryAgain` to `false`. The program then jumps out of the try/catch construct. Because `tryAgain` is now `false`, the loop will not repeat.

The same strategy is used in lines 37 through 56 to get and validate the rectangle's length.

Extracting Data from the Exception Class

Sometimes we might want an exception object to pass data back to the exception handler. For example, suppose we would like the `Rectangle` class not only to signal when a negative value has been given, but also to pass the value back. This can be accomplished by giving the exception class members in which data can be stored.

In our next modification of the `Rectangle` class, the `NegativeWidth` and `NegativeLength` classes have been expanded, each with a member variable and a constructor. Here is the code for the `NegativeWidth` class:

```
class NegativeWidth
{
private:
   double value;
public:
   NegativeWidth(double val)
      { value = val; }

   double getValue() const
      { return value; }
};
```

When we throw this exception, we want to pass the invalid value as an argument to the class's constructor. This is done in the `setWidth` member function with the following statement:

```
throw NegativeWidth(w);
```

This `throw` statement creates an instance of the `NegativeWidth` class and passes a copy of the w variable to the constructor. The constructor then stores this number in `NegativeWidth`'s member variable, `value`. The class instance carries this member variable to the catch block that intercepts the exception.

In the catch block, the value is extracted with code such as

```
catch (Rectangle::NegativeWidth e)
{
   cout << "Error: " << e.getValue()
        << " is an invalid value for the"
        << " rectangle's width.\n";
}
```

Notice that the catch block defines a parameter object named e. This is necessary because we want to call the class's getValue function to retrieve the value that caused the exception.

Here is the code for the NegativeLength class:

```cpp
class NegativeLength
{
private:
   double value;
public:
   NegativeLength(double val)
      { value = val; }

   double getValue() const
      { return value; }
};
```

This class also has a member variable named value, and a constructor that initializes the variable. When we throw this exception, we follow the sane general steps that were just described for the NegativeWidth exception. The complete code for the revised Rectangle class is shown here. Program 16-5 demonstrates these classes. (These files are stored in the Student Source Code Folder Chapter 16\Rectangle Version 3.)

Contents of Rectangle.h (Version 3)

```cpp
 1  // Specification file for the Rectangle class
 2  #ifndef RECTANGLE_H
 3  #define RECTANGLE_H
 4
 5  class Rectangle
 6  {
 7     private:
 8        double width;      // The rectangle's width
 9        double length;     // The rectangle's length
10     public:
11        // Exception class for a negative width
12        class NegativeWidth
13        {
14        private:
15           double value;
16        public:
17           NegativeWidth(double val)
18              { value = val; }
19
20           double getValue() const
21              { return value; }
22        };
23
24        // Exception class for a negative length
25        class NegativeLength
26        {
27        private:
28           double value;
```

```
29          public:
30              NegativeLength(double val)
31                  { value = val; }
32
33              double getValue() const
34                  { return value; }
35          };
36
37          // Default constructor
38          Rectangle()
39              { width = 0.0; length = 0.0; }
40
41          // Mutator functions, defined in Rectangle.cpp
42          void setWidth(double);
43          void setLength(double);
44
45          // Accessor functions
46          double getWidth() const
47              { return width; }
48
49          double getLength() const
50              { return length; }
51
52          double getArea() const
53              { return width * length; }
54      };
55      #endif
```

Contents of `Rectangle.cpp` (Version 3)

```
 1    // Implementation file for the Rectangle class.
 2    #include "Rectangle.h"
 3
 4    //**********************************************************
 5    // setWidth sets the value of the member variable width.   *
 6    //**********************************************************
 7
 8    void Rectangle::setWidth(double w)
 9    {
10       if (w >= 0)
11          width = w;
12       else
13          throw NegativeWidth(w);
14    }
15
16    //**********************************************************
17    // setLength sets the value of the member variable length. *
18    //**********************************************************
19
20    void Rectangle::setLength(double len)
21    {
22       if (len >= 0)
23          length = len;
24       else
25          throw NegativeLength(len);
26    }
```

Program 16-5

```cpp
1   // This program demonstrates Rectangle class exceptions.
2   #include <iostream>
3   #include "Rectangle.h"
4   using namespace std;
5
6   int main()
7   {
8      double width;
9      double length;
10
11     // Create a Rectangle object.
12     Rectangle myRectangle;
13
14     // Get the width and length.
15     cout << "Enter the rectangle's width: ";
16     cin >> width;
17     cout << "Enter the rectangle's length: ";
18     cin >> length;
19
20     // Store these values in the Rectangle object.
21     try
22     {
23        myRectangle.setWidth(width);
24        myRectangle.setLength(length);
25        cout << "The area of the rectangle is "
26             << myRectangle.getArea() << endl;
27     }
28     catch (Rectangle::NegativeWidth e)
29     {
30        cout << "Error: " << e.getValue()
31             << " is an invalid value for the"
32             << " rectangle's width.\n";
33     }
34     catch (Rectangle::NegativeLength e)
35     {
36        cout << "Error: " << e.getValue()
37             << " is an invalid value for the"
38             << " rectangle's length.\n";
39     }
40
41     cout << "End of the program.\n";
42     return 0;
43  }
```

Program Output with Example Input Shown in Bold
```
Enter the rectangle's width: -1 [Enter]
Enter the rectangle's length: 10 [Enter]
Error: -1 is an invalid value for the rectangle's width.
End of the program.
```
(program output continues)

Program 16-5   *(continued)*

Program Output with Different Example Input Shown in Bold
```
Enter the rectangle's width: 5 [Enter]
Enter the rectangle's length: -1 [Enter]
Error: -1 is an invalid value for the rectangle's length.
End of the program.
```

Unwinding the Stack

Once an exception has been thrown, the program cannot jump back to the throw point. The function that executes a throw statement will immediately terminate. If that function was called by another function, and the exception is not caught, then the calling function will terminate as well. This process, known as *unwinding the stack*, continues for the entire chain of nested function calls, from the throw point, all the way back to the try block.

If an exception is thrown by the member function of a class object, then the class destructor is called. If statements in the try block or branching from the try block created any other objects, their destructors will be called as well.

Rethrowing an Exception

It is possible for try blocks to be nested. For example, look at this code segment:

```
try
{
    doSomething();
}
catch(exception1)
{
    // code to handle exception 1
}
catch(exception2)
{
    // code to handle exception 2
}
```

In this try block, the function doSomething is called. There are two catch blocks, one that handles exception1, and another that handles exception2. If the doSomething function also has a try block, then it is nested inside the one shown.

With nested try blocks, it is sometimes necessary for an inner exception handler to pass an exception to an outer exception handler. Sometimes, both an inner and an outer catch block must perform operations when a particular exception is thrown. These situations require that the inner catch block *rethrow* the exception so the outer catch block has a chance to catch it.

A catch block can rethrow an exception with the throw; statement. For example, suppose the doSomething function (called in the throw block above) calls the doSomethingElse function, which potentially can throw exception1 or exception3. Suppose doSomething does not want to handle exception1. Instead, it wants to rethrow it to the outer block. The following code segment illustrates how this is done:

```
try
{
    doSomethingElse();
}
catch(exception1)
{
    throw; // Rethrow the exception
}
catch(exception3)
{
    // Code to handle exception 3
}
```

When the first catch block catches exception1, the throw; statement simply throws the exception again. The catch block in the outer try/catch construct will then handle the exception.

Handling the bad_alloc Exception

Recall from Chapter 9 that when the new operator fails to allocate memory, an exception is thrown. Now that you've seen how to handle exceptions, you can write code that determines whether the new operator was successful.

When the new operator fails to allocate memory, C++ throws a bad_alloc exception. The bad_alloc exception type is defined in the new header file, so any program that attempts to catch this exception should have the following directive:

```
#include <new>
```

The bad_alloc exception is in the std namespace, so be sure to have the using namespace std; statement in your code as well.

Here is the general format of a try/catch construct that catches the bad_alloc exception:

```
try
{
    // Code that uses the new operator
}
catch (bad_alloc)
{
    // Code that responds to the error
}
```

Program 16-6 shows an example. The program uses the new operator to allocate a 10,000-element array of doubles. If the new operator fails, an error message is displayed.

Program 16-6

```
1  // This program demonstrates the bad_alloc exception.
2  #include <iostream>
3  #include <new>        // Needed for bad_alloc
4  using namespace std;
5
```

(program continues)

Program 16-6   *(continued)*

```
 6  int main()
 7  {
 8     double *ptr;   // Pointer to double
 9
10     try
11     {
12        ptr = new double [10000];
13     }
14     catch (bad_alloc)
15     {
16        cout << "Insufficient memory.\n";
17     }
18
19     return 0;
20  }
```

 Checkpoint

myprogramminglab   *www.myprogramminglab.com*

16.1   What is the difference between a try block and a catch block?

16.2   What happens if an exception is thrown, but not caught?

16.3   If multiple exceptions can be thrown, how does the catch block know which
        exception to catch?

16.4   After the catch block has handled the exception, where does program execution
        resume?

16.5   How can an exception pass data back to the exception handler?

 16.2   # Function Templates

> **CONCEPT:** A function template is a "generic" function that can work with any data
> type. The programmer writes the specifications of the function, but
> substitutes parameters for data types. When the compiler encounters a
> call to the function, it generates code to handle the specific data type(s)
> used in the call.

Introduction

Overloaded functions make programming convenient because only one function name
must be remembered for a set of functions that perform similar operations. Each of the
functions, however, must still be written individually, even if they perform the same operation. For example, suppose a program uses the following overloaded `square` functions.

```
int square(int number)
{
   return number * number;
}
```

```
double square(double number)
{
    return number * number;
}
```

The only differences between these two functions are the data types of their return values and their parameters. In situations like this, it is more convenient to write a *function template* than an overloaded function. Function templates allow you to write a single function definition that works with many different data types, instead of having to write a separate function for each data type used.

A function template is not an actual function, but a "mold" the compiler uses to generate one or more functions. When writing a function template, you do not have to specify actual types for the parameters, return value, or local variables. Instead, you use a *type parameter* to specify a generic data type. When the compiler encounters a call to the function, it examines the data types of its arguments and generates the function code that will work with those data types. (The generated code is known as a *template function*.)

Here is a function template for the square function:

VideoNote

Writing a Function Template

```
template <class T>
T square(T number)
{
    return number * number;
}
```

The beginning of a function template is marked by a *template prefix*, which begins with the key word `template`. Next is a set of angled brackets that contains one or more generic data types used in the template. A generic data type starts with the key word `class` followed by a parameter name that stands for the data type. The example just given only uses one, which is named `T`. (If there were more, they would be separated by commas.) After this, the function definition is written as usual, except the type parameters are substituted for the actual data type names. In the example the function header reads

```
T square(T number)
```

`T` is the type parameter, or generic data type. The header defines `square` as a function that returns a value of type `T` and uses a parameter, `number`, which is also of type `T`. As mentioned before, the compiler examines each call to `square` and fills in the appropriate data type for `T`. For example, the following call uses an `int` argument:

```
int y, x = 4;
y = square(x);
```

This code will cause the compiler to generate the function

```
int square(int number)
{
    return number * number;
}
```

while the following statements

```
double y, f = 6.2
y = square(f);
```

will generate the function

```cpp
double square(double number)
{
    return number * number;
}
```

Program 16-7 demonstrates how this function template is used.

Program 16-7

```cpp
 1   // This program uses a function template.
 2   #include <iostream>
 3   #include <iomanip>
 4   using namespace std;
 5
 6   // Template definition for square function.
 7   template <class T>
 8   T square(T number)
 9   {
10       return number * number;
11   }
12
13   int main()
14   {
15       int userInt;        // To hold integer input
16       double userDouble;  // To hold double input
17
18       cout << setprecision(5);
19       cout << "Enter an integer and a floating-point value: ";
20       cin >> userInt >> userDouble;
21       cout << "Here are their squares: ";
22       cout << square(userInt) << " and "
23            << square(userDouble) << endl;
24       return 0;
25   }
```

Program Output with Example Input Shown in Bold
```
Enter an integer and a floating-point value: 12 4.2 [Enter]
Here are their squares: 144 and 17.64
```

NOTE: All type parameters defined in a function template must appear at least once in the function parameter list.

Because the compiler encountered two calls to square in Program 16-7, each with a different parameter type, it generated the code for two instances of the function: one with an int parameter and int return type, the other with a double parameter and double return type. This is illustrated in Figure 16-3.

Notice in Program 16-7 that the template appears before all calls to square. As with regular functions, the compiler must already know the template's contents when it encounters

Figure 16-3

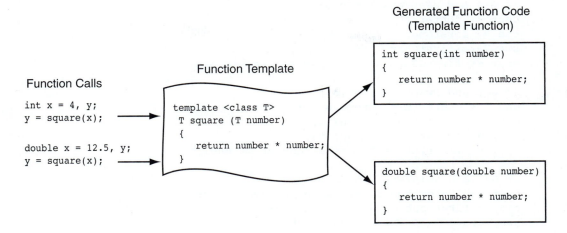

a call to the template function. Templates, therefore, should be placed near the top of the program or in a header file.

NOTE: A function template is merely the specification of a function and by itself does not cause memory to be used. An actual instance of the function is created in memory when the compiler encounters a call to the template function.

Program 16-8 shows another example of a function template. The function, swapVars, uses two references to type T as parameters. The function swaps the contents of the variables referenced by the parameters.

Program 16-8

```
1   // This program demonstrates the swapVars function template.
2   #include <iostream>
3   using namespace std;
4
5   template <class T>
6   void swapVars(T &var1, T &var2)
7   {
8       T temp;
9
10      temp = var1;
11      var1 = var2;
12      var2 = temp;
13  }
14
15  int main()
16  {
17      char firstChar, secondChar;      // Two chars
18      int firstInt, secondInt;         // Two ints
19      double firstDouble, secondDouble; // Two doubles
20
```

(program continues)

Program 16-8 *(continued)*

```
21      // Get and swapVars two chars
22      cout << "Enter two characters: ";
23      cin >> firstChar >> secondChar;
24      swapVars(firstChar, secondChar);
25      cout << firstChar << " " << secondChar << endl;
26
27      // Get and swapVars two ints
28      cout << "Enter two integers: ";
29      cin >> firstInt >> secondInt;
30      swapVars(firstInt, secondInt);
31      cout << firstInt << " " << secondInt << endl;
32
33      // Get and swapVars two doubles
34      cout << "Enter two floating-point numbers: ";
35      cin >> firstDouble >> secondDouble;
36      swapVars(firstDouble, secondDouble);
37      cout << firstDouble << " " << secondDouble << endl;
38      return 0;
39   }
```

Program Output with Example Input Shown in Bold
```
Enter two characters: A B [Enter]
B A
Enter two integers: 5 10 [Enter]
10 5
Enter two floating-point numbers: 1.2 9.6 [Enter]
9.6 1.2
```

Using Operators in Function Templates

The square template shown earlier uses the * operator with the number parameter. This works well as long as number is of a primitive data type such as int, float, etc. If a user-defined class object is passed to the square function, however, the class must contain code for an overloaded * operator. If not, the compiler will generate a function with an error.

Always remember that a class object passed to a function template must support all the operations the function will perform on the object. For instance, if the function performs a comparison on the object (with >, <, ==, or another relational operator), those operators must be overloaded by the class object.

Function Templates with Multiple Types

More than one generic type may be used in a function template. Each type must have its own parameter, as shown in Program 16-9. This program uses a function template named larger. This template uses two type parameters: T1 and T2. The sizes of the function parameters, var1 and var2, are compared and the function returns the number of bytes occupied by the larger of the two. Because the function parameters are specified with different types, the function generated from this template can accept two arguments of different types.

Program 16-9

```cpp
1   // This program demonstrates a function template
2   // with two type parameters.
3   #include <iostream>
4   using namespace std;
5
6   template <class T1, class T2>
7   int largest(const T1 &var1, T2 &var2)
8   {
9      if (sizeof(var1) > sizeof(var2))
10        return sizeof(var1);
11     else
12        return sizeof(var2);
13  }
14
15  int main()
16  {
17     int i = 0;
18     char c = ' ';
19     float f = 0.0;
20     double d = 0.0;
21
22     cout << "Comparing an int and a double, the largest\n"
23          << "of the two is " << largest(i, d) << " bytes.\n";
24
25     cout << "Comparing a char and a float, the largest\n"
26          << "of the two is " << largest(c, f) << " bytes.\n";
27
28     return 0;
29  }
```

Program Output

```
Comparing an int and a double, the largest
of the two is 8 bytes.
Comparing a char and a float, the largest
of the two is 4 bytes.
```

 NOTE: Each type parameter declared in the template prefix must be used somewhere in the template definition.

Overloading with Function Templates

Function templates may be overloaded. As with regular functions, function templates are overloaded by having different parameter lists. For example, there are two overloaded versions of the sum function in Program 16-10. The first version accepts two arguments, and the second version accepts three.

Program 16-10

```
 1   // This program demonstrates an overloaded function template.
 2   #include <iostream>
 3   using namespace std;
 4
 5   template <class T>
 6   T sum(T val1, T val2)
 7   {
 8      return val1 + val2;
 9   }
10
11   template <class T>
12   T sum(T val1, T val2, T val3)
13   {
14      return val1 + val2 + val3;
15   }
16
17   int main()
18   {
19      double num1, num2, num3;
20
21      // Get two values and display their sum.
22      cout << "Enter two values: ";
23      cin >> num1 >> num2;
24      cout << "Their sum is " << sum(num1, num2) << endl;
25
26      // Get three values and display their sum.
27      cout << "Enter three values: ";
28      cin >> num1 >> num2 >> num3;
29      cout << "Their sum is " << sum(num1, num2, num3) << endl;
30      return 0;
31   }
```

Program Output with Example Input Shown in Bold
```
Enter two values: 12.5 6.9 [Enter]
Their sum is 19.4
Enter three values: 45.76 98.32 10.51 [Enter]
Their sum is 154.59
```

There are other ways to perform overloading with function templates as well. For example, a program might contain a regular (nontemplate) version of a function as well as a template version. As long as each has a different parameter list, they can coexist as overloaded functions.

16.3 Focus on Software Engineering: Where to Start When Defining Templates

Quite often, it is easier to convert an existing function into a template than to write a template from scratch. With this in mind, you should start designing a function template by writing it first as a regular function. For example, the swapVars template in Program 16-8 would have been started as something like the following:

```
void swapVars(int &var1, int &var2)
{
    int temp;

    temp = var1;
    var1 = var2;
    var2 = temp;
}
```

Once this function is properly tested and debugged, converting it to a template is a simple process. First, the template <class T> header is added, then all the references to int that must be changed are replaced with the data type parameter T.

 ## Checkpoint

 www.myprogramminglab.com

16.6   When does the compiler actually generate code for a function template?

16.7   The following function accepts an int argument and returns half of its value as a double:

```
double half(int number)
{
    return number / 2.0;
}
```

Write a template that will implement this function to accept an argument of any type.

16.8   What must you be sure of when passing a class object to a function template that uses an operator, such as * or >?

16.9   What is the best method for writing a function template?

16.4 Class Templates

CONCEPT: Templates may also be used to create generic classes and abstract data types. Class templates allow you to create one general version of a class without having to duplicate code to handle multiple data types.

Recall the IntArray class from Chapter 14. By overloading the [ ] operator, this class allows you to implement int arrays that perform bounds checking. But suppose you would like to have a version of this class for other data types? Of course, you could design specialized classes such as LongArray, FloatArray, DoubleArray, and so forth. A better solution, however, is to design a single class template that works with any primitive data type. In this section, we will convert the IntArray class into a generalized template named SimpleVector.

Declaring a class template is very similar to declaring a function template. First, a template prefix, such as template<class T>, is placed before the class declaration. As with function templates, T (or whatever identifier you choose to use) is a data type parameter. Then, throughout the class declaration, the data type parameter is used where you wish to support any data type. Below is the `SimpleVector` class template declaration.

Contents of `SimpleVector.h`

```
 1   // SimpleVector class template
 2   #ifndef SIMPLEVECTOR_H
 3   #define SIMPLEVECTOR_H
 4   #include <iostream>
 5   #include <new>          // Needed for bad_alloc exception
 6   #include <cstdlib>      // Needed for the exit function
 7   using namespace std;
 8
 9   template <class T>
10   class SimpleVector
11   {
12   private:
13      T *aptr;            // To point to the allocated array
14      int arraySize;      // Number of elements in the array
15      void memError();    // Handles memory allocation errors
16      void subError();    // Handles subscripts out of range
17
18   public:
19      // Default constructor
20      SimpleVector()
21         { aptr = 0; arraySize = 0;}
22
23      // Constructor declaration
24      SimpleVector(int);
25
26      // Copy constructor declaration
27      SimpleVector(const SimpleVector &);
28
29      // Destructor declaration
30      ~SimpleVector();
31
32      // Accessor to return the array size
33      int size() const
34         { return arraySize; }
35
36      // Accessor to return a specific element
37      T getElementAt(int position);
38
39      // Overloaded [] operator declaration
40      T &operator[](const int &);
41   };
42
43   //*********************************************************
44   // Constructor for SimpleVector class. Sets the size of the *
45   // array and allocates memory for it.                       *
46   //*********************************************************
47
```

```
48   template <class T>
49   SimpleVector<T>::SimpleVector(int s)
50   {
51      arraySize = s;
52      // Allocate memory for the array.
53      try
54      {
55         aptr = new T [s];
56      }
57      catch (bad_alloc)
58      {
59         memError();
60      }
61
62      // Initialize the array.
63      for (int count = 0; count < arraySize; count++)
64         *(aptr + count) = 0;
65   }
66
67   //*******************************************
68   // Copy Constructor for SimpleVector class. *
69   //*******************************************
70
71   template <class T>
72   SimpleVector<T>::SimpleVector(const SimpleVector &obj)
73   {
74      // Copy the array size.
75      arraySize = obj.arraySize;
76
77      // Allocate memory for the array.
78      aptr = new T [arraySize];
79      if (aptr == 0)
80         memError();
81
82      // Copy the elements of obj's array.
83      for(int count = 0; count < arraySize; count++)
84         *(aptr + count) = *(obj.aptr + count);
85   }
86
87   //************************************
88   // Destructor for SimpleVector class.   *
89   //************************************
90
91   template <class T>
92   SimpleVector<T>::~SimpleVector()
93   {
94      if (arraySize > 0)
95         delete [] aptr;
96   }
97
98   //********************************************************
99   // memError function. Displays an error message and      *
100  // terminates the program when memory allocation fails. *
101  //********************************************************
102
```

```
103    template <class T>
104    void SimpleVector<T>::memError()
105    {
106       cout << "ERROR:Cannot allocate memory.\n";
107       exit(EXIT_FAILURE);
108    }
109
110    //**********************************************************
111    // subError function. Displays an error message and        *
112    // terminates the program when a subscript is out of range. *
113    //**********************************************************
114
115    template <class T>
116    void SimpleVector<T>::subError()
117    {
118       cout << "ERROR: Subscript out of range.\n";
119       exit(EXIT_FAILURE);
120    }
121
122    //**********************************************************
123    // getElementAt function. The argument is a subscript.    *
124    // This function returns the value stored at the           *
125    // subcript in the array.                                  *
126    //**********************************************************
127
128    template <class T>
129    T SimpleVector<T>::getElementAt(int sub)
130    {
131       if (sub < 0 || sub >= arraySize)
132          subError();
133       return aptr[sub];
134    }
135
136    //**********************************************************
137    // Overloaded [] operator. The argument is a subscript. *
138    // This function returns a reference to the element      *
139    // in the array indexed by the subscript.                *
140    //**********************************************************
141
142    template <class T>
143    T &SimpleVector<T>::operator[](const int &sub)
144    {
145       if (sub < 0 || sub >= arraySize)
146          subError();
147       return aptr[sub];
148    }
149    #endif
```

 NOTE: The arraySize member variable is declared as an int. This is because it holds the size of the array, which will be an integer value, regardless of the data type of the array. This is also why the size member function returns an int.

Defining Objects of the Class Template

Class template objects are defined like objects of ordinary classes, with one small difference: the data type you wish to pass to the type parameter must be specified. Placing the data type name inside angled brackets immediately following the class name does this. For example, the following statements create two SimpleVector objects: intTable and doubleTable.

```
SimpleVector<int> intTable(10);
SimpleVector<double> doubleTable(10);
```

In the definition of intTable, the data type int will be used in the template everywhere the type parameter T appears. This will cause intTable to store an array of ints. Likewise, the definition of doubleTable passes the data type double into the parameter T, causing it to store an array of doubles. This is demonstrated in Program 16-11.

Program 16-11

```cpp
 1  // This program demonstrates the SimpleVector template.
 2  #include <iostream>
 3  #include "SimpleVector.h"
 4  using namespace std;
 5
 6  int main()
 7  {
 8     const int SIZE = 10;     // Number of elements
 9     int count;               // Loop counter
10
11     // Create a SimpleVector of ints.
12     SimpleVector<int> intTable(SIZE);
13
14     // Create a SimpleVector of doubles.
15     SimpleVector<double> doubleTable(SIZE);
16
17     // Store values in the two SimpleVectors.
18     for (count = 0; count < SIZE; count++)
19     {
20        intTable[count] = (count * 2);
21        doubleTable[count] = (count * 2.14);
22     }
23
24     // Display the values in the SimpleVectors.
25     cout << "These values are in intTable:\n";
26     for (count = 0; count < SIZE; count++)
27       cout << intTable[count] << " ";
28     cout << endl;
29     cout << "These values are in doubleTable:\n";
30     for (count = 0; count < SIZE; count++)
31       cout << doubleTable[count] << " ";
32     cout << endl;
33
```

(program continues)

Program 16-11   *(continued)*

```
34       // Use the standard + operator on the elements.
35       cout << "\nAdding 5 to each element of intTable"
36            << " and doubleTable.\n";
37       for (count = 0; count < SIZE; count++)
38       {
39          intTable[count] = intTable[count] + 5;
40          doubleTable[count] = doubleTable[count] + 5.0;
41       }
42
43       // Display the values in the SimpleVectors.
44       cout << "These values are in intTable:\n";
45       for (count = 0; count < SIZE; count++)
46          cout << intTable[count] << " ";
47       cout << endl;
48       cout << "These values are in doubleTable:\n";
49       for (count = 0; count < SIZE; count++)
50          cout << doubleTable[count] << " ";
51       cout << endl;
52
53       // Use the standard ++ operator on the elements.
54       cout << "\nIncrementing each element of intTable and"
55            << " doubleTable.\n";
56       for (count = 0; count < SIZE; count++)
57       {
58          intTable[count]++;
59          doubleTable[count]++;
60       }
61
62       // Display the values in the SimpleVectors.
63       cout << "These values are in intTable:\n";
64       for (count = 0; count < SIZE; count++)
65          cout << intTable[count] << " ";
66       cout << endl;
67       cout << "These values are in doubleTable:\n";
68       for (count = 0; count < SIZE; count++)
69          cout << doubleTable[count] << " ";
70       cout << endl;
71
72       return 0;
73    }
```

Program Output

```
These values are in intTable:
0 2 4 6 8 10 12 14 16 18
These values are in doubleTable:
0 2.14 4.28 6.42 8.56 10.7 12.84 14.98 17.12 19.26
```

```
Adding 5 to each element of intTable and doubleTable.
These values are in intTable:
5 7 9 11 13 15 17 19 21 23
These values are in doubleTable:
5 7.14 9.28 11.42 13.56 15.7 17.84 19.98 22.12 24.26

Incrementing each element of intTable and doubleTable.
These values are in intTable:
6 8 10 12 14 16 18 20 22 24
These values are in doubleTable:
6 8.14 10.28 12.42 14.56 16.7 18.84 20.98 23.12 25.26
```

Class Templates and Inheritance

Inheritance can easily be applied to class templates. For example, in the following template, SearchableVector is derived from the SimpleVector class.

Contents of `SearchableVector.h`

```
1   #ifndef SEARCHABLEVECTOR_H
2   #define SEARCHABLEVECTOR_H
3   #include "SimpleVector.h"
4
5   template <class T>
6   class SearchableVector : public SimpleVector<T>
7   {
8   public:
9       // Default constructor
10      SearchableVector() : SimpleVector<T>()
11          {}
12
13      // Constructor
14      SearchableVector(int size) : SimpleVector<T>(size)
15          { }
16
17      // Copy constructor
18      SearchableVector(const SearchableVector &);
19
20      // Accessor to find an item
21      int findItem(const T);
22  };
23
24  //*****************************************************
25  // Copy constructor                                  *
26  //*****************************************************
27
28  template <class T>
29  SearchableVector<T>::SearchableVector(const SearchableVector &obj) :
30                      SimpleVector<T>(obj.size())
31  {
32      for(int count = 0; count < this->size(); count++)
33          this->operator[](count) = obj[count];
34  }
```

```
35
36   //*********************************************************
37   // findItem function                                      *
38   // This function searches for item. If item is found      *
39   // the subscript is returned. Otherwise -1 is returned.    *
40   //*********************************************************
41
42   template <class T>
43   int SearchableVector<T>::findItem(const T item)
44   {
45      for (int count = 0; count <= this->size(); count++)
46      {
47         if (getElementAt(count) == item)
48            return count;
49      }
50      return -1;
51   }
52   #endif
```

This class template defines a searchable version of the `SimpleVector` class. The member function `findItem` accepts an argument, and performs a simple linear search to determine whether the argument's value is stored in the array. If the value is found in the array, its subscript is returned. Otherwise, −1 is returned.

Notice that each time the name `SimpleVector` is used in the class template, the type parameter `T` is used with it. For example, here is the first line of the class declaration, in line 6, which names `SimpleVector` as the base class:

```
class SearchableVector : public SimpleVector<T>
```

Also, here are the function headers for the class constructors:

```
SearchableVector() : SimpleVector<T>()
SearchableVector(int size) : SimpleVector<T>(size)
```

Because `SimpleVector` is a class template, the type parameter must be passed to it.

Program 16-12 demonstrates the class by storing values in two `SearchableVector` objects and then searching for a specific value in each.

Program 16-12

```
1    // This program demonstrates the SearchableVector template.
2    #include <iostream>
3    #include "SearchableVector.h"
4    using namespace std;
5
6    int main()
7    {
8       const int SIZE = 10;    // Number of elements
9       int count;              // Loop counter
10      int result;             // To hold search results
11
```

```
12       // Create two SearchableVector objects.
13       SearchableVector<int> intTable(SIZE);
14       SearchableVector<double> doubleTable(SIZE);
15
16       // Store values in the objects.
17       for (count = 0; count < SIZE; count++)
18       {
19          intTable[count] = (count * 2);
20          doubleTable[count] = (count * 2.14);
21       }
22
23       // Display the values in the objects.
24       cout << "These values are in intTable:\n";
25       for (count = 0; count < SIZE; count++)
26          cout << intTable[count] << " ";
27       cout << endl << endl;
28       cout << "These values are in doubleTable:\n";
29       for (count = 0; count < SIZE; count++)
30          cout << doubleTable[count] << " ";
31       cout << endl;
32
33       // Search for the value 6 in intTable.
34       cout << "\nSearching for 6 in intTable.\n";
35       result = intTable.findItem(6);
36       if (result == -1)
37          cout << "6 was not found in intTable.\n";
38       else
39          cout << "6 was found at subscript " << result << endl;
40
41       // Search for the value 12.84 in doubleTable.
42       cout << "\nSearching for 12.84 in doubleTable.\n";
43       result = doubleTable.findItem(12.84);
44       if (result == -1)
45          cout << "12.84 was not found in doubleTable.\n";
46       else
47          cout << "12.84 was found at subscript " << result << endl;
48       return 0;
49    }
```

Program Output
```
These values are in intTable:
0 2 4 6 8 10 12 14 16 18

These values are in doubleTable:
0 2.14 4.28 6.42 8.56 10.7 12.84 14.98 17.12 19.26

Searching for 6 in intTable.
6 was found at subscript 3

Searching for 12.84 in doubleTable.
12.84 was found at subscript 6
```

The `SearchableVector` class demonstrates that a class template may be derived from another class template. In addition, class templates may be derived from ordinary classes, and ordinary classes may be derived from class templates.

Specialized Templates

Suppose you have a template that works for all data types but one. For example, the `SimpleVector` and `SearchableVector` classes work well with numeric, and even character, data. But they will not work with C-strings. Situations like this require the use of *specialized templates*. A specialized template is one that is designed to work with a specific data type. In the declaration, the actual data type is used instead of a type parameter. For example, the declaration of a specialized version of the `SimpleVector` class might start like this:

```
class SimpleVector<char *>
```

The compiler would know that this version of the `SimpleVector` class is intended for the `char *` data type. Anytime an object is defined of the type `SimpleVector<char *>`, the compiler will use this template to generate the code.

 ## Checkpoint

myprogramminglab *www.myprogramminglab.com*

16.10   Suppose your program uses a class template named `List`, which is defined as

```
template<class T>
class List
{
    // Members are declared here…
};
```

Give an example of how you would use `int` as the data type in the definition of a `List` object. (Assume the class has a default constructor.)

16.11   As the following `Rectangle` class is written, the `width` and `length` members are `doubles`. Rewrite the class as a template that will accept any data type for these members.

```
class Rectangle
{
    private:
        double width;
        double length;
    public:
        void setData(double w, double l)
            { width = w; length = l;}
        double getWidth()
            { return width; }
        double getLength()
            { return length; }
        double getArea()
            { return width * length; }
};
```

16.5 Introduction to the Standard Template Library (STL)

CONCEPT: The Standard Template Library contains many templates for useful algorithms and data structures.

NOTE: Section 7.12 of Chapter 7 presents a concise introduction to the Standard Template Library, and discusses the `vector` data type. This discussion is continued in Section 8.5 of Chapter 8. If you have not already studied those sections, do so now.

In addition to its runtime library, which you have used throughout this book, C++ also provides a library of templates. The *Standard Template Library* (or STL) contains numerous generic templates for implementing abstract data types (ADTs) and algorithms. In this section you will be introduced to the general types of ADTs and algorithms that may be found in the STL.

Abstract Data Types

The most important data structures in the STL are *containers* and *iterators*. A container is a class that stores data and organizes it in some fashion. An iterator is an object that behaves like a pointer. It is used to access the individual data elements in a container.

There are two types of container classes in the STL: *sequence* and *associative*. A sequence container organizes data in a sequential fashion similar to an array. The three sequence containers currently provided are listed in Table 16-1.

Table 16-1

Container Name	Description
vector	An expandable array. Values may be added to or removed from the end or middle of a `vector`.
deque	Like a `vector`, but allows values to be added to or removed from the front.
list	A doubly linked list of data elements. Values may be inserted to or removed from any position. (You will learn more about linked lists in Chapter 17.)

Performance Differences Between `vectors`, `deques`, and `lists`

There is a difference in performance between `vectors`, `deques`, and `lists`. When choosing one of these templates to use in your program, remember the following points:

- A `vector` is capable of quickly adding values to its end. Insertions at other points are not as efficient.
- A `deque` is capable of quickly adding values to its front and its end. `deques` are not efficient at inserting values at other positions, however.
- A `list` is capable of quickly inserting values anywhere in its sequence. `lists` do not, however, provide random access.

An associative container uses keys to rapidly access elements. (If you've ever used a relational database, you are probably familiar with the concept of keys.) The four associative containers currently supported are shown in Table 16-2.

Table 16-2

Container Name	Description
set	Stores a set of keys. No duplicate values are allowed.
multiset	Stores a set of keys. Duplicates are allowed.
map	Maps a set of keys to data elements. Only one key per data element is allowed. Duplicates are not allowed.
multimap	Maps a set of keys to data elements. Many keys per data element are allowed. Duplicates are allowed.

Iterators are generalizations of pointers and are used to access data stored in containers. The types of iterators are shown in Table 16-3.

Table 16-3

Iterator Type	Description
Forward	Can only move forward in a container (uses the ++ operator).
Bidirectional	Can move forward or backward in a container (uses the ++ and – operators).
Random-access	Can move forward and backward, and can jump to a specific data element in a container.
Input	Can be used with an input stream to read data from an input device or a file.
Output	Can be used with an output stream to write data to an output device or a file.

Iterators are associated with containers. The type of container you have determines the type of iterator you use. For example, vectors and deques require random-access iterators, while lists, sets, multisets, maps, and multimaps require bidirectional iterators.

Algorithms

The algorithms provided by the STL are implemented as function templates, and perform various operations on elements of containers. There are many algorithms in the STL, but Table 16-4 lists a few of them. (The table gives only general descriptions.)

Table 16-4

Algorithm	Description
binary_search	Performs a binary search for an object and returns true if the object is found. *Example:* binary_search(iter1, iter2, value); In this statement, iter1 and iter2 point to elements in a container. (iter1 points to the first element in the range and iter2 points to the last element in the range.) The statement performs a binary search on the range of elements, searching for value. The binary_search function returns true if the element was found, and false if the element was not found.

(table continues)

Table 16-4   *(continued)*

Algorithm	Description
count	Returns the number of times a value appears in a range.
	Example: iter3 = count(iter1, iter2, value); In this statement, iter1 and iter2 point to elements in a container. (iter1 points to the first element in the range and iter2 points to the last element in the range.) The statement returns the number of times value appears in the range of elements.
find	Finds the first object in a container that matches a value and returns an iterator to it.
	Example: iter3 = find(iter1, iter2, value); In this statement, iter1 and iter2 point to elements in a container. (iter1 points to the first element in the range and iter2 points to the last element in the range.) The statement searches the range of elements for value. If value is found, the function returns an iterator to the element containing it.
for_each	Executes a function for each element in a container.
	Example: for_each(iter1, iter2, func); In this statement, iter1 and iter2 point to elements in a container. (iter1 points to the first element in the range and iter2 points to the last element in the range.) The third argument, func, is the name of a function. The statement calls the function func for each element in the range, passing the element as an argument.
max_element	Returns an iterator to the largest object in a range.
	Example: iter3 = max_element(iter1, iter2); In this statement, iter1 and iter2 point to elements in a container. (iter1 points to the first element in the range and iter2 points to the last element in the range.) The statement returns an iterator to the element containing the largest value in the range.
min_element	Returns an iterator to the smallest object in a range.
	Example: iter3 = min_element(iter1, iter2); In this statement, iter1 and iter2 point to elements in a container. (iter1 points to the first element in the range and iter2 points to the last element in the range.) The statement returns an iterator to the element containing the smallest value in the range.

(table continues)

Table 16-4 *(continued)*

Algorithm	Description
random_shuffle	Randomly shuffles the elements of a container.
	Example: random_shuffle(iter1, iter2); In this statement, iter1 and iter2 point to elements in a container. (iter1 points to the first element in the range and iter2 points to the last element in the range.) The statement randomly reorders the elements in the range.
sort	Sorts a range of elements.
	Example: sort(iter1, iter2); In this statement, iter1 and iter2 point to elements in a container. (iter1 points to the first element in the range and iter2 points to the last element in the range.) The statement sorts the elements in the range in ascending order.

Example Programs Using the STL

Now that you have been introduced to the types of data structures and algorithms offered by the STL, let's look at some simple programs that use them.

Containers

Program 16-13 provides a limited demonstration of the vector class template. The member functions of vector used in this program are listed in Table 16-5.

Table 16-5

Member Function	Description
size()	Returns the number of elements in the vector.
push_back()	Accepts as an argument a value to be inserted into the vector. The argument is inserted after the last element. (Pushed onto the back of the vector.)
pop_back()	Removes the last element from the vector.
operator[]	Allows array-like access of existing vector elements. (The vector must already contain elements for this operator to work. It cannot be used to insert new values into the vector.)

The vector class template has many more member functions, but these are enough to demonstrate the class.

Program 16-13

```
1   // This program provides a simple demonstration of the
2   // vector STL template.
3   #include <iostream>
4   #include <vector> // Include the vector header
5   using namespace std;
6
```

```
 7   int main()
 8   {
 9       int count;   // Loop counter
10
11       // Define a vector object.
12       vector<int> vect;
13
14       // Use the size member function to get
15       // the number of elements in the vector.
16       cout << "vect starts with " << vect.size()
17           << " elements.\n";
18
19       // Use push_back to push values into the vector.
20       for (count = 0; count < 10; count++)
21           vect.push_back(count);
22
23       // Display the size of the vector now.
24       cout << "Now vect has " << vect.size()
25           << " elements. Here they are:\n";
26
27       // Use the [] operator to display each element.
28       for (count = 0; count < vect.size(); count++)
29           cout << vect[count] << " ";
30       cout << endl;
31
32       // Use the pop_back member function.
33       cout << "Popping the values out of vect...\n";
34       for (count = 0; count < 10; count++)
35           vect.pop_back();
36
37       // Display the size of the vector now.
38       cout << "Now vect has " << vect.size() << " elements.\n";
39       return 0;
40   }
```

Program Output
```
vect starts with 0 elements.
Now vect has 10 elements. Here they are:
0 1 2 3 4 5 6 7 8 9
Popping the values out of vect...
Now vect has 0 elements.
```

VideoNote
Storing Objects in a vector

Notice the inclusion of the vector header file in line 4, which is required for the vector container. vectors are one of the simplest types of containers in the STL. In following chapters, you will see examples using other types of containers.

Iterators

In Program 16-13, the vector's elements were accessed by the container's member functions. Iterators may also be used to access and manipulate container elements. Program 16-14 demonstrates the use of an iterator with a vector object.

Program 16-14

```
 1   // This program provides a simple iterator demonstration.
 2   #include <iostream>
 3   #include <vector>      // Include the vector header
 4   using namespace std;
 5
 6   int main()
 7   {
 8      int count;   // Loop counter
 9
10      // Define a vector object.
11      vector<int> vect;
12
13      // Define an iterator object.
14      vector<int>::iterator iter;
15
16      // Use push_back to push values into the vector.
17      for (count = 0; count < 10; count++)
18      vect.push_back(count);
19
20      // Step the iterator through the vector,
21      // and use it to display the vector's contents.
22      cout << "Here are the values in vect: ";
23      for (iter = vect.begin(); iter < vect.end(); iter++)
24      {
25         cout << *iter << " ";
26      }
27
28      // Step the iterator through the vector backwards.
29      cout << "\nand here they are backwards: ";
30      for (iter = vect.end() - 1; iter >= vect.begin(); iter--)
31      {
32         cout << *iter << " ";
33      }
34      return 0;
35   }
```

Program Output
```
Here are the values in vect: 0 1 2 3 4 5 6 7 8 9
and here they are backwards: 9 8 7 6 5 4 3 2 1 0
```

The definition of an iterator is closely related to the definition of the container it is to be used with. For example, Program 16-14 defines a vector of ints as:

```
vector<int> vect;
```

The iterator that will work with the vector is defined as:

```
vector<int>::iterator iter;
```

This definition creates an iterator specifically for a vector of ints. The compiler automatically chooses the right type (in this case, a random-access iterator).

The second for loop in lines 23 through 26 causes the iterator to step through each element in the vector:

```
for (iter = vect.begin(); iter < vect.end(); iter++)
```

The loop's initialization expression uses the container's `begin()` member function, which returns an iterator pointing to the beginning of the `vector`. The statement

```
iter = vect.begin();
```

causes `iter` to point to the first element in the `vector`. The test expression uses the `end()` member function, which returns an iterator pointing to the location just past the end of the container:

```
iter < vect.end();
```

As long as `iter` points to an element prior to the end of the `vector`, this statement will be true.

The loop's update expression uses the `++` operator to increment the iterator. This causes the iterator to point to the next element in the vector.

The body of the loop uses a `cout` statement in line 25 to display the element that the iterator points to:

```
cout << *iter << " ";
```

Like a pointer, iterators may be dereferenced with the `*` operator. The statement above causes the value pointed to by `iter` to be displayed.

Back to the `vector` Template

Table 16-6 lists several more member functions of the `vector` class template. Some of these accept iterators as arguments and/or return an iterator.

Table 16-6

Member Function	Examples and Description
`at(element)`	Returns the value of the element located at *element* in the vector.
	Example: `x = vect.at(5);` This statement assigns the value of element 5 of `vect` to `x`.
`back()`	Returns a reference to the last element in the vector.
	Example: `cout << vect.back() << endl;`
`begin()`	Returns an iterator pointing to the vector's first element.
	Example: `iter = vect.begin();`
`capacity()`	Returns the maximum number of elements that may be stored in the vector without additional memory being allocated. (This is not the same value as returned by the `size` member function.)
	Example: `x = vect.capacity();` This statement assigns the capacity of `vect` to `x`.

(table continues)

Table 16-6 *(continued)*

Member Function	Examples and Description
clear()	Clears a vector of all its elements.
	Example: `vect.clear();` This statement removes all the elements from `vect`.
empty()	Returns true if the vector is empty. Otherwise, it returns false.

	Example:
	`if (vect.empty())`
	`    cout << "The vector is empty.";`
	This statement displays the message if `vect` is empty.

end()	Returns an iterator pointing to the vector's last element.
	Example: `iter = vect.end();`
erase()	Causes the vector element pointed to by the iterator `iter` to be removed.
	Example: `vect.erase(iter);`
erase(*iter1, iter2*)	Causes all the vector elements from the iterator `iter1` to the iterator `iter2` to be removed.
	Example: `vect.erase(firstIter, secondIter);`
front()	Returns a reference to the vector's first element.
	Example: `cout << vector.front() << endl;`
insert (*iter, value*)	Inserts a value into a `vector`.
	Example: `vect.insert(iter, 22);` This statement inserts the value 22 into `vect`. The value is inserted into the element before the one pointed to by `iter`.
resize(*n, value*)	Resizes a vector by *n* new elements. The elements are initialized with *value*.
	Example: `vect.resize(10, 0);` This statement adds ten new elements to `vect` and initializes the new elements with the value 0.
reverse()	Reverses the order of the items stored in a vector.
	Example: `vect.reverse();`

Algorithms

There are many algorithms in the STL, implemented as function templates. Program 16-15 demonstrates `random_shuffle`, `sort`, and `binary_search`.

Program 16-15

```cpp
1   // A simple demonstration of STL algorithms
2   #include <iostream>
3   #include <vector>    // Required for the vector type
4   #include <algorithm> // Required for STL algorithms
5   using namespace std;
6
7   int main()
8   {
9       int count;         // Loop counter
10
11      // Define a vector object.
12      vector<int> vect;
13
14      // Use push_back to push values into the vector.
15      for (count = 0; count < 10; count++)
16          vect.push_back(count);
17
18      // Display the vector's elements.
19      cout << "The vector has " << vect.size()
20           << " elements. Here they are:\n";
21      for (count = 0; count < vect.size(); count++)
22          cout << vect[count] << " ";
23      cout << endl;
24
25      // Randomly shuffle the vector's contents.
26      random_shuffle(vect.begin(), vect.end());
27
28      // Display the vector's elements.
29      cout << "The elements have been shuffled:\n";
30      for (count = 0; count < vect.size(); count++)
31          cout << vect[count] << " ";
32      cout << endl;
33
34      // Now sort the vector's elements.
35      sort(vect.begin(), vect.end());
36
37      // Display the vector's elements again.
38      cout << "The elements have been sorted:\n";
39      for (count = 0; count < vect.size(); count++)
40          cout << vect[count] << " ";
41      cout << endl;
42
43      // Now search for an element with the value 7.
44      if (binary_search(vect.begin(), vect.end(), 7))
45          cout << "The value 7 was found in the vector.\n";
46      else
47          cout << "The value 7 was not found in the vector.\n";
48      return 0;
49  }
```

(program output continues)

Program 16-15 *(continued)*

Program Output
```
The vector has 10 elements. Here they are:
0 1 2 3 4 5 6 7 8 9
The elements have been shuffled:
4 3 0 2 6 7 8 9 5 1
The elements have been sorted:
0 1 2 3 4 5 6 7 8 9
The value 7 was found in the vector.
```

NOTE: The STL algorithms require the `algorithm` header file.

The `random_shuffle` function rearranges the elements of a container. In line 26 of Program 16-15, it is called in the following manner:

```
random_shuffle(vect.begin(), vect.end());
```

The function takes two arguments, which together represent a range of elements within a container. The first argument is an iterator to the first element in the range. In this case, `vect.begin()` is used. The second argument is an iterator to the last element in the range. Here we have used `vect.end()`. These arguments tell `random_shuffle` to rearrange all the elements from the beginning to the end of the `vect` container.

The `sort` algorithm also takes iterators to a range of elements. Here is the function call that appears in line 35:

```
sort(vect.begin(), vect.end());
```

All the elements within the range are sorted in ascending order.

The `binary_search` algorithm searches a range of elements for a value. If the value is found, the function returns `true`. Otherwise, it returns `false`. For example, the following function call, which appears in line 44, searches all the elements in `vect` for the value 7.

```
binary_search(vect.begin(), vect.end(), 7)
```

Program 16-16 demonstrates the count algorithm.

Program 16-16

```
1   // This program demonstrates the STL count algorithm.
2   #include <iostream>
3   #include <vector>    // Needed to define the vector
4   #include <algorithm> // Needed for the count algorithm
5   using namespace std;
6
7   int main()
8   {
9      // Define a vector object.
10     vector<int> values;
11
```

```
12        // Define an iterator for the vector.
13        vector<int>::iterator iter;
14
15        // Store some values in the vector.
16        values.push_back(1);
17        values.push_back(2);
18        values.push_back(2);
19        values.push_back(3);
20        values.push_back(3);
21        values.push_back(3);
22
23        // Display the values in the vector.
24        cout << "The values in the vector are:\n";
25        for (iter = values.begin(); iter < values.end(); iter++)
26           cout << *iter << " ";
27        cout << endl << endl;
28
29        // Display the count of each number.
30        cout << "The number of 1s in the vector is ";
31        cout << count(values.begin(), values.end(), 1) << endl;
32        cout << "The number of 2s in the vector is ";
33        cout << count(values.begin(), values.end(), 2) << endl;
34        cout << "The number of 3s in the vector is ";
35        cout << count(values.begin(), values.end(), 3) << endl;
36        return 0;
37    }
```

Program Output

```
The values in the vector are:
1 2 2 3 3 3

The number of 1s in the vector is 1
The number of 2s in the vector is 2
The number of 3s in the vector is 3
```

Program 16-17 demonstrates the max_element and min_element algorithms.

Program 16-17

```
1    // A demonstration of the max_element and min_element algorithms
2    #include <iostream>
3    #include <vector>    // Needed to define the vector
4    #include <algorithm> // Needed for the algorithms
5    using namespace std;
6
7    int main()
8    {
9        // Define a vector object.
10       vector<int> numbers;
11
```

(program continues)

Program 16-17 *(continued)*

```
12      // Define an iterator for the vector.
13      vector<int>::iterator iter;
14
15      // Store some numbers in the vector.
16      for (int count = 0; count < 10; count++)
17         numbers.push_back(count);
18
19      // Display the numbers in the vector.
20      cout << "The numbers in the vector are:\n";
21      for (iter = numbers.begin(); iter != numbers.end(); iter++)
22         cout << *iter << " ";
23      cout << endl << endl;
24
25      // Find the largest value in the vector.
26      iter = max_element(numbers.begin(), numbers.end());
27      cout << "The largest value in the vector is " << *iter << endl;
28
29      // Find the smallest value in the vector.
30      iter = min_element(numbers.begin(), numbers.end());
31      cout << "The smallest value in the vector is " << *iter << endl;
32      return 0;
33   }
```

Program Output

```
The numbers in the vector are:
0 1 2 3 4 5 6 7 8 9

The largest value in the vector is 9
The smallest value in the vector is 0
```

Program 16-18 demonstrates the `find` algorithm.

Program 16-18

```
1   // A demonstration of the STL find algorithm.
2   #include <iostream>
3   #include <vector>    // Needed to define the vector
4   #include <algorithm> // Needed for the find algorithm
5   using namespace std;
6
7   int main()
8   {
9      // Define a vector object.
10     vector<int> numbers;
11
12     // Define an iterator for the vector.
13     vector<int>::iterator iter;
14
```

```
15      // Store some numbers in the vector.
16      for (int x = 0; x < 10; x++)
17        numbers.push_back(x);
18
19      // Display the numbers in the vector.
20      cout << "The numbers in the vector are:\n";
21      for (iter = numbers.begin(); iter != numbers.end(); iter++)
22        cout << *iter << " ";
23      cout << endl << endl;
24
25      // Find the number 7 in the vector.
26      iter = find(numbers.begin(), numbers.end(), 7);
27      cout << *iter << endl;
28      return 0;
29   }
```

Program Output

```
The numbers in the vector are:
0 1 2 3 4 5 6 7 8 9

7
```

Program 16-19 demonstrates the for_each algorithm.

Program 16-19

```
1    // A demonstration of the for_each algorithm.
2    #include <iostream>
3    #include <vector>     // Needed to define the vector
4    #include <algorithm>  // Needed for the for_each algorithm
5    using namespace std;
6
7    // Function prototype
8    void doubleValue(int &);
9
10   int main()
11   {
12      // Define a vector object.
13      vector<int> numbers;
14
15      // Define an iterator for the vector.
16      vector<int>::iterator iter;
17
18      // Store some numbers in the vector.
19      for (int x = 0; x < 10; x++)
20        numbers.push_back(x);
21
```

(program continues)

Program 16-19 (continued)

```
22      // Display the numbers in the vector.
23      cout << "The numbers in the vector are:\n";
24      for (iter = numbers.begin(); iter != numbers.end(); iter++)
25         cout << *iter << " ";
26      cout << endl << endl;
27
28      // Double the values in the vector.
29      for_each(numbers.begin(), numbers.end(), doubleValue);
30
31      // Display the numbers in the vector again.
32      cout << "Now the numbers in the vector are:\n";
33      for (iter = numbers.begin(); iter != numbers.end(); iter++)
34         cout << *iter << " ";
35      cout << endl;
36      return 0;
37   }
38
39   //********************************************************
40   // Function doubleValue. This function accepts an int    *
41   // reference as its argument. The value of the argument  *
42   // is doubled.                                           *
43   //********************************************************
44
45   void doubleValue(int &val)
46   {
47      val *= 2;
48   }
```

Program Output

```
The numbers in the vector are:
0 1 2 3 4 5 6 7 8 9

Now the numbers in the vector are:
0 2 4 6 8 10 12 14 16 18
```

In line 29, the following statement calls `for_each`:

```
for_each(numbers.begin(), numbers.end(), doubleValue);
```

The first and second arguments specify a range of elements. In this case, the range is the entire vector. The third argument is the name of a function. The `for_each` algorithm calls the function once for each element in the range, passing the element as an argument to the function.

The programs in this section give you a brief introduction to using the STL by demonstrating simple operations on a vector. In the remaining chapters you will be given specific examples of how to use other STL containers, iterators, and algorithms.

Review Questions and Exercises

Short Answer

1. What is a throw point?

2. What is an exception handler?

3. Explain the difference between a try block and a catch block.

4. What happens if an exception is thrown, but not caught?

5. What is "unwinding the stack"?

6. What happens if an exception is thrown by a class's member function?

7. How do you prevent a program from halting when the new operator fails to allocate memory?

8. Why is it more convenient to write a function template than a series of overloaded functions?

9. Why must you be careful when writing a function template that uses operators such as [ ] with its parameters?

10. What is a container? What is an iterator?

11. What two types of containers does the STL provide?

12. What STL algorithm randomly shuffles the elements in a container?

Fill-in-the-Blank

13. The line containing a throw statement is known as the _____.

14. The _____ block contains code that directly or indirectly might cause an exception to be thrown.

15. The _____ block handles an exception.

16. When writing function or class templates, you use a(n) _____ to specify a generic data type.

17. The beginning of a template is marked by a(n) _____.

18. When defining objects of class templates, the _____ you wish to pass into the type parameter must be specified.

19. A(n) _____ template works with a specific data type.

20. A(n) _____ container organizes data in a sequential fashion similar to an array.

21. A(n) _____ container uses keys to rapidly access elements.

22. _____ are pointer-like objects used to access data stored in a container.

23. The _____ exception is thrown when the new operator fails to allocate the requested amount of memory.

Algorithm Workbench

24. Write a function that searches a numeric array for a specified value. The function should return the subscript of the element containing the value if it is found in the array. If the value is not found, the function should throw an exception.

25. Write a function that dynamically allocates a block of memory and returns a `char` pointer to the block. The function should take an integer argument that is the amount of memory to be allocated. If the `new` operator cannot allocate the memory, the function should return a null pointer (a pointer to address 0).

26. Make the function you wrote in Question 24 a template.

27. Write a template for a function that displays the contents of an array of any type.

28. A program has the following definition statements:

    ```
    vector<int> numbers;
    vector<int>::iterator iter;
    ```

    Write code that uses the iterator to display all the values stored in the vector.

29. Write a statement that performs the STL `binary_search` algorithm on the vector defined in Question 28.

30. A program has the following definition:

    ```
    vector<double> numbers;
    ```

    The same program also has the following function:

    ```
    void display(double n)
    {
        cout << n << endl;
    }
    ```

    Write code that uses the STL `for_each` algorithm to display the elements of the `numbers` vector using the `display` function.

True or False

31. T F There can be only one catch block in a program.

32. T F When an exception is thrown, but not caught, the program ignores the error.

33. T F Data may be passed with an exception by storing it in members of an exception class.

34. T F Once an exception has been thrown, it is not possible for the program to jump back to the throw point.

35. T F All type parameters defined in a function template must appear at least once in the function parameter list.

36. T F The compiler creates an instance of a function template in memory as soon as it encounters the template.

37. T F A class object passed to a function template must overload any operators used on the class object by the template.

38. T F Only one generic type may be used with a template.

39. T F In the function template definition, it is not necessary to use each type parameter declared in the template prefix.

40. T F It is possible to overload two function templates.

41. T F It is possible to overload a function template and an ordinary (nontemplate) function.

42. T F A class template may not be derived from another class template.

43. T   F   A class template may not be used as a base class.

44. T   F   Specialized templates work with a specific data type.

45. T   F   When defining an iterator from the STL, the compiler automatically creates the right kind, depending upon the container it is to be used with.

46. T   F   STL algorithms are implemented as function templates.

Find the Error

Each of the following declarations or code segments has errors. Locate as many as possible.

47.
```
catch
{
    quotient = divide(num1, num2);
    cout << "The quotient is " << quotient << endl;
}
try (string exceptionString)
{
    cout << exceptionString;
}
```

48.
```
try
{
    quotient = divide(num1, num2);
}
cout << "The quotient is " << quotient << endl;
catch (string exceptionString)
{
    cout << exceptionString;
}
```

49.
```
template <class T>
T square(T number)
{
    return T * T;
}
```

50.
```
template <class T>
int square(int number)
{
    return number * number;
}
```

51.
```
template <class T1, class T2>
T1 sum(T1 x, T1 y)
{
    return x + y;
}
```

52. Assume the following definition appears in a program that uses the `SimpleVector` class template presented in this chapter.

```
int <SimpleVector> array(25);
```

53. Assume the following statement appears in a program that has defined `valueSet` as an object of the `SimpleVector` class presented in this chapter. Assume that `valueSet` is a vector of ints, and has 20 elements.

```
cout << valueSet<int>[2] << endl;
```

Programming Challenges

myprogramminglab

Visit www.myprogramminglab.com to complete many of these Programming Challenges online and get instant feedback.

1. **Date Exceptions**

   Modify the Date class you wrote for Programming Challenge 1 of Chapter 13. The class should implement the following exception classes:

InvalidDay	Throw when an invalid day (< 1 or > 31) is passed to the class.
InvalidMonth	Throw when an invalid month (< 1 or > 12) is passed to the class.

   Demonstrate the class in a driver program.

2. **Time Format Exceptions**

   Modify the MilTime class you created for Programming Challenge 4 of Chapter 15. The class should implement the following exceptions:

BadHour	Throw when an invalid hour (< 0 or > 2359) is passed to the class.
BadSeconds	Throw when an invalid number of seconds (< 0 or > 59) is passed to the class.

   Demonstrate the class in a driver program.

3. **Minimum/Maximum Templates**

   Write templates for the two functions minimum and maximum. The minimum function should accept two arguments and return the value of the argument that is the lesser of the two. The maximum function should accept two arguments and return the value of the argument that is the greater of the two. Design a simple driver program that demonstrates the templates with various data types.

4. **Absolute Value Template**

   Write a function template that accepts an argument and returns its absolute value. The absolute value of a number is its value with no sign. For example, the absolute value of −5 is 5, and the absolute value of 2 is 2. Test the template in a simple driver program.

5. **Total Template**

   Write a template for a function called total. The function should keep a running total of values entered by the user, then return the total. The argument sent into the function should be the number of values the function is to read. Test the template in a simple driver program that sends values of various types as arguments and displays the results.

6. **IntArray Class Exception**

   Chapter 14 presented an IntArray class that dynamically creates an array of integers and performs bounds checking on the array. If an invalid subscript is used with the class, it displays an error message and aborts the program. Modify the class so it throws an exception instead.

7. **TestScores** Class

Write a class named `TestScores`. The class constructor should accept an array of test scores as its argument. The class should have a member function that returns the average of the test scores. If any test score in the array is negative or greater than 100, the class should throw an exception. Demonstrate the class in a program.

8. **SimpleVector** Modification

Modify the `SimpleVector` class template presented in this chapter to include the member functions `push_back` and `pop_back`. These functions should emulate the STL vector class member functions of the same name. (See Table 16-5.) The `push_back` function should accept an argument and insert its value at the end of the array. The `pop_back` function should accept no argument and remove the last element from the array. Test the class with a driver program.

9. **SearchableVector** Modification

Modify the `SearchableVector` class template presented in this chapter so that it performs a binary search instead of a linear search. Test the template in a driver program.

10. **SortableVector** Class Template

Write a class template named `SortableVector`. The class should be derived from the `SimpleVector` class presented in this chapter. It should have a member function that sorts the array elements in ascending order. (Use the sorting algorithm of your choice.) Test the template in a driver program.

11. Inheritance Modification

Assuming you have completed Programming Challenges 9 and 10, modify the inheritance hierarchy of the `SearchableVector` class template so it is derived from the `SortableVector` class instead of the `SimpleVector` class. Implement a member function named `sortAndSearch`, both a sort and a binary search.

12. Specialized Templates

In this chapter, the section *Specialized Templates* within Section 16.4 describes how to design templates that are specialized for one particular data type. The section introduces a method for specializing a version of the `SimpleVector` class template so it will work with strings. Complete the specialization for both the `SimpleVector` and `SearchableVector` templates. Demonstrate them with a simple driver program.

13. Rainfall **vector**

Modify Programming Challenge 2 in Chapter 7 (Rainfall Statistics) to use an STL vector instead of an array. Refer to the information in Tables 16-5 and 16-6 if you wish to use any of the member functions.

14. Test Scores **vector**

Modify Programming Challenge 2 in Chapter 9 (Test Scores #1) to use an STL vector instead of a dynamically allocated array. Refer to the information in Tables 16-5 and 16-6 if you wish to use any of the member functions.

15. STL Binary Search

Modify programming Challenge 1 in Chapter 8 (Change Account Validation) so it uses a `vector` instead of an array. Also, modify the program so it uses the STL `binary_search` algorithm to locate valid account numbers.

VideoNote
**Solving the
Exception
Project
Problem**

16. **Exception Project**

This assignment assumes you have completed Programming Challenge 1 of Chapter 15 (Employee and ProductionWorker Classes). Modify the Employee and ProductionWorker classes so they throw exceptions when the following errors occur:

- The Employee class should throw an exception named InvalidEmployeeNumber when it receives an employee number that is less than 0 or greater than 9999.
- The ProductionWorker class should throw an exception named InvalidShift when it receives an invalid shift.
- The ProductionWorker class should throw an exception named InvalidPayRate when it receives a negative number for the hourly pay rate.

Write a driver program that demonstrates how each of these exception conditions works.

17. **Phone Book Vector**

This chapter has an accompanying video note that shows how to store an object in a vector. After you view that video, write a class named PhoneBookEntry that has members for a person's name and phone number. Then write a program that creates at least five PhoneBookEntry objects and stores them in a vector. After the objects are stored in the vector, use a loop to display the contents of each object in the vector.

17 Linked Lists

17.1 Introduction to the Linked List ADT

CONCEPT: Dynamically allocated data structures may be linked together in memory to form a chain.

A linked list is a series of connected *nodes*, where each node is a data structure. A linked list can grow or shrink in size as the program runs. This is possible because the nodes in a linked list are dynamically allocated. If new data need to be added to a linked list, the program simply allocates another node and inserts it into the series. If a particular piece of data needs to be removed from the linked list, the program deletes the node containing that data.

Advantages of Linked Lists over Arrays and `vectors`

Although linked lists are more complex to code and manage than arrays, they have some distinct advantages. First, a linked list can easily grow or shrink in size. In fact, the programmer doesn't need to know how many nodes will be in the list. They are simply created in memory as they are needed.

One might argue that linked lists are not superior to `vectors` (found in the Standard Template Library), because `vectors`, too, can expand or shrink. The advantage that linked lists have over `vectors`, however, is the speed at which a node may be inserted into or deleted from the list. To insert a value into the middle of a `vector` requires all the elements below the insertion point to be moved one position toward the `vector`'s end, thus making room for the new value. Likewise, removing a value from a `vector` requires all the elements below the removal point to be moved one position toward the `vector`'s beginning. When a node is inserted into or deleted from a linked list, none of the other nodes have to be moved.

The Composition of a Linked List

Each node in a linked list contains one or more members that represent data. (Perhaps the nodes hold inventory records, or customer names, addresses, and telephone numbers.) In addition to the data, each node contains a pointer, which can point to another node. The makeup of a node is illustrated in Figure 17-1.

Figure 17-1

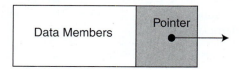

A linked list is called "linked" because each node in the series has a pointer that points to the next node in the list. This creates a chain where the first node points to the second node, the second node points to the third node, and so on. This is illustrated in Figure 17-2.

Figure 17-2

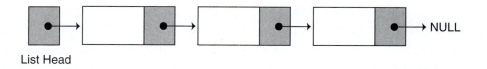

List Head

The list depicted in Figure 17-2 has three nodes, plus a pointer known as the *list head*. The head simply points to the first node in the list. Each node, in turn, points to the next node in the list. The first node points to the second node, which points to the third node. Because the third node is the last one in the list, it points to the NULL address (address 0). This is usually how the end of a linked list is signified—by letting the last node point to NULL.

 NOTE: Figure 17-2 depicts the nodes in the linked list as being very close to each other, neatly arranged in a row. In reality, the nodes may be scattered around various parts of memory.

Declarations

So how is a linked list created in C++? First you must declare a data structure that will be used for the nodes. For example, the following `struct` could be used to create a list where each node holds a `double`:

```
struct ListNode
{
    double value;
    ListNode *next;
};
```

The first member of the `ListNode` structure is a `double` named `value`. It will be used to hold the node's data. The second member is a pointer named `next`. The pointer can hold the address of any object that is a `ListNode` structure. This allows each `ListNode` structure to point to the next `ListNode` structure in the list.

Because the `ListNode` structure contains a pointer to an object of the same type as that being declared, it is known as a *self-referential data structure*. This structure makes it possible to create nodes that point to other nodes of the same type.

The next step is to define a pointer to serve as the list head, as shown here.

```
ListNode *head;
```

Before you use the `head` pointer in any linked list operations, you must be sure it is initialized to NULL, because that marks the end of the list. Once you have declared a node data structure and have created a NULL `head` pointer, you have an empty linked list. The next step is to implement operations with the list.

Checkpoint

myprogramminglab *www.myprogramminglab.com*

17.1   Describe the two parts of a node.

17.2   What is a list head?

17.3   What signifies the end of a linked list?

17.4   What is a self-referential data structure?

17.2   Linked List Operations

> **CONCEPT:** The basic linked list operations are appending a node, traversing the list,
> inserting a node, deleting a node, and destroying the list.

In this section we will develop an abstract data type that performs basic linked list operations using the `ListNode` structure and `head` pointer defined in the previous section. We will use the following class declaration, which is stored in `NumberList.h`.

Contents of `NumberList.h`

```
1   // Specification file for the NumberList class
2   #ifndef NUMBERLIST_H
3   #define NUMBERLIST_H
4
5   class NumberList
6   {
```

```
 7   private:
 8      // Declare a structure for the list
 9      struct ListNode
10      {
11         double value;          // The value in this node
12         struct ListNode *next; // To point to the next node
13      };
14
15      ListNode *head;           // List head pointer
16
17   public:
18      // Constructor
19      NumberList()
20         { head = NULL; }
21
22      // Destructor
23      ~NumberList();
24
25      // Linked list operations
26      void appendNode(double);
27      void insertNode(double);
28      void deleteNode(double);
29      void displayList() const;
30   };
31   #endif
```

Notice that the constructor initializes the head pointer to NULL. This establishes an empty linked list. The class has member functions for appending, inserting, and deleting nodes, as well as a displayList function that displays all the values stored in the list. The destructor destroys the list by deleting all its nodes. These functions are defined in NumberList.cpp. We will examine the member functions individually.

Appending a Node to the List

VideoNote
Appending a Node to a Linked List

To append a node to a linked list means to add the node to the end of the list. The appendNode member function accepts a double argument, num. The function will allocate a new ListNode structure, store the value in num in the node's value member, and append the node to the end of the list. Here is a pseudocode representation of the general algorithm:

```
Create a new node.
Store data in the new node.
If there are no nodes in the list
   Make the new node the first node.
Else
   Traverse the list to find the last node.
   Add the new node to the end of the list.
End If.
```

Here is the actual C++ code for the function:

```
11   void NumberList::appendNode(double num)
12   {
13      ListNode *newNode;  // To point to a new node
14      ListNode *nodePtr;  // To move through the list
15
```

```
16        // Allocate a new node and store num there.
17        newNode = new ListNode;
18        newNode->value = num;
19        newNode->next = NULL;
20
21        // If there are no nodes in the list
22        // make newNode the first node.
23        if (!head)
24           head = newNode;
25        else  // Otherwise, insert newNode at end.
26        {
27           // Initialize nodePtr to head of list.
28           nodePtr = head;
29
30           // Find the last node in the list.
31           while (nodePtr->next)
32              nodePtr = nodePtr->next;
33
34           // Insert newNode as the last node.
35           nodePtr->next = newNode;
36        }
37   }
```

Let's examine the statements in detail. In lines 13 and 14 the function defines the following local variables:

```
ListNode *newNode;  // To point to a new node
ListNode *nodePtr;  // To move through the list
```

The newNode pointer will be used to allocate and point to the new node. The nodePtr pointer will be used to travel down the linked list, in search of the last node.

The following statements, in lines 17 through 19, create a new node and store num in its value member:

```
newNode = new ListNode;
newNode->value = num;
newNode->next = NULL;
```

The statement in line 19 is important. Because this node will become the last node in the list, its next pointer must point to NULL.

In line 23, we test the head pointer to determine whether there are any nodes already in the list. If head points to NULL, we make the new node the first in the list. Making head point to the new node does this. Here is the code:

```
if (!head)
    head = newNode;
```

If head does not point to NULL, however, there are nodes in the list. The else part of the if statement must contain code to find the end of the list and insert the new node. The code, in lines 25 through 36, is shown here:

```
else
{
    // Initialize nodePtr to head of list.
    nodePtr = head;
```

```
        // Find the last node in the list.
        while (nodePtr->next)
            nodePtr = nodePtr->next;

        // Insert newNode as the last node.
        nodePtr->next = newNode;
    }
```

The code uses `nodePtr` to travel down the list. It does this by first assigning `nodePtr` to head in line 28:

```
    nodePtr = head;
```

The `while` loop in lines 31 and 32 is then used to *traverse* (or travel through) the list searching for the last node. The last node will be the one whose `next` member points to NULL:

```
    while (nodePtr->next)
        nodePtr = nodePtr->next;
```

When `nodePtr` points to the last node in the list, we make its `next` member point to `newNode` in line 35 with the following statement.

```
    nodePtr->next = newNode;
```

This inserts `newNode` at the end of the list. (Remember, `newNode->next` already points to NULL.)

Program 17-1 demonstrates the function.

Program 17-1

```
 1   // This program demonstrates a simple append
 2   // operation on a linked list.
 3   #include <iostream>
 4   #include "NumberList.h"
 5   using namespace std;
 6
 7   int main()
 8   {
 9       // Define a NumberList object.
10       NumberList list;
11
12       // Append some values to the list.
13       list.appendNode(2.5);
14       list.appendNode(7.9);
15       list.appendNode(12.6);
16       return 0;
17   }
```

(This program displays no output.)

Let's step through the program, observing how the `appendNode` function builds a linked list to store the three argument values used.

The `head` pointer is declared as a private member variable of the `NumberList` class. `head` is initialized to 0 (NULL) by the `NumberList` constructor, which indicates that the list is empty.

The first call to `appendNode` in line 13 passes 2.5 as the argument. In the following statements, a new node is allocated in memory, 2.5 is copied into its `value` member, and NULL is assigned to the node's `next` pointer:

```
newNode = new ListNode;
newNode->value = num;
newNode->next = NULL;
```

Figure 17-3 illustrates the state of the `head` pointer and the new node.

Figure 17-3

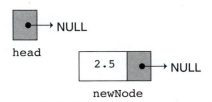

The next statement to execute is the following `if` statement:

```
if (!head)
    head = newNode;
```

Because `head` points to NULL, the condition `!head` is true. The statement `head = newNode;` is executed, making `newNode` the first node in the list. This is illustrated in Figure 17-4.

Figure 17-4

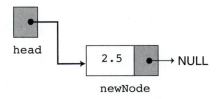

There are no more statements to execute, so control returns to function `main`. In the second call to `appendNode`, in line 14, 7.9 is passed as the argument. Once again, the first three statements in the function create a new node, store the argument in the node's `value` member, and assign its `next` pointer to NULL. Figure 17-5 illustrates the current state of the list and the new node.

Figure 17-5

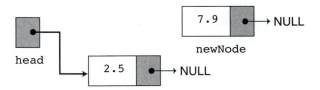

Because `head` no longer points to NULL, the `else` part of the `if` statement executes:

```
else    // Otherwise, insert newNode at end.
{
        // Initialize nodePtr to head of list.
        nodePtr = head;

        // Find the last node in the list.
        while (nodePtr->next)
            nodePtr = nodePtr->next;

        // Insert newNode as the last node.
        nodePtr->next = newNode;
}
```

The first statement in the `else` block assigns the value in `head` to `nodePtr`. This causes `nodePtr` to point to the same node that `head` points to. This is illustrated in Figure 17-6.

Figure 17-6

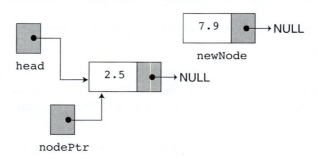

Look at the `next` member of the node that `nodePtr` points to. Its value is NULL, which means that `nodePtr->next` also points to NULL. `nodePtr` is already at the end of the list, so the `while` loop immediately terminates. The last statement, `nodePtr->next = newNode;` causes `nodePtr->next` to point to the new node. This inserts `newNode` at the end of the list as shown in Figure 17-7.

Figure 17-7

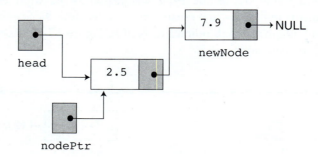

The third time `appendNode` is called, in line 15, 12.6 is passed as the argument. Once again, the first three statements create a node with the argument stored in the `value` member. This is shown in Figure 17-8.

Figure 17-8

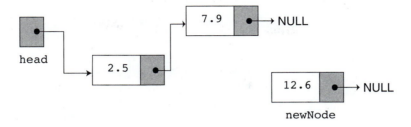

Next, the `else` part of the `if` statement executes. As before, `nodePtr` is made to point to the same node as `head`, as shown in Figure 17-9.

Figure 17-9

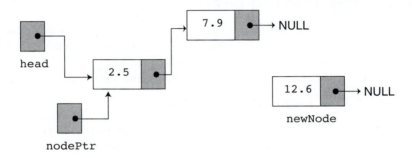

Because `nodePtr->next` is not NULL, the `while` loop will execute. After its first iteration, `nodePtr` will point to the second node in the list. This is shown in Figure 17-10.

Figure 17-10

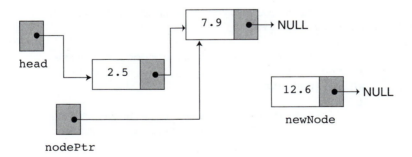

The `while` loop's conditional test will fail after the first iteration because `nodePtr->next` now points to NULL. The last statement, `nodePtr->next = newNode;` causes `nodePtr->next` to point to the new node. This inserts `newNode` at the end of the list as shown in Figure 17-11.

Figure 17-11

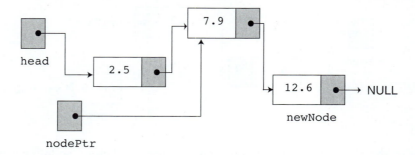

Figure 17-11 depicts the final state of the linked list.

Traversing a Linked List

The appendNode function demonstrated in the previous section contains a while loop that traverses, or travels through the linked list. In this section we will demonstrate the displayList member function that traverses the list, displaying the value member of each node. The following pseudocode represents the algorithm.

```
Assign List head to node pointer.
While node pointer is not NULL
    Display the value member of the node pointed to by node pointer.
    Assign node pointer to its own next member.
End While.
```

The function is shown here:

```cpp
45  void NumberList::displayList() const
46  {
47      ListNode *nodePtr;  // To move through the list
48
49      // Position nodePtr at the head of the list.
50      nodePtr = head;
51
52      // While nodePtr points to a node, traverse
53      // the list.
54      while (nodePtr)
55      {
56          // Display the value in this node.
57          cout << nodePtr->value << endl;
58
59          // Move to the next node.
60          nodePtr = nodePtr->next;
61      }
62  }
```

Program 17-2, a modification of Program 17-1, demonstrates the function.

Program 17-2

```cpp
 1   // This program demonstrates the displayList member function.
 2   #include <iostream>
 3   #include "NumberList.h"
 4   using namespace std;
 5
 6   int main()
 7   {
 8      // Define a NumberList object.
 9      NumberList list;
10
11      // Append some values to the list.
12      list.appendNode(2.5);
13      list.appendNode(7.9);
14      list.appendNode(12.6);
15
16      // Display the values in the list.
17      list.displayList();
18      return 0;
19   }
```

Program Output
```
2.5
7.9
12.6
```

Usually, when an operation is to be performed on some or all the nodes in a linked list, a traversal algorithm is used. You will see variations of this algorithm throughout this chapter.

Inserting a Node

Appending a node is a straightforward procedure. Inserting a node in the middle of a list, however, is more involved. For example, suppose the values in a list are sorted and you wish all new values to be inserted in their proper position. This will preserve the order of the list. Using the `ListNode` structure again, the following pseudocode shows an algorithm for finding a new node's proper position in the list and inserting it there. The algorithm assumes the nodes in the list are already in order.

VideoNote
Inserting a Node in a Linked List

```
Create a new node.
Store data in the new node.
If there are no nodes in the list
    Make the new node the first node.
Else
    Find the first node whose value is greater than or equal to the new
        value, or the end of the list (whichever is first).
    Insert the new node before the found node, or at the end of the list
        if no such node was found.
End If.
```

Notice that the new algorithm finds the first node whose value is greater than or equal to the new value. The new node is then inserted before the found node. This will require the use of two node pointers during the traversal: one to point to the node being inspected and another to point to the previous node. The code for the traversal algorithm is as follows. (As before, num holds the value being inserted into the list.)

```
// Position nodePtr at the head of list.
nodePtr = head;

// Initialize previousNode to NULL.
previousNode = NULL;

// Skip all nodes whose value is less than num.
while (nodePtr != NULL && nodePtr->value < num)
{
   previousNode = nodePtr;
   nodePtr = nodePtr->next;
}
```

This code segment uses the ListNode pointers nodePtr and previousNode. previousNode always points to the node before the one pointed to by nodePtr. The entire insertNode function is shown here:

```
69   void NumberList::insertNode(double num)
70   {
71      ListNode *newNode;            // A new node
72      ListNode *nodePtr;            // To traverse the list
73      ListNode *previousNode = NULL; // The previous node
74
75      // Allocate a new node and store num there.
76      newNode = new ListNode;
77      newNode->value = num;
78
79      // If there are no nodes in the list
80      // make newNode the first node
81      if (!head)
82      {
83         head = newNode;
84         newNode->next = NULL;
85      }
86      else   // Otherwise, insert newNode
87      {
88         // Position nodePtr at the head of list.
89         nodePtr = head;
90
91         // Initialize previousNode to NULL.
92         previousNode = NULL;
93
94         // Skip all nodes whose value is less than num.
95         while (nodePtr != NULL && nodePtr->value < num)
96         {
97            previousNode = nodePtr;
98            nodePtr = nodePtr->next;
99         }
100
101        // If the new node is to be the 1st in the list,
102        // insert it before all other nodes.
103        if (previousNode == NULL)
104        {
```

```
105              head = newNode;
106              newNode->next = nodePtr;
107         }
108         else  // Otherwise insert after the previous node.
109         {
110              previousNode->next = newNode;
111              newNode->next = nodePtr;
112         }
113    }
114 }
```

Program 17-3 is a modification of the Program 17-2. It uses the `insertNode` member function to insert a value in its ordered position in the list.

```
 1  // This program demonstrates the insertNode member function.
 2  #include <iostream>
 3  #include "NumberList.h"
 4  using namespace std;
 5
 6  int main()
 7  {
 8     // Define a NumberList object.
 9     NumberList list;
10
11     // Build the list with some values.
12     list.appendNode(2.5);
13     list.appendNode(7.9);
14     list.appendNode(12.6);
15
16     // Insert a node in the middle of the list.
17     list.insertNode(10.5);
18
19     // Display the list
20     list.displayList();
21     return 0;
22  }
```

Program Output

```
2.5
7.9
10.5
12.6
```

Like Program 17-2, Program 17-3 calls the `appendNode` function three times to build the list with the values 2.5, 7.9, and 12.6. The `insertNode` function is then called, with the argument 10.5.

In `insertNode`, a new node is created and the function argument is copied to its `value` member. Because the list already has nodes stored in it, the `else` part of the `if` statement will execute. It begins by assigning `nodePtr` to `head`. Figure 17-12 illustrates the state of the list at this point.

Figure 17-12

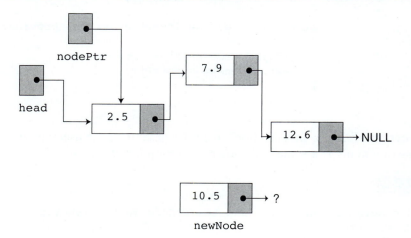

Because nodePtr is not NULL and nodePtr->value is less than num, the while loop will iterate. During the iteration, previousNode will be made to point to the node that nodePtr is pointing to. nodePtr will then be advanced to point to the next node. This is shown in Figure 17-13.

Figure 17-13

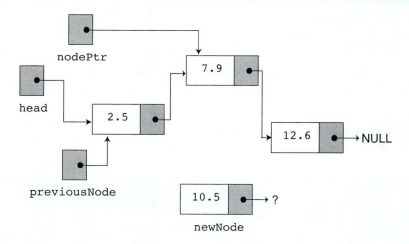

Once again, the loop performs its test. Because nodePtr is not NULL and nodePtr->value is less than num, the loop will iterate a second time. During the second iteration, both previousNode and nodePtr are advanced by one node in the list. This is shown in Figure 17-14.

Figure 17-14

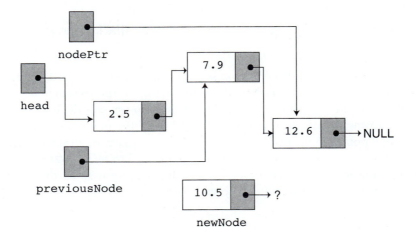

This time, the loop's test will fail because `nodePtr->value` is not less than `num`. The statements after the loop will execute, which cause `previousNode->next` to point to `newNode`, and `newNode->next` to point to `nodePtr`. This is illustrated in Figure 17-15.

Figure 17-15

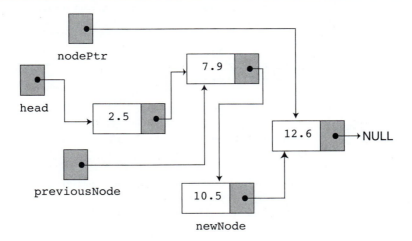

This leaves the list in its final state. If you follow the links, from the `head` pointer to the NULL, you will see that the nodes are stored in the order of their `value` members.

 Checkpoint

myprogramminglab *www.myprogramminglab.com*

17.5 What is the difference between appending a node to a list and inserting a node into a list?

17.6 Which is easier to code: appending or inserting?

17.7 Why does the `insertNode` function shown in this section use a `previousNode` pointer?

Deleting a Node

Deleting a node from a linked list requires two steps:

1. Remove the node from the list without breaking the links created by the next pointers.

2. Delete the node from memory.

VideoNote
**Deleting a
Node from a
Linked List**

The deleteNode member function searches for a node containing a particular value and deletes it from the list. It uses an algorithm similar to the insertNode function. Two node pointers, nodePtr and previousNode, are used to traverse the list. previousNode always points to the node whose position is just before the one pointed to by nodePtr. When nodePtr points to the node that is to be deleted, previousNode->next is made to point to nodePtr->next. This removes the node pointed to by nodePtr from the list. The final step performed by this function is to free the memory used by the node with the delete operator. The entire function is shown below.

```
122   void NumberList::deleteNode(double num)
123   {
124      ListNode *nodePtr;        // To traverse the list
125      ListNode *previousNode;   // To point to the previous node
126
127      // If the list is empty, do nothing.
128      if (!head)
129         return;
130
131      // Determine if the first node is the one.
132      if (head->value == num)
133      {
134         nodePtr = head->next;
135         delete head;
136         head = nodePtr;
137      }
138      else
139      {
140         // Initialize nodePtr to head of list
141         nodePtr = head;
142
143         // Skip all nodes whose value member is
144         // not equal to num.
145         while (nodePtr != NULL && nodePtr->value != num)
146         {
147            previousNode = nodePtr;
148            nodePtr = nodePtr->next;
149         }
150
151         // If nodePtr is not at the end of the list,
152         // link the previous node to the node after
153         // nodePtr, then delete nodePtr.
154         if (nodePtr)
155         {
156            previousNode->next = nodePtr->next;
157            delete nodePtr;
158         }
159      }
160   }
```

Program 17-4 demonstrates the function by first building a list of three nodes, and then deleting them one by one.

Program 17-4

```
1    // This program demonstrates the deleteNode member function.
2    #include <iostream>
3    #include "NumberList.h"
4    using namespace std;
5
6    int main()
7    {
8        // Define a NumberList object.
9        NumberList list;
10
11       // Build the list with some values.
12       list.appendNode(2.5);
13       list.appendNode(7.9);
14       list.appendNode(12.6);
15
16       // Display the list.
17       cout << "Here are the initial values:\n";
18       list.displayList();
19       cout << endl;
20
21       // Delete the middle node.
22       cout << "Now deleting the node in the middle.\n";
23       list.deleteNode(7.9);
24
25       // Display the list.
26       cout << "Here are the nodes left.\n";
27       list.displayList();
28       cout << endl;
29
30       // Delete the last node.
31       cout << "Now deleting the last node.\n";
32       list.deleteNode(12.6);
33
34       // Display the list.
35       cout << "Here are the nodes left.\n";
36       list.displayList();
37       cout << endl;
38
39       // Delete the only node left in the list.
40       cout << "Now deleting the only remaining node.\n";
41       list.deleteNode(2.5);
42
43       // Display the list.
44       cout << "Here are the nodes left.\n";
45       list.displayList();
46       return 0;
47   }
```

(program output continues)

Program 17-4 *(continued)*

Program Output
```
Here are the initial values:
2.5
7.9
12.6

Now deleting the node in the middle.
Here are the nodes left.
2.5
12.6

Now deleting the last node.
Here are the nodes left.
2.5

Now deleting the only remaining node.
Here are the nodes left.
```

To illustrate how deleteNode works, we will step through the first call which deletes the node containing 7.9 as its value. This node is in the middle of the list.

In the deleteNode function, look at the else part of the second if statement. This is lines 138 through 159. This is where the function will perform its action since the list is not empty, and the first node does not contain the value 7.9. Just like insertNode, this function uses nodePtr and previousNode to traverse the list. The while loop in lines 145 through 149 terminates when the value 7.9 is located. At this point, the list and the other pointers will be in the state depicted in Figure 17-16.

Figure 17-16

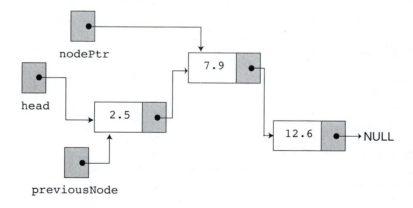

Next, the following statement in line 156 executes:

```
previousNode->next = nodePtr->next;
```

This statement causes the links in the list to bypass the node that `nodePtr` points to. Although the node still exists in memory, this removes it from the list, as illustrated in Figure 17-17.

Figure 17-17

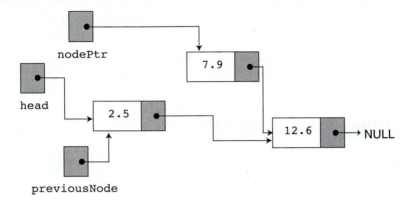

The statement in line 157 uses the `delete` operator to complete the total deletion of the node.

Destroying the List

It's important for the class's destructor to release all the memory used by the list. It does so by stepping through the list, deleting one node at a time. The code is shown here:

```
167   NumberList::~NumberList()
168   {
169      ListNode *nodePtr;    // To traverse the list
170      ListNode *nextNode;   // To point to the next node
171
172      // Position nodePtr at the head of the list.
173      nodePtr = head;
174
175      // While nodePtr is not at the end of the list...
176      while (nodePtr != NULL)
177      {
178         // Save a pointer to the next node.
179         nextNode = nodePtr->next;
180
181         // Delete the current node.
182         delete nodePtr;
183
184         // Position nodePtr at the next node.
185         nodePtr = nextNode;
186      }
187   }
```

Notice the use of `nextNode` instead of `previousNode`. The `nextNode` pointer is used to hold the position of the next node in the list, so that it will be available after the node pointed to by `nodePtr` is deleted.

Checkpoint

myprogramminglab *www.myprogramminglab.com*

17.8 What are the two steps involved in deleting a node from a linked list?

17.9 When deleting a node, why can't you just use the `delete` operator to remove it from memory? Why must you take the steps you listed in response to Question 17.8?

17.10 In a program that uses several linked lists, what might eventually happen if the class destructor does not destroy its linked list?

 17.3 **A Linked List Template**

CONCEPT: A template can be easily created to store linked lists of any type.

The limitation of the `NumberList` class is that it can only hold `double` values. The class can easily be converted to a template that will accept any data type, as shown in the following code. (This file is stored in the Student Source Code Folder `Chapter 17\ LinkedList Template Version 1.`)

Contents of `LinkedList.h` (Version 1)

```
 1  // A class template for holding a linked list.
 2  #ifndef LINKEDLIST_H
 3  #define LINKEDLIST_H
 4  #include <iostream>      // For cout and NULL
 5  using namespace std;
 6
 7  template <class T>
 8  class LinkedList
 9  {
10  private:
11     // Declare a structure for the list.
12     struct ListNode
13     {
14        T value;                 // The value in this node
15        struct ListNode *next;   // To point to the next node
16     };
17
18     ListNode *head;   // List head pointer
19
20  public:
21     // Constructor
22     NumberList()
23        { head = NULL; }
24
25     // Destructor
26     ~NumberList();
27
```

```
28      // Linked list operations
29      void appendNode(T);
30      void insertNode(T);
31      void deleteNode(T);
32      void displayList() const;
33   };
34
35
36   //**************************************************
37   // appendNode appends a node containing the value  *
38   // passed into newValue, to the end of the list.   *
39   //**************************************************
40
41   template <class T>
42   void LinkedList<T>::appendNode(T newValue)
43   {
44      ListNode *newNode;  // To point to a new node
45      ListNode *nodePtr;  // To move through the list
46
47      // Allocate a new node and store num there.
48      newNode = new ListNode;
49      newNode->value = num;
50      newNode->next = NULL;
51
52      // If there are no nodes in the list
53      // make newNode the first node.
54      if (!head)
55         head = newNode;
56      else  // Otherwise, insert newNode at end.
57      {
58         // Initialize nodePtr to head of list.
59         nodePtr = head;
60
61         // Find the last node in the list.
62         while (nodePtr->next)
63            nodePtr = nodePtr->next;
64
65         // Insert newNode as the last node.
66         nodePtr->next = newNode;
67      }
68   }
69
70   //**************************************************
71   // displayList shows the value                     *
72   // stored in each node of the linked list          *
73   // pointed to by head.                             *
74   //**************************************************
75
76   template <class T>
77   void LinkedList<T>::displayList()
78   {
79      ListNode *nodePtr;  // To move through the list
80
81      // Position nodePtr at the head of the list.
82      nodePtr = head;
```

```
 83
 84       // While nodePtr points to a node, traverse
 85       // the list.
 86       while (nodePtr)
 87       {
 88          // Display the value in this node.
 89          cout << nodePtr->value << endl;
 90
 91          // Move to the next node.
 92          nodePtr = nodePtr->next;
 93       }
 94  }
 95
 96  //***************************************************
 97  // The insertNode function inserts a node with      *
 98  // newValue copied to its value member.             *
 99  //***************************************************
100
101  template <class T>
102  void LinkedList<T>::insertNode(T newValue)
103  {
104     ListNode *newNode;               // A new node
105     ListNode *nodePtr;               // To traverse the list
106     ListNode *previousNode = NULL;   // The previous node
107
108     // Allocate a new node and store num there.
109     newNode = new ListNode;
110     newNode->value = num;
111
112     // If there are no nodes in the list
113     // make newNode the first node.
114     if (!head)
115     {
116        head = newNode;
117        newNode->next = NULL;
118     }
119     else   // Otherwise, insert newNode.
120     {
121        // Position nodePtr at the head of list.
122        nodePtr = head;
123
124        // Initialize previousNode to NULL.
125        previousNode = NULL;
126
127        // Skip all nodes whose value is less than num.
128        while (nodePtr != NULL && nodePtr->value < num)
129        {
130           previousNode = nodePtr;
131           nodePtr = nodePtr->next;
132        }
133
```

```
134         // If the new node is to be the 1st in the list,
135         // insert it before all other nodes.
136         if (previousNode == NULL)
137         {
138            head = newNode;
139            newNode->next = nodePtr;
140         }
141         else  // Otherwise insert after the previous node.
142         {
143            previousNode->next = newNode;
144            newNode->next = nodePtr;
145         }
146      }
147  }
148
149  //*********************************************************
150  // The deleteNode function searches for a node           *
151  // with searchValue as its value. The node, if found,    *
152  // is deleted from the list and from memory.             *
153  //*********************************************************
154
155  template <class T>
156  void LinkedList<T>::deleteNode(T searchValue)
157  {
158     ListNode *nodePtr;        // To traverse the list
159     ListNode *previousNode;   // To point to the previous node
160
161     // If the list is empty, do nothing.
162     if (!head)
163        return;
164
165     // Determine if the first node is the one.
166     if (head->value == num)
167     {
168        nodePtr = head->next;
169        delete head;
170        head = nodePtr;
171     }
172     else
173     {
174        // Initialize nodePtr to head of list.
175        nodePtr = head;
176
177        // Skip all nodes whose value member is
178        // not equal to num.
179        while (nodePtr != NULL && nodePtr->value != num)
180        {
181           previousNode = nodePtr;
182           nodePtr = nodePtr->next;
183        }
184
185        // If nodePtr is not at the end of the list,
186        // link the previous node to the node after
187        // nodePtr, then delete nodePtr.
```

```
188          if (nodePtr)
189          {
190              previousNode->next = nodePtr->next;
191              delete nodePtr;
192          }
193      }
194  }
195
196  //**************************************************
197  // Destructor                                      *
198  // This function deletes every node in the list.   *
199  //**************************************************
200
201  template <class T>
202  LinkedList<T>::~LinkedList()
203  {
204      ListNode *nodePtr;    // To traverse the list
205      ListNode *nextNode;   // To point to the next node
206
207      // Position nodePtr at the head of the list.
208      nodePtr = head;
209
210      // While nodePtr is not at the end of the list...
211      while (nodePtr != NULL)
212      {
213          // Save a pointer to the next node.
214          nextNode = nodePtr->next;
215
216          // Delete the current node.
217          delete nodePtr;
218
219          // Position nodePtr at the next node.
220          nodePtr = nextNode;
221      }
222  }
223  #endif
```

Note that the template uses the ==, !=, and < relational operators to compare node values, and it uses the << operator with cout to display node values. Any type passed to the template must support these operators.

Now let's see how the template can be used to create a list of objects. Recall the FeetInches class that was introduced in Chapter 14. That class overloaded numerous operators, including ==, <, and <<. In the Chapter 17\LinkedList Template Version 1 folder we have included a modified version of the FeetInches class that also overloads the != operator. Program 17-5 is stored in that same folder. This program uses the LinkedList template to create a linked list of FeetInches objects.

Program 17-5

```
 1   // This program demonstrates the linked list template.
 2   #include <iostream>
 3   #include "LinkedList.h"
 4   #include "FeetInches.h"
 5   using namespace std;
 6
 7   int main()
 8   {
 9      // Define a LinkedList object.
10      LinkedList<FeetInches> list;
11
12      // Define some FeetInches objects.
13      FeetInches distance1(5, 4); // 5 feet 4 inches
14      FeetInches distance2(6, 8); // 6 feet 8 inches
15      FeetInches distance3(8, 9); // 8 feet 9 inches
16
17      // Store the FeetInches objects in the list.
18      list.appendNode(distance1); // 5 feet 4 inches
19      list.appendNode(distance2); // 6 feet 8 inches
20      list.appendNode(distance3); // 8 feet 9 inches
21
22      // Display the values in the list.
23      cout << "Here are the initial values:\n";
24      list.displayList();
25      cout << endl;
26
27      // Insert another FeetInches object.
28      cout << "Now inserting the value 7 feet 2 inches.\n";
29      FeetInches distance4(7, 2);
30      list.insertNode(distance4);
31
32      // Display the values in the list.
33      cout << "Here are the nodes now.\n";
34      list.displayList();
35      cout << endl;
36
37      // Delete the last node.
38      cout << "Now deleting the last node.\n";
39      FeetInches distance5(8, 9);
40      list.deleteNode(distance5);
41
42      // Display the values in the list.
43      cout << "Here are the nodes left.\n";
44      list.displayList();
45      return 0;
46   }
```

(program output continues)

Program 17-5   *(continued)*

Program Output
```
Here are the initial values:
5 feet, 4 inches
6 feet, 8 inches
8 feet, 9 inches

Now inserting the value 7 feet 2 inches.
Here are the nodes now.
5 feet, 4 inches
6 feet, 8 inches
7 feet, 2 inches
8 feet, 9 inches

Now deleting the last node.
Here are the nodes left.
5 feet, 4 inches
6 feet, 8 inches
7 feet, 2 inches
```

Using a Class Node Type

In the `LinkedList` class template, the following structure was used to create a data type for the linked list node.

```
struct ListNode
{
   T value;
   struct ListNode *next;
};
```

Another approach is to use a separate class template to create a data type for the node. Then, the class constructor can be used to store an item in the `value` member and set the next pointer to NULL. Here is an example:

```
template <class T>
class ListNode
{
public:
   T value;               // Node value
   ListNode<T> *next;     // Pointer to the next node

   // Constructor
   ListNode (T nodeValue)
      { value = nodeValue;
        next = NULL;}
};
```

The `LinkedList` class template can then be written as the following:

```
template <class T>
class LinkedList
{
private:
   ListNode<T> *head;    // List head pointer
```

```
public:
   // Constructor
   LinkedList()
      { head = NULL; }

   // Destructor
   ~LinkedList();

   // Linked list operations
   void appendNode(T);
   void insertNode(T);
   void deleteNode(T);
   void displayList() const;
};
```

Because the `ListNode` class constructor assigns a value to the `value` member and sets the next pointer to NULL, some of the code in the `LinkedList` class can be simplified. For example, the following code appears in the previous version of the `LinkedList` class template's appendNode function:

```
newNode = new ListNode;
newNode->value = newValue;
newNode->next = NULL;
```

By using the `ListNode` class template with its constructor, these three lines of code can be reduced to one:

```
newNode = new ListNode<T>(newValue);
```

(This file is stored in the Student Source Code Folder `Chapter 17\LinkedList Template Version 2`.)

Contents of `LinkedList.h` (Version 2)

```
 1 // A class template for holding a linked list.
 2 // The node type is also a class template.
 3 #ifndef LINKEDLIST_H
 4 #define LINKEDLIST_H
 5
 6 //*********************************************
 7 // The ListNode class creates a type used to  *
 8 // store a node of the linked list.           *
 9 //*********************************************
10
11 template <class T>
12 class ListNode
13 {
14 public:
15    T value;           // Node value
16    ListNode<T> *next; // Pointer to the next node
17
18    // Constructor
19    ListNode (T nodeValue)
20       { value = nodeValue;
21          next = NULL;}
22 };
23
```

```
24 //*********************************************
25 // LinkedList class                           *
26 //*********************************************
27
28 template <class T>
29 class LinkedList
30 {
31 private:
32    ListNode<T> *head;    // List head pointer
33
34 public:
35    // Constructor
36    LinkedList()
37       { head = NULL; }
38
39    // Destructor
40    ~LinkedList();
41
42    // Linked list operations
43    void appendNode(T);
44    void insertNode(T);
45    void deleteNode(T);
46    void displayList() const;
47 };
48
49
50 //*************************************************
51 // appendNode appends a node containing the value  *
52 // passed into newValue, to the end of the list.   *
53 //*************************************************
54
55 template <class T>
56 void LinkedList<T>::appendNode(T newValue)
57 {
58    ListNode<T> *newNode;  // To point to a new node
59    ListNode<T> *nodePtr;  // To move through the list
60
61    // Allocate a new node and store newValue there.
62    newNode = new ListNode<T>(newValue);
63
64    // If there are no nodes in the list
65    // make newNode the first node.
66    if (!head)
67       head = newNode;
68    else  // Otherwise, insert newNode at end.
69    {
70       // Initialize nodePtr to head of list.
71       nodePtr = head;
72
73       // Find the last node in the list.
74       while (nodePtr->next)
75          nodePtr = nodePtr->next;
76
```

```
 77            // Insert newNode as the last node.
 78            nodePtr->next = newNode;
 79        }
 80  }
 81
 82  //****************************************************
 83  // displayList shows the value stored in each node *
 84  // of the linked list pointed to by head.          *
 85  //****************************************************
 86
 87  template <class T>
 88  void LinkedList<T>::displayList() const
 89  {
 90      ListNode<T> *nodePtr;  // To move through the list
 91
 92      // Position nodePtr at the head of the list.
 93      nodePtr = head;
 94
 95      // While nodePtr points to a node, traverse
 96      // the list.
 97      while (nodePtr)
 98      {
 99          // Display the value in this node.
100          cout << nodePtr->value << endl;
101
102          // Move to the next node.
103          nodePtr = nodePtr->next;
104      }
105  }
106
107  //****************************************************
108  // The insertNode function inserts a node with      *
109  // newValue copied to its value member.            *
110  //****************************************************
111
112  template <class T>
113  void LinkedList<T>::insertNode(T newValue)
114  {
115      ListNode<T> *newNode;                // A new node
116      ListNode<T> *nodePtr;                // To traverse the list
117      ListNode<T> *previousNode = NULL; // The previous node
118
119      // Allocate a new node and store newValue there.
120      newNode = new ListNode<T>(newValue);
121
122      // If there are no nodes in the list
123      // make newNode the first node.
124      if (!head)
125      {
126          head = newNode;
127          newNode->next = NULL;
128      }
```

```
129       else   // Otherwise, insert newNode.
130       {
131          // Position nodePtr at the head of list.
132          nodePtr = head;
133
134          // Initialize previousNode to NULL.
135          previousNode = NULL;
136
137          // Skip all nodes whose value is less than newValue.
138          while (nodePtr != NULL && nodePtr->value < newValue)
139          {
140             previousNode = nodePtr;
141             nodePtr = nodePtr->next;
142          }
143
144          // If the new node is to be the 1st in the list,
145          // insert it before all other nodes.
146          if (previousNode == NULL)
147          {
148             head = newNode;
149             newNode->next = nodePtr;
150          }
151          else   // Otherwise insert after the previous node.
152          {
153             previousNode->next = newNode;
154             newNode->next = nodePtr;
155          }
156       }
157 }
158
159 //********************************************************
160 // The deleteNode function searches for a node          *
161 // with searchValue as its value. The node, if found,  *
162 // is deleted from the list and from memory.           *
163 //********************************************************
164
165 template <class T>
166 void LinkedList<T>::deleteNode(T searchValue)
167 {
168    ListNode<T> *nodePtr;         // To traverse the list
169    ListNode<T> *previousNode;    // To point to the previous node
170
171    // If the list is empty, do nothing.
172    if (!head)
173       return;
174
175    // Determine if the first node is the one.
176    if (head->value == searchValue)
177    {
178       nodePtr = head->next;
179       delete head;
180       head = nodePtr;
181    }
```

```
182    else
183    {
184       // Initialize nodePtr to head of list
185       nodePtr = head;
186
187       // Skip all nodes whose value member is
188       // not equal to num.
189       while (nodePtr != NULL && nodePtr->value != searchValue)
190       {
191          previousNode = nodePtr;
192          nodePtr = nodePtr->next;
193       }
194
195       // If nodePtr is not at the end of the list,
196       // link the previous node to the node after
197       // nodePtr, then delete nodePtr.
198       if (nodePtr)
199       {
200          previousNode->next = nodePtr->next;
201          delete nodePtr;
202       }
203    }
204 }
205
206 //***************************************************
207 // Destructor                                      *
208 // This function deletes every node in the list.   *
209 //***************************************************
210
211 template <class T>
212 LinkedList<T>::~LinkedList()
213 {
214    ListNode<T> *nodePtr;    // To traverse the list
215    ListNode<T> *nextNode;   // To point to the next node
216
217    // Position nodePtr at the head of the list.
218    nodePtr = head;
219
220    // While nodePtr is not at the end of the list...
221    while (nodePtr != NULL)
222    {
223       // Save a pointer to the next node.
224       nextNode = nodePtr->next;
225
226       // Delete the current node.
227       delete nodePtr;
228
229       // Position nodePtr at the next node.
230       nodePtr = nextNode;
231    }
232 }
233 #endif
```

17.4   Variations of the Linked List

CONCEPT: There are many ways to link dynamically allocated data structures together. Two variations of the linked list are the doubly linked list and the circular linked list.

The linked list examples that we have discussed are considered *singly linked lists*: Each node is linked to a single other node. A variation of this is the *doubly linked list*. In this type of list, each node points not only to the next node, but also to the previous one. This is illustrated in Figure 17-18.

Figure 17-18

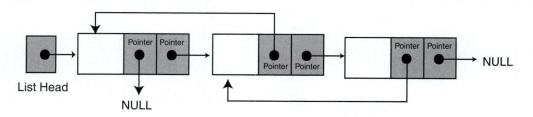

In Figure 17-18, the last node and the first node in the list have pointers to the NULL address. When the program traverses the list it knows when it has reached either end.

Another variation is the *circularly linked list*. The last node in this type of list points to the first, as shown in Figure 17-19.

Figure 17-19

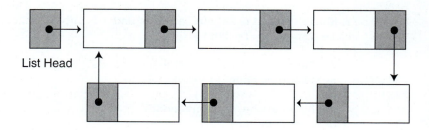

17.5   The STL list Container

CONCEPT: The Standard Template Library provides a linked list container.

The list container, found in the Standard Template Library, is a template version of a doubly linked list. STL lists can insert elements or add elements to their front quicker than vectors can, because lists do not have to shift the other elements. lists are also efficient at adding elements at their back because they have a built-in pointer to the last element in the list (no traversal required).

Table 17-1 describes some of the list member functions.

Table 17-1

Member Function	Examples and Description
back	`cout << list.back() << endl;` The back member function returns a reference to the last element in the list.
empty	`if (list.empty())` The empty member function returns true if the list is empty. If the list has elements, it returns false.
end	`iter = list.end();` end returns a bidirectional iterator to the end of the list.

erase	`list.erase(iter);`
	`list.erase(firstIter, lastIter)`
	The first example causes the list element pointed to by the iterator iter to be removed. The second example causes all of the list elements from firstIter to lastIter to be removed.

front	`cout << list.front() << endl;` front returns a reference to the first element of the list.
insert	`list.insert(iter, x)` The insert member function inserts an element into the list. This example inserts an element with the value x, just before the element pointed to by iter.
merge	`list1.merge(list2);` merge inserts all the items in list2 into list1. list1 is expanded to accommodate the new elements plus any elements already stored in list1. merge expects both lists to be sorted. When list2 is inserted into list1, the elements are inserted into their correct position, so the resulting list is also sorted.
pop_back	`list.pop_back();` pop_back removes the last element of the list.
pop_front	`list.pop_front();` pop_front removes the first element of the list.
push_back	`list.push_back(x);` push_back inserts an element with value x at the end of the list.
push_front	`list.push_front(x);` push_front inserts an element with value x at the beginning of the list.

(table continues)

Table 17-1 *(continued)*

Member Function	Examples and Description
reverse	`list.reverse();` reverse reverses the order in which the elements appear in the list.
size	Returns the number of elements in the `list`.
swap	`list1.swap(list2)` The swap member function swaps the elements stored in two `lists`. For example, assuming `list1` and `list2` are `lists`, this statement will exchange the values in the two lists.
unique	`list.unique();` unique removes any element that has the same value as the element before it.

Program 17-6 demonstrates some simple operations with the list container.

Program 17-6

```cpp
 1   // This program demonstrates the STL list container.
 2   #include <iostream>
 3   #include <list>       // Include the list header.
 4   using namespace std;
 5
 6   int main()
 7   {
 8      // Define a list object.
 9      list<int> myList;
10
11      // Define an iterator for the list.
12      list<int>::iterator iter;
13
14      // Add values to the list.
15      for (int x = 0; x < 100; x += 10)
16         myList.push_back(x);
17
18      // Display the values.
19      for (iter = myList.begin(); iter != myList.end(); iter++)
20         cout << *iter << " ";
21      cout << endl;
22
23      // Now reverse the order of the elements.
24      myList.reverse();
25
26      // Display the values again.
27      for (iter = myList.begin(); iter != myList.end(); iter++)
28         cout << *iter << " ";
29      cout << endl;
30      return 0;
31   }
```

Program Output

```
0 10 20 30 40 50 60 70 80 90
90 80 70 60 50 40 30 20 10 0
```

Review Questions and Exercises

Short Answer

1. What are some of the advantages that linked lists have over arrays?

2. What advantage does a linked list have over the STL `vector`?

3. What is a list head?

4. What is a self-referential data structure?

5. How is the end of a linked list usually signified?

6. Name five basic linked list operations.

7. What is the difference between appending a node and inserting a node?

8. What does "traversing the list" mean?

9. What are the two steps required to delete a node from a linked list?

10. What is the advantage of using a template to implement a linked list?

11. What is a singly linked list? What is a doubly linked list? What is a circularly linked list?

12. What type of linked list is the STL `list` container?

Fill-in-the-Blank

13. The _____ points to the first node in a linked list.

14. A data structure that points to an object of the same type as itself is known as a(n) _____ data structure.

15. After creating a linked list's head pointer, you should make sure it points to _____ before using it in any operations.

16. _____ a node means adding it to the end of a list.

17. _____ a node means adding it to a list, but not necessarily to the end.

18. _____ a list means traveling through the list.

19. In a(n) _____ list, the last node has a pointer to the first node.

20. In a(n) _____ list, each node has a pointer to the one before it and the one after it.

Algorithm Workbench

21. Consider the following code:

```
struct ListNode
{
    int value;
    struct ListNode *next;
};

ListNode *head;   // List head pointer
```

Assume that a linked list has been created and `head` points to the first node. Write code that traverses the list displaying the contents of each node's `value` member.

22. Write code that destroys the linked list described in Question 21.

23. Write code that defines an STL `list` container for holding `float` values.

24. Write code that stores the values 12.7, 9.65, 8.72, and 4.69 in the `list` container you defined for Question 23.

25. Write code that reverses the order of the items you stored in the `list` container in Question 24.

True or False

26. T F The programmer must know in advance how many nodes will be needed in a linked list.

27. T F It is not necessary for each node in a linked list to have a self-referential pointer.

28. T F In physical memory, the nodes in a linked list may be scattered around.

29. T F When the head pointer points to NULL, it signifies an empty list.

30. T F Linked lists are not superior to STL vectors.

31. T F Deleting a node in a linked list is a simple matter of using the `delete` operator to free the node's memory.

32. T F A class that builds a linked list should destroy the list in the class destructor.

Find the Error

Each of the following member functions has errors in the way it performs a linked list operation. Find as many mistakes as you can.

33.
```cpp
void NumberList::appendNode(double num)
{
    ListNode *newNode, *nodePtr;
    // Allocate a new node & store num
    newNode = new listNode;
    newNode->value = num;

    // If there are no nodes in the list
    // make newNode the first node.
    if (!head)
        head = newNode;
    else        // Otherwise, insert newNode.
    {
        // Find the last node in the list.
        while (nodePtr->next)
            nodePtr = nodePtr->next;
        // Insert newNode as the last node.
        nodePtr->next = newNode;
    }
}
```

34.
```cpp
void NumberList::deleteNode(double num)
{
    ListNode *nodePtr, *previousNode;
    // If the list is empty, do nothing.
    if (!head)
        return;
    // Determine if the first node is the one.
    if (head->value == num)
```

```
            delete head;
        else
        {
            // Initialize nodePtr to head of list.
            nodePtr = head;

            // Skip all nodes whose value member is
            // not equal to num.
            while (nodePtr->value != num)
            {
                previousNode = nodePtr;
                nodePtr = nodePtr->next;
            }
            // Link the previous node to the node after
            // nodePtr, then delete nodePtr.
            previousNode->next = nodePtr->next;
            delete nodePtr;
        }
    }
35. NumberList::~NumberList()
    {
        ListNode *nodePtr, *nextNode;
        nodePtr = head;
        while (nodePtr != NULL)
        {
            nextNode = nodePtr->next;
            nodePtr->next = NULL;
            nodePtr = nextNode;
        }
    }
```

Programming Challenges

Visit www.myprogramminglab.com to complete many of these Programming Challenges online and get instant feedback.

myprogramminglab

1. Your Own Linked List

Design your own linked list class to hold a series of integers. The class should have member functions for appending, inserting, and deleting nodes. Don't forget to add a destructor that destroys the list. Demonstrate the class with a driver program.

2. List Print

Modify the linked list class you created in Programming Challenge 1 to add a print member function. The function should display all the values in the linked list. Test the class by starting with an empty list, adding some elements, and then printing the resulting list out.

3. List Copy Constructor

Modify your linked list class of Programming Challenges 1 and 2 to add a copy constructor. Test your class by making a list, making a copy of the list, and then displaying the values in the copy.

4. **List Reverse**

   Modify the linked list class you created in the previous programming challenges by adding a member function named reverse that rearranges the nodes in the list so that their order is reversed. Demonstrate the function in a simple driver program.

5. **List Search**

   Modify the linked list class you created in the previous programming challenges to include a member function named search that returns the position of a specific value in the linked list. The first node in the list is at position 0, the second node is at position 1, and so on. If x is not found on the list, the search should return −1. Test the new member function using an appropriate driver program.

VideoNote

Solving the Member Insertion by Position Problem

6. **Member Insertion by Position**

   Modify the list class you created in the previous programming challenges by adding a member function for inserting a new item at a specified position. A position of 0 means that the value will become the first item on the list, a position of 1 means that the value will become the second item on the list, and so on. A position equal to or greater than the length of the list means that the value is placed at the end of the list.

7. **Member Removal by Position**

   Modify the list class you created in the previous programming challenges by adding a member function for deleting a node at a specified position. A value of 0 for the position means that the first node in the list (the current head) is deleted. The function does nothing if the specified position is greater than or equal to the length of the list.

8. **List Template**

   Create a list class template based on the list class you created in the previous programming challenges.

9. **Rainfall Statistics Modification**

   Modify Programming Challenge 2 in Chapter 7 (Rainfall Statistics) to let the user decide how many months of data will be entered. Use a linked list instead of an array to hold the monthly data.

10. **Payroll Modification**

    Modify Programming Challenge 10 in Chapter 7 (Payroll) to use three linked lists instead of three arrays to hold the employee IDs, hours worked, and wages. When the program starts, it should ask the user to enter the employee IDs. There should be no limit on the number of IDs the user can enter.

11. **List Search**

    Modify the LinkedList template shown in this chapter to include a member function named search. The function should search the list for a specified value. If the value is found, it should return a number indicating its position in the list. (The first node is node 1, the second node is node 2, and so forth.) If the value is not found, the function should return 0. Demonstrate the function in a driver program.

12. **Double Merge**

    Modify the `NumberList` class shown in this chapter to include a member function named `mergeArray`. The `mergeArray` function should take an array of `doubles` as its first argument, and an integer as its second argument. (The second argument will specify the size of the array being passed into the first argument.)

    The function should merge the values in the array into the linked list. The value in each element of the array should be inserted (not appended) into the linked list. When the values are inserted, they should be in numerical order. Demonstrate the function with a driver program. When you are satisfied with the function, incorporate it into the `LinkedList` template.

13. **Rainfall Statistics Modification #2**

    Modify the program you wrote for Programming Challenge 9 so that it saves the data in the linked list to a file. Write a second program that reads the data from the file into a linked list and displays it on the screen.

14. **Overloaded [ ] Operator**

    Modify the linked list class that you created in Programming Challenge 1 (or the `LinkedList` template presented in this chapter) by adding an overloaded [ ] operator function. This will give the linked list the ability to access nodes using a subscript, like an array. The subscript 0 will reference the first node in the list, the subscript 1 will reference the second node in the list, and so forth. The subscript of the last node will be the number of nodes minus 1. If an invalid subscript is used, the function should throw an exception.

15. **pop and push Member Functions**

    The STL list container has member functions named `pop_back`, `pop_front`, `push_back`, and `push_front`, as described in Table 17-1. Modify the linked list class that you created in Programming Challenge 1 (or the `LinkedList` template presented in this chapter) by adding your own versions of these member functions.

18 Stacks and Queues

TOPICS

18.1 Introduction to the Stack ADT

CONCEPT: A stack is a data structure that stores and retrieves items in a last-in-first-out manner.

Definition

Like an array or a linked list, a stack is a data structure that holds a sequence of elements. Unlike arrays and lists, however, stacks are *last-in, first-out (LIFO)* structures. This means that when a program retrieves elements from a stack, the last element inserted into the stack is the first one retrieved (and likewise, the first element inserted is the last one retrieved).

When visualizing the way a stack works, think of a stack of plates at the beginning of a cafeteria line. When a cafeteria worker replenishes the supply of plates, the first one he or she puts on the stack is the last one taken off. This is illustrated in Figure 18-1.

The LIFO characteristic of a stack of plates in a cafeteria is also the primary characteristic of a stack data structure. The last data element placed on the stack is the first data retrieved from the stack.

Figure 18-1

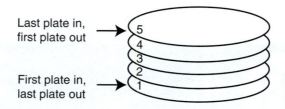

Last plate in, first plate out →

First plate in, last plate out →

Applications of Stacks

Stacks are useful data structures for algorithms that work first with the last saved element of a series. For example, computer systems use stacks while executing programs. When a function is called, they save the program's return address on a stack. They also create local variables on a stack. When the function terminates, the local variables are removed from the stack and the return address is retrieved. Also, some calculators use a stack for performing mathematical operations.

Static and Dynamic Stacks

There are two types of stack data structure: static and dynamic. Static stacks have a fixed size, and are implemented as arrays. Dynamic stacks grow in size as needed, and are implemented as linked lists. In this section you will see examples of both static and dynamic stacks.

Stack Operations

A stack has two primary operations: *push* and *pop*. The push operation causes a value to be stored, or pushed onto the stack. For example, suppose we have an empty integer stack that is capable of holding a maximum of three values. With that stack we execute the following push operations.

```
push(5);
push(10);
push(15);
```

Figure 18-2 illustrates the state of the stack after each of these push operations.

Figure 18-2

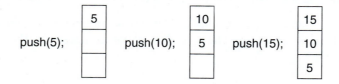

push(5);   push(10);   push(15);

The pop operation retrieves (and hence, removes) a value from the stack. Suppose we execute three consecutive pop operations on the stack shown in Figure 18-2. Figure 18-3 depicts the results.

Figure 18-3

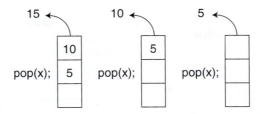

As you can see from Figure 18-3, the last pop operation leaves the stack empty.

For a static stack (one with a fixed size), we will need a Boolean isFull operation. The isFull operation returns true if the stack is full, and false otherwise. This operation is necessary to prevent a stack overflow in the event that a push operation is attempted when all the stack's elements have values stored in them.

For both static and dynamic stacks we will need a Boolean isEmpty operation. The isEmpty operation returns true when the stack is empty, and false otherwise. This prevents an error from occurring when a pop operation is attempted on an empty stack.

A Static Stack Class

Now we examine a class, IntStack, that stores a static stack of integers and performs the isFull and isEmpty operations. The class has the member variables described in Table 18-1.

Table 18-1

Member Variable	Description
stackArray	A pointer to int. When the constructor is executed, it uses stackArray to dynamically allocate an array for storage.
stackSize	An integer that holds the size of the stack.
top	An integer that is used to mark the top of the stack.

The class's member functions are listed in Table 18-2.

Table 18-2

Member Functions	Description
Constructor	The class constructor accepts an integer argument that specifies the size of the stack. An integer array of this size is dynamically allocated, and assigned to stackArray. Also, the variable top is initialized to –1.
Destructor	The destructor frees the memory that was allocated by the constructor.
isFull	Returns true if the stack is full and false otherwise. The stack is full when top is equal to stackSize − 1.
isEmpty	Returns true if the stack is empty, and false otherwise. The stack is empty when top is set to –1.

(table continues)

Table 18-2 *(continued)*

Member Functions	Description
pop	The pop function uses an integer reference parameter. The value at the top of the stack is removed and copied into the reference parameter.
push	The push function accepts an integer argument, which is pushed onto the top of the stack.

 NOTE: Even though the constructor dynamically allocates the stack array, it is still a static stack. The size of the stack does not change once it is allocated.

The code for the class follows.

Contents of `IntStack.h`

```
 1   // Specification file for the IntStack class
 2   #ifndef INTSTACK_H
 3   #define INTSTACK_H
 4
 5   class IntStack
 6   {
 7   private:
 8      int *stackArray;   // Pointer to the stack array
 9      int stackSize;     // The stack size
10      int top;           // Indicates the top of the stack
11
12   public:
13      // Constructor
14      IntStack(int);
15
16      // Copy constructor
17      IntStack(const IntStack &);
18
19      // Destructor
20      ~IntStack();
21
22      // Stack operations
23      void push(int);
24      void pop(int &);
25      bool isFull() const;
26      bool isEmpty() const;
27   };
28   #endif
```

Contents of `IntStack.cpp`

```
 1   // Implementation file for the IntStack class
 2   #include <iostream>
 3   #include "IntStack.h"
 4   using namespace std;
 5
```

```cpp
 6   //*********************************************
 7   // Constructor                              *
 8   // This constructor creates an empty stack. The *
 9   // size parameter is the size of the stack.     *
10   //*********************************************
11
12   IntStack::IntStack(int size)
13   {
14      stackArray = new int[size];
15      stackSize = size;
16      top = -1;
17   }
18
19   //*********************************************
20   // Copy constructor                            *
21   //*********************************************
22
23   IntStack::IntStack(const IntStack &obj)
24   {
25      // Create the stack array.
26      if (obj.stackSize > 0)
27         stackArray = new int[obj.stackSize];
28      else
29         stackArray = NULL;
30
31      // Copy the stackSize attribute.
32      stackSize = obj.stackSize;
33
34      // Copy the stack contents.
35      for (int count = 0; count < stackSize; count++)
36         stackArray[count] = obj.stackArray[count];
37
38      // Set the top of the stack.
39      top = obj.top;
40   }
41
42   //*********************************************
43   // Destructor                                  *
44   //*********************************************
45
46   IntStack::~IntStack()
47   {
48      delete [] stackArray;
49   }
50
51   //*********************************************
52   // Member function push pushes the argument onto  *
53   // the stack.                                     *
54   //*********************************************
55
56   void IntStack::push(int num)
57   {
58      if (isFull())
59      {
60         cout << "The stack is full.\n";
61      }
```

```
62       else
63       {
64          top++;
65          stackArray[top] = num;
66       }
67   }
68
69   //*****************************************************
70   // Member function pop pops the value at the top      *
71   // of the stack off, and copies it into the variable *
72   // passed as an argument.                             *
73   //*****************************************************
74
75   void IntStack::pop(int &num)
76   {
77      if (isEmpty())
78      {
79         cout << "The stack is empty.\n";
80      }
81      else
82      {
83         num = stackArray[top];
84         top--;
85      }
86   }
87
88   //*****************************************************
89   // Member function isFull returns true if the stack  *
90   // is full, or false otherwise.                      *
91   //*****************************************************
92
93   bool IntStack::isFull() const
94   {
95      bool status;
96
97      if (top == stackSize - 1)
98         status = true;
99      else
100        status = false;
101
102     return status;
103  }
104
105  //*****************************************************
106  // Member function isEmpty returns true if the stack *
107  // is empty, or false otherwise.                     *
108  //*****************************************************
109
110  bool IntStack::isEmpty() const
111  {
112     bool status;
113
114     if (top == -1)
115        status = true;
```

```
116        else
117            status = false;
118
119        return status;
120    }
```

The class has two constructors, one that accepts an argument for the stack size (lines 12 through 17 of IntStack.cpp) and a copy constructor (lines 23 through 40). The first constructor dynamically allocates the stack array in line 14, initializes the stackSize member variable in line 15, and initializes the top member variable in line 16. Remember that items are stored to and retrieved from the top of the stack. In this class, the top of the stack is actually the end of the array. The variable top is used to mark the top of the stack by holding the subscript of the last element. When top holds –1, it indicates that the stack is empty. (See the isEmpty function, which returns true if top is –1, or false otherwise.) The stack is full when top is at the maximum subscript, which is stackSize − 1. This is the value that isFull tests for. It returns true if the stack is full, or false otherwise.

Program 18-1 is a simple driver that demonstrates the IntStack class.

Program 18-1

```
1    // This program demonstrates the IntStack class.
2    #include <iostream>
3    #include "IntStack.h"
4    using namespace std;
5
6    int main()
7    {
8        int catchVar; // To hold values popped off the stack
9
10       // Define a stack object to hold 5 values.
11       IntStack stack(5);
12
13       // Push the values 5, 10, 15, 20, and 25 onto the stack.
14       cout << "Pushing 5\n";
15       stack.push(5);
16       cout << "Pushing 10\n";
17       stack.push(10);
18       cout << "Pushing 15\n";
19       stack.push(15);
20       cout << "Pushing 20\n";
21       stack.push(20);
22       cout << "Pushing 25\n";
23       stack.push(25);
24
25       // Pop the values off the stack.
26       cout << "Popping...\n";
27       stack.pop(catchVar);
28       cout << catchVar << endl;
29       stack.pop(catchVar);
30       cout << catchVar << endl;
31       stack.pop(catchVar);
32       cout << catchVar << endl;
```

(program continues)

Program 18-1 *(continued)*

```
33      stack.pop(catchVar);
34      cout << catchVar << endl;
35      stack.pop(catchVar);
36      cout << catchVar << endl;
37      return 0;
38   }
```

Program Output

Pushing 5
Pushing 10
Pushing 15
Pushing 20
Pushing 25
Popping...
25
20
15
10
5

In Program 18-1, the constructor is called with the argument 5. This sets up the member variables as shown in Figure 18-4. Because top is set to –1, the stack is empty.

Figure 18-4

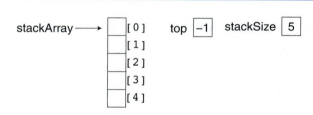

Figure 18-5 shows the state of the member variables after the push function is called the first time (with 5 as its argument). The top of the stack is now at element 0.

Figure 18-5

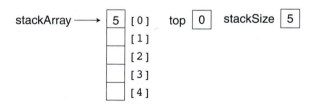

Figure 18-6 shows the state of the member variables after all five calls to the push function. Now the top of the stack is at element 4, and the stack is full.

Figure 18-6

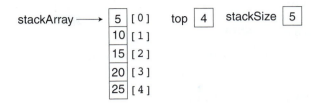

Notice that the pop function uses a reference parameter, num. The value that is popped off the stack is copied into num so it can be used later in the program. Figure 18-7 depicts the state of the class members, and the num parameter, just after the first value is popped off the stack.

Figure 18-7

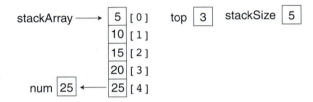

The program continues to call the pop function until all the values have been retrieved from the stack.

Implementing Other Stack Operations

More complex operations may be built on the basic stack class previously shown. In this section, we will discuss a class, MathStack, that is derived from IntStack. The MathStack class has two member functions: add() and sub(). The add() function pops the first two values off the stack, adds them together, and pushes the sum onto the stack. The sub() function pops the first two values off the stack, subtracts the second value from the first, and then pushes the difference onto the stack. The class declaration is as follows.

Contents of `MathStack.h`

```
 1   // Specification file for the MathStack class
 2   #ifndef MATHSTACK_H
 3   #define MATHSTACK_H
 4   #include "IntStack.h"
 5
 6   class MathStack : public IntStack
 7   {
 8   public:
 9      // Constructor
10      MathStack(int s) : IntStack(s) {}
11
```

```
12        // MathStack operations
13        void add();
14        void sub();
15    };
16    #endif
```

The definitions of the member functions are shown here:

Contents of `MathStack.cpp`

```
 1    // Implementation file for the MathStack class
 2    #include "MathStack.h"
 3
 4    //************************************************
 5    // Member function add. add pops             *
 6    // the first two values off the stack and    *
 7    // adds them. The sum is pushed onto the stack. *
 8    //************************************************
 9
10    void MathStack::add()
11    {
12        int num, sum;
13
14        // Pop the first two values off the stack.
15        pop(sum);
16        pop(num);
17
18        // Add the two values, store in sum.
19        sum += num;
20
21        // Push sum back onto the stack.
22        push(sum);
23    }
24
25    //************************************************
26    // Member function sub. sub pops the         *
27    // first two values off the stack. The       *
28    // second value is subtracted from the       *
29    // first value. The difference is pushed     *
30    // onto the stack.                           *
31    //************************************************
32
33    void MathStack::sub()
34    {
35        int num, diff;
36
37        // Pop the first two values off the stack.
38        pop(diff);
39        pop(num);
40
41        // Subtract num from diff.
42        diff -= num;
43
44        // Push diff back onto the stack.
45        push(diff);
46    }
```

The class is demonstrated in Program 18-2, a simple driver.

Program 18-2

```
 1   // This program demonstrates the MathStack class.
 2   #include <iostream>
 3   #include "MathStack.h"
 4   using namespace std;
 5
 6   int main()
 7   {
 8      int catchVar;   // To hold values popped off the stack
 9
10      // Create a MathStack object.
11      MathStack stack(5);
12
13      // Push 3 and 6 onto the stack.
14      cout << "Pushing 3\n";
15      stack.push(3);
16      cout << "Pushing 6\n";
17      stack.push(6);
18
19      // Add the two values.
20      stack.add();
21
22      // Pop the sum off the stack and display it.
23      cout << "The sum is ";
24      stack.pop(catchVar);
25      cout << catchVar << endl << endl;
26
27      // Push 7 and 10 onto the stack
28      cout << "Pushing 7\n";
29      stack.push(7);
30      cout << "Pushing 10\n";
31      stack.push(10);
32
33      // Subtract 7 from 10.
34      stack.sub();
35
36      // Pop the difference off the stack and display it.
37      cout << "The difference is ";
38      stack.pop(catchVar);
39      cout << catchVar << endl;
40      return 0;
41   }
```

Program Output

```
Pushing 3
Pushing 6
The sum is 9

Pushing 7
Pushing 10
The difference is 3
```

It will be left as a Programming Challenge for you to implement the `mult()`, `div()`, and `mod()` functions that will complete the `MathStack` class.

A Static Stack Template

The stack classes shown previously in this chapter work only with integers. A stack template can be easily designed to work with any data type, as shown by the following example:

Contents of `Stack.h`

```
 1  #ifndef STACK_H
 2  #define STACK_H
 3  #include <iostream>
 4  using namespace std;
 5
 6  // Stack template
 7  template <class T>
 8  class Stack
 9  {
10  private:
11     T *stackArray;
12     int stackSize;
13     int top;
14
15  public:
16     // Constructor
17     Stack(int);
18
19     // Copy constructor
20     Stack(const Stack&);
21
22     // Destructor
23     ~Stack();
24
25     // Stack operations
26     void push(T);
27     void pop(T &);
28     bool isFull();
29     bool isEmpty();
30  };
31
32  //*************************************************
33  //   Constructor                                 *
34  //*************************************************
35
36  template <class T>
37  Stack<T>::Stack(int size)
38  {
39     stackArray = new T[size];
40     stackSize = size;
41     top = -1;
42  }
43
```

```
44   //*************************************************
45   //   Copy constructor                             *
46   //*************************************************
47
48   template <class T>
49   Stack<T>::Stack(const Stack &obj)
50   {
51      // Create the stack array.
52      if (obj.stackSize > 0)
53         stackArray = new T[obj.stackSize];
54      else
55         stackArray = NULL;
56
57      // Copy the stackSize attribute.
58      stackSize = obj.stackSize;
59
60      // Copy the stack contents.
61      for (int count = 0; count < stackSize; count++)
62         stackArray[count] = obj.stackArray[count];
63
64      // Set the top of the stack.
65      top = obj.top;
66   }
67
68   //*************************************************
69   //   Destructor                                   *
70   //*************************************************
71
72   template <class T>
73   Stack<T>::~Stack()
74   {
75      if (stackSize > 0)
76         delete [] stackArray;
77   }
78
79   //*********************************************************
80   // Member function push pushes the argument onto          *
81   // the stack.                                             *
82   //*********************************************************
83
84   template <class T>
85   void Stack<T>::push(T item)
86   {
87      if (isFull())
88      {
89         cout << "The stack is full.\n";
90      }
91      else
92      {
93         top++;
94         stackArray[top] = item;
95      }
96   }
97
```

```
 98 //**************************************************************
 99 // Member function pop pops the value at the top              *
100 // of the stack off, and copies it into the variable          *
101 // passed as an argument.                                      *
102 //**************************************************************
103
104 template <class T>
105 void Stack<T>::pop(T &item)
106 {
107    if (isEmpty())
108    {
109       cout << "The stack is empty.\n";
110    }
111    else
112    {
113       item = stackArray[top];
114       top--;
115    }
116 }
117
118 //**************************************************************
119 // Member function isFull returns true if the stack           *
120 // is full, or false otherwise.                               *
121 //**************************************************************
122
123 template <class T>
124 bool Stack<T>::isFull()
125 {
126    bool status;
127
128    if (top == stackSize - 1)
129       status = true;
130    else
131       status = false;
132
133    return status;
134 }
135
136 //**************************************************************
137 // Member function isEmpty returns true if the stack          *
138 // is empty, or false otherwise.                              *
139 //**************************************************************
140
141 template <class T>
142 bool Stack<T>::isEmpty()
143 {
144    bool status;
145
146    if (top == -1)
147       status = true;
148    else
149       status = false;
150
151    return status;
152 }
153 #endif
```

Program 18-3 demonstrates the Stack template. It creates a stack of strings, and then presents a menu that allows the user to push an item onto the stack, pop an item from the stack, or quit the program.

Program 18-3

```cpp
1 // This program demonstrates the Stack template.
2 #include <iostream>
3 #include <string>
4 #include "Stack.h"
5 using namespace std;
6
7 // Constants for the menu choices
8 const int PUSH_CHOICE = 1,
9          POP_CHOICE = 2,
10         QUIT_CHOICE = 3;
11
12 // Function prototypes
13 void menu(int &);
14 void getStackSize(int &);
15 void pushItem(Stack<string>&);
16 void popItem(Stack<string>&);
17
18 int main()
19 {
20     int stackSize; // The stack size
21     int choice;    // To hold a menu choice
22
23     // Get the stack size.
24     getStackSize(stackSize);
25
26     // Create the stack.
27     Stack<string> stack(stackSize);
28
29     do
30     {
31         // Get the user's menu choice.
32         menu(choice);
33
34         // Perform the user's choice.
35         if (choice != QUIT_CHOICE)
36         {
37             switch (choice)
38             {
39                 case PUSH_CHOICE:
40                     pushItem(stack);
41                     break;
42                 case POP_CHOICE:
43                     popItem(stack);
44             }
45         }
46     } while (choice != QUIT_CHOICE);
47
48     return 0;
49 }
```

(program continues)

Program 18-3   (continued)

```
50
51  //***********************************************
52  // The getStackSize function gets the desired   *
53  // stack size, which is assigned to the         *
54  // reference parameter.                         *
55  //***********************************************
56  void getStackSize(int &size)
57  {
58      // Get the desired stack size.
59      cout << "How big should I make the stack? ";
60      cin >> size;
61
62      // Validate the size.
63      while (size < 1)
64      {
65          cout << "Enter 1 or greater: ";
66          cin >> size;
67      }
68  }
69
70  //***********************************************
71  // The menu function displays the menu and gets *
72  // the user's choice, which is assigned to the  *
73  // reference parameter.                         *
74  //***********************************************
75  void menu(int &choice)
76  {
77      // Display the menu and get the user's choice.
78      cout << "\nWhat do you want to do?\n"
79           << PUSH_CHOICE
80           << " - Push an item onto the stack\n"
81           << POP_CHOICE
82           << " - Pop an item off the stack\n"
83           << QUIT_CHOICE
84           << " - Quit the program\n"
85           << "Enter your choice: ";
86      cin >> choice;
87
88      // Validate the choice
89      while (choice < PUSH_CHOICE || choice > QUIT_CHOICE)
90      {
91          cout << "Enter a valid choice: ";
92          cin >> choice;
93      }
94  }
95
96  //***********************************************
97  // The pushItem function gets an item from the  *
98  // user and pushes it onto the stack.           *
99  //***********************************************
100 void pushItem(Stack<string> &stack)
```

Program 18-3   *(continued)*

```
101 {
102     string item;
103
104     // Get an item to push onto the stack.
105     cin.ignore();
106     cout << "\nEnter an item: ";
107     getline(cin, item);
108     stack.push(item);
109 }
110
111 //*****************************************************
112 // The popItem function pops an item from the stack *
113 //*****************************************************
114 void popItem(Stack<string> &stack)
115 {
116     string item = "";
117
118     // Pop the item.
119     stack.pop(item);
120
121     // Display the item.
122     if (item != "")
123         cout << item << " was popped.\n";
124 }
```

Program Output with Example Input Shown in Bold

How big should I make the stack? **3 [Enter]**

What do you want to do?
1 - Push an item onto the stack
2 - Pop an item off the stack
3 - Quit the program
Enter your choice: **1 [Enter]**

Enter an item: **The Adventures of Huckleberry Finn [Enter]**

What do you want to do?
1 - Push an item onto the stack
2 - Pop an item off the stack
3 - Quit the program
Enter your choice: **1 [Enter]**

Enter an item: **All Quiet on the Western Front [Enter]**

What do you want to do?
1 - Push an item onto the stack
2 - Pop an item off the stack
3 - Quit the program
Enter your choice: **1 [Enter]**

Enter an item: **Brave New World [Enter]**

(program output continues)

Program 18-3   *(continued)*

```
What do you want to do?
1 - Push an item onto the stack
2 - Pop an item off the stack
3 - Quit the program
Enter your choice: 2 [Enter]
Brave New World was popped.

What do you want to do?
1 - Push an item onto the stack
2 - Pop an item off the stack
3 - Quit the program
Enter your choice: 2 [Enter]
All Quiet on the Western Front was popped.

What do you want to do?
1 - Push an item onto the stack
2 - Pop an item off the stack
3 - Quit the program
Enter your choice: 2 [Enter]
The Adventures of Huckleberry Finn was popped.

What do you want to do?
1 - Push an item onto the stack
2 - Pop an item off the stack
3 - Quit the program
Enter your choice: 2 [Enter]
The stack is empty.

What do you want to do?
1 - Push an item onto the stack
2 - Pop an item off the stack
3 - Quit the program
Enter your choice: 3 [Enter]
```

18.2   Dynamic Stacks

CONCEPT: A stack may be implemented as a linked list, and expand or shrink with each **push** or **pop** operation.

A dynamic stack is built on a linked list instead of an array. A linked list–based stack offers two advantages over an array-based stack. First, there is no need to specify the starting size of the stack. A dynamic stack simply starts as an empty linked list, then expands by one node each time a value is pushed. Second, a dynamic stack will never be full, as long as the system has enough free memory.

In this section we will look at a dynamic stack class, `DynIntStack`. This class is a dynamic version of the `IntStack` class previously discussed. The class declaration is shown here:

Contents of `DynIntStack.h`

```
1   // Specification file for the DynIntStack class
2   #ifndef DYNINTSTACK_H
3   #define DYNINTSTACK_H
4
5   class DynIntStack
6   {
7   private:
8       // Structure for stack nodes
9       struct StackNode
10      {
11          int value;          // Value in the node
12          StackNode *next;    // Pointer to the next node
13      };
14
15      StackNode *top;         // Pointer to the stack top
16
17  public:
18      // Constructor
19      DynIntStack()
20          {  top = NULL; }
21
22      // Destructor
23      ~DynIntStack();
24
25      // Stack operations
26      void push(int);
27      void pop(int &);
28      bool isEmpty();
29  };
30  #endif
```

The `StackNode` structure is the data type of each node in the linked list. It has a `value` member and a `next` pointer. Notice that instead of a `head` pointer, a `top` pointer is defined. This member will always point to the first node in the list, which will represent the top of the stack. It is initialized to NULL by the constructor, to signify that the stack is empty.

The definitions of the other member functions are shown here:

Contents of `DynIntStack.cpp`

```
1   #include <iostream>
2   #include "DynIntStack.h"
3   using namespace std;
4
5   //*****************************************************
6   // Destructor                                         *
7   // This function deletes every node in the list.      *
8   //*****************************************************
9
10  DynIntStack::~DynIntStack()
11  {
12      StackNode *nodePtr, *nextNode;
13
```

```
14      // Position nodePtr at the top of the stack.
15      nodePtr = top;
16
17      // Traverse the list deleting each node.
18      while (nodePtr != NULL)
19      {
20         nextNode = nodePtr->next;
21         delete nodePtr;
22         nodePtr = nextNode;
23      }
24   }
25
26   //***********************************************
27   // Member function push pushes the argument onto *
28   // the stack.                                     *
29   //***********************************************
30
31   void DynIntStack::push(int num)
32   {
33      StackNode *newNode; // Pointer to a new node
34
35      // Allocate a new node and store num there.
36      newNode = new StackNode;
37      newNode->value = num;
38
39      // If there are no nodes in the list
40      // make newNode the first node.
41      if (isEmpty())
42      {
43         top = newNode;
44         newNode->next = NULL;
45      }
46      else  // Otherwise, insert NewNode before top.
47      {
48         newNode->next = top;
49         top = newNode;
50      }
51   }
52
53   //***************************************************
54   // Member function pop pops the value at the top      *
55   // of the stack off, and copies it into the variable *
56   // passed as an argument.                             *
57   //***************************************************
58
59   void DynIntStack::pop(int &num)
60   {
61      StackNode *temp; // Temporary pointer
62
63      // First make sure the stack isn't empty.
64      if (isEmpty())
65      {
66         cout << "The stack is empty.\n";
67      }
68      else  // pop value off top of stack
```

```
69      {
70          num = top->value;
71          temp = top->next;
72          delete top;
73          top = temp;
74      }
75  }
76
77  //****************************************************
78  // Member function isEmpty returns true if the stack *
79  // is empty, or false otherwise.                     *
80  //****************************************************
81
82  bool DynIntStack::isEmpty()
83  {
84      bool status;
85
86      if (!top)
87          status = true;
88      else
89          status = false;
90
91      return status;
92  }
```

Let's look at the push operation in lines 31 through 51 of `DynIntStack.cpp`. First, in lines 36 and 37, a new node is allocated in memory and the function argument is copied into its value member:

```
newNode = new StackNode;
newNode->value = num;
```

Next in line 41, an `if` statement calls the `isEmpty` function to determine whether the stack is empty:

```
if (isEmpty())
{
    top = newNode;
    newNode->next = NULL;
}
```

If `isEmpty` returns `true`, `top` is made to point at the new node, and the new node's `next` pointer is set to NULL. After these statements execute, there will be one node in the list (and one value on the stack).

If `isEmpty` returns `false` in the `if` statement, the following statements in lines 46 through 50 are executed.

```
else    // Otherwise, insert newNode before top
{
    newNode->next = top;
    top = newNode;
}
```

Notice that `newNode` is being inserted in the list before the node that `top` points to. The `top` pointer is then updated to point to the new node. When this is done, `newNode` is at the top of the stack.

Now let's look at the pop function in lines 59 through 75. Just as the push function must insert nodes at the head of the list, pop must delete nodes at the head of the list. First, the function calls isEmpty in line 64 to determine whether there are any nodes in the stack. If there are none, an error message is displayed:

```
if (isEmpty())
{
    cout << "The stack is empty.\n";
}
```

If isEmpty returns false, then the following statements in lines 68 through 74 are executed.

```
else    // pop value off top of stack
{
    num = top->value;
    temp = top->next;
    delete top;
    top = temp;
}
```

First, the value member of the top node is copied into the num reference parameter. This saves the value for later use in the program. Next, a temporary StackNode pointer, temp, is made to point to top->next. If there are other nodes in the list, this causes temp to point to the second node. (If there are no more nodes, this will cause temp to point to NULL.) Now it is safe to delete the top node. After the top node is deleted, the top pointer is set equal to temp. This action moves the top pointer down the list by one node. The node that was previously second in the list becomes first.

The isEmpty function, in lines 82 through 92, is simple. If top is NULL, then the list (the stack) is empty.

Program 18-4 is a driver that demonstrates the DynIntStack class.

Program 18-4

```
 1  // This program demonstrates the dynamic stack.
 2  // class DynIntClass.
 3  #include <iostream>
 4  #include "DynIntStack.h"
 5  using namespace std;
 6
 7  int main()
 8  {
 9      int catchVar;  // To hold values popped off the stack
10
11      // Create a DynIntStack object.
12      DynIntStack stack;
13
14      // Push 5, 10, and 15 onto the stack.
15      cout << "Pushing 5\n";
16      stack.push(5);
17      cout << "Pushing 10\n";
18      stack.push(10);
19      cout << "Pushing 15\n";
20      stack.push(15);
```

```
21
22      // Pop the values off the stack and display them.
23      cout << "Popping...\n";
24      stack.pop(catchVar);
25      cout << catchVar << endl;
26      stack.pop(catchVar);
27      cout << catchVar << endl;
28      stack.pop(catchVar);
29      cout << catchVar << endl;
30
31      // Try to pop another value off the stack.
32      cout << "\nAttempting to pop again... ";
33      stack.pop(catchVar);
34      return 0;
35  }
```

Program Output
```
Pushing 5
Pushing 10
Pushing 15
Popping...
15
10
5

Attempting to pop again... The stack is empty.
```

A Dynamic Stack Template

The dynamic stack class shown previously in this chapter works only with integers. A dynamic stack template can be easily designed to work with any data type, as shown by the following example:

Contents of `DynamicStack.h`

```
 1 #ifndef DYNAMICSTACK_H
 2 #define DYNAMICSTACK_H
 3 #include <iostream>
 4 using namespace std;
 5
 6 // Stack template
 7 template <class T>
 8 class DynamicStack
 9 {
10 private:
11    // Structure for the stack nodes
12    struct StackNode
13    {
14       T value;          // Value in the node
15       StackNode *next;  // Pointer to the next node
16    };
```

```
17
18      StackNode *top;      // Pointer to the stack top
19
20  public:
21      //Constructor
22      DynamicStack()
23      { top = NULL; }
24
25      // Destructor
26      ~DynamicStack();
27
28      // Stack operations
29      void push(T);
30      void pop(T &);
31      bool isEmpty();
32  };
33
34  //***************************************************
35  //   Destructor                                     *
36  //***************************************************
37  template <class T>
38  DynamicStack<T>::~DynamicStack()
39  {
40      StackNode *nodePtr, *nextNode;
41
42      // Position nodePtr at the top of the stack.
43      nodePtr = top;
44
45      // Traverse the list deleting each node.
46      while (nodePtr != NULL)
47      {
48          nextNode = nodePtr->next;
49          delete nodePtr;
50          nodePtr = nextNode;
51      }
52  }
53
54  //***********************************************************
55  // Member function push pushes the argument onto           *
56  // the stack.                                              *
57  //***********************************************************
58
59  template <class T>
60  void DynamicStack<T>::push(T item)
61  {
62      StackNode *newNode; // Pointer to a new node
63
64      // Allocate a new node and store num there.
65      newNode = new StackNode;
66      newNode->value = item;
67
68      // If there are no nodes in the list
69      // make newNode the first node.
70      if (isEmpty())
```

```
 71      {
 72         top = newNode;
 73         newNode->next = NULL;
 74      }
 75      else  // Otherwise, insert NewNode before top.
 76      {
 77         newNode->next = top;
 78         top = newNode;
 79      }
 80  }
 81
 82  //****************************************************************
 83  // Member function pop pops the value at the top            *
 84  // of the stack off, and copies it into the variable       *
 85  // passed as an argument.                                  *
 86  //****************************************************************
 87
 88  template <class T>
 89  void DynamicStack<T>::pop(T &item)
 90  {
 91      StackNode *temp; // Temporary pointer
 92
 93      // First make sure the stack isn't empty.
 94      if (isEmpty())
 95      {
 96         cout << "The stack is empty.\n";
 97      }
 98      else  // pop value off top of stack
 99      {
100         item = top->value;
101         temp = top->next;
102         delete top;
103         top = temp;
104      }
105  }
106
107  //****************************************************************
108  // Member function isEmpty returns true if the stack       *
109  // is empty, or false otherwise.                           *
110  //****************************************************************
111
112  template <class T>
113  bool DynamicStack<T>::isEmpty()
114  {
115      bool status;
116
117      if (!top)
118         status = true;
119      else
120         status = false;
121
122      return status;
123  }
124  #endif
```

Program 18-5 demonstrates the `DynamicStack` template. This program is a modification of Program 18-3. It creates a stack of strings, and then presents a menu that allows the user to push an item onto the stack, pop an item from the stack, or quit the program.

Program 18-5

```
 1 #include <iostream>
 2 #include <string>
 3 #include "DynamicStack.h"
 4 using namespace std;
 5
 6 // Constants for the menu choices
 7 const int PUSH_CHOICE = 1,
 8           POP_CHOICE = 2,
 9           QUIT_CHOICE = 3;
10
11 // Function prototypes
12 void menu(int &);
13 void getStackSize(int &);
14 void pushItem(DynamicStack<string> &);
15 void popItem(DynamicStack<string> &);
16
17 int main()
18 {
19     int choice;     // To hold a menu choice
20
21     // Create the stack.
22     DynamicStack<string> stack;
23
24     do
25     {
26         // Get the user's menu choice.
27         menu(choice);
28
29         // Perform the user's choice.
30         if (choice != QUIT_CHOICE)
31         {
32             switch (choice)
33             {
34                 case PUSH_CHOICE:
35                     pushItem(stack);
36                     break;
37                 case POP_CHOICE:
38                     popItem(stack);
39             }
40         }
41     } while (choice != QUIT_CHOICE);
42
43     return 0;
44 }
45
46 //************************************************
47 // The menu function displays the menu and gets  *
48 // the user's choice, which is assigned to the   *
49 // reference parameter.                          *
50 //************************************************
```

```
51  void menu(int &choice)
52  {
53      // Display the menu and get the user's choice.
54      cout << "What do you want to do?\n"
55           << PUSH_CHOICE
56           << " - Push an item onto the stack\n"
57           << POP_CHOICE
58           << " - Pop an item off the stack\n"
59           << QUIT_CHOICE
60           << " - Quit the program\n"
61           << "Enter your choice: ";
62      cin >> choice;
63
64      // Validate the choice
65      while (choice < PUSH_CHOICE || choice > QUIT_CHOICE)
66      {
67          cout << "Enter a valid choice: ";
68          cin >> choice;
69      }
70  }
71
72  //********************************************
73  // The pushItem function gets an item from the   *
74  // user and pushes it onto the stack.            *
75  //********************************************
76  void pushItem(DynamicStack<string> &stack)
77  {
78      string item;
79
80      // Get an item to push onto the stack.
81      cin.ignore();
82      cout << "\nEnter an item: ";
83      getline(cin, item);
84      stack.push(item);
85  }
86
87  //**********************************************
88  // The popItem function pops an item from the stack *
89  //**********************************************
90  void popItem(DynamicStack<string> &stack)
91  {
92      string item = "";
93
94      // Pop the item.
95      stack.pop(item);
96
97      // Display the item.
98      if (item != "")
99          cout << item << " was popped.\n";
100 }
```

(program output continues)

Program 18-5 *(continued)*

Program Output with Example Input Shown in Bold

```
What do you want to do?
1 - Push an item onto the stack
2 - Pop an item off the stack
3 - Quit the program
Enter your choice: 1 [Enter]

Enter an item: The Catcher in the Rye [Enter]

What do you want to do?
1 - Push an item onto the stack
2 - Pop an item off the stack
3 - Quit the program
Enter your choice: 1 [Enter]

Enter an item: Crime and Punishment [Enter]
What do you want to do?
1 - Push an item onto the stack
2 - Pop an item off the stack
3 - Quit the program
Enter your choice: 2 [Enter]
Crime and Punishment was popped.

What do you want to do?
1 - Push an item onto the stack
2 - Pop an item off the stack
3 - Quit the program
Enter your choice: 2 [Enter]
The Catcher in the Rye was popped.

What do you want to do?
1 - Push an item onto the stack
2 - Pop an item off the stack
3 - Quit the program
Enter your choice: 2 [Enter]
The stack is empty.

What do you want to do?
1 - Push an item onto the stack
2 - Pop an item off the stack
3 - Quit the program
Enter your choice: 3 [Enter]
```

18.3 The STL stack Container

CONCEPT: The Standard Template Library offers a stack template, which may be implemented as a **vector**, a **list**, or a **deque**.

VideoNote

Storing Objects in an STL stack

So far, the STL containers you have learned about are vectors and lists. The STL stack container may be implemented as a vector or a list. (It may also be implemented as a deque, which you will learn about later in this chapter.) Because the stack container is used to adapt these other containers, it is often referred to as a *container adapter*.

Here are examples of how to define a stack of ints, implemented as a vector, a list, and a deque.

```
stack< int, vector<int> > iStack;    // Vector stack
stack< int, list<int> > iStack;      // List stack
stack< int > iStack;                 // Default — deque stack
```

> **NOTE:** Be sure to put spaces between the angled brackets that appear next to each other. This will prevent the compiler from mistaking > > for the stream extraction operator, >>.

Table 18-3 lists and describes some of the stack template's member functions.

Table 18-3

Member Function	Examples and Description
empty	`if (myStack.empty())` The empty member function returns true if the stack is empty. If the stack has elements, it returns false.
pop	`myStack.pop();` The pop function removes the element at the top of the stack.
push	`myStack.push(x);` The push function pushes an element with the value x onto the stack.
size	`cout << myStack.size() << endl;` The size function returns the number of elements in the list.
top	`x = myStack.top();` The top function returns a reference to the element at the top of the stack.

> **NOTE:** The pop function in the stack template does not retrieve the value from the top of the stack, it only removes it. To retrieve the value, you must call the top function first.

Program 18-6 is a driver that demonstrates an STL stack implemented as a vector.

Program 18-6

```cpp
1   // This program demonstrates the STL stack
2   // container adapter.
3   #include <iostream>
4   #include <vector>
5   #include <stack>
6   using namespace std;
7
8   int main()
9   {
10     const int MAX = 8;   // Max value to store in the stack
11     int count;           // Loop counter
12
13     // Define an STL stack
14     stack< int, vector<int> > iStack;
15
16     // Push values onto the stack.
17     for (count = 2; count < MAX; count += 2)
18     {
19        cout << "Pushing " << count << endl;
20        iStack.push(count);
21     }
22
23     // Display the size of the stack.
24     cout << "The size of the stack is ";
25     cout << iStack.size() << endl;
26
27     // Pop the values off the stack.
28     for (count = 2; count < MAX; count += 2)
29     {
30        cout << "Popping " << iStack.top() << endl;
31        iStack.pop();
32     }
33     return 0;
34  }
```

Program Output

```
Pushing 2
Pushing 4
Pushing 6
The size of the stack is 3
Popping 6
Popping 4
Popping 2
```

 Checkpoint

myprogramminglab   *www.myprogramminglab.com*

18.1   Describe what LIFO means.

18.2   What is the difference between static and dynamic stacks? What advantages do dynamic stacks have over static stacks?

18.3   What are the two primary stack operations? Describe them both.

18.4   What STL types does the STL stack container adapt?

18.4 Introduction to the Queue ADT

CONCEPT: A queue is a data structure that stores and retrieves items in a first-in-first-out manner.

Definition

Like a stack, a queue (pronounced "cue") is a data structure that holds a sequence of elements. A queue, however, provides access to its elements in *first-in, first-out (FIFO)* order. The elements in a queue are processed like customers standing in a grocery checkout line: The first customer in line is the first one served.

Application of Queues

Queue data structures are commonly used in computer operating systems. They are especially important in multiuser/multitasking environments where several users or tasks may be requesting the same resource simultaneously. Printing, for example, is controlled by a queue because only one document may be printed at a time. A queue is used to hold print jobs submitted by users of the system, while the printer services those jobs one at a time.

Communications software also uses queues to hold data received over networks and dial-up connections. Sometimes data is transmitted to a system faster than it can be processed, so it is placed in a queue when it is received.

Static and Dynamic Queues

Just as stacks are implemented as arrays or linked lists, so are queues. Dynamic queues offer the same advantages over static queues that dynamic stacks offer over static stacks. In fact, the primary difference between queues and stacks is the way data elements are accessed in each structure.

Queue Operations

Just like check-out lines in a grocery store, think of queues as having a front and a rear. This is illustrated in Figure 18-8.

Figure 18-8

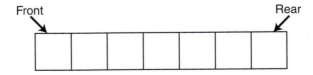

When an element is added to a queue, it is added to the rear. When an element is removed from a queue, it is removed from the front. The two primary queue operations are *enqueuing* and *dequeuing*. To enqueue means to insert an element at the rear of a queue, and to dequeue means to remove an element from the front of a queue. There are several different algorithms for implementing these operations. We will begin by looking at the most simple.

Suppose we have an empty static integer queue that is capable of holding a maximum of three values. With that queue we execute the following enqueue operations.

```
enqueue(3);
enqueue(6);
enqueue(9);
```

Figure 18-9 illustrates the state of the queue after each of these enqueue operations.

Figure 18-9

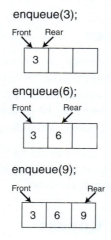

Notice in this example that the front index (which is a variable holding a subscript or perhaps a pointer) always references the same physical element. The rear index moves forward in the array as items are enqueued. Now let's see how dequeue operations are performed. Figure 18-10 illustrates the state of the queue after each of three consecutive dequeue operations.

Figure 18-10

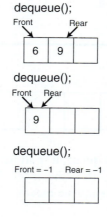

In the dequeuing operation, the element at the front of the queue is removed. This is done by moving all the elements after it forward by one position. After the first dequeue operation, the value 3 is removed from the queue and the value 6 is at the front. After the second dequeue operation, the value 6 is removed and the value 9 is at the front. Notice that when only one value is stored in the queue, that value is at both the front and the rear.

When the last dequeue operation is performed in Figure 18-10, the queue is empty. An empty queue can be signified by setting both front and rear indices to –1.

The problem with this algorithm is its inefficiency. Each time an item is dequeued, the remaining items in the queue are copied forward to their neighboring element. The more items there are in the queue, the longer each successive dequeue operation will take.

Here is one way to overcome the problem: Make both the front and rear indices move in the array. As before, when an item is enqueued, the rear index is moved to make room for it. But in this design, when an item is dequeued, the front index moves by one element toward the rear of the queue. This logically removes the front item from the queue and eliminates the need to copy the remaining items to their neighboring elements.

With this approach, as items are added and removed, the queue gradually "crawls" toward the end of the array. This is illustrated in Figure 18-11. The shaded squares represent the queue elements (between the front and rear).

Figure 18-11

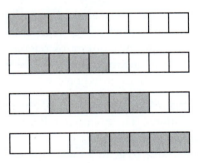

The problem with this approach is that the rear index cannot move beyond the last element in the array. The solution is to think of the array as circular instead of linear. When an item moves past the end of a circular array, it simply "wraps around" to the beginning. For example, consider the queue depicted in Figure 18-12.

Figure 18-12

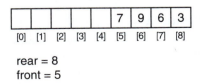

					7	9	6	3
[0]	[1]	[2]	[3]	[4]	[5]	[6]	[7]	[8]

rear = 8
front = 5

The value 3 is at the rear of the queue, and the value 7 is at the front of the queue. Now, suppose an enqueue operation is performed, inserting the value 4 into the queue. Figure 18-13 shows how the rear of the queue wraps around to the beginning of the array.

Figure 18-13

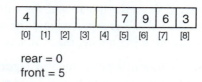

rear = 0
front = 5

So, what is the code for wrapping the rear marker around to the opposite end of the array? One straightforward approach is to use an `if` statement such as

```
if (rear == queueSize - 1)
   rear = 0;
else
   rear++;
```

Another approach is with modular arithmetic:

```
rear = (rear + 1) % queueSize;
```

This statement uses the `%` operator to adjust the value in `rear` to the proper position. Although this approach appears more elegant, the choice of which code to use is yours.

Detecting Full and Empty Queues with Circular Arrays

One problem with the circular array algorithm is that, because both the front and rear indices move through the array, detecting whether the queue is full or empty is a challenge. When the rear index and the front index reference the same element, does it indicate that only one item is in the queue, or that the queue is full? A number of approaches are commonly taken, two of which are listed below.

- When moving the rear index backward, always leave one element empty between it and the front index. The queue is full when the rear index is within two positions of the front index.
- Use a counter variable to keep a total of the number of items in the queue.

Because it might be helpful to keep a count of items in the queue anyway, we will use the second method in our implementation.

A Static Queue Class

The declaration of the `IntQueue` class is as follows:

Contents of `IntQueue.h`

```
1  // Specification file for the IntQueue class
2  #ifndef INTQUEUE_H
3  #define INTQUEUE_H
4
```

```
 5   class IntQueue
 6   {
 7   private:
 8       int *queueArray;   // Points to the queue array
 9       int queueSize;     // The queue size
10       int front;         // Subscript of the queue front
11       int rear;          // Subscript of the queue rear
12       int numItems;      // Number of items in the queue
13   public:
14       // Constructor
15       IntQueue(int);
16
17       // Copy constructor
18       IntQueue(const IntQueue &);
19
20       // Destructor
21       ~IntQueue();
22
23       // Queue operations
24       void enqueue(int);
25       void dequeue(int &);
26       bool isEmpty() const;
27       bool isFull() const;
28       void clear();
29   };
30   #endif
```

Notice that in addition to the operations discussed in this section, the class also declares a member function named `clear`. This function clears the queue by resetting the `front` and `rear` indices, and setting the `numItems` member to 0. The member function definitions are listed below.

Contents of `IntQueue.cpp`

```
 1   // Implementation file for the IntQueue class
 2   #include <iostream>
 3   #include "IntQueue.h"
 4   using namespace std;
 5
 6   //*************************************************************
 7   // This constructor creates an empty queue of a specified size. *
 8   //*************************************************************
 9
10   IntQueue::IntQueue(int s)
11   {
12       queueArray = new int[s];
13       queueSize = s;
14       front = -1;
15       rear = -1;
16       numItems = 0;
17   }
18
```

```
19   //*************************************************************
20   // Copy constructor                                            *
21   //*************************************************************
22
23   IntQueue::IntQueue(const IntQueue &obj)
24   {
25      // Allocate the queue array.
26      queueArray = new int[obj.queueSize];
27
28      // Copy the other object's attributes.
29      queueSize = obj.queueSize;
30      front = obj.front;
31      rear = obj.rear;
32      numItems = obj.numItems;
33
34      // Copy the other object's queue array.
35      for (int count = 0; count < obj.queueSize; count++)
36         queueArray[count] = obj.queueArray[count];
37   }
38
39   //*************************************************************
40   // Destructor                                                  *
41   //*************************************************************
42
43   IntQueue::~IntQueue()
44   {
45      delete [] queueArray;
46   }
47
48   //*************************************************************
49   // Function enqueue inserts a value at the rear of the queue.  *
50   //*************************************************************
51
52   void IntQueue::enqueue(int num)
53   {
54      if (isFull())
55         cout << "The queue is full.\n";
56      else
57      {
58         // Calculate the new rear position
59         rear = (rear + 1) % queueSize;
60         // Insert new item
61         queueArray[rear] = num;
62         // Update item count
63         numItems++;
64      }
65   }
66
67   //*************************************************************
68   // Function dequeue removes the value at the front of the queue *
69   // and copies t into num.                                      *
70   //*************************************************************
71
```

```cpp
72    void IntQueue::dequeue(int &num)
73    {
74       if (isEmpty())
75          cout << "The queue is empty.\n";
76       else
77       {
78          // Move front
79          front = (front + 1) % queueSize;
80          // Retrieve the front item
81          num = queueArray[front];
82          // Update item count
83          numItems--;
84       }
85    }
86
87    //***************************************************************
88    // isEmpty returns true if the queue is empty, otherwise false. *
89    //***************************************************************
90
91    bool IntQueue::isEmpty() const
92    {
93       bool status;
94
95       if (numItems)
96          status = false;
97       else
98          status = true;
99
100      return status;
101   }
102
103   //***************************************************************
104   // isFull returns true if the queue is full, otherwise false.  *
105   //***************************************************************
106
107   bool IntQueue::isFull() const
108   {
109      bool status;
110
111      if (numItems < queueSize)
112         status = false;
113      else
114         status = true;
115
116      return status;
117   }
118
119   //***************************************************************
120   // clear sets the front and rear indices, and sets numItems to 0. *
121   //***************************************************************
122
```

```
123   void IntQueue::clear()
124   {
125      front = queueSize - 1;
126      rear = queueSize - 1;
127      numItems = 0;
128   }
```

Program 18-7 is a driver that demonstrates the IntQueue class.

Program 18-7

```
 1   // This program demonstrates the IntQueue class.
 2   #include <iostream>
 3   #include "IntQueue.h"
 4   using namespace std;
 5
 6   int main()
 7   {
 8      const int MAX_VALUES = 5;   // Max number of values
 9
10      // Create an IntQueue to hold the values.
11      IntQueue iQueue(MAX_VALUES);
12
13      // Enqueue a series of items.
14      cout << "Enqueuing " << MAX_VALUES << " items...\n";
15      for (int x = 0; x < MAX_VALUES; x++)
16         iQueue.enqueue(x);
17
18      // Attempt to enqueue just one more item.
19      cout << "Now attempting to enqueue again...\n";
20      iQueue.enqueue(MAX_VALUES);
21
22      // Dequeue and retrieve all items in the queue
23      cout << "The values in the queue were:\n";
24      while (!iQueue.isEmpty())
25      {
26         int value;
27         iQueue.dequeue(value);
28         cout << value << endl;
29      }
30      return 0;
31   }
```

Program Output

```
Enqueuing 5 items...
Now attempting to enqueue again...
The queue is full.
The values in the queue were:
0
1
2
3
4
```

A Static Queue Template

The queue class shown previously works only with integers. A queue template can be easily designed to work with any data type, as shown by the following example:

Contents of `Queue.h`

```
 1 #ifndef QUEUE_H
 2 #define QUEUE_H
 3 #include <iostream>
 4 using namespace std;
 5
 6 // Stack template
 7 template <class T>
 8 class Queue
 9 {
10 private:
11     T *queueArray;     // Points to the queue array
12     int queueSize;     // The queue size
13     int front;         // Subscript of the queue front
14     int rear;          // Subscript of the queue rear
15     int numItems;      // Number of items in the queue
16 public:
17     // Constructor
18     Queue(int);
19
20     // Copy constructor
21     Queue(const Queue &);
22
23     // Destructor
24     ~Queue();
25
26     // Queue operations
27     void enqueue(T);
28     void dequeue(T &);
29     bool isEmpty() const;
30     bool isFull() const;
31     void clear();
32 };
33
34 //*************************************************************
35 // This constructor creates an empty queue of a specified size. *
36 //*************************************************************
37 template <class T>
38 Queue<T>::Queue(int s)
39 {
40     queueArray = new T[s];
41     queueSize = s;
42     front = -1;
43     rear = -1;
44     numItems = 0;
45 }
46
```

```cpp
47  //**************************************************************
48  // Copy constructor                                            *
49  //**************************************************************
50  template <class T>
51  Queue<T>::Queue(const Queue &obj)
52  {
53     // Allocate the queue array.
54     queueArray = new T[obj.queueSize];
55
56     // Copy the other object's attributes.
57     queueSize = obj.queueSize;
58     front = obj.front;
59     rear = obj.rear;
60     numItems = obj.numItems;
61
62     // Copy the other object's queue array.
63     for (int count = 0; count < obj.queueSize; count++)
64        queueArray[count] = obj.queueArray[count];
65  }
66
67  //**************************************************************
68  // Destructor                                                  *
69  //**************************************************************
70  template <class T>
71  Queue<T>::~Queue()
72  {
73     delete [] queueArray;
74  }
75
76  //**************************************************************
77  // Function enqueue inserts a value at the rear of the queue.  *
78  //**************************************************************
79  template <class T>
80  void Queue<T>::enqueue(T item)
81  {
82     if (isFull())
83        cout << "The queue is full.\n";
84     else
85     {
86        // Calculate the new rear position
87        rear = (rear + 1) % queueSize;
88        // Insert new item
89        queueArray[rear] = item;
90        // Update item count
91        numItems++;
92     }
93  }
94
95  //**************************************************************
96  // Function dequeue removes the value at the front of the queue *
97  // and copies t into num.                                      *
98  //**************************************************************
99  template <class T>
100 void Queue<T>::dequeue(T &item)
```

```
101 {
102    if (isEmpty())
103       cout << "The queue is empty.\n";
104    else
105    {
106       // Move front
107       front = (front + 1) % queueSize;
108       // Retrieve the front item
109       item = queueArray[front];
110       // Update item count
111       numItems--;
112    }
113 }
114
115 //***************************************************************
116 // isEmpty returns true if the queue is empty, otherwise false. *
117 //***************************************************************
118 template <class T>
119 bool Queue<T>::isEmpty() const
120 {
121    bool status;
122
123    if (numItems)
124       status = false;
125    else
126       status = true;
127
128    return status;
129 }
130
131 //***************************************************************
132 // isFull returns true if the queue is full, otherwise false.   *
133 //***************************************************************
134 template <class T>
135 bool Queue<T>::isFull() const
136 {
137    bool status;
138
139    if (numItems < queueSize)
140       status = false;
141    else
142       status = true;
143
144    return status;
145 }
146
147 //***************************************************************
148 // clear sets the front and rear indices, and sets numItems to 0. *
149 //***************************************************************
150 template <class T>
151 void Queue<T>::clear()
152 {
153    front = queueSize - 1;
154    rear = queueSize - 1;
155    numItems = 0;
156 }
157 #endif
```

Program 18-8 demonstrates the `Queue` template. It creates a queue that can hold strings, and then prompts the user to enter a series of names that are enqueued. The program then dequeues all of the names and displays them.

Program 18-8

```
 1  // This program demonstrates the Queue template.
 2  #include <iostream>
 3  #include <string>
 4  #include "Queue.h"
 5  using namespace std;
 6
 7  const int QUEUE_SIZE = 5;
 8
 9  int main()
10  {
11      string name;
12
13      // Create a Queue.
14      Queue<string> queue(QUEUE_SIZE);
15
16      // Enqueue some names.
17      for (int count = 0; count < QUEUE_SIZE; count++)
18      {
19          cout << "Enter a name: ";
20          getline(cin, name);
21          queue.enqueue(name);
22      }
23
24      // Dequeue the names and display them.
25      cout << "\nHere are the names you entered:\n";
26      for (int count = 0; count < QUEUE_SIZE; count++)
27      {
28          queue.dequeue(name);
29          cout << name << endl;
30      }
31      return 0;
32  }
```

Program Output with Example Input Shown in Bold

```
Enter a name: Chris [Enter]
Enter a name: Kathryn [Enter]
Enter a name: Alfredo [Enter]
Enter a name: Lori [Enter]
Enter a name: Kelly [Enter]

Here are the names you entered:
Chris
Kathryn
Alfredo
Lori
Kelly
```

18.5 Dynamic Queues

CONCEPT: A queue may be implemented as a linked list, and expand or shrink with each enqueue or dequeue operation.

Dynamic queues, which are built around linked lists, are much more intuitive to understand than static queues. A dynamic queue starts as an empty linked list. With the first enqueue operation, a node is added, which is pointed to by the `front` and `rear` pointers. As each new item is added to the queue, a new node is added to the rear of the list, and the `rear` pointer is updated to point to the new node. As each item is dequeued, the node pointed to by the `front` pointer is deleted, and `front` is made to point to the next node in the list. Figure 18-14 shows the structure of a dynamic queue.

Figure 18-14

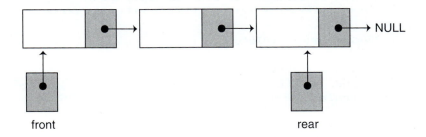

A dynamic integer queue class is listed here.

Contents of `DynIntQueue.h`

```
1   #ifndef DYNINTQUEUE_H
2   #define DYNINTQUEUE_H
3
4   class DynIntQueue
5   {
6   private:
7      // Structure for the queue nodes
8      struct QueueNode
9      {
10        int value;       // Value in a node
11        QueueNode *next; // Pointer to the next node
12     };
13
14     QueueNode *front;  // The front of the queue
15     QueueNode *rear;   // The rear of the queue
16     int numItems;      // Number of items in the queue
17  public:
18     // Constructor
19     DynIntQueue();
20
```

```
21       // Destructor
22       ~DynIntQueue();
23
24       // Queue operations
25       void enqueue(int);
26       void dequeue(int &);
27       bool isEmpty() const;
28       bool isFull() const;
29       void clear();
30  };
31  #endif
```

Contents of `DynIntQueue.cpp`

```
 1  #include <iostream>
 2  #include "DynIntQueue.h"
 3  using namespace std;
 4
 5  //*******************************************
 6  // The constructor creates an empty queue.   *
 7  //*******************************************
 8
 9  DynIntQueue::DynIntQueue()
10  {
11      front = NULL;
12      rear = NULL;
13      numItems = 0;
14  }
15
16  //*******************************************
17  // Destructor                               *
18  //*******************************************
19
20  DynIntQueue::~DynIntQueue()
21  {
22      clear();
23  }
24
25  //*******************************************
26  // Function enqueue inserts the value in num *
27  // at the rear of the queue.                *
28  //*******************************************
29
30  void DynIntQueue::enqueue(int num)
31  {
32      QueueNode *newNode;
33
34      // Create a new node and store num there.
35      newNode = new QueueNode;
36      newNode->value = num;
37      newNode->next = NULL;
38
39      // Adjust front and rear as necessary.
40      if (isEmpty())
41      {
42          front = newNode;
43          rear = newNode;
```

```
44       }
45    else
46    {
47       rear->next = newNode;
48       rear = newNode;
49    }
50
51    // Update numItems.
52    numItems++;
53 }
54
55 //**********************************************
56 // Function dequeue removes the value at the   *
57 // front of the queue, and copies it into num. *
58 //**********************************************
59
60 void DynIntQueue::dequeue(int &num)
61 {
62    QueueNode *temp;
63
64    if (isEmpty())
65    {
66       cout << "The queue is empty.\n";
67    }
68    else
69    {
70       // Save the front node value in num.
71       num = front->value;
72
73       // Remove the front node and delete it.
74       temp = front;
75       front = front->next;
76       delete temp;
77
78       // Update numItems.
79       numItems--;
80    }
81 }
82
83 //**********************************************
84 // Function isEmpty returns true if the queue *
85 // is empty, and false otherwise.             *
86 //**********************************************
87
88 bool DynIntQueue::isEmpty() const
89 {
90     bool status;
91
92    if (numItems > 0)
93       status = false;
94    else
95       status = true;
96    return status;
97 }
98
```

```
 99  //*******************************************
100  // Function clear dequeues all the elements  *
101  // in the queue.                             *
102  //*******************************************
103
104  void DynIntQueue::clear()
105  {
106      int value;    // Dummy variable for dequeue
107
108      while(!isEmpty())
109          dequeue(value);
110  }
```

Program 18-9 is a driver that demonstrates the DynIntQueue class.

Program 18-9

```
 1   // This program demonstrates the DynIntQueue class.
 2   #include <iostream>
 3   #include "DynIntQueue.h"
 4   using namespace std;
 5
 6   int main()
 7   {
 8       const int MAX_VALUES = 5;
 9
10       // Create a DynIntQueue object.
11       DynIntQueue iQueue;
12
13       // Enqueue a series of numbers.
14       cout << "Enqueuing " << MAX_VALUES << " items...\n";
15       for (int x = 0; x < 5; x++)
16           iQueue.enqueue(x);
17
18       // Dequeue and retrieve all numbers in the queue
19       cout << "The values in the queue were:\n";
20       while (!iQueue.isEmpty())
21       {
22           int value;
23           iQueue.dequeue(value);
24           cout << value << endl;
25       }
26       return 0;
27   }
```

Program Output
```
Enqueuing 5 items...
The values in the queue were:
0
1
2
3
4
```

A Dynamic Queue Template

The dynamic queue class shown previously in this chapter works only with integers. A dynamic queue template can be easily designed to work with any data type, as shown by the following example:

Contents of `DynamicQueue.h`

```cpp
 1 #ifndef DYNAMICQUEUE_H
 2 #define DYNAMICQUEUE_H
 3 #include <iostream>
 4 using namespace std;
 5
 6 // DynamicQueue template
 7 template <class T>
 8 class DynamicQueue
 9 {
10 private:
11    // Structure for the queue nodes
12    struct QueueNode
13    {
14       T value;          // Value in a node
15       QueueNode *next; // Pointer to the next node
16    };
17
18    QueueNode *front;  // The front of the queue
19    QueueNode *rear;   // The rear of the queue
20    int numItems;       // Number of items in the queue
21 public:
22    // Constructor
23    DynamicQueue();
24
25    // Destructor
26    ~DynamicQueue();
27
28    // Queue operations
29    void enqueue(T);
30    void dequeue(T &);
31    bool isEmpty() const;
32    bool isFull() const;
33    void clear();
34 };
35
36 //*******************************************
37 // The constructor creates an empty queue.   *
38 //*******************************************
39 template <class T>
40 DynamicQueue<T>::DynamicQueue()
41 {
42    front = NULL;
43    rear = NULL;
44    numItems = 0;
45 }
46
```

```
47  //**********************************************
48  // Destructor                                  *
49  //**********************************************
50  template <class T>
51  DynamicQueue<T>::~DynamicQueue()
52  {
53     clear();
54  }
55
56  //**********************************************
57  // Function enqueue inserts the value in num *
58  // at the rear of the queue.                   *
59  //**********************************************
60  template <class T>
61  void DynamicQueue<T>::enqueue(T item)
62  {
63     QueueNode *newNode;
64
65     // Create a new node and store num there.
66     newNode = new QueueNode;
67     newNode->value = item;
68     newNode->next = NULL;
69
70     // Adjust front and rear as necessary.
71     if (isEmpty())
72     {
73        front = newNode;
74        rear = newNode;
75     }
76     else
77     {
78        rear->next = newNode;
79        rear = newNode;
80     }
81
82     // Update numItems.
83     numItems++;
84  }
85
86  //************************************************
87  // Function dequeue removes the value at the    *
88  // front of the queue, and copies it into num.  *
89  //************************************************
90  template <class T>
91  void DynamicQueue<T>::dequeue(T &item)
92  {
93     QueueNode *temp;
94
95     if (isEmpty())
96     {
97        cout << "The queue is empty.\n";
98     }
99     else
100    {
101       // Save the front node value in num.
102       item = front->value;
```

```
103
104         // Remove the front node and delete it.
105         temp = front;
106         front = front->next;
107         delete temp;
108
109         // Update numItems.
110         numItems--;
111     }
112 }
113
114 //*********************************************
115 // Function isEmpty returns true if the queue *
116 // is empty, and false otherwise.             *
117 //*********************************************
118 template <class T>
119 bool DynamicQueue<T>::isEmpty() const
120 {
121     bool status;
122
123     if (numItems > 0)
124         status = false;
125     else
126         status = true;
127     return status;
128 }
129
130 //*********************************************
131 // Function clear dequeues all the elements   *
132 // in the queue.                              *
133 //*********************************************
134 template <class T>
135 void DynamicQueue<T>::clear()
136 {
137     T value;    // Dummy variable for dequeue
138
139     while(!isEmpty())
140         dequeue(value);
141 }
142 #endif
```

Program 18-10 demonstrates the DynamicQueue template. This program is a modification of Program 18-8. It creates a queue that can hold strings, and then prompts the user to enter a series of names that are enqueued. The program then dequeues all of the names and displays them. (The program's output is the same as that of Program 18-8.)

Program 18-10

```
1 // This program demonstrates the DynamicQueue template.
2 #include <iostream>
3 #include <string>
4 #include "DynamicQueue.h"
5 using namespace std;
6
```

(program continues)

Program 18-10   *(continued)*

```
 7 const int QUEUE_SIZE = 5;
 8
 9 int main()
10 {
11     string name;
12
13     // Create a Queue.
14     DynamicQueue<string> queue;
15
16     // Enqueue some names.
17     for (int count = 0; count < QUEUE_SIZE; count++)
18     {
19         cout << "Enter a name: ";
20         getline(cin, name);
21         queue.enqueue(name);
22     }
23
24     // Dequeue the names and display them.
25     cout << "\nHere are the names you entered:\n";
26     for (int count = 0; count < QUEUE_SIZE; count++)
27     {
28         queue.dequeue(name);
29         cout << name << endl;
30     }
31     return 0;
32 }
```

Program Output
(Same as Program 18-8's output.)

18.6   The STL deque and queue Containers

CONCEPT: The Standard Template Library provides two containers, deque and
queue, for implementing queue-like data structures.

In this section we will examine two ADTs offered by the Standard Template Library:
deque and queue. A deque (pronounced "deck" or "deek") is a double-ended queue. It is
similar to a vector, but allows efficient access to values at both the front and the rear. The
queue ADT is like the stack ADT: It is actually a container adapter.

The deque Container

Think of the deque container as a vector that provides quick access to the element at its
front as well as at the back. (Like vector, deque also provides access to its elements with
the [ ] operator.)

Programs that use the deque ADT must include the deque header. Because we are concentrating on its queue-like characteristics, we will focus our attention on the push_back, pop_front, and front member functions. Table 18-4 describes them.

Table 18-4

Member Function	Examples and Description
push_back	`iDeque.push_back();` Accepts as an argument a value to be inserted into the deque. The argument is inserted after the last element. (Pushed onto the back of the deque.)
pop_front	`iDeque.pop_front();` Removes the first element of the deque.
front	`cout << iDeque.front() << endl;` front returns a reference to the first element of the deque.

Program 18-11 demonstrates the deque container.

Program 18-11

```
1   // This program demonstrates the STL deque container.
2   #include <iostream>
3   #include <deque>
4   using namespace std;
5
6   int main()
7   {
8      const int MAX = 8;    // Max value
9      int count;            // Loop counter
10
11     // Create a deque object.
12     deque<int> iDeque;
13
14     // Enqueue a series of numbers.
15     cout << "I will now enqueue items...\n";
16     for (count = 2; count < MAX; count += 2)
17     {
18        cout << "Pushing " << count << endl;
19        iDeque.push_back(count);
20     }
21
22     // Dequeue and display the numbers.
23     cout << "I will now dequeue items...\n";
24     for (count = 2; count < MAX; count += 2)
25     {
26        cout << "Popping "<< iDeque.front() << endl;
27        iDeque.pop_front();
28     }
29     return 0;
30  }
```

(program output continues)

Program 18-11 *(continued)*

Program Output
```
I will now enqueue items...
Pushing 2
Pushing 4
Pushing 6
I will now dequeue items...
Popping 2
Popping 4
Popping 6
```

The queue Container Adapter

VideoNote

**Storing
Objects in an
STL queue**

The queue container adapter can be built upon vectors, lists, or deques. By default, it uses deque as its base.

The insertion and removal operations supported by queue are the same as those supported by the stack ADT: push, pop, and top. There are differences in their behavior, however. The queue version of push always inserts an element at the rear of the queue. The queue version of pop always removes an element from the structure's front. The top function returns the value of the element at the front of the queue.

Program 18-12 demonstrates a queue. Because the definition of the queue does not specify which type of container is being adapted, the queue will be built on a deque.

Program 18-12

```cpp
1   // This program demonstrates the STL queue container adapter.
2   #include <iostream>
3   #include <queue>
4   using namespace std;
5
6   int main()
7   {
8      const int MAX = 8;   // Max value
9      int count;           // Loop counter
10
11     // Define a queue object.
12     queue<int> iQueue;
13
14     // Enqueue a series of numbers.
15     cout << "I will now enqueue items...\n";
16     for (count = 2; count < MAX; count += 2)
17     {
18        cout << "Pushing "<< count << endl;
19        iQueue.push(count);
20     }
21
22     // Dequeue and display the numbers.
23     cout << "I will now dequeue items...\n";
24     for (count = 2; count < MAX; count += 2)
```

```
25      {
26          cout << "Popping "<< iQueue.front() << endl;
27          iQueue.pop();
28      }
29      return 0;
30  }
```

Program Output

```
I will now enqueue items...
Pushing 2
Pushing 4
Pushing 6
I will now dequeue items...
Popping 2
Popping 4
Popping 6
```

Review Questions and Exercises

Short Answer

1. What does LIFO mean?

2. What element is always retrieved from a stack?

3. What is the difference between a static stack and a dynamic stack?

4. Describe two operations that all stacks perform.

5. Describe two operations that static stacks must perform.

6. The STL `stack` is considered a container adapter. What does that mean?

7. What types may the STL `stack` be based on? By default, what type is an STL `stack` based on?

8. What does FIFO mean?

9. When an element is added to a queue, where is it added?

10. When an element is removed from a queue, where is it removed from?

11. Describe two operations that all queues perform.

12. What two queue-like containers does the STL offer?

Fill-in-the-Blank

13. The _____ element saved onto a stack is the first one retrieved.

14. The two primary stack operations are _____ and _____.

15. _____ stacks and queues are implemented as arrays.

16. _____ stacks and queues are implemented as linked lists.

17. The STL stack container is an adapter for the _____, _____, and _____ STL containers.

18. The _____ element saved in a queue is the first one retrieved.

19. The two primary queue operations are _____ and _____.

20. The two ADTs in the Standard Template Library that exhibit queue-like behavior are _____ and _____.

21. The queue ADT, by default, adapts the _____ container.

Algorithm Workbench

22. Suppose the following operations are performed on an empty stack:

```
push(0);
push(9);
push(12);
push(1);
```

Insert numbers in the following diagram to show what will be stored in the static stack after the operations above have executed.

```
┌─────┐  Top of Stack
│     │
├─────┤
│     │
├─────┤
│     │
├─────┤
│     │
└─────┘  Bottom of Stack
```

23. Suppose the following operations are performed on an empty stack:

```
push(8);
push(7);
pop();
push(19);
push(21);
pop();
```

Insert numbers in the following diagram to show what will be stored in the static stack after the operations above have executed.

```
┌─────┐  Top of Stack
│     │
├─────┤
│     │
├─────┤
│     │
├─────┤
│     │
└─────┘  Bottom of Stack
```

24. Suppose the following operations are performed on an empty queue:

```
enqueue(5);
enqueue(7);
enqueue(9);
enqueue(12);
```

Insert numbers in the following diagram to show what will be stored in the static stack after the operations above have executed.

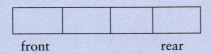

front   rear

25. Suppose the following operations are performed on an empty queue:

```
enqueue(5);
enqueue(7);
dequeue();
enqueue(9);
enqueue(12);
dequeue();
enqueue(10);
```

Insert numbers in the following diagram to show what will be stored in the static stack after the operations above have executed.

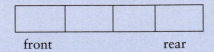

front   rear

26. What problem is overcome by using a circular array for a static queue?

27. Write two different code segments that may be used to wrap an index back around to the beginning of an array when it moves past the end of the array. Use an `if/else` statement in one segment and modular arithmetic in the other.

True or False

28. T   F   A static stack or queue is built around an array.

29. T   F   The size of a dynamic stack or queue must be known in advance.

30. T   F   The push operation inserts an element at the end of a stack.

31. T   F   The pop operation retrieves an element from the top of a stack.

32. T   F   The STL stack container's pop operation does not retrieve the top element of the stack, it just removes it.

Programming Challenges

Visit www.myprogramminglab.com to complete many of these Programming Challenges online and get instant feedback.

1. **Static Stack Template**

   Write your own version of a class template that will create a static stack of any data type. Demonstrate the class with a driver program.

2. **Dynamic Stack Template**

   Write your own version of a class template that will create a dynamic stack of any data type. Demonstrate the class with a driver program.

3. **Static Queue Template**

Write your own version of a class template that will create a static queue of any data type. Demonstrate the class with a driver program.

4. **Dynamic Queue Template**

Write your own version of a class template that will create a dynamic queue of any data type. Demonstrate the class with a driver program.

5. **Error Testing**

The `DynIntStack` and `DynIntQueue` classes shown in this chapter are abstract data types using a dynamic stack and dynamic queue, respectively. The classes do not currently test for memory allocation errors. Modify the classes so they determine whether new nodes cannot be created by handling the `bad_alloc` exception.

 NOTE: If you have already done Programming Challenges 2 and 4, modify the templates you created.

6. **Dynamic String Stack**

Design a class that stores strings on a dynamic stack. The strings should not be fixed in length. Demonstrate the class with a driver program.

7. **Dynamic MathStack**

The `MathStack` class shown in this chapter only has two member functions: `add` and `sub`. Write the following additional member functions:

Function	Description
`mult`	Pops the top two values off the stack, multiplies them, and pushes their product onto the stack.
`div`	Pops the top two values off the stack, divides the second value by the first, and pushes the quotient onto the stack.
`addAll`	Pops all values off the stack, adds them, and pushes their sum onto the stack.
`multAll`	Pops all values off the stack, multiplies them, and pushes their product onto the stack.

Demonstrate the class with a driver program.

8. **Dynamic MathStack Template**

Currently the `MathStack` class is derived from the `IntStack` class. Modify it so it is a template, derived from the template you created in Programming Challenge 2.

9. **File Reverser**

Write a program that opens a text file and reads its contents into a stack of characters. The program should then pop the characters from the stack and save them in a second text file. The order of the characters saved in the second file should be the reverse of their order in the first file.

10. **File Filter**

    Write a program that opens a text file and reads its contents into a queue of characters. The program should then dequeue each character, convert it to uppercase, and store it in a second file.

11. **File Compare**

    VideoNote
    Solving the File Compare Problem

    Write a program that opens two text files and reads their contents into two separate queues. The program should then determine whether the files are identical by comparing the characters in the queues. When two nonidentical characters are encountered, the program should display a message indicating that the files are not the same. If both queues contain the same set of characters, a message should be displayed indicating that the files are identical.

12. **Inventory Bin Stack**

    Design an inventory class that stores the following members:

`serialNum:`	An integer that holds a part's serial number.
`manufactDate:`	A member that holds the date the part was manufactured.
`lotNum:`	An integer that holds the part's lot number.

    The class should have appropriate member functions for storing data into, and retrieving data from, these members.

    Next, design a stack class that can hold objects of the class described above. If you wish, you may use the template you designed in Programming Challenge 1 or 2.

    Last, design a program that uses the stack class described above. The program should have a loop that asks the user if he or she wishes to add a part to inventory, or take a part from inventory. The loop should repeat until the user is finished.

    If the user wishes to add a part to inventory, the program should ask for the serial number, date of manufacture, and lot number. The data should be stored in an inventory object, and pushed onto the stack.

    If the user wishes to take a part from inventory, the program should pop the top-most part from the stack and display the contents of its member variables.

    When the user finishes the program, it should display the contents of the member values of all the objects that remain on the stack.

13. **Inventory Bin Queue**

    Modify the program you wrote for Programming Challenge 12 so it uses a queue instead of a stack. Compare the order in which the parts are removed from the bin for each program.

14. **Balanced Parentheses**

    A string of characters has balanced parentheses if each right parenthesis occurring in the string is matched with a preceding left parenthesis, in the same way that each right brace in a C++ program is matched with a preceding left brace. Write a program that uses a stack to determine whether a string entered at the keyboard has balanced parentheses.

15. **Balanced Multiple Delimiters**

A string may use more than one type of delimiter to bracket information into "blocks." For example, A string may use braces { }, parentheses ( ), and brackets [ ] as delimiters. A string is properly delimited if each right delimiter is matched with a preceding left delimiter of the same type in such a way that either the resulting blocks of information are disjoint, or one of them is completely nested within the other. Write a program that uses a single stack to check whether a string containing braces, parentheses, and brackets is properly delimited.

19 Recursion

TOPICS

19.1 Introduction to Recursion

CONCEPT: A recursive function is one that calls itself.

You have seen instances of functions calling other functions. Function A can call function B, which can then call function C. It's also possible for a function to call itself. A function that calls itself is a *recursive function*. Look at this message function:

```
void message()
{
    cout << "This is a recursive function.\n";
    message();
}
```

This function displays the string "This is a recursive function.\n", and then calls itself. Each time it calls itself, the cycle is repeated. Can you see a problem with the function?

There's no way to stop the recursive calls. This function is like an infinite loop because there is no code to stop it from repeating.

> **NOTE:** The function example `message` will eventually cause the program to crash. Do you remember learning in Chapter 18 that the system stores temporary data on a stack each time a function is called? Eventually, these recursive function calls will use up all available stack memory, and cause it to overflow.

Like a loop, a recursive function must have some method to control the number of times it repeats. The following is a modification of the `message` function. It passes an integer argument, that holds the number of times the function is to call itself.

```
void message(int times)
{
   if (times > 0)
   {
      cout << "This is a recursive function.\n";
      message(times - 1);
   }
}
```

This function contains an `if` statement that controls the repetition. As long as the `times` argument is greater than zero, it will display the message and call itself again. Each time it calls itself, it passes `times - 1` as the argument. For example, let's say a program calls the function with the following statement:

```
message(5);
```

The argument, 5, will cause the function to call itself five times. The first time the function is called, the `if` statement will display the message and then call itself with 4 as the argument. Figure 19-1 illustrates this:

Figure 19-1

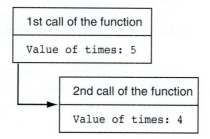

The diagram in Figure 19-1 illustrates two separate calls of the `message` function. Each time the function is called, a new instance of the `times` parameter is created in memory. The first time the function is called, the `times` parameter is set to 5. When the function calls itself, a new instance of `times` is created, and the value 4 is passed into it. This cycle repeats until, finally, zero is passed to the function. This is illustrated in Figure 19-2.

Figure 19-2

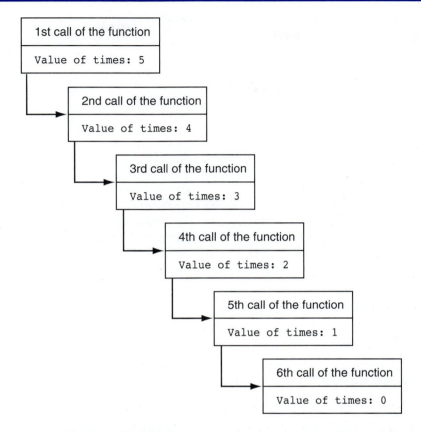

As you can see from Figure 19-2 the function is called a total of six times. The first time it is called from `main`, and the other five times it calls itself, so the *depth of recursion* is five. When the function reaches its sixth call, the `times` parameter will be set to 0. At that point, the `if` statement's conditional expression will be false, so the function will return. Control of the program will return from the sixth instance of the function to the point in the fifth instance directly after the recursive function call:

```
void message (int times)
{
    if (times > 0
    {
        cout << "This is a recursive function.\n"
        message (times - 1);       ◄──────── Recursive call
    }
}  ◄──────── Control returns here from the recursive call,
             causing the function to return.
```

Because there are no more statements to be executed after the function call, the fifth instance of the function returns control of the program back to the fourth instance. This repeats until all instances of the function return. Program 19-1 demonstrates the recursive `message` function.

Program 19-1

```
 1   // This program demonstrates a simple recursive function.
 2   #include <iostream>
 3   using namespace std;
 4
 5   // Function prototype
 6   void message(int);
 7
 8   int main()
 9   {
10      message(5);
11      return 0;
12   }
13
14   //*********************************************************
15   // Definition of function Message. If the value in times is *
16   // greater than 0, the message is displayed and the        *
17   // function is recursively called with the argument        *
18   // times - 1.                                              *
19   //*********************************************************
20
21   void message(int times)
22   {
23      if (times > 0)
24      {
25         cout << "This is a recursive function.\n";
26         message(times - 1);
27      }
28   }
```

Program Output

```
This is a recursive function.
This is a recursive function.
This is a recursive function.
This is a recursive function.
This is a recursive function.
```

To further illustrate the inner workings of this recursive function, let's look at another version of the program. In Program 19-2, a message is displayed each time the function is entered, and another message is displayed just before the function returns.

Program 19-2

```
 1   // This program demonstrates a simple recursive function.
 2   #include <iostream>
 3   using namespace std;
 4
 5   // Function prototype
 6   void message(int);
 7
```

```
 8   int main()
 9   {
10      message(5);
11      return 0;
12   }
13
14   //************************************************************
15   // Definition of function message. If the value in times is  *
16   // greater than 0, the message is displayed and the function *
17   // is recursively called with the argument times - 1.        *
18   //************************************************************
19
20   void message(int times)
21   {
22      cout << "message called with " << times << " in times.\n";
23
24      if (times > 0)
25      {
26         cout << "This is a recursive function.\n";
27         message(times - 1);
28      }
29
30      cout << "message returning with " << times;
31      cout << " in times.\n";
32   }
```

Program Output
```
message called with 5 in times.
This is a recursive function.
message called with 4 in times.
This is a recursive function.
message called with 3 in times.
This is a recursive function.
message called with 2 in times.
This is a recursive function.
message called with 1 in times.
This is a recursive function.
message called with 0 in times.
message returning with 0 in times.
message returning with 1 in times.
message returning with 2 in times.
message returning with 3 in times.
message returning with 4 in times.
message returning with 5 in times.
```

19.2 Solving Problems with Recursion

CONCEPT: A problem can be solved with recursion if it can be broken down into successive smaller problems that are identical to the overall problem.

Programs 19-1 and 19-2 in the previous section show simple demonstrations of *how* a recursive function works. But these examples don't show us *why* we would want to write a recursive function. Recursion can be a powerful tool for solving repetitive problems and is an important topic in upper-level computer science courses. What might not be clear to you yet is how to use recursion to solve a problem.

First, it should be noted that recursion is never absolutely required to solve a problem. Any problem that can be solved recursively can also be solved iteratively, with a loop. In fact, recursive algorithms are usually less efficient than iterative algorithms. This is because a function call requires several actions to be performed by the C++ runtime system. These actions include allocating memory for parameters and local variables, and storing the address of the program location where control returns after the function terminates. These actions, which are sometimes referred to as *overhead*, take place with each function call. Such overhead is not necessary with a loop.

Some repetitive problems, however, are more easily solved with recursion than with iteration. Where an iterative algorithm might result in faster execution time, the programmer might be able to design a recursive algorithm faster.

In general, a recursive function works like this:

- If the problem can be solved now, without recursion, then the function solves it and returns.
- If the problem cannot be solved now, then the function reduces it to a smaller but similar problem and calls itself to solve the smaller problem.

VideoNote
Reducing a Problem with Recursion

In order to apply this approach, we first identify at least one case in which the problem can be solved without recursion. This is known as the *base case*. Second, we determine a way to solve the problem in all other circumstances using recursion. This is called the *recursive case*. In the recursive case, we must always reduce the problem to a smaller version of the original problem. By reducing the problem with each recursive call, the base case will eventually be reached and the recursion will stop.

Example: Using Recursion to Calculate the Factorial of a Number

Let's take an example from mathematics to examine an application of recursion. In mathematics, the notation $n!$ represents the factorial of the number n. The factorial of a non-negative number can be defined by the following rules:

If $n = 0$ then $n! = 1$
If $n > 0$ then $n! = 1 \times 2 \times 3 \times \ldots \times n$

Let's replace the notation *n*! with factorial(*n*), which looks a bit more like computer code, and rewrite these rules as

If *n* = 0 then   factorial(*n*) = 1
If *n* > 0 then   factorial(*n*) = 1 × 2 × 3 × ... × *n*

These rules state that when *n* is 0, its factorial is 1. When *n* is greater than 0, its factorial is the product of all the positive integers from 1 up to *n*. For instance, factorial(6) is calculated as 1 × 2 × 3 × 4 × 5 × 6.

When designing a recursive algorithm to calculate the factorial of any number, we first identify the base case, which is the part of the calculation that we can solve without recursion. That is the case where *n* is equal to 0:

If *n* = 0 then   factorial(*n*) = 1

This tells how to solve the problem when *n* is equal to 0, but what do we do when *n* is greater than 0? That is the recursive case, or the part of the problem that we use recursion to solve. This is how we express it:

If *n* > 0 then   factorial(*n*) = *n* × factorial(*n* − 1)

This states that if *n* is greater than 0, the factorial of *n* is *n* times the factorial of *n* − 1. Notice how the recursive call works on a reduced version of the problem, *n* − 1. So, our recursive rule for calculating the factorial of a number might look like this:

If *n* = 0 then   factorial(*n*) = 1
If *n* > 0 then   factorial(*n*) = *n* × factorial(*n* − 1)

The following pseudocode shows how we might implement the factorial algorithm as a recursive function:

```
factorial(n)
   If n is 0 then
      return 1.
   else
      return n times the factorial of n - 1.
end factorial.
```

Here is the C++ code for such a function:

```cpp
int factorial(int n)
{
   if (n == 0)
      return 1;                        // Base case
   else
      return n * factorial(n - 1);  // Recursive case
}
```

Program 19-3 demonstrates the recursive factorial function.

Program 19-3

```
 1   // This program demonstrates a recursive function to
 2   // calculate the factorial of a number.
 3   #include <iostream>
 4   using namespace std;
 5
 6   // Function prototype
 7   int factorial(int);
 8
 9   int main()
10   {
11      int number;
12
13      // Get a number from the user.
14      cout << "Enter an integer value and I will display\n";
15      cout << "its factorial: ";
16      cin >> number;
17
18      // Display the factorial of the number.
19      cout << "The factorial of " << number << " is ";
20      cout << factorial(number) << endl;
21      return 0;
22   }
23
24   //*********************************************************
25   // Definition of factorial. A recursive function to calculate *
26   // the factorial of the parameter n.                          *
27   //*********************************************************
28
29   int factorial(int n)
30   {
31      if (n == 0)
32         return 1;                         // Base case
33      else
34         return n * factorial(n - 1);  // Recursive case
35   }
```

Program Output with Example Input Shown in Bold
```
Enter an integer value and I will display
its factorial: 4 [Enter]
The factorial of 4 is 24
```

In the example run of the program, the `factorial` function is called with the argument 4 passed into n. Because n is not equal to 0, the `if` statement's `else` clause executes the following statement, in line 34:

```
return n * factorial(n - 1);
```

Although this is a `return` statement, it does not immediately return. Before the return value can be determined, the value of `factorial(num - 1)` must be determined. The `factorial` function is called recursively until the fifth call, in which the n parameter will be set to zero. The diagram in Figure 19-3 illustrates the value of n and the return value during each call of the function.

Figure 19-3

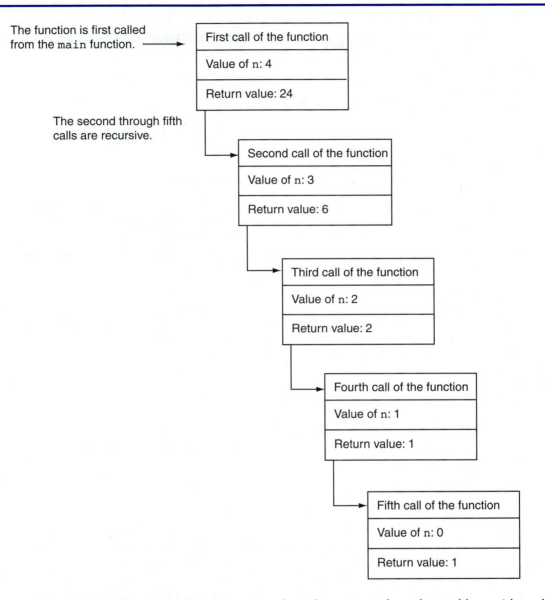

The function is first called from the `main` function. →

First call of the function

Value of n: 4

Return value: 24

The second through fifth calls are recursive.

Second call of the function

Value of n: 3

Return value: 6

Third call of the function

Value of n: 2

Return value: 2

Fourth call of the function

Value of n: 1

Return value: 1

Fifth call of the function

Value of n: 0

Return value: 1

This diagram illustrates why a recursive algorithm must reduce the problem with each recursive call. Eventually the recursion has to stop in order for a solution to be reached. If each recursive call works on a smaller version of the problem, then the recursive calls work toward the base case. The base case does not require recursion, so it stops the chain of recursive calls.

Usually, a problem is reduced by making the value of one or more parameters smaller with each recursive call. In our `factorial` function, the value of the parameter n gets closer to 0 with each recursive call. When the parameter reaches 0, the function returns a value without making another recursive call.

Example: Using Recursion to Count Characters

Let's look at another simple example of recursion. The following function counts the number of times a specific character appears in a string. The line numbers are from Program 19-4, which we will examine momentarily.

```
29   int numChars(char search, string str, int subscript)
30   {
31      if (subscript >= str.length())
32      {
33         // Base case: The end of the string is reached.
34         return 0;
35      }
36      else if (str[subscript] == search)
37      {
38         // Recursive case: A matching character was found.
39         // Return 1 plus the number of times the search
40         // character appears in the rest of the string.
41         return 1 + numChars(search, str, subscript+1);
42      }
43      else
44      {
45         // Recursive case: A character that does not match the
46         // search character was found. Return the number of times
47         // the search character appears in the rest of the string.
48         return numChars(search, str, subscript+1);
49      }
50   }
```

The function's parameters are

- `search`: The character to be searched for and counted
- `str`: a `string` object containing the string to be searched
- `subscript`: The starting subscript for the search

When this function examines a character in the string, three possibilities exist:

- The end of the string has been reached. This is the base case because there are no more characters to search.
- A character that matches the search character is found. This is a recursive case because we still have to search the rest of the string.
- A character that does not match the search character is found. This is also a recursive case because we still have to search the rest of the string.

Let's take a closer look at the code. The first `if` statement, in line 31, determines whether the end of the string has been reached:

```
if (subscript >= str.length())
```

Reaching the end of the string is the base case of the problem. If the end of the string has been reached, the function returns 0, indicating that 0 matching characters were found. Otherwise, the following `else if` clause, in lines 36 through 42, is executed:

```
    else if (str[subscript] == search)
    {
        // Recursive case: A matching character was found.
        // Return 1 plus the number of times the search
        // character appears in the rest of the string.
        return 1 + numChars(search, str, subscript+1);
    }
```

If str[subscript] contains the search character, then we have found one matching character. But because we have not reached the end of the string, we must continue to search the rest of the string for more matching characters. So, at this point the function performs a recursive call. The return statement returns 1 plus the number of times the search character appears in the string, starting at subscript+1. In essence, this statement returns 1 plus the number of times the search character appears in the rest of the string.

Finally, if str[subscript] does not contain the search character, the following else clause in lines 43 through 49 is executed:

```
    else
    {
        // Recursive case: A character that does not match the
        // search character was found. Return the number of times
        // the search character appears in the rest of the string.
        return numChars(search, str, subscript+1);
    }
```

The return statement in line 48 makes a recursive call to search the remainder of the string. In essence, this code returns the number of times the search character appears in the rest of the string. Program 19-4 demonstrates the function.

Program 19-4

```
 1  // This program demonstrates a recursive function for counting
 2  // the number of times a character appears in a string.
 3  #include <iostream>
 4  #include <string>
 5  using namespace std;
 6
 7  // Function prototype
 8  int numChars(char, string, int);
 9
10  int main()
11  {
12      string str = "abcddddef";
13
14      // Display the number of times the letter
15      // 'd' appears in the string.
16      cout << "The letter d appears "
17          << numChars('d', str, 0) << " times.\n";
18
19      return 0;
20  }
21
```

(program continues)

Program 19-4   *(continued)*

```
22   //************************************************
23   // Function numChars. This recursive function     *
24   // counts the number of times the character        *
25   // search appears in the string str. The search    *
26   // begins at the subscript stored in subscript.    *
27   //************************************************
28
29   int numChars(char search, string str, int subscript)
30   {
31      if (subscript >= str.length())
32      {
33         // Base case: The end of the string is reached.
34         return 0;
35      }
36      else if (str[subscript] == search)
37      {
38         // Recursive case: A matching character was found.
39         // Return 1 plus the number of times the search
40         // character appears in the rest of the string.
41         return 1 + numChars(search, str, subscript+1);
42      }
43      else
44      {
45         // Recursive case: A character that does not match the
46         // search character was found. Return the number of times
47         // the search character appears in the rest of the string.
48         return numChars(search, str, subscript+1);
49      }
50   }
```

Program Output

```
The letter d appears 4 times.
```

Direct and Indirect Recursion

The examples we have discussed so far show recursive functions that directly call themselves. This is known as *direct recursion*. There is also the possibility of creating *indirect recursion* in a program. This occurs when function A calls function B, which in turn calls function A. There can even be several functions involved in the recursion. For example, function A could call function B, which could call function C, which calls function A.

 Checkpoint

myprogramminglab *www.myprogramminglab.com*

19.1   What happens if a recursive function never returns?

19.2   What is a recursive function's base case?

19.3   What will the following program display?

```
#include <iostream>
using namespace std;
```

```
// Function prototype
void showMe(int arg);

int main()
{
    int num = 0;

    showMe(num);
    return 0;
}

void showMe(int arg)
{
    if (arg < 10)
        showMe(++arg);
    else
        cout << arg << endl;
}
```

19.4   What is the difference between direct and indirect recursion?

Focus on Problem Solving and Program Design: The Recursive gcd Function

CONCEPT: The gcd function uses recursion to find the greatest common divisor (GCD) of two numbers.

Our next example of recursion is the calculation of the greatest common divisor, or GCD, of two numbers. Using Euclid's algorithm, the GCD of two positive integers, x and y, is:

> $\gcd(x, y) = y$;   if y divides x evenly
> $\gcd(y,$ remainder of x/y);   otherwise

The definition above states that the GCD of x and y is y if x/y has no remainder. Otherwise, the answer is the GCD of y and the remainder of x/y. Program 19-5 shows the recursive C++ implementation:

Program 19-5

```
1  // This program demonstrates a recursive function to calculate
2  // the greatest common divisor (gcd) of two numbers.
3  #include <iostream>
4  using namespace std;
5
6  // Function prototype
7  int gcd(int, int);
8
```

(program continues)

Program 19-5   *(continued)*

```cpp
 9   int main()
10   {
11      int num1, num2;
12
13      // Get two numbers.
14      cout << "Enter two integers: ";
15      cin >> num1 >> num2;
16
17      // Display the GCD of the numbers.
18      cout << "The greatest common divisor of " << num1;
19      cout << " and " << num2 << " is ";
20      cout << gcd(num1, num2) << endl;
21      return 0;
22   }
23
24   //*********************************************************
25   // Definition of gcd. This function uses recursion to     *
26   // calculate the greatest common divisor of two integers, *
27   // passed into the parameters x and y.                    *
28   //*********************************************************
29
30   int gcd(int x, int y)
31   {
32      if (x % y == 0)
33         return y;                // Base case
34      else
35         return gcd(y, x % y);   // Recursive case
36   }
```

Program Output with Example Input Shown in Bold
Enter two integers: **49 28 [Enter]**
The greatest common divisor of 49 and 28 is 7

19.4 Focus on Problem Solving and Program Design: Solving Recursively Defined Problems

CONCEPT: Some mathematical problems are designed for a recursive solution.

Some mathematical problems are designed to be solved recursively. One well-known example is the calculation of *Fibonacci numbers*. The Fibonacci numbers, named after the Italian mathematician Leonardo Fibonacci (born circa 1170), are the following sequence:

0, 1, 1, 2, 3, 5, 8, 13, 21, 34, 55, 89, 144, 233, ...

Notice that after the second number, each number in the series is the sum of the two previous numbers. The Fibonacci series can be defined as

$$F_0 = 0$$
$$F_1 = 1$$
$$F_N = F_{N-1} + F_{N-2} \text{ for } N \geq 2.$$

A recursive C++ function to calculate the nth number in the Fibonacci series is shown here:

```cpp
int fib(int n)
{
   if (n <= 0)
      return 0;
   else if (n == 1)
      return 1;
   else
      return fib(n - 1) + fib(n - 2);
}
```

The function is demonstrated in Program 19-6, which displays the first 10 numbers in the Fibonacci series.

Program 19-6

```cpp
 1  // This program demonstrates a recursive function
 2  // that calculates Fibonacci numbers.
 3  #include <iostream>
 4  using namespace std;
 5
 6  // Function prototype
 7  int fib(int);
 8
 9  int main()
10  {
11     cout << "The first 10 Fibonacci numbers are:\n";
12     for (int x = 0; x < 10; x++)
13        cout << fib(x) << " ";
14     cout << endl;
15     return 0;
16  }
17
18  //*****************************************
19  // Function fib. Accepts an int argument  *
20  // in n. This function returns the nth    *
21  // Fibonacci number.                      *
22  //*****************************************
23
24  int fib(int n)
25  {
26     if (n <= 0)
27        return 0;                         // Base case
28     else if (n == 1)
29        return 1;                         // Base case
30     else
31        return fib(n - 1) + fib(n - 2); // Recursive case
32  }
```

(program output continues)

Program 19-6   *(continued)*

Program Output
```
The first 10 Fibonacci numbers are:
0 1 1 2 3 5 8 13 21 34
```

Another such example is Ackermann's function. A Programming Challenge at the end of this chapter asks you to write a recursive function that calculates Ackermann's function.

19.5 Focus on Problem Solving and Program Design: Recursive Linked List Operations

CONCEPT: Recursion can be used to traverse the nodes in a linked list.

Recall that in Chapter 17 we discussed a class named `NumberList` that holds a linked list of `double` values. In this section we will modify the class by adding recursive member functions. The functions will use recursion to traverse the linked list and perform the following operations:

- Count the number of nodes in the list.

To count the number of nodes in the list by recursion, we introduce two new member functions: `numNodes` and `countNodes`. `countNodes` is a private member function that uses recursion, and `numNodes` is the public interface that calls it.

- Display the value of the list nodes in reverse order.

To display the nodes in the list in reverse order, we introduce two new member functions: `displayBackwards` and `showReverse`. `showReverse` is a private member function that uses recursion, and `displayBackwards` is the public interface that calls it.

The class declaration, which is saved in `NumberList.h`, is shown here:

```cpp
 1   // Specification file for the NumberList class
 2   #ifndef NUMBERLIST_H
 3   #define NUMBERLIST_H
 4
 5   class NumberList
 6   {
 7   private:
 8      // Declare a structure for the list
 9      struct ListNode
10      {
11         double value;
12         struct ListNode *next;
13      };
14
15      ListNode *head;      // List head pointer
16
17      // Private member functions
18      int countNodes(ListNode *) const;
19      void showReverse(ListNode *) const;
20
```

```
21   public:
22      // Constructor
23      NumberList()
24         { head = NULL; }
25
26      // Destructor
27      ~NumberList();
28
29      // Linked List Operations
30      void appendNode(double);
31      void insertNode(double);
32      void deleteNode(double);
33      void displayList() const;
34      int numNodes() const
35         { return countNodes(head); }
36      void displayBackwards() const
37         { showReverse(head); }
38   };
39   #endif
```

Counting the Nodes in the List

The numNodes function is declared inline. It simply calls the countNodes function and passes the head pointer as an argument. (Because the head pointer, which is private, must be passed to countNodes, the numNodes function is needed as an interface.)

The function definition for countNodes is shown here:

```
173   int NumberList::countNodes(ListNode *nodePtr) const
174   {
175      if (nodePtr != NULL)
176         return 1 + countNodes(nodePtr->next);
177      else
178         return 0;
179   }
```

The function's recursive logic can be expressed as:

```
If the current node has a value
   Return 1 + the number of the remaining nodes.
Else
   Return 0.
End If.
```

Program 19-7 demonstrates the function.

Program 19-7

```
1   // This program counts the nodes in a list.
2   #include <iostream>
3   #include "NumberList.h"
4   using namespace std;
5
```

(program continues)

Program 19-7   *(continued)*

```
 6  int main()
 7  {
 8     const int MAX = 10;  // Maximum number of values
 9
10     // Define a NumberList object.
11     NumberList list;
12
13     // Build the list with a series of numbers.
14     for (int x = 0; x < MAX; x++)
15        list.insertNode(x);
16
17     // Display the number of nodes in the list.
18     cout << "The number of nodes is "
19          << list.numNodes() << endl;
20     return 0;
21  }
```

Program Output

```
The number of nodes is 10
```

Displaying List Nodes in Reverse Order

The technique for displaying the list nodes in reverse order is designed like the node counting procedure: A public member function, which serves as an interface, passes the head pointer to a private member function. The public displayBackwards function, declared inline, is the interface. It calls the showReverse function and passes the head pointer as an argument. The function definition for showReverse is shown here:

```
187  void NumberList::showReverse(ListNode *nodePtr) const
188  {
189     if (nodePtr != NULL)
190     {
191        showReverse(nodePtr->next);
192        cout << nodePtr->value << " ";
193     }
194  }
```

The base case for the function is nodePtr being equal to NULL. When this is true, the function has reached the last node in the list, so it returns. It is not until this happens that any instances of the cout statement execute. The instance of the function whose nodePtr variable points to the last node in the list will be the first to execute the cout statement. It will then return, and the previous instance of the function will execute its cout statement. This repeats until all the instances of the function have returned.

The modified class declaration is stored in NumberList.h, and its member function implementation is in NumberList.cpp. The remainder of the class implementation is unchanged from Chapter 17, so it is not shown here. Program 19-8 demonstrates the function.

Program 19-8

```cpp
1   // This program demonstrates the recursive function
2   // for displaying the list's nodes in reverse.
3   #include <iostream>
4   #include "NumberList.h"
5   using namespace std;
6
7   int main()
8   {
9      const double MAX = 10.0;  // Upper limit of values
10
11     // Create a NumberList object.
12     NumberList list;
13
14     // Add a series of numbers to the list.
15     for (double x = 1.5; x < MAX; x += 1.1)
16        list.appendNode(x);
17
18     // Display the values in the list.
19     cout << "Here are the values in the list:\n";
20     list.displayList();
21
22     // Display the values in reverse order.
23     cout << "Here are the values in reverse order:\n";
24     list.displayBackwards();
25     return 0;
26  }
```

Program Output

```
Here are the values in the list:
1.5
2.6
3.7
4.8
5.9
7
8.1
9.2
Here are the values in reverse order:
9.2 8.1 7 5.9 4.8 3.7 2.6 1.5
```

Focus on Problem Solving and Program Design: A Recursive Binary Search Function

CONCEPT: The binary search algorithm can be defined as a recursive function.

In Chapter 8 you learned about the binary search algorithm and saw an iterative example written in C++. The binary search algorithm can also be implemented recursively. For example, the procedure can be expressed as

```
If array[middle] equals the search value, then the value is found.
```

Else, if array[middle] is less than the search value, perform a binary search on the upper half of the array.

Else, if array[middle] is greater than the search value, perform a binary search on the lower half of the array.

The recursive binary search algorithm is an example of breaking a problem down into smaller pieces until it is solved. A recursive binary search function is shown here:

```
int binarySearch(int array[], int first, int last, int value)
{
    int middle;    // Midpoint of search

    if (first > last)
        return -1;
    middle = (first + last) / 2;
    if (array[middle] == value)
        return middle;
    if (array[middle] < value)
        return binarySearch(array, middle+1,last,value);
    else
        return binarySearch(array, first,middle-1,value);
}
```

The first parameter, array, is the array to be searched. The next parameter, first, holds the subscript of the first element in the search range (the portion of the array to be searched). The next parameter, last, holds the subscript of the last element in the search range. The last parameter, value, holds the value to be searched for. Like the iterative version, this function returns the subscript of the value if it is found, or –1 if the value is not found. Program 19-9 demonstrates the function.

Program 19-9

```
 1   // This program demonstrates the recursive binarySearch function.
 2   #include <iostream>
 3   using namespace std;
 4
 5   // Function prototype
 6   int binarySearch(int [], int, int, int);
 7
 8   const int SIZE = 20;  // Array size
 9
10   int main()
11   {
12       // Define an array of employee ID numbers
13       int tests[SIZE] = {101, 142, 147, 189, 199, 207, 222,
14                          234, 289, 296, 310, 319, 388, 394,
15                          417, 429, 447, 521, 536, 600};
16       int empID;     // To hold an ID number
17       int results;   // To hold the search results
18
```

```
19        // Get an employee ID number to search for.
20        cout << "Enter the Employee ID you wish to search for: ";
21        cin >> empID;
22
23        // Search for the ID number in the array.
24        results = binarySearch(tests, 0, SIZE - 1, empID);
25
26        // Display the results of the search.
27        if (results == -1)
28            cout << "That number does not exist in the array.\n";
29        else
30        {
31            cout << "That ID is found at element " << results;
32            cout << " in the array\n";
33        }
34        return 0;
35    }
36
37    //*****************************************************************
38    // The binarySearch function performs a recursive binary search *
39    // on a range of elements of an integer array passed into the   *
40    // parameter array. The parameter first holds the subscript of  *
41    // the range's starting element, and last holds the subscript   *
42    // of the range's last element. The parameter value holds the   *
43    // search value. If the search value is found, its array        *
44    // subscript is returned. Otherwise, -1 is returned indicating  *
45    // the value was not in the array.                              *
46    //*****************************************************************
47
48    int binarySearch(int array[], int first, int last, int value)
49    {
50        int middle; // Midpoint of search
51
52        if (first > last)
53            return -1;
54        middle = (first + last)/2;
55        if (array[middle]==value)
56            return middle;
57        if (array[middle]<value)
58            return binarySearch(array, middle+1,last,value);
59        else
60            return binarySearch(array, first,middle-1,value);
61    }
```

Program Output with Example Input Shown in Bold
```
Enter the Employee ID you wish to search for: 521 [Enter]
That ID is found at element 17 in the array
```

19.7 The Towers of Hanoi

CONCEPT: The repetitive steps involved in solving the Towers of Hanoi game can be easily implemented in a recursive algorithm.

The Towers of Hanoi is a mathematical game that is often used in computer science textbooks to illustrate the power of recursion. The game uses three pegs and a set of discs with holes through their centers. The discs are stacked on one of the pegs as shown in Figure 19-4.

Figure 19-4   The pegs and discs in the Towers of Hanoi game

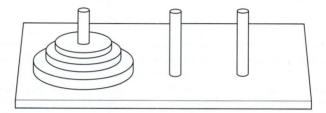

Notice that the discs are stacked on the leftmost peg, in order of size with the largest disc at the bottom. The game is based on a legend in which a group of monks in a temple in Hanoi have a similar set of pegs with 64 discs. The job of the monks is to move the discs from the first peg to the third peg. The middle peg can be used as a temporary holder. Furthermore, the monks must follow these rules while moving the discs:

- Only one disc may be moved at a time.
- A disc cannot be placed on top of a smaller disc.
- All discs must be stored on a peg except while being moved.

According to the legend, when the monks have moved all of the discs from the first peg to the last peg, the world will come to an end.

To play the game, you must move all of the discs from the first peg to the third peg, following the same rules as the monks. Let's look at some example solutions to this game, for different numbers of discs. If you only have one disc, the solution to the game is simple: move the disc from peg 1 to peg 3. If you have two discs, the solution requires three moves:

- Move disc 1 to peg 2.
- Move disc 2 to peg 3.
- Move disc 1 to peg 3.

Notice that this approach uses peg 2 as a temporary location. The complexity of the moves continues to increase as the number of discs increases. To move three discs requires the seven moves shown in Figure 19-5.

Figure 19-5

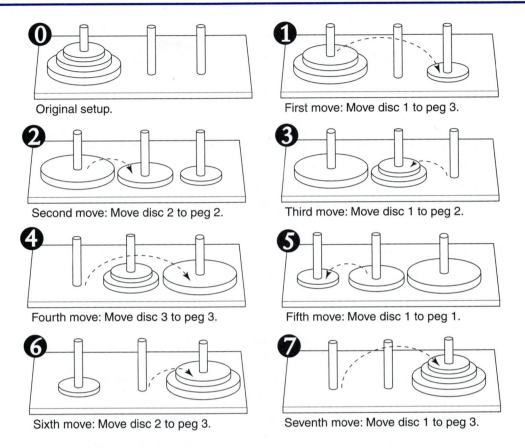

0 | Original setup.

1 | First move: Move disc 1 to peg 3.

2 | Second move: Move disc 2 to peg 2.

3 | Third move: Move disc 1 to peg 2.

4 | Fourth move: Move disc 3 to peg 3.

5 | Fifth move: Move disc 1 to peg 1.

6 | Sixth move: Move disc 2 to peg 3.

7 | Seventh move: Move disc 1 to peg 3.

The following statement describes the overall solution to the problem:

Move n discs from peg 1 to peg 3 using peg 2 as a temporary peg.

The following algorithm can be used as the basis of a recursive function that simulates the solution to the game. Notice that in this algorithm we use the variables *A*, *B*, and *C* to hold peg numbers.

To move n discs from peg A to peg C, using peg B as a temporary peg:
If n > 0 Then
    Move n – 1 discs from peg A to peg B, using peg C as a temporary peg.
    Move the remaining disc from the peg A to peg C.
    Move n – 1 discs from peg B to peg C, using peg A as a temporary peg.
End If

The base case for the algorithm is reached when there are no more discs to move. The following code is for a function that implements this algorithm. Note that the function does not actually move anything, but displays instructions indicating all of the disc moves to make.

```
void moveDiscs(int num, int fromPeg, int toPeg, int tempPeg)
{
    if (num > 0)
    {
        moveDiscs(num - 1, fromPeg, tempPeg, toPeg);
        cout << "Move a disc from peg " << fromPeg
            << " to peg " << toPeg << endl;
        moveDiscs(num - 1, tempPeg, toPeg, fromPeg);
    }
}
```

This function accepts arguments into the following three parameters:

num   The number of discs to move.

fromPeg   The peg to move the discs from.

toPeg   The peg to move the discs to.

tempPeg   The peg to use as a temporary peg.

If num is greater than 0, then there are discs to move. The first recursive call is

```
moveDiscs(num - 1, fromPeg, tempPeg, toPeg);
```

This statement is an instruction to move all but one disc from fromPeg to tempPeg, using toPeg as a temporary peg. The next statement is

```
cout << "Move a disc from peg " << fromPeg
    << " to peg " << toPeg << endl;
```

This simply displays a message indicating that a disc should be moved from fromPeg to toPeg. Next, another recursive call is executed:

```
moveDiscs(num - 1, tempPeg, toPeg, fromPeg);
```

This statement is an instruction to move all but one disc from tempPeg to toPeg, using fromPeg as a temporary peg. Program 19-10 demonstrates this function.

Program 19-10

```
 1  // This program displays a solution to the Towers of
 2  // Hanoi game.
 3  #include <iostream>
 4  using namespace std;
 5
 6  // Function prototype
 7  void moveDiscs(int, int, int, int);
 8
 9  int main()
10  {
11     const int NUM_DISCS = 3;    // Number of discs to move
12     const int FROM_PEG = 1;     // Initial "from" peg
13     const int TO_PEG = 3;       // Initial "to" peg
14     const int TEMP_PEG = 2;     // Initial "temp" peg
15
```

```
16        // Play the game.
17        moveDiscs(NUM_DISCS, FROM_PEG, TO_PEG, TEMP_PEG);
18        cout << "All the pegs are moved!\n";
19        return 0;
20    }
21
22    //****************************************************
23    // The moveDiscs function displays a disc move in    *
24    // the Towers of Hanoi game.                         *
25    // The parameters are:                               *
26    //    num:     The number of discs to move.          *
27    //    fromPeg: The peg to move from.                 *
28    //    toPeg:   The peg to move to.                    *
29    //    tempPeg: The temporary peg.                     *
30    //****************************************************
31
32    void moveDiscs(int num, int fromPeg, int toPeg, int tempPeg)
33    {
34        if (num > 0)
35        {
36            moveDiscs(num - 1, fromPeg, tempPeg, toPeg);
37            cout << "Move a disc from peg " << fromPeg
38                 << " to peg " << toPeg << endl;
39            moveDiscs(num - 1, tempPeg, toPeg, fromPeg);
40        }
41    }
```

Program Output

```
Move a disc from peg 1 to peg 3
Move a disc from peg 1 to peg 2
Move a disc from peg 3 to peg 2
Move a disc from peg 1 to peg 3
Move a disc from peg 2 to peg 1
Move a disc from peg 2 to peg 3
Move a disc from peg 1 to peg 3
All the pegs are moved!
```

19.8 Focus on Problem Solving and Program Design: The QuickSort Algorithm

CONCEPT: The QuickSort algorithm uses recursion to efficiently sort a list.

The QuickSort algorithm is a popular general-purpose sorting routine developed in 1960 by C.A.R. Hoare. It can be used to sort lists stored in arrays or linear linked lists. It sorts a list by dividing it into two sublists. Between the sublists is a selected value known as the *pivot*. This is illustrated in Figure 19-6.

Figure 19-6

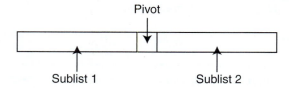

Notice in the figure that sublist 1 is positioned to the left of (before) the pivot, and sublist 2 is positioned to the right of (after) the pivot. Once a pivot value has been selected, the algorithm exchanges the other values in the list until all the elements in sublist 1 are less than the pivot, and all the elements in sublist 2 are greater than the pivot.

Once this is done, the algorithm repeats the procedure on sublist 1, and then on sublist 2. The recursion stops when there is only one element in a sublist. At that point the original list is completely sorted.

The algorithm is coded primarily in two functions: `quickSort` and `partition`. `quickSort` is a recursive function. Its pseudocode is shown here:

```
quickSort:
If Starting Index < Ending Index
      Partition the List around a Pivot.
      quickSort Sublist 1.
      quickSort Sublist 2.
End If.
```

Here is the C++ code for the `quickSort` function:

```cpp
void quickSort(int set[], int start, int end)
{
   int pivotPoint;

   if (start < end)
   {
      // Get the pivot point.
      pivotPoint = partition(set, start, end);
      // Sort the first sublist.
      quickSort(set, start, pivotPoint - 1);
      // Sort the second sublist.
      quickSort(set, pivotPoint + 1, end);
   }
}
```

This version of `quickSort` works with an array of integers. Its first argument is the array holding the list that is to be sorted. The second and third arguments are the starting and ending subscripts of the list.

The subscript of the pivot element is returned by the `partition` function. `partition` not only determines which element will be the pivot, but also controls the rearranging of the other values in the list. Our version of this function selects the element in the middle of the list as the pivot, then scans the remainder of the list searching for values less than the pivot.

The code for the `partition` function is shown here:

```cpp
int partition(int set[], int start, int end)
{
    int pivotValue, pivotIndex, mid;

    mid = (start + end) / 2;
    swap(set[start], set[mid]);
    pivotIndex = start;
    pivotValue = set[start];
    for (int scan = start + 1; scan <= end; scan++)
    {
        if (set[scan] < pivotValue)
        {
            pivotIndex++;
            swap(set[pivotIndex], set[scan]);
        }
    }
    swap(set[start], set[pivotIndex]);
    return pivotIndex;
}
```

NOTE: The `partition` function does not initially sort the values into their final order. Its job is only to move the values that are less than the pivot to the pivot's left, and move the values that are greater than the pivot to the pivot's right. As long as that condition is met, they may appear in any order. The ultimate sorting order of the entire list is achieved cumulatively, though the recursive calls to `quickSort`.

There are many different ways of partitioning the list. As previously stated, the method shown in the function above selects the middle value as the pivot. That value is then moved to the beginning of the list (by exchanging it with the value stored there). This simplifies the next step, which is to scan the list.

A `for` loop scans the remainder of the list, and when an element is found whose value is less than the pivot, that value is moved to a location left of the pivot point.

A third function, `swap`, is used to swap the values found in any two elements of the list. The function is shown below.

```cpp
void swap(int &value1, int &value2)
{
    int temp = value1;
    value1 = value2;
    value2 = temp;
}
```

Program 19-11 demonstrates the QuickSort algorithm shown here.

Program 19-11

```
1   // This program demonstrates the QuickSort Algorithm.
2   #include <iostream>
3   using namespace std;
4
5   // Function prototypes
6   void quickSort(int [], int, int);
7   int partition(int [], int, int);
8   void swap(int &, int &);
9
10  int main()
11  {
12     const int SIZE = 10;   // Array size
13     int count;             // Loop counter
14     int array[SIZE] = {7, 3, 9, 2, 0, 1, 8, 4, 6, 5};
15
16     // Display the array contents.
17     for (count = 0; count < SIZE; count++)
18        cout << array[count] << " ";
19     cout << endl;
20
21     // Sort the array.
22     quickSort(array, 0, SIZE - 1);
23
24     // Display the array contents.
25     for (count = 0; count < SIZE; count++)
26        cout << array[count] << " ";
27     cout << endl;
28     return 0;
29  }
30
31  //************************************************
32  // quickSort uses the quicksort algorithm to     *
33  // sort set, from set[start] through set[end].    *
34  //************************************************
35
36  void quickSort(int set[], int start, int end)
37  {
38     int pivotPoint;
39
40     if (start < end)
41     {
42        // Get the pivot point.
43        pivotPoint = partition(set, start, end);
44        // Sort the first sublist.
45        quickSort(set, start, pivotPoint - 1);
```

```
46            // Sort the second sublist.
47            quickSort(set, pivotPoint + 1, end);
48        }
49    }
50
51    //************************************************************
52    // partition selects the value in the middle of the         *
53    // array set as the pivot. The list is rearranged so         *
54    // all the values less than the pivot are on its left        *
55    // and all the values greater than pivot are on its right.   *
56    //************************************************************
57
58    int partition(int set[], int start, int end)
59    {
60        int pivotValue, pivotIndex, mid;
61
62        mid = (start + end) / 2;
63        swap(set[start], set[mid]);
64        pivotIndex = start;
65        pivotValue = set[start];
66        for (int scan = start + 1; scan <= end; scan++)
67        {
68            if (set[scan] < pivotValue)
69            {
70                pivotIndex++;
71                swap(set[pivotIndex], set[scan]);
72            }
73        }
74        swap(set[start], set[pivotIndex]);
75        return pivotIndex;
76    }
77
78    //*****************************************
79    // swap simply exchanges the contents of  *
80    // value1 and value2.                     *
81    //*****************************************
82
83    void swap(int &value1, int &value2)
84    {
85        int temp = value1;
86
87        value1 = value2;
88        value2 = temp;
89    }
```

Program Output

```
7 3 9 2 0 1 8 4 6 5
0 1 2 3 4 5 6 7 8 9
```

19.9   Exhaustive Algorithms

CONCEPT: An exhaustive algorithm is one that finds a best combination of items by looking at all the possible combinations.

Recursion is helpful if you need to examine many possible combinations and identify the best combination. For example, consider all the different ways you can make change for $1.00 using our system of coins:

1 dollar piece, or
2 fifty-cent pieces, or
4 quarters, or
1 fifty-cent piece and 2 quarters, or
3 quarters, 2 dimes, and 1 nickel, or
... there are many more possibilities.

Although there are many ways to make change for $1.00, some ways are better than others. For example, you would probably rather give a single dollar piece instead of 100 pennies.

An algorithm that looks at all the possible combinations of items in order to find the best combination of items is called an exhaustive algorithm. Program 19-12 presents a recursive function that exhaustively tries all the possible combinations of coins. The program then displays the total number of combinations that can be used to make the specified change, and the best combination of coins.

Program 19-12

```
 1 // This program demonstrates a recursive function that exhaustively
 2 // searches through all possible combinations of coin values to find
 3 // the best way to make change for a specified amount.
 4 #include <iostream>
 5 using namespace std;
 6
 7 // Constants
 8 const int MAX_COINS_CHANGE = 100; // Max number of coins to give in change
 9 const int MAX_COIN_VALUES = 6;    // Max number of coin values
10 const int NO_SOLUTION = INT_MAX;  // Indicates no solution
11
12 // Function prototype
13 void makeChange(int, int, int[], int);
14
15 // coinValues - global array of coin values to choose from
16 int coinValues[MAX_COIN_VALUES] = {100, 50, 25, 10, 5, 1 };
17
18 // bestCoins - global array of best coins to make change with
19 int bestCoins[MAX_COINS_CHANGE];
20
```

```
21  // Global variables
22  int numBestCoins = NO_SOLUTION,   // Number of coins in bestCoins
23      numSolutions = 0,             // Number of ways to make change
24      numCoins;                     // Number of allowable coins
25
26
27  int main()
28  {
29     int coinsUsed[MAX_COINS_CHANGE], // List of coins used
30         numCoinsUsed = 0,             // The number of coins used
31         amount;                       // The amount to make change for
32
33     // Display the possible coin values.
34     cout << "Here are the valid coin values, in cents: ";
35     for (int index = 0; index < 5; index++)
36        cout << coinValues[index] << " ";
37     cout << endl;
38
39     // Get input from the user.
40     cout << "Enter the amount of cents (as an integer) "
41          << "to make change for: ";
42     cin >> amount;
43     cout << "What is the maximum number of coins to give as change? ";
44     cin >> numCoins;
45
46     // Call the recursive function.
47     makeChange(numCoins, amount, coinsUsed, numCoinsUsed);
48
49     // Display the results.
50     cout << "Number of possible combinations: " << numSolutions << endl;
51     cout << "Best combination of coins:\n";
52     if (numBestCoins == NO_SOLUTION)
53        cout << "\tNo solution\n";
54     else
55     {
56        for (int count = 0; count < numBestCoins; count++)
57           cout << bestCoins[count] << " ";
58     }
59     cout << endl;
60     return 0;
61  }
62
63  //*************************************************************************
64  // Function makeChange. This function uses the following parameters:   *
65  // coinsLeft - The number of coins left to choose from.                *
66  // amount - The amount to make change for.                             *
67  // coinsUsed - An array that contains the coin values used so far.     *
68  // numCoinsUsed - The number of values in the coinsUsed array.         *
69  //                                                                     *
70  // This recursive function finds all the possible ways to make change  *
71  // for the value in amount. The best combination of coins is stored in *
72  // the array bestCoins.                                                *
73  //*************************************************************************
```

(program continues)

Program 19-12   *(continued)*

```
74
75  void makeChange(int coinsLeft, int amount, int coinsUsed[],
76                  int numCoinsUsed)
77  {
78     int coinPos,    // To calculate array position of coin being used
79         count;      // Loop counter
80
81     if (coinsLeft == 0)    // If no more coins are left
82        return;
83     else if (amount < 0)   // If amount to make change for is negative
84        return;
85     else if (amount == 0)  // If solution is found
86     {
87        // Store as bestCoins if best
88        if (numCoinsUsed < numBestCoins)
89        {
90           for (count = 0; count < numCoinsUsed; count++)
91              bestCoins[count] = coinsUsed[count];
92           numBestCoins = numCoinsUsed;
93        }
94        numSolutions++;
95        return;
96     }
97
98     // Find the other combinations using the coin
99     coinPos = numCoins - coinsLeft;
100    coinsUsed[numCoinsUsed] = coinValues[coinPos];
101    numCoinsUsed++;
102    makeChange(coinsLeft, amount - coinValues[coinPos],
103             coinsUsed, numCoinsUsed);
104
105    // Find the other combinations not using the coin.
106    numCoinsUsed--;
107    makeChange(coinsLeft - 1, amount, coinsUsed, numCoinsUsed);
108 }
```

Program Output with Example Input Shown in Bold

```
Here are the valid coin values, in cents: 100 50 25 10 5 1
Enter the amount of cents (as an integer) to make change for: 62 [Enter]
What is the maximum number of coins to give as change? 6 [Enter]
Number of possible combinations: 77
Best combination of coins:
50 10 1 1
```

19.10

Focus on Software Engineering: Recursion vs. Iteration

CONCEPT: Recursive algorithms can also be coded with iterative control structures. There are advantages and disadvantages to each approach.

20 Binary Trees

TOPICS

20.1 Definition and Applications of Binary Trees

CONCEPT: A binary tree is a nonlinear linked structure in which each node may point to two other nodes, and every node but the root node has a single predecessor. Binary trees expedite the process of searching large sets of data.

A standard linked list is a linear data structure in which one node is linked to the next. A *binary tree* is a nonlinear linked structure. It is nonlinear because each node can point to two other nodes. Figure 20-1 illustrates the organization of a binary tree.

The data structure is called a tree because it resembles an upside-down tree. It is anchored at the top by a *tree pointer*, which is like the head pointer in a standard linked list. The first node in the list is called the *root node*. The root node has pointers to two other nodes, which are called *children*, or *child nodes*. Each of the children has its own set of two pointers, and can have its own children. Notice that not all nodes have two children. Some point to only one node, and some point to no other nodes. A node that has no children is called a *leaf node*. All pointers that do not point to a node are set to NULL.

Figure 20-1

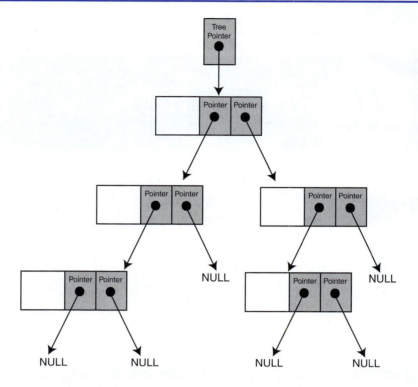

Binary trees can be divided into *subtrees*. A subtree is an entire branch of the tree, from one particular node down. For example, Figure 20-2 shows the left subtree from the root node of the tree shown in Figure 20-1.

Figure 20-2

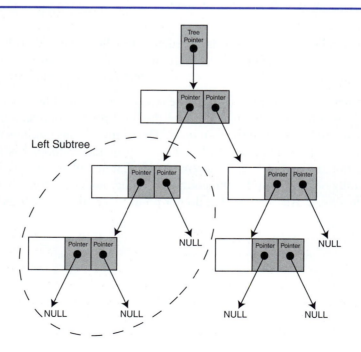

Applications of Binary Trees

Searching any linear data structure, such as an array or a standard linked list, is slow when the structure holds a large amount of data. This is because of the sequential nature of linear data structures. Binary trees are excellent data structures for searching large amounts of data. They are commonly used in database applications to organize key values that index database records. When used to facilitate searches, a binary tree is called a *binary search tree*. Binary search trees are the primary focus of this chapter.

Data are stored in binary search trees in a way that makes a binary search simple. For example, look at Figure 20-3.

Figure 20-3

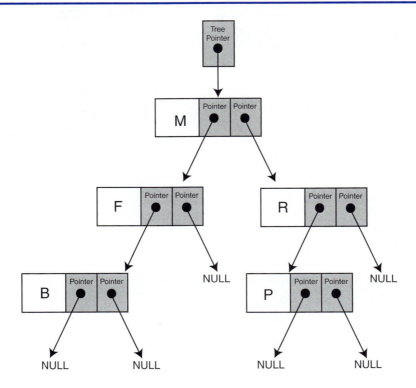

The figure depicts a binary search tree where each node stores a letter of the alphabet. Notice that the root node holds the letter M. The left child of the root node holds the letter F, and the right child holds R. Values are stored in a binary search tree so that a node's left child holds data whose value is less than the node's data, and the node's right child holds data whose value is greater than the node's data. This is true for all nodes in the tree that have children.

It is also true that *all* the nodes to the left of a node hold values less than the node's value. Likewise, all the nodes to the right of a node hold values that are greater than the node's data. When an application is searching a binary tree, it starts at the root node. If the root node does not hold the search value, the application branches either to the left or right child, depending on whether the search value is less than or greater than the value at the root node. This process continues until the value is found. Figure 20-4 illustrates the search pattern for finding the letter P in the binary tree shown.

Figure 20-4

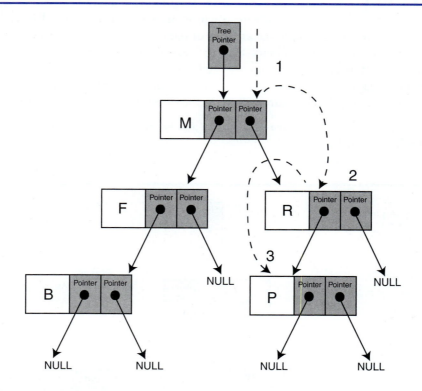

 ## Checkpoint

myprogramminglab *www.myprogramminglab.com*

20.1   Describe the difference between a binary tree and a standard linked list.

20.2   What is a root node?

20.3   What is a child node?

20.4   What is a leaf node?

20.5   What is a subtree?

20.6   Why are binary trees suitable for algorithms that must search large amounts of data?

 # 20.2   Binary Search Tree Operations

CONCEPT: There are many operations that may be performed on a binary search tree. In this section we will discuss creating a binary search tree and inserting, finding, and deleting nodes.

In this section you will learn some basic operations that may be performed on a binary search tree. We will study a simple class that implements a binary tree for storing integer values.

Creating a Binary Tree

We will demonstrate the fundamental binary tree operations using a simple ADT: the IntBinaryTree class. The basis of our binary tree node is the following struct declaration:

```
struct TreeNode
{
   int value;
   TreeNode *left;
   TreeNode *right;
};
```

Each node has a value member for storing its integer data, as well as left and right pointers. The struct is implemented in the class declaration shown here:

Contents of IntBinaryTree.h

```
 1   // Specification file for the IntBinaryTree class
 2   #ifndef INTBINARYTREE_H
 3   #define INTBINARYTREE_H
 4
 5   class IntBinaryTree
 6   {
 7   private:
 8      struct TreeNode
 9      {
10         int value;          // The value in the node
11         TreeNode *left;     // Pointer to left child node
12         TreeNode *right;    // Pointer to right child node
13      };
14
15      TreeNode *root;        // Pointer to the root node
16
17      // Private member functions
18      void insert(TreeNode *&, TreeNode *&);
19      void destroySubTree(TreeNode *);
20      void deleteNode(int, TreeNode *&);
21      void makeDeletion(TreeNode *&);
22      void displayInOrder(TreeNode *) const;
23      void displayPreOrder(TreeNode *) const;
24      void displayPostOrder(TreeNode *) const;
25
26   public:
27      // Constructor
28      IntBinaryTree()
29         { root = NULL; }
30
31      // Destructor
32      ~IntBinaryTree()
33         { destroySubTree(root); }
34
35      // Binary tree operations
36      void insertNode(int);
37      bool searchNode(int);
38      void remove(int);
39
```

```
40    void displayInOrder() const
41       { displayInOrder(root); }
42
43    void displayPreOrder() const
44       { displayPreOrder(root); }
45
46    void displayPostOrder() const
47       { displayPostOrder(root); }
48 };
49 #endif
```

The `root` pointer will be used as the tree pointer. Similar to the head pointer in a linked list, root will point to the first node in the tree, or to NULL if the tree is empty. It is initialized in the constructor, which is declared inline. The destructor calls `destroySubTree`, a private member function that recursively deletes all the nodes in the tree.

Inserting a Node

The code to insert a node into the tree is fairly straightforward. The public member function `insertNode` is called with the number to be inserted passed as an argument. The code for the function, which is in `IntBinaryTree.cpp`, is shown here:

VideoNote
Inserting a Node in a Binary Tree

```
27  void IntBinaryTree::insertNode(int num)
28  {
29     TreeNode *newNode;       // Pointer to a new node.
30
31     // Create a new node and store num in it.
32     newNode = new TreeNode;
33     newNode->value = num;
34     newNode->left = newNode->right = NULL;
35
36     // Insert the node.
37     insert(root, newNode);
38  }
```

First, a new node is allocated in line 32 and its address stored in the local pointer variable newNode. The value passed as an argument is stored in the node's `value` member in line 33. The node's `left` and `right` child pointers are set to NULL in line 34 because all nodes must be inserted as leaf nodes. Next, the private member function `insert` is called in line 37. Notice that the `root` pointer and the `newNode` pointer are passed as arguments. The code for the `insert` function is shown here:

```
12  void IntBinaryTree::insert(TreeNode *&nodePtr, TreeNode *&newNode)
13  {
14     if (nodePtr == NULL)
15        nodePtr = newNode;                    // Insert the node.
16     else if (newNode->value < nodePtr->value)
17        insert(nodePtr->left, newNode);    // Search the left branch.
18     else
19        insert(nodePtr->right, newNode);   // Search the right branch.
20  }
```

In general, this function takes a pointer to a subtree and a pointer to a new node as arguments. It searches for the appropriate location in the subtree to insert the node, and then makes the insertion. Notice the declaration of the first parameter, `nodePtr`:

```
TreeNode *&nodePtr
```

The nodePtr parameter is not simply a pointer to a TreeNode structure, but a *reference* to a pointer to a TreeNode structure. This means that any action performed on nodePtr is actually performed on the argument that was passed into nodePtr. The reason for this will be explained momentarily.

The if statement in line 14 determines whether nodePtr points to NULL:

```
if (nodePtr == NULL)
    nodePtr = newNode;   // Insert the node.
```

If nodePtr points to NULL, it is at the end of a branch and the insertion point has been found. nodePtr is then made to point to newNode, which inserts newNode into the tree. This is why the nodePtr parameter is a reference. If it weren't a reference, this function would be making a copy of a node point to the new node, not the actual node in the tree.

If nodePtr doesn't point to NULL, the following else if statement in line 16 executes:

```
else if (newNode->value < nodePtr->value)
    insert(nodePtr->left, newNode);   // Search the left branch.
```

If the new node's value is less than the value pointed to by nodePtr, the insertion point is somewhere in the left subtree. If this is the case, the insert function is recursively called in line 17 with nodePtr->left passed as the subtree argument.

If the new node's value is not less than the value pointed to by nodePtr, the else statement in line 18 executes:

```
else
    insert(nodePtr->right, newNode);   // Search the right branch.
```

The else statement recursively calls the insert function called with nodePtr->right passed as the subtree argument.

Program 20-1 demonstrates these functions.

Program 20-1

```
 1  // This program builds a binary tree with 5 nodes.
 2  #include <iostream>
 3  #include "IntBinaryTree.h"
 4  using namespace std;
 5
 6  int main()
 7  {
 8      IntBinaryTree tree;
 9
10      cout << "Inserting nodes. ";
11      tree.insertNode(5);
12      tree.insertNode(8);
13      tree.insertNode(3);
14      tree.insertNode(12);
15      tree.insertNode(9);
16      cout << "Done.\n";
17
18      return 0;
19  }
```

Figure 20-5 shows the structure of the binary tree built by Program 20-1.

Figure 20-5

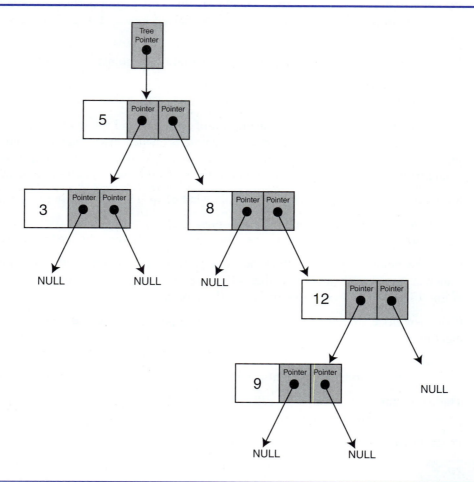

 NOTE: The shape of the tree is determined by the order in which the values are inserted. The root node in the diagram above holds the value 5 because that was the first value inserted. By stepping through the function, you can see how the other nodes came to appear in their depicted positions.

 NOTE: If the new value being inserted into the tree is equal to an existing value, the insertion algorithm inserts it to the right of the existing value.

Traversing the Tree

There are three common methods for traversing a binary tree and processing the value of each node: *inorder*, *preorder*, and *postorder*. Each of these methods is best implemented as a recursive function. The algorithms are described as follows:

- *Inorder traversal*
  1. The current node's left subtree is traversed.
  2. The current node's data is processed.
  3. The current node's right subtree is traversed.
- *Preorder traversal*
  1. The current node's data is processed
  2. The current node's left subtree is traversed.
  3. The current node's right subtree is traversed.
- *Postorder traversal*
  1. The current node's left subtree is traversed.
  2. The current node's right subtree is traversed.
  3. The current node's data is processed.

The `IntBinaryTree` class can display all the values in the tree using all three of these algorithms. The algorithms are initiated by the following inline public member functions:

```
void displayInOrder() const
   { displayInOrder(root); }

void displayPreOrder() const
   { displayPreOrder(root); }

void displayPostOrder() const
   { displayPostOrder(root); }
```

Each of the public member functions calls an overloaded recursive private member function, and passes the root pointer as an argument. The recursive functions, which are very simple and straightforward, are shown here:

```
149   //***********************************************************
150   // The displayInOrder member function displays the values    *
151   // in the subtree pointed to by nodePtr, via inorder traversal.  *
152   //***********************************************************
153
154   void IntBinaryTree::displayInOrder(TreeNode *nodePtr) const
155   {
156      if (nodePtr)
157      {
158         displayInOrder(nodePtr->left);
159         cout << nodePtr->value << endl;
160         displayInOrder(nodePtr->right);
161      }
162   }
163
164   //***********************************************************
165   // The displayPreOrder member function displays the values    *
166   // in the subtree pointed to by nodePtr, via preorder traversal. *
167   //***********************************************************
168
169   void IntBinaryTree::displayPreOrder(TreeNode *nodePtr) const
170   {
171      if (nodePtr)
172      {
173         cout << nodePtr->value << endl;
174         displayPreOrder(nodePtr->left);
```

```
175              displayPreOrder(nodePtr->right);
176         }
177   }
178
179   //************************************************************
180   // The displayPostOrder member function displays the values    *
181   // in the subtree pointed to by nodePtr, via postorder traversal.*
182   //************************************************************
183
184   void IntBinaryTree::displayPostOrder(TreeNode *nodePtr) const
185   {
186      if (nodePtr)
187      {
188         displayPostOrder(nodePtr->left);
189         displayPostOrder(nodePtr->right);
190         cout << nodePtr->value << endl;
191      }
192   }
```

Program 20-2, which is a modification of Program 20-1, demonstrates each of the traversal methods.

Program 20-2

```
1    // This program builds a binary tree with 5 nodes.
2    // The nodes are displayed with inorder, preorder,
3    // and postorder algorithms.
4    #include <iostream>
5    #include "IntBinaryTree.h"
6    using namespace std;
7
8    int main()
9    {
10      IntBinaryTree tree;
11
12      // Insert some nodes.
13      cout << "Inserting nodes.\n";
14      tree.insertNode(5);
15      tree.insertNode(8);
16      tree.insertNode(3);
17      tree.insertNode(12);
18      tree.insertNode(9);
19
20      // Display inorder.
21      cout << "Inorder traversal:\n";
22      tree.displayInOrder();
23
24      // Display preorder.
25      cout << "\nPreorder traversal:\n";
26      tree.displayPreOrder();
27
28      // Display postorder.
29      cout << "\nPostorder traversal:\n";
30      tree.displayPostOrder();
31      return 0;
32   }
```

Program Output
```
Inserting nodes.
Inorder traversal:
3
5
8
9
12

Preorder traversal:
5
3
8
12
9

Postorder traversal:
3
9
12
8
5
```

Searching the Tree

The `IntBinaryTree` class has a public member function, `searchNode`, that returns `true` if a value is found in the tree, or `false` otherwise. The function simply starts at the `root` node and traverses the tree until it finds the search value, or runs out of nodes. The code is shown here.

```
63  bool IntBinaryTree::searchNode(int num)
64  {
65      TreeNode *nodePtr = root;
66
67      while (nodePtr)
68      {
69          if (nodePtr->value == num)
70              return true;
71          else if (num < nodePtr->value)
72              nodePtr = nodePtr->left;
73          else
74              nodePtr = nodePtr->right;
75      }
76      return false;
77  }
```

Program 20-3 demonstrates this function.

Program 20-3

```
 1   // This program builds a binary tree with 5 nodes.
 2   // The SearchNode function is demonstrated.
 3   #include <iostream>
 4   #include "IntBinaryTree.h"
 5   using namespace std;
 6
 7   int main()
 8   {
 9      IntBinaryTree tree;
10
11      // Insert some nodes in the tree.
12      cout << "Inserting nodes.\n";
13      tree.insertNode(5);
14      tree.insertNode(8);
15      tree.insertNode(3);
16      tree.insertNode(12);
17      tree.insertNode(9);
18
19      // Search for the value 3.
20      if (tree.searchNode(3))
21         cout << "3 is found in the tree.\n";
22      else
23         cout << "3 was not found in the tree.\n";
24
25      // Search for the value 100.
26      if (tree.searchNode(100))
27         cout << "100 is found in the tree.\n";
28      else
29         cout << "100 was not found in the tree.\n";
30      return 0;
31   }
```

Program Output

```
Inserting nodes.
3 is found in the tree.
100 was not found in the tree.
```

Deleting a Node

VideoNote

Deleting a Node from a Binary Tree

Deleting a leaf node is not difficult. We simply find its parent and set the child pointer that links to it to NULL, then free the node's memory. But what if we want to delete a node that has child nodes? We must delete the node while at the same time preserving the subtrees that the node links to.

There are two possible situations to face when deleting a nonleaf node: the node has one child, or the node has two children. Figure 20-6 illustrates a tree in which we are about to delete a node with one subtree.

Figure 20-6

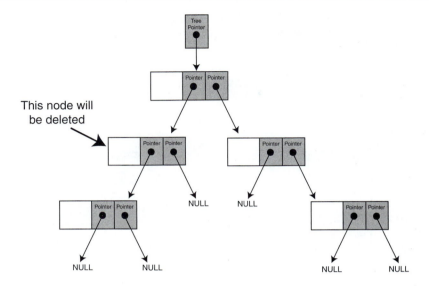

Figure 20-7 shows how we will link the node's subtree with its parent:

Figure 20-7

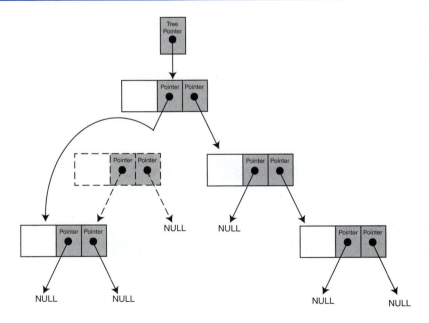

The problem is not as easily solved, however, when the node we are about to delete has two subtrees. For example, look at Figure 20-8:

Figure 20-8

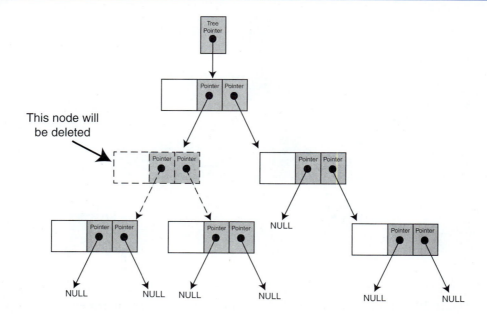

Obviously, we cannot attach both of the node's subtrees to its parent, so there must be an alternative solution. One way of addressing this problem is to attach the node's right subtree to the parent, then find a position in the right subtree to attach the left subtree. The result is shown in Figure 20-9.

Figure 20-9

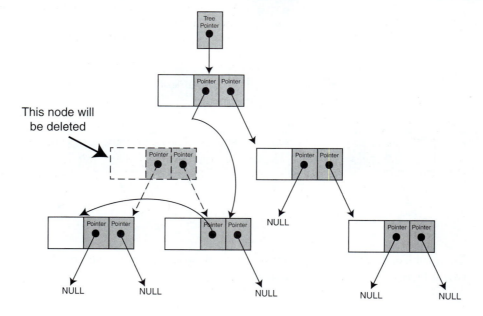

Now we will see how this action is implemented in code. To delete a node from the `IntBinaryTree`, call the public member `remove`. The argument passed to the function is the value of the node you wish to delete. The `remove` member function is shown here:

```
84   void IntBinaryTree::remove(int num)
85   {
86      deleteNode(num, root);
87   }
```

The `remove` member function calls the `deleteNode` member function. It passes the value of the node to delete and the `root` pointer. The `deleteNode` member function is shown here:

```
95   void IntBinaryTree::deleteNode(int num, TreeNode *&nodePtr)
96   {
97      if (num < nodePtr->value)
98         deleteNode(num, nodePtr->left);
99      else if (num > nodePtr->value)
100        deleteNode(num, nodePtr->right);
101     else
102        makeDeletion(nodePtr);
103  }
```

Notice that this function's arguments are references to pointers. Like the `insert` function, the `deleteNode` function must have access to an actual pointer in the tree. You will see why momentarily.

The `deleteNode` function uses an `if/else if` statement. The first part of the statement is in lines 97 and 98:

```
if (num < nodePtr->value)
   deleteNode(num, nodePtr->left);
```

This code compares the parameter num with the `value` member of the node that `nodePtr` points to. If num is less, then the value being searched for will appear somewhere in `nodePtr`'s left subtree (if it appears in the tree at all). In this case, the `deleteNode` function is recursively called with num as the first argument and `nodePtr->left` as the second argument.

If num is not less than `nodePtr->value`, the `else if` in lines 99 and 100 statement is executed:

```
else if (num > nodePtr->value)
   deleteNode(num, nodePtr->right);
```

If num is greater than `nodePtr->value`, then the value being searched for will appear somewhere in `nodePtr`'s right subtree (if it appears in the tree at all). So, the `deleteNode` function is recursively called with num as the first argument, and `nodePtr->right` as the second argument.

If num is equal to nodePtr->value, then neither of the if statements will find a true condition. In this case, nodePtr points to the node that is to be deleted, and the trailing else in lines 101 and 102 will execute:

```
else
    makeDeletion(nodePtr);
```

The trailing else statement calls the makeDeletion function, and passes nodePtr as its argument. The makeDeletion function actually deletes the node from the tree, and must reattach the deleted node's subtrees as shown in Figure 20-9. Therefore, it must have access to the actual pointer, in the binary tree, to the node that is being deleted (not just a copy of the pointer). This is why the nodePtr parameter in the deleteNode function is a reference. It must pass to makeDeletion the actual pointer, in the binary tree, to the node that is to be deleted. The makeDeletion function's code is as follows:

```
112    void IntBinaryTree::makeDeletion(TreeNode *&nodePtr)
113    {
114        // Define a temporary pointer to use in reattaching
115        // the left subtree.
116        TreeNode *tempNodePtr;
117
118        if (nodePtr == NULL)
119            cout << "Cannot delete empty node.\n";
120        else if (nodePtr->right == NULL)
121        {
122            tempNodePtr = nodePtr;
123            nodePtr = nodePtr->left;    // Reattach the left child.
124            delete tempNodePtr;
125        }
126        else if (nodePtr->left == NULL)
127        {
128            tempNodePtr = nodePtr;
129            nodePtr = nodePtr->right;  // Reattach the right child.
130            delete tempNodePtr;
131        }
132        // If the node has two children.
133        else
134        {
135            // Move one node to the right.
136            tempNodePtr = nodePtr->right;
137            // Go to the end left node.
138            while (tempNodePtr->left)
139                tempNodePtr = tempNodePtr->left;
140            // Reattach the left subtree.
141            tempNodePtr->left = nodePtr->left;
142            tempNodePtr = nodePtr;
143            // Reattach the right subtree.
144            nodePtr = nodePtr->right;
145            delete tempNodePtr;
146        }
147    }
```

Program 20-4 demonstrates these functions.

Program 20-4

```cpp
 1    // This program builds a binary tree with 5 nodes.
 2    // The DeleteNode function is used to remove two of them.
 3    #include <iostream>
 4    #include "IntBinaryTree.h"
 5    using namespace std;
 6
 7    int main()
 8    {
 9        IntBinaryTree tree;
10
11        // Insert some values into the tree.
12        cout << "Inserting nodes.\n";
13        tree.insertNode(5);
14        tree.insertNode(8);
15        tree.insertNode(3);
16        tree.insertNode(12);
17        tree.insertNode(9);
18
19        // Display the values.
20        cout << "Here are the values in the tree:\n";
21        tree.displayInOrder();
22
23        // Delete the value 8.
24        cout << "Deleting 8...\n";
25        tree.remove(8);
26
27        // Delete the value 12.
28        cout << "Deleting 12...\n";
29        tree.remove(12);
30
31        // Display the values.
32        cout << "Now, here are the nodes:\n";
33        tree.displayInOrder();
34        return 0;
35    }
```

Program Output

```
Inserting nodes.
Here are the values in the tree:
3
5
8
9
12
Deleting 8...
Deleting 12...
Now, here are the nodes:
3
5
9
```

For your reference, the entire contents of `IntBinaryTree` file are shown below.

Contents of `IntBinaryTree.cpp`

```
1   // Implementation file for the IntBinaryTree class
2   #include <iostream>
3   #include "IntBinaryTree.h"
4   using namespace std;
5
6   //**********************************************************
7   // insert accepts a TreeNode pointer and a pointer to a node. *
8   // The function inserts the node into the tree pointed to by  *
9   // the TreeNode pointer. This function is called recursively. *
10  //**********************************************************
11
12  void IntBinaryTree::insert(TreeNode *&nodePtr, TreeNode *&newNode)
13  {
14     if (nodePtr == NULL)
15        nodePtr = newNode;                    // Insert the node.
16     else if (newNode->value < nodePtr->value)
17        insert(nodePtr->left, newNode);    // Search the left branch.
18     else
19        insert(nodePtr->right, newNode);   // Search the right branch.
20  }
21
22  //**********************************************************
23  // insertNode creates a new node to hold num as its value, *
24  // and passes it to the insert function.                   *
25  //**********************************************************
26
27  void IntBinaryTree::insertNode(int num)
28  {
29     TreeNode *newNode;         // Pointer to a new node.
30
31     // Create a new node and store num in it.
32     newNode = new TreeNode;
33     newNode->value = num;
34     newNode->left = newNode->right = NULL;
35
36     // Insert the node.
37     insert(root, newNode);
38  }
39
40  //**********************************************************
41  // destroySubTree is called by the destructor. It    *
42  // deletes all nodes in the tree.                     *
43  //**********************************************************
44
45  void IntBinaryTree::destroySubTree(TreeNode *nodePtr)
46  {
47     if (nodePtr)
48     {
49        if (nodePtr->left)
50           destroySubTree(nodePtr->left);
```

```
51          if (nodePtr->right)
52             destroySubTree(nodePtr->right);
53          delete nodePtr;
54       }
55  }
56
57  //*******************************************************
58  // searchNode determines whether a value is present in *
59  // the tree. If so, the function returns true.          *
60  // Otherwise, it returns false.                         *
61  //*******************************************************
62
63  bool IntBinaryTree::searchNode(int num)
64  {
65     TreeNode *nodePtr = root;
66
67     while (nodePtr)
68     {
69        if (nodePtr->value == num)
70           return true;
71        else if (num < nodePtr->value)
72           nodePtr = nodePtr->left;
73        else
74           nodePtr = nodePtr->right;
75     }
76     return false;
77  }
78
79  //*********************************************
80  // remove calls deleteNode to delete the     *
81  // node whose value member is the same as num. *
82  //*********************************************
83
84  void IntBinaryTree::remove(int num)
85  {
86     deleteNode(num, root);
87  }
88
89
90  //*********************************************
91  // deleteNode deletes the node whose value    *
92  // member is the same as num.                 *
93  //*********************************************
94
95  void IntBinaryTree::deleteNode(int num, TreeNode *&nodePtr)
96  {
97     if (num < nodePtr->value)
98        deleteNode(num, nodePtr->left);
99     else if (num > nodePtr->value)
100       deleteNode(num, nodePtr->right);
101    else
102       makeDeletion(nodePtr);
103 }
104
105
```

```
106   //**************************************************************
107   // makeDeletion takes a reference to a pointer to the node    *
108   // that is to be deleted. The node is removed and the         *
109   // branches of the tree below the node are reattached.        *
110   //**************************************************************
111
112   void IntBinaryTree::makeDeletion(TreeNode *&nodePtr)
113   {
114      // Define a temporary pointer to use in reattaching
115      // the left subtree.
116      TreeNode *tempNodePtr;
117
118      if (nodePtr == NULL)
119         cout << "Cannot delete empty node.\n";
120      else if (nodePtr->right == NULL)
121      {
122         tempNodePtr = nodePtr;
123         nodePtr = nodePtr->left;    // Reattach the left child.
124         delete tempNodePtr;
125      }
126      else if (nodePtr->left == NULL)
127      {
128         tempNodePtr = nodePtr;
129         nodePtr = nodePtr->right;  // Reattach the right child.
130         delete tempNodePtr;
131      }
132      // If the node has two children.
133      else
134      {
135         // Move one node to the right.
136         tempNodePtr = nodePtr->right;
137         // Go to the end left node.
138         while (tempNodePtr->left)
139            tempNodePtr = tempNodePtr->left;
140         // Reattach the left subtree.
141         tempNodePtr->left = nodePtr->left;
142         tempNodePtr = nodePtr;
143         // Reattach the right subtree.
144         nodePtr = nodePtr->right;
145         delete tempNodePtr;
146      }
147   }
148
149   //****************************************************************
150   // The displayInOrder member function displays the values       *
151   // in the subtree pointed to by nodePtr, via inorder traversal. *
152   //****************************************************************
153
154   void IntBinaryTree::displayInOrder(TreeNode *nodePtr) const
155   {
156      if (nodePtr)
157      {
158         displayInOrder(nodePtr->left);
159         cout << nodePtr->value << endl;
160         displayInOrder(nodePtr->right);
161      }
162   }
```

```
163
164   //****************************************************************
165   // The displayPreOrder member function displays the values      *
166   // in the subtree pointed to by nodePtr, via preorder traversal. *
167   //****************************************************************
168
169   void IntBinaryTree::displayPreOrder(TreeNode *nodePtr) const
170   {
171      if (nodePtr)
172      {
173         cout << nodePtr->value << endl;
174         displayPreOrder(nodePtr->left);
175         displayPreOrder(nodePtr->right);
176      }
177   }
178
179   //****************************************************************
180   // The displayPostOrder member function displays the values     *
181   // in the subtree pointed to by nodePtr, via postorder traversal.*
182   //****************************************************************
183
184   void IntBinaryTree::displayPostOrder(TreeNode *nodePtr) const
185   {
186      if (nodePtr)
187      {
188         displayPostOrder(nodePtr->left);
189         displayPostOrder(nodePtr->right);
190         cout << nodePtr->value << endl;
191      }
192   }
```

 Checkpoint

myprogramminglab *www.myprogramminglab.com*

20.7   Describe the sequence of events in an inorder traversal.

20.8   Describe the sequence of events in a preorder traversal.

20.9   Describe the sequence of events in a postorder traversal.

20.10   Describe the steps taken in deleting a leaf node.

20.11   Describe the steps taken in deleting a node with one child.

20.12   Describe the steps taken in deleting a node with two children.

20.3 Template Considerations for Binary Search Trees

CONCEPT: Binary search trees may be implemented as templates, but any data types used with them must support the <, >, and == operators.

When designing a binary tree template, remember that any data types stored in the binary tree must support the <, >, and == operators. If you use the tree to store class objects, these operators must be overridden.

The following code shows an example of a binary tree template. Program 20-5 demonstrates the template. It creates a binary tree that can hold strings, and then prompts the user to enter a series of names that are inserted into the tree. The program then displays the contents of the tree using inorder traversal.

Contents of `BinaryTree.h`

```
 1  #ifndef BINARYTREE_H
 2  #define BINARYTREE_H
 3  #include <iostream>
 4  using namespace std;
 5
 6  // Stack template
 7  template <class T>
 8  class BinaryTree
 9  {
10  private:
11     struct TreeNode
12     {
13        T value;          // The value in the node
14        TreeNode *left;   // Pointer to left child node
15        TreeNode *right;  // Pointer to right child node
16     };
17
18     TreeNode *root;       // Pointer to the root node
19
20     // Private member functions
21     void insert(TreeNode *&, TreeNode *&);
22     void destroySubTree(TreeNode *);
23     void deleteNode(T, TreeNode *&);
24     void makeDeletion(TreeNode *&);
25     void displayInOrder(TreeNode *) const;
26     void displayPreOrder(TreeNode *) const;
27     void displayPostOrder(TreeNode *) const;
28
29  public:
30     // Constructor
31     BinaryTree()
32        { root = NULL; }
33
34     // Destructor
35     ~BinaryTree()
36        { destroySubTree(root); }
37
38     // Binary tree operations
39     void insertNode(T);
40     bool searchNode(T);
41     void remove(T);
42
43     void displayInOrder() const
44        { displayInOrder(root); }
45
46     void displayPreOrder() const
47        { displayPreOrder(root); }
48
```

```
49      void displayPostOrder() const
50         { displayPostOrder(root); }
51  };
52
53  //**********************************************************
54  // insert accepts a TreeNode pointer and a pointer to a node. *
55  // The function inserts the node into the tree pointed to by  *
56  // the TreeNode pointer. This function called recursively. *
57  //**********************************************************
58  template <class T>
59  void BinaryTree<T>::insert(TreeNode *&nodePtr, TreeNode *&newNode)
60  {
61     if (nodePtr == NULL)
62        nodePtr = newNode;                     // Insert the node
63     else if (newNode->value < nodePtr->value)
64        insert(nodePtr->left, newNode);    // Search the left branch
65     else
66        insert(nodePtr->right, newNode);   // Search the right branch
67  }
68
69  //**********************************************************
70  // insertNode creates a new node to hold num as its value, *
71  // and passes it to the insert function.                   *
72  //**********************************************************
73  template <class T>
74  void BinaryTree<T>::insertNode(T item)
75  {
76     TreeNode *newNode;        // Pointer to a new node
77
78     // Create a new node and store num in it.
79     newNode = new TreeNode;
80     newNode->value = item;
81     newNode->left = newNode->right = NULL;
82
83     // Insert the node.
84     insert(root, newNode);
85  }
86
87  //**********************************************************
88  // destroySubTree is called by the destructor. It    *
89  // deletes all nodes in the tree.                     *
90  //**********************************************************
91  template <class T>
92  void BinaryTree<T>::destroySubTree(TreeNode *nodePtr)
93  {
94     if (nodePtr)
95     {
96        if (nodePtr->left)
97           destroySubTree(nodePtr->left);
98        if (nodePtr->right)
99           destroySubTree(nodePtr->right);
100       delete nodePtr;
101    }
102 }
103
```

```cpp
104  //****************************************************
105  // searchNode determines if a value is present in   *
106  // the tree. If so, the function returns true.       *
107  // Otherwise, it returns false.                      *
108  //****************************************************
109  template <class T>
110  bool BinaryTree<T>::searchNode(T item)
111  {
112     TreeNode *nodePtr = root;
113
114     while (nodePtr)
115     {
116        if (nodePtr->value == item)
117           return true;
118        else if (item < nodePtr->value)
119           nodePtr = nodePtr->left;
120        else
121           nodePtr = nodePtr->right;
122     }
123     return false;
124  }
125
126  //*********************************************
127  // remove calls deleteNode to delete the     *
128  // node whose value member is the same as num. *
129  //*********************************************
130  template <class T>
131  void BinaryTree<T>::remove(T item)
132  {
133     deleteNode(item, root);
134  }
135
136  //*********************************************
137  // deleteNode deletes the node whose value    *
138  // member is the same as num.                 *
139  //*********************************************
140  template <class T>
141  void BinaryTree<T>::deleteNode(T item, TreeNode *&nodePtr)
142  {
143     if (item < nodePtr->value)
144        deleteNode(item, nodePtr->left);
145     else if (item > nodePtr->value)
146        deleteNode(item, nodePtr->right);
147     else
148        makeDeletion(nodePtr);
149  }
150
151  //****************************************************************
152  // makeDeletion takes a reference to a pointer to the node   *
153  // that is to be deleted. The node is removed and the        *
154  // branches of the tree below the node are reattached.       *
155  //****************************************************************
156  template <class T>
157  void BinaryTree<T>::makeDeletion(TreeNode *&nodePtr)
158  {
```

```
159      // Define a temporary pointer to use in reattaching
160      // the left subtree.
161      TreeNode *tempNodePtr;
162
163      if (nodePtr == NULL)
164         cout << "Cannot delete empty node.\n";
165      else if (nodePtr->right == NULL)
166      {
167         tempNodePtr = nodePtr;
168         nodePtr = nodePtr->left;    // Reattach the left child
169         delete tempNodePtr;
170      }
171      else if (nodePtr->left == NULL)
172      {
173         tempNodePtr = nodePtr;
174         nodePtr = nodePtr->right;  // Reattach the right child
175         delete tempNodePtr;
176      }
177      // If the node has two children.
178      else
179      {
180         // Move one node to the right.
181         tempNodePtr = nodePtr->right;
182         // Go to the end left node.
183         while (tempNodePtr->left)
184            tempNodePtr = tempNodePtr->left;
185         // Reattach the left subtree.
186         tempNodePtr->left = nodePtr->left;
187         tempNodePtr = nodePtr;
188         // Reattach the right subtree.
189         nodePtr = nodePtr->right;
190         delete tempNodePtr;
191      }
192 }
193
194 //*************************************************************
195 // The displayInOrder member function displays the values    *
196 // in the subtree pointed to by nodePtr, via inorder traversal. *
197 //*************************************************************
198 template <class T>
199 void BinaryTree<T>::displayInOrder(TreeNode *nodePtr) const
200 {
201    if (nodePtr)
202    {
203       displayInOrder(nodePtr->left);
204       cout << nodePtr->value << endl;
205       displayInOrder(nodePtr->right);
206    }
207 }
208
209 //*************************************************************
210 // The displayPreOrder member function displays the values    *
211 // in the subtree pointed to by nodePtr, via preorder traversal. *
212 //*************************************************************
213 template <class T>
214 void BinaryTree<T>::displayPreOrder(TreeNode *nodePtr) const
```

```
215 {
216    if (nodePtr)
217    {
218       cout << nodePtr->value << endl;
219       displayPreOrder(nodePtr->left);
220       displayPreOrder(nodePtr->right);
221    }
222 }
223
224 //************************************************************
225 // The displayPostOrder member function displays the values   *
226 // in the subtree pointed to by nodePtr, via postorder traversal.*
227 //************************************************************
228 template <class T>
229 void BinaryTree<T>::displayPostOrder(TreeNode *nodePtr) const
230 {
231    if (nodePtr)
232    {
233       displayPostOrder(nodePtr->left);
234       displayPostOrder(nodePtr->right);
235       cout << nodePtr->value << endl;
236    }
237 }
238 #endif
```

Program 20-5

```
1 // This program demonstrates the BinaryTree class template.
2 // It builds a binary tree with 5 nodes.
3 #include <iostream>
4 #include "BinaryTree.h"
5 using namespace std;
6
7 const int NUM_NODES = 5;
8
9 int main()
10 {
11    string name;
12
13    // Create the binary tree.
14    BinaryTree<string> tree;
15
16    // Insert some names.
17    for (int count = 0; count < NUM_NODES; count++)
18    {
19       cout << "Enter a name: ";
20       getline(cin, name);
21       tree.insertNode(name);
22    }
23
24    // Display the values.
25    cout << "\nHere are the values in the tree:\n";
26    tree.displayInOrder();
27    return 0;
28 }
```

Program Output with Example Input Shown in Bold
```
Enter a name: David [Enter]
Enter a name: Geri [Enter]
Enter a name: Chris [Enter]
Enter a name: Samantha [Enter]
Enter a name: Anthony [Enter]

Here are the values in the tree:
Anthony
Chris
David
Geri
Samantha
```

Review Questions and Exercises

Short Answer

1. Each node in a binary tree may point to how many other nodes?

2. How many predecessors may each node other than the root node have?

3. What is a leaf node?

4. What is a subtree?

5. What initially determines the shape of a binary tree?

6. What are the three methods of traversing a binary tree? What is the difference between these methods?

Fill-in-the-Blank

7. The first node in a binary tree is called the _____.

8. A binary tree node's left and right pointers point to the node's _____.

9. A node with no children is called a(n) _____.

10. A(n) _____ is an entire branch of the tree, from one particular node down.

11. The three common types of traversal with a binary tree are _____, _____, and _____.

Algorithm Workbench

12. Write a pseudocode algorithm for inserting a node in a tree.

13. Write a pseudocode algorithm for the inorder traversal.

14. Write a pseudocode algorithm for the preorder traversal.

15. Write a pseudocode algorithm for the postorder traversal.

16. Write a pseudocode algorithm for searching a tree for a specified value.

17. Suppose the following values are inserted into a binary tree, in the order given:

    12, 7, 9, 10, 22, 24, 30, 18, 3, 14, 20

    Draw a diagram of the resulting binary tree.

18. How would the values in the tree you sketched for Question 17 be displayed in an inorder traversal?

19. How would the values in the tree you sketched for Question 17 be displayed in a pre-order traversal?

20. How would the values in the tree you sketched for Question 17 be displayed in a postorder traversal?

True or False

21. T F Each node in a binary tree must have at least two children.

22. T F When a node is inserted into a tree, it must be inserted as a leaf node.

23. T F Values stored in the current node's left subtree are less than the value stored in the current node.

24. T F The shape of a binary tree is determined by the order in which values are inserted.

25. T F In inorder traversal, the node's data is processed first, then the left and right nodes are visited.

Programming Challenges

Visit www.myprogramminglab.com to complete many of these Programming Challenges online and get instant feedback.

VideoNote
Solving the Node Counter Problem

1. Binary Tree Template

Write your own version of a class template that will create a binary tree that can hold values of any data type. Demonstrate the class with a driver program.

2. Node Counter

Write a member function, for either the template you designed in Programming Challenge 1 or the `IntBinaryTree` class, that counts and returns the number of nodes in the tree. Demonstrate the function in a driver program.

3. Leaf Counter

Write a member function, for either the template you designed in Programming Challenge 1 or the `IntBinaryTree` class, that counts and returns the number of leaf nodes in the tree. Demonstrate the function in a driver program.

4. Tree Height

Write a member function, for either the template you designed in Programming Challenge 1 or the `IntBinaryTree` class, that returns the height of the tree. The height of the tree is the number of levels it contains. For example, the tree shown in Figure 20-10 has three levels.

Figure 20-10

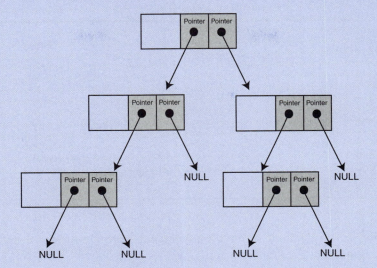

Demonstrate the function in a driver program.

5. **Tree Width**

   Write a member function, for either the template you designed in Programming Challenge 1 or the `IntBinaryTree` class, that returns the width of the tree. The width of the tree is the largest number of nodes in the same level. Demonstrate the function in a driver program.

6. **Tree Assignment Operator and Copy Constructor**

   Design an overloaded assignment operator and a copy constructor for either the template you designed in Programming Challenge 1 or the `IntBinaryTree` class. Demonstrate them in a driver program.

7. **Queue Converter**

   Write a program that stores a series of numbers in a binary tree. Then have the program insert the values into a queue in ascending order. Dequeue the values and display them on the screen to confirm that they were stored in the proper order.

8. **Employee Tree**

   Design an `EmployeeInfo` class that holds the following employee information:

Employee ID Number:	an integer
Employee Name:	a string

   Next, use the template you designed in Programming Challenge 1 to implement a binary tree whose nodes hold an instance of the `EmployeeInfo` class. The nodes should be sorted on the Employee ID number.

Test the binary tree by inserting nodes with the following information.

Employee ID Number	Name
1021	John Williams
1057	Bill Witherspoon
2487	Jennifer Twain
3769	Sophia Lancaster
1017	Debbie Reece
1275	George McMullen
1899	Ashley Smith
4218	Josh Plemmons

Your program should allow the user to enter an ID number, then search the tree for the number. If the number is found, it should display the employee's name. If the node is not found, it should display a message indicating so.

A Getting Started with Alice

Alice is an innovative software system that allows you to create 3D animations and computer games while learning fundamental programming concepts. With Alice you place graphical objects such as people, animals, buildings, cars, and so on inside 3D virtual worlds. Then you create programming statements that make the objects perform actions. Alice's drag-and-drop program editor makes it easy to create animations with rich interactions between objects.

This appendix serves as a quick reference for using Alice versions 2.0 or 2.2. If you need a complete text that teaches programming using the Alice software, see *Starting Out with Alice: A Visual Introduction to Programming*, also published by Addison-Wesley.

Downloading and Installing Alice

Alice is free software, available from Carnegie Mellon University. You can download the latest version from http://www.alice.org. When you download Alice 2.2 (the recommended version at the time this appendix was written) to your system, you get a file named *Alice2.2.zip*. There is no installation wizard with Alice; you simply extract the contents of this file in the location where you want to install the software.

When you extract the contents of *Alice2.2.zip* you will get a folder named *Alice2.2*. Inside this folder you will find an executable file named *Alice.exe*. Double-click this file to run Alice.

 TIP: You will probably want to create a shortcut to the *Alice.exe* file on your desktop. Right-click the file and then select *Send To Desktop (create shortcut)* from the menu. To start Alice double-click the shortcut that appears on the desktop.

Using the *Welcome to Alice!* Dialog Box

When you start Alice the splash screen shown in Figure A-1 will display for a few seconds. When the software is fully loaded you should see the *Welcome to Alice!* dialog box, as shown in Figure A-2.

Figure A-1 The Alice splash screen

Figure A-2 The *Welcome to Alice!* dialog box

 NOTE: If you do not see the *Welcome to Alice!* dialog box on your system, then Alice has been configured so it will not display the dialog box at startup, which might be the case in a shared computer lab. You can display the dialog box by clicking *File* on the menu bar, and then clicking the *New World* or *Open World...* menu items.

Note that at the bottom of the *Welcome to Alice!* dialog box there is a *Show this dialog at start* check box. Make sure this check box is checked so the dialog box will be displayed each time you start Alice.

Near the top of the *Welcome to Alice!* dialog box you will see a set of tabs labeled *Tutorial, Recent Worlds, Templates, Examples,* and *Open a world.* The following are brief descriptions of what you get when you click these tabs:

Tutorial—Click this tab and you will see a set of four Alice worlds that work as tutorials. These tutorial worlds guide you through the basic features of Alice. If you want to run the tutorials, click the *Start the Tutorial* button to execute them in order, or select and open any of the worlds individually.

Recent Worlds—Click this tab and you will see thumbnail images of the worlds that were most recently opened on your system. You can quickly open any world shown in this tab by selecting its thumbnail image and then clicking the *Open* button. You will not see any worlds listed here if you have not yet opened any worlds.

Templates—Click this tab and you will see a set of templates that you can use to create a new world. The templates are named *dirt, grass, sand, snow, space,* and *water.* Each template gives you a ground surface and a sky color.

Examples—Click this tab and you will see thumbnail images of example worlds that have been created by the developers of Alice.

Open a world—Click this tab and you will see a dialog box that allows you to open an Alice world. With this tab you can browse your local system or any attached network drive for Alice worlds. Note that Alice worlds are saved in files that end with the *.a2w* extension. (The *.a2w* extension signifies that the file contains an Alice version 2.0 or 2.2 world.)

The Alice Environment

In Alice the screen that you work with is referred to as the *Alice environment.* The Alice environment is divided into the following areas: the Toolbar, the World View Window, the Object Tree, the Details Panel, the Method Editor, and the Events Editor. In addition, the toolbar area provides a trashcan icon and one or more clipboard icons. The locations of these different areas and icons are shown in Figure A-3. In the figure, *SnowLove,* one of the example worlds, is opened. Brief descriptions of each area in the Alice environment follow:

Toolbar—The toolbar provides a *Play* button that plays your virtual world, an *Undo* button that undoes the previous operation, and a *Redo* button that repeats the operation that was most recently undone.

Trashcan—Next to the buttons on the toolbar there is a trashcan icon. You delete items by dragging them to the trashcan.

Clipboards—The clipboard provides a place to store a copy of something. In Alice clipboards you can store copies of objects, instructions, methods, and events. To store a copy of an item in a clipboard, you click and drag the item to the clipboard. When a clipboard contains an item, it appears as if it has a white sheet of paper on it. In Figure A-3 the left-most clipboard shows an example. To paste the item that is stored in a clipboard, you click and drag the clipboard icon to the location where you want to paste the item. If you want to empty a clipboard, you click and drag it to the trashcan.

By default, Alice shows only one clipboard. To change the number of available clipboards you click the *Edit* menu and then click *Preferences*. On the dialog box that appears, you click the *Seldom Used* tab and then change the number that appears next to *number of clipboards*.

World View Window—The World View Window shows a view of your virtual world. Each virtual world has a camera; the World View Window acts as the camera's viewfinder and also provides controls for moving and rotating the camera.

Object Tree—The Object Tree holds a list of all the objects in the world. Each object in the world is represented by a *tile*, which is simply a small rectangular icon. Tiles are used extensively in the Alice environment to represent numerous things.

Details Panel—The Details Panel shows detailed information about an object that has been selected in the World View Window or in the Object Tree.

Method Editor—The Method Editor is where you create methods (a set of instructions that causes some action to take place). You create methods by arranging tiles in the Method Editor.

Events Editor—An event is some action that takes place while the world is playing, such as clicking the mouse or pressing a key. Alice is able to detect when various events take place. You can use the Events Editor to specify an action that is to take place when a specific event occurs.

Figure A-3 Parts of the Alice environment

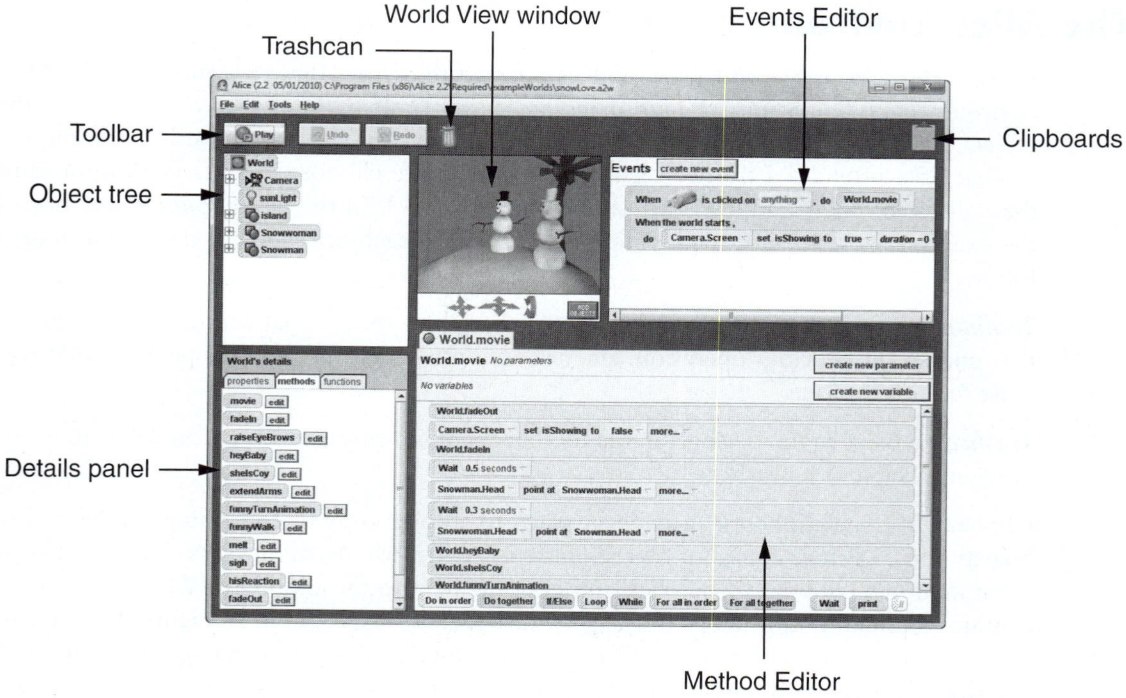

Playing a World

When you click the *Play* button, a separate *World Running...* window appears and the world's animation will play out in that window. For example, Figure A-4 shows the *Snow-Love* example world playing.

Figure A-4 The *SnowLove* world playing

Notice the toolbar at the top of the *World Running...* window. The following are brief descriptions of the items that appear on the toolbar:

Speed Slider Control—This controls the speed at which the world is played. When the slider is set to 1x, the world plays at normal speed. Moving the slider to the right increases the speed up to 10 times its normal speed.

Pause Button—Clicking the *Pause* button causes the world to pause.

Play Button—Once a world has been paused with the *Pause* button, you can click the *Play* button to resume playing.

Restart Button—Clicking the *Restart* button causes the world to start playing again.

Stop Button—Clicking the *Stop* button causes the world to stop playing and closes the *World Running...* window.

Take Picture Button—Clicking the *Take Picture* button captures an image from the world and saves it in a file. The dialog box that appears when you click the *Take Picture* button reports the name and path of the file containing the image.

Creating a New World and Adding Objects to It

To create a new world, you click *File* on the menu bar and then click the *New World...* menu item. This displays the *Welcome to Alice!* dialog box, as shown in Figure A-2. (By default, this dialog box is also displayed when you start Alice.) Make sure the *Templates* tab is selected, as shown in Figure A-5.

The *Templates* tab shows a set of templates named *dirt*, *grass*, *sand*, *snow*, *space*, and *water* that you can use to create a new world. When you select a template from this dialog box and then click the *Open* button, Alice will create a ground surface and set the color of the sky. For example, Figure A-6 shows a world that was created with the sand template.

Figure A-5 The *Welcome to Alice!* dialog box

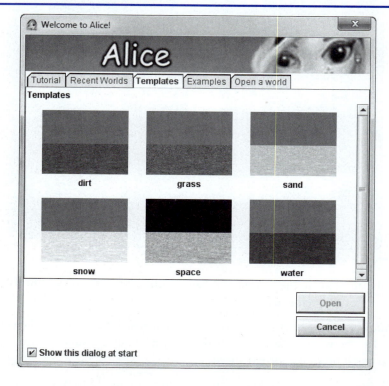

Figure A-6 shows the *Add Objects* button just below the World View Window. When you click this button the Alice environment changes to scene editor mode and opens a gallery, as shown in Figure A-7. A *gallery* is an assortment of different *types* of objects and is organized into various collections of objects such as animals, buildings, furniture, and people.

Alice provides two galleries: a local gallery and a Web gallery. The *local gallery* is stored on your computer and is installed with the Alice software. It provides a good sampling of object types and should be adequate for many of your projects. The *Web gallery* is maintained by the creators of Alice and may be accessed if your computer is connected to the Internet. It provides a much more extensive collection of object types than the local gallery.

Figure A-6 A world created with the sand template

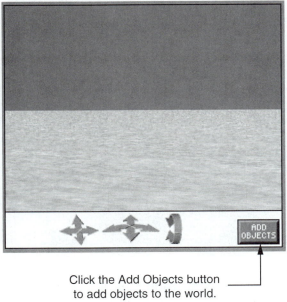

Click the Add Objects button
to add objects to the world.

Figure A-7 Alice in scene editor mode

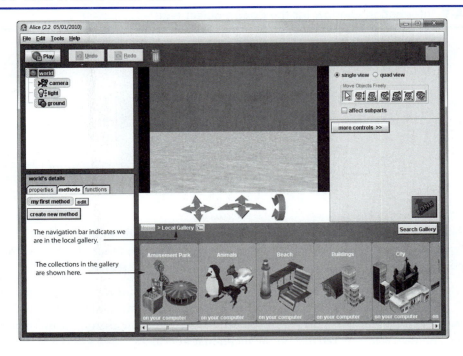

Figure A-7 points out a navigation bar that indicates which gallery and collection is currently displayed. Below the navigation bar are thumbnail images for the collections in the gallery. To open a collection and see the object types it contains, you click the collection's thumbnail image. For example, one of the collections is named *People*. It contains various types of people objects, as shown in Figure A-8.

Figure A-8 Some of the object types in the `People` collection

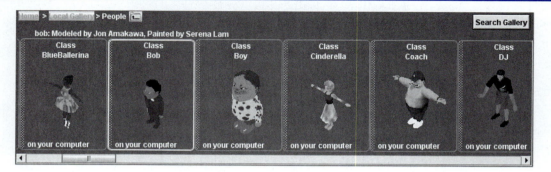

One way to add an object to the world is to click the thumbnail for that object type. You will then see an information window for the object. For example, if you click the thumbnail for the `Coach` object type, you will see the information window shown, as shown in Figure A-9. Click the *Add instance to world* button to add an object of this type to the world.

Figure A-9 Information window for the `Coach` object type

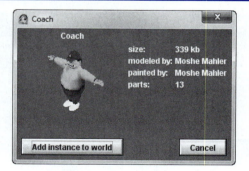

Another way to add an object to the world is to click and drag the thumbnail for the object type into the World View Window. When you release the mouse button (with the mouse pointer inside the World View Window) an object will be created.

After you add an object to a world, you should see a tile for the object in the Object Tree, as shown in Figure A-10. Each object in a world has a name, and the object's tile will show the name that Alice assigned to the object. You can rename the object by right-clicking its tile and then selecting *rename* on the menu that appears.

Figure A-10 An object is added to the world

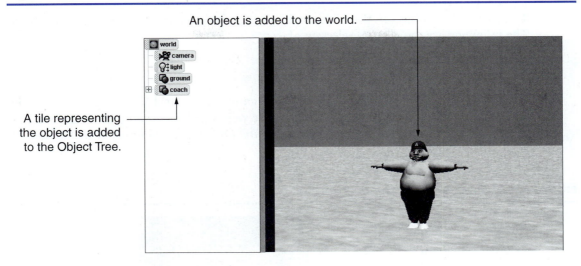

An object is added to the world.

A tile representing the object is added to the Object Tree.

Moving the Camera in the Alice Environment

The three camera controls shown in Figure A-11 appear just below the World View Window. You use these controls to move the camera around in the world and point it in different directions. The control on the left moves the camera up, down, left, and right. The control in the center moves the camera forward and backward, and rotates the camera left and right. The control on the right tilts the camera up and down.

Notice that each of the controls shows a set of arrows. You manipulate these controls by clicking and dragging the arrow that points in the direction that you want to move, rotate, or tilt the camera. You can make the camera move faster by dragging the mouse pointer away from the center of the camera control. The farther you drag the pointer away from the center of the camera control, the faster the camera will move.

Figure A-11 Camera controls

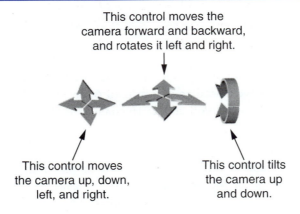

This control moves the camera forward and backward, and rotates it left and right.

This control moves the camera up, down, left, and right.

This control tilts the camera up and down.

Selecting Objects

To work with an object in the Alice environment, often you first have to select the object. The following are the ways to select an object:

- Click its tile in the Object Tree
- Click the object in the World View Window

When you select an object, a box appears around it in the World View Window, as shown in Figure A-12. (On your screen the box will be yellow.) This *bounding box* indicates that the object is selected. Also, the object's tile in the Object Tree will appear highlighted, as shown in the figure.

Figure A-12 The coach object is selected

Object Subparts

Objects are commonly made of other objects, which are referred to as *subparts*. When a plus sign appears next to an object tile in the Object Tree, it means that the object is made of subparts. For example, look at the Object Tree shown in Figure A-12 and notice that a plus sign appears next to the tile for the coach object. You can click the plus sign next to an object to expand the tree and see the tiles for the subparts. The plus sign then turns into a minus sign, which hides the inner objects when clicked.

Figure A-13 shows the Object Tree expanded to reveal that the coach object is composed of numerous subparts. One of these subparts, the head, is selected.

Properties

Each object in an Alice world has *properties*, which are values that specify the object's characteristics. Once you have placed an object in an Alice world, you can adjust its properties until it has the characteristics you desire. To change an object's property you perform the following steps:

- Select the object
- In the Details Panel select the *properties* tab, as shown in Figure A-14
- Change the value of the desired property (to change a property's value, click the down-arrow that appears next to the property's value)

Figure A-13 An object subpart selected

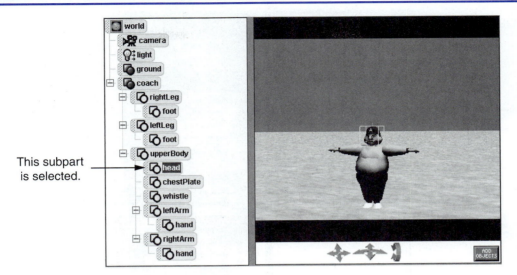

This subpart is selected.

Figure A-14 Properties displayed in the Details Panel

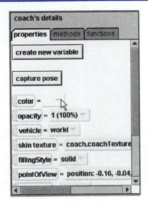

Primitive Methods

A *method* is a set of instructions that causes some action to take place. In Alice all objects have a common set of built-in methods for performing basic actions. These methods, which are known as *primitive methods*, cause objects to move, turn, change size, and do other fundamental operations.

While you are creating an Alice world you can immediately execute an object's primitive methods by right-clicking the object in the World View Window or the object's tile in the Object Tree. Then you select *methods* from the menu that appears. Another menu appears showing a list of methods that you can immediately execute in the World View Window. Figure A-15 shows an example of these menus. Table A-1 describes each of the primitive methods shown on the menu.

Figure A-15 Selecting a primitive method

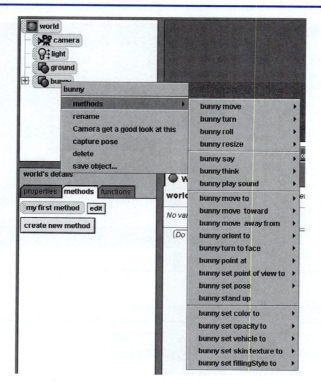

Table A-1 Primitive methods

Method Name	Description
move	This method causes the object to move up, down, left, right, forward, or backward. You specify the direction and distance that you want the object to move.
turn	This method causes the object to turn toward the left, right, forward, or backward. You specify the amount you want the object to turn in revolutions.
roll	This method causes the object to roll toward the left or the right. You specify the amount you want the object to roll in revolutions.
resize	This method changes the object's size by a specified amount.
say	This method causes a cartoon-like speech bubble containing a message to be displayed, as if the object were saying the message.
think	This method causes a cartoon-like thought bubble containing words to be displayed, as if the object were thinking the words.
play sound	This method plays a sound. You can specify one of the sounds that Alice provides or you can import any MP3 or WAV file.

(continues)

Table A-1 Primitive methods (*continued*)

Method Name	Description
move to	This method causes the object to move to another object. When the method completes, both objects' center points will be in the same location.
move toward	This method causes the object to move in the direction of another object. You specify the distance to move in meters.
move away from	This method causes the object to move away from another object. You specify the distance to move in meters.
orient to	This method orients the object in the same direction as another specified object. When this method executes the object will turn so its up, right, and forward axes are aligned with the axes of the specified object.
turn to face	This method causes the object to turn so it is facing another object.
point at	This method is similar to the turn to face method, except the object will be tilted so its forward axis is "aiming" at the specified object's center point.
set point of view to	This method sets the object's point of view to that of another object. It is commonly used with the camera to move it to the location of another object, and give a view from that object's point of view.
set pose	Alice allows you to position an object and its subparts in a certain way and then capture that as a pose. This method causes the object to assume a pose that was previously captured.
stand up	This method makes the object "stand up" by aligning the object's up axis with the world's up axis.
set color to	This method sets the object's color property to a specified color, making the object appear in that color.
set opacity to	This method sets the object's opacity property, which determines the object's transparency. You set this property to some value between 0 percent and 100 percent, where 0 is completely invisible and 100 is completely opaque.
set vehicle to	This method sets the object's vehicle property. The vehicle property couples the object with another object. When the other object moves, this object moves with it.
set skin texture to	This method sets the object's skin texture property. The skin texture property specifies a graphic image to be displayed on the object.
set fillingStyle to	The fillingStyle property determines how the object is displayed. It has three settings: solid, wireframe, and points. The default setting is solid, which causes the object to be displayed as a solid. When the fillingStyle property is set to wireframe, the object is displayed as a wire skeleton that you can see through. When the fillingStyle property is set to points, the object is displayed as a set of points.

Most of the primitive methods require that you specify additional pieces of information. For example, the move method causes the object to move, and it requires that you specify two pieces of information: a direction and an amount. These pieces of information are known as arguments—pieces of information that a method requires in order for it to execute.

Deleting Objects

You can delete an object in an Alice world by performing any of the following operations:

- Right-click the object in the World View Window and then select delete from the menu that appears
- Right-click the object's tile in the Object Tree and then select delete from the menu that appears
- Click and drag the object's tile from the Object Tree to the trashcan

Modifying Objects in Scene Editor Mode

When you click the *Add Objects* button, which appears below the World View Window, Alice goes into scene editor mode, in which you can use the mouse to modify the objects in your Alice world. For example, you can use the mouse to move objects, resize objects, rotate objects, and copy objects. Figure A-16 shows the location of the *mouse mode buttons*, which determine the action that can be performed with the mouse.

Figure A-16 Location of the mouse mode buttons

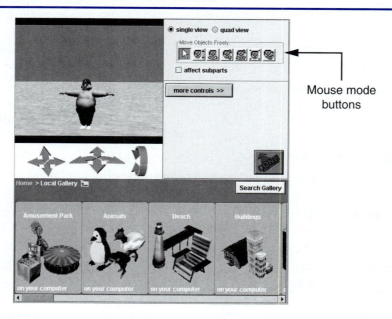

Mouse mode buttons

Figure A-17 shows the purposes of the buttons. The following are brief descriptions of each:

Move Freely—When this button is selected the mouse can be used to move an object freely in the world. Here are the actions that you can perform:
- To move an object horizontally within the world you simply click and drag it
- To move an object straight up or down, you hold down the (Shift) key while clicking and dragging the object
- To rotate an object left or right, you hold down the (Ctrl) key while clicking and dragging the object
- To tumble an object (rotate it left, right, forward, backward, or any combination of these directions), you hold down the (Ctrl) and (Shift) keys while clicking and dragging the object

Move Up and Down—When this button is selected you can move an object straight up or straight down by clicking and dragging the object.

Turn Left and Right—When this button is selected you can rotate an object toward the left or the right by clicking and dragging the object.

Turn Forward and Backward—When this button is selected you can rotate an object forward or backward by clicking and dragging the object.

Tumble—When this button is selected you can tumble an object by clicking and dragging the object. This means you can rotate the object right, left, forward, backward, or in any combination of these directions.

Resize—When this button is selected you can make an object larger or smaller by clicking and dragging the object.

Copy—When this button is selected you can make a copy of an object by clicking the object.

Figure A-17 The purposes of the mouse mode buttons

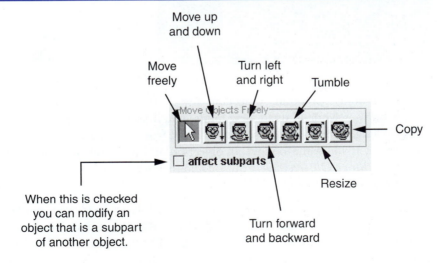

Notice that just below the buttons a check box labeled *affect subparts* appears. By default, this is not checked. When it is not checked the modifications that you make to an object using the *mouse mode* buttons are applied to the entire object. However, if you check the *affect subparts* check box, the modifications are applied only to one of the object's subparts.

Single View and Quad View Modes

When Alice is in scene editor mode, you can switch the display of the world between single view mode and quad view mode. So far we have been using *single view mode*, which is the default display mode. In single view mode you have one view of the world—the World View Window. In *quad view mode* you have four views of the world: the World View Window, a view from the top, a view from the right, and a view from the front. Figure A-18 shows an example of these views and points out the *quad view* button, which you click to switch to quad view mode.

Figure A-18 Quad view

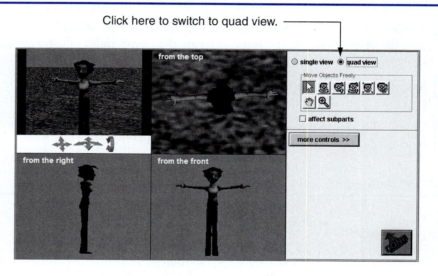

You can use the mouse to modify objects in any of the views. If you look carefully at the *mouse mode* buttons while in quad view mode, you'll notice that the *Move Up and Down* button ⬛ no longer appears because the right and front viewing windows support up and down movement. If you want to move an object up or down while in quad view mode, you simply select the *Move Objects Freely* button and then move the object up or down in either the right view or the front view.

You will also notice that two new buttons appear while in quad view mode: The *Scroll View* button ✋ and the *Zoom* button 🔍. Often, when you switch to quad view mode the objects in the world will not be fully visible in all of the views. To remedy this you can use the *Scroll View* button to scroll the top, right, or front view. To use the button, follow these steps:

1. Select the *Scroll View* button; the mouse pointer changes into a hand tool
2. Move the mouse pointer into the view you wish to scroll
3. Click and drag the view in the direction you wish to scroll

The *Zoom* button allows you to zoom into or out of the top, right, and front views. To use it, follow these steps:

1. Select the *Zoom* button; the mouse pointer changes into a zoom tool
2. Move the mouse pointer into the desired view and position it over the point that you wish to zoom into or zoom out from
3. Zoom by clicking and dragging; if you want to zoom in, drag down or to the right, if you want to zoom out, drag up or to the left

Writing Methods in Alice

Recall that a method is a set of instructions that causes some action to take place. If you want an action to take place when an Alice world is played, you have to write a method. Figure A-19 shows the location of the Method Editor in the Alice environment, where you write the methods that perform actions in an Alice world.

Figure A-19 The Method Editor

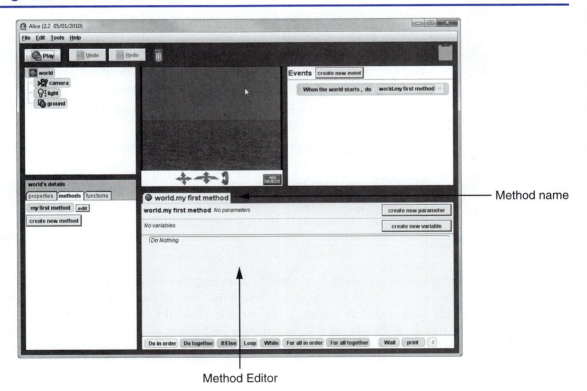

Notice that a *world.my first method* tab appears at the top of the Method Editor in Figure A-19. All methods have a name, and world.my first method is the name of the method that is currently open in the editor. When you create a new world Alice automatically creates an empty method named `world.my first method`. By default, this method is automatically executed when you play the world.

In Figure A-19 notice that a group of tiles appears at the bottom of the Method Editor. Each of these tiles is an instruction that you can place in the method. Table A-2 describes the instructions represented by these tiles.

Table A-2 Alice instructions

Instruction	Description
Do in order	You place other instructions inside a `Do in order` instruction. The instructions that you place inside a `Do in order` instruction are executed in the order that they appear.
Do together	You place other instructions inside a `Do together` instruction. The instructions that you place inside a `Do together` instruction are executed simultaneously.
If/Else	The `If/Else` instruction tests a condition, which is anything that gives a true or false value. If the value is true, then one set of instructions is executed. If the value is false, then a different set of instructions is executed.
Loop	The `Loop` instruction causes one or more other instructions to repeat a specific number of times.
While	The `While` instruction causes one or more other instructions to repeat as long as a condition is true.
For all in order	The `For all in order` instruction steps through the items in a list, one item at a time, performing the same operation on each item.
For all together	The `For all together` instruction performs the same operation on all the items in a list simultaneously.
Wait	The `Wait` instruction causes the method to pause for a specified number of seconds.
print	The `print` instruction displays a message in a special area at the bottom of the *World Running...* window.
//	The `//` tile allows you to insert a comment into a method.

In Alice you place instructions in a method by dragging tiles into the Method Editor. For example, if you want to place a `Wait` instruction in the method that you are currently writing, you simply click and drag the `Wait` tile into the Method Editor, as shown in Figure A-20. When you drop the tile (by releasing the mouse button) the `Wait` instruction will be created in the method.

In addition to using the instructions that you see at the bottom of the Method Editor, you can also create instructions that execute an object's primitive methods. Once you have added an object to a world, you can see tiles for all of the methods that the object can perform by doing the following:

1. Select the object
2. In the Details Panel select the *methods* tab to display a set of tiles representing the object's methods

Figure A-20 Dragging the `Wait` instruction into the Method Editor

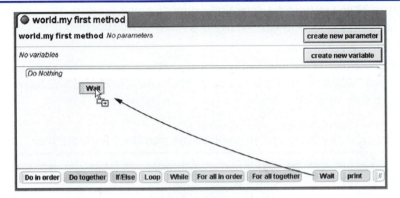

For example, Figure A-21 shows an Alice world with an instance of the `Hare` class (which is in the *Animals* collection). The object, which is named `hare`, is selected. The *methods* tab is selected in the Details Panel, and a set of tiles for the `hare` object's primitive methods is displayed.

Figure A-21 Methods displayed in the Details Panel

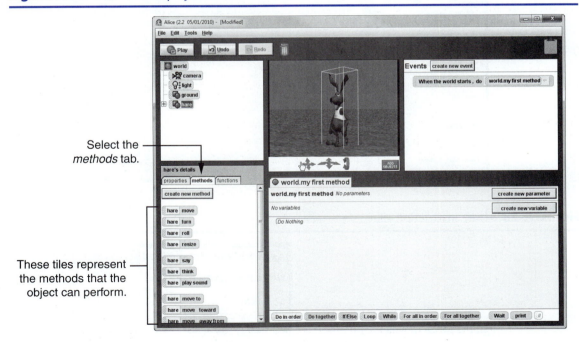

To create an instruction that executes a primitive method in the method that you are currently writing, simply drag the primitive method's tile and drop it into the Method Editor.

For example, Figure A-22 shows tile for the `hare` object's `move` method being dragged into the Method Editor.

Most of the primitive methods require that you specify arguments. For example, when you drop the tile for the `move` method into the Method Editor, a pop-up menu appears allowing you to select a direction. The allowable directions are up, down, left, right, forward, and backward. After you select a direction, another menu appears allowing you to select an amount, which is the distance that the object moves. In Alice distances are always measured in meters.

Figure A-23 shows an example of `world.my first method` after three instructions have been created. When the world containing this method is played, the `hare` object will move up 1 meter, then turn left 1 revolution, and then move down 1 meter.

Figure A-22 Dragging the `hare.move` method tile into the Method Editor

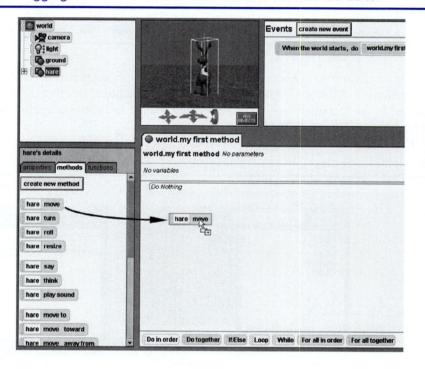

Figure A-23 Three instruction tiles

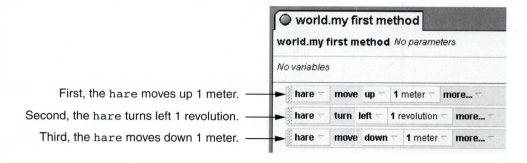

Copying and Deleting Instructions

To make a copy of an instruction tile within the same method, you right-click the tile and then select *make copy* from the menu that appears. To copy an instruction so that you can paste it into a different method, you drag the instruction to the clipboard. Then you open the method that you want to paste the instruction into, and click and drag the clipboard icon to the location where you want to paste the instruction. To delete an instruction tile that you have created in the Method Editor, you drag the tile to the trashcan.

Creating Methods

When you first create an Alice world, a method named `world.my first method` is automatically created in the `world` object. You are not limited to this one method in the world, however. Follow these steps to create a new method in the `world`:

1. Select the `world` in the Object Tree.
2. In the Details Panel, under the *methods* tab, click the *create new method* button, as shown in Figure A-24.
3. A dialog box will appear asking for the new method's name. Enter a name in the dialog box and click the *OK* button. A tile for the new method will appear in the Details Panel, above the *create new method* button. For example, the Details Panel in Figure A-25 shows three world-level methods.
4. Create the instructions for the method in the Method Editor.

Figure A-24 The *create new method* button

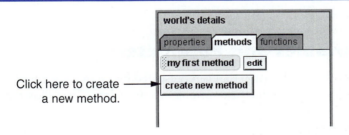

Figure A-25 An example of a world with three world-level methods

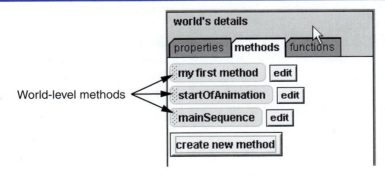

Once you have created the new method, you can call it from other methods by dragging the new method's tile from the Details Panel into the Method Editor and dropping it at the point where you wish to call the method.

You can also create your own custom methods in the objects that you place in your world. In Alice the methods that are part of an object are referred to as *class-level methods*. If an object doesn't provide all of the methods that you need, you can easily add your own methods for that object. You write custom class-level methods in Alice by following these steps:

1. Create the desired object.
2. Select the object.
3. In the Details Panel, under the *methods* tab, click the *create new method* button.
4. A dialog box will appear asking for the new method's name. Enter a name in the dialog box and click the *OK* button. A tile for the new method will appear in the Details Panel, above the *create new method* button.
5. Create the instructions for the method in the Method Editor.

Once you have created the new method, you can call it from other methods in the usual way: by dragging the new method's tile into the Method Editor and dropping it at the point where you wish to call the method.

Renaming Methods

To rename a method, you simply right-click the method's tile and select *Rename* from the menu that appears. After you do this, you will be able to edit the name that appears on the method's tile directly.

Creating Variables and Parameters

A variable is a storage location that is represented by a name. Like traditional programming languages, Alice allows you to use variables to store data. The following variable categories are available in Alice:

- **Local Variables**—A *local variable* belongs to a specific method and can be used only in the instructions in that method. When a method stops executing, its local variables cease to exist in memory.
- **World-Level Variables**—A *world-level variable* belongs to the world object, and exists as long as the world is playing.
- **Class-Level Variables**—A *class-level variable* belongs to a specific object, and exists as long as the object exists. Class-level variables are like properties.
- **Parameter Variables**—A *parameter variable* is used to hold an argument that is passed to a method when the method is called. Once you create a parameter variable in a method, you must provide an argument for that parameter whenever you call the method.

Before you can use a variable, you have to create it. To create a local variable or a parameter variable in a method, you open the method in the Method Editor and then you click the *create new variable* button or the *create new parameter* button. Figure A-26 shows the locations of these buttons.

Figure A-26 The *create new variable* button

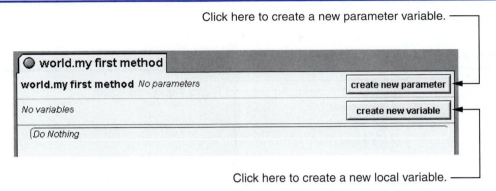

When you click either of these buttons, a dialog box appears requiring you to enter more information about the variable. In the dialog box you enter the variable's name and select the variable's type and initial value. Figure A-27 shows the *Create New Local Variable* dialog box, which appears when you click the *create new variable* button. When you click the *create new parameter* button, a dialog box that is virtually identical to the one in Figure A-27 is displayed.

After you provide a name for the variable, select its type, specify its initial value, and click the *OK* button, a tile for the variable is created in the method.

Figure A-27 The *Create New Local Variable* dialog box

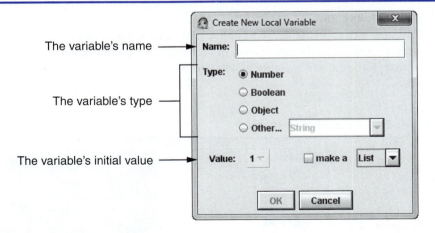

To create a world-level variable you perform the following steps:

1. Select the `world` object in the Object Tree.
2. In the Details Panel select the *properties* tab.

3. Click the *create new variable* button, which appears at the top of the *properties* tab, as shown in Figure A-28.

4. Enter the variable's name, type, and initial value in the *create new variable* dialog box, which is similar to the one shown in Figure A-27. When you click the dialog box's *OK* button, a tile for the variable will be created in the Details Panel, under the *properties* tab.

Figure A-28 Creating a world-level variable

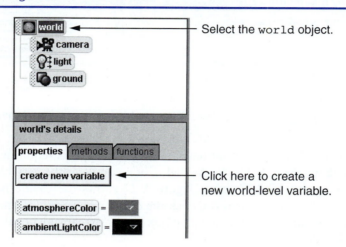

Select the `world` object.

Click here to create a new world-level variable.

To create a class-level variable in an object you perform the following steps:

1. Select the object in the Object Tree.
2. In the Details Panel select the *properties* tab.
3. Click the *create new variable* button, which appears at the top of the *properties* tab, as shown in Figure A-29.
4. Enter the variable's name, type, and initial value in the *create new variable* dialog box, which is similar to the one shown in Figure A-27. When you click the dialog box's *OK* button, a tile for the variable will be created in the Details Panel, under the *properties* tab.

Figure A-29 Creating a class-level variable

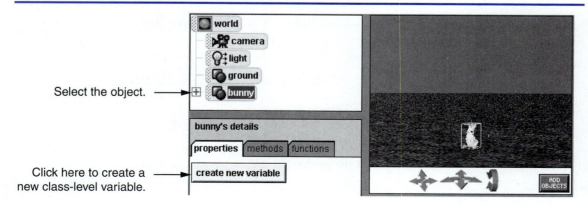

Select the object.

Click here to create a new class-level variable.

Variable Assignment

When you create a variable, you give it an initial value. The initial value will remain in the variable until you store a different value in the variable. In an Alice method you can create *set instructions* that store different values in the variable. A set instruction simply "sets" a variable to a new value.

To create a set instruction for a variable, you drag the variable tile and drop it into the Method Editor at the point where you want the set instruction to occur. A menu appears, and you select *set value*. Another menu appears that allows you to specify the value you wish to store in the variable. As a result, a set instruction is created.

Events

An event is an action that takes place while a program is running. When Alice worlds are running, they are capable of detecting several different types of events. For example, an event occurs when the user clicks an object with the mouse. An event also occurs when the user types a key on the keyboard. Table A-3 describes all of the events that an Alice world can detect while it is running.

Table A-3 Events that Alice can detect

Event	Description
When the world starts	This event occurs immediately when the world is started. It happens only once, each time the world is played.
When a key is typed	When the user types a key on the keyboard, this event occurs when the key is released.
When the mouse is clicked on something	This event occurs when the user clicks an object in the world with the mouse.
While something is true	When a condition that you have specified becomes true, this event occurs as long as the condition remains true.
When a variable changes	This event occurs when a variable's value changes.
Let the mouse move <objects>	This event allows the user to move an object in the world by clicking and dragging it with the mouse.
Let the arrow keys move <subject>	This event allows the user to move an object in the world by typing the arrow keys on the keyboard.
Let the mouse move the camera	This event allows the user to move the camera through the world by clicking and dragging the mouse.
Let the mouse orient the camera	This event allows the user to change the camera's orientation (the direction in which it is pointing) by clicking and dragging the mouse.

When any of the events listed in Table A-3 occur, your Alice world can perform an action in response to that event, such as calling a method.

At the top right of the screen in the Alice environment, you see an area labeled *Events*, as shown in Figure A-30. This area is called the *Events Editor*. When you create an Alice world, a tile appears in the Events Editor that reads as follows:

```
When the world starts, do world.my first method
```

This tile specifies that when the world starts, the method `world.my first method` will be executed. The left portion of the tile shows the name of an event, `When the world starts`, and the right portion of the tile is a drop-down box that shows the name of the method that will be executed when the event occurs. You can click the down arrow on the drop-down box to select a different method. Any method that is selected in this tile will be automatically executed when the world starts.

Figure A-30 The Events Editor

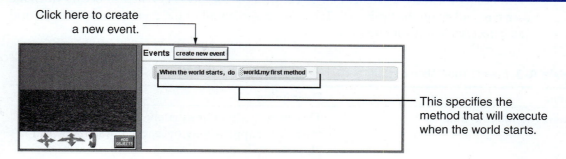

The process of responding to an event is commonly called *handling the event*. In order for an Alice world to handle an event, a tile for that event must appear in the Events Editor. When a world is first created, the only tile that appears in the Events Editor is for the `When the world starts` event. If you want the world to handle any other events, you must create a new tile for the event in the Events Editor. To create a new event tile, you click the *create new event* button, as shown in Figure A-30. A menu of available events will appear next. You select the event that you want to handle from this menu. A tile for the event will then be created in the Events Editor.

Most event tiles require that you specify additional arguments, such as the method that you want to execute in response to the event. A method that is executed in response to an event is commonly referred to as an *event handler*. For example, the event tile that is shown in Figure A-30 specifies that when the world starts, `world.my first method` is called. The method `world.my first method` is the event handler.

Figure A-31 shows another example of an event tile. Assume that this tile appears in a world that has an object named `fridge` (a refrigerator object). The event tile specifies that when the mouse is clicked on the `fridge` object's `fridgeDoor` subpart, the `fridgeDoor` will turn left 0.25 revolutions.

Figure A-31 Example of an event tile

B The ASCII Character Set

Nonprintable ASCII Characters					Printable ASCII Characters			
Dec	Hex	Oct	Name of Character		Dec	Hex	Oct	Character
0	0	0	NULL		32	20	40	(Space)
1	1	1	SOTT		33	21	41	!
2	2	2	STX		34	22	42	"
3	3	3	ETY		35	23	43	#
4	4	4	EOT		36	24	44	$
5	5	5	ENQ		37	25	45	%
6	6	6	ACK		38	26	46	&
7	7	7	BELL		39	27	47	'
8	8	10	BKSPC		40	28	50	(
9	9	11	HZTAB		41	29	51	)
10	a	12	NEWLN		42	2a	52	*
11	b	13	VTAB		43	2b	53	+
12	c	14	FF		44	2c	54	,
13	d	15	CR		45	2d	55	-
14	e	16	SO		46	2e	56	.
15	f	17	SI		47	2f	57	/
16	10	20	DLE		48	30	60	0
17	11	21	DC1		49	31	61	1
18	12	22	DC2		50	32	62	2
19	13	23	DC3		51	33	63	3
20	14	24	DC4		52	34	64	4
21	15	25	NAK		53	35	65	5
22	16	26	SYN		54	36	66	6
23	17	27	ETB		55	37	67	7
24	18	30	CAN		56	38	70	8
25	19	31	EM		57	39	71	9
26	1a	32	SUB		58	3a	72	:
27	1b	33	ESC		59	3b	73	;
28	1c	34	FS		60	3c	74	<
29	1d	35	GS		61	3d	75	=
30	1e	36	RS		62	3e	76	>
31	1f	37	US		63	3f	77	?
127	7f	177	DEL		64	40	100	@
					65	41	101	A
					66	42	102	B
					67	43	103	C

Printable ASCII Characters			
Dec	Hex	Oct	Character
68	44	104	D
69	45	105	E
70	46	106	F
71	47	107	G
72	48	110	H
73	49	111	I
74	4a	112	J
75	4b	113	K
76	4c	114	L
77	4d	115	M
78	4e	116	N
79	4f	117	O
80	50	120	P
81	51	121	Q
82	52	122	R
83	53	123	S
84	54	124	T
85	55	125	U
86	56	126	V
87	57	127	W
88	58	130	X
89	59	131	Y
90	5a	132	Z
91	5b	133	[
92	5c	134	\
93	5d	135	]
94	5e	136	^
95	5f	137	_
96	60	140	`
97	61	141	a

Printable ASCII Characters			
Dec	Hex	Oct	Character
98	62	142	b
99	63	143	c
100	64	144	d
101	65	145	e
102	66	146	f
103	67	147	g
104	68	150	h
105	69	151	i
106	6a	152	j
107	6b	153	k
108	6c	154	l
109	6d	155	m
110	6e	156	n
111	6f	157	o
112	70	160	p
113	71	161	q
114	72	162	r
115	73	163	s
116	74	164	t
117	75	165	u
118	76	166	v
119	77	167	w
120	78	170	x
121	79	171	y
122	7a	172	z
123	7b	173	{
124	7c	174		
125	7d	175	}
126	7e	176	~

APPENDIX C

Operator Precedence and Associativity

The operators are shown in order of precedence, from highest to lowest.

Operator	Associativity
`::`	unary: left to right
	binary: right to left
`()  []  ->  .`	left to right
`++  −  +  −  !  ~  (type)  *  &  sizeof`	right to left
`*  /  %`	left to right
`+  −`	left to right
`<<  >>`	left to right
`<  <=  >  >=`	left to right
`==  !=`	left to right
`&`	left to right
`^`	left to right
`|`	left to right
`&&`	left to right
`||`	left to right
`?:`	right to left
`=  +=  −=  *=  /=  %=  &=  ^=  |=  <<=  >>=`	right to left
`,`	left to right

C++ Quick Reference

C++ Data Types

Data Type	Description
`char`	Character
`unsigned char`	Unsigned Character
`int`	Integer
`short int`	Short integer
`short`	Same as `short int`
`unsigned short int`	Unsigned short integer
`unsigned short`	Same as `unsigned short int`
`unsigned int`	Unsigned integer
`unsigned`	Same as `unsigned int`
`long int`	Long integer
`long`	Same as `long int`
`unsigned long int`	Unsigned long integer
`unsigned long`	Same as `unsigned long int`
`float`	Single precision floating point
`double`	double precision floating point
`long double`	Long double precision floating point

Forms of the `if` Statement

Simple if | Example
```
if (expression)
    statement;
```
```
if (x < y)
    x++;
```

if/else | Example
```
if (expression)
    statement;
else
    statement;
```
```
if (x < y)
    x++;
else
    x--;
```

if/else if | Example
```
if (expression)
    statement;
else if (expression)
    statement;
else
    statement;
```
```
if (x < y)
    x++;
else if (x < z)
    x--;
else
    y++;
```

To conditionally-execute more than one statement, enclose the statements in braces:

Form | Example
```
if (expression)
{
    statement;
    statement;
}
```
```
if (x < y)
{
    x++;
    cout << x;
}
```

Web Sites

For the *Starting Out with C++* Companion Web Site
www.pearsonhighered.com/gaddis
For Addison-Wesley Computing
www.pearsonhighered.com/cs

Commonly Used Operators

Assignment Operators
`=`	Assignment
`+=`	Combined addition/assignment
`-=`	Combined subtraction/assignment
`*=`	Combined multiplication/assignment
`/=`	Combined division/assignment
`%=`	Combined modulus/assignment

Arithmetic Operators
`+`	Addition
`-`	Subtraction
`*`	Multiplication
`/`	Division
`%`	Modulus (remainder)

Relational Operators
`<`	Less than
`<=`	Less than or equal to
`>`	Greater than
`>=`	Greater than or equal to
`==`	Equal to
`!=`	Not equal to

Logical Operators
`&&`	AND
`||`	OR
`!`	NOT

Increment/Decrement
`++`	Increment
`--`	Decrement

Conditional Operator ?:

Form:

expression ? *expression* : *expression*

Example:
```
x = a < b ? a : b;
```
The statement above works like:
```
if (a < b)
    x = a;
else
    x = b;
```

The `while` Loop

Form: | Example:
```
while (expression)
    statement;
```
```
while (x < 100)
    cout << x++ << endl;
```

```
while (expression)
{
    statement;
    statement;
}
```
```
while (x < 100)
{
    cout << x << endl;
    x++;
}
```

The do-while Loop

Form: | Example:
```
do
    statement;
while (expression);
```
```
do
    cout << x++ << endl;
while (x < 100);
```

```
do
{
    statement;
    statement;
} while (expression);
```
```
do
{
    cout << x << endl;
    x++;
} while (x < 100);
```

C++ Quick Reference (continued)

The *for* Loop
Form:
```
for (initialization; test; update)
    statement;

for (initialization; test; update)
{
    statement;
    statement;
}
```

Example:
```
for (count = 0; count < 10; count++)
    cout << count << endl;

for (count = 0; count < 10; count++)
{
    cout << "The value of count is ";
    cout << count << endl;
}
```

The *switch/case* Construct
Form:
```
switch (integer-expression)
{
    case integer-constant:
        statement(s);
        break;
    case integer-constant:
        statement(s);
        break;
    default :
        statement;
}
```

Example:
```
switch (choice)
{
    case 0 :
        cout << "You selected 0.\n";
        break;
    case 1 :
        cout << "You selected 1.\n";
        break;
    default :
        cout << "You did not select 0 or 1.\n";
}
```

Using *cout*
Requires `<iostream>` header file.

Commonly used stream manipulators

Name	Description
endl	advances output to the beginning of the next line.
fixed	sets fixed point notation
left	sets left justification
right	sets right justification
setprecision	sets the number of significant digits
setw	sets field width
showpoint	forces decimal point & trailing zeros to display

Example:
```
cout << setprecision(2) << fixed
     << left << x << endl;
```

Member functions for output formatting

Name	Description
.precision	sets the number of significant digits
.setf	sets one or more ios flags
.unsetf	clears one or more ios flags
.width	sets field width

Example:
```
cout.precision(2);
```

Using *cin*
Requires `<iostream>` header file

Commonly used stream manipulators

Name	Description
setw	sets field width

Member functions for specialized input

Name	Description
.getline	reads a line of input as a C-string
.get	reads a character
.ignore	ignores the last character entered
.width	sets field width

Some Commonly Used Library Functions

Name	Description
(The following require <cstdlib>)	
atof	Converts C-string to float
atoi	Converts C-string to int
atol	Converts C-string to long int
rand	Generates a pseudo-random number
srand	Sets seed value for random numbers
(The following require <cctype>)	
islower	Returns true if char argument is lowercase
isupper	Returns true if char argument is uppercase
tolower	Returns the lowercase equivalent of the char argument
toupper	Returns the uppercase equivalent of the char argument
(The following require <cmath>)	
pow	Raises a number to a power
sqrt	Returns square root of a number
(The following require <cstring>)	
strcat	Appends a C-string to another C-string
strcpy	Copies a C-string
strlen	Returns the length of a C-string

Index